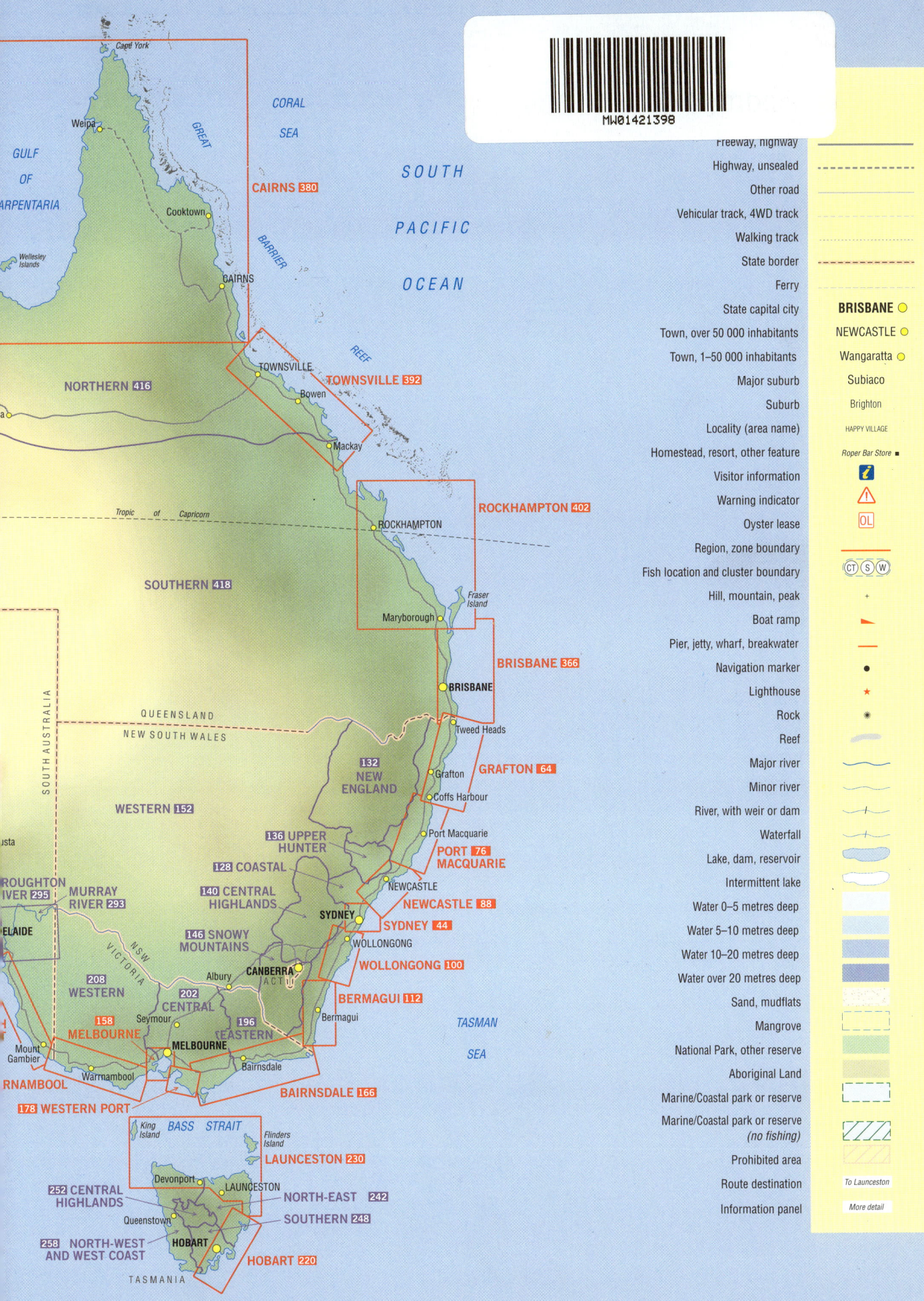

FISH
AUSTRALIA

FISH
AUSTRALIA

VIKING

Viking
A division of Penguin Books Australia Ltd
250 Camberwell Road, Camberwell, Victoria 3124, Australia
Penguin Books Ltd
Harmondsworth, Middlesex, England
Penguin Putnam Inc.
375 Hudson Street, New York, New York 10014, USA
Penguin Books Canada Limited
10 Alcorn Avenue, Toronto, Ontario, Canada M4V 3B2
Penguin Books (N.Z.) Ltd
Cnr Rosedale and Airborne Roads, Albany, Auckland, New Zealand
Penguin Books (South Africa) (Pty) Ltd
24 Sturdee Avenue, Rosebank, Johannesburg 2196, South Africa
Penguin Books India (P) Ltd
11, Community Centre, Panchsheel Park, New Delhi 110 017, India

Second edition published by Penguin Books Australia Ltd, 2002
First published 1995
Reprinted 1997

Copyright © Penguin Books Australia Ltd, 2002

2 4 6 8 10 9 7 5 3 1

ISBN 0 670 91145 3

All rights reserved. Without limiting the rights under copyright reserved above, no part of this publication may be reproduced, stored in or introduced into a retrieval system, or transmitted in any form or by any means (electronic, mechanical, photocopying, recording or otherwise) without the prior written permission of both the copyright owner and the above publisher of this book.

Printed in China by Midas Printing (Asia) Ltd

Publisher's Note: Every effort has been made to ensure that the information in this book is accurate at the time of going to press. The publisher welcomes information and suggestions for correction or improvement. Email: cartog@penguin.com.au

Disclaimers: The publisher cannot accept responsibility for any errors or omissions. The representation on the maps of water features – depths, buoys, etc. – is intended as a guide to fishing spots only. These maps should not be used as a navigational aid. The publisher recommends the Australian Admiralty Charts prepared by the Hydrographic Services of the Royal Australian Navy be used for navigational information. The representation on the maps of any road or track is not necessarily evidence of public right of way.

Acknowledgements

Much of the material in this book originally appeared in **Fish Australia**, published by Penguin Books, 1995, where full acknowledgements for individual contributions appear.

The Publisher would also like to acknowledge the following individuals and organisations:

GENERAL EDITOR
Steve Cooper

PROJECT MANAGER
Astrid Browne

DESIGN
Cover design
Susannah Low, Penguin Design Studio

Internal design
Adrian Saunders and Susannah Low, Penguin Design Studio

CARTOGRAPHY
Damien Demaj, Colin Critchell

PAGE LAYOUT AND TYPESETTING
Post Pre-press Group, Brisbane

EDITORIAL ASSISTANCE
Saskia Adams, Fay Donlevy

PICTURE RESEARCH
Heidi Marfurt

MAP CHECKING
Michael Archer, Simon Hrabe, Julie Sheridan

PRODUCTION
Sue Van Velsen

SPECIALIST CONSULTANTS
Victoria
Philip Weigall
Paul Worsteling

New South Wales
Peter Horrobin
Jim Harnwell

Queensland
Steve Morgan
David Green

South Australia
Greg Brown
Phill Heitmann

Western Australia
Kurt Blanksby

Northern Territory
Alex Julius

Tasmania
Greg French
Mike Stevens

Fish species and common names
Julian Pepperell

Bait, tackle, knots and rigs
Geoff Wilson

ASSISTANCE WITH MAP RESEARCH
Boat ramps
Neil Grose and Fishnet.com.au Pty Ltd

Victoria
Department of Natural Resources and Environment
Parks Victoria

New South Wales
NSW Fisheries
Marine Parks Authority
National Parks and Wildlife Service
Port Macquarie Visitor Information & Booking Centre

Queensland
Great Barrier Reef Marine Park Authority
Queensland Parks and Wildlife Service

South Australia
Primary Industries and Resources
Department for Environment and Heritage

Western Australia
Department of Conservation and Land Management
Department of Fisheries

Northern Territory
Department of Primary Industry and Fisheries

Tasmania
Department of Primary Industries, Water and Environment

ILLUSTRATIONS
Fish illustrations are by Roger Swainston (some previously published in Roger Swainston and Barry Hutchins, *Sea Fishes of Southern Australia*, Swainston Publishing, Perth, 1986) and Walter Stackpool (reproduced with permission from Jack Pollard, *The Complete Illustrated Guide to Fish*, Transworld, Sydney, 1991).

PHOTOGRAPHY
Front cover
TOP:
Surf fishing for tailor, Sunshine Coast, Qld
Jock Dyason

BOTTOM (LEFT TO RIGHT):
Paul Worsteling with albacore
Paul Worsteling

Cristi Duncan with snapper
Paul Worsteling

Philip Weigall with brown trout
Philip Weigall

Back cover
Fishing off Fishermans Wharf, Darwin Harbour, NT
Alex Julius

Spine
Paul Worsteling with albacore
Paul Worsteling

Half-title page
Trout fishing on the Ouse River, Tas.
Rob Sloane

Title page
Fishing at dawn, Hawks Nest, NSW
J.P. & E.S. Baker

Other photography credits
ANT Photo Library (Bill Bachman, J.P. & E.S. Baker, Jocelyn Burt, Ralph & Daphne Keller, Natfoto, Peter Walton); Jack Atley; AUSCAPE (Brett Gregory); Australian Picture Library (Douglass Baglin, J.P. & E.S. Baker, John Carnemolla, Sean Davey, Craig Lamotte, Jonathan Marks, Leo Meier, Fritz Prenzel, Wayne Stead); Bill Bachman; J.P. & E.S. Baker; Ross Barnett; Dave Buckley; Kaj Busch; Andrew Chapman; Bill Classon; Peter Cochrane; Gene & Gwen Dundon; Jock Dyason; Greg French; Jane Gardner; Brian Gilkes; David Green; Simon Griffiths; Harding's Studio; Rod Harrison; Anne Heazlewood; Peter Horrobin; Richard I'Anson; Instock Photo Library (Adam Bruzzone); Alex Julius; Peta Kowalski; Neville Lester; Lochman Transparencies (Jiri Lochman, Dennis Sarson, Neil Wehlack); Shane Mensforth; Steve Morgan; Percy Munchenberg; Chris Parkinson; Trevor Percival; PhotoDisk; photolibrary.com; Bruce Postle; Michael Rayner; Christo Reid; Retrospect (Dale Mann); David Roche; Mike Roennfeldt; Margot Seares; Don Skirrow; Rob Sloane; Robin Smith; South Australian Tourism Commission; Ken Stepnell; Warren Steptoe; Stock Photos (Bill Bachman, David Bassett, Trevern Dawes, Robert Della-Piana, Neil Follett, Robert Gray, Great Western Images, Gary Howard, Owen Hughes, John Jenkins, Noeline Kelly, Ern Mainka, Lance Nelson, Bruce Peebles, Otto Rogge, Ken Stepnell); The Photo Library (Peter Walton); Rob Torelli; Peter Walton; Philip Weigall; Geoff Wilson; Paul Worsteling

Contents

ACKNOWLEDGEMENTS v
HOW TO USE THIS BOOK x
INTRODUCTION xiii

HOW TO FISH 1

Estuary and Bay Fishing	2
Rock and Beach Fishing	6
Offshore Fishing	10
Inland Fishing	14
Rods and Reels	18
Hooks, Lines and Sinkers	22
Lures and Flies	26
Knots and Rigs	28
All About Bait	30
Fishing Safely	34
Caring for the Environment	36

WHERE TO FISH 39

New South Wales 40

COASTAL FISHING 42

SYDNEY REGION 44
- Brisbane Water 46
- Hawkesbury 48
- Northern Beaches 52
- Sydney Harbour 54
- Sydney South and Botany Bay 60
- Kurnell and Port Hacking 62

GRAFTON REGION 64
- Tweed Coast 66
- Brunswick Heads to Whites Head 68
- Ballina and Evans Head 70
- Shark Bay to Minnie Water 72
- Wooli to Coffs Harbour 74

PORT MACQUARIE REGION 76
- Sawtell to Nambucca Heads 78
- South West Rocks to Hat Head 80
- Port Macquarie 82
- Camden Haven and Manning River 84
- Tuncurry to Charlotte Head 86

NEWCASTLE REGION 88
- Seal Rocks and Myall Lakes 90
- Port Stephens 92
- Newcastle and Lake Macquarie 94
- Coastal Lakes 96
- Terrigal 98

WOLLONGONG REGION 100
- Royal National Park 102
- Wollongong 103
- Lake Illawarra 104
- Minnamurra to Culburra 106
- Jervis Bay to Lake Conjola 108
- Ulladulla to Durras Lake 110

BERMAGUI REGION 112
- Batemans Bay to Broulee 114
- Moruya to Kianga Lake 116
- Narooma to Wallaga Lake 118
- Bermagui to Wapengo Lake 120
- Tathra to Pambula 122
- Eden to Green Cape 124

INLAND FISHING 126

COASTAL REGION 128
- North Coast 129
- Central Coast 130
- South Coast 131

NEW ENGLAND REGION 132
- Highlands 134
- Western Slopes 135

CONTENTS

UPPER HUNTER REGION 136
   Barrington Tops 137
   Hunter River 138

CENTRAL HIGHLANDS REGION 140
   Mudgee 142
   Bathurst 143
   Goulburn 144
   Yass 145

SNOWY MOUNTAINS REGION 146
   Central Monaro and Cooma 148
   Southern Monaro 149
   Snowy Mountains 150

WESTERN REGION 152

BAIRNSDALE REGION 166
   Mallacoota 168
   Tamboon and Bemm River 170
   Marlo and Lake Tyers 171
   Gippsland Lakes East 172
   Lake Victoria 174
   Port Albert 176
   Corner Inlet 177

WESTERN PORT REGION 178
   Waratah Bay 180
   Anderson Inlet 181
   Western Port South 182
   Western Port North 184

WARRNAMBOOL REGION 186
   Anglesea to Apollo Bay 188
   Cape Otway to Port Fairy 190
   Portland Bay to Nelson 192

INLAND FISHING 194
EASTERN REGION 196
   East Gippsland 198
   Tambo–Mitchell Rivers 199
   Murray–Kiewa Rivers 200

CENTRAL REGION 202
   Ovens–Broken Rivers 204
   Goulburn–Campaspe Rivers 205
   West Gippsland 206
   Yarra–Maribyrnong Rivers 207

WESTERN REGION 208
   Loddon–Avoca Rivers 210
   Moorabool–Curdies Rivers 212
   Hopkins River Basin 213
   Moyne–Glenelg Rivers 214
   Wimmera and Mallee 215

Tasmania 216

COASTAL FISHING 218
HOBART REGION 220
   Swansea to Maria Island 222
   Tasman Peninsula 224
   Derwent Estuary 226
   D'Entrecasteaux Channel 228

Victoria 154

COASTAL FISHING 156
MELBOURNE REGION 158
   Port Phillip South-east 160
   Port Phillip East 161
   Port Phillip North 162
   Corio Bay 164
   Bellarine Peninsula 165

CONTENTS

Duck–Blythe Rivers	262
Leven–Mersey Rivers	263

South Australia 264

COASTAL FISHING 266
ADELAIDE REGION 268
- Cape Jervis to Port Adelaide 270
- Yorke Peninsula 272
- Kangaroo Island 274

SOUTH EAST REGION 276
- Port MacDonnell to Kingston 278
- The Coorong 280
- Victor Harbor 282

PORT LINCOLN REGION 284
- North Spencer Gulf 286
- Port Lincoln 288
- Coffin Bay to Cape Nuyts 290

INLAND FISHING 292
MURRAY RIVER REGION 293

ONKAPARINGA RIVER REGION 294

BROUGHTON RIVER REGION 295

Western Australia 296

COASTAL FISHING 298
PERTH REGION 300
- Perth Beaches 302
- Swan River 304
- Rottnest Island 305
- Guilderton to Kalbarri 306

ALBANY REGION 308
- Israelite Bay to Munglinup Beach 310
- Hopetoun to Torbay Head 312
- Denmark to Point Nuyts 314
- Augusta to Cape Naturaliste 316
- Bunbury and Mandurah 318

GASCOYNE–KIMBERLEY REGION 320
- Shark Bay 322
- Carnarvon to Exmouth 324
- Dampier Coast 326
- Broome to Cambridge Gulf 328

INLAND FISHING 330
SOUTH-WEST REGION 332

KIMBERLEY REGION 333

LAUNCESTON REGION 230
- Hunter Island to Devonport 232
- Port Sorell to Bridport 234
- Ansons Bay to Bicheno 236
- King Island 238
- Flinders Island 239

INLAND FISHING 240
NORTH-EAST REGION 242
- Far North-east 244
- East Coast 245
- Esk System 246

SOUTHERN REGION 248
- East Derwent 250
- West Derwent 251

CENTRAL HIGHLANDS REGION 252
- Great Lake–Arthurs Lake 254
- Bronte–Echo 255
- Western Lakes 256
- Cradle Mountain–Lake St Clair 257

NORTH-WEST AND WEST COAST REGION 258
- Franklin–Gordon 260
- Queenstown–Arthur River 261

CONTENTS

Northern Territory 334

COASTAL FISHING 336
DARWIN REGION 338
- Cape Scott to Bynoe Harbour 340
- Port Darwin and Shoal Bay 342
- Bathurst and Melville Islands 344
- Van Diemen Gulf 346

GOVE REGION 348
- East Arnhem Land 350

INLAND FISHING 352
WEST COAST RIVERS REGION 354

ADELAIDE–MARY RIVERS REGION 356

KAKADU REGION 358

EAST COAST RIVERS REGION 360

Queensland 362

COASTAL FISHING 364
BRISBANE REGION 366
- Tin Can Inlet and Sunshine Coast 368
- Moreton Bay and Brisbane River 372
- Jumpinpin and Gold Coast 376

CAIRNS REGION 380
- Gulf and Cape York 382
- Cooktown to Cairns 386
- Innisfail–Mourilyan Area 390
- Hinchinbrook Island Area 391

TOWNSVILLE REGION 392
- Halifax Bay and Palm Islands 394
- Townsville and Bowling Green Bay 395
- Ayr to Bowen 396
- The Whitsundays 398
- St Helens Bay to Yarrawonga Point 400

ROCKHAMPTON REGION 402
- Shoalwater Bay to Fitzroy River 404
- Port Alma to Gladstone 406
- Tannum Sands to Burnett Heads 408
- Hervey Bay and Fraser Island 410

INLAND FISHING 414
NORTHERN REGION 416

SOUTHERN REGION 418

IDENTIFYING YOUR CATCH 421

COOKING YOUR CATCH 443

- Hook to Cook 444
- Cuts for Cooking 446
- Cooking Methods 448
- Recipes 449

INDEX OF PLACE NAMES 455

ix

How to Use This Book

The page illustrated shows a typical fishing area and explains the various features of text and maps

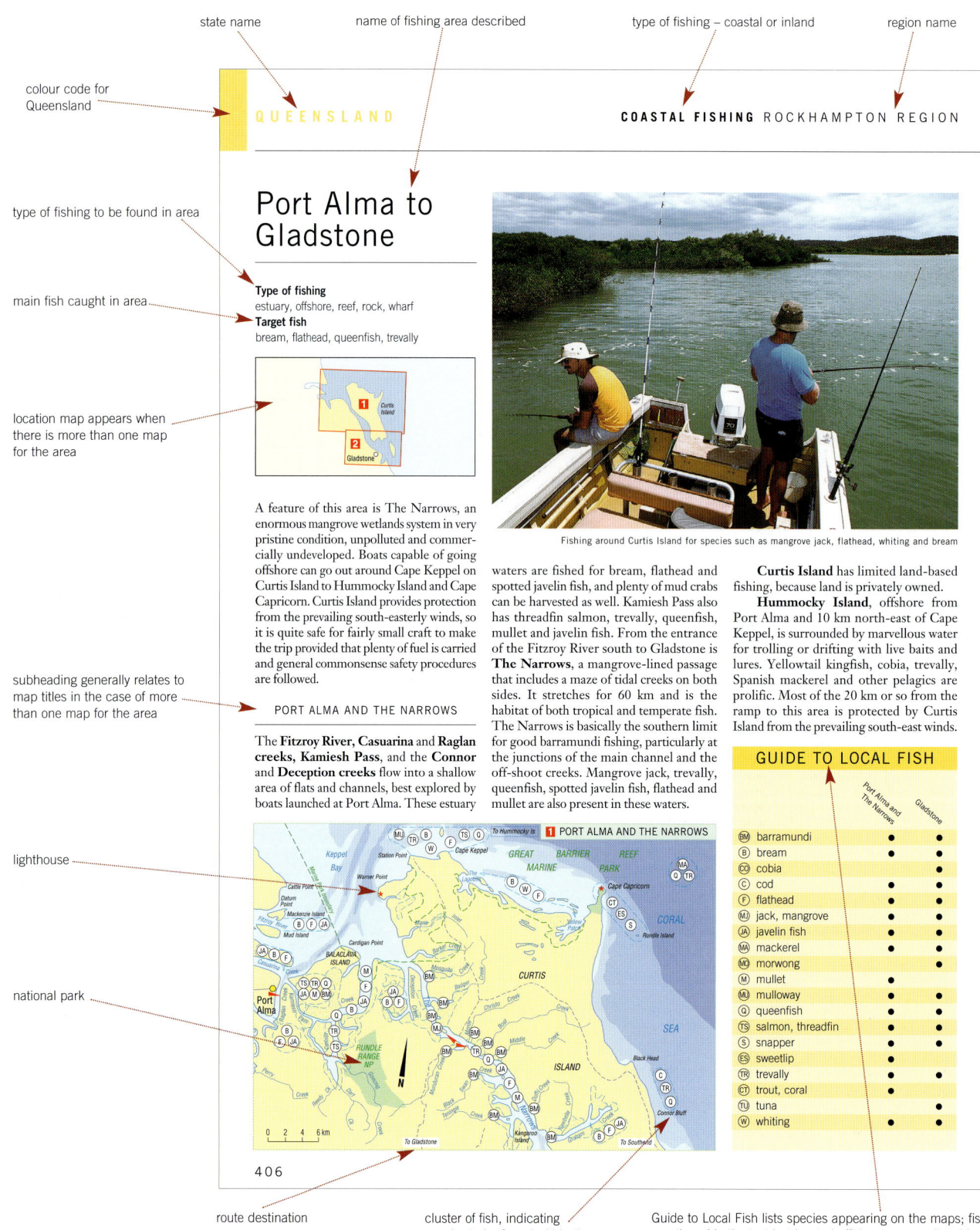

boat ramp

pier/jetty/wharf/breakwater

mangrove area

fish symbol, identified in Guide to Local Fish on adjoining page

COASTAL FISHING ROCKHAMPTON REGION   QUEENSLAND

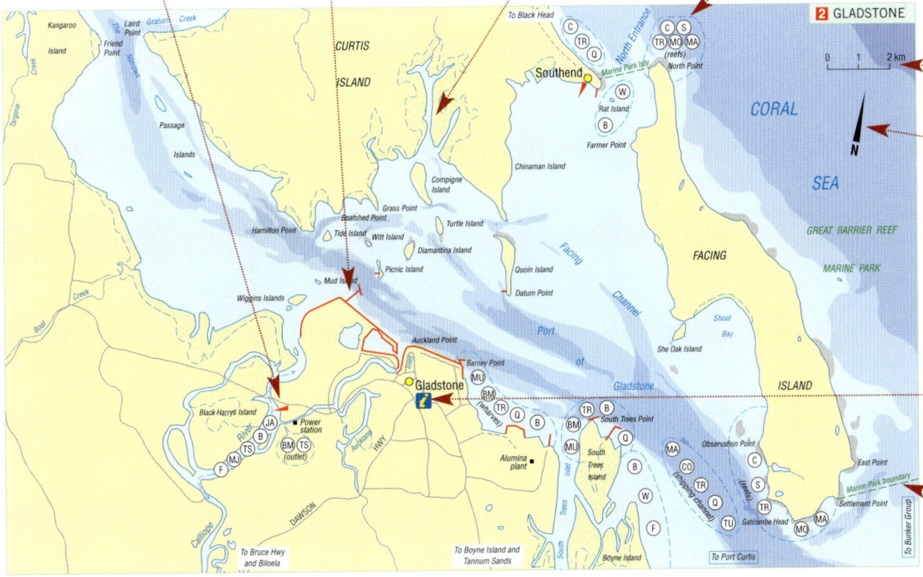

map corresponds to numbered area on location map

scale bar

north point

visitor information centre

marine/coastal park or reserve boundary

From Station Point to **Cape Keppel**, mulloway and trevally are the main fish, along with whiting, bream, flathead, threadfin salmon and queenfish. South-east of Cape Keppel, in two inlets known as **The Lagoons** and **Yellow Patch**, there are some protected waters where bream, whiting and flathead find shelter. At **Cape Capricorn**, at the north-east of the island, and nearby **Rundle Island** there is bottom fishing over reefs for coral trout, sweetlip and snapper. Offshore from Cape Capricorn there is deep water ideal for trolling for mackerel, trevally and queenfish.

GLADSTONE

The **Calliope River** reaches the coast near the big industrial city of Gladstone, creating a delta of mangrove creeks and sand flats. The hot water outlet from the power station near the boat ramp is a top spot for barramundi and threadfin salmon. Flathead, mangrove jack, bream and spotted javelin fish can also be found in this area.

To reach the northern waters of the port, boat anglers have to navigate the channels through the sandbanks. There is a car ferry service from Gladstone to Southend on Curtis Island on Friday, Saturday and Sunday. All roads on the island are suitable only for four-wheel-drive vehicles. The long stretch from Black Head down to North Entrance is ideal for anglers seeking cod, trevally and queenfish. North Entrance, especially around tiny **Rat Island**, is excellent for bream and whiting.

Facing Island shelters the Port of Gladstone. The island has rocks and a number of reefs at its north and south ends that attract fish like cod, snapper and trevally; morwong and mackerel are possible catches around the reef fringes.

The deeper port area has good land-based angling, particularly from **Barney Point** and **South Trees wharves**, with mulloway and barramundi the main targets, along with trevally, queenfish and bream. There is some good fishing around **South Trees Island** and **Boyne Island**. Whiting are among the weed patches, and there are discernible gutters for flathead and bream around the shorelines. Ramps at Boyne Island and Tannum Sands provide the easiest launching for the deep shipping channel, which runs through **Port Curtis** and carries school mackerel, cobia, trevally, queenfish and tuna. Gladstone is the best launching place for boat anglers wanting access to the offshore reefs. Charter fishing vessels regularly leave here for the Swain Reefs, 210 km north-east of Rosslyn Bay (see Shoalwater Bay to Fitzroy River area).

About 60 km east of Gladstone are a chain of reefs and islands generally known as the **Capricorn** and **Bunker groups** which include the **Fairfax Islands, Lady Musgrave Island** and **Lady Elliot Island**. There are certain areas around Lady Musgrave and Lady Elliot islands where you are not permitted to fish. Charter boats visit the area regularly. Over the reefs there are red emperor, sweetlip, snapper and cod, and the surrounding waters, according to the season, have Spanish and school mackerel, yellowtail kingfish, trevally, cobia and tuna.

Prawns
There are a number of prawn species in Australia, inhabiting mangrove areas, mud flats, sand channels, sea grass and open waters. They can be collected by dragging the area with a scoop net and are an ideal bait for fish such as bream, whiting, barramundi and mangrove jack.

special feature providing additional information relevant to fishing in the Port Alma to Gladstone area

maps are a guide only and show fishing information for the area but must not be used for marine navigation; such information is available from published hydrographic charts and visiting anglers should always check local information centres for danger spots and sand weather warnings

bold type indicates a fishing spot

Introduction

'Have you ever had the pleasure of landing a blackfish on a rod and reel? If you have, then you know the thrill that passes through one as you see your quill disappear. A gentle "strike" tells you that you have hooked one and the fight begins. Fight advisedly, as there is no greater fighter, size for size, in the seven seas ...'

– *Jock Scott, c. 1920*

Three mighty oceans, extensive coral reefs, a massive coastline providing thousands of kilometres of beaches and cliffs, large estuaries, a network of coastal and inland rivers, together with a benign climate enabling anglers to fish most days of the year make Australia great for fishing.

Fishing, like any other sport, has its fraternity of enthusiasts, but in Australia the fishing crowds are bigger than in any other country. An estimated four million Australians go fishing every year. Allowing for a lot of 'few times a year' holiday anglers, there remains a huge and dedicated band, who seek to renew their battle with the fish as often as possible. Whether they are learning, semi-skilled or expert, their appetite for knowledge is unabated.

Fishing is a sport with so many facets that even the experts do not know everything. If you ever get abreast of all the fishing tackle available – and you probably never will – you will have mastered just one aspect of the great sport of fishing. But it is the place that is most important. Every dedicated angler has their favourite fishing spot, often a closely guarded secret. Fish Australia takes you to some of these 'secret' locations as well as providing a guide to the better-known fishing places. It directs you to the best place, what fish to target in that place, the new techniques for different fish, and the time and tide. This is what fishing is all about, and why anglers are prepared to get up early in the morning, in any weather, to drive for hours and go for a long, bumpy ride in a boat before they get a line in the water. This is why they will stand for hours, drenched by saltwater spray, casting into the foaming eddies around the rocks for the close-in fish like luderick, silver drummer, groper and bream, or casting out into the deep for passing pelagic fish, such as tuna, yellowtail kingfish, Spanish mackerel, cobia and trevally. This is why they will spend a day on the beach, or even half the night, exploring the gutters and channels for flathead, whiting, trevally, tailor and other species moving about in these inshore highways. This is why they will jockey a four-wheel-drive vehicle along rough bush tracks, and even backpack a few kilometres, to get to a remote stretch of river where trout might be sought in untested water.

Ocean, rock, beach, river and lake – these are just a few of the types of location that attract anglers. There are those who love fishing the usually placid coastal lakes and estuaries, and those who enjoy the camaraderie of the pier and the occasional boil-ups of excitement when the fish are 'on'. Some fish the slower, inland rivers, while others find excitement on the great water storage lakes. The busy water close to major cities, such as the Brisbane River, Sydney Harbour and Port Phillip, have their devotees and yield to those who know the 'what, where and how' of their area.

Then there are the anglers who work the offshore holes, gravel patches, weeds, rocks, reefs, bomboras and known fish highways, anywhere from just offshore out to the continental shelf. And the big game anglers, who seek to test their skill and strength against fighting game fish like marlin and yellowfin tuna.

The fishing, and the fish, is as varied as the habitats in a continent that stretches from the cool temperate south to the tropical north. The saltwater species of the south – flathead, bream, whiting and snapper – give way to the kings of the north – barramundi, queenfish, mangrove jack and fingermark. Some fish migrate with the seasons, and are at the limit of their zone at various times of the year. A few, like flathead, can be found anywhere.

Fish Australia, with its maps of the fishing waterways, aims to help all Australian anglers to find the fish. With the input of its consultants and an immense store of fishing advice, it shows you the areas and spots where you are likely to catch the various fish species. Its maps, accompanied by notes on the fishing experience of each area, also locate the boat ramps, piers, channels, reefs, bait collecting areas, land fishing spots and danger points. The onshore facilities like boat hire, bait and tackle shops, marine dealers and tourist information centres are also mapped.

Before you get to the State, regional and area maps, there is a comprehensive introductory section. It covers all aspects of fishing from specific techniques for the fish that inhabit the various environments, to rods and reels, and bait and berley. There is also an illustrated guide to the major fish species and their habitats, and information on how to clean and cook fish.

Fish Australia tells you how, where and what to catch. It is the essential companion for anglers, whether beginners or experts, locals or visitors.

A spectacular catch off the southern New South Wales coast

HOW TO FISH

HOW TO FISH

Estuary and Bay Fishing

Half of Australia's estimated four million anglers fish in estuaries and bays, because they offer easy access to a variety of fish in safety and comfort, and a range of locations and habitats. You can fish from the shore, or a small boat, and once you are aware of available fishing spots, best baits and local techniques, you should enjoy success.

Estuary and bay anglers fish from land, from land-based structures such as piers, wharves, jetties and bridges, or from boats. Estuaries exist in bays, inlets, lakes, lagoons and tidal rivers, wherever fresh water meets salt, resulting in brackish water. Many fish spend their entire lives in the estuary, but it is also a spawning ground, nursery and feeding area for fish from the open ocean or the lower reaches of freshwater rivers and streams.

WHEN TO FISH

Most fish inhabiting estuaries and bays feed at dawn and dusk; their behaviour is also strongly influenced by tides. For the angler, forward planning is important and should include: deciding on the species you are trying to catch, collecting bait, preparing berley, setting suitable tackle, and considering the effect that tide and time of day will have on where you fish.

Dawn and dusk feeders, such as bream, flathead, whiting, snapper and mulloway, will feed in the shallows in low light, but are inclined to seek safer depths during the day, especially in busy waterways. City anglers who cannot get away to fish during the day mid-week can use this dawn and dusk routine to advantage. Mullet, leatherjacket and luderick are less demanding about time of day, but still their behaviour is influenced by the tides.

Fish are habitual creatures with seasonal cycles of spawning and forage migrations, and certain habitat preferences. In temperate climes, for example, snapper, hairtail, luderick, mullet and bream move in and out of the sheltered waters of bays and estuaries according to season and locality. Generally, fishing is best during the warmer months, from September through to April, sometimes May. During winter many estuary dwellers move out of the estuaries to deeper offshore waters, returning in spring to spawn. In the tropics, species like barramundi, trevally, threadfin salmon and mangrove jack also move according to season and locality. However, the seasons in this region are predominantly the Wet and the Dry. During the Wet, which starts around November and lasts through to March or April, there are fish to be caught, but the Dry season is more conducive to fishing the northern estuaries.

WHERE TO FISH

Fish within estuaries and bays tend to base their lives around structures – whether artificial, like wharves, bridges, rock walls, oyster leases and buoys, or natural ones, like weed beds, gutters, channels, points and holes. Such places provide the fish with a reference point, with food and with relative safety. You will do much better fishing these areas than those that are featureless.

Sand or mudflats that are exposed at low tide are excellent areas to explore when the tide is rising. In southern estuaries, whiting, bream and flathead will search for food there, and trevally, shark and even barramundi will hunt through the shallows feeding on bait fish, attracted by the food sources on the flats. The best fishing occurs on flats that have a deep channel or gutter running alongside. A good flat will have around one metre or more of water over it at high tide.

In many bays and estuaries, you can fish quite effectively from shoreline features such as river banks, beaches and rocky points, or from structures such as piers or breakwalls. Such access becomes more difficult the further north you go; in the

A boat is usually necessary to fish Australia's northern estuaries

FISHING FETISHES

Knowing some basic rules about fish behaviour will help you to put your bait in the right place in the bay or estuary.

Fish face upstream or into the tidal flow in order to breathe more easily. This position also allows them to see their prey as they await the flow of food towards them.

Fish save energy by lurking just off the main current flow. Here they can hold position and grab food as it swirls past. They may also find shelter behind a rock or log, still close to the current.

Fish are attracted to structures such as rocks, logs, islands and trees, and to channels and shelving drop-offs, as they provide shelter.

Fish avoid shallow, clear water in daylight hours to protect themselves from the sun and animal predators – and anglers!

Fish use the tide to bring them food or allow them access to food-rich areas such as weed patches, encrusted pylons and yabby banks that are above water at low tide.

HOW TO FISH

mangrove-lined estuaries of the far north, a boat is almost essential.

Piers – wharves, jetties, call them what you will – are usually more common in bays and lakes, but are also found in some rivers. In many estuarine rivers, however, breakwalls do much the same job, providing deepwater access for land-based angling. Bridges also are often good spots, provided that fishing is allowed from them.

Wherever you fish from the shore, you need to take into account your lack of mobility. Choose places where the fish have some reason to gather, or at least have to pass by. It also helps if you incorporate some form of berleying into your strategy, to attract passing fish or to encourage those already resident to feed.

The keys to successful land-based fishing are to be prepared, have the right tackle and bait for the species you are after, and work the tides so you are there at the same time as the fish.

BAIT

Fish tend to favour the food items commonly found in whatever habitat they are in, so when fishing in estuaries and bays, as elsewhere, locally available baits are often the best choice. To ease the pressure on bait stocks, especially near cities and towns, only gather as much bait as you need for immediate use.

A type of burrowing shrimp found in southern estuaries, variously called 'yabby',

Piers often provide deepwater access for land-based angling

BAY AND ESTUARY FISH

barracouta	Vic., Tas., SA, WA, Qld
barramundi	WA, NT, Qld
bream, black	NSW, Vic., Tas., SA, WA
bream, pikey	NT, Qld
bream, yellowfin	NSW, Vic., Qld
catfish, blue	NSW, Qld
catfish, eel-tailed	NSW, Vic., Qld
catfish, estuary	NSW, SA, WA
catfish, fork-tailed	WA, Qld
cod, estuary	WA, NT, Qld
elephant fish	NSW, Vic., Tas., SA
fingermark	NSW, Vic., Tas., Qld
flathead, dusky	NSW, Vic., Qld
flathead, sand	NSW, Vic., Tas., SA, WA
flounder, bay	NSW, Vic., Tas., SA, WA
garfish	NSW, Vic., Tas., SA, WA, Qld
garfish, northern	WA, NT, Qld
hairtail	NSW, WA, Qld
jack, mangrove	NSW, WA, NT, Qld
jewfish, black	WA, NT, Qld
kingfish, yellowtail	NSW, Vic., Tas., SA, WA, Qld
leatherjacket	NSW, Vic., Tas., SA, WA, Qld
ling, rock	NSW, Vic., Tas., SA, WA
luderick	NSW, Vic., Tas., Qld
mackerel, horse	NSW, Vic., SA, WA, Qld
mullet, flat-tail	NSW, Vic., SA, WA
mullet, sand	NSW, SA, WA, Qld
mullet, sea	All States and NT
mulloway	NSW, Vic., SA, WA, Qld
perch, estuary	NSW, Vic., Tas., SA
pike, long-finned	NSW, Vic., Tas., SA, WA
queenfish	WA, NT, Qld
salmon, Atlantic	Tas.
salmon, Australian	NSW, Vic., Tas., SA, WA
salmon, threadfin	WA, NT, Qld
snapper	NSW, Vic., SA, WA, Qld
snook	NSW, Vic., Tas., SA, WA
tailor	NSW, Vic., Tas., SA, WA, Qld
tarwhine	NSW, Vic., Tas., SA, WA, Qld
trevally, bigeye	NSW, WA, NT, Qld
trevally, giant	NSW, WA, NT, Qld
trevally, golden	WA, NT, Qld
trevally, gold-spotted	WA, NT, Qld
trevally, sand	Vic., Tas., SA, WA
trevally, silver	NSW, Vic., Tas., SA, WA
whiting, King George	NSW, Vic., Tas., SA, WA
whiting, sand	NSW, Vic., Tas., Qld
whiting, trumpeter	NSW, WA, NT, Qld
whiting, yellow-finned	SA, WA

HOW TO FISH

'bass yabby' or 'pink nipper', lives in tidal sand flats and can be gathered with a suction pump. Similar 'green nippers' found in more northern regions can be 'puddled' by treading shallow weed beds and scooping them from the surface, or found under rocks and logs exposed by a falling tide. Bloodworms and squirt worms can be dug or pumped, using a bait pump, from exposed tidal flats. Prawns, shrimp, small fish and squid are good baits, as are cockles, oysters and mussels.

Other useful baits for estuary species include the various whitebaits, pilchards and bluebaits. They are best for flathead, though large flathead prefer tiny live mullet caught in a small bait trap. Baits of fresh striped tuna and squid are also effective and chicken gut is very popular for bream in Queensland.

You do not need bait for all species of fish. Many will attack lures, and tackle shops can often advise which lures work best on the fish in their locality.

TARGET FISH

Nationally, the six most common estuary species are bream, flathead, mullet, mulloway, snapper and whiting. Others, such as barramundi, estuary perch, flounder, garfish, hairtail, mangrove jack, tailor and trevally, are important on a regional or seasonal basis.

Bream are likely to be found almost anywhere in an estuary or bay, but prefer areas offering a structure and shelter. The three main species are black bream, yellowfin bream and pikey bream. Unlike most other estuarine species, bream stay in the estuary over winter and, rather than migrating offshore, they move up the estuary to where fresh water meets salt and spawn there.

Flathead come in more than a dozen forms, but three commonly encountered species are sand flathead, a widespread inshore species; dusky flathead, the most common species in temperate estuaries kind; and tiger flathead, a heavily built version common in southern bays. In estuaries, flathead favour the edges of sandbanks, scattered patches of weed and any place where the current is deflected into eddies. In bays, they congregate where tidal flows meet, and offshore, they gather in depths around 40 m – wherever currents combine to form food lanes.

Mullet are one of the most widespread families of fish in Australia, one species or another appearing in the estuaries and bays of every State. Common types include: sea mullet, fantail (silver), yelloweye, flat-tail, tiger, diamond-scale, pop-eye and sand mullet (lano, tallegalane). Of these, the most easily line-caught types are the sand, yelloweye and tiger mullets. While others can be sometimes line-caught, they are more commonly netted by professionals.

Some of the **mulloway** (jewfish) found in bays and estuaries are residents, others are only occasional visitors. They frequent areas around bridges, points, holes and creek mouths, where they hunt or ambush their favoured foods of small fish, prawns or squid. Live or dead baits of these are effective, as are large minnow-style lures. Mulloway are found in estuaries at any time of the year, their whereabouts being dependent on the presence of prawns, squid and schools of pilchard, mullet and whitebait on which they feed.

Juvenile **snapper** live in temperate bays and estuaries along the east coast of New South Wales and Queensland, while adult fish spend much of their time around offshore reefs. Periodically, however, big fish

Tuna and kingfish are the target at the Merimbula Wharf

Fishing from breakwalls is effective

WORKING THE TIDES

Estuary anglers must allow for the reversal every six hours of tidal flow, and alter their fishing spots accordingly. The most productive ends of reefs, structures, channels and gutters reverse with the tide. The sea entrance to an estuary is a good place to fish on a running tide, as fish passing from the estuary to the sea, or vice versa, must use this corridor.

As the tide falls, small fish, prawns and crabs leave the shelter of sand flats, weed areas and mangrove roots, and return to the channels, where the larger fish are waiting for them. A selected bait, cast into a channel at the right time, is likely to be grabbed by a fish expecting to feed. The main areas to fish at low tide are around structures, gutters and drop-offs, with the deepest holes carrying the best fish. Predatory fish such as flathead face the run of the tide, lurking around the edges of sandbars, gutters and channels waiting for smaller fish, prawns and food scraps to be drawn towards them.

At high tide the small fish, prawns and shellfish spread out, and the larger fish go after them and also the worms, crabs and other types of food that live around the flats and mangrove banks. This expands the range of fishing but makes it harder to pinpoint the spots where the fish are feeding. Structures, holes and gutters still exist and should remain the target.

Some fish break the rules and stay close to shelter behind structures and often close to overhanging banks or mangrove stands. Mangrove jack, for example, has to be sought in these sheltered spots.

Tides have less effect in the middle of an estuary or bay as the movement of water is not so strong.

Make sure you have a current tide chart for your area. The chart times relate to certain major points such as a port or headland. Work out the time variation of high and low tides between the places you normally fish and those named on the chart, and plan your trips around the tides.

One strategy is to gather bait at low tide and begin to fish along the channel edges and drop-offs as the tide rises and the water floods out of the channels. Equally, you could time your fishing to just before high tide, and fish the edges of the channels and drop-offs as the water recedes and the small creatures begin to be drawn back into the channels. In very shallow estuaries you must time your departure to avoid being left high and dry on a sandbank!

HOW TO FISH

Mullet

Mullet, of which there are many species, are found in estuaries and bays Australia wide. The sea mullet is mainly estuarine, moving out to sea to spawn.

do move into sheltered waters, usually in spring and summer, and are reasonably easy to catch. In summer, numbers of large adults are also found in Port Phillip and Western Port, in Victoria, and Gulf St Vincent and Spencer Gulf in South Australia.

There are some eight common species of **whiting**; of these the best known are the trumpeter and sand whiting of the eastern seaboard (a trumpter species is also found in Western Australia), the yellow-finned whiting of Western Australia and South Australia, and the King George whiting, plentiful in South Australia and Victoria, but less abundant in New South Wales, Tasmania and Western Australia. Whiting are a warm weather fish and leave estuaries in winter.

Barramundi and **mangrove jack** often co-exist in mangrove-lined tidal creeks, frequenting the intersections of main and feeder streams, as well as rocky points on bays and inshore islands.

Garfish are a common catch in estuaries and bays and, if you do not mind the small bones, are delicious food. They are even better as bait for larger fish. They can be berleyed up with bread or pollard and caught on tiny baits of uncooked prawn, fish flesh or bread dough. Use a light line attached to a slender float and small long-shanked hooks.

Leatherjacket are delicious to eat and easy to catch in good numbers once you have found their hiding places. These include deep water underneath jetties and alongside weed beds, and quiet corners of bays over mixed rock, weed and sand bottoms. Bait up with small baits on long-shanked hooks and periodically toss in a small handful of berley to keep them on the go.

Luderick mainly inhabit the east coast of New South Wales, Victoria and northern Tasmania. The adult fish are residents of the wash areas fronting ocean rocks. Luderick also spend much of their lives inside estuaries, bays and coastal lakes. Here, as juveniles up to about 30 cm, they stay and grow until ready for their run to the sea to spawn. After spawning migrations, some of them re-enter their home estuaries, others remain along the coastal shoreline or find new estuaries to call home. They take baits of green weed, sea-lettuce, squirt worms and pink nippers, and are usually best fished with a long flexible rod, light line and a float.

Tailor are common through New South Wales and southern Queensland, rare along the continent's southern coast, but in good numbers from the south to mid-coast of Western Australia. Known as the 'poor man's game fish', they are related to the bluefish of America, which grow to over 15 kg, but Australian tailor are usually under 2 kg. Most estuary tailor, known as 'choppers', are less than half that, but despite their size, they attack bait schools ferociously and will readily take either baits or lures.

Trevally frequent many estuaries, the silver variety being common in temperate zones, and species such as giant, golden, gold-spotted and bigeye usually found further north. Most trevally will take lures; all will take baits of small fish. Silvers will also take various worms, crustaceans and shellfish. Larger trevally are usually caught offshore.

Occasionally, but mainly in spring and summer, big, fast, ocean fish like **tuna** and **yellowtail kingfish** come into bays and large estuaries chasing schools of bait fish that are flushed in and out by warming waters and big tides. They can be a bit of a handful for beginners, being difficult to hook and even harder to land. Be aware that they exist, or you may wonder what kind of bream can rip 100 m of line off a reel – and then break free – all in a matter of seconds!

In the tropical north, estuaries can yield **pikey bream**, **barramundi**, **threadfin salmon**, **mangrove jack**, several types of **trevally**, **black jewfish (mulloway)**, **estuary cod** and **fingermark**. The list is longer, but these are the species you will most likely target and encounter. Lures are readily taken by all these species, but they also like to eat small live fish or large live prawns, so these make excellent baits. Because of the generally greater tidal range in the tropics, a tide chart is indispensable if you expect to catch anything worthwhile. Also the nature of tropical estuaries and creeks is such that you may find them easier to fish on the smaller neap tides than the much larger spring tides, which can scatter fish up into the mangrove forests where they become too hard to reach.

WORKING THE BAIT

Rather than casting your bait into the water and waiting passively for a bite, you will catch more fish if you have a more searching and aggressive approach.

Think about your casting spot: a shrimp sent towards a piece of sunken timber will be in a place where shrimps are numerous; a pilchard will look more normal 'swimming' along the edge of a gutter than lying inactive on the bottom.

Think about the way your bait will move. All marine creatures move; your bait should be lightly weighted so that it moves naturally in the currents of the water and at the depth appropriate for it. Sending a bomb weight to the deep will not attract many takers. Fish do not expect to see pieces of food, prawns or small fish coming towards them against the current. Your bait should look as if it is moving with the forces of the water.

Hold the rod so that you can feel the bite.

5

HOW TO FISH

Rock and Beach Fishing

Land-based saltwater fishing offers anglers the opportunity to roam and seek out a special place, often in remote and beautiful surroundings, perhaps to have a private battle with wind, wave and water or to enjoy the camaraderie of other experts. The fishing can range from a gentle beach activity to the challenge of ocean-ravaged rocks and cliffs.

The vast ocean shoreline of Australia affords land-based anglers great opportunities. Rocky ledges and headlands all along the coast are interspersed with long stretches of beach, often away from population centres and providing a fishing paradise for anglers.

Most capital cities in Australia are within easy reach of ocean beaches, readily accessed by two-wheel-drive vehicles. Visiting anglers can have a rod in the water within an hour or two of leaving home, and be back in time to provide the catch of the day for the evening meal. This book directs you to the best spots to fish within easy reach of your capital city.

For the more intrepid angler there are beaches in remote parts of the country, particularly in the west, north and north-east of Australia. A four-wheel-drive will often be required to reach these places that are 'off the beaten track'.

Rock fishing should always be approached with care. Some of the rocky platforms that front deep ocean water are exciting places to fish, but also demand that anglers exercise good sense and caution. When fishing from rocks at sea level, most of the threat comes from the water itself. Large waves can mount the rocks and wash the unwary in, and natural growths of weed and algae can make surfaces extremely slippery underfoot.

The dangers of high-cliff fishing are obvious. There are also hidden traps, such as sandstone ledges that can be worn treacherously thin by erosion and weakened by saltwater absorption. You need to approach any climb-in spots with particular caution. There are injuries and fatalities each year among anglers who have been careless or inexperienced.

WHEN TO FISH

When fishing this 'edge of Australia', the tides come into play in a marked way. Low water can virtually obliterate holes and gutters on a beach, sending fish out to deeper water. On the rocks, low tide can create a stretch of broken rock between you and the water into which you want to cast. High tides can improve the fishing opportunities or wipe them out – it all depends on the terrain and the weather.

By intelligently using tide charts and some knowledge of local terrain, you can prepare fishing plans that use the tides to best effect, and place you within safe and comfortable casting distance of fish that have been moved about by the changing water levels. An understanding of the feeding habits of your target species can help you focus your efforts on those times and places when the fish are likely to be in the greatest numbers.

The time of year is another important factor. The fishing from beach and rocks along the east coast of Australia is best from November to May. This period coincides with the warmer Pacific currents moving closer to shore, bringing with them the rich plankton, the bait fish and the larger fish that chase the bait schools. The further north you go the more extensive the fishing season becomes. The Great Barrier Reef protects the inshore waters and fish are present and active all year round, only being affected by the wet season.

The west coast is exposed to the big Indian Ocean swells. Here, pelagics such as

Channels and gutters form around wrecks providing productive fishing areas

HOW TO FISH

Time, tide, weather and terrain affect the success and safety of the rock angler

mackerel, tuna and shark can be taken all year round. The intense heat of summer can be very difficult for the angler north of Geraldton and Shark Bay, but plenty of fish are still present.

South from Perth, across the Bight to South Australia and into Victoria, the rock fishing is not as good, but there is excellent surf fishing in the cooler months for such species as tailor, Australian salmon, mulloway and gummy shark.

ROCK FISHING

Fish do not live in an environmental vacuum. They gather in places where it is easy, safe and productive to feed. These places relate to the underwater shape of the seabed. It is not always possible to see these bottom features clearly as the surging water off ocean rocks is often roiled and opaque.

Holes and gutters, and inshore reefs, which break the force of the surging water, attract and hold fish around the rocks. They allow fish to use eddies and back currents to keep their position near food. Rock crevices,

ROCK FISHING SAFETY

When you are rock fishing it is important to have a sure footing and to be constantly aware of your surroundings. A larger-than-normal wave can throw you off balance. Once you are off a ledge and in the sea, rescue can be difficult. It is wise to have an emergency procedure agreed between a fishing group so that equipment is at hand and there is no time lost if someone goes in.

Non-slip shoes and comfortable, waterproof clothing that is easy to remove if you go into the water, are part of the rock-hopper's gear.

Many high cliffs are of sandstone with overhangs that can be weakened by centuries of erosion and absorption of salt water. Never stand on thin ledges that overhang the cliff face, and be careful of wind gusts that could push you off balance.

If you are fishing close to the sea always keep an eye on the tide, waves and weather, as the pattern of waves can change quickly and a large wave can wash you into the water. Many victims were experienced anglers who had grown used to their location and become complacent about safety. If the safety rules are observed, cliff and rock fishing is basically a safe sport and a thrilling one.

ROCK AND BEACH FISH

barracouta	NSW, Vic., Tas., SA, WA
barracuda	WA, NT, Qld
barramundi	WA, NT, Qld
bonito	NSW, WA, Qld
bream, black	NSW, Vic., Tas., SA, WA, Qld
bream, pikey	WA, NT, Qld
bream, yellowfin	NSW, WA, Qld
cobia	NSW, WA, NT, Qld
cod, black	NSW
cod, coral	WA, NT, Qld
dart, swallowtail	NSW, Vic., SA, WA, Qld
drummer, silver	NSW, Vic., Tas., SA, WA
fingermark	WA, NT, Qld
flathead, dusky	NSW, Qld
flathead, sand	NSW, Vic., Tas., SA, WA, Qld
garfish	NSW, Vic., Tas., SA, WA, NT, Qld
groper	NSW, Tas., SA, WA, NT, Qld
gurnard	NSW, Vic., Tas., WA, Qld
jewfish, black	WA, NT, Qld
kingfish, yellowtail	NSW, Vic., Tas., SA, WA, Qld
ling	NSW, Vic., Tas., SA, WA
luderick	NSW, Vic., Tas., Qld
mackerel, grey	NSW, WA, NT, Qld
mackerel, school	NSW, WA, NT, Qld
mackerel, Spanish	NSW, WA, NT, Qld
mackerel, spotted	NSW, WA, NT, Qld
mullet, sea	NSW, Vic., Tas., SA, WA, NT, Qld
mullet, yelloweye	NSW, Vic., Tas., SA, WA
mulloway	NSW, Vic., SA, WA, Qld
parrotfish	NSW, Tas., WA, NT, Qld
pike, long-finned	NSW, Vic., Tas., SA, WA
queenfish	WA, NT, Qld
salmon, Australian	NSW, Vic., SA, WA
salmon, threadfin	WA, NT, Qld
shark, gummy	NSW, Vic., Tas., SA, WA
shark, school	NSW, Vic., Tas., SA, WA
shark, whaler	NSW, Vic., Tas., SA, WA, Qld
shark, white*	NSW, Vic., Tas., SA, WA
snapper	NSW, Vic., Tas., SA, WA, Qld
snook	NSW, Vic., Tas., SA, WA
sweep	NSW, Vic., Tas., SA, WA
tailor	NSW, Vic., Tas., SA, WA, Qld
trevally, bigeye	NSW, WA, NT, Qld
trevally, giant	NSW, WA, NT, Qld
trevally, golden	WA, NT, Qld
trevally, silver	NSW, Vic., Tas., SA, WA, Qld
tuna, mackerel	NSW, WA, NT, Qld
tuna, northern bluefin	NSW, WA, NT, Qld
tuna, southern bluefin	NSW, Vic., Tas., SA, WA
tuna, yellowfin	NSW, Vic., Tas., SA, WA, NT, Qld
whiting, King George	NSW, Vic., Tas., SA, WA
whiting, sand	NSW, Vic., Tas., Qld
whiting, trumpeter	NSW, Qld

*Denotes protected species

HOW TO FISH

READING THE BEACH

The most important element in beach fishing is being able to 'read' the beach and understand the undersea formations that make fish gather in search of food. Waves on an ocean beach will scour channels and make holes, gutters, sandbars and spits, creating natural places for feeding and predation.

Surf anglers take time to study a beach at low tide to see the patterns of the exposed sands and reefs, and again at high tide to look for the feeding places indicated by changes in colour and the movement of the waves. Swelling, unbroken waves indicate deeper water, while those that curl over and break indicate shallows. Rips or run-outs create gutters, which are detectable by short, choppy waves and the movement of white water out to sea.

Channels are the main arterial roads of the undersea system. They are deep water formations parallel to the beach, often extending well past the shoreline. Gutters are the minor roads, which fish use to travel between channels, into holes or shallow waters near the beach. The banks of the channels are the drop-offs where the predators wait, out of the main wave action, for their food. Sandbars and flats are indicated by breaking waves and foaming water that spread across them, sweeping small fish and food items into the drop-off areas. Holes can be identified by darker green or blue water, and in the way the wave formation is interrupted.

Regulars always check their favourite beach to see the changes that time and weather have wrought since their last visit. In rough weather tonnes of sand can be moved around in a few hours. A high vantage point, polaroids and binoculars are good aids in reading the beach, as the best time for reconnaissance is when the sun is high and the scene is not distorted by shadows.

Tailor is one of the main targets for beach anglers

stands of kelp and weed, and the foamy blanket of white water provide places to hide from predators. Small fish, including yellowtail, garfish and sweep, tend to school quite close to the rocks, but usually at some depth. Larger foraging species, such as bream, blackfish, drummer and groper, skirt the rock face and work in close under the line of white water. More active fish, like snapper, yellowtail kingfish, tailor and Australian salmon, roam a little further out, calling in to the shoreline to make feeding raids or to get away from larger predators. The big surface fish of the summer months, such as longtail and yellowfin tuna, shark and even marlin, will also move in close to the rocks in season, but spend most of their time in clear open water, travelling from one patch of concentrated food to another. Mulloway (jewfish), on the other hand, tend to keep close to particular reefs, caves and gutters, usually venturing out on hunting sprees at first or last light, or during the hours of darkness.

Basically there are two types of rock fishing practised around Australia. The first could be called baitfishing for species for the table. In southern Australia these species include parrotfish, sweep and pike, and further north along the New South Wales coast, luderick, rock blackfish, drummer, groper and even snapper are the more common catches.

The other method of rock fishing practised is often referred to as land-based game fishing, and ranges from high-speed spinning for tuna to various live-bait fishing techniques for species such as tuna, yellowtail kingfish, mackerel, giant trevally and even marlin. The species just depends on where you are fishing – Quobba on the west coast or the Pulpit on the east coast.

Your tackle should be appropriate for the fish and the conditions. It is helpful if rods are around 3 m or more. Your line should be a little heavier than that used in sheltered waters, both to withstand the punishment of the terrain, and also to control the fish, which will often be larger than those found in estuaries.

There will be times when your rod and line will not be strong enough to land some fish and, in these instances, a gaff on a suitably long pole is a practical fishing tool. Anglers fishing from high cliffs are faced with unique problems in landing fish, and they may need to use a grapnel or flying gaff to secure their played-out fish and hoist it up.

BEACH FISHING

In the same way that fish are attracted to depth and rock areas, and feed most freely around such features, they are selective and at least partly predictable in their use of various seabed structures when they visit ocean beaches.

There are differences, however, between the productive fishing areas around rocks and those around beaches. Rocky terrain may include gradually shallowing bottom shapes, steeply rising bomboras or even cliff-like rock walls; whatever form it takes, it remains a more or less permanent feature of that locality. In the case of beaches, however, the

HOW TO FISH

Watch the water when rock fishing at sea level

marine life. There may be channels, gutters, drop-offs and banks close inshore as well as further out. The tideline and close-in areas are the likely spots for foraging fish such as whiting, luderick and bream, while the gutters and holes are popular places of concealment for predators such as mulloway, salmon, tailor and flathead.

Gutters inside offshore sandbanks are excellent for whiting and bream, as the wave action over the bank dislodges amounts of sand and the food within it to the foraging fish. Whiting will surf with a wave over a sandbank and into a gutter to seek this sort of food.

Tailor, bream, flathead and salmon are very common beach fish and tend to inhabit the midline between the inshore waters and the outer gutters. Mulloway favour the deeper channels and holes, and are mostly night feeders, while shark and stingray can be encountered at any time, but also have their peak activity at night.

Beach fishing tackle, suitable for tailor, Australian salmon, bream and whiting, usually consists of a 3 to 3.5-m rod, and a reel of your choice spooled with 4 to 8-kg line. If targeting larger fish, such as mulloway or gummy shark, or fishing close to the rocky corners at either end of a beach, you may need heavier tackle or at least a trace of heavier line for insurance. These rocky corners are often good for bream, tailor, flathead or whiting, but also sometimes provide bonuses, such as rock blackfish, trevally and snapper, if you can fish close enough to the rock shelves running into deeper water.

BAIT

In many cases, the best baits available will be lying buried beneath the sand you are standing on – baits such as beachworms, sand crabs, or the ubiquitous shellfish known in various locales as pipis, eugaries or cockles. Other excellent beach baits include bait fish, such as pilchards, whitebait and bluebait and strip baits of fish such as tuna, squid and mussels.

Often, if you arrive at low tide, or the last of the run-out, you can gather your bait from the beach before you start to fish. The intertidal area inhabited by these sand dwellers is then freshly exposed and they are still close to the surface.

Be aware of the vulnerability of the stocks of these intertidal creatures, and observe any bag limits or prohibitions that may apply to a particular area. Such regulations are not there just to inconvenience you; they are part of an overall management system to protect the resource – for the benefit of you and other anglers.

operative fish-attracting features are anything but permanent, often changing from week to week, or in heavy weather, being altered completely in a matter of hours.

This means that on any given day, it is likely you will have to check the beach before fishing it to see what changes have occurred. In periods of stable weather, or in seas that are somewhat sheltered, formations may persist for a long time, only being worn away gradually by water movement. On more exposed beaches (which often fish better), the changes can be sudden and dramatic, and the unobservant angler is likely to pay by catching few fish or none at all.

Australia's classic deep beaches extend from Fraser Island on the east coast, south to Victoria, across the Bight then north along the coast of Western Australia to Shark Bay. North of Fraser Island and Shark Bay, the beaches become much shallower.

Beaches are not natural habitats for fish, but are more like highways and feeding places through which the fish pass. In the tideline areas there is an abundance of

TARGET FISH

Around the southern perimeter of Australia, beach species include bream, whiting, flathead, tailor, Australian salmon and mulloway, as well as various rays, skates and shark. From the rocks, you can add groper, drummer, rock blackfish, luderick, snapper, yellowtail kingfish and mackerel, and occasional visitors such as trevally, sweetlip, cobia, sailfish, marlin and yellowfin tuna, as well as various other surface speedsters such as bonito and striped and mackerel tuna.

THE BITE

This is the most exciting or frustrating part of the day, depending on your skill and luck. Some fish seem to catch themselves, some get away from even the most expert strike. While fishing, hold your finger on the line so that you can feel any bites. Keep the line slack so that you give the fish a chance to move with the bait. Most fish take the bait with an intake of water and then expel the water. The fish that does this hooks itself unless it senses trouble (a tight line or a tug) and expels the lot.

Once you feel you have a fish, lift the rod tip smartly (but not wildly) or give a steady pull on a handline (to set the hook). If you are in whiting territory do not waste time, as they are one-hit feeders and need to be hooked instantly.

HOW TO FISH

Offshore Fishing

Many boat anglers enjoy the adventure and variety of the ocean waters beyond the shore. Fishing around reefs and rocks, or over gravel beds, sand or mud; fishing the bottom with a heavy sinker and hooks on droppers; fishing with unweighted baits; drifting; trolling or fishing from an anchored position – all are options for the offshore angler.

Broadly, offshore fishing in Australia encompasses trolling for game and sportfish, bottom fishing with bait, jigging lures for reef-dwelling species or lure casting for sportfish around structures such as bomboras, reefs and washes. The size of the boat will depend on the seas likely to be encountered.

Most offshore fishing is done in proximity to land, near reefs, islands or the mainland shore itself. However, there is also good fishing to be had in more open water, where the influence of the structure of the seabed may not be so evident, but where the food-rich ocean currents play the major role in attracting offshore pelagic fish.

READING THE WATER

Inshore, around shallow reefs, headlands and islands, it is easy to recognise areas where fish might be gathered, but out in open water, it is different. Fish will be spread over a wide area and their whereabouts must be gauged by guesswork and intuition. Atmospheric conditions, such as light levels, wind and barometric pressure, and factors such as the clarity, turbulence, temperature and oxygen content of the water – all have an influence on fish presence

Islands can be viewed as enlarged structures, providing an ideal habitat for many fish species

OFFSHORE SAFETY

Fishing in the open sea, no matter how close to shore, demands attention to boat equipment. You need to have life jackets for all on board, a reliable motor, flares for attracting attention, and enough anchor rope or chain and ground tackle to anchor in water up to 60 m deep. You should always inform a responsible person of your fishing plans.

Caution is imperative when fishing around reefs, bomboras and exposed rocks, as waves can rise up and break from an apparently flat sea, or surge suddenly and push boats around – at worst onto rocks or coral. It is wise to keep the engine running in potentially dangerous situations, so that the boat can be instantly manoeuvred should trouble threaten. In calm water it is sometimes possible to anchor to a bombora, and then drift your baits and berley back into the eddy area behind the structure.

and behaviour, and all of these can affect the availability of food and the fish's willingness to bite. It is also important that you consider the prevailing conditions when deciding which baits and lures to use, and how to go about presenting them.

The colour of the water indicates temperature changes: warm water appears to be bluish, and colder water has a greener tinge. However, just how warm or cold the water is depends on where you are. Off Bermagui (south coast of New South Wales), a water temperature of 21 (Celsius might be considered warm, but off Townsville (north coast of Queensland) it would be regarded as a cold snap.

General light levels and the angle at which light falls on the water can also affect fish distribution and the willingness of fish to bite. Many species of fish prefer to feed under the cover of darkness, or at least at half light. Some fish that would not go anywhere near shallow water during the day, can be attracted by the half light of dawn or dusk, or the darkness of night to move into water barely deep enough to cover them, provided the pickings are rich enough to warrant the trouble. Others, in particular the pelagics like tuna and marlin, seem not to be affected by light.

The roughness of the sea not only determines your ability to venture offshore, it also affects general fish behaviour. A moderate degree of wind and wave action is beneficial to fishing, as the associated white water and wind chop allows fish to move about with reduced risk from predators.

Turbulence can also stimulate feeding, as there is often more to eat at such times. Wave action tears food loose from reefs and rock ledges. Prey species are driven by currents and wind into concentrations, providing an easily harvested food supply. Broken water also offers another prompt to fish activity: the ruptured surface film of the water allows higher than normal levels of oxygen from the atmosphere to be absorbed by the water. This boost in oxygen content both encourages and enables fish to maintain higher levels of sustained effort.

Fish that have a high metabolic rate feed almost constantly, and have a correspondingly high level of oxygen demand. Many surface-feeding species must roam extensively to find food; they burn up vast amounts of oxygen just

HOW TO FISH

Game fishing often requires the use of a harness and heavy tackle

to survive. Such species include mackerel, yellowtail kingfish, marlin, tailor and especially those frenetic speed merchants, the tunas.

Other more sedentary species, such as snapper, bream or mulloway, have generally slower metabolic rates, and less continuous periods of activity. They often browse, rest or drift with the moving water, generally close to cover and always where they are most comfortable. But when the occasion demands, they can move like lightning, either to feed, to drive off intruders or to flee from danger.

A shift of some kind in the surrounding conditions usually triggers localised reef fish to exert themselves and feed vigorously. It might be a tide change, a flush of warm current, the onset of bumpy weather, a different moon phase or the sudden arrival of an attractive, easily harvested food supply.

GAME FISHING

Game fishing is a popular pastime and places such as Cairns, Port Stephens, Bermagui, Port Fairy and Rottnest Island are well-known locations, some with an international reputation.

Thirty years ago most game fishing in Australia was conducted from large professional charter boats catering for a select few devotees. Nowadays there is an even larger and thriving charter-boat industry in addition to thousands of anglers who fish offshore in private craft from around 4 to 20 m in length.

Large game fish are likely to be where there are warm, blue, ocean currents pushing southwards from the tropics. Other indicators are surface-feeding schools of intermediate predators, such as striped tuna or frigate mackerel. These gather where currents and wind concentrate dense schools of tiny bait fish, juvenile squid or other planktonic larvae, such as those of crabs or lobsters. In turn, big fish, such as yellowfin tuna, marlin or shark, move in to feed and these smaller predators then become the prey.

Feeding pods of fish are often signposted by wheeling flocks of sea birds, but you can also stumble across them by trolling along current lines. Generally, the more current

OFFSHORE FISH	
albacore	NSW, Vic., Tas., SA, WA
amberjack	NSW, Vic., Tas., SA, WA, Qld
barracouta	NSW, Vic., Tas., SA, WA
barracuda	WA, NT, Qld
bonito	NSW, WA, Qld
cobia	NSW, WA, NT, Qld
cod, coral	WA, NT, Qld
dart	NSW, Vic., SA, WA, Qld
dolphin fish	NSW, WA, NT, Qld
emperor, red	WA, NT, Qld
emperor, spangled	WA, NT, Qld
grenadier, blue	NSW, Vic., Tas., SA, WA
gurnard	NSW, Vic., Tas., WA, Qld
jewfish, Westralian	WA
Job-fish	WA, NT, Qld
john dory	NSW, Vic., Tas., SA, WA
kingfish, yellowtail	NSW, Vic., Tas., SA, WA, Qld
mackerel, grey	NSW, WA, NT, Qld
mackerel, school	NSW, WA, NT, Qld
mackerel, Spanish	NSW, Tas., WA, NT, Qld
mackerel, spotted	NSW, WA, NT, Qld
marlin, black	NSW, Vic., Tas., WA, NT, Qld
marlin, blue	NSW, Vic., Tas., WA, Qld
marlin, striped	NSW, Vic., Tas., WA, Qld
morwong	NSW, Vic., Tas., SA, WA, Qld
mulloway	NSW, Vic., SA, WA, Qld
nannygai	NSW, Vic., Tas., SA, Qld
perch, pearl	NSW, WA, Qld
perch, sea	WA, NT, Qld
queenfish	WA, NT, Qld
sailfish	WA, NT, Qld
salmon, Australian	NSW, Vic., Tas., SA, WA
samson fish	NSW, WA, Qld
shark, gummy	NSW, Vic., Tas., SA, WA
shark, school	NSW, Vic., Tas., SA, WA
shark, others	NSW, Vic., Tas., SA, WA, NT, Qld
snapper	NSW, Vic., Tas., SA, WA, Qld
snapper, saddletail	NSW, WA, NT, Qld
spearfish, shortbill	NSW, WA, Qld
sweep	NSW, Vic., Tas., SA, WA
sweetlip, grass	WA, NT, Qld
sweetlip, red-throated	NSW, WA, NT, Qld
swordfish, broadbill	NSW, Vic., Tas., SA, WA, Qld
teraglin	NSW, Vic., Qld
trevalla, blue-eye	NSW, Vic., Tas., SA
trevally, bigeye	NSW, WA, NT, Qld
trevally, giant	NSW, WA, NT, Qld
trout, coral	WA, NT, Qld
trumpeter, bastard	NSW, Vic., Tas., SA, WA
trumpeter, real bastard	Tas.
trumpeter, Tasmanian	NSW, Vic., Tas., SA, WA
tuna, longtail	NSW, WA, NT, Qld
tuna, mackerel	NSW, WA, NT, Qld
tuna, southern bluefin	NSW, Vic., Tas., SA
tuna, striped	NSW, Vic., Tas., WA, Qld
tuna, yellowfin	NSW, Vic., Tas., SA, WA, NT, Qld
tuskfish	NSW, WA, NT, Qld
wahoo	NSW, WA, Qld
warehou	NSW, Vic., Tas., SA

HOW TO FISH

Islands provide excellent fishing conditions

ISLAND FISHING

Islands provide particularly good fishing conditions, as they are really an enlarged version of a structure and thus provide the feeding, resting and ambushing areas that are part of the pattern of predator and victim. They can be rocks in the ocean, like Montague Island, off New South Wales, or have their own beaches, reefs, estuaries and bays, like Kangaroo Island, South Australia.

The bulk of the island creates a break in the ocean current, in the same way as a log in a river has the water eddying around it. This produces a pressure-free zone on the upcurrent side of the island where predators can wait for the concentrations of food swept in by the current. The washes, rocks and holes are natural feeding stations for predatory fish.

The best island fishing is usually on the rougher, upcurrent side and along the currents that sweep around an island. Headlands and reefs create secondary concentrations of fish, while the lee side still has potential, as fish will rest and wait off the current for food.

---

lines and the warmer and bluer the water, the better. When such oceanic streams converge, they create ideal conditions, attracting whole food chains into specific areas.

Game fishing methods include trolling lures, trolling dead 'skip' baits, trolling live baits, fishing live or dead baits from a drifting boat and at times (although rarely) fishing baits from an anchored boat. Trolling lures or bait is by far the most popular method. Fast trolling large dead scad or tuna off Cairns accounts for the huge black marlin caught in those waters.

Further south the preferred method for larger marlin and yellowfin tuna is to slow troll live striped tuna. Other areas have other methods depending on the fish targeted.

REEF FISHING

Not everyone who fishes offshore, however, will set their sights on game fish, nor do they need to. Many other species of offshore fish cost less to catch, provide plenty of fishing fun and supply good seafood for the family table into the bargain. Fish, such as emperor, snapper, yellowtail kingfish, cobia, mackerel, tailor and mulloway, inhabit inshore reefs, headland and island areas, and can be pursued with smaller boats and less sophisticated tackle.

In southern Australia, fishing for such species does not require travelling far out to sea as most reef dwellers are found within a couple of kilometres of shore. Further north in Queensland and the top half of Western Australia this situation changes due to the shallowness of the inshore waters, and a run of many kilometres may be required.

While fishing offshore reefs for a variety of species on the bottom, there is often an opportunity to pursue many sportfish that come past. Small mackerel tuna, snook, queenfish, trevally and barracouta are some of the sportfish found around offshore reefs.

USING BERLEY OFFSHORE

While you can not change the water temperature or the weather, much less control the moon, you can time your trips to take advantage of them. Similarly, even though seasonal movements of bait and injections of storm-washed foods are beyond your organisational ability, you can fake such events by the use of berley. Berley is used in all forms of offshore fishing including game and sportfishing as well as fishing over a reef for bottom dwellers. Sending down a cloud of easily-gathered food among a bunch of sleepy fish can change their attitude dramatically.

Offshore berley can be made from pieces of fish flesh and various fish oils, either used alone, or mixed together and extended with some kind of cereal product,

HOW TO FISH

Yellowtail kingfish
This species, also known as yellowtail and kingfish, is found in southern Australian waters, from southern Queensland around to Shark Bay in Western Australia. Smaller specimens are caught from December to February but larger fish are best targeted in October and November.

such as bread, laying mash or stock-food pellets. It can be dispensed in various ways: through a berley bucket or berley bomb, or simply tossed over the side, a little at a time.

One technique used in game fishing for such species as yellowfin tuna is called 'cubing'. Small cubes of fresh tuna, 2 x 2 cm in size, are dropped into the ocean current from a drifting game boat. This sets up a long 'freeway' of enticing tid-bits, which after a couple of hours will stretch for a couple of kilometres. Tuna coming across the trail will simply follow it to the back of the boat, where the waiting angler is ready with live bait or a hook impaled cube. More conventional berleying techniques over reefs also produce results when the fish are not on the bite.

The key with berley is to use the right type and just enough to get the job done. A little, in a constant stream, is better than a big slug of it, then nothing. This is especially important offshore, where currents can take the berley away from you, and the fish with it. Remember do not feed the fish! Berley should only stimulate them.

Saltwater fly casting for tuna in the Gulf of Carpentaria

LOCATING THE CATCH

Regardless of the style of offshore fishing you pursue, it is important to fish in the right place, where all the hungry fish are congregated. Finding hungry fish in all that water relies on knowing the kinds of places fish frequent and how those places can be located.

A depth sounder can be a big advantage offshore and not only to tell the angler the depth of the water. Good sounders can easily pinpoint offshore reefs in 20 m of water and often locate fish over that structure as well. Used in conjunction with hydrographic charts, sounders enable anglers to return to the same location, particularly when out of sight of identifiable landmarks.

Having found your fish, all that is required is to determine the best rig and approach. While the 'right' tackle and baits remain fairly constant for certain species, the way you rig and go about presenting them will vary according to location and conditions. You do not need a rod and rig for every fish in the ocean, but you do need to take into account that fish differ in size, aggression and eating habits, and have a range of tackle on board to be adequately prepared. With much offshore fishing one needs a fair bit of lead to get down to the bottom.

At the simple end of things, you could get away with a set of light and heavy handlines, but by rod fishing you give yourself added versatility, being able to cast, troll, drift or bottom fish with a variety of baits or lures, or fish in a number of places for a range of species, from those that are small and slow to big fast deepwater game fish.

HANDLING

If you plan to return your catch to the water, handle it as little as possible because the slime coating of the fish protects it from disease. If you are intending to eat your catch, your first task is to kill the fish immediately, either by a sharp blow with a blunt instrument (the heel of your knife or a small hammer) between or above the eyes, a knife-stab in the same spot, or by breaking the bridge across the throat and bending the head back. The last process helps to bleed the fish, which improves the final eating quality of some species.

It is advisable to have an old towel to hold a landed fish, and a pair of pliers to remove the hook. This is a tricky process, as some fish such as flathead have protective spines and spurs that can inflict a wound. Many tropical fish, such as stonefish, red rock cod, butterfly cod and fortescue, have poisonous spines that can cause severe illness.

You should immediately remove the gut and the gills of the fish, but leave the scales on to keep the flesh moist. Gutting is simply done by making a shallow cut from the throat to the anus and scooping out the entrails with your knife. Run the knife along each side of the backbone to remove any remaining pockets of blood. Don't cut into the gut. The fish should be washed to remove external slime and placed on ice; within 5 to 15 minutes of capture in the tropics, where fish flesh degenerates rapidly.

At the end of the day you must complete the job of cleaning the fish and preparing it for the table. You need a scaling tool, a strong working knife and a fine, sharp scaling knife. Once you have scaled the fish the easiest way to fillet it is to cut the fish behind the head down to the backbone and then flatten the knife and cut along the bone towards the tail with a sawing motion, taking the fillet and the skin at the same time. Next you can remove the skin by making a cut at the tail and, while holding the skin with one hand, cut along the skin with a flattened knife. (See Cooking Your Catch.) Many fish have oily skins that affect the taste of the flesh.

Finally, wash and dry the fillet thoroughly and, if refrigeration is not at hand, roll it in plastic to keep it airtight. In Australia's hot climate it is mandatory to keep fish refrigerated or on ice at all times.

HOW TO FISH

Inland Fishing

To many, fly fishing is the pinnacle of fishing, the consummate battle between a skilled and patient angler and a noble opponent. But fly fishing is just one of the wide variety of freshwater fishing experiences available in Australia, each with its own excitement, fascination and keen devotees.

Australia is one of the driest continents on earth and the majority of its land mass is classed as desert. At first glance, it would seem that Australia is not well placed to provide a worthwhile freshwater fishery. After all, rain is needed for rivers and lakes – the habitat for freshwater fish.

Fortunately, while much of the Australian inland is very dry and virtually devoid of permanent waterways, the greater part of the coastal fringe enjoys good rainfall, and a resultant abundance of rivers and lakes. Even better, most of Australia's population lives on this fringe, giving them easy access to these same waterways, and some great freshwater fishing!

While there is no denying that inland waterways are beset by their share of environmental problems, a relatively small population (and a growing sense of environmental responsibility) means they have escaped the devastation that has claimed so many freshwater fisheries on other parts of the globe. Most inland waters remain public property and Australian anglers generally enjoy a right of access to rivers and lakes that would be the envy of those in many parts of the world, where huge fees can be paid for the 'privilege' of fishing in privately owned waters.

Most fresh water can be fished for the price of a licence. From the premier trout fisheries of Tasmania, to the giant barramundi of northern Australia, there is something for every angling taste. And whether your preference is for fly fishing, lure casting or baitfishing, there is sure to be a fishery not far away to indulge your sport.

BAITFISHING

At its most basic, baitfishing is the simplest and most widely known form of freshwater fishing. Even non-anglers are familiar with the concept of sitting beside a river holding a rod rigged with a sinker and a hook baited with a worm! Nowadays, baitfishing can be quite complex. For example, bait drifting – the casting and retrieving of virtually unweighted baits – requires perfectly tuned equipment and a good knowledge of natural baits.

Another form of baitfishing called coarse angling has all but developed into a distinct sport on its own, although the dividing line between it and conventional baitfishing is somewhat blurred. Coarse angling uses berley extensively: quantities of bread crumbs and similar mixtures to lure fish into the area the angler is fishing. Originally developed in the United Kingdom and Europe to fish for 'coarse' or non-game fish such as carp and tench, it is now very popular in Australia, where the techniques work on a wide range of species – even 'game' fish like trout. Many coarse anglers employ highly specialised equipment such as long and very sensitive rods and finely tuned floats, and choose from an array of surprisingly small hooks. Baits are also quite different to those normally used by regular bait fishers, and include maggots (gents), corn kernels and dough.

Despite the complexities of bait drifting and coarse angling, basic baitfishing remains a great technique for the casual angler, beginners and children. There is a delightful simplicity in a rod and threadline reel. Rigged with 3-kg line and either a small sinker or a float about half to one metre above a hook baited with a common bait like worms or shrimp, it remains a cheap, easy and quite effective method for catching many species. Redfin, eel, golden and silver perch, river blackfish, catfish, trout and sooty grunter are some fish that fall to basic baitfishing.

Of course learning about where to go, what type of water to fish, targeting a particular species, and the best way to present the right bait – all will help improve your catch. Fish cannot hear your yelling and screaming but they will be scared away by splashing, heavy vibrations and lots of movement on the bank such as waving arms especially if covered in bright clothes. Most successful anglers have learned that finesse; using light gear and carefully approaching the water helps success. Watch an accomplished angler at work and you will soon discover that the notion of fishing being based on luck is a myth!

LURE CASTING AND TROLLING LURES

Lure casting involves casting and retrieving lures: artificial creations made from metal, wood or plastic that either mimic bait fish and other fish food, or simply 'trigger' an attack response in fish. Trolling works on the same principle, only the lure is towed behind a moving boat. Lure casting and trolling work best on active predators including barramundi, sooty grunter, redfin, golden perch, Australian bass, trout and Murray cod.

Fly fishing is the art of casting almost weightless artificial lures called flies

HOW TO FISH

Like baitfishing, lure casting and trolling have become increasingly sophisticated in recent years. There are now endless varieties of lures on the market, including models that dive to great depth or wriggle along the surface. There are also spinners that have a flashing revolving blade, and even lures that contain a rattle to attract fish by vibrations. These days, anglers can purchase a range of Australian-made lures that are designed to appeal particularly to native species such as Murray cod, barramundi and bass.

Lure fishing can be as simple as trolling a wobbler behind a moving boat, or as complex as casting just the right lure to just the right location, and retrieving it at just the right speed and depth. Once again, experienced anglers target a particular fish species, and use gear that is not unnecessarily heavy.

FLY FISHING

Fly fishing is the art of casting almost weightless artificial lures called flies, which are made from materials such as fur and feather or modern substitutes. Because these flies have so little weight, conventional casting does not work. Instead, fly fishers use comparatively heavy lines (usually plastic wrapped around a braided core) and long flexible rods. The fly line is cast back and forth in the air until sufficient line speed is built up to enable the fly to be presented to the desired target.

The fly line is too thick to attach a hook, so a leader (a length of tapered fishing line) is linked to the end of the fly line, and to this is tied the fly itself. It takes practice to learn the timing and technique required to keep the fly line airborne and then deliver the final cast and present the fly. It is this element that has given rise to much of the mystique that surrounds fly fishing. Actually, a few days of informed practice is usually enough to cast well enough to begin catching fish, and some 'naturals' pick up fly casting in a few hours. It is worth noting

Baitfishing for species such as Murray cod and golden perch in the Condamine River, Queensland

FRESHWATER FISH

barramundi	WA, NT, Qld
Bass, Australian	NSW, Vic., Qld
blackfish, river	NSW, Vic., Tas., SA
bream, black	NSW, Vic., Tas., SA, WA
bream, bony	NSW, Vic., SA, WA, NT, Qld
carp, European	NSW, Vic., SA
catfish, eel-tailed	NSW, Vic., WA, Qld
catfish, fork-tailed	WA, NT, Qld
cod, eastern	NSW
cod, Mary River	Qld
cod, Murray	NSW, Vic., SA, Qld
eel, long-finned	NSW, Vic., Tas., Qld
eel, short-finned	NSW, Vic., Tas., Qld
fish, archer	WA, NT, Qld
garfish, northern	WA, NT, Qld
goldfish	NSW, Vic., SA, Qld
grayling, Australian	NSW*, Vic.*, Tas.*
grunter, leathery	Qld
grunter, sooty	WA, NT, Qld
herring, freshwater	All States (Vic.*)
jack, mangrove	WA, NT, Qld
long tom, freshwater	Qld
mullet, freshwater	NSW, Qld
perch, estuary	NSW, Vic., Tas.
perch, golden	NSW, Vic., SA, Qld
perch, jungle	Qld
perch, Macquarie	NSW*, Vic.
perch, silver	NSW, Vic., SA, Qld
redfin	NSW, Vic., Tas., SA, WA
roach	NSW, Vic., WA, NT, Qld
salmon, Atlantic	NSW, Vic., Tas., SA, WA
salmon, Chinook	NSW, Vic., Tas., SA
saratoga, northern	NT, Qld
saratoga, southern	Qld
sawfish	NSW, WA, NT, Qld
tench	Vic., Tas., SA
trout, brook	NSW, Vic., Tas.
trout, brown	NSW, Vic., Tas., SA, WA
trout, rainbow	NSW, Vic., Tas., SA, WA

*Species totally protected in this State

that baitfishing and lure casting, in addition to being productive in their own right, can provide a good grounding for anglers wishing to take up fly fishing.

Until recently, freshwater fly fishing was regarded as the sole domain of the trout angler. While trout are still the number one target of fly fishers, more anglers are discovering that nearly every fish that swims can be caught on the fly. Fly fishing for trout will always remain especially popular because trout respond so well to the technique. Trout frequently feed on small insects like mayflies or caddis that may be only fingernail size, floating on the surface. When 'rising' to such tiny, buoyant insects, trout are all but uncatchable to anyone but fly fishers using dry (floating) artificial flies – lure casters and bait fishers are driven mad at such times!

Wet (sinking) flies can be used for trout and many other species. The huge diversity of wet fly patterns available means that just about every form of aquatic life is realistically copied. It is the clever use of wet flies that has led to a recent boom in fly fishing for species such as Murray cod and golden perch. Unlike dry flies, which are usually left to drift naturally on lake or stream, wet flies are normally retrieved to impart a swimming motion that matches that of the organism being imitated.

Normanby River, Cape York: Northern Australia is renowned for its diversity of freshwater species

READING THE WATER

Despite all the other skills needed, the most important ingredient in freshwater fishing is reading the water: knowing where to lay that cast or run that bait or lure.

The habits of fish, either in fresh water or salt water, are predictable and this helps you to know where to seek them in rivers and lakes. They tend to position themselves near the main current flow, but not in it, and face into the current so that they can snatch up any morsels drifting with the current.

The biggest fish in any given area will take up the prized positions, in shelter but with the first chance at oncoming food. In rivers and streams they will be in the deeper, slower flowing sections – the pools or holes – and usually close to rapids or shallower sections that are washing food into the pools. The path of floating leaves or debris shows the natural places where the current is floating insects and other food.

In the heat of summer most fish, trout particularly, tend to go into the deeper water. The depth of pools can usually be gauged by the banks of rivers and lakes. A steeply sloping bank usually indicates deeper water. Fish like cover and protection, and some, such as Australian bass, estuary perch, Murray cod and barramundi, prefer the protection of underwater timber and overhanging branches. In apparently featureless water the smallest log may provide the hiding place for a fish.

Whether using wet or dry flies, fly fishers sometimes utilise an interesting technique called polaroiding. Polarised sunglasses remove much of the glare and reflection from the water surface, enabling much clearer vision beneath it. If light conditions and water clarity are favourable, fly fishers wearing polaroids can locate their target fish, and present their fly to the right spot. Polaroiding is particularly effective for trout anglers, but is gaining popularity among those chasing other species, such as golden perch. Although it sounds simple, polaroiding takes practice to perfect – most fish are well camouflaged, and skilled fly fishers often rely on little more than an unusual movement or the flash of a white mouth to locate their quarry.

Fly fishing is arguably the most complex style of freshwater fishing, particularly where trout are concerned, but it is also a lot of fun!

SOUTH-EASTERN AUSTRALIA

New South Wales, Victoria and Tasmania have abundant freshwater fishing on offer. The Great Dividing Range, which arcs south then west through New South Wales and Victoria, is the source of every significant river in these States. It is in and around these hills and mountains, in cool, clean water, that the trout, the most sought-after freshwater sportfish, is found. Trout are often erroneously described as 'alpine' fish, but in fact they are confined to very elevated habitat only in northern New South Wales. Further south they are found at lower elevations. In Victoria, trout thrive in many waters at or near sea level, and a long way from true mountain country. Across Bass Strait, Tasmania has arguably the cream of Australian trout fishing. This large island has proved an ideal habitat for trout, and most freshwater lakes and streams (and many estuaries) hold good numbers.

In all three States, trout are the only significant angling species in the true alpine country, but as the elevation decreases, trout begin to share their habitat with other angling species. Redfin co-exist with trout in many lakes and rivers, and extend beyond this range to inhabit many of the slower, warmer waters of the inland. Because of their abundance, redfin are a popular angling species, but they can dominate some waters because of their prolific breeding habits and voracious appetites. Also caught from immediately outside the alpine country through to the edge of the warm inland waters are two sought-after native fish: Macquarie perch and river blackfish. Macquarie perch is the rarer of the two, and does best in Victoria (it is protected in New South Wales). The totally protected trout cod is rarer again, and should always be carefully returned to the water alive if caught.

Three superb warm-water natives, Murray cod, golden perch and silver perch, are making a strong comeback in many inland waters in Victoria and New South Wales, particularly those that flow west into the Murray–Darling system. Modern breeding programs and efforts to improve habitat mean that these fish are once more a viable angling option in south-eastern Australia. They are also making a comeback into several impoundments that previously held only trout and redfin. Lakes such as Burrinjuck, Hume and Eildon now offer a blend of cool and warm-water species.

HOW TO FISH

The coastal streams of New South Wales contain another top native sportfish, the Australian bass. As one moves into coastal Victoria, these fish are replaced by a less well-known relative, the estuary perch. Bass, in particular, have returned to sportfishing prominence in recent years, thanks in part to a major scientific breakthrough that has enabled large-scale hatchery breeding, and the stocking of artificial lakes.

Of the four south-eastern States, South Australia is the poorest for freshwater fishing, simply because so much of it is desert country devoid of permanent lakes and rivers. However, the Murray River does offer fishing for golden perch, silver perch, Murray cod and redfin, and smaller streams around Adelaide contain some trout stocks, especially after a succession of wet years.

As well as the species already mentioned, anglers in south-eastern freshwater areas may also encounter eel and tench, and that most destructive invader, the European carp. Carp are considered to be responsible for damaging the habitat of many south-eastern waters, and every care should be taken to ensure they do not spread beyond their present range. Any carp caught should be killed immediately.

WESTERN AUSTRALIA

The largest State provides an enormous variety of freshwater fishing commensurate with its range of freshwater environments. The south-western corner has a temperate climate similar to Victoria and southern New South Wales. Not surprisingly, this area is the home of the west's trout fishery. Though not as successful as in the eastern States, trout have done quite well in a number of rivers and lakes, and some very big trout are caught each year.

Redfin are very successful in the south-west, and frequently overlap with trout. Native angling species of significance are rare in the area, although the locals enjoy catching a delicious crustacean called marron.

From just north of Perth through to the start of the Kimberley, freshwater fishing is limited. The country is very dry and there are few permanent waterways. Small natives provide the only freshwater fishing.

There is an abrupt change for the better once the remote tropics of the Kimberley are reached. Heavy monsoonal rains over summer feed a number of major rivers, and many permanent and semi-permanent lagoons. These waters are home to numerous tropical species, the most famous of which is the barramundi, one of Australia's premier sportfish. As well as barramundi, freshwater anglers may encounter species as diverse as long tom, giant catfish and various species of perch.

NORTHERN AUSTRALIA

The Top End of the Northern Territory, Queensland's Cape York Peninsula and the Gulf Country that separates the two, provide a continuation of the excellent tropical freshwater fishing found in the Kimberley. Barramundi continues to be the most prized sportfish, with species like sooty grunter and saratoga also popular. But the list of potential angling species is endless, as this area has perhaps the greatest diversity of fish in the country. Much of the tropical north is very difficult to access due to the lack of roads and, by southern standards, freshwater areas are relatively free from fishing pressure.

Moving south from Cape York Peninsula, Queensland freshwater fishing changes. Barramundi becomes less common, and ambitious stocking programs for impoundments have improved freshwater fishing significantly. Lake Tinaroo on the Atherton Tableland is showing great promise for land-locked barramundi, and consistently produces enormous sooty grunter. Further south, stocking with other species like golden perch, bass and saratoga is proving successful.

The Darling River feeder streams west of the Great Divide provide native fish like those found further down the system, with golden perch especially abundant. Catfish are found in eastern-flowing streams, with jungle perch in some tropical mountain streams in the north, and Mary River cod in the Maryborough area. South of the Noosa River, Australian bass can be caught in the coastal rivers where the habitat is suitable.

THE INLAND

Beyond the coastal rivers and the Murray–Darling system lies the dry inner core of Australia, containing rare small pockets of water inhabited by tiny, hardy fish that have no angling appeal. In a few places with slightly higher rainfall, mountain gorges or the termination of distant catchments provide larger waterholes where tough natives such as golden perch survive. The quality of the fishing most of the time would not be enough to warrant the long, difficult journey.

LANDING THE FISH

Do not try to reel the fish in and land it. The reel is not for dragging fish, but for taking up the slack or playing out line while you fight the fish and eventually bring it in.

A fish is never caught until it is in the boat or on the wharf. A last flurry of energy at any time close to retrieval may well dislodge a hook that is not fully set.

Jetty anglers are at peril of losing the fish if the pier platform is a long way above the water. It is best if the fish is exhausted so that it remains passive at the critical point when it leaves the water and its full weight comes onto the line as you bring it in. It is likely to make a last run under the jetty, so you have to be prepared to play out line and begin the process of bringing it back to the point of retrieval.

Fish should not be lifted from the water on a line if it can be avoided. For boat anglers a net or a short gaff (a large hook connected to a piece of cane) can be employed to secure the fish. On a jetty a long gaff, flying gaff or grapnel can be used.

If you use a gaff, align the hook with the side of the fish and insert it into the flesh, bringing it in at an angle that easily penetrates the protective scales. Aim for the bulkiest part of the fish but avoid touching the belly.

If your fish is too small, a species that you would prefer to release or one more than you need for the day, slip it back into the water as gently as possible. There are usually pier steps that will get you closer to the water level for this.

Remember that our fisheries are a precious resource. The only reason for killing a fish is for bait, for the table or if it is a pest species.

Underwater timber provides protection for native species

HOW TO FISH

Rods and Reels

The perfect fishing outfit will be chosen for a certain style of fishing while retaining some versatility. The rod will be neither too heavy nor too light for the line and vice versa, and the reel and terminal tackle will complement both. Overall, a good outfit will feel comfortable and balanced in the hand. Your angling abilities should be enhanced by the gear you choose, not diminished.

A wide variety of fishing styles has created a staggering array of equipment, each designed for a particular purpose. Before you buy, you will need to work out your fishing preferences. It is best to know something about all the components of a fishing outfit and then find the particular combinations to suit your needs.

RODS

There are hundreds of different types of fishing rods available. Twenty years ago, multi-purpose rods were common; today, rods are made of space-age materials and usually designed for specific uses. Some rods can be used for two or three applications. For example a double-handed, pistol-grip rod can be used for lure casting for barramundi, bait fishing for snapper and drifting for flathead. When selecting a rod, its length, action and power should be considered.

Rods can be broadly classified as light, medium and heavy, but within these categories there is also a variety of types usually made for particular reels.

Long, heavier rods are used for beach fishing

LIGHT RODS

Light rods are the most common type, as they are generally used in the popular pursuits of freshwater and estuary angling. Among the light rods are single-handed spinning rods, single-handed plugs and fly rods. They should have a whippy tip that will easily cast lightweight lures and sinkers, and should have a solid feel at the base.

Generally, the shortest rods are for baitcaster reels, which are designed for accurate lure or light bait casting. These rods usually have a pistol grip for controlled casting. Single-handed light rods are used to cast light baits and lures.

MEDIUM RODS

Medium rods include double-handed plugs, double-handed spinning rods and boat rods. A medium rod, measuring between 2.5 and 3.3 m, is very versatile and can be used for either heavier estuary and bay fishing, or for beach and rock work. It can give a longer cast when necessary, but retain enough sensitivity for accuracy. It should have a tip responsive enough to cast a bait or lure as little as 50 g in weight. These rods are often used with threadline and sidecast reels. Rods in this category will easily cast distances between 50 and 80 m due to their length and power, if matched with appropriate line diameter.

HEAVY RODS

Rock and surf threadlines, overhead and sidecast threadlines, game rods and jig rods are examples of heavy rods. A heavy, long outfit is used for beach, rock and jetty casting. Measuring between 2.8 and 3.8 m, it needs good weight in the lower half and a tip rigid enough to throw a rig weighing up to 100 g, with a line up to 20-kg breaking strain. They are used mainly with sidecast and overhead reels.

REELS

Just as there is no such thing as an all-purpose rod, there is no all-purpose reel. Nobody would put a huge reel on a light rod or vice versa; matching a rod and reel is very important. Your selection has to be based on your perceived needs and personal preference. This is an important choice and advice from a reputable retailer or experienced angler should be considered. The rod, when placed on one hand just ahead of the reel, should be at the point of balance, neither tip-heavy nor butt-heavy.

THREADLINES

These reels are more accurately described as fixed-spool reels and are mounted underneath the rod. They are versatile and easy to use, and excellent for general fishing. Threadlines suit

ROD TALK

The way the rod curves when it is under load is called its action. The way it narrows from its butt to its tip is called its taper. The most common rods have a medium taper and medium action, bending down to about two-thirds of the rod under pressure and being easier to cast for the less expert angler.

Rods that taper gradually from butt to tip are called slow taper rods and have a parabolic action, with the entire rod bending as the load pressure increases. They are favoured by fly and luderick anglers as they cast more gently and accurately, and exert minimum pressure on a hooked fish.

Fast action rods taper quickly at the top from a thick butt. Under pressure, the top third of the rod bends while the butt is not affected. They are popular with boat anglers for trolling, jigging, spinning and lure casting; and with rock and beach anglers. They deliver a long, fast cast. Light fast-taper rods are used in light-line spinning.

SOME TACKLE COMBINATIONS

Rod	Reel	Line	Casting weight	Swivel size	Hook size
1.5–2.2	baitcast	1.3 kg	6–30 g	16–10	12–1/0
	threadline	3–5 kg	10–50 g	2–8	6–5/0
1.7–2.8	threadline	4–8 kg	20–70 g	10–8	4–4/0
	sidecast	6–10 kg	30–80 g	0–6	4–6/0
2.5–3.7	sidecast	6–15 kg	50–120 g	6–4	1–8/0
	overhead	8–20 kg	70–150 g	6–4	2/0–10/0

HOW TO FISH

Spinning rods with threadline reels
Designed to cast all types of artificial lures, spinning rods need to be as light as possible for angler comfort during hours of repetitive casting and retrieving. A medium-action rod is best for general spinning. Anglers concentrating on fishing surface lures require a stiffer tip-actioned rod. Light threadline reels are ideal for spinning with the lightest of lures and cast more efficiently than baitcaster/overhead reels. The long butt section on the third model makes the rod more suitable for trolling in fresh water or estuaries, and is useful for longer casts in salt water.

Fly rod and reel
Designed specifically for casting a fly line as far as possible, fly rods bend with a gradual curve to deliver the fly line smoothly. It is vital to match reel and line with the rod. Fly rods are from 1.8 to 3.3 m long. A simple centre-pin reel is used with a drag to prevent line over-run when casting. Fly reels are often drilled to lessen the weight and to provide ventilation for the line to dry.

Double-handed pistol grip rod with baitcaster reel
These rods are used for casting lures accurately for medium to heavy-weight fish such as barramundi and Murray cod. Matching reels are medium to heavy-weight baitcasters.

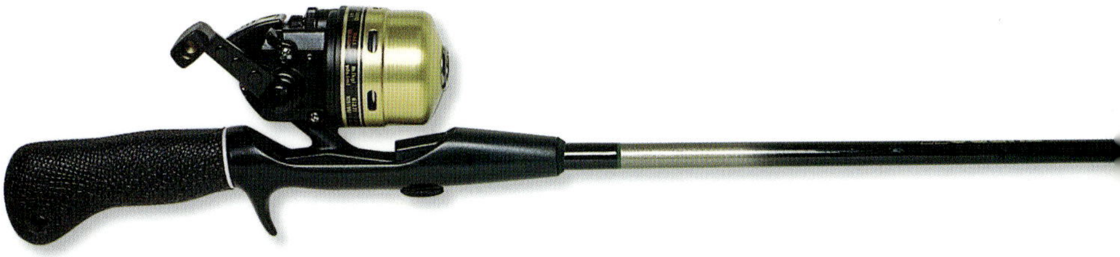

Single-handed pistol grip rod and closed-face reel
Used for estuary and light freshwater angling for fish such as Australian bass and bream. Suitable reels for use with this type of rod are small baitcasters, or closed-face reels.

19

HOW TO FISH

Young anglers quickly learn the fundamentals of fishing

Offshore rods are designed to handle maximum stress. A rod bucket is a useful support

fishing with lures or bait, and can handle most freshwater, estuary and some beach and rock fishing; they work best with an 8-kg breaking strength line or less. When cast, line must travel across the edge of the spool, and thin line offers less resistance.

Since their spools are relatively small, using thick line on threadlines means you cannot fit much line on the reel. Heavy line will not help you get the best out of such gear; it will simply inhibit the reel's casting ability and reduce the amount of line you have to play out.

OVERHEAD REELS

So called because they are mounted on top of, or 'over', the rod, these come in a range of sizes from small baitcasters, through medium-sized surf or jig reels, to heavy-duty trolling reels. Baitcasters can cast lures over short distances with great accuracy, while surf or jig reels suit beach, rock or boat spinning, bottom fishing, jigging or light tackle live-baiting. Game fishing or trolling reels are the big models in this group and are used to capture the large pelagics such as tuna and marlin.

One type of overhead will not suit all fishing jobs. For example, you would not chase large game fish on a baitcaster, or try to cast any distance with a large, heavy-spooled game reel. You might be able to use a baitcaster or a mid-sized, good quality jig reel, for both a bit of light tackle fishing and maybe some ambitious fishing for a few heavyweights (provided you have the skill and some luck).

SIDECAST REELS

The sidecast reel is an Australian innovation made by the Brisbane-based Alvey reel company. Sidecasts are popular with beach and rock anglers, and also many boat anglers. The reel has some advantages over both threadlines and overheads. To cast, the spool is rotated 90°, allowing the line to flow off the reel almost unimpeded. Unlike an overhead, there is no spool inertia to overcome, so light casting weights can be easily flicked out. Their main advantage is that unweighted baits, which so often attract big fish, can be fished on line that is heavy enough to keep hooked whoppers under control.

MAINTENANCE

Rods and reels should be separated when not in use and stored out of the weather. After each outing they should be washed with warm fresh water and dried, and the moving parts of the reels oiled regularly. If you do not feel competent to repair a faulty mechanism, take it to a tackle shop. You might also want the shop to strip, clean and oil your reel every year or so.

The mechanical advantage of a sidecast's direct drive and large spool diameter enables you to wind line in against considerable pressure. Small fish can be brought in quickly, and hefty fish can be battled and beaten, then winched from the water.

CLOSED-FACE REELS

Sometimes called 'pushbutton' or 'spincast' reels, these small reels sit on top of the rod like a baitcaster, have a fixed spool like a threadline, but differ in that the spool is enclosed behind a front cover, which has a hole in the middle through which the line can pass.

Closed-face reels can be used with either lures or bait, and are very simple to operate, but since they have very limited line capacity, they are only suitable for freshwater and light saltwater use.

HANDCASTER

The simplest system of all is the handline or handcaster. Handlines can be as simple as line on a cylinder of cork, and these are commonly available in tackle shops. A plastic ring with a curved spooling lip is more generally favoured, as the larger diameter of the ring allows line to be more easily wound in. To cast, you can strip a couple of metres of line from the lip and throw your tackle out, holding the lipped side of the ring towards the casting area. The line will play out over the lip and any slack can easily be wound back.

Rods and reels need to be compatible with line sizes, casting weights and rigs in use, and all should suit the fish and the terrain.

DRAGS ON REELS

Most reels have drag systems of various kinds which prevent a hooked fish from running effortlessly. The drag system requires a running fish to haul the line from the reel, thus (theoretically!) preventing the fish from making line-breaking jolts or pulls against immovable resistance. The drag also tires the fish and allows it to be 'played'. The drag setting should be well below the line strength, say at 4 kg for a 10-kg line.

HOW TO FISH

Leger rod with threadline reel

Leger rods are most commonly used for advanced baitfishing techniques in fresh water and estuaries. They usually have a solid glass nibble tip for the last 30 cm of the rod. Threadline reels are a popular reel type for use with leger rods.

Float rod with threadline reel

Float rods around 3.7 to 4 m in length are used mostly for freshwater bait fishing. Longer rods, between 4.3 and 4.6 m, are better when fishing salt water and for species such as luderick. Threadline reels work best with these rods: in fresh water, with lines between 1 and 3 kg; in salt water, with lines between 3 and 6 kg.

Game and sportfishing rods with overhead reels

These rods are designed to handle maximum stress and to apply maximum leverage for powerful game fish. Usually 1.6 to 2 m long, they are highly specialised, single-purpose rods. Game fishing reels are large overhead reels used for bluewater fishing where strength, enormous line capacity, heavy-duty braking and an efficient, heat dissipating drag system are necessary.

Sidecast rod with Alvey reel

These rods most commonly range in length between 3.5 to 4 m. Sidecast rods with a slow taper are needed for soft baits and float rigs. Fast tapered rods are required for big baits and big fish. They are popular with beach, rock and boat anglers. A sidecast reel is often used with this rod because of the way it allows line to flow off the reel, although practice is necessary to avoid line twist and tangles.

Surf rod with threadline reel

Surf rods are usually heavier and longer to assist casting over long distances. This particular reel is designed for heavy duty spinning in either salt or fresh water.

21

HOW TO FISH

Hooks, Lines and Sinkers

Hooks and sinkers are part of a host of items that are described as terminal tackle. Despite their simple functions, their design is often complex and there are innumerable variations available, each designed for a particular purpose. Work out your fishing preferences, then find the particular combinations to suit your needs. The golden rule is to keep it simple.

HOOKS

Hooks used for fishing range from size 14 to size 1 in the smaller sizes, the larger number designating the smaller hook. Larger hooks range upwards from size 1/0 to 20/0. Specialized hooks, some much smaller than size 14, are used for tying very small flies.

A detailed discourse on hook patterns or designs is not appropriate here as is clearly indicated by the fact that leading hook manufacturer, Mustad of Norway, currently has the capacity to produce some 25,000 different hook patterns.

Dedicated anglers seeking large, or trophy-size fish, usually sharpen their hooks. However, the recent introduction of hardened steel, pre-sharpened hooks, which are usually marketed as chemically sharpened hooks, has made the sharpening stone redundant by anglers using them.

The point on chemically sharpened hooks is created by a brew of corrosive chemicals that is applied to hooks to get rid of irregularities and produce a smooth needle-point that maximises penetrating power. It is more like polishing than sharpening, although by improving the penetration power of the point it can accurately be said to sharpen the hook.

The recent introduction of small, light-gauge 'circle' hooks has also benefited anglers because of their superior holding capacity over 'J' pattern hooks. However, care needs to be taken when baiting circles so that the gap between point and shank is not obscured.

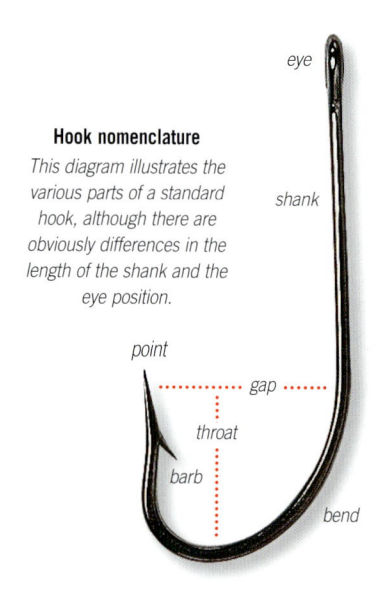

Hook nomenclature
This diagram illustrates the various parts of a standard hook, although there are obviously differences in the length of the shank and the eye position.

Sliced-shanks
These can be suicides or other styles; what makes them special is that there are barbs formed in the shank. These help bait presentation by holding the bait up and preventing it sliding down and bunching unnaturally in the bend of the hook.

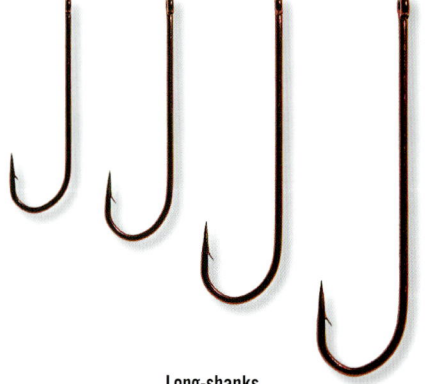

Long-shanks
These suit fish with teeth that can bite through line. Fish such as leatherjacket need sizes 12 to 8, and flathead, sizes 2/0 to 5/0. They can also be used to catch small bait fish.

Suicides
These are recurved or 'beak' hooks with a turned up eye and fairly short shank. Sizes 2 to 10 are for carrying trout baits like mudeyes, shrimp and earthworms; for bream, sizes 1 to 2/0 carry baits like prawns, fish strips and pipis; and for snapper, mulloway and yellowtail kingfish, use sizes 3/0 to 6/0.

Forged hooks
This hook has a flattened shank, which helps resist damage by the fish's jaws. Forged hooks generally suit heavy rather than light tackle. This hook type works well for groper, drummer, rock blackfish, snapper and mulloway; or open water speedsters like mackerel, trevally, yellowtail kingfish, tuna and marlin.

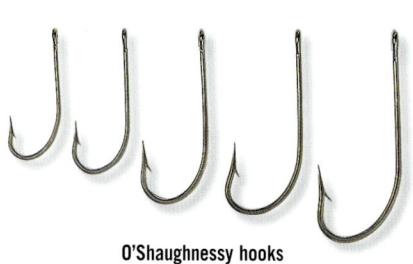

O'Shaughnessy hooks
These stainless steel, multi-purpose hooks can be used anytime and anywhere, in fresh or salt water. They are most commonly used in salt water for snapper, Australian salmon and flathead.

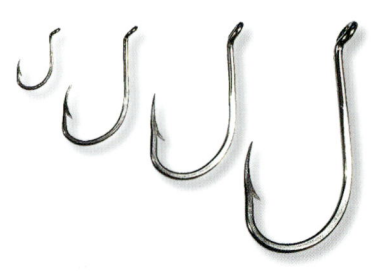

Treble hooks
Treble hooks are designed for use on lures and need to be replaced, along with the split rings holding them, regularly. Any suggestion that a treble hook gives the angler three times the chance of hooking a fish is simply wrong.

HOW TO FISH

LINES

Nylon monofilament fishing lines have dominated the fishing line market for more than fifty years in all sizes and can usually be joined or rigged, using just a few basic knots.

The chief disadvantage of nylon monofilament is its elasticity. This becomes a problem when there is lot of line out, for example when playing a very large fish, or when fishing on the bottom in very deep water.

Woven dacron lines with minimal stretch are available but are more expensive than monofilament. Dedicated game-fishermen who use dacron lines readily attest to the advantages of reduced elasticity which permits large game fish like marlin to be subdued more quickly, an especially important consideration if the fish is to be released.

Polyethylene gelspun fishing lines are much stronger than other fishing lines of comparable diameter. This coupled with their low stretch and high sensitivity makes them ideal for bottom fishing in deep water. However, careful attention needs to be made when tying knots or unexpected separations may occur.

Specialized lines, like those used for fly-fishing, and dedicated leader materials, are separate subjects and require a more detailed description than space allows for here.

monofilament
monofilament
co-polymer
braided dacron
polyethylene gel-spun braid
polyethylene-spun braid with monofilament core
fly line
monofilament
polyethylene gel-spun braid

SINKERS

Sinkers come in a wide range of weights and designs. Some have a ring or eye at one end so that they can be tied to the end of the line. These are called fixed sinkers. Others have a hole through the centre through which the line is threaded so they slide along the line. These are called running sinkers.

Split shot are small lead spheres which are split half way through so that they may be clamped onto the line, often to provide additional weight to ballast a float, or to sink a buoyant bait. With these factors in mind, choosing a sinker of the correct design is fairly easy.

Choosing the correct type and weight of sinker is a matter of judgement which comes with experience, but the use of a sinker which is either too heavy or too light, is soon indicated by difficulty in casting or holding bottom.

Several dozen barrel sinkers are sometimes threaded onto hand-lines used for trolling. They are then crimped at close intervals along the line so that the bait or lure is presented some distance below the surface of the water.

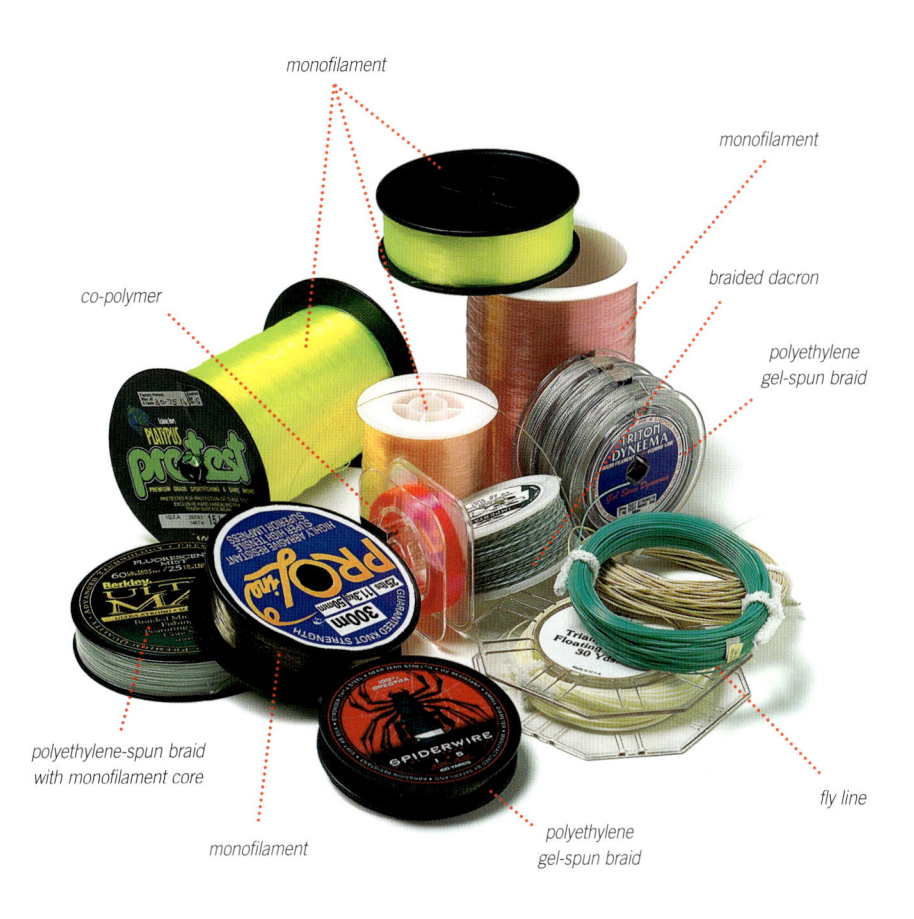

A general range of all-purpose sinkers for use in saltwater and freshwater situations; beans (top left and bottom); barrels (left); balls (top right and mid right); bug (centre)

Star sinkers, used for surf fishing. These come in a large range of sizes

Bomb or teardrop sinkers used for saltwater fishing; the largest ones in surf, rock or boat situations, the smaller variety with either heavy or light tackle in heavy or light saltwater situations

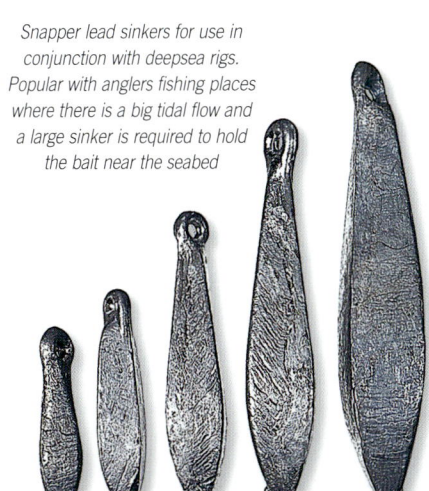

Snapper lead sinkers for use in conjunction with deepsea rigs. Popular with anglers fishing places where there is a big tidal flow and a large sinker is required to hold the bait near the seabed

23

HOW TO FISH

FLOATS

The primary function of a float is to suspend bait at a predetermined depth. When the depth at which the bait is to be presented is modest, say not more than 1.5 metres, a fixed float is used.

When the depth is greater than that allowed by a fixed float, then a running float, which is free to slide along the line between two stoppers, is used.

A running float enables the angler to cast out with the float resting on the bottom stopper. However, when the rig hits the water, the bait sinks, drawing line through the float until the top stopper comes to rest at the top of the float.

A variation of the running float is the bubble float, which is rigged in tandem with a second smaller float as a bottom stopper. The bubble itself is partially filled with water to make it heavy enough to cast out. When a fish takes the bait, only the small float submerges, the line being free to pass through the larger bubble float without resistance.

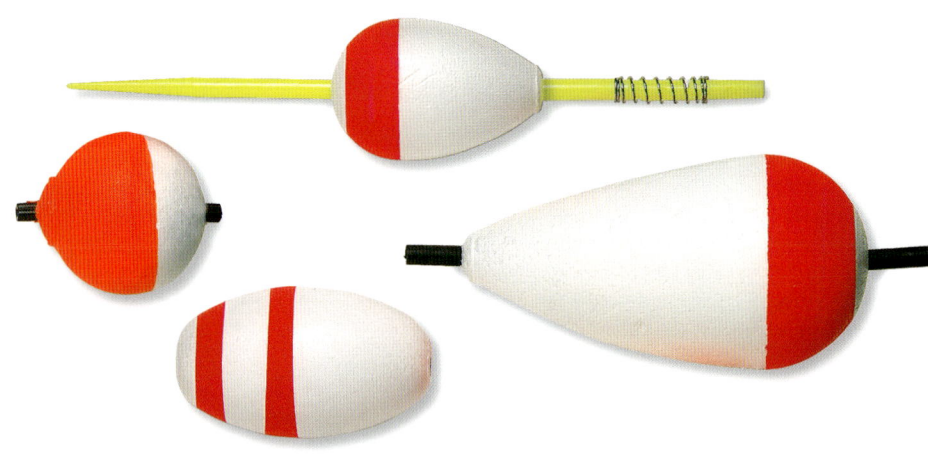

Polystyrene floats
These torpedo-shaped floats are particularly suited to live baiting off the rocks. Designed for heavier baits, the larger pear-shaped versions work well in rough seas when fishing for tailor, drummer or snapper.

Bubble floats
Bubble floats, usually made of plastic, are designed to be partially filled with water to assist casting. They are mainly used for baitfishing in fresh water. Some are coloured or luminous to aid visibility.

Coarse angling: Stick floats
These floats are used mainly in moving fresh water such as rivers and creeks. The line is usually attached to the top and the bottom with the aid of a small plastic grommet. Split shot is used to weigh them so that 80 to 90 per cent is submerged.

Coarse angling: Waggler floats
These are used in fresh still waters such as lakes and impoundments. The line is attached to the bottom of the float only, via a ring. The line is pinned either side with split shot, weighted so only the tip shows above the water. This prevents fast drifting in high winds.

HOW TO FISH

SWIVELS AND RINGS

The primary objectives of swivels are to eliminate line twist and provide a point to which the line may be tied.

Unfortunately, even the best swivels do not eliminate line twist completely, and their efficiency is further reduced as the size of the swivel increases in comparison to the line being used.

Swivels sometimes incorporate additional features like a third eyelet, as in the case of a cross-line swivel, or a wire snap-lock to enable the easy attachment of a pre-rigged leader.

Game fishers often use ball-bearing snap-lock swivels. These are designed for heavy fishing applications where the amount of pressure likely to be applied through the line could pull a normal snap swivel free. Snaps are suitable for quick changing ready-made terminal rigs or lures when trolling or spinning.

Swivel sizes are categorized like hooks with the smallest swivels beginning at number 14 and increasing in size to number 1, then 1/0, 2/0 etc.

Black barrel swivels of various sizes, used to keep the twist out of the line, as a link or join, and as a sinker stop.

Black ball bearing swivels. Larger sizes are used in heavy saltwater and game fishing and the smaller sizes for light to medium saltwater fishing.

Brass swivels. The larger variety incorporate a barrel with safety snap; the smaller ones have an interlock snap. Snap swivels are used in conjunction with bladed lures.

Black snap swivels, used in conjunction with minnow lures or bladed lures. Swivels allow the lures to move around without the line twisting.

Brass barrel swivels and three-way crossline swivels. The latter are multi-purpose, allowing for various attachments to the rig. Use in salt and fresh water depending on size.

Black ball bearing snap-lock swivel, which can be used in conjunction with traces and lures. The black colour is preferable to the brass in some situations for camouflage reasons.

TRACES AND LEADERS

The term trace and leader are interchangeable, but in common usage, the term leader usually refers to an extended length or separate length of heavier line on which a lure or hook is rigged as is the practice when game fishing.

The term 'trace' usually refers to a separate, often quite short length of line to which a hook is tied. When sharks, or other fish with sharp teeth are sought, then a wire trace or leader may be used to reduce the chance of being bitten off.

Wire is also incorporated in some commercially prepared terminal rigs for bottom fishing. These are also constructed with wire snap-locks at their extremities, so hooks and sinkers may be easily attached. These rigs make no concession to timid fish, but will take the occasional fish when they are abundant and 'on the bite'.

In some situations, the leader on which the hook is tied is lighter than the main line. The best example is in freshwater fly-fishing where the fly, which is really a 'dressed' hook, is tied to the fine end of a tapered leader.

Nylon trace encompasses any heavier than normal main line traces. Often used for snapper, barramundi, tuna and marlin.

Nylon-coated pre-rigged wire trace, available in various lengths and breaking strains, is most often used in conjunction with lures. At times used with bait but only recommended if fish are aggressive and traces are required.

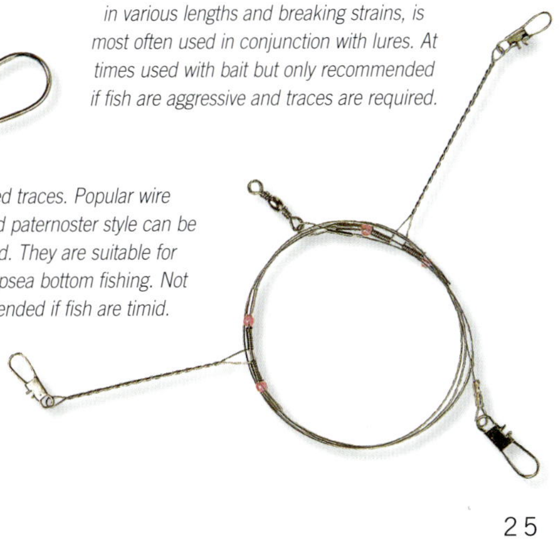

Pre-rigged traces. Popular wire traces rigged paternoster style can be purchased. They are suitable for surf to deepsea bottom fishing. Not recommended if fish are timid.

25

HOW TO FISH

Lures and Flies

At one time, lures and flies were carefully fashioned to imitate as closely as possible the prey of the target fish. Today, many lures and flies are unrecognisable as prey; some even come in fluorescent colours. But they are 'real' to the target fish, which can be duped into taking a lure or a fly providing it looks appealing, behaves correctly and is presented in the right place at the right time in the right way.

LURES

There are thousands of different types of lures made. There are floating lures, sinking lures, huge half-metre-long lures for marlin and tiny micro jigs for trout. There are lures for trolling, casting, jigging, flipping, pitching and just about any other style of fishing one can imagine.

Whatever the type, the principle remains the same: a lure is used in the hope that it represents the prey of the target fish such that it will fool the fish into making a strike. Thus it is critical that the lure matches in some way the natural food of the fish. A lure need not be an exact resemblance of the prey in appearance; as long as it represents particular features of the prey such as movement and colour, it will be successful.

The main groups of lures are minnows, surface lures, soft plastics, skirted trolling lures, spinner blade lures, spoons and slices, Tassie lures and jigs. Of these, the minnow group is one of the most popular styles of lures that are available.

Spinner blade lures
One of the best styles of lure for trout is the basic spinner. These spinners are designed to be cast and retrieved, but are rarely trolled as they can produce excessive line twist.

Soft plastics
Classic soft plastic fishing involves slow jigging or jerking of the lure over the bottom structure. As the hook is embedded in the soft plastic itself, the lure is virtually snag proof. Soft plastics work well on native fish such as Murray cod, golden perch and impoundment bass.

Jigs
Jigs, despite the variety of shapes and sizes, are all designed to be worked or jigged vertically. Small marabou jigs are excellent for trout in rivers, but remember to free drift and not retrieve them. Larger and heavier bucktail jigs account for dozens of fish species in salt water from snapper to many other reef dwellers.

FLIES

The term artificial flies describes a huge range of fish deceiving creations, primarily constructed with fur and feathers, or artificial substitutes. Most are so light they are unable to be cast; they must be presented using a fly line where the weight of the line takes the fly to the fish.

The different types of flies are often categorised by whether the fly floats or sinks, and by the type of food imitated. Dry flies float on the water surface; wet flies are designed to fish below the surface.

Flies are most popular for trout fishing in fresh water, but many other species including Australian bass, Murray cod, barramundi, tuna, flathead and bream will take a fly.

Saltwater fly fishing has become popular. Most saltwater flies are wet, and are usually larger than freshwater flies.

Red Humpy   *Kelly's Hopper*   *Gum Beetle*   *Red Tag*

Freshwater dry flies: Terrestrial
This group represents terrestrial insects, ranging from tiny midges to large beetles, that fall onto the water surface.

Barry Lodge's Emerger   *Blue Dun*   *Black Spinner*   *Elk Hair Caddis*

Freshwater dry flies: Aquatic
These represent insects that live underwater during their nymphal stage and then hatch on or return to, the water surface as airborne insects, such as mayfly, caddis and damselflies.

HOW TO FISH

Skirted trolling lures
These lures are used almost exclusively as trolling lures and almost always in salt water. They are trolled fast behind a boat in offshore fishing grounds for pelagic fish such as tuna, marlin or sailfish.

Tassie lures
The Tassie lure is an Australian invention that combines a minnow profile with an enticing action all of its own. They are primarily designed to be trolled in fresh water for trout and are easily one of the most effective designs for this type of fishing. They account for many fish taken in salt water as well, but are yet to gain widespread acceptance by saltwater anglers.

Spoons and slices
These are primarily designed to be cast and retrieved at a range of retrieve speeds. The more slim the profile, the faster the retrieve; the larger and wider the profile, the slower the retrieve. These lures can catch almost any fish that swims in salt or fresh water.

Minnows
This group is designed to resemble and behave like prey that will entice a strike from a larger predator. There are a variety of general types: floating divers, sinking divers, floating deep divers and neutral buoyancy lures. Minnow lures will catch many species of fish in both salt and fresh water, and they can either be cast or trolled behind a boat.

Surface lures
Surface lures are designed mainly to be cast and retrieved, and are rarely trolled behind a boat. They float on or near the surface and make a considerable disturbance on the surface when retrieved. This disturbance often attracts predator fish to the surface to smash the lure, sometimes in a spectacular fashion.

Bead-head Nymph   *Damselfly Nymph*   *Brown Nymph*

Freshwater wet flies: Nymphs
These patterns are particularly successful with trout. They represent the aquatic nymphal stage of some freshwater insects including mudeyes (dragonfly nymphs) and caddis.

Mrs Simpson   *Craigs Nightime*   *Tom Jones*

Freshwater wet flies: General
These represent aquatic animals such as bait fish (like galaxias), tadpoles, water beetles and shrimp.

Weed Wizard   *Green Lizard*   *Deep Pink Thing*

Red Marabou   *G. D. Deceiver*

Saltwater flies
Wet flies: These are used in salt water for fish ranging from barramundi to flathead, and bream to marlin. Wet flies usually represent such prey as bait fish and cephalopods.
Poppers: These are dry flies used in both salt and fresh water. They are designed to stimulate a fish's propensity to strike a food source on the surface; for example, a Deer Hair Muddler for trout, a big polystyrene popper for marlin or sailfish.

Knots and Rigs

Practical knots are essential for successful angling and it is absolutely necessary to have a series of knots at your disposal to cater for the various rigging situations required for the different styles of fishing.

KNOTS

The full blood knot is probably the strongest to use for tying a hook, ring, or swivel to nylon monofilament. Limitations are only experienced when the line or leader is too heavy, or stiff, to permit the knot to be pulled tight.

The perfection loop is used for tying lure to leader because it does not impede the action of the lure. It is also useful for attaching fly to leader or tippet because it lays straight and does not cock to one side.

The double blood knot is useful for joining nylon monofilament lines of the same or similar size. Limitations are experienced when attempting to join lines of markedly different sizes.

RIGS

The basic rig is the Paternoster rig – one that is useful offshore, in bays and estuaries, and occasionally in fresh water. To make this rig correctly, you must learn the simple techniques of tying a tagless dropper loop and a blood bight loop, then all you do is put them together.

Another useful rig is the running sinker rig, which may be constructed in a number of ways using rings, swivels and even patented 'easy' running devices. These rigs are very suitable for estuary and freshwater fishing.

Perfection Loop

Attaching a lure to a heavy monofilament leader is the main use of the perfection loop.

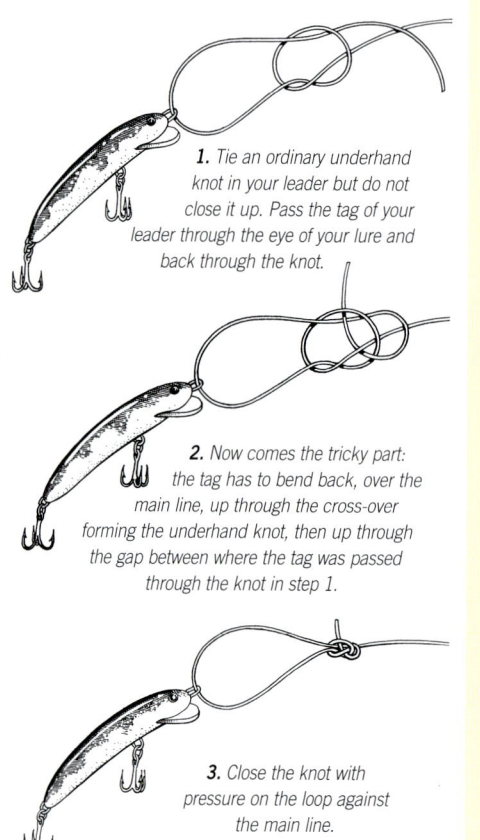

1. Tie an ordinary underhand knot in your leader but do not close it up. Pass the tag of your leader through the eye of your lure and back through the knot.

2. Now comes the tricky part: the tag has to bend back, over the main line, up through the cross-over forming the underhand knot, then up through the gap between where the tag was passed through the knot in step 1.

3. Close the knot with pressure on the loop against the main line.

FULL BLOOD KNOT

If bay and estuary anglers were limited to using one knot, the full blood knot would be a good choice. At its best in lines from 3 to 30 kg, this knot is easy to tie and retains around 80 per cent of the line's strength.

Pass the tag of the line to be tied through the eye of the hook.

Pass it through a second time so that a circle within a loop is formed. This circle-loop formation should be retained through the following steps for the best results.

Wrap the tag around the main line as shown. Do this three to six times; more for lighter line, less for heavier line.

Having completed the required number of wraps, pass the tag back through the central loop and pull the knot tight.

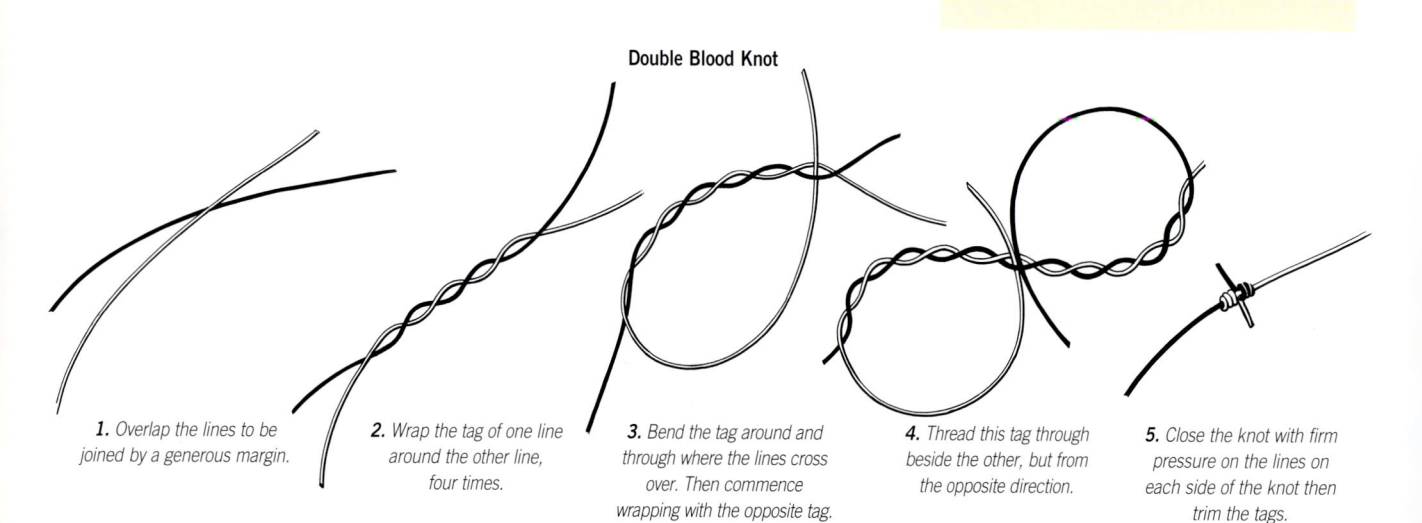

Double Blood Knot

1. Overlap the lines to be joined by a generous margin.

2. Wrap the tag of one line around the other line, four times.

3. Bend the tag around and through where the lines cross over. Then commence wrapping with the opposite tag.

4. Thread this tag through beside the other, but from the opposite direction.

5. Close the knot with firm pressure on the lines on each side of the knot then trim the tags.

HOW TO FISH

Paternoster rig

To put together the rig, first tie a tagless dropper loop. This can be tied anywhere along the line enabling the angler to use multiple droppers. To attach the sinker and the dropper line to the hook, tie a blood bight loop.

Tagless Dropper Loop

This method allows the angler to tie a loop that will not slip anywhere along the line.

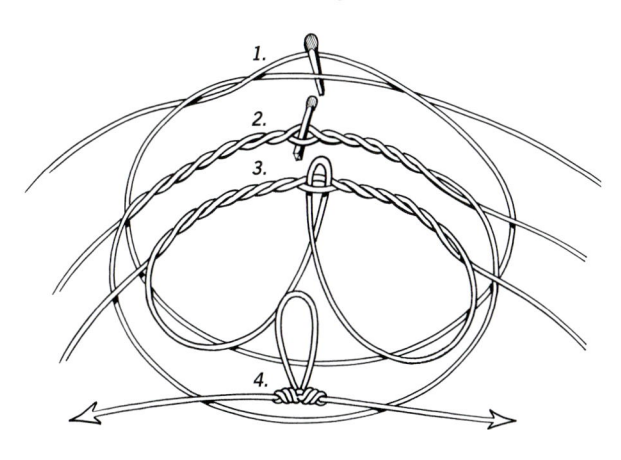

1. Make a loop in your line and insert a match or something similar to one side of the crossover.

2. Rotate the match through three or four complete turns.

3. Remove the match and insert the loop through the same wrap from where you removed the match.

4. Close the knot with pressure on each side of the loop.

Blood Bight Loop

This is a loop for attaching droppers or snoods to a dropper loop in the main line.

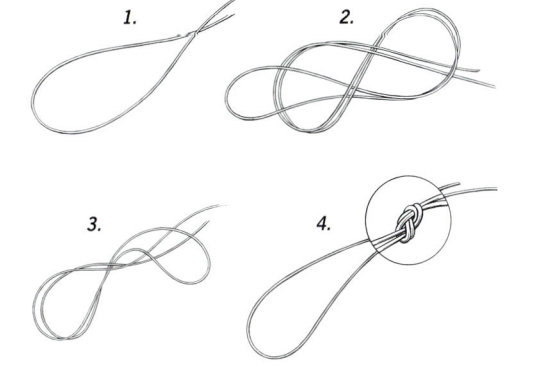

1. Make a loop in the opposite end of the dropper to the hook.

2. Bend the loop back on itself to form a second loop.

3. Thread the first loop through the second so that you have a figure-of-eight configuration.

4. Pull the knot up and trim the tag. The inset shows the appearance of the knot.

Making a Paternoster rig

Join the two loops together by interlocking.

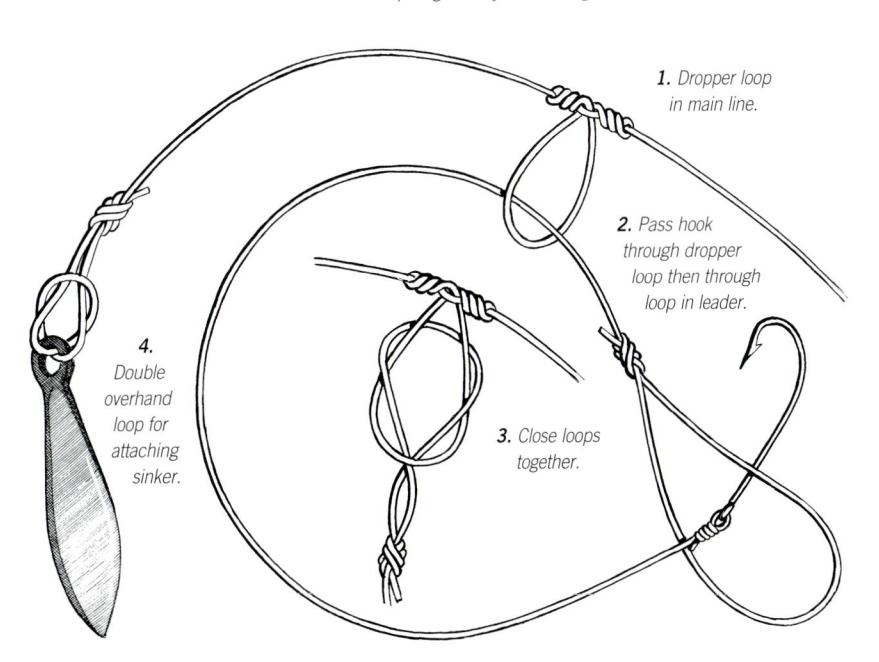

1. Dropper loop in main line.

2. Pass hook through dropper loop then through loop in leader.

3. Close loops together.

4. Double overhand loop for attaching sinker.

Running Sinker rig

The purpose of a running sinker rig is to allow the line to run freely through the sinker when a fish picks up and then pulls on the bait. Sinkers used for this rig should have a hole through them, the larger the better.

Shown is a running sinker rig in its simplest form with a small ball sinker threaded onto the line and running all the way down to the hook. This rig works well but has no provision for a heavier leader. As well, only very small sinkers can be used to avoid damage to the bait when casting out.

This rig employs a swivel stop above the hook enabling the use of a wider range of sinker weights and leader strengths.

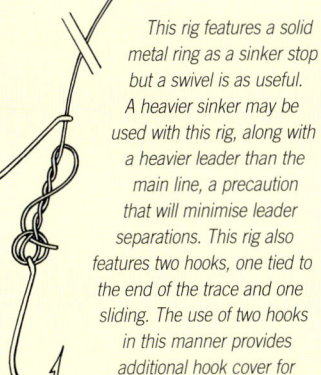

This rig features a solid metal ring as a sinker stop but a swivel is as useful. A heavier sinker may be used with this rig, along with a heavier leader than the main line, a precaution that will minimise leader separations. This rig also features two hooks, one tied to the end of the trace and one sliding. The use of two hooks in this manner provides additional hook cover for larger baits.

Shown is the Ezy rig by Symmetric Sinkers, which features a plastic barrel threaded onto the line in the same manner as a running sinker. The clip on the plastic barrel permits heavier or lighter sinkers to be used as the tidal stream increases or slows. The bomb style sinker is most suited for use with the Ezy rig.

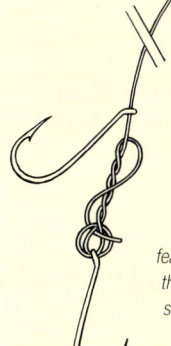

29

HOW TO FISH

All About Bait

Fish will respond best to a bait that is presented as naturally and attractively as possible. It should be a bait that offers no reason for the fish to become suspicious or alarmed and, preferably, one that is a naturally occurring food item in the habitat of the target fish.

SALTWATER BAITS

A fussy fish, and there are many of these, will often baulk at something that seems unnatural in the water, is unfamiliar or stale. A well presented bait freshly procured from the bait grounds where one is fishing works almost every time.

A fish's attraction to bait is partly visual, but mostly has to do with taste, smell and touch. For this reason, contaminants such as sun cream, insect repellent and some kinds of food, such as bananas, onion and oranges, can turn fish off. Even some human odours, such as pherenomes exuded from the skin and pores, can have a detrimental effect. There is a good reason to use masking substances such as various fish attractant solutions, or simply 'washing' your hands with bait, much like you would with soap.

Fresh and live baits work best because they secrete various chemical signals that stimulate fish to feed. These natural chemicals are, however, labile; that is, they become dispersed and destroyed on contact with air and water. Dead or cut baits lose their attraction very rapidly, while live baits continue to exude chemical strike triggers for a short time but, as fatigue and stress mount, the production of these attractants slows down. This is why you can often get a result by pulling in a bait that has lain untouched for some time and replacing it with a fresh one.

The key to baitfishing is to realise that you are talking about food. Fish food, it is true, but food nonetheless, and to understand the importance of top grade bait, look no further than your own preference for fresh and attractively presented food.

Anchovies
Good estuary bait. Use for snapper, tailor and other estuary-type species.

Mussels
A good bait for whiting and bream. The shell and remains can be used as berley.

Whitebait
A popular bait fish that attracts a wide range of estuary species.

Beachworm
Use for bream, luderick and whiting.

Squid (bottley squid shown here)
A good general purpose bait for snapper, flathead and whiting.

Pilchards or mulies
One of Australia's most widely used bait fish.

Prawns
Use for estuary and bay fishing.

Pippis
One of the better all-round baits. Target fish are whiting, bream and Australian salmon.

30

HOW TO FISH

POPULAR SALTWATER BAITS

Description	Location	Method of catching	Buying	Storage	Target fish
Bait fish (whole dead or live garfish, pilchards, hardyheads, whitebait, slimy mackerel, poddy mullet, fish strips, cubes, slabs)	Estuaries over sand flats and weed beds or in deep water near wharves; close to ocean rocks.	Line fishing, scoop netting, trapping.	Fresh or frozen from most bait outlets.	Keep alive for a day or overnight in broad, shallow container, open to the air. Refrigerate dead fish overnight; salt or freeze for longer periods.	Dead: drift or cast whole fish or pieces for flathead, large bream, tailor, snapper, mulloway, barramundi, tuna, mackerel; rig and troll large whole fish for pelagics. Live: drift or troll for tuna, mackerel, shark, john dory, flathead, barramundi.
Beachworms	Intertidal area of shelving ocean beaches.	Entice to surface with 'stink' bait of dead fish; look for 'V' wake as wave recedes, grab with fingers or worming pliers.	Available live, frozen and preserved from bait outlets.	Roll live worms in dry sand for temporary storage; keep cool in covered shallow dish overnight.	Bream, flathead, whiting, luderick, Australian salmon, mulloway, dart, javelin fish.
Crabs (whole, live or dead; or dead, cut into pieces)	Intertidal shoreline of estuary mud and sand flats; rocks on coastal shoreline.	By hand.	Difficult to buy.	Keep live overnight in 8 cm of water in bucket with aerator. Dead crabs do not keep well.	Bream in estuaries, groper and big bream from ocean rocks.
Cunjevoi (cunje)	Intertidal zone of ocean rocks and rocky shoreline of open bays.	Cut casing with strong knife and remove flesh of animal.	Some bait outlets.	Freeze in sealed containers or use same day; keep cool and damp.	Bream, drummer, groper.
Estuarine worms (bloodworms, squirt worms, tube worms blubber worms)	Saltwater creeks, tidal mud and sand flats, exposed weedbeds.	Dig blood and tube worms; pump or pressurise squirt worms; dig tube worms and blubber worms.	Preserved and live bloodworms available from bait outlets.	Live worms best used immediately; refrigerate preserved worms.	Bream, flathead, whiting, Australian salmon, luderick, mulloway, javelin fish.
Green nippers (green shrimp, mud shrimp, pistol prawn, snapping shrimp)	Intertidal mudflats and seagrass beds; under logs, rocks and debris exposed by falling tide.	Pump as for pink nippers; tread shallows over weed beds until shrimp float to top of muddy water; turn over debris.	Rarely available for sale.	Overnight in bucket of clean aerated sea water.	All estuary species and some inshore species.
Green weed	Estuary shorelines, quiet bays especially; some ocean or bay rock platforms.	Rake or by hand.	Bait outlets. Wrap in paper, not plastic.	Foam Esky, or wrapped in newspaper and kept cool in fridge.	Luderick in estuaries and from ocean rocks; also rock blackfish.
Mussels	Wharf and bridge pylons, oyster rack timbers.	Hand pick or use mussel rake to remove from beds.	Bait outlets, fish shops.	Keep live for 2 to 3 days in sealed container in fridge; freeze as dead baits.	Most estuary species, especially whiting when slit into thin strips.
Pink nippers (bass yabbies, yabbies, ghost shrimp)	Intertidal estuary sand and mudflats.	Pump from sand by placing yabby pump over holes.	Sold live from some bait outlets.	Overnight in bucket of clean aerated sea water.	All estuary species and some inshore species.
Pippis (eugaries, wongs, Goolwa cockles in SA)	Intertidal zone of surf beaches.	Hand-dig under raised mounds, or look for twin siphon holes and 'V' wake as wave recedes.	Most bait outlets.	Keep live for 2 to 3 days in sealed container in fridge; freeze as dead baits.	Bream, flathead, whiting, tailor, garfish, mullet, Australian salmon.
Prawns	Estuaries and coastal lakes.	As for shrimp; or with lights and scoop, or drag nets at night when no moon.	Bait outlets.	Live: in wet weed and hessian or in aerated bucket. Dead: on ice for 1 to 2 days, or freeze for longer.	All estuary fish, and also inshore species. Peeled prawns good offshore for morwong and snapper.
Sea cabbage (cabbage, sea lettuce)	Intertidal zone of ocean rocks.	Pick by hand.	Rarely available for sale.	As for green weed.	As for green weed.
Shrimp	Weed beds, tidal creeks.	Push prawn scoop through weed beds, or disturb with garden rake and scoop up escaping shrimp.	Difficult to buy, but seasonally available in some localities.	Live: in wet weed and hessian or in aerated bucket. Dead: on ice for 1 to 2 days, or freeze for longer.	All estuary fish.
Squid (calamari, flying squid)	Offshore or bays near rocks or jetties.	Yo Zuri squid jig or baited squid jig.	From bait outlets.	Freeze or refrigerate.	Whole squid for pelagics; strips for estuary species.

HOW TO FISH

FRESHWATER BAITS

As with saltwater baits, the best freshwater baits are those that are gathered fresh from the area where you are fishing. They should be presented live if practical and as naturally as possible.

A very interesting side of baitfishing emerges when angling in fresh water that runs down into estuarine rivers and lakes. Here, marine baits, such as prawns and shrimp, can be taken by bass from one spot and bream from another only metres downstream.

In some Victorian lakes, saltwater whitebait have been used with success on land-locked salmon and, in various large New South Wales water storages, trout have fallen to cooked saltwater prawns. The counterpoint is that bream have been seen smashing live cicadas from the surface, just like a bass. There are some universal baits that 'travel' well, and they will work just about anywhere. This does not, however, invalidate the principle of selecting baits that the fish might expect to see in their habitat.

The traditional trout fishing ploy of examining the stomach contents of captured fish is wonderfully enlightening, once you wash and sift through the contents to identify what it is that the fish have been eating. Such examinations will often reveal that much of the diet of freshwater fish is insects and, because it is so difficult to mount all but the largest of insects on a hook, one can see why artificial fly fishing came into being.

Large insects, like grasshoppers, mudeyes, beetles, cicadas, and various larvae of moths, beetles and so on, are all prime candidates for freshwater baits. So are small foragers, such as galaxias, gudgeons and many others. Crustaceans are important too. Various forms of shrimp and yabbies work on everything from barramundi to trout. Worms and grubs – the quintessential bait of small children and truant executives alike – are dynamite on a range of freshwater fish. There are even various shellfish found inside captured fish, but these present rigging difficulties which mean they are seldom used.

As with saltwater baitfishing, bait selection, rigging and methods of presentation are of paramount importance. The same rules apply: show the fish something it likes to eat and expects to see, and put it where it can be eaten without risk to the fish.

When baitfishing in either fresh or salt water, care should be taken to prevent the escape of live baits not taken from the same water you are fishing. Leftover live baits should be returned to the water from whence they came.

Maggots
Used for a range of freshwater fishing particularly for smaller species. Especially popular when coarse fishing for trout, redfin and tench.

Earthworms
A popular bait that attracts most freshwater species including trout, redfin, silver perch and eel.

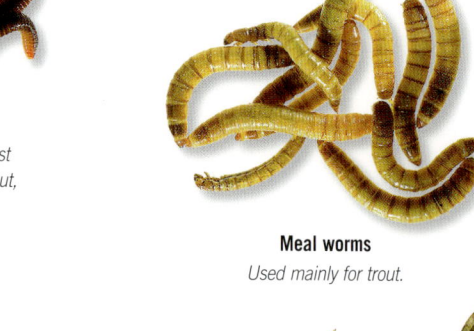

Mudeyes
These larvae of dragonflies are one of the most effective trout baits. Sometimes expensive, or difficult to find, especially during winter.

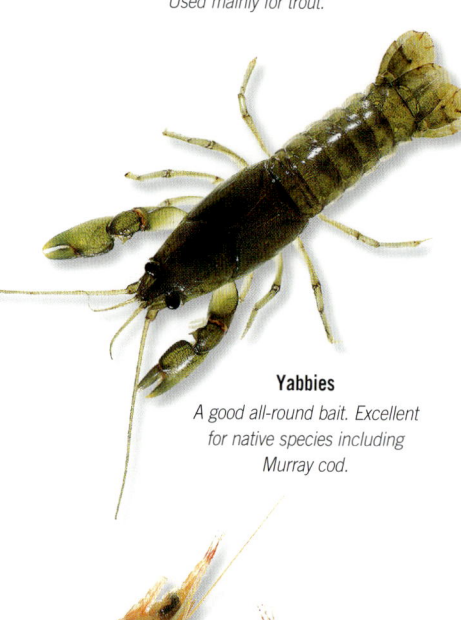

Glassies
Inhabit salt water but best for freshwater fishing, especially when chinook salmon and rainbow trout are the targets.

Mussels
A good bait for whiting and bream. The shell and remains can be used as berley.

Meal worms
Used mainly for trout.

Yabbies
A good all-round bait. Excellent for native species including Murray cod.

Shrimp
A multi-purpose bait, good for trout and native species, and the northern estuary dwellers such as barramundi and sooty grunter.

POPULAR FRESHWATER BAITS

Description	Location	Method of catching	Buying	Storage	Target fish
Crickets (black and sand, or 'mole')	Black crickets in paddocks under cow dung, rotting vegetation; mole crickets buried in riverside sand banks.	Turn over mulch and dung for black crickets; dig for mole crickets or gather them whenever they swarm on hot summer nights.	Rarely available.	Push gently down into old sock, which lets them breathe but traps them until required.	Australian bass, perch, trout, cod, redfin.
Grasshoppers	Any grassy area, usually the sunny side of hills.	Catch by hand (best early morning, before dew evaporates, as grasshoppers cannot fly until wings are dry).	Not generally available.	Push gently down into old sock, which lets them breathe but traps them until required.	Australian bass, perch, trout, cod, redfin.
Grubs (bardi grubs, witchetty grubs)	Burrows or holes around gum trees, river banks and river flats.	Either dig or use bardi cable.	Most bait outlets.	Containers of cool damp earth or canvas boxes that allow grubs to breathe.	Trout, Murray cod, perch, catfish; bream and whiting in estuaries.
'Kitchen' baits (sweet corn, potato, bread, dough)	Home kitchen or grocery store.	Kitchen scraps.	Supermarket.	As for normal food storage.	European carp, freshwater mullet, sometimes trout.
Maggots (blowfly larvae, gentles)	Home grown.	Hang pieces of meat outside to attract blowflies.	Good bait outlets.	Keep cool to delay pupation.	Trout and other freshwater species; popular with coarse anglers.
Mudeyes (larvae of common dragonfly)	Small, weedy farm dams; lake shores at night.	Fine mesh net dragged through likely habitat, or scooping insects and plucking them from reed stems, etc., as they migrate to shore during hatches.	Good bait outlets.	Keep refrigerated, or in cool damp environment.	Trout, redfin, perch, Australian bass, cod.
Mussels	Mud bottom of large rivers, particularly in cooler climates.	Collect from river bottom.	Not generally available.	Keep alive for 2 to 3 days in sealed container in refrigerator, or freeze as dead baits for longer periods.	Catfish, eels, European carp; bream in estuarine areas.
Shrimp	Weed beds in dams, creeks and rivers.	Scoop net; shrimp trap, baited with soap or luncheon meat.	Not widely available.	Cool damp bag or canvas box; cover loosely with freshly cut weed, use as soon as possible.	Perch, Australian bass, cod, trout, redfin, barramundi, saratoga, catfish, sooty grunter.
Whole dead baitfish (gambusia, galaxias, glassies, gudgeons, bony bream, marine whitebait)	Small dams, creeks, ponds, backwaters, edges of lakes and rivers (except marine baitfish).	Fish traps; scoop netting; berley; and in case of bony bream, tiny baited hooks.	Can be bought frozen, chilled or preserved from bait outlets.	Refrigerate or freeze in sealed plastic packs, or preserve in salt.	Trout, Australian bass, perch, barramundi (fresh best), cod.
Worms (earthworms, tiger worms, scrub worms)	Under rotting vegetation in home gardens or gullies below dairies. Scrub worms from well-watered rock and sand slopes, or under leaf litter.	Lift mulch, rocks and logs, or dig.	Most bait outlets.	Containers filled with cool damp earth and mulch, or dampened canvas boxes that allow the baits to breathe.	Redfin, trout, Australian bass, cod, perch, catfish and European carp; bream and whiting in estuarine areas.
Yabbies (crayfish)	Mud banks of large rivers and dams, rock piles and edges of weed beds.	Piece of meat on string in farm dams (scoop up as feelers break the surface); spotlight at night in sandy lake shallows.	Good bait outlets.	Damp, cool aerated bag or canvas box.	Big trout, Australian bass, perch, barramundi, saratoga, redfin, catfish, sooty grunter.

HOW TO FISH

Fishing Safely

Fishing is one of the safer sports. Rock anglers are the most vulnerable; their keenness can lead them to make foolhardy decisions. When accidents happen they can usually be traced to foolishness or inexperience.

THE WEATHER

Weather has a lot of bearing on water safety, so whether you are fishing from a boat or from land, be aware of the weather forecast and watch for changes.

Wind is the single greatest threat to fishing safety. Offshore winds (blowing from land to sea) can occur any time but are most common in winter. They blow up quickly and often violently, and pose most threat to boats, especially those with mechanical problems, inadequate horsepower or marginal sea ability. A disabled boat can be blown kilometres out to sea.

Cool changes, too, can come through with a rush, usually from the south. They can whip up seas in a matter of minutes, threatening boat anglers or rock hoppers. Onshore winds also affect rock and boat anglers, but tend to give more notice in that they often blow gently from daybreak and strengthen as the day progresses. However, any wind that increases force perceptibly needs to be treated with respect. Boat anglers should quit early and run home in reasonable conditions, rather than wait until the squall hits and have to battle their way back.

Watch weather reports on television each night, phone your local boating weather information service before you go out, and keep an eye on the sky during the day yourself. Indications of developing low pressure cells and associated winds show up on weather maps as a lot of lines (isobars) compressed together. Recorded phone weather information is usually a few hours old by the time you hear it, so bear in mind that a system that is a couple of hundred kilometres away at night might be just about to hit next morning. Look for dense cloud banks developing on the horizon, or seabirds flying low and fast – and all in the same direction – both of which are natural signs nearly always heralding that strong winds are to follow.

ROCK FISHING

When fishing the rocks, especially in an unfamiliar place, keep the following in mind.

- On arrival always first work out where you might be able to swim to and climb out, should you fall or be washed in. If there is the slightest risk of going in and you have any doubt about your ability to get safely back out again, do not fish that spot. There are plenty of fish in less dangerous places.
- Be aware of swell sizes and the way changing weather or tide levels can affect particular locations. Many spots are sheltered from one direction but exposed to another. Pick your spots to suit the weather.
- Watch the sea for at least twenty minutes to assess the safety of the platform, before you venture down to sea level.
- Look for hazard signs such as wet rock surfaces or substantial growths of weed. These areas are sure to be covered with water at times and can be slippery.
- Use suitable footwear: on weedy rocks, wear rock plates or at least studded plastic sandals. Sneakers are fine on dry rock, but can be dangerous on slime. Leather-soled shoes are suicidal.
- Never fish the rocks alone.

BOATING

Safety in boats means not placing yourself or your boat in situations beyond your control. Bigger boats are more stable than smaller ones, but the safety of both depends on responsible and accomplished boating ability. You need to maintain the boat's balance by sensible loading, avoid water too rough for the boat to handle, and have the safety gear required by law, for whatever environment you are fishing – including lifejackets for everyone on board, especially children.

Many rivers are tranquil, and aside from possible collisions you should encounter few risks. Punts and tiny craft suitable for placid water should not be used in rough conditions or where fast currents exist. Spend enough time in calm water to become familiar with your boat's capabilities before venturing into open and rough water. Ease yourself gradually into more demanding conditions over several outings; don't just trust to luck and tackle the big stuff right away.

Shallow waters such as bays, estuaries and large lakes can become extremely choppy in windy conditions, and a small boat can get into difficulties very quickly. Beyond

Bar crossing can be particularly hazardous for boat anglers

POSITION FINDERS

Most offshore boats are equipped with depth sounders; some are also equipped with a global positioning satellite (GPS) navigation system. Basically this is a receiver that allows you to lock onto several satellites that are constantly orbiting the earth, and obtain a 'fix' of your position quickly and precisely. Hand-held models are available.

A GPS receiver also has the advantage of enabling you to locate a fishing spot, once you have 'fixed' its position, or once its co-ordinates are known. Further information is available from your supplier.

HOW TO FISH

HOOK REMOVAL

While the most common fishing accident is a cut or graze, the next is the one that the angler most fears: being impaled by a fish hook. If such a misfortune occurs, and the barb is protruding, you can cut it off and withdraw the hook easily. If the barb is embedded in the flesh, seek medical attention if possible; if not, put a line around the throat of the hook and, when downward pressure is placed on the shank, pull the hook straight out. The downward pressure brings the barb out through the hole already in the flesh, enlarging it somewhat, but not making a ragged tear. If two people can perform this service for the sufferer, so much the better. The one pulling on the cord should not be kind, but get the hook out in one swift pull. Once the hook has been removed, follow standard first-aid procedures.

Ensure junior anglers wear lifejackets at all times

sheltered waters, the open ocean beckons many anglers but the risks are greater. Offshore boating demands a larger boat, more experience and a greater level of preparedness to cope with the risks involved.

The entrances between estuaries and the ocean can be particularly hazardous places for boat anglers. These entrances, called bars, are where tidal flows, offshore weather and the shallowing sea floor combine to create steep breaking seas and dangerous currents. They are most dangerous when a strong outgoing tide runs against an onshore wind.

Anglers in boats under 4 m should not contemplate bar crossings in anything but the calmest of conditions. Since conditions can quickly change, boats of 5 or 6 m are a more realistic minimum offshore size. Even large boats can get into trouble if their skippers plan poorly and return to port to face a run-out tide and onshore wind. Storms increase the hazards, of course.

Open boats will expose their occupants to the elements more than boats with cabins or at least covers of some sort. But one of the greatest safety aids is being able to see where you are going and covers that obscure vision are not safe at all. Your boat engine should be regularly serviced, and a backup engine is sensible too – either as a smaller auxiliary or a twin engine set-up. A marine radio is an essential safety item, enabling you to radio for help in a variety of situations.

To gain the best idea you can of the water you are fishing, start with Admiralty charts of the area, supplemented by fishing information on various locality maps. These will help you avoid known hazards and increase your fishing success as well. Always tell someone where you are going and what time you expect to be back, and if you change your mind, tell them again. Staying out later or coming in early without signing off can have a lot of people worried for nothing.

Alcohol and boats do not mix any better than alcohol and cars. Alcohol will cloud your judgement, impair your ability to control the boat and slow down your response to emergencies. Save your hard drinking for dry land; water or soft drinks are the way to go while in charge of a boat.

CLOTHING

Carry adequate clothing. Temperatures can drop quickly overnight or even in the middle of the day if there is a sudden change of weather. Being caught in a rainstorm and chilled by wind can lead to hypothermia.

Extra clothing can be stowed in the boat until required and even land-based anglers can roll up a lightweight rain jacket, or keep a jumper on hand for emergencies.

Minimise the discomfort of sunburn and the risk of skin cancer with suitable clothing, a hat and a 15+ sunscreen. Carry an insect repellent too as many good fishing areas attract insects such as mosquitoes.

FIRST AID

Anyone going fishing needs some first aid training and a basic first-aid kit. When an accident happens, it is likely you will be some distance away from help. First-aid kits should include band-aids, wound dressings, antiseptic, a clean surgical blade or scissors, and a pressure bandage.

HOW TO FISH

Caring for the Environment

Recreational fishing is great fun – lots of fresh air, beautiful scenery, peace and quiet, and with a bit of luck a fish or two! It certainly seems like a sport with a low impact on the environment, and responsible angling can be just that. A solitary angler fishing off a jetty or wandering a river bank may not seem capable of doing any significant harm, but multiply that impact by the millions of Australians who fish every year and the story is quite different.

Everybody who ventures out with a rod and line should remember one important fact: Australia's fisheries are very much a finite resource.

A big school of tailor off a beach, a rock platform covered with shellfish, or a heavy 'rise' on a trout lake may each give the illusion of endless abundance, but an illusion is all it is. Australia's fisheries are slowly but surely shrinking, and they were never particularly rich in the first place. Scientists state that Australian coastal waters have always been less fertile than waters found in many other parts of the globe. The relative lack of inland rivers and lakes has also limited the productivity of the freshwater fisheries.

Since European settlement, three dangers have steadily encroached on Australia's fragile fisheries: habitat depletion, pollution and fishing pressure. While ruthless industries, urban sprawl or commercial anglers might be blamed for the decline, the sad fact is that the humble recreational angler has done, and continues to do, a share of the damage. Harsh words, but the good news is that with a bit of care and a sense of responsibility, fishing can be virtually harmless to the environment. The following information shows how anglers can enjoy fishing without damaging the fishery.

OBEY FISHING REGULATIONS

Recreational fishing should never be seen as a 'free-for-all'. Regulations prescribing bag and size limits, closed seasons, closed waters and protected species are there for a reason. Many fish are vulnerable, especially at spawning (breeding) time, and fish populations can be, and have been, decimated by greedy or ignorant anglers. Other species are slow to breed, or have had their habitat so reduced that they cannot rebuild large populations.

Some fish that are especially vulnerable to over-fishing include Australian bass, Murray cod, gummy and school shark, southern bluefin tuna and snapper. Others, like trout cod and Australian grayling, are now so rare they are totally protected. Even seemingly abundant species, such as trout, bream and whiting, are vulnerable in some locations.

Regulations also apply to the equipment you may use – the number of rods and hooks, and (where permitted at all) the size and shape of nets. Fortunately, the use of destructive set-lines and set-nets is largely illegal now, and offenders risk heavy penalties in many parts of Australia.

It is the responsibility of all anglers to know the regulations pertaining to the waters they choose to fish. Many shellfish and crustaceans are also the subject of regulations. Take the wrong species, or too many, and you may be breaking the law. The regulations outlined in this book are intended as a guide only; contact your nearest State fisheries office or consult the guide issued with your fishing licence for up-to-date information.

An abalone inspector looks out for poachers. Avoid breaking the law – know the regulations

LIMIT YOUR CATCH

Throughout Australia, a welcome trend has appeared over the last decade or two: anglers are starting to release fish, even where no limits apply or bag limits have not been met. Many anglers now realise that most legal limits are extremely generous. Australia lags far behind many western nations, where limits of just one or two fish per angler per day are now commonplace. While a few pest species like carp need heavy culling by anglers, for the vast majority of species there is a growing realisation that overloaded bags of fish are a loss Australian waters – fresh or salt – can no longer withstand. Keeping a couple of fish for dinner is usually okay, but otherwise, fish should be carefully released.

Line-caught fish can usually be released with a high chance of survival if the following recommendations are observed.

- Handle the fish as gently and as little as possible, with wet hands.
- Keep it out of the water for a minimal time. If the hook is too deep to easily wriggle free, cut it off with clippers as close to the hook eye as possible.

LITTER

Discarded bottles, cans and wrappers are an eyesore in otherwise beautiful fishing environments. Six-pack rings and discarded fishing line are killers – fish and numerous aquatic animals become tangled in these and die by the thousands each year.

POLLUTION

Anglers are most likely to risk polluting waters when boating or camping. The obvious threat from boats is oil and petrol leaks, and spills, so motors, tanks and lines should be checked regularly. Campers can inadvertently pollute lakes and streams by the use of soaps and detergents, which even in small quantities can upset the chemical balance of the waters. The safest solution is to do the dishes and any washing in basins or buckets back at camp. Incidentally, if camp site toilets are not available, burying human waste 50 m or more from waterways will help avoid possible contamination. Of course, driving off-road vehicles and motorbikes for any distance along stream beds is physically and chemically damaging. Crossing a stream via the shortest practical route is the

HOW TO FISH

When gathering bait, only take as much as you need for immediate use

only acceptable method, and if a bridge is available nearby, use it.

Finally, berleying is beginning to cause concern as coarse fishing becomes more popular. While not likely to pose too many problems in the ocean, berleying on confined inland waters may have a negative impact on the environment if large quantities are used. For this reason, berleying is illegal on some inland waters. It is totally prohibited on Tasmanian inland waters.

NOXIOUS SPECIES AND DISEASE

Noxious fish such as European carp have done tremendous damage to Australia's inland fisheries. With few natural enemies, incredible breeding abilities and destructive feeding habits, they are the 'aquatic rabbit' of inland waters. Ironically, it was the illegal release of these fish for angling that caused the problem. While carp have grabbed the spotlight, numerous other fish, even natives, can cause great damage if introduced into the wrong aquatic environments. Not only does the translocation of the fish themselves carry risks, there is also a danger of spreading fish diseases in the process.

Anglers most commonly distribute undesirable fish species in two ways: inadvertently through the careless use of live bait, or deliberately through illegal stocking. Both can have equally devastating consequences. Great care should be taken to prevent the escape of any live baits not taken from the same water you are fishing. Under no circumstances should carp, redfin, gambusia or aquarium fish ever be used as live bait. Note that using live bait is prohibited in some waters. Needless to say, stocking of any species of fish is usually illegal without the approval of State fisheries departments.

GATHERING BAIT

As well as the environmental risks of using live fish baits outlined above, anglers should be aware of the damage that gathering other baits can cause. Concentrated digging for the humble earthworm has caused substantial damage on several inland waterways. Similar damage on a smaller scale can result from anglers turning over logs and rocks when bait collecting. On the subject of bait collecting, it should be noted that frogs are now a prohibited bait in some areas.

All the above do's and don'ts might seem to suggest that anglers are an uncaring lot where the environment is concerned, but usually the reverse is true. Most have a vested interest in ensuring the environment is well cared for – after all, a healthy environment equals more fish to catch!

All over the country, anglers are not only acting with environmental responsibility, they are also taking positive steps to actually mend the damage done by others in years gone by. Many angling clubs in particular are doing plenty of good work to rehabilitate the waterways, with restocking programs, streamside revegetation schemes, and the lobbying of governments for better care of fisheries and other activities. If you are not content with merely avoiding damage to the environment, call your local club and see what projects they are involved in – you may get an opportunity to help your local fisheries, and directly improve your fishing in the process.

WHERE TO FISH

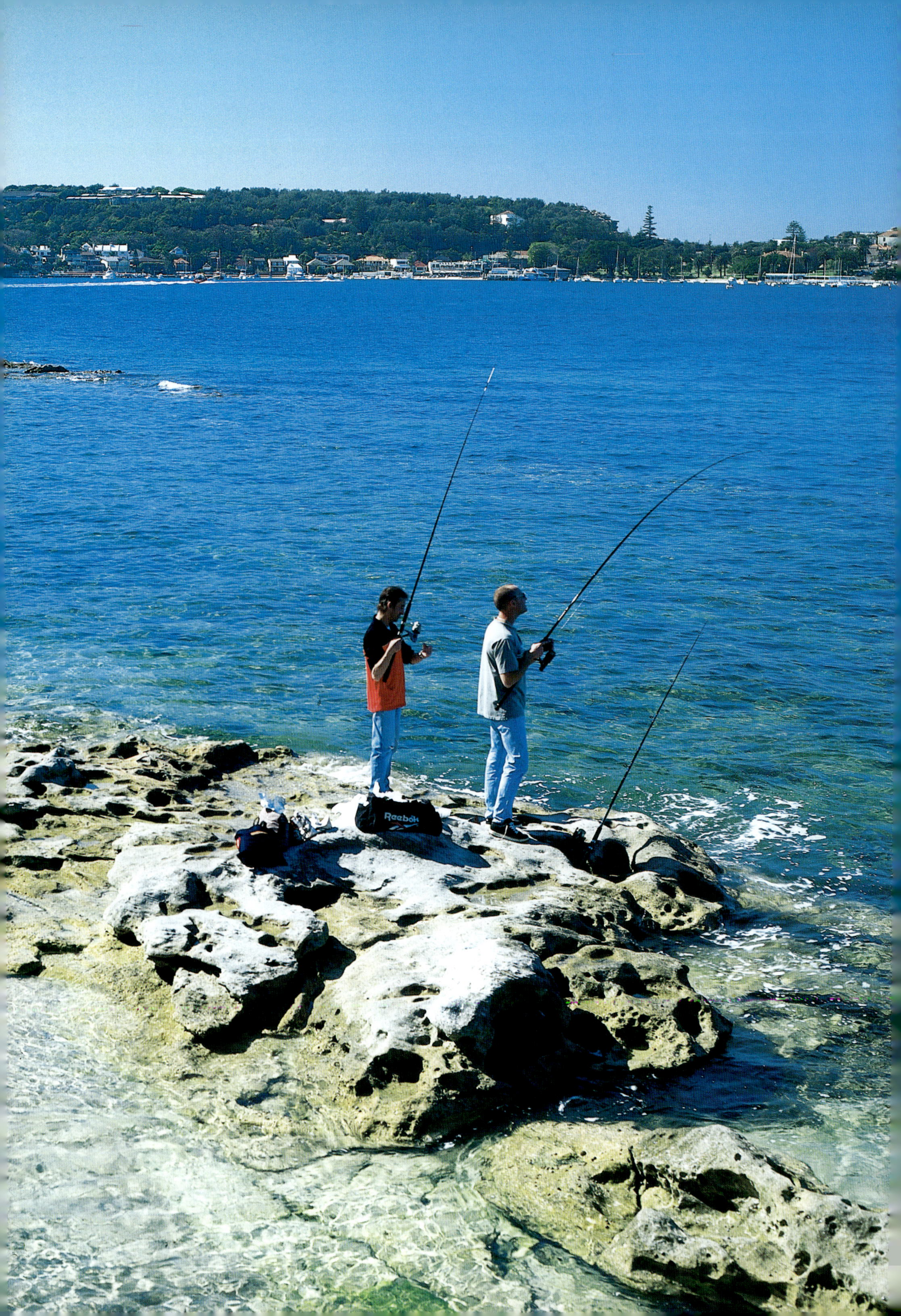
Reebok

Contents

Coastal Fishing

Sydney Region	44
Grafton Region	64
Port Macquarie Region	76
Newcastle Region	88
Wollongong Region	100
Bermagui Region	112

Inland Fishing

Coastal Region	128
New England Region	132
Upper Hunter Region	136
Central Highlands Region	140
Snowy Mountains Region	146
Western Region	152

New South Wales

New South Wales is a big fishing state, with its offshore, coastal and inland waters diverse enough to provide wonderful fishing across a whole range of styles. Rock and beach fishing is more heavily practised here than in other States, and there are some superb locations to attract the highly skilled devotees to this branch of the sport. Trout and native streams are the most extensive in the country.

There are reefs offshore for the 'outside' boat anglers, and big game in the oceanic currents that come within the range of the experienced and well-equipped sports anglers.

The lower reaches of the big rivers of the north, and the superb estuarine lakes of the south, can be explored for Australia's best known table fish – flathead, whiting and bream.

Inland, there are plentiful supplies of natives like golden perch in the warmer waters. Trout abound in the cooler lakes and rivers from the New England tablelands right down south to the famous Snowy Mountains' fisheries. The long, slow-flowing rivers in the west of the State provide a more relaxed style of freshwater fishing. Holiday makers here will find fishing just one of the attractions.

Rock fishing in Port Jackson

NEW SOUTH WALES

Coastal Fishing

The estuaries and shores, rocks, beaches, outcrops and offshore reefs along the coast provide varied fishing. The Sydney Region is Australia's busiest fishing area. Explore the Newcastle Region's inland waterways, the rivers of the Grafton Region, and the rock ledges, beaches, estuaries and offshore and inshore spots around Wollongong. Bermagui is legendary for its game fishing.

State regulations

To fish anywhere in New South Wales, whether in fresh or saltwater, you must have a recreational fishing licence, unless you are exempt on grounds of age, aboriginality or are the holder of a specific Government exemption. There are several Aquatic Reserves within New South Wales and within these, various fishing restrictions apply. For further details, to purchase a licence or check whether you qualify for any current exemption, contact NSW Fisheries on 1300 369 365, or visit their website at www.fisheries.nsw.gov.au

Protected species

The following fish are totally protected in New South Wales. If you catch one it must be carefully returned to the water. Marine species are: giant Queensland groper, estuary cod, black rock cod (or saddletail rock cod), eastern blue devil fish, elegant wrasse, grey nurse shark, Herbsts nurse shark, the great white shark, Ballina angelfish, weedy sea dragon (or common sea dragon).

Boating rules

Any person who drives a mechanically propelled recreational vessel on New South Wales waters at 10 knots or more must be licensed. Most categories of recreational vessels in New South Wales must also be registered and carry a Hull Identification Number (HIN) also known as Boatcode. For information regarding licensing, registration and Boatcode, contact NSW Waterways on 13 1256 or visit their website at www.waterways.nsw.gov.au

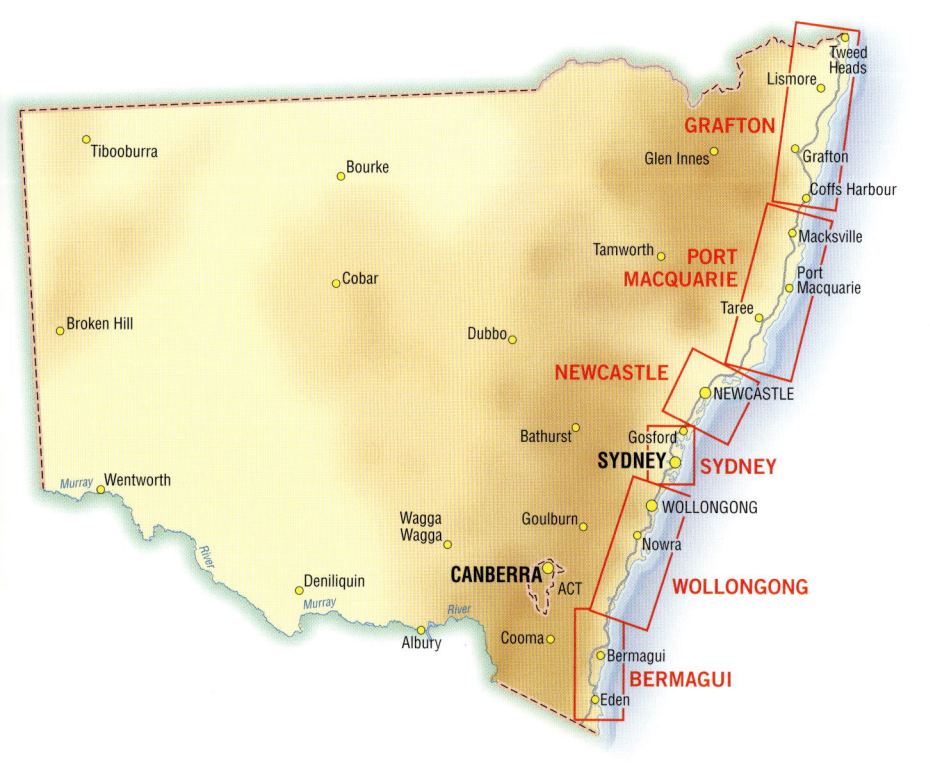

COASTAL FISHING

WHERE TO FISH

Along the coast

SYDNEY REGION ● 44
This is Australia's busiest fishing area, with superb rock and beach spots all along the coast. There is good fishing in Broken Bay, the Hawkesbury, Sydney Harbour, Botany Bay, the Georges River and Port Hacking.

GRAFTON REGION ● 64
The big rivers, such as the Tweed, Brunswick, Richmond, Sandon and Wooli, fish well and there are fine rock spots, beaches and offshore reefs. The Solitary Islands mark the transition point between temperate and tropical waters.

PORT MACQUARIE REGION ● 76
This region provides great coastal fishing with arguably the best rock areas in the State. There is also fine estuary fishing and wonderful wharves and walls for shore-based anglers.

NEWCASTLE REGION ● 88
The major features of this area are the big coastal waterways – Lake Macquarie, Myall Lakes, Port Stephens and Tuggerah Lake.

WOLLONGONG REGION ● 100
Royal National Park to Wollongong has rock ledges and quiet beaches. Fishing inshore and offshore from Kiama to Gerroa is excellent as is estuary fishing in the Shoalhaven and offshore fishing at the Sir Joseph Young Banks.

BERMAGUI REGION ● 112
The far south coast is a legendary place for its game fishing grounds. It also offers rocks, beaches, estuaries and good inshore grounds. The Tathra wharf is famous and Eden and Merimbula are very busy, especially during school holidays.

Weather

Weather forecasts can be obtained by ringing the Weather Bureau on (02) 9296 1555 or 1900 155 361 for recorded information. To receive weather reports via fax, put your machine on receive and dial 019 725 220 for coastal waters forecasts and reports, and 019 725 222 for the Sydney area. Weather forecasts are also available at: www.bom.gov.au/weather/nsw

COASTAL FISHING   NEW SOUTH WALES

GUIDE TO LOCAL FISH

(AC)	albacore	(LJ)	leatherjacket	(SM)	samson fish
(AJ)	amberjack	(LU)	luderick	(GS)	shark, school
(BC)	barracouta	(MA)	mackerel, slimy	(S)	snapper
(BA)	bass, Australian	(MA)	mackerel, Spanish	(SW)	sweep
(B)	bream, black	(MA)	mackerel, spotted	(T)	tailor
(B)	bream, yellowfin	(MJ)	mangrove jack	(TR)	trevally, others
(CO)	cobia	(ML)	marlin, black	(TR)	trevally, giant
(DA)	dart	(ML)	marlin, blue	(TR)	trevally, golden
(DO)	dolphin fish	(ML)	marlin, striped	(TR)	trevally, silver
(D)	drummer, silver	(MO)	morwong, jackass	(TP)	trumpeter
(F)	flathead, dusky	(MO)	morwong, red	(TU)	tuna, bigeye
(F)	flathead, sand	(MO)	morwong, rubberlip	(TU)	tuna, frigate mackerel
(F)	flathead, tiger	(M)	mullet, sand	(TU)	tuna, mackerel
(F)	flathead, others	(M)	mullet, sea or bully	(TU)	tuna, longtail
(FL)	flounder	(MU)	mulloway	(TU)	tuna, southern bluefin
(G)	garfish	(NG)	nannygai	(TU)	tuna, striped
(GR)	groper	(EP)	perch, estuary	(TU)	tuna, yellowfin
(GU)	gurnard	(PP)	perch, pearl	(WH)	wahoo
(HT)	hairtail	(PI)	pike, long-finned	(W)	whiting, King George
(DR)	john dory	(RB)	rock blackfish	(W)	whiting, sand
(KI)	kingfish, yellowtail	(SA)	salmon, Australian	(W)	whiting, trumpeter

Bag and size limits apply. Consult NSW Fisheries on (02) 9527 8411, or 'Saltwater Recreational Fishing in New South Wales' for details.

Tailor, salmon and kingfish are the main target fish from the Merimbula Wharf

FISHING TIP

Ever wonder why so many boats seem to congregate around channel beacons and old pilings? The answer is simple: old pilings have collected all manner of vegetation and crustacean life over the years and the natural build up creates a vertical reef that provides cover and food. Small fish come to feed on even smaller marine animals, and wherever you find small fish you are sure to find bigger fish. Species such as yellowtail kingfish, john dory, Australian salmon and bonito are some of the fish that find channel beacons and piers attractive.

FURTHER INFORMATION

Fishing For fishing regulations, contact NSW Fisheries at 202 Nicholson Pde, Cronulla, tel. (02) 9527 8411, its regional offices or check the website, www.fisheries.nsw.gov.au. There is a Fisheries Information Service on tel. (02) 9566 7802. Obtain Fisheries publications from its offices, bait and tackle shops or its website.

Boating The Waterways Authority is at James Craig Rd, Rozelle, tel. (02) 9563 8511. It produces a variety of boating maps and guides and videos on waterways regulations and boat safety. Available from Waterways offices and some marine supply shops. Also check its website, www.waterways.nsw.gov.au.

NEW SOUTH WALES

COASTAL FISHING SYDNEY REGION

Sydney Region

Despite the mass of population around Sydney, the fishing is mainly in clean waterways. Sydney Harbour and Botany Bay, while severely affected by crowds and industry, nevertheless maintain reasonable fish stocks.

The Hawkesbury is a magnificent, safe waterway for varied fishing. Sydney Harbour is best fished at dawn and dusk. It is then very good for boat and shore fishing as the wash of thousands of craft is not churning up the water.

The northern coastline has rock and beach fishing, and the coast from South Head to Botany Bay and then on to the Kurnell Peninsula is a mecca for rock anglers. Georges River and Port Hacking are relatively quiet southern estuaries, especially popular with boat anglers.

Boat ramp tips

- Before launching your boat, have the bungs in, all ropes, lights, and tie-downs off and the bow-lead attached
- To help you back the trailer straight, attach a high, clearly-seen stick to one or both rear corners of the boat
- When you park the car and trailer, pull the winch cable down to the rear of the trailer and position the hook where you can reach it when retrieving the boat later

WHERE TO FISH

Sydney Region

BRISBANE WATER ● 46
This waterway, with its sandbanks, weed beds, channels and oyster leases, offers a variety of fishing. The best area is the southern section, especially in autumn and summer. Whiting, flathead, flounder, mulloway, bream and garfish are the targets. There are plenty of good land-based spots.

HAWKESBURY ● 48
The clear waters of the Hawkesbury are ideal for trouble-free fishing. Try for whiting, bream, luderick, mulloway and flathead. Pittwater has fine drifting runs and Cowan Creek provides a highlight with hairtail in winter. Mangrove Creek is a tranquil paradise. Bass are available further up the Hawkesbury.

NORTHERN BEACHES ● 52
There is a great diversity of ocean fishing from rocks, headlands and beaches in this area. Whiting, flathead, bream and other estuary fish can be caught at the eastern end of Narrabeen Lakes. Fish from either a boat or land.

SYDNEY HARBOUR ● 54
Australia's busiest waterway is still very productive. There are plenty of wharves and rocky points in Port Jackson for shore-based anglers, and hot spots for boat anglers like the Sow and Pigs reef and the Wedding Cakes (shipping markers). Fishing at dawn and dusk is best in these busy waters. Middle Harbour is sheltered and more tranquil.

SYDNEY SOUTH AND BOTANY BAY ● 60
The coast from Sydney to Botany Bay is a great place for rock anglers. There are towering sandstone cliffs with rock spots at many levels, and fine trolling grounds and close-in reefs. Botany Bay and the Georges River have good shore and boat fishing, and the breakwalls in Botany Bay are very popular with land-based anglers.

KURNELL AND PORT HACKING ● 62
Although access is somewhat restricted, there are classic rock spots on the Kurnell Peninsula, and good surf fishing from the beaches around Cronulla. The weed areas in Port Hacking provide typical estuary fishing, and there are great boating facilities.

COASTAL FISHING SYDNEY REGION

NEW SOUTH WALES

Typical winter run bream from the north coast

Baitfishing tips

- Fresh bait is best – whatever type of bait you use, always try to ensure that it is as fresh as possible
- Ensure that all hooks are sharp, clean and securely attached with appropriate knots
- Always wash your hands over the side after handling fuel, insect repellants or sunscreen
- Rig baits so they appear as natural and enticing as possible
- Try not to let baits slump down into the bend of the hook so they don't block the hook point

GUIDE TO LOCAL FISH

bass, Australian
bonito
bream
drummer, silver
flathead
flounder
garfish
groper
hairtail
john dory
kingfish, yellowtail
leatherjacket
luderick
mackerel
mullet
mulloway
perch, estuary
rock blackfish
salmon, Australian
shark
snapper
tailor
tarwhine
teraglin
trevally
tuna
whiting

Weather

Do not venture out in low pressure systems unless you have a large, well-equipped boat as conditions can get rough, and always keep an eye out for signs of a change in the weather. Best times for fishing are early morning and late afternoon unless you are going offshore in a boat of 5 m or more. You can check weather details with the Weather Bureau on tel. (02) 9296 1555, or the local Coast Guard or Coastal Patrol.

Boating

Be aware of boating hazards like the Sow and Pigs reef, just inside South Head; the cardinal markers that warn of dangerous areas; and all wash zones and speed limits. For offshore fishing, be aware of the East Australian current running south and present all year. During the summer months it can run at up to 4 knots. If you are fishing in areas like Long Reef or north of Pittwater, speak to a local first and ensure your boat has all the necessary safety equipment. In some areas, the fish are contaminated by pollution and should not be eaten. Look out for warning signs and return these fish to the water. For further information, contact the Waterways Authority offices.

FURTHER INFORMATION

Fishing and boating New South Wales Fisheries has two offices in the Sydney Metropolitan area, Northern Beaches at 12 Shirley Rd, Wollstonecraft, tel. (02) 9438 5046 or (02) 9439 3148 and Sydney South Metropolitan at 1 Water St, Sans Souci, tel. (02) 9529 4293. The Waterways Authority issues publications with information for boaters and has a number of offices in the Sydney area.
Head office is at James Craig Rd, Rozelle, Sydney, tel. (02) 9563 8511. Others are at: 5/15-17 Kildare Rd, Blacktown, tel. (02) 9831 7200; 131 Donnison St, Gosford, tel. (02) 4323 7171; 4 Bridge St, Hornsby, tel. (02) 9477 6600; and 207 Kent St, Sydney, tel. (02) 9241 6307. The Royal Volunteer Coastal Patrol has radio bases at Botany Bay, Sydney Harbour and Mosman, tel. (02) 9960 3311; the Hawkesbury, tel. (02) 9985 9012; Broken Bay, tel. (02) 9999 3554 and Terrey Hills, tel. (02) 9450 2468. The Coast Guard's main base in Sydney is at South Head, tel. (02) 9337 5033.

Tourist centres Tourism Hawkesbury, Ham Common, Bicentenary Park, Richmond Rd, Clarendon, tel. (02) 4588 5895; Sydney Harbour Foreshore Authority, tel. (02) 9240 8500; Rotary Park, Terrigal Dr, Terrigal, tel. (02) 4385 4430; Ocean Beach, South Steyne, Manly, tel. (02) 9977 1088; Sydney Visitor Centre, 106 George St, The Rocks, tel. (02) 9255 1788; Peninsula Chamber of Commerce Visitors Centre, cnr Bulleen St and West St, Umina, tel. (02) 4344 2200.

Davidson's oyster farm gives a rustic charm to the banks of the Hawkesbury; waters around oyster leases invariably offer good fishing in the Sydney Region

NEW SOUTH WALES　　COASTAL FISHING SYDNEY REGION

Brisbane Water

Type of fishing
beach, estuary
Target fish
bream, flathead, luderick, whiting

Brisbane Water is an estuary system within a system as it feeds into the northern side of Broken Bay and runs some 6 km up to Gosford, through a labyrinth of fascinating fishing waters. There are sandbanks, weed beds, channels and oyster leases, providing varied types of fishing.

It is productive and safe water, well supplied with launching ramps, mostly in Gosford and Woy Woy, the main population centres. Hire boats, tackle and bait are abundantly available. Live baits can be gathered from sandbanks and from bays and shallows close to shore.

The Rip Ridge area is a narrow part of the waterway and has perhaps the strongest tidal flow on the whole New South Wales coast. Boat anglers should be wary of this area, and when they cross the bar at Wagstaff Point, near the entrance to Broken Bay.

Summer and autumn are the best fishing times, with the waters yielding whiting, flathead, flounder, mulloway, tailor, luderick, young snapper and garfish. The tidal areas are best fished at the top or bottom of the tide.

Lure casting for bream can be as successful as bait fishing, especially near the oyster leases at Gosford

There is good fishing outside the Brisbane Water entrance, with garfish and whiting off **Lobster Beach**, and luderick outside **Wagstaff Point** on a run-out tide.

On the other side of the entrance, **Ocean Beach** can be fished for mulloway in January and February, and bream and whiting from June to September, but only at night as the surfers are in charge during the day. The sandbar at the end of the beach is good for flathead and whiting.

Favoured land spots inside the estuary are Wagstaff Jetty, Hardys Bay Jetty, The Rip Bridge, St Huberts Island Bridge, and Woy Woy public wharves.

The most popular approach in this estuary system is to fish out of a small craft. The bottom half of the estuary, up to Lintern Channel, at the top of **Rileys Island**, provides the best fishing. Luderick and bream can be caught in the channel off Wagstaff Point. From Kourung Gourung Point, across Hardys Bay and into The Rip, the target species are whiting, flathead and bream. Right under The Rip Bridge are bream, mulloway and sharks, but the area can only be fished at slack tide.

The area west of Rileys Island and into Lintern Channel is very productive, with good quantities of bream, whiting and flathead. It is a night area for bream. Around the corner, in **Cockle Channel** and at **Empire Bay**, there is drifting for flathead and bream.

About half-way across Lintern Channel from the **Woy Woy ramp** is a mulloway hole. The edges of the oyster leases are good bream spots at night, and also home to luderick, which go for the weed around the oyster poles and frames. The best bream baits are chicken gut, live mullet and yellowtail. Blue pilchards are the best bait shop offerings.

The top of Brisbane Water does not fish so well as there are few features to attract fish. Flathead and bream are fished inshore, or in **Narara Creek**, which runs into the system near Gosford.

Land-based angling from jetties and piers on Brisbane Water is almost as popular as boat fishing

GUIDE TO LOCAL FISH

B	bream
F	flathead
FL	flounder
G	garfish
LJ	leatherjacket
LU	luderick
M	mullet
MU	mulloway
SH	shark
S	snapper
T	tailor
W	whiting

COASTAL FISHING SYDNEY REGION

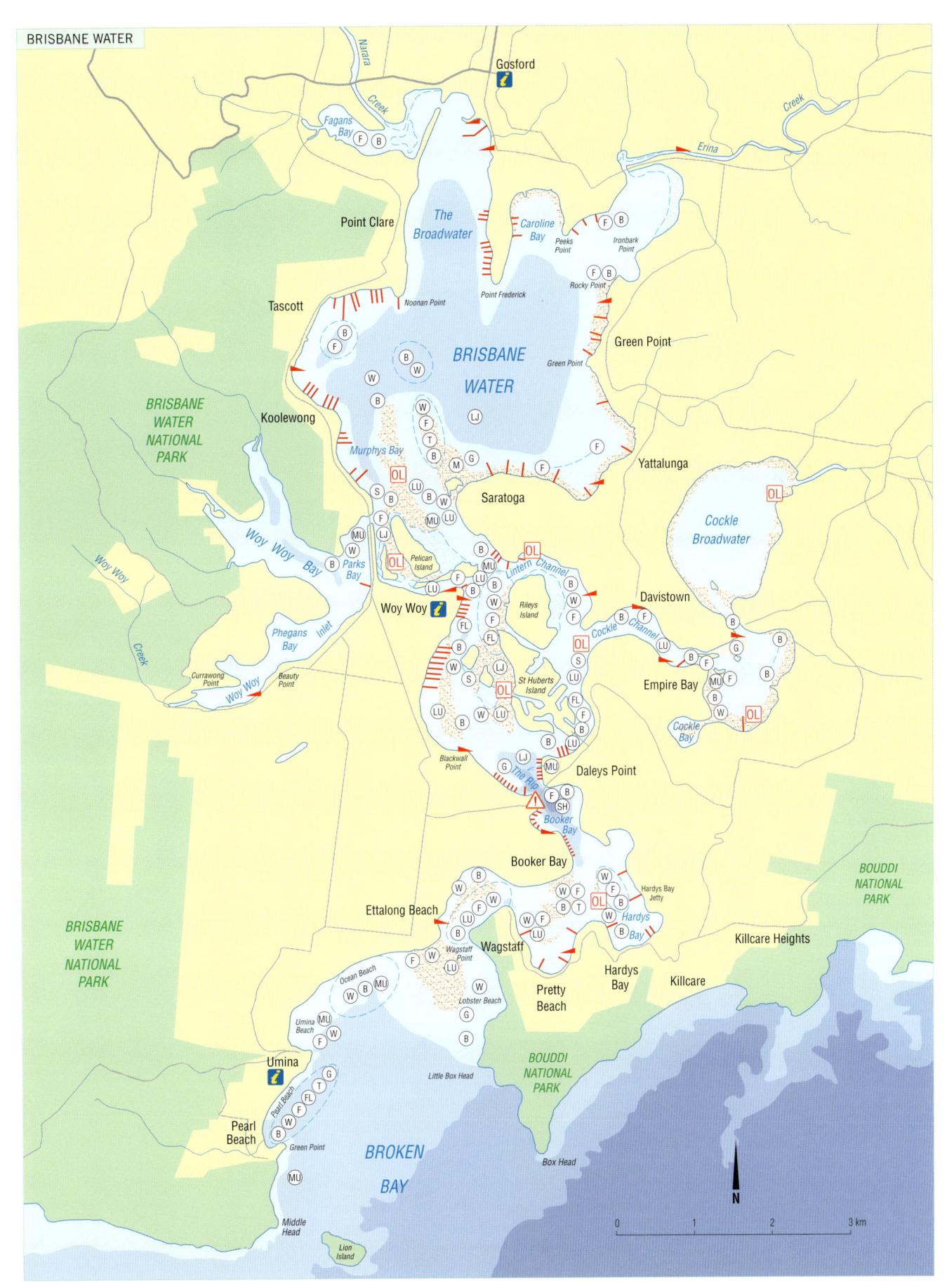

NEW SOUTH WALES

BRISBANE WATER

(Map of Brisbane Water and surrounding area, New South Wales)

Labeled locations and features:
- Gosford
- Narara Creek
- Fagans Bay
- Erina Creek
- Point Clare
- The Broadwater
- Caroline Bay
- Peeks Point
- Ironbark Point
- Tascott
- Noonan Point
- Point Frederick
- Rocky Point
- Green Point
- BRISBANE WATER
- BRISBANE WATER NATIONAL PARK
- Koolewong
- Murphys Bay
- Saratoga
- Yattalunga
- Cockle Broadwater
- Woy Woy Bay
- Parks Bay
- Pelican Island
- Lintern Channel
- Davistown
- Woy Woy
- Rileys Island
- Cockle Channel
- Empire Bay
- Phegans Bay
- St Huberts Island
- Cockle Bay
- Currawong Point
- Beauty Point
- Blackwall Point
- Daleys Point
- The Rip
- Booker Bay
- BOUDDI NATIONAL PARK
- Ettalong Beach
- Hardys Bay Jetty
- Wagstaff Point
- Wagstaff
- Hardys Bay
- Killcare Heights
- BRISBANE WATER NATIONAL PARK
- Ocean Beach
- Lobster Beach
- Pretty Beach
- Hardys Bay
- Killcare
- Umina Beach
- Little Box Head
- BOUDDI NATIONAL PARK
- Umina
- Pearl Beach
- Green Point
- Box Head
- BROKEN BAY
- Middle Head
- Lion Island

Scale: 0 — 1 — 2 — 3 km

47

Hawkesbury

Type of fishing
bay, estuary, river

Target fish
bass, bream, estuary perch, flathead, hairtail, mulloway, whiting

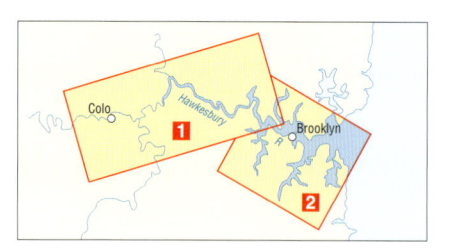

GUIDE TO LOCAL FISH

B	bream
D	drummer, silver
F	flathead
FL	flounder
GR	groper
HT	hairtail
DR	john dory
KI	kingfish, yellowtail
LJ	leatherjacket
LU	luderick
MA	mackerel
MU	mulloway
SA	salmon, Australian
S	snapper
T	tailor
TR	trevally
W	whiting

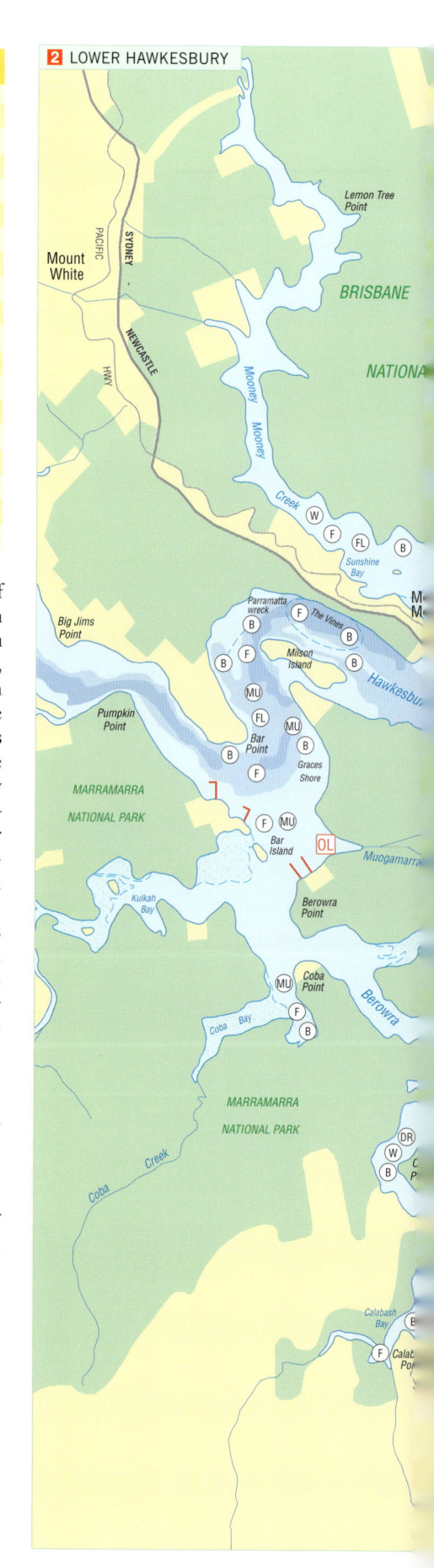

The Hawkesbury flows through Sydney's western suburbs as the Nepean River, becomes the Hawkesbury at Windsor, and then turns into a broadwater, with many waterways branching off into wooded valleys. Eventually it flows past Brisbane Water and Pittwater to enter the sea at Broken Bay. Its clean and clear waters are ideal for trouble-free fishing and there are many access points, boat ramps and facilities. Houseboats for hire provide the most comfortable fishing platforms.

LOWER HAWKESBURY

Pittwater is a clear waterway, so is best fished with fine line and lightly weighted baits. At the entrance to Pittwater, near **Barrenjoey Head**, groper and drummer can be taken on the full tide. The best places for luderick are at the top reaches of Pittwater, near **Scotland Island**. Off the jetties at Scotland Island there is a chance of yellowtail kingfish, and snapper and black bream near **Longnose Point** around dawn and dusk. But the best way of fishing Pittwater is to drift in the middle reaches, not too far from shore.

The Lower Hawkesbury has the influence of sea and tides. Around **Flint and Steel Bay**, just west of the entrance to Pittwater, there are many places to moor and seek black bream, juvenile snapper, flathead and mulloway, all on the ebb tide, although school mulloway are prevalent in many areas.

Cowan Creek, a drowned river valley, is a beautiful place, surrounded by the bush of the Ku-ring-gai Chase National Park. Fish for hairtail with blue pilchards or live yellowtail and with a wire trace to resist their razor sharp teeth. On a crisp winter night, there are few better experiences than watching the phosphorescent flashes of hooked hairtail in the clear depths. Fish a suspended or slow-sinking bait until you find how deep the school is congregating, then fish at that depth, experimenting when the bite slackens off. The best spots are **Waratah Bay**, **Jerusalem Bay**, **Yeomans Bay** and **Akuna Bay**. The arms of the Cowan Creek system usually end in sandy bays – good for flathead and whiting – while the rocky shores are haunts for bream, leatherjacket, luderick and mulloway. Winter anglers also find john dory a good catch.

There are luderick haunts at **Soldiers Point**, **West Head**, **Refuge Bay** and **Gunyah Point**. Close to **Juno Point** is a good spot for mulloway on the rising tide. Mooring from **Eleanor Bluffs** to **Green Point** on a high tide is productive for bream, flathead and mulloway, as it is on the other side of the river, off **Little Wobby Beach** and around **Dangar Island**.

Behind Dangar Island, the fishing is best on the ebb tide. There are also some superb bream grounds, particularly off **Cow Rock**, just past Peats Ferry Bridge; at **The Vines**, on the north shore from Milson Island; around the *Parramatta* wreck; at **Graces Shore**; and at **Bar Point**.

Berowra Creek is similar in style to Cowan Creek, but it is shallower and generally yields fewer fish. The only road access is from the Berowra Waters ferry.

Coba Point, at the Berowra Creek mouth, has mulloway, flathead and bream to be fished at the top of the tide. Further down the inlet, Calabash Bay and Joe Crafts Creek offer the same fare.

COASTAL FISHING SYDNEY REGION

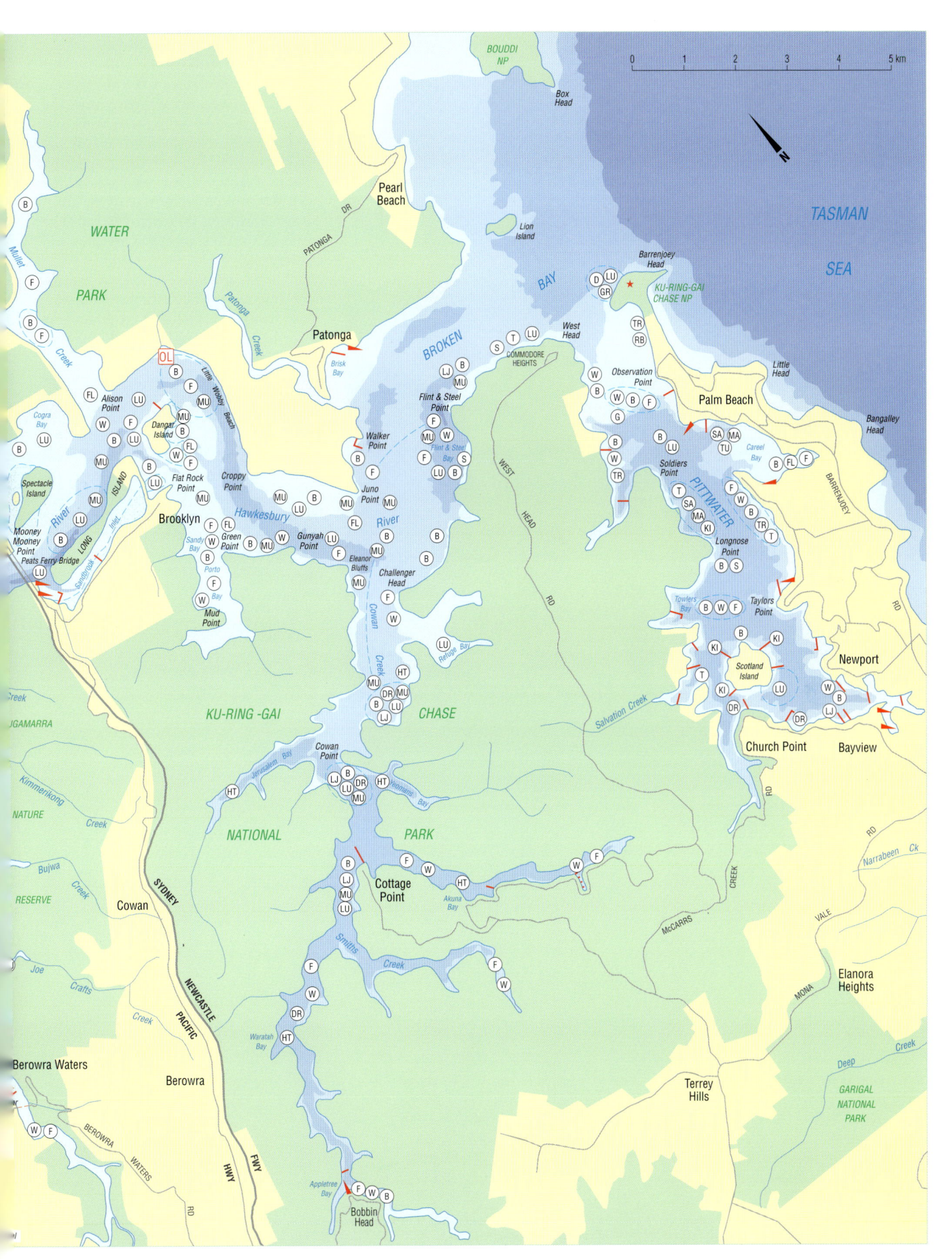

NEW SOUTH WALES

NEW SOUTH WALES

COASTAL FISHING SYDNEY REGION

UPPER HAWKESBURY

The fishing resources of the picturesque Upper Hawkesbury keep pace with the productive richness of the river flats. The best fishing time is spring, and the best way to fish is by boat, although there are plenty of spots for land-based fishing from the roads that run on either side of the river, downstream from **Wisemans Ferry**. The target fish in this waterway are bass and estuary perch.

There is productive drifting for flathead near **Spencer**, while school mulloway, bream, and the odd luderick are around the oyster lease at **Triangle Island**. **Spencer Wharf** and the nearby pontoon landing is a good mulloway spot, particularly with live yellowtail bait at dusk and night.

Mangrove Creek has bream, flathead and mulloway, and an abundance of mud crabs. The entrances to **Tarbay Gully** and **Scotchmans Creek** are similar. Bream are off the mud bank at the beach of **Neverfail Island**, and flathead, bream and mulloway are in midstream. You will find these fish again upriver at the **Popran Creek** entrance and at the **Wisemans Ferry** road bridge.

GUIDE TO LOCAL FISH

BA	bass, Australian
B	bream
F	flathead
LU	luderick
M	mullet
MU	mulloway
EP	perch, estuary

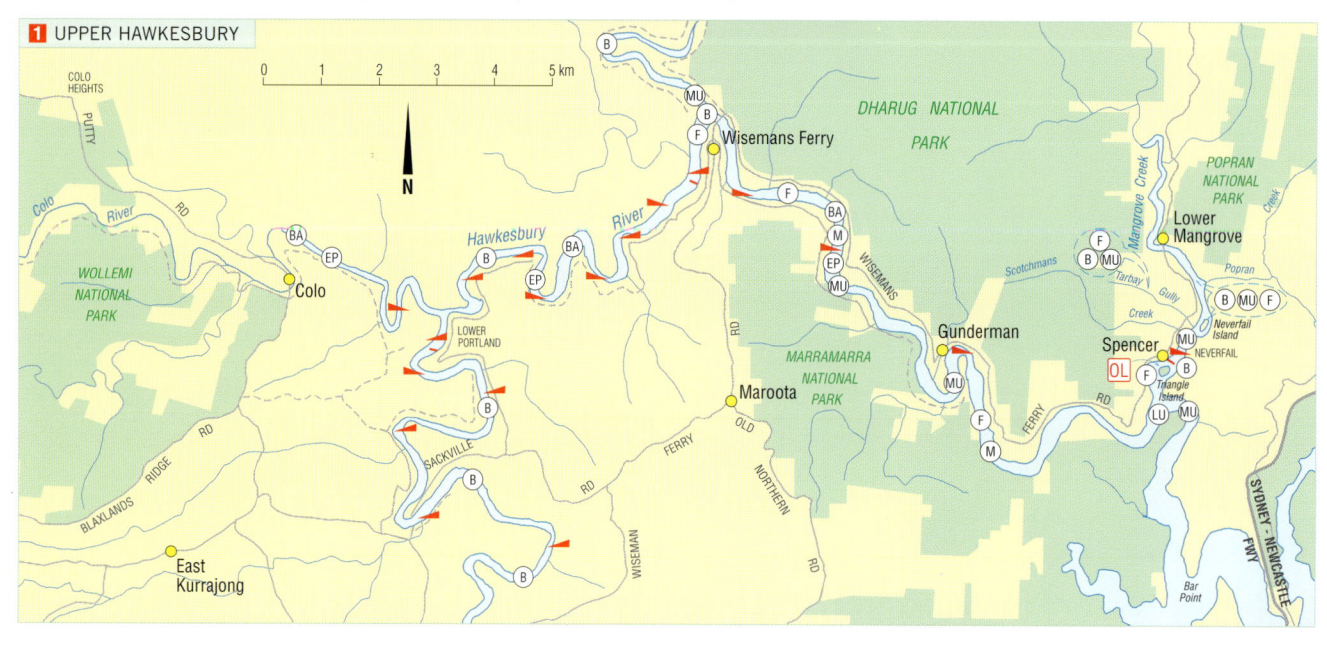

Anglers launch a boat in the early morning on the Hawkesbury River near Wisemans Ferry

1 UPPER HAWKESBURY

50

COASTAL FISHING SYDNEY REGION　　　　　　　　　　　　　　　　　　　　　NEW SOUTH WALES

Jurassic jewfish*

What's 140 km long, flanked by visible rock strata over 160 million years old, is known to carry over 7 million megalitres of water in a single year and lies within two hours drive of any part of Greater Sydney?

Give up? The answer is – the Hawkesbury River – a huge complex of mother flow and feeder streams, flung casually across the Sydney flood plain like a great gnarled geological tree. If its trunk is in the Pacific Ocean near Broken Bay, its limbs and branches reach deep into the heartland of the south and west. Here, its waters rise in places as diverse and far-flung as Goulburn, Katoomba, and the Colo wilderness.

The upper extremities of the river are near the crossing known as Yarramundi, where the Grose River runs in from the eastern slopes of the Blackheath–Katoomba Rim. Above Yarramundi, the river is known as the Nepean, and is a purely freshwater system. The fresh water continues down for some distance into the Hawkesbury itself, however – for about another 40 km, to Sackville Reach. But even then, there is still a good hundred kilometres of main saltwater river and nearly five times that again in tributaries for estuarine anglers to enjoy.

Estimates of the number of anglers who visit the Hawkesbury annually approach the one million mark, but it is still possible to find your own quiet corner to chase bass, flathead, bream, whiting, tailor, leatherjacket, luderick, or that mystical target species of all serious river anglers, the large and elusive mulloway. If the Hawkesbury is famous for one species above all the other fish available throughout its length, it is for its large and plentiful jewfish.

Each of the bends and stretches of the Hawkesbury is famed for one kind of fish or another: Sentry Box and Haycock reaches, Spencer and its environs, all produce fish. Creeks, such as Mangrove, Berowra, Cowan and Coal and Candle are all known treasure troves. The points, too, are famed, and worthy of it. Examples include Prickly, Green, Cottage, Juno and Flint and Steel points. There are hundreds of bays – try Illawong, Yeomans, and Jerusalem bays, not to mention massive and productive waters within Broken Bay and Pittwater.

Nowhere else in Sydney, and in few places within New South Wales, could you find such a rich and varied estuarine system as the Hawkesbury. What is more, that it survives after two centuries of environmental abuse and sometimes rapacious fishing is something of a miracle.

But when you consider that the Permian outcrops of rock on the river's western escarpments have peered down over the ebb and flow of dinosaurs, indigenous peoples, white settlers, agriculture, commerce and urbanisation, you sort of get the feeling that the Hawkesbury is in it for the long haul.

Fishing through the chill of a foggy winter's night, and seeing the sun come up through the mist and labyrinth of riverside gorges, you do get a different perspective on how much beauty, richness and grandeur can be summed up in that one simple word 'estuary'.

Even though there's room for debate about whether the Hawkesbury will survive us, or we it – to sit in a gently rocking boat and take in the magic glow of a sun-fired cliff as the bush comes to life around you – it's easier to think if we do change our ways enough, maybe we'll both be around for some time to come.

– Peter Horrobin

*Throughout this book jewfish are referred to as mulloway.

NEW SOUTH WALES

COASTAL FISHING SYDNEY REGION

Northern Beaches

Type of fishing
beach, estuary, rock

Target fish
bream, flathead, luderick, tailor, whiting

The coastal area north of Sydney offers a wide variety of fishing. There are plenty of good spots from the beaches and off the rocky headlands from Palm Beach down to North Head. Just inland, at Narrabeen Lakes, there is a change of pace with estuary fishing on offer.

There is a huge variety of ocean fishing from the rocks, headlands and beaches north of Sydney. Luderick hunters have ample rocky washes to work around, with rock blackfish and bream also available, and tailor in winter. From the rocks you can fish with live bait for yellowtail kingfish, tuna and salmon, with whiting, bream and small tailor available from the beaches. Many beaches are popular with surfers and fishing is best done at dawn and dusk, but anglers can usually find an end of a beach to themselves. Some of the most favoured beach spots are **Palm Beach**, a reliable summer whiting and flathead beach; **Bilgola and Bungan beaches** (both yielding bait); off **Narrabeen** and **Collaroy** for whiting, tailor, bream, flathead and mulloway; and **Dee Why Beach**.

Popular rock spots include under the lighthouse at **Barrenjoey Head**, Little Head at **Whale Beach**, the Hole in the Wall at **Avalon**, the rocks north of **Bilgola Head**, the flat outcrops south of **Bilgola**, the rocks south of **Newport** near Little Reef, the **Warriewood Ledges** at Turimetta Head and the headlands at the entrance to **Narrabeen Lakes**.

The rocky headlands between Mona Vale and North Head carry a lot of fishing traffic. **Long Reef Point** is an Aquatic Reserve and restrictions apply. All other headlands offer less restricted fishing for luderick, drummer, rock blackfish, bream and snapper fishing, and spinning for tailor. Care must be taken on a rising sea as these headlands are dangerous, but not quite to the extent of Suicide Point at **Turimetta Head** and the **Mona Vale Headland**.

There are many other spots, each with their devotees. If you are fishing a place for the first time, it pays to let the locals take up their customary stands and to allow yourself to blend quietly into the scene. It is also important to look after these busy locations, leaving them clean for the next people who happen along.

Safety comes first on the rocks. To that end take a few minutes to study the waves before venturing down.

Dee Why Beach still fishes well: the rule is to be up with the joggers and fish an incoming tide at dawn

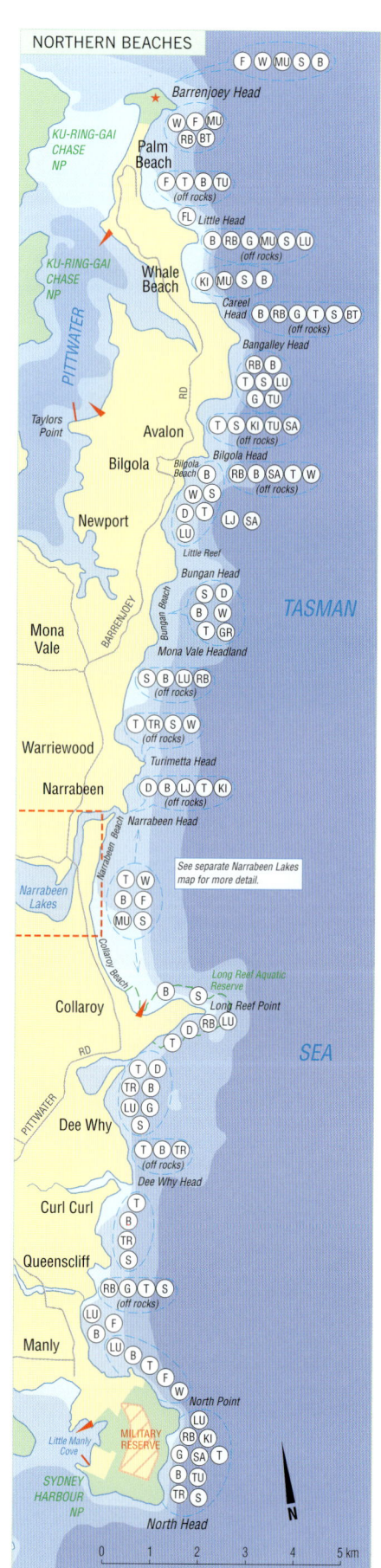

COASTAL FISHING SYDNEY REGION

NEW SOUTH WALES

Estuary entrances are always good surf fishing areas; the southern spit at North Narrabeen is popular due to its easy access and the availability of bait in the intertidal zone

NARRABEEN LAKES

The only estuary within the busy north Sydney metropolitan region, **Narrabeen Lakes** has plenty of fishing opportunities. At the eastern end, whiting, flathead and bream can be taken, with bait in the form of nippers pumped on the sand flats around the **Ocean Street Bridge**. Luderick are generally found around the edges of the weed beds and are most active on the run-out tide.

The **Pittwater Road Bridge** area carries flathead, tailor and luderick, and there is good fishing for whiting and bream around the eastern side of the islands, on either side of the bridge, with luderick in the northern channel. Around the corner from the Picnic Reserve on the point is a stretch known as **Dark Hole**, where the bream are prolific. The sandbar at **Pipeclay Point** is an ideal platform for prawners between October and February, with whiting over the weed beds, and flathead and bream lurking in the drop-offs. Bream and mullet are close to the opposite shore.

The western end of the lakes opens out into drifting grounds for very big flathead, with whiting, flounder and mullet also plentiful. Live poddy mullet are a great attraction to the flathead, which can be up to 5 kg, and mullet gut is good for the bream. Mullet can also be caught at the creek entrances and in Deep Creek, while you may find an estuary perch further up the creek.

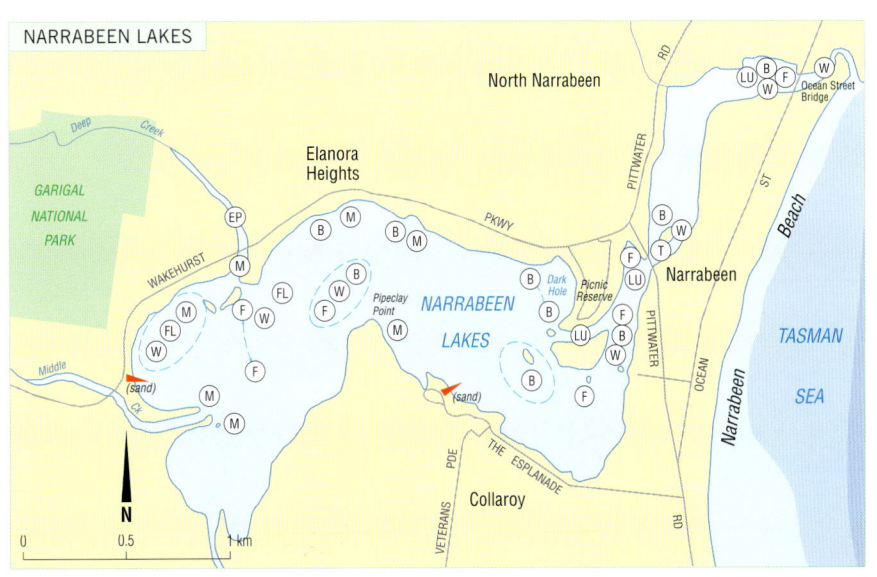

GUIDE TO LOCAL FISH

	Northern Beaches	Narrabeen Lakes
(BT) bonito	●	
(B) bream	●	●
(D) drummer, silver	●	
(F) flathead	●	●
(FL) flounder	●	●
(G) garfish	●	
(GR) groper	●	
(KI) kingfish, yellowtail	●	
(LJ) leatherjacket	●	
(LU) luderick	●	●
(M) mullet	●	●
(MU) mulloway	●	
(EP) perch, estuary		●
(RB) rock blackfish	●	
(SA) salmon, Australian	●	
(S) snapper	●	
(T) tailor	●	●
(TR) trevally	●	
(TU) tuna	●	
(W) whiting	●	●

NEW SOUTH WALES — COASTAL FISHING SYDNEY REGION

Sydney Harbour

Type of fishing
beach, harbour, rock
Target fish
bream, flathead, leatherjacket, luderick, tailor, trevally, whiting

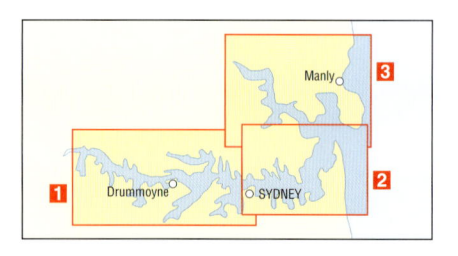

Sydney Harbour can be neatly divided into three major areas. Middle Harbour is comparatively unspoilt by industry or shipping and is the cleanest Sydney Harbour arm. Port Jackson is the busiest Australian waterway and one of the most heavily fished sections of water, while the upper harbour, west of the bridge, is overlooked by the city and bound by the grimy structures of industry. It does not look too enticing, but once you discover the points of access and action it is a huge and productive fishery.

MIDDLE HARBOUR

Middle Harbour is more sheltered than the harbour proper, and a delightful place to fish, particularly for the big population of bream that abounds within its waters.

All migratory fish visiting Middle Harbour must pass under Spit Bridge

This is where shore-based anglers come into their own as there are many pleasant and accessible spots from which to cast a line. Look for rocks, pylons, wharves, rocky outcrops and other features that attract the fish. You will need to be here early or late, as the fish take off for the deeper water in the middle of the day.

The ideal gear is a 2-m rod with a light tip for casting and a solid butt for lifting; a 2-kg line with a heavier shock trace; little or no weight; and a number 1 or 1/0 hook, which is needle sharp. Baits include local black crabs, mussels, clams and worms. The water you are fishing should be berleyed.

Inner **North Head** is a favoured place for close-in fishing, with mulloway, tailor, yellowtail kingfish and bream the targets. The North Harbour area, from Quarantine Beach to Dobroyd Head, contains the **North Harbour Aquatic Reserve**, where restrictions apply – consult NSW Fisheries for details. **Manly Point** and **Forty Baskets Beach** offer good fishing, with bream, john dory, leatherjacket and luderick on the agenda. Boat drifting from **Quarantine Beach** can yield good catches of flathead, flounder, bream and trevally. **Manly Wharf** is a good bait catching ground, with john dory a possibility in winter using live yellowtail for bait. Out in the swell of the

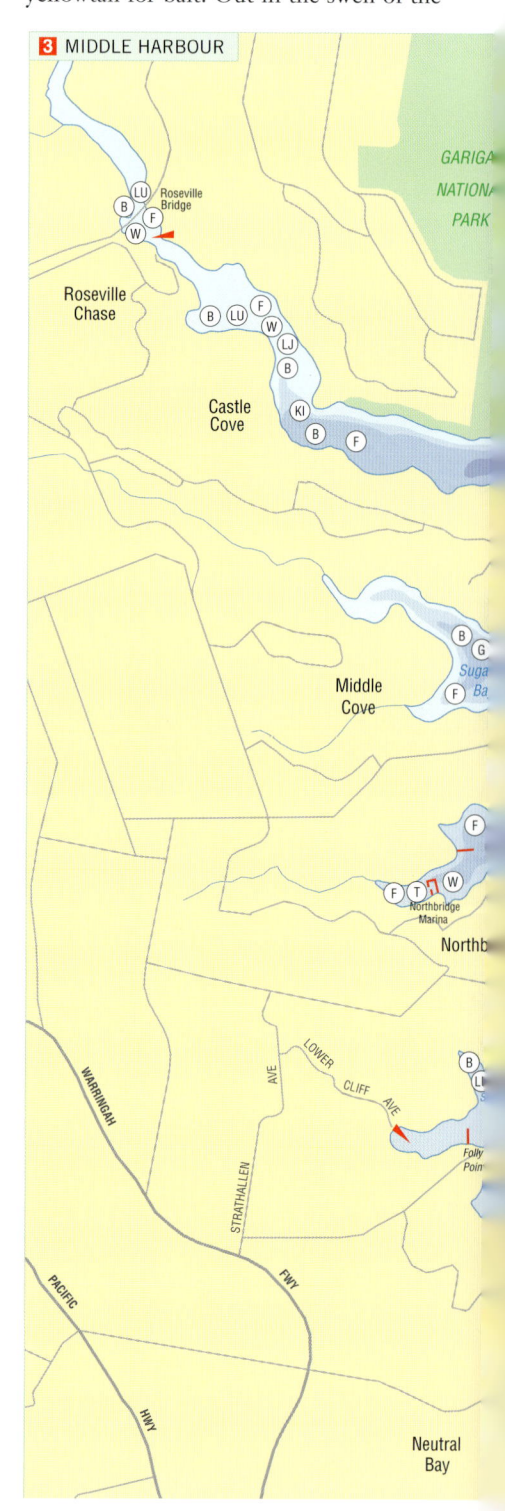

GUIDE TO LOCAL FISH

B	bream
F	flathead
FL	flounder
G	garfish
DR	john dory
KI	kingfish, yellowtail
LJ	leatherjacket
LU	luderick
M	mullet
MU	mulloway
S	snapper
T	tailor
TR	trevally
W	whiting

COASTAL FISHING SYDNEY REGION — NEW SOUTH WALES

Dobroyd Head area, near the bombora markers, is a good boat spot for bream, snapper, trevally and tailor, but only when the seas are calm. Similarly, rock fishing for bream or luderick should only be tried on the calmest days. Anywhere off **Grotto Point** is equally good for bream and mulloway.

Top spots in Middle Harbour are in **Pearl Bay**, at **Beauty Point** and **Quakers Hat**, in **Willoughby Bay**, at **Folly Point**, around the wreck in **Salt Pan Creek**, at **Fig Tree Point**, **Northbridge Marina**, and the reserve adjoining the **Roseville Bridge**.

All migratory fish that visit the area must pass under **Spit Bridge**, so anglers do well to fish around the bridge or moor close to it. The deep holes at **Bluff Head** are mulloway haunts. Further into the harbour, **Sailors**, **Sugarloaf** and **Bantry** bays are good drifting areas for whiting, bream and flathead.

Middle Harbour is also home to mulloway around the rocks and holes, and to luderick, flathead, whiting, flounder and tailor, with yellowtail kingfish in the more ocean-influenced Spit area. There are plenty of yellowtail, mullet and garfish to provide the live bait needed for mulloway and kingfish, as well as being targets in their own right.

NEW SOUTH WALES

COASTAL FISHING SYDNEY REGION

Rose Bay is a popular boat harbour for big game craft

PORT JACKSON

Fishing is particularly difficult on weekends in Port Jackson, so it is important to be up early before the boat traffic churns the waters to a froth. The land-based anglers, who take up a lot of space on wharves and rocky points, are mainly rigged for bream, fishing in shallow water at dawn and dusk, and casting into the deep during the day, usually with bloodworm or fresh prawn baits. Other targets are tailor, leatherjacket, luderick, flathead and trevally. Whiting can

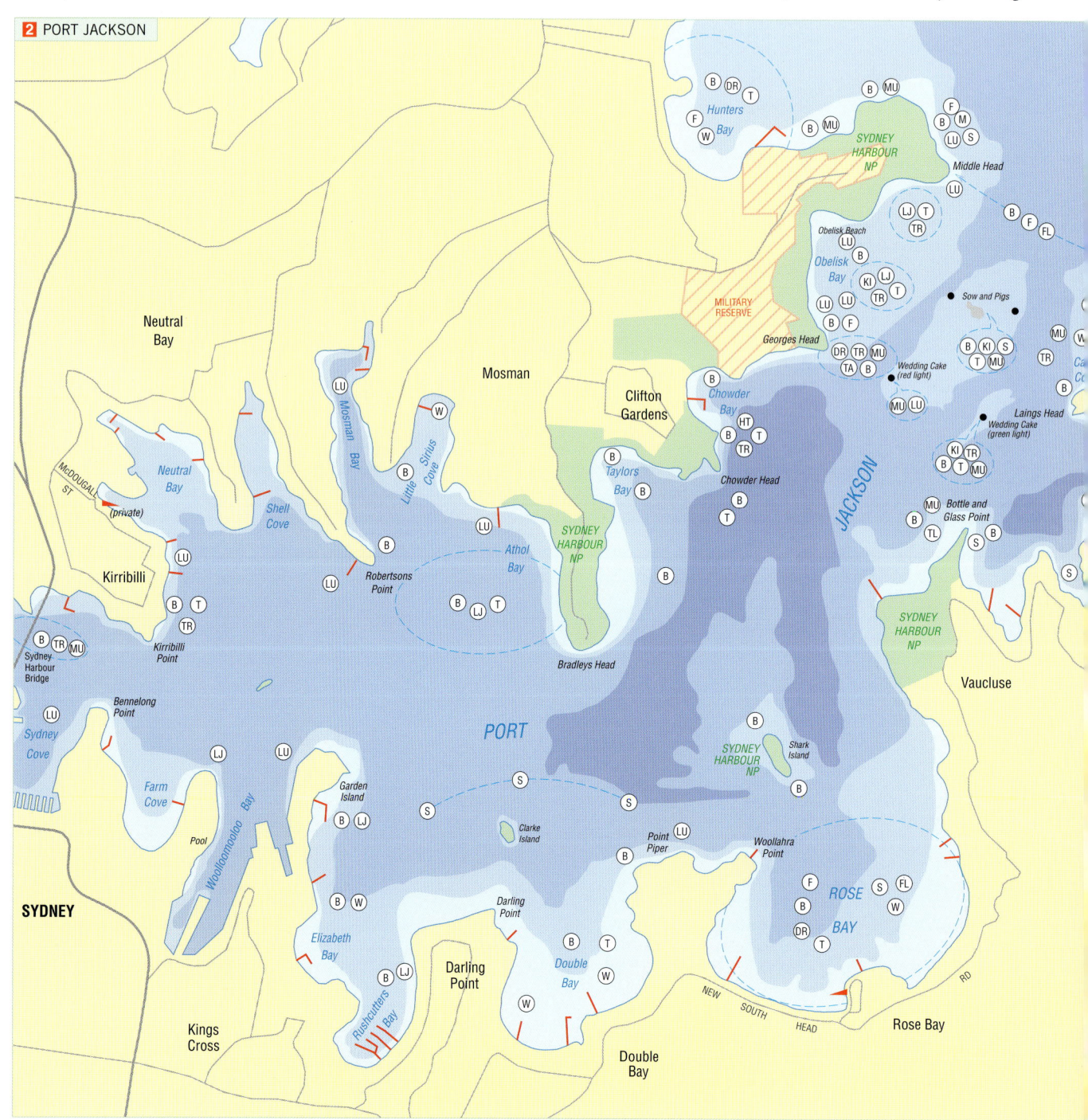

2 PORT JACKSON

56

COASTAL FISHING SYDNEY REGION   NEW SOUTH WALES

be sought in bays like **Camp Cove**, **Rose Bay**, **Double Bay** and **Little Sirius Cove** on the northern shore.

Rose Bay is merely one of the bays harbouring big game craft that fish for pelagic species offshore. Inside South Head, boat anglers can get out to some very hot places, notably the Sow and Pigs reef off Obelisk Beach and the Wedding Cakes structures that mark the shipping lane into Sydney. When fishing these and other channel markers, you are obliged and advised to stay out of the channel, or you risk being run down. The best fishing practice is to anchor away from the channel and run your bait down to the markers, where the fish tend to congregate. In a strong southerly the dawn to dusk rules are overturned, and in these weather conditions the fish tend to bite all day. However, it is also a time for boating caution.

The drift from outside **South Head** to the inside of **Middle Head** is rewarding for bream, flathead and flounder on worm baits, while just off South Head, fishing an inward tide in summer and anchoring firmly on the rough bottom, you may harvest yellowtail kingfish and mulloway, along with bream.

The inside of South Head is great fishing water for land or boat anglers. Bream and luderick can be fished from the rocks at **Lady Beach**, bream off the rocks at **Camp Cove**, and trevally and mulloway offshore. You can also find bream and snapper off the rocks at **Bottle and Glass Point**, with bream, mulloway and teraglin nearby.

The **Green Light Wedding Cake**, offshore from Bottle and Glass Point, is a great spot for yellowtail kingfish, bream, trevally, mulloway and tailor. There are bream at **Shark Island**; flathead, whiting, flounder, john dory and tailor drifting at **Rose Bay**; luderick and bream at **Point Piper**; and year-round boat and shore angling for bream across the harbour at **Taylors Bay** and **Chowder Head**. Hairtail are attracted to a deep hole to the north-east of **Chowder Head**, and bream, tarwhine and mulloway are at **Georges Head**. Here you should moor according to the wind. Luderick are at the northern end of **Obelisk Beach**, with a good bream hole 60 m out.

Offshore from Georges Head is the famous **Sow and Pigs reef**, well known for tailor catches in winter, and bream, yellowtail kingfish and mulloway all year. On a run-in tide moor on the north side and fish towards the reef, vice versa on an outgoing tide. You can also drift the area and troll around it, according to your fancy. Nearby is the **Red Light Wedding Cake**, with mulloway and luderick.

There are good rocks for luderick fishing between Georges Head and Middle Head (again take care with the weather), and more luderick at the end of the beach running to Georges Head. Bream and flathead are noted inhabitants of the drop-off out from Middle Head. Moor and fish with berley, or drift with the right wind and tide. Continue on to the wharf just east of **Hunters Bay** for good bream and mulloway grounds.

GUIDE TO LOCAL FISH

B	bream
F	flathead
FL	flounder
HT	hairtail
DR	john dory
KI	kingfish, yellowtail
LJ	leatherjacket
LU	luderick
M	mullet
MU	mulloway
S	snapper
T	tailor
TA	tarwhine
TL	teraglin
TR	trevally
W	whiting

Fishing on the harbour below the Royal Botanic Gardens

NEW SOUTH WALES

COASTAL FISHING SYDNEY REGION

WEST OF THE BRIDGE

In comparison with the lower reaches of Sydney Harbour, the upper harbour area has the advantage of fewer pleasure craft disturbing the waters on weekends. Wharves, jetties, parklands and rocky points are there for the shore-based angler, with whiting and flathead on the sandy-bottomed regions, and bream, luderick and leatherjacket amid the rocks and rubble.

Some of the best shore-based locations are **Dawes Point** and **McMahons Point**, just west of the bridge, where long casts may find bream, trevally and school mulloway; **Luna Park** for luderick; opposite at **Walsh Bay** for luderick, bream and leatherjacket around the pylons, and bream around the boats; **Pyrmont wharves** where tailor and leatherjacket can be caught; **Balls Head** on the northern side of the harbour for leatherjacket and luderick; the seawall at **Clarkes Point Reserve** for bream, luderick and leatherjacket; around to **Kellys Bush Reserve**, a good place for bream at night; opposite at the **Dawn Fraser Pool** for trevally; and then around to the **Wolseley Street Wharf** for bream, trevally, tailor and leatherjacket; **Old Gladesville Bridge** at Five Dock Point, for bream and leatherjacket; **Abbotsford Wharf** for mullet, leatherjacket and bream; and **Cabarita Point** for bream and leatherjacket.

Hen and Chicken Bay and **Half Moon Bay** on the southern side, and **Tarban Creek** on the northern shore are all excellent locations for prawning and crabbing, and the shallow, weedy sand flats attract bream, whiting and flathead.

Boat anglers, either drifting or anchoring out from the rocky shores, will find variety and action. Those after bream should anchor and berley heavily, then use light tackle and lightly weighted baits. Luderick can be taken, especially using the favoured Parramatta River weed baits, some 4 to 5 m under floats, and berleying with a chopped weed and sand mixture. Drifters for bream, trevally, whiting, flathead and school

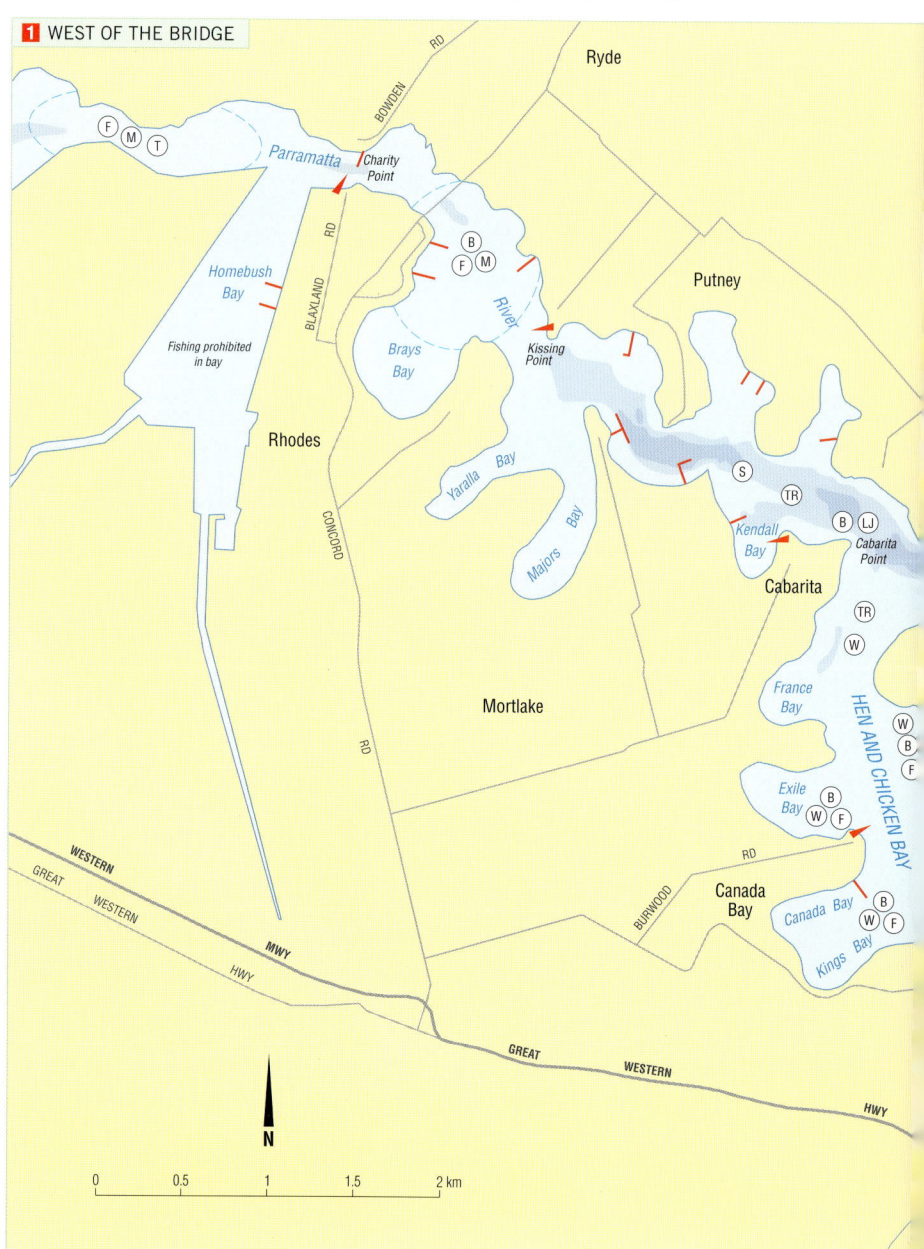

GUIDE TO LOCAL FISH

B	bream
F	flathead
LJ	leatherjacket
LU	luderick
M	mullet
MU	mulloway
S	snapper
T	tailor
TR	trevally
W	whiting

The Parramatta River, starting at the Gladesville Bridge, produces good schools of fish

COASTAL FISHING SYDNEY REGION

NEW SOUTH WALES

mulloway should bait up with prawn or bloodworm. Top areas are between **Goat Island** and **Balmain**, drifting for tailor; west of Goat Island for trevally, bream and tailor; **Balls Head** light beacon for big mulloway, trevally and tailor; **Greenwich Sailing Club** for bream from boat or shore; between **Cockatoo and Spectacle islands**, drifting for bream and trevally; **Pulpit Point**, either moored for bream, trevally and school mulloway, or drifting to **Wrights Point** for flathead and whiting; **Gladesville Bridge**, drifting for bream, flathead, trevally and tailor; the **Blackwall Point** mussel bed for school mulloway, bream and trevally on the run-out tide; and up into the **Lane Cove River**, drifting for school mulloway, bream, tailor and flathead.

Jetties around Five Dock and Gladesville often see young anglers casting for the estuary dwellers

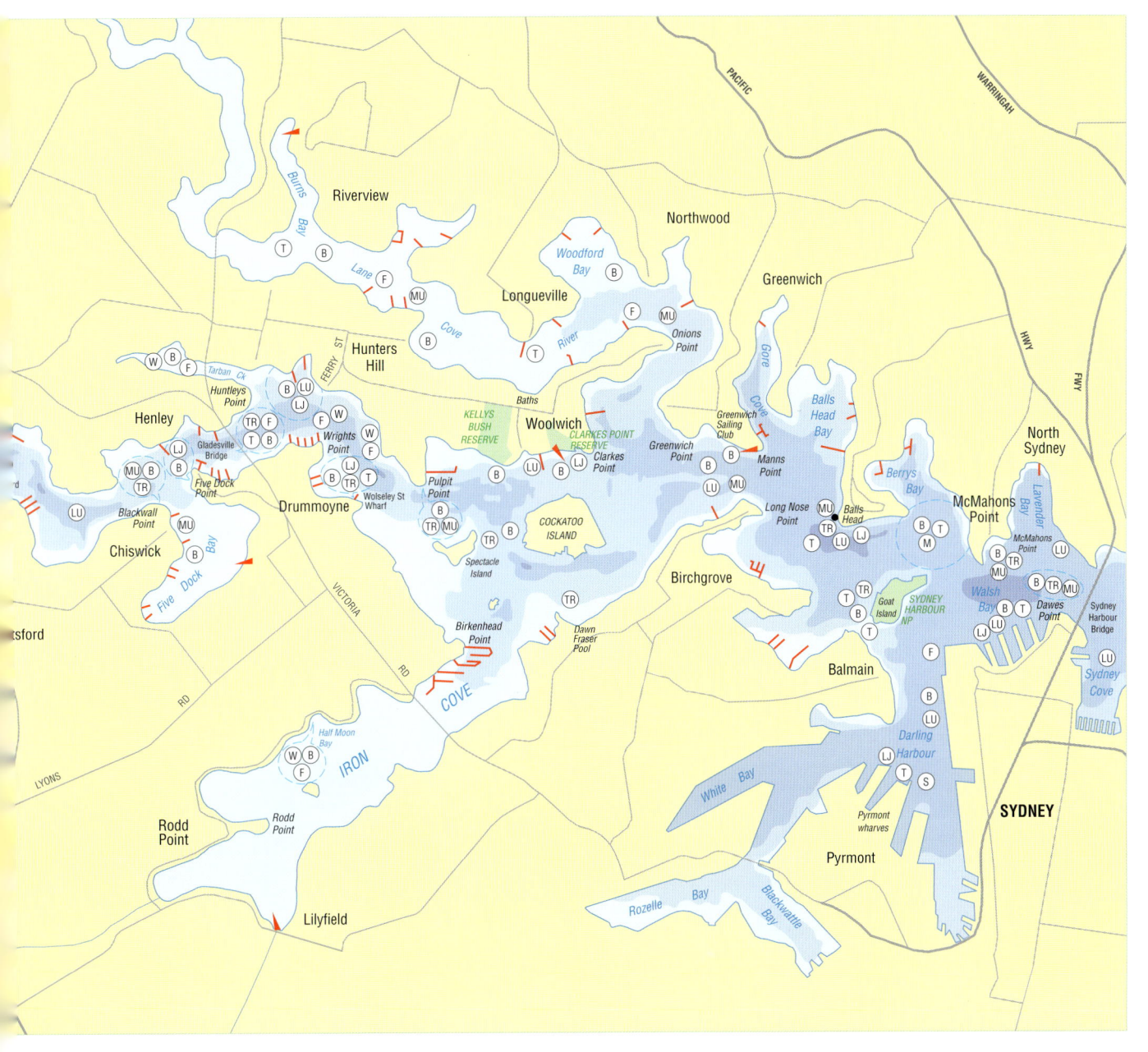

NEW SOUTH WALES
COASTAL FISHING SYDNEY REGION

Sydney South and Botany Bay

Type of fishing
bay, beach, estuary, rock

Target fish
bream, flathead, luderick, rock blackfish, whiting

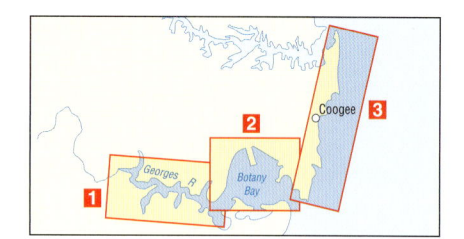

The coastline from Sydney to Botany has everything for the rock angler, with its towering sandstone cliffs containing rocky platforms at various levels, including many that are pounded by the sea at high tides. Botany Bay itself is surrounded by the airport, industry and suburbia. It is heavily fished and ever threatened by pollution and dredging, but it is still a reasonable fishing water.

SOUTHERN BEACHES

This area is a place for local knowledge about safety. Many fishing locations are easily accessible, while others may involve climbing ropes and ladders. The uninitiated should begin with safe and easily reached locations. Luderick, bream and rock blackfish inhabit the rocky washes, with tailor, Australian salmon, snapper and trevally also possible.

Mulloway and yellowtail kingfish can be caught outside **South Head** using live yellowtail for bait. South Head's best place in calmer seas is **Elephant Rock**. The targets are bream, rock blackfish, luderick and tailor. From **The Gap** to **Rosa Gully** is all high cliffs, but there is a steel ladder down to Rosa Gully. However, the spots are only good in calm weather. Again try for rock blackfish, luderick, bream and tailor.

Ben Buckler, the northern point of Bondi Beach, provides a wide variety of fishing – rock blackfish, luderick, bream, tailor, salmon – while it is mainly bream and rock blackfish at **Mackenzies Point**. One of the best spots is **Shark Point**, which can provide catches of luderick, bream, rock blackfish, Australian salmon, tailor and groper, with the occasional yellowtail kingfish for lure casters. In rough weather there is still a good chance of luderick on the rocks near **Clovelly Baths**. Well protected from the ocean swell, **Coogee Beach** is the best beach fishing location along this stretch.

The Stakes at the northern end of **Maroubra Beach** is great for luderick and rock blackfish, and in the winter there is excellent fishing with live bait for tailor, Australian salmon, trevally and bream. There are three good ledges further south (**Little Greeny**, **Big Greeny** and **The Blessings**), all excellent for luderick and rock blackfish.

South to **Cape Banks** is excellent rock fishing territory, particularly for luderick specialists, although bream, Australian salmon and tailor are also caught. This is a particularly dangerous area, and iron stakes have been driven into the rocks to provide a hold if a wave washes over. Rock plates are advised for shoes. Some of the well-known spots include Donkeys and Julieann (access north from Little Beach); The Gutter, Doctors Rocks, The Trap and The Pinnacle (south from Little Beach); and **Jolong** and **Shakey**, which are on the Cape.

BOTANY BAY

Botany Bay was once outstanding, but its future for fishing is in the balance. There are some very busy parts of the bay, with anglers, sailors, workboats and ships all taking up space, so it pays to be alert and to check your position.

A popular land-based spot is the **Cooks River** breakwall, where bream, luderick, flathead, tailor and the occasional mulloway are available. Other good land locations are **Bare Island**, the retaining wall at **Molineaux Point**, **Brighton Wharf**, **Lady Robinsons Beach**, **Ramsgate Baths** and **Dolls Point**. Generally Botany Bay is best fished at the start of a run-in tide, but the **Towra Point** area is best on the run-out.

Fishing the rocks outside South Head can be dangerous but often rewarding

COASTAL FISHING SYDNEY REGION   NEW SOUTH WALES

GUIDE TO LOCAL FISH

	Southern Beaches	Botany Bay	Georges River
(B) bream	•	•	•
(D) drummer, silver	•	•	
(F) flathead		•	•
(FL) flounder			•
(G) garfish	•		
(GR) groper	•	•	
(HT) hairtail		•	
(KI) kingfish, yellowtail	•	•	
(LJ) leatherjacket	•		•
(LU) luderick	•	•	•
(MU) mulloway	•	•	•
(RB) rock blackfish	•		
(SA) salmon, Australian	•		
(S) snapper	•	•	
(T) tailor	•	•	
(TR) trevally	•	•	
(TU) tuna	•		
(W) whiting		•	•

Sunrise over Botany Bay and the best time to catch fish from one of the many piers on the western side of the bay

Inshore fishing all around the bay is mainly for bream, whiting, tailor and mulloway, and drifting for flathead is a popular exercise. One of the best inshore spots is 200 to 300 m out from **Silver Beach**.

Out into the bay, the end of the new airport runway is a yellowtail kingfish haunt; off **Molineaux Point**, there is deep water for mulloway, hairtail, snapper, yellowtail kingfish, tailor, whiting and bream; and **Watts Reef**, off Kurnell Peninsula, is a renowned big bream spot at night. The Aquatic Reserve at Towra Point has restrictions applying. To the southwest, in **Woolooware Bay**, the weed beds around the oyster leases attract bream, flathead and luderick.

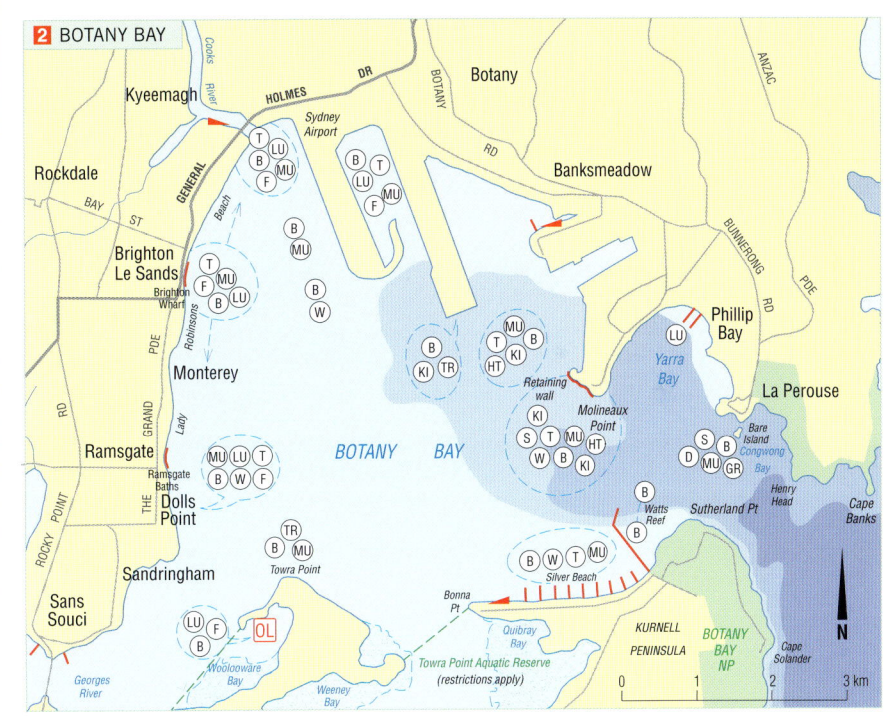

GEORGES RIVER

Georges River has a lot to offer. Just inside the entrance is a good flathead drifting area, while its lower reaches have popular stands from either shore for bream, luderick and flathead. The **Captain Cook Bridge** area is fished for bream, again from either shore, and there are some noted mulloway holes between here and the **Georges River Bridge**. Bream, flathead and whiting can be caught all along the river, with bloodworms the best bait. Luderick are plentiful further upstream, particularly around the mouth of the **Woronora River**, but berley and a run-out tide are essential. **Jewfish Bay** and **Jewfish Point** have mulloway residing in some deepwater areas.

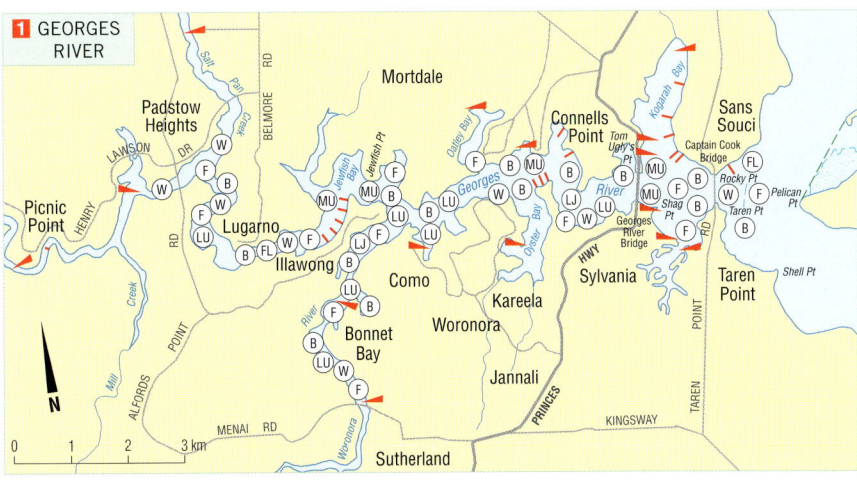

61

NEW SOUTH WALES

COASTAL FISHING SYDNEY REGION

Kurnell and Port Hacking

Type of fishing
bay, beach, estuary, rock

Target fish
bream, flathead, luderick, mulloway, tailor, whiting

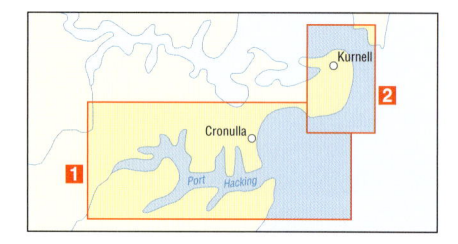

Access to the rocky Kurnell Peninsula is limited by the security of the nearby refinery and the national park, but the park gates open at about 7 a.m. The fishing produces luderick, rock blackfish, bream, trevally, Australian salmon, tailor and groper, but care must be taken on the often dangerous rock ledges. The beaches in the Cronulla area create a long stretch for surf fishing. Port Hacking has estuary fishing, with weed areas, sandbanks and channels.

KURNELL PENINSULA

Cape Solander Drive leads to great fishing nearby at **Inscription Point**, where there are comparatively safe rock ledges from which to seek luderick and rock blackfish. Others facing the sea are dangerous, even in reasonably calm weather. From Sir Joseph Banks Drive, roads branch off towards the coast – one towards the **Tabbigai** area, and another south to **Potter Point**. Again a weather watch is essential, but this is great rock blackfish, luderick and bream water. Potter Point is heavy with luderick, but it is one of the most dangerous places in the area. It is better to move around the corner to **Boat Harbour** to try for bream, whiting and tailor.

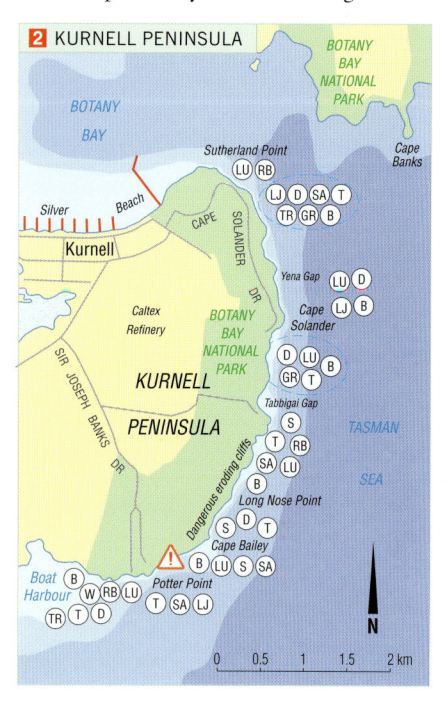

CRONULLA AND PORT HACKING

Outside Port Hacking, tailor, flathead, whiting and bream are the predominant fish at the **Cronulla beaches**, with the chance of mulloway in the deeper gutters at night. Fishing on a high tide in the evenings provides good catches of bream on the rocks south of **Sandshoes Beach** towards the entrance to Port Hacking.

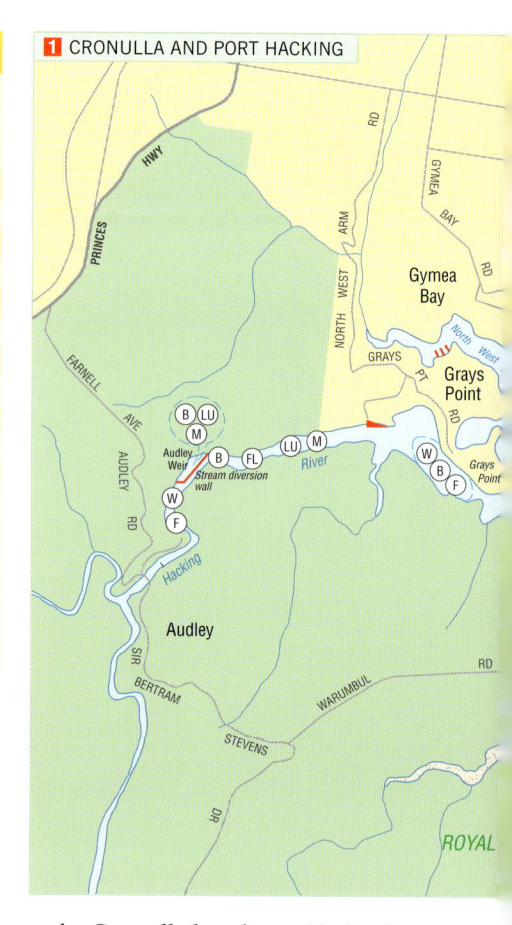

Port Hacking is essentially a boating water as there are few accessible land-based fishing points on the rocky shores. Low tide, when the fish retreat from the flats to the channels, is the best time to fish, but at high tide, fishing inshore will also bring

GUIDE TO LOCAL FISH

		Kurnell Peninsula	Cronulla and Port Hacking
B	bream	●	●
D	drummer, silver	●	●
F	flathead		●
FL	flounder		●
GR	groper	●	
DR	john dory		●
KI	kingfish, yellowtail		●
LJ	leatherjacket	●	●
LU	luderick	●	●
M	mullet		●
MU	mulloway		●
RB	rock blackfish	●	
SA	salmon, Australian	●	●
S	snapper	●	●
T	tailor	●	●
TR	trevally	●	●
W	whiting	●	●

The dramatic sea cliffs and rock platforms at Cape Solander should be approached with caution

COASTAL FISHING SYDNEY REGION   NEW SOUTH WALES

Mulloway or jewfish fall to beach, rock and offshore anglers as well as estuary fishers

good yields. There is an Aquatic Reserve at Shiprock, near Little Turriel Point, where fishing restrictions apply.

The best all-round spot is at the **Ballast Heap**, on the western point of Fishermans Bay, where the sand flat runs into Maianbar. The fishery also includes visitors like snapper, mulloway, trevally, tailor, yellowtail kingfish and john dory.

Some of the other good places in Port Hacking are **Hungry Point** for luderick; **Gunnamatta Bay** for shore-based catches of flathead, bream and trevally in winter; **Bonnievale Spit** for snapper on an outgoing tide; **Dolans Bay Wharf** for bream and flathead, and bait of yellowtail and mullet; **South West Arm**, for mulloway and yellowtail kingfish as well as flathead and bream; and **Lilli Pilli Baths** for bream, trevally, yellowtail kingfish, tailor and school mulloway.

The ideal baits for Port Hacking are pink nippers and squirt worms, which can be gathered on the sand flats at Maianbar. It is illegal to remove shellfish, just as any kind of fish trap or net is illegal in Port Hacking.

In the **Hacking River**, Grays Point is a great whiting, flathead and bream spot. At the stream diversion wall and **Audley Weir**, the river yields bream, luderick and mullet.

NEW SOUTH WALES

COASTAL FISHING GRAFTON REGION

Grafton Region

Big rivers weave through the beautiful northern coastal country of New South Wales, providing a major focus for fishing in the towns. Flathead, whiting and bream are in these waters, but mulloway and more tropical species may surprise. Bass and estuary perch are further upriver.

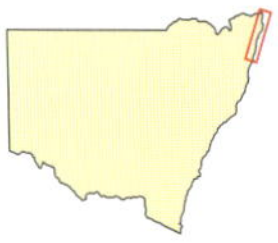

The facilities, climate and an abundance of fish make this region a popular resort all year round. A variety of rock and beach fishing is all along the coast, and there are some rewarding platforms for angling. There is also great game fishing in the area, with wahoo, mackerel and tuna, in particular, caught offshore from Cape Byron, east of Byron Bay. Further south, between Wooli and Coffs Harbour, several reefs can be fished for cobia and Spanish mackerel. For estuary anglers, flathead and bream are the targets at the Evans River entrance, with bream, tailor and mulloway available in the Clarence River estuary, between Iluka and Yamba. The Clarence River above Grafton is one of the best bass rivers in New South Wales.

At Yamba, looking up the tremendously productive Clarence River

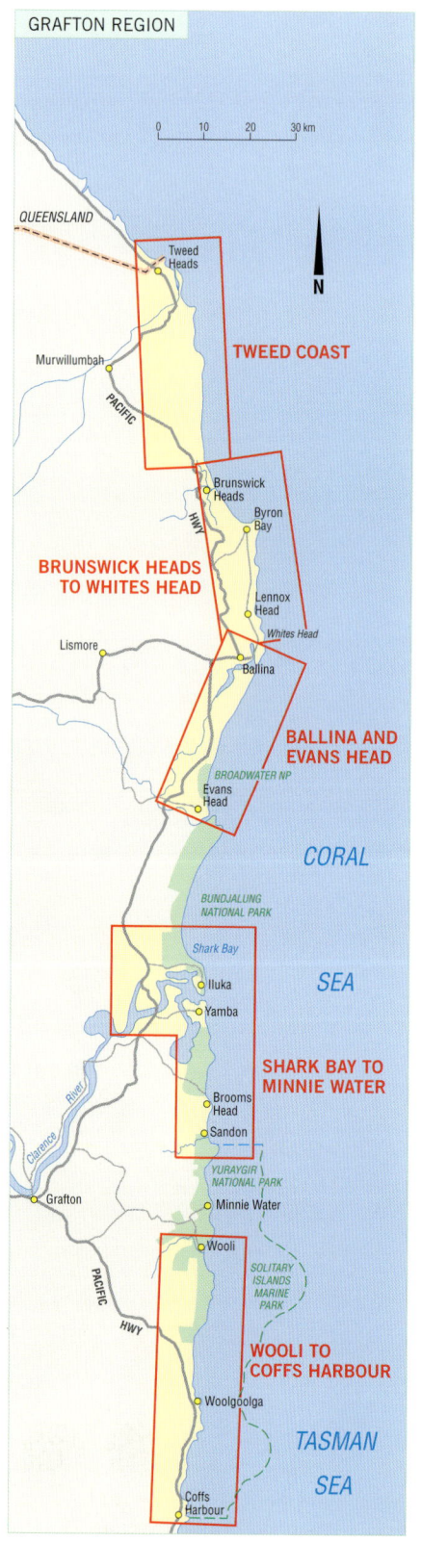

WHERE TO FISH

Grafton Region

TWEED COAST ● 66
This is a good area for river fishing, with whiting, flathead and bream the target fish. Breakwall and bridge fishing are options for mulloway and mangrove jack. There is a great variety of rock fishing, with Fingal Head the best spot. Beaches and offshore reefs are also possible locations.

BRUNSWICK HEADS TO WHITES HEAD ● 68
Brunswick Heads has long and productive surf beaches, and great wall and boat fishing in and around the Brunswick River. Cape Byron has good rock fishing, and is a vantage point for the gutters at Suffolk Park Beach. Lennox Head is also a top rock spot. There is great game fishing offshore at the Julian Rocks Aquatic Reserve.

BALLINA AND EVANS HEAD ● 70
The big Richmond River is a superb and varied fishing area, and Ballina has both rock and breakwall fishing for land anglers. The beach fishing offshore is excellent. The Evans River is a productive area for estuary fishing, with more rock and beach fishing outside the heads.

SHARK BAY TO MINNIE WATER ● 72
The Clarence River is ideal for estuary anglers, with many land-based spots at the entrance. The Yamba–Iluka coastline has excellent rock and beach spots, and the Sandon River–Minnie Water area is a great fishing hideaway.

WOOLI TO COFFS HARBOUR ● 74
This part of the coast has a delightful combination of estuaries, beaches, headlands, rock platforms and offshore islands.

Rock blackfish
The distribution of rock blackfish is along the entire New South Wales coast and into southern Queensland. They should not be confused with luderick (also known as blackfish). They are excellent fighting fish, sometimes called 'pigs' as well as 'black drummer'.

COASTAL FISHING GRAFTON REGION   NEW SOUTH WALES

GUIDE TO LOCAL FISH

- amberjack
- bass, Australian
- bream, yellowfin
- bream, black
- cobia
- dart
- dolphin fish
- drummer, silver
- flathead
- flounder
- garfish
- groper
- kingfish, yellowtail
- luderick
- mackerel, Spanish
- mackerel, spotted
- mackerel, slimy
- mangrove jack
- marlin, black
- marlin, blue
- marlin, striped
- mullet
- mulloway
- perch, estuary
- perch, pearl
- pike, yellow-finned sea
- rock blackfish
- samson fish
- snapper
- tailor
- tarwhine
- teraglin
- trevally, giant
- trevally, golden
- trevally, silver
- tuna, mackerel
- tuna, longtail
- tuna, striped
- tuna, yellowfin
- wahoo
- whiting, sand
- whiting, trumpeter

FISHING TIP

Northern New South Wales can offer surprisingly good snapper fishing in winter, usually out over deeper offshore reefs. Tackle needs to be scaled down as the fish are shyer in the clear cold water, and braided line helps here, offering increased breaking strength for greatly reduced line diameter and low stretch to help feel tentative bites. After heavy southerly weather, winter snapper move inshore, to feast on cuttlefish, or to prey on dense shoals of baitfish pushed inshore by the rough seas. At such times, big schools of migrating tailor also sometimes attack these inshore bait schools and snapper can be found underneath this carnage.

The Clarence River at Iluka: a recent move by prawn trawlers here to fit fish exclusion devices to their nets should see greater survival of juveniles such as mulloway

Weather

North-easterlies are the prevailing winds in this region in early summer, and can reach 15 to 20 knots. From July to September west winds can be very rough, and southerlies are prevalent in winter. Always watch for sudden changes, especially when the 'Southerly Buster' comes in during the afternoon, or when crossing the bars at Ballina, Brunswick Heads, Evans Head and Tweed Heads. For up-to-date weather information, contact the Weather Bureau on (02) 9296 1555 or the local Coast Guard or Coastal Patrol.

Boating

Offshore, there are washes and rocks around South Solitary Island (part of a marine reserve, off Emerald Beach and just north of Coffs Harbour) and three large surface-level bomboras, which are not easily visible and should be checked from charts. For specific conditions in particular areas, check with the Waterways Authority officer or the local Coastal Patrol.

FURTHER INFORMATION

Fishing and boating NSW Fisheries has offices at 5 Regatta Ave, Ballina, tel. (02) 6686 2018; Coffs Harbour Jetty, Coffs Harbour, tel. (02) 6651 9522; 18A River St, Maclean, tel. (02) 6645 2147; and 10/12 Greenway Dr, Tweed Heads, tel. (07) 5523 1822. The Waterways Authority has offices at 36 Marina Dr, Coffs Harbour Jetty, Coffs Harbour, tel. (02) 6651 3400; Tweed City Arcade, 69 Wharf St, Tweed Heads, tel. (07) 5536 1001, open Mondays, Thursdays and Fridays; and Shop 6, Ballina Boulevard, 70 River St, Ballina, tel. (02) 6686 4180, open Mondays, Thursdays and Fridays. The Coast Guard's main bases are at Ballina, tel. (02) 6681 4700 and Iluka, tel. (02) 6646 6311. The Coastal Patrol has bases at Byron Bay, tel. (02) 6685 5474 and at Coffs Harbour, tel. (02) 6652 3155.

Tourist centres Cnr River St and Las Balsa Plaza, Ballina, tel. (02) 6686 3484; 80 Jonson St, Byron Bay, tel. (02) 6685 8050; Pacific Hwy, Coffs Harbour, tel. (02) 6652 1522; The Professionals Real Estate, 9 Oak St, Evans Head, tel. (02) 6682 4611; Lower Clarence Visitors Centre, Ferry Park, Pacific Hwy, tel. (02) 6645 4121; World Heritage Rainforest Centre, cnr Pacific Hwy and Alma St, Murwillumbah, tel. (02) 6672 1340; 4 Wharf St, Tweed Heads, tel. (07) 5536 4244.

NEW SOUTH WALES

COASTAL FISHING GRAFTON REGION

Tweed Coast

Type of fishing
beach, offshore, river, rock, wall

Target fish
bream, flathead, mulloway, whiting

There is a wonderful variety of rock and beach fishing all along the coast from Tweed Heads to Brunswick Heads, and the huge Tweed River system is one of the most attractive and well-serviced fishing areas in New South Wales.

TWEED COAST

Fingal Beach, on the south side of the wall, is a good start for beach anglers as it has a long gutter for about a third of its length, yielding tailor, bream and sometimes mulloway. Fingal Head is the best rock spot in the area, but the Giants Causeway must be carefully negotiated. Big bream, tailor and mulloway are the general reward, but pelagics are also attracted to this rich food source.

The washes around Marys Rock on the north side of **Cook Island** carry yellowtail kingfish and tailor, while mulloway, wahoo and marlin are on the lee side in summer. North-east of Cook is **Fidos Reef**. It can be quite dangerous in heavy weather, but provides a bonanza of snapper, yellowtail kingfish, Spanish mackerel, cobia and other pelagics. **Nine Mile Reef**, a further 8 km east, is an underwater cliff that reaches to within 6 m of the surface, again dangerous in heavy weather. It attracts dolphin fish, wahoo, tuna, yellowtail kingfish and marlin in the summer.

Dreamtime Beach, at Wommin Bay, and **Kingscliff Beach** are subject to changing gutters, but may reward with whiting, bream and dart. The Kingscliff bar at the mouth of Cudgen Creek can provide people in boats with an alternative access to the ocean when the dangerous Tweed Heads bar is subject to south-easterlies. In calm conditions there is good fishing for tailor, mulloway and bream on the rocks below the Kingscliff south wall, at the mouth of the creek.

Bogangar Beach has good gutters. The southern end is known for quality whiting, and Towners Hole and Spencers Hole are popular for big mulloway and tailor. Norries Head has good rock spots for tailor and bream, but they can be very dangerous.

There are rock platforms near **Hastings Point** that fish well for tailor or snapper. The most comfortable of them is Flat Rock, just off the southern point of Cudgera Creek. Pottsville, Mooball and Wooyung beaches will have tailor, bream, whiting and mulloway if there are good sand formations in place. The Black Rocks, several kilometres offshore between Pottsville and Wooyung, is a good spot for bream, tailor and mulloway, with whiting in the gutters on either side.

A reef about 2 km offshore from New Brighton has snapper, yellowtail kingfish, school tailor in winter, and spotted and Spanish mackerel in abundance in summer.

GUIDE TO LOCAL FISH

		Tweed Coast	Tweed River
B	bream	●	●
CO	cobia	●	
DA	dart	●	
F	flathead		●
KI	kingfish, yellowtail	●	
LU	luderick		●
MA	mackerel	●	
MU	mangrove jack		●
ML	marlin	●	
MU	mulloway	●	●
PP	perch, pearl		●
S	snapper	●	
T	tailor	●	●
TL	teraglin	●	
TR	trevally	●	●
TU	tuna	●	
WH	wahoo	●	
W	whiting	●	●

Tweed Heads entrance with Fingal Beach in the background – a good start for the visiting land-based angler as there are bream, tailor and often mulloway to be caught here

COASTAL FISHING GRAFTON REGION   NEW SOUTH WALES

TWEED RIVER

The broad reaches of the **Lower Tweed** provide all-round action, starting with the breakwalls and headlands around the entrance, which are renowned for luderick, and for tailor in the autumn and winter. Mulloway are in this area when the tailor are schooling and during the poddy mullet run in spring.

Whiting and bream are the main targets in the river. Flathead are also often present, as are big mulloway from October to March, particularly around the **Blue Hole** at the head of Ukerebagh Island, the **Boyds Bay and Barneys Point bridges**, **Tonys Island** and **Lillies Island**. The bridges are also good for jigging with feathered lures, with trevally the target, while the wooded edges of Barneys Point are haunts for mangrove jack. In the summer months, whiting and bream are more likely to be caught after rain or at dawn or dusk. Flathead, however, will be in holes and drop-offs close to the water's edge as the tide recedes.

Bream in the Tweed appear to prefer strips of fish flesh, especially tailor, rather than the prawns fancied in waters around Brisbane. Nippers can also be pumped from sand and mudflats along the edges of the waterways, and will be grabbed by the flathead.

The Tweed has good fishing all the way to Murwillumbah, some 30 km from Tweed Heads, and beyond. **Chinderah**, opposite the caravan park, is a good spot for whiting, and luderick around the banks. North of **Dodds Island** is a reef where bream and mulloway are present, and the shallow sandy stretch up to **Stotts Island** is whiting territory. The river has to be carefully navigated as there are shallow areas, particularly between Tumbulgum (just upstream from Stotts Island) and Murwillumbah, and you have to look out for waterskiers by day and dredges by night. The southern side of the river is generally deeper. Whiting, flathead and mulloway are the targets in this busy area.

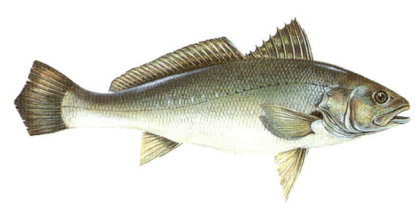

The waters of the upper Tweed near Murwillumbah, navigable by boat although there are shallow areas

Mulloway
Colloquially known as jewfish, the mulloway is a popular game and table fish throughout the southern regions of Australia. It is often confused with teraglin or northern mulloway.

NEW SOUTH WALES   COASTAL FISHING GRAFTON REGION

Brunswick Heads to Whites Head

Type of fishing
beach, estuary, offshore, river, rock
Target fish
bream, flathead, mulloway, tailor, whiting

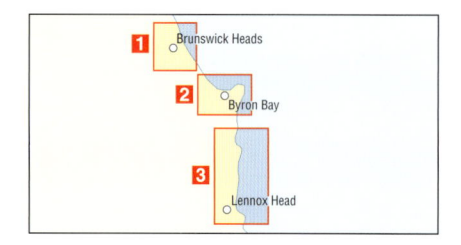

The fishing is reliable at Brunswick Heads, either in the Brunswick River or around its entrance. Byron Bay's popularity as a surfing area can be limiting to fishing on the long surf beaches that stretch out on either side of the town. There is good offshore fishing along the coast.

BRUNSWICK HEADS

The main targets in the **Brunswick River** and nearby beaches are tailor, bream, whiting and mulloway, with flathead, whiting and bream in the estuary. The estuary breaks into Marshalls and Simpsons creeks, known as the north and south arms, which are shallow and require knowledge of the channels.

A particularly good land-based angling place for bream, flathead, luderick and school mulloway is the **Spur Wall**, at the inland entrance of the south arm. Bream and luderick are the main quarries further west at the **Memorial Wall**, and bream make for the boat harbour, just west of the wall, when the prawn trawlers arrive with their catch. Further into the estuary, whiting, flathead and bream continue to abound. Oyster leases provide good fishing areas.

Land anglers also do well on the breakwalls at the river entrance. The seaward side of the **North Wall** is good for tailor and mulloway, with bream, whiting and luderick on the sheltered side. Bream, tailor and mulloway are around both sides of the **South Wall**, with some flathead on the river side. **Seagull Rocks** offer whiting, bream, tailor and luderick in the rocky washes, while the 10-km long **South Beach** has good formations for whiting, tailor and bream. Boat anglers should be aware that the bar is dangerous.

The oyster beds in the Brunswick River harbour good populations of bream that live and feed in and around the leases

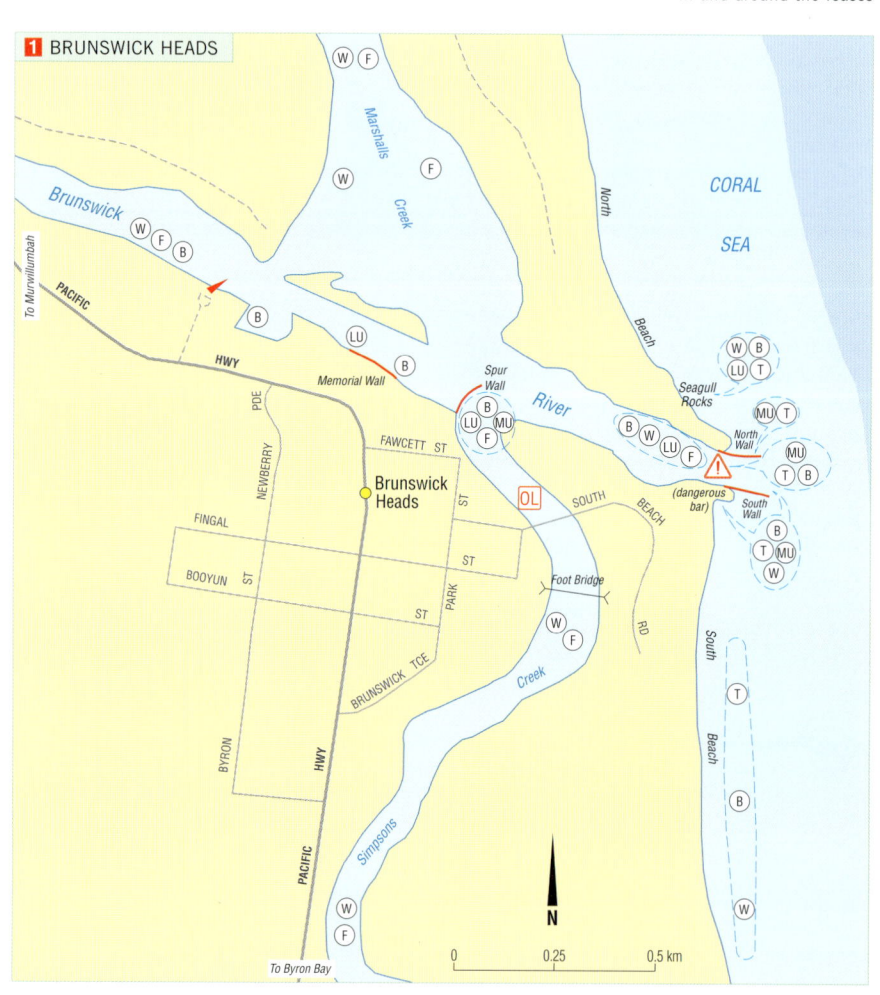

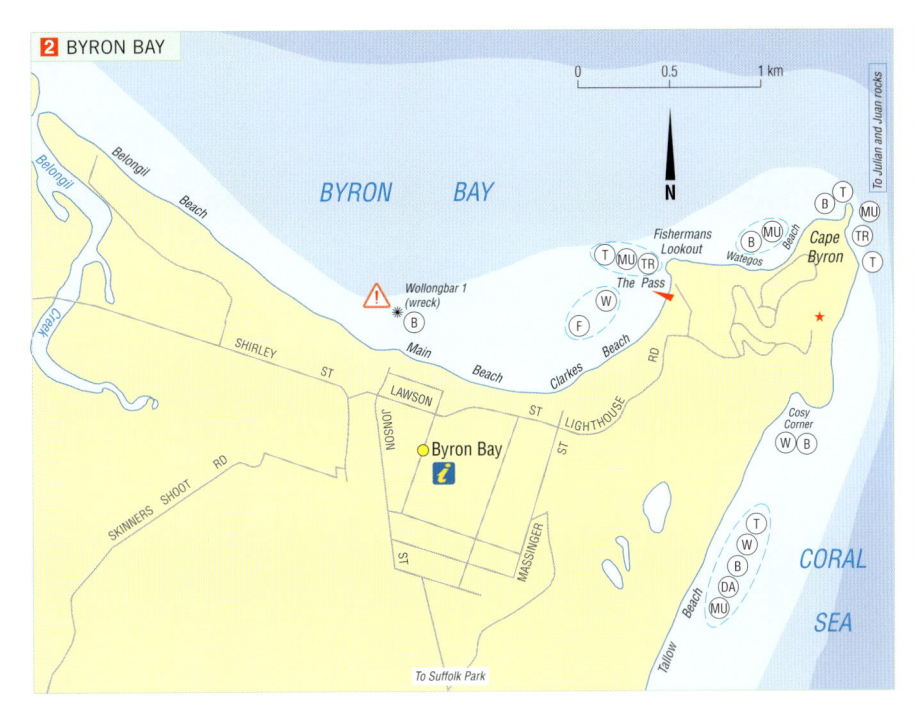

COASTAL FISHING GRAFTON REGION　　　　　　　　　　　　　NEW SOUTH WALES

2 BYRON BAY

GUIDE TO LOCAL FISH

	Brunswick Heads to Byron Bay	Tallow Beach to Whites Head
B　bream	●	●
DA　dart	●	●
D　drummer, silver		●
F　flathead	●	●
LU　luderick	●	
MA　mackerel		●
MU　mulloway	●	●
RB　rock blackfish		●
S　snapper	●	●
T　tailor	●	●
TR　trevally	●	
TU　tuna		●
W　whiting	●	●

BYRON BAY

Some 40 m offshore from Main Beach lies the wreck of the *Wollongbar 1*, which can be a good bream spot in rough weather. However, people in boats anchor at their peril, as the waves here are unpredictable. The main swimming areas in Byron Bay, **Clarkes Beach** and **Wategos Beach**, are seldom fished by day, but the former has flathead, and big whiting in the autumn, while the rocks around Wategos can be good for bream and mulloway in poor weather. **The Pass** at the Cape Byron end of Clarkes Beach offers the only boat-launching facility, and four-wheel drives are recommended. You will need to be fit and determined to get down to the rocks on the seaward side of the rugged cape, but the rewards of tailor and mulloway are sometimes enhanced by summer visits of tropical trevally, a rare happening in New South Wales.

Offshore there are two rocky outcrops about 4 km north-east of the cape, known as **Julian and Juan rocks**. These are brilliant game fishing locations for wahoo, mackerel, tuna, snapper, bream, mulloway, teraglin, pearl perch and trevally, but as the area is a marine reserve, only one line and one hook per angler are allowed.

TALLOW BEACH TO WHITES HEAD

The **Tallow Beach and Suffolk Park area** has gutters with tailor, whiting, dart, bream and mulloway sometimes present, while further south **Broken Head** is good for bream, tailor, mulloway, rock blackfish and drummer.

Seven Mile Beach requires a vehicle permit, but provides a ready source of bait with worms, pippis and crabs for the bream, whiting and mulloway in the gutters and holes. The area in front of the surf club is recommended. **Lennox Head** is a great place for tailor and big bream, and **The Point** has big tailor, but is virtually unfishable by day because of surfers. **The Ledge**, on the southern side of Lennox Head, requires a stiff climb to the high platform, but good rock anglers will enjoy the tailor, mulloway, luderick and passing pelagics, along with snapper after a heavy blow. **Shag Rock** has tailor and rock blackfish. The **Iron Peg** is a narrow finger of rock over deep water. This is a dangerous spot in any weather, but can yield an abundance of fish. **Skennars Head** is for the fit and experienced, as it requires a rope descent.

3 TALLOW BEACH TO WHITES HEAD

Tallow Beach provides good surf fishing for bream, whiting, tailor and sometimes even dart

NEW SOUTH WALES — COASTAL FISHING GRAFTON REGION

Ballina and Evans Head

Type of fishing
beach, estuary, river, rock, wall

Target fish
bream, flathead, luderick, mulloway, tailor

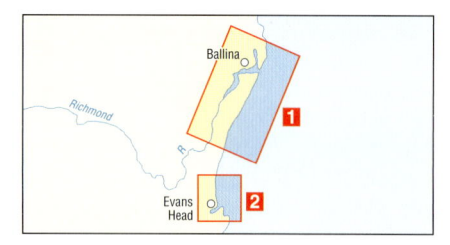

Ballina is a great place for fishing with good rock, breakwall and beach angling around the town, highly productive fishing and prawning in the Richmond River, and some excellent offshore spots. Evans Head is one of the best snapper ports in New South Wales, with quality mulloway, teraglin and diminishing pearl perch to be found.

BALLINA

Outside and north of Ballina, the action starts at **Sharps Beach**, with a good hole at the northern end of the beach for bream and school mulloway. At the southern end, **Flat Rock** headland has some rocky gutters on the northern side, attracting bream, luderick, rock blackfish, trevally and tailor.

South of Flat Rock, **Angels Beach** has productive holes and gutters for whiting, flathead and mulloway, with **Pontoon Rocks** in the middle of the beach making a good platform for bream, tailor and mulloway. Further south, **Black Head** is also a popular spot, with mulloway, bream and whiting close in, and mackerel and marlin possibilities in summer. **Ballina Head** and the beaches on either side have bream, whiting and mulloway as their main targets.

Around the walls of the **Richmond River** there are bream, mulloway and tailor, with the occasional mackerel and bluefin tuna coming close in summer. The North Wall fishes well on the outside for bream, tailor and mulloway, and on the inside for bream sheltering from a north-easterly. Low tide is best. The end of the South Wall is great for mulloway and bream.

Just inside the entrance is the landlocked but tidal **Shaws Bay**, which carries very big tailor, mangrove jack, bream and luderick. It is best at dusk with a floating prawn bait. The mangrove-lined **North Creek** requires knowledge of the channels and shallows, but is terrific for big flathead, whiting, bream and occasionally mangrove jack. The **Missingham Bridge** over the creek entrance is a fine place to try for luderick, bream, whiting and flathead, while the **Porpoise Wall** has bream and luderick

GUIDE TO LOCAL FISH

		Ballina	Evans Head
B	bream	●	●
D	drummer, silver		●
F	flathead	●	●
LU	luderick	●	●
MA	mackerel	●	●
MJ	mangrove jack	●	●
ML	marlin	●	
MU	mulloway	●	●
RB	rock blackfish	●	●
S	snapper	●	●
T	tailor	●	●
TR	trevally	●	
TU	tuna	●	●
W	whiting	●	●

COASTAL FISHING GRAFTON REGION   NEW SOUTH WALES

on the channel side and flathead and whiting in the shallows on the other side.

Just out from the Apex boat ramp on the north shore is a bream hole that attracts a lot of boats seeking the fish that abound there in winter. The hole is best fished around sunset.

The river continues to be one of Australia's finest areas for bream, whiting, school mulloway and flathead, all the way down to **Pimlico Island**. Some of the best places are the **Co-op Wharf**, **Riverview Park**, **Burns Point** and **Emigrant Creek**. Further upriver, bream can be caught around the structures, while drifting for big flathead continues all the way to Wardell.

The 20-km long beach on the south side of the Richmond River entrance has four-wheel drive access for those with permits from the Ballina Shire Council; worms and pippis for the taking; and gutters carrying whiting, tailor, bream and mulloway. For boat anglers, the **North and South Riordan shoals** are about 2.5 km off the beach and 3 km apart. They are hard to find, but the snapper and trevally are abundant.

EVANS HEAD

Airforce Beach at **Evans Head** often has a hole in front of the surf club, which is best fished at dawn and dusk for bream and whiting. The **North Wall** fishes very well after rain, with bream, whiting, tailor and mulloway on the seaward side, luderick and bream inside. Nearby, the **Little Wall** is renowned for autumn and winter bream. The **South Wall** is also worth trying for bream, whiting, tailor and flathead. There are some hot spots in the deep lower estuary and the boat ramp and bridge area, with flathead as the main target, while the boat harbour attracts big bream when the prawn fleet arrives in the morning. The beach on the seaward side of the bridge is a good fishing spot, and also a great bait spot for yabbies.

A little further upstream, whiting and flathead are caught off the sand flats around the island, and the flats here are also crawling with yabbies. Inland from the island the stream narrows, and the old iron floodgates (which have given the area its name, Iron Gates) are a great place for bream. A little further along, a bay in the river has a good mulloway hole and is also a reliable spot for mangrove jack, bream and flathead.

There are many good rock places around the headland on the southern side of the river. South-east of Little Beach is **Half Tide Inlet**, where mulloway and bream are the main targets. **Joggly Point** can only be reached by walking or four-wheel drive and

The Richmond River at Ballina, permanently open to the ocean, provides a port for many professional boats

is a dangerous place in a swell, but on a good day it can be fished for mulloway, bream, tailor, drummer and luderick. Bream is the main target from the sandy bottom beneath a series of rocks called the **Piano Rocks**. The **Red Hill headland** is for walkers only, but can have mulloway, bream, tailor and rock blackfish.

Chinamans Beach and **New Zealand Beach**, both good for bream, tailor and whiting, are split by some rocks, which are best fished in rough conditions for bream and tailor. **Snapper Rock** has a low ledge on its seaward side, to be avoided in a swell, but in good weather try for bream, luderick, rock blackfish, mulloway and pelagics such as mackerel and longtail tuna. An exposed bombora called **Chaos** can be seen to the south-east and is known for its big Spanish mackerel and yellowtail kingfish.

71

NEW SOUTH WALES

COASTAL FISHING GRAFTON REGION

Shark Bay to Minnie Water

Type of fishing
beach, estuary, offshore, river, rock, wall

Target fish
bream, flathead, mulloway, tailor, whiting

There is good outside fishing in the Yamba–Iluka area, with plenty of rock and beach spots. The Clarence River is a mecca for anglers in New South Wales, and further south, the village of Minnie Water has good rock fishing for bream and tailor, and beach fishing for mulloway, flathead and whiting.

SHARK BAY TO BROOMS HEAD

At **Shark Bay**, you can fish from North Beach for tailor, flathead, whiting and bream. The rocks at Woody Head are a fine platform for varied fishing, with tailor and mulloway the main targets. **Frasers Rock** and **Second Bluff** are the closest rock spots to Iluka, but there is easy access to all the north shore rocks. Mulloway are again the prime target from all these rocks.

In the south, **Pippi Beach** has good fishing for flathead, bream and tailor, with mulloway around Flat Rock at the beach's southern end. The rocks around Green Point and Angourie Point attract rock blackfish, luderick and sometimes mackerel, but the main targets are mulloway, bream and tailor.

Angourie Beach is productive and runs to a rocky formation known as **One Man Rock**, a dangerous place in rough weather, but with mulloway, groper and drummer. **Shelly Beach Head** carries a similar variety of fish, but is accessible only by walking. **Brooms Head** has good fishing for luderick, bream, rock blackfish, groper, mackerel and tailor, with snapper in summer. There is reef fishing offshore, and it is possible to beach-launch from the lee of the headland.

CLARENCE RIVER

The Clarence River has tailor and mulloway around the entrance; bream and luderick around the piers and rock walls; and flathead and whiting on the sand flats along the river. The townships of Yamba and Iluka on either side of the entrance have excellent facilities for boat launching, boat hire and bait and tackle supply.

The walls at the entrance extend well out to sea, and bream, mulloway, luderick and tailor are the regular catches. **Middle Wall**, on the southern side of the river, is noted for prolific catches of bream and luderick in winter, and the same fish are targets on the northern side at **Turkeys Nest Wall** and **Collis Wall**.

Inside the river is a complex of channels, islands and sand flats. Most of the fishing is drifting for flathead and whiting, with bream and luderick around rocky banks and structures like walls and piers. The flathead and whiting are distributed up the river as far as the town of **Maclean**, but some of the best spots are downriver from **Freeburn Island**, around Sleeper Point on **Palmers Island**, where mulloway hold the deeper water, and in the oyster channel running along the eastern side of **Micalo Island** to **Wooloweyah Lagoon**. The lagoon, a popular place for mud crabbing, carries a lot of flathead and bream.

The best times to fish the Clarence are dawn and dusk. A falling tide will enhance prospects of taking the flathead and whiting in the channels.

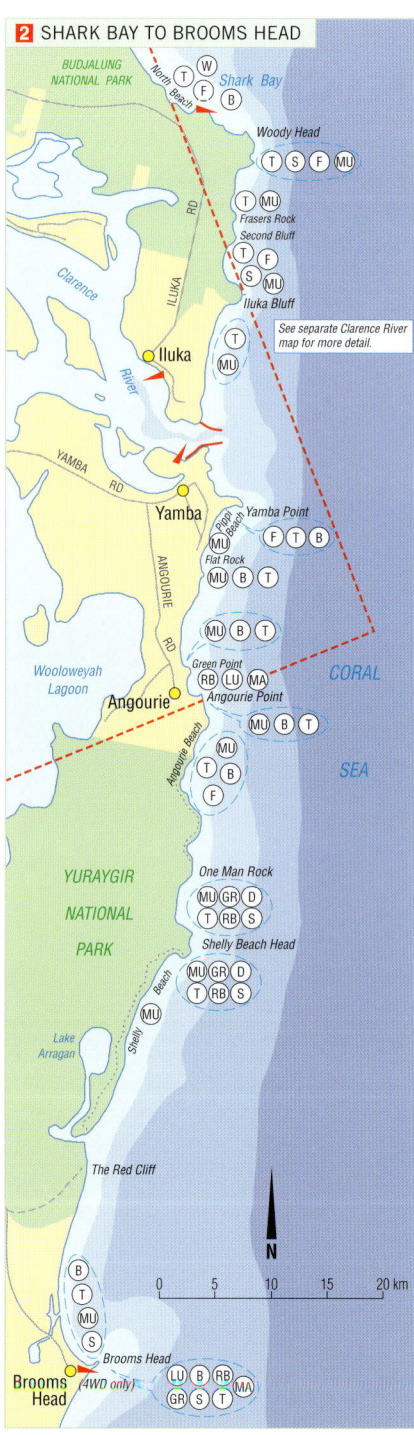

Young anglers on the lower Clarence River

GUIDE TO LOCAL FISH

		Shark Bay to Brooms Head	Clarence River	Sandon River
B	bream	•	•	•
D	drummer, silver	•	•	•
F	flathead	•	•	•
FL	flounder			•
GR	groper	•		•
LU	luderick	•	•	•
MA	mackerel	•	•	
MU	mulloway	•	•	•
RB	rock blackfish	•		•
S	snapper	•		•
T	tailor	•	•	•
TU	tuna		•	
W	whiting	•	•	•

COASTAL FISHING GRAFTON REGION NEW SOUTH WALES

1 CLARENCE RIVER

3 SANDON RIVER

SANDON RIVER

The Sandon River region is a great fishing hideaway. The seclusion of Sandon township allows for some peaceful fishing in the river exploration of the rock and beach spots.

On the northern side of the entrance, **Plover Island**, which is connected to the mainland, can be fished from the rocks or a boat for tailor, bream and drummer, with occasional mulloway and snapper in rough weather. Boat fishing around the southern headland for the likes of rock blackfish, groper, mulloway, bream and tailor is popular. Inside the entrance, whiting and flathead are abundant around the sand flats, with the whiting best after rain. Bream and luderick are around the river mouth in winter.

Near the entrance to **Toumbaal Creek**, where the rocky bar is close to the surface, there can be good catches of school mulloway, bream and flathead on a run-out tide. The bend in the main river leads to oyster leases, and the likelihood of bream. Around the island and on to the forks in the river there are flathead, whiting in summer, and luderick and bream around rocky banks and structures. The river is shallow throughout.

The sheltered lagoon at **Minnie Water** is a fish nursery habitat and therefore a fishing drawcard, carrying bream, tarwhine, pike, sand whiting and many tropical species in the summer. Sandon and Minnie Water are part of the Solitary Islands Marine Reserve, which is subject to the control of the New South Wales Department of Fisheries and New South Wales National Parks.

NEW SOUTH WALES — COASTAL FISHING GRAFTON REGION

Wooli to Coffs Harbour

Type of fishing
beach, creek, estuary, offshore, river, rock

Target fish
bream, mulloway, tailor, whiting

The waters between Wooli and Coffs Harbour are a delightful combination of estuaries, beaches, headlands, rock platforms and offshore islands. They include the Wooli Wooli River, which runs parallel to the coast behind Wooli, and the all-weather harbour at Coffs Harbour, one of the best established towns for fishing in Australia. A number of small rivers also run down this stretch of coast, with sand flats, channels and seagrass patches creating a varied habitat for mullet, bream, luderick, whiting and flathead. From north to south, they are **Station Creek**, **Saltwater Creek**, **Corindi River**, **Arrawarra Creek**, **Woolgoolga Creek** and **Moonee Creek**.

Fishing from the various headlands can yield snapper, tailor, groper, yellowtail kingfish, Spanish mackerel and tuna, while the main beach species are tailor, bream, whiting, flathead and mulloway. The most commonly fished headlands are at the **Station Creek** entrance, **Red Rock**, **Arrawarra**, **Woolgoolga** and **Bare Bluff**, while **Corindi**, **Woolgoolga** and **Moonee** are outstanding among the beaches along the coast.

The **Solitary Islands** are a chain of islands and other outcrops, the northernmost offshore from Wooli and the furthest south just past Moonee Beach. The warm, southward flowing current bathes the islands, creating a habitat for temperate fish and for tropical fish not found elsewhere in New South Wales. This area is a reserve, under strict controls, but line fishing is allowed in all but a few designed sanctuary zones.

North Solitary Island has snapper, yellowtail kingfish, teraglin, mulloway, pearl perch, tailor, groper, rock blackfish, silver drummer, Spanish mackerel and tuna. On the western side of the island fishing is prohibited for 200 m. **North Rock** is 3 km north of Red Rock headland, but the nearest launching places are the Wooli Wooli River and Corindi River, both with bar crossings that can only be attempted in calm water at high tide. North Rock is really twin rocks, with a sand-bottomed gutter fished for yellowtail kingfish, snapper, pearl perch, tailor, Spanish mackerel, longtail tuna and other pelagics.

North West Solitary, **South West Solitary** (known locally as Groper Islet), **South Solitary and Split Solitary islands** all have closed waters and other areas restricted to line fishing, and carry the same diversity of temperate and tropical bottom fish and pelagic species. South Solitary has the best fishing of all the islands. It is really three islands, and the northernmost, Birdie Island, often has a number of the protected grey nurse sharks in its waters.

GUIDE TO LOCAL FISH

	Wooli to Coffs Harbour	Coffs Harbour	Wooli
(AJ) amberjack	●		
(B) bream	●	●	●
(CO) cobia	●		
(DA) dart			●
(D) drummer, silver	●	●	●
(F) flathead	●	●	●
(GR) groper	●	●	●
(KI) kingfish, yellowtail	●	●	●
(LU) luderick	●		●
(MA) mackerel	●	●	●
(M) mullet	●		
(MU) mulloway	●	●	●
(PP) perch, pearl	●	●	
(RB) rock blackfish	●	●	
(SM) samson fish	●		
(S) snapper	●		●
(T) tailor	●	●	●
(TL) teraglin	●		
(TU) tuna	●		●
(WH) wahoo	●		
(W) whiting	●	●	●

COASTAL FISHING GRAFTON REGION — NEW SOUTH WALES

WOOLI

The **Wooli Wooli River** is shallow and the boat channel fairly winding, so care is needed. Both sides of the entrance are good for mulloway, bream, tailor and luderick. The bar is passable in southerly weather but dangerous in a north-easterly, particularly on a run-out tide. Seek local advice before attempting a crossing. A picnic area on the town side of the river has easy fishing for whiting and flathead, but there are many more spots along the river. The **Co-op Wharf** is an excellent place for bream when the fishing boats return. On the opposite side of the river, the oyster shell dumps create a habitat for large bream.

Other good spots are underneath the powerlines that cross the river near the most southerly boat ramp for flathead; around the oyster posts towards Rum Island for flathead; and in the channel on the western side of Rum Island for whiting. In its upper reaches, the river becomes a closed sanctuary zone from the point where the river branches, known as The Forks.

COFFS HARBOUR

At **Diggers Beach**, whiting, dart, bream and tailor are the main targets, with snapper around the headlands. The rock locations around **Macauleys Headland** have a variety of fish, including rock blackfish, luderick, groper, mulloway, bream and flathead.

The main surfing beach, **Park Beach**, has good gutter formations along its length for hauls of whiting, bream, school mulloway, tailor and dart. **Coffs Creek** enters the beach here, and is fished down to the Pacific Highway for flathead, and for whiting and luderick near the entrance. Offshore is **Little Muttonbird Island**, which can be reached on foot at low tide, for snapper and tailor.

Tailor abound along the State's beaches year round, with seasonal peaks in late summer and winter

Muttonbird Island was joined to the mainland in 1925 to form the northern breakwater for Coffs Harbour, and is one of the best rock fishing spots in the area, with snapper and tailor, and pelagics like Spanish mackerel, tuna and yellowtail kingfish.

The **North Wall**, which joins the island to the mainland, is fished on the ocean side for bream, tailor, snapper and drummer. The harbour is busy, but there are good hauls of yellowtail kingfish and luderick around the marina, and whiting and bream from **Jetty Beach** and the jetty itself.

The **East Wall** is fished for Spanish mackerel and mulloway on the seaward side, and bream, whiting and flathead on the harbour side. The rocks of the southern headland have many good spots to fish for mulloway, tailor, bream, luderick and snapper, including an excellent spot at the southern extremity called the Bream Hole.

Boambee Beach is another accessible and ideal fishing beach, with a plentiful supply of beach worms and pippis, and good catches of tailor, bream, whiting and school mulloway along its length.

With a good harbour and plenty of islands and reefs, Coffs Harbour offers a lot of attraction for offshore fishing. One close-in spot is the **Park Beach Bombora**, which can be located by broken water in anything from a moderate swell. Snapper, spotted and Spanish mackerel and longtail tuna are among the pelagic species here.

Offshore, the **Changte Shoal**, straight out from the harbour, is a large reef area rising to within 6 m of the surface. The reef fish include teraglin, yellowtail kingfish, cobia and snapper, and there can be good runs of school mulloway. Pelagic fish like Spanish mackerel, various tunas and even black marlin come to the shoal.

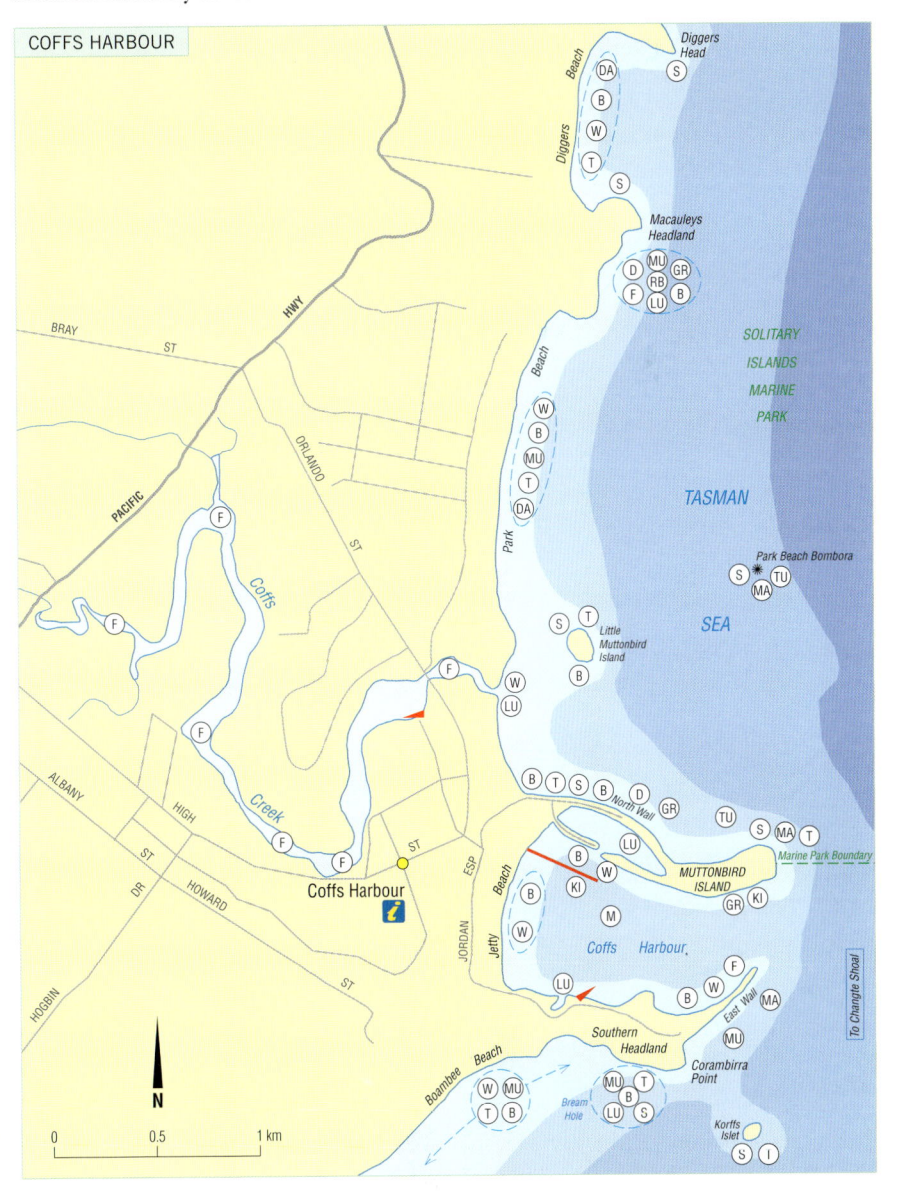

NEW SOUTH WALES

COASTAL FISHING — PORT MACQUARIE REGION

Port Macquarie Region

The combination of rock, beach, estuary and offshore fishing around Port Macquarie places this region at the forefront of Australian fishing.

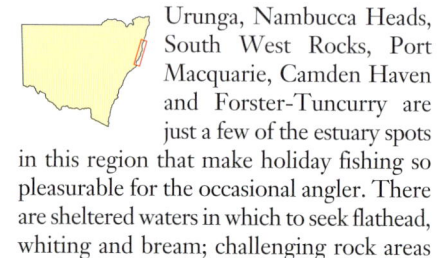

Urunga, Nambucca Heads, South West Rocks, Port Macquarie, Camden Haven and Forster-Tuncurry are just a few of the estuary spots in this region that make holiday fishing so pleasurable for the occasional angler. There are sheltered waters in which to seek flathead, whiting and bream; challenging rock areas that attract both pelagics and inshore species; and beaches with channels and gutters to try for fish such as flathead and tailor.

Boat anglers go out to the reefs, rocks, islands and bomboras for fish like snapper, pearl perch and morwong, and to the game fishing grounds for wahoo, dolphin fish, tuna and shark.

Nambucca River viewed from Nambucca Heads

WHERE TO FISH

Port Macquarie Region

SAWTELL TO NAMBUCCA HEADS ● 78
Boambee Head and Boambee Beach are a good fishing combination. Sawtell has beach, rock and river fishing, with lure fishing upriver for bream and mangrove jack. There is great land fishing around Urunga and the Kalang River. Nambucca Heads has excellent offshore and beach fishing, as well as good estuary and wall spots.

SOUTH WEST ROCKS TO HAT HEAD ● 80
The Macleay River estuary is brilliant all the way, with big mulloway at the mouth, particularly after a flood. South West Rocks is the base for some of the best light-tackle game fishing in New South Wales, with cobia caught all year round. Fish Rock, off Smoky Cape, is one of the best offshore places along this coast. The rock and beach fishing is also magical, with some superb rock spots around Hat Head.

PORT MACQUARIE ● 82
Boat anglers find wonderful sport in the Hastings River, and fine mulloway fishing around the entrance walls. There are ocean beaches on either side of Port Macquarie and reef areas close to shore, with blue water game fishing only a few kilometres out. For lovers of rock fishing, Queens Head, between Port Macquarie and Crescent Head, is the place for rock blackfish and luderick.

CAMDEN HAVEN AND MANNING RIVER ● 84
Camden Haven is a tranquil and easily fished estuary area, with big mulloway around the walls and good beach and rock areas nearby. Point Perpendicular is one of the best rock areas in the State, with high ledges and platforms over deep water. The Manning River is full of sand flats and channels for flathead and whiting.

TUNCURRY TO CHARLOTTE HEAD ● 86
The huge Wallis Lake area at Forster-Tuncurry has fine breakwall and bridge fishing. The two towns were once fishing villages, but are now boom towns. The deep-shelving rocks and cliffs around Charlotte Head allow casting with overhead and side-cast rigs for longtail tuna, yellowfin tuna, cobia and kingfish in season, while there is regular fare of tailor, bream, mulloway, whiting and salmon passing through the area during their annual migrations.

COASTAL FISHING PORT MACQUARIE REGION — NEW SOUTH WALES

GUIDE TO LOCAL FISH

- Australian salmon
- bonito
- bream, black
- bream, yellowfin
- cobia
- dolphin fish
- drummer, silver
- flathead
- flounder
- garfish
- groper
- kingfish, yellowtail
- luderick
- mackerel, slimy
- mackerel, Spanish
- mackerel, spotted
- mangrove jack
- marlin, black
- marlin, blue
- marlin, striped
- morwong
- mullet
- mulloway
- perch, pearl
- rock blackfish
- shark
- snapper
- tailor
- teraglin
- trevally, giant
- trevally, golden
- trevally, silver
- tuna, longtail
- tuna, striped
- tuna, yellowfin
- wahoo
- whiting, sand
- whiting, trumpeter

Fishing boats moored at South West Rocks

FURTHER INFORMATION

Fishing and boating NSW Fisheries has offices at 14 John St, Port Macquarie, tel. (02) 6583 1102; and 59 Pitt Chatham St, Taree, tel. (02) 6552 6799. The Waterways Authority has an office at Shop 3, Port Marina, Port Macquarie, tel. (02) 6583 1007. The Coastal Patrol has bases at South West Rocks, tel. (02) 6566 5240; and Forster, tel. (02) 6554 5458.

Tourist centres Great Lakes Tourism, Little St, Forster, tel. (02) 6554 8799; Harrington Service Station, 85 Beach St, Harrington, tel. (02) 6556 1188; Pacific Hwy, South Kempsey, tel. (02) 6563 1555; 4 Pacific Hwy, Nambucca Heads, tel. (02) 6568 6954; cnr Clarence St and Hay St, Port Macquarie, tel. (02) 6581 8000; Ocean Ave, South West Rocks, tel. (02) 6566 7099; Pacific Hwy, Urunga, tel. (02) 6655 5711.

Weather

Prevailing winds in the summer months are north-north-easterlies, with westerlies dominating the winter season. The Port Macquarie region is prone to localised thunderstorms, which can bring hail, so always keep an eye out for cloud build-up to warn of impending change. The Weather Bureau can be reached on tel. (02) 9296 1555.

FISHING TIP

Over shallow tidal sand flats on a rising tide, schools of 'lano' or sand mullet can be berleyed into a reckless feeding binge with fragments of white bread. If you cast small, white, floating flies among these fish, they will readily grab them, providing fast-paced and effective fishing.

Boating

Port Macquarie has a bar, which must be carefully navigated. Local authorities always advise visitors to stay within the navigational markers. The bar is especially dangerous at ebb tides if the wind is north-easterly. The Macleay River has no navigational markers and must be negotiated with extreme caution. Laurieton, in the Camden Haven area, has a safe entrance to the sea via the Camden Haven Inlet. Further south, the two natural entrances to the Manning River are dangerous to use. For safe shelter and access to the Manning River area, use the man-made harbour and triple boat ramp at Crowdy Head, 8 km north of Harrington. This also gives the best access to Mermaid Reef. For further information, contact the local Waterways Authority office.

NEW SOUTH WALES

COASTAL FISHING PORT MACQUARIE REGION

Sawtell to Nambucca Heads

Type of fishing
beach, offshore, river, rock, wall

Target fish
bream, flathead, luderick, Spanish mackerel

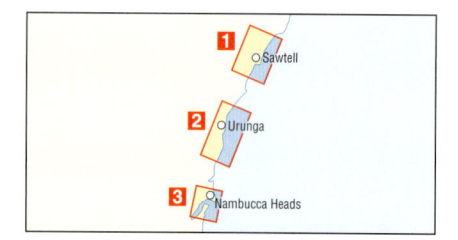

The tiny settlement of Boambee offers a smaller version of the fishing variety to the north at Coffs Harbour. Sawtell is another well-established fishing town. The Urunga area has superb river fishing just behind the coast, excellent bank and boat access, and a combination of beach, wall and rock fishing. Nambucca Heads is a major tourist town, with its river at the centre of the fishing action.

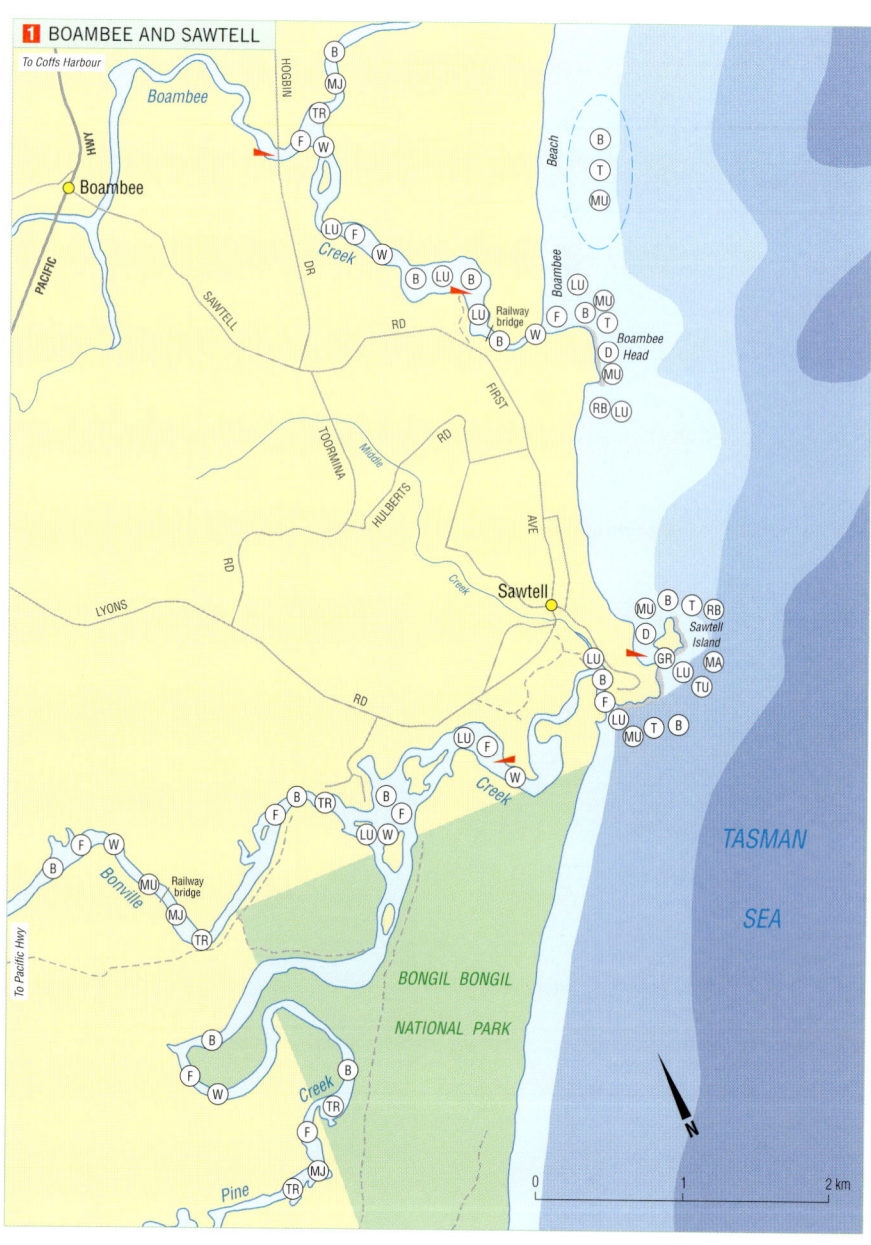

BOAMBEE AND SAWTELL

Boambee Beach has good gutters for bream, tailor and mulloway, while just inside the entrance of **Boambee Creek**, the railway bridge pylons attract bream and luderick. Past the bridge in the wider part of the creek, there are weed beds and channels where drifting can reward with flathead and whiting, and you can lure cast for bream, and flat fish for luderick.

The sand flats on the southern side of the creek, where yabbies can be pumped, have flathead and whiting. The creek narrows and forks, with mangroves along its slender northern channel providing a habitat for bream, mangrove jack and trevally in summer. There is a ramp on the southern side of the lower branch, giving access to these productive upper reaches of the creek.

Boambee Head is a combination of rock platforms and sandy gutters, with fishing for tailor, bream and mulloway. The mulloway bite best on a run-out tide, particularly after heavy rain. The southern side of the headland is rockier and provides a habitat for rock blackfish and luderick.

The headland at **Sawtell** has rock spots from which to seek tailor and mulloway, with luderick in the calmer weather. **Sawtell Island** has a good spinning platform for luderick, rock blackfish and groper, as well as tailor, silver drummer and mulloway.

Bonville Creek and its tributary **Pine Creek** get a lot of attention, as the fishing is reliable for bream, flathead, whiting in summer, and mulloway in winter.

Just inside the sheltered entrance at Sawtell, along the southern side, is an ideal luderick spot. Weed for bait can be gathered on the northern side. The creek takes a bend around a high finger of land, creating a sheltered spot, where weed and shellfish encourage the presence of bream and luderick. Opposite, there are drop-offs from the sand flats, and big flathead. A broader stretch continues this ideal situation up to the confluence of the two creeks, which is a hot spot for all these species and a great place to gather yabbies for bait. As the creeks go inland, there is lure fishing for the mangrove jack and tropical trevally that mingle with the whiting and bream.

There are school mulloway in the holes around the railway bridge over Bonville Creek, and small bass in the upper reaches, but they are too small to eat and the stock is limited so they are best released, as are the protected estuary cod, which show up occasionally further downstream.

URUNGA

The mouth of the **Bellinger River** has excellent fishing for mulloway, bream, flathead, whiting and tailor, while the southern wall is a great spot for mulloway, luderick, and large bream on a falling tide.

COASTAL FISHING PORT MACQUARIE REGION   NEW SOUTH WALES

The footbridge is also a great fishing spot. The walls on either side of the confluence of the Bellinger and Kalang rivers are excellent for luderick, bream, flathead and whiting. **Yellow Rock Inlet** has good fishing for flathead, whiting and bream.

Further upriver near **Tuckers Island**, there are whiting and flathead, with good yabbies in the sand flats. Access is by boat from the township of Mylestom. Downstream, some 300 m from **Repton**, there is a hole for mulloway, and bream, mangrove jack and school mulloway abound in the area. Towards the road bridge, there is a sandy channel with good whiting and flathead.

The best spots on the **Kalang River** are near the bridge. You can fish from the bank or by boat for flathead and bream. A boat will take you on to the Snapper Hole, where a tributary branches off, and where mangrove jack, bream and mulloway can be in big numbers.

There is fine rock and beach fishing on either side of the estuary. The beaches produce tailor, flathead, mulloway, bream and whiting on worm and pippi baits from the sand, while snapper, rock blackfish and luderick add to the targets around Hungry Head.

NAMBUCCA HEADS

Shelly Beach has bream, flathead, tailor and mulloway among the rocks, and there is a good mulloway hole at the southern end.

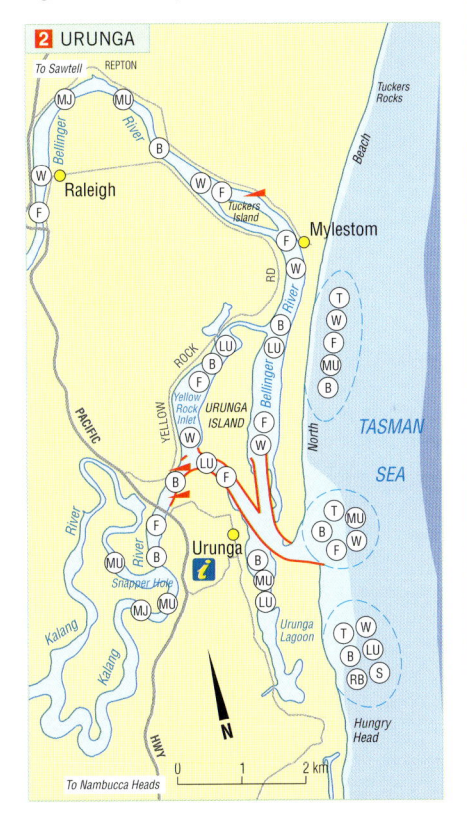

Nambucca River is silted and shallow at the river mouth, so those attracted by the prolific offshore fishing must launch from Shelly Beach. Locals can offer some good advice on the location of the reefs, which are east and north-east of the river mouth. These are worth seeking for snapper, teraglin, mulloway, pearl perch and morwong.

The headlands at the river entrance are good for spotted and Spanish mackerel in summer. The North Wall is very popular, mainly for bream, luderick and mulloway.

The wall swings south at **Vee Beach**, and creates a sheltered area where flathead and whiting come in. The action for bream, luderick and mulloway continues right along the upstream training wall. In the main channels of the river and in **Warrell Creek**, a southern tributary, the targets are flathead, whiting and bream.

South of Nambucca Heads, the beaches around **Scotts Head** and **Grassy Head** fish well, while the many offshore reefs are haunts of Spanish and spotted mackerel as well as mulloway, kingfish, cobia and teraglin. A depth sounder will help in locating these reefs and it pays to use a GPS unit to mark the reefs for future reference.

GUIDE TO LOCAL FISH

		Boambee and Sawtell	Urunga	Nambucca Heads
B	bream	●	●	●
D	drummer, silver	●		●
F	flathead	●	●	●
GR	groper	●		
LU	luderick	●	●	●
MA	mackerel	●		●
MJ	mangrove jack	●	●	
MO	morwong			●
MU	mulloway	●	●	●
PP	pearl perch			●
RB	rock blackfish	●	●	
S	snapper		●	●
T	tailor	●	●	●
TL	teraglin			●
TR	trevally	●		
TU	tuna	●		
W	whiting	●	●	●

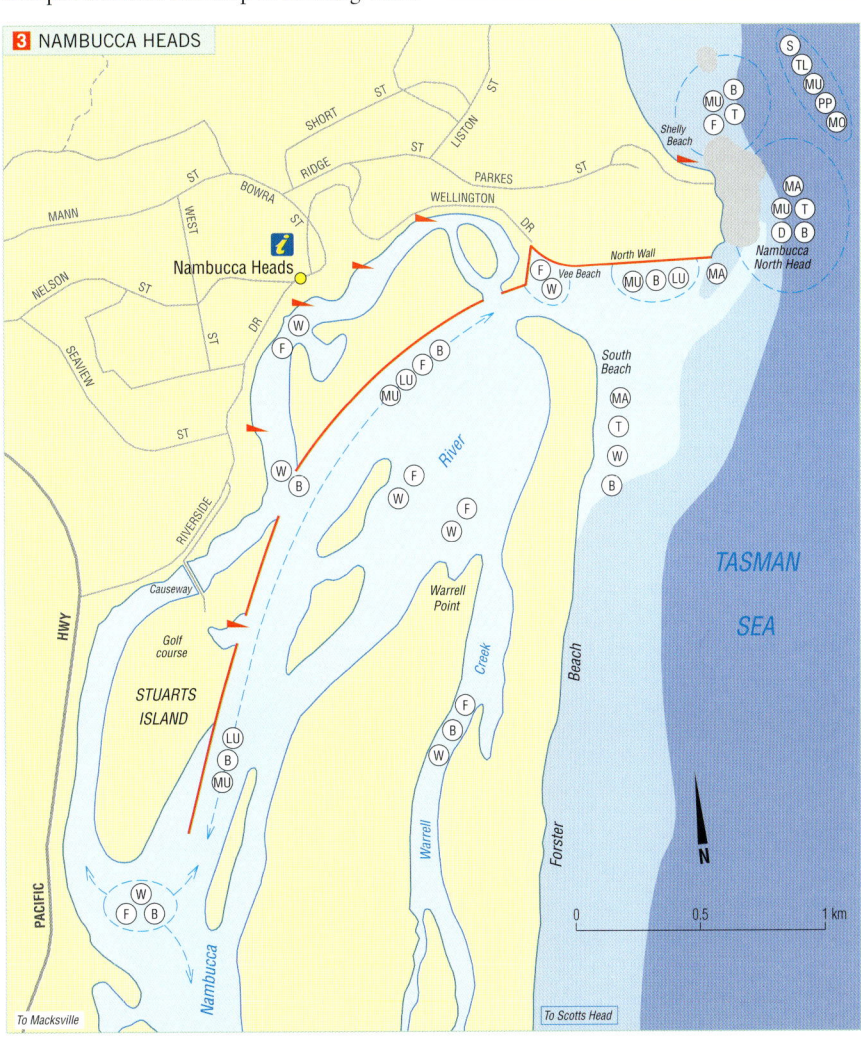

NEW SOUTH WALES

COASTAL FISHING PORT MACQUARIE REGION

South West Rocks to Hat Head

Type of fishing
beach, estuary, offshore, rock

Target fish
bream, luderick, whiting, yellowtail kingfish

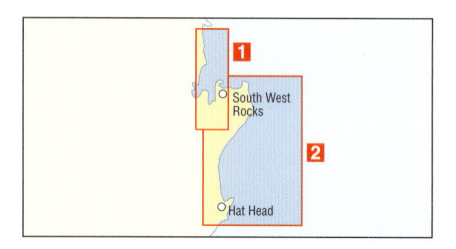

The Macleay River estuary is very productive, even into the freshwater reaches above Kempsey. South West Rocks has excellent light-tackle game fishing, with tropical and temperate fish species in the area according to the season. The coastline south of South West Rocks has some of the most magical rock and beach fishing in New South Wales.

MACLEAY RIVER ESTUARY

The action starts at the mouth of the **Macleay River**, particularly after a flood, when there can be a run of big mulloway. The mulloway anglers on the long entrance walls use up to 40-kg line with live baits or lures, and fish the area where the muddy fresh water reaches the clean ocean water. Here, the mulloway are in wait for prey washed out of the river.

The **North Wall** is best, but both this and the **South Wall** fish consistently in season for Spanish mackerel, luderick, flathead, bream and tailor. On the north side, the channels that run to the wall are fished for flathead, luderick and bream. The inner end of the wall in the north is called **Kemps Corner**, and opens into the northern stretch of the river, one of the best fishing areas. With **Shark Island** on one side and sandbanks and channels on the other, it is a great place to drift for whiting and flathead, exploring the deeper water for mulloway, and the rocks and banks for bream and luderick.

The Bay at the top of Shark Island yields bream, flathead and luderick at high tide. Further on near the oyster leases, there are channels for bream, flathead and whiting. The long run up to **Stuarts Point** may be rewarded with luderick and bream on either side of high tide. All the sandbanks in this area are great spots for collecting pink nippers.

South again, it pays to drift with pilchards in the deep channel beside **Little Shark Island**. There is an extensive weed bank at the northern end of the island, where whiting, flathead and luderick are best fished on either side of low tide. To the south, the next two sand islands have similar conditions at their northern ends. The **Clybucca Creek** entrance is excellent to drift for whiting and flathead.

Flathead Spit, on the run down to Jerseyville Bridge, is excellent drifting and spinning water, and the bridge itself attracts bream, school mulloway, flathead and tailor. It fishes well at night. The main river continues to be good for drifting for flathead, with bream and luderick around the bridges, and there are plenty of sandbanks and drop-offs yielding flathead and whiting.

Below South West Rocks, a tributary of the main river called **Spencers Creek** has flathead at the entrance, and luderick and bream along the banks, while the footbridge over **Back Creek** – known as The Spot – is reputedly the best location for luderick, and is easily accessed from South West Rocks township.

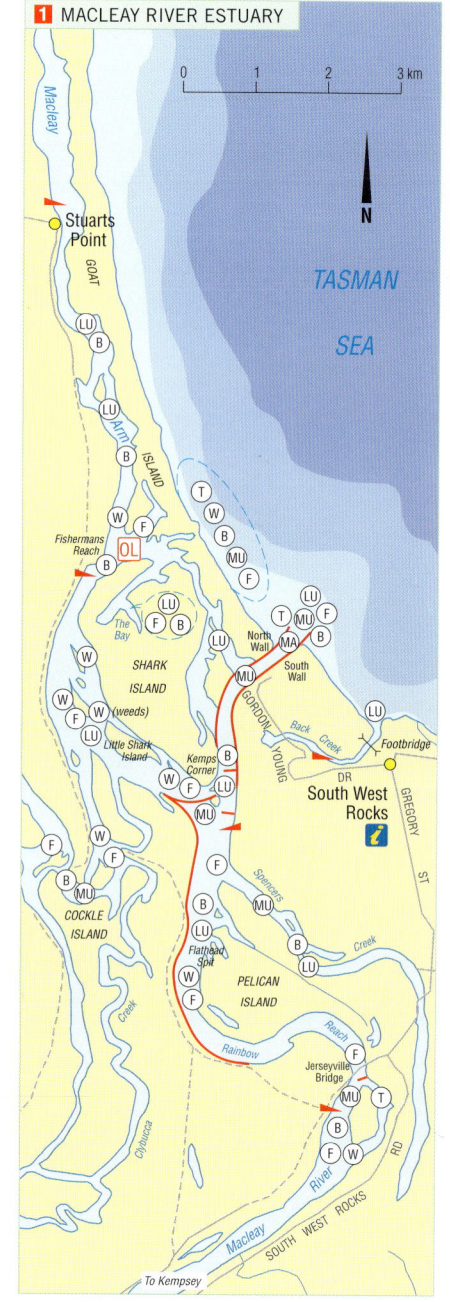

Trial Bay Beach is a popular surf fishing venue

SOUTH WEST ROCKS TO HAT HEAD

Species common on the **South West Rocks** coast are Spanish and spotted mackerel from February to May, and marlin, tuna, dolphin fish, wahoo, kingfish and shark in high summer. Cobia are a lucky year-round catch.

There are also some wonderful rock spots, with the fishing peaking in autumn and winter for tailor and rock blackfish. Bream, whiting, mulloway, mackerel, drummer, luderick, snapper, kingfish and bonito are also caught from Monument Point to Smoky Cape. Some specific rock locations are the Trial Bay Gaol; Little Bay; the deep narrow bay past Green Island; the

COASTAL FISHING PORT MACQUARIE REGION — NEW SOUTH WALES

GUIDE TO LOCAL FISH

	Macleay River Estuary	South West Rocks to Hat Head
(BT) bonito		●
(B) bream	●	●
(CO) cobia		●
(DO) dolphin fish		●
(D) drummer, silver		●
(F) flathead	●	●
(KI) kingfish, yellowtail		●
(LU) luderick	●	●
(MA) mackerel	●	●
(ML) marlin		●
(MU) mulloway	●	●
(RB) rock blackfish		●
(SH) shark		●
(S) snapper		●
(T) tailor	●	●
(TU) tuna		●
(WH) wahoo		●
(W) whiting	●	●

2 SOUTH WEST ROCKS TO HAT HEAD

bay between Green Island and Smoky Cape; and when conditions allow safe fishing, Gibraltar Rock, just off the lighthouse point.

Fish Rock, south-east of Smoky Cape, is one of the best offshore locations along this coast, as it sits on the edge of the blue water current and has everything from game fish, such as marlin, wahoo, cobia, kingfish and tuna, to bottom fish like mulloway and snapper. Further south is **Black Rocks**. A bombora in its north-west corner is good for snapper and bream, and pinnacles just south of the rock attract mulloway and snapper. The eastern side has good trolling for Spanish mackerel, cobia, kingfish and bonito.

Smoky Cape Beach has good deep gutters, holding tailor, bream and whiting, and can be accessed with four-wheel drive.

Little Beach, just before Hat Head, is sheltered from the southerlies, and is an excellent bream spot. Tailor, whiting, flathead, luderick and the occasional mulloway are also present.

The north side of **Korogoro Point** can only be reached by walking track, and allows casting into deep water for bonito, Spanish mackerel, kingfish and tuna, while closer in, there are rock blackfish, bream and mulloway in the rocky gutters. Around the point is the **Death Hole**, which requires ropes and care, but rewards with tailor, bream, silver drummer and mulloway. A series of bays to the south have deepwater rock fishing for the same species.

A spot called **The Island** is accessible only at low water, but is a great all-round area for rock fishing. Beyond there are some high ledges, and catches of mulloway, tailor and bream will require gaff work to bring them up. **Gap Beach** after a storm is a terrific area for luderick, rock blackfish, silver drummer, whiting, bream, tailor and mulloway. The next point south has high ledges and remains excellent for big tailor, mulloway, luderick, rock blackfish and bream.

Connors Beach has a deep gutter, protected by a sandbar, and **Third Beach** has continual wave action, so they both yield big tailor, bream and mulloway. The little finger of land between the beaches offers deepwater fishing for bream, tailor and mulloway.

The rocks around **Windy Gap** have fish, but catches can be hard to lift up onto the high ledges. The best areas are at the southern end of the point at **Twin Holes**, **Kemps Corner** and **The Jew Bite**.

Offshore from Hat Head are bomboras that provide a focus for Spanish mackerel, cobia, kingfish, tuna and shark. Out from Hat Head are **Close Reef** (4 km) and **Wide Reef** (8 km), which are good for bottom fishing for snapper, teraglin, pearl perch and dolphin fish. Off Kemps Corner, about 8 km and 9 km, are another two reef areas, which invite drifting for snapper, teraglin, morwong and pearl perch.

81

NEW SOUTH WALES

COASTAL FISHING PORT MACQUARIE REGION

Port Macquarie

Type of fishing
beach, offshore, rock, wall

Target fish
bream, luderick, mulloway, rock blackfish

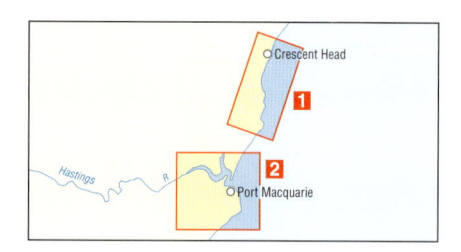

The excellent beach and rock fishing continues down this section of coast, and Port Macquarie – a historic town founded as a convict settlement – is one of New South Wales' most popular holiday resorts, offering a wonderful variety of fishing.

CRESCENT HEAD TO QUEENS HEAD

The area from Racecourse Head to Queens Head is dotted with many safe rock fishing spots. Tailor from 1 to 3 kg are common, and rock blackfish are a regular catch in the washes. Bream, luderick, drummer and mulloway are around in good numbers. The best fishing is in autumn and winter.

Racecourse Head allows fishing into a gutter at the end of the beach for flathead and whiting, as well as rock blackfish and luderick behind the reef in rough waters. Similar conditions exist on **Racecourse Island**, which can be waded to at low tide. **Big Hill Point** has rugged rock formations above reefs and gutters. Two favourite bream and mulloway spots are **The Arch**, accessible at low tides, and **The Stairs**, reached by following a narrow path.

The beach to the north of **Point Plomer** is sheltered in a southerly and is excellent for bream. The north side of the point is easy to fish for tailor, bream, luderick, rock blackfish, mulloway and groper. On the seaward side, fishing is for tailor off the point, and luderick and bream in the gutters. The beach on the southern side has good gutters for bream and whiting.

Barrys Bay is ideal for inshore fishing from a boat, and anglers can cast for the prime target fish caught here – Spanish mackerel, cobia and longtail tuna.

Neverfail is two rocky spurs surrounded by gutters, and is accessible in all but the biggest seas for luderick and rock blackfish close in, and bream, tailor and mulloway further out. **Queens Head** is the place for rock blackfish and luderick specialists.

PORT MACQUARIE

Of the ocean stretches near Port Macquarie, **North Beach** is just one area renowned for wonderful whiting catches on beach worm in summer, and tailor on pilchards, garfish or lures in winter.

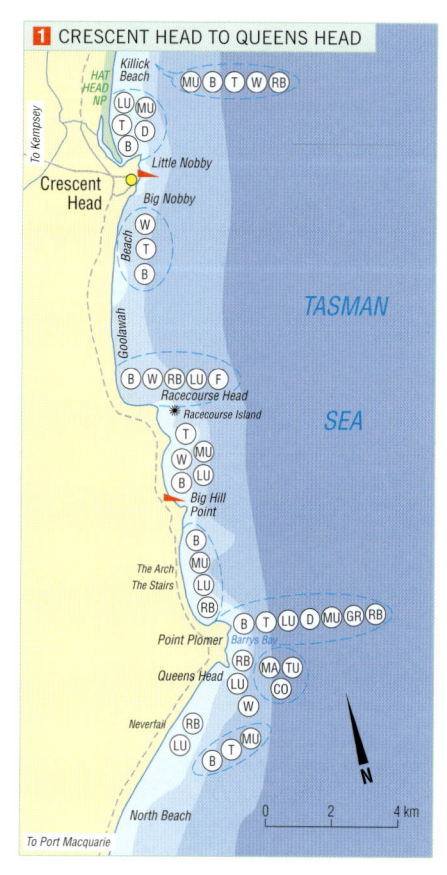

Fishing boats at Port Macquarie where the waters provide excellent fishing over autumn and winter

The **Hastings River** estuary provides great sport for whiting, flounder, flathead, bream and mulloway, and the weed-eating luderick, with some big tailor near the entrance in the winter.

Luderick are along the deeper banks and around the weed beds throughout the system. The best bait for them is either weed (available from local bait shops) or pink nippers, which are plentiful on the sandbanks.

The most popular fishing, however, is drifting for flathead and whiting along the

GUIDE TO LOCAL FISH

		Crescent Head to Queens Head	Port Macquarie
B	bream	●	●
CO	cobia	●	
DO	dolphin fish		●
D	drummer, silver	●	●
F	flathead	●	●
FL	flounder		●
GR	groper	●	
KI	kingfish, yellowtail		●
LU	luderick	●	●
MA	mackerel	●	
ML	marlin		●
MO	morwong		●
M	mullet		●
MU	mulloway	●	●
RB	rock blackfish	●	●
SH	shark		●
S	snapper		●
T	tailor	●	●
TU	tuna	●	
WH	wahoo		●
W	whiting	●	●

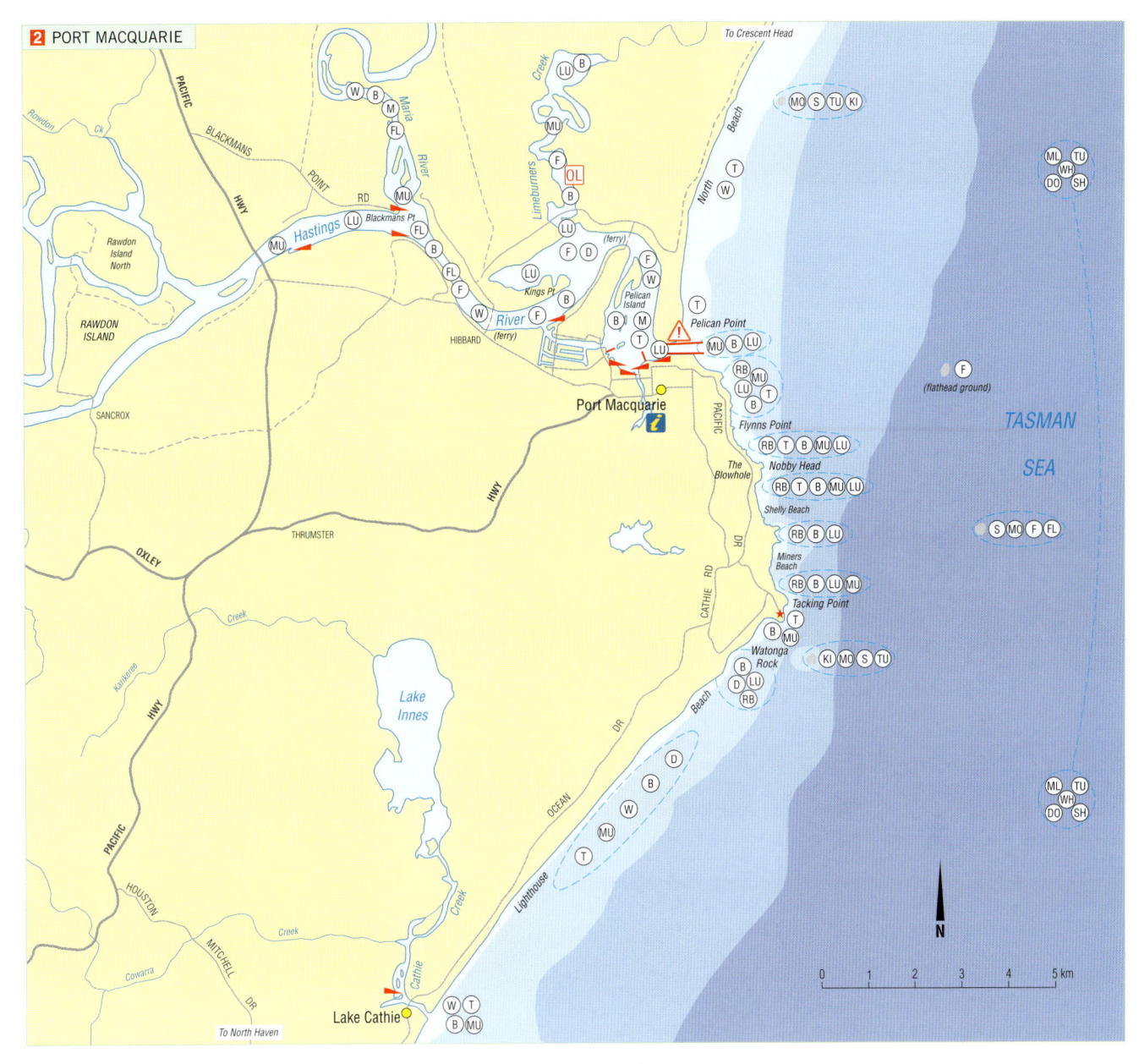

COASTAL FISHING PORT MACQUARIE REGION — NEW SOUTH WALES

channels and drop-offs, and over weed beds, with nippers or pilchards as bait. There are also bream, mulloway and mullet throughout the system.

Most of the mulloway are taken by fishing from the training walls at the entrance to the river with live mullet or luderick as bait, as they are the food the mulloway are naturally seeking in the area. These mulloway are big fish, requiring 20-kg line or more, with a beach rod and a big side cast or overhead reel to manage hooked fish in the tough terrain.

As the river swings north and then south inside the entrance, the water is mostly bream, flathead and whiting territory, with luderick along the banks. **Limeburners Creek** has oyster leases in the area close to its junction with the river. In the channels of the creek are big flathead, with bream in the upper reaches. In the Hastings River, the biggest mulloway are often found further upstream in deep water, past the confluence with the **Maria River**.

The rock and beach areas on the southern side of the town are convenient, offering tailor, rock blackfish, luderick, mulloway and bream. A good rock spot, though dangerous in big seas is **The Blowhole. Shelly Beach** offers excellent beach fishing.

Reefs north and south of Port Macquarie hold a good quotient of bottom and surface fish. Snapper is the prime target on the inshore reefs, taken by drifting baits down a berley stream. Straight in front of the town, from 5 to 7 km out, is a very big flathead ground. Off Shelly Beach, some 4 to 6 km, is a large area of rubble and reef attracting snapper, morwong, flathead and other reef fish.

Blue water game fishing off Port Macquarie is a growing sport, with the boats working out to areas 100 fathoms deep and more. Summer targets are marlin, wahoo, dolphin fish, yellowfin tuna and shark, and winter and early spring bring big catches of mako shark. Makos are known for their tremendous leaps from the water when hooked.

The entrance to Port Macquarie can be dangerous, particularly on a run-out tide when strong north winds are blowing. Boats can launch from Shelly Beach, or from Big Hill Point or Crescent Head for more northern offshore grounds.

83

Camden Haven and Manning River

Type of fishing
beach, estuary, rock, wall
Target fish
bream, flathead, luderick, mulloway

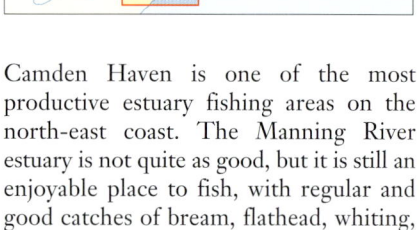

Fishing for luderick at Pilot Headland

Camden Haven is one of the most productive estuary fishing areas on the north-east coast. The Manning River estuary is not quite as good, but it is still an enjoyable place to fish, with regular and good catches of bream, flathead, whiting, school mulloway and luderick.

CAMDEN HAVEN

The fishing delights in this estuary are many. As always on the New South Wales coast, the big mulloway are around the entrance walls, particularly when rain has flushed the system and carried prey out to the estuary mouth. Bream and tailor are also common. There are ample launching ramps, and the added thoughtfulness of cleaning tables and running water to make the fishing experience at 'The Haven' as good as you can find.

The river quickly becomes shallow inside the entrance. The southern wall allows access to **Gogleys Lagoon**, also known as Lake Hope, a shallow lagoon with plenty of yabbies to gather on the sand flats. These will be taken by the flathead and whiting that congregate in the area. The main entrance to the lagoon is at **Gogleys Creek**, where big bream can be found. An Australian record bream of 4.45 kg was caught here.

Under the **North Haven Bridge**, there is a good chance for big flathead and bream. Further along this arm are channels for flathead and whiting, with bream and luderick around the rocks and banks. Because of extensive ill-marked oyster leases at the entrance to Queens Lake, the passage is difficult to negotiate, except on a high tide.

Down towards Laurieton, there are luderick around **Camden Point**, and bream on the north shore towards the Laurieton launching ramp. Weed beds, sandbars and more oyster leases all the way to **Watson Taylors Lake** ensure productive drifting for whiting and flathead.

There are some good outside areas including **Grants Beach**, an excellent spot for whiting, bream and tailor, and **Dunbogan Beach**, with its long gutters carrying whiting, flathead, bream, tailor and mulloway. **Pilot Beach**, just outside the southern wall, is a reliable whiting spot and a pleasant, sheltered place to fish.

Point Perpendicular is one of the State's best rock spots, with high ledges and platforms fronting deep water that can

GUIDE TO LOCAL FISH

		Camden Haven	Manning River
B	bream	●	●
CO	cobia	●	
D	drummer, silver	●	
F	flathead	●	●
KI	kingfish, yellowtail	●	
LU	luderick	●	●
MA	mackerel	●	
MU	mulloway	●	●
RB	rock blackfish	●	●
T	tailor	●	●
TU	tuna	●	
W	whiting	●	●

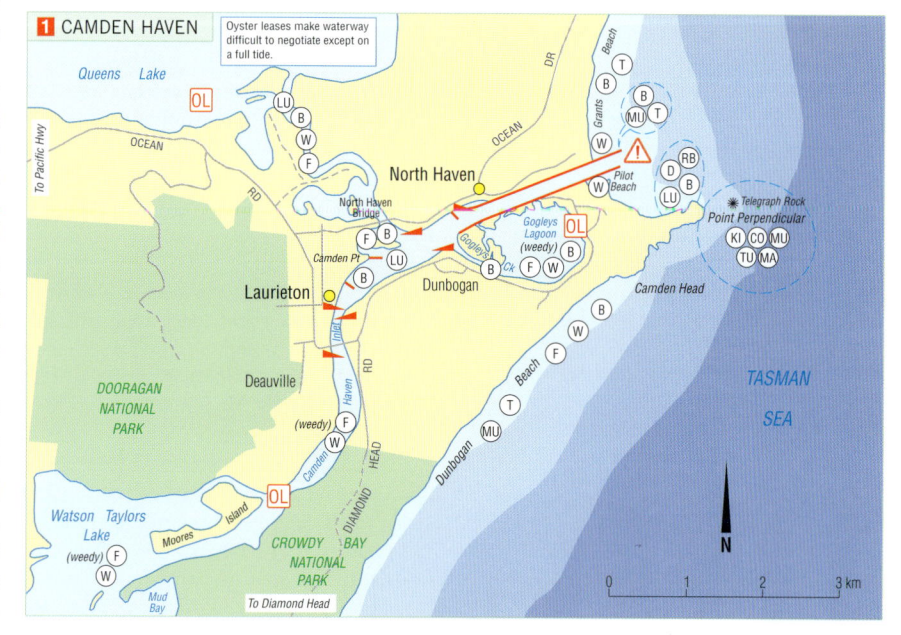

COASTAL FISHING PORT MACQUARIE REGION   NEW SOUTH WALES

carry an abundance of yellowtail kingfish, cobia, longtail tuna, Spanish mackerel and mulloway. Bream, rock blackfish, silver drummer and luderick are among the smaller species found here. Further to the south, **Diamond Head** is another great rock fishing spot.

MANNING RIVER

The **Manning River** estuary is full of sand flats and channels, and so requires careful navigation, but these are ideal conditions to drift for flathead and whiting. School mulloway are in the deeper holes, while luderick are close to the shore, especially in weedy areas or near rocks.

At **Harrington**, the north section of the sea wall is fished for bream and tailor, with mulloway particularly active after heavy rain. Rock blackfish and luderick will bite on cunjevoi or weed at the bend, while the southern section of the wall fishes well for flathead and whiting. Mulloway, bream and luderick are the targets around **Manning Point**, a perfect jumping-off point for exploration of the river.

Cattai Bridge, on the road from Coopernook to Harrington, is an excellent land spot for bream, luderick and flathead, particularly on its eastern side. The river between **Jones and Mitchells islands** is good for boat fishing, and the best place for bream, flathead and mulloway is just out from the channel marker pole, about 500 m from Croki. **Dumaresq Island Bridge**, at Cundletown, is also productive. Beyond Dumaresq Island and just upstream from the Fishermens Co-op is a good spot for luderick.

Scotts Creek and the **Manning River South Channel** flow around Oxley Island and into **Farquhar Inlet**, a shallow sand flat and weed area, which provides great boat fishing for whiting, bream, luderick and flathead. The bridges on either creek are good land spots for bream, flathead and mulloway.

This entrance is unsafe. Small boats can launch off the beach at Old Bar, but most seagoing boats launch from Crowdy Head, 5 km north of Harrington, where there is a protected anchorage and a triple boat ramp. This also gives best access to the highly productive **Mermaid Reef**, 2 km offshore and 6 km north-east of Crowdy Head. The reef has a large number of fish, such as snapper, kingfish, mulloway, bream and bonito, and summer visits from surface pelagics like striped tuna, marlin, shark, wahoo and yellowfin tuna.

East of Crowdy Head, there are many reef formations extending some 10 km out, again with a variety of reef and game fish. Crowdy Head has great rock fishing.

The Manning River at Taree is particularly scenic although the fishing is better in the lower reaches

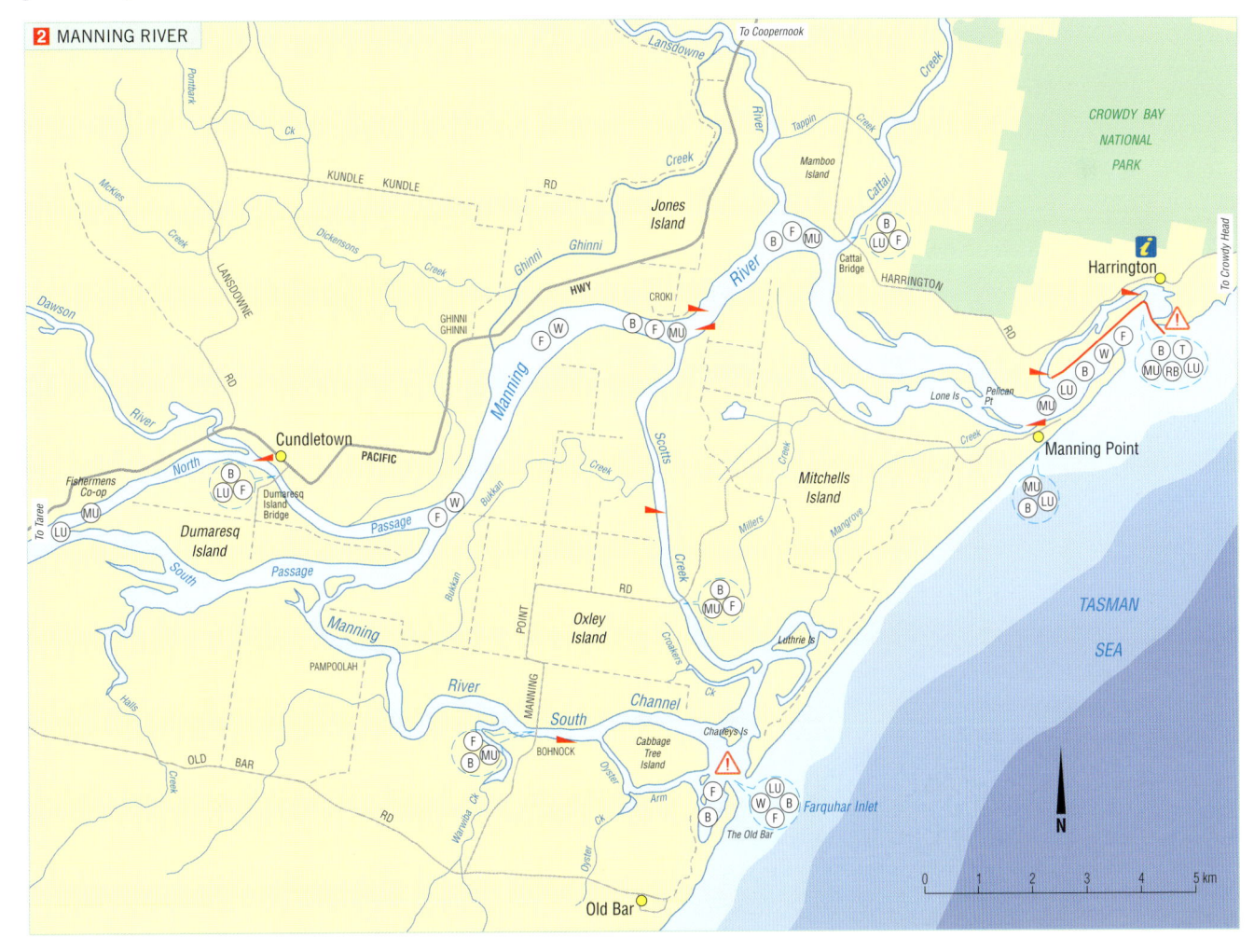

NEW SOUTH WALES

COASTAL FISHING PORT MACQUARIE REGION

Tuncurry to Charlotte Head

Type of fishing
beach, estuary, offshore, rock, wall

Target fish
bream, flathead, luderick, whiting

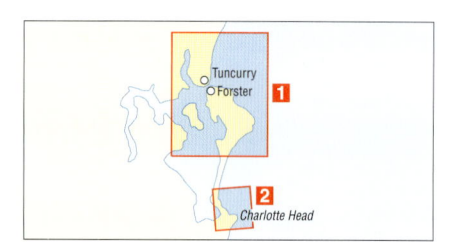

The bonanza of estuary fishing on the New South Wales coast continues at Forster–Tuncurry, once two sleepy fishing villages but now boom towns. The attractions are many, including good rock and beach areas outside the entrance to the lake, keen offshore fishing, and wonderful estuary fishing in the huge Wallis Lake area. South of Forster, Charlotte Head juts into the sea and creates an unusual combination of rock and beach fishing close to the deeper game waters.

TUNCURRY AND FORSTER

The breakwalls on both sides of the entrance fish exceptionally well for bream, tailor and flathead, while the North Wall is a mulloway hot spot. The South Wall and the southern channel attract the luderick anglers, despite the rough bottom, which can claim a lot of tackle. The **Fishermans**

Boats moored at Forster harbour

Co-op on the north side draws the bream when the fleet comes in.

Inside the entrance there is a bridge linking the two towns, which is usually productive for bream, tailor, flathead, whiting and garfish, but the fishing really hits the heights at night on a run-out tide. The sand spit near the bridge is a great spot to lure cast for flathead.

Straight on from the bridge is a big area of oyster leases, set in a maze of channels, which are a haven for bream and, to a lesser extent, luderick. There are many other equally productive oyster lease areas in the northern end of **Wallis Lake**.

Breckenridge Channel is one of the most consistent luderick-producing areas in the State, as it combines weed beds with the proximity of oyster leases. The **Forster Channel**, on the northern side of Godwin Island and around the south-east of Cockatoo Island, is a wonderful stretch of water for drifting for flathead, whiting and bream.

The hot spot is a channel called **Hells Gate**, in the narrows between Godwin and Wallis islands.

This area, from Hells Gate to and beyond the bridge, is filled with boats at the time of the new moon on summer nights, as the channels are thick with prawns moving out to sea on a run-out tide.

South-east of **Regatta Island**, a vast area of channels and sand and weed flats is ideal for drifting for flathead, and also a great spot for whiting, bream and flounder.

The undoubted pick of the lake is on the eastern side of **Wallis Island**. One enters a rocky area called **The Stockyard**, where luderick and bream are the targets, and then continues south through barely navigable water to reach **The Step**, where the sand level at the entrance shelves into the main body of the lake. This is a magnificent location for tailor, flathead, bream and mulloway. These predatory fish wait here for small fish and crustaceans to

COASTAL FISHING PORT MACQUARIE REGION   NEW SOUTH WALES

Wallis Lake, a large and productive waterway, provides excellent estuary fishing, especially around the oyster leases

be swept over the edge towards them on the rising tide. Anglers should stay on the shallow side and feed their baits with the current into the drop-off area. Live poddy mullet, pilchards, whitebait or prawns, properly presented, will be snapped up. Blue swimmer crabs, common throughout the lake, are abundant in this stretch.

Offshore anglers should be wary of the Forster-Tuncurry entrance, but there are large hauls of flathead to be had outside. The reef areas are well north and south of the entrance. **Black Head**, 8 km to the north, has an extension of reefs, which carry a lot of snapper. **The Pinnacles**, east of Cape Hawke, are good for snapper, teraglin, mulloway and kingfish.

CHARLOTTE HEAD

Seven Mile Beach is renowned for tailor, which come close inshore on the steeply shelving beach as they drive the bait fish into the shallows. Bream, mulloway, whiting and salmon also come close in to this area.

The rock areas, between Booti Booti and Elizabeth Beach, are fished mainly for luderick, rock blackfish and bream among the washes, but are also good for bait casting for tailor. **Elizabeth Beach** is a good place for summer whiting, and also big mulloway, and its southern end is the place to launch boats over the sand. The headland at the southern end of the beach is easily reached from a carpark, and offers mostly bream and tailor.

The small **Shelly Beach** is protected. Big mulloway are a feature here, along with bream, tailor and whiting. Nearby **Seagull Point** is a safe place to fish in all but southerly blows and has reef fish varieties, like snapper, yellowtail kingfish, cobia and mulloway. The rocks and cliffs on the north side of **Charlotte Head** are hard to reach and exposed to the south, but can be fished in moderate weather for drummer and bream. Anglers can also target yellowfin tuna and yellowtail kingfish with lures, or by drifting out live baits.

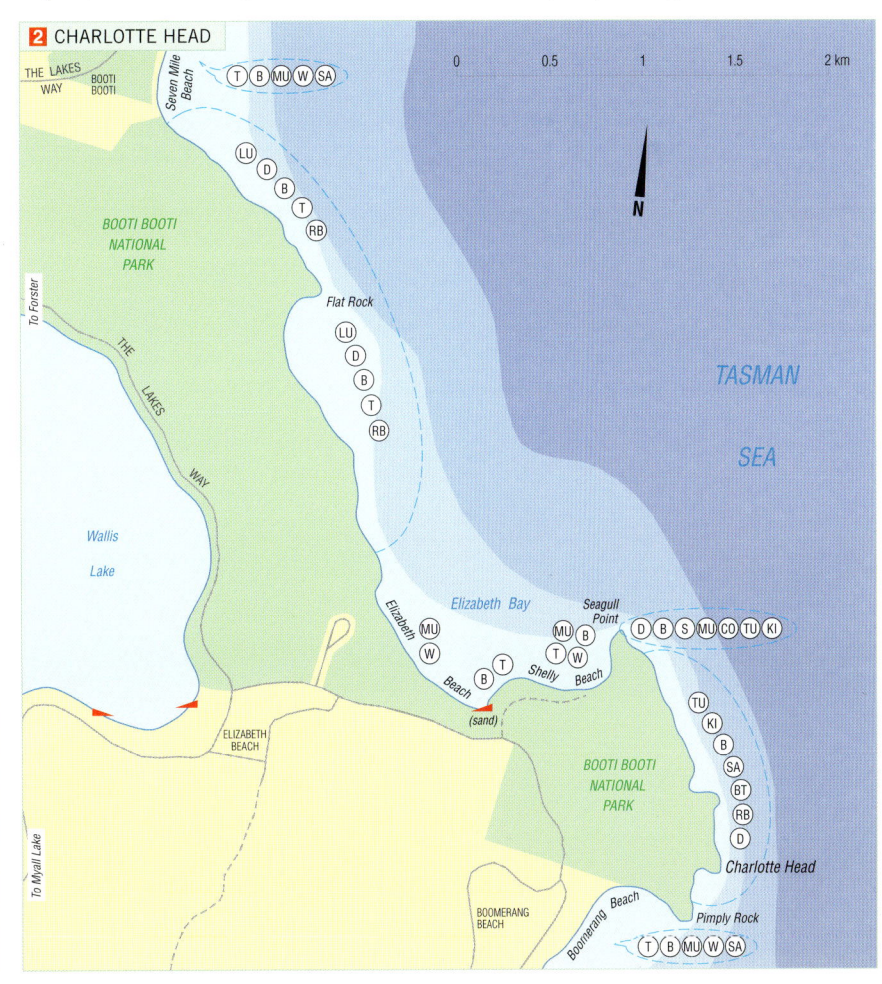

GUIDE TO LOCAL FISH

		Tuncurry and Forster	Charlotte Head
BT	bonito		●
B	bream	●	●
CO	cobia		●
D	drummer, silver	●	●
F	flathead	●	
FL	flounder	●	
G	garfish	●	
KI	kingfish, yellowtail		●
LU	luderick	●	●
MU	mulloway	●	●
RB	rock blackfish	●	●
SA	salmon, Australian	●	●
S	snapper		●
T	tailor	●	●
TU	tuna		●
W	whiting	●	●

2 CHARLOTTE HEAD

NEW SOUTH WALES

Newcastle Region

The Myall Lakes and Lake Macquarie are the main geographic and scenic features of the Newcastle region, and the fishing they offer is tranquil. Flathead, whiting, bream and luderick are usually found around the sea entrances. Outside, there is reliable beach fishing.

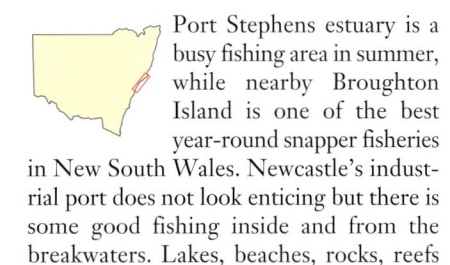

Port Stephens estuary is a busy fishing area in summer, while nearby Broughton Island is one of the best year-round snapper fisheries in New South Wales. Newcastle's industrial port does not look enticing but there is some good fishing inside and from the breakwaters. Lakes, beaches, rocks, reefs and wrecks add to the variety.

An angler fishing The Entrance for luderick, at the mouth of Tuggerah Lake

COASTAL FISHING NEWCASTLE REGION

WHERE TO FISH

Newcastle Region

SEAL ROCKS AND MYALL LAKES ● 90
There is some exhilarating boat fishing near the tiny village of Seal Rocks – around the headland, offshore rocks, pinnacles and reefs. The lakes system is vast and shallow and fish can be hard to find, but there are some reliable reefs and drifts for boat anglers, and some good shore fishing places. The nearby Myall River carries flathead, whiting and luderick.

PORT STEPHENS ● 92
The Port Stephens estuary has a lot of summer fishing traffic. The Hawks Nest area is excellent for both land-based and boat fishing, and there is great rock fishing near the port entrance. Offshore islands and reefs are another attraction, with Broughton Island superb for snapper.

NEWCASTLE AND LAKE MACQUARIE ● 94
There is interesting fishing in Newcastle Harbour, from land or sea. Hairtail are caught here in winter. The entrance and Stockton Beach are well worth fishing, as are the offshore wrecks and reefs. The best fishing in Lake Macquarie is at the entrance, as the lake itself is generally featureless. However, five artificial reefs placed around the lake have attracted fish.

COASTAL LAKES ● 96
Munmorah and Budgewoi lakes have little tidal influence so the best fishing is around structures. The entrances to the power station channels are ideal spots in both lakes. Good offshore points include Birdie Beach and Wybung Head. In Tuggerah Lake, there is great fishing for the family from the park at Picnic Point, at The Entrance; and the North Channel, running between The Entrance North and Terilbah Island, is ideal for boat fishing.

TERRIGAL ● 98
Protected rocks and beaches attract big predatory fish, including tuna, bonito and yellowtail kingfish. When the lagoon is open, flathead, bream and tailor are found inside the entrance, and beaches nearby have bream, tailor and mulloway. The Terrigal coast is a good rock and beach fishery, attracting many anglers with its accessible rock platforms and varied and plentiful fish. The best rock area is The Skillion.

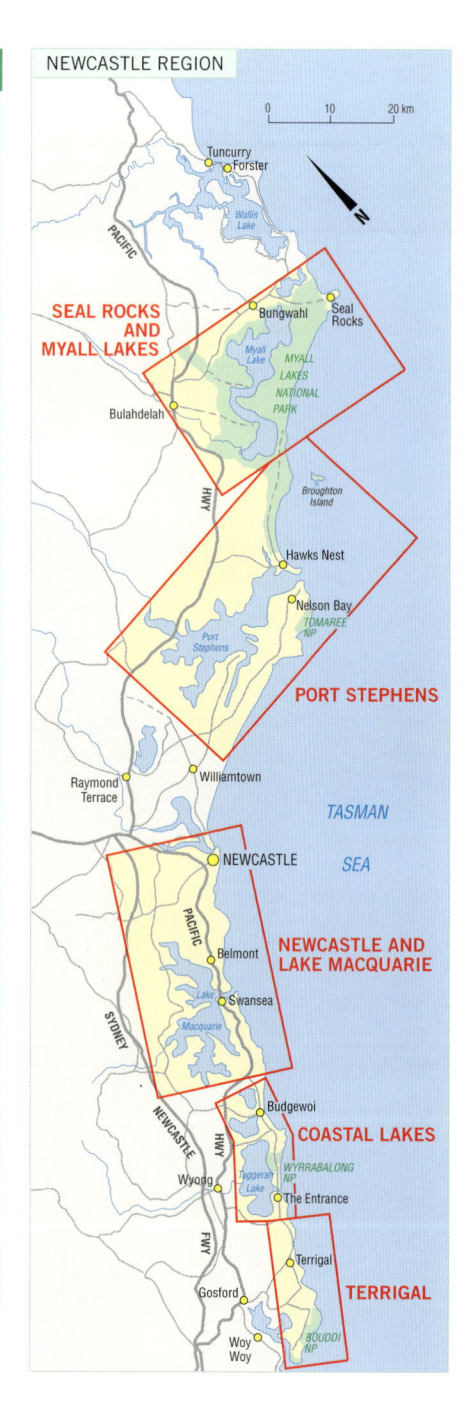

FISHING TIP

One of the best kept 'secret baits' for bream fishing is plain white bread. Some anglers prefer to use dry hard crusty bread, while others use bread as fresh as they can get it. By adding judicious amounts of water, and kneading the bread into small dollops, it is possible to return it to a dough-like texture that can be moulded onto a hook and withstand the stresses of casting. The bream often take it quite well.

COASTAL FISHING NEWCASTLE REGION   NEW SOUTH WALES

GUIDE TO LOCAL FISH

- bass, Australian
- bonito
- bream, black
- bream, yellowfin
- cobia
- drummer, silver
- flathead
- flounder
- garfish
- groper
- hairtail
- john dory
- kingfish, yellowtail
- leatherjacket
- luderick
- marlin, black
- marlin, blue
- marlin, striped
- morwong
- mullet
- mulloway
- rock blackfish
- salmon, Australian
- shark
- snapper
- tailor
- tarwhine
- teraglin
- trevally, silver
- tuna, frigate mackerel
- tuna, longtail
- tuna, mackerel
- tuna, striped
- tuna, yellowfin
- whiting, sand
- whiting, trumpeter

Rods and net poised for action as the sun sets over Lake Macquarie

Weather

The prevailing winds are north-easterlies, which can reach forces up to 20 knots, creating dangerous and choppy conditions on Lake Macquarie. In summer, southerlies can come in, causing even more dangerous conditions. When boating on Lake Macquarie, always look out for these southerly changes as they can come in quickly and fiercely. For coastal forecasts, ring the Weather Bureau on tel. (02) 9296 1555 or contact local Coast Guards or the Coastal Patrol.

Boating

Boat anglers should be cautious of the bar at the entrance to the channel at Swansea Heads; it is dangerous at low tide when a north-easterly is blowing. If your vessel is too big to pass under Swansea Bridge, you will need to give the Coast Guards at least one hour's notice for the bridge to be lifted. Never anchor too close to the bridge, as tidal waters are extremely strong and could sweep your craft away. Commonsense should prevail when on the water. Apart from the obvious weather check, see what the tide is doing and understand what effect the wind will have on the direction of tidal flow. Never anchor in shipping channels and always use navigation lights at night. For further information, contact the local Waterways Authority office.

Luderick
Luderick, often called blackfish, are found in estuaries, near rock walls, and in open water where there are rocky foreshores. A good specimen will weigh 1 kg.

FURTHER INFORMATION

Fishing and boating NSW Fisheries have offices at Taylors Beach Rd, Taylors Beach, tel. (02) 4982 1311; 97 Hannell St, Wickham, tel. (02) 4927 6548; 55 Lambton Pde, Swansea, tel. (02) 4971 1201; and Marine Dr, Tea Gardens, tel. (02) 4997 0214. The Waterways Authority has a Newcastle office at 8 Cowper St Sth, Carrington, tel. (02) 4940 0198. The Coast Guard has depots at Newcastle, tel. (02) 4927 8237; Port Stephens, tel. (02) 4982 4981; Shoal Bay, tel. (02) 4981 3585; and Swansea, tel. (02) 4971 3498. The Coastal Patrol has bases at Port Stephens, tel. (02) 4981 3585; Lake Macquarie, tel. (02) 4971 3723; Gosford, tel. (02) 4325 7929; and Terrigal, tel. (02) 4384 5577.

Tourist centres Lake Macquarie Visitors' Information Centre, 72 Pacific Hwy, Blacksmiths, tel. (02) 4972 1172; Great Lakes Tourism, Little St, Forster, tel. (02) 6554 8799; Victoria Pde, Nelson Bay, tel. (02) 4981 1579; Wheeler Pl, 363 Hunter St, Newcastle, tel. (02) 4974 2999; Central Coast Tourism, Rotary Park, Terrigal Dr, Terrigal, tel. (02) 4385 4430; Memorial Park, Marine Pde, The Entrance, tel. (02) 4385 4430.

NEW SOUTH WALES

COASTAL FISHING NEWCASTLE REGION

Seal Rocks and Myall Lakes

Type of fishing
beach, lake, offshore, reef, river, rock

Target fish
bream, flathead, luderick, tailor, yellowtail kingfish

The tiny fishing village of Seal Rocks is the jumping-off point for some exhilarating boat fishing around the headlands, offshore rocks, pinnacles and reefs in the area. The Myall Lakes, surrounded by national park, have many boat ramps and camping places to allow leisurely and rewarding fishing expeditions. The long outside beach is hard to reach, but fishes very well. The Big Gibber Headland is a fine rock spot.

SEAL ROCKS

Boat launching is from the sheltered beach at Sugarloaf Bay, basic but effective for craft up to about 6 m with a suitable launching vehicle. **Baby Reef**, 5 km to the north-east of Sugarloaf Bay offers an extensive reef area. It generally rewards those drifting and bottom fishing for snapper and bream, or surface fishing for kingfish and tailor, with scope for other species.

Sugarloaf Point is an excellent rock fishing area, with good ledges that are reasonably safe and allow comfortable fishing for luderick, snapper, tailor (especially in autumn), bream, rock blackfish and mulloway. The pelagic game fish come close in past this point, and yellowtail kingfish, bonito, yellowfin tuna, longtail and mackerel tuna are just some of the species prevalent in the area. The best time to chase these pelagics is between December and April although, depending on water currents, they can be present in the winter months as well.

Boat anglers can fish the rocky islets off the point, and **Treachery Head** to the south, for snapper, bream, tailor and kingfish. Treachery Head is well named, as the waves close to shore can rise unexpectedly.

Sugarloaf Bay, looking towards Seal Rocks – a good area to fish in a southerly, with surf-dwelling species available

MYALL LAKES

The **Myall River** winds up from Port Stephens, carrying a good complement of flathead, whiting and luderick, before it runs through the vast and shallow **Myall Lakes** system, a nursery ground for many species of fish. It has good quantities of bream, mullet and luderick. Small boats and, at times, with care, even stable canoes can be used in the lakes as the waters are generally placid. There are a number of shore fishing spots, notably at Mungo Brush in the south; along the difficult road east of the Bombah Broadwater; at Nerong; the northern river mouth; Bombah Point; around the lake to Violet Hill; Neranie Head; and near Smiths Lake, in the northern-most part of the system.

The best fishing places for boat anglers are off Pigeon Point; around Sheep and Goat islands on the Boolambayte Lake; off Mayers Point; on the drift from

COASTAL FISHING NEWCASTLE REGION — NEW SOUTH WALES

GUIDE TO LOCAL FISH

		Seal Rocks	Myall Lakes
BA	bass, Australian		•
BT	bonito	•	
B	bream	•	•
D	drummer, silver	•	
F	flathead	•	•
FL	flounder		•
KI	kingfish, yellowtail	•	
LU	luderick	•	•
M	mullet		•
MU	mulloway	•	•
RB	rock blackfish	•	
SA	salmon, Australian	•	
S	snapper	•	
T	tailor	•	•
TA	tarwhine	•	
TU	tuna	•	
W	whiting	•	•

Stinging Tree Point to Burrah Burrah Point; around the oyster leases in the middle of the main lake; and on the eastern side, around Shelly Point, Blossom Point and Long Point.

The coastal side of the park has long stretches of beach, which can be reached by four-wheel drive by branching off from the rather rudimentary Hawks Nest–Seal Rocks Road. However, beach access for four-wheel drives is strictly limited and you should contact the Great Lakes Shire Council for information. The beach anglers' favourite fish – bream, flathead, whiting, mulloway and tailor – are in bountiful supply along these lonely shores. An accessible spot for beach anglers is the **Sand Bar Beach** near Smiths Lake, which can also fish well at times.

Offshore, some 5 km north of Seal Rocks, are the exposed **Skeleton Rocks**, a good spot for snapper, bream, mulloway and yellowtail kingfish. On calm days the best fishing is between the rocks. South-west of Seal Rocks, the **Yagon Reef** is about 1 km off the Yagon Gibber Headland and is a good place for mulloway and flathead.

Little Seal Rocks can be seen some 3 km to the south-east of Sugarloaf Point (see Seal Rocks map). Big snapper are caught here, particularly after a heavy sea, and there is also a strong possibility of mulloway. The abundant surface fish include kingfish, yellowfin tuna, and tailor and salmon (in good years) in winter.

A little to the south-west of Seal Rocks is **Edith Breaker**, which is easily found as it rises to just below the surface and creates clearly visible waves in all but the calmest seas. Fish the sides of the reef for the plentiful snapper, bonito and yellowtail kingfish.

The long beach stretching from Yagon Gibber Headland to Port Stephens offers whiting, tailor, flathead, and mulloway, while one of the best rock spots in New South Wales, the **Big Gibber Headland**, attracts bream, whiting, rock blackfish, mulloway and tailor.

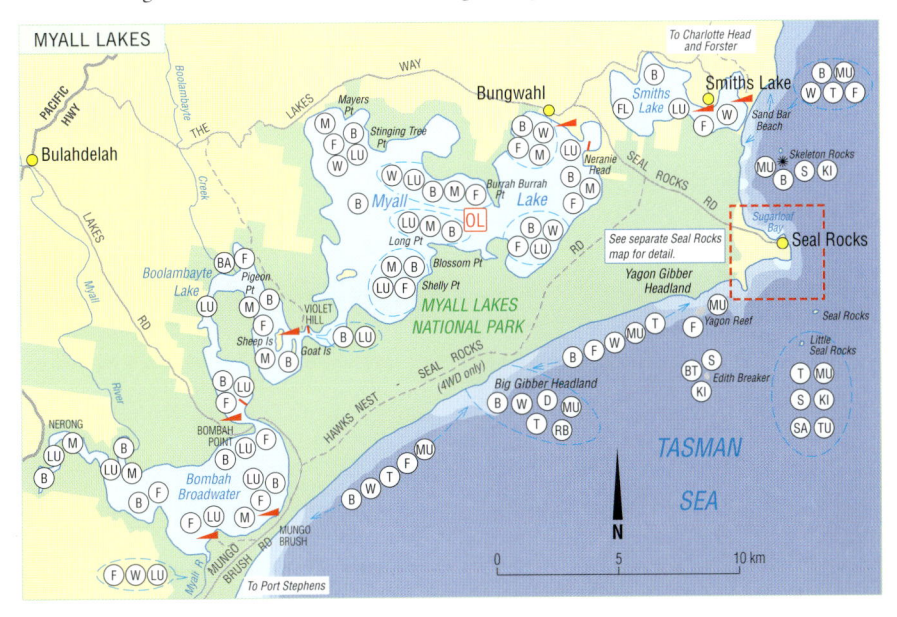

Myall Lakes is steeped in history and this extensive estuary complex has been home to anglers and their craft for over one hundred years

NEW SOUTH WALES

COASTAL FISHING NEWCASTLE REGION

Port Stephens

Type of fishing
beach, estuary, jetty, offshore, reef, river, rock

Target fish
bream, flathead, marlin, mulloway, snapper, tuna

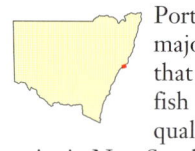

Port Stephens has become a major holiday destination that offers many types of fish in great abundance. A quality snapper fishery is a rarity in New South Wales waters, but the hard-bottomed reefs, washes and drop-offs at Broughton Island create ideal conditions.

PORT STEPHENS

The estuary holds up against considerable summer traffic, and at various times of the year provides good catches of mulloway, bream, flathead, whiting, flounder, tailor, crabs and other estuary species. Whiting are particularly prolific in summer, mostly around **Lemon Tree Passage**. They can be caught, along with flathead and bream on fresh baits of worms and yabbies, which can be collected at low tide on the sand and mudflats. Lure casting near oyster leases can also reward with flathead and bream.

Once a yearly event, the springtime invasion by striped and mackerel tuna is now rare. Mulloway can be caught in the deeper holes, particularly those around the Nelson Bay **Marina Breakwall**, the channel marker at Dutchmans beach, the wreck in Salamander Bay, and around **Dowardee** and **Middle islands**. Further upstream, there are good holes and channels in the mouth of the Karuah River.

One of the most accessible and exciting areas of the port is the entrance to the **Myall River**, near the twin north-shore towns of Hawks Nest and Tea Gardens. The Myall's main channel and the sand flats around it are ideal places to fish for bream, whiting, flathead and mulloway.

The jetty at **Hawks Nest** is over deep water and allows good land-based fishing for a variety of species, even for beginners. Fronting the ocean, **Bennetts Beach** provides great fishing for bream, flathead, tailor and occasional mulloway. Worms and pippis for bait are plentiful.

There are excellent rock platforms on either side of the entrance to Port Stephens. **Yacaaba Head** on the northern side is rugged and risky in rough weather, but offers bream, tailor and silver drummer. **Tomaree Head**, on the southern side, produces these same species, plus snapper and trevally, and big fish such as tuna, yellowtail kingfish, cobia, shark and even the odd marlin.

Port Stephens has outstanding attractions for offshore anglers, with reefs and islands close inshore for small boats, and excellent game fishing, from close grounds to the edge of the continental shelf, 40 km out. Close in are Cabbage Tree Island, Little Island and Boondelbah or Big Island. The eastern side of **Little Island** can produce marlin, snapper, mulloway, kingfish, bonito and various tunas, and at **Cabbage Tree Island** there are garfish, bream, snapper, rock blackfish, bonito, tuna and live bait grounds.

Inshore reefs here carry teraglin, snapper, flathead, morwong and sundry other reef fish. In spring, large schools of big silver trevally visit a lot of Port Stephens' reefs. Among these is **Gunsight**

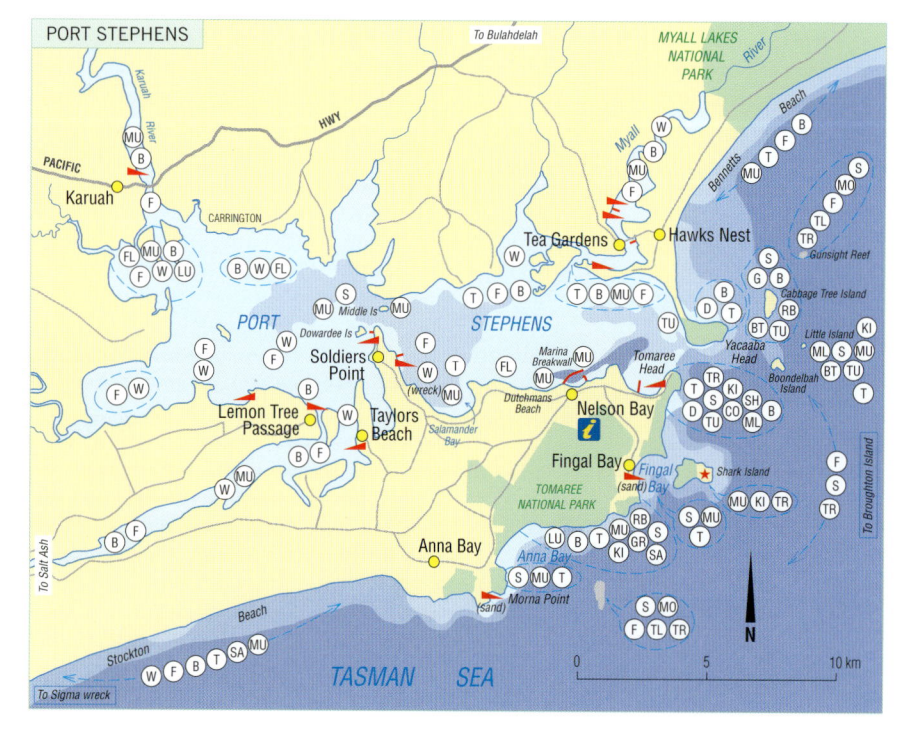

Port Stephens is highly regarded for its quality bream

Beachworm

Beachworms are a favoured and highly prized bait. They are caught on the beach in sand on the receding wash. A berley bag is swished over the sand and as the wash carries the scent back, the beachworms poke their heads out. While experienced anglers use thumb and forefinger to extract the worms, most find it easier to use a pair of worm pliers to pull them out smoothly. They are one of the strongest and sturdiest worms available and are perfect for surf casting.

COASTAL FISHING NEWCASTLE REGION   NEW SOUTH WALES

GUIDE TO LOCAL FISH

		Port Stephens	Broughton Island
(BT)	bonito	•	•
(B)	bream	•	
(CO)	cobia	•	
(D)	drummer, silver	•	
(F)	flathead	•	
(FL)	flounder	•	
(G)	garfish	•	
(GR)	groper	•	
(KI)	kingfish, yellowtail	•	•
(LU)	luderick	•	
(ML)	marlin	•	•
(MO)	morwong	•	•
(MU)	mulloway	•	•
(RB)	rock blackfish	•	
(SA)	salmon, Australian	•	
(SH)	shark	•	
(S)	snapper	•	•
(T)	tailor	•	
(TL)	teraglin	•	
(TR)	trevally	•	•
(TU)	tuna	•	•
(W)	whiting	•	

Reef, north of Cabbage Tree, where trevally up to 5 kg have been caught.

To the south, **Shark Island** has mulloway, kingfish and trevally around its eastern and south-eastern coast. Flathead and snapper can be found drifting between the islands, and trolling in the area will be well repaid.

A string of bays, beaches, rocky points and headlands runs from **Fingal Bay** to **Anna Bay**. The rock areas around the beaches are great casting spots for luderick, bream, salmon, tailor and mulloway. This coastline also offers superb fishing for kingfish, rock blackfish, snapper and groper. Calamari can be taken on squid jigs, and bait fish like slimy mackerel, yellowtail and garfish are seasonally abundant close in. Boats can be launched from the beaches of Fingal Bay and Anna Bay, and from Morna Point.

Stockton Beach has deep holes and gutters promising everything from whiting, flathead and bream to tailor and salmon, and big mulloway for those who put in the time.

Offshore, there are wrecks as well as reefs to hold the fish. The *Sigma* wreck has its own attractions, but serves as a mark for Carls Reef and The Gravel, which are good snapper, kingfish and mulloway areas. To the south-east of the *Sigma* is a renowned mulloway spot known as 'the mudhole'.

In recent years the offshore waters have achieved international recognition as one of the world's premier salt water fly destinations for marlin. Anglers from all over the world have come here in search of world records, and many new benchmarks have been established.

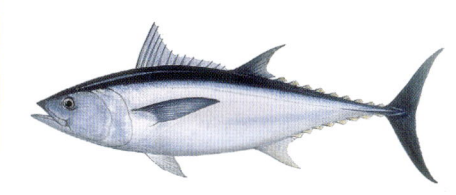

Longtail tuna is a popular inshore species keenly sought by shore-based anglers who specialise in fishing with live baits or high-speed spinning. Although this species can grow to 40 kg, it is most commonly caught from 10 to 15 kg.

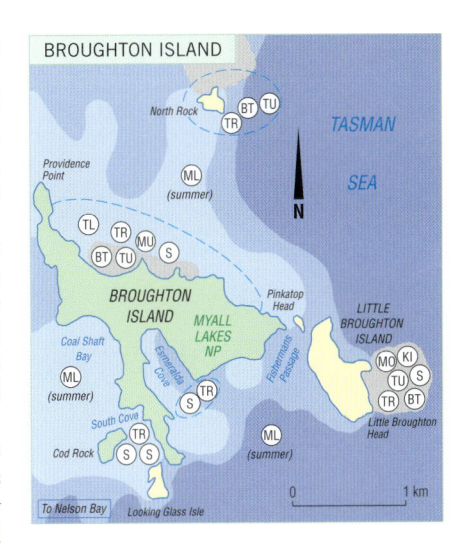

FISHING TIP

Birds can often be one of the most effective ways of finding schools of fish. A flock of birds sitting close together on the water is not often the sign of fish, but birds flying in circles, and diving into the water is a sure sign that there are fish beneath the surface. Shearwaters or muttonbirds are great hunters and a favourite for fishermen looking for schools of pelagic fish. But not all birds are as helpful. Seagulls can look like they are working when in fact all they are doing is haggling between themselves over a few scraps of orange peel.

BROUGHTON ISLAND

Apart from the snapper that are found around the island for most of the year, there are a lot of trevally, particularly in spring, as well as bonito and tuna over the reefs. These shallow reef areas can be drifted, or fished at anchor, and best results usually come from using light line and unweighted baits. Broughton has the advantage of some sheltered spots at Esmeralda Cove and South Cove in bad weather. The northern side has broad expanses of shallow reefs as well as deep holes and caves, which will reward with mulloway.

Fishing from the jetty at Nelson Bay

NEW SOUTH WALES

COASTAL FISHING NEWCASTLE REGION

Newcastle and Lake Macquarie

Type of fishing
beach, estuary, lake, rock, wall, wharf

Target fish
bream, flathead, hairtail, luderick, mulloway

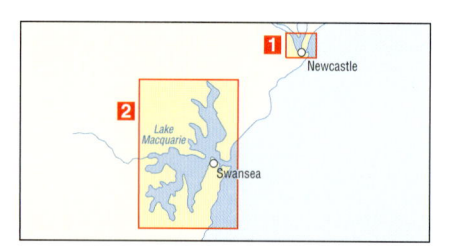

The Newcastle area boasts a good fishery that varies from rock and surf to inside fishing in the lake, estuary and harbour. The Hunter River is surprisingly resilient to the effects of heavy industry. Despite the vastness of the Lake Macquarie waterway, some of the best action is in the relatively small area around the entrance.

NEWCASTLE

Bream and school mulloway are the staple catch, but the highlight of the year is the invasion of hairtail, in winter. The harbour then becomes crowded with boats, night fishing with live and slab baits under light sticks on floats.

The two long breakwaters at the entrance to the harbour provide a good platform for fishing. The **Northern Breakwater** allows good ocean rock fishing on the outside, with a wreck as an added bonus, and estuary fishing on the inside. The best place to fish the wreck is towards the stern, and the quarry here are bream, flathead, yellowtail kingfish, tailor, morwong and john dory. Elsewhere on the wall, trevally and bream are the targets. The estuary side has bream, luderick and occasionally mulloway, with the head of the wall being the best mulloway spot in the area. There is a strong tidal flow through here, but it abates as the river bends north, allowing excellent land-based fishing from the Stockton ferry wharf for bream, flathead, mulloway and luderick.

On the southern side of the entrance, the peninsula and a constructed wall join to form a long breakwater, which offers great fishing inside and out. Snapper, tailor, mulloway, tuna and kingfish can be found at the ocean end, but the sloping rocky bottom demands that you fish beneath a float. Just inside the wall there is a deep hole, which is favoured for bream, snapper and occasionally mulloway. Luderick can be caught all the way down to the wharves.

Half-way along the breakwater, at **Stony Point**, anglers can walk out to the edge of the stones at low tide and cast a lightly weighted bait for bream and tailor. Flathead and whiting are caught from **Horse Shoe Beach**. At the end of the beach is the small harbour breakwall with bream, tailor, mulloway and flathead, and a small beach attracting tailor, flathead and whiting.

Further west, at **Queens Wharf** and other wharves nearby, there is fishing for bream, flathead and school mulloway. Further up the Hunter River, good bream, flathead, whiting and school mulloway can be taken, particularly at drop-offs and smaller creeks and channel mouths on a dropping tide.

Along the outer edge of the Southern Breakwater and stretching south-west to Nobbys Beach is a reefy area, which is ideal for snapper, particularly after a blow. Bream and luderick are also caught here. Further out is a peaked reef known as Big Ben Rock, which appears at low tide. The area should be avoided in heavy weather, but on a calm morning you can be sure of pulling snapper, mulloway and kingfish into the boat.

Inner reefs that are good for snapper, mulloway and bream are the **Middle Reef**, straight out from the port, and the **'dumping ground'**, 3 to 5 km out, where rubble from dredging the harbour has been deposited.

A popular beach fishing technique is to cast lightly weighted pilchards for tailor on sidecast tackle

There are some fine rock and beach spots to the south. **Newcastle and Merewether beaches** are good for luderick, bream, Australian salmon, tailor and mulloway.

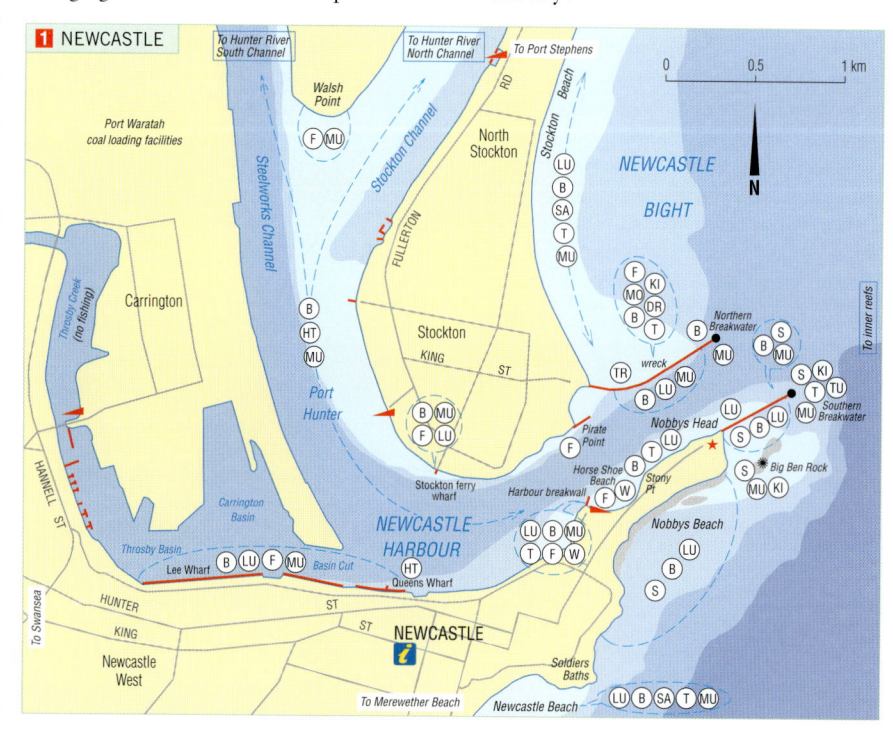

94

COASTAL FISHING NEWCASTLE REGION — NEW SOUTH WALES

LAKE MACQUARIE AND SWANSEA

Lake Macquarie has little tidal movement, and this reduces its value as a fishery as there are few places where the fish naturally gather on the tides to feed. An attempt to enhance the fishery has been made with the placement of five artificial reefs: four just north-west of Swansea and one in Warners Bay. Bream is the main reef species.

But, generally, the target fish in the lake are bream, luderick, flathead and whiting, with the bonus of tailor and mulloway in some places. Other spots to try are around headlands or at the head of the many bays in the system. Dora Creek, entering the lake on its western side, produces bream, flathead, mulloway and luderick.

The fast flowing **Swansea Channel** carries good numbers of truly big flathead, bream, whiting, luderick, mulloway and even yellowtail kingfish. The area around the bridge is particularly good for all these species, while luderick and bream are best found around the walls at the entrance. The best spot of all is at the western end of the channel, where there is a big drop-off from the shallow channel to the floor of the lake. The biggest flathead in the State can wait here for their prey to reach them on the incoming tide, and often that prey is yellowtail or small tailor, which can be caught for live bait. The channel is also noted for its prawn runs, and prawns can be scoop netted in the two or three days either side of a new moon over summer.

GUIDE TO LOCAL FISH

		Newcastle	Lake Macquarie	Swansea
B	bream	●	●	●
F	flathead	●	●	●
HT	hairtail	●		
DR	john dory	●		
KI	kingfish, yellowtail	●		●
LJ	leatherjacket			●
LU	luderick	●	●	●
MO	morwong	●		
M	mullet	●		
MU	mulloway	●	●	●
SA	salmon, Australian	●		
S	snapper	●		
T	tailor	●	●	●
TR	trevally	●		
TU	tuna	●		
W	whiting	●	●	●

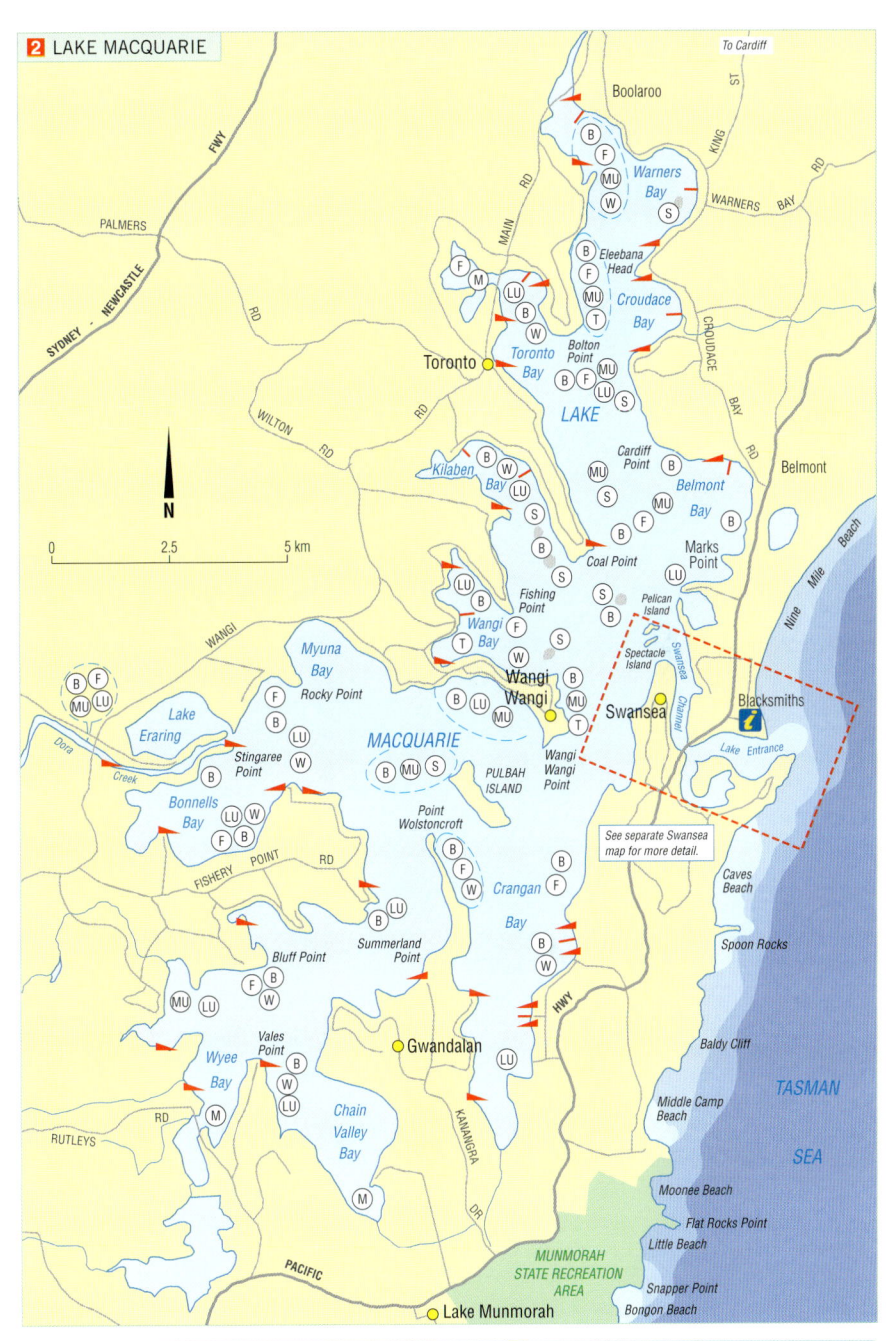

NEW SOUTH WALES

COASTAL FISHING NEWCASTLE REGION

Coastal Lakes

Type of fishing
beach, lake, offshore, river, rock
Target fish
bream, flathead, luderick, tailor, whiting

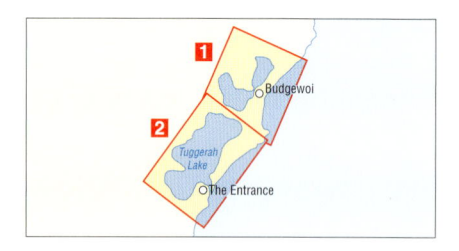

Flathead, bream, whiting and luderick are the target fish from the jetties at The Entrance

Munmorah and Budgewoi lakes, now in a built-up area within easy reach of Sydney, are fairly busy waterways. Tuggerah Lake is the most interesting fishery, with the entrance on the ocean side creating a tidal flow, as well as sand flats and channels.

MUNMORAH AND BUDGEWOI LAKES

Lake Munmorah is the northernmost and deepest of the central coast lakes and offers good fishing for flathead, bream and tailor, mostly around the banks. Because there is little tidal influence in these lakes, berley can be important, as the fish tend to gather around power station flow points and other structures around the lake rather than waiting for food washed to them by the tides.

The power station inlet, in the north-west corner, attracts luderick and bream, and the occasional tailor. Shore-based anglers can have a bonanza here at the right time. Access, however, involves a creek crossing so a four-wheel drive is needed to get to the inlet. The next best place for both boat and bank fishing in Lake Munmorah is in the south, at the entrance to Budgewoi Lake. The bridge over the entrance is a good luderick and bream spot, and the whole channel carries bream, luderick and tarwhine. It is a place for light line and minimum weights. There are some deep areas north of the entrance where it is possible to catch very big tailor.

Bream, the biggest catch in **Budgewoi Lake**, are best sought at dusk using lightly weighted baits, while drifting along the northern banks can yield good catches of whiting and flathead, and prawns. The north-west part of the lake has similar conditions to Munmorah, but here the water heated in the power station is expelled, creating a thermal attraction for a variety of species. The hot water outlet is built into a rock wall that extends into the north-west lobe of the lake and is only accessible by boat. Bream can be caught in big numbers here, but special care should be taken to release the large number of small fish that can also be taken. The immediate surrounds of the outlet are closed to fishing from May to August.

A little to the west is **Wallarah Creek**, particularly good when rough water in the lake sends fish into calmer areas. Bloodworms are easy to pump and gather in this area.

The ocean fishing is good around **Snapper Point** and **Wybung Head** to the north. This great rock location is part of the Munmorah State Recreation Area, and access is by tracks most suited to walking or four-wheel drive. Wybung is probably the best rock fishing area on the central coast, with great deepwater angling over boulders or gravel. Mulloway and snapper are the main hope, but bream, groper, luderick, rock blackfish and tailor are all in good supply around these rocks. At Birdie Beach, adjacent to Lake Munmorah, there is good

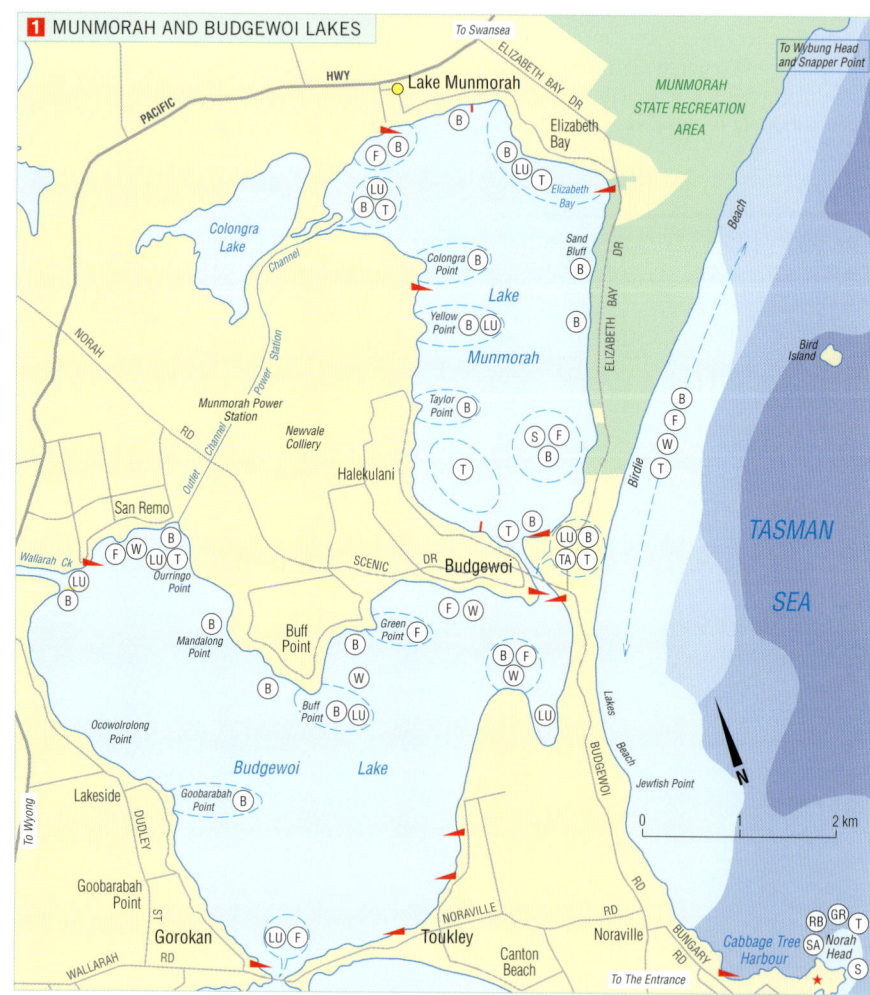

COASTAL FISHING NEWCASTLE REGION NEW SOUTH WALES

surf fishing. To the south at Norah Head, the fishing is also good for rock blackfish, snapper, groper, tailor and Australian salmon.

TUGGERAH LAKE

The mouth of **Tuggerah Lake**, known as The Entrance, is fast flowing on any tide, and should not be navigated. Fish from the land here for luderick. Prawning on a moonless night is best done when the tide is slack or turning. The sand flats just inside are good for collecting yabby and worm baits, and fishing for whiting, flathead and bream.

There is a net and trap exclusion zone in Tuggerah Lake, extending west from Picnic Point, northward past Pelican Island and eastward toward the Two-Shores Caravan Park. Bank fishing into the south channel from the park at **Picnic Point** is an ideal family pastime, as children can find other safe activities if they lose interest in the fishing. The North Channel is an ideal luderick spot on a run-out tide, with a weed bank in the shallows to provide instant bait and berley. Another channel runs past **Pelican Island** on its western side, with a drop-off ideal for boat anglers, who can anchor nearby and drift baits on light lines into the channel. Drifting past the island for flathead can be very productive.

As with the other lakes, the fishing gets harder where the tidal influence is less, and the central area of the lake does not make good fishing. The best inflow area is at **Chittaway Point**, where Ourimbah Creek runs in, and provides bream, luderick, mullet and flathead over the sand and weed flats. The fishing is excellent after heavy rain, when fish are pushed down by the fresh water. The situation is similar where the **Wyong River** enters the lake at Tacoma, and there is the extra bonus that this river can be navigated in a small boat and has surprisingly good bass fishing upstream. **Canton Beach** in the north-east is a good whiting, bream and flathead area. Bream and luderick are the main targets along the eastern side of the lake.

Outside, **Tuggerah Beach** is backed by Wyrrabalong National Park, so walking is required for those seeking the main beach fare of tailor, whiting and mulloway. Offshore, a large area of reef, known as The Shallows, runs south to Pelican Point at the northern end of Tuggerah Beach and carries snapper, mulloway and yellowtail kingfish. You can also wade to the drop-off at low tide from **Pelican Point**, provided the sea is calm, and try for tailor and mulloway. You can only fish for a short while, however, as the rising tide can cut you off from the mainland.

The best mulloway fishing is just north of The Entrance, and usually on a run-out tide, while there are snapper, drummer and mulloway on the southern side.

Further south, **Toowoon Point** creates a sheltered fishing area in Toowoon Bay, so fish back to the beach for bream and the big whiting that come into the bay. The rocky washes at the end of the point carry luderick and rock blackfish, and there are some good mulloway holes on the southern side.

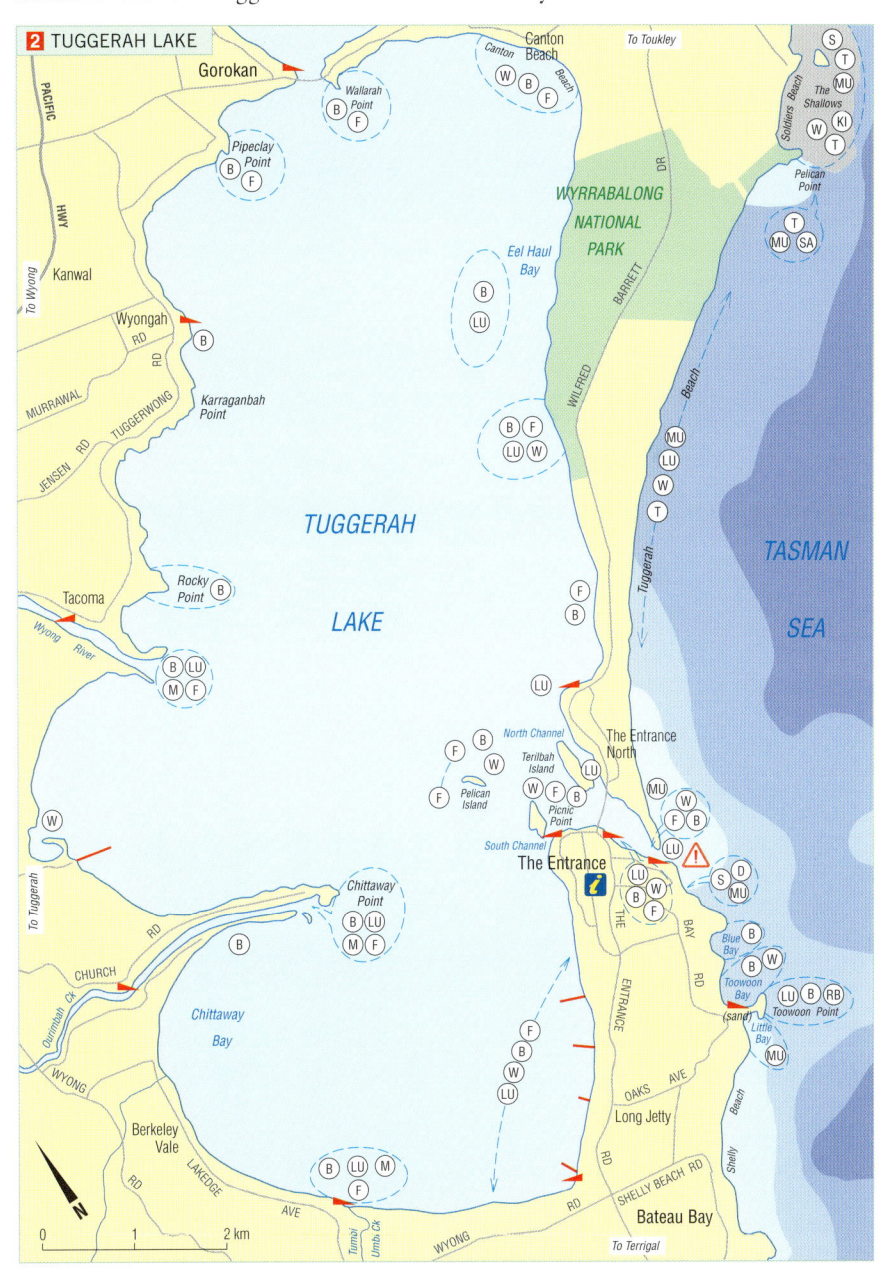

GUIDE TO LOCAL FISH

		Munmorah and Budgewoi Lakes	Tuggerah Lake
(B)	bream	●	●
(D)	drummer, silver		●
(F)	flathead	●	●
(GR)	groper	●	
(KI)	kingfish, yellowtail		●
(LU)	luderick	●	●
(M)	mullet		●
(MU)	mulloway	●	●
(RB)	rock blackfish	●	●
(SA)	salmon, Australian	●	
(S)	snapper	●	●
(T)	tailor	●	●
(TA)	tarwhine	●	
(W)	whiting	●	●

NEW SOUTH WALES

COASTAL FISHING NEWCASTLE REGION

Terrigal

Type of fishing
beach, lagoon, rock

Target fish
bream, rock blackfish, tailor, tuna

The rock and beach areas running from Bateau Bay to Box Head are heavily fished by anglers due to their proximity to Sydney and the excellent and varied fishing that they provide. More specifically, the fishing at Terrigal and Terrigal Haven features good access to the rocks and beaches and plenty of opportunities for big fish.

BATEAU BAY TO BOX HEAD

Crackneck Point and **Yumbool Point** have good rock spots, though they require some serious walking from Bateau Bay township. A few are a little low and dangerous in high seas, but in calm conditions they can offer snapper, rock blackfish, bream and groper.

Forresters Beach is very good for whiting at its southern end, particularly if the bait is beachworm taken from the beach. A high, safe rock ledge at **Wamberal Point** has good fishing for snapper, luderick, tailor, rock blackfish and bream, and the little beach beyond has bream, particularly when the swimmers are not around. When Wamberal Lagoon is open, the long stretch of **Wamberal and Terrigal beaches** fishes best near the entrance. Mulloway and tailor wait here for prey to be swept from the

GUIDE TO LOCAL FISH

		Bateau Bay to Box Head	Terrigal
BT	bonito		●
B	bream	●	●
D	drummer, silver	●	●
F	flathead	●	●
GR	groper	●	●
KI	kingfish, yellowtail	●	●
LU	luderick	●	●
MU	marlin		●
MU	mulloway	●	●
RB	rock blackfish	●	●
SA	salmon, Australian	●	●
S	snapper	●	●
T	tailor	●	●
TU	tuna	●	●
W	whiting	●	

98

COASTAL FISHING NEWCASTLE REGION — NEW SOUTH WALES

Hooked up on The Skillion

lagoon. Otherwise, the beaches are best fished wherever the gutters are at the time, and for bream, flathead, whiting and tailor.

The large headland at **Avoca Beach** is a popular rock area as there is car parking close by. The seas have to be watched on the north side, but to the south, a long, flat ledge takes over, dropping into deep water over a sand bottom. This area is fished for flathead, bream, rock blackfish, silver drummer, snapper and mulloway. Tuna, Australian salmon, kingfish and tailor are among the surface fish that come in here, and even marlin are not out of the question. Most regulars either use lures or live bait for the bigger fish. Bream, rock blackfish and luderick are also in the washes along the rocks of this big headland area.

The rock platform at The Skillion provides a great fishing spot for anglers targeting pelagic species

MacMasters Beach is backed by a large lagoon, known as **Cockrone Lake**. This is sometimes open to the sea and is a good place to get small mullet as bait. Whiting and mulloway are the main catches off the beach, with tailor and salmon in winter. Part of the scenic Bouddi National Park – the stretch from Bombi Point to Gerrin Point – is a marine reserve and is closed to fishing. To the south-west, **Putty Beach** can be easily reached for whiting and mulloway, but the big action for rock anglers requires a long walk to **Box Head**. This is at its best when the Hawkesbury River is in flood and the mulloway prowl after fish flushed from the river. At other times, Box Head generally fishes well for bream and tailor.

TERRIGAL

The comparatively protected waters of the Haven attract some big surface fish from offshore, like frigate mackerel, bonito and yellowtail kingfish. The frigates are most prevalent around February and March. They can be fished from the shore on the inner side of the headland, if you can find standing room, and by casting small metal lures. This promontory is also good for bream and tailor, particularly in the rocky washes after a southerly blow. Luderick, rock blackfish and silver drummer are also around the rocks.

Terrigal Lagoon is often closed at the beach, but when it is open flathead, bream and tailor are caught around the entrance, and the beach fishing becomes more active for bream, tailor and mulloway. At the southern end of the beach is a high rock known as **Grannys**, which can be fished safely, with bream as the main target.

Around the headland, there are good rock spots known as the Cod Hole, Flat Rock and Splashy, and bream, luderick and rock blackfish can be caught here, particularly after a southerly swell. Flat Rock can only be fished in calmer conditions.

One of the most crowded spots in this popular rock area is **The Skillion**, which can be reached by walking through parkland. Fishing for bonito, tailor, kingfish and striped and mackerel tuna is done with lures or live baits, and the place is generally crowded at the peak fishing times of early morning and tide changes. Those with more modest ambitions can still fish close in for luderick, rock blackfish and bream. The ledges here extend around the point, creating shelter from north-east winds, and the fishing is good for bream, tailor, luderick and rock blackfish.

NEW SOUTH WALES

COASTAL FISHING WOLLONGONG REGION

Wollongong Region

The beach and rock fishing in the Wollongong region starts in the unspoiled Royal National Park, within an hour's drive of Sydney, and continues in great variety all the way to Durras lake. The Shoalhaven is the only big river in the region, and the islands, sand flats, creeks and channels in its estuary are fascinating to explore by boat.

There are close-in reefs all down the coast carrying fish such as snapper, morwong, trevally, yellowtail kingfish and tuna. Minnamurra, Kiama, Gerringong and Gerroa are among a chain of fishing towns down this coast, and one of the best rock fishing spots in the region is Bass Point, which juts out into deep water. Further south a string of rock platforms, beaches, harbours, estuaries, rivers, channels and sand flats offer wonderful fishing.

Weather

As is the case along the rest of this coast, prevailing winds in the summer months are north-north-easterlies, with a tendency to swing sharply to the south unexpectedly. Always keep an eye on the cloud cover to ensure you are not taken by surprise. It is usually better to fish on the southern side of headlands, except during southerlies, when the northern aspect is obviously preferable. For information, ring the Weather Bureau on tel. (02) 9296 1555 or contact the local Coast Guard or Coastal Patrol. Detailed weather information can be found at: www.bom.gov.au

Boating

Tidal surges can cause problems at the Bellambi (Wollongong) and Kiama boat ramps, and the Shellharbour boat ramp is adequate, but not great. Generally anglers use Port Kembla, which has calm waters. There are bomboras off Wollongong and at the entrance to Shellharbour, so check the Admiralty Chart maps for water levels. Lake Illawarra and the Minnamurra River have bars close to their entrances, and Lake Illawarra is very shallow in parts. For local information, check with the Coast Guards, Waterways Authority and local maps.

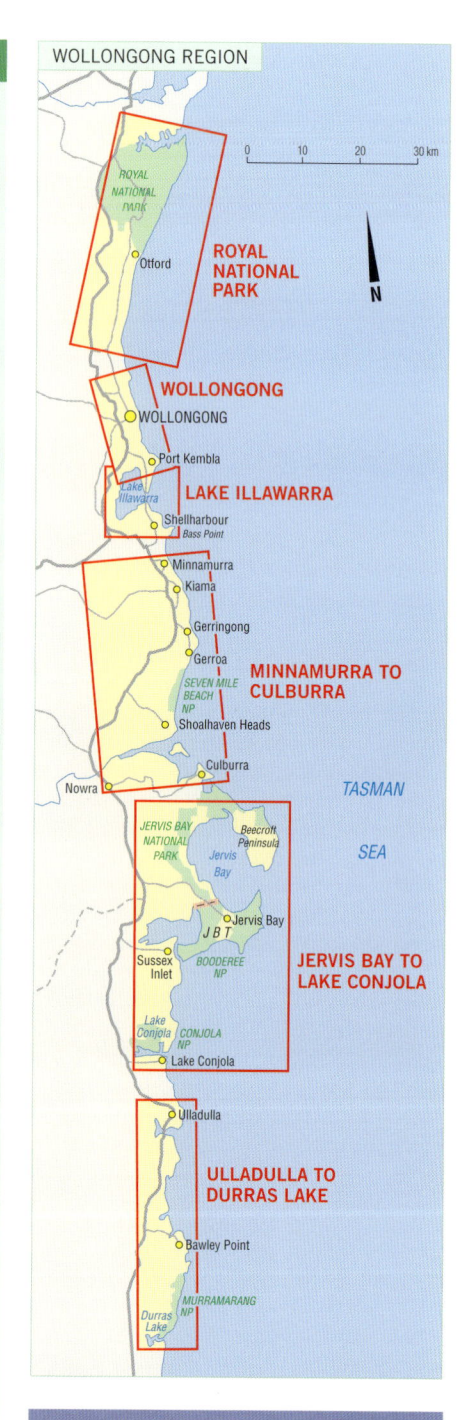

WHERE TO FISH

Wollongong Region

ROYAL NATIONAL PARK • 102
There is camping in the national park, and walking to some spectacular deep-water rock spots and secluded beaches. One attraction is The Gulf, a deep gutter frequented by a variety of pelagics.

WOLLONGONG • 103
Port Kembla harbour has fine breakwater fishing. There are great rock and beach locations on either side of Port Kembla and Wollongong, and extensive reefs close to shore.

LAKE ILLAWARRA • 104
Lake Illawarra is very shallow and best fished near the entrance, with outstanding prawn runs in summer. Nearby Windang Island is prolific for numerous species, while Bass Point juts a long way out into the sea and attracts big surface fish as well as the close-in rock species.

MINNAMURRA TO CULBURRA • 106
This is a beautiful stretch of coast, with harbour fishing at Kiama, some great beach spots, and rock fishing at places such as Blowhole Point and Black Head at Gerroa. The Shoalhaven River is a fascinating estuary, with numerous islands, sandbars, bays and canals near the coast, creating some prime fishing locations.

JERVIS BAY TO CONJOLA • 108
There is excellent rock fishing on the Beecroft Peninsula, and good, safe land spots in Jervis Bay. Boat fishing is rewarding but unsafe in a southerly. Sir Joseph Young Banks is a large, productive reef 4 km out from the peninsula, while Sussex Inlet is good for both land and boat fishing. Lake Conjola is famous for its big flathead.

ULLADULLA TO DURRAS LAKE • 110
This area offers a combination of beach, rock, harbour and estuary fishing, while the offshore islands can teem with snapper and yellowtail kingfish.

FISHING TIP

Cunjevoi is a superb bait for a number of species including snapper and bream. Also known as sea-squirts or cunje, these animals are more like plants and live in colonies along the tidal zone of rock platforms and on pier pilings. Although tough on the outside, once opened the flesh is a rich orange to purple and should be scooped out. A few cunje will generally last a reasonable period. Rather than take too many, try taking just enough because they don't breed as fast as anglers can remove them.

COASTAL FISHING WOLLONGONG REGION

NEW SOUTH WALES

GUIDE TO LOCAL FISH

albacore
bonito
bream, black
bream, yellowfin
drummer, silver
flathead
flounder
garfish
groper
hairtail
john dory
kingfish, yellowtail
leatherjacket
luderick
mackerel, slimy
marlin, black
marlin, blue
marlin, striped
morwong
mullet, sand
mullet, sea
mulloway
nannygai
rock blackfish
salmon, Australian
snapper
tailor
teraglin
trevally, silver
tuna, mackerel
tuna, striped
tuna, yellowfin
whiting, King George
whiting, sand
whiting, trumpeter

FURTHER INFORMATION

Fishing and boating NSW Fisheries has offices at 43 Reddall Pde, Lake Illawarra South, tel. (02) 4295 1809; and 64 North St, Nowra, tel. (02) 4423 2200. The Waterways Authority has an office at Unit 5, cnr Kembla St and Beach St, Wollongong, tel. (02) 4227 3644. The Coast Guard's main bases are at Bellambi (Wollongong), tel. (02) 4284 8822; Port Kembla tel. (02) 4274 4455 and Shellharbour, tel. (02) 4297 3999. The Coastal Patrol has bases at Wollongong, tel. (02) 4229 3434; Jervis Bay, tel. 0402 079 838; Sussex Inlet, tel. (02) 4441 1444; Kiola, tel. (02) 4457 1109; and Ulladulla, tel. (02) 4455 3403.

Tourist centres Shoalhaven Tourist Centre, 254 Princes Hwy, Bomaderry, tel. (02) 4421 0778; Blowhole Point Rd, Kiama, tel. (02) 4232 3322; Princes Hwy, Ulladulla, tel. (02) 4455 1269; 93 Crown St, Wollongong, tel. (02) 4228 0300.

Garie Beach area: the high elevation enables this angler to cast out to the back of the breakers

NEW SOUTH WALES

COASTAL FISHING WOLLONGONG REGION

Royal National Park

Type of fishing
beach, offshore, rock

Target fish
Australian salmon, bream, snapper, tailor

Although close to Sydney, Royal National Park is a largely unspoilt paradise for the rock and beach angler. You must be prepared to walk to your fishing spot, to carry your supplies, and to get a permit if you want to camp overnight. The good news is that the bushwalking is pleasant and the fishing wonderful.

The northernmost fishing area, known as **The Cobblers**, can be reached from the walking track that runs from Bundeena to Marley Beach. This area can be very dangerous in big seas and the high ledges make a cliff gaff essential. There is good fishing for luderick and rock blackfish in the washes and, further out, for tailor, Australian salmon and snapper.

Marley Head and the rocky ledges south of Marley Beach are good luderick, bream and rock blackfish territory. The adjoining **Marley and Little Marley beaches** are bream and whiting grounds, with tailor and salmon in winter. The ledges south of Little Marley are good casting platforms for snapper further out, and for spinning in summer for yellowtail kingfish, tuna, salmon and tailor.

The sheltered **Wattamolla Bay** can provide bream and tailor. At **Curracurrang** there is inshore fishing for luderick, rock blackfish, bream, groper and leatherjacket, with snapper, tailor, salmon and kingfish further out. A track from the Wattamolla road leads to **The Gulf**, a deep gutter running back to a large rock platform. Marlin, tuna and kingfish can be caught on live baits, while tailor, salmon, trevally, snapper and bream are targets for those spinning and baitfishing in the washes.

Further south, trevally, tailor, bream, snapper and salmon can be caught from the rocks at the north point of Garie Beach. The beaches at **South Era** are good for flathead, whiting and bream.

Offshore, there are Jibbon Bombora in the north, Marley Head, Little Marley Beach, Wattamolla and Curracurrang. There are no boat ramps in the park but boats may be launched at Cronulla. Snapper, mulloway, tailor, morwong and nannygai are likely to be caught over reefs, while there is good drifting for flathead along the entire coast. South of Royal National Park, there are extensive reefs offshore from Austinmer and Bellambi Point, with kingfish, bonito and yellowfin tuna the main catches.

GUIDE TO LOCAL FISH

	Royal National Park	Wollongong
(B) bream	•	•
(F) flathead	•	•
(GR) groper	•	•
(HT) hairtail		•
(DR) john dory		•
(KI) kingfish, yellowtail	•	•
(LJ) leatherjacket	•	•
(LU) luderick	•	•
(ML) marlin	•	•
(MO) morwong	•	•
(MU) mulloway	•	•
(NG) nannygai	•	•
(RB) rock blackfish	•	•
(SA) salmon, Australian	•	•
(S) snapper	•	•
(T) tailor	•	•
(TL) teraglin	•	•
(TR) trevally	•	•
(TU) tuna	•	•
(W) whiting	•	•

COASTAL FISHING WOLLONGONG REGION   NEW SOUTH WALES

Wollongong

Type of fishing
beach, harbour, offshore, rock

Target fish
bream, luderick, mulloway, snapper, tailor

Flagstaff Point is a good spot for luderick, rock blackfish, tailor and bream, while **Wollongong Beach**, running to Port Kembla, will yield tailor, salmon and flathead. There is good fishing all around the Wollongong area, particularly in and around Port Kembla Harbour.

Like many other port locations, with piers, buoys and other structures attracting fish, **Port Kembla Harbour** has a lot to offer the land-based angler. The best spot is the Northern Breakwater, where mulloway, snapper, bream, luderick and tailor are plentiful, particularly at dawn and dusk. Hairtail are caught here at times. Those who fish outside the retaining wall, running to the breakwater, will be fishing over sand for luderick, rock blackfish, school mulloway and tailor. The Southern Breakwater is almost as good, while in the harbour the shipping wharves can be fished for school mulloway, john dory and yellowtail kingfish when ships are not tied up. The walls on both sides of the inner harbour entrance provide great locations for luderick fishing.

The rocks at **Battery Point**, near the Southern Breakwater, are great luderick and rock blackfish spots, with good weed on the rocks but a sandy bottom to protect your rig. Between Battery Point and Red Point, flathead, bream, whiting and tailor are found off the beaches.

Further south, the headland at the north end of **Perkins Beach** has good rock fishing for snapper, tailor and Australian salmon, but it must only be fished in calm seas, as it is not called Dead Mans Hole for nothing.

The offshore fishing in the region is consistent, without being spectacular, for those who know the right locations and tactics. There are gravel patches with good snapper possibilities about 1.5 km out from Wollongong Harbour, and a snapper reef another 1 km out. Similar gravel areas run from west of Big Island.

Off Port Kembla, The Five Islands, which include **Flinders and Bass islets** and **Big Island**, have kingfish, snapper and mulloway, with bream, tailor and salmon in the inshore washes. Boat launching can be made from Wollongong or Shellharbour, but avoid the entrance to Lake Illawarra.

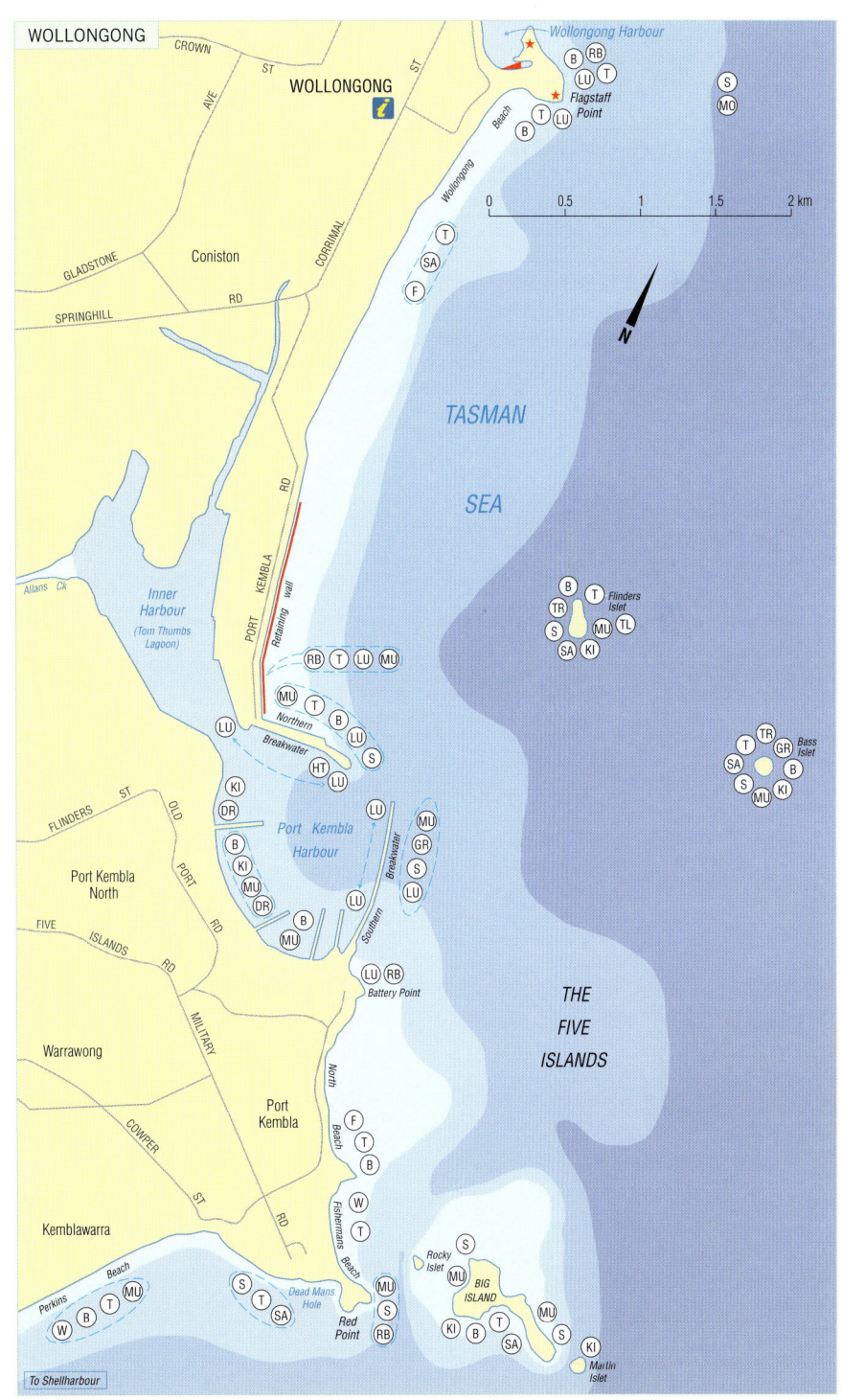

Tailor

The tailor is one of Australia's most popular saltwater sportfish. It is found in inshore and close offshore waters from Fraser Island, in Queensland, right round the south coast to Shark Bay in Western Australia. It is a great fighting fish, requiring the use of a wire trace or ganged hooks. It will readily hit trolled or cast lures as well as static or moving baits. As a table fish, tailor is best bled immediately after capture and tastiest when freshly cooked. It does not freeze well.

NEW SOUTH WALES

COASTAL FISHING WOLLONGONG REGION

Lake Illawarra

Type of fishing
beach, lake, rock

Target fish
bream, flathead, luderick, rock blackfish, tailor, whiting

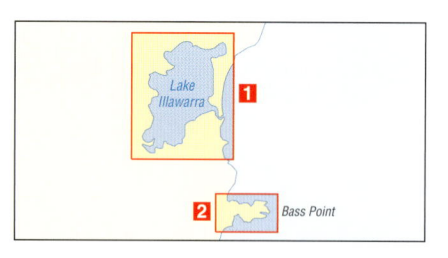

Lake Illawarra is very shallow, less than 4 m at its deepest, but it yields a lot of fish year after year, despite the pressure from both professional and recreational fishers. The best fishing along the whole Wollongong coast is at Bass Point, a wedge of land jutting into the sea just south of Shellharbour.

LAKE ILLAWARRA

Lake Illawarra's best fishing is at the entrance and around the shore, although its very shallowness makes its central waters productive also – sandbanks and gutters close in are good for whiting, using live worms or yabbies as bait. The lake can be dangerous in high winds, as the choppy conditions can easily overturn small craft. Nevertheless, the hire boats available around the lake attest to the popularity of this waterway and its general safety.

The entrance is the most prolific and crowded area of the lake, producing whiting, flathead, mullet, luderick, bream and tailor for both boat and shore anglers. The prawn runs around the entrance in summer, on the new moon, are outstanding, and hundreds of people wade the shallows with strong lights and dip nets to reap the rewards. Others operate out of boats. There are prawning areas all along the north-eastern side of the lake. On the northern shore, just inside the entrance, the flathead fishing can be good, particularly at dusk on a falling tide. Persistent holiday-makers often get their evening meal at a flathead mark just north of **Cudgeree Island**, or a bucket of prawns a little further north and near the bank. Straight in from the entrance is **Bevans Island**, which has luderick on the north side. Whiting, flathead and bream can be caught all around the island.

Several creeks run into the lake on its western side. Near their entrances, these waters provide reliable fishing for bream, and luderick, mullet and flathead are also prevalent. Fishing outside the creek entrances after heavy rain can yield big bream catches at **Mullet Creek**, **Duck Creek** and **Macquarie Rivulet**.

Outside, Windang Island is connected to the mainland by a changing tidal sandbar that sometimes blocks the southerly outflow. When this occurs, **Perkins Beach** (known locally as Windang Beach), which is one of the best south coast beaches, becomes even more prolific for mulloway, as well as bream, flathead, salmon, whiting and tailor.

Windang Island is a great place to fish, with the rocky shores attracting bream, luderick, rock blackfish, drummer and tailor to its washes, and its deep, sandy-bottomed surrounds making casting and spinning a pleasure. It is known as a bream hot spot, particularly in winter, and the best bream area is on its south-eastern shore. The north-eastern area of the island is best for snapper, while luderick can be caught from the northern shore, along with tailor and rock blackfish.

Warilla Beach fishes very well if the lake is flowing out south of Windang

Suitable tackle for the Lake Illawarra estuary

COASTAL FISHING WOLLONGONG REGION   NEW SOUTH WALES

Island. The target fish are whiting, bream, tailor and mulloway. At the southern end of the beach, **Barrack Point** has rock fishing for bream and luderick, using bait under floats in the washes close-in, tailor further out, again with bait under a float, and snapper by casting well out on the bottom.

BASS POINT

The peninsula juts out into the passing currents and is a perfect venue to fish for pelagics such as tailor and tuna as well as bream, leatherjacket, luderick, rock blackfish, snapper and silver drummer attracted to the rocky washes and gutters. Baits like cunjevoi, crabs and cabbage weed are easily gathered, and there are two boat ramps in the area for those wishing to fish the currents out from the island. The ramp at Shellharbour, to the north, is the safer of the two as boat launching at Bass Point is subject to rough seas.

On the north-east shore of Bass Point, a carpark allows good access to rocky gutters that produce yellowtail kingfish, snapper and trevally. Bream, luderick and leatherjacket are also here. The eastern-most point of the peninsula, near the bombora, is the best spot to cast out for tuna, tailor, kingfish and other pelagics.

A cove, known as **Bushrangers Bay**, on the south-east corner of the point, is an aquatic reserve nursery for juvenile fish species and other marine life, and is completely protected. On the southern side there is a group of rock ledges that allows high and safe casting for the inshore rock fish, and tailor, salmon and snapper.

Lake Illawarra is a well-known estuary for land-based locations

GUIDE TO LOCAL FISH

		Lake Illawarra	Bass Point
BT	bonito		●
B	bream	●	●
D	drummer, silver	●	●
F	flathead	●	
G	garfish		●
GR	groper		●
KI	kingfish, yellowtail		●
LJ	leatherjacket		●
LU	luderick	●	●
M	mullet	●	
MU	mulloway	●	
RB	rock blackfish	●	●
SA	salmon, Australian	●	●
S	snapper	●	●
T	tailor	●	●
TU	tuna		●
W	whiting	●	

NEW SOUTH WALES

COASTAL FISHING WOLLONGONG REGION

Minnamurra to Culburra

Type of fishing
bay, beach, estuary, offshore, rock

Target fish
bream, flathead, snapper, whiting

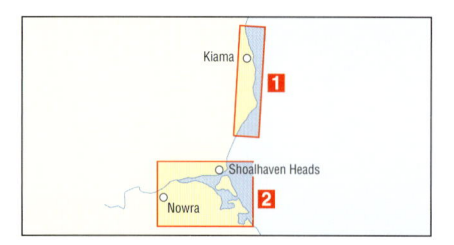

Fishing is a great part of the life of the townsfolk, retirees and vacationers on the beautiful stretch of coast from Minnamurra to Culburra. A string of rock platforms and beaches offers wonderful fishing, providing that the rock-hoppers take care as most of the locations are near sea level and very dangerous. The Shoalhaven River has many islands, sandbars, bays and canals near the coast, creating some prime fishing spots.

MINNAMURRA TO SEVEN MILE BEACH

The Minnamurra River provides relaxing fishing for luderick, bream and whiting on nippers and flathead near the mouth spinning. **Boyds Beach** is a good spot for luderick, rock blackfish and snapper, with gutters for bream and whiting from the beach. **The Boneyard** is protected, and when the huge southerlies are rolling in can still be fished for bream, luderick and snapper. **Bombo**, **Surf** and **Kendalls beaches** are all good for bream and whiting.

Land-based anglers get the best of **Kiama Harbour** after a big southerly sea, when bream, luderick and snapper come into these protected waters. For reef fishing, snapper and morwong are the main targets. Further out you can troll for striped and yellowfin tuna and marlin, with albacore out off the shelf.

Blowhole Point is one of the finest rock fishing spots on the coast, and one of the easiest to reach by road. Live baits, which can be caught in the harbour, are drifted off the point for kingfish and tuna, while snapper and salmon are also taken.

South of Kiama, **Marsden Head** is the next great spot, with big trevally in the winter, spinning for tuna and kingfish, and salmon, tailor and snapper. Further south, **Werri Beach** and **Walkers Beach** have deep gutters holding salmon and tailor, with good summer catches of bream, whiting and flathead. Big fish can be caught off the rocks all the way to Gerroa, with top places including **Big Rock**, south of

GUIDE TO LOCAL FISH

		Minnamurra to Seven Mile Beach	Shoalhaven River
BA	bass, Australian		●
B	bream	●	●
D	drummer, silver	●	
F	flathead	●	●
FL	flounder	●	●
G	garfish	●	●
GR	groper	●	
KI	kingfish, yellowtail	●	
LU	luderick	●	●
ML	marlin	●	
MO	morwong	●	
MU	mulloway	●	
RB	rock blackfish	●	
SA	salmon, Australian	●	●
S	snapper	●	
T	tailor	●	●
TR	trevally	●	
TU	tuna	●	
W	whiting	●	●

Fishing the rocks at Black Head near Gerroa

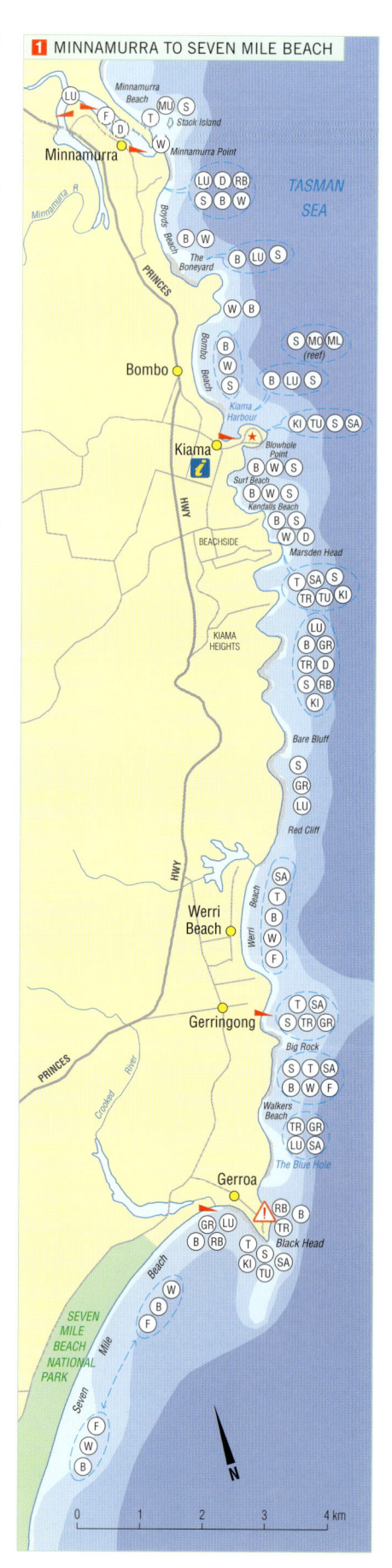

COASTAL FISHING WOLLONGONG REGION — NEW SOUTH WALES

Gerringong; **The Blue Hole**, past Walkers Beach; and **Black Head**, at Gerroa. Small boats can be launched from the protected northern end of the **Seven Mile Beach** at Gerroa, and this most popular beach is wonderful for whiting and bream and the odd flathead in the summer.

SHOALHAVEN RIVER

Shoalhaven River provides a lot of interest for boat anglers who are after great estuary fare like whiting, flathead, bream, luderick, tailor and even mulloway. The best baits are right there on the sand flats – squirt worms and nippers are abundant and will catch anything you might encounter. The **Shoalhaven entrance** is often closed but sometimes opens after big floods. Fishing inside the entrance or from the beaches will yield whiting, bream and flathead, with nipper available all around the inner shore. The reef near O'Keefes Point and **Berrys Canal** are the best places for big mulloway. The canal runs down to the entrance of the Crookhaven River and its island-filled estuary, Curleys Bay, where bream, flathead and luderick are in good numbers. One hot spot for luderick is **Greenwell Point**, just south of the boat ramps, and the flathead drifting is good from Greenwell Point to the wharf just inside the entrance. Comerong Bay, behind the entrance, is very shallow, but there is drifting for flathead and good bream water near the shore. Outside, anglers will do well on the beaches in either direction, seeking whiting, bream, tailor and salmon.

Into the Shoalhaven proper there is an excellent flathead drifting run on the incoming tide from **O'Keefes Point** to the **Broughton Creek** entrance. The river is then split by islands and sandbars. Anchor in the sand flats east of **Numbaa Island** to catch flathead on a rising tide. Past the island, a buoy marks a sand flat that is exposed at low tide. In this area there is good drifting for flathead along the northern shore on a run-out tide. Bream, luderick, whiting and flathead are at the eastern head of **Pig Island**. On the northern bank there is a high paper mill that marks a prime spot for bream and luderick, and some really big mulloway. Beyond the island is a reef, dangerous for boating but excellent for luderick and bream at night. The Shoalhaven is well served for boat ramps.

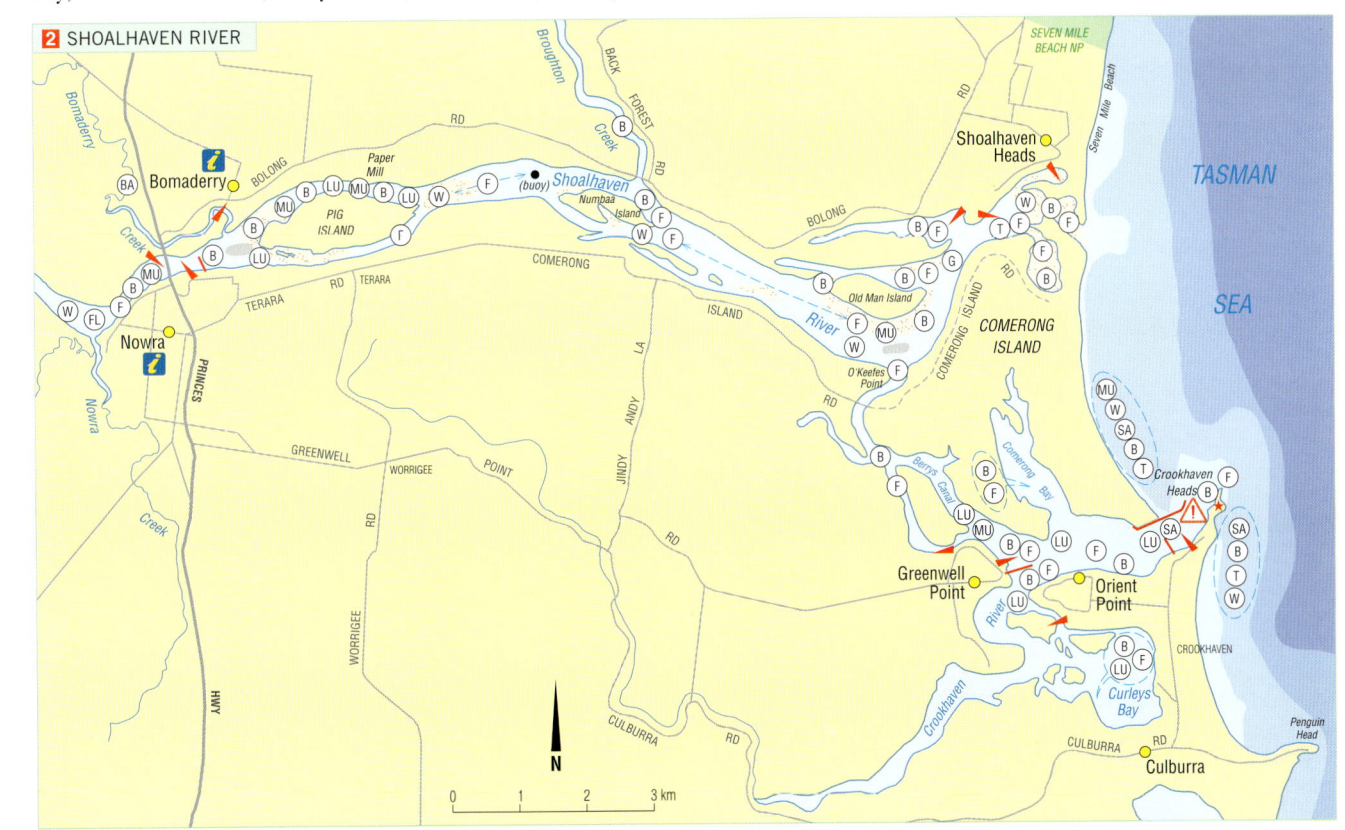

Typical shoreline around the Shoalhaven district

NEW SOUTH WALES

COASTAL FISHING WOLLONGONG REGION

Jervis Bay to Lake Conjola

Type of fishing
bay, beach, lake, offshore, reef, rock

Target fish
bream, flathead, luderick, whiting, yellowtail kingfish

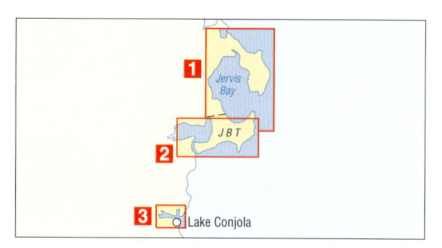

Jervis Bay offers a combination of good rock, boat and land fishing in the bay itself, and excellent offshore fishing at the Sir Joseph Young Banks. In the Sussex Inlet area, the excavation of canals has expanded the fishing water. Lake Conjola, a relatively quiet estuary, rates as one of the most pleasant places to fish in New South Wales.

JERVIS BAY

The Jervis Bay area has top rate rock fishing on the low rock ledges among the high cliffs of the **Beecroft Peninsula**. Surface fish such as kingfish, bonito and tuna are the targets, with marlin a welcome surprise, along with snapper and rock blackfish in the washes. Rock fishing at Beecroft Head, Eves Ravine, Never Fail, Devils Gorge and The Ladders is only for those with experience who can deal with the hazards of using ropes and ladders and carrying large fish.

The entrance to Jervis Bay has a reef known as the **Middle Ground**, a good drifting area for flathead and bream, but also carrying tuna, tailor, kingfish, bonito and trevally. Inside, on the south-western side of the Beecroft Peninsula, there is good land and boat fishing for snapper, rock blackfish, salmon, bream, trevally and an abundance of garfish. Further north, inshore drifting offers flathead, bream, flounder and whiting, but any southerly blow funnels through here and makes boating hazardous.

The rest of the bay is good and safe fishing, mainly from the beaches, for whiting, bream and flathead, though other species are also present.

Jervis Bay is now a marine park with the likelihood that areas within the bay will be closed to fishing. Contact Jervis Bay Marine Park on (02) 4441 7752 for details.

The greatest attraction of the Jervis Bay area is the big offshore reef known as the **Sir Joseph Young Banks**, lying about 4 km north-east of Beecroft Head and best fished from October to May. The northern end of the reef is good for snapper and big kingfish, and the outer side of the reef is frequented by marlin and tuna. Over the reef there is bottom fishing for snapper, morwong, trevally and kingfish.

Two other offshore spots are the **Nowra Hill Ground**, 4 km north-east of Penguin Head (snapper, mulloway, teraglin, kingfish) and **The Shallows** to the north of Currarong (kingfish, snapper, mulloway).

SUSSEX INLET

Access to the coast is difficult between Jervis Bay and Cape St George and the area is not heavily fished. Rock spots around **Green Rock** have luderick, rock blackfish and bream. **Cave Beach** is renowned for its salmon.

The beaches around the entrance to Sussex Inlet provide brilliant fishing for bream, salmon and tailor, while the rock platforms on the southern side of the inlet fish very well at dawn and dusk for these same fish, and also luderick.

Sussex Inlet carries bream, whiting and flathead in large numbers, with luderick in the weed beds and around rocky areas,

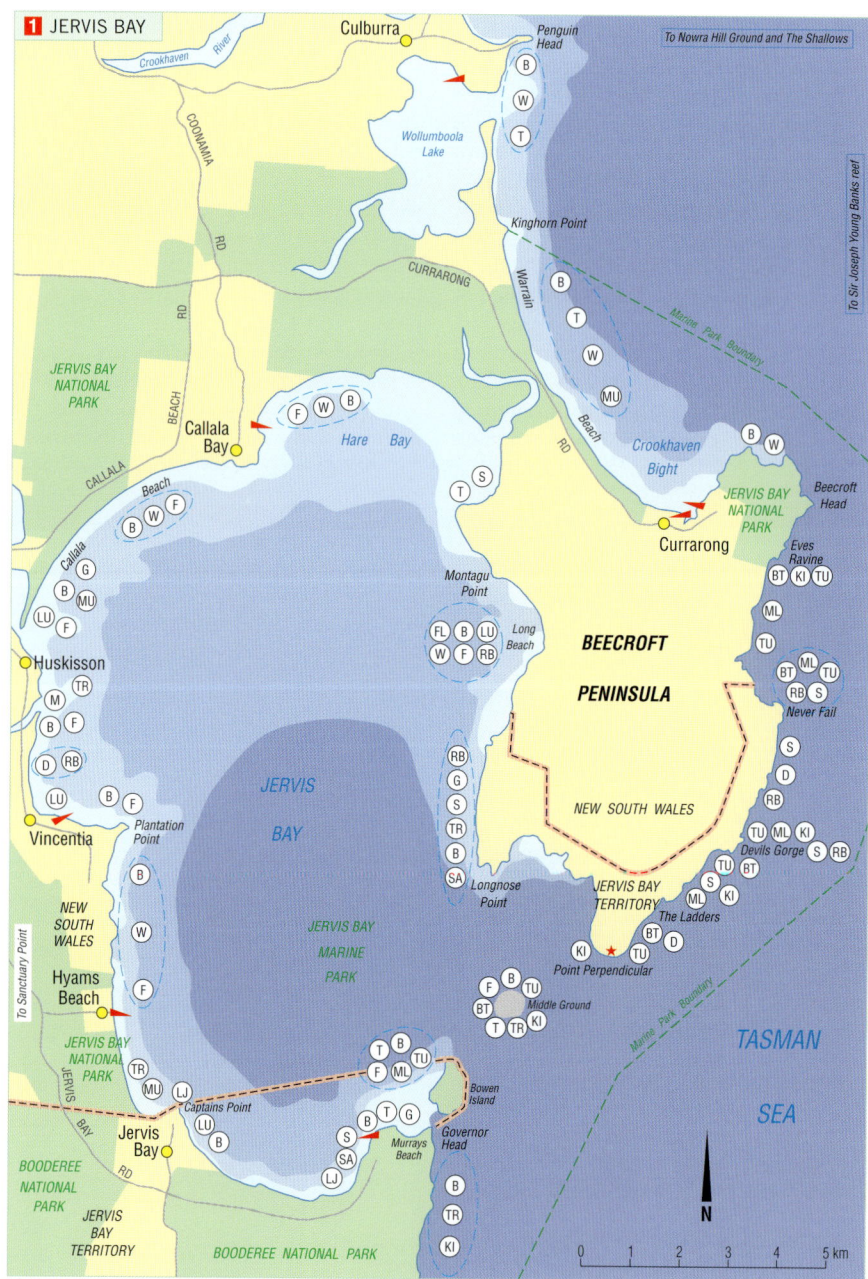

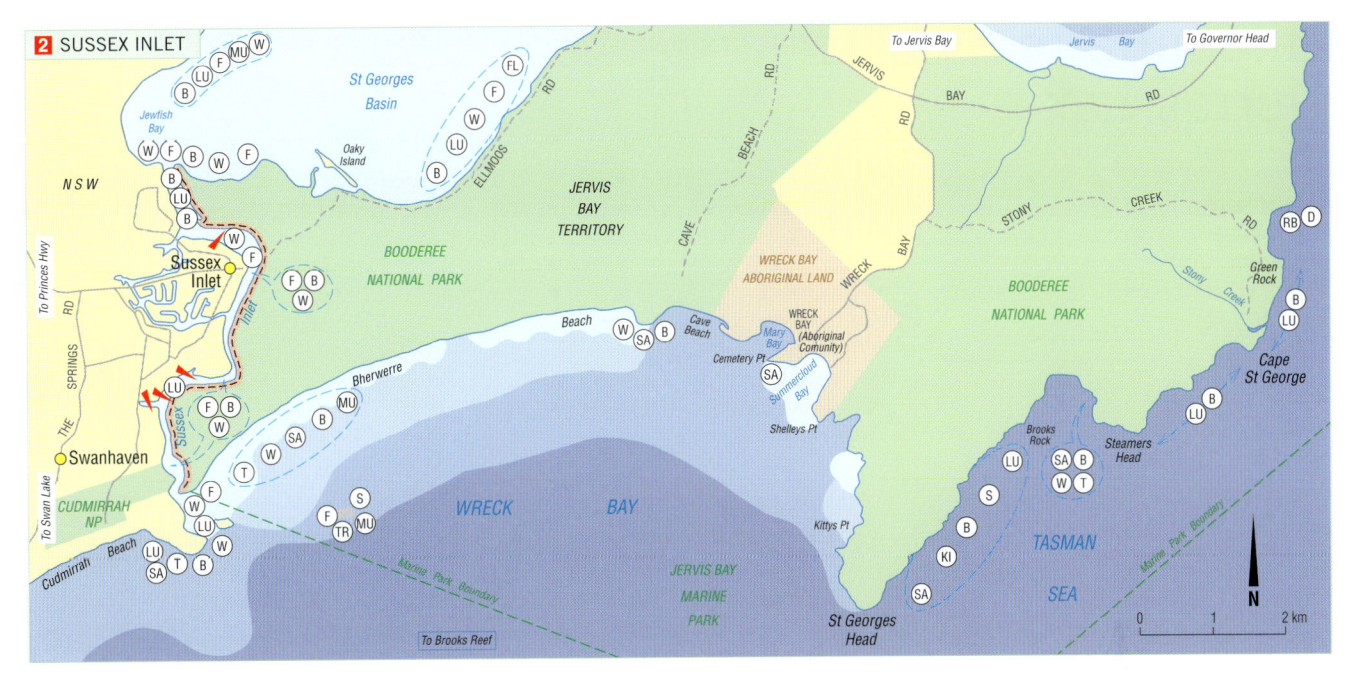

COASTAL FISHING WOLLONGONG REGION   NEW SOUTH WALES

especially near the entrance. Boat fishing and shore-based angling will be rewarded here, particularly at slack water on a high tide.

St Georges Basin is best where the inlet enters the lake, either for shore angling or drifting, mainly for flathead. The shores of the lake offer good fishing, with marshes and mud banks creating natural food sources for bream, luderick, flathead and whiting. Nearby **Swan Lake** has similar fishing, with bream the target fish.

About 1 km offshore, an extensive gravelly area is ideal for drifting for snapper, morwong, flathead and trevally, and further out Brooks Reef attracts kingfish, morwong, snapper and tuna.

LAKE CONJOLA

Lake Conjola is part of a lake system entering the sea at Cunjurong, south of Sussex Inlet. The attraction on the sand flats of the lower part of Lake Conjola are big flathead, while flounder, garfish, bream, luderick and mullet are also on the menu. The upper lake fishes well for bream, flathead, mulloway and whiting, particularly in summer. The prime position in the lake is The Steps, at the entrance to the channel between the lakes, where a drop into deep water creates an ambush point for flathead and bream.

Outside the lake is Green Island, separated from the land by a shallow sand spit. Anglers can walk across to the island on low tide or wade through chest-deep water at high tide. On the ocean side of the island groper can be caught, along with snapper, bream, luderick and rock blackfish. **Conjola Beach** is a favoured place for anglers pursuing flathead, whiting, salmon, tailor, bream and occasionally mulloway.

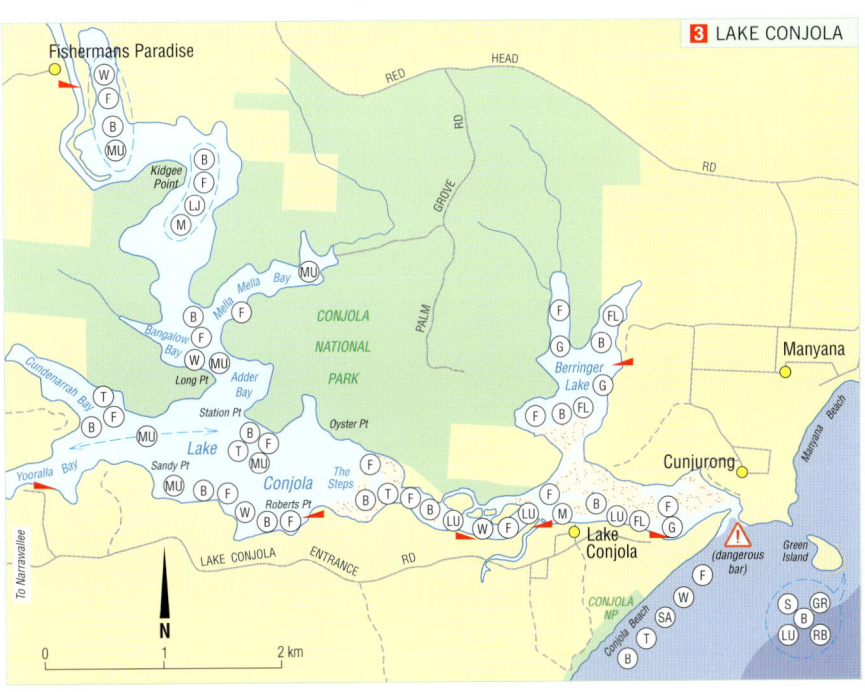

GUIDE TO LOCAL FISH

		Jervis Bay	Sussex Inlet	Lake Conjola
BT	bonito	●		
B	bream	●	●	●
D	drummer	●	●	
F	flathead	●	●	●
FL	flounder	●	●	●
G	garfish	●		●
GR	groper	●		●
KI	kingfish, yellowtail	●	●	
LJ	leatherjacket	●		●
LU	luderick	●	●	●
ML	marlin	●		
M	mullet	●	●	●
MU	mulloway	●	●	●
RB	rock blackfish	●	●	●
SA	salmon, Australian	●	●	●
S	snapper	●	●	●
T	tailor	●	●	●
TR	trevally	●	●	
TU	tuna	●		
W	whiting	●	●	●

109

NEW SOUTH WALES

COASTAL FISHING WOLLONGONG REGION

Ulladulla to Durras Lake

Type of fishing
beach, estuary, harbour, lake, rock

Target fish
Australian salmon, bream, flathead, luderick, snapper, tailor, whiting

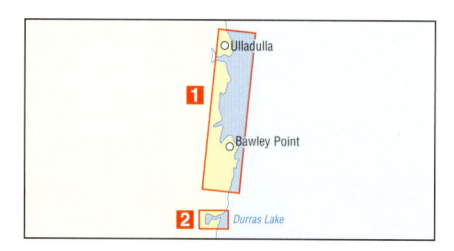

GUIDE TO LOCAL FISH

		Ulladulla to Point Upright	Tabourie Lake	Durras Lake
B	bream	•	•	•
F	flathead	•	•	•
GR	groper	•		
KI	kingfish, yellowtail	•	•	
LU	luderick	•	•	•
MO	morwong	•		
M	mullet			•
MU	mulloway	•		•
RB	rock blackfish	•		•
SA	salmon, Australian	•		
S	snapper	•		
T	tailor	•	•	
TR	trevally	•		
TU	tuna	•	•	
W	whiting	•	•	•

Anglers flock to this part of the New South Wales coast for the combination of beach, rock, harbour and estuary fishing. The offshore islands between Bawley Point and Point Upright reward boat anglers with yellowtail kingfish, tuna, snapper and morwong.

ULLADULLA TO POINT UPRIGHT

North of Ulladulla, **Mollymook Beach** is a great spot for salmon, tailor, bream and flathead. **Ulladulla Harbour** should not be overlooked by anglers, as bream, tailor and salmon abound there, with luderick, rock blackfish and bream around the harbour rocks. The harbour fishes best when white water is breaking on the outer reef. Outside the reef are salmon, mulloway, snapper and trevally, but these are best sought by boat, as fishing from the exposed reef is dangerous.

There are good rock ledges around Ulladulla for tailor, bream, luderick and rock blackfish, particularly at **Warden Head**. Two of the best fishing beaches in the area are **Rennies Beach**, especially after a storm, for bream and mulloway, and **Racecourse Beach** for salmon and tailor.

Further south is the wide entrance to **Burrill Lake**, with bream and luderick the main targets from **Horseshoe Beach**, on the coast, up to the lake itself. This is a very good area for land fishing, with the **Princes Highway Bridge** excellent for bream and the odd mulloway. The sand flats and channels in the lake produce whiting and big flathead, best caught with live poddy mullet, lures or worms and yabbies taken from the sand flats. Luderick and bream are around the lake shores. Three boat ramps in the lake provide good access for boat fishing.

Lagoon Head is another of the top rock fishing spots on the coast. Fishing off the ledges here can yield tailor, bream, luderick and rock blackfish.

The very best of beach and rock fishing can be found in the beautiful stretch of

Ulladulla Harbour has resident populations of bream, luderick, rock blackfish, tailor and salmon

COASTAL FISHING WOLLONGONG REGION
NEW SOUTH WALES

coastline from Bawley Point to south of Point Upright. The rock platforms are high and safe, and they front deep water. Offshore, many small islands attract kingfish, snapper and various tunas. Many rocks are accessible for the collection of bait like cunjevoi, crabs, shellfish and cabbage weed, while the beaches abound with pippis and worms.

Bawley Point is not typical as the rock slopes down to the sea, and it requires long casts. Luderick, snapper, trevally and groper are among the many species to be caught here. **Murramarang Beach** is best for tailor, salmon and mulloway, with some whiting and bream. Offshore, **Brush Island** often teems with snapper and yellowtail kingfish.

Merry Beach is an outstanding rock fishing area. The rocks form a crescent and the main area, known as **The Horseshoe**, is a place for experienced devotees with cliff gaffs seeking big snapper, groper, tailor, salmon, luderick and rock blackfish. **Snapper Point** is a moderately high platform with deep water close in. It attracts big fish from their offshore highway, and some notable catches of tuna and kingfish are made on live bait. There is also potential for catches of snapper, tailor, salmon, rock blackfish and luderick.

Further south, offshore from Depot Beach and around Grasshopper Island, you may be rewarded with large numbers of tailor and salmon, along with bream, flathead and snapper. Big flathead are taken on the drift outside Point Upright.

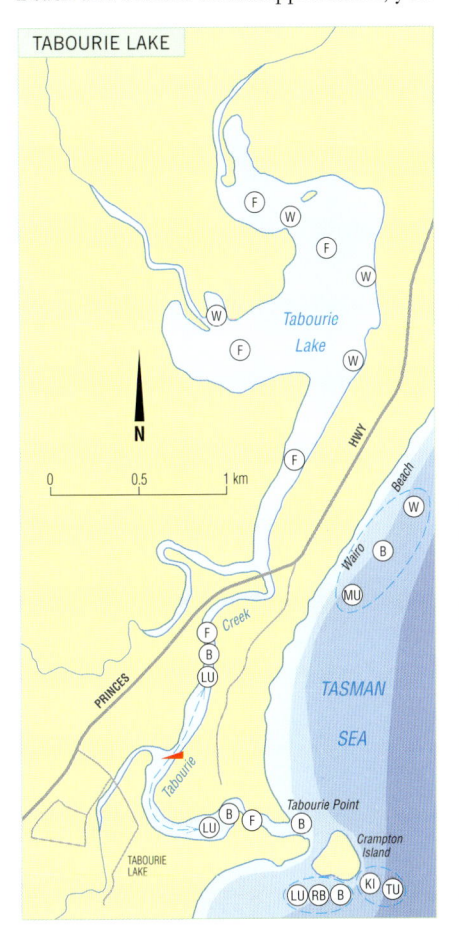

Near Lagoon Head the surf fishing from the beach is productive, especially at dawn and dusk

TABOURIE LAKE

Stretching south from Lagoon Head to Tabourie Point, **Wairo Beach** is good for whiting, bream and mulloway. **Crampton Island** can be reached across the sand at low tide, and has high cliffs on the south-eastern side, allowing spinning for kingfish and tuna. There are luderick, rock blackfish and bream close in on the south-east.

Along **Tabourie Creek** luderick, flathead and bream are the main targets. There is a safe launching ramp on the creek bank near the entrance. In the lake, drift for flathead along the channels between the sand flats, and seek whiting around weed patches.

DURRAS LAKE

Throughout the year, Durras Lake is among the best bream spots along the whole New South Wales coast, although the fish have a tendency at times to retreat to the deep channels in the upper reaches. The lake is also an excellent producer of flathead, whiting and mullet. When it is open to the sea, the prawning runs on the new moon summer nights can be terrific. The lake abuts a superb surf beach, which is excellent for whiting in the summer, and is bounded by national park and bushland, which provides a tranquil fishing experience. Boats can be launched into the lake from the southern shore near the entrance.

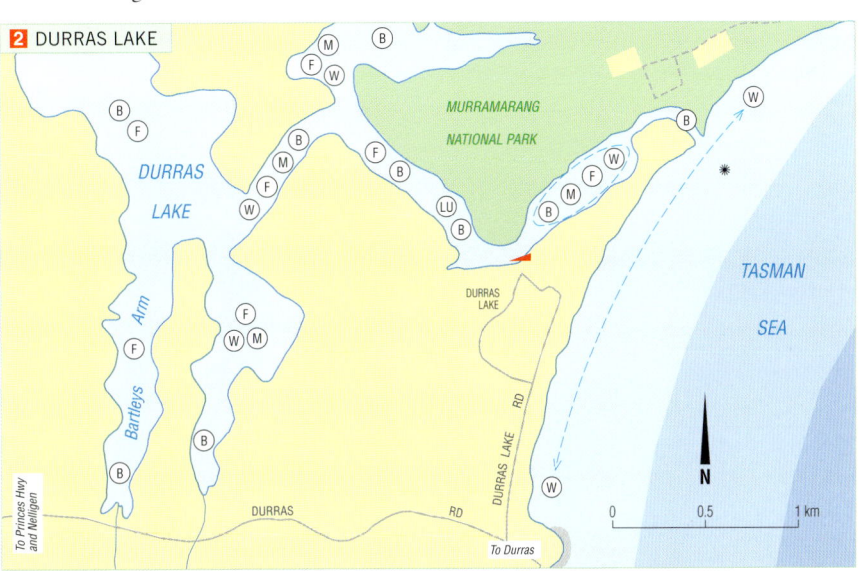

111

NEW SOUTH WALES

COASTAL FISHING BERMAGUI REGION

Bermagui Region

The stunningly beautiful far south coast of New South Wales is not only easy on the eye but is also almost perfect for fishing in all forms (lake, estuary, offshore and big game). Anglers can enjoy the spectacularly rugged coastline, the frequently mist-covered mountains and the unspoiled countryside.

The bays and headlands provide virtually continuous rock and beach fishing, and there are many close-in gravel patches and reefs to be explored by inshore boat anglers. The beautiful estuaries are the joy of the southern scene for most anglers, with bream flathead and whiting as the main targets, and mulloway the cream on the cake. Offshore, the southern game fishing grounds are inhabited by various tunas, bonito, kingfish, blue and black marlin and sharks.

Weather

Watch out for north-easterlies, as they can be dangerous for small craft if winds are over 15 knots. Generally conditions are good, but be aware of south-west changes, which can come in very fast. The best time for fishing is early morning, from daybreak to about 10.30 a.m., before the wind comes

Boat fishing on the Clyde River at Nelligen near Batemans Bay

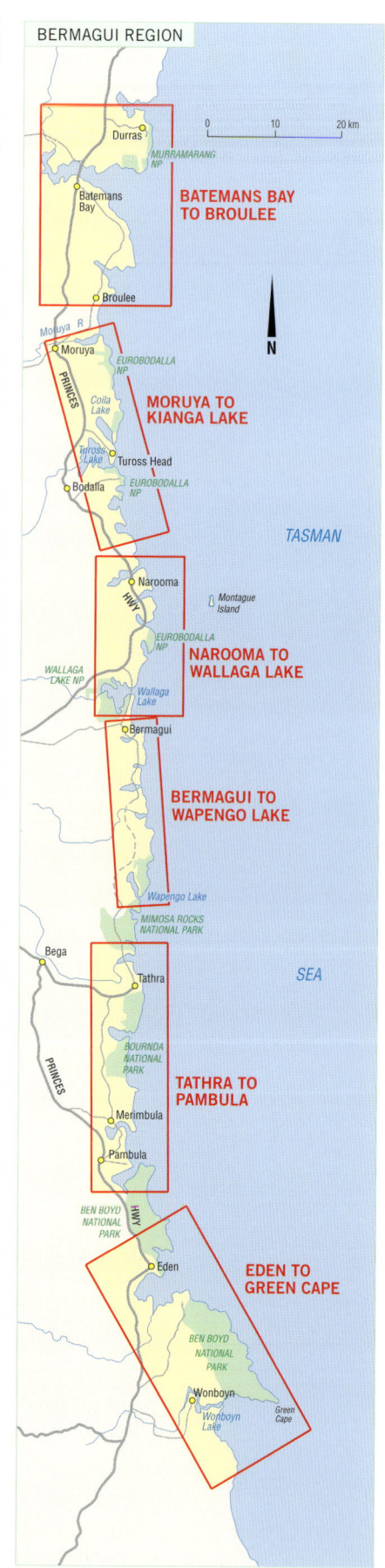

WHERE TO FISH
Bermagui Region

BATEMANS BAY TO BROULEE ● 114
Clyde River is an easy estuary to fish, and there is good shore fishing south of Batemans Bay. Jimmies Island provides a land and boat bonanza, and there is access to reef fishing in Broulee Bay.

MORUYA TO KIANGA LAKE ● 116
Moruya River is a perfect estuary for both land and boat fishing, with bass upstream. Tuross and Coila lakes are complex and picturesque, with plenty of fish.

NAROOMA TO WALLAGA LAKE ● 118
At Narooma, there is plenty of action in Wagonga Inlet, and good beach and rock fishing nearby. Montague Island is a mecca for boat fishers.

BERMAGUI TO WAPENGO LAKE ● 120
A succession of rocks, headlands, beaches and inlets makes this one of the most interesting stretches of fishing coastline in New South Wales.

TATHRA TO PAMBULA ● 122
Tathra has good beach, estuary and bay fishing, but the high Tathra Wharf is the supreme fishing spot in the area. Good bay, river, lake, rock and beach angling prevail along the coast, with reef fishing offshore.

EDEN TO GREEN CAPE ● 124
The wharves at Eden are very popular with holiday anglers, Twofold Bay has a huge and sheltered inshore area with deepwater fishing, and there is great and rugged rock fishing at Green Cape.

COASTAL FISHING BERMAGUI REGION — NEW SOUTH WALES

GUIDE TO LOCAL FISH

- barracouta
- bass, Australian
- bonito
- bream, black
- bream, yellowfin
- drummer, silver
- flathead
- flathead, dusky
- flounder
- garfish
- groper
- gurnard
- john dory
- kingfish, yellowtail
- leatherjacket
- luderick
- mackerel, slimy
- marlin, black
- marlin, blue
- marlin, striped
- morwong
- mullet
- mulloway
- nannygai
- pike, striped sea
- rock blackfish
- salmon, Australian
- shark
- snapper
- sweep
- tailor
- tarwhine
- teraglin
- trevally, silver
- trumpeter
- tuna, bigeye
- tuna, mackerel
- tuna, longtail
- tuna, southern bluefin
- tuna, striped
- tuna, yellowfin
- wahoo
- whiting, King George
- whiting, sand
- whiting, trumpeter

Many large sharks have been caught from the Tathra Wharf as well as smaller resident fish such as trevally, yellowtail, salmon and tailor

up. At Eden, the north-easterly blows in mid-morning, but the area generally has calm water inshore and rough water out wide. Contact the Coast Guard, Coastal Patrol, or Weather Bureau on tel. (02) 9296 1555 or visit the website: www.bom.gov.au

Boating

It is worth investing in Admiralty charts if you are navigating this coast, as there are dozens of bomboras and hazardous rocky headlands and features such as Black Rock, near Batemans Bay. There are a considerable number of dangerous bar crossings: the bar at Tuross Lake should never be attempted by boat; the Narooma bar at the entrance to Wagonga Inlet can be fearsome and should only be attempted by experienced boaters; the bars at Merimbula and Pambula require careful navigation; and the bar at Wonboyn Lake is shallow and hazardous.

Safety comes first when you have to negotiate a bar crossing. Some bars, such as the one at Merimbula, can appear relatively calm but you should never go out to sea with the idea that crossing any bar will be easy. It pays to observe the bar before attempting passage. If you haven't crossed the bar before then seek local advice and check with a local Waterways Authority officer.

FURTHER INFORMATION

Fishing and boating NSW Fisheries has offices at Suite 8, Braysyth Bldg, Cnr Beach Rd and Orien St, Batemans Bay, tel. (02) 4472 4032; Eden Wharf, Snug Cove, tel. (02) 6496 1377; and Riverside Drive, Narooma, tel. (02) 4476 2072. The Waterways Authority has an office at 95 Campbell St, Narooma, tel. (02) 4476 2006, open on Fridays. The Coast Guard has a base at Bermagui, tel. (02) 6493 4506. The Coastal Patrol has bases at Batemans Bay, tel. (02) 4472 6595; Moruya Heads, tel. (02) 4474 2770; Narooma, tel. (02) 4476 1443; Merimbula, tel. (02) 6495 3331; and Eden, tel. (02) 6496 2167.

Tourist centres Cnr Princes Hwy and Beach Rd, Batemans Bay, tel. (02) 4472 6900; Princes Hwy, Bega, tel. (02) 6492 2045; Lamont St, Bermagui, tel. (02) 6493 3054; Princes Hwy, Eden, tel. (02) 6496 1953; Beach St, Merimbula, tel. (02) 6495 1129; Princes Hwy, Narooma, tel. (02) 4476 2881.

NEW SOUTH WALES

COASTAL FISHING BERMAGUI REGION

Batemans Bay to Broulee

Type of fishing
bay, beach, estuary, offshore, reef, river, rock

Target fish
Australian salmon, bream, flathead, luderick, snapper

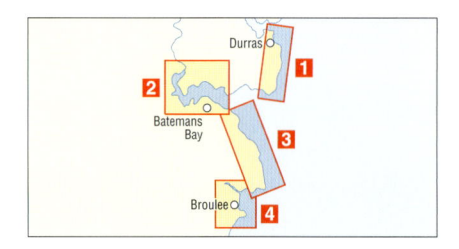

The remote coastal country between Durras and Batemans Bay allows solitary and rewarding fishing for adventurous anglers, while Batemans Bay itself, with its wide but sheltered bay, its navigable river entrance and a vast and sheltered estuary region, is one of the most popular fishing areas of the south coast. Batehaven to Burrewarra Point is great flathead drifting territory.

DURRAS TO NORTH HEAD

Four-wheel drive and walking tracks provide the only access to the rugged rock locations and small beaches in this area, where snapper, Australian salmon, bream, tailor, luderick and rock blackfish can be sought.

Wasp Island lies off the southern end of Beagle Bay. Boat anglers can catch snapper close to the island, while morwong, teraglin and kingfish can be taken on the drift on the eastern side. Further out is good live bait or trolling water for yellowfin tuna and marlin. The shoal area to the south of Wasp Head should only be fished in calm conditions, but it does carry a lot of snapper.

Along this stretch of coast, the most accessible places are **Flat Rock Island** for big luderick, rock blackfish, snapper and bream; **Myrtle Beach** for snapper, salmon and tailor; **Green Point** for snapper, bream, luderick and rock blackfish; **Richmond Beach** for salmon and tailor, with snapper and groper off the rocks; **Oaky Beach** for salmon, tailor and snapper, and the rocks at its southern end for luderick, drummer, snapper and groper; **North Head** for snapper, groper, luderick, bream and tailor; and **Acheron Ledge**, where snapper and kingfish are the main targets.

BATEMANS BAY AND CLYDE RIVER

Batemans Bay is a big camping and accommodation centre, and the supply of bait, tackle, boat hire and ramps leaves little for the angler to desire. Boating provides enormous variety, but there are plenty of productive places for land anglers.

Square Head, at the northern entrance to the bay, is a good land spot for yellowtail kingfish, tailor, bream and whiting. On the opposite shore, in the township of **Batemans Bay**, fishing from the rock will yield flathead, mulloway and luderick.

The river and estuary area is exciting. The caravan park beach is a good spot for bream and whiting, and ideal for children on their first forays into fishing. The jetties on the southern bank are also good, particularly for bream.

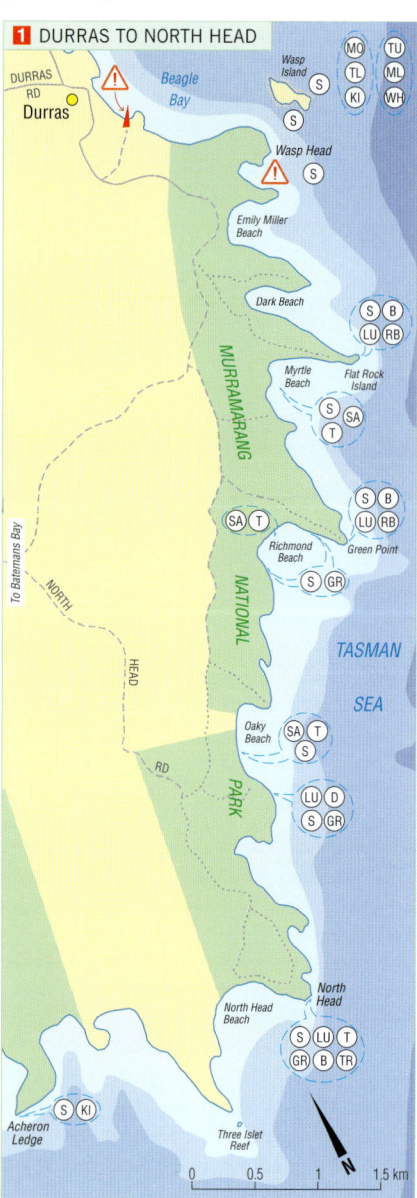

Most of the estuary is best tackled by boat anglers, and can be fished as far up as Nelligen and beyond. The Clyde River Bridge, fished by boat on a falling tide, can produce some large mulloway. Between the bridge and the powerlines is best for bream, with good possibilities for flathead, mulloway and whiting. Beyond the powerlines are the oyster leases, always a haunt for bream, especially at high tide.

The estuary narrows to **Chinamans Point**, where shallow reefs are frequented by mulloway, and in the bay on the opposite shore there is a deep hole carrying very big flathead and mulloway.

Drifting for flathead will take you up the estuary, past the navigable eastern side of **Big Island**, where it may pay to anchor on the falling tide and baitfish for flathead. Further along the Clyde to Nelligen, anglers can try for bream, flathead, flounder and mulloway. Beyond Nelligen there is some of the best water for bass.

BATEHAVEN TO BURREWARRA POINT

The south-west side of **Snapper Island** is excellent for bream and the eastern side produces flathead and whiting. When boating in this area beware of breaking waves. There is land-based angling at Observation Head.

The run down from the southern end of Batemans Bay to Burrewarra Point has some good shore fishing spots. **Corrigans Beach**, on the west side of Observation Head, is particularly good for tailor, and trolling close to the shore between Point Pleasure and Denhams Beach can yield yellowtail kingfish.

Offshore, about 4 km east of Denhams Beach, are the **Tollgate Islands**, where good numbers of flathead are taken on the shallow sands to the south and east of the islands. Snapper and morwong may be caught closer in, while there are often large numbers of bait fish sheltering between the islands. Trolling out to the east can yield good catches of yellowfin and mackerel tuna, wahoo and marlin.

The headland at **Lilli Pilli** has a rough bottom and a float will be required, although a cast of 70 m on the southern side will drop a bait into a deep snapper hole. Tailor, salmon, bream and rock blackfish are the close-in fish. About 1 km offshore, **Black Rock** has a reef extending out to the east, again good for snapper and morwong.

Mosquito Bay, which has a launching ramp, and **Garden Bay** are great spots for garfish and bream. **South Head** has a rough area close inshore, but this attracts snapper,

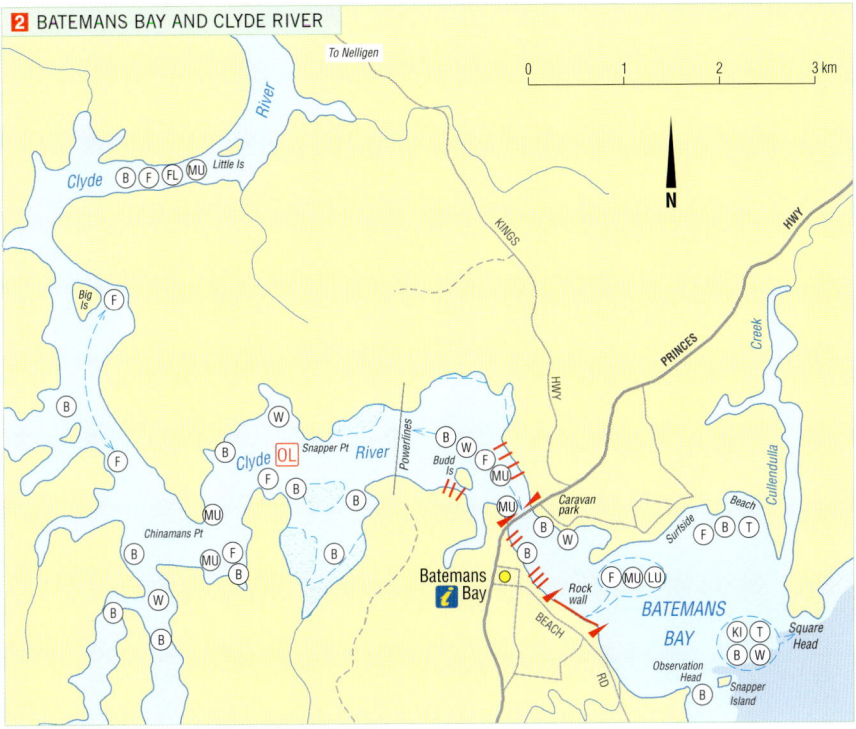

COASTAL FISHING BERMAGUI REGION   NEW SOUTH WALES

2 BATEMANS BAY AND CLYDE RIVER

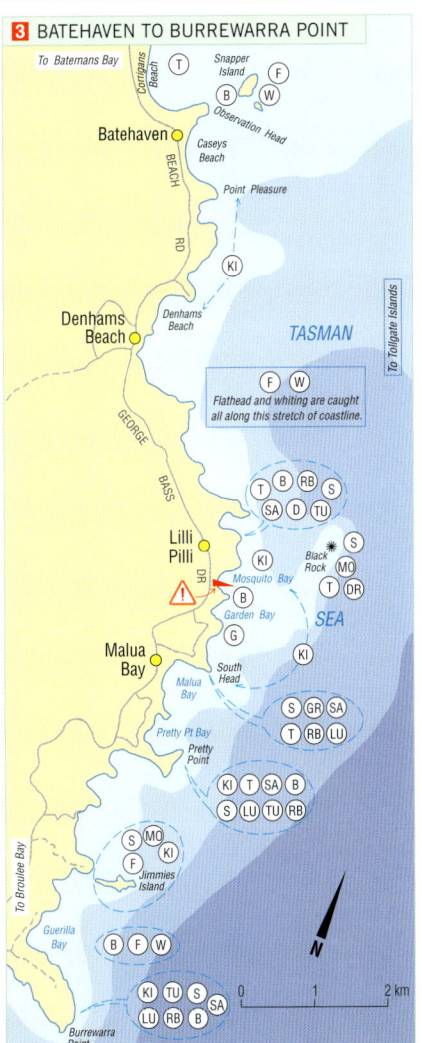

3 BATEHAVEN TO BURREWARRA POINT

4 BROULEE

groper, salmon and tailor, along with weed-eating rock blackfish and luderick.

South Head attracts the inshore rock fish, but boat anglers can take big hauls of kingfish just offshore. **Pretty Point** is a rope and ladder location for the hardy, but they can lure cast or baitfish for kingfish and tuna, as well as going after the good numbers of salmon, tailor, bream, luderick, snapper and rock blackfish.

Jimmies Island, connected to the mainland, is surrounded by mixed reef and sand bottom, making it a great spot for land and boat anglers alike. Snapper, morwong, flathead and kingfish are the main targets in an area that can provide a bonanza at times. At **Guerilla Bay** you can launch your boat from the beach to head north to Jimmies Island, or fish within this delightful bay for bream and flathead, with whiting a possibility in autumn and winter.

Burrewarra Point projects well to the east and attracts ocean fish. Kingfish and tuna are the targets for spinning, and it can produce snapper, bream, Australian salmon, luderick and rock blackfish close inshore. It is a long walk to the point but the effort can be well worthwhile.

BROULEE

The main catch in the **Tomaga River** is bream, but there are luderick around weed beds and on the rocky parts of the shore, and flathead and whiting around the sand flats. The river provides safe access to the sea for boats and a relatively sheltered bay outside (except in a southerly), where there is good reef fishing for snapper, morwong and trevally, and drifting for flathead. Boat anglers can fish for the snapper, luderick, rock blackfish and groper close in to **Broulee Island**.

Broulee Beach is ideal for whiting, using the worms that are plentiful on the beach. There are also tailor, Australian salmon and bream off the beach, and luderick, rock blackfish and some silver drummer around the headland, which also creates a sheltered place for beach launching.

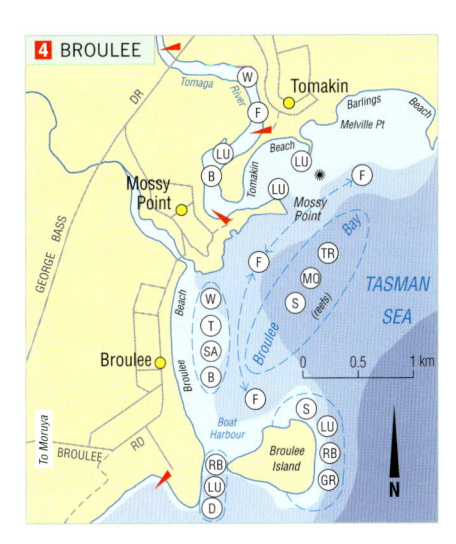

GUIDE TO LOCAL FISH

		Batehaven to Burrewarra Point	Batemans Bay and Clyde River	Durras to North Head	Broulee
B	bream	●	●	●	●
D	drummer, silver		●		●
F	flathead	●	●	●	●
FL	flounder		●		
G	garfish				●
GR	groper	●		●	●
DR	john dory				●
KI	kingfish, yellowtail	●	●		●
LU	luderick	●	●		●
ML	marlin		●		
MO	morwong	●			●
MU	mulloway		●		
RB	rock blackfish	●	●		●
SA	salmon, Australian	●	●		●
S	snapper	●	●	●	●
T	tailor	●	●		●
TL	teraglin		●		
TR	trevally	●	●		●
TU	tuna	●	●		
WH	wahoo		●		
W	whiting	●	●		●

115

NEW SOUTH WALES   COASTAL FISHING BERMAGUI REGION

Moruya to Kianga Lake

Type of fishing
beach, estuary, lake, reef, river, rock
Target fish
Australian salmon, bream, flathead, tailor, yellowtail kingfish

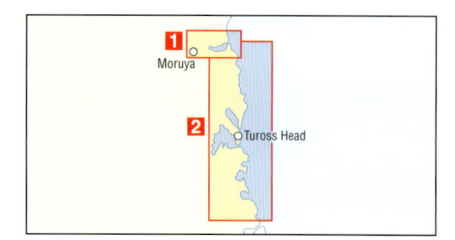

A feature of **Congo Point** is a long low rock shelf, and anglers must be aware of the tide and any build-up of waves. The shelf takes the angler to the trevally, bream and drummer, with snapper prevalent in winter.

Mullimburra Point attracts bream, rock blackfish, luderick, snapper and mulloway, with Australian salmon and tailor in summer. But the most popular rock location is **Bingie Bingie Point**, a low headland of rock, which is protected from north and south winds and has reliable fishing for salmon and tailor.

Past the Tuross Lake complex is **Potato Point**, where there are good rock platforms. Yellowtail kingfish come in over the summer period and can be caught on live baits, fish strips or lures. There are rock blackfish, sweep, salmon and tailor close in, and salmon and tailor are the targets from the beach north of Potato Point. There are reefs all around, creating good snapper and morwong grounds. Pinnacles due east of the point provide a focus for the best fishing.

Tarourga, Brou and Mummuga lakes are seldom open to the sea, but still carry flathead, whiting and bream. When the lakes are first open each year, the bream gather around the lake entrances to spawn, and the hauls are large. East of the lakes is **Brou Beach**, where there are plenty of worms for bait, and tailor and salmon are again the target fish. A reef about 1 km out from the beach attracts schools of bait fish and, in turn, kingfish, yellowfin tuna, marlin and shark.

Off Yellow Head, at **Dalmeny**, a reef extends 2 km or so out to sea, again providing good snapper and morwong fishing. The Dalmeny boat ramp is exposed to the ocean swell and is unsuitable in north-easterlies.

Outside the reef areas, drifting about 500 m offshore will produce big flathead and whiting over the sand and weed areas. The rock ledges at Dalmeny are dangerous in high seas, but the fish variety is great, including rock blackfish, luderick, sweep, salmon, bream, tailor, snapper and small kingfish.

The beaches between Dalmeny and Narooma are very popular as they are easy to reach. One of the best spots is a rock ledge near **Kianga Lake**, which allows casting behind the breakers.

MORUYA

The **Moruya River** winds down from deep in the hinterland and has bass fishing in the upper reaches. Its estuary fans out near the coast through oyster leases, channels and patches of sand, mud and mangrove, providing perfect conditions for flathead, whiting, bream, luderick and mulloway. The rock walls on both sides of the entrance are great platforms for seeking bream and flathead, while the channels and sandbanks running down to the river mouth are best in summer, when flathead and whiting are particularly prolific. Boating newcomers must take care because some sandbanks are just covered by water at high tide. The entrance to **Malabar Creek** on the northern side is the only exit for prawns when they are running with the new moon. The Princes Highway Bridge is also a fish attractor, with flathead, mulloway and schools of mullet.

Outside Moruya Heads, the **Bengello Beach** stretches some 5 km to the north, and it is known as a good spot for Australian salmon and tailor on pilchard bait, with flathead and john dory also present. Two parallel reefs, out from the airport and some 2 km offshore, create a wonderful kingfish ground. There is trolling for yellowfin tuna, and snapper and morwong between the reefs. On the south side of the heads, **Toragy Point** can be a good place for rock blackfish, salmon and snapper, with yellowtail kingfish a possibility. A long reef runs from Toragy Point to Pedro Point, and kingfish and snapper abound in this area, from about 500 m to 1.5 km out. Beyond that is fairly shallow sand, ideal for flathead, with some deeper holes for morwong.

GUIDE TO LOCAL FISH

		Moruya to Kianga Lake	Moruya	Tuross and Coila Lakes
B	bream	●	●	●
D	drummer, silver	●		
F	flathead	●	●	●
FL	flounder			●
G	garfish			●
DR	john dory		●	
KI	kingfish, yellowtail	●	●	
LU	luderick	●	●	●
ML	marlin	●		
MO	morwong	●		
M	mullet		●	
MU	mulloway	●	●	
RB	rock blackfish	●	●	
SA	salmon, Australian	●	●	
SH	shark	●		
S	snapper	●	●	
SW	sweep	●		
T	tailor	●	●	
TR	trevally	●		
TU	tuna	●		
W	whiting	●	●	●

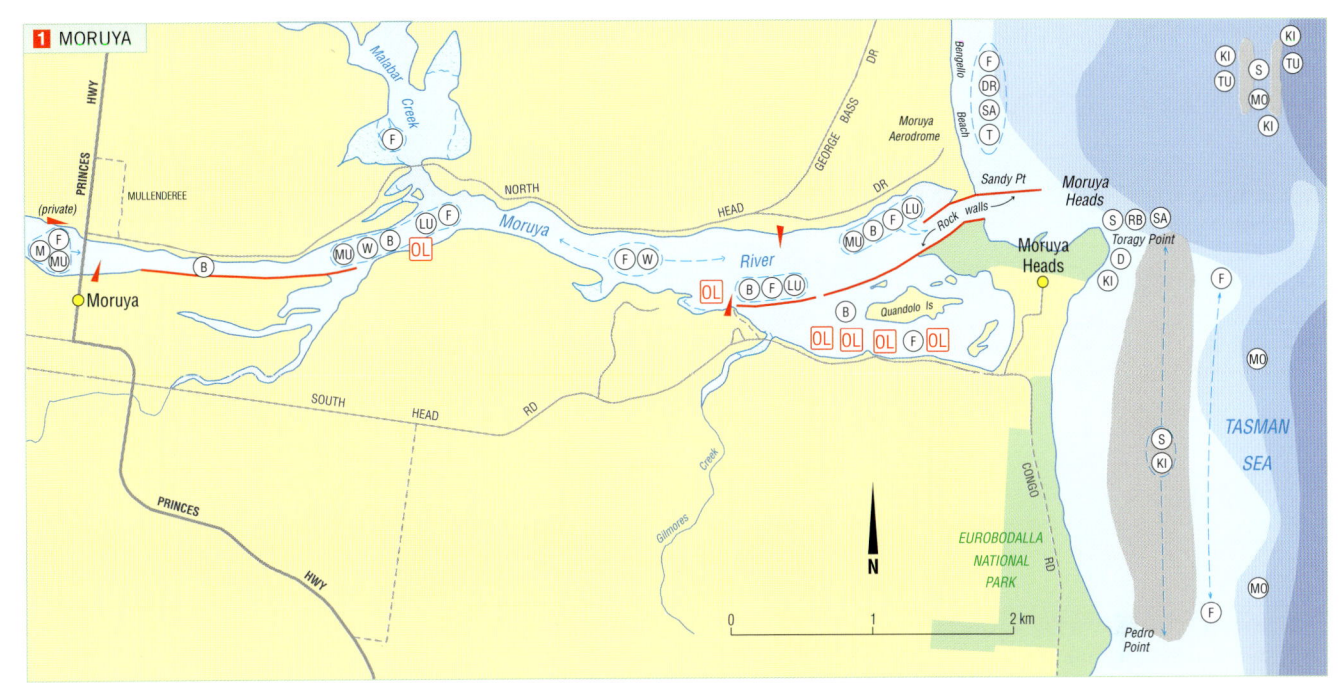

COASTAL FISHING BERMAGUI REGION   NEW SOUTH WALES

1 MORUYA

TUROSS AND COILA LAKES

The Tuross area, a complex and picturesque waterway, has everything for the estuary angler – hire boats, tackle and bait supplies, bait gathering spots and a variety of holiday accommodation. Coila Lake is often closed to the sea, but when it is open, particularly after heavy rain, the bream move down from Coila Creek. The target fish in the lake are bream, flathead, whiting and flounder. **Coila Creek**, running into the north-west of the lake, is great for bream, particularly if you fish from the southern bank in the Princes Highway Bridge area. Prawn or mullet gut baits, and berleying, will yield the best results.

Tuross Lake is sometimes closed, but even when it is open the bar should never be attempted by boat. **Sandy Point** is hailed as the best luderick spot in the State, while the channel past **Horse Island** carries big mulloway. The oyster leases north of Reedy Island are thick with bream on a high tide, while **Four Ways**, between Reedy and Cooper islands, attracts flathead, bream, luderick, whiting, flounder and mulloway. The **Tuross River** is good drifting for garfish and flathead before it branches into **Borang Lake**. This lake is very shallow and requires some careful navigation, but fishing the channels of the southern bank for enormous flathead is an exhilarating experience. The Tuross River becomes a bass haunt beyond the Princes Highway Bridge (not shown on the map).

Near the entrances to the lakes, anglers can fish for flathead, whiting, mulloway, bream and Australian salmon.

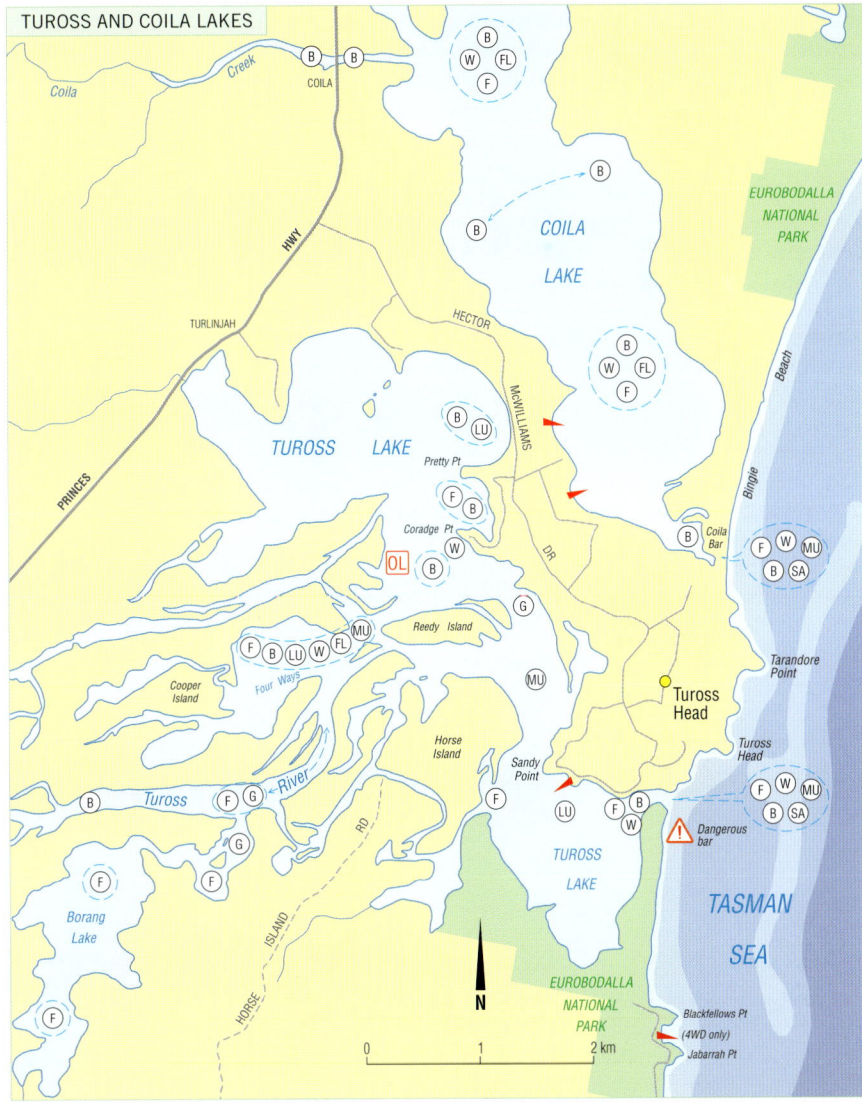

NEW SOUTH WALES

COASTAL FISHING BERMAGUI REGION

Narooma to Wallaga Lake

Type of fishing
bay, beach, estuary, lake, offshore, rock, wharf
Target fish
bream, flathead, whiting

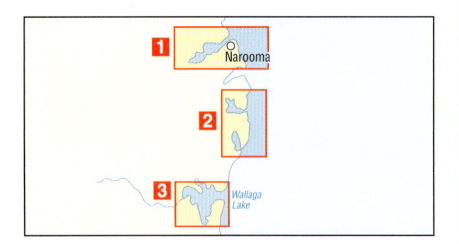

Montague Island is one of the most famous game fishing spots on the south coast

Wagonga Inlet, and further south, Corunna Lake, have large and varied fish populations, with plenty of bait. But the real action is at Montague Island or out past the reefs and onto the 100-fathom line, about 20 km out, which is legendary kingfish, tuna, marlin and general game fish territory. The shallow but extensive waters of Wallaga Lake, north of Bermagui, are popular for estuary fishing.

NAROOMA

Wagonga Inlet provides plenty of action for shore anglers and those people in boats who prefer estuary fishing to braving the Narooma bar. The sand flats, running from the entrance to the Princes Highway Bridge, are mainly flathead and whiting grounds, while the trawler wharf is a good luderick spot, and the trainer walls at the entrance are platforms for bream and tailor fishing.

West of the bridge, there are abundant flathead in the channels and some big mulloway in the holes, bream around the oyster leases, and some whiting and garfish. The inlet is well sheltered and the whole area has fine boat launching, boat hire and fishing facilities.

Outside, there is easy rock fishing from **Wagonga Head**, with tailor, bream, luderick and rock blackfish the main targets, while **Bar Beach** and **Narooma Beach** have Australian salmon, tailor and flathead, with bream and whiting in the gutters. Offshore, Narooma Beach also has fine flathead drifting over the sand for around 3 km. Similar conditions occur offshore from Little Dromedary Mountain down to Wallaga Lake.

The jewel of the coast between Narooma and Bermagui is **Montague Island**, 6 km east of Narooma and 22 km north of Bermagui. Narooma is the closest access, but its bar is dangerous and only those with experience or those prepared to listen to local advice should attempt the crossing.

Once at the island you will find an abundance of fish, particularly large yellowtail kingfish around the north-west side. The north shore generally produces yellowfin tuna, marlin, wahoo, dolphin fish and kingfish, with snapper plentiful for the bottom anglers. Schools of kingfish congregate in the south-east, and yellowfin tuna and marlin can be trolled on the eastern side. The **Aughinish Rocks**, south of the island and 3 m under water, can reward close-in anglers with snapper. Care should be taken in heavier weather, as waves can break over the reef.

CORUNNA LAKE AREA

This stretch of coast is secluded and difficult to access. The best of the coastal features are **Bogola Head** for tailor, salmon and bream; **Mystery Bay** for these same fish and also

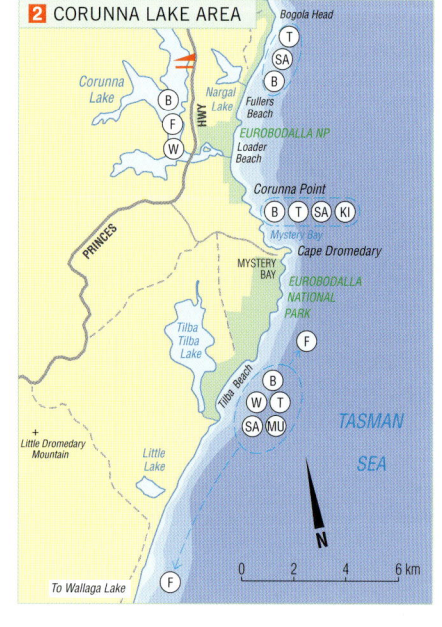

COASTAL FISHING BERMAGUI REGION   NEW SOUTH WALES

3 WALLAGA LAKE

yellowtail kingfish; and **Tilba Beach** for bream, whiting, salmon, flathead, tailor and mulloway. There is a boat ramp at Mystery Bay suitable for small craft up to 4.5 m. Access to offshore grounds is possible from here. **Corunna Lake** is a poor fishery, but an excellent place to find weed bait for luderick. The lake itself can offer bream, flathead and whiting.

WALLAGA LAKE

Wallaga Lake is not always open to the sea, and the entrance is impassable at any time. When it is newly opened the fishing can be excellent. It is known for its flathead, which can reach 2 to 3 kg. The lake is wide and exposed, presenting a problem for small boat anglers in the wind, as it becomes very choppy.

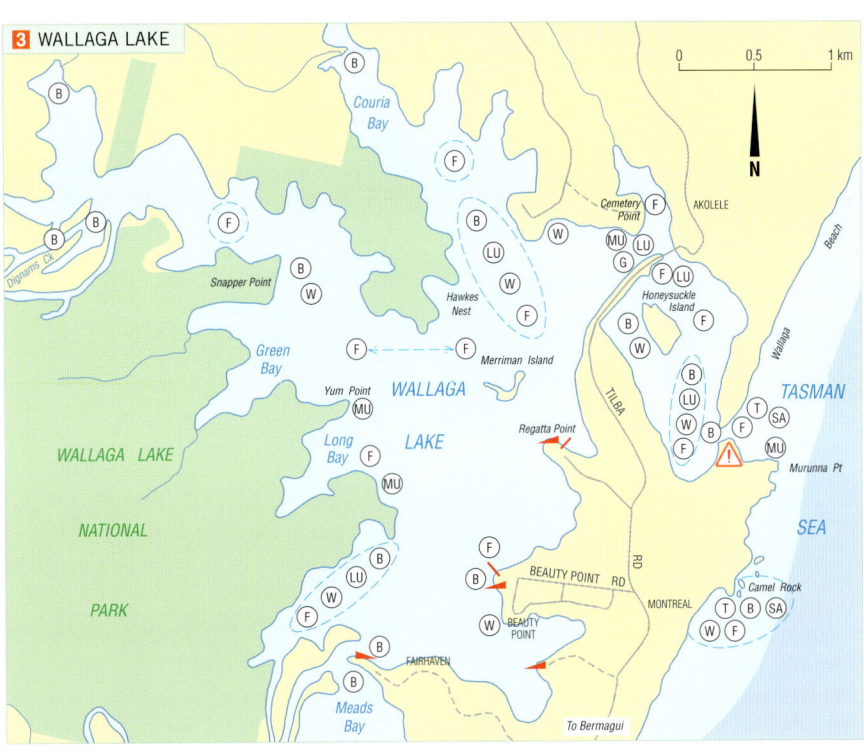

There are some good spots for shore-based anglers all around the estuary, but the best areas are in the entrance to the lake, between Honeysuckle Island and the bridge, and along the channel, which skirts along the northern shores of the lake and is deepest off Cemetery Point. Bream and sand whiting are taken on the incoming tide, while flathead are best caught on the outgoing tide. Sand flats at low tide are revealed around the entrance area, where nippers can be pumped.

Mulloway are not prolific in the lake, but they can be fished at low tide in the deeper areas off **Cemetery Point** and around **Yum Point**, on the southern side.

Luderick and garfish are sought near the **Tilba Road Bridge**. Use a float rig and bread or weed for bait. Bream tend to retreat into the remote and shallow arms of the lake – **Dignams Creek** contains bream, but the mouth is difficult to navigate. The easiest spot for land-based anglers is the **Beauty Point Road Jetty**, where flathead may also be taken.

Outside the lake, to the south, **Camel Rock** is a good location for tailor, bream, Australian salmon, whiting and flathead.

Camel Rock, to the south of Wallaga Lake entrance, is a popular beach fishing area

GUIDE TO LOCAL FISH

	Narooma Corunna Lake Area	Wallaga Lake
(B) bream	•	•	•
(F) flathead	•	•	•
(G) garfish	•		•
(KI) kingfish, yellowtail		•	
(LU) luderick	•		•
(MU) mulloway	•	•	•
(RB) rock blackfish	•		
(SA) salmon, Australian	•	•	•
(T) tailor	•	•	•
(W) whiting	•	•	•

119

NEW SOUTH WALES

COASTAL FISHING BERMAGUI REGION

Bermagui to Wapengo Lake

Type of fishing
estuary, lake, offshore, reef, rock

Target fish
bream, flathead, whiting, yellowfin tuna

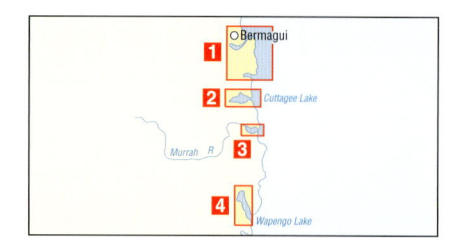

Bermagui is legendary for its fishing. It is the home of the first game fishing club in Australia and to a big trawler fleet, which can take advantage of the proximity of the deep waters beyond the continental shelf. The Bermagui River has something to offer both the land and boat angler.

BERMAGUI TO BARAGOOT POINT

Bermagui is the best place for those wishing to take yellowfin tuna, as the offshore waters contain the hottest areas for these majestic and hard-fighting fish. Many anglers prefer the longer run to Montague Island from Bermagui to avoid the Narooma bar, as the Bermagui bar is more predictable. There is plenty of boat action over the three reefs situated out from Bermagui. **Four Mile Reef** is straight out from Keatings Headland, and can be fished for snapper, morwong, tuna and marlin. **Six Mile Reef** attracts these same fish, while the long **Twelve Mile Reef** abounds in snapper, morwong, marlin, shark and yellowfin tuna.

Game fishing craft crowd each other to catch live bait in Horseshoe Bay prior to motoring offshore

On either side of the entrance of the **Bermagui Harbour**, some 500 m out there is fine flathead drifting. Close in to **Bermagui Point** there is good bait fishing in the kelp beds. The entrance has various rock breakwalls, and tailor, bream and luderick can be taken there at most times of the year. Mullet are also plentiful.

Upriver is pleasant drifting in the channels for flathead and whiting, but the water becomes too shallow for boating about 2 km from the entrance. Bream concentrate around the trawling fleet when it returns to harbour.

From Bermagui south to Baragoot Point there are a number of rock and beach spots worth trying. Outside Bermagui Harbour, Bermagui Point is good for yellowtail kingfish, slimy mackerel and tailor caught on bait, while **The Slot** has rock blackfish, groper and tailor. Around the headland, the rocks from Point Dickinson to Beares Beach are good for rock blackfish, luderick, tailor and snapper. **Beares Beach** has Australian salmon and tailor, while **Jerimbut Point** has the same species, and luderick and rock blackfish in the washes. The next safe area is **Jaggers Beach**, which attracts snapper, luderick, rock blackfish, salmon and tailor.

CUTTAGEE, MURRAH AND WAPENGO LAKES

Cuttagee, Murrah and Wapengo lakes all have whiting, flathead and bream present.

COASTAL FISHING BERMAGUI REGION — NEW SOUTH WALES

GUIDE TO LOCAL FISH

	Bermagui to Baragoot Point	Cuttagee Lake	Murrah Lagoon	Wapengo Lake
(B) bream	●	●	●	●
(D) drummer, silver	●			
(F) flathead		●	●	●
(FL) flounder			●	●
(GR) groper	●			
(KI) kingfish, yellowtail	●			
(LU) luderick	●	●	●	●
(MA) mackerel, slimy	●			
(M) mullet			●	●
(MU) mulloway			●	
(RB) rock blackfish	●			
(SA) salmon, Australian	●	●	●	●
(S) snapper	●			●
(T) tailor	●	●	●	●
(TA) tarwhine				●
(TR) trevally		●		●
(W) whiting	●	●	●	●

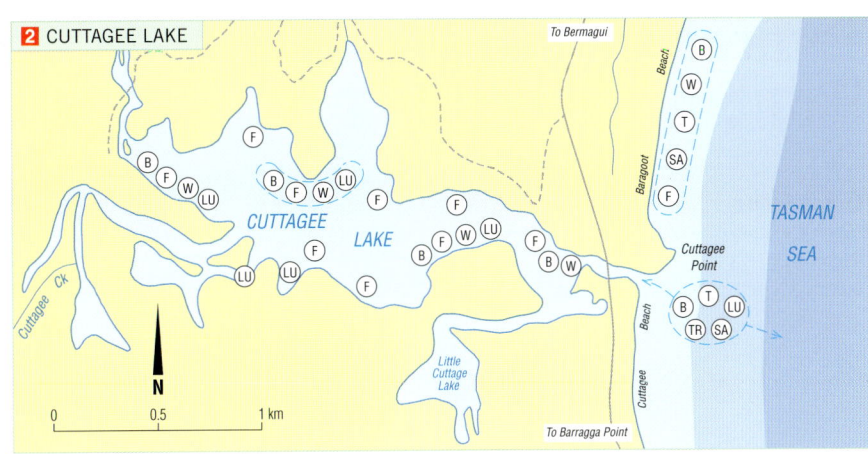

These waters are best for shore-based fishing as they are reached from the coastal road, which branches off the Princes Highway. Worm and nipper baits can be found on the sand flats, and bait fish like poddy mullet can be trapped. Wading the sand flats with fresh bait, or spinning with a lure, can be very worthwhile.

Although usually open to the sea, a breakthrough of a temporary closure of **Cuttagee Lake** gets fish moving and improves fishing near the mouth. An outgoing tide can see a gathering of predators on the ocean side of the entrance and an incoming tide will bring bream, tailor, luderick, trevally and Australian salmon inside the entrance. The staple fish for anglers, however, are bream, flathead, whiting and luderick. The weedy areas around the edges of the lake are fine for luderick fishing, while the channels and sand flats close to the shores are a haven for flathead. Outside the lake's entrance, the long **Baragoot Beach** is good for collecting worms and catching flathead, salmon, tailor, whiting and bream. South of Cuttagee Beach, **Barragga Point** has rock fishing for salmon, tailor, bream, rock blackfish and luderick.

Murrah Lagoon is bounded by private properties and can only be reached by a rough road to the southern shore, near the mouth, where small boats can be launched. Flathead congregate near the entrance on the end of a rising tide, and retreat to the sand flats and channels at the head of the lake as the tide recedes. Fishing in this area with nippers, worms or prawns can bring catches of flathead, bream, flounder, luderick and salmon. Fishing the deeper holes with small live mullet can yield some very big flathead. Outside at **Murrah Head**, and south of the inlet at **Goalen Head**, there is good rock fishing for a variety of species, including snapper and mulloway.

Wapengo is the biggest of the lakes, and a small boat is almost mandatory. Launching is over the sand near the oyster farmers' sheds, half-way down the eastern shore of the estuary. The variety of fish is overwhelming, as anything from big flathead, bream, snapper, flounder, luderick, trevally, tailor, salmon or tarwhine may be caught and, very rarely, gurnard. There are oyster leases all around the lake, many close to shore, so that shore anglers may cast near them on a high tide, with an unweighted prawn bait used with berley to get quick bream action. Boat anglers can use the same technique. The sandbanks in the lower half of the lake require some negotiation, but the flathead are in the channels on an ebb tide. For boat anglers, drifting the upper lake from north to south will produce flathead. Outside the entrance and to the north, **Bunga Head** has good rock fishing.

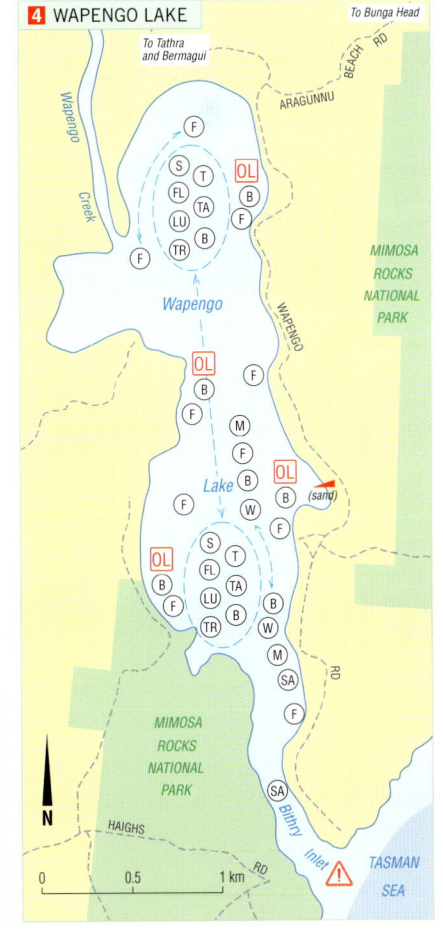

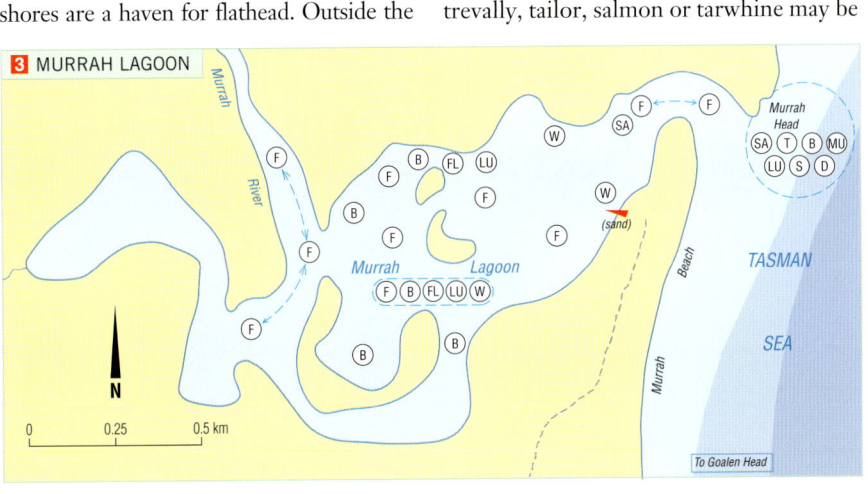

NEW SOUTH WALES

COASTAL FISHING BERMAGUI REGION

Tathra to Pambula

Type of fishing
beach, estuary, offshore, reef, rock, wharf

Target fish
Australian salmon, bream, flathead, tailor, tuna, yellowtail kingfish

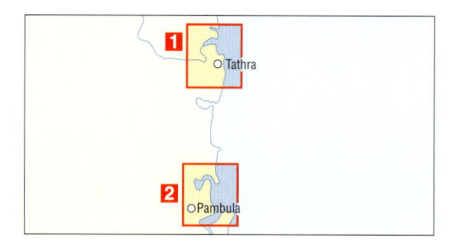

There is little to surpass the beauty and fishing variety of the short strip of coastline north of Tathra. Rocky headlands plunging into deep, clean-bottomed water, long ocean beaches, the peaceful and productive Bega River and many lakes and lagoons create an angling paradise. Tathra Wharf is the best fishing spot, closely followed by the wharf at Merimbula.

Tathra to Merimbula is forest country, for the most part, and the tracks to the coast can be a bit rough. One of the best rock places south of Tathra is **Kangarutha Point**, which has a reef, and is good for Australian salmon, tailor, snapper, bream, rock blackfish and leatherjacket. **Turingal Head** can also be reached by a track. The rocks require an awkward climb down, but it is worth fishing for the salmon and tailor around the entrance of Wallagoot Lake, when it is open.

There is a close-in area from Kianinny Bay, near Tathra, down to Turingal Head, for leatherjacket, snapper and morwong. Turingal Head marks a good spot, about 2 km out, for yellowfin tuna and marlin. **Wallagoot** is usually open to the sea and is ideal for flathead, bream and prawns. The beach outside carries whiting, bream, salmon and tailor. **Bournda Island** is attached to the beach at low tide, and has prolific tailor fishing on the north side, but the south should be avoided in big seas. Rock blackfish and bream are close to the rocks.

Tura Head works so well for rock anglers that, despite the rough drive in, overcrowding can be a problem in summer. There are bream, rock blackfish, tailor, salmon and luderick, and deep water is close in, with kingfish, bonito and yellowfin tuna.

Flathead grounds are found about 1 km out from Tura Head. **Short Point Beach** is best at its northern corner, near Tura Head, and near the rock outcrop halfway down the beach. The target fish are whiting, bream, salmon and tailor.

TATHRA

To the north of Tathra, **Middle Beach** has good beach fishing for bream, flathead and salmon, and when **Middle Lagoon** is open this is enhanced after heavy rain with bream, mulloway, tailor and flathead around the lagoon entrance. **Gillards Beach** and **Cowdroys Beach** are split by a rock formation, particularly good for snapper and silver drummer after heavy weather. The best fishing at **Baronda Head** is on its north side, for luderick, rock blackfish and snapper.

Nelson Lagoon is small and remote but it has plenty of flathead, luderick and bream, with whiting near the mouth in summer. Overall the fishing is good, but a small boat or canoe is required as there is no launching ramp. Anglers must drive in and carry their craft across the sand.

Wajurda Point has snapper, leatherjacket and rock blackfish in close, and attracts tuna and kingfish and other pelagics. The rocks running down to **Mogareka Inlet** are excellent for spinning for salmon and tailor, but are dangerous in a southerly.

The **Bega River**, running from Mogareka Inlet, feeds two lagoons, which abound in bream and flathead. There are a number of holes for night fishing for mulloway, bream and flathead. The river can be drifted for flathead. A particularly good spot for big flathead is the mouth of **Chinnock Lagoon**. There is good bass fishing upstream, but silting has affected the quality.

Tathra Beach has salmon, tailor, bream, flathead and mulloway, and whiting at its northern end.

Tathra Wharf has been described as being like a land-based boat, but it is better than that as fish congregate around it in big numbers. Yellowtail, trevally, pike and slimy mackerel swarm under the pier at dawn and dusk but devotees are more interested in the sharks, very big tuna, snapper, salmon, mulloway and yellowtail kingfish.

COASTAL FISHING BERMAGUI REGION — NEW SOUTH WALES

GUIDE TO LOCAL FISH

		Tathra	Merimbula to Pambula
BT	bonito	●	●
B	bream	●	●
D	drummer, silver	●	●
F	flathead	●	●
G	garfish	●	●
GR	groper	●	
DR	john dory		●
KI	kingfish, yellowtail	●	●
LJ	leatherjacket	●	●
LU	luderick	●	●
MA	mackerel, slimy	●	
ML	marlin		●
MO	morwong	●	●
M	mullet	●	
MU	mulloway	●	●
NG	nannygai		●
PI	pike	●	●
RB	rock blackfish	●	●
SA	salmon, Australian	●	●
SH	shark	●	
S	snapper	●	●
SW	sweep		●
T	tailor	●	●
TR	trevally	●	●
TU	tuna	●	●
W	whiting	●	●

2 MERIMBULA TO PAMBULA

The most unusual anglers on the wharf are the shark hunters, who use the biggest of tackle and make a practice of paddling their bait out into the bay by canoe or surf ski. The wharf can get very crowded in peak summer months, so patience waiting for fishing spots and dealing with tangled lines is important. It is essential to have a long-handled net or cliff gaff, as the platform is around 6 m above the water, depending on the tide.

Tathra Head is a good deepwater spot, with tailor, salmon, big bream, groper, bonito and snapper the targets, and rock blackfish and luderick close in. It is dangerous in a heavy swell. In the small bay to the south anglers can spin or fish with live bait as the water is very deep and carries morwong and groper, along with salmon, tailor, tuna, rock blackfish and luderick.

Kianinny Bay is protected from the weather and is a good shore fishing location when there is not too much boat traffic from the angling club ramp. Fish and berley in the channel on the southern side for bream, luderick and rock blackfish. Schools of garfish and mullet may be berleyed at the head of the inlet.

Offshore fishing in this area originates mostly from the Kianinny Bay ramp, as the Merimbula entrance is for experts only.

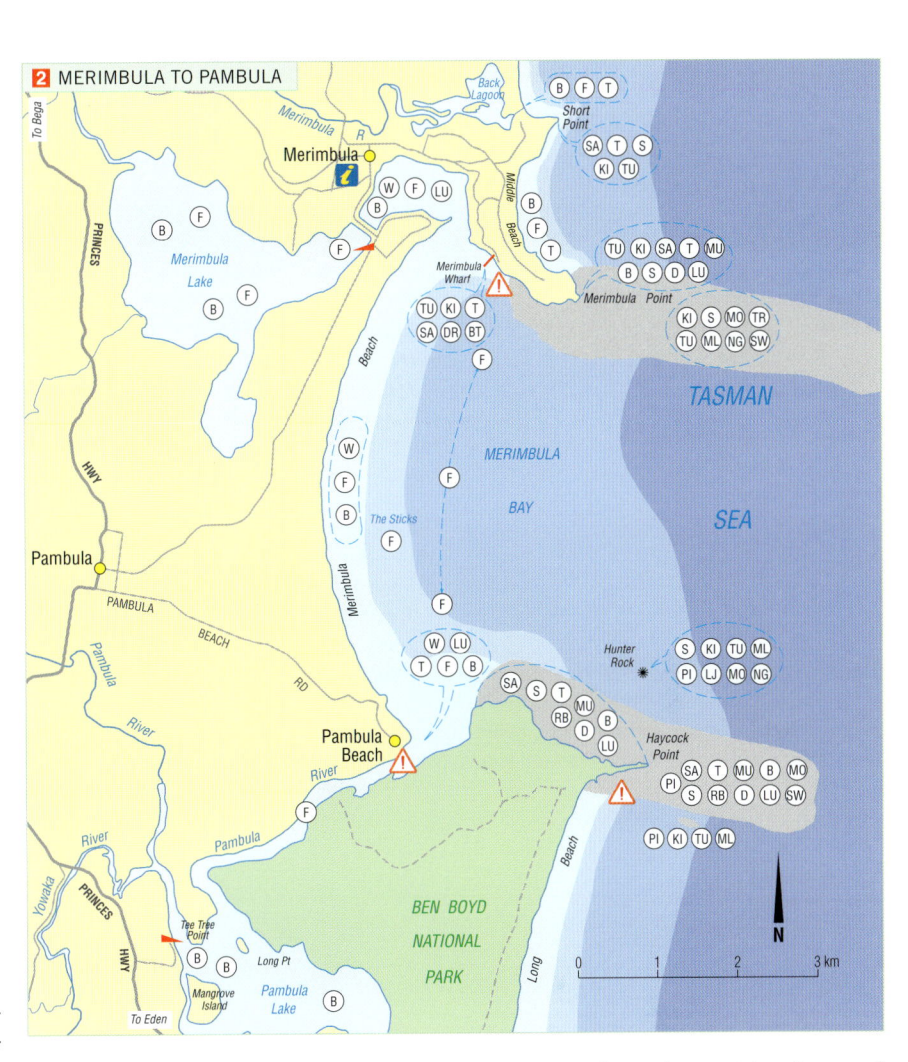

MERIMBULA TO PAMBULA

Merimbula has excellent and varied fishing even during crowded summer periods. Just north of the town is **Back Lagoon**, a hot spot for bream, flathead and tailor when the lagoon occasionally breaks out onto the beach. **Middle Beach** has the same fish, plus snapper, and is bounded by two rocky points, **Short Point** and **Merimbula Point**. These should be fished in calm seas, for salmon, tailor, snapper, kingfish and tuna. There are reefs off Merimbula Point running east with pinnacles and drop-offs, which attract yellowtail kingfish, sweep, snapper, morwong, trevally, tuna, marlin and nannygai.

The channel into **Merimbula Lake** is terrific for whiting, flathead and luderick, with the causeway concentrating the prawns into a narrow run-out area on nights of the new moon. Past the causeway, flathead are almost certain, and Merimbula Lake abounds in bream and flathead.

Merimbula Wharf is just outside the entrance and is almost as famous as Tathra Wharf. Targets are mainly tuna and kingfish, but there is also a wide range of smaller fish, including tailor, salmon, john dory and bonito. **Merimbula Beach** is relatively sheltered, good for collecting worms and pippis for bait, and producing whiting, flathead and bream. Offshore, **Merimbula Bay** is fished for flathead, and the best area is **The Sticks**, 800 m out from a prominent patch of dead trees half-way along the beach.

Tailor, flathead, bream, whiting and luderick are concentrated at the entrance to the **Pambula River**, while **Pambula Lake** has many good areas for bream, with the best place being around **Tee Tree Point**. The lake has launching facilities for offshore fishing, but the bar needs caution.

Rock anglers can fish from **Haycock Point**, near Pambula, which is safe on its north side and provides a wide range of fish – salmon, tailor, mulloway, bream, snapper, rock blackfish, silver drummer and luderick. The point is also surrounded by extensive reefs. A bombora 150 m south-east of the point, dangerous in any sea, is a good fishing area, as well as **Hunter Rock**, 1 km north of the point, which breaks in heavy seas. Snapper, kingfish, tuna, marlin, pike, leatherjacket and morwong can all be caught here.

123

NEW SOUTH WALES

COASTAL FISHING BERMAGUI REGION

Eden to Green Cape

Type of fishing
bay, beach, jetty, offshore, reef, rock

Target fish
Australian salmon, bream, flathead, tuna, yellowtail kingfish

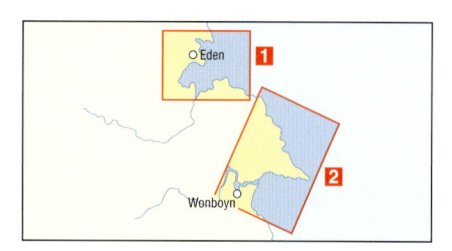

Eden provides anglers with rock, beach, jetty and boat fishing in and around the large expanse of Twofold Bay. The coastline from Twofold Bay to Green Cape and Disaster Bay is rugged national park bushland, with a vehicle and walking tracks. It is a place for people who love fishing and the bush and don't mind a bit of hardship and exercise.

EDEN AND TWOFOLD BAY

There are some top rock fishing places north of the town of Eden, although they should only be considered in calm seas. Bream, snapper, sweep, trevally, rock blackfish, pike, luderick, Australian salmon and tailor abound, while floating live baits may take tuna, kingfish or shark.

Worang Point, at the southern end of the Ben Boyd National Park, fishes well for all rock species. This whole area is dangerous in easterly or southerly weather. **Aslings Beach** is a fine fishing spot for salmon, tailor, bream and whiting. Boat fishing behind the breaks yields flathead. The small **Curalo Lagoon**, west of the beach, offers bank fishing for bream and flathead and is ideal for youngsters and beginners. It is also an excellent prawning area in summer.

The fishing wharves at **Eden** are popular with holiday anglers, and are very productive. With the aid of berley, some mullet gut or prawn bait, there is a good chance of bream, flathead, leatherjacket and trevally. Shore anglers can also fish from the headlands and beaches in sheltered **Quarantine Bay**, where flathead and bream are the main catches, and snapper and yellowtail kingfish are a chance. At the south of Twofold Bay is Kiah Inlet, fed by the Towamba River. Access is by boat across the bay as there is extensive private land around the estuary. It holds flathead, bream, garfish and mullet. Outside Kiah Inlet there is excellent boat fishing from **Whale Beach** for whiting, flathead, bream and snapper, with occasional schools of tailor and salmon. Trolling for salmon and tailor in the bay can be very productive. Flathead and whiting can be taken from **Fisheries Beach**.

On the south-east side of the bay there is some rock fishing for bream, snapper,

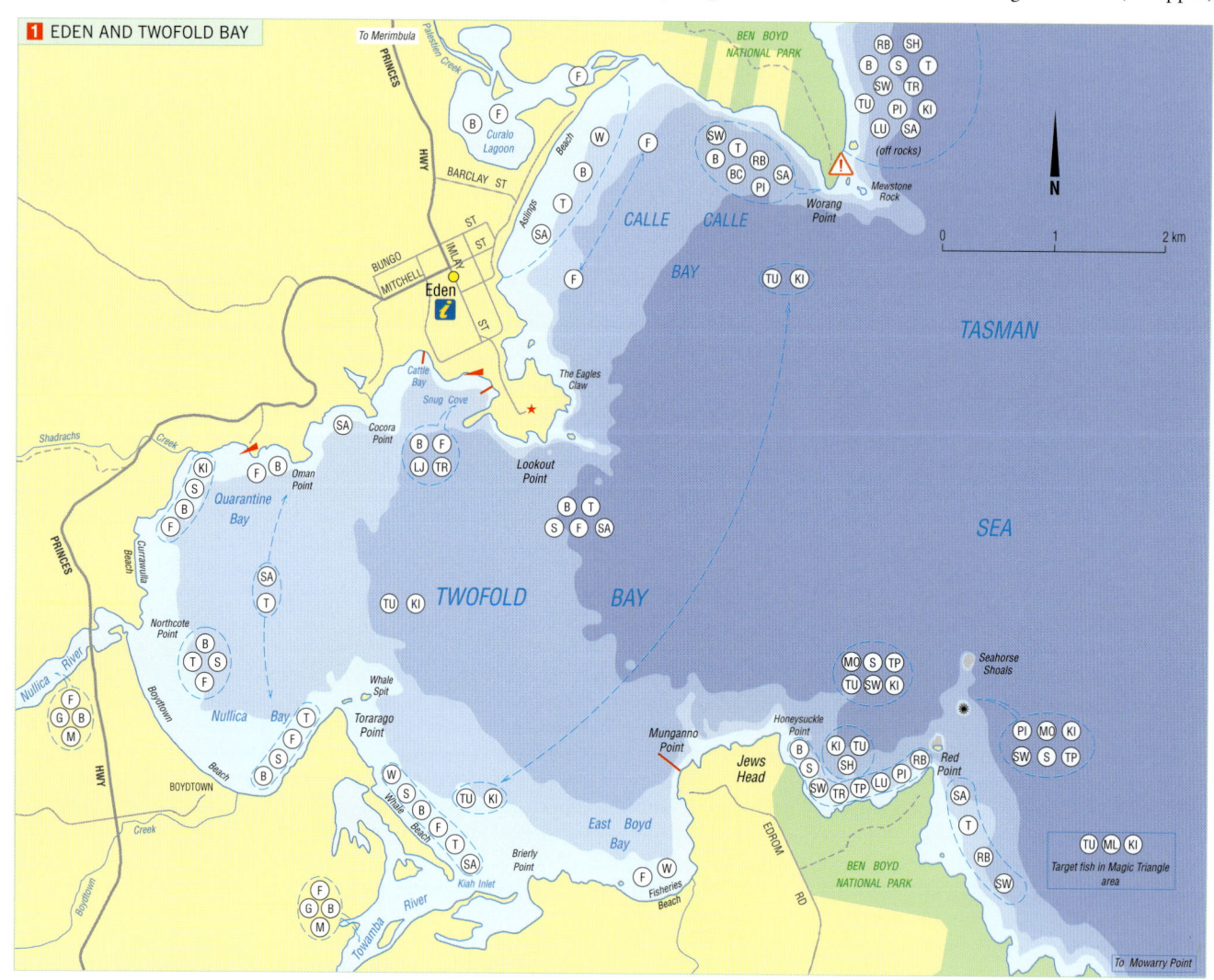

COASTAL FISHING BERMAGUI REGION — NEW SOUTH WALES

sweep, trevally, rock blackfish, luderick and pike close in, and kingfish, tuna and shark for heavy tackle anglers. **Jews Head** and **Red Point** are the main fishing places, but conditions must be calm. Red Point has a rough bottom, so float rigs with bait and lure casting are the best ways to fish.

Twofold Bay is very deep, so boat anglers seeking the deepwater species do not have to stray outside the line from Worang Point to Red Point, and those operating in the south will be in the most protected water. A depth sounder will help locate the reefs where morwong, kingfish, trumpeter and snapper are the main catches. Trolling in the bay will yield catches of tuna and kingfish.

For those boat anglers who venture outside the bay, the action starts at the **Magic Triangle**, which is an area between Red Point and Morwarry Point. Game fish abound here, and the main catches are bonito, yellowfin tuna, kingfish and marlin.

GREEN CAPE AND WONBOYN LAKE

This is one of the most exciting areas in Australia for land-based game fishing, with some brilliant offshore action for prudent boat people. However, it is also a place where the weather has to be watched, from land or sea.

Pulpit Rock on Green Cape: hundreds of large tuna and kingfish have been hooked, lost or landed here

Morwarry Point has tailor, Australian salmon, snapper in the washes, and tuna and yellowtail kingfish for boat anglers. A reef 1 km from Mowarry Point holds a lot of snapper and morwong on the bottom, and kingfish and tuna near the surface. **Saltwater Creek** is reached from Green Cape Road. The beach there carries salmon, tailor and bream. The rocks to the north of the beach have bream, silver drummer, and sweep close in, and are good platforms for spinning for tailor, salmon, pike and bonito. Offshore, there is trolling near the southern headland for bonito and salmon.

Bittangabee Bay also has road access, a camping area and a place to launch small boats straight off the beach in good weather. The inlet carries mainly bream and flathead, and there is bait on the mud and sand flats. The rocks on the north side can produce snapper and rock blackfish or try spinning for tailor, salmon, bonito and other pelagics. Similar fishing can be had along rocks to the south of the bay, reached by a walking track. For boat anglers, Bittangabee Bay is a welcome place to run to if weather conditions change, and a reef about 300 m offshore carries snapper, morwong and leatherjacket.

Pulpit Rock is reached by track from the Green Cape Road. It is renowned as one of Australia's best rock fishing platforms for game fish. Lure casting and live baiting are the practice here, for tuna, kingfish, shark, and occasionally marlin.

Green Cape is easily reached from the picnic spot near the lighthouse. Fishing at the tip of Green Cape is not recommended. On the south side is City Rocks, another famous platform for pelagic species, and offshore there is good game fishing. **Disaster Bay** holds pelagics as well as being an excellent drift for flathead.

Wonbyn Lake is in a remote area and runs out at Disaster Bay. It is favoured by the small band of devotees who go there every year. They camp or stay at the resort, and boat hire is available. Mulloway can be caught off the northern shores of the lake. The lower lake, with its dangerous bar, is very shallow and requires careful negotiation, but there are big flathead on the banks and luderick among the weed. Oyster leases yield bream particularly at dawn and dusk on a rising tide. Yabbies and sandworms are readily available on the banks. A prominent red rock on the edge of the channel is a good spot for all the fish inhabiting the lake – flathead, mulloway, luderick, whiting, tailor, mullet and bream. At the end of the channel, a sand spit is a hot spot for whiting. Fishing the spit is also good, as is the drop-off for flathead, whiting and bream. The upper lake is well stocked with tailor, and bream is the main catch in the **Wonboyn River**.

On the coast, **Wonboyn Beach** is good for flathead, tailor and salmon on the north side, and mostly salmon in the south. The beach is best reached by boat, tying up inside the entrance.

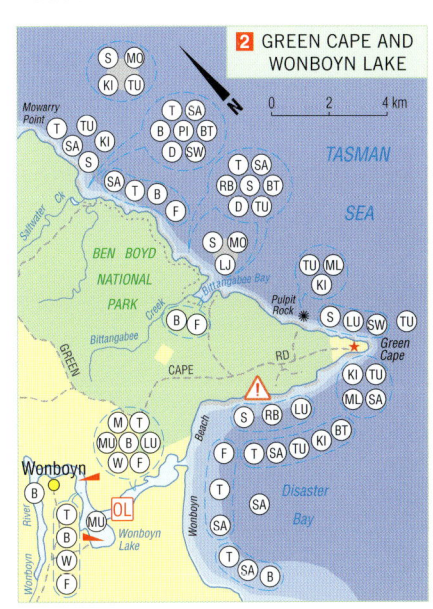

GUIDE TO LOCAL FISH

		Eden and Twofold Bay	Green Cape and Wonboyn Lake
BC	barracouta		●
BT	bonito	●	●
B	bream	●	●
D	drummer, silver	●	●
F	flathead	●	●
G	garfish	●	
KI	kingfish, yellowtail	●	●
LJ	leatherjacket	●	●
LU	luderick	●	●
ML	marlin	●	●
MO	morwong	●	●
M	mullet	●	●
MU	mulloway		●
PI	pike	●	●
RB	rock blackfish	●	●
SA	salmon, Australian	●	●
SH	shark	●	●
S	snapper	●	●
SW	sweep	●	●
T	tailor	●	●
TR	trevally	●	
TP	trumpeter	●	
TU	tuna	●	●
W	whiting	●	●

NEW SOUTH WALES

Inland Fishing

Golden perch to 10 kg, Murray cod up to 50 kg, excellent trout fishing and the best bass fishing in Australia, New South Wales has it all. You can fish quietly on a mighty western river or fly cast in the Snowy Mountains – New South Wales provides variety as well as quality in freshwater fishing.

Land shape and climatic peculiarities within New South Wales mean that the bulk of freshwater fishing is concentrated within quite a small proportion of the State. Some 60 per cent, or nearly 500 000 sq km, is open, generally flat country, only sparsely laced with rivers, and lacking the steeply folded landforms needed to trigger rainfall, or accumulate and conserve water.

The Great Dividing Range is the geographic feature that determines the freshwater fishing in New South Wales. The coastal strip to the east of the Divide has a regular rainfall and the easterly flowing rivers are significant waterways despite their relatively short length.

The mountain range is the home base of the great New South Wales trout fisheries. In the north and centre of the Divide, the New England, Upper Hunter and Central Highlands regions have trout lakes and rivers, and in the south the Snowy Mountains and Monaro boast numerous trout lakes and streams. The impoundments on the western slopes provide some of the best native species fishing for golden perch, Murray cod, silver perch and redfin, and trout in higher dams.

To the west of the Divide, the rainfall is erratic and the major rivers are wider, with slower flows and long, deep pools. Trout and bass are replaced here by Murray cod, golden perch, silver perch, redfin, carp and catfish.

The State also encircles the Australian Capital Territory, with some significant fisheries in substantial dams near Canberra, stocked with trout and native fish species.

From March 2001, anglers were required to have a licence to fish all waters in New South Wales. Check with your local fisheries office for up-to-date information on these regulations.

Protected species

In New South Wales, four species of fish are totally protected. They are trout cod, eastern freshwater cod, Macquarie perch and Australian grayling. These fish must be released unharmed.

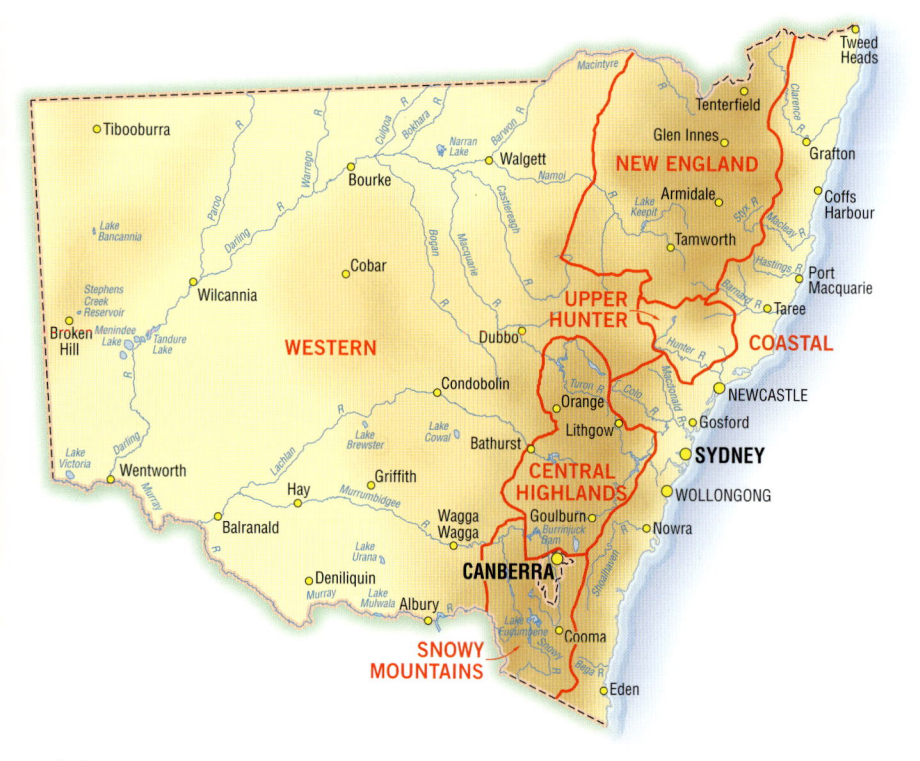

WHERE TO FISH

Inland

COASTAL REGION ● 128

Along more than 1000 km of coast, the main freshwater species is Australian bass. There are catfish, mullet and the endangered eastern freshwater cod in the north, mullet and catfish along the central coast, and mullet and the now rare Australian grayling on the south coast.

NEW ENGLAND REGION ● 132

The New England Region blends history, great fishing and a variety of spectacular scenery among rich grazing lands, plateau forests and fertile lowland farms. The region is dominated by trout in the rivers. There is some good fishing in reservoirs and several of the rivers for native fish.

UPPER HUNTER REGION ● 136

This freshwater fishery comprises about eight major rivers and four dams. Numerous small trout inhabit the cool streams of the Barrington Tops, while bass, herring, mullet, catfish and carp thrive in the eastern and southern waters. The region's dams hold trout, bass, silver and golden perch, catfish and eels.

CENTRAL HIGHLANDS REGION ● 140

This region embraces pine-clad snowline peaks, rugged sandstone escarpments, eucalypt forests and rolling grasslands. Most rivers are small, but hold either brown or rainbow trout. In warmer reaches, there are native species such as catfish, Murray cod, golden and silver perch. There is some fantastic stillwater fishing in the region.

SNOWY MOUNTAINS REGION ● 146

Here is some of the best trout fishing in mainland Australia. The slow, weedy Monaro streams provide blue-ribbon fly fishing that attracts visitors from all over the world. The huge Snowy Mountains' impoundments offer a totally different fishing experience. In addition to fly fishing, they are especially suited to bait fishing, trolling and spinning.

WESTERN REGION ● 152

This large region includes a few incredibly productive dams and rivers. It is the home of Murray cod and golden and silver perch, although the introduced European carp can be a nuisance in some areas.

INLAND FISHING

NEW SOUTH WALES

Trolling on Lake Jindabyne

Fishing regulations

There are some 15 common freshwater angling species of fin fish available within New South Wales. Four of these are totally protected: trout cod, eastern freshwater cod, Australian grayling and Macquarie perch. If caught, none of these protected fish may be kept, but must immediately and carefully be returned to the water unharmed.

GUIDE TO LOCAL FISH
bass, Australian
blackfish, river
carp, European
catfish, eel-tailed
cod, Murray
crayfish, Murray
eel, long-finned
herring, freshwater
mullet, bully
mullet, pinkeye
perch, estuary
perch, golden
perch, redfin
perch, silver
perch, spangled
salmon, Atlantic
trout, brook
trout, brown
trout, rainbow

Other threatened species, such as the purple-spotted gudgeon, may have little direct angling significance, but are nonetheless important, as they provide part of the forage base for fish that anglers do catch. All recreational anglers within New South Wales are required to hold a current 'all-waters' fishing licence. Some exemptions do apply to certain age groups and various holders of Government exemption cards. Details are available from New South Wales Fisheries. New South Wales recreational fishing licences are available from several outlets, including Fisheries offices and authorised fishing tackle shops, or by phoning 1300 369 365. All enquiries regarding current fishing regulations can be made by phoning NSW Fisheries on (02) 9527 8411 or by visiting the NSW Fisheries website at www.fisheries.nsw.gov.au

Boating regulations

All powered craft, capable of speeds greater than 10 knots, must be registered with the New South Wales Waterways Authority and to drive such vessel, you must be licensed by Waterways. All craft registered within New South Wales must also carry a hull identification number, known as a 'Boat Code'. Enquiries regarding Boat Code, licensing procedures, registration of power craft, required safety gear and 'rules of the road' can be made by contacting New South Wales Waterways on 13 1236 or by visiting the Waterways website at www.waterways.nsw.gov.au

---

FURTHER INFORMATION

Fishing For full details of fishing regulations, contact NSW Fisheries at 202 Nicholson Pde, Cronulla, tel. (02) 9527 8411, its regional offices or its website, www.fisheries.nsw.gov.au. The authority operates a Fisheries Information Service on tel. (02) 9566 7802. Obtain Fisheries publications from its offices, bait and tackle shops or its website.

Boating The Waterways Authority is at James Craig Rd, Rozelle, tel. (02) 9563 8511, and has many regional offices. It produces a variety of boating maps, guides and videos on waterways regulations and boat safety that are available from Waterways offices. Also see its website, www.waterways.nsw.gov.au. Weather forecasts and information are available from the Bureau of Meteorology, tel. 1900 926 113.

An excellent catch of Murray cod

NEW SOUTH WALES

INLAND FISHING COASTAL REGION

Coastal Region

Along more than 1000 km of coastline, the principal freshwater species on offer is Australian bass – a pugnacious, cover-loving species with the endearing tendency to strike at anything that comes within range.

Bass move around during the year, migrating downstream to the brackish water in late autumn and winter to spawn. In spring, they work their way upstream again, to feed during summer in the best stretches they can find. Their upstream progress is generally halted when they encounter a major obstruction, such as a weir or a waterfall, as nearly all major New South Wales streams and rivers, except the Clyde River, have been damned or altered in some way. Bass are frequently caught on lures, either by trolling or casting. In recent years bass numbers have increased as a result of intensive stocking programmes in suitable impoundments. This in turn has led to a growth in bass fishing tournaments.

Sometimes a canoe and four-wheel drive are needed to get to the best water

WHERE TO FISH

Coastal Region

NORTH COAST ● 127
The pristine Timbarra and Nymboida rivers, below the falls, are home for bass and the protected eastern cod.

CENTRAL COAST ● 128
This area fishes well for bass, freshwater herring, pinkeye and bully mullet, and catfish. Bass and eel are found in many impoundments, while mullet and some bass can be caught within the Sydney area.

SOUTH COAST ● 129
The Shoalhaven River offers limited bass fishing from about Burrier to as far up as the Tallowa Dam wall. Further south is the Clyde River, and there are a host of dams, such as the Brogo Reservoir near Bega.

GUIDE TO LOCAL FISH

bass, Australian
catfish, eel-tailed
eel, long-finned
eel, short-finned
herring, freshwater
mullet, bully
mullet, pinkeye
perch, estuary
perch, golden
perch, silver
redfin
trout, rainbow

FURTHER INFORMATION

Fishing and boating For details of coastal offices of NSW Fisheries and Waterways Authority offices, see Coastal Fishing Further Information listings: Sydney Region, page 45; Grafton Region, page 65; Port Macquarie Region, page 77; Newcastle Region, page 89; Wollongong Region, page 101; and Bermagui Region, page 113.

Tourist centres Cnr Princes Hwy and Beach Rd, Batemans Bay, tel. (02) 4472 6900; Pacific Hwy, Coffs Harbour, tel. (02) 6652 1522; Princes Hwy, Eden, tel. (02) 6496 1953; Great Lakes Tourism, Little St, Forster, tel. (02) 6554 8799; Central Coast Tourism, Rotary Park, Terrigal Dr, Terrigal, tel. (02) 4385 4430; cnr Ballina St and Molesworth St, Lismore, tel. (02) 6622 0122; Wheeler Pl, 363 Hunter St, Newcastle, tel. (02) 4974 2999; cnr Spring St and Pacific Hwy, South Grafton, tel. (02) 6642 4677.

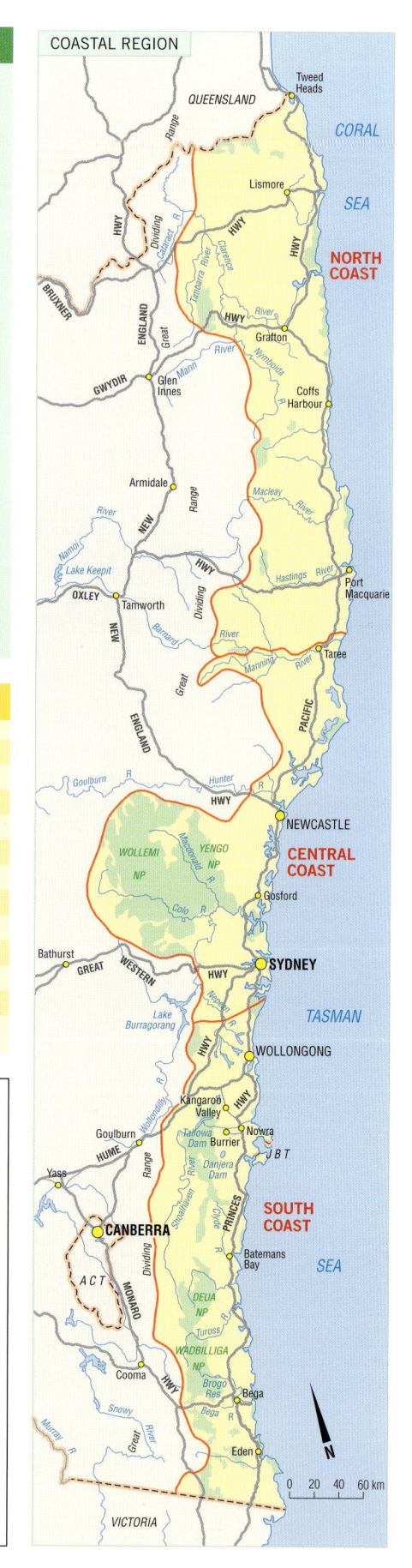

INLAND FISHING COASTAL REGION

NEW SOUTH WALES

North Coast

Type of fishing
dam, lake, river
Target fish
bass

The remote north-western pristine rivers such as the **Timbarra** and **Nymboida** are wilderness fisheries, mainly accessible by raft or canoe. Catch and release, self-restraint, and the use of barbless hooks all go a long way towards experiencing this wilderness fishery without damaging it. Responsible professional guiding outfits also operate in the area.

Bass inhabit much of the freshwater reaches of the **Brunswick, Richmond, Orara, Bellinger, Nambucca, Macleay, Wilson, Hastings, Camden Haven, Stewarts** and **Lansdowne rivers**. The eastern cod is still found in the upper Clarence and Nymboida and has been stocked back into the Richmond system. It is, however, a protected species. It is superficially similar in appearance but more aggressive than the Murray cod, which is a native of the western plains and slopes. The eastern cod is slow growing and, with its aggression, is very vulnerable. This species, which nearly became extinct before a breeding program stocked important waters, was once so common it was used as pig food.

More accessible bass rivers include the Bellinger, Nambucca, Wilson, Brunswick and lower Clarence. In fishing these waters a small craft is very handy, and lures – either trolled past rock walls or deep snags or cast close to cover – produce very good results. The very best way to catch the large hard fighting bass is to drift a live shrimp about 2 m deep under a light float, along rock edges or snags. Hang on because these bruisers will try to bury you very quickly. Most of these rivers have a measure of accessible bank angling.

Freshwater herring occur as far north as the **upper Richmond**, but these fish are more often found in the central and southern sectors. *Tandanus tandanus*, a species of eel-tailed catfish, is native to the freshwater sections of most coastal rivers and found wherever de-snagging, pollution, or fishing pressure has not wiped them out. Mullet are widespread along the coast, both the true freshwater pinkeye and also juveniles of the marine bully species.

Freshwater dams in this area include **Clarrie Hall Dam**, south of Murwillumbah (bass and golden perch), and **Toonumbar Dam**, west of Kyogle (silver perch, bass and catfish). All these dams rely on stocking.

GUIDE TO LOCAL FISH

bass, Australian
catfish
eel, long-finned
herring, freshwater
mullet, bully
mullet, pinkeye
perch, golden
perch, silver

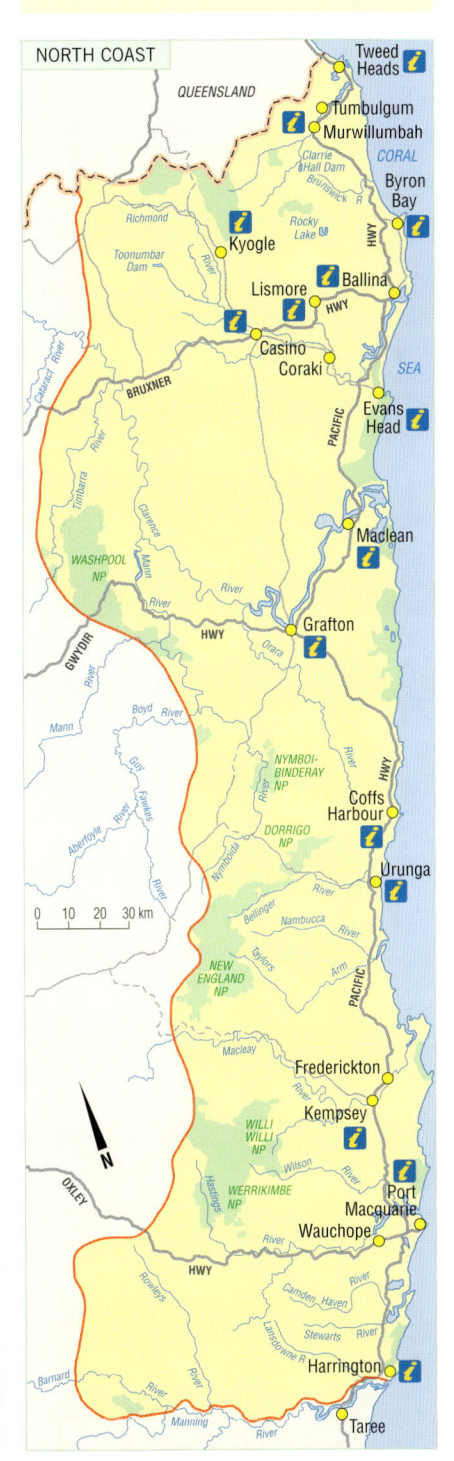

Bass country on the upper Clarence River

NEW SOUTH WALES

INLAND FISHING COASTAL REGION

Central Coast

Type of fishing
dam, lake, river

Target fish
bass, catfish, mullet

The riverine fresh water of the Central Coast, from the Manning River to the Sydney area, offers bass, freshwater herring, pinkeye and bully mullet, and catfish. It is noticeable, however, that the closer you get to heavily populated areas, the more anglers there are and the harder it is to catch fish.

Despite this, the fishing is worthwhile in streams such as the **Wallamba**, near Nabiac, the upper **Karuah**, and the **Williams River**, on which **Seaham Weir** is located. The weir has bass, mullet, catfish and eels. There is very good bass fishing downstream of Seaham Weir during late winter and early spring. The fishing is also worthwhile in **Dora and Wyong creeks**, which run into the central coast lakes, in the **Colo River**, and in the **Nepean and upper Hawkesbury system**. The upper Hawkesbury above Wisemans Ferry is a major freshwater fishery for Australian bass, with some surprisingly large fish still taken. Various tributaries, such as **Mangrove, Cattai** and **Webbs creeks**, are all classic bass and mullet habitats. Both **Nortons** and **Bents basins**, on the Nepean River at Wallacia, carry bass, mullet, catfish and herring.

A boat is a useful asset when fishing the central coast rivers, and lure fishing an excellent technique to bag a bass. These areas are heavily fished and suffer decreasing water quality due to urban sprawl and pollution. There is still good bass fishing available and those who experiment with deep diving, surface and soft plastic lures as well as flies and bait will most often take these educated fish. Dawn and dusk and into the night during warmer months are the best times. Surface lures on a warm summer night can provide some of the most exciting fishing imaginable as bass crash into lures, shattering the silence. In cooler weather, fish closer to brackish water, using small diving lures or bait.

The bass is a territorial fish. One method of encouraging a strike on surface lures is to cast the lure and allow it to sit for 10 or 15 seconds before starting the retrieve.

Central coast impoundments, such as **Grahamstown Dam, Brooklyn Dam** and **Lake Parramatta** have bass and eels in them. **Manly Dam** also has redfin and silver perch. Check boating regulations as outboard motors are generally disallowed.

Within the Sydney metropolitan area, the **upper Georges River** near Liverpool, and the **Hacking River**, above Audley Weir, have mullet – and some very educated bass.

Some coastal freshwater pondages, like this one south of Taree, have been stocked with bass and golden perch

GUIDE TO LOCAL FISH

	Central Coast	South Coast
bass, Australian	●	●
catfish	●	
eel	●	●
herring, freshwater	●	
mullet	●	●
redfin	●	
perch, estuary		●
perch, silver	●	
trout, rainbow		●

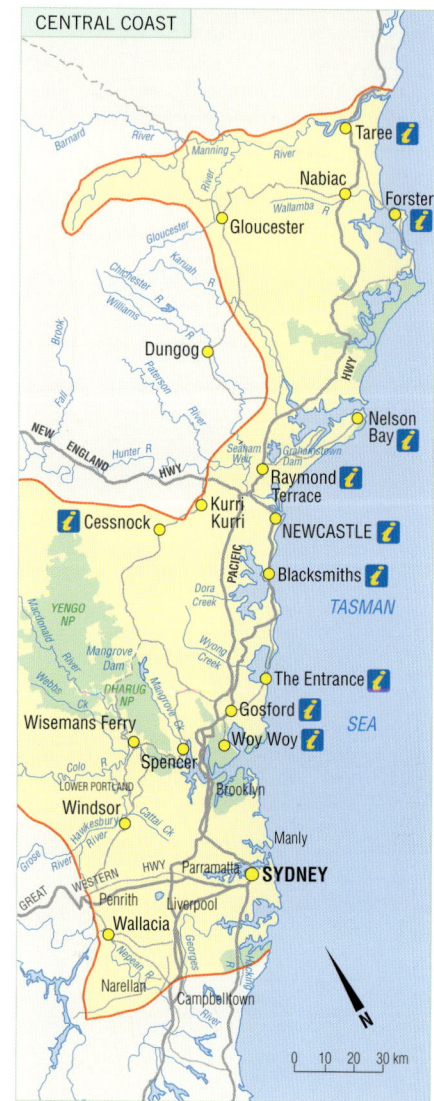

Eel-tailed catfish
The Tandanus tandanus *species of catfish is found throughout the island and coastal fresh water of much of south and eastern Australia. The dorsal and pectoral spines can inflict nasty wounds.*

INLAND FISHING COASTAL REGION   NEW SOUTH WALES

South Coast

Type of fishing
dam, river

Target fish
bass, estuary perch, mullet

Some of the best water here cannot be fished. Sydney water supply dams are closed to fishing, which means that the productive Cataract Dam is not accessible. Near Nowra, the **Shoalhaven River** offers quality bass fishing from about Burrier, as far up as the Tallowa Dam wall. **Broughton Creek** can yield bass up towards Berry.

Stocking **Tallowa Dam** with bass in recent years has seen the emergence of a 'put and take' fishery to offset the loss of the Shoalhaven's capacity to self-regenerate its bass following construction of the dam, which stopped bass migrating. It is early days, but indications of the new fishery are promising.

Further south, there are short freshwater stretches in **Wandandian** and **Conjola creeks**, but the next major freshwater stream southwards is the **Clyde**, where bass are present. The best section begins around Shallow Crossing and extends to the Budawang Range. The Clyde produces large numbers of small bass, but big fish, though present, are difficult to catch.

The **Deua River**, upstream of Moruya, and the **Tuross** above Bodalla, are also good streams to try. The **Murrah** and **Brogo rivers** have mullet, and sketchy populations of bass, while there are both these fish and estuary perch in the **Bega** and **Towamba rivers**, and estuary perch in the **Wallagaraugh**.

South coast dams include **Fitzroy Falls Reservoir**, above Kangaroo Valley, **Tallowa** and **Danjera dams** near Nowra, and **Brogo Reservoir**, near Bega. There are bass in Tallowa, Danjera and Brog and rainbow trout in Fitzroy Falls Reservoir, where canoe access (no motors) is available exclusively to members of the Campbelltown Sportfishing Club and then only from September through October. There is however about a kilometre of bank access on Fitzroy's eastern shore for public angling.

Fitzroy Falls, Morton National Park

NEW SOUTH WALES

New England Region

There are two separate and recognisable sectors within this region, divided by a central spine of granite-studded highlands running generally north and south with cool streams, which drain east and west.

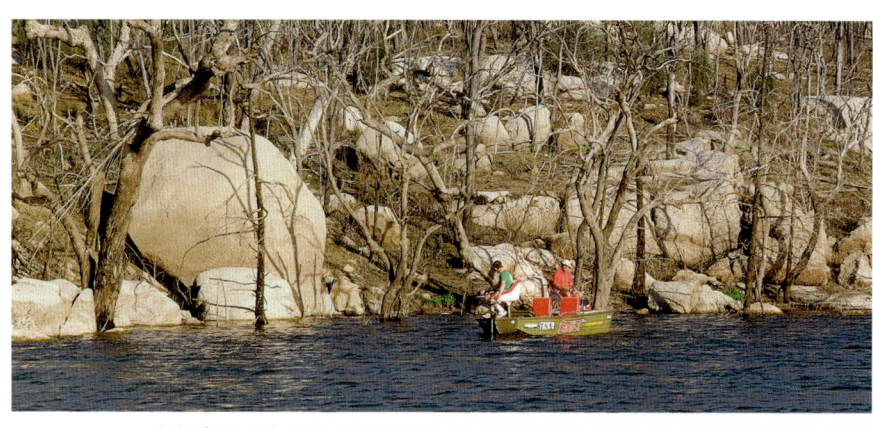

INLAND FISHING NEW ENGLAND REGION

Lake Copeton is well known for its large golden perch, which are caught near rocky points

These cool rivers are the adopted homes of brown and rainbow trout. To the west and south, among the slopes and foothills, a scattering of key dams are fed by warmer rivers that carry Murray cod, catfish, golden and silver perch, and redfin.

However, many of the dams were built for irrigation and are subject to fluctuations in water levels that can be dramatic in drought years. Some of the best fishing is along the original river beds, and where the feeder streams flow into these dams. The tourist value of many of these dams is highlighted by the accommodation available, much of it aimed at the families who fish.

Many of the west-flowing rivers enter and continue beyond impoundments, some of them having good populations of native fish both above and below the dam walls, as a result of either natural breeding or restocking. These north-western river systems eventually feed into the mighty Murray–Darling river complex, the breeding heartland of our Murray cod and golden perch fisheries.

Rainbow trout have been acclimatised to the high plateau streams of the New England Region, and are also stocked in numerous private farm dams

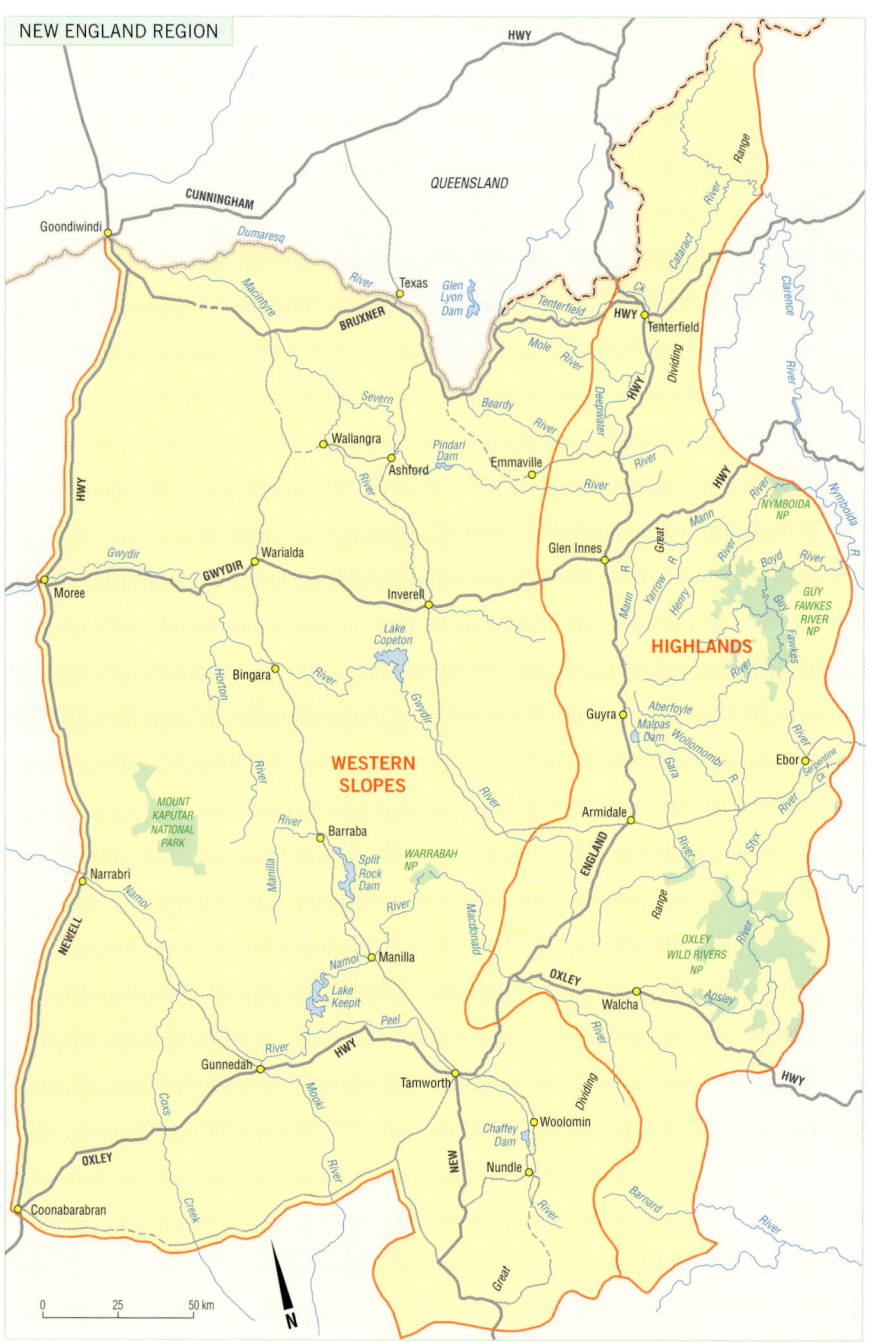

INLAND FISHING NEW ENGLAND REGION • NEW SOUTH WALES

WHERE TO FISH

New England Region

HIGHLANDS • 134

Good trout waters in this area include the Deepwater in the north, the Gara and Wollomombi rivers near Guyra, and the Apsley, Styx, Serpentine and Guy Fawkes rivers. Bass have been stocked into Malpas Dam, near Guyra, where there are also redfin.

WESTERN SLOPES • 135

Water temperatures are often too warm here for trout. Most likely fish are native species such as Murray cod, golden and silver perch and catfish. Redfin and carp are also found. Productive native fish streams include Tenterfield Creek, and the Mole, Severn, Dumaresq, Macintyre and Gwydir rivers. There is also excellent fishing in major dams and lakes such as Chaffey, Keepit, Copeton, Split Rock and Pindari.

GUIDE TO LOCAL FISH

bass, Australian
carp, European
catfish
cod, Murray
eel
herring, freshwater
redfin
perch, golden
perch, silver
trout, brown
trout, rainbow

FURTHER INFORMATION

Fishing and boating NSW Fisheries offices at 24 Andrews St, Inverell, tel. (02) 6722 1129 and at 72 Gunnedah St, Tamworth, tel. (02) 6765 4591. The Waterways Authority office at Shop 16, Tamworth Arcade, Peel St, Tamworth, tel. (02) 6766 9839.

Tourist centres 82 Marsh St, Armidale, tel. 1800 627 736; 116 Queen St, Barraba, tel. (02) 6782 1255; Newell Hwy, Coonabarabran, tel. (02) 6842 1441; Church St, Glen Innes, tel. (02) 6732 2397; Water Towers Complex, Campbell St, Inverell, tel. (02) 6728 8161; Lyle Houlihan Park, Cnr Newell and Gwydir hwys, Moree, tel. (02) 6757 3350; cnr Peel St and Murray St, Tamworth, tel. (02) 6755 4300; 157 Rouse St, Tenterfield, tel. (02) 6736 1082.

Mann River landscape

NEW SOUTH WALES

INLAND FISHING NEW ENGLAND REGION

Highlands

Type of fishing
dam, river

Target fish
trout

The trout angler has a good chance of catching trout in the many highland rivers that have been stocked with fish produced at the Dutton Trout Hatchery at Ebor. Between one and two million trout fingerlings and fry per year are stocked into the New England and Barrington Tops area. However, remember that these waters are subject to low flows in drought years and the quality of the trout angling will deteriorate in these conditions.

Trout rivers of the area include the **Deepwater**, which runs through the town of Deepwater, south of Tenterfield. Downstream from the New England Highway, golden perch and cod can be caught along with trout. Other trout streams are the **Wollomombi and Gara rivers**, east of the New England Highway, the **Styx**, which begins in the Oxley Wild Rivers National Park and the **Apsley**, which rises near Walcha. The **Guy Fawkes River**, a major trout stream of the area, draws water from the Aberfoyle and Sara rivers and runs northward through rugged forest country in the eastern section of the New England plateau. There is good fishing near the Chandler River, Oaky River and Serpentine Falls. Further south, the **Macdonald River** rises to the east of Niangala and runs westward, to eventually flow into the Namoi River. All these rivers can be accessed by road.

The rivers mentioned above, and some other smaller streams, have cool temperatures for trout, especially in their upper reaches, enabling them to contribute something to the overall trout fishery of New England.

Beardy Waters, just east of Glen Innes, contains large numbers of redfin, which are also found in a number of other waters. Malpas Dam, south of Guyra, has been largely unsuccessful for trout and contains redfin. In an attempt to establish this fishery it has now been stocked with bass.

Lower Allans Water near Ebor

GUIDE TO LOCAL FISH

	Highlands	Western Slopes
bass, Australian		
carp, European		●
catfish		●
cod, Murray	●	●
eel		
redfin	●	●
perch, golden	●	●
perch, silver		●
trout	●	●

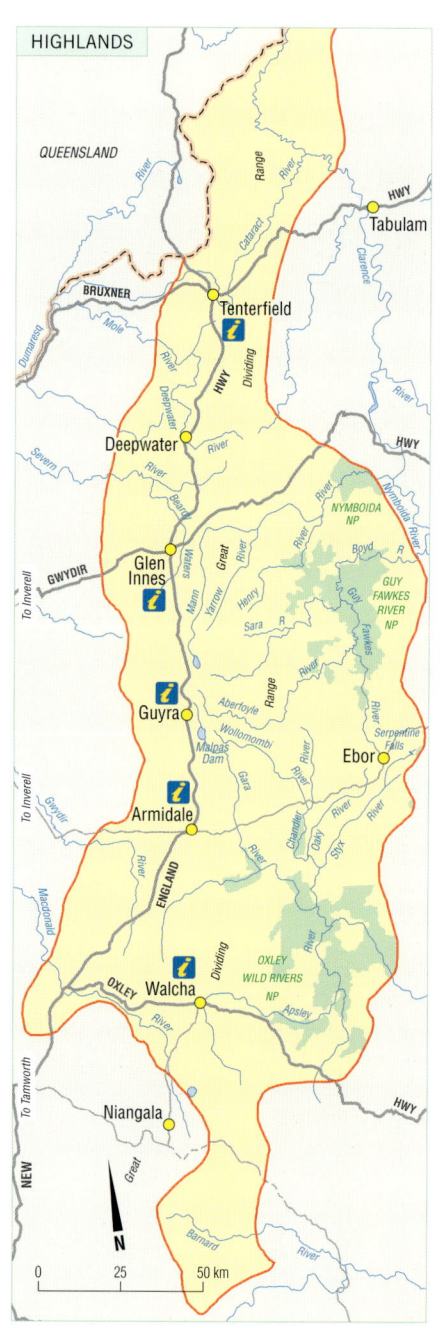

134

INLAND FISHING NEW ENGLAND REGION — NEW SOUTH WALES

Western Slopes

Type of fishing
dam, lake, river

Target fish
catfish, golden perch, Murray cod, silver perch

The **Dumaresq River** has many productive rocky stretches where Murray cod or golden perch can be trolled or spun from snags and corners. Good streams for native fish include **Tenterfield Creek**, which holds some excellent Murray cod.

The **Mole River**, rising south of Tenterfield, can hold trout in its upper waters, but for much of its length is best fished for natives. The **Severn**, rising in the ranges north of Glen Innes, feeds Pindari Dam, before joining the **Macintyre River** just north of Wallangra. All these waters hold native species like Murray cod and golden perch, which can be readily taken on lures when the rivers run clear, but when the water is coloured by heavy rain, species such as silver perch and catfish may be better sought with baits. Few of these rivers are boating propositions. There is fantastic fishing in rock granite gorges, although access is difficult. Keen anglers should refer to topographical maps and seek local advice. There is also great fishing in the Severn near Emmaville and in the Gwydir near Bingara because of the tremendous efforts of locals.

Pindari Dam, near Ashford, has been enlarged by five times, and has native species like golden and silver perch, Murray cod and catfish, as well as redfin. **Lake Inverell**, near the town of Inverell, has catfish, as well as golden and silver perch, while nearby **Lake Copeton** has a full complement of native species – Murray cod, catfish, golden and silver perch and large numbers of redfin. The fishing for giant golden perch is excellent in Copeton, but overcommitment to irrigators sees its level drop alarmingly over summer, which can turn the fish off. Boating is allowed on Pindari and Copeton – casting lures, trolling lures or bait fishing are all successful. In spring, land-based anglers should fish the rocky shores of these impoundments, near the dam walls, for golden perch.

The **Gwydir River** supplies Lake Copeton, and has Murray cod and golden perch. There is reasonable trout fishing in the Macintyre River above Lake Inverell where, around Elsmore, cod and trout can be taken together.

Split Rock Dam, which is fed by the Manilla River, and **Lake Keepit**, which is most easily approached from the Oxley Highway, are strongholds for golden perch. Bait fishers in Keepit generally 'bob' yabbies over submerged treetops along the old riverbed of the Namoi. Lure fishers work those same areas or troll or cast around points and ledges, and jig bladed spinners or rattling plugs over any horizontal sunken timber they can find to take goldens and cod. Keepit is now stocked with cod, golden and silver perch.

South-east of Tamworth is **Chaffey Dam**. Chaffey has Murray cod, golden and some quality silver perch and catfish. Its numerous large European carp will take wet flies and nymphs.

All these dams fish best in spring and early summer, before irrigation drawdown is greatest. They fish well again in autumn until about Easter. The State's stocking program for natives in impoundments is terrific and will ensure continued quality fishing.

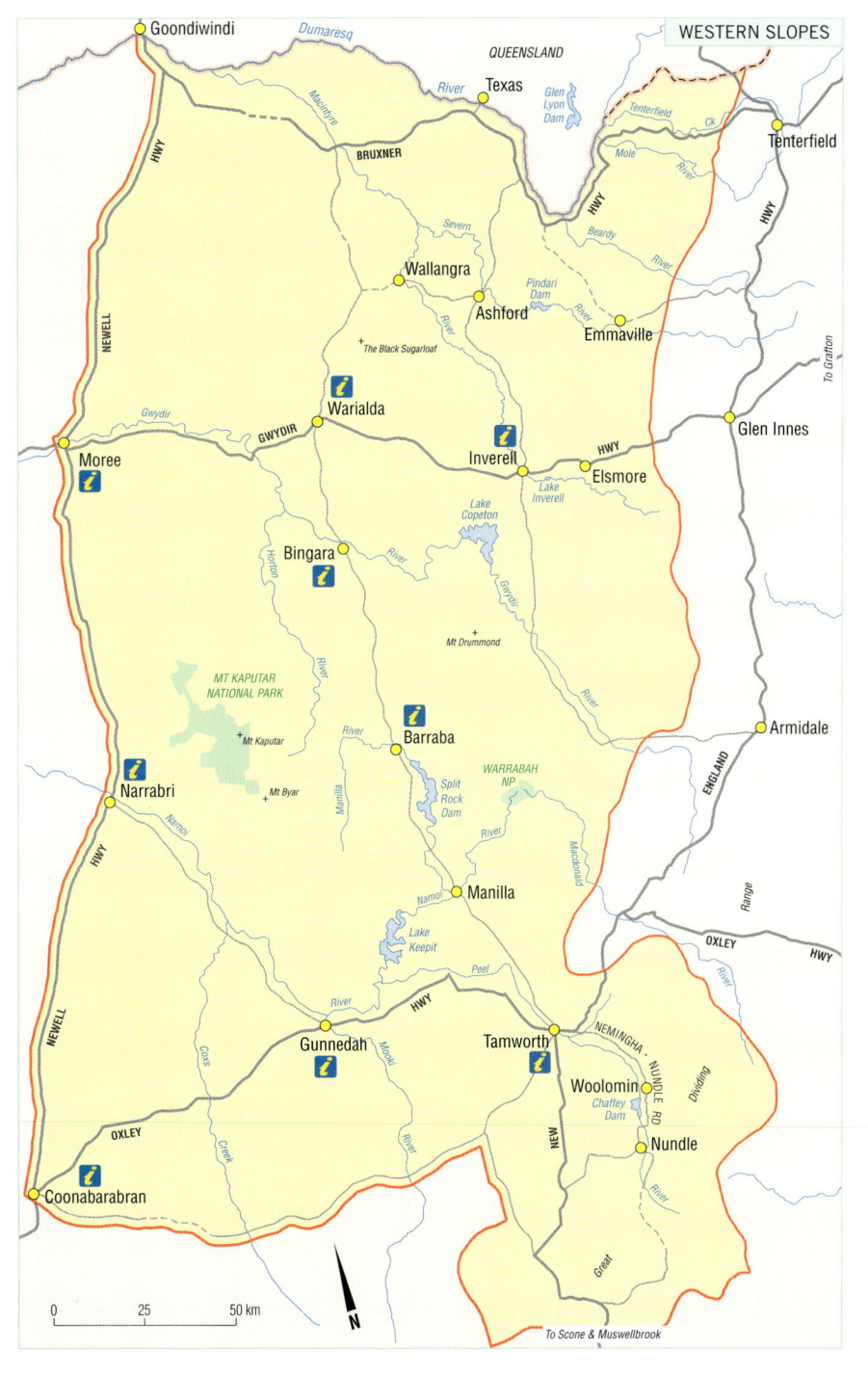

NEW SOUTH WALES

INLAND FISHING UPPER HUNTER REGION

Upper Hunter Region

The countryside of this region changes in character as you descend – from semi-alpine summits, belts of wet sclerophyll and temperate rainforest where trout can be caught, down through rolling grasslands to the coastal flood plain, a section that yields native fish in abundance.

The Upper Hunter's rivers, streams and dams contain both trout and native species. Freshwater impoundments, such as Lake St Clair, Glenbawn and Lostock dams, can provide fishing for golden perch and Australian bass.

Most of the region's freshwater starts in the complex of peaks and ridges known as the Tops. The Barrington and Gloucester Tops extend, like a spread hand, roughly south, west and east from the junction of the Liverpool and Hastings ranges.

Trout have been long-time imports to the highland streams of the Top district, but it is rare for them to achieve any great size. Carp, on the other hand, present in various warm lowland streams, often reach 3 kg or more. Bass have been stocked in dams and streams, as well as catfish. While the introduced bass seem to grow rapidly in these impoundments, they cannot breed. Catfish, on the other hand, do breed and have done so very well.

In common with many other parts of New South Wales, much of the land adjacent to streams in the upper Hunter region is privately owned. While inhospitality is rare, landowners can by law deny access across their property to fish a river. Aside from public right of way, the title of rural land in New South Wales most often only extends to the high water mark, but in a handful of cases, can also include the river bed beneath the water as well, to the middle of the stream. In theory this can preclude even wading the river. However, if the stream is large enough to support a canoe or small boat, you can avoid such problems and fish the river quite legally, never needing to touch the bank or the bottom.

WHERE TO FISH

Upper Hunter Region

BARRINGTON TOPS ● 137

The eastern slopes of the Tops can be fished for trout, and the lowland reaches of the Barrington, Moppy and Gloucester rivers provide anglers with bass, catfish and mullet. The Chichester, Allyn, Williams and Paterson rivers rise on the southern slopes and hold trout in their upper reaches.

HUNTER RIVER ● 138

In the east, the southern side of the Tops (encompassing the Chichester, Williams, Allyn and Paterson rivers) has trout up high and natives down low. Dams and lakes have bass, catfish, mullet, golden perch and eels. The rest of this area essentially follows the floor of the Hunter, where bass and mullet are predominant. Glenbawn Dam has mullet, bass, golden and silver perch, Murray cod and catfish; the Hunter down to Maitland has the odd bass.

GUIDE TO LOCAL FISH

- bass, Australian
- carp, European
- catfish
- cod, Murray
- eel
- herring, freshwater
- mullet, pinkeye
- perch, golden
- perch, silver
- trout, brown
- trout, rainbow

FURTHER INFORMATION

Fishing and boating NSW Fisheries has an office at the Newcastle Fishermen's Co-op Building, 97 Hannell St, Wickham, tel. (02) 4927 6548 and at 55 Lambton Pde, Swansea, tel. (02) 4971 1201; The Waterways Authority has an office at 8 Cowper St Sth, Carrington, tel. (02) 4940 0198.

Tourist centres Cnr Brown and Dowling St, Dungog, tel. (02) 4992 2212; 27 Denison St, Gloucester, tel. (02) 6558 1408; cnr New England Hwy and High St, Maitland, tel. (02) 4933 2611; 87 Hill St, Muswellbrook, tel. (02) 6541 4050; cnr Susan St and Kelly St, Scone, tel. (02) 6545 1526; Shire Offices, Queen St, Singleton, tel. (02) 6578 7267.

INLAND FISHING UPPER HUNTER REGION

NEW SOUTH WALES

Barrington Tops

Type of fishing
river
Target fish
bass, catfish, mullet, trout

The rivers and streams of the Tops can be a challenge to fish. Access is limited by the rugged topography of the Barrington Tops National Park. The best tactic is to walk a kilometre or so from an access point before starting to fish. These streams warm up in summer so fish in the aerated water of riffles and at the heads of pools as the season progresses. Flies, jigs and spinners work well in the tight waters.

East-flowing streams such as the **Moppy, Barrington** and **Gloucester rivers** and their tributaries rise in the Tops district, and hold brown and rainbow trout in their upper reaches, but rainbows are the most commonly caught. The water temperature in these streams rises as they reach lower country and, providing no obstructions exist to prevent free movement from downstream, bass, mullet and catfish can start to put in an appearance. Even though, in strict drainage terms, the rivers mentioned do not fall within the Upper Hunter system (they feed the Karuah's system, not the Hunter's), they are commonly regarded as being within the Hunter's angling scope and promoted as such in tourist and angling literature.

Some streams are overstocked and have large numbers of small fish. Anything over the old pound mark can be considered a good catch, but this is challenging fishing and very enjoyable and rewarding.

One of several small streams carrying trout in the Barrington Tops area. The fish are rarely large, but thrive on a diet of terrestrial and aquatic insects in this picturesque country

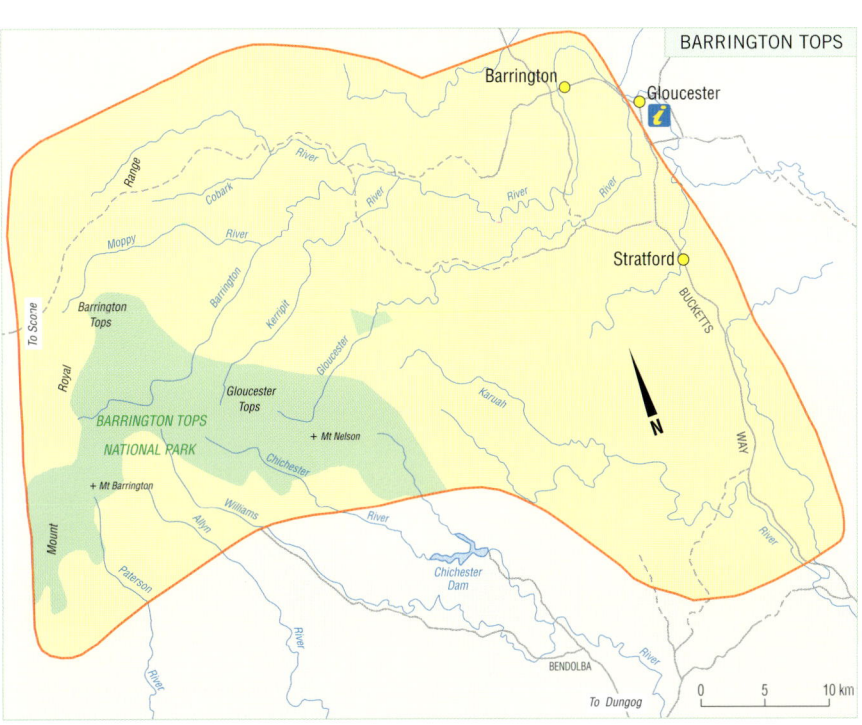

Elk Hair Caddis
The Elk Hair is a good imitation of one of our most important trout stream insects.

GUIDE TO LOCAL FISH

bass, Australian
catfish
mullet
trout, brown
trout, rainbow

NEW SOUTH WALES

INLAND FISHING UPPER HUNTER REGION

Hunter River

Type of fishing
dam, lake, river
Target fish
bass, catfish, golden perch, mullet, trout

GUIDE TO LOCAL FISH

	Williams–Paterson Rivers	Hunter River
bass, Australian	●	●
carp, European		●
catfish	●	●
cod, Murray		●
eel	●	●
herring, freshwater		●
mullet	●	●
perch, golden		●
silver perch		●
trout	●	●

The Hunter River rises above Glenbawn Dam, picks up the Paterson River at Morpeth and receives tribute from other rivers rising in the Barringtons, such as the Chichester and Williams, where the Williams River joins the Hunter at Raymond Terrace before flowing to the coast. Other south-flowing streams from the Barrington Tops, such as the Paterson and its tributaries, feed the Hunter at Morpeth.

WILLIAMS–PATERSON RIVERS

This sector contains an interesting collection of rivers and dams. The **Chichester, Williams, Allyn** and **Paterson rivers** hold trout in their upper reaches, and have quality bass, mullet and catfish further down.

Angling is prohibited in Chichester Dam, and the Hunter Water Corporation, which controls the Chichester Catchment Area, actively discourages entry.

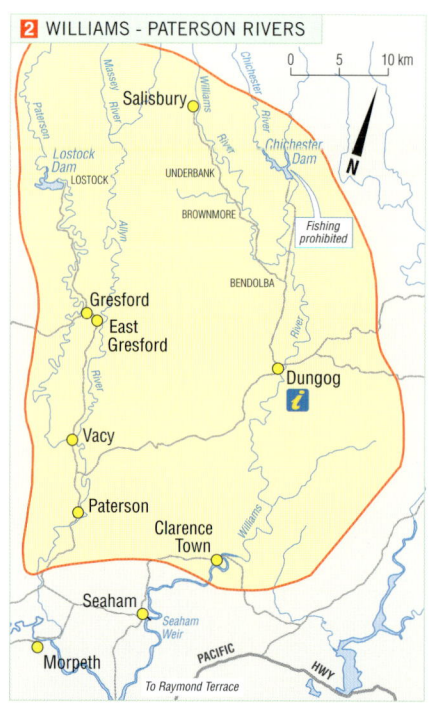

The **Williams River** runs alongside small farming communities between Salisbury and Bendolba, but fishes best from Dungog down, continuing through Clarence Town and on to Raymond Terrace.

The **lower Allyn River** can produce some good mullet fishing as far down as its junction with the Paterson River near Vacy, on the road between Paterson and East Gresford. The Paterson feeds **Lostock Dam**, a small irrigation impoundment that has been stocked with bass, and also has catfish. Although Lostock is improving, fish don't come easily.

Below Lostock, the **Paterson River** continues roughly south-east to Morpeth, and in this stretch it has good numbers of freshwater mullet, with some good bass water downstream towards its junction with the Hunter.

HUNTER RIVER

From the west-facing peaks of the Barrington Tops, **Polblue Creek** and **Moonan** and **Omadale brooks** run towards the headwaters of the Hunter River, carrying trout as far down as about 800 m elevation. The fishing is often patchy though, because the western streams warm more quickly than their eastern counterparts, and for much of the year they have temperatures unsuitable

Lake St Clair, near Singleton, suits small boat fishing and supports an excellent fishery of bass and golden perch, with some catfish, mullet and eel as well

INLAND FISHING UPPER HUNTER REGION
NEW SOUTH WALES

for trout. The **Hunter River**, with its source in the Liverpool–Hastings range, picks up these tributaries and irrigates the fertile valley that bears its name. Flowing south, and to the east of Scone, the Hunter supplies Glenbawn Dam, above which it carries little except mullet.

Glenbawn Dam itself holds Australian bass, golden and silver perch, Murray cod (which have been stocked illegally), mullet and catfish. It is by far the biggest and most heavily fished impoundment in the area. Catfish, in particular, have found Glenbawn to their liking. The bass are mostly chunky middleweights, but some are large and powerful fish. While the silver perch fishery is not remarkable, the goldens make up for it, with 2-kg fish being common. A huge 16-kg golden perch was caught from this dam and fish over 8 kg are taken by those who put in the time. Glenbawn's obvious potential as a bass and golden perch fishery is fast becoming legend. Land-based angling is limited to the lower section of the dam, but boating is allowed and is usually rewarding. Glenbawn is one of the State's few impoundments where access is permitted along the dam wall. Trolling or casting the wall is most productive, although rocky points are also good.

Below **Glenbawn Dam**, the Hunter sweeps through stock and crop country past Muswellbrook, then, through Denman, eastward to Singleton and Maitland, before picking up the Williams River at Raymond Terrace – the freshwater extent of the system. The freshwater species on offer are principally mullet, bass, herring, catfish and European carp.

Freshwater fishing in the Hunter is no longer as good as its size might suggest. This once-great river is only a shadow of its former self. Massive demands on its water frequently reduce its volume and water quality markedly, and that it survives to be worth fishing in its lower freshwater reaches is due largely to the inflow of the comparatively unscathed Paterson and Williams rivers.

Lake St Clair, fed by Carrow Brook and the now-drowned Glennies Creek, has catfish, eels, bass and golden perch. It is the best of the still waters in the area and boats are permitted. Glennies Creek below the dam can be very sandy and shallow, but reasonably good fishing can be found by casting to small, deep pockets of cover. Try the crossing a few kilometres downstream of the dam wall and around Aberdeen for better results, although bass can be caught around Muswellbrook, Denman and Jerrys Plains for those who make the effort.

Glenbawn Dam offers good fishing for Australian bass, golden perch and some Murray cod

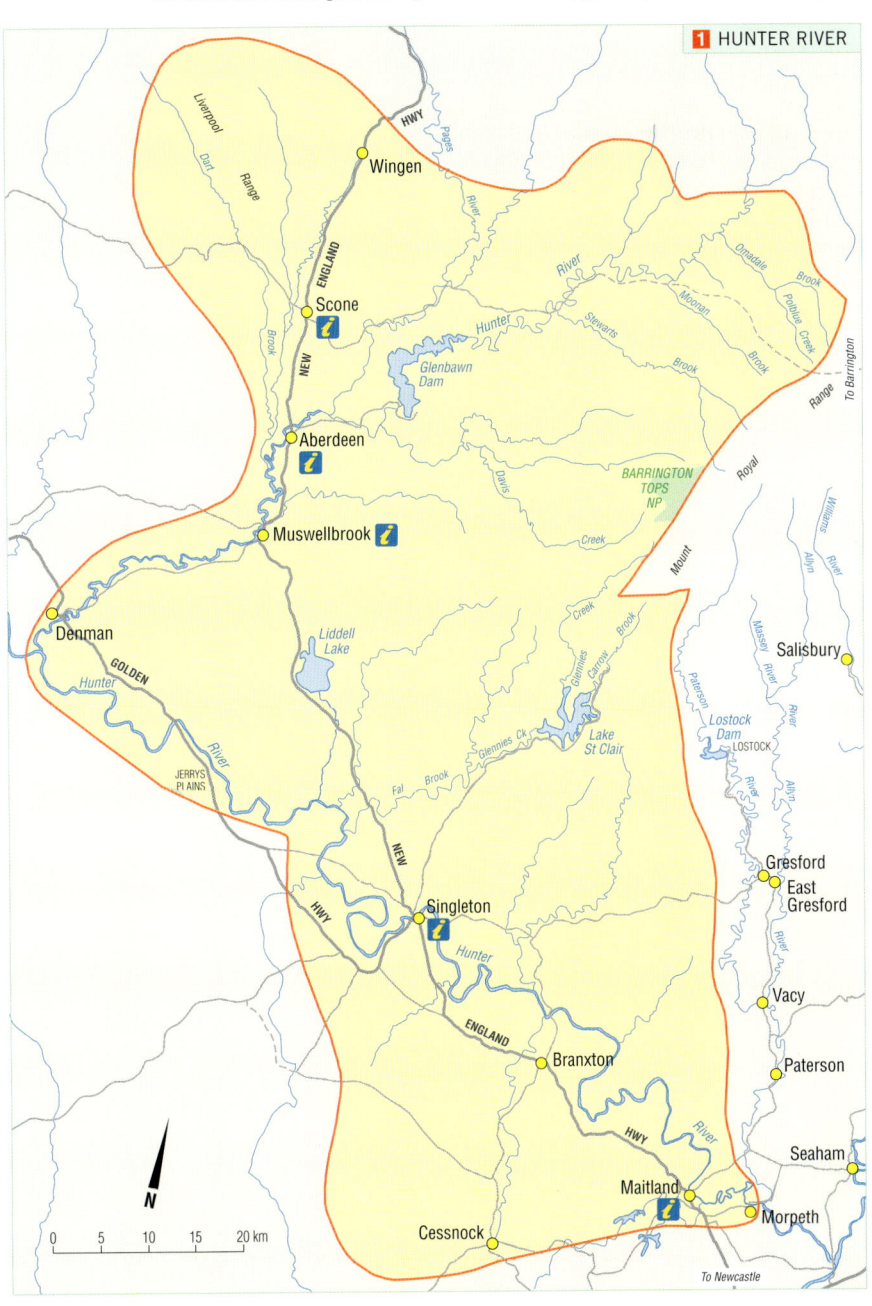

1 HUNTER RIVER

NEW SOUTH WALES

INLAND FISHING CENTRAL HIGHLANDS REGION

Central Highlands Region

This region offers tremendous variety, with small fly fishing waters for educated trout, larger rivers and tailraces where trophy trout can be found and some fantastic impoundment fishing for trout and native species.

When heavy rain falls, some waters become turbid because of run-off, but this usually clears quickly. In dry spells, the same rivers can nearly stop flowing, and suffer from algal blooms. Given regular rain, however, most streams in the area provide good fishing for much of the season.

Access to the streams in the region can be difficult. The bulk of the best water runs through private property, so reaching it often means getting through gates, and good fishing relies heavily on grace and favour arrangements with local landowners. Many farmers, however, have had bad experiences with anglers in the past and are cautious about allowing them on their properties. While riparian rights legislation in New South Wales provides theoretical access to all rivers, real life access depends on finding out who owns or controls the land, making the necessary overtures to gain permission, and getting your public relations skills up to speed.

The difficulty of accessing these rivers encourages many people to fish the many large dams in the region. Wyangala and Burrinjuck lakes have trout and native fish species.

There are three superb trout fishing lakes in the Lithgow district. Lake Lyell on the Cox's River near Bowenfels is the largest, Lake Wallerawang (Lake Wallis) at Wallerawang is next in size and Thompsons Creek Dam, also near Wallerawang is both the newest and the smallest. Powerboats are allowed on Lake Lyell but not on Lake Wallerawang and no boats of any description are allowed on Thompson Creek Dam.

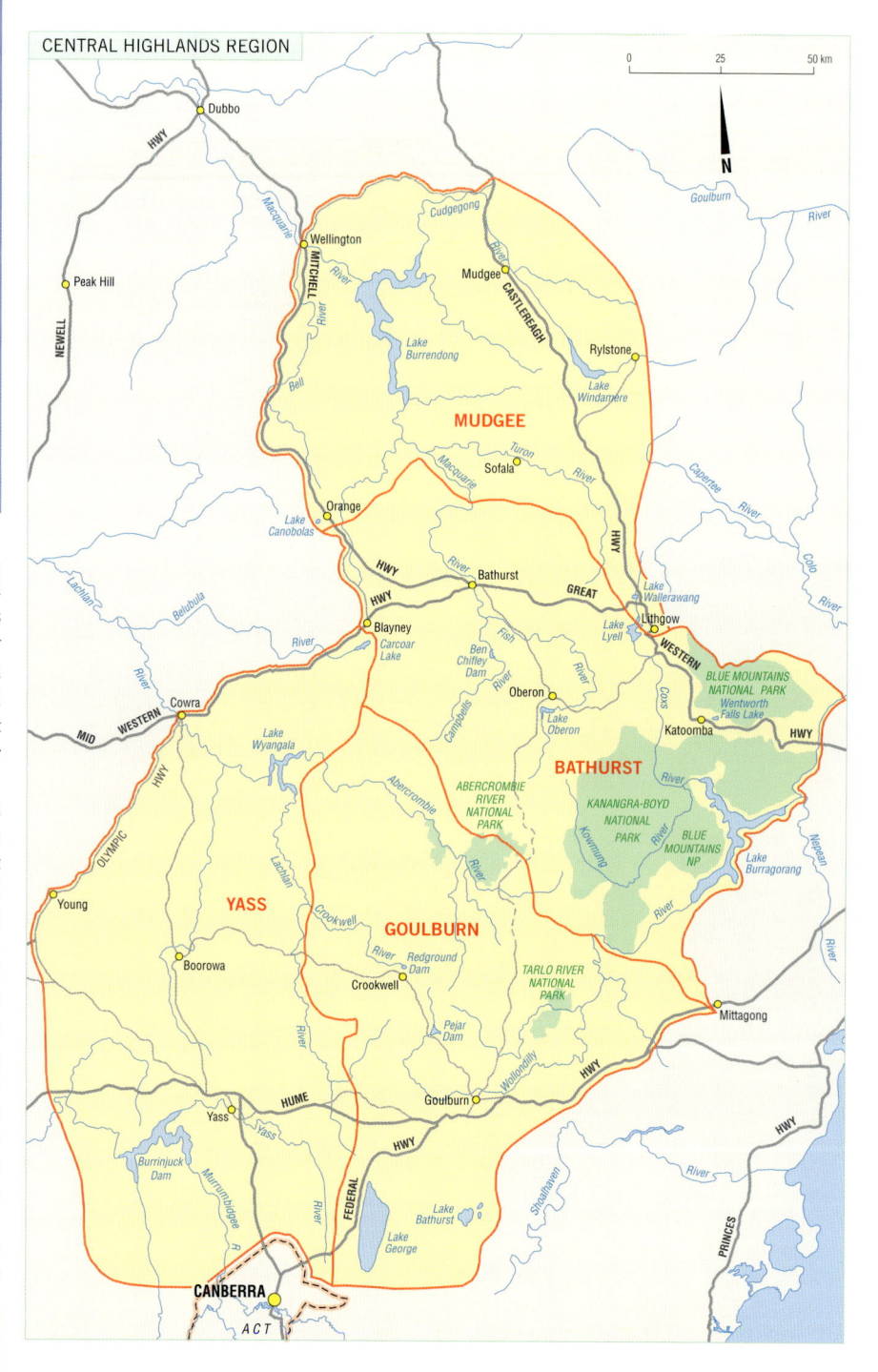

GUIDE TO LOCAL FISH

Atlantic salmon
blackfish, river
carp, European
catfish
cod, Murray
crayfish, Murray
redfin
perch, golden
perch, silver
trout, brown
trout, rainbow

Brown trout

This fish, considered a great sporting challenge, was introduced to Australia from Europe in the 1880s. Those caught by most anglers average around 1 kg, although large specimens can reach 10 kg. They are brown to blackish brown in colour, with red and black spots covering their sides.

INLAND FISHING CENTRAL HIGHLANDS REGION

NEW SOUTH WALES

WHERE TO FISH

Central Highlands Region

MUDGEE • 142

Lake Windamere, Rylstone Weir and Lake Burrendong are great native fisheries, as are the Cudgegong and Macquarie rivers, which feed these impoundments. Lake Wallerawang near Lithgow, and its tributary streams, hold brown and rainbow trout, as does the Macquarie below Burrendong.

BATHURST • 143

This area forms the nucleus of the Central Highland's freshwater fishery, with the complex of rivers that feed Lake Burragorang providing some of the best trout waters in the State. There are natives and redfin in some rivers and dams.

GOULBURN • 144

Streams such as the Wollondilly, Crookwell and Abercrombie have trout, as do some of their tributaries. Lake George has native fish, and there are trout in both the Pejar and Redground dams.

YASS • 145

Lake Wyangala and Burrinjuck Dam hold native fish and trout. Both have excellent tailrace fisheries for larger trout. There are redfin and golden perch in Carcoar Lake to the north.

FURTHER INFORMATION

Fishing and boating NSW Fisheries has offices at Research Station Dr, Bathurst, tel. (02) 6331 1428; Commonwealth Bank Building, Suite 1, Lot 7 Namina Crt, Wellington, tel. (02) 6845 4438; and at 254 Comur St, Yass, tel. (02) 6226 3867. The nearest Waterways Authority office is at 2/43 Macquarie St, Dubbo, tel. (02) 6884 5355.

Tourist centres 28 William St, Bathurst, tel. (02) 6332 1444 or 1800 681 000; Shire Council, 91 Adelaide St, Blayney, tel. (02) 6368 2104; 44 Goulburn St, Crookwell, tel. (02) 4832 1988; Great Western Hwy, Glenbrook, tel. 1300 653 408; Sloane St, Goulburn, tel. (02) 4823 4492; Echo Point, Katoomba, tel. (02) 4739 6266; 285 Main St, Lithgow, tel. (02) 6351 2307; 84 Market St, Mudgee, tel. (02) 6372 1020; Civic Gardens, Byng St, Orange, tel. (02) 6361 5226; Bridge View Inn, Louee St, Rylstone, tel. (02) 6379 1132; Cameron Park, Nanima Crs, Wellington, tel. (02) 6845 1733; Coronation Park, Comur St, Yass, tel. (02) 6226 2557; 2 Short St, Young, tel. (02) 6382 3394.

Casting from shore at Lake Windamere is an excellent fishing method for golden perch, the resident sportfish

NEW SOUTH WALES
INLAND FISHING CENTRAL HIGHLANDS REGION

Mudgee

Type of fishing
dam, lake, river

Target fish
golden perch, silver perch, trout

The **Cudgegong River** rises above **Lake Windamere**. Below Windamere, it runs through Mudgee and into **Lake Burrendong**, which has Murray cod, golden and silver perch, catfish and countless redfin. **Rylstone Weir** will take small boats, and has golden perch, catfish and river blackfish. It is ostensibly a picnic spot, with angling as an added attraction.

Lake Windamere, near Mudgee, by contrast is a spectacular and versatile fishery. Access is good and you can fish from a boat, from the shores – reached by road – or from the road rock walls. The dominant species are golden and silver perch, with an improving Murray cod fishery and no carp or redfin. Goldens and silvers can be caught here in reasonable numbers and are of good size. Baits, lures or flies work, and while trolling is popular, one of the best ways to fish – for goldens in particular – is to walk the banks while wearing polarised sunglasses to spot fish before casting to them. Murray cod introduced into the lake are starting to do well, with catch rates climbing all the time.

This area also takes in the headwaters of the south-flowing **Coxs River**, the source for Lake Wallerawang, and further to the north, the west-flowing **Turon River**, which joins the Macquarie north of Bathurst. Both these rivers are excellent trout fisheries. **Lake Wallerawang** holds brown and rainbow trout, most of which are less than 1 kg, although there are occasional trophy-sized specimens. The banks fish particularly well for big rainbows in the evening with fly.

There is also good fishing around Orange and Molong in the small creeks. Lake Canobolas was once a small but premier trout fishery before redfin were introduced. It is now stocked with golden perch to supplement the trout and redfin. The protected trout cod has been stocked into the upper reaches of the Turon River and should be returned to the water if caught.

The Macquarie River, in the waters below Burrendong, holds both brown and rainbow trout. Good cod are also caught in the river, especially around Long Point.

Lake Windamere, where the angler can fish from a boat, from shore or from the road rock walls

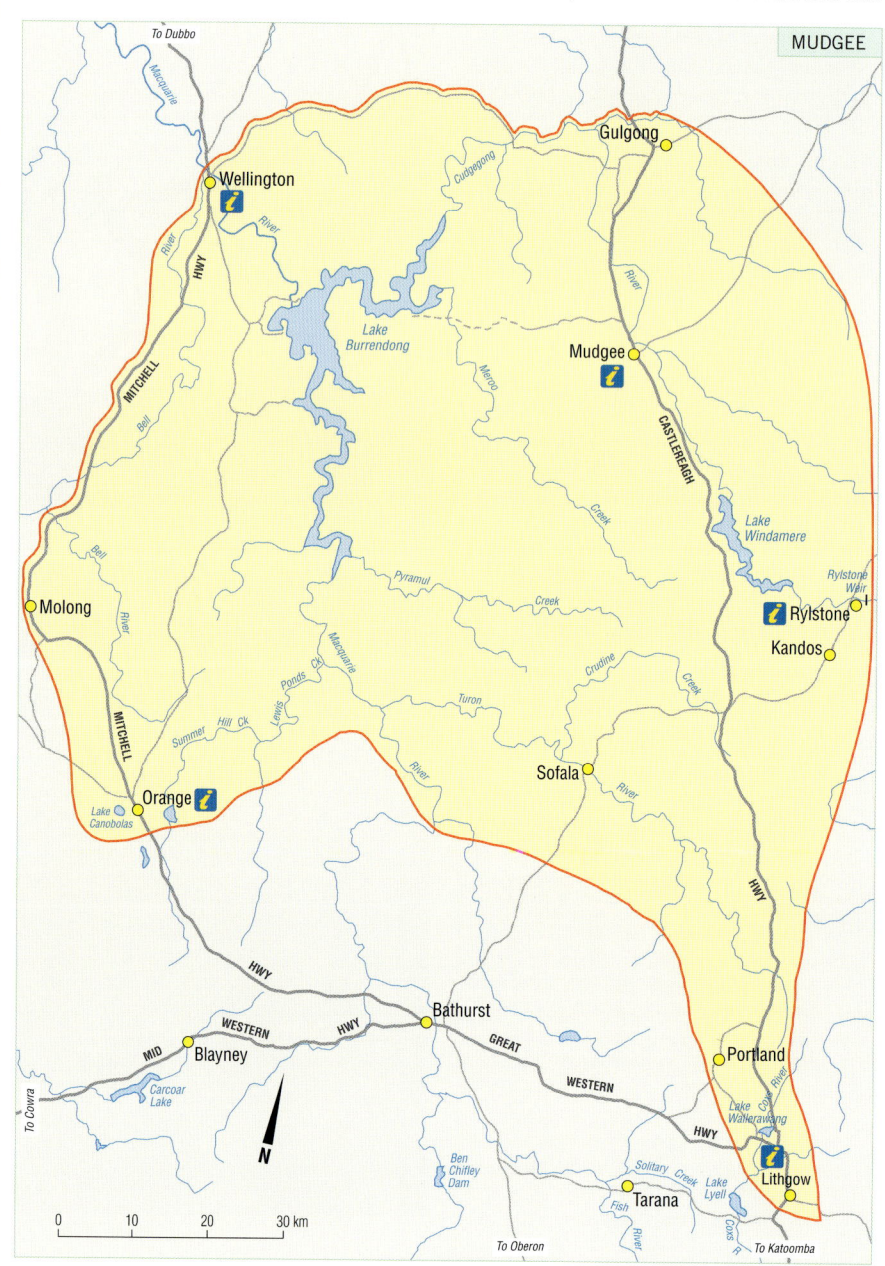

INLAND FISHING CENTRAL HIGHLANDS REGION NEW SOUTH WALES

Bathurst

Type of fishing
dam, lake, river
Target fish
trout

In this area, the major towns of Bathurst, Lithgow and Oberon are centres for trout fishing, and most of the trout streams are within a day-trip of these towns. The upland streams forming the nucleus of the Central Highlands' freshwater fishery rise in high forests to the south of Oberon. The **Fish, Duckmaloi** and **Campbells rivers** all drain roughly northward and are all trout waters.

At **Lake Oberon** (near the town), fishing from boats is not allowed, but the lake can be fished from the banks right through the year. It yields good-sized browns and rainbows on lures, baits or fly.

Ben Chifley Dam, south of Bathurst, can be fished from bank or boat, and has some brown but mostly rainbow trout, a few Murray cod and golden perch, and heaps of tiny redfin.

In the south-west, the Isabella and Retreat (also known as Little) rivers flow southwards, their waters eventually running into Lake Wyangala. These south-flowing streams also carry trout. In the north-west the lower reaches of the Macquarie River is a trout water, but carries native species, too.

In the east, the other major drainage system in the area comprises the Kedumba, Coxs, Jenolan, Tuglow, Kowmung, Tonalli, Wollondilly and Nattai rivers and the Blackheath and Butchers creeks, which all wind up in Lake Burragorang, Sydney's main water supply dam. The lake itself is prohibited to public access but the vast bulk of the huge canyons and extensive rivers above it are not. The principal stream in this complex is the **Coxs River** which, with the **Jenolan, Tuglow** and **Kowmung rivers**, forms Burragorang's northern catchment. Access to these upper reaches is limited to dirt tracks, suitable only for four-wheel drive vehicles. Some more remote sections can only be reached by hiking. On the Coxs River, near Lithgow, **Lake Lyell** holds brown and rainbow trout, as does Lake Wallerawang and the Thompson Creek Dam.

In the northern reaches of the Kedumba River, the **lake at Wentworth Falls**, near Katoomba, has both brown and rainbow trout.

An idyllic Central Highlands trout stream: Solitary Creek near Tarana

GUIDE TO LOCAL FISH

	Mudgee	Bathurst
blackfish, river	●	
catfish	●	
cod, Murray	●	●
redfin	●	●
perch, golden	●	●
perch, silver	●	
trout, brown	●	●
trout, rainbow	●	●

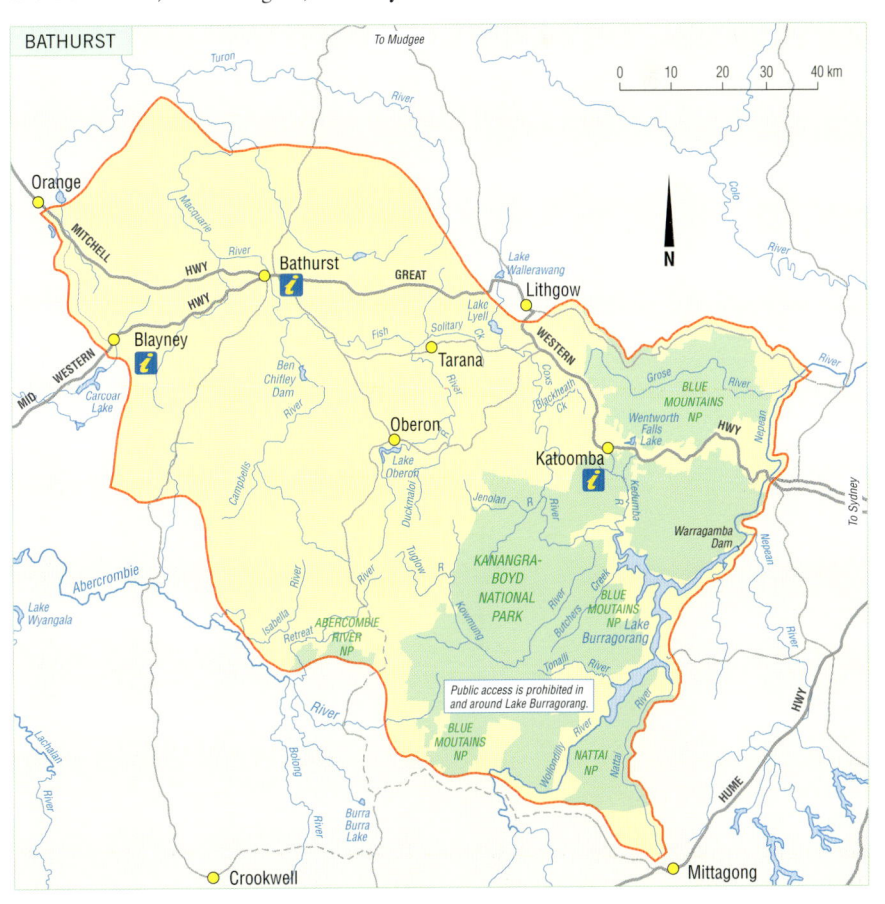

143

NEW SOUTH WALES

INLAND FISHING CENTRAL HIGHLANDS REGION

Goulburn

Type of fishing
dam, lake, river

Target fish
golden perch, silver perch, trout

The rivers in this area hold good numbers of both brown and rainbow trout, with fishing best in cooler months although good results can be had during the summer hopper season, especially by walking some distance from major roads before starting to fish.

Two major trout rivers have their headwaters in the southern highlands around Goulburn and Crookwell: the **Wollondilly**, which runs north into Lake Burragorang; and the **Crookwell**, which runs north-west into the Lachlan River.

To the north, the **Abercrombie River** also has trout, and natives such as silver, golden and Macquarie perch. The Macquaries and recently stocked trout cod are protected, however, and must be released alive if caught.

Redground Dam, or Crookwell Reservoir, near Crookwell, has trout, Murray cod, golden and silver perch and catfish. **Pejar Dam**, north-west of Goulburn, offers excellent fly fishing for large trout in the cooler months. While power boats are not permitted on the dam, some anglers use float-tubes to reach otherwise inaccessible banks and are rewarded with large fish. Lake Sooley is the water supply dam for the town of Goulburn, and no fishing is allowed. To the south of Goulburn, **Lake Bathurst** holds few fish.

Lake George, which periodically dries up, has been stocked with golden perch, silver perch and Murray cod. Fishing can be very good for those who find deeper water with cover that holds fish.

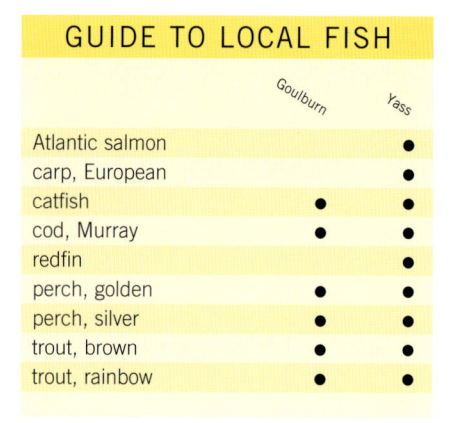

There are plenty of back country streams in this area holding some beautiful trout

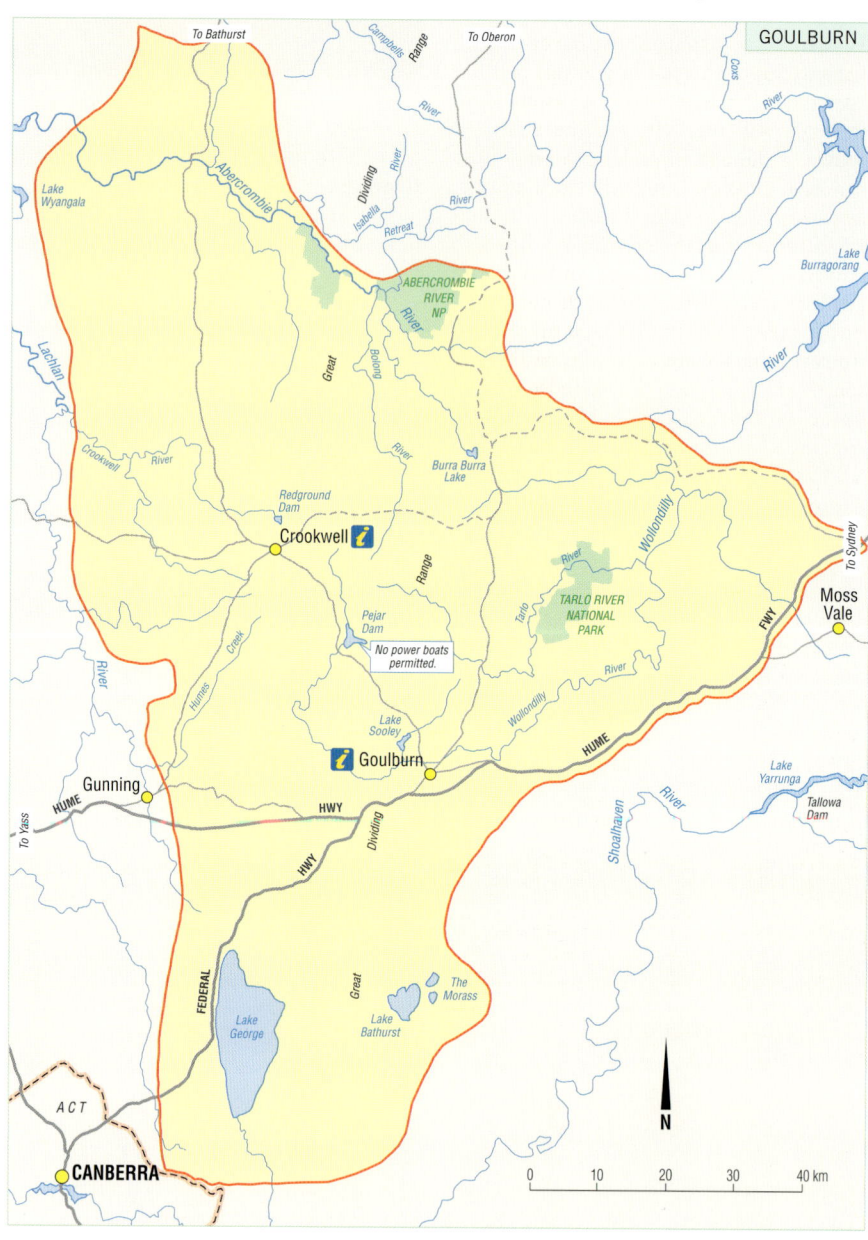

GUIDE TO LOCAL FISH

	Goulburn	Yass
Atlantic salmon		•
carp, European		•
catfish	•	•
cod, Murray	•	•
redfin		•
perch, golden	•	•
perch, silver	•	•
trout, brown	•	•
trout, rainbow	•	•

INLAND FISHING CENTRAL HIGHLANDS REGION   NEW SOUTH WALES

Yass

Type of fishing
dam, lake, river

Target fish
Atlantic salmon, golden perch, Murray cod, silver perch, trout

Lake Wyangala and Burrinjuck Dam are fed by extensive catchments, while Carcoar Lake is more modest. **Carcoar Lake** accepts boats and bank anglers, but is relatively featureless and sometimes malodorous. Its major attraction is tonnes of redfin, some of which can be sizeable. It carries some golden perch and recent stockings of Murray cod. While the goldens are known to eat redfin, the survival of the cod fingerlings is as yet unproven. If they do become established, they too will feed well on the abundant redfin. If the cod fingerlings survive, they will have plenty of redfin to eat, so growth rates may prove to be excellent.

Lake Wyangala, near Cowra, has both golden and silver perch, and Murray cod. It also has a rainbow trout fishery that is at times excellent, and Atlantic salmon and brown trout in the cool tailrace water below the dam wall. This dam is one of the most popular west of Sydney, with good facilities for boat anglers and plenty of access to the shores for land-based enthusiasts. Bush camping is allowed all around the lake and there are a number of excellent caravan parks.

The **Lachlan River**, which flows through Lake Wyangala, and the Abercrombie River, hold trout in the reaches above the lake. Sizeable fish can be found at Reids Flat early and late in the season, but they are either there in numbers or not at all. Below the lake the Lachlan tailrace contains some trophy brown trout, as well as large, hard-fighting rainbow trout. Atlantic salmon have also been stocked here.

Burrinjuck Dam, is a huge reservoir that offers golden and silver perch, Murray cod, carp, redfin, catfish, trout and Atlantic salmon. Macquarie perch are also here, but this protected species must be released alive if taken. Land-based angling is popular but the best results are from a boat. The Murrumbidgee offers good fishing above and below the lake, while the Yass is a mediocre stream.

Further south, the Goodradigbee River at Wee Jasper is a well-known trout area and contains monster cod in lower reaches during the closed season.

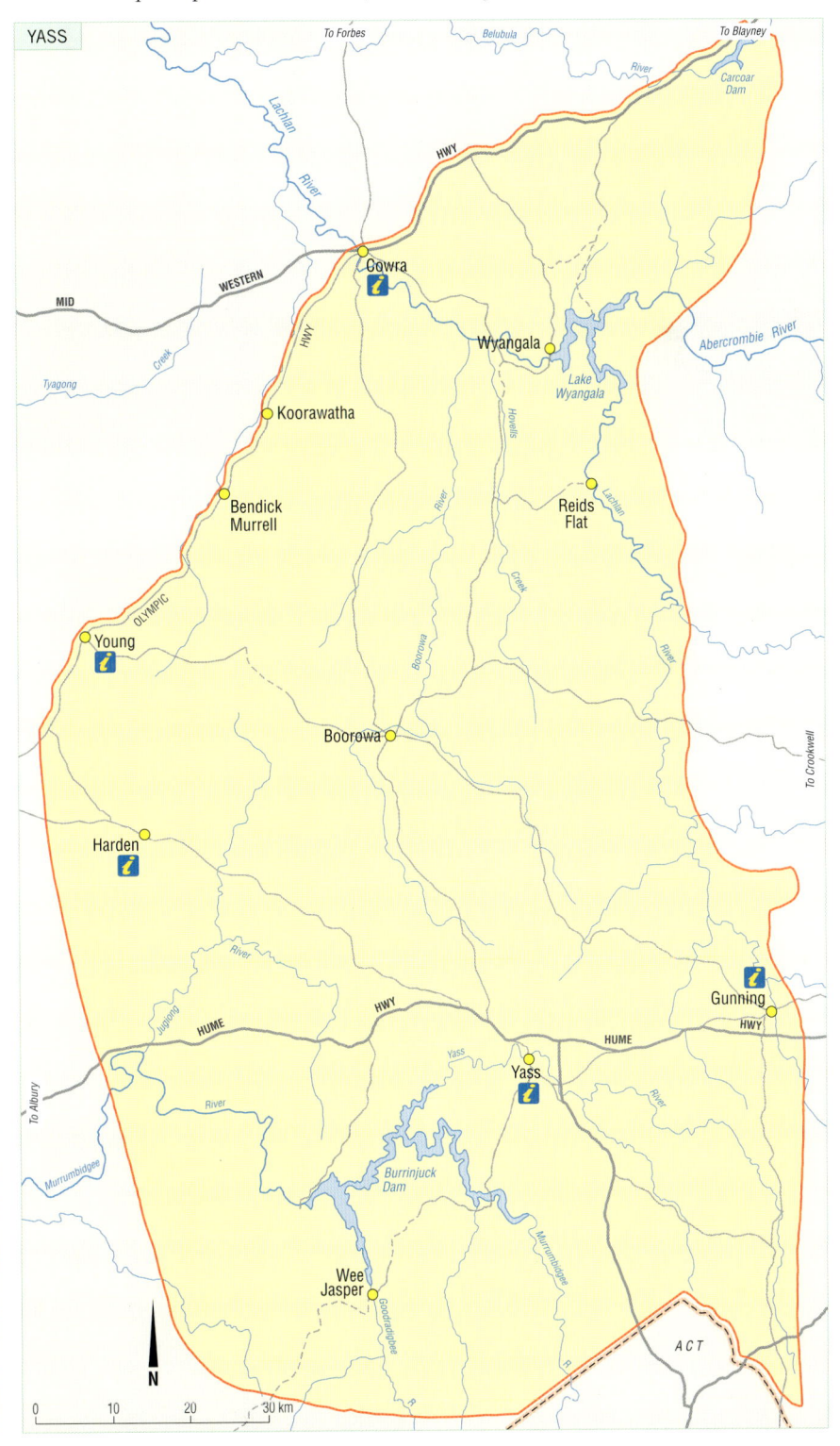

Wyangala Dam contains both native fish and trout

NEW SOUTH WALES

INLAND FISHING SNOWY MOUNTAINS REGION

Snowy Mountains Region

This area is the premier trout fishery in New South Wales. Views of the snow-covered peaks of the main range are commonplace and the scenery is spectacular. The large impoundments provide fishing fun for thousands of anglers every year, and attract large numbers of boat anglers. The big waters are well suited to the practice of trolling artificial lures behind boats, a method of fishing that is easy and relaxing for the whole family.

The highest mountains in Australia provide the run-off for the streams and rivers of this region. Rivers such as the Thredbo and the Eucumbene are swift and cold and they feed the huge, cool Jindabyne and Eucumbene lakes. There are other smaller dams, built as part of the Snowy Mountains Hydro Scheme, such as Tantangara, Island Bend and Talbingo, and these waters, too, often produce exciting trout fishing. On the Monaro plateau the rivers and creeks are more sedate, and the Murrumbidgee, Maclaughlin, Kybeyan and Numeralla rivers, and the Rock Flat, Bobundara, Kydra and Cambalong creeks, meander along in a series of weedy pools.

Trout are the main quarry for anglers in the region and the two main species present are browns and rainbows. The rainbow trout is an important contributor to the impoundment fisheries and the brown is the blue-ribbon target of the fly fisher in the streams. The flowing waters offer a wide range of fishing options, with the large gravel-bottomed rivers favouring spin and fly fishing amidst rugged mountain scenery, the high plains streams catering for the true fly enthusiast, and the headwaters of the eastern-flowing creeks offering a pleasant diversion for the casual spin fisher. Atlantic salmon are also found in Lake Jindabyne and brook trout are a rare catch in Lake Jindabyne and other waters.

The western slopes hold good native populations and the Murray crayfish is a tasty catch from the Murrumbidgee River.

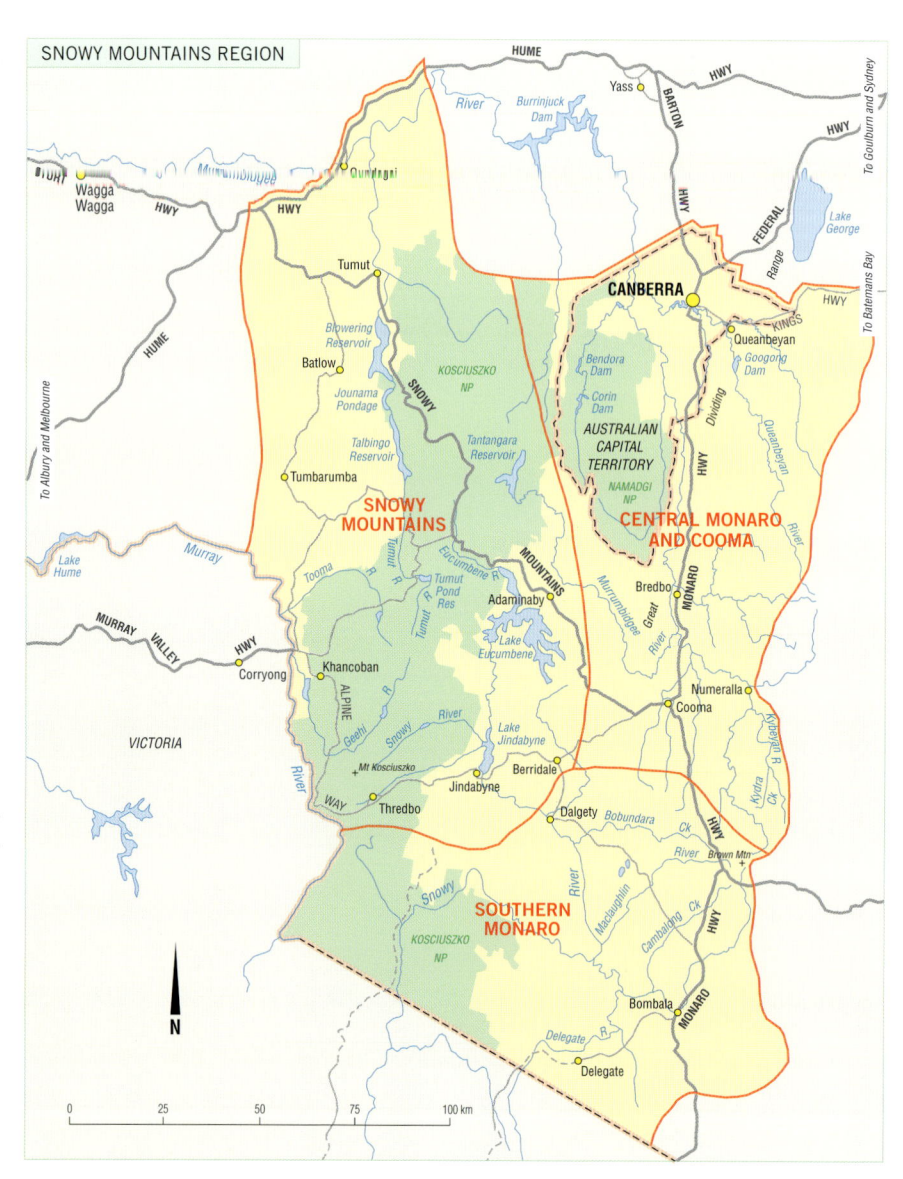

The lakes and ponds of the Snowy Mountains offer great fly fishing in summer

INLAND FISHING SNOWY MOUNTAINS REGION

NEW SOUTH WALES

WHERE TO FISH

Snowy Mountains Region

CENTRAL MONARO AND COOMA • 148

This area lies between the mountains and the coastal escarpment, with the Australian Capital Territory within its western boundary. This is one of Australia's most challenging trout fisheries and the Monaro rivers offer some of the best fly fishing in the world. Many of the streams here can be affected by low summer flows.

SOUTHERN MONARO • 149

The Southern Monaro straddles a steep escarpment: to the east, the lower streams flow to the Tasman Sea and they can be marginal for trout because of high temperatures. West of Brown Mountain there are high growth-rate basalt streams that fly fishers rate highly. The fishing can be technical and difficult but to a keen devotee of the sport this only makes it more desirable. There is a small hydro lake known as Cochrane Dam at the top of Brown Mountain, however, that is well stocked with small rainbows, and this venue is suitable for beginners.

SNOWY MOUNTAINS • 150

Many of the region's rivers have been dammed to form the famous Snowy scheme, and the resultant impoundments have achieved high status as trout waters. The streams in this area are cool and fast-flowing, with gravelly bottoms and rapids. Trout are smaller than in the Monaro streams, but generally more abundant. This area is magnificent and encompasses one of the finest all-round fisheries in the country. Native fish can be caught in Blowering Reservoir and the lower Murrumbidgee River.

GUIDE TO LOCAL FISH

Atlantic salmon
carp, European
cod, Murray
crayfish, Murray
redfin
perch, golden
perch, silver
trout, brook
trout, brown
trout, rainbow

Fly fishing the Thredbo River

Special status streams

Several streams in the Snowy Mountains have been classified as 'catch and release only' or have reduced bag limits. For details contact NSW Fisheries.

Rainbow trout

The rainbow trout, native to America, can reach 10 kg, but 2-kg specimens are more likely. It is greenish in colour on its back, with red markings along its sides, which brighten in the breeding season. The underbelly is silver.

FURTHER INFORMATION

Fishing and boating NSW Fisheries has offices at 39 Bombala St, Cooma, tel. (02) 6452 3996; Gippsland St, Jindabyne, tel. (02) 6456 2115; and 89 Clarke St, Tumut, tel. (02) 6947 9028. The Waterways Authority has an office at 1/1 Buttle St, Queanbeyan, tel. (02) 6297 4985, open Thursday and Fridays.

Tourist centres 119 Sharp St, Cooma, tel. (02) 6450 1742; Canberra Visitors Centre, Northbourne Ave, Dickson (Canberra), tel. (02) 6205 0044; Snowy Region Visitor Centre, Kosciuszko Rd, Jindabyne, tel. (02) 6450 5600; National Parks and Wildlife Service, Scott St, Khancoban, tel. (02) 6076 9373; cnr Farrer Pl and Lowe St, Queanbeyan, tel. (02) 6298 0241; This 'n' That, 31 The Parade, Tumbarumba, tel. (02) 6948 3444; Old Butter Factory Tourist Complex, Adelong Rd, (Snowy Mountains Hwy), Tumut, tel. (02) 6947 1849.

NEW SOUTH WALES

INLAND FISHING SNOWY MOUNTAINS REGION

Central Monaro and Cooma

Type of fishing
dam, river

Target fish
brown trout, rainbow trout

Googong Dam catchment, south-east of Queanbeyan, is a fine fishery, with brown trout, rainbow trout, golden perch, Murray cod and the protected Macquarie perch. Redfin now make up the bulk of the catch. Trolling is the preferred method here as the banks are steep and difficult to access. Boats may be powered with electric motors or oars – petrol motors are banned.

The **Murrumbidgee River** is an excellent stream that has a good head of rainbow and brown trout, as well as small pockets of the protected trout cod. Murray cod and silver perch are also present. Popular spots include Pine Island and Casuarina Sands. In the main, the section of river that flows through this area is fished for trout. Bait drifting with natural grasshoppers is popular and there are regular evening hatches of aquatic insects to keep the fly fisher happy. Spinning for the rainbows with Celta-style lures or jigs also works well in the faster water. The majority of the fish are small, with the average being well under 1 kg, but there have been some large brown trout over 3 kg taken from this water. European carp are now seen in the lower reaches.

Small brown and rainbow trout are taken from the **Bredbo River**, but the lower reaches tend to overheat and it doesn't have a high reputation. The **Numerella River** is formed when the Kydra and the Kybeyan join and it then flows into the Murrumbidgee. Both rainbow and brown trout can be taken and small lures and flies are the best producers. The river forms long shallow pools with gravel runs between them.

Kydra Creek winds its way through thick tussock country and wooded hills, and carries brightly coloured small brown trout. The occasional fish does reach 1 kg but the stream is fished fairly hard and big ones are rare. There are good rises to mayflies and grasshoppers, and the Kydra is a delightful dry fly stream if rainfall has been reasonable.

Running through extremely fertile country, the **Kybeyan River** is sometimes almost choked up with weed. The dense weed, however, provides great cover for brown trout and plenty of food in the form of mayfly nymphs, damsel flies and caddis. The fish run up to 1.5 kg, with the odd bigger one showing up at times. Warm spring days often herald frantic action as fish jump for mayfly 'spinners'.

Another of the slow weedy creeks that often produce outsized brown trout, **Big Badja River** is predominantly a fly fishing water featuring rich weed beds crawling with insect life. Good fishing depends to a large degree on the rainfall – if the seasons have been good for a few years the Badja can fish brilliantly, but significant fish-kills during droughts often reduce the fish population.

Rock Flat Creek is a fertile stream plagued by a low water flow. In good seasons both brown and rainbow trout rise freely to mayflies and beetles. Fish can attain a good size here and some approaching 4.5 kg have been taken. The area is most suited to fly fishing. While not being a recognised water, **Cooma Creek** does have a trout population.

Near the western border of the Australian Capital Territory and within easy reach of Canberra, the **Goodradigbee River** is heavily fished, but it is possible to take brown trout and rainbows in picturesque settings. Summer fishing with grasshoppers and their imitations can be very successful.

The Molonga River can be patchy, but produces reasonable trout as well as Macquarie perch.

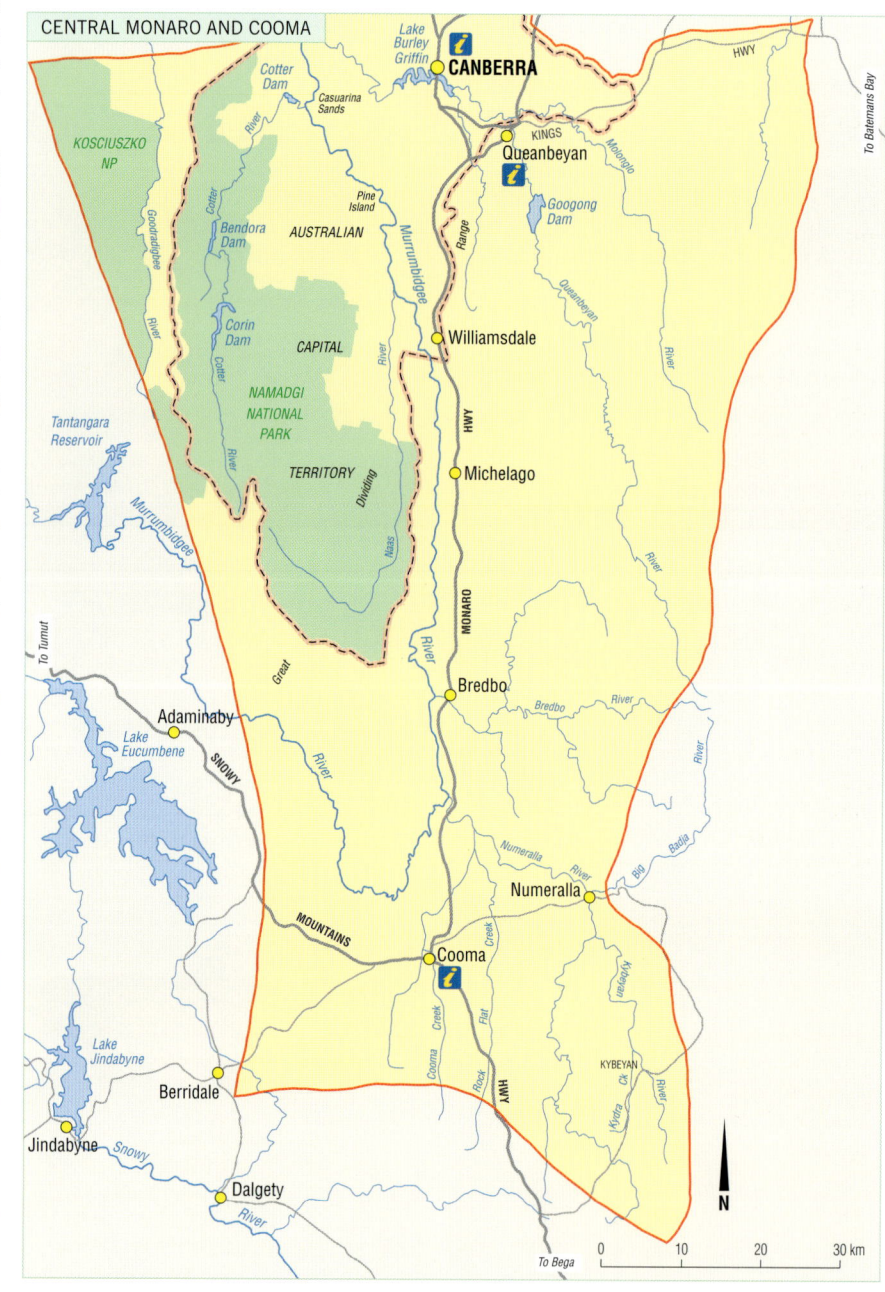

INLAND FISHING SNOWY MOUNTAINS REGION — NEW SOUTH WALES

Southern Monaro

Type of fishing
river

Target fish
brown trout, rainbow trout

This whole area is lightly populated but there is increasing fishing pressure because trout fishing is undergoing something of a boom and the Southern Monaro is recognised as a prime location. Scenically, the area is very attractive and it has enormous potential for ecotourism activities.

The **Maclaughlin River** is affectionately known as the 'Mac' and is a prominent attraction. It is a stream made up of shallow stony runs and long still pools. It produces brown trout with an average weight of around 1 kg and occasional specimens over 3 kg. Fly fishing is the most successful method. Small nymphs and dry flies are recommended here. Public access points are few but landowners will generally allow entry to responsible anglers prepared to seek permission.

Cambalong Creek has a mixed population of brown and rainbow trout in its deep still pools – best fished with nymphs and small dries as well as small bladed lures. Some of the rainbows can reach significant size. Often affected by dry conditions, the **Bombala River** is slow and weedy and has a reasonable population of brown trout. Fly fishers often do well on ant patterns as much of the river has timbered banks.

The **Coolumbooka River** suffers from a small catchment area and is in an unreliable rainfall pocket. Shallow areas allow the river to heat up quickly and it only holds quantities of reasonable-sized fish in wet seasons. A marginal brown trout water with fish up to 1 kg in high rainfall years, **Saucy Creek** can have a heavy weed growth problem.

Only a short section of the **Little Plains River** flows through New South Wales before it runs into the Delegate, but it maintains a good head of smaller brown trout that rise freely to grasshopper-pattern flies and take small lures.

The **Delegate River** rises in Victoria, in high rainfall country, so it fishes well when other rivers in the southern Monaro are drought-affected. Early morning and especially evening hatches of mayflies can be spectacular. Tiger snakes abound in the marshy areas above Delegate township.

Fishing in the **Snowy River** has suffered from a restricted flow since the Jindabyne dam was completed, but in wet seasons there are brown trout in the section from the junction with Bobundara Creek to the base of the dam wall. Extensive erosion has also shallowed the river and decreased its potential as a good fishery.

In good seasons, **Bobundara Creek** produces large brown trout from its slow weedy pools. It has acquired a reputation as a tough but rewarding water for the dedicated fly fisher. Large hatches of turkey brown mayflies offer exceptional fishing in the spring if water levels have been high. Unfortunately this productive stream suffers badly in times of drought.

An angler at Bobundara Creek plays a strong Monaro brown

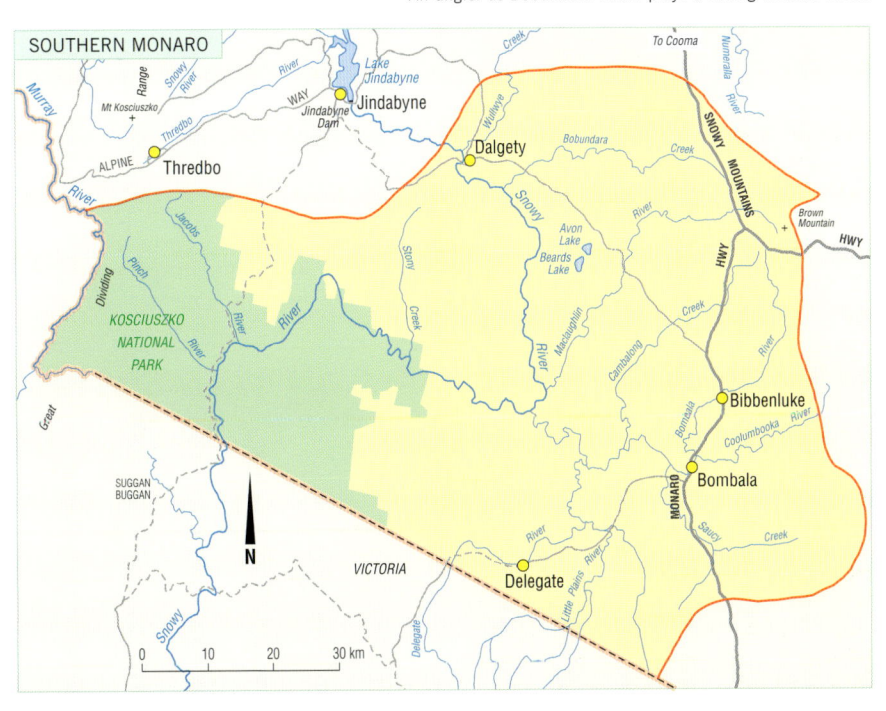

GUIDE TO LOCAL FISH

	Central Monaro and Cooma	Southern Monaro
carp, European	●	
cod, Murray	●	
redfin	●	
perch, golden	●	
perch, silver	●	
trout, brown	●	●
trout, rainbow	●	●

NEW SOUTH WALES

INLAND FISHING SNOWY MOUNTAINS REGION

Snowy Mountains

Type of fishing
dam, lake, river
Target fish
trout

The rivers draining the western side of the Snowy Mountains are snow plain waters in their upper reaches, steep and rocky in their middle reaches, grading to medium-paced with gravel beds further down. The Indi (upper Murray), Geehi, Swampy Plains and Tumut are all very good trout streams, with the last two benefiting from tailrace influence in their lower sections. The Tooma is also a reasonable river, as are the Goobarragandra, Yarrangobilly and Paddys rivers.

Blowering Reservoir has rainbow trout, brown trout and redfin, and native fish such as golden perch and Murray cod. Fishing from the bank in spring is the best way to find trout, while the natives, particularly golden perch and Murray cod, respond well to trolled lures when the water heats up in the summer. The tailrace below Blowering can produce huge trout but flows vary due to irrigation demand, while further down native fish and Murray crayfish are found.

Talbingo Reservoir is a steep-sided, crystal clear body of water, mainly suited to boat trolling for trout. Access is limited to the dam wall and at the top end known as Sue City. Redfin and the protected trout cod (must be released alive) can also be caught.

The eastern slopes are generally less precipitous than those further west. Gravel and rock bottomed streams of moderate gradient dominate. The upper Murrumbidgee and its major tributaries like

GUIDE TO LOCAL FISH

cod, Murray
crayfish, Murray
perch, golden
redfin
salmon, Atlantic
trout, brook
trout, brown
trout, rainbow

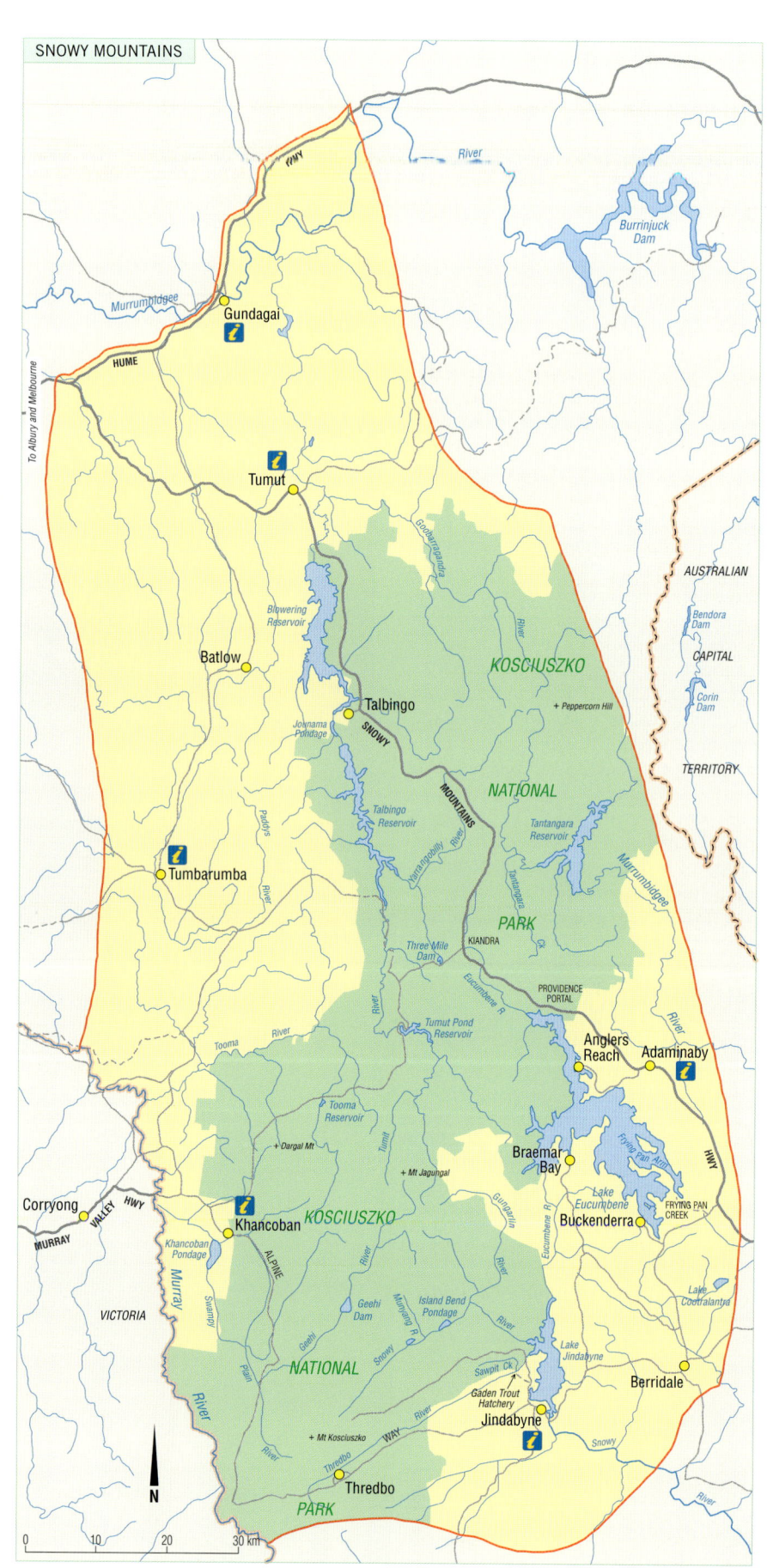

INLAND FISHING SNOWY MOUNTAINS REGION — NEW SOUTH WALES

Tantangara Creek are good trout streams, while the upper Snowy and tributaries like the Munyang and Gungarlin contain plenty of smallish trout. The Eucumbene River and Thredbo River are major spawning streams, and contain large lake fish for a period in autumn and early winter prior to their seasonal closure. The Eucumbene, in particular, continues to offer good fishing during the warmer months.

Tantangara Reservoir is one of the most exposed lakes in the area. Although subject to sudden rises and falls, this water has fair populations of both brown and rainbow trout. In spring, when the tunnel through to Lake Eucumbene is closed, the lake tends to fill fast and good fishing can be had from the bank. At other times, trolling from boats is the favoured option.

Lake Eucumbene is a huge lake where brown trout and rainbow trout are both prolific, but the rainbows are the main targets for the trollers and bait fishers that flock to its shores. Mudeyes and scrubworms are the most common baits employed here, but wood grubs and small yabbies also work well. The stealthy brown trout are a prized catch for the fly fishers who stalk the shores, and large fish are taken on a fairly regular basis. The average fish is likely to be around 500 g. Fish caught from Lake Eucumbene often have bright red flesh and make delicious eating.

The barren shores of **Lake Jindabyne** belie the lake's productivity. Brown trout are prolific and each year fish in the old-fashioned double-figure (pounds) are landed. There are also plenty of rainbows in the lake, and they grow fat on a diet of midges, caddis, snails and yabbies. Small but significant populations of Atlantic salmon and brook trout are also present. Bait fishing, fly fishing and trolling are all successful techniques here.

The trout in **Geehi Dam**, one of New South Wales' most remote impoundments, are generally small rainbows and browns, and they take surface food readily. The best methods are mudeyes under a bubble float, trolling, or lure casting near the river entrances. A small craft is necessary.

Rainbows and browns inhabit the scenic **Khancoban Pondage**, but the fishing does not seem to be as good as it once was. Trolling from boats is the favoured method of fishing this water. Other quality waters such as Three Mile Dam, Tooma and Happy Jacks Pondage all have their devotees.

You can rely on the Pan

Hearing the mighty wallops and seeing the heavy boils of feeding fish is reason enough for many anglers to return to the Frying Pan year after year.

Frying Pan Arm on Lake Eucumbene is about the most reliable place I know to catch trout – its sheltered bays suit just about any fishing technique – and it offers easy access. An affordable lakeside caravan park offers anglers basic accommodation and boats can be launched from the park or from an old gravel road that runs straight into the lake opposite.

You can fish the 'Pan' with artificial flies or natural bait or lures cast from the shore or your boat. If you decide to try some lure trolling from a boat, the best tactics involve trolling slow Flatfish-style lures up the main arm of Frying Pan Creek in front of the park, and as far up the creek as you can comfortably run your boat. Under high water conditions the arm extends a long way up the creek, but when the lake is low your options are more limited.

If there is a wind blowing down the lake, this area is difficult to fish, so it pays to head for sheltered Muzzelwood Inlet, less than 10 minutes from the caravan park by boat. The best lures for trolling in this area include small Flatfish in Frog and Perch Scale colours, Tassie Devils in hot pink, and green and gold, Old Cobbers in No. 26 and a black and white spotted colour scheme known as Corroboree. The best trolling speed for the Flatfish is dead slow, but you can increase your speed for the Devil-style lures until your rod tip is performing a distinct nod. This indicates that the lure has achieved optimum speed and is darting around enticingly. If you go too fast the lure will spin and your rod will buckle over in a steady curve. Make sure that you set a light drag on your reel because the fish often hit hard.

The 'Pan' is a great place to fish with bait off the bank. Even the kids can get into the act here as it isn't hard to rig up a small hook and a running sinker and heave the whole thing out into the lake. The best baits to use on the bottom are scrubworms and wood grubs. If the lake is rising in the spring, plenty of scrubworms can be found around the edges of the water right in front of the park. Another successful tactic is to rig a mudeye 50 cm or so under a partly-filled clear plastic bubble float. This works particularly well early in the morning or late in the evening during the warmer months. If the action is slow you can continually cast this rig out and carefully wind it in to attract extra strikes. Substituting a wet fly for a natural mudeye can also give outstanding results. You don't need deep water to catch trout on bait, and the shallow flats directly opposite the caravan park often produce good fishing.

During the summer and autumn months the Frying Pan draws fly anglers like a magnet. When conditions are right there are spectacular hatches of caddis moths and midges, while sporadic falls of beetles and ants occur on hot thundery days. In a good year the mudeye migration is an exciting event that brings some of the big brown trout that Eucumbene is famous for into the shallows. Hearing the mighty wallops and seeing the heavy boils of feeding fish is reason enough for many anglers to return year after year.

Time seems to stand still at the park as you are lulled to sleep by the not-so-distant barking of dogs and the weird cries of peacocks. The rest of the world flies past but nothing ever changes here! Long may it be so. I guess the whole charm of one of my favourite spots is that it is just a good honest fishing spot where everyone gets to have some fun.

– Kaj Busch

NEW SOUTH WALES

Western Region

The western rivers invite a more relaxed style of fishing that often attracts repeat visits year after year. Holiday makers camping on the banks of these slow but beautiful waters will find fishing is just one of the attractions.

Type of fishing
dam, river

Target fish
catfish, golden perch, Murray cod, redfin, silver perch

The western rivers, in particularly the **Barwon**, **Bokhara** and **Culgoa** in the north, as well as the **Warrego** and **Paroo**, all hold Murray cod, golden perch, silver perch, European carp and catfish, as do the northward flowing **Bogan**, **Macquarie** and **Castlereagh**. All these rivers eventually flow into the Darling, which joins the Murray River at Wentworth, before continuing on to South Australia. In the Riverina belt, the Murray is also joined by the **Murrumbidgee**, and around Wagga Wagga, Narrandera and Hay you know you are in serious fishing country. Those with local knowledge do particularly well for goldens, cod and redfin. **Lake Albert** in Wagga provides quality angling as can **Lake Talbot** at Narrandera and **Lake Centenary** at Temora.

The **Lachlan** is the other major tributary of the Murray–Darling system. It provides the worst fishing generally and cod numbers have been seriously depleted. Carp is the main species caught and Lake Cargelligo, Lake Brewster and Lake Caval average 10 to 20 huge carp for every golden perch. **Lake Forbes** provides good native fishing.

The **Murray** itself still provides some quality fishing in spite of intensive river management. The best area is above Hume to around Tocumwal, with the area downstream of Lake Hume producing some of the largest brown trout in the State as well as good golden perch fishing.

Lake Mulwala is one of the best Murray cod fisheries in the country, and the river downstream of the Yarrawonga Weir offers some of the best river fishing for native species in the region and is one of the last strongholds of the protected trout cod.

The fishing downstream of Tocumwal is less predictable, but there is still good fishing in the **Edward** (upper reaches are good for crayfishing), **Wakool** and **Niemur rivers**. From Echuca, the fishing is fairly poor.

Up north, where the **Darling** and its tributaries flow through seemingly interminable dry plains, the drainage is typified by sluggish flows for much of the year. But when heavy rains come down from Queensland and fill them, these rivers can unleash awesome power. Fishing these rising rivers can be very productive. One of the best spots in the whole Western Region is the regulator at **Menindee Lakes**, where golden perch can congregate in large numbers. The much degraded Darling River still produces some quantities of native fish (as well as blue-green algae) and a week-long trip beyond 'the back of Bourke' is a must-do for serious freshwater fishers.

In the northern reaches of the Darling River and in other northern streams, small spangled perch can be taken. Although not a popular sportfish they play an important role as food for larger species.

When the western rivers of the vast open plains swell in flood, they spread over a huge area, filling creeks, depressions and dried billabongs, providing native fish, such as Murray cod and perch, with a brief opportunity to spawn in the warm shallows and swollen feeder creeks before the waters subside again.

These rivers can be turbid for much of the year, so local practice is usually to baitfish them, but they can be successfully lure fished too. The most effective lures are usually those that send out strong sonic pulses. In slightly less dirty water, lures with fluorescent or metallic hues can work, as can those with inbuilt rattles, or the sonic beat and visual attraction of revolving blades. Baits in the region include live yabbies, worms, bardi grubs, and big insects, like crickets and grasshoppers.

In long slow reaches of inland rivers, the only visible sign of fish-holding territory might be the top of a fallen tree sticking out of the water. Or it could be a stand of river gums, which offer tangled roots and fallen limbs underwater, and shade above it.

Bends in the stream create deeper holes on their outside curves, and creek mouths, rock bars, or any narrowing of the river bed can provide fish with convenient places to feed or rest. Actively fishing such features will prove far more productive than merely soaking a setline along just any old stretch of river.

FISHING TIP

Murray cod are not reckless fish but they are fearless. Many experienced anglers contend you need to 'wake up' these essentially lazy fish by bumping the boat or lures into the snags where they lie. Another part of that same approach is to present large, noisy lures, repeatedly, in areas of likely looking water. If you see fish on an echo sounder, or deduce from the terrain that cod are likely to be present in an area, it can pay to persevere, making repeated casts or trolling passes to goad the fish into striking.

GUIDE TO LOCAL FISH

carp, European
catfish
cod, Murray
redfin
perch, golden
perch, silver
perch, spangled
trout, brown

FURTHER INFORMATION

Fishing and boating NSW Fisheries has offices at 3/556 Macauley St, Albury, tel. (02) 6021 2954; 31 Darling St, Bourke, tel. (02) 6872 2481; and 360 Whitelock St, Deniliquin, tel. (03) 5881 6036. The Waterways Authority has offices at 440 Swift St, Albury, tel. (02) 6021 7188; 159A Eighth St, Mildura, tel. (03) 5023 4610; and 104/110 Banna Ave, Griffith, tel. (02) 6964 0417.

Tourist centres cnr Blende St and Bromide St, Broken Hill, tel. (08) 8087 6077; Railway Station, Hovell St, Cootamundra, tel. (02) 6942 4212; 88 Sanger St, Corowa, tel. (02) 6033 3221; Peppin Heritage Centre, George St, Deniliquin, tel. (03) 5881 2878; cnr Erskine St and Macquarie St, Dubbo, tel. (02) 6884 1422; cnr Banna Ave and Jondaryan Ave, Griffith, tel. (02) 6962 4145; 407 Moppett St, Hay, tel. (02) 6993 4045; 10 Yanco Ave, Leeton, tel. (02) 6953 6481; Kelly Reserve, Newell Hwy, Parkes, tel. (02) 6862 4365; Tarcutta St, Wagga Wagga, tel. (02) 6926 9621; McCann Park, Newell Hwy, West Wyalong, tel. (02) 6972 3645; Shire Offices, Reid St, Wilcannia, tel. (02) 8091 5909; Gateway Visitor Information Centre, Lincoln Causeway, Wodonga, tel. (02) 6041 3875.

INLAND FISHING WESTERN REGION

NEW SOUTH WALES

The Darling River at Wentworth. This much degraded river still produces good quantities of native fish

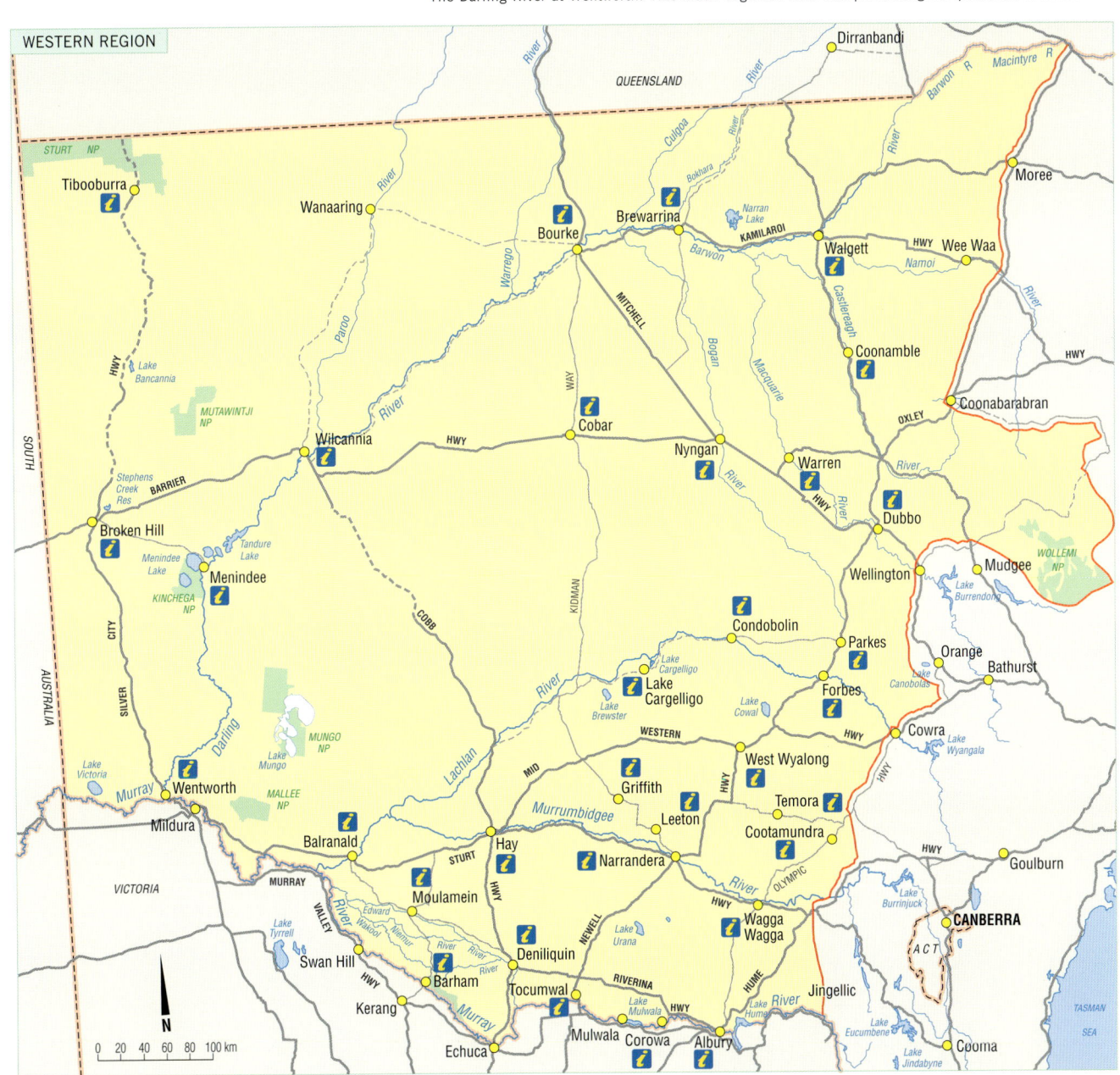

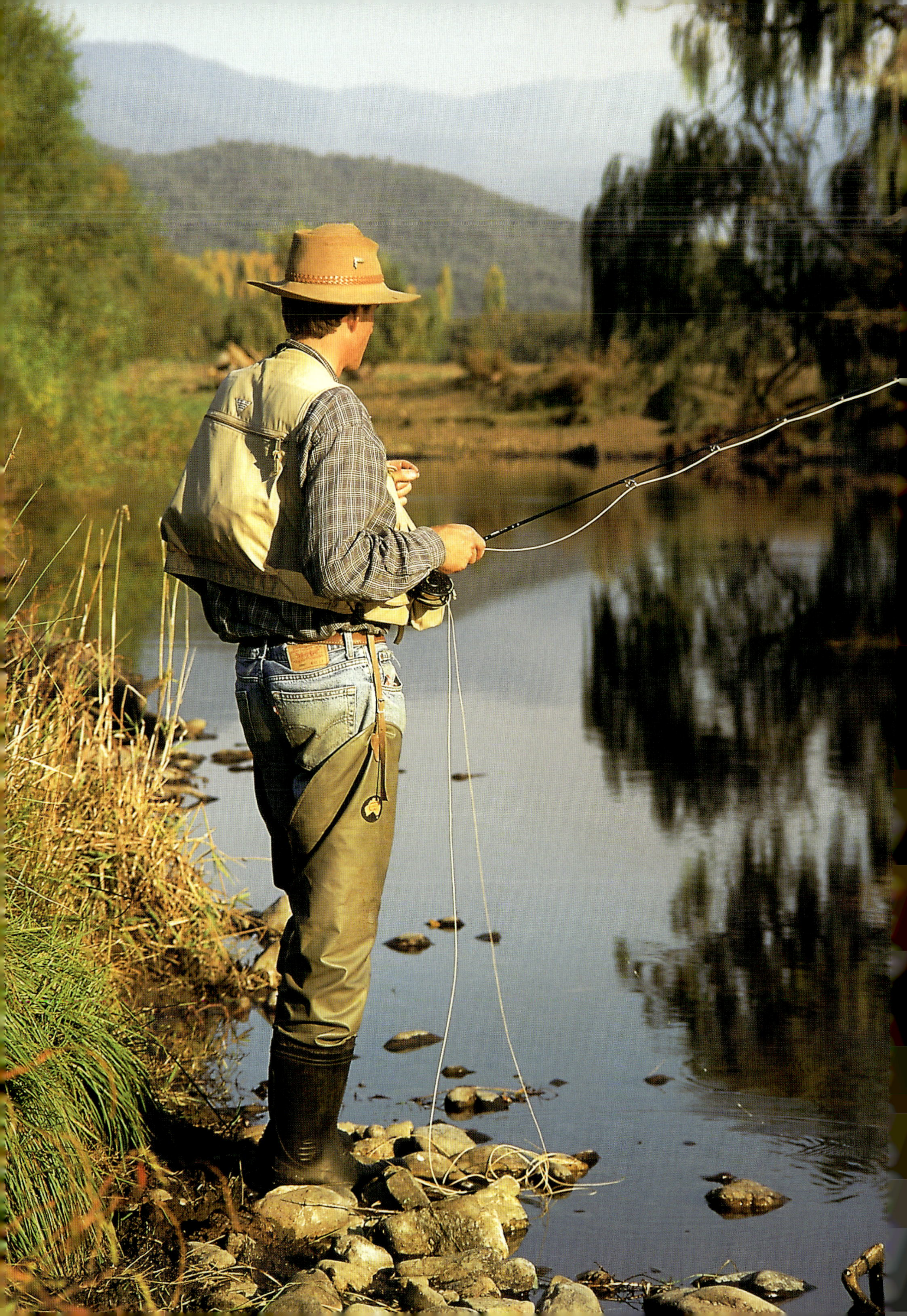

Contents

Coastal Fishing

Melbourne Region	158
Bairnsdale Region	166
Western Port Region	178
Warrnambool Region	186

Inland Fishing

Eastern Region	196
Central Region	202
Western Region	208

Victoria

There is something for every angler in Victoria. The ocean, the big bays, the estuaries and coastal rivers create a network for saltwater fishing all along the coast, and the inland rivers and lakes offer a variety of fishing for trout or native fish. Whether you prefer to fish inland or along the coast, there are plenty of good places for shore fishing, and safe waters for those who want to fish without fighting the elements.

Fly fishing the Mitta Mitta River

Ocean fishing rewards with tuna – such as southern bluefin, striped tuna, albacore and even yellowfin – shark and yellowtail kingfish. The best land-based ocean fishing is from the surf beaches, where Australian salmon, flathead, mullet, mulloway, gummy shark and tailor provide a challenge.

The large bays, Port Phillip and Western Port, provide good catches of Australia's most sought-after fish, the snapper, particularly when the fish are running from October to May. The King George whiting that inhabits Port Phillip, Western Port and the huge Corner Inlet–Port Albert system is the major prize from January to April.

Estuary fishing is best in East Gippsland, where a chain of lakes from Mallacoota to the huge Gippsland Lakes complex offers a wide range of locations. Between these lakes and Western Port are the productive and protected areas of Corner Inlet, Waratah Bay and Andersons Inlet.

Inland fishing is widely varied, with Victoria rich in streams, rivers, lakes, dams and pondages for the freshwater angler.

VICTORIA

Coastal Fishing

Whether you are sampling the variety of ocean, estuary and river fishing available along Victoria's west coast, fishing the huge estuaries of the east, or taking advantage of a city pier, you will find marine and bait suppliers, boats for hire and a wide variety of accommodation.

Fishing regulations

An all waters Recreational Fishing Licence is required to fish in Victoria, in both salt and fresh water. The licence costs $20 a year, but short-term licences are also available. The cost is $10 for a 28-day licence and $5 for a 48-hour licence. There are many exemptions including Seniors cardholders, age and invalid pensioners and children under 18 years of age. Licences are available from over 1000 outlets including Natural Resources and Environment offices and tackle shops.

Further information regarding licences can be obtained from NRE on 13 6186, or at their web site: www.nre.vic.gov.au/fisheries

NRE also produces the 'Victorian Recreational Fishing Guide', which can be obtained free where you purchase your licence. Fishing regulations in Victoria have undergone a series of changes in recent years and it is recommended that you consult the guide before planning a trip.

Marine parks

Victoria has a number of marine parks and marine reserves and has plans to introduce more in the future. The parks and reserves, and the rules regarding fishing in them, are listed in the 'Victorian Recreational Fishing Guide'.

Further information can be obtained from the department of Natural Resources and Environment on 13 6186, or at their web site: www.nre.vic.gov.au/fisheries

COASTAL FISHING

WHERE TO FISH
Along the coast

MELBOURNE REGION ● 158
The most immediate fishing water for Melbourne's anglers, this region is heavily fished over but by no means fished out. Stay close to shore for the big three – snapper, King George whiting and flathead.

BAIRNSDALE REGION ● 166
Establish a base then explore the range of fishing this region has to offer. The vast Gippsland Lakes system alone could take months, but there are equal attractions in the prolific Corner Basin area, at Mallacoota, in the big rivers, the inlets, and at Lake Tyers.

WESTERN PORT REGION ● 178
Western Port is a big expanse of water with a huge tidal flow – tricky but rewarding if you work with the tides. After Port Phillip, this is one of Victoria's best snapper grounds. There is fine beach fishing at Woolamai, Venus Bay and Waratah Bay, and good rock fishing on the ocean side of Phillip Island.

WARRNAMBOOL REGION ● 186
The Southern Ocean sweeps in upon this region's beaches and rocks, wave-cut cliffs and headlands, much of it backed by mountainous forest country – an inspiring backdrop for the pursuit of fishing. Bay and estuary fishing is more limited here than in other parts of the State but the charm of the location and quality of the catch should more than satisfy.

COASTAL FISHING   VICTORIA

Weather

A thorough understanding of the weather and how it affects an area you intend fishing is important. Watch for weather updates on television and radio news and get on line with the Bureau of Meteorology: www.bom.gov.au/weather/vic

Recreational boating licences

The Victorian Government has announced boat licensing laws will apply from the 2001–2002 boating season. The new laws are designed to increase safety awareness.

Powerboats must be registered and operators under 21 years of age will need licences for the 2001–2002 summer; remaining operators will need licences by late 2002–2003. Under the proposed regulations, anybody operating a recreational powerboat will need to be licensed.

Interstate licences will be automatically recognised in Victoria and will be valid for three years after the commencement date of licensing, and Victorian licences will be recognised interstate.

Restricted licences will be available for powerboat operators over the age of 12 and under 16 years of age. Victorian licences will be recognised interstate.

For further information regarding these and other boating and safety regulations call the Marine Board of Victoria on (03) 9655 3399.

FURTHER INFORMATION

Fishing For full details of Victoria's fishing regulations, contact Natural Resources and Environment at 8 Nicholson St, East Melbourne, tel. 136 186, or at any of its regional offices. The department produces an annual booklet, the 'Victorian Recreational Fishing Guide', which is available from its offices and at most bait and tackle shops.

Boating The Marine Board of Victoria is at Level 11, 80 Collins Street, Melbourne, tel. (03) 9655 3399. It produces a comprehensive guide to boating rules, safety, navigation signals and accident procedure, which is available from the council, its website, www.marineboard.vic.gov.au, and most marine dealers. The Water Police, tel. (03) 9534 7361, also provide advice on State boating rules.

GUIDE TO LOCAL FISH

BC	barracouta
BA	bass, Australian
B	bream
C	cod, rock
EL	elephant fish
F	flathead
FL	flounder
G	garfish
GU	gurnard
KI	kingfish, yellowtail
LJ	leatherjacket
L	ling
LU	luderick
MA	mackerel, horse
ML	marlin
MO	morwong
M	mullet, yelloweye
MU	mulloway
EP	perch, estuary
PI	pike, long-finned
SA	salmon, Australian
GS	shark, gummy
GS	shark, school
SH	shark, others
S	snapper
SN	snook
SO	sole
SW	sweep
T	tailor
TR	trevally, silver
TU	tuna
WA	warehou
W	whiting, grass
W	whiting, King George

Size and bag limits apply. Consult the 'Victorian Recreational Fishing Guide' for details.

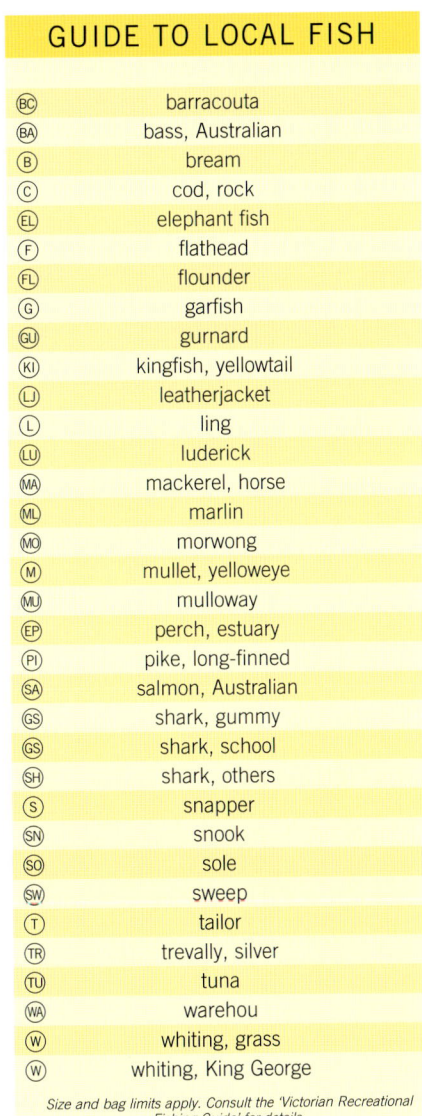

Anglers at Johanna Beach, one of the west coast's renowned surf fishing beaches

VICTORIA

Melbourne Region

Melbourne has a population of well over three million and suburbs that stretch half-way around the huge Port Phillip, but it is still possible to fish in relative peace. An hour's drive will take you to the coastal towns on either side of Port Phillip.

Snapper is the real prize in this region, respected by anglers for its appearance, fighting spirit when hooked and table qualities. While it can grow to 1.3 m and reach 20 kg, sizes in Port Phillip now only average 4 kg. Snapper come into the bay to spawn as early as September and stay until around May, and although a creature of varied habitat and appetite, it seems to favour channels and gutters, behind sand flats, around rocks or over rubble or weed.

Snapper circle Port Phillip, coming in on the east side, exiting around the west, with a lot of congregation in Corio Bay. The best time to fish is before sunrise or at sunset and then into the night. This time can be more rewarding if there is a change of tide. Snapper feed in shallow water in the morning, moving into deeper water as the day progresses. Fishing at night is rewarding, but sea lice can strip your bait quickly so make regular checks.

Weather

Southerlies and easterlies blow in winter, and summer westerly changes on hot, north wind days can be very dangerous for boating. The Bureau of Meteorology gives information on local weather: bays and coast, tel. 1900 926 110; three-day forecast, tel. 1900 926 109; country, tel. 1900 926 111. There is a special tide information line, Tide Times, tel. 1900 930 200.

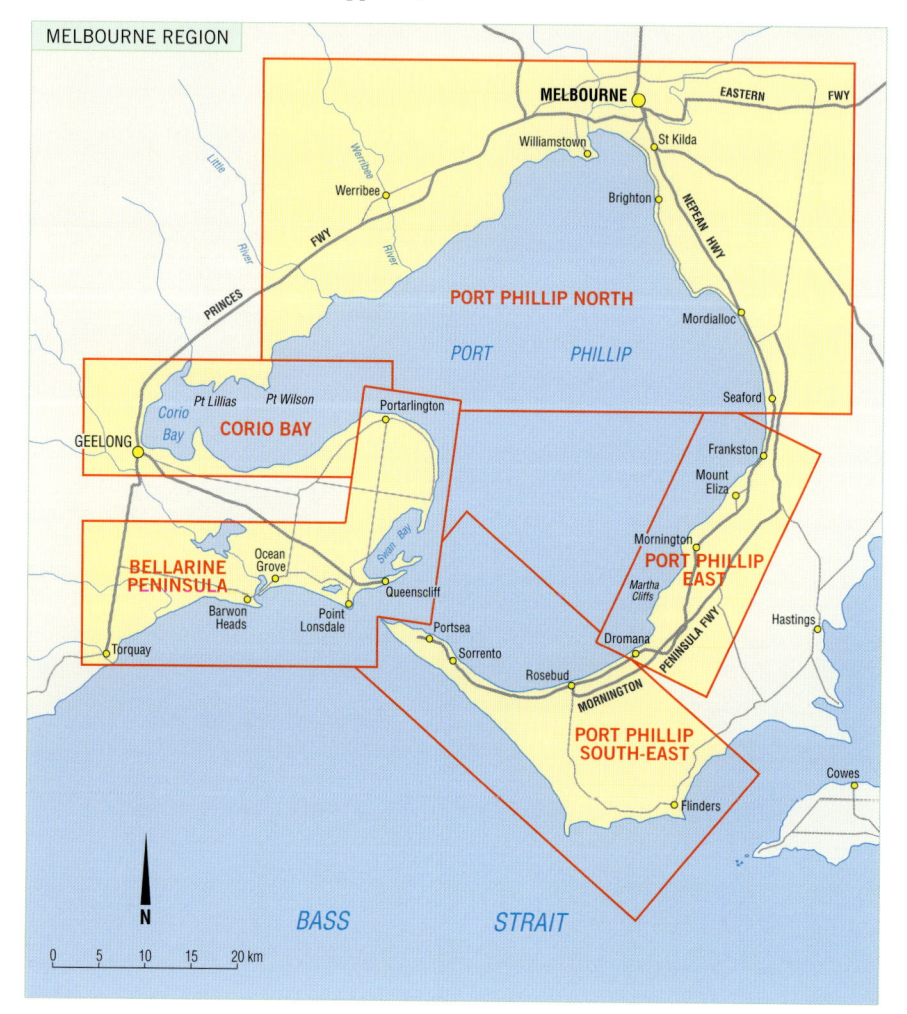

COASTAL FISHING MELBOURNE REGION

WHERE TO FISH

Melbourne Region

PORT PHILLIP SOUTH-EAST ● 160
Fish the Hovell Pile, off Rosebud, for snapper, or along the coast from Sorrento to Portsea for whiting and flathead. There's snapper here, too, and sometimes yellowtail kingfish in the South Channel.

PORT PHILLIP EAST ● 161
The long 18-metre line that extends from Mount Eliza to Mount Martha, marks the place where snapper congregate. The artificial reef in Balcombe Bay and Morrisons Fault Line are also reliable fishing spots. Try torchlight floundering in Dromana Bay. The Mornington Pier is the most productive to baitfish.

PORT PHILLIP NORTH ● 162
Whiting, snapper and flathead are the main catches in Victoria's busiest fishing water. Fish the waters of the Werribee, Yarra, Maribyrnong and Patterson rivers for bream and mullet.

CORIO BAY ● 164
Corio Bay holds fish all year round. Snapper, whiting and Australian salmon are at the head of the bay and around the shipping channel. Land anglers should try the rocks on the eastern side of Point Lillias, Limeburners Bay, North Shore rocks or St Helens.

BELLARINE PENINSULA ● 165
There are prolific whiting grounds from Portarlington to Queenscliff, and Port Phillip's biggest flathead are in Swan Bay. Pier fish at Queenscliff in summer or from the Barwon Heads bridge, and rock fish at Point Lonsdale at the change of tides.

Snapper
Snapper is the main target fish in Port Phillip Bay. It can grow to 1.3 m and reach 20 kg, but those caught in Victorian waters average 4 kg. The annual snapper run commences in spring and lasts through until late autumn.

COASTAL FISHING MELBOURNE REGION

VICTORIA

The tranquil harbour at Williamstown provides a peaceful setting for an evening's fishing

Boating

Anchoring in a **defined shipping channel** in the bays is prohibited, as is tying up to any buoy or beacon. A shallow spit off **Wedge Point** carries less than 1 m at low tide and extends 1.5 m out. There are boulders just beneath the surface at **RAAF Pier**, Point Cook, so stay 200 m from the pier. There is a reef at **Elwood Canal**, which is exposed at low tide and marked by pylons, and another between **Brighton Pier** and **Dendy Street**, which is marked by Bonnet Rock. Take care when entering **Mordialloc** or **Kananook creeks** in heavy seas at low tide, and steer clear of the shelf in front of the **Red Bluff Hotel** and the rocky ledge between **Black Rock** ramp and **Cerberus Breakwater**.

FISHING TIP

Ever wonder why boats congregate around channel beacons and old pilings? The answer is simple. Old pilings have collected all manner of vegetation and crustacean life over many years and the natural build up creates a vertical reef. Small fish come to feed on even smaller marine animals, and wherever you find small fish, you will eventually find bigger fish.

GUIDE TO LOCAL FISH

- barracouta
- bream
- flathead
- flounder
- garfish
- gurnard
- kingfish, yellowtail
- leatherjacket
- luderick
- mackerel, horse
- mullet, yelloweye
- mulloway
- pike, long-finned
- salmon, Australian
- shark, gummy/school
- shark, others
- snapper
- snook
- sweep
- tailor
- trevally, silver
- tuna
- warehou
- whiting, King George

Silver trevally

A hard fighting fish that feeds around piers and inshore reefs, silver trevally offer anglers great sport from winter through to spring. Most of the trevally caught would weigh from 400 grams to about 1kg. Trevally are attracted by berley trails and the best baits include pippis, bluebait and pilchard strips.

FURTHER INFORMATION

Fishing information There are NRE offices in East Melbourne, tel. 136 186, and Geelong, tel. (03) 5226 4667.

Visitor information Nepean Hwy, Dromana, tel. (03) 5987 3078; National Wool Museum, Moorabool St, Geelong, tel. (03) 5222 2900; Victorian Visitor Information Centre, cnr Little Collins and Swanston Sts, Melbourne, tel. 132 842, cnr Main and Elizabeth Sts, Mornington, tel. (03) 5975 1644; St Albans Way, Sorrento, tel. (03) 5984 5678; Surf World, Surf Coast Plaza, cnr Geelong and Beach Rd, Torquay, tel. (03) 5261 4219.

VICTORIA — COASTAL FISHING MELBOURNE REGION

Port Phillip South-east

Type of fishing
bay, beach, pier

Target fish
flathead, salmon, snapper, squid, whiting

From **Portsea to Sorrento**, there are whiting and flathead in the shallow inshore waters, and snapper offshore. This area is not net fished because of the tides so there are plenty of fish for the dedicated amateur. The tides are such that heavy sinkers are needed to hold bottom so use long leaders. Whiting is the target from **Portsea and Sorrento piers**.

Out from the **Portsea Pier**, and outside the anchor restriction zone, there are good spots for yellowtail kingfish. A kilometre out from Portsea Pier is a drop-off into deeper water, easily detected with a depth sounder, with big snapper and flathead, and occasionally gummy shark. The water off **Point Nepean** is also good for Australian salmon, but shore-based fishing is prohibited.

Inside the bay to the north-east there are snapper around the Hovell Pile, off **Rosebud**. Further south is Capel Sound, a deep area where flathead and snapper cruise around the rubble and reefs and whiting congregate closer to shore. A kilometre off **Blairgowrie**, Capel Sound terminates in the Shark Hole, a very reliable snapper area. The weedy holes between the South Channel Pile and South Channel Fort are good whiting grounds.

Mud Island, scheduled for marine park status, with lots of rubble, sand holes and weed, is an excellent fishing area. You can seek snapper or on a still day at low tide ground your boat on a sandbar and lure cast for whiting. There is also great fishing for flathead by drifting baits in the channels. Around Mud Island are the Pinnace, Loelia and Symonds channels, reliable for snapper.

Boating in **The Rip** must be approached with caution, especially on a run-out tide, when dangerous pressure waves can form. On the slack tide, you can drop for snapper, but the area is mainly fished for Australian salmon by trolling skirted lures. Yellowtail kingfish used to be caught here in large numbers, but the big schools of kingfish haven't returned since the late 1980s.

Outside the entrance, the Portsea to Flinders coast is a rugged combination of beach, rock and cliffs, with the strength of Bass Strait coming in behind the usual southerlies. For the surf angler, Australian salmon, mullet and flathead are the main catches from Portsea Surf Beach, Rye Ocean Beach, St Andrews and Gunnamatta.

Wild seas off the rocks at Portsea Surf Beach

GUIDE TO LOCAL FISH

		Port Phillip South-east	Port Phillip East
BC	barracouta	●	●
F	flathead	●	●
FL	flounder		●
G	garfish		●
GU	gurnard	●	
KI	kingfish, yellowtail	●	
LJ	leatherjacket	●	●
MA	mackerel, horse	●	
M	mullet, yelloweye	●	●
MU	mulloway	●	
SA	salmon, Australian	●	
GS	shark, gummy/school	●	
SH	shark, others	●	
S	snapper	●	●
SN	snook	●	
SW	sweep	●	
T	tailor	●	
W	whiting, King George	●	●

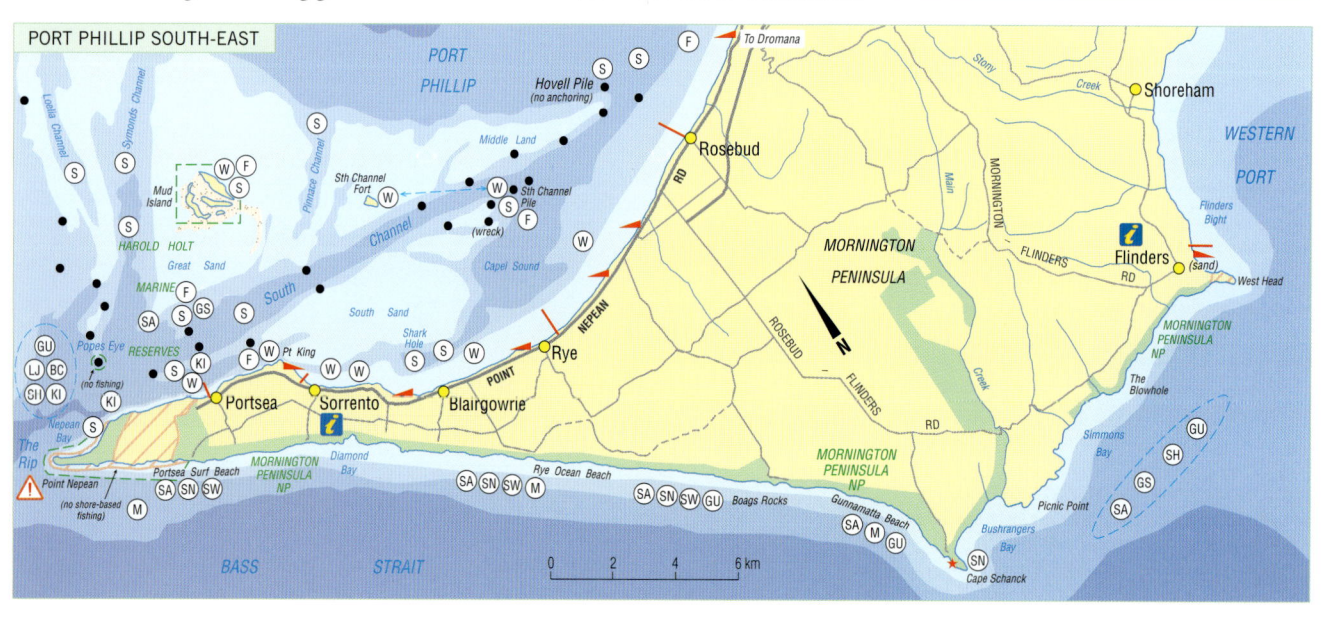

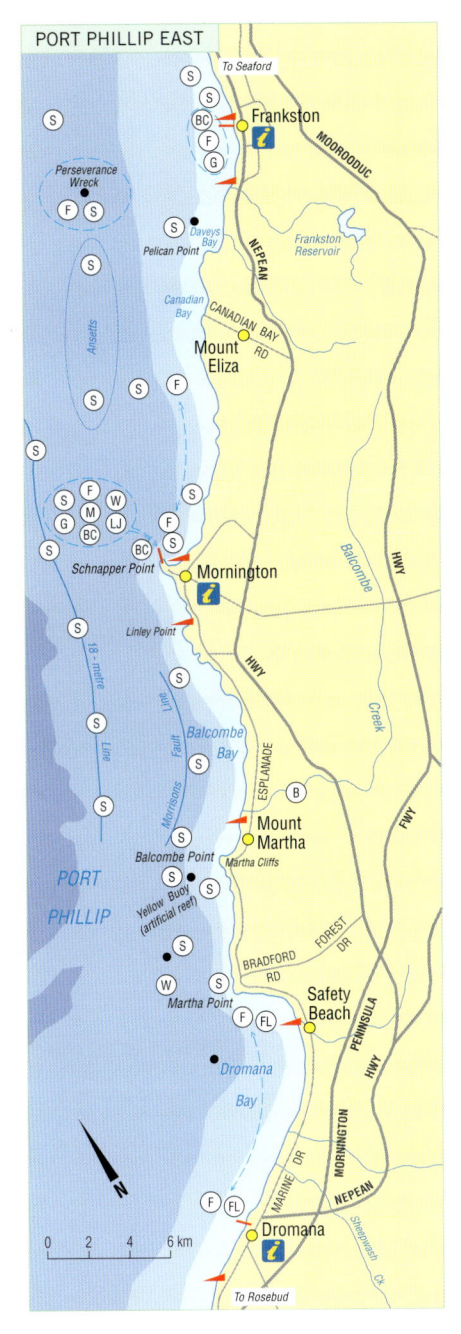

COASTAL FISHING MELBOURNE REGION   VICTORIA

Port Phillip East

Type of fishing
bay, beach, pier

Target fish
flathead, garfish, snapper, whiting

Whiting and flathead are abundant in this area, and snapper abound from October to May. The flat and shallow waters of **Dromana Bay** are good for inshore flathead, but best for torchlight flounder. The piles in the shipping channel are fishing marks. **Dromana Pier** is a focal point in the area, with flathead the target. Flounder are also a possibility in the vicinity of the pier.

Morrisons Fault Line, 2 km from Linley Point and stretching to Martha Cliffs, **Mount Martha**, is also good for snapper. A yellow buoy marks the artificial reef off Martha Cliffs.

Further towards **Frankston**, the best marks are the 18-metre Line (offshore and extending from **Mount Martha** to **Mount Eliza**), Ansetts and the *Perseverance* wreck.

Mornington Pier is one of the best piers on the bay with something always available. Flathead can be taken all year round from the deeper half of the pier, particularly in calmer weather. Snapper becomes the target when the westerlies and northerlies blow. Garfish and the occasional whiting, leatherjacket and mullet are possible catches. Barracouta are less common than they once were, but a few smaller ones can still be caught from the pier. King George whiting are a favourite during the spring and autumn.

Squid
Squid is a good, general-purpose bait, used cut or whole for a variety of saltwater fish including snapper, flathead, whiting and leatherjacket. To prepare strips, cut open, remove guts and skin, and slice the flesh.

Flathead
Flathead is one of Australia's most popular fish to eat. Anglers should watch out for the spines on either side of its head as they are the cause of one of Australia's most common fishing injuries.

King George whiting
A prized table fish, whiting is usually found in sandy shallows. It can be caught from a beach, jetty or boat.

The rocky point at Mornington provides shelter for pier anglers intent on flathead and snapper

VICTORIA
COASTAL FISHING MELBOURNE REGION

Port Phillip North

Type of fishing
bay, pier
Target fish
flathead, snapper, whiting

In the city itself, industrial pollution has abated in the **Yarra** and **Maribyrnong rivers** and they can now be fished right into the suburbs, with bream moving into the river around September and October. West of the Yarra the fishing extends to Point Wilson at the entrance to Corio Bay.

EAST OF THE YARRA

There is the chance of mulloway at the mouth of the **Yarra** and in the area out from the piers at **Port Melbourne** called 'Siberia', so named for its bleak surroundings. Here, you are also in line for the biggest snapper in the bay.

Sandridge Beach, in front of the BP station at Port Melbourne, is the only bay beach where long surf-casting rods come into play, as anglers go after the large flathead that come here to spawn in summer. There is always action, if not fish, at the areas on **Station Pier** and **Princes Pier** that are set aside for anglers, and at **Lagoon Pier** and **St Kilda Pier**. Flathead, bream, mullet, garfish and perhaps snapper are on the agenda here. At 'The Magpie', a noted spot some 900 m out from the **Kerferd Road Pier**, a black buoy signifies snapper and whiting.

The **Brighton Breakwall and Pier** are popular with land-based anglers, with whiting, flathead and small snapper the target from the end of the pier, and mullet and garfish off the middle section. At 'Outer Spuds', 3 km off **Brighton Pier**, the rubble bottom makes a haven for snapper. Garfish can be taken in the Dendy Street shallows, in north and easterly winds, using breadcrumbs as berley. The Anonyma Shoal, off Half Moon Bay at **Sandringham**, marked by a green buoy, is good for snapper, small Australian salmon, yellowtail kingfish and whiting; the Fawkner Beacon, about 5 km off the **Sandringham Breakwater**, for snapper; and the 'Aquarium Hole', about 800 m out from the clock tower at Balcombe Road, **Black Rock**, is noted for snapper but named because of the variety of fish in the area. A float is needed at **Black Rock Pier** in Half Moon Bay, as the seabed is very rocky, but there are garfish, mullet and leatherjacket, particularly in late summer.

At Quiet Corner, **Ricketts Point**, there are snapper inshore and offshore near the gas pipe. Boat anglers should also try off Table Rock, at the entrance to **Beaumaris Bay**, near the Mentone Hotel, where rough seabed areas some 300 to 400 m out attract snapper, flathead and whiting. Try for the same species in summer from the **Beaumaris Yacht Squadron Pier**, and the estuarine dwellers, bream and mullet, from **Mordialloc Pier** near Mordialloc Creek. There is snapper inshore at **Aspendale** opposite the CSIRO beacon, and around the beacon itself.

The shores of the Patterson Lakes are largely privately owned so it is best to fish from a small boat for the school salmon and prolific mullet that congregate around the entrance. The system is also one of the few bream waters around the bay.

The **Carrum Drain** and **Seaford Pier** mark two offshore snapper areas, some 2 km out. Further out from the Carrum Drain is the outer artificial reef, which is another place for snapper. The area from **Mordialloc** to **Frankston** provides summer snapper.

WEST OF THE YARRA

Land-based anglers line up at the **'Warmies'**, where warm water from the Newport power station attracts bream, mullet and tailor in large numbers, and the occasional mulloway. Bream can also be taken from the banks under the **West Gate Bridge**, as well as the odd big snapper and mulloway.

GUIDE TO LOCAL FISH

B	bream
F	flathead
G	garfish
KI	kingfish, yellowtail
LJ	leatherjacket
M	mullet, yelloweye
MU	mulloway
SA	salmon, Australian
GS	shark, gummy/school
S	snapper
T	tailor
TR	trevally, silver
W	whiting, King George

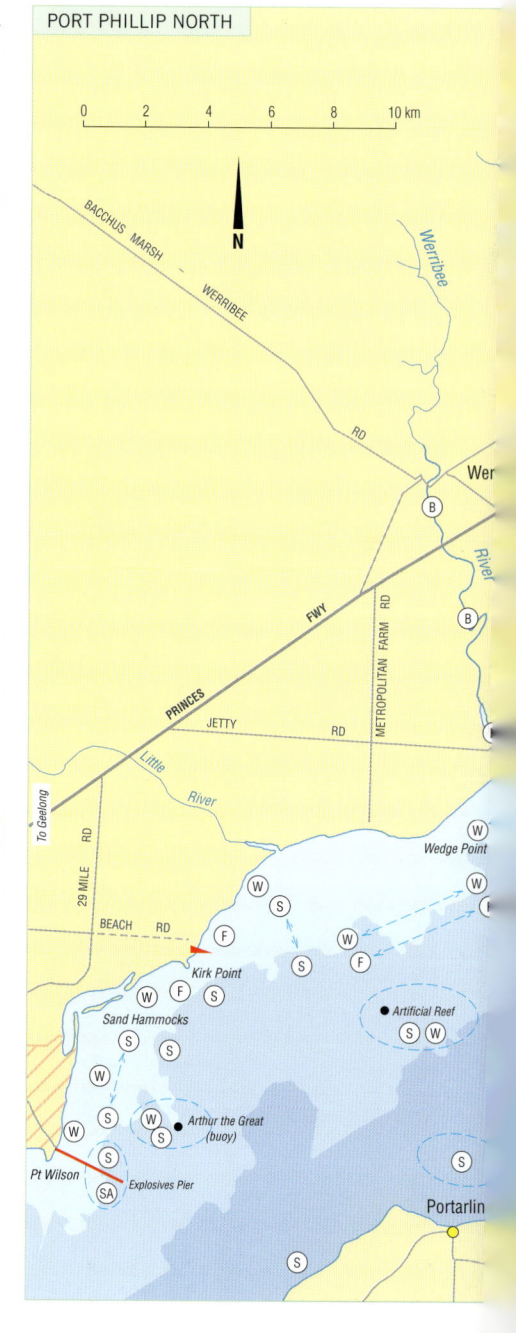

COASTAL FISHING MELBOURNE REGION

VICTORIA

A gathering of pier anglers at dawn in Port Phillip

The area around **Williamstown** is noted for big snapper up to the end of December, and school snapper into the autumn. At Gem Pier, Williamstown, you can fish in sheltered waters for bream and mullet. Off Point Gellibrand is the Gellibrand Shoal, a sometime producer of big snapper. The rocks near Breakwater Pier face into the southerly winds, which is the time to try for snapper. 'The Butts', offshore from the new Rifle Range housing estate, is known whiting and snapper water.

Offshore from the RAAF jetty at **Point Cook** there are productive whiting and snapper grounds, with more snapper in the target buoy area. Some of the bay's largest flathead inhabit this area. Around Point Cook and immediately into **Altona Bay**, whiting and flathead are generally available. The P2 buoy (yellow), which marks the gas pipeline between **Williamstown** and **Mordialloc**, is a prime snapper spot.

From the **Werribee River** to **Wedge Point** is mainly whiting territory, although there is a noted snapper mark 6 km offshore. The Werribee River, easily accessible, is a prolific bream estuary. Flathead and whiting are 2 to 3 km out from the mouth of the river. Further to the south-west, the artificial reef about 10 km off **Kirk Point** is marked with a yellow buoy. This is a reliable spot for snapper and whiting.

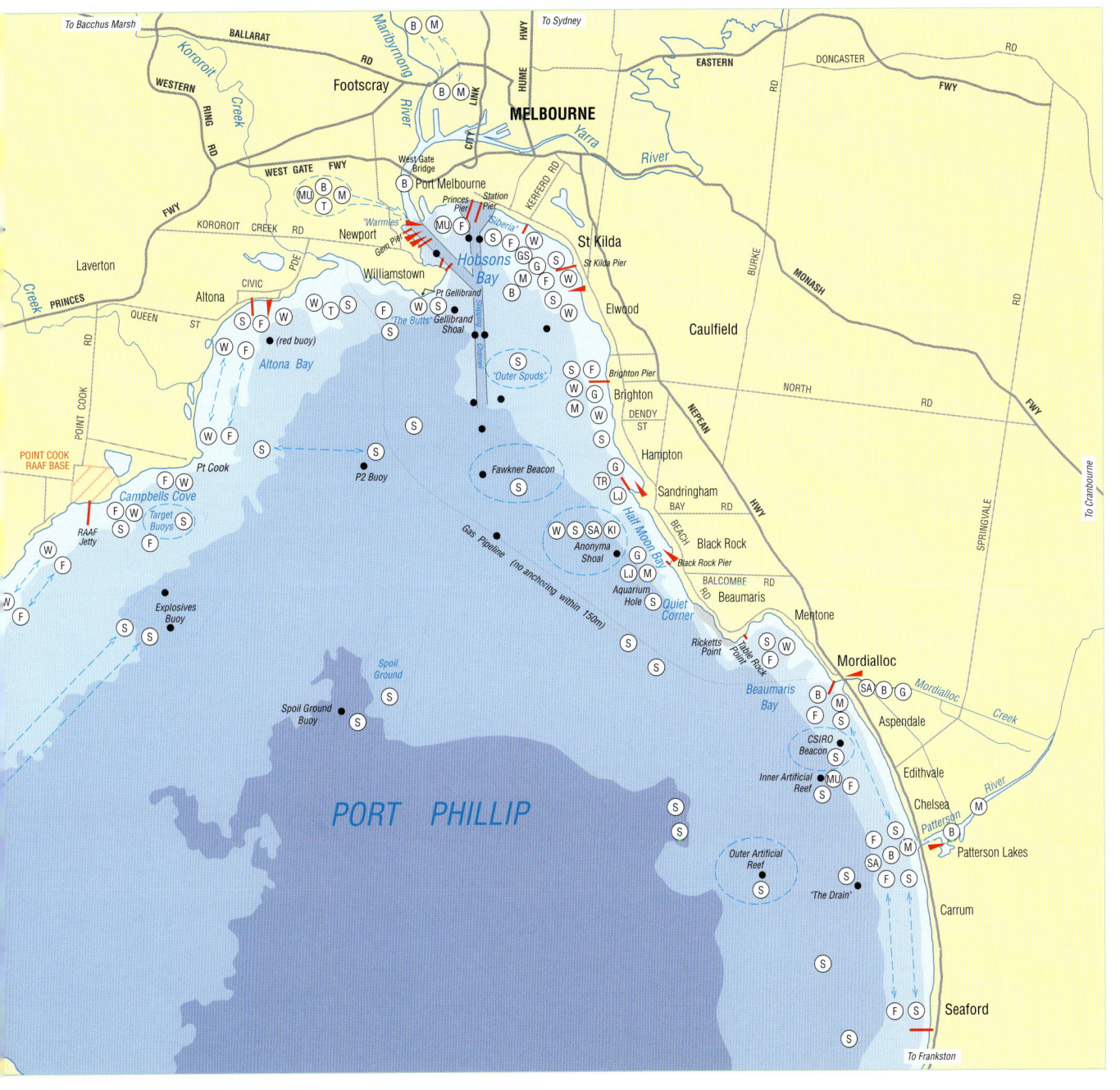

163

VICTORIA
COASTAL FISHING MELBOURNE REGION

Corio Bay

Type of fishing
bay, pier

Target fish
flathead, garfish, snapper, trevally, whiting

Corio Bay is a year-round snapper area, as a good number of this usually migratory species lodge here for the winter. The bay acts as a natural fish trap, funnelling schools of fish down towards Geelong instead of the entrance to Port Phillip.

There are often snapper, whiting and Australian salmon at the head of the bay and around the shipping channel.

The **Bellarine Bank** is a daylight snapper area. The drift along this bank to **Point Henry**, at the entrance to the inner harbour, is good for snapper and whiting, with flathead and whiting close to shore. A beacon known as 'The Chair' marks a snapper spot on this south side of the channel, and schools move through the area and through Corvette Hole on the north side of the channel.

Limeburners Bay, near the Geelong Grammar School, is known for its big snapper in the winter and spring, as well as mullet, flathead, bream and flounder. Whiting grounds from **Avalon** to **Point Wilson** are interspersed with snapper spots around **Point Lillias** and the wreck of the *Anneaura*.

At the long **Explosives Pier**, you can troll for surface salmon or fish the bottom for snapper. Around the point is the Arthur the Great buoy and sandspit, a great fishing spot, particularly in autumn and winter with whiting on the banks and snapper in deeper water.

There are a number of good places for land anglers. The rocks on the eastern side of **Point Lillias** are good for snapper while there are whiting, trevally, bream and snapper from the rocks along the north shore. In Geelong, **Rippleside Jetty** produces garfish and whiting, while the retaining wall between the **Western Beach** boatsheds and **Cunningham Pier** has snapper, flathead, bream and whiting.

A good snapper catch in Corio Bay

GUIDE TO LOCAL FISH

	Corio Bay	Portarlington to Point Lonsdale	Ocean Grove to Torquay
(BC) barracouta		●	●
(B) bream	●	●	●
(F) flathead	●	●	●
(FL) flounder	●	●	
(G) garfish	●	●	●
(GU) gurnard			●
(KI) kingfish, yellowtail	●	●	●
(LJ) leatherjacket		●	
(LU) luderick			●
(M) mullet, yelloweye	●	●	●
(MU) mulloway			●
(PI) pike, long-finned		●	●
(SA) salmon, Australian	●	●	●
(GS) shark, gummy/school	●	●	●
(SH) shark, others	●	●	
(S) snapper	●	●	●
(SN) snook		●	●
(SW) sweep		●	●
(T) tailor	●		
(TR) trevally, silver	●	●	●
(TU) tuna			●
(W) whiting, King George	●	●	●

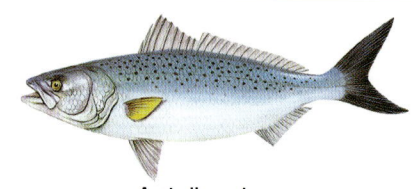

Australian salmon
Australian salmon are found generally in southeastern waters, and are popular with anglers for their sporting prowess.

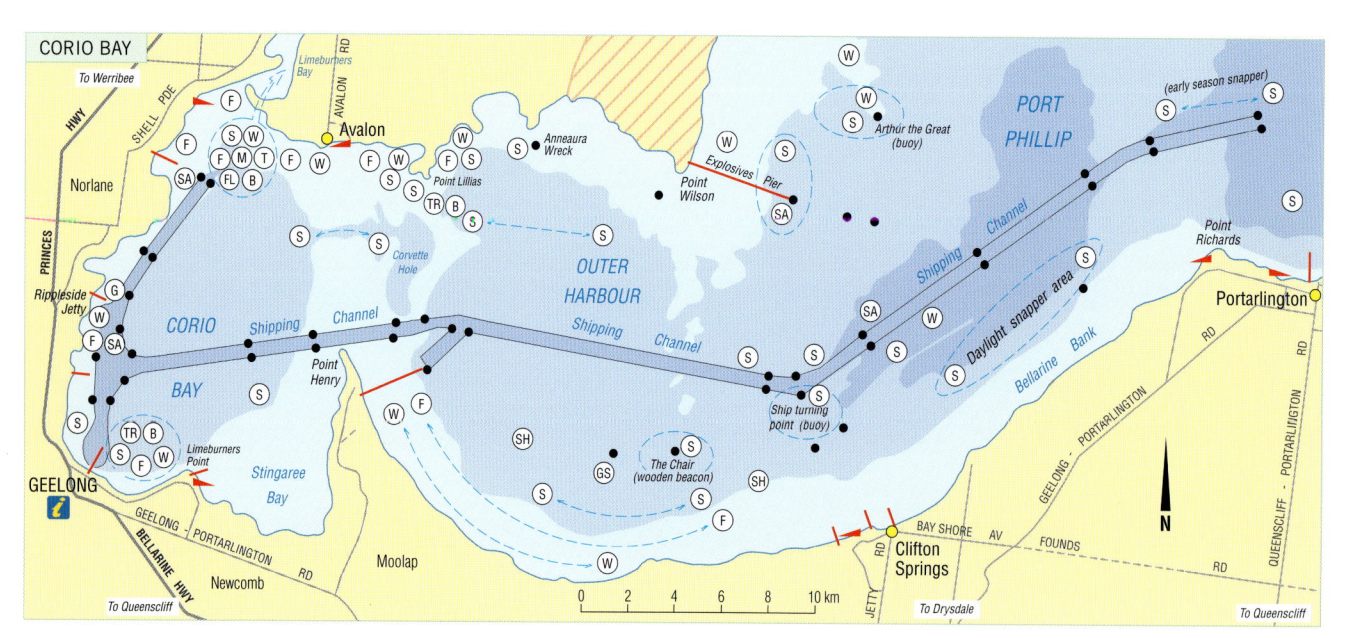

COASTAL FISHING MELBOURNE REGION

VICTORIA

Bellarine Peninsula

Type of fishing
bay, beach, pier

Target fish
flathead, snapper, whiting

The peninsula provides a wide variety of fishing. Fish from any of the numerous piers along the coast, in the sheltered bays, or there is good beach fishing from Barwon Heads to Torquay.

PORTARLINGTON TO POINT LONSDALE

Try the **Portarlington Pier** in rough weather for snapper, or for garfish, whiting and flathead in summer, but move to the nearby **St Leonards Pier** for a more likely summer catch of snapper, squid and whiting.

Prince George Light, about 4 km from **Grassy Point**, is the first snapper mark. Fish the banks west and south-west for whiting.

There are whiting grounds from **Portarlington** all the way to **Queenscliff**. Drift in Swan Bay for Port Phillip's yank flathead, especially around Edwards Point and Duck Island. Catch trevally and whiting in the harbour on a rising tide.

Pier fishing at **Queenscliff** is best in summer. Coles Channel light on the Swan Island Point is noted for its gummy shark; Bell Reef, at Shortland Bluff at Queenscliff, is a great haunt for trevally and Australian salmon; and Lonsdale Bay has whiting, trevally and snapper, and trolling for yellowtail kingfish.

Point Lonsdale has rock fishing at change of tides, although anglers are warned about the strong and dangerous currents. Mullet, Australian salmon, barracouta and the occasional whiting can be caught from the pier, which is a favourite spot for land-based shark fishing.

OCEAN GROVE TO TORQUAY

At Ocean Grove there is surf fishing for snapper, mulloway and gummy shark. In summer, join the continuous line of anglers on the bridge linking **Ocean Grove** to **Barwon Heads**; on **Fishermens Jetty**, closer to the Barwon River entrance; or on the **Ozone Jetty**, upstream from the bridge. The tidal current and weed can make fishing difficult, but when the water clears there is a good chance of catching bream, luderick, salmon and trevally, with mulloway as the big prize. At **Torquay** there is more snapper, and whiting near the ramp.

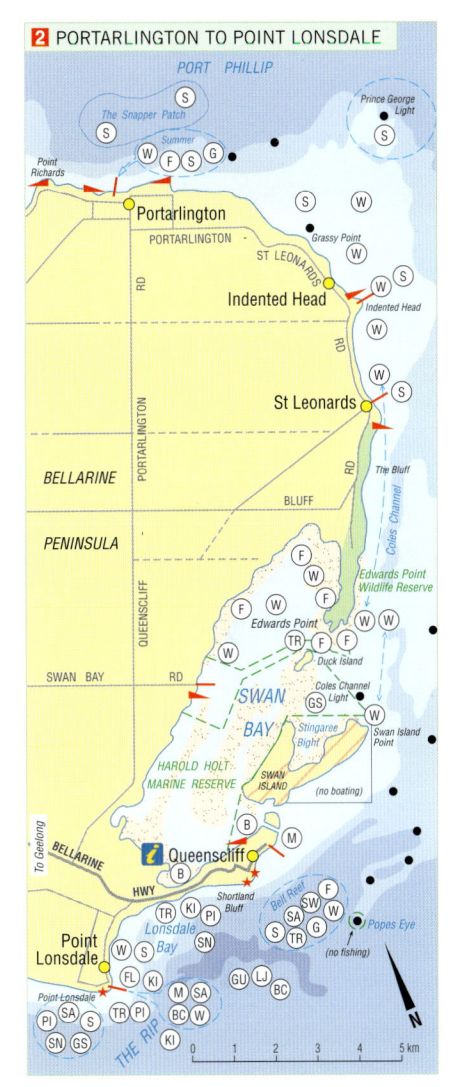

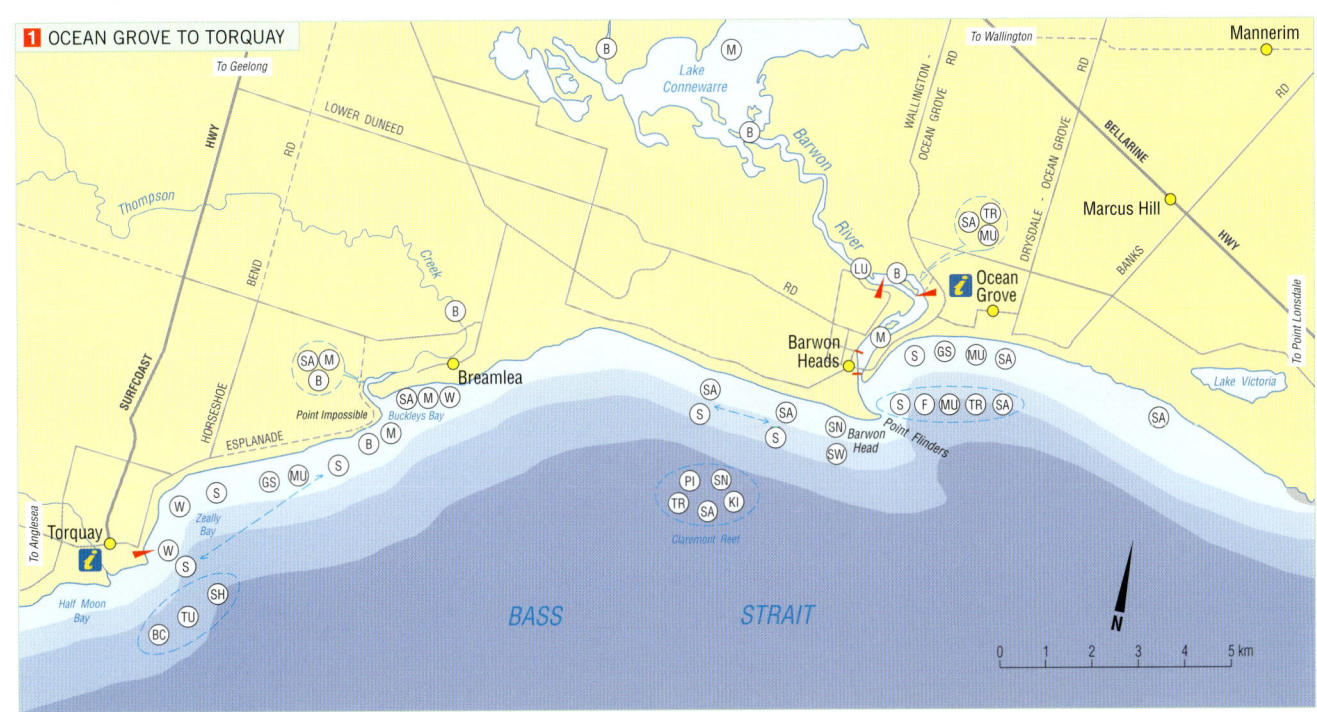

VICTORIA

COASTAL FISHING BAIRNSDALE REGION

Bairnsdale Region

Fishing is a big part of the holiday attraction of the East Gippsland region. The vast Gippsland Lakes system could occupy anglers for months, but there are equal attractions in the prolific Corner Inlet area, at Mallacoota, in the big rivers, in the Wingan, Tamboon and Sydenham inlets, in Lake Tyers and around the coastal town of Marlo.

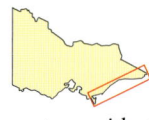

The towns on the Gippsland Lakes – Lakes Entrance, Metung, Paynesville and Loch Sport – are fishing centres, with plenty of advice available from the locals, boats for hire and well-tested shore fishing spots.

In particular, watch for the snapper in the Snake and Midge channels near Port Albert during November, the superb bream fishing after heavy rain in the Nicholson, Mitchell and Tambo rivers, which run into Lake King; and McLoughlins Beach near Port Albert, which is regarded as one of the best snapper fishing areas in the State.

A popular way to fish the Tambo River estuary for bream is to tie your boat up to the bank

WHERE TO FISH

Bairnsdale Region

MALLACOOTA ● 168
The mecca for many anglers, Mallacoota inlet is more sheltered than the Gippsland Lakes and a few degrees warmer. There is estuary and river fishing and surf beach access. Fish from boat or shore for bream, flathead, whiting and mulloway.

TAMBOON AND BEMM RIVER ● 170
There is both estuary and river fishing at the isolated Tamboon Inlet and good boating if approached with care. Try for bream, flathead, whiting, trevally and snapper. The Sydenham Inlet is famous for its bream fishing, and the Bemm River provide bass, estuary perch and the odd brown trout.

MARLO AND LAKE TYERS ● 171
From the quiet fishing town of Marlo, there is access to estuary and river fishing, with surf fishing as a further option. There are plenty of bream, flathead, whiting, mulloway and bass.

GIPPSLAND LAKES EAST ● 172
Lakes Entrance is the focus for this magnificent stretch of fishing water. There are large numbers of bream, tailor, flathead, whiting and mullet in Lake King.

LAKE VICTORIA ● 174
Mullet and bream are the main species in the McMillan Strait. Lake Victoria has good land angling for mullet and bream from the jetty at Loch Sport during the day, tailor for lure casters, and flounder for those with a light and spear in the evenings. Try McLennan Strait for big bream, flathead, estuary perch, luderick and mulloway.

PORT ALBERT ● 176
Port Albert is famous for catches of big snapper from October to March, with good whiting after Christmas. Flathead are always present. There is great offshore fishing, with resident schools of yellowtail kingfish, a big population of snook, occasional southern bluefin and striped tuna and more snapper.

CORNER INLET ● 177
This vast tidal lagoon with a huge variety of fish can be very rewarding. Your catch could include flathead, whiting, mullet, trevally, gummy shark, snapper, pike, barracuta, Australian salmon and flounder.

GUIDE TO LOCAL FISH

- barracouta
- bass, Australian
- bream
- flathead
- flounder
- garfish
- gurnard
- kingfish, yellowtail
- luderick
- marlin
- mullet, yelloweye
- mulloway
- perch, estuary
- pike, long-finned
- salmon, Australian
- shark, gummy/school
- shark, others
- snapper
- snook
- sweep
- tailor
- trevally, silver
- trout, brown
- tuna
- whiting, King George

Black bream
An estuarine species, bream are also found in large congregations in the Gippsland Lakes. They can be finicky feeders and are best sought using local baits including prawns, shell, shrimp, crab and sandworms.

BAIRNSDALE REGION

COASTAL FISHING BAIRNSDALE REGION

VICTORIA

Fishing off the rocks in the Croajingolong National Park near Mallacoota

Weather

Most inshore areas are comparatively sheltered, but are subject to strong southerlies, particularly in winter, and strong northerlies in summer. There are potentially rough seas offshore and on exposed coasts all year. Summer conditions are subject to sudden changes, particularly on hot days with northerly winds. Weather reports are issued by the Coast Guard, Loch Sport (VH3 LAG) and Paynesville Rescue Squad (VH3 AAR) over channel 88 first, then over channel 86, from 6.05 a.m. to 7.05 p.m.

Boating

Extreme caution should be taken in crossing the bars at **Lakes Entrance**, **Mallacoota**, **McLoughlins Beach** and **Port Albert**. Avoid crossing with an outgoing tide and an onshore wind. The passage out of **Corner Inlet** can be slow and arduous in choppy to rough seas. The exposed waters of the **Gippsland Lakes, Lake King** and **Lake Wellington** are very shallow and subject to extremely choppy seas in a wind. Boating in these conditions is very dangerous. Offshore conditions are often rough in winter and subject to violent change in summer. Inexperienced sailors are advised not to use the boat ramp at Cape Conran.

FURTHER INFORMATION

Fishing information NRE offices: 7 Service St, Bairnsdale, tel. (03) 5152 0400; off Princes Hwy, Cann River, tel. (03) 5158 2100; Main St, Foster, tel. (03) 5682 2133; 1 Bullock Island Rd, Lakes Entrance, tel. (03) 5155 1539; cnr Buckland and Allan Dr, Mallacoota, tel. (03) 5158 0219; 171 Nicholson St, Orbost, tel. (03) 5161 1222; 310 Commercial Rd, Yarram, tel. (03) 5183 9100.

Visitor information 240 Main St, Bairnsdale, tel. (03) 5152 3444; cnr The Esplanade and Marine Pde, Lakes Entrance, tel. (03) 5155 1966; cnr Buckland and Allan Dr, Mallacoota, tel. (03) 5158 0219; The Slab Hut, cnr Lochiel and Browning St, Orbost, tel. (03) 5154 2424; Paynesville Marine Services and Supplies, The Esplanade, Paynesville, tel. (03) 5156 6554; Court House, Rodger St, Yarram, tel. (03) 5182 6553.

FISHING TIP

If you are after finicky fish, consider using a solid or quiver tip rod. A selection of interchangeable tips will make the rod more adaptable to different fishing applications.

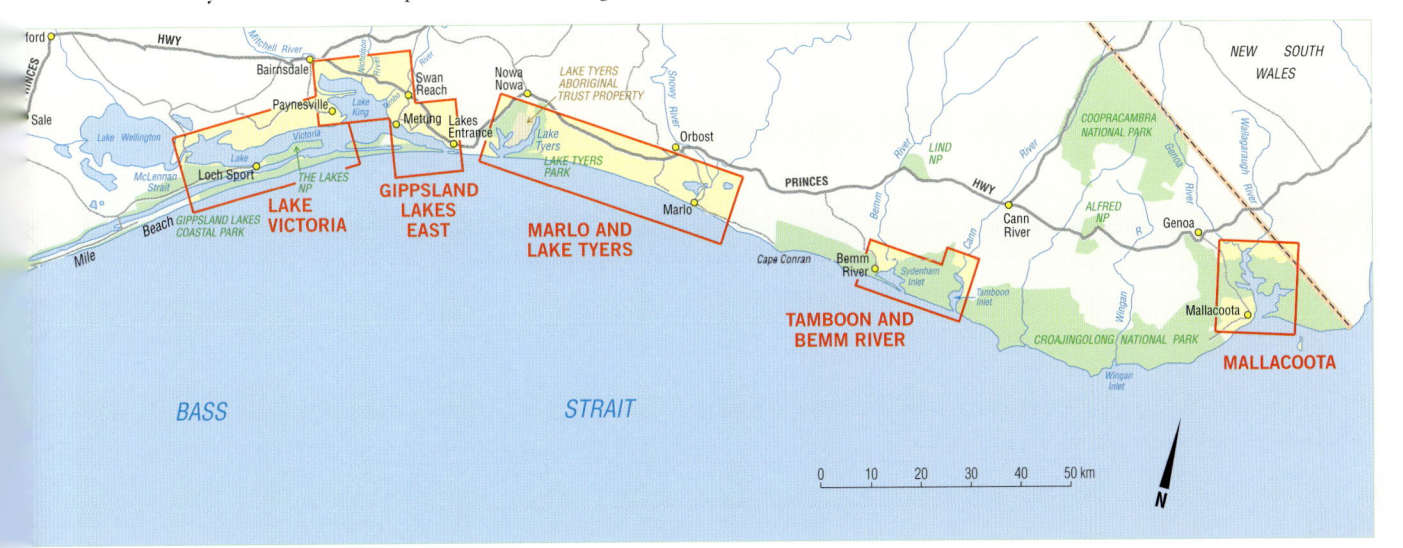

VICTORIA
COASTAL FISHING BAIRNSDALE REGION

Mallacoota

Type of fishing
beach, estuary, offshore, river

Target fish
bream, flathead, mulloway

There are five main fishing areas within the **Mallacoota inlet**: Bottom Lake, The Narrows, Top Lake and the Genoa and Wallagaraugh rivers. Beach fishing from either side of the entrance or at the mouth of the **Betka River** can yield Australian salmon and tailor. Boats, except the shark cats of the abalone divers, tend to avoid the potentially turbulent entrance.

The **Betka River** estuary is a lovely spot to fish from the banks for flathead and bream, while there are estuary perch further upstream. Best access is from the road bridge.

At **Mallacoota**, 24 km from the Princes Highway, luderick can be taken along the rocks near the boat ramp and at **Captains Point**. The navigation aid in the **Bottom Lake**, known as the John Bull Light, is a popular fishing spot for flathead, snapper and bream. Flathead are caught all over this lake; the best method is to drift in a boat and fish with small live mullet or fresh or frozen pilchards.

The far reaches of the Bottom Lake, at **Cemetery Bight**, produce flathead in the morning before the waterskiers (in summer) get going. **The Narrows**, a deep channel between the lakes, is famous for its large mulloway, active over summer and autumn. The beautiful **Double Creek Arm** has many coves and inlets, with bream and garfish just outside the weed area.

Gipsy Point, a tiny but beautiful village boasting a hotel and store, gives the best access to the upper reaches of the system. The smaller **Top Lake** has mostly bream and flathead, and it runs up to Cape Horn, a deep area where mulloway, bream and flathead abound. Schools of bream move into the **Genoa and Wallagaraugh rivers** between August and November. The large hole on the Wallagaraugh, known as the Bull Ring, yields the most prolific catches of each year, while the specialists for estuary perch and bass look further down the Wallagaraugh, in the Back Water and in the Genoa River.

The **offshore** fishing at Mallacoota is among the best in Victoria, sometimes good catches of tuna and marlin are made in summer and autumn. Other fish caught offshore include flathead, gummy sharks and snapper. Extreme caution should be exercised when passing through the entrance or launching from the ramp at Bastion Point. The rugged **Tallaberga and Gabo islands** have Australian salmon, tailor, yellowtail kingfish and gummy shark.

GUIDE TO LOCAL FISH

BA	bass, Australian
B	bream
F	flathead
G	garfish
KI	kingfish, yellowtail
LU	luderick
ML	marlin
MU	mulloway
EP	perch, estuary
SA	salmon, Australian
GS	shark, gummy
SH	shark, others
S	snapper
T	tailor
TU	tuna
W	whiting, King George

In spring and autumn, Mallacoota's climate is almost perfect and the locality exhibits some of Victoria's best fishing without the crowds

COASTAL FISHING BAIRNSDALE REGION

VICTORIA

MALLACOOTA

Tamboon and Bemm River

Type of fishing
bay, beach, estuary, river

Target fish
bass, bream, estuary perch, flathead, snapper, whiting

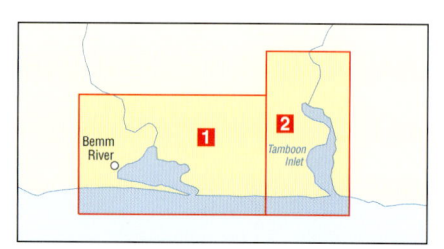

Boats are almost a necessity in East Gippsland's inlets. To fish the Tamboon Inlet, many people launch at Furnell, where a concrete boat ramp will take medium-sized boats. Keep to the eastern side of the river. The water level is low when the inlet is open to the sea and rocks create a boating hazard for the unwary. A similar situation occurs in the Sydenham Inlet. Small 'tinnies' are ideal in this waterway as they offer better access. At high tide you can launch from the boat ramp or beside the jetty.

A quiet moment at Wingan Inlet

TAMBOON INLET

Tamboon Inlet is a remote fishing and camping spot, which although offering the minimum in facilities (even drinking water needs to be brought in) has excellent fishing. **Peach Tree Creek**, south of Furnell, is another popular camping spot. Boat-based camping around the inlet is also available. Along the western side there are long stretches of sandy beach, and bait fishing at night will produce flathead and bream. A channel runs down the eastern side of the inlet to the entrance, and the most effective way to take fish during the day is to anchor off the channel and try for flathead and bream, with the possibility of whiting, snapper and silver trevally. Estuary perch are keenly sought by lure fishers.

GUIDE TO LOCAL FISH

	Tamboon Inlet	Bemm River	Lake Tyers Marlo
(BA) bass, Australian		●	● ●
(B) bream	●	●	● ●
(F) flathead	●	●	● ●
(G) garfish			● ●
(LU) luderick	●	●	
(M) mullet, yelloweye	●	●	● ●
(MU) mulloway		●	
(EP) perch, estuary	●	●	●
(SA) salmon, Australian	●	●	●
(GS) shark, gummy/school	●	●	
(S) snapper	●		●
(SW) sweep		●	●
(T) tailor	●	●	●
(TR) trevally, silver	●	●	
(BT) trout, brown		●	
(W) whiting, King George	●	●	

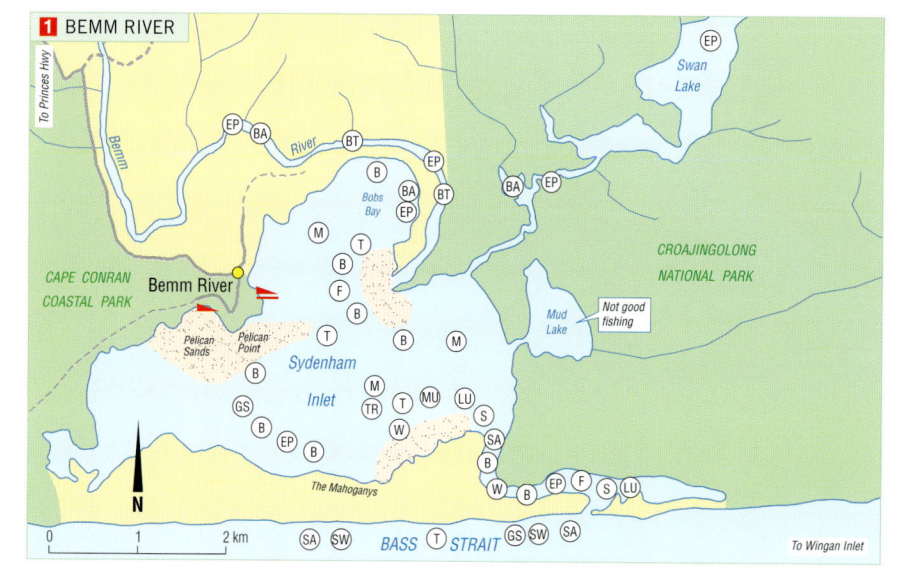

BEMM RIVER

This area is noted for its beautiful coastal scenery and regarded by many as Victoria's premier estuary. Try for bass and estuary perch in the **Bemm River**, and from the Sydenham Inlet bank in the spawning season of October and November. Large flathead and bream are abundant at the mouth of the river. Other popular spots for bream are **Bobs Bay**, **The Mahoganys**, **Pelican Point** and the channel with fresh prawn and sandworm by far the best baits.

Near the inlet entrance there are a number of rocky outcrops and substantial weed beds, with the possibility of luderick, snapper, whiting, silver trevally and bream. Sometimes tailor, Australian salmon and mulloway come in from the sea to feed on prawns, and this can create a fishing bonanza.

The surf beach at the mouth of the inlet is easily reached by pulling the boat up in the estuary and walking to the beach. A deep gutter formation runs in close to the beach. Tailor and Australian salmon are available by day, gummy shark at night.

The **Wingan Inlet** is one of the most peaceful estuaries on the coast, permanently open to the sea and with a large fish population, varied by season and water conditions. Access is from the Princes Highway, 24 km east of Cann River.

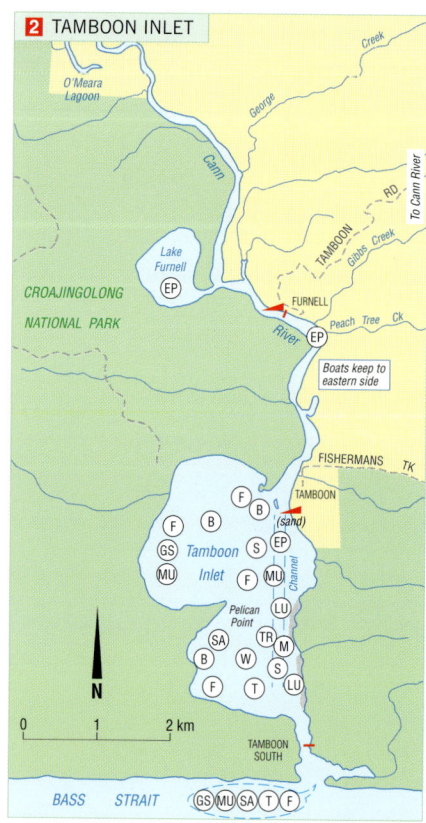

COASTAL FISHING BAIRNSDALE REGION

VICTORIA

Marlo and Lake Tyers

Type of fishing
beach, estuary, jetty, river

Target fish
bass, bream, estuary perch, flathead, luderick

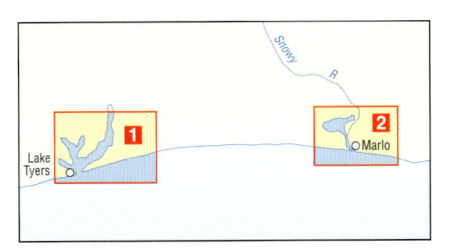

Marlo, a quiet fishing town is the jumping-off point for an adventure in estuary and river fishing, with beach fishing another option, while further west, the fishing in **Lake Tyers** is comparable to that of any Victorian estuary.

MARLO

The Snowy River joins the **Brodribb River** to bring a body of water down to **Lake Corringle** and through a sheltered arm to the sea entrance. The Brodribb River is also fed by **Cabbage Tree Creek**, a peaceful coastal waterway. There are launching ramps at Marlo and near the Marlo Road on the Brodribb River. The Marlo ramp is near an L-shaped jetty, where shore-based anglers have a good chance at bream, estuary perch, flathead and mullet.

Anglers with boats have ample scope in both the inlet and adjacent estuaries for bream, estuary perch and luderick. Fallen timber and rocks create havens for estuary perch and bass. Big flathead are present in the shallow water areas towards the mouth of the inlet and in **Frenchs Narrows**. Prawns are abundant in the inlet in summer and autumn and are prized for bait. Surf fishing near the river mouth is popular at night for mulloway, and productive during the day for flathead and Australian salmon.

Cape Conran, 19 km east of Marlo, is a popular beach fishing spot, with plenty of flathead, Australian salmon, tailor and gummy shark. There is a concrete boat ramp at West Cape, but be sure to check the weather conditions before launching into Bass Strait. When it is too windy offshore or on the beach, the nearby **Yeerung Estuary** offers bream, mullet, trevally and estuary perch.

LAKE TYERS

Lake Tyers has the advantage of good boating water over the whole lake system, as the entrance is seldom open to the sea and the depths remain fairly constant. There are several caravan parks in the town, and flats, houseboats and fishing boats available for hire.

The lake is an extensive estuary system broken up into three sections: the lake itself; the **Toorloo and Blackfellows arms**; and the long arm that goes to the township of Nowa Nowa, on the Princes Highway. This **Nowa Nowa Arm** is generally the most popular fishing area, as it has deeper water. The stretch between **Gordon Bight** and **Big Bight** is 7 m deep in places, and contains bream, tailor, mullet, flathead and garfish. Further upstream, at **Devils Hole** and **Florence Bay**, the water is home to giant flathead, luderick and bream.

In the main lake, west of the **Mud Islands**, there is good trolling for tailor and a chance of flathead. **Fishermans Landing Arm** is noted for flathead, bream and garfish. When the lake entrance is closed, the lower lake has garfish, mullet, tailor and the odd luderick. The jetty is the most productive spot and best fished at dawn or dusk. The **Toorloo Arm**, particularly upstream towards Burnt Bridge, is very rewarding for garfish, bream and flathead. Out on **Ninety Mile Beach**, surf anglers can find Australian salmon, bream, mullet and tailor.

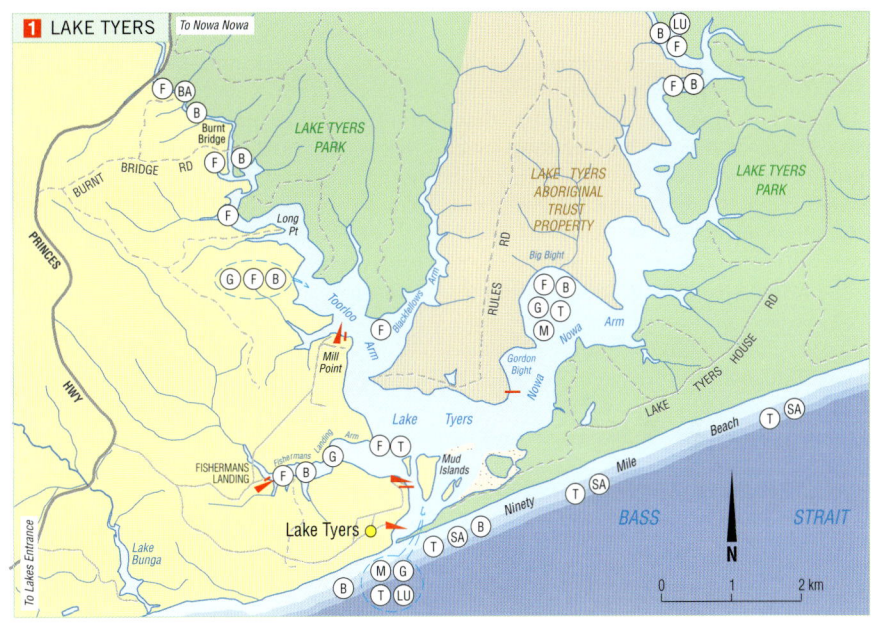

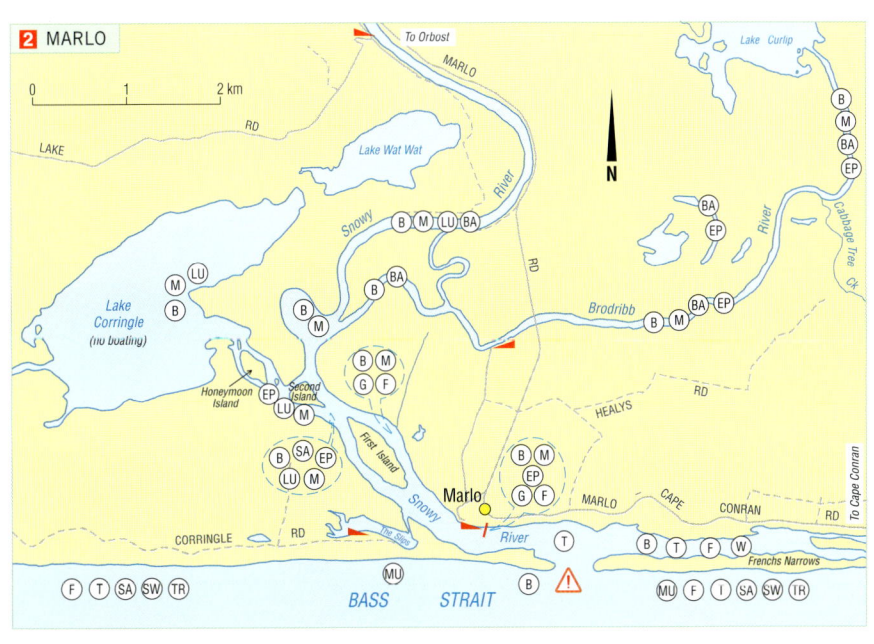

171

Gippsland Lakes East

Type of fishing
beach, estuary, jetty

Target fish
Australian salmon, bream, tailor, trevally

The township of Lakes Entrance is the focus for this magnificent stretch of fishing water, which covers an area of more than 400 sq km. It is a big holiday town, and provides good access to the lakes, and Ninety Mile Beach via a bridge across the Cunninghame Arm.

LAKES ENTRANCE TO METUNG

The entrance is the only outlet for the biggest inland water system in Australia. It can be treacherous at all times, tides and weather, but especially dangerous with an onshore wind and outgoing tide. Fishing at slack tide in the channel can, however, yield a bonanza in the season from October to April. Tailor, bream, luderick, Australian salmon, mullet and silver trevally move through here. Beware of the anchoring restrictions.

The jetties in **Cunninghame Arm** provide great fishing for children and casual anglers, with bream and mullet abounding. The eastern ocean beach section south of the Cunninghame Arm causeway has a productive gutter close to the beach, where mullet and small Australian salmon can be caught. Night anglers try here for gummy shark.

The channel below the **Bullock Island Bridge** is also very popular because of easy access, and is still good for mullet, tailor and bream. Lure casting from the light on Bullock Island produces Australian salmon and tailor, bream and luderick are also common here. There is a strong tidal flow between **Bullock and Rigby islands**, so large sinkers are required to hold baits on the lake bed in the middle of the stream. Snapper and mulloway are also present, but masses of crabs create frustration as they plunder the large fish baits.

Opposite Bullock Island on the mainland is **Jemmys Point**, easily accessible for luderick anglers. They can supplement their bait from the rocks along the Kalimna Wall. The nearby jetty at **Kalimna** offers good fishing for a variety of fish, including luderick, barracouta, flathead, mullet, bream, silver trevally, snapper, Australian salmon and tailor. The channel between Rigby Island and the mainland, known as The Narrows, carries snapper, Australian salmon and mulloway, with boat fishing for bream at the entrance of Maringa Creek.

The channel on the seaward side of Rigby Island, known as **Hopetoun Channel** or the Barrier, can give good results at first and last light, when the boat traffic has died down. Fishing around the rocks at the eastern end of **Rigby Island** can be good for bream.

The more open water of the **South Channel** is good for drifting for whiting and flounder, while the Reeve Channel, on the other side of the long Flannagan Island, is prime water for whiting, flathead and bream, particularly in the early hours of an ebb tide. Luderick can be found close to the island. **Nungurner** faces a bay where sheltered fishing can proceed if the winds and tides of Reeve Channel become difficult.

Bancroft Bay, on the western side of Bell Point, is also protected from winds

GUIDE TO LOCAL FISH

		Lakes Entrance to Metung	Lake King
BC	barracouta	●	
BA	bass, Australian		●
B	bream	●	●
F	flathead	●	●
FL	flounder	●	●
G	garfish	●	●
LU	luderick	●	●
M	mullet, yelloweye	●	●
MU	mulloway	●	
EP	perch, estuary	●	●
SA	salmon, Australian	●	
GS	shark, gummy/school	●	
S	snapper	●	
SN	snook	●	
T	tailor	●	●
TR	trevally, silver	●	●
W	whiting, King George	●	●

COASTAL FISHING BAIRNSDALE REGION   VICTORIA

and provides some of the best fishing in the area, as the drop-offs from the sandbanks carry bream, garfish, mullet and flathead. Bream can also be plentiful under the cliffs on the eastern side of Bell Point.

Shaving Point, easily reached from the lovely boating village of Metung, is good for shore fishing and boat drifting, for flathead and whiting. Occasional mulloway are taken on the eastern side of the point.

LAKE KING

The excellent fishing in **Lake King** is due to the large numbers of bream, tailor, flathead, whiting and mullet that move in and out of the Tambo, Nicholson and Mitchell rivers. Leaving Metung, there is a flathead drift to **Tambo Bluff**, and beneath the bluff there are snapper, flathead and bream in the close-in water, and tailor further out. At the entrances to the rivers, flathead and bream are the main catch, with Australian salmon a possibility in deeper water. The lake entrances and lower river reaches fish best after heavy rain.

The most popular boating river is the meandering **Tambo**, which has 20 km of fishable water with some notable hot spots. Many boat anglers launch at Johnsonville, about 3 km upriver. The Tambo is great for bream, particularly further upriver after a long hot spell. Luderick, flathead and mulloway are also good at certain spots.

The mouth of the **Nicholson** is very weedy, and a float will be needed for the bream. Upriver is a good summer section for bream, luderick and estuary perch.

Fishing off one of the jetties on the Mitchell River, Bairnsdale

The **Mitchell** is remarkable for its silt jetties, which extend 6 km into Lake King. Boat users can enter the river at The Cut, on the northern side of the jetties, or use the boat ramp at **Eagle Point**. The river, good for land-based anglers because the Paynesville-Bairnsdale Road runs beside it, provides winter fishing for bream, and mid-summer fishing on a high tide in the late afternoon.

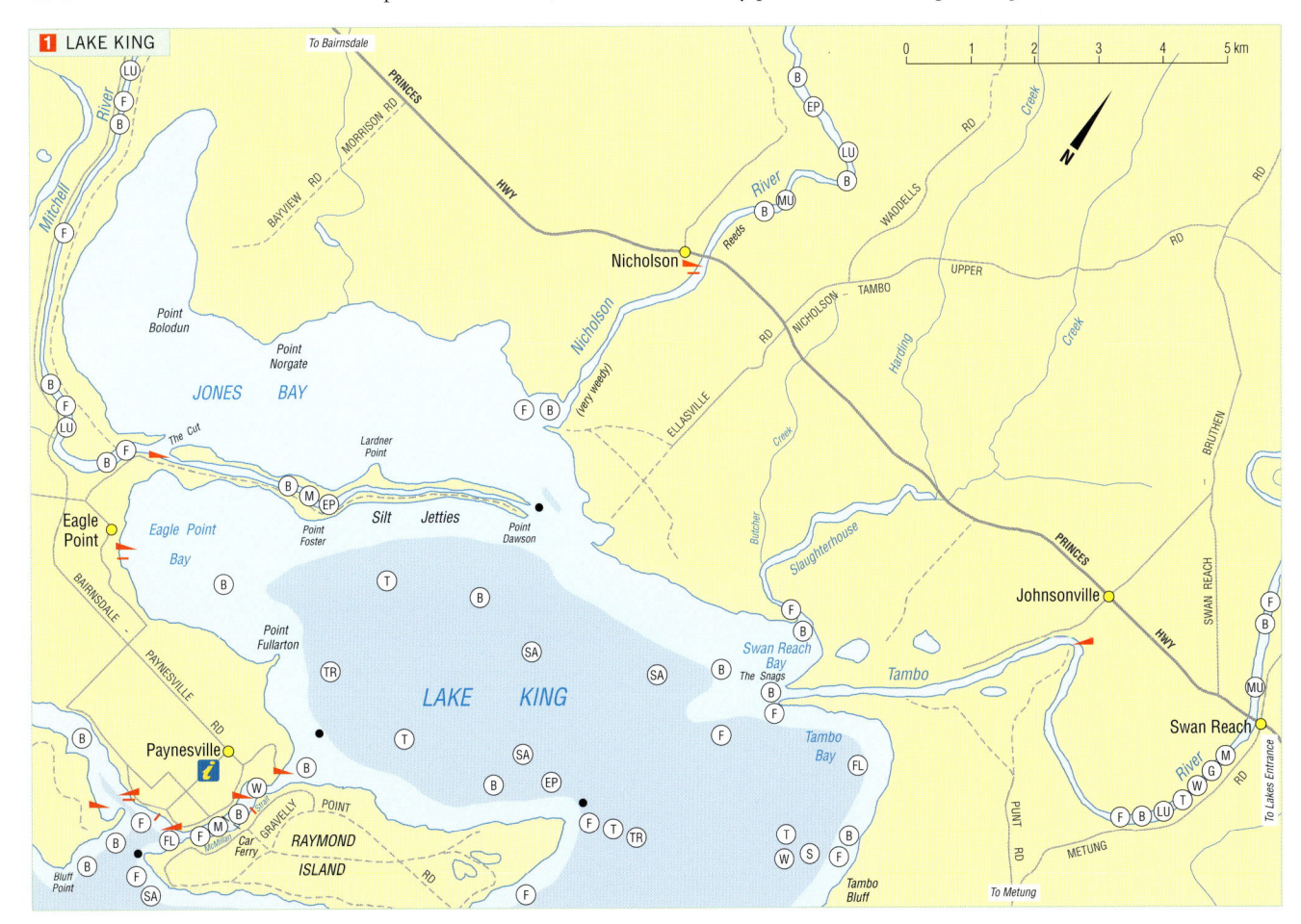

173

Lake Victoria

Type of fishing
beach, estuary, jetty, river
Target fish
bream, flathead, salmon, tailor, whiting

Paynesville, a fast-growing holiday and boating centre, is virtually split in two by McMillan Strait. Boats tie up in the strait and in Newlands Arm, so the waters around the town are very busy in summer. The hardy flathead and bream seem to be fish that can stand the activity, although the odd whiting is possible. Land anglers still use the old Fisherman's Co-operative Wharf as the best spot in this crowded area.

Opposite **Raymond Island** is the Aurora Channel, which runs to Ocean Grange, and the narrow strip of land separating the lakes from the Ninety Mile Beach. There are flathead and bream in the channel. A jetty here allows you to tie up and walk to the surf fishing beaches, mostly for flathead, mulloway and tailor. **Campbell Channel**, on the seaward side of Raymond Island, provides good fishing for flathead, bream and whiting, with silver trevally in the deeper areas, and Australian salmon and tailor further out.

This is the pattern along **Lake Victoria**, with most of the action on the deeper landward side. From Bluff Point, Lady Bay extends into the sheltered waters of **Duck Arm and Picnic Arm**, where there is peaceful fishing for flathead and bream. These remain the target fish all along the shore waters to Steel Bay, with Australian salmon and tailor in the centre of the lake, and bream and whiting on the opposite side, mostly around Wilson Point and Walker Point.

GUIDE TO LOCAL FISH	
(BC)	barracouta
(B)	bream
(F)	flathead
(FL)	flounder
(LU)	luderick
(M)	mullet, yelloweye
(MU)	mulloway
(EP)	perch, estuary
(SA)	salmon, Australian
(T)	tailor
(TR)	trevally, silver
(W)	whiting, King George

Boats moored in McMillan Strait at Paynesville

Lake Victoria becomes progressively shallower past the holiday town of **Loch Sport** and towards the south-western shore at Hollands Landing. Loch Sport has excellent boating facilities and is a good starting point for excursions north and west into Lake Victoria. There is land fishing from the jetty for mullet and bream, with tailor possible for lure casters in the evening. The shallow shores around the town bring out those who seek flounder with a torch and spear.

COASTAL FISHING BAIRNSDALE REGION — VICTORIA

The wharf and retaining wall at **Hollands Landing**, fished at dawn and dusk, produce some big bream. Here the narrow **McLennan Strait** leads to Lake Wellington. It is less than 100 m wide for most of its 9-km length, but the water depth averages 4 m and the fishing is good for both bank and boat anglers launching from the villages of Seacombe, Loch Sport or Hollands Landing. The target fish are bream and flathead, but mullet are plentiful, and estuary perch, luderick and school mulloway have been taken by anglers using the appropriate rigs. The current is strong at times. The waters round both entrances to McLennan Strait are good bream areas, with some flathead and whiting.

Lake Wellington, 8 km wide and 16 km long, is the largest of the lakes and the outlet for the Avon River, and for the Thompson, La Trobe and Macalister rivers, which join up and enter the lake through the La Trobe River mouth. The lake is very shallow and exposed, presenting danger for boats in choppy conditions. The only real area of interest for fishing in the lake is at the entrance to the Avon River, where bream, flathead and whiting are occasionally taken.

Fishing from the sands of the Ninety Mile Beach

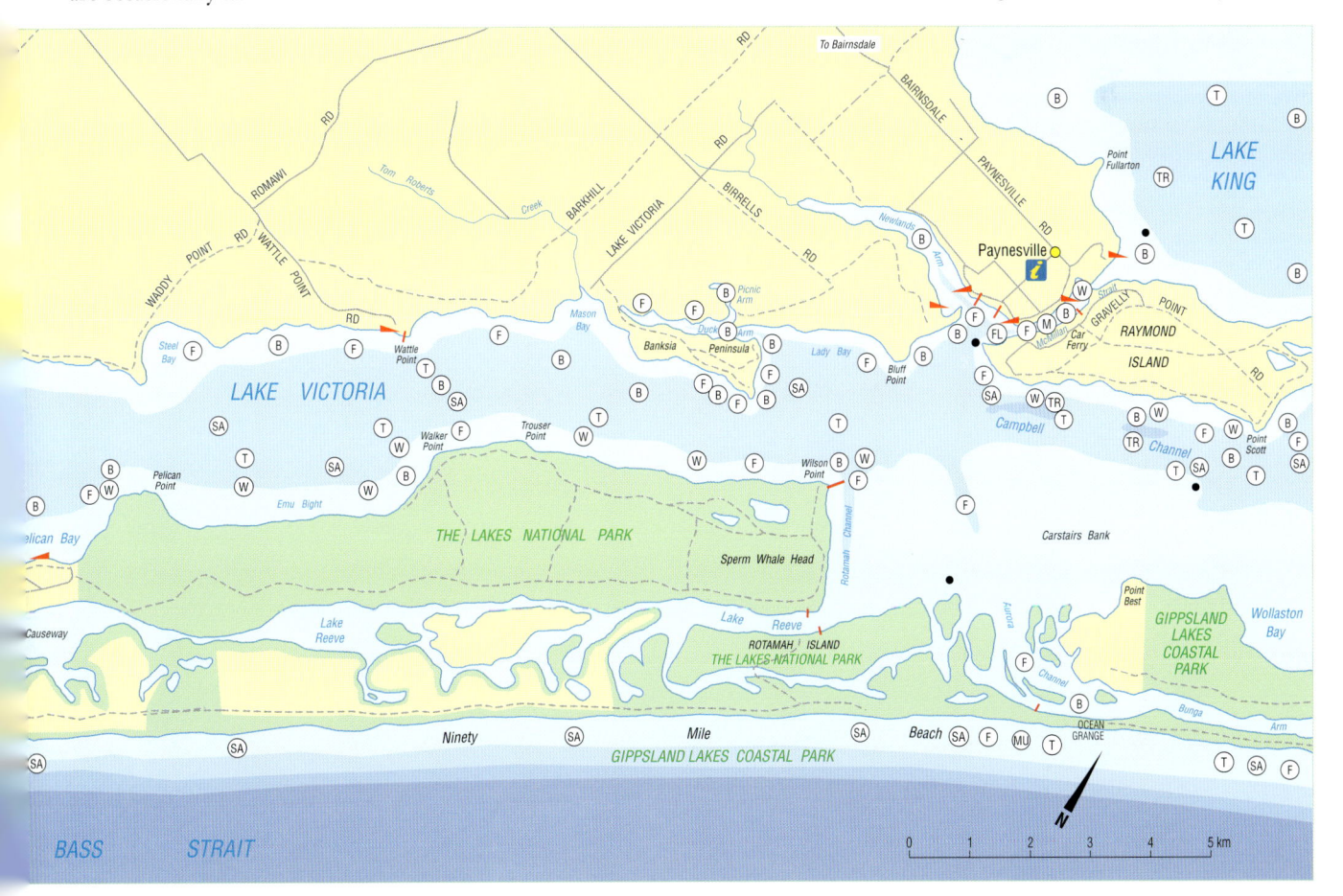

VICTORIA

COASTAL FISHING BAIRNSDALE REGION

Port Albert

Type of fishing
beach, estuary, jetty, offshore
Target fish
flathead, snapper, whiting

The historic township of **Port Albert**, once the supply port for Gippsland, is now a fishing town, with a hotel that caters especially for anglers, a caravan park, a fishing co-operative and bait supply, a boat ramp and numerous jetties and wharves.

This vast estuary system is famous for its big run of snapper in November. The best areas are the northern tip of **Sunday Island** in the channel, and the channel areas near the Port Albert entrance. The run is followed by good possibilities for King George whiting, fished on a run-out tide. Strong tides call for a heavy sinker and long leader. Flathead are ever-present, but other fish in these waters include gummy shark, Australian salmon, bream, pike, trevally, school shark, gurnard, flounder and snook.

Robertsons Beach and **Manns Beach** offer excellent fishing for whiting, flathead, Australian salmon, pike and snook. There is a boat ramp further east at **McLoughlins Beach**, but the fishing is restricted to channels in the shallow area, with whiting and big flathead available. There is a notable run of prawns in the summer months.

Port Albert boasts access to the offshore via the Port Albert entrance. It is a long entrance and can be very dangerous in rough weather. There are prolific snapper reefs around the **Seal Island** group, where there are resident schools of yellowtail kingfish and a big population of snook. There are also occasional captures of southern bluefin and striped tuna. On the south coast of **Snake Island**, off Bentley Point, snook, yellowtail kingfish, snapper and Australian salmon are the target fish.

Port Albert is the launching point for estuary waters containing whiting, snapper and flathead

Gummy shark
The mainstay of the Australian fish and chip trade, gummy sharks have flattened teeth, live on the sea bottom, average about one metre in length, and are ash grey in colour with white spots on the back. Most are caught in the surf and inlets.

GUIDE TO LOCAL FISH

		Port Albert	Corner Inlet
BC	barracouta		●
B	bream	●	●
F	flathead	●	●
FL	flounder	●	●
G	garfish	●	●
GU	gurnard	●	
KI	kingfish, yellowtail	●	●
M	mullet, yelloweye	●	
PI	pike, long-finned	●	●
SA	salmon, Australian	●	●
GS	shark, gummy/school	●	●
SH	shark, others		●
S	snapper	●	●
SN	snook	●	●
TR	trevally, silver	●	●
TU	tuna	●	
W	whiting, King George	●	●

176

COASTAL FISHING BAIRNSDALE REGION　　　　　VICTORIA

Corner Inlet

Type of fishing
estuary, jetty

Target fish
flathead, gummy shark, snapper, trevally, whiting

Corner Inlet is a vast tidal lagoon that holds a variety of fish. The inlet can become very choppy and unsafe for small craft on windy days, but in calm seas fishing is good in the upper reaches. Flathead, whiting, mullet, silver trevally, gummy shark, snapper, pike, Australian salmon and flounder are there in abundance, and are best fished from December to April. Flathead like the upper reaches of the channels in 2 to 4 m of water, while King George whiting are prolific in 2 to 5 m of water around weed beds. Large snapper enter the area around October and leave in March. The best areas for them are in the deeper channels, such as the **Singapore Deep** and the **Franklin Channel**.

Port Welshpool has long been a major fishing port, and now services the oil and gas rigs of Bass Strait. The best fishing is in the relatively sheltered Lewis Channel, in the eastern reaches towards Port Albert, where King George whiting is the target. The two jetties are good for land-based fishing – try for whiting, flathead, mullet, flounder and garfish in summer, and for trevally and pike in winter. The long jetty gives generally better results. Port Welshpool's ramp has three lanes and can carry boats of all sizes.

There is an excellent concrete ramp at **Toora**, suitable for all-sized trailer boats, although some difficulty may be experienced at the bottom of the lowest tides. The ramp at Yanakie Landing, accessible from Foley Road, is suitable for medium-sized boats, but is only usable at half to full tide.

Access to offshore and the eastern side of Wilsons Promontory is through Corner Inlet Channel. Beware of strong northerly, easterly and southerly winds. Boats can be chartered at Port Welshpool.

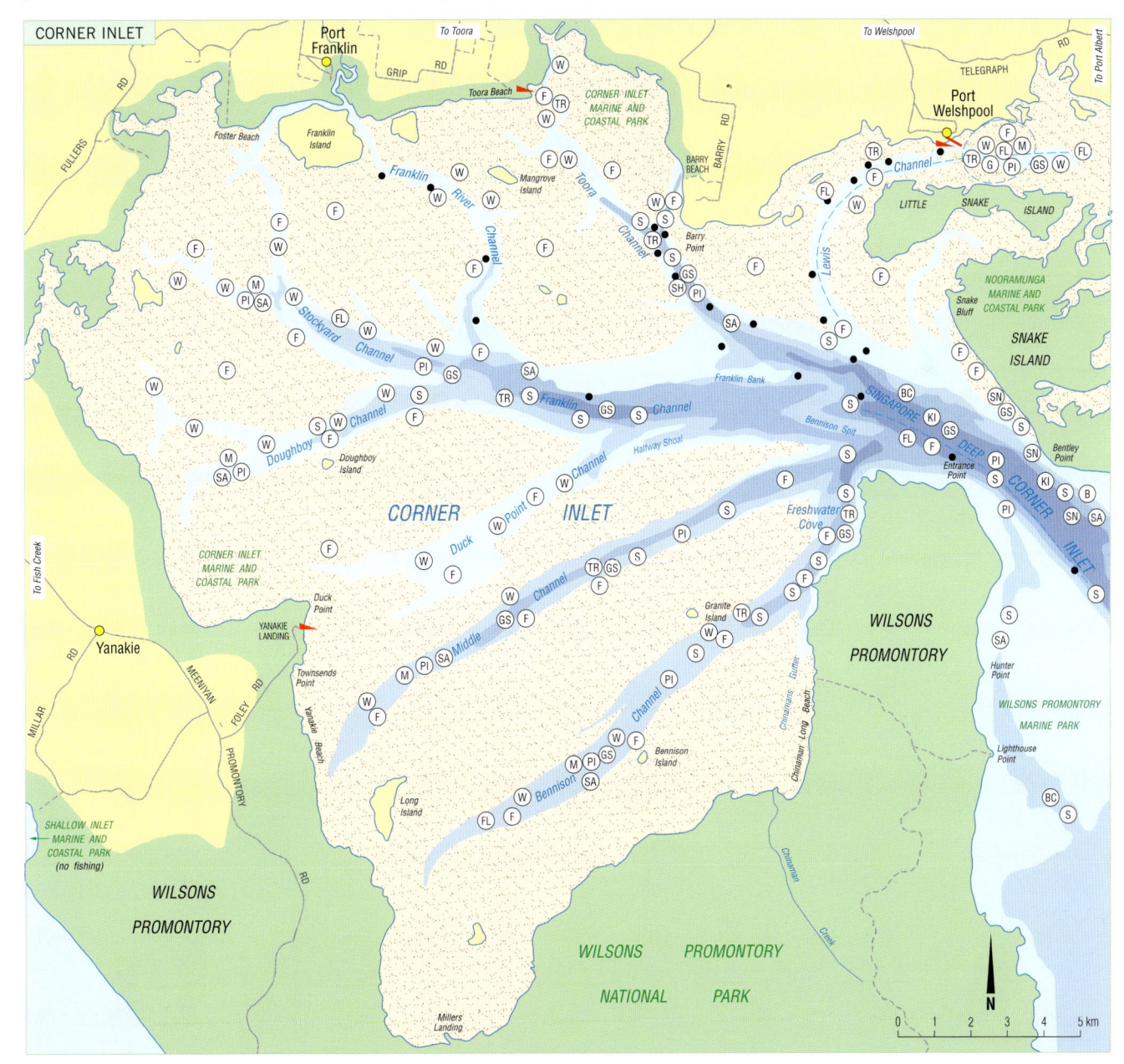

177

VICTORIA

COASTAL FISHING WESTERN PORT REGION

Western Port Region

Western Port is a big expanse of water with a huge tidal flow – tricky but rewarding once you learn to work with the tides. Other highly productive waterways are Anderson Inlet, Waratah Bay and Shallow Inlet.

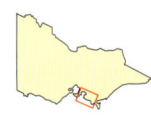

Anderson Inlet and Shallow Inlet are enclosed waters that are relatively safe for boating. Both inlets contain King George whiting, mullet, Australian salmon and estuary perch. Waratah Bay is fairly sheltered and small boats can be launched off the beach. Again the target is whiting, which can be taken all year round. There is fine beach fishing at Woolamai, Cemetery Beach Kilcunda, Williamsons Beach Wonthaggi, Baxters Beach, Venus Bay and Waratah Bay.

Phillip Island has spectacular coastal country with the bleak, rolling hills breaking into abrupt cliffs, sometimes pounded by the wild Bass Strait waters. One of the best places to experience the Phillip Island atmosphere is The Nobbies at the south-western end of the island. Here, the high cliff sits above a pathway to a booming blowhole, and looks over a large island of rock, which can be reached at low tide. Extreme caution must be taken when fishing at The Nobbies, and while rock fishing along the ocean side of the island. Western Port holds good numbers of large snapper from September to April. The big fish come in mid-September and may be caught in the deep sections and channels, while the smaller ones run from December to March. And only a few kilometres away is one of Australia's best-known tourist destinations, the Penguin Parade at Phillip Island. Cowes is the main town here, a favoured holiday resort with pleasant beaches and a jetty that is popular with anglers.

GUIDE TO LOCAL FISH

- barracouta
- bream
- elephant fish
- flathead
- garfish
- kingfish, yellowtail
- leatherjacket
- ling
- mackerel, horse
- mullet, yelloweye
- mulloway
- perch, estuary
- pike, long-finned
- salmon, Australian
- shark, gummy/school
- shark, others
- snapper
- snook
- sweep
- tailor
- trevally, silver
- whiting, King George
- zebra fish

WHERE TO FISH

Western Port Region

WARATAH BAY • 180

A sheltered bay, this area offers safe boating offshore in the right winds. At the eastern end is the estuary, Shallow Inlet. There are flathead and whiting in the bay and estuary, and Australian salmon, tailor, barracouta and trevally inside the inlet entrance. Rock fishing is also an option at the south-western end of the bay.

ANDERSON INLET • 181

There are a wide variety of fish available in Anderson Inlet and the Tarwin River, including mullet, trevally, bream, Australian salmon, snapper, flathead, snook, mulloway, estuary perch and whiting. The boating is safe but the entrance is always dangerous. Large sand areas are exposed at low tide. There is good fishing from the jetty at Inverloch, and excellent winter surf fishing from the beaches of Venus Bay.

WESTERN PORT SOUTH • 182

The eastern channels around Corinella and the fishing town of Rhyll have summer snapper. Yellowtail kingfish and Australian salmon are near the entrances. The piers at San Remo and Cowes are best at slack tide, morning or evening. There is varied rock, beach and boat fishing along Phillip Island's ocean coast, and sheltered bay fishing in the lee of the island.

WESTERN PORT NORTH • 184

This is a huge fishing area, with sand flats and channels harbouring snapper, whiting, gummy shark and snook. Mussels, pippis, sandworms and bass yabbies are available for bait. Boating care is needed to avoid being stranded on sandbanks on the tidal run-out. Many launching ramps are out of the water at low tide.

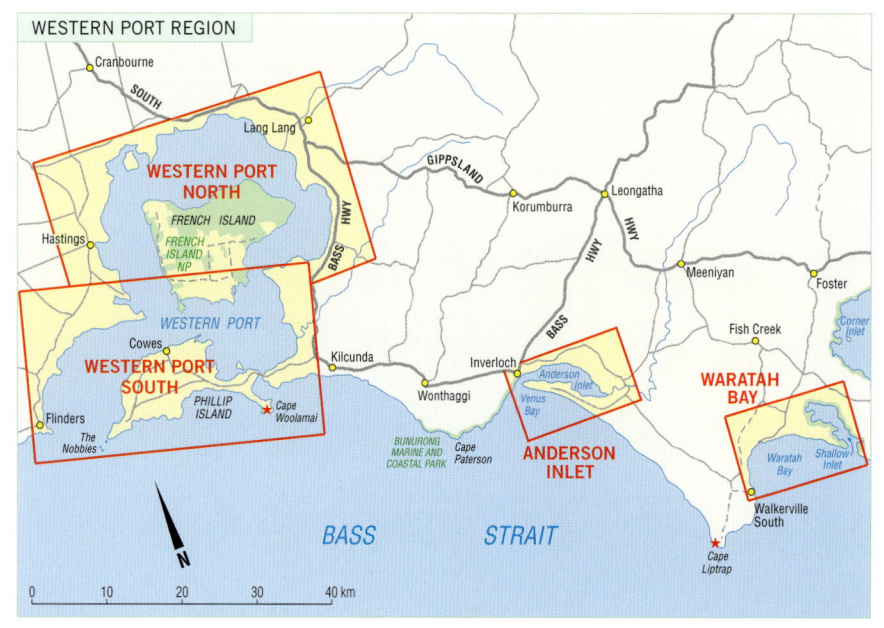

Pippis

A burrowing, bivalve mullusc, pippis are one of the better all-round baits. They are often exposed by waves or can be uncovered by digging with your feet in the sand. Target fish are whiting, bream and salmon.

COASTAL FISHING WESTERN PORT REGION   VICTORIA

Aerial view of Phillip Island: view to Churchill Island and the mainland

Weather

The coastline is exposed to Bass Strait. Waratah Bay is sheltered except in southerlies, while Anderson Inlet and Shallow Inlet are generally sheltered. Western Port is reasonably sheltered from Bass Strait, but becomes treacherous when the wind opposes the flow of the tide. The area is subject to strong southerlies, particularly in winter, and high seas. A southerly change on hot north-wind days can create dangerous squalls. Information on local weather is available from the Bureau of Meteorology: bays and coast, tel. 1900 926 110; 3-day forecast, tel. 1900 926 109; country, tel. 1900 926 111. There is a special tide information line, Tide Times, tel. 1900 930 200.

Boating

Crossing from **Mornington Peninsula** to **Phillip Island** can be hazardous because of the shallow Middle Bank, where seas break without warning. The safest route is via the marked shipping channel. There are strong tidal flows throughout the area. Shallow waters, particularly around **French Island**, can cause boats to run aground. Avoid having to return to boat ramps at low tide. The best plan is to fish when the tide is about

Fishing from the beach at Flinders

two-thirds out, so the channels can be seen, returning in the flood tide. Navigation hazards in Western Port are marked with Association of Lighthouse Authorities (ALA) symbols. Keep watch for shipping. Bars to **Anderson Inlet** and **Shallow Inlet** are dangerous.

FISHING TIP

If fishing Western Port in a boat for the first time, take the time at low tide to explore areas you may wish to fish. Not only will you find some great spots but you will also reduce your chances of running aground.

FURTHER INFORMATION

Fishing information NRE offices: cnr Chapel St and Osborne Ave, Cowes, tel. (03) 5952 5910. Other local fishing information is available from San Remo Fishermen's Co-operative Society, tel. (03) 5678 5206 or Venus Bay Outdoor Store, tel. (03) 5663 7222.

Visitor information Thompson Ave, Cowes, tel. (03) 5952 2650; William St, Inverloch, tel. (03) 5674 2706; Information Centre, Phillip Island Tourist Rd, Newhaven, tel. (03) 5956 7447.

VICTORIA

COASTAL FISHING WESTERN PORT REGION

Waratah Bay

Type of fishing
bay, beach, estuary, rock

Target fish
Australian salmon, barracouta, flathead, whiting

Waratah Bay is one of the few places where King George whiting spend the winter. The bay is a recess in the coastline about 10 km long, and its waters are largely protected from south-westerlies by Cape Liptrap on one side and Wilsons Promontory on the other.

The launching beach is on the western end of the bay near the small community of Walkerville South. There is a concrete road that leads to a hard-packed beach from which boats up to 4.5 m can be launched. There are similar launching systems at Walkerville and Waratah Bay, and two concrete ramps into the water on either side of Shallow Inlet, which adjoins Waratah Bay.

The greatest attraction of Waratah Bay is the close inshore whiting grounds, which extend for about 3 km along the shore and up to 500 m out. There are also snook in this inshore water.

There is good flathead fishing up to 2 km out, but still well within the sheltered waters of the bay. Barracouta frequent the deeper waters, and schools of Australian salmon can come into the bay.

Looking south from Shallow Inlet, with a view to Darby Beach and the west side of the Yanakie Isthmus, Wilsons Promontory National Park

Shallow Inlet is aptly named, but the channel that runs down to the entrance, with hard-sand boat launching, provides the fishing action. On the Sandy Point side boats must be hauled over sand flats at low tide to reach the channel. The upper reaches of the channel are whiting and flathead water but close to the entrance the scene changes, and trevally, barracouta, tailor and Australian salmon are the likely catches. The narrow entrance can be crossed, but it is a dangerous process and not recommended. The best baits are sourced locally. Bass yabbies are found on the sand flats, while pippis can be gathered at low tide.

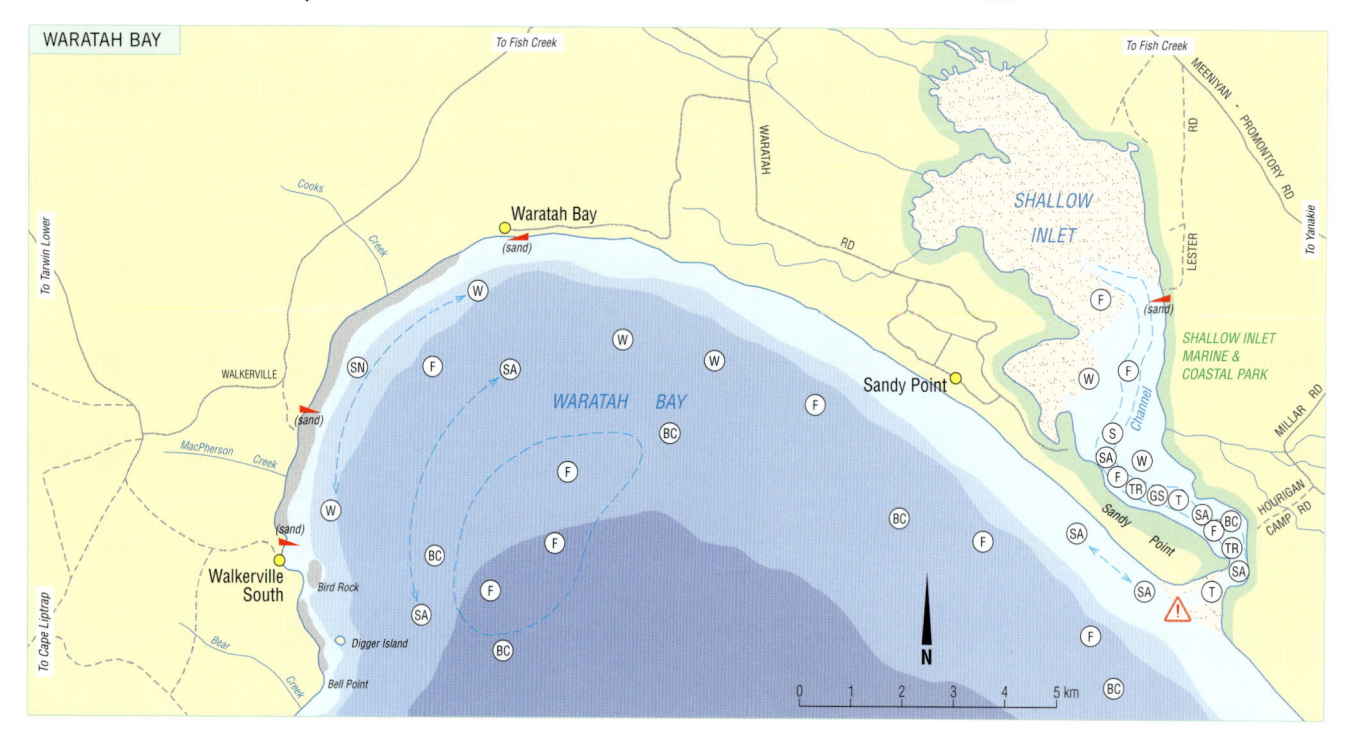

COASTAL FISHING WESTERN PORT REGION   VICTORIA

Anderson Inlet

Type of fishing
beach, estuary, jetty

Target fish
Australian salmon, estuary perch, flathead, snapper, whiting

Anderson Inlet is another shallow inlet, fed by the Tarwin River at the eastern end and by a narrow and extremely dangerous sandbar entrance to the sea at the western end. The inlet is the most southerly habitat of mangroves. At low tide the water is reduced almost to mudflats, but there are extensive channels and they provide very good fishing, even in winter. Try for King George whiting, pinkie snapper, silver trevally and Australian salmon. The tide scours near the entrance can shift hundreds of tonnes of sand overnight, so it is good to get the advice of locals on the location of the channels. Heavy rain can lead to strong outflows of muddy water from the Tarwin, and interrupt proceedings for a few days.

The **Tarwin River**, however, provides a bonus, as estuary perch are found along its length, in its entrance and in the channel running from the estuary. These fish can be taken by casting near visible snags with bait like shrimp, and by using trolling lures. A boat is almost a necessity to fish the river. Within the estuary channels is a wide variety of fish including mullet, trevally, bream, flathead, Australian salmon, snapper, snook, mulloway and whiting.

The Tarwin River estuary, while not noted as a bream fishery, can at times surprise the angler by providing good numbers of these fish using bass yabbies, found locally, as bait.

The small seaside resort of **Inverloch** has long stretches of beach. The town provides the angler with most fishing needs. The drive to Cape Paterson, through the Bunurong Marine Park, is well worth it for the views, which rival those on the Great Ocean Road. There are three boat ramps within the inlet – at Inverloch (near Point Hughes), Mahers Landing and Fishermans Landing – and a fourth in the Tarwin estuary, accessed from Venus Bay. There is also a jetty at Inverloch, which can be fished comfortably when the tide is not running too fast. Snapper can be caught at the entrance or in the deeper tide scours and channels. King George whiting are also prolific in summer and are often taken in shallow water on the edge of the channels on a run-out tide.

Surf fishing is excellent on the back beaches of Anderson Inlet and access is from the town of **Venus Bay**. Australian salmon, mullet and trevally are the main target fish. The surf beaches are identified locally by numbers 1 to 5. The most consistent catches are to be had at beaches 1, 4 and 5, which yield Australian salmon, mullet and trevally. There is a fair tidal variation at these surf beaches and they usually fish best between the rising tide to one hour after high tide.

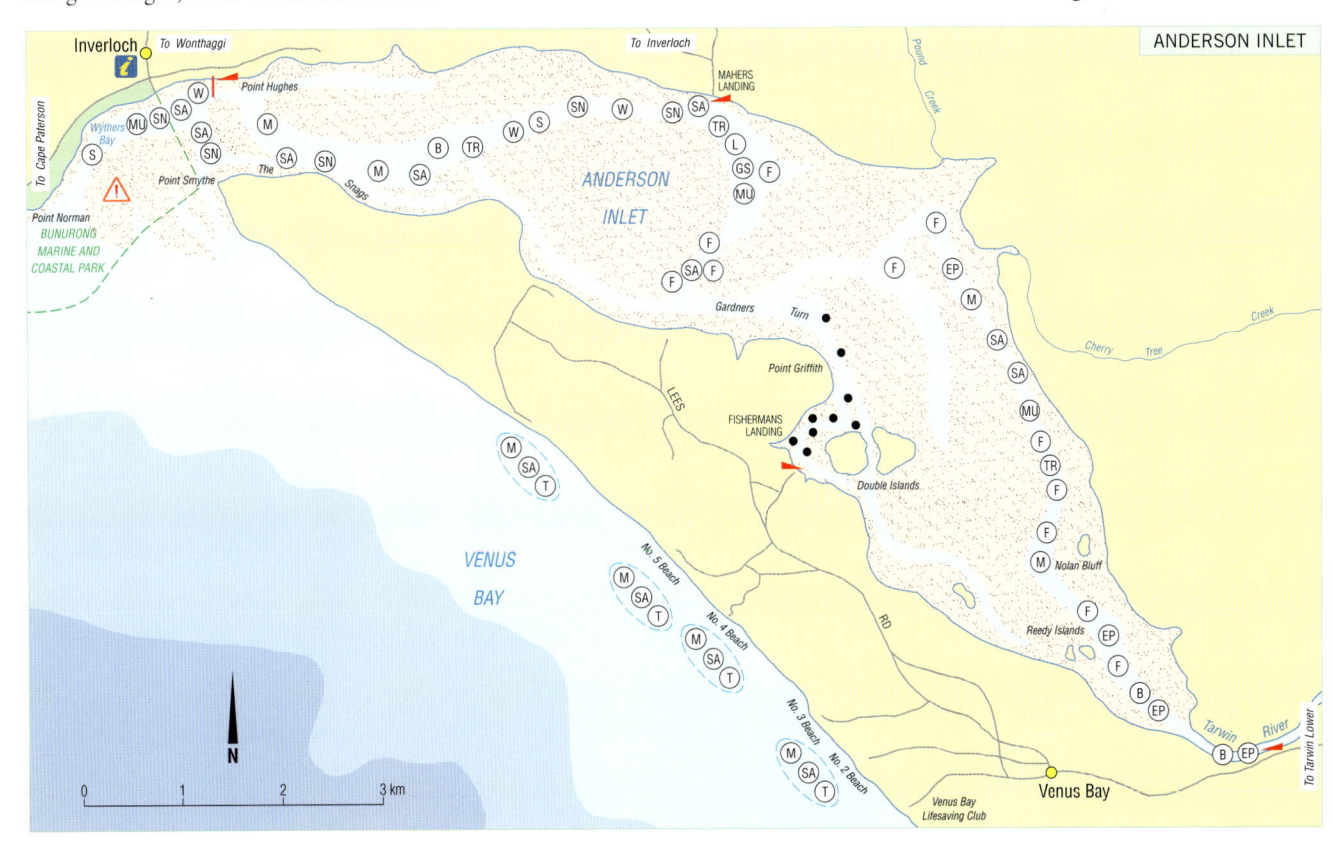

GUIDE TO LOCAL FISH

		Waratah Bay	Andersons Inlet
BC	barracouta	•	
B	bream		•
F	flathead	•	•
L	ling		•
M	mullet, yelloweye		•
MU	mulloway		•
EP	perch, estuary		•
SA	salmon, Australian	•	•
GS	shark, gummy/school	•	•
S	snapper	•	•
SN	snook	•	•
T	tailor	•	•
TR	trevally, silver	•	•
W	whiting, King George	•	•

VICTORIA

COASTAL FISHING WESTERN PORT REGION

Western Port South

Type of fishing
bay, beach, pier, rock

Target fish
Australian salmon, elephant fish, flathead, garfish, gummy and other sharks, snapper, squid, whiting

Fishing the shallow water of Western Port requires a quality anchor and at least half a boat length of chain to hold firmly against the tidal flow. To attract whiting, berley with crushed mussels, with plenty of shell to hold the meat. They will drift with the tide along the seabed. In deeper water, when fishing for snapper, berley is of little use, except at slack water.

BOAT FISHING

The shallow and intensely tidal waterway from **Stony Point** to **Corinella** truly presents the angler with a 'riddle of the sands'. It is not a place to drop the boat in and hope for the best. The maximum tide rise, occurring during spring, can be 3 m. The amount of water in the bay can shrink by a third over a period of six hours, sometimes leaving anglers and their boats trapped in the shallows. So you should always fish Western Port armed with a tide chart. All ramps in this area present difficulties at low tide.

The Corinella ramp gives access to **Corinella Channel** and the eastern coast of French Island. In this area snapper and whiting are the targets from October to April.

The area from Somers to Balnarring Beach in **Flinders Bight** is dotted with reefs and sand holes where the whiting linger. The area from Balnarring Beach to Flinders has some whiting banks.

Phillip Island seascape

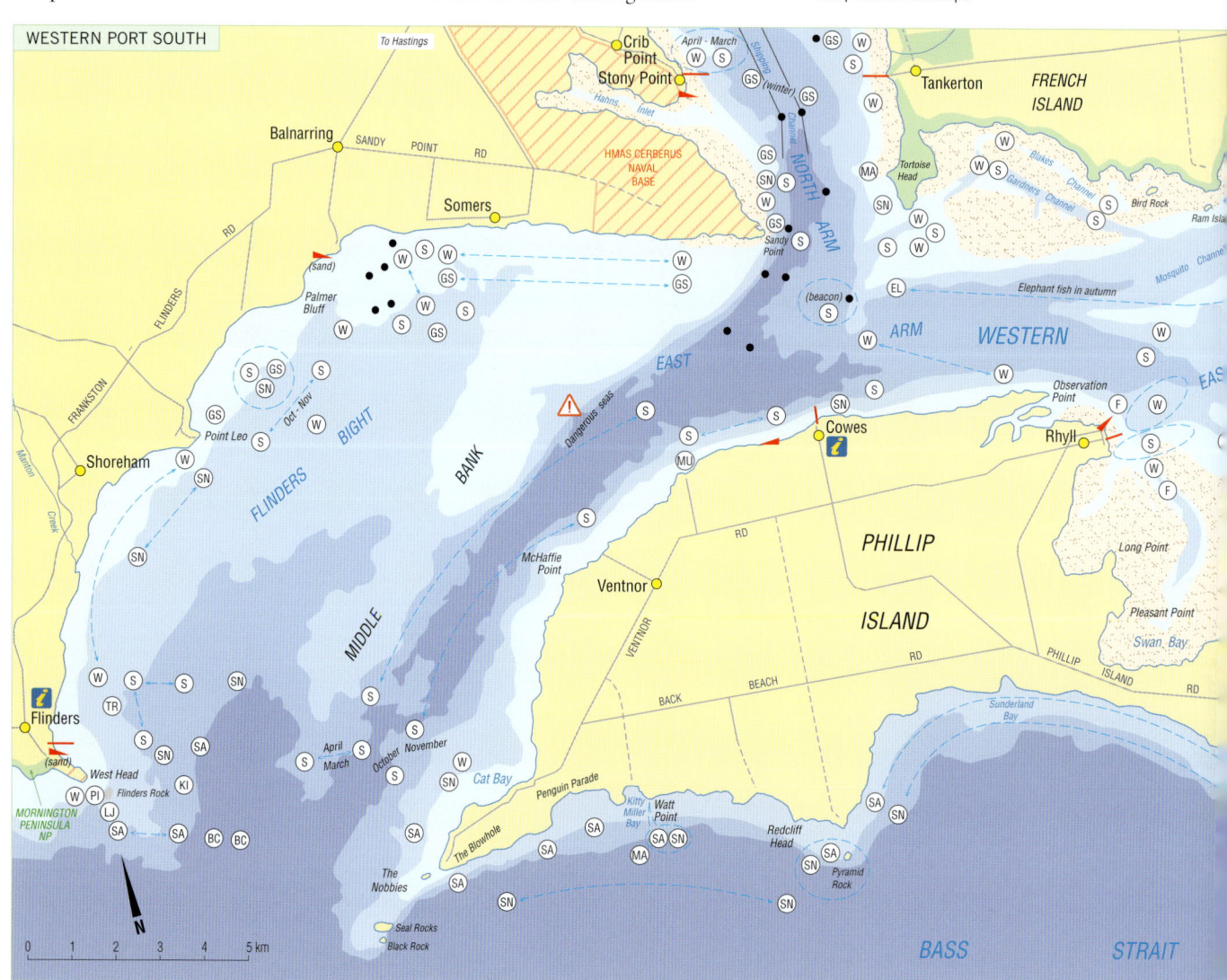

182

COASTAL FISHING WESTERN PORT REGION — VICTORIA

Boat fishing around **Phillip Island** is exciting, particularly on the ocean side. Fishing around the rocks and the Blowhole will produce an assortment of reef fish, but should only be done on calm days, and then with an eye on the sea. The waters of **Kitty Miller Bay Beach** are similarly productive. Silver trevally and Australian salmon are the main fish here, but there are possibilities all along the coast.

On the bay side, **Cat Bay**, well protected when the southerlies blow, can be good for whiting, squid and snapper. Off **McHaffief Point** are two large reef areas, best found by sounder. These are good for snapper. A buoy out from **Cowes Pier** marks where the North and East arms meet; this is good snapper territory in the deeper water, with whiting further inshore. Near **French Island**, Gardners and Blakes channels are good for whiting and snapper. Also try in the Mosquito and Elizabeth channels.

Rhyll is the fishing town of Phillip Island, with extensive sand flats but a navigable channel to deep water. The best launching facilities on the island are here. There is good fishing for whiting and flathead in the channels.

As most fishing in Western Port is for snapper and whiting, some other fish are missed. Trevally are rarely hooked by those after snapper and whiting. Garfish are abundant but overlooked. Attract them with berley over grass beds. Yellowtail kingfish are taken near the entrances, but those hooked by anglers seeking snapper are usually lost through inadequate tackle. Mulloway lurk in the channels, but those hooked are usually lost for the same reason. There are also good populations of pike and barracouta in the southern sections of the bay.

A regular autumn visitor from the ocean is the elephant fish, a shark-like creature that swims like a state, undulating its pectoral fins. It is likely to be an incidental catch in the East Arm, particularly in the waters from Tortoise Head, on the southwest tip of French Island, to Corinella.

LAND-BASED SPOTS

Land locations include the **San Remo Pier** at high tide; **Bass River**, north-east of San Remo, which is the only bream water in the area; **Tankerton Jetty**, which is the ferry stop for French Island; and **Stony Point**. **Flinders Pier** is popular but the pickings are slim. Serious land-based anglers should try the rocks at **West Head** for whiting, pike and leatherjacket. There are beach and rock locations along the Flinders Bight foreshore.

On Phillip Island, fish from **Cowes Pier** at high tide and slack water; the **Red Point** platforms on rugged Cape Woolamai (these are a 40-minute walk from Newhaven and full of mutton-bird holes, but some of the best rock fishing is here) for barracouta, Australian salmon and big flathead; and the south end of Phillip Island and **The Nobbies**, on both the ocean and bay side. The ocean side has sloping cliffs down to rock ledges, but some ledges extend too far underwater to make fishing practical.

GUIDE TO LOCAL FISH

(BC)	barracouta
(B)	bream
(EL)	elephant fish
(F)	flathead
(G)	garfish
(KI)	kingfish, yellowtail
(LJ)	leatherjacket
(MA)	mackerel, horse
(M)	mullet, yelloweye
(MU)	mulloway
(EP)	perch, estuary
(PI)	pike, long finned
(SA)	salmon, Australian
(GS)	shark, gummy/school
(SH)	shark, others
(S)	snapper
(SN)	snook
(SW)	sweep
(TR)	trevally, silver
(W)	whiting, King George

VICTORIA

COASTAL FISHING WESTERN PORT REGION

Western Port North

Type of fishing
bay, estuary

Target fish
flathead, gummy shark, mullet, snapper, whiting

The main target species in the many channels in the northern Western Port area is the King George whiting, closely followed by snapper. The whiting season extends from December through to March and the snapper season from September through to the end of autumn.

The whiting inhabit the sand flats around the entire northern area and can be taken on pippis, mussels and fresh squid that has been softened. Anchoring and berleying is the best tactic, and due to the variation in tidal flow it is wise to rig so that the sinker weight can be quickly changed in response to an increase or decrease in flow. When snapper are the target – they are best in November – the most rewarding baits include tuna, pilchard and squid.

There are many channels running eastwards towards **Lang Lang**, including the **Cockyanes**, **Lyalls**, **Boulton** and **Bouchier** channels, producing great catches through summer to mid-autumn of whiting, flathead, mullet and sometimes snapper and gummy shark. Each channel is marked by spit buoys. In the central waters, to the west of where these channels converge, is a hazard marker indicating a submerged sandy area known as **Joes Island**. Fishing around the island on either side of the tide can result in catches of snapper, gummy shark and bronze whaler sharks.

Running south-east from Joes Island is the **Inside Channel**, the closest to French Island. It is shallow and runs into mudflats, so can only be fished at high tide, but provides excellent catches of flathead, trevally and whiting. The Post Office gutter runs from the channel towards the island, and produces whiting and snapper. **Crawfish Rock**, directly north of Scrub Point on the north-west tip of French Island, has deep water, often with snapper and gummy shark.

On the eastern side of Western Port you take off from ramps at Corinella, Grantville and south-west of Lang Lang near Bluff Point. The north-flowing channels here cut out south of Lang Lang. There are gummy shark and Australian salmon to be caught, but the main fishing

The channel to the Hastings boat ramp is always navigable, even at low tide

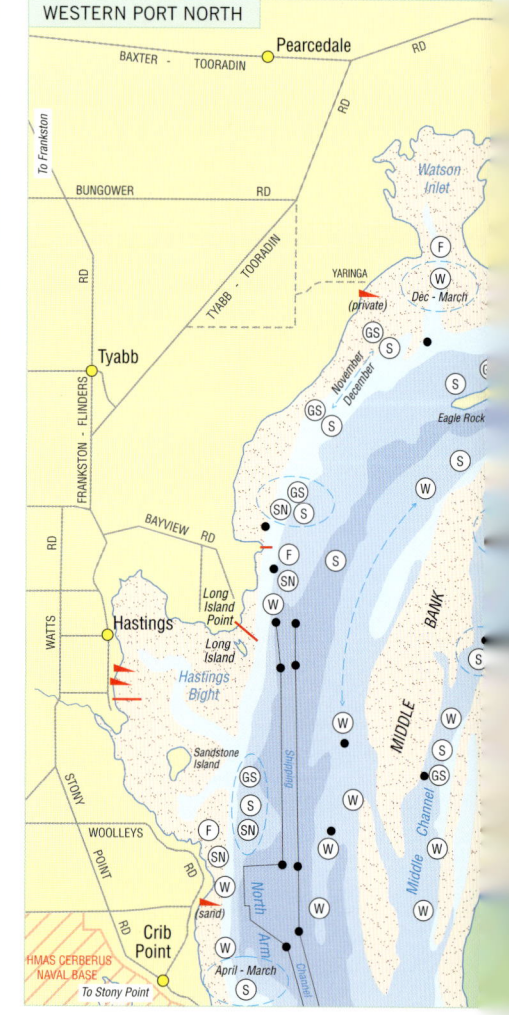

GUIDE TO LOCAL FISH

B	bream
F	flathead
M	mullet, yelloweye
SA	salmon, Australian
GS	shark, gummy/school
S	snapper
SN	snook
TR	trevally, silver
W	whiting, King George

Elephant fish are keenly sought in Western Port

184

COASTAL FISHING WESTERN PORT REGION　　　　　　　　　　　　　　　　　　　　　　　　　　**VICTORIA**

is for whiting and snapper. The best fishing is experienced on either side of both low and high slack water, when the influence of the strong tidal run is reduced.

The boat ramps in the northernmost section of Western Port are at Tooradin, Blind Bight and Warneet, and you are virtually straight into fishing water. **Tooradin** is the main fishing centre. Boats are moored here in the Sawtell River and up the creeks of the flat hinterland. Access in and out of the river is best at half to full tide. The Tooradin Channel is the longest of the northern channels and is marked with port and starboard piles. Whiting are usually here from November to April.

A lot of gutters empty into this channel, washing feed off the banks, so it pays to anchor at the mouth of a gutter at the end of an ebb tide, when the fish will be feeding. **Gentle Anne Channel** runs from the Blind Bight ramp at the Tooradin Channel, and produces good fishing for whiting up until Christmas. A beacon known as **The Basket**, where the two channels meet, has a deep hole that carries big snapper.

There is land-based action at Tooradin and Warneet two hours either side of high tide. Fish the foreshores of the river inlets for whiting and mullet.

Another popular fishing area is the **Middle Channel**, a large body of water on the western side of French Island, extending south to Stony Point. In recent years, fishing for sharks, particularly seven gill and bronze whalers, has taken on a renewed popularity in this bay.

Yaringa Harbour is private and access is by arrangement only, tel. (03) 5977 4154. Boat ramps at Yaringa Harbour and Warneet enable anglers to choose either the Middle Channel or the North Arm, which carries tankers to the refinery at Crib Point. Here it is important to have a peep over the shoulder now and then to see if a tanker is coming, as some overly absorbed anglers have had some narrow escapes in this area. The main catches in and around the shipping channel are whiting and snapper, with snook and gummy shark good alternatives, and the occasional flathead.

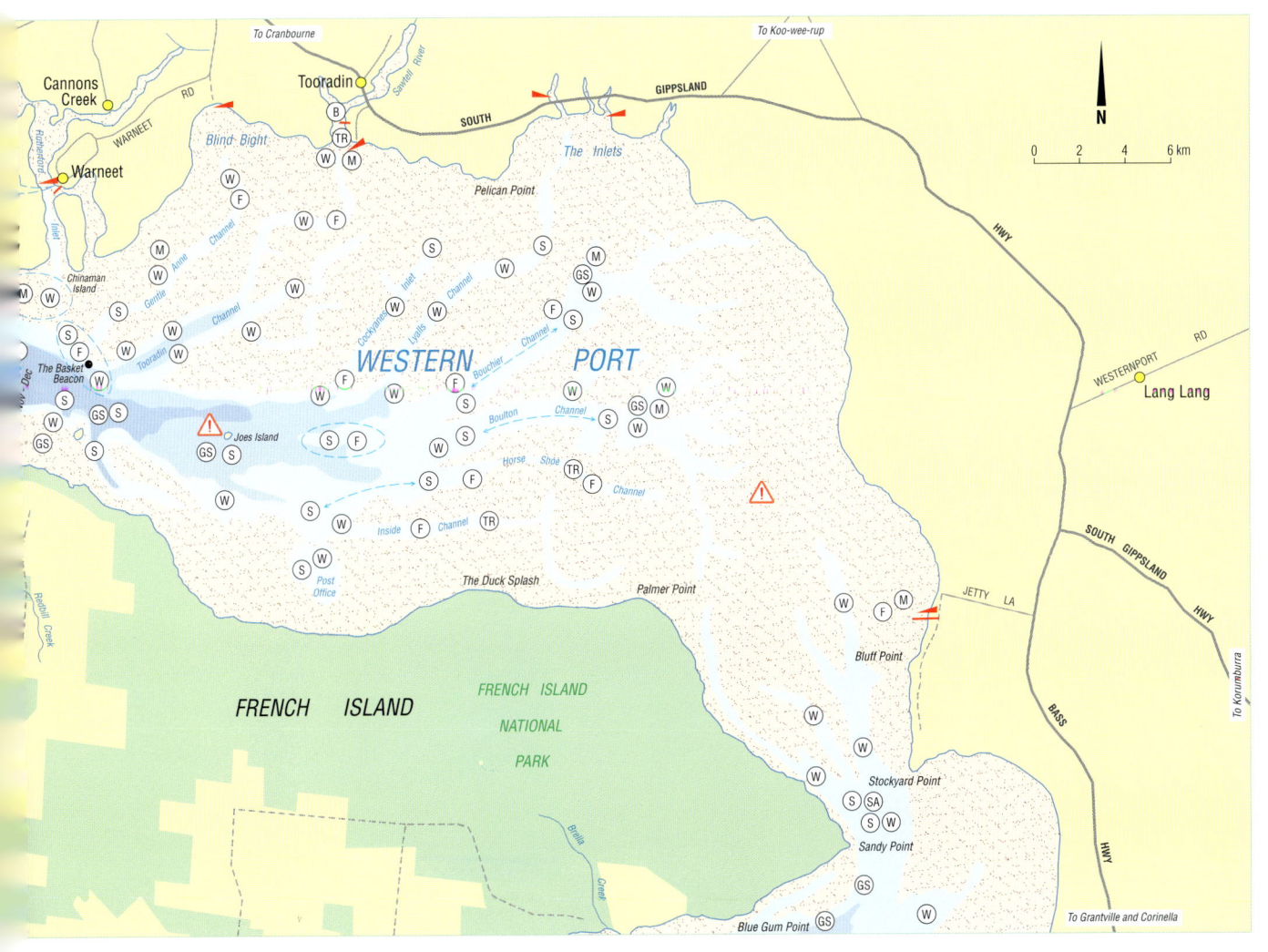

185

VICTORIA

COASTAL FISHING WARRNAMBOOL REGION

Warrnambool Region

The western Victorian coast has a wild grandeur that creates an inspiring backdrop for the pursuit of fishing. Mountainous forest country rises above the beaches, rocks, wave-cut cliffs and headlands that are swept by the waters of the Southern Ocean.

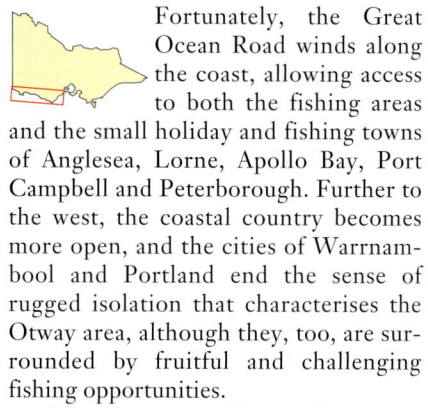

Setting out to fish the Hopkins River at Jubilee Park near Allansford

Fortunately, the Great Ocean Road winds along the coast, allowing access to both the fishing areas and the small holiday and fishing towns of Anglesea, Lorne, Apollo Bay, Port Campbell and Peterborough. Further to the west, the coastal country becomes more open, and the cities of Warrnambool and Portland end the sense of rugged isolation that characterises the Otway area, although they, too, are surrounded by fruitful and challenging fishing opportunities.

The west coast of Victoria has mostly surf, rock and offshore fishing. Snapper is still one of the main catches from November to April offshore from Warrnambool. Whiting is prevalent in bays around Port Fairy, Portland, Warrnambool, Peterborough and Port Campbell, while Australian salmon, tailor, trevally, flathead and gummy shark are among surf targets. Trevally often school around breakwaters and piers.

You will find mullet, bream and garfish in protected estuary waters, which although less common in this part of the State, should more than satisfy because of their charming locations and quality of the catch. Common among the big game fish offshore are yellowtail kingfish and southern bluefin tuna, with Portland the best area. There is also great fishing from the beaches between Warrnambool and Portland.

Australian salmon, King George whiting, yelloweye mullet, gummy sharks, mulloway and even snapper are regular captures.

WHERE TO FISH

Warrnambool Region

ANGLESEA TO APOLLO BAY ● 188
This area has mostly rock fishing with some beach fishing and a few bays and rivers. Ingoldsby Reef at Anglesea has whiting, snapper, Australian salmon and yellowtail kingfish, while the small creeks between Lorne and Apollo Bay have mullet and Australian salmon in the estuary areas. Apollo Bay has river, beach and boat fishing, and the best offshore fishing on this coast.

CAPE OTWAY TO PORT FAIRY ● 190
This wild and rugged area provides beach and rock fishing, some creek and estuary fishing, and bays and coves that have garfish, whiting and snapper. This is also crayfish coast. Peterborough and Port Campbell have great close-in fishing for snapper and whiting. Warrnambool has a magnificent combination of beach, bay, offshore, estuary and trout fishing, while Port Fairy has fine estuary and bay fishing.

PORTLAND BAY TO NELSON ● 192
Beach fishing is very good at Narrawong, and there are snapper and mulloway off the Surrey River mouth. Portland has beach, bay and offshore fishing. Snapper, whiting, Australian salmon, yellowtail kingfish and pike are the target fish for shore-based and bay anglers. The Glenelg River is a classic for mulloway, bream and mullet in the estuary, and estuary perch in the higher reaches.

COASTAL FISHING WARRNAMBOOL REGION

VICTORIA

GUIDE TO LOCAL FISH

- barracouta
- bream
- flathead
- garfish
- kingfish, yellowtail
- luderick
- mackerel, horse
- morwong
- mullet, yelloweye
- mulloway
- perch, estuary
- pike, long-finned
- salmon, Australian
- shark, gummy/school
- shark, others
- snapper
- snook
- sweep
- trevally, silver
- tuna
- warehou
- whiting, King George

Crayfish pots on the jetty at Apollo Bay

Weather

The coast is exposed to the Southern Ocean, with few ports, bays and estuaries for shelter. It is subject to strong southerly blows and swells. Winds are predominantly south-west to south-east in summer, creating choppy to rough seas. Best conditions are during north to north-east breezes. In northerlies, beware the forecast of westerly changes, because they can produce wild wind gusts and squalls. Seek out local advice before making a decision.

Boating

There best safe launching ramp along this coastline is at Apollo Bay. There are boat ramps in the river estuaries of the Curdies, Hopkins and Merri rivers, and makeshift launching for small craft on the Gellibrand and Aire rivers. Most boating accidents occur in shallow ocean waters, where a run of waves can build up to break around a boat. Offshore anglers should team up with an experienced party en route to fishing grounds, particularly those going to Lady Julia Percy Island.

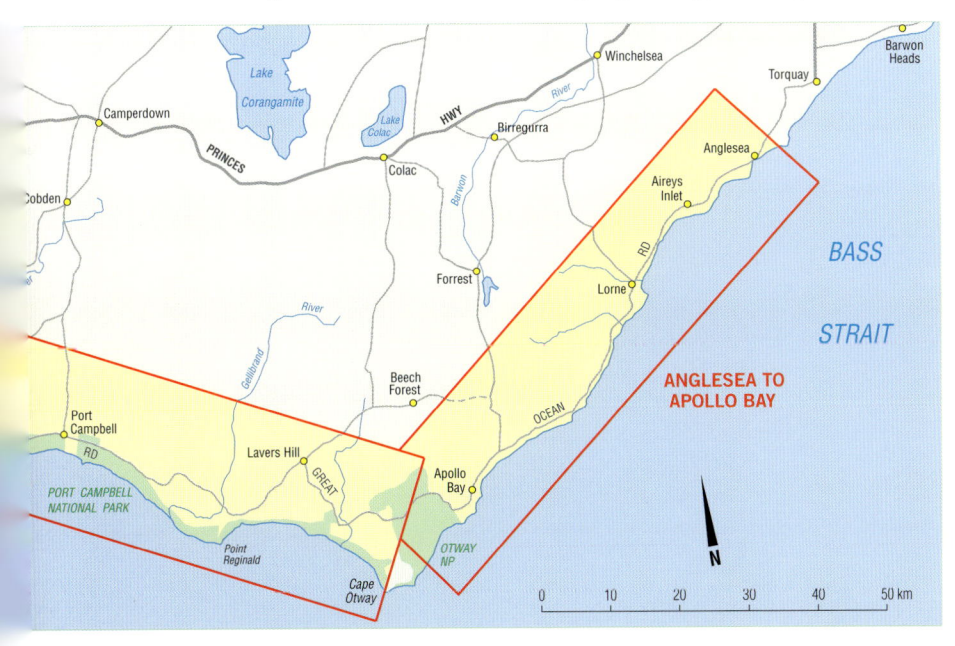

The Hopkins River at Warrnambool has shallow reef areas so maintain a slow speed and note warning signs. 'The Pass' near Jubilee Park has rocks just below the surface when the river is low. Run-outs, rips, reefs and channels make Marengo near Apollo Bay another place for boating caution. At Warrnambool and Port Fairy there are marine radio base channels on 27-880.

FISHING TIP

Barracouta are often prolific offshore and are most often caught trolling skirted lures. But when these fish are not on the surface, use your sounder to locate the schools down deep and then try jigging for them with heavy metal lures. When you bring a fish to the surface, many others will often follow it up.

FURTHER INFORMATION

Fishing information There are Natural Resources and Environment offices at Oak Ave, Apollo Bay, tel. (03) 5237 6889; 83 Gellibrand St, Colac, tel. (03) 5233 5533; 8–12 Julia St, Portland, tel. (03) 5523 3232; 78 Henna St, Warrnambool, tel. (03) 5561 9950.

Visitor information Great Ocean Rd Visitor Information Centre, 100 Great Ocean Rd, Apollo Bay, tel. (03) 5237 6529; Bank St, Port Fairy, tel. (03) 5568 2682; Portland Foreshore Lee Breakwater Rd, Portland, tel. (03) 5523 2671; 600 Raglan Pde, Warrnambool, tel. (03) 5564 7837.

VICTORIA
COASTAL FISHING WARRNAMBOOL REGION

Anglesea to Apollo Bay

Type of fishing
bay, beach, offshore, river, rock

Target fish
Australian salmon, barracouta, flathead, sharks, snapper, whiting, yellowtail kingfish

The Great Ocean Road runs along one of the most beautiful stretches of coastline in the world, with the hills and cliffs creating a backdrop for spectacular rock formations, sweeping beaches and rolling surf.

In mild weather Anglesea's best fishing is at **Ingoldsby Reef**, about 1 km out from the cliff between the Eumeralla Scout Camp and Anglesea. The sand holes on the inshore side of the reef produce really big whiting and some snapper. Other species around the reef are Australian salmon, yellowtail kingfish, snook and pike.

Anglesea River has good fishing, especially in the evening, for bream, estuary perch, mullet, Australian salmon and trevally. In winter, the best fishing is in the river mouth; in the summer, upstream.

The beach at **Hutt Gully** is good for Australian salmon, especially when there is a channel running away from the beach. You will also find snapper and trevally on the exposed reef at low tide. At the western end of this long beach is **Urquhart Bluff**, which has a deep hole and run-out under the bluff – a good spot for Australian salmon. Nearby, anglers target snapper, whiting and salmon at Nathans Point, especially in early summer, and at dusk on a rising tide.

It is mainly rock and beach fishing from Anglesea to Lorne. **Aireys Inlet** has a headland beneath the cliffs, known as Eagle Rock, which can be fished at low tide for snapper, whiting and Australian salmon. About 1 km out to sea from the lighthouse is an obvious drop-off that is good for snapper. Fish the end of the beach, to the right of the lighthouse, for mullet and Australian salmon.

The **Painkalac Creek** at Aireys Inlet is best when the entrance is open, with bream and the elusive estuary perch the target. Fishing near the entrance is good in summer, while the favoured winter area is where the road to Bambra runs alongside the stream.

The long **Fairhaven Beach** has some good spots: at night, a broken channel past the Life Saving Club for Australian salmon and gummy shark; Moggs Creek beach for Australian salmon; Moggs Creek estuary for bream; and Moggs Ledge, a drop-off that carries snapper in November.

Eastern View is a noted night fishing spot for Australian salmon; offshore fishing behind the breaker line gives good whiting and snapper with bait or Australian salmon with lures. There is excellent rock fishing around the entrance to Grassy Creek.

Fishing boats in the harbour at Apollo Bay

GUIDE TO LOCAL FISH

		Anglesea to Apollo Bay	Lorne	Apollo Bay
BC	barracouta	•	•	•
B	bream		•	
F	flathead	•		
G	garfish	•	•	•
KI	kingfish, yellowtail	•		
MA	mackerel, horse	•		
M	mullet, yelloweye	•	•	•
MU	mulloway	•		
EP	perch, estuary	•	•	•
PI	pike, long-finned	•		
SA	salmon, Australian	•	•	•
GS	shark, gummy/school	•	•	
SH	shark, others	•		
S	snapper	•	•	•
SN	snook	•		
SW	sweep			•
TR	trevally, silver	•	•	•
WA	warehou			•
W	whiting, King George	•	•	•

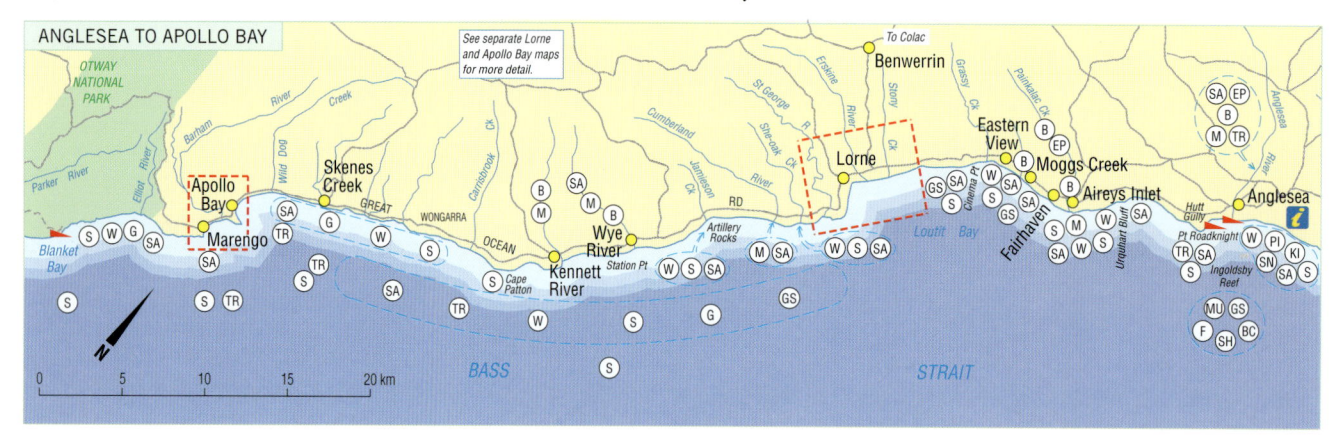

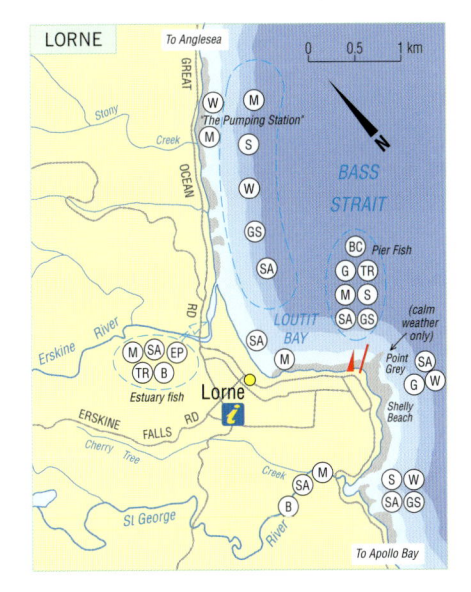

COASTAL FISHING WARRNAMBOOL REGION

VICTORIA

worth trying for whiting, snapper, Australian salmon and garfish. A reef 1.5 km off Cape Patton produces good numbers of small snapper, while **offshore** from White Crests Guest House on the eastern side of Wongarra is a deep ledge, which can be located by depth sounder, with great boat fishing for snapper and trevally.

To get to the entrances of the **Elliot and Parker rivers**, west of Apollo Bay, you must go off the Great Ocean Road. Neither river has great fishing, but at Elliot the rock fishing yields acceptable catches of whiting, Australian salmon, snapper and garfish. The same varieties can be sought from the rock platforms at the Parker.

LORNE

The beautiful coastal town of **Lorne** is on Loutit Bay, where evening fishing may produce gummy shark, snapper and Australian salmon. The Pumping Station, a rock ledge, is best fished in the evening on a high tide.

Lorne Pier is considered the best pier on the west coast. Mullet, garfish and trevally can be taken on lighter rigs, whereas long casters can try for Australian salmon and barracouta. Some heavy-gear anglers try for shark with tuna bait. Best fishing is at dusk.

The rocks at **Point Grey**, only good on a calm day, can produce whiting and garfish when the tide is out, particularly in the evening. The **Erskine River**, at Lorne, in its lower reaches is good for mullet, Australian salmon, trevally, bream and estuary perch, before it gives way to brown trout water.

South-west of Lorne, **She-oak Creek** is good for Australian salmon, snapper and whiting, but only in calm conditions at low tide. Near the carpark at the Ninety Mile marker is a safer platform, but the target is a reef 100 m out – only an option for long casters. The **Cumberland River** estuary is shallow, but you can bait fish for mullet and Australian salmon.

From the **Artillery Rocks**, past the Jamieson Creek, you can surf cast for snapper, whiting and Australian salmon. Bream, mullet and Australian salmon are estuary targets at **Wye River**. There are good rock platforms to the west of the river and at Station Point. Similar shallow estuary conditions are at **Kennett River** and **Carisbrook, Skenes and Wild Dog creeks**. The coastal rock formations all along here are

Surf anglers near the mouth of Moggs Creek

The estuary of the **St George River** is shallow, but produces mullet and Australian salmon when the tide is full. Offshore from the river mouth are good catches of whiting and snapper, with the occasional gummy shark, but launching is very difficult.

APOLLO BAY

Apollo Bay Beach, abutting the Barham River and sheltered by a reef, produces the rare ideal situation in which children can fish in the estuary while their parents take on the surf. Upstream the Barham has bream, estuary perch and brown trout – three wily species to test the experts. But the boat harbour at Apollo Bay is a land angler's dream. The harbour walls give access to barracouta, Australian salmon, trevally and big flathead, while the jetties are good for slimy mackerel, trevally, barracouta and warehou. The ramp is sheltered from all but easterlies, but if it is too rough to go out there is still good boat fishing in the harbour. Best time is at dusk.

Past Apollo Bay, the water is wilder again. **Mounts Bay** is best at high tide, particularly if it coincides with the evening. **Marengo** has run-outs and rips and is interspersed with reefs and channels. Boat anglers like the gap in **Hayley Reef**, off Marengo. The direction of the tide flow determines which side of the reef you should fish for the big whiting. There is whiting to be caught from the Marengo Beach, but thick kelp is a hindrance. The eastern end of the beach is an excellent spot for trevally and Australian salmon, but only at dawn and dusk. The **Rifle Butts**, for garfish and sweep, is a rock platform west of Marengo, while fine **offshore** spots include the Bunbury Reef and the flathead grounds past Hayley Reef.

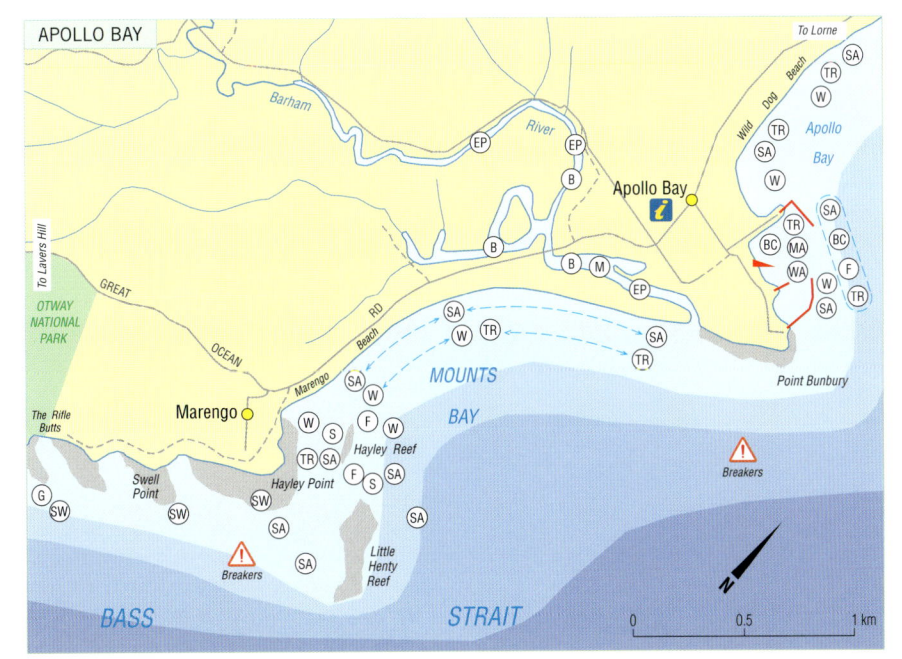

VICTORIA

COASTAL FISHING WARRNAMBOOL REGION

Cape Otway to Port Fairy

Type of fishing
bay, beach, creek, estuary, offshore, pier, river, rock

Target fish
Australian salmon, gummy shark, snapper, tailor, trevally, yellowtail kingfish

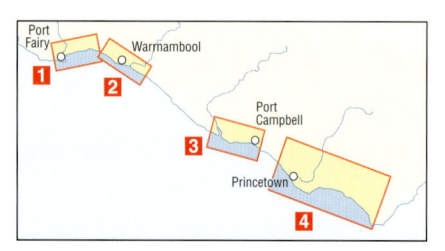

This grand stretch of coast, with its magnificent cliffs, rock formations and peaceful villages, provides some of the most varied coastal fishing in Australia. From Cape Otway an early stop is the **Aire River**, reached by a detour from Hordern Vale. You can fish upstream for brown trout or in **Lake Craven** for bream and estuary perch. A small aluminium boat is handy but the lower reaches of the river are accessible from shore. The beach on the east side of the river is one of the State's best beach fishing spots. Fish at night for catches of the abundant Australian salmon, mulloway, gummy shark and snapper.

The detour road takes you to Glenaire. Try for trout in the **Ford River**, near the main road bridge, or fish for Australian salmon and snapper from the beach at **Castle Cove**. Another detour takes you down to **Johanna**, a renowned surf beach. The night fishing here is excellent, but you must have checked the rips, reefs and gutters by daylight to know where to cast.

The great charm of **Princetown** is the fishing at the junction of the La Trobe Creek and Gellibrand River. Small mullet, bream and Australian salmon can be caught between the bridge and the carpark – a safe, but exciting place for children. The river is deep and wide enough to launch a dinghy.

Gibsons Steps are signposted some 4.5 km past Princetown. The best daytime fishing is among the obvious sandy areas within the reef and weed, to the left of the long, steep steps. At night, it is long casting for Australian salmon, gummy shark and snapper.

Young anglers fishing on the Aire River

PORT CAMPBELL

Port Campbell is a popular fishing spot, although the launching ramp is very steep and subject to strong ocean swells. Many locals prefer to winch their boats from the jetty. The jetty yields a variety of fish, including whiting, snapper, trevally and the occasional crayfish. Campbells Creek can be fished for bream and mullet from a boat for 1.5 km upstream. The channel in Port Campbell Bay is the recognised fishing ground for snapper and whiting.

Curdies River at Peterborough is often closed to the sea, but the shallow inlet produces bream, and Australian salmon and mullet near the mouth. The river can be navigated by small boat for several kilometres, and is one of the best bream fisheries on the west coast. The reef areas in the centre of the bay at Peterborough provide a base for casting into the sand and seagrass for whiting.

WARRNAMBOOL

Warrnambool is a big, handsome city on the water – an ideal place for anglers, with all types of fishing close at hand. There is good estuary fishing in the Hopkins River, trout in the Merri River and Lake Gillear, surf and offshore fishing, as well as pier and limited rock fishing.

The **Hopkins River** offers both good land-based and boat angling. It is a prolific estuary, with large populations of bream and estuary perch, and a seasonal run of mulloway from 3 kg to just over 20 kg. Best bait for bream are shrimp, marine worm and 'greyback' minnows. Estuary perch will take baits such as shrimp or worm under a float, and can also be taken on lures and wet flies.

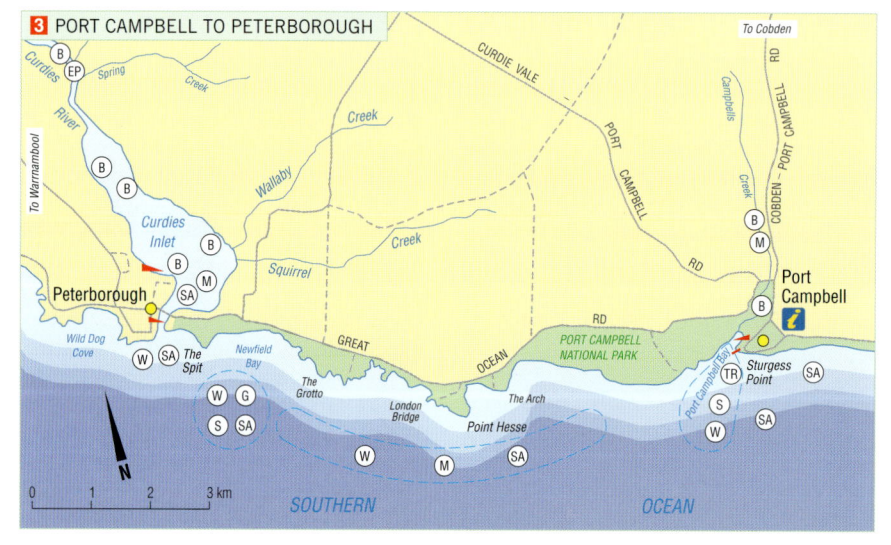

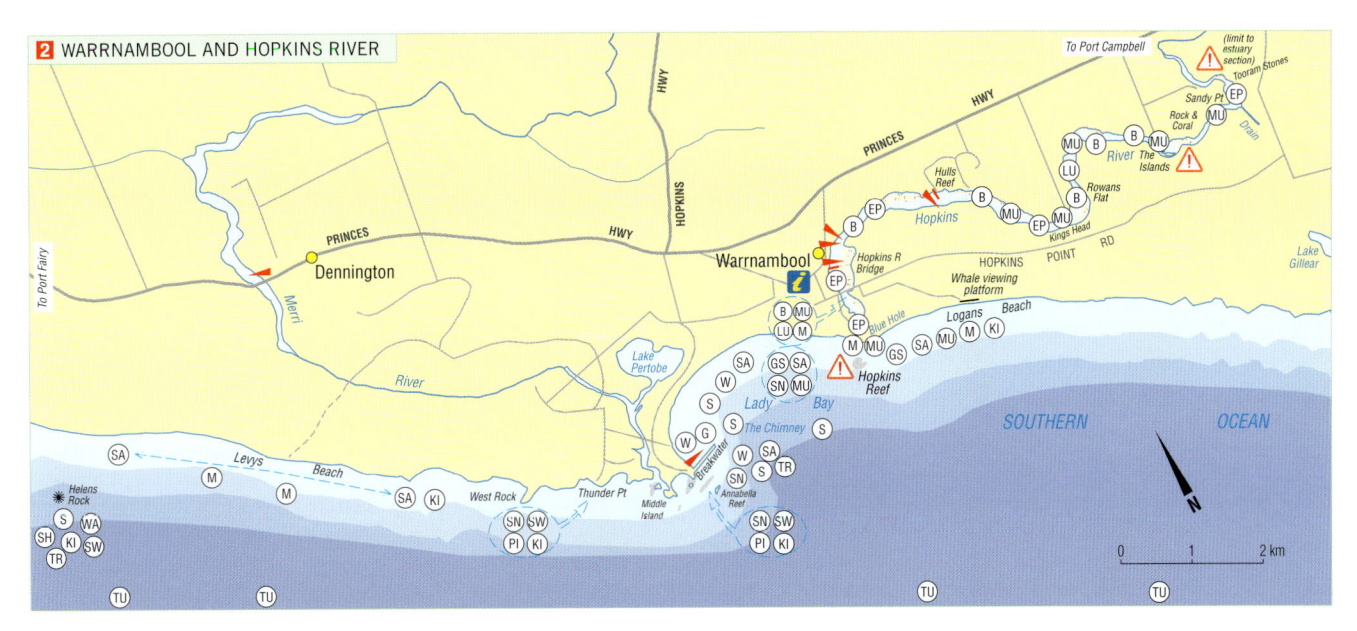

COASTAL FISHING WARRNAMBOOL REGION

VICTORIA

2 WARRNAMBOOL AND HOPKINS RIVER

The Hopkins estuary winds through the country near Warrnambool for some 9 km, until it reaches rapids at Tooram Stones. Just inside the estuary entrance, the Blue Hole is a place for mulloway and estuary perch. Bream, mullet, mulloway, perch and sometimes luderick can be had throughout the estuary, but the great mulloway holes further upriver are not productive in a hot summer as the water loses oxygen. Fish nearer the mouth in winter and spring, and fish the whole river in summer and autumn, especially for estuary perch at night after a hot day.

Land-based anglers prefer the **Lady Bay Breakwater**, while **Logans Beach** and **Levys Beach** provide surf fishing for Australian salmon and mullet. About 2.5 km offshore from the west end of Levys is **Helens Rock**, a pinnacle beneath the surface. You can locate it on rough days from the spray, but a depth sounder would be required to find it on calm days. Sometimes the following species can be caught in summer: snapper, yellowtail kingfish, trevally and thresher shark. Garfish school in the bay in winter, and bream also emerge in times of flood.

Offshore you can seek reef fish behind **Annabella Reef** and west towards Thunder Point, or east from the Hopkins River mouth. There are a number of good snapper marks in and out from Lady Bay over summer.

PORT FAIRY

At historic **Port Fairy**, the Moyne River estuary is home to mullet and bream, with some Australian salmon, trevally, luderick and occasional mulloway. The best estuary fishing is around the **Garden St Bridge**. There is an excellent ramp and the entrance to the ocean is very safe. The breakwater produces Australian salmon, bream and snapper.

There is beach fishing between The Cutting and Killarney Beach for whiting, salmon and yelloweye mullet, while the reef off Basin Point can be reached by shore casters for snapper and, at times, yellowtail kingfish. **Killarney Beach** offers reef fishing from the surf, the rocks or a boat for King George whiting, snapper, silver trevally and Australian salmon. Small boats can be launched from the beach and a 4wd vehicle is advised.

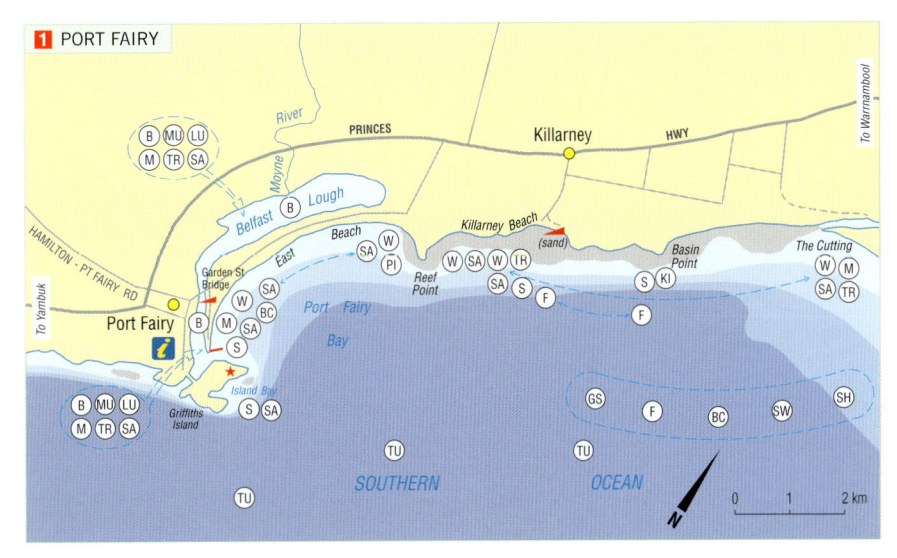

GUIDE TO LOCAL FISH

	Cape Otway and Princetown	Port Campbell to Peterborough	Warrnambool and Hopkins River	Port Fairy
BC barracouta				●
B bream		●	●	●
F flathead				●
G garfish			●	●
KI kingfish, yellowtail			●	●
LU luderick			●	●
M mullet, yelloweye	●		●	●
MU mulloway		●	●	
EP perch, estuary	●	●	●	
PI pike, long-finned			●	●
SA salmon, Australian	●	●	●	●
GS shark, gummy/school	●		●	●
SH shark, others			●	●
S snapper	●	●	●	●
SN snook			●	●
SW sweep			●	●
TR trevally, silver	●		●	●
TU tuna				●
WA warehou			●	
W whiting, King George	●	●	●	●

1 PORT FAIRY

VICTORIA

COASTAL FISHING WARRNAMBOOL REGION

Portland Bay to Nelson

Type of fishing
bay, beach, offshore, river

Target fish
Australian salmon, snapper, whiting, yellowtail kingfish

There is a great variety of fishing around **Portland**, site of the first European settlement in Victoria in 1834. The beach and port waters are protected from southerly squalls by Cape Sir William Grant and carry snapper, flathead, whiting, sweep, trevally and Australian salmon. There is game fishing offshore for shark, yellowtail kingfish and bluefin tuna. Portland's launching ramp is the best in the area. It is totally protected, with cleaning tables and jetties.

A particular phenomenon is the movement of sharks into **Portland Bay** to mate from October to December. They can be caught by boat anglers all along the coast from just north of the harbour to the Fitzroy River, near Tyrendarra East, using wire

Small boats are ideal to fish the Glenelg River, almost necessary, as bank access is very limited

traces and strong, sharp hooks in the range of 6/0 to 10/0. Species include blue, mako, thresher, bronze whaler, school and gummy sharks. From October to May, sharks tend to congregate off the Fitzroy River mouth and out to sea, off Cape Nelson.

Of the more generally prolific species, whiting, snapper and flathead are the common inshore targets around Portland. The best snapper time is November to April. Some of the bigger catches for shore anglers have been from the **Lee Breakwater** and the marina wharf in the port, and along the rock wall to the north of the port. Boat anglers should try over the **Minerva Reef**, offshore from the Surrey River mouth. But the whole bay has possibilities, either for drifting or for anchoring over sand holes or rubble areas. Some 3 to 4 km off the harbour entrance (in line with Lady Julia Percy Island) is a submerged patch of limestone known as the **Cod Splat**, a fine snapper mark.

Whiting congregate around **Blacknose Point** and **Point Danger**, in the port and along the north shore to Minerva Reef. The best season is from December to April, but there is sometimes a run outside the Lee Breakwater from July to August.

Long-finned pike, in Portland Bay all year round, and out from Point Danger around **Lawrence Rocks**, is the particular target fish for anglers trolling small silver lures behind paravanes. In calm conditions pike can be caught drifting over reefs using whitebait.

Sweep are close to shore in the rocky headlands and rougher water around Point Danger, Lawrence Rocks, Cape Sir William Grant and Cape Nelson, but they

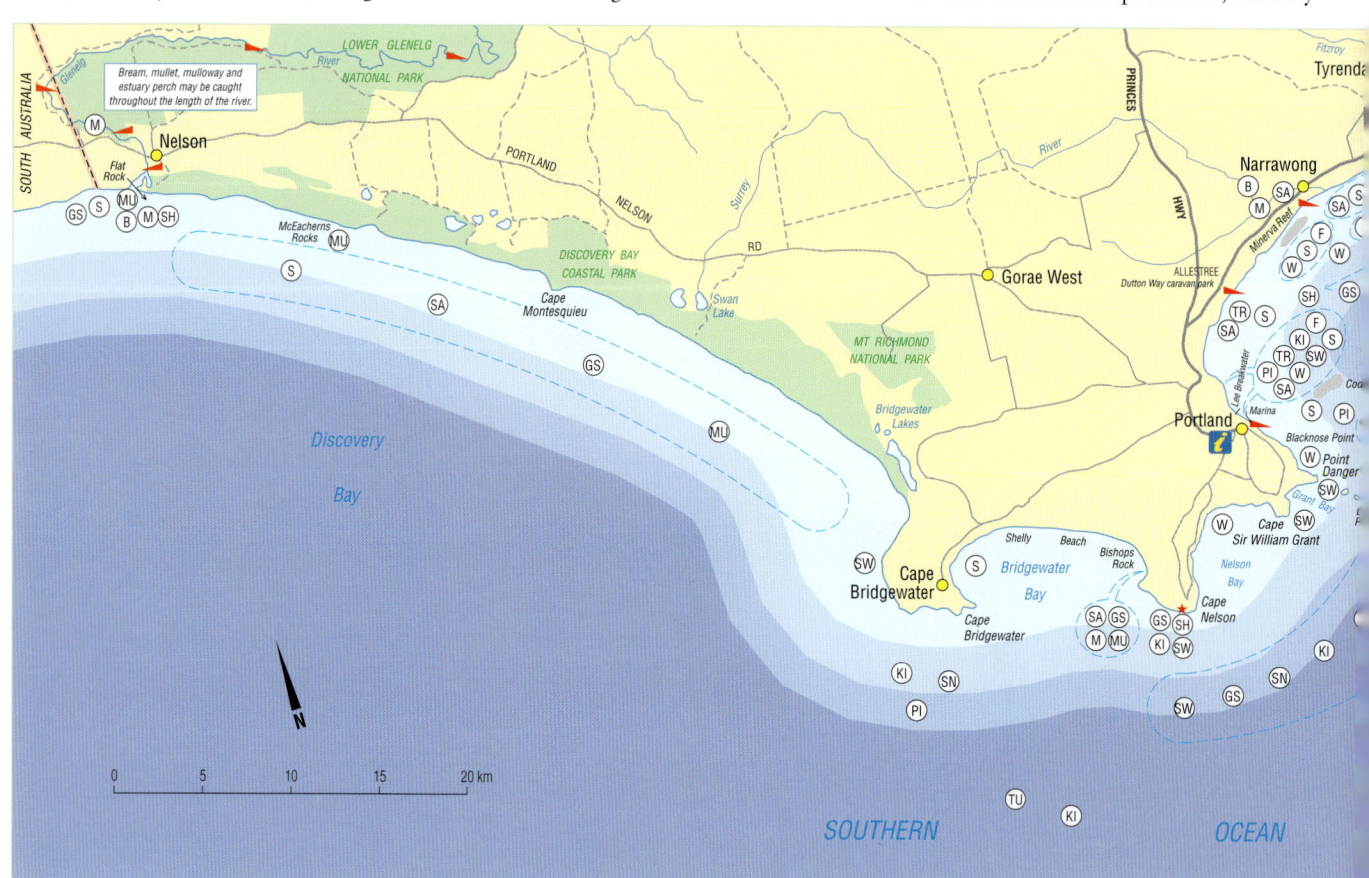

192

COASTAL FISHING WARRNAMBOOL REGION

VICTORIA

can also be caught at the end of the Lee Breakwater. Australian salmon can be caught all year round from the breakwaters, wharves, boats and the shore, while there are yellowtail kingfish inshore from January to late March, and then out around the capes and Lawrence Rocks.

To the east of Portland, at **Yambuk**, there is surf fishing for Australian salmon and snapper. Offshore at Mills Reef are snook, yellowtail kingfish and sweep. Weedy Yambuk Lake is fished for mullet and bream. Butchers Jetty and O'Briens Point, just north of the boat ramp, are popular spots. Offshore is **Lady Julia Percy Island**, which harbours a large seal colony. The waters around the island provide great game fishing on a calm day for yellowtail kingfish, trevally, sweep, warehou and bluefin tuna, as well as snapper and morwong on the reef. Off the Surrey River mouth, in line with Lady Julia Percy Island and around 400 to 500 m out, is an area producing big snapper and school mulloway.

The beach at **Narrawong**, 19 km east of Portland, is excellent for surf fishing. Australian salmon and even snapper and mulloway are present over the summer months. It is also reasonably sheltered from the prevailing south-westerlies. The beach is quite shallow, so should be checked during the day for gutters and fished from dusk to dawn. The locals don't ignore the bream, mullet and occasional schools of Australian salmon that enter the **Surrey River** here and further east at the **Fitzroy River**. The beach at Fitzroy River is also productive for gummy shark, salmon and snapper.

West of Portland, at **Shelly Beach**, on the western end of Bridgewater Bay, snapper can occasionally be seen by torchlight with their tails up feeding head down in the sand. Bishops Rock, at the eastern end of the bay near Cape Nelson, is a productive fishing platform in calm conditions.

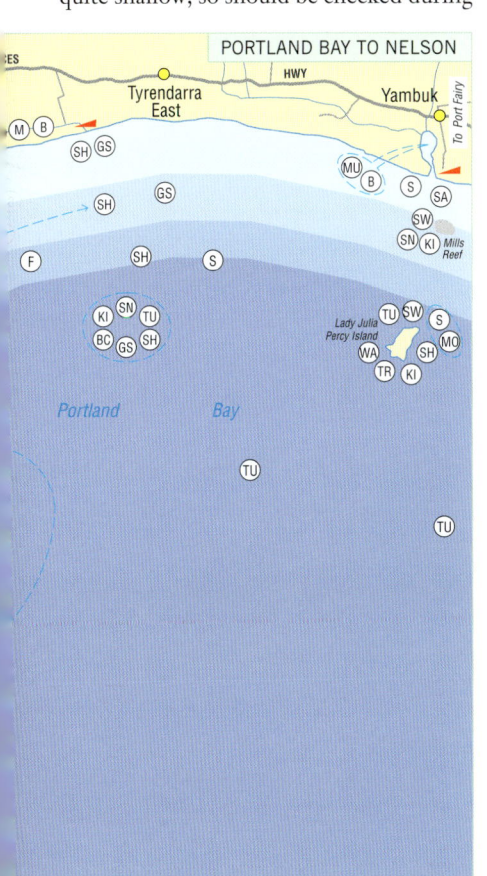

Surf casting off Narrawong Beach, east of Portland. This beach produces some solid gummy shark and Australian salmon, as well as the normal run of surf species

Discovery Bay is noted for big Australian salmon, but snapper, gummy shark and the odd mulloway are taken as well. You can reach the beach from the Swan Lake picnic area using a 1.5-km, four-wheel drive track (although you are not permitted to drive on the beach), or from 2 km further along the highway.

The picturesque town of **Nelson** nestles sleepily on the shores of the Glenelg River, which winds its way down through farmland and bush from its source in the Grampians National Park, above the Rocklands Reservoir. The **Glenelg River** estuary at Nelson is well known for catches of mulloway, bream and mullet, as well as estuary perch in the higher reaches. The big mulloway are not as prevalent as they once were, but there are still many school mulloway. Trolling bait between Flat Rock and McEacherns Rocks is the way to entice a mulloway. Rowing is preferred, as always in quiet waters but the use of electric motors is growing. Flat Rock is a good fishing platform in calm weather.

Upstream there are kilometres of bream water. Finding the bream can be difficult due to their migratory habits and the length of the river; fish alongside the banks near structures rather than midstream.

The entire river can be navigated by boat. Land-based access is available in certain areas and fishing from the many small jetties can be productive. Best baits are fresh shrimp, sandworm and bass yabbies.

There is good surf fishing for mulloway, snapper and shark from the beach on either side of the **Glenelg River** mouth.

GUIDE TO LOCAL FISH

BC	barracouta
B	bream
F	flathead
KI	kingfish, yellowtail
MO	morwong
M	mullet, yelloweye
MU	mulloway
EP	perch, estuary
PI	pike, long-finned
SA	salmon, Australian
GS	shark, gummy/school
SH	shark, others
S	snapper
SN	snook
SW	sweep
TR	trevally, silver
TU	tuna
WJ	warehou
W	whiting, King George

193

VICTORIA

Inland Fishing

Victoria is rich in streams, rivers, lakes, dams and pondages for the freshwater angler. Most of the larger rivers flow northwards into the dominant inland water system of Australia, the Murray-Darling, and a smaller number flow southwards. The fast-flowing rivers in the east run from the mountains to the sea; the rivers of the flatter western country take a more meandering course. Then there are the classic coastal streams that contain a wonderful diversity of fish species. There are many lakes of natural origin, and storage dams and reservoirs that have vastly extended the boat and shore-based fishing potential of the inland areas.

The Great Dividing Range, twisting through the east of the State, is laced with temperate streams, fast-flowing rivers and large water-storage areas – perfect for trout, redfin, blackfish, and native fish like Macquarie perch. Small populations of Murray cod exist in places. It is spectacular country, with forested ranges giving way to green fingers of valleys that contain accessible fishing water. The Kiewa, Mitta Mitta, Howqua, Jamieson and upper King rivers are renowned for fly fishing. But there are many other rivers and streams, some easily accessible, others not.

There are large rivers at the foothills of the Divide like the Goulburn and Ovens rivers, which carry trout and other cold-water species in their upper reaches before giving way to the warmer, slower waters that are the major habitat of Australian native fish. The average size and number of some natives have dwindled and restocking efforts are under way. Serious anglers are also helping by limiting their catch to the requirements of the table and releasing the rest.

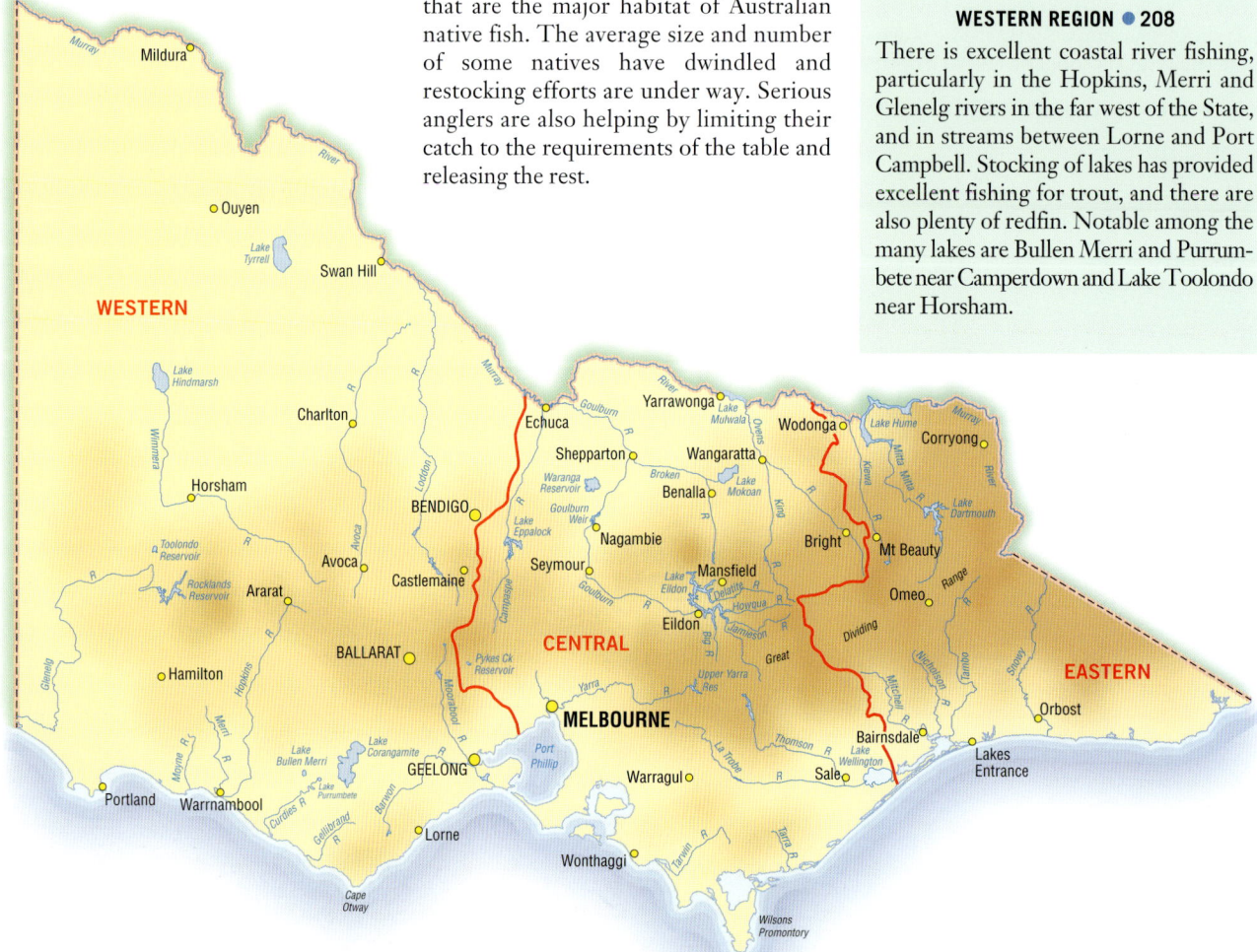

INLAND FISHING

WHERE TO FISH

Inland

EASTERN REGION ● 196

The Murray above Lake Hume provides excellent trout fishing, with plenty of trout in feeder streams like the Cudgewa and Nariel creeks. The Mitta Mitta and tributaries are productive trout fisheries and the river flows into two well-stocked storage areas – Lake Dartmouth and Lake Hume. The Snowy, Tambo, Mitchell and Nicholson rivers all contain reasonable to good trout fishing in their upper reaches.

CENTRAL REGION ● 202

The Goulburn River and its tributaries are the most popular inland fishing waters in Victoria. There is trout fishing in the upper Campaspe basin, particularly in the water storages. Native fish predominate further inland as the rivers run to the Murray. Major fishing lakes include Eildon and Lake Eppalock, the Waranga Reservoir near Shepparton and the Goulburn Weir near Nagambie.

WESTERN REGION ● 208

There is excellent coastal river fishing, particularly in the Hopkins, Merri and Glenelg rivers in the far west of the State, and in streams between Lorne and Port Campbell. Stocking of lakes has provided excellent fishing for trout, and there are also plenty of redfin. Notable among the many lakes are Bullen Merri and Purrumbete near Camperdown and Lake Toolondo near Horsham.

INLAND FISHING

VICTORIA

The beautiful rivers of north-east Victoria consist of alternate stretches of fast broken water and quiet shingle-bottomed pools like this one

Protected species

In Victoria, 21 species, including four crustaceans, are listed as threatened. They are: Murray cod, Macquarie perch, trout cod, silver perch, freshwater catfish, Australian grayling, freshwater herring, Tasmanian mudfish, Murray hardyhead, non-speckled hardyhead, barred galaxias, dwarf galaxias, Cox's gudgeon, southern purple-spotted gudgeon, Agassiz's chanda perch, variegated pygmy perch, Yarra pygmy perch, Orbost spiny crayfish, and the Mallacoota, Warragul and Narracan burrowing crayfish. Of the listed species, regulations permit angling for Murray cod, Macquarie perch, silver perch and freshwater catfish. However, restrictions such as season, bag and size limits apply. This list is under constant review and is subject to change at any time. The changes may only apply to specific fish communities. In some waters it will be legal to catch the same fish, but in others, due to population declines, restrictions may be introduced until the fishery is declared safe. If fishing in the Murray river, check New South Wales regulations.

Fishing regulations

An all waters Recreational Fishing Licence is required to fish in Victoria. The licence costs $20 a year, but short-term licences are also available. The cost is $10 for a 28-day licence and $5 for a 48-hour licence. There are many exemptions including Seniors cardholders, age and invalid pensioners and children under 18 years of age.

Licences are available from over 1000 outlets including Natural Resources and Environment offices and tackle shops.

Further information regarding licences can be obtained from NRE on 13 6186, or at their website: www.nre.vic.gov.au/fisheries.

NRE also produces the 'Victorian Recreational Fishing Guide', which can be obtained free where you purchase your licence.

Fishing regulations in Victoria have undergone a series of changes in recent years and most fish are now subject to bag and size limit restrictions. Some native fish are protected and there are closed seasons for Murray cod, Macquarie perch, and river blackfish. There is also a closed season for trout in rivers, so consult the guide before planning a trip.

Boating regulations

All powered boats used in Victoria are required to be registered and carry safety equipment. Various other regulations apply on Victorian waterways including speed limits, blood alcohol limits and restricted boating zones.

The Victorian Government has announced boat licensing laws will apply from the 2001–2002 boating season. Powerboat operators under 21 years of age will need to be licensed for the 2001–2002 summer, while remaining operators will be licensed in late 2002–2003.

Under the proposed regulations, anybody operating a recreational powerboat will need to be licensed. Interstate licences will be automatically recognised in Victoria and will be valid for three years after the commencement date of licensing, and Victorian licences will be recognised interstate.

Restricted licences will be available for powerboat operators over the age of 12 and under 16 years of age. Victorian licences will be recognised interstate.

Full details of Victorian boating rules and regulations can be found in 'The Victorian Boating Guide', produced by the Marine Board of Victoria. For further information regarding this and other boating and safety regulations call the Marine Board of Victoria on (03) 9655 3399.

GUIDE TO LOCAL FISH

bass, Australian
blackfish, river
carp
catfish
cod, Murray
eel, long-finned
eel, short-finned
goldfish
perch, estuary
perch, golden
perch, Macquarie
perch, silver
redfin
roach
salmon, chinook
spiny freshwater crayfish
tench
trout, brown
trout, rainbow
tupong

Consult the 'Victorian Recreational Fishing Guide' for size, bags and seasons.

Weather

A thorough understanding of the weather and how it affects an area you intend fishing is important. Watch for weather updates on television and radio news and get on line with the Bureau of Meteorology: www.bom.gov.au/weather/vic

FISHING TIP

Always use your powers of observation when fishing for trout. For example, fly fishers talk about 'matching the hatch' when selecting flies. This means choosing a fly that resembles the insects the trout are feeding on at the time. It is a rule that also works for bait fishers, particularly when large insects such as crickets or grasshoppers are abundant, or perhaps the trout are feeding on smalt ('smelting') or mudeyes.

FURTHER INFORMATION

Fishing For full details of Victoria's inland fishing regulations contact Natural Resources and Environment at the State Government Offices, Cnr Fenwick and Little Malop Sts, tel. (03) 5226 4667 or 8 Nicholson St, East Melbourne, tel. 13 6186. See also the department's publication the 'Victorian Recreational Fishing Guide', which is available at most bait and tackle shops.

Boating 'The Victorian Boating Guide' is a pamphlet produced by the Marine Board of Victoria, which is at Level 11, 80 Collins St, Melbourne, tel. (03) 9655 3399.

VICTORIA

INLAND FISHING EASTERN REGION

Eastern Region

The east of the State is dominated by the Great Dividing Range, reaching across from the eastern border to the ranges on the outskirts of Melbourne. On one side of the Divide rivers flow north into the Murray and on the other rivers flow towards the coast.

GUIDE TO LOCAL FISH

- bass, Australian
- blackfish, river
- carp
- cod, Murray
- eel
- grayling, Australian
- perch, golden
- perch, Macquarie
- redfin
- spiny freshwater crayfish
- trout, brown
- trout, rainbow
- tupong

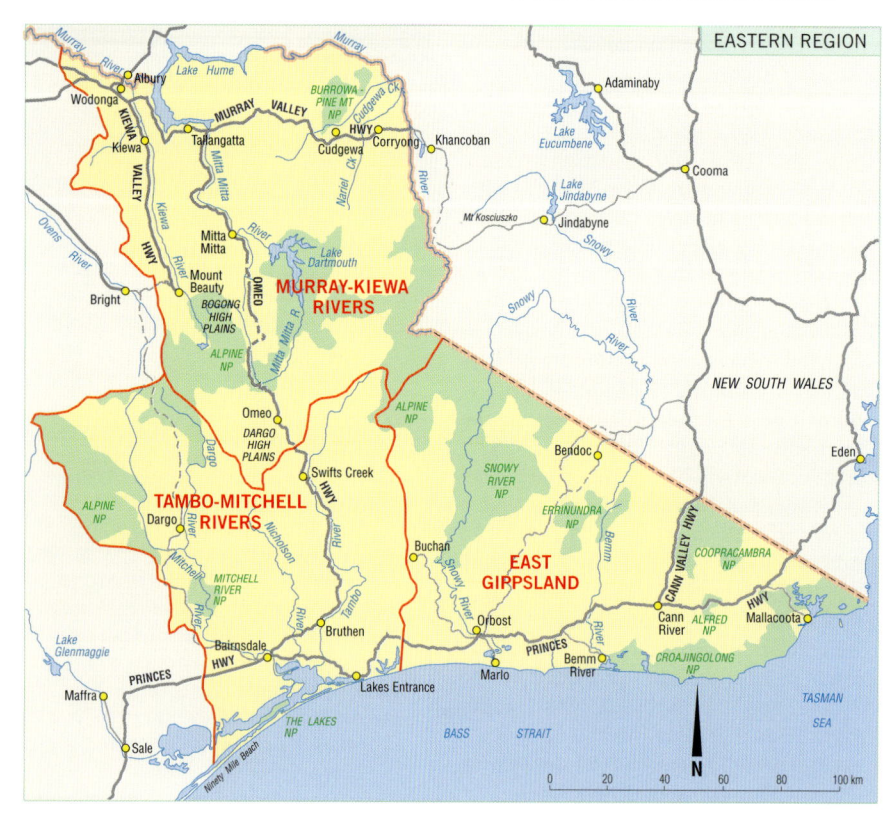

WHERE TO FISH

Eastern Region

EAST GIPPSLAND ● 198

Access is generally difficult in the inland region of the Snowy River basin, but for those who have established a route to a favourite river, the fishing can be very good. Brown trout and bass are the main catch. There is a high fire danger in these remote forests over summer. In the extreme east the fishing is generally poor, with only a few decent-sized trout and Australian bass in the rivers. Again, beware of the fire risk.

TAMBO–MITCHELL RIVERS ● 199

Brown trout, short-finned eels and long-finned eels and tupong are the main freshwater fish in the Tambo basin. Although only four-wheel drives and walking will get you to most areas of the Mitchell River and the numerous small streams and rivers that run into it, the fishing is often very good once you are there.

MURRAY–KIEWA RIVERS ● 200

The upper Murray area – high country rivers fed by small streams – is perfect water for self-sustaining brown trout and rainbow trout populations, and the Mitta Mitta River and others nearby are simply 'trout heaven'. Murray cod are a chance in the slower and deeper parts of the Kiewa, while Lake Dartmouth carries good numbers of big brown trout, rainbow trout and Macquarie perch.

The upper Murray River above Lake Hume has a well-deserved reputation as a trout fishery. Some native species, including Murray cod, are also present. The major tributary of the upper Murray is the Mitta Mitta, a first-class trout stream above and below Lake Dartmouth. The lake itself offers good fishing for trout and Macquarie perch.

South of the Divide, the Tambo, Snowy, Mitchell and Nicholson rivers all provide fair to good trout fishing. The rivers of the far east generally offer poor fishing for trout but rate much better for Australian bass.

Australian bass

Australian bass are sometimes confused with estuary perch. While the two species bear a close resemblance to one another, there are distinct differences. The most marked difference is where the fish are caught. Australian bass are a freshwater fish, while estuary perch, as the name implies, is a saltwater fish. And Gippsland marks the eastern boundary for bass, while estuary perch can be caught in estuaries in the west of the state.

FURTHER INFORMATION

Fishing information There are Natural Resources and Environment offices at 7 Service St, Bairnsdale, tel. (03) 5152 0400; 1 Bullock Island Rd, Lakes Entrance, tel. (03) 5155 1539; cnr Buckland and Allan Drs, Mallacoota, tel. (03) 5158 0219; 171 Nicholson St, Orbost, tel. (03) 5161 1222; 1 McKoy St, Wodonga, tel. (02) 6055 6111.

Visitor information 240 Main St, Bairnsdale, tel. (03) 5152 3444; General store, Main St, Buchan, tel. (03) 5155 9202; Parks Victoria Information Centre, Princes Hwy, Cann River, tel. (03) 5158 6351; Corryong Visitor Information Centre, 50 Hanson St, Corryong, tel. (02) 6076 2277; cnr The Esplanade and Marine Pde, Lakes Entrance, tel. (03) 5155 1966; cnr Buckland and Allan Dr, Mallacoota, tel. (03) 5158 0219. The Slab Hut, cnr Lochiel and Browning St, Orbost, tel. (03) 5154 2424; Lincoln Causeway, Wodonga, tel. (02) 6041 3875.

INLAND FISHING EASTERN REGION   VICTORIA

One in a Thousand

'The blackest brown trout I have ever seen leapt clear from the water, as if to show me beyond doubt its massive bulk.'

In any trout water, among the thousands of fish there are always a few – just a handful – that grow to an exceptional size. How this comes to be is often a mystery. Why does nature allow one or two trout to keep growing and thriving far beyond the average? Is it cold, hard genetic superiority, or simply good fortune smiling on a single trout and providing the best possible combination of food and shelter year after year? Perhaps it is a blend of the two.

Late one evening on the upper Murray River near Towong, I encountered such a fish. As the gentle autumn sun slipped behind the pale yellow hills, the Kosciuszko mayfly began to hatch. From among the nooks and crannies in the gravel beneath the swift, cold current the aquatic mayfly nymphs started to make their life or death dash for the surface. Here, they would float in the current and emerge from their nymphal husks in a remarkable transition that would see them transformed into a winged flying insect called a dun. The duns would drift in the current until their wings dried, then flutter to the bank-side bushes to shed their skin, mate and die.

But at every stage prior to take-off from the surface, the duns were vulnerable to the Murray trout. In the pink glow of sunset, the fish slashed like sharks at their fluttering prey. Many were caught, never to fulfil their final quest. However, the duns numbered hundreds, maybe thousands, and some escaped.

Within this flurry of activity, one trout ignored the frantic splashing out in the main current. Against a steep bank, hemmed in almost entirely by a clutter of logs and sticks, was a small back eddy. I had the good luck to locate this table-sized pocket, discreetly hidden away from obvious view. Here some of the duns were swept aside and became trapped, swirling around and around like broken aircraft doomed never to fly.

The old giant of a trout, two-thirds of a metre long and over 3 kg in weight, knew of this place. His massive hooked jaws snipped the hapless insects off the surface with a gentle efficiency that belied his great size. Crouching low, I slipped and stumbled along the steep gravel bank to within a few metres of the backwater. Scarcely daring to breathe, I watched the huge dark shape cruise lazily around its tiny beat, continuing to consume the many duns with ease. I judged my moment, and flicked my fawn deer-hair dry fly. It fell gently among the naturals not 5 m away. Though not an exact replica, it took all of my concentration to focus on my fly among the real duns silhouetted in the twilight.

The trout was sipping again, closer, closer. A dun not 30 cm from my fly disappeared in a swirl, then an instant later a dark snout clipped my deer hair off the surface. I paused for a heartbeat, then lifted my powerful Sage rod into an explosion of power. The blackest brown trout I have ever seen leapt clear from the water, as if to show me beyond doubt its massive bulk. Next, I felt incredible tension as the fish throbbed for the sanctuary of the log jam. I anticipated this move, and applied all the side-strain that I dared.

Briefly the trout turned and shook its head in panicked confusion. I relaxed for an instant, and that was my downfall. The great fish sensed its chance, and lunged again. I frantically tried to turn it, but this time I felt the sickening rasp of line on wood... then nothing. With shaking hands, I retrieved my slack, torn line. The exceptional trout, that one in a thousand, was gone forever.

– *Philip Weigall*

VICTORIA

INLAND FISHING EASTERN REGION

East Gippsland

Type of fishing
river

Target fish
bass, blackfish, brown trout

The **Combienbar River** north of Club Terrace is one of the few easily accessible freshwater streams in the far east of this area. It flows through grazing land, carrying small brown and rainbow trout, eels and blackfish. Some of the best fishing is in late summer and autumn, using techniques such as lure casting and bait drifting with live grasshoppers and crickets. The adjoining **Errinundra River**, with a gravel and sand bottom and flowing mostly through forested country, should be fished in the same way.

The **Bemm River**, below Club Terrace, contains some brown trout, bass, spiny freshwater crayfish and blackfish, but is difficult to access.

To the north, the **Bendoc River** at Bendoc offers good trout angling for most of the year, but can be unsuitable in a dry summer because of the low water flow.

In the same area are the **Queensborough**, **Delegate** and **Deddick rivers**. A four-wheel drive vehicle is needed to reach some sections of these streams. They are all lightly fished and provide good angling. The Delegate has brown trout up to 1.5 kg and some rainbow trout, while the Queensborough carries one of the best blackfish populations in East Gippsland, as well as brown trout and redfin.

The nearby **Bonang River** can be reached in a number of places from the Bonang Highway. Like many surrounding streams, it can be affected by a low summer flow and is difficult to fish because of overhanging vegetation, but it carries abundant brown trout, small rainbow trout, blackfish and short-finned eels.

The **Brodribb River** in the south is a handsome stream flowing through partly cleared forested country. It is best reached from the Bonang Highway. It carries brown trout, particularly in the upper reaches, and some eels.

The **Snowy River**, north of Bete Bolong, is generally hard to reach and lightly fished. The Snowy River often becomes too warm in its lower reaches for trout – this section is more likely to produce bass. Only above the junction with the Deddick does the river become cool enough to contain viable populations of trout. In the far west of the area, the **Buchan River** at Buchan has its best fishing in the more remote areas, where four-wheel-drive tracks are closed during the winter. It carries brown trout, eels, tupong, blackfish and bass in lower reaches.

Most trout in the East Gippsland area are of modest size, but sometimes much larger fish are caught, like this 2-kg brown

GUIDE TO LOCAL FISH

	East Gippsland	Tambo-Mitchell Rivers
bass, Australian	●	●
blackfish, river	●	●
eel	●	●
redfin	●	
spiny freshwater crayfish	●	
trout, brown	●	●
trout, rainbow	●	
tupong	●	●

INLAND FISHING EASTERN REGION   VICTORIA

Tambo–Mitchell Rivers

Type of fishing
river
Target fish
blackfish, brown trout

The **Timbarra River**, in the east, is one of the best waters for trout fishing in the area. It flows in mountain country and often through steep gorges, and although walking is necessary to fish most of the river, it is still popular. It also has a good population of blackfish, eels and tupong.

The **Tambo** and **Nicholson rivers** flow through forested, mountain country. The Tambo is well-accessed by the Omeo Highway but is disappointing below

The scenery is spectacular in the middle reaches of the Mitchell River

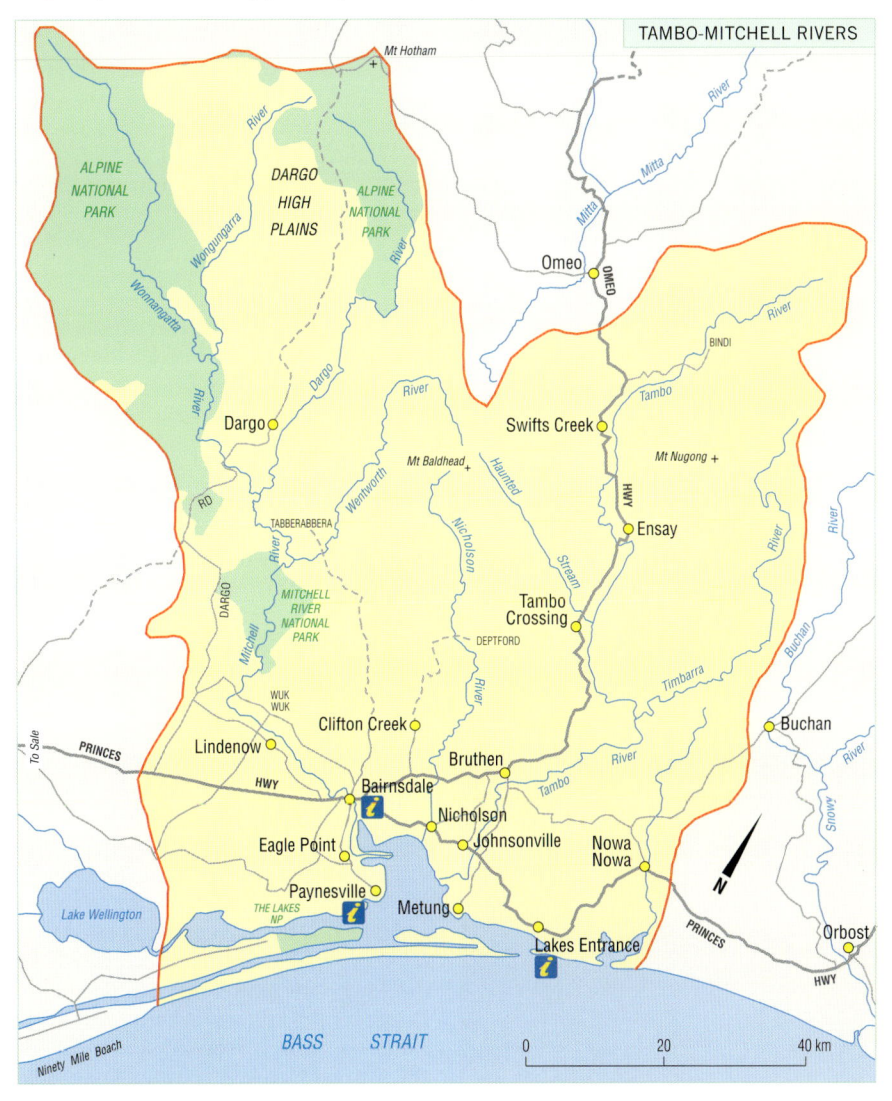

Bindi. It is thought that a concentration of toxic material may be responsible. **Haunted Stream**, a tributary of the Tambo, holds a lot of small trout to 500 g. Access is difficult along most of the Nicholson's length. Brown trout, long-finned and short-finned eels and tupong are the main freshwater fish. The upper Nicholson offers better trout fishing than the upper Tambo. The Nicholson is hard to reach upstream from Deptford but has a fine blackfish population, brown trout and spiny freshwater crayfish.

Numerous creeks and rivers join the **Mitchell River** in its upper reaches and run through heavily timbered mountain country. The area has only one major road, the Dargo Road, and only four-wheel drives and walking will get you to many sections of the rivers. But the fishing is good for brown trout. The middle reaches of the Mitchell River are spectacular in their scenery and contain brown trout and Australian bass.

The **Dargo River** flows from the mountains of the Alpine National Park to grazing land and joins the Mitchell River. Access is by car to Tabberabbera and by walking tracks. It contains brown trout, blackfish, bass and eels, and is most productive in the cooler months.

The **Wentworth River** is reached by a forestry track and is a good trout stream with a gravel bottom, while further north the **Wongungarra** and **Wonnangatta rivers** are well-regarded, if remote, trout streams.

VICTORIA

INLAND FISHING EASTERN REGION

Murray–Kiewa Rivers

Type of fishing
lake, river

Target fish
Macquarie perch, Murray cod, brown trout, rainbow trout

The Murray in its upper reaches, often referred to as the **Indi River** above the Bringenbrong Bridge, flows through mountain country and is fed by many small streams. This is perfect water for self-sustaining brown and rainbow trout populations, accessible by the Murray Valley Highway and via towns such as Corryong, Tintaldra, Walwa and Nariel.

The best small streams for trout are the **Cudgewa** and **Nariel creeks**, both of which have gravel and rock beds. The Cudgewa, easily reached from the Cudgewa–Tintaldra Road, carries brown and rainbow trout, abundant blackfish, spiny freshwater crayfish, with redfin and occasional Murray cod in the lower reaches. Wading is difficult in places, but there is excellent bank fishing. The Nariel Creek, with trout and blackfish, flows from forest to farmland. With its gravel bed, it is excellent for wading, as well as bank fishing.

The little **Koetong Creek** has been stocked with the protected trout cod, which must be returned to the water if caught. North of Koetong the creek is easily accessible and trout of more than 1 kg are present. The **Walwa Creek** also carries small trout.

Buckwong and **Limestone creeks** are remote and beautiful trout streams. Buckwong Creek is reached from the Alpine Way. Limestone Creek can be reached by a four-wheel drive track just south of Suggan Buggan.

The **Murray River**, winding north and west to Lake Hume, carries good numbers of brown and rainbow trout, redfin and occasional Murray cod. The biggest trout are present in the Murray between Lake Hume and the Bringenbrong Bridge, but plenty of trout exist upstream of this point in the Indi River. Excellent fishing places include Towong, Tintaldra, Walwa and Jingellic.

The **Mitta Mitta River** area is 'trout heaven', with granite and gravel-bottomed streams running through forested mountain country into the main river, itself a productive and easily accessed water. Some of the feeder streams are accessible only to four-wheel-drive vehicles and walkers, and some are so remote that they are fished only by people who have 'secret' camps by their favourite stretches of water. Brown trout are abundant, with Macquarie perch in the deeper water.

The **Cobungra**, **Bundara** and **Big rivers** all converge to form the Mitta Mitta, which then flows into Lake Dartmouth. The best trout streams are the Cobungra and Bundara rivers, near Anglers Rest on the Omeo Highway. Both are difficult to reach in most sections without four-wheel drive, but carry abundant brown trout, rainbow trout and blackfish. Their gravel beds are ideal for wading and fly fishing.

Other fishing waters, reached from the Omeo Highway and the Benambra Road, are the upper reaches of the Mitta Mitta, the **Gibbo River**, **Benambra Creek** and **Morass Creek**. Again local knowledge

Small tributaries like Middle Creek usually hold plenty of modest-sized trout

INLAND FISHING EASTERN REGION

VICTORIA

GUIDE TO LOCAL FISH
blackfish, river
carp
cod, Murray
perch, golden
perch, Macquarie
redfin
spiny freshwater crayfish
trout, brown
trout, rainbow

is required but the effort is worth it, as there are many large brown trout and smaller rainbow trout and blackfish to be caught in these delightful streams, with rubble and gravel beds.

Lake Dartmouth now covers the confluence of the Mitta Mitta and the **Dart River** and extends some 40 km from the retaining wall to its furthest point up the Mitta Mitta River. This terrific boating water carries very good numbers of big brown trout, rainbow trout, Macquarie perch, some big carp and the occasional Murray cod. The road route is from the Dartmouth township, where there is a caravan park and most facilities.

There is good fishing for trout in the **Snowy Creek**, near the town of Mitta Mitta. The lower Mitta Mitta River, as it runs to Lake Hume below Dartmouth Dam, carries redfin, brown trout up to 2 kg, and some rainbows and carp. There are blackfish in some places. Trout fishing in the pondage just below the Dartmouth wall is very productive. The section of the river between Mitta Mitta township and about halfway to Lake Hume is a superb tailrace fishery for trout.

Lake Hume, a huge reservoir surrounded by cleared land, contains many carp. However, there are abundant redfin and also brown trout, Murray cod and golden perch. Most trout are caught from early winter to late spring, during rising water.

The **Kiewa River** flows northwards from the Bogong High Plains to the Murray River. Several water storages have been built in the upper reaches of the river, as part of the Kiewa hydro-electric scheme. The most reliable is Rocky Valley Dam, a productive summer trout fishery. The best trout fishing is in the clear waters of the Kiewa River below the Mt Beauty Pondage. There are few streams running into the Kiewa, but the **Yackandandah Creek** at Yackandandah, while not easy to reach, contains abundant brown trout, small rainbow trout and redfin. Further down the Kiewa becomes slower and deeper and contains some Murray cod.

The Mitta Mitta has a reputation for big trout, particularly downstream from Lake Dartmouth

VICTORIA

INLAND FISHING CENTRAL REGION

Central Region

The Goulburn River and its tributaries are the most popular inland fishing waters in Victoria, with trout as the main target fish.

Major fishing lakes in the region include Eildon (brown trout, rainbow trout and natives), Lake Eppalock near Heathcote (natives, redfin and a few trout), the Waranga Reservoir near Shepparton (natives and redfin) and the Goulburn Weir at Nagambie (natives and redfin).

Evening on the Delatite

WHERE TO FISH

Central Region

OVENS–BROKEN RIVERS ● 204

The Ovens is an important river system in this area, with fine trout streams including the King, Buffalo and Buckland rivers. Lake William Hovell provides reasonable still-water trout fishing. Some of the best trout fishing is had in the more isolated stretches. The lower Ovens and tributaries are better suited to redfin and natives.

GOULBURN–CAMPASPE RIVERS ● 205

The Goulburn River and its tributaries above Seymour are well-regarded trout fisheries. Lake Eildon offers good fishing for a wide range of species including brown and rainbow trout, Murray cod and golden perch. Lake Eppalock is an important redfin and native fishery.

WEST GIPPSLAND ● 206

The Macalister River and its major tributaries like the Thomson provide good trout fishing. Other significant trout rivers include the La Trobe and Morwell, with Blue Rock Lake providing fair trout fishing and plenty of monster carp.

YARRA–MARIBYRNONG RIVERS ● 207

Although many waters have been degraded by urban development, there are still reasonable fishing prospects. The Yarra and Maribyrnong offer trout and redfin upstream and carp and redfin downstream. The Werribee River contains similar species in its lower reaches and trout in its upper reaches.

GUIDE TO LOCAL FISH

blackfish, river
carp
catfish
cod, Murray
eel
goldfish
perch, golden
perch, Macquarie
redfin
spiny freshwater crayfish
tench
trout, brown
trout, rainbow
tupong

INLAND FISHING CENTRAL REGION

VICTORIA

Brown trout
Brown trout were introduced into Australia from Europe in 1864. So successful have they been that many Victorian streams now have self-sustaining populations. Browns take baits such as worms and mudeyes, minnow and small bladed lures and flies.

Rainbow trout
An attractively coloured fish, rainbow trout are a native of the Pacific coast of North America from Mexico to Alaska. Rainbow trout were introduced to Victoria in 1894 from New Zealand. This species can be caught on baits, lures and flies, and is particularly susceptible to trolling.

Murray cod
This fish is distinguished from trout cod by its shorter snout. Numbers have significantly declined and to protect this most prized of inland native species during spawning there is a closed season in New South Wales and Victoria.

FURTHER INFORMATION

Fishing information There are NRE offices at 46 Aitken St, Alexandra, tel. (03) 5772 0200; 57 Bridge St West, Benalla, tel. (03) 5761 1611; 1 Lacey St, Sale, tel. (03) 5144 3048; 71 Hotham St, Traralgon, tel. (03) 5172 2111; Ford St, Wangaratta, tel. (03) 5720 1750; Symes Rd, Woori Yallock, tel. (03) 5964 7088; 310 Commercial Rd, Yarram, tel. (03) 5183 9100.

Visitor information 14 Mair St, Benalla, tel. (03) 5762 1749; 119 Gavan St, Bright, tel. (03) 5755 2275; 2 Station St, Cobram, tel. (03) 5872 2132; 2 Heygarth St, Echuca, tel. (03) 5480 7555; Old Courthouse, Harker St, Healesville, tel. (03) 5962 2600; cnr Silkstone Rd and Sth Gippsland Hwy, Korumburra, tel. (03) 5655 2233; old Mansfield Railway Station, Maroondah Hwy, Mansfield, tel. (03) 5775 1464; cnr Swanston and Little Collins Sts, Melbourne, tel. 132 842; Lloyd St, Moe, tel. (03) 5127 3082; 145 High St, Nagambie, tel. (03) 5794 2647; 8 Foster St, Sale, tel. (03) 5144 1108; Wyndham St, Shepparton, tel. (03) 5831 4400; cnr Tone Rd and Handley St, Wangaratta, tel. (03) 5721 5711; 1 Main St, Warburton, tel. (03) 5966 2071; Warburton Hwy, Woori Yallock, tel. (03) 5964 7404; Irvine Pde, Yarrawonga, tel. (03) 5744 1989.

The Howqua River through the seasons

'Only if you stare patiently into the water's crystal clarity might you see the flicker of a brown trout or the flash of a rainbow's red sash among the stones.'

There are still streams scattered here and there that bear few scars of human interference, and the Howqua River is one of them. Rising on the precipitous slopes of Mount Howitt on Victoria's Great Divide, the Howqua tumbles through forested mountains almost all the way to Lake Eildon. It has a deserved reputation as a prolific trout stream and has changed little in twenty-five years. Perhaps the most evocative memories for me are those concerned with the changing seasons of this beautiful place.

Winter, during the closed season for trout fishing, is the frame for an icy cold and seemingly lifeless river. Only if you stare patiently into the water's crystal clarity might you see the flicker of a brown trout or the flash of a rainbow's red sash among the stones.

The flowering daffodils among the clearings near the ancient cattlemen's huts announce spring. In early September, the first shafts of sunlight reach the valley floor and in no time the snow on the surrounding mountains is melting. The valley is filled with a constant roar as a mass of green water thunders down the river. Now the streamlined shape of the trout stands them in good stead as they hug the river bed and edges. But the time of semi-hibernation is over and periodically they dash out into the current to seize a morsel of food. The angler fishing deep with a lure or wet fly may well be rewarded with a powerful strike. Howqua trout are seldom large, but they fight with a vigour that matches their environment.

The last trickle of snowmelt departs the highest peaks and soon after summer arrives in the Howqua Valley. Mostly the nights are cool but the days are warm or even hot. The river settles down to a more pedestrian flow, and a profusion of life on and under the surface brings prolonged activity from the trout. During the heat of the day, they rest quietly on the stream bed, but at other times they may leap clear from the water for dragonflies or sip quietly in the shade on a windfall of beetles or grasshoppers. Equal numbers of rainbows and browns will fall to a fly fisher gently floating a Royal Wulff or Red Tag down the rapids and runs, or the baitcaster quietly prospecting with a juicy grasshopper.

Autumn comes with the turning leaves of the poplars and willows, planted by miners and settlers who left this valley long ago. Now the river is low and gin clear. The trout are made edgy by their exposed position, but at the same time they must feed up for the rigours of winter and spawning. If the angler can present his offering with sufficient stealth, there is a good chance of a take.

Eventually, the last leaves blow from the poplars. The nights are cold and frosty, and the weak sun barely reaches the valley floor. The first dusting of snow touches the highest peaks and the trout will again vanish among the river rocks.

– Philip Weigall

Ovens–Broken Rivers

Type of fishing
lake, river

Target fish
blackfish, golden perch, Macquarie perch, Murray cod, redfin, brown trout, rainbow trout

The **Ovens River** and its tributaries begin their journeys in mountain country. The best trout streams are in the high country between Bright and Mansfield. The **King River** joins the Ovens River at Wangaratta. It rises in forest country and is a classic trout stream, containing brown trout, rainbow trout, blackfish, a few redfin and Macquarie perch.

The **Rose River**, running to the tiny township of Dandongadale, is a popular fishing water, with big brown and rainbow trout in the headwaters. The **Dandongadale River**, relatively remote, offers excellent and tranquil fishing for brown trout, redfin and the occasional freshwater catfish.

The **Buffalo River**, a popular stream that can be mostly accessed by conventional vehicles, contains brown trout up to 2 kg, blackfish and redfin, with the occasional Macquarie perch and Murray cod in the bigger pools. North of Lake Buffalo, the Buffalo River flows through grazing land and is fished for trout and Murray cod.

The **Buckland River** provides reliable fishing for trout except in dry summers.

The **Ovens River** is a good fishing river right along its length, with plenty of trout in the swifter upper regions. As it runs to Wangaratta, it carries big redfin, brown trout, some Murray cod, golden perch, blackfish and spiny freshwater crayfish. Murray cod become more common as the river runs on to **Lake Mulwala**, which is one of the best Murray cod fisheries along the Victorian–New South Wales border. The middle reaches of the Ovens River are more suited to bait fishing for natives and redfin.

One of the better boating waters in the area is **Lake William Hovell** on the King River. Motor usage is limited to 10 hp, which minimises disturbance to the fish. The reservoir contains brown trout to 4 kg, large blackfish, some Macquarie perch and redfin. Best trout fishing is at the top end of the lake.

The **Broken River** has mediocre trout fishing in its upper reaches. Some tributaries offer better prospects. There are trout above and immediately below Lake Nillahcootie, but as it runs to Benalla and Shepparton the river becomes sluggish, with deep pools and runs. It carries Murray cod, golden perch, redfin, carp and blackfish. Occasionally, very big Murray cod are caught.

The **Broken Creek**, a channel-like river with a few deep holes, has good fishing for Murray cod and golden perch between Numurkah and Barmah. **Lake Mokoan**, near Benalla, provides good boat fishing for big carp, redfin, golden perch, an occasional trout and a rare Murray cod. Boat and bank fishing are both productive at **Lake Nillahcootie**, mainly for redfin. Scrubworms, yabbies and bladed lures are popular.

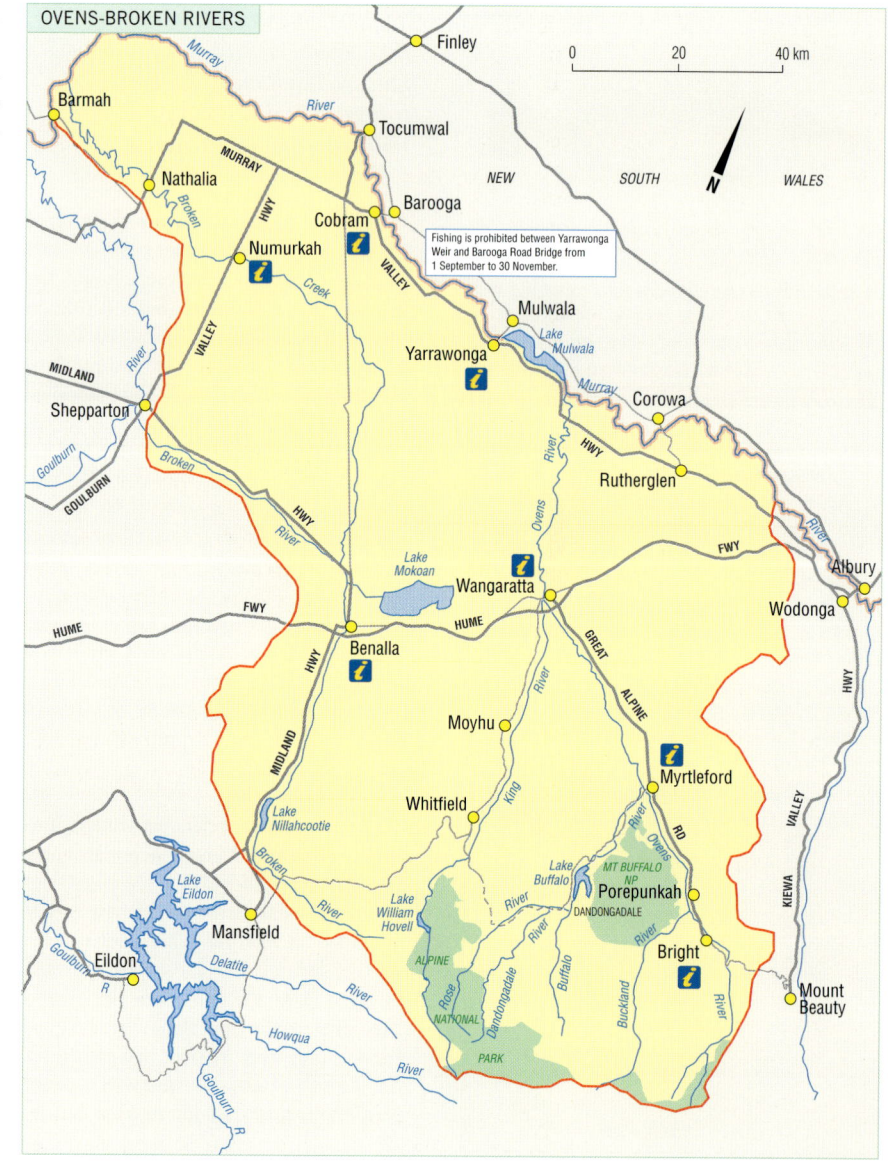

GUIDE TO LOCAL FISH

	Ovens–Broken Rivers	Goulburn–Campaspe Rivers
blackfish, river	•	•
carp		
catfish	•	
cod, Murray	•	•
goldfish		
perch, golden	•	•
perch, Macquarie	•	•
redfin	•	•
spiny freshwater crayfish	•	
tench		•
trout, brown	•	•
trout, rainbow	•	•

INLAND FISHING CENTRAL REGION

VICTORIA

Goulburn–Campaspe Rivers

Type of fishing
lake, river

Target fish
golden perch, Murray cod, redfin, brown trout, rainbow trout

The **Goulburn River** and its tributaries are the most popular inland fishing waters in Victoria, the main attraction being the trout water between Seymour and Lake Eildon. Spiny freshwater crayfish are also abundant and reach their biggest size in the **Waranga Reservoir** and **Goulburn Weir**.

The **Howqua** and **Jamieson rivers** flow almost entirely through forested mountains and carry abundant stocks of rainbow and brown trout. The **Delatite** contains brown trout, some rainbow trout, redfin, small blackfish, spiny freshwater crayfish and Murray cod in the lower reaches. The **Big River** can be reached by road or by boat from Lake Eildon, and is an excellent trout stream, particularly in its upper reaches.

The huge aquatic playground of **Lake Eildon** has many wide and deep arms that are ideal for trolling. Brown trout are plentiful and up to 4 kg, with lesser numbers of rainbow trout up to 1.5 kg. The lake also contains stocks of Murray cod and Macquarie perch, and large numbers of carp and tench.

The section of the **Rubicon** above its junction with the Goulburn holds many brown trout, especially when the Goulburn is flowing high and cold during the summer irrigation season.

The **Royston River**, which flows into the Rubicon, contains small trout, while the **King Parrot Creek** and **Murrindindi River** fish well for trout and contain redfin, blackfish and Macquarie perch. The **Acheron River** is also a good trout stream.

North of Eildon is **Seven Creeks**, a small deep stream carrying Macquarie perch, blackfish and a few trout. On this stream, Polly McQuinn Dam to Watchbox Creek is completely closed to angling to protect a population of the endangered trout cod.

Lake Nagambie, Goulburn Weir and the **Waranga Reservoir** contain native fish and redfin. The Goulburn itself holds good numbers of native fish all the way to its confluence with the Murray River.

The main fishing waters in north-central Victoria are the Campaspe River, which drains into the Murray River at Echuca, the Lauriston and Malmsbury reservoirs, the Coliban River and Lake Eppalock.

In the **Campaspe**, fair brown trout fishing exists in places from Kyneton down to Lake Eppalock, with rainbow trout in a small area near the Turpin Falls. North of Lake Eppalock the Campaspe mostly contains big carp, golden perch and redfin, with some large brown trout within a few kilometres of the dam. The weir at Elmore is one of the best fishing areas along the river, with golden perch and Murray cod.

The **Coliban River** near Kyneton is a narrow, gravel-bed stream flowing through grazing country. It is lightly fished. Species include blackfish and redfin, and some catches of brown trout.

Lake Eppalock is a large reservoir where anglers have to compete with water-skiers. It has become an excellent golden perch fishery, and is suited to lure fishing. Murray cod are present in good numbers, along with carp and redfin. Trout are scarce.

The **Malmsbury Reservoir** near Kyneton is popular for both redfin and trout. No boating is allowed. The **Lauriston** and **Upper Coliban reservoirs** are situated above Malmsbury, and contain trout and redfin.

Fly fishing the Jamieson River

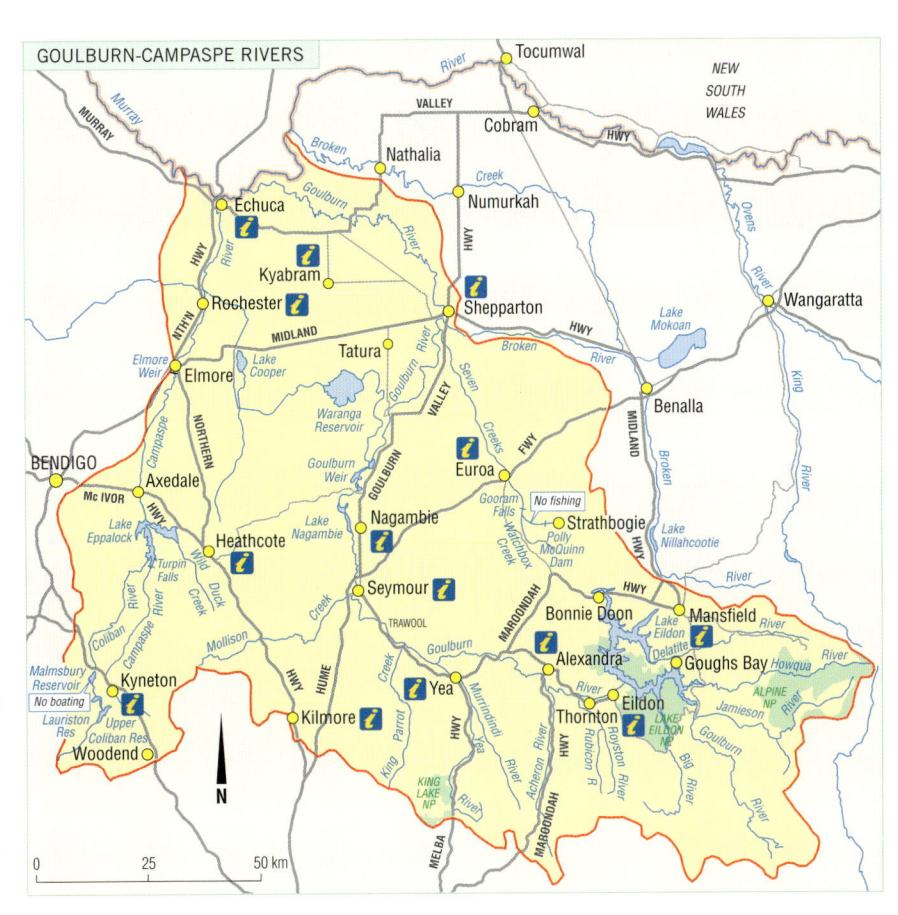

VICTORIA

INLAND FISHING CENTRAL REGION

West Gippsland

Type of fishing
lake, river

Target fish
blackfish, redfin, brown trout, rainbow trout

The upper **Macalister River** has extensive pools and fast runs containing brown trout and redfin, blackfish, spiny freshwater crayfish, carp and eels. The best fishing is in spring and autumn. Some trout are caught in the river below **Lake Glenmaggie**, early and late in the season.

Lake Tali Karng at the head of the **Wellington River** is a small mountain lake that is ideal for bank fishing but access is by hiking only. The river itself offers trout fishing. The **Shaw Creek** at Glencairn, a tributary of the Macalister, is popular with fly anglers because it flows mainly through button grass plains and has a population of small trout that will rise readily to the fly. It contains brown trout, rainbow trout, blackfish and freshwater crayfish.

The Macalister River runs into **Lake Glenmaggie**, an irrigation storage lake where camping and boating are permitted. Fishing by boat or from the shore is best in spring and summer for redfin, carp and the occasional trout. The **Thomson Reservoir** is part of the Melbourne Water storage and cannot be fished. Streams within the catchment area may be fished, but restrictions apply (contact Melbourne Water for details).

Above the reservoir, the **Thomson River** contains brown trout, some rainbow trout and blackfish. Most of the river can be waded, although there are some deep holes. Contact Melbourne Water for the latest advice on fishing restrictions. The river below the reservoir continues to carry brown trout, blackfish and other freshwater species.

Most of the streams in the **La Trobe River** area run through open country around the Gippsland towns of Moe, Morwell, Yallourn and Warragul, but they rise in steep, forested country where the fishing is good but hard to reach. Brown trout are plentiful, but the most established fish is the undesirable carp.

The upper reaches of the La Trobe River are clear and fast-flowing, and are accessible via the Willowgrove–Noojee Road. The best fishing is around Noojee, for brown trout, blackfish and redfin. The river also carries eels, tench, redfin and spiny freshwater crayfish.

The upper section of the **Morwell River**, which rises near Mirboo North, contains small brown trout, blackfish, carp, tupong and redfin. It is particularly good for fly fishing.

The **Tanjil River** is good trout water both above and below **Blue Rock Lake**. Some carp in the Blue Rock Lake are up to 6 kg, while trout in the lake are up to 1.3 kg. The reputation of this water storage has declined in recent years but there are plans to stock Australian bass.

The South Gippsland area has short, fast streams that run down from the hills and give way to slower coastal rivers and their estuaries. There is fair trout fishing in the area, particularly in the headwaters of the **Tarwin River** and the upper **Tarra River**.

GUIDE TO LOCAL FISH

	Yarra–Maribyrnong Rivers	West Gippsland
blackfish, river	●	●
carp	●	●
eel	●	●
redfin	●	●
spiny freshwater crayfish	●	
tench	●	
trout, brown	●	●
trout, rainbow	●	●
tupong		●

Blue Rock Lake is a popular area to troll for trout

INLAND FISHING CENTRAL REGION

VICTORIA

Yarra–Maribyrnong Rivers

Type of fishing
lake, river

Target fish
blackfish, eels, Macquarie perch, Murray cod, redfin, roach, brown trout, rainbow trout

Sugarloaf Reservoir on the outer edge of the Melbourne metropolitan area is a fantastic place to coarse fish during the day or fly fish in early morning or late evening

The freshwater fishing waters around Melbourne are linked to the two major rivers flowing into the city, the **Yarra** and the **Maribyrnong**. The Yarra headwaters are in forested mountain country and flow through varying terrain to the estuarine waters below Dights Falls, Collingwood. The best fishing for blackfish and brown trout in the Yarra is from below the Upper Yarra Reservoir through to Warburton, Woori Yallock, and from Healesville to Warrandyte. The middle and lower reaches of the Yarra also contain redfin, carp, roach, Macquarie perch and a few Murray cod. Tributaries above Warburton are small, gravel-bottomed streams carrying trout, blackfish and eels. The **Don River** and **Little Yarra River** at Launching Place and the **Olinda Creek** at Lilydale contain small trout and have become popular after work venues.

The only reservoir along the Yarra open to fishing is the **Sugarloaf Reservoir** at Christmas Hills, reached from the Eltham–Yarra Glen Road. It is subject to opening and closing hours and delineated fishing areas. The main angling targets are carp and redfin.

In the east of this area, north of Warragul, the **Tarago River** above the Tarago Reservoir is hard to reach, but has good brown trout fishing in a sand and gravel-bottomed river. The reservoir is closed to fishing. The **Bunyip River** offers fair trout fishing and blackfish.

The **Maribyrnong River** and its tributaries, including **Emu Creek, Deep Creek** and **Jacksons Creek**, flow through grazing land and access is mostly limited to road crossings. The **Hanging Rock Lake**, inside the racecourse, is a 1 ha dam, stocked regularly with brown trout.

Further west, the **Werribee River** runs into Port Phillip, and has small trout, redfin and blackfish in its upper reaches. The **Lerderderg River** contains a good number of trout although much of its length is in rugged gorge country and it therefore has limited access. **Pykes Creek Reservoir**, near Bacchus Marsh, provides reasonable fishing for trout and redfin.

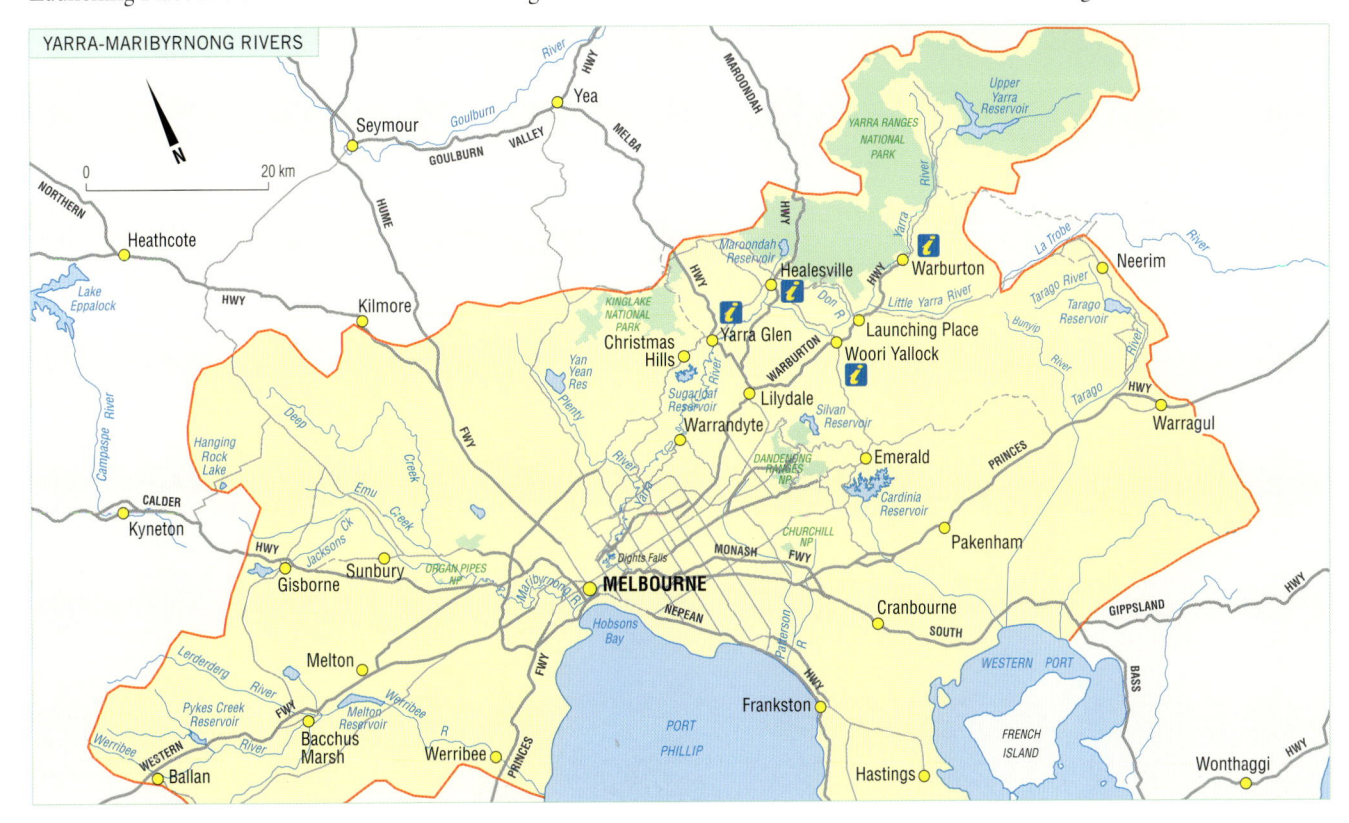

VICTORIA

INLAND FISHING WESTERN REGION

Western Region

Although generally drier than the rest of the State, this area contains its fair share of trout waters. Lakes like Toolondo, Fyans and Cairn Curran are all capable of producing fine trout fishing, with the Merri one of the region's best trout rivers.

Apart from the trout, redfin are abundant, especially in lakes like Rocklands Reservoir and Burrumbeet. The Loddon–Avoca system holds natives like Murray cod and golden perch in its northern reaches, as does the Wimmera system. Access to individual rivers and lakes is often restricted by private property, so please ask permission. Coastal river fishing in the area is excellent, and a network of small to medium-sized towns provides a range of fishing services.

Four of these coastal rivers, the Aire, Ford, Gellibrand, and Curdies, are renowned for producing exceptionally large brown trout to 7 kg. These rivers also host solid populations of river blackfish, and during the warmer months, it is common to see anglers fishing with light sticks on their floats for these tricky native battlers.

Eel-tailed catfish

Prized as a table fish, eel-tailed or freshwater catfish are capable of growing to 2 kg. Anglers must handle them with caution due to the dorsal and pectoral spines that can inflict nasty wounds. It is illegal to catch catfish in any Victorian waters other than those within the Wimmera River Basin.

The lower Hopkins River produces some impressive trout, and a favourite location is the area around Hopkins Falls

WHERE TO FISH

Western Region

LODDON–AVOCA RIVERS ● 210

The north-flowing waters of both the Loddon and Avoca rivers, in the central west of the State, carry trout in their headwaters and native fish in their lower waters, which run through dry grazing land. There are some good trout lakes in the area, including Cairn Curran Reservoir, Newlyn Reservoir and Hepburn Lagoon.

MOORABOOL–CURDIES RIVERS ● 212

The lakes in this area provide accessible fishing: Lake Murdeduke has big rainbows and chinook salmon while Lake Modewarre has browns and rainbows. Further west, lakes Bullen Merri, Purrumbete and Tooliorook have stocks of rainbow trout and periodically brown trout are also stocked. Lake Purrumbete also has chinook salmon. The Barwon River and creeks of the Otway Ranges have small to medium size brown trout; the Curdies, Gellibrand and Aire rivers carry some big trout.

HOPKINS RIVER BASIN ● 213

The Hopkins River basin has excellent fishing in some of its rivers and lakes. The lower Hopkins is a respected estuary perch fishery, while freshwater species further upstream include brown trout and blackfish. The Merri River is one of the best trout waters in the region. The better fishing lakes are the tiny Lake Gillear, lakes Bolac and Burrumbeet, and Lake Learmonth, which is regularly stocked with trout.

MOYNE–GLENELG RIVERS ● 214

Most of the rivers in this area are short – only the Glenelg begins deep inland. It carries a few trout, redfin and blackfish in its upper reaches. The Rocklands Reservoir, through which the Glenelg flows, has abundant redfin, and trout to 2 kg. A great trout water in the area is the small Konong Wootong Reservoir near Coleraine.

WIMMERA AND MALLEE ● 215

Although generally dry, there is some good fishing in the south of this area, near The Grampians. Lake Fyans has brown trout to 2 kg, rainbows to 1.5 kg, redfin and tench. Other popular fishing waters include the Toolondo Reservoir – one of the finest trout lakes in Victoria – Pine and Dock lakes, and near the weirs on the Wimmera River where Murray cod, golden perch and redfin are sometimes available.

INLAND FISHING WESTERN REGION

VICTORIA

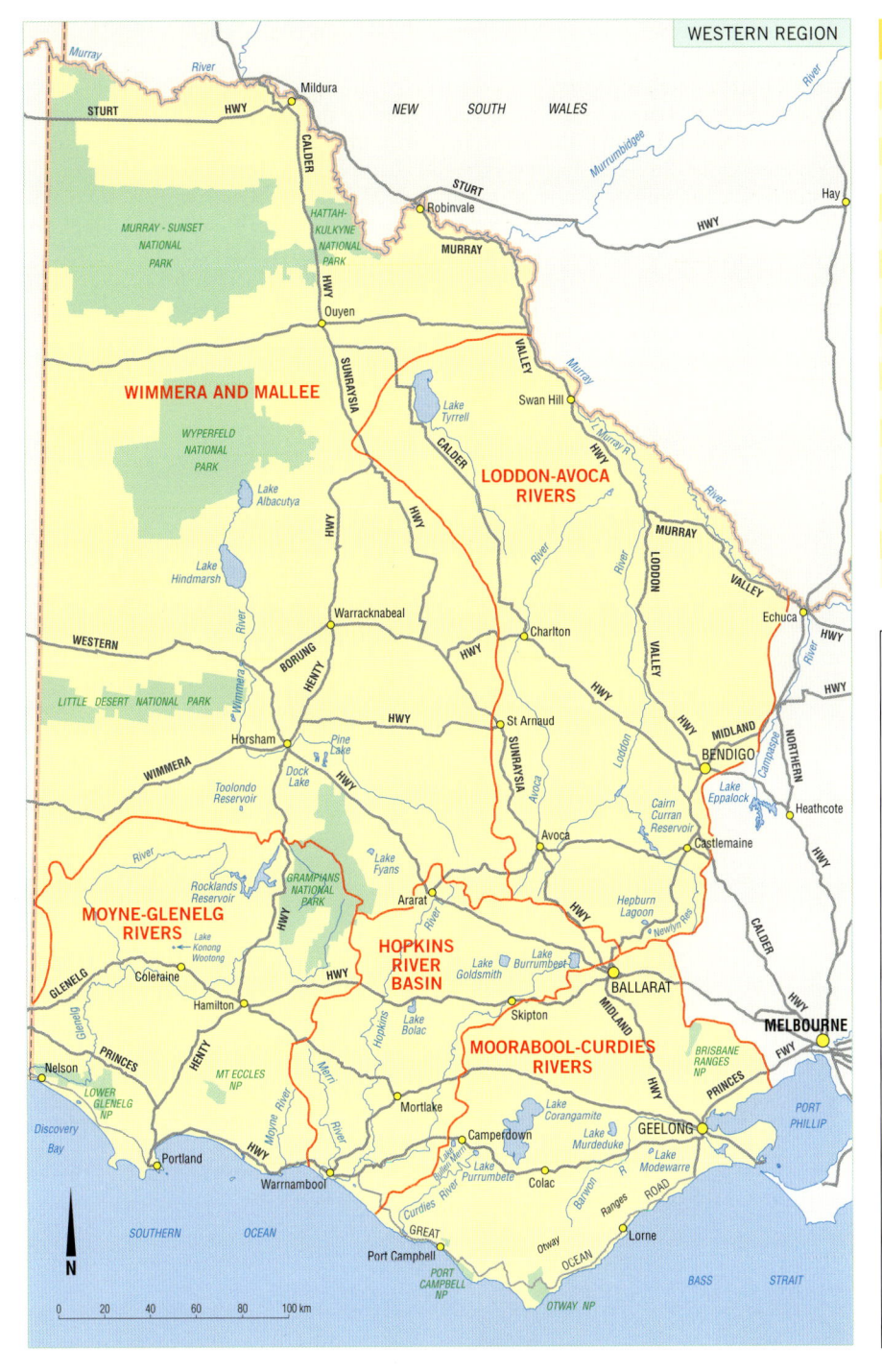

GUIDE TO LOCAL FISH

- blackfish, river
- carp
- cod, Murray
- eel
- goldfish
- perch, estuary
- perch, golden
- perch, Macquarie
- perch, silver
- redfin
- roach
- salmon, chinook
- spiny freshwater crayfish
- tench
- trout, brown
- trout, rainbow
- tupong

FURTHER INFORMATION

Fishing information There are NRE offices at cnr Mair St and Doveton St, Ballarat, tel. (03) 5333 6782; cnr Hargreaves St and Mundy St, Bendigo, tel. (03) 5444 6666; 83 Gellibrand St, Colac, tel. (03) 5233 5533; 21 McLachlan St, Horsham, tel. (03) 5381 1255; 26 Wellington St, Kerang, tel. (03) 5452 1266; 87 Langtree Ave, Mildura, tel. (03) 5022 4300.

Visitor information High St, Ararat, tel. (03) 5352 2096; High St, Avoca, tel. (03) 5465 3767; cnr Sturt St and Albert St, Ballarat, tel. (03) 5320 5741; Historic Post Office, Pall Mall, Bendigo, tel. (03) 5444 4445; The Court House, Manifold St, Camperdown, tel. (03) 5593 3390; Shiels Tce, Casterton, tel. (03) 5581 2070; cnr Murray St and Queen St, Colac, tel. (03) 5231 3730; National Wool Museum, Moorabool St, Geelong, tel. (03) 5222 2900; Lonsdale St, Hamilton, tel. (03) 5572 3746; 20 O'Callaghan Pde, Horsham, tel. (03) 5382 1832; Railway Station Tourist Complex, Maryborough, tel. (03) 5460 4511; 180–190 Deakin Ave, Mildura, tel. (03) 5021 4424; Portland Foreshore, Lee Breakwater Rd, Portland, tel. (03) 5523 2671; 50–52 Western Hwy, Stawell, tel. (03) 5358 2314; 306 Campbell St, Swan Hill, tel. (03) 5032 3033; 119 Scott St, Warracknabeal, tel. (03) 5398 1632; 600 Raglan Pde, Warrnambool, tel. (03) 5564 7837.

Barry Lodge's Emerger
A good fly during mayfly hatches.

Highland Hopper
A deadly fly when trout are feeding on grasshoppers on windy summer days.

Red Tag
A popular general-purpose dry, and great when trout are taking beetles.

Royal Wulff
Excellent dry fly in fast or broken water.

Loddon–Avoca Rivers

Type of fishing
lake, river

Target fish
golden perch, Murray cod, redfin, brown trout, rainbow trout

The **Loddon** and **Avoca rivers**, in the central west of the State, flow north. Rising in hilly country, both rivers carry trout in their headwaters – though the Loddon is the most significant in this regard – before running through dry grazing land, where they provide the classic habitat for native species.

In the upper reaches of the Loddon, before Cairn Curran reservoir, there are abundant brown trout to 1.7 kg – though most are smaller – and rainbow trout. Further north are Murray cod, redfin, golden and silver perch, carp and tench.

Cairn Curran Reservoir at Newstead has excellent boating facilities. It is a good trout lake but it is often drawn down for irrigation so fishes best in cool weather, especially for fly fishing. It is stocked annually with brown trout, and fish to 2 kg are not uncommon. Redfin are present and golden perch are now being stocked for the summer fishery.

For the boat angler good results can be had on Cairn Curran Reservoir by trolling near the dam wall for the aforementioned trout and redfin. For those braving the cold weather in winter on this large expanse of water, many a good bag of trout can be caught using Tassie Devils and small minnows. In summer this same dam wall area is productive, but often the troller needs to employ downriggers or lead core in order to get the lures down to the deeper, cooler water, which the trout prefer.

There are a number of lakes in the south of this area, all of which are stocked with trout and have good fishing at times. They include **Cosgrove Reservoir** (brown trout), **Newlyn Reservoir** (brown trout), **Dean Reservoir** (brown trout), **Hepburn Lagoon** (brown and rainbow trout), **Talbot Reservoir** (brown trout and redfin) and **Harcourt Reservoir** (brown trout). In many of these waters wading and boating is illegal, and a special permit may be required. Check with the local NRE

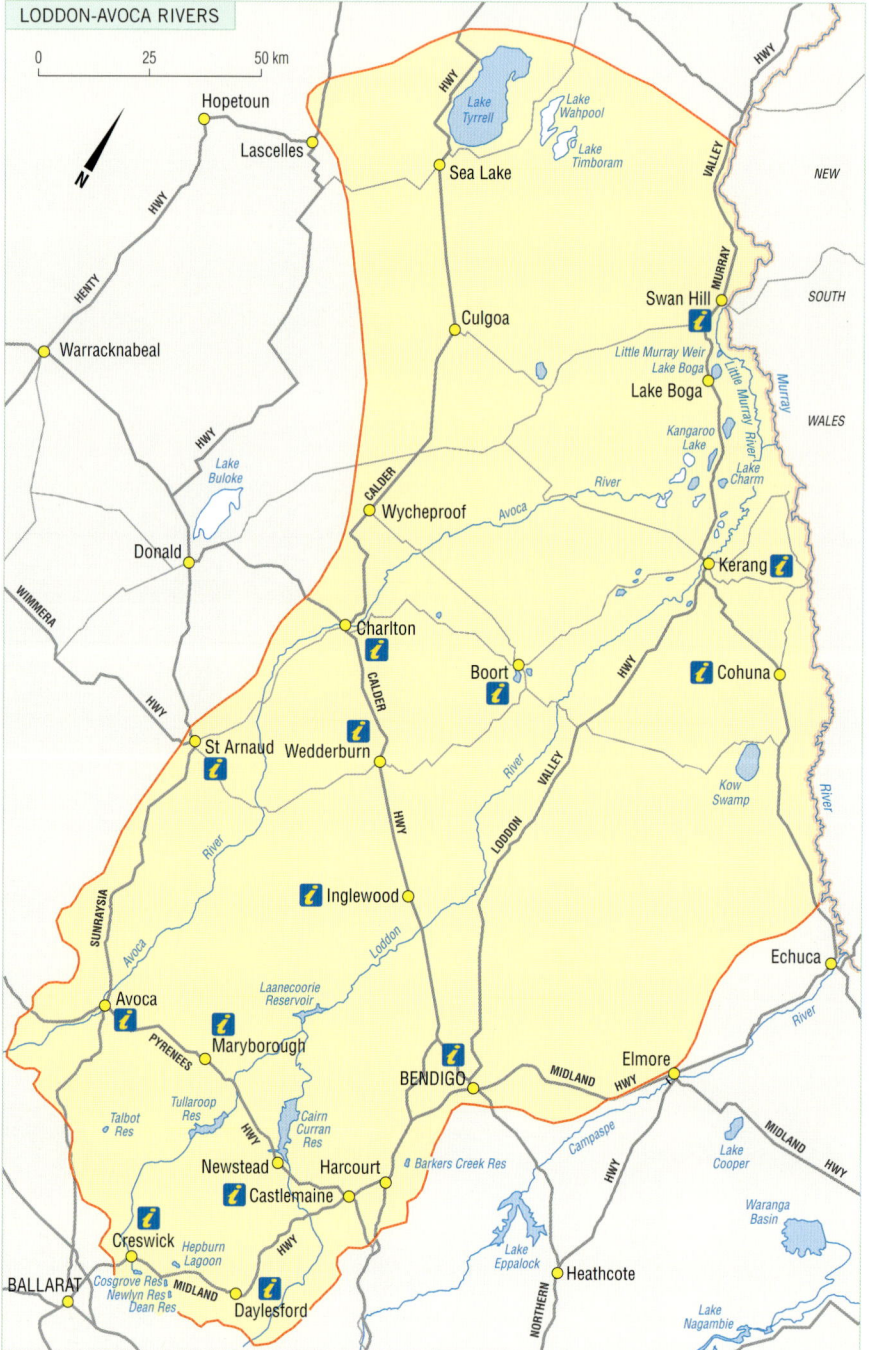

Hepburn Lagoon can be difficult fishing, but some very large trout reward perseverance

INLAND FISHING WESTERN REGION

VICTORIA

Cairn Curran Reservoir is often drawn down for irrigation, exposing a perimeter scar, but the trout fishing is good during the cooler months, and redfin catches are excellent over summer

office. All these lakes are ideal land-based fisheries.

Cosgrove Reservoir is a small impoundment often underrated as a fishery. Access by vehicle is possible to the dam wall, but beyond there one must walk. All forms of angling are popular, including fly, lure and bait fishing. Harcourt is another small but beautiful reservoir. Again it supports all forms of angling but fly fishing is very popular.

Dean Reservoir is yet another pocket-sized storage that contains some large trout but they are difficult to catch. This water has been frequently closed to fishing in recent years. Talbot Reservoir, further to the west near Clunes, is small but very popular with fly fishers, but trout are also taken on bait, especially mudeyes fished under a bubble float.

Newlyn Reservoir and Hepburn Lagoon are two larger lakes in this area. Both are close to the township of Newlyn and anglers can move from one lake to the other in search of fish. Newlyn Reservoir is stocked with brown trout, while Hepburn Lagoon is stocked with both brown and rainbow trout. Both fish well in winter, when the trout feed on the growing minnow populations. However, when the insects are hatching, spring and summer rises do occur.

These larger reservoirs are very popular with fly fishers, but nonetheless the bait fisher can do well too.

The **Tullaroop Reservoir**, east of Maryborough, contains brown trout and abundant redfin and tench. Only bank fishing is allowed but access to the shoreline by vehicle is reasonable.

The northern run of the **Loddon** is through flat and dry land. The Loddon and the **Little Murray River**, which joins it near its confluence with the Murray, contain Murray cod, redfin, carp, blackfish, golden and silver perch. Some good fishing in the Loddon is around the town of Kerang and in the Little Murray for some 9 km below the Little Murray Weir. The best season is from January to May.

A chain of lakes around the Murray Valley Highway carries native species and redfin, and the best of the lakes are **Lake Boga, Kangaroo Lake, Lake Charm** and, near Cohuna, **Kow Swamp**. Dense weed makes boating necessary on all these lakes.

The **Avoca River** is sluggish and often dry in its northern reaches, but is fished in its cooler southern waters for small redfin, brown trout, tench, carp and blackfish.

GUIDE TO LOCAL FISH

blackfish, river
carp
cod, Murray
perch, golden
perch, silver
redfin
tench
trout, brown
trout, rainbow

Mrs Simpson
A good choice for prospecting lakes and large rivers – especially under low light conditions.

VICTORIA
INLAND FISHING WESTERN REGION

Moorabool–Curdies Rivers

Type of fishing
lake, river

Target fish
blackfish, redfin, brown trout, rainbow trout

Trolling for chinook salmon on Lake Bullen Merri

Two major rivers, the **Moorabool** and **Barwon**, join near the city of Geelong. Most of their upper waters are in grazing land and, although they carry brown trout and other introduced and native species, the most easily reached fishing is in the lakes and reservoirs. Moorabool and Gong Gong reservoirs are controlled by Central Highlands Water in Ballarat and a permit is required to fish them. These waters have trout and redfin.

The best fishing in the **Barwon** is between Buckley Falls and Inverleigh, where brown trout to 1 kg, blackfish, spiny freshwater crayfish and redfin are the most likely species to be encountered. The inaccessible headwaters contain small trout in good numbers.

Lake Modewarre fishes well when the water level is high. It carries brown trout up to 4.5 kg, rainbows to 3 kg, tench and carp. **Lake Murdeduke** is much bigger and contains rainbow trout to 5 kg and periodically chinook salmon. The lake has submerged reefs on its western shore, and becomes very rough in windy conditions. **Lake Wendouree**, a shallow, weedy lake in the heart of Ballarat, carries mainly brown trout, redfin, tench and goldfish. Best fishing for trout is in the evenings.

Further west, lakes **Colac** at Colac, **Bullen Merri** and **Purrumbete** near Camperdown, and **Tooliorook** at Lismore are interesting fisheries. Purrumbete and Bullen Merri have stocks of rainbow trout, and at times both also carry chinook salmon and brown trout. Lake Colac has large redfin. Tooliorook (or Lake Ettrick) contains large redfin and rainbow trout. Nearby at Derrinollum, **Deep Lake** can provide great trout fishing, but it is a poor option in dry seasons.

The Otway ranges create a host of small coastal streams between Lorne and Cape Otway. Their estuaries are well stocked with marine fish, while the upper reaches carry small brown trout. The **Gellibrand** and **Aire** rivers, are more substantial propositions, carrying large brown trout and the largest blackfish in the State. Both rivers fish well at night. The **Curdies River** north of Curdie Vale carries a few big trout, but access is limited by grazing land and bank vegetation. A small boat provides the best access to the upper reaches.

Lake Elingamite, near Cobden, has brown and rainbow trout to 2 kg and redfin, but weed around the shore makes a boat desirable.

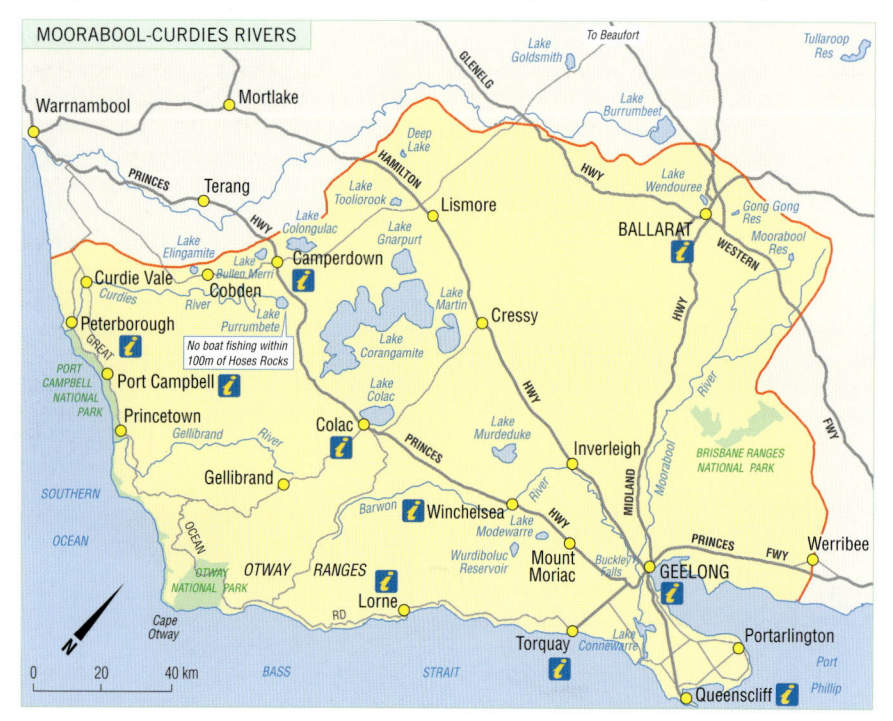

GUIDE TO LOCAL FISH

	Moorabool–Curdies Rivers	Hopkins River Basin
blackfish, river	●	●
carp	●	●
eel		●
goldfish	●	●
perch, estuary		●
perch, golden		●
redfin	●	●
roach		●
salmon, chinook	●	
spiny freshwater crayfish	●	
tench	●	●
trout, brown	●	●
trout, rainbow	●	●
tupong		●

INLAND FISHING WESTERN REGION   VICTORIA

Hopkins River Basin

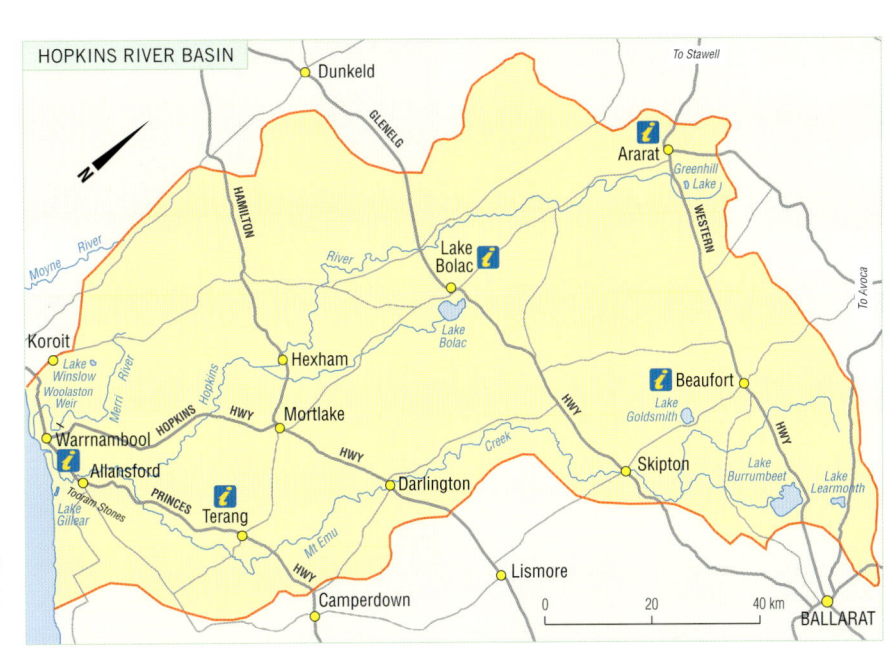

Type of fishing
lake, river

Target fish
golden perch, redfin, brown trout, rainbow trout

The **Hopkins River**, which flows into the sea at Warrnambool, drains a large river basin that is mainly comprised of grazing land. There is excellent fishing for freshwater species in many rivers and lakes in the basin, with good access to the water in a number of places. The Hopkins River has 11 km of estuary water from its mouth at Warrnambool to Tooram Stones, and is then a reasonable freshwater stream to the town of Hexham on the Hamilton Highway. This section contain brown trout, blackfish, short-finned eels, estuary perch, tench, goldfish, tupong and some redfin and grayling. The lower Hopkins is one of the most respected estuary perch fisheries in the State.

The **Merri River**, also at Warrnambool, carries both brown trout and redfin as well as estuary perch, bream and mullet in its estuary waters. The river upstream to **Woolaston Weir**, some 11 km from the sea, is considered one of the best trout waters in the west of the State, with brown trout to 4 kg and averaging 1.3 kg. It is excellent fly fishing water, but also suitable for boating and other fishing methods. Above the Woolaston Weir, the river is suitable for bank angling only. It flows through bush and grazing land with pools and runs over a mud and rock bottom. The trout are smaller, but fish to 2 kg are caught from time to time.

The **Mount Emu Creek**, running through Skipton, Darlington and Terang to join the Hopkins near the sea, has varied fishing for brown trout, blackfish, redfin, tupong, tench and goldfish. The main fishing access is from road bridges. Fishing lakes in the area include tiny lakes Gillear and Winslow near Warrnambool, Lake Bolac at the town of the same name, Greenhill Lake at Ararat, and the lakes Burrumbeet and Learmonth near Ballarat.

Lake Gillear is popular with fly and bait anglers, but access can be difficult in wet conditions. A small boat is useful. It carries brown trout to 2 kg and rainbow trout to 1.7 kg, along with redfin, tench and short-finned eels. **Lake Winslow** holds trout and redfin and fishes well from the shore or in a boat.

Lake Bolac is large and shallow, so is subject to rough water in windy conditions. It is a popular boat fishing lake, with redfin the predominant species and carp, short-finned eels and sometimes brown trout are also present.

Burrumbeet is another shallow lake surrounded by grazing land, and a popular boat fishing lake. It is often subject to discolouring and algal bloom. Redfin is the major species and reach 2.5 kg, while eels, roach, tench, carp and goldfish make a not so agreeable mixture of targets. From time to time, it also carries trout depending on stocking.

Lake Learmonth has a similar mixture, but is regularly stocked with trout. It is sometimes used for high-speed boating competitions, making fishing difficult on occasions.

Greenhill Lake at Ararat contains brown trout, redfin and golden perch, and is ideal for boat and bank fishing, fly fishing, bait fishing, lure casting and trolling. Both Greenhill and Learmonth have suffered badly from low water levels in recent years.

Lake Winslow near Warrnambool provides trout and redfin fishing

VICTORIA

INLAND FISHING WESTERN REGION

Moyne–Glenelg Rivers

Type of fishing
lake, river
Target fish
redfin, brown trout, rainbow trout

The main rivers in the south-western corner of Victoria are the Glenelg, Wannon, Fitzroy, Surrey, Shaw and Moyne. Most are short rivers; only the **Glenelg** has its source deep inland. It flows through the huge Rocklands Reservoir, Balmoral, Harrow, Casterton and Dartmoor. Estuary fish continue in the Glenelg for some 60 km upstream. The river, once pristine fishing water along its length, has been affected by erosion, landslip and silting. Access is also varied as it runs through much private property. However, it does carry a few brown and rainbow trout, redfin and blackfish. The other rivers in the area carry similar combinations of short-finned eels, redfin, blackfish, tupong and tench, with brown trout in small numbers.

Boat fishing near the bank, on the Glenelg River

Rocklands Reservoir has abundant redfin to 2.3 kg, brown trout to 2 kg and rainbow trout to 1 kg. Trout can be caught in the Glenelg River where it flows into the reservoir and in the dam wall area.

The **Wannon** has also been affected by erosion and silting, and is best between the Nigretta and Wannon Falls, where there are blackfish, redfin and some Macquarie perch, and below the Wannon Falls, which has trout, golden perch and tupong. The Tahara Bridge area below Coleraine is popular with anglers seeking golden perch.

A good fly water is the small **Konong Wootong Reservoir** near Coleraine. No power boats are permitted, with brown trout and redfin to 2 kg, carp and tench the dominant fish species.

Lake Hamilton, a 25-ha lake within the city boundary, is popular with local anglers and contains brown trout and redfin to 2.5 kg, golden perch to 1 kg and large tench.

GUIDE TO LOCAL FISH

	Moyne–Glenelg Rivers	Wimmera and Mallee
blackfish, river	●	
cod, Murray		●
eel	●	
goldfish	●	
perch, golden	●	●
perch, Macquarie	●	
redfin	●	●
tench	●	
trout, brown	●	●
trout, rainbow	●	●
tupong	●	

INLAND FISHING WESTERN REGION

VICTORIA

Wimmera and Mallee

Type of fishing
lake, river

Target fish
golden perch, Murray cod, redfin, brown trout, rainbow trout

Ideal fly fishing conditions at Lake Wartook in early spring

The Wimmera and the Mallee make up the State's more arid central border region. The wheat-growing area of the Wimmera is dry in the north but with some good fishing water in the south, near the Grampians, an isolated spur of the Great Dividing Range. There is a growing emphasis on native fish, and anglers should not be surprised if some traditional trout waters become Murray cod and golden perch fisheries in future years.

Lake Wartook is one of the most attractive waters in the Wimmera and Mallee. It lies in a high basin in the Grampians, surrounded by forested mountains. It is well regarded for trout fishing, particularly by bait and fly fishers, and also produces some good-sized redfin.

Lake Fyans, near Halls Gap, is a popular boating and fly fishing water, with brown trout to 2 kg, rainbow trout to 1.5 kg, redfin and tench.

When water levels are moderate to high, the **Toolondo Reservoir** is one of Victoria's finest trout lakes, with consistent brown trout on bait, fly and trolling as well. The lake also holds big redfin. **Pine** and **Dock lakes** near Horsham have a similar mixture and size of fish, and are also popular fishing waters. Boating facilities are good at Toolondo and Pine Lake.

The best fishing places on the **Wimmera River** are in and near the weirs, particularly at Antwerp and Jeparit, where Murray cod, golden perch and redfin are the sought after catches.

West of Goroke, the **Booroopki Swamp** and **Lake Charlegrark** are noted for big Murray cod in the 20-kg class, along with redfin. The fishing has suffered in recent years due to low water levels.

Lake Wallace at Edenhope is a good boating and fly fishing lake, carrying rainbow trout to 1.3 kg, brown trout to 2 kg, redfin and tench. Aquatic weed can make it difficult to keep the fish on the hook.

The **Murray River** is the major fishing river of south-eastern Australia; it is covered in the New South Wales section.

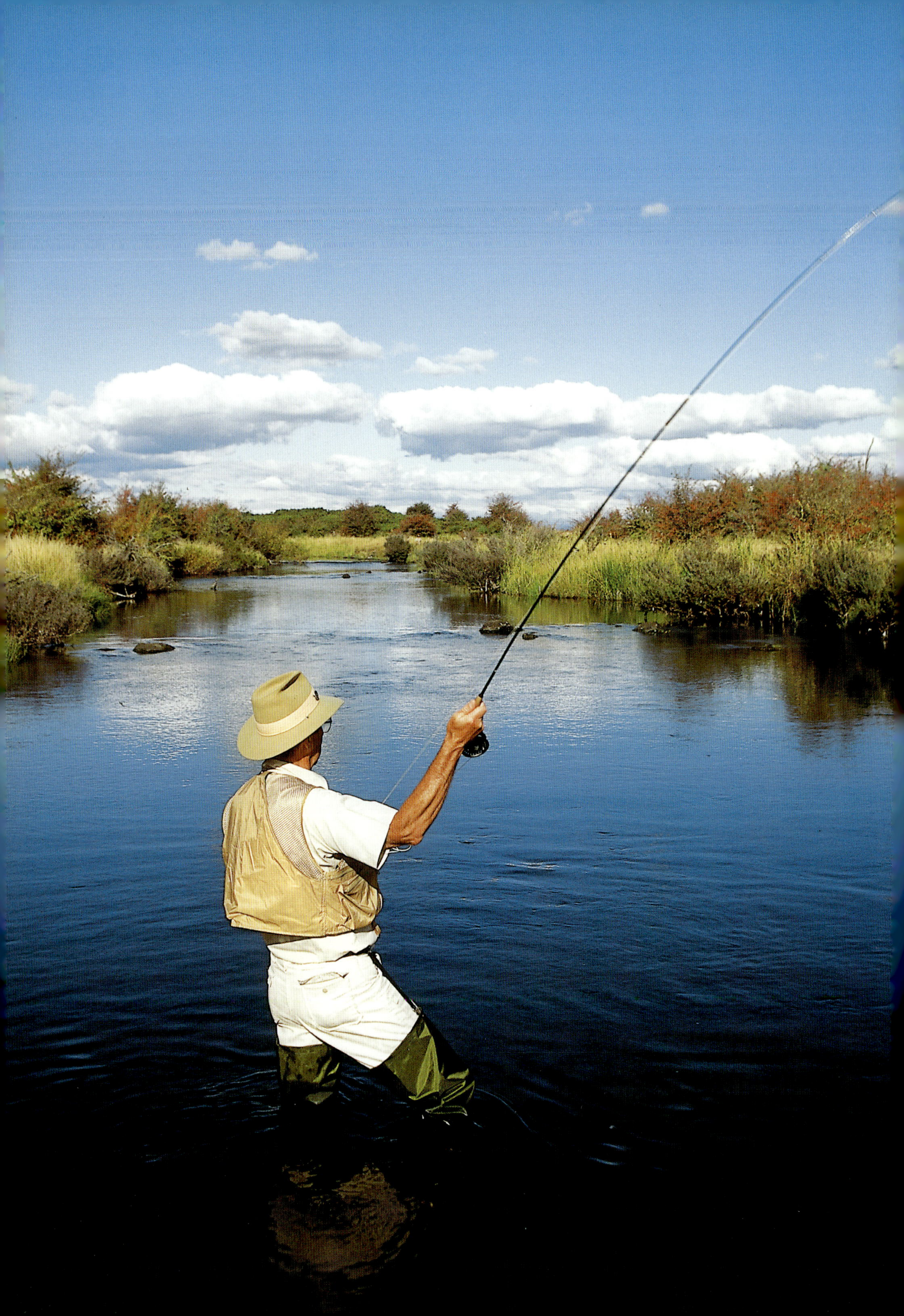

Contents

Coastal Fishing
Hobart Region	220
Launceston Region	230

Inland Fishing
North-east Region	242
Southern Region	248
Central Highlands Region	252
North-west and West Coast Region	258

Tasmania

Tasmania is internationally renowned for its freshwater fishing – its wild brown trout fishery is widely regarded as one of the best in the world. For the saltwater angler, numerous bays, estuaries, beaches and islands around the coastline offer good fishing for a variety of species. Fresh or saltwater, the angler in Tasmania can expect a delightfully uncrowded fishing environment.

Trout fishing on the
Macquarie River near Cressy

Fishing off the beaches and jetties, Australian salmon, whiting, flathead and mullet are some of the species to be caught, while bream and good sea-run brown trout are found in many estuaries. Ocean fishing, accessed from the coast or islands, provides plenty of possibilities. The offshore enthusiast may tangle with sportfish like tuna or marlin. Journey inland, and most rivers and lakes offer trout fishing, with excellent sport in the highlands and the midlands south of Launceston. Although trout are the feature species in Tasmanian freshwater, blackfish, redfin and eel are also found in many waters.

TASMANIA

Coastal Fishing

The options are many around Tasmania's coast. There are sheltered estuaries and bays for those after the inshore fish, beaches for surf anglers, thriving offshore waters for those who like a challenge, and plenty of rock sites and islands. Fishing from the rocks can be rewarding, but care must be taken as the rocks are often dangerous in exposed areas.

The east coast of Tasmania is sprinkled with small holiday and fishing villages set on lovely bays and estuaries. There are islands and reefs and the waters of the offshore game fishing grounds. The complex of peninsulas and bays in the south leads into the sheltered and beautiful estuary of the Derwent, with land and boat fishing right on Hobart's doorstep. The D'Entrecasteaux Channel, Bruny Island's shores, the Huon River estuary, the sandy banks of Bass Strait in the north, the Mersey River and the Tamar River estuary – these are some of the enticing places for Tasmanian saltwater fishing. The renown of the freshwater should not diminish the quality of the salt-water fishing in any way – but it does make the waterways less crowded and lightly fished. The dominant species are different from the mainland. Trevally, trumpeter, salmon and cod are more likely to be talked about than the same old 'flathead, whiting and bream'. But those three stalwarts are there as well. And for some real 'off the track' fishing there are the abundant coasts of Flinders and King islands.

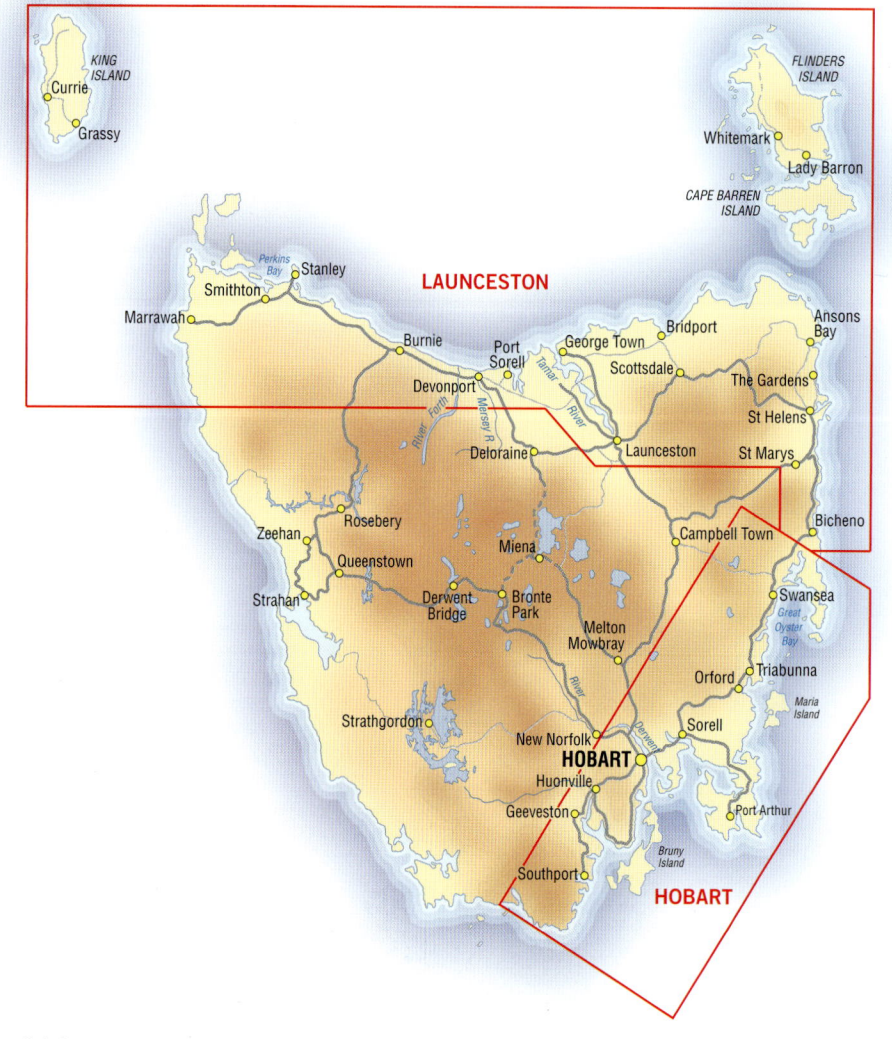

COASTAL FISHING

WHERE TO FISH

Along the coast

HOBART REGION ● 220

The Great Oyster Bay area has both shore-based and boat fishing, with the sheltered Coles Bay probably the most popular boat fishing place in Tasmania. Triabunna and Orford have estuary and bay fishing, and sheltered waters in Mercury Passage. The Derwent is a productive estuary with many pelagic species plus sea-run trout and excellent bream fishing. There are quiet estuary waters on the Huon River peninsula, and fishing on the Tasman Peninsula and on either side of Bruny Island.

LAUNCESTON REGION ● 230

The north coastal waters of Tasmania are often exposed to rough weather in Bass Strait, but there are sheltered waters in Perkins and Duck bays, the River Forth and the Mersey. Port Sorell and Port Dalrymple, at the mouth of the Tamar River, are good, safe fisheries and the river offers shore-based and estuary fishing. Bridport is a fishing town, with a combination of beach and boat angling. Ansons Bay, St Helens and Bicheno are the fishing centres of the delightful east coast. Flinders and King islands have jetties, beaches, rocks and estuaries, and a chance for some exciting charter boat fishing in Bass Strait.

State regulations

Recreational rod and line fishing licences are not required for angling in salt water in Tasmania. Licences are required for taking fish with nets as well as for abalone and rock lobster by any method.

Tasmania's marine fishing regulations have undergone a lot of changes over the last few years and most bays, rivers and estuaries are now 'no netting' areas.

Rules for marine waters are constantly changing and are subject to legislative review every few years so make sure you are familiar with any changes. There are often special rules that only apply in some areas as well.

Regulations regarding netting, bag limits, rock lobster, abalone, scale-fish and marine parks should be checked before planning to fish an area.

Excellent information on current regulations for fishing and boating is available

COASTAL FISHING

TASMANIA

GUIDE TO LOCAL FISH

Code	Fish	Code	Fish	Code	Fish
AC	albacore	LU	luderick	S	snapper
BC	barracouta	MA	mackerel	SN	snook
B	bream	ML	marlin	SW	sweep
C	cod	MO	morwong, banded	T	tailor
D	drummer	MO	morwong, other	TR	trevally, silver
EL	elephant fish	M	mullet		trout, sea-run
F	flathead	PF	parrotfish	TP	trumpeter, bastard
FL	flounder	PI	pike	TP	trumpeter, real bastard
G	garfish	AS	salmon, Atlantic	TP	trumpeter, Tasmanian
BG	grenadier, blue	SA	salmon, Australian	TU	tuna, southern bluefin
GU	gurnard	SF	sawfish	TU	tuna, striped
KI	kingfish, yellowtail	GS	shark, gummy	WA	warehou
LJ	leatherjacket	GS	shark, school	W	whiting
L	ling	SH	shark, others		

Bag and size limits apply. Check the government fishing guide 'Recreational Scalefishing' for details.

from the Tasmanian government's Service Tasmania outlets located around the State. Many post offices also have information on marine fishing regulations.

Boating regulations

All boats/vessels powered by 4 hp or more, are required, by law, to be registered. The operator must also hold a current speed boat licence. Tasmania does recognise equivalent endorsements from other States.

It is a requirement for all registered and unregistered motor boats to carry the minimum required safety equipment.

For full details of boating rules, contact the closest Service Tasmania outlet, or Marine and Safety Tasmania (MAST) on (03) 6233 8801. MAST's Safe Boating Handbook outlines the regulations.

FISHING TIP

The fishing line is the weakest link in the connection between angler and fish, so it pays to spend a couple of minutes to make sure everything is in order before starting to fish. The first thing you should do is check the first couple of metres of line before and during fishing. Constant casting or bottom fishing causes persistent wear and tear, and it is wise to cut off any line which is frayed or nicked. Nor should you leave your line in the sun for too long as this causes it to dry out and deteriorate. A wet rag can be squeezed to keep the line moist while some anglers place a cover over their line to ensure it is shaded. Before casting out your bait always check to see that the line is not wrapped around the rod tip. It might seem obvious, but in the heat of the action when a hot bite is on, even experienced anglers sometimes forget this – at their own cost.

Snook
A member of the pike family, the snook or shortfinned seapike inhabits inshore waters around southern Australia. Found mainly around weedy areas and along drop offs where it seeks out smaller fish, snook can grow to more than 4 kg. They are known for staying in the same area for extended periods.

FURTHER INFORMATION

Fishing For full details of Tasmania's coastal fishing regulations, contact the Fisheries Division of the Department of Primary Industries, Water & Environment, tel. 1300 368 550. The department's website at www.dpiwe.tas.gov.au also contains information on regulations, permits, licences, maps, and 'Fish Facts' information sheets. Information on recreational fishing is also available at www.fishonline.tas.gov.au

Boating Marine & Safety Tasmania (MAST) is on the 1st floor, 7-9 Franklin Wharf, Hobart, tel. (03) 6233 8801 and it oversees boating safety and registration. See its website at www.mast.tas.gov.au for information on trip preparation and speed limits, as well as boating registration, licences and ownership forms. For weather information, contact the Marine & Safety Tasmania Telephone Boating Weather Service, which is updated three times daily. For Southern Tasmania tel. (03) 6233 9955; Northern Tasmania tel. (03) 6323 2555; Eastern Tasmania tel. (03) 6376 0555; and North-West Tasmania tel. (03) 6498 7755. For information from the Bureau of Meteorology call its Weathercall service, tel. 1900 926 113. You can also get coastal forecasts and reports on the Weather By Fax service, fax. 1902 935 240, and for marine warnings fax 1902 935 049.

The north and east coasts of Tasmania offer extensive, well-protected shallow bays for fishing and boating

TASMANIA   COASTAL FISHING HOBART REGION

Hobart Region

Hobart is a convenient base from which to access coastal fisheries in the south-east part of the State. The many protected estuaries, islands and channels provide anglers with beach, rock and boat fishing, and there are numerous protected bays for small boats, as well as the more open waterways like Storm Bay, where larger boats, perhaps chartered, are needed. Drive an hour or so out of Hobart and there are many possibilities.

The rocky shores of Maria Island

The Great Oyster Bay area has both land and boat fishing, with the sheltered Coles Bay being one of the most popular fishing places in Tasmania. Triabunna and Orford have estuary and bay fishing, and the waters in Mercury Passage are sheltered by Maria Island. There are offshore opportunities for anglers seeking shark, marlin and tuna.

The convoluted coastline of the south creates sheltered bays, points and promon-tories for land and boat anglers. The Derwent is a productive estuary, at its best at the end of winter when sea-run trout and bream come to the fore. Access is very good with plenty of land spots right in the city.

Anglers checking lobster pots on the Freycinet Peninsula

The quiet estuaries south of Hobart, the D'Entrecasteaux Channel and the fishing on either side of Bruny Island, add to the varied fishing of the region.

Weather

Predominant winds in this area are westerlies, but on almost any day it is possible to find sheltered bays suitable for fishing. However watch out for sudden weather changes, which are frequent. On hot days, a strong sea breeze can be expected most afternoons. Marine and Safety Tasmania (MAST) provide regional weather reports; tel. (03) 6233 8801 for details.

Boating

There are a number of local regulations, so check them before you head off. It is law that all registered and unregistered motor boats carry the minimum required safety equipment. Unregistered motor boats are

WHERE TO FISH
Hobart Region

SWANSEA TO MARIA ISLAND ● 222
Great Oyster Bay and its surrounds is a staggeringly beautiful area that provides a range of fishing possibilities. There is boat fishing on the bay itself, beach fishing from the isolated Wineglass Bay in the Freycinet National Park, and respected tuna fishing offshore. The Swan River and Little Swanport offer some of the State's best bream fishing.

TASMAN PENINSULA ● 224
The bays around the Tasman Peninsula have superb fishing, mainly for flathead and striped trumpeter. These waters are largely sheltered and are well serviced by the many small towns that hug the shores. Professional fishing fleets are based here, and are often joined by amateurs in the hunt for the shark, marlin and tuna that are found offshore.

DERWENT ESTUARY ● 226
There is fishing right in Hobart's central business area, with mackerel, cod, flathead, Australian salmon and bream usually available, and barracouta and warehou in season. Good fishing continues in both directions, with bays and rocks towards the ocean, and plenty of cod and flathead upriver.

D'ENTRECASTEAUX CHANNEL ● 228
Shore fishing is as rewarding in this area as boat fishing, with the wharves and jetties and natural fishing spots within reach of the deep shelves found here. Escapees from the Atlantic salmon farms are an added bonus in the estuary waters. Calamari and arrow squid can be caught seasonally.

all motorised vessels of less than 4 hp. These vessels must carry the minimum required safety equipment, which includes a fire extinguisher, bailer or bilge pump, flares, an anchor with the correct length of chain and rope and oars or paddles. Maximum speed within 60 m of the Tasman Bridge is 5 knots and no boats can tie up to the bridge or anchor or lie within 150 m on either side. There are dangerous bars at Southport Lagoon, Prosser River at Orford, Carlton River, which flows into the Frederick Henry Bay, and Marion Bay Narrows at the entrance to Blackman Bay.

COASTAL FISHING HOBART REGION

TASMANIA

HOBART REGION

GUIDE TO LOCAL FISH

- albacore
- barracouta
- bream
- cod
- drummer
- elephant fish
- flathead
- flounder
- garfish
- grenadier, blue
- gurnard
- kingfish, yellowtail
- leatherjacket
- ling
- luderick
- mackerel
- marlin
- morwong, banded
- morwong, other
- mullet
- parrotfish
- pike
- salmon, Atlantic
- salmon, Australian
- shark, gummy
- shark, school
- shark, other
- snapper
- snook
- sweep
- trevally, silver
- trumpeter, bastard
- trumpeter, real bastard
- trumpeter, Tasmanian
- tuna, southern bluefin
- tuna, striped
- warehou
- whiting

FURTHER INFORMATION

Fishing and boating The Fisheries Division of the Department of Primaries, Water & Environment has an office at the Marine Board Building, 1 Franklin Wharf, Hobart, tel. 1300 368 550, website www.dpiwe.tas.gov.au Boating information is available from Marine & Safety Tasmania, tel. (03) 6233 8801, website www.mast.tas.gov.au

Tourist centres Officers' Mess, off Arthur Hwy, Eaglehawk Neck, tel. (03) 6250 3635; Forest and Heritage Centre, Church St, Geeveston, tel. (03) 6297 1836; Cnr Davey and Elizabeth sts, Hobart, tel. (03) 6230 8233; Bruny D'Entrecasteaux Visitor Centre, Ferry Rd, Kettering, tel. (03) 6267 4494; Orford Riverside Cottages, Old Convict Road, Orford, tel. (03) 6257 1655; Swansea Bark Mill & East Coast Museum, 96 Tasman Hwy, Swansea, tel. (03) 6257 8382; Cnr Charles St and Esplanade West, Triabunna, tel. (03) 6257 4090.

TASMANIA

COASTAL FISHING HOBART REGION

Swansea to Maria Island

Type of fishing
bay, beach, estuary, offshore, river, rock

Target fish
Australian salmon, barracouta, bream, flathead, tuna

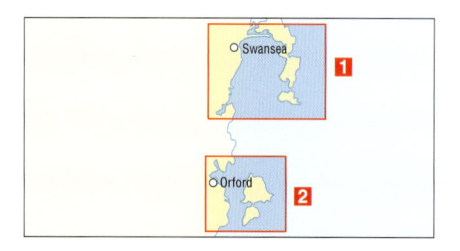

Great Oyster Bay and the country around it is almost too beautiful to be true, with its white beaches, rocky headlands and low granite peaks. Triabunna is a small fishing port on Spring Bay, a deep and sheltered inlet, which is further protected by the offshore bulk of Maria Island, a national park and former penal colony. A daily ferry runs from Orford to the ruins of Darlington on the island.

No tourist vehicles are permitted on the island, which is a refuge for over eighty species of birds.

Offshore fishing can yield albacore, southern bluefin tuna and striped tuna, along with mackerel and barracouta and the occasional yellowtail kingfish. Charter fishing boats can be hired in Triabunna.

GREAT OYSTER BAY

Wineglass Bay, on the ocean side of the Freycinet Peninsula, is a delicately shaped bay, ideal for peaceful beach fishing, netting and crayfishing. The catch can include flathead, cod, mackerel and shark, Australian salmon and barracouta in good numbers in season, and warehou in autumn.

Schouten Passage is sometimes turbulent, but is an outstanding fishery for large flathead, Australian salmon, barracouta in season, bastard trumpeter, a few ling and the occasional luderick.

The popular fishing area of **Coles Bay** has flathead, cod, mackerel, shark, Australian salmon, barracouta, occasional yellowtail kingfish and warehou in autumn. The water here is clear, deeply shelving, and sheltered from anything but a howling south-westerly. It is ideal for small boat fishing, which can be extended out into Great Oyster Bay in calm conditions.

Nine Mile Beach, at the head of Great Oyster Bay, is backed by a narrow strip of land. Moulting Lagoon, to the north, is full of small bait fish. The channel running from the bay behind Nine Mile Beach can be

GUIDE TO LOCAL FISH

		Great Oyster Bay	Maria Island Area
(AC)	albacore	●	
(BC)	barracouta	●	●
(B)	bream	●	●
(C)	cod	●	●
(F)	flathead	●	●
(FL)	flounder	●	
(G)	garfish	●	●
(K)	kingfish, yellowtail	●	
(L)	ling	●	●
(LU)	luderick	●	●
(MA)	mackerel	●	●
(MO)	morwong		●
(M)	mullet	●	●
(PF)	parrotfish	●	●
(SA)	salmon, Australian	●	●
(SH)	shark	●	●
(TR)	trevally	●	●
(TP)	trumpeter	●	●
(TU)	tuna	●	●
(WA)	warehou	●	●
(W)	whiting	●	●

COASTAL FISHING HOBART REGION

TASMANIA

fished from land for bream, flathead, Australian salmon and flounder, and the **Swan River**, which empties into this channel, provides bream fishing equal to the best.

Swansea has a sheltered boat ramp at Jubilee Beach. Both the beach and the jetty are good fishing venues, with the likely catches being flounder, garfish, flathead, whiting, bream and mullet. There is another boat ramp at the end of Gordon Street, with flathead, mullet and whiting for boats drifting or trolling close to the shoreline.

The rocks and beaches along the west coast of the bay have flathead, cod, mackerel and shark, warehou in autumn, and seasonal Australian salmon and barracouta. Particular fishing places are **Waterloo Point**, **Webber Point**, **Buxton Point** and **Point Bailly**. Bream are in the creeks and rivers along this coast, and particularly around the entrances after rain. The estuary of the **Little Swanport River** is the place for bream specialists, who can launch at Little Swanport ramp at the mouth of the river.

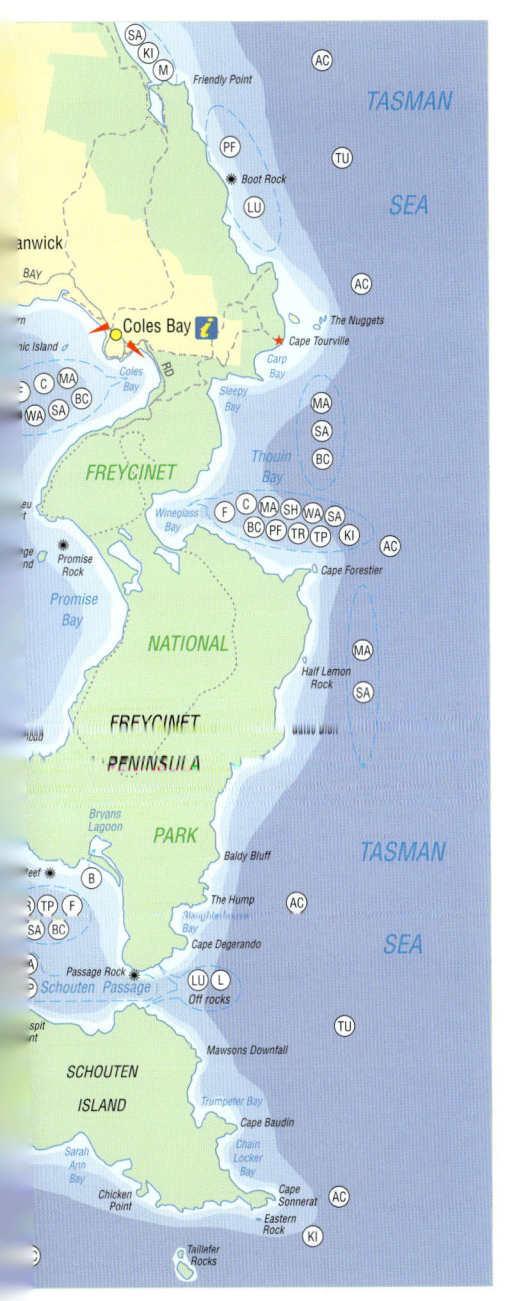

Fishing action at Coles Bay

MARIA ISLAND AREA

The best close-in boat area is just outside Spring Bay to the east of **Freestone Point**, where tuna, Australian salmon, trevally, trumpeter, flathead and cod can be found. At **Triabunna**, Spring Bay can be fished for flathead, mullet, cod and bream. Fishing activity increases when the commercial fleet is just in and food scraps are being hosed into the water. There are also whiting, mackerel and Australian salmon in the bay for boat anglers.

Prosser Bay has Australian salmon, flathead, whiting, barracouta and cod. There are bream in the entrance of the **Prosser River** and trout upstream, and in the Orford Rivulet nearby.

The **Mercury Passage**, which is sheltered by Maria Island, has flathead, whiting, cod and trevally. The island is a major attraction for anglers, with excellent flathead drifting in the clear, shallow waters along the western shores. There are also Australian salmon and barracouta in season. In the open waters to the east of Maria Island, amateurs and professionals alike troll for tuna. Cod, ling and morwong can be caught off the rocky shores.

223

TASMANIA   COASTAL FISHING HOBART REGION

Tasman Peninsula

Type of fishing
bay, beach, offshore

Target fish
Australian salmon, flathead, flounder, shark, trevally, trumpeter, whiting

There are several sheltered bays on the ocean side of the Forestier and Tasman peninsulas. There are parrotfish in huge numbers around the kelp beds and reefs along this entire coast. Gurnard are present in the reef systems and rocky bottom areas.

Blackman Bay, reached by canal from Norfolk Bay at Dunalley, has big flathead, particularly around Boomer Island and Green Point. Flounder are in the shallows. **Pirates Bay** is the main base for the game fishing boats used to hunt tuna, marlin and shark. These charter boats give amateurs a safe chance of catching prized blue-water fish. Pirates Bay also has easily reached inshore waters, where flathead, Australian salmon, barracouta, bastard trumpeter, silver trevally and morwong are sought.

The remote **Fortescue Bay** is worth the journey through the forest from the Arthur Highway. Boats can be launched from the boat ramp at Cape Hauy and the likely catches include trumpeter, cod, Australian salmon, flathead, trevally, yellowtail kingfish and mackerel. Luderick are around the rocks, and beach anglers can try for Australian salmon and mackerel.

Offshore from Tasman Island there are good numbers of Tasmanian trumpeter, gurnard and morwong.

The remains of the convict settlement at **Port Arthur** have made it Tasmania's major tourist attraction, so it is very accessible to campers and anglers. Once away from the shore the solitude of this beautiful inlet makes fishing a memorable experience. The likely fish are flathead, Australian salmon, trumpeter, trevally, barracouta, mackerel, garfish and cod. Land anglers can cast into deep water from Garden Point, Point Puer and Stand Up Point.

Storm Bay, on the west side of the Tasman Peninsula, has more exposed water, but there is safe boating and fishing in **Parsons Bay**. Flathead, cod, whiting, ling and leatherjacket, and trout and Atlantic salmon – escapees from local fish farms – are often caught here. There are barracouta further out. Boats can be launched at Nubeena. In the deeper offshore waters, schools of southern bluefin tuna are the target for professional and game anglers from March until June. Albacore and small striped tuna are also present in good numbers, along with marlin and shark.

There is superb bay fishing in the waters sheltered by the Forestier and Tasman peninsulas. Norfolk Bay, Frederick Henry Bay and Pitt Water have a convoluted coastline of bays, points and promontories, creating good shore fishing locations and interesting boat fishing. The prime target is undoubtedly flathead, but flounder and shark are also present, particularly in the shallows of Pitt Water, near the town of Lewisham. The flounder are pursued beyond dusk, by wading in the shallows with a torch and spear. Sometimes flathead are also taken this way.

Norfolk Bay fishing spots are reached mostly from the Tasman Peninsula, launching at Saltwater River, Taranna and Eaglehawk Neck. Australian salmon, mullet, whiting and flathead are sought by boat anglers.

Frederick Henry Bay has launching facilities at places such as Primrose Sands, Dodges Ferry, Lauderdale, in the west of the bay, and Cremorne. The **Carlton River**, between Primrose Sands and Dodges Ferry, is a prime Australian salmon spot, either trolled around the entrance or in the estuary, where bait, lure and fly will all produce good results. There are flathead, trumpeter, trevally, Australian salmon and whiting around **Sloping Island** and in **Lime Bay**. **Cremorne Bay** is a good flounder spot. The bay also produces good numbers of squid in season. Bream fishing in this region has advanced beyond bait and many anglers now use lures and flies.

GUIDE TO LOCAL FISH

(AC)	albacore
(BC)	barracouta
(B)	bream
(C)	cod
(F)	flathead
(FL)	flounder
(G)	garfish
(GU)	gurnard
(KI)	kingfish, yellowtail
(LJ)	leatherjacket
(L)	ling
(LU)	luderick
(MA)	mackerel
(ML)	marlin
(MO)	morwong
(M)	mullet
(PF)	parrotfish
(AS)	salmon, Atlantic
(SA)	salmon, Australian
(SH)	shark
(S)	snapper
(TR)	trevally
(TP)	trumpeter
(TU)	tuna
(W)	whiting

The waters of the beautiful inlet at historic Port Arthur contain flathead, Australian salmon and barracouta

COASTAL FISHING HOBART REGION

TASMANIA

TASMAN PENINSULA

TASMANIA
COASTAL FISHING — HOBART REGION

Derwent Estuary

Type of fishing
estuary, jetty, river, rock

Target fish
Australian salmon, cod, flathead, warehou

The Derwent estuary brings fishing to the very doorstep of Tasmania's capital city, Hobart. There are many jetties and fishing spots for land anglers on both sides of this beautiful waterway, which remains tranquil despite being surrounded by city and suburbs. But it is boat anglers who get the best of the Derwent.

One of the most prevalent fish in the autumn months is the warehou. Huge schools move into the estuary and fishing is rewarding either from land or boat. The other main species are flathead, bream, Australian salmon, mackerel, cod and barracouta. Elephant fish, also known locally as elephant shark or ghost shark, are here in considerable numbers, and squid are also present. Sea-run trout often run in August. In some years juvenile blue grenadier can be found from Opossum Bay in the south-east of the estuary to as far north as Berriedale. Marine worms, mussels and crabs are favoured baits for bream in the river, while fish pieces and locally caught bait fish are used for other species.

On the south-eastern side of the estuary, around **South Arm**, boat anglers seek trevally, trumpeter, Australian salmon, pike, flathead and cod. Australian salmon and pike can be caught outside the estuary, around the headlands in Storm Bay.

Ralphs Bay is noted for its large flathead, but Australian salmon, flounder and whiting are also caught. Out from Tranmere is **Punchs Reef**, which has morwong, silver trevally and cod.

On the western side of the estuary, boat anglers fish from **Piersons Point** to **Taroona**. There are whiting and flathead in the bays, and Australian salmon, pike, mackerel, cod, trumpeter and trevally off the rocky shores between the bays. There are crayfish available from north of Piersons Point to Crayfish Point at Taroona.

Towards the city, the **Sandy Bay** area is fished by shore and boat anglers for flathead, whiting, flounder, garfish, trumpeter and small morwong. Silver trevally is the target on the eastern shore, north-east of Sandy Bay, and can reach up to 3 kg in the area between Droughty Point and the Tasman Bridge. Crayfish Point is a research area and closed to fishing. Cod and flathead are the main mid-river catches south of the **Tasman Bridge**, with a few trevally, morwong and Australian salmon also around. Elephant fish can be caught right up to the Bowen Bridge.

A short walk from the centre of Hobart to the wharves will get you in the thick of things, and there are also good fishing stands nearby at the jetties around **Secheron Point**, in the **Queens Domain** and at **Selfs Point**. The main jetty fish in this area are mackerel, cod and flathead, with barracouta, bream and warehou plentiful at times.

There are trevally, cod and flathead on the northern side of the bridge and into **Elwick and Berriedale bays**. Sea-run trout and Atlantic salmon can be caught in the upper reaches of the river in autumn, with favoured spots including **Otago Bay**, **Old Beach**, **Herdsmans Cove** and around the **Bridgewater Causeway**. Cod and flathead are in mid-river.

There are plenty of boat ramps all along the Derwent and the conditions are such that there are few days unsuitable for fishing.

Silver trevally is one of the main target fish in the Tasman Bridge area of the Derwent estuary

Mussels
Mussels are one of the best baits to use for the many bay and estuary species in Australia, particularly bream and whiting. Mussels can be collected from pylons, piers and rocks.

GUIDE TO LOCAL FISH

BC	barracouta
B	bream
C	cod
EL	elephant fish
F	flathead
FL	flounder
G	garfish
BG	grenadier, blue
MA	mackerel
MO	morwong
M	mullet
PI	pike
AS	salmon, Atlantic
SA	salmon, Australian
TR	trevally
TP	trumpeter
WA	warehou
W	whiting

COASTAL FISHING HOBART REGION

TASMANIA

DERWENT ESTUARY

For fish in Pitt Water and Frederick Henry Bay see Tasman Peninsula map on page 225.

Juvenile blue grenadier can be found in some years from around Berriedale to Opossum Bay.

227

TASMANIA

COASTAL FISHING HOBART REGION

D'Entrecasteaux Channel

Type of fishing
bay, beach, estuary, jetty, offshore, rock

Target fish
Australian salmon, cod, flathead, whiting

The jetty angler is just as likely to catch a swag of fish as those in boats in the estuaries that indent this quiet southern coastline. The **Huon River** and **Port Cygnet**, **Port Esperance**, **Southport** and **Recherche Bay** all have some area of deeply shelving waters, reached from the natural fishing points, and the wharves and jetties. The most common catches are flathead, Australian salmon, whiting and cod, but Atlantic salmon, sea-run brown trout and barracouta are also often caught. Trevally and trumpeter are found in the deeper water. Flounder are spread throughout the shallows, inviting night exploration with torch and spear.

There are a number of fish farms in these estuaries nurturing the highly regarded Atlantic salmon, and escapees can often be caught around the fish farm areas and in the estuaries, but only if they are in open waters and outside the areas marked by buoys.

Around the Huon River and Port Cygnet (the major waterway here), the towns are Huonville, Franklin, Port Huon and Cygnet. Huge trout to 10 kg are caught around Huonville every year. The fishing centres further south are Dover, Southport and Cockle Creek. These are small towns in a quiet countryside, with the heavy forests and mountains of the Hartz Mountains National Park and the South West National Park off to the west.

The mainland coast and the west coast of **Bruny Island** give boating access to excellent fishing in the D'Entrecasteaux Channel. The island is one of the world's most peaceful and unpolluted places, with a population of under 400 and a long coastline with many interesting fishing possibilities. The only vehicular access to the island is by ferry, which operates daily from the town of Kettering, 65 km south of Hobart. Boat ramps at Alonnah and Lunawanna give access to the fishing grounds in the D'Entrecasteaux Channel, with a spur road running to Adventure Bay in the east and a boat ramp, near East Cove, for launching into the bay.

Atlantic salmon
Atlantic salmon are farmed in Tasmania's estuaries. The species is grown in pens or cages, but a number escape each year and form an important but limited sport fishery. They are best taken by lure casting or trolling.

The fishing in the channel concentrates on trevally, flathead, Australian salmon, cod, squid and trumpeter. The shallow waters of **Isthmus Bay**, **Little Taylors Bay** and **Great Taylors Bay** are productive flounder grounds. **Cloudy Bay**, at the south of the island, has more varied fishing for flathead, Australian salmon, barracouta, pike, trevally, trumpeter and cod.

The east coast of the island gives access to the productive southern bluefin tuna grounds for which Tasmania's offshore waters are renowned. These tuna are consistently the largest bluefin caught in Australian waters by anglers and game fishers have been known to come from all over the globe when the tuna season is a good one. Trevally, trumpeter, flathead and mackerel are closer inshore, notably in **Trumpeter Bay** in the north and in the big expanse of **Adventure Bay**. The long beach in Adventure Bay is one of the few beach fishing venues in this southern Tasmanian region. The bay carries morwong, cod, whiting, flathead, pike, trevally, trumpeter and mackerel. There are bream in the small creeks that empty into Adventure Bay. These fish can be caught on lures and flies, as well as bait.

Lure casting in the lower reaches of the Huon River. Here many anglers chase the Atlantic salmon escapees from the fish farms of the lower estuaries and bays

GUIDE TO LOCAL FISH

BC	barracouta
B	bream
C	cod
F	flathead
FL	flounder
MA	mackerel
MO	morwong
PI	pike
AS	salmon, Atlantic
SA	salmon, Australian
TR	trevally
	trout, brown
TP	trumpeter
TU	tuna
W	whiting

COASTAL FISHING HOBART REGION

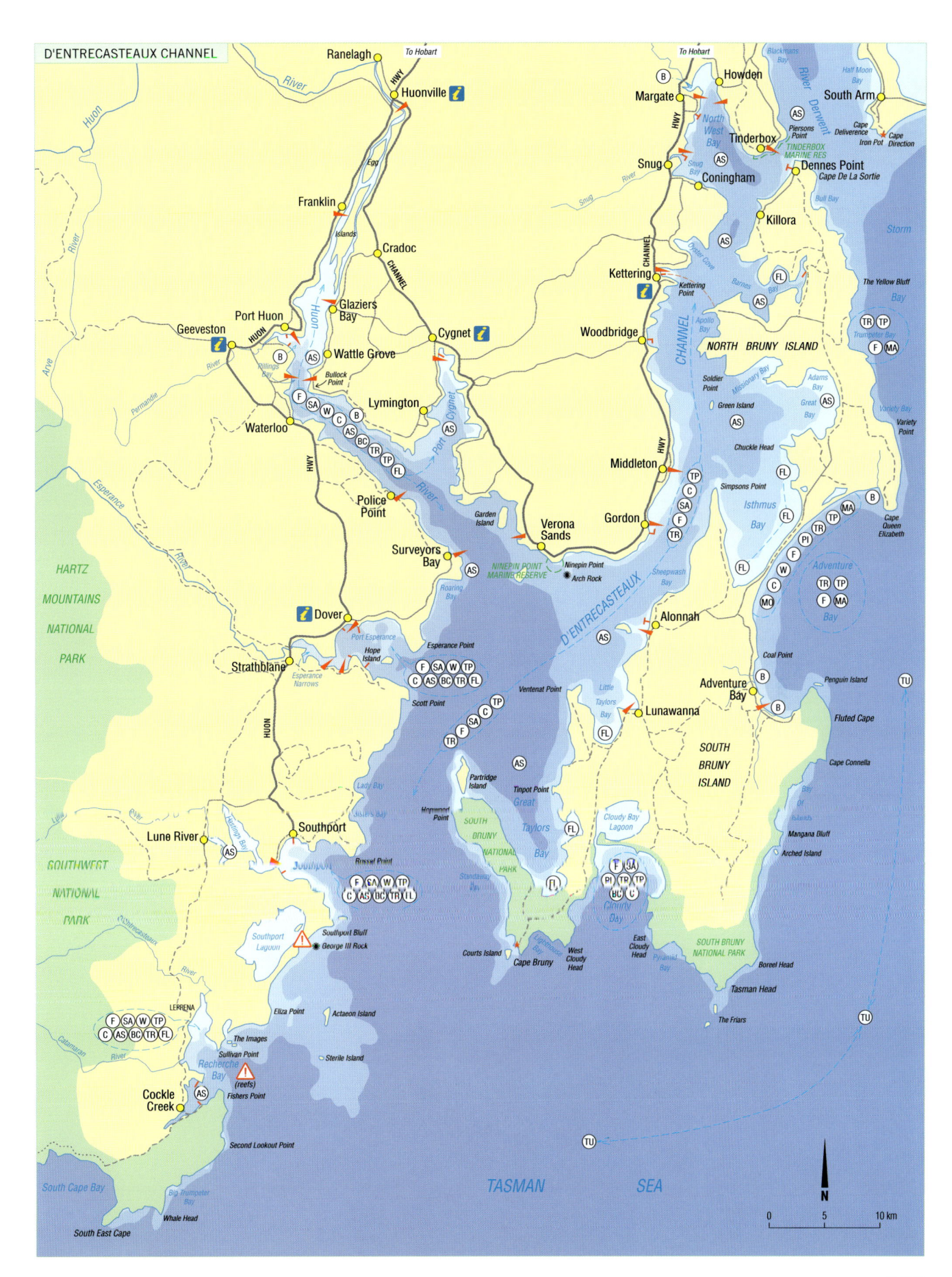

TASMANIA

TASMANIA

Launceston Region

The north of Tasmania has a little of everything for the angler – rivers and estuaries, bays and beaches, rocks and islands. Fish from the land, small boats, or large charter boats – you'll come across a good variety of species to suit your taste.

The coastal waters of northern Tasmania are often exposed to the rough weather of Bass Strait, but there are sheltered waters in Perkins and Duck bays in the far north-west, and in the Forth and Mersey rivers. Towards Launceston, the shelving sand-bottomed waters of the strait hold Australian salmon, trevally and trumpeter among many other species.

Port Sorell and Port Dalrymple are good, safe fisheries and the Tamar River offers 65 km of land-based and boat fishing. In recent years, the Tamar River has been blessed with many excellent pontoons. Designed for boats, the pontoons are ideal fishing platforms. In the north-east, Bridport offers a combination of beach, boat and jetty fishing.

Ansons Bay, The Gardens, St Helens and Bicheno are the fishing centres of the delightful north-east coast, and put professionals and game anglers within reach of the warm East Australian Current.

Flinders and King islands have jetties, beaches, rocks and estuaries, and a chance for some exciting charter fishing in Bass Strait.

Weather

Weather conditions on the north coast can be treacherous, so it is important to be vigilant at all times. Around the lower Tamar River, there is a strong tidal effect on the ebb tide, making the sea choppy. However, the coast is generally protected from huge ocean swells. In the summer months, a strong north-west breeze comes in and can reach 15 to 20 knots. Overall, the best time for boating is from February to April. For weather information contact Marine and Safety Tasmania, tel. (03) 6233 8801.

GUIDE TO LOCAL FISH

- barracouta
- bream
- cod
- drummer
- flathead
- flounder
- garfish
- gurnard
- kingfish, yellowtail
- leatherjacket
- ling
- luderick
- mackerel
- marlin
- morwong
- mullet
- parrotfish
- pike
- salmon, Australian
- sawfish
- shark, gummy
- shark, others
- snapper
- snook
- sweep
- tailor
- trevally, silver
- trumpeter, bastard
- tuna
- warehou
- whiting

Boating

Boating can be hazardous in this region as the coastline is generally shallow and rocky, creating a choppy sea. The Tamar River can be dangerous, with reefs near its mouth, although they are marked with river lights. There are launching facilities all along the Tamar, and at most of the coastal towns.

Georges Bay at St Helens have dangerous bars. For full details on boating hazards and other information, contact local marine authorities in the area.

Barracouta

Barracouta is a common species in Tasmania's southern bays as well as being present offshore. They school and will hit lures or baits with abandon. The average size is 1 to 2 kg but fish can grow to 5 kg.

COASTAL FISHING LAUNCESTON REGION

WHERE TO FISH

Launceston Region

HUNTER ISLAND TO DEVONPORT ● 232
The best fishing along this stretch of coast is in the sheltered bays, channels and rivers. From the islands off the north-west tip to the shallow waters of the Mersey River, a large variety of fish is available, with common catches including Australian salmon, flathead, barracouta and whiting.

PORT SORELL TO BRIDPORT ● 234
Port Sorell is a quiet estuary holding a variety of fish, and the Tamar River has 65 km of well-serviced fishing waters. Outside, the best fishing is on the reefs and sandy surfaces found around the river entrances.

ANSONS BAY TO BICHENO ● 236
Saltwater anglers love this north-eastern coast of Tasmania, with its sheltered inlets, beaches and fine rock fishing spots. But one of its greatest assets is the warm East Australian Current that flows down the coast, attracting large numbers of fish.

KING ISLAND ● 238
King Island's north is fringed by beaches and headlands, while its rugged south-west has good fishing off the rocks for sweep.

FLINDERS ISLAND ● 239
You may need to charter a boat when on a trip to Flinders Island if you want access to the great fishing around the offshore rocks and smaller islands, where you will find shark, yellowtail kingfish, trevally and morwong, and tuna and barracouta in season.

The Bass Strait islands

King and Flinders islands are the two main Bass Strait islands. King Island, at the western end of the strait, has picturesque, rugged terrain with an unspoiled coastline of beautiful sandy beaches on the east and north coasts, contrasting with the forbidding cliffs of Seal Rocks and the lonely coast to the south. The surf fishing is particularly productive. Flinders Island is renowned for its fishing – it is the main industry of the tiny community of Lady Barron to the south, a port village overlooking Franklin Sound and Cape Barren Island. The best way to

COASTAL FISHING LAUNCESTON REGION

TASMANIA

LAUNCESTON REGION

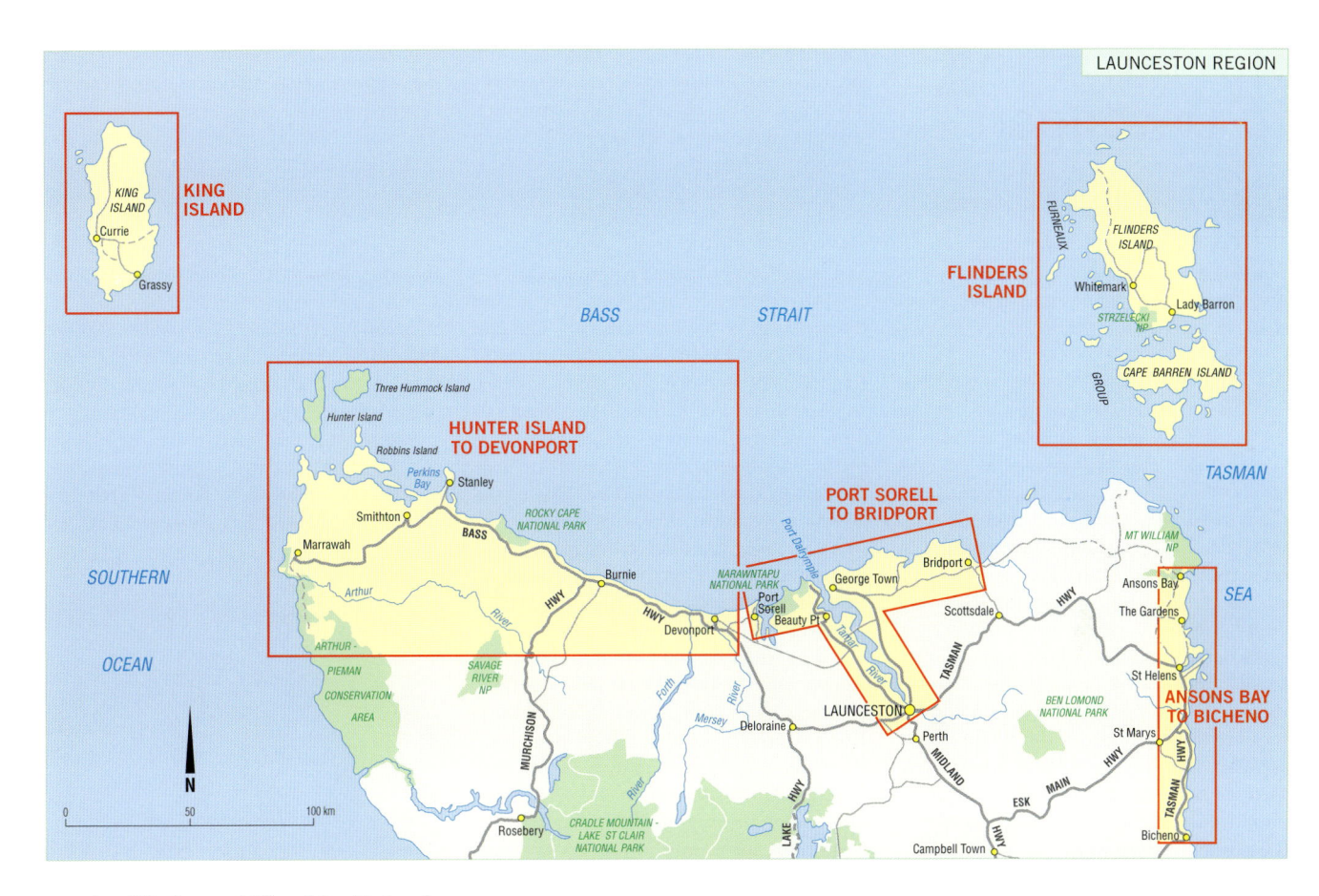

Currie Harbour, King Island

travel to Flinders and King Island is by air. There are regular flights by regional airlines to King and Flinders islands, from Tasmania and Victoria. The airlines cater for travelling anglers but you should find out the size of the rod tube you are allowed to carry and the best way to pack your tackle.

FURTHER INFORMATION

Boating and fishing The Fisheries Division of the Department of Primary Industries, Water & Environment has an information line, tel. 1300 368 550. There are port authorities in Burnie, tel. (03) 6434 7300; Devonport, tel. (03) 6424 0911; Grassy (King Island), tel. (03) 6461 1155; and Launceston, tel. (03) 6332 0111.

Tourist centres Tasman Hwy, Bicheno, tel. (03) 6375 1333; Civic Centre Plaza, Little Alexander St, Burnie, tel. (03) 6434 6111; 92 Formby Rd, Devonport, tel. (03) 6424 4466; Main Rd, Exeter, tel. (03) 6394 4454; Cnr Main Rd and Victoria St, George Town, tel. (03) 6382 1700; Cnr St John and Paterson sts, Launceston, tel. (03) 6336 3133; St Helens History Room, 61 Cecilia St, St Helens, tel. (03) 6376 1744; The Nut Chairlift, Browns Rd, Stanley, tel. (03) 6458 1286; Council Offices, Goldie St, Smithton, tel. (03) 6452 1265; Cnr Hogg and Goldie sts, Wynyard, tel. (03) 6442 4143.

TASMANIA

COASTAL FISHING LAUNCESTON REGION

Hunter Island to Devonport

Type of fishing
bay, beach, estuary, jetty, river, rock

Target fish
Australian salmon, barracouta, flathead, pike, snapper, whiting

The north-west coast of Tasmania does not offer great fishing in areas exposed to the shallow and often stormy waters of Bass Strait, but there are a number of comparatively sheltered areas where fishing is extraordinary in the right weather conditions.

In the far west, the **Arthur River** is a popular holiday resort and fishing spot, where large Australian salmon and some tailor are caught at the river mouth. Around the north-west tip, extreme boating care is required by those going out to the island complex of **Hunter, Three Hummock, Walker and Robbins islands**, but there is good fishing in the channels around there. The fishing is based on Australian salmon, barracouta, flathead, cod, trevally, trumpeter, pike and whiting, with flounder in some shallow areas. **Walker Channel** and **Robbins Passage**, both within easy reach of the Tasmanian mainland, are the main fishing grounds in this area.

Duck Bay and **Perkins Bay** are relatively sheltered from the westerlies by these islands. There are flounder and garfish in the shallow inshore waters of the bays, and flathead, whiting, barracouta, snapper and Australian salmon for boat anglers. In Duck Bay there are good land-based angling prospects at the wharf at Smithton and the Duck River, with big catches of mullet, Australian salmon, tailor and large flathead in the channels.

Moving east from Perkins Bay, around North Point to Godfreys Beach, Circular Head (known locally as The Nut), Sawyer Bay and Tatlows Beach, shore-based and boat anglers can try for flathead, Australian salmon, mackerel, warehou, pike, barracouta in season, and the occasional yellowtail kingfish. Stanley wharf is sometimes closed when commercial boats are in. The wharf is a real 'hot spot' and the fishing for warehou is legendary. Best time is from January to June. East and West inlets on either side of the Nut offer opportunities for land-based anglers.

The rocks around **Circular Head** give an opportunity for luderick and parrotfish, and these vegetarian species are also around **Rocky Cape**, to the east. **Sisters Beach** and **Boat Harbour** have squid, luderick, cod, flathead, Australian salmon and barracouta. Offshore in this region, Australian salmon, barracouta, mackerel and pike are the most common catches, with the occasional tailor.

Burnie is Tasmania's fourth-largest town and is situated on Emu Bay. Its busy deep-water port serves the west coast mining centres. There is no fishing allowed from the wharf at Burnie. East of the town there is a boat ramp and breakwater where land-based fishing can be excellent. Parrotfish, leatherjacket, cod and squid can be caught from the rocky stretches of coast. The whole area is largely fished from boats. In deeper water the main fish are Australian salmon and flathead, found on the sandy bottom, with some barracouta and snook. Offshore from Burnie, anglers will find barracouta, pike and Australian salmon.

Around **Ulverstone**, there is some sheltered fishing in the inlet for Australian salmon, flathead, mullet and cod, and at The Fish Pond, a small U-shaped bay which attracts parrotfish, mullet and Australian salmon.

All along this coast there is offshore boat fishing for flathead, salmon, barracouta, whiting and pike. The **River Forth** has Australian salmon at its mouth, and flathead

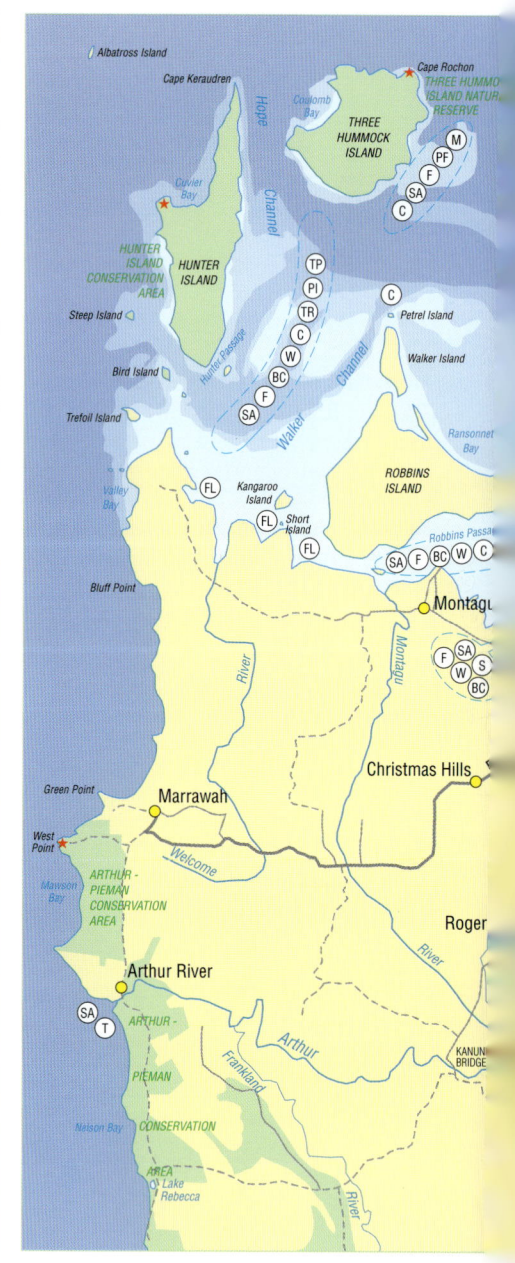

Fishing boats in the harbour at Stanley

GUIDE TO LOCAL FISH

BC	barracouta
C	cod
F	flathead
FL	flounder
G	garfish
KI	kingfish, yellowtail
LJ	leatherjacket
LU	luderick
MA	mackerel
MO	morwong
M	mullet
PF	parrotfish
PI	pike
SA	salmon, Australian
S	snapper
SN	snook
T	tailor
TR	trevally
TP	trumpeter
WA	warehou
W	whiting

COASTAL FISHING LAUNCESTON REGION — TASMANIA

and tailor on the sandy spots. There are a few trout in the river's upper reaches.

Around Devonport there are good numbers of fish in the sheltered, shallow waters of **East Devonport Beach**, beside the **Mersey River** entrance. Flathead and whiting are plentiful here, along with Australian salmon, barracouta, pike and trevally – some snapper, too, if you can tap local knowledge. Past the ferry terminal, where the *Spirit of Tasmania* ferry to mainland Australia turns around, there are cod, mackerel and morwong along the western shores of the river, and flathead and Australian salmon in the water running to the Bass Highway Bridge. Mullet can be caught throughout the whole length of the river – as far as brackish water runs.

Circular Head is known locally as The Nut. Here boat anglers can fish for flathead and Australian salmon

HUNTER ISLAND TO DEVONPORT

TASMANIA   COASTAL FISHING LAUNCESTON REGION

Port Sorell to Bridport

Type of fishing
bay, beach, estuary, jetty, reef, river
Target fish
barracouta, cod, flounder, mullet, snapper, yellowtail kingfish

The central point in this area is George Town, at the mouth of the Tamar River. In the west, near Devonport, the town of Port Sorell is the oldest township on the north-west coast. It is situated at the entrance to the large waterway of Port Sorell, which is also the estuary of the Rubicon River. Bridport, on the north-east coast, is a fishing town, providing beach, river, sea and lake fishing.

PORT SORELL TO BRIDPORT

The sand bottom in the area immediately outside **Port Sorell** produces some good boat fishing. Flathead and whiting are the main target fish, along with Australian salmon, barracouta and pike. There is excellent fishing inside this estuary for flathead, mullet, cod, Australian salmon, trevally and whiting, with flounder in the shallows and the occasional tailor.

Bass Strait remains shallow and sandy to **Port Dalrymple**, at the head of the Tamar estuary. The fishing along this coast is as good as outside Port Sorell. Near **Low Head**, on the eastern side of the entrance, there are flathead, Australian salmon, cod, yellowtail kingfish and snapper on the outside reefs, with garfish and barracouta in season.

From Port Dalrymple to Bridport, there are a number of small creeks running back from the coast, such as **Pipers River**, **Little Forester River** and **Brid River**. Australian salmon are found at the entrances of most of the rivers and creeks along this coastline. The whole area has a sandy floor, with the gutters and formations, holes and weed areas a habitat for many species, including flathead, whiting and cod, with flounder on the sand. The area is not known for its reef fishing but the occasional rocky outcrop will yield yellowtail kingfish, snapper and barracouta in autumn. It is mainly boating water, with some protection in **Noland Bay** and **Anderson Bay**, although beach fishing is popular on the Anderson Bay beaches. Flathead, cod, whiting and flounder are usually here in good numbers, with leatherjacket and ling caught in the rocky areas. Again, Australian salmon and barracouta are common in season.

Bridport is a fishing town, with a professional fishing fleet operating from the wharf in the Brid River. Flathead, mullet and whiting can be caught from the jetties. In the entrance to the river, there is usually a congregation of Australian salmon, flathead and mullet, while the fishing wharf is a reliable place for bream.

TAMAR RIVER

Within the Tamar estuary, which runs some 65 km inland to the northern city of Launceston, there are flathead, cod, mullet,

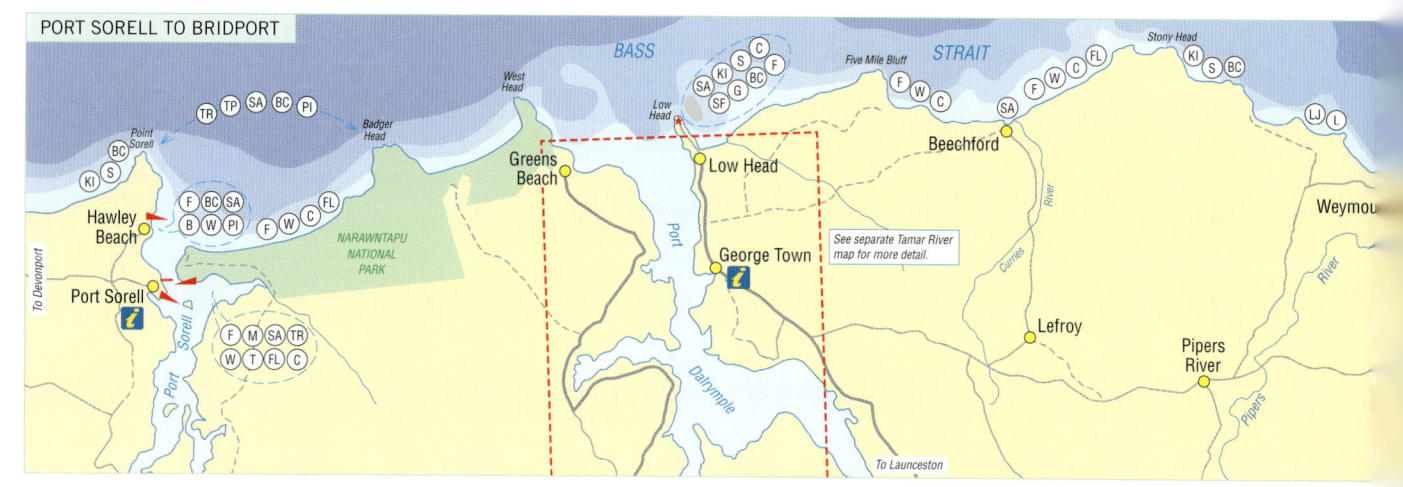

The Tamar is one of Tasmania's larger river estuaries and contains flathead, whiting and snapper in the lower reaches

COASTAL FISHING LAUNCESTON REGION

TASMANIA

whiting, a few snapper, tailor and silver trevally, with warehou around in autumn. Flathead, cod and whiting are predominant further in, and there are some deep holes where snapper can be caught. Australian salmon come into the estuary in big schools, and sometimes there are runs of tailor to make for exciting fishing. Best fishing in the Tamar is below Windermere, although some sea-run trout are caught in the upper reaches – especially at the Trevallyn Tailrace near Launceston. There are small towns dotted along the whole length of the Tamar, with wharves and jetties at places such as **George Town**, **Beauty Point** and **Windermere**. They are reliable fishing places for cod, mullet and Australian salmon, with spotted mackerel in the autumn and always a chance of flathead.

There are many boat ramps along the length of the estuary. The mouth of the river can be dangerous and boats need to watch out for the reefs, although they are marked with river lights.

GUIDE TO LOCAL FISH

		Port Sorell to Bridport	Tamar River
(BC)	barracouta	●	
(B)	bream	●	
(C)	cod	●	●
(F)	flathead	●	●
(FL)	flounder	●	
(G)	garfish	●	
(KI)	kingfish, yellowtail	●	
(LJ)	leatherjacket	●	
(L)	ling	●	
(MA)	mackerel		●
(M)	mullet	●	●
(PI)	pike	●	
(SA)	salmon, Australian	●	●
(SF)	sawfish	●	
(S)	snapper	●	●
(T)	tailor	●	●
(TR)	trevally	●	●
(TP)	trumpeter	●	
(WA)	warehou		●
(W)	whiting	●	

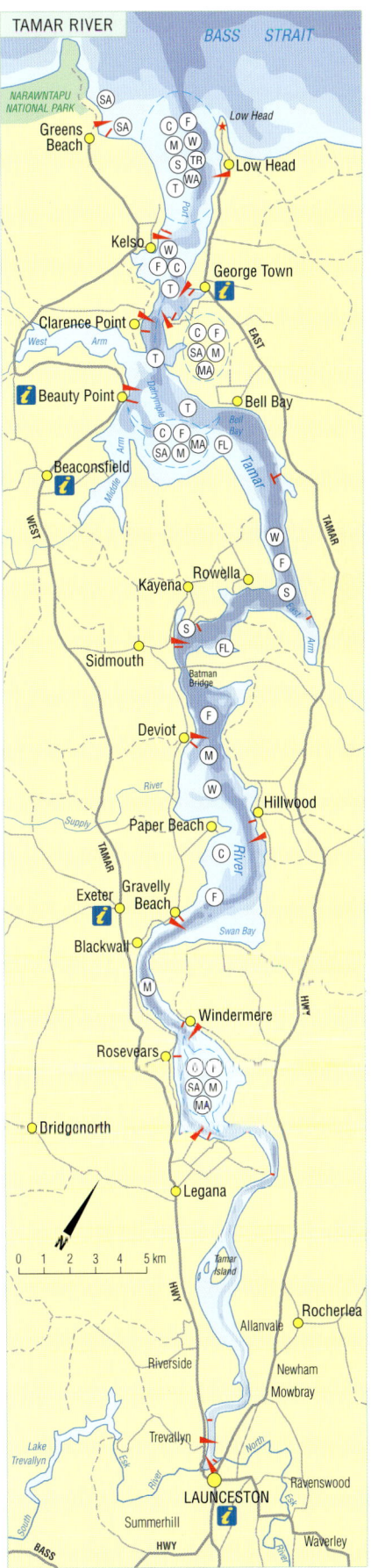

TASMANIA COASTAL FISHING LAUNCESTON REGION

Ansons Bay to Bicheno

Type of fishing
bay, beach, estuary, offshore, reef, river, rock
Target fish
Australian salmon, bream, flathead, marlin, trumpeter, tuna

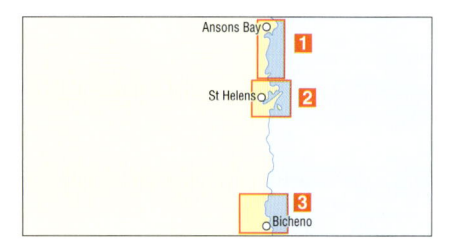

The east coast is the preferred fishing area for Tasmania's saltwater anglers, with its sheltered inlets and beach and rock fishing potential. There are easy launching facilities to the productive offshore waters, which are affected by the warm East Australian Current flowing right down the coast.

ANSONS BAY TO BIG LAGOON

The most northerly fishing area on this stretch of coast is **Ansons Bay**, a shallow estuary of the Ansons River, with channels, sandbanks and weedy areas that make for a good day's fishing. There are Australian salmon and flathead in the entrance to the estuary and garfish in the bay in autumn, with large bream in the river proper. It is regarded by many as Tasmania's 'big bream' water. Bream to 2 kg can be expected. In the inshore waters outside the estuary, there are Australian salmon, silver trevally, mackerel, flathead and whiting, and barracouta in autumn.

Between Ansons Bay and The Gardens, there is offshore fishing for yellowtail kingfish, Australian salmon, snook, barracouta, morwong, parrotfish, trevally and cod.

South of Ansons Bay, but more accessible from St Helens, is the area known as **The Gardens**. The target fish here are cod, the weed-eating parrotfish, flathead and mullet. **Sloop Reef** is about 5 km to the south near Sloop Lagoon, and flathead, Australian salmon, trumpeter and whiting can be prolific here.

BINALONG BAY AND ST HELENS

The town of **St Helens** is a jumping-off point for those heading out to fish in the East Australian Current for tuna, marlin and shark. But there is plenty for land-based and inshore anglers as well, as the town is set at the head of **Georges Bay**, a long and narrow estuary. Jetties near the town, and the Golden Fleece Bridge, which spans the entrance to Medeas Cove, provide plenty of opportunities to try for the flathead, cod, Australian salmon, silver trevally, bream, mullet and garfish that congregate here. There are tailor and trevally in Georges Bay, and luderick are also present. The locals call them butterfish and they are often caught by accident by anglers bream fishing the lagoons and lower reaches of the rivers.

On the north side of the bay, the entrances to **Colchis Creek** and the **George River** are also good for bream. There are trout, too, not far upstream. Beach anglers have a prime spot at the settlement of **Stieglitz**, on the southern side of the bay. The beach is right beside the road and there is great fishing for whiting, flathead, Australian salmon, elephant fish, mullet and garfish.

The beach fishing continues on the coast outside the bay, for Australian salmon, flathead, yellowtail kingfish and barracouta. The headlands of the bay, **Grants Point** and **St Helens Point**, can be fished for luderick, Australian salmon, flathead, leatherjacket and warehou, with yellowtail kingfish also a possibility off St Helens Point.

Heading south, the coast from St Helens Point to Bicheno provides a long string of beautiful headlands and beaches. The

Georges Bay is a large bay with several jetties offering land-based fishing

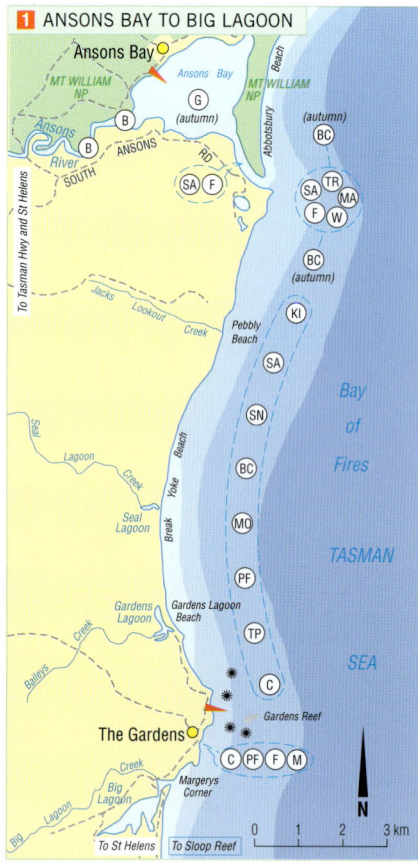

GUIDE TO LOCAL FISH

	Ansons Bay to Big Lagoon	Binalong Bay and St Helens	Bicheno
(BC) barracouta	•	•	•
(B) bream	•	•	•
(C) cod	•	•	•
(D) drummer			•
(F) flathead	•	•	•
(G) garfish	•	•	
(KI) kingfish, yellowtail	•	•	
(LE) leatherjacket		•	•
(L) ling			•
(LU) luderick		•	•
(MA) mackerel	•		
(ML) marlin			•
(MO) morwong	•		•
(M) mullet	•	•	
(PF) parrotfish	•	•	
(SA) salmon, Australian	•	•	•
(SH) shark		•	
(SN) snook	•		
(T) tailor		•	
(TR) trevally	•	•	•
(TP) trumpeter			•
(TU) tuna		•	
(WA) warehou		•	
(W) whiting	•	•	•

COASTAL FISHING LAUNCESTON REGION — TASMANIA

Crayfish boil at Bicheno

Leatherjacket
There are over fifty species of leatherjacket in Australia. Most have little colour but the toothbrush species illustrated here is quite striking. Leatherjacket is found in weed and reef areas of southern Australia.

BICHENO

A delightful holiday village, Bicheno has a good combination of beach, bay and rock fishing. The coast is rocky, so there are many fishing places to choose from. Boat anglers can fish **MacLean Bay** for trevally, trumpeter, cod, whiting and Australian salmon. Further out there are good possibilities for mullet, whiting, flathead, Australian salmon, barracouta, mackerel and trevally, and there may be a few ling on the inshore reefs. There are flathead, cod and Australian salmon at **Redbill Beach**, on the north side of the town, and mullet and garfish close in at **Waubs Bay**.

Waubs Gulch, a narrow waterway between the rocky mainland shores and Governor Island, is a marine reserve. Parrotfish and drummer inhabit the area, along with morwong, silver trevally, leatherjacket, bastard trumpeter and cod, and very occasionally luderick, so fishing from the rocks can be a very rewarding experience, although strong swells through the channel can make the rocks dangerous.

Tasman Highway runs right along this coast, so there is plenty of opportunity for beach anglers to survey the beach formations and pick some likely spots, and for rock anglers to look for deep water shelving down from a headland or the weedy rock gutters that attract luderick and parrotfish, such as those at **Ironhouse Point**. Among other prominent rock fishing places are **Wardlaws, Piccaninny and Long points**. There are rivers and creeks, too, with bream in the lower reaches and entrances. Some to try are the **Avenue River** at Scamander, and the **Henderson Lagoon** and the **Douglas River** at Falmouth. Flathead, Australian salmon, barracouta, cod, sweep and pike are among the inshore fish for the boat anglers who go out in calm conditions.

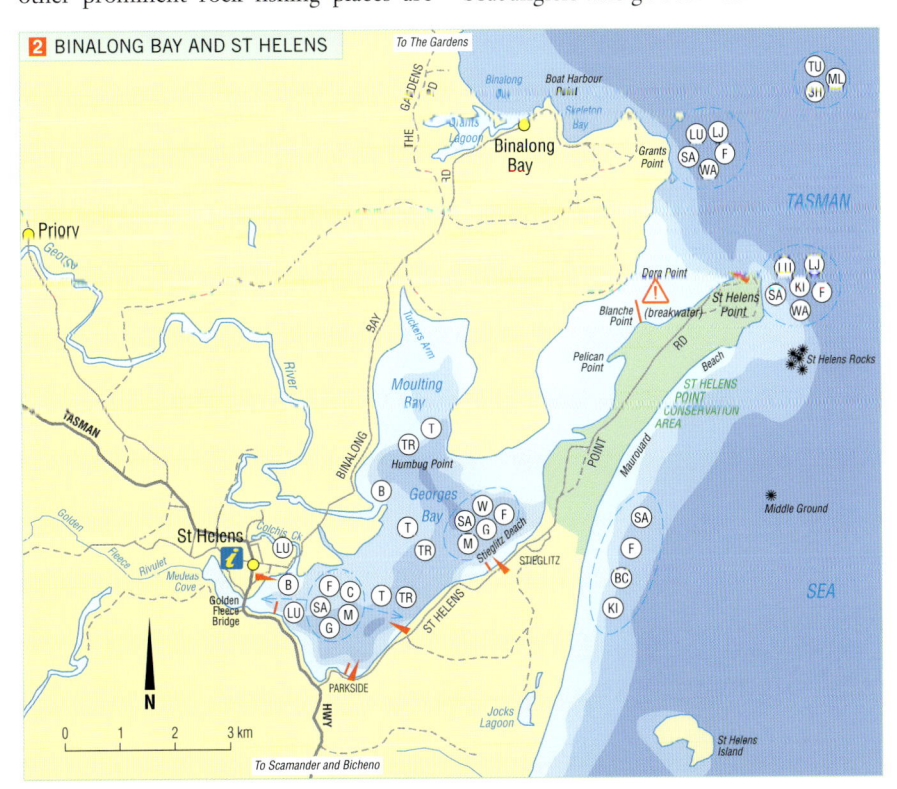

2 BINALONG BAY AND ST HELENS

3 BICHENO

TASMANIA

COASTAL FISHING LAUNCESTON REGION

King Island

Type of fishing
bay, beach, jetty, offshore, reef, rock
Target fish
Australian salmon, flathead, mullet, sweep, whiting

Off the north-west coast of Tasmania, King Island is a place of contrast, in both the landscape and the fishing. The verdant, rolling grassland of the north, renowned for its dairy products, is fringed by superb sandy beaches and headlands, while the rugged south-west coast has good fishing off the rocks for sweep.

The only way to reach King Island is by air. Three airlines operate regular services between the island and various coastal cities and towns in Victoria and Tasmania.

In the island's north, there is excellent fishing, particularly on the eastern side, which is sheltered from the prevailing westerlies and the swell of the ocean. Beach anglers can fish for Australian salmon, flathead, whiting, mullet, parrotfish and gurnard, while there are good rock stands at **Boulder Point** and **Lavinia Point**.

Further south, at **Naracoopa**, jetty anglers can seek Australian salmon, squid and barracouta, and the old mining town of

Flathead are a plentiful offshore species, particularly on the north-east coast

Grassy has a wharf and breakwater, which are fished for squid, barracouta, trevally and sweep. There are boat ramps at both towns, and a fishing charter boat operates out of Naracoopa in season.

In the south-west sweep are the target, particularly from Surprise Point and Cataraqui Point. Some 6 km south of the main town of Currie is the **British Admiral Reef**. Morwong, warehou, yellowtail kingfish and squid can be caught by boat anglers over and around the reef. There is a boat ramp at **Currie**, bait and tackle and also a charter boat operation for those who wish to fish offshore with the experts. The jetty is a popular angling spot, with morwong, squid, warehou, and garfish in autumn.

Phoques Bay in the north-west also has good beach fishing for Australian salmon, flathead, whiting and mullet, with boat action centred around **New Year and Christmas islands** and **Whistler Point**.

King Island takes the brunt of some heavy ocean weather, particularly on its west coast, and all boat anglers should pay attention to weather forecasts and local advice.

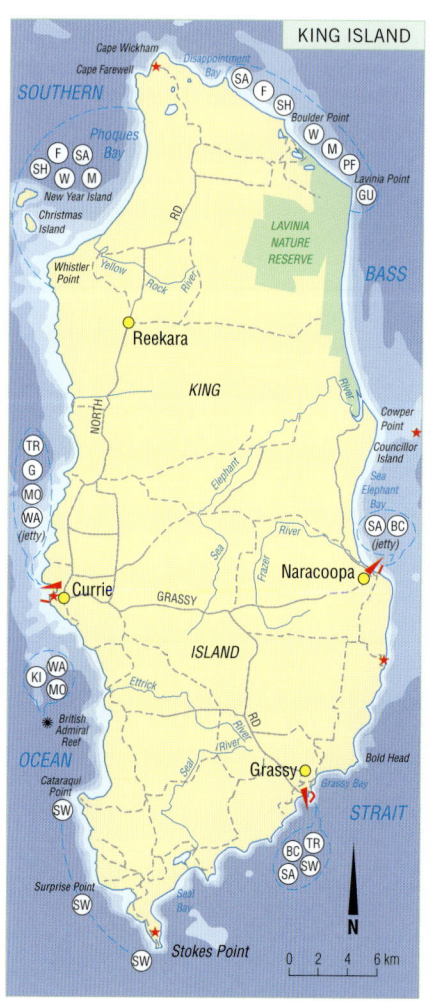

Beach fishing on King Island for Australian salmon

Sweep
The sea sweep, probably more common in Victorian, South Australian and southern Western Australian waters, is caught in reasonable numbers around the coastal reef areas of King Island.

GUIDE TO LOCAL FISH

		King Island	Flinders Island
BC	barracouta	●	●
C	cod		●
F	flathead	●	●
FL	flounder		●
G	garfish	●	●
GU	gurnard	●	
KI	kingfish, yellowtail	●	
MO	morwong	●	
M	mullet	●	●
PF	parrotfish	●	●
SA	salmon, Australian	●	●
SH	shark	●	
GS	shark, gummy		●
S	snapper		●
SW	sweep	●	
T	tailor		●
TR	trevally	●	●
TP	trumpeter		●
TU	tuna		●
WA	warehou	●	
W	whiting	●	●

COASTAL FISHING LAUNCESTON REGION   TASMANIA

Flinders Island

Type of fishing
bay, beach, estuary, offshore, rock
Target fish
Australian salmon, barracouta, flathead, tuna, whiting

Flinders Island, the main island of the Furneaux Group, lies off the north-east coast of Tasmania. It is an unspoiled place of farm and bushland, backed by mountains and with a beautiful shoreline of bays, beaches and coves overlooking rocks and smaller islands that beckon the boat angler. Charter boat operators are in demand here, as the average angler comes by plane from Melbourne or the Tasmanian 'mainland' and does not have a craft to explore these offshore waterways. The professional fishing fleet sends out its catches by air.

The excellent beach, bay and rock fishing has plenty to occupy the land-based angler, with flathead, whiting, cod, mullet and Australian salmon among the inshore fish. A fine fishing area in the north is the estuary of the **North East River**, completely sheltered and renowned for cod, Australian salmon, big flathead, flounder and gummy shark, and with an excellent camping ground right by the water. Further south, on the east side, **Patriarch Inlet** and **Cameron Inlet** have sheltered land and boat fishing.

The main fishing centre on the island is at **Lady Barron**, in the sheltered Adelaide Bay, and around the many islands in **Franklin Sound**. Apart from the crayfish and abalone specialists, the commercial fishing fleet concentrates on shark, yellowtail kingfish, trevally and morwong, and tuna and barracouta in season. The fishermen's wharf here is a popular place for casual anglers and they may be rewarded with mullet, cod and flathead.

A popular land-based fishing and camping spot is **Trousers Point**, in the south-west of the island, where the rock ledges make ideal stands for seeking Australian salmon, trevally and the occasional tailor.

The settlement of **Wybalenna**, with Arthur Bay on the south side of Settlement Point and Port Davies on the north, is a centre for bay fishing. **Killiecrankie Bay**, to the north, is sheltered from south-easterlies. Shore-based or boat fishing is mainly for mullet, flathead, salmon and garfish close to shore, and trevally and trumpeter in the bays. You may also encounter the odd snapper and in recent times striped tuna have been caught in good numbers during February.

There is plenty of scope for rock fishing on Flinders Island

239

TASMANIA

Inland Fishing

Tasmania is by far the smallest Australian state, at only 68 331 km², but it provides a wealth of trout fishing opportunities to rival any of the mainland states in both quality and quantity. The cool maritime climate of Tasmania, coupled with mountainous terrain, has adorned this large island with numerous rivers and streams that have proved to be ideal habitat for trout. As good as the river fishing is, Tasmania is probably better known internationally for its huge number of trout-filled lakes, both natural and artificial. Other freshwater species such as redfin, tench and blackfish are also present, but few anglers target these fish in view of the abundant trout fishing available. Carp have recently been found in Tasmania. Along with redfin, they are regarded as a serious threat to inland fisheries, and heavy penalties exist for translocation of these species.

Although rainbow trout have done well in several waters, and maintain at least a presence in many others, it is the wild brown trout that has truly thrived. Virtually every water has been infiltrated by this fish, with only steep waterfalls preventing colonisation of a few remote lakes. Brook trout is the least successful of the three species, with this fish available in only a handful of waters where the other two are absent.

The major geographical feature of Tasmania is the wild Central Highlands. Comprising a high plateau in the east, jagged mountains in the west and gentle

WHERE TO FISH

Inland

NORTH-EAST REGION ● 242
The catchments of the North and South Esk rivers are justifiably renowned for the quality of the trout fishing, with waters of high quality such as the Macquarie, Break O'Day and Meander rivers, and the half-river, half-lake – Brumbys Creek. The north-east corner is less impressive, but good stream fishing is possible in rivers like the Great Forester and upper Ringarooma. The east coast is perhaps the poorest area, but if its waters were on the mainland, they would still be heavily visited because the lower Forester is very good.

SOUTHERN REGION ● 248
Southern Tasmania provides good to excellent stream fishing, particularly on the western River Derwent tributaries like the Tyenna River, while Mount Field National Park offers some small trout lakes in remote and rugged country. More accessible lakes like Meadowbank in the Derwent Valley also produce good trout. Streams flowing into the Derwent from the east such as the Clyde and Ouse have fewer but bigger fish than those found in the western tributaries.

CENTRAL HIGHLANDS REGION ● 252
This area is famous for the wild trout that inhabit literally thousands of lakes and tarns, along with connecting streams. Although bushwalking is the only option to reach many lakes in this wilderness, plenty of the most famous waters, such as Arthurs Lake, Great Lake, Little Pine Lagoon and Lake King William, can be reached by road. The stream fishing seldom measures up to the standard of the lakes.

NORTH-WEST AND WEST COAST REGION ● 258
Barrington and Rowallan are probably the most popular lakes in north-west Tasmania, and there are plenty of reasonable trout streams, with the Leven and the Mersey among the most appealing. In western Tasmania, some rivers and lakes are so remote they remain largely unexplored. However, there are a number of first-class trout waters easily accessible by car or a short walk, including Lake Pedder, Lake Burbury near Queenstown, and the Pieman and Henty rivers in their lower reaches.

INLAND FISHING

TASMANIA

Sea-run brown trout are worth chasing during spring in the lower reaches of several west coast rivers, such as the Henty

foothills in the south, this region is a trout fishing nirvana of lakes and tarns that number in the thousands, although access is not always straightforward.

The theme of rugged, remote country is even more pronounced on the west of the island. Here the massive rainfall provides countless rivers and streams, many containing trout, but usually all but inaccessible. An annual highlight in the lower reaches is the migration of sea-run brown trout (sea trout) in spring, while huge hydro dams on the upper reaches provide very good fishing.

Outside of the centre and west, Tasmania is more 'civilised', with towns and services easy to find, and good roads provide access to most of the better rivers and lakes. However, these parts still remain largely unspoiled and uncrowded by mainland standards, despite a benign climate and gentle landscape. High quality trout fishing, especially on rivers and streams, is commonplace.

Tasmania is blessed with abundant wild trout stocks, but the visiting angler should beware. Although plentiful, the Tassie trout are as wily as anywhere, particularly in the lakes, and plenty of patience and persistence is usually required to bring them undone. They won't just jump into your lap. If you don't have time to work it out for yourself, hiring one of the island's professional trout guides is the best option. Finally, remember that restrictions on certain fishing techniques apply on some waters – check the regulations that are provided with your fishing licence. Most Tasmanian inland waters are closed from May until the end of July.

Licences

The government authority responsible for the management of inland waters is the Inland Fisheries Service. Anyone may fish in Tasmania's inland waters provided they have a current angling licence from the Inland Fisheries Service and they fish at approved inland waters with a rod, reel and line during the open season. A special licence is required for the taking of whitebait.

Protected species

Of Tasmania's 25 species of native fish, the 12 recognised as being 'threatened' are now wholly protected and cannot be taken by anglers. These include the Australian grayling (also known as cucumber herring) and 11 species of galaxiid (being all galaxiid species except the jollytail, climbing galaxias, spotted galaxies and Tasmanian mudfish). The giant freshwater crayfish is now wholly protected. Fishing for all other species of freshwater crayfish is restricted.

Open seasons

The trout season starts at the beginning of August, though several waters are not opened until October or November.

Most waters are closed at the end of April, though some do not close until the end of May and a handful are now open all year round. Regulations for individual waters can change frequently and anglers are advised to check the current *Angling Code* (issued free with licences) for specific dates.

State regulations

For the first time in Tasmania's history, regulations are being tailored to reflect the unique requirements of different waters. Specific fishing regulations for bag and size limits as well as fishing techniques (artificial lures only and fly only) are gradually being phased-in for sensitive waters. These regulations may well be refined in subsequent seasons depending upon environmental and social outcomes. Consequently, Tasmania's inland angling regulations are now in a state of flux and potentially subject to annual change. A summary of the year's *Angling Code* is included in the *Inland Fisheries Handbook*, issued free with licences.

Boating

All boats of 4 hp or more are required to be registered. Operators of a boat powered by 4 hp or more are also required to have a *Speed Boat Licence*. Details on how and where you can obtain a licence and/or register a boat are available from Marine and Safety Tasmania.

GUIDE TO LOCAL FISH

blackfish, river
bream
eel, long-finned
eel, short-finned
flounder
redfin
salmon, Atlantic
tench
trout, brook
trout, brown
trout, rainbow

Bag and size limits apply. See the 'Inland Fisheries Handbook' for details.

FISHING TIP

If you want to catch a trout, first you must know where to fish and what they are feeding on. Trout in streams try to conserve energy by sitting where the current will bring food to them. Most anglers know that trout adopt what are known as feeding lanes in rivers, but did you know that these fish are more often found feeding in low-pressure areas in front of rocks rather than behind them? Most waterways fish well after flooding. The water level rises and floods over the grassy banks offering up a selection of untapped food such as snails and beetles. Big trout often only feed at night. In lakes they will come into the shallows to hunt and the best time is after the moon has gone down.

FURTHER INFORMATION

Fishing For full details of Tasmania's inland fishing regulations, contact the Inland Fisheries Service at 6B Lampton Ave, Derwent Park, tel. (03) 6233 4140, website www.ifs.tas.gov.au. The Service publishes an annual guide for anglers which is available from its offices and from bait and tackle shops.

Boating For full details on boating regulations, contact the marine board or port authority operating in the area. For information on boating safety and registration, contact Marine & Safety Tasmania (MAST), 1st floor, 7–9 Franklin Wharf, Hobart, tel. (03) 6233 8801, website www.mast.tas.gov.au

TASMANIA

North-east Region

In contrast to much of western Tasmania, this area is characterised by a mild climate, large areas of cleared agricultural land and numerous towns and roads.

Mountains and forests still exist, but not on the scale of the west. Visitors will find most fishing access comfortable and straightforward, though of course permission should be sought before crossing private property.

Undoubtedly the best fishing is in the famed meadow streams of the South Esk catchment, notably the Macquarie, Break O'Day and Meander, all of which flow across flat pasture. Brumbys Creek, a tail-race fishery, which receives cold water from the Central Highlands, is another highlight.

Apart from these rivers, you can also try Lake Leake, Tooms Lake and the tidal reaches of the Great Forester, Scamander and Apsley rivers. This region attracts fly fishers from mainland Australia and overseas. Much of the tourism is based on recreational fishing needs so the travelling angler is well catered for in most areas.

INLAND FISHING NORTH-EAST REGION

WHERE TO FISH

North-east Region

FAR NORTH-EAST ● 244

Some of the best trout come from tidal reaches of coastal rivers while Blackmans Lagoon produces trophy fish during springtime. Otherwise the fishing is largely confined to fast-flowing streams with gravel beds where the trout are numerous but generally small.

EAST COAST ● 245

The East Coast is one of the driest areas in Tasmania, and the fishing does not match that found in other parts of the State.

ESK SYSTEM ● 246

The catchment of the North and South Esk rivers is arguably the best place for stream fishing in Tasmania. Both rivers are good fisheries in their own right, but many tributaries provide picturesque stream fishing, and rivers such as the Macquarie, Lake and Break O'Day produce larger fish, especially on the fly. The famous Brumbys Creek can provide idyllic fishing conditions.

GUIDE TO LOCAL FISH

blackfish, river
eel, long-finned
eel, short-finned
redfin
tench
trout, brown
trout, rainbow

FURTHER INFORMATION

Fishing and Boating There is an Inland Fisheries Service inspector at St Leonards, tel. (03) 6339 1794, or contact the head office on tel. (03) 6233 4140. For boating enquiries, contact the Port of Launceston Authority, tel. (03) 6382 0111.

Tourist centres Tasman Hwy, Bicheno, tel. (03) 6375 1333; 18 High St, Evandale, tel. (03) 6391 8128; Main Rd, Exeter, tel. (03) 6394 4454; Cnr Main Rd and Victoria St, George Town, tel. (03) 6382 1700; Cnr St John and Paterson sts, Launceston, tel. (03) 6336 3133; Orford Riverside Cottages, Old Convict Rd, Orford, tel. (03) 6357 1655; Tasmanian Wool Centre, Church St, Ross, tel. (03) 6381 5466; St Helens History Room, 61 Cecilia St, St Helens, tel. (03) 6376 1744; Lyric Snack Bar, 27 King St, Scottsdale, tel. (03) 6352 3235; Swansea Bark Mill & East Coast Museum, 96 Tasman Hwy, Swansea, tel. (03) 6257 8382; Cnr Charles St and Esplanade West, Triabunna, tel. (03) 6257 4090.

Macquarie River Broadwater

'The nights were chilly, the days sunny and humid, and Macquarie spinners filled the air. Just about everything felt right...'

Some years ago I took my parents to Tasmania for a holiday. It was early April, and we hoped to catch a few trout while we were in the north-east of the State. We stopped at Noel and Lois Jetson's tackle shop in Cressy to get licences, buy a few flies, and wheedle a bit of local knowledge out of them. The conversation was rather guarded, but towards the end Lois mumbled something about a little fishing shack for hire on the Macquarie River about half-way to Campbell Town. When pressed, she said we probably wouldn't like it because it was quite a way off the road and you had to take your own food, and anyway it might already be booked.

But we found the entrance of Barton Station, and the small sign pointing the way to the homestead and to 'Broadwater Cabin', and 5 km, four gates, and a thousand or so sheep later, we pulled up at the Broadwater itself – a huge, still waterhole on the Macquarie River.

I like to describe the Broadwater as the bulge in the python – you know, when it has swallowed a goat but is still a few days away from digesting it. From the air and on most maps, that is exactly what it looks like.

Out in the middle it is very deep, but above and below the Broadwater the Macquarie is a regular river, with pools and runs and ripples. It is easily fished in thigh waders. Upstream it winds through grazing country, with grassy banks and willowy bends. Downstream it is a little brisker, and for a kilometre or so bubbles along through a charming valley of open tea-tree scrub and towering moribund eucalypts before widening out into bigger, lazier water once again.

At the right time of year – usually late November through to early December and likewise in March and April – it is known for prodigious hatches of Macquarie spinners, but the visitors' book at the cabin did not promote great optimism. 'Plenty of trophy-sized possums, but where are all the fish?' was the typical entry.

Still, I had that feeling we were going to do well right away. We got there at 1 o'clock in the afternoon – not exactly prime time for trout – but the surface of the Broadwater was blooming with concentric circles, and within 20 minutes the old man had caught a 1.5-kg brown, and 10 minutes later pulled in its twin brother.

We stayed for three and a half days. It was early autumn, but the water was surprisingly fresh for so late in the year. The nights were chilly, the days sunny and humid, and Macquarie spinners filled the air. In other words, just about everything felt right, and to prove it, three of us caught two dozen more fish, and lost half as many more.

A year and a half later I went back to the Broadwater with some friends. This time it was early December – supposedly peak season – but I knew we were in trouble as soon as we arrived. Part of it was that sixth sense, but there were some obvious signs too. Only a quarter of the normal rainfall for the year had fallen in the district, and the river was low, sluggish and weedy.

The relatively few rises we saw were short-lived, and hard to fish to because the water was so clear and quiet. There was plenty of insect life, but try as we might, we just couldn't crack the code. In the end, four of us, all good anglers, could only manage five pretty ordinary fish in as many days.

But that's the way it is sometimes – and as my mother-in-law is fond of saying, one should always leave a place knowing there is something left for next time.

– *Bill Bachman*

TASMANIA

INLAND FISHING NORTH-EAST REGION

Far North-east

Type of fishing
lake, river
Target fish
brown trout, rainbow trout

The trout fishing in this area consists largely of fast-flowing creeks and rivers that run through partly forested mountain and hill country. Although the quality of fishing does not generally compare with that found elsewhere in Tasmania, anglers can still enjoy good trouting. Most waters can be reached by conventional car.

The **Ringarooma River**, flowing into Ringarooma Bay on the north coast, is despoiled by siltation from mining in its lower reaches, but the upper section is a good trout stream that can be comfortably waded.

The **Great Forester**, with its mouth in Anderson Bay, provides some sea-trout in its lower reaches. The overgrown middle section features difficult conditions for fishing, but some trout reach a large size. The upper reaches are more comfortable and better suited to fly fishing, with fish of more modest proportions.

Rainbows can be found in some Far North-east streams, but they are usually small

Such trout are also typical of the **Little Forester**, further to the west, the exception being the sluggish lower reaches where some quite large trout occur. Both the **Brid River**, in between the two Foresters, and the **George River**, flowing into Georges Bay on the east coast, can provide fast stream fishing for smallish trout, with the odd sea-trout in their lowest sections. Most other creeks in the area hold trout, but they are generally of little interest to serious anglers. It is worth noting that populations of blackfish exist in most streams in this area, particularly those containing plenty of submerged timber.

The area is largely devoid of still waters, but three small lakes make an exception. **Blackmans Lagoon**, near Waterhouse, is essentially a springtime fishery. Having no spawning facilities, it is reliant on regular stocking. Some fish grow to 4 kg or more, and Blackmans is noted as a trophy trout water. The lake can be very weedy, and considerable persistence is usually required to hook a fish, but the big trout receive the attention of serious anglers. Nearby **Big Waterhouse Lake** is disappointing; **Little Waterhouse Lake** is a much better trout fishing option.

INLAND FISHING NORTH-EAST REGION   TASMANIA

East Coast

Type of fishing
lake, river
Target fish
brown trout, rainbow trout

By the time Tasmania's prevailing westerly airflow has reached the east coast, it has crossed many mountain ranges which have sucked most of the moisture from the clouds. The area is thus comparatively dry, and also enjoys the mildest climate in the State. Unfortunately, the quality of the trout fishing falls short of that found elsewhere – the area lacks the large lakes and strongly flowing streams typical of other parts of Tasmania.

Even so, average river fishing can be found on some rivers. Anglers prepared to stalk the deeper pools and broadwaters with fly or bait have a chance of landing the better trout. Small pools and riffles are unlikely to produce decent fish during the lengthy periods of low flow over summer and autumn. Of the specific rivers, the **Scamander**, in the north, the **Apsley**, west of Bicheno, and the **Prosser**, in the south, are all capable of yielding some well-conditioned browns of 1 kg or more, although the average size is smaller. The Apsley also contains blackfish. Of the three, the Prosser is probably the best and produces some very nice browns to skilled anglers. Two tributaries, the **Bluff River** and **Tea Tree Rivulet**, produce a few reasonable browns to dedicated anglers. Good sea-trout occur from time to time in the lower reaches of the major rivers, especially during spring. Sea-run trout are often brighter in colour and in better condition than trout which have stayed in the rivers.

A few good sea-trout can be caught in the lower reaches of the **Swan River**, which runs into Great Oyster Bay, near Swansea. The upper reaches of the Swan River are not so highly regarded as they provide limited trout fishing in shallow water. Large numbers of tench and redfin are found in the **Little Swanport River**, north of Triabunna, along with some trout. Most other streams on the east coast carry resident populations of trout, but poor summer and autumn flows limit their appeal. It is worth remembering that the much more productive waters of the upper Esk system are within easy striking distance of here.

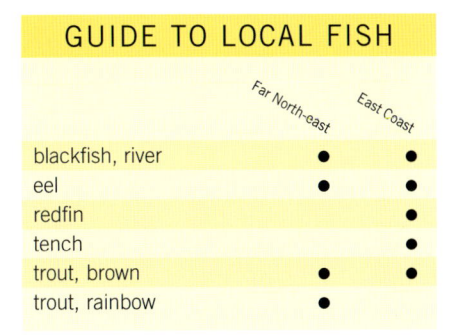

Although small trout are the norm for the East Coast streams, some better fish can reward the patient angler

Mudeyes

Throughout Australia mudeyes are regarded as one of the best trout baits, and Tasmania is no different. Fished under a float on lakes, or simply drifted unweighted down a stream, the mudeye accounts for numerous Tasmanian trout each season. No live bait of any kind (including mudeyes) may be brought into Tasmania. If collecting mudeyes for bait, they should be taken from the water you intend to fish. It is illegal to transfer species into waters in which they do not already occur.

GUIDE TO LOCAL FISH

	Far North-east	East Coast
blackfish, river	●	●
eel	●	●
redfin		●
tench		●
trout, brown	●	●
trout, rainbow	●	

245

TASMANIA

INLAND FISHING NORTH-EAST REGION

Esk System

Type of fishing
lake, river

Target fish
brown trout, rainbow trout

The enormous network of rivers feeding the North and South Esk rivers provides some of the finest stream fishing in the State. In contrast to the rugged country and inhospitable weather that dominates much of Tasmania, there are gentle pastures, a mild climate and good road networks.

The **North Esk River** is smaller than its southern cousin, but is still an impressive stream offering good fishing: riffles and pools in its upper reaches, rocky and rough in the middle reaches, and slower again in the lower sections. There is an approximate increase in the average size of the trout as one moves downstream. The beautiful forest-shrouded **St Patricks**, a tributary of the North Esk, produces few big trout, but is popular for its idyllic setting and numerous fish.

The **South Esk** is a massive river in its lower reaches towards Lake Trevallyn, and even the gorge below the lake, in Launceston, produces trout despite its urban surrounds. All the way to its source, the river provides reasonable to very good trout fishing. Arguably the best section is from Ormley to Mathinna, though the slow, weedy pools and backwaters from Clarendon to Epping Forest also offer fine sport.

A number of tributaries are at least as highly regarded as the river itself. The **Meander**, flowing from the north-west, is a fast-water stream above Deloraine, but slower and weedier below. Both sections are very good, with bigger fish more common in the lower part. To the south, the **Liffey** has roughly the same characteristics on a smaller scale.

Near Westbury are two purpose-built public fisheries, **Brushy Lagoon** and **Four Springs Lake**. Both are popular, but the fishing is mediocre compared to most highland waters.

Feeding the lower South Esk and flowing northwards, the **Macquarie** is an excellent trout stream, especially for fly fishers who revere the spring mayfly hatches. Its lazy course through flat farmland encourages a rich growth of aquatic weed and insects in its slightly discoloured waters. The water below Brumbys Creek is a tailrace fishery, which provides consistently good sport. Upstream as far as Ross, the summer flows are unreliable and the fishing is usually best in spring. A major tributary rising in the west from Arthurs Lake, the **Lake River** is a smaller, swifter version of the main river. In addition to trout, it holds a reasonable head of blackfish. Blackfish occur at a few other locations in this area, favouring snaggy streams.

East of the South Esk, the **Break O'Day** and **St Pauls** are again held in high regard by fly fishers seeking good-sized stream fish in their weedy runs and still broadwaters. A couple of lesser rivers in the system – the **Nile** and **Elizabeth** – still provide worthwhile trouting at times.

Brumbys Creek, near Cressy, is a good, if overgrown, stream, but the name is generally applied in referring to a series of three weirs on its lower reaches. The system is a tailrace fishery which receives cool water from the Central Highlands and provides relatively consistent fishing throughout the year. Fly fishing is especially popular, though lure casting does well at times. Many trout are of only average size, but there is a considerable head of larger (and wilier) specimens.

Of the true stillwaters, **Tooms Lake** and **Lake Leake** on the upper Macquarie system are well-regarded. **Lake Trevallyn** offers fishing on the edge of Launceston, but is overshadowed by other fine waters in the area. **Curries River Dam**, near George Town, produces some good trout, and is quite popular with local anglers.

A number of slower waters in the Esk system contain redfin and tench.

Runs and riffles complement the still broadwaters on many Esk System rivers

GUIDE TO LOCAL FISH

blackfish, river
redfin
tench
trout, brown
trout, rainbow

INLAND FISHING NORTH-EAST REGION

TASMANIA

Brumbys Creek near Cressy is great fly fishing water, especially in November during the early mayfly hatches

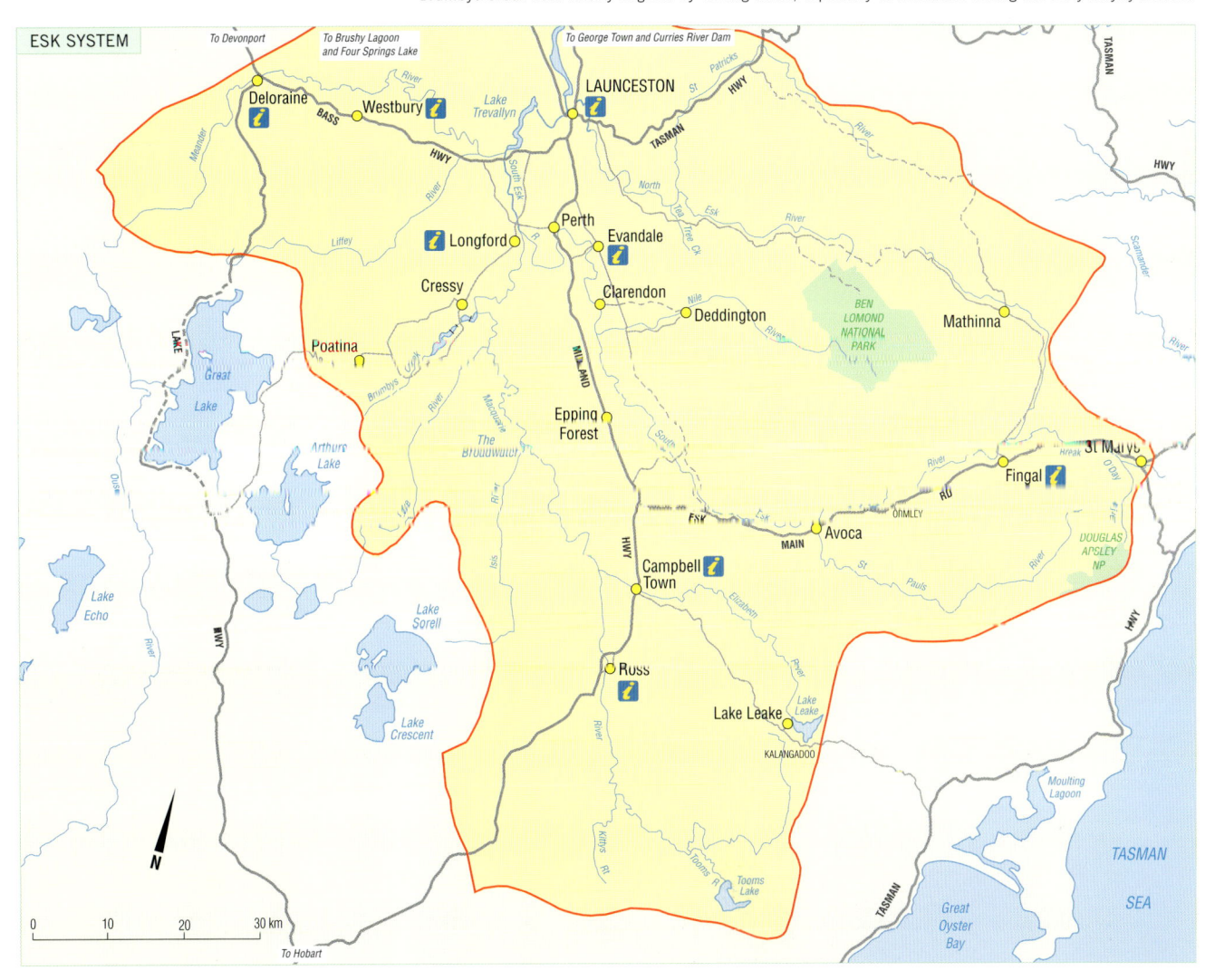

ESK SYSTEM

TASMANIA

INLAND FISHING SOUTHERN REGION

Southern Region

The eastern half of this region has comparatively mild weather and low rainfall and features slower flowing streams in a rural setting. The western half is typically cold and wet, with extensive mountainous country and large, swift streams.

Road access and services are abundant in the east but restricted in the west. As well as the river and stream fishing, this region offers some good stillwater trout fishing, especially in the Derwent Valley lakes.

In spring the sea-trout fishing in the Derwent and Huon estuaries can be superb. Later in the season, quality fastwater fishing is to be experienced in tributaries such as the Weld, Styx and Tyenna rivers. The best of the lowland impoundments are Meadowbank Lake and Craigbourne Dam while those looking for pristine waters will delight in the sub-alpine lakes and tarns in Mount Field National Park.

Fishing in the rugged wilderness of Mount Field National Park

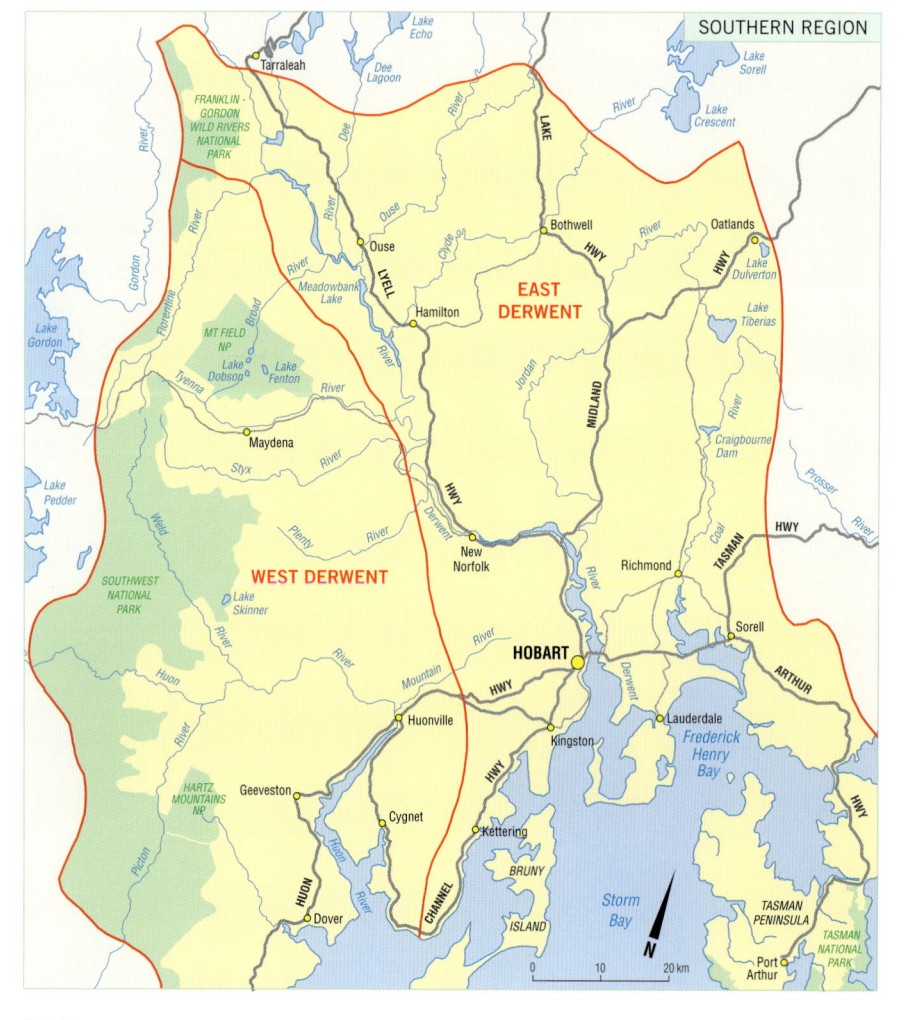

WHERE TO FISH

Southern Region

EAST DERWENT ● 250

The Derwent River and several hydro dams along its course are the dominant features of this area. All contain trout but the most popular is Meadowbank Lake which also benefits from annual liberations of large Atlantic salmon. Of the Derwent's eastern tributaries, the Ouse and Clyde rivers are the best trout fisheries. Further east, the Craigbourne Dam and the Coal River are worth a look. The Derwent estuary is good in spring when the sea trout are about.

WEST DERWENT ● 251

To the west of the Derwent, the country is more mountainous and forested. Several clean, fast streams flow in from the west, including the Tyenna, Styx and Plenty. The Huon's lower reaches produce several monster browns of 5 kg or more each season, while the fast upper sections contain more average stream trout. The remote Weld River is one of the few Tasmanian rivers dominated by rainbows. Mount Field National Park contains a number of reasonable trout lakes, though all but Lake Dobson require walking to reach.

GUIDE TO LOCAL FISH

blackfish, river
eel, long-finned
eel, short-finned
redfin
salmon, Atlantic
tench
trout, brown
trout, rainbow

FURTHER INFORMATION

Fishing and Boating The Inland Fisheries Service head office is at 6B Lampton Ave, Derwent Park, tel. (03) 6233 4010. A senior inspector is available after hours on tel. 0408 145 768. Marine & Safety Tasmania (MAST) is on the 1st floor, 7–9 Franklin Wharf, Hobart, tel. (03) 6233 8100.

Tourist centres Australasian Golf Museum, Market Pl, Bothwell, tel. (03) 6259 4033; Forest and Heritage Centre, Church St, Geeveston, tel. (03) 6297 1836; Cnr Davey and Elizabeth sts, Hobart, tel. (03) 6230 8233; Bruny D'Entrecasteaux Visitor Centre, Ferry Rd, Kettering, tel. (03) 6267 4494; Council Offices, 12 Summerville St, Sorell, tel. (03) 6265 2201.

The Ouse

'Despite its shrunken stature, the Ouse still carries trout and at times offers quite good sport to the angler searching its quiet pools and murmuring runs.'

In 1933, the Ouse River etched its place in Tasmanian angling lore when an 8-kg (17 lb 10 oz) rainbow trout was caught in its upper reaches. To this day, that trout remains the largest authenticated rainbow from Tasmanian waters.

Many years ago, the Ouse was a mighty river. Its headwaters lay among the vast network of lakes and streams on the alpine moors of the Central Plateau. Once its strength had been mustered from the rain and snow of this harsh highland, the river gouged an ever-deepening ravine as it moved southward to join the Derwent. Along the way, the Shannon tumbled down to swell its already powerful flow.

But in the early part of this century, work began to harness the hydro-electric value of these swift rivers. Dams were constructed, and flows were diverted for maximum power yield. Though few anglers would begrudge the angling waters directly and indirectly created by the hydro scheme, the Ouse itself and its main tributary gradually shrivelled to comparative trickles.

Today, the Ouse is a gentle, subdued stream. However, if you look closely, you will see hints of the former strength of this river. Note the water scars high on the bare rock faces above the present river level, and the huge water-worn boulders lying well up the bank, perhaps partly hidden by willows.

Despite its shrunken stature, the Ouse still carries trout and at times offers quite good sport to the angler searching its quiet pools and murmuring runs. In its lower reaches, at least, it may be that the reduced flows have made it a somewhat richer stream, allowing weedbeds and the like to grow where previously the stream bed would have been swept clean by the angry floods of winter and spring.

I have fished the Ouse a few times. During bursts of savage highland weather, a trip down into the sheltered Ouse valley can offer respite from the biting winds. On other occasions, my angling journeys from lake to lake have taken me past the river, and I have been unable to resist a spot of stream fishing so conveniently offered.

On a bright summer's day with low flows, the Ouse can seem devoid of any reasonable trout. But in overcast weather or at dusk some surprisingly good fish quietly emerge from their lies between the submerged boulders and undercut banks.

At these times, a good tactic is to sit by a large pool, watching and waiting. With luck, a decent fish may begin to cruise its domain, searching for errant insects lying trapped on the surface. These trout usually have a 'beat' – a set course which they patrol. Having established this beat, you can cast a small dry fly like a Red Tag in ambush. Hopefully, sipping rises will come closer and closer, until your fly is suddenly gone. When you lift your rod, you may find a good trout attached. It may not be an 8-kg monster like that rainbow from 1933, but in fishing, you can never be quite sure!

– *Philip Weigall*

TASMANIA

INLAND FISHING SOUTHERN REGION

East Derwent

Type of fishing
lake, river

Target fish
brown trout

The Derwent Valley dominates this area, which consists largely of cleared, gently sloping country, changing to forested hills toward the upper end. Road networks are good, with numerous small towns throughout the district, and the city of Hobart situated on the lowest reaches of the **River Derwent**. This waterway has been extensively dammed by a string of hydro storages of varying fishing quality. Between and downstream of these lakes, the river itself offers a range of fishing environments. The estuary from the Tasman Bridge at Hobart to New Norfolk and beyond is a superb spring sea-trout fishery. Further upstream, powerful fastwater sections can produce reasonable numbers of medium-sized resident trout, while the slower broadwaters hold a few larger fish.

One of the better lakes on the Derwent is **Meadowbank**. This picturesque lake is set in farmland between Ouse and Hamilton and offers many flatter shores suitable for fly fishing, as well as deeper water for lure casting, trolling and bait fishing. It also receives annual liberations of very large Atlantic salmon (up to 7 or 8 kg) – surplus brood stock donated by Saltas. Upstream, **Cluny Lagoon** is a smaller version of Meadowbank, while **Repulse** and **Catagunya** are steep-sided and not popular. **Wayatinah Lagoon** has a reasonable reputation for trolling, but other methods also produce fish.

Flowing into the Derwent from the east are the **Ouse and Clyde rivers**. The Ouse slows down as it approaches the Derwent and contains larger fish here than up in the hill country. The Clyde usually contains small fish in its generally slow and weedy pools, but good trout are sometimes taken in the middle and upper parts. Both rivers have been infiltrated by redfin.

To the north and east of Hobart are the **Jordan and Coal rivers** respectively. Although it is prone to warm water and very low flows during summer and autumn, the Jordan holds a few respectable trout amongst its eels, tench and redfin. The Coal, on the other hand, is a respectable trout fishery, especially downstream of the Craigbourne dam where steady flows of cool water are assured.

The **Craigbourne Dam** on the upper Coal is a popular fishery. Near Oatlands lies the shallow **Lake Dulverton**. It periodically dries up, but when full for a few consecutive years, becomes a noted water for big trout.

The tiny creeks of the **Tasman Peninsula** hold equally tiny trout, and are hardly worth serious attention.

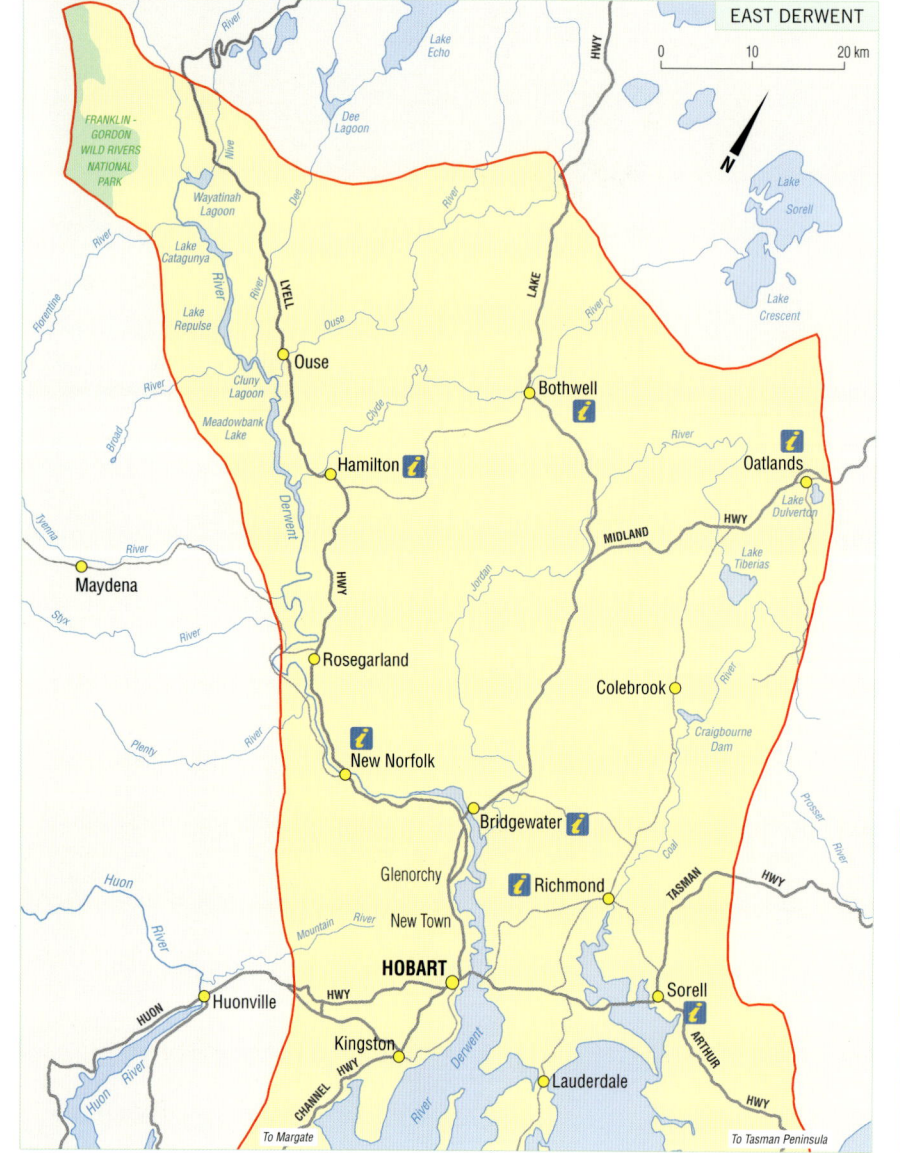

Though not as popular as trout, redfin are common in some Tasmanian waters like the Coal River

GUIDE TO LOCAL FISH

	East Derwent	West Derwent
blackfish, river	●	●
eel	●	●
redfin	●	●
salmon, Atlantic	●	
tench	●	●
trout, brown	●	●
trout, rainbow	●	●

INLAND FISHING SOUTHERN REGION   TASMANIA

West Derwent

Type of fishing
lake, river
Target fish
brown trout, rainbow trout

The character of the country to the west of the River Derwent is quite different to the east. There are high mountains, thick forests and the climate is cool and wet. Road access is still reasonable near the major valleys, but deteriorates in remote areas.

Several clean, fast mountain streams flow into the Derwent from the west. The **Florentine River** supports a large head of small to medium sized trout though it is located in production forest and the access roads are gated (contact Forestry Tasmania for details on how to obtain an access permit). The **Tyenna** is highly regarded, and holds one of the highest trout densities of any Tasmanian river. Excellent spinning and fly fishing is common, and although most trout are little more than pan-size, some much bigger trout surprise anglers from time to time. The **Styx and Plenty rivers** cannot compete with the Tyenna, but still hold a good head of typical stream fish.

The major river to the west of the Derwent is the **Huon**. A 29-lb (13-kg) brown caught here over a hundred years ago remains the largest authenticated Tasmanian trout – but only just. The lower reaches still produce several huge browns of 5 kg or more each season, while the fast-flowing upper sections contain stream trout of more typical proportions. A tributary, the remote and beautiful **Weld River**, is hemmed by thick rainforest and is one of the few Tasmanian rivers dominated by rainbow trout. Most are small, but a few reach a good size. The **Picton River**, another tributary, is difficult to fish due to deep water and thick scrub lining its banks. It carries only fair quality trout, mainly browns.

The alpine plateau contained within the Mount Field National Park features a number of trout lakes. Sadly, Lake Fenton is now closed to fishing. **Lake Dobson** can be reached by car and holds big fish. Several other trout lakes require walking to reach, but can be worth the trip if the fish are active. Walkers should be well-prepared for harsh weather.

Blackfish may be encountered in the West Derwent area, particularly in streams containing the snaggy habitat favoured by this species.

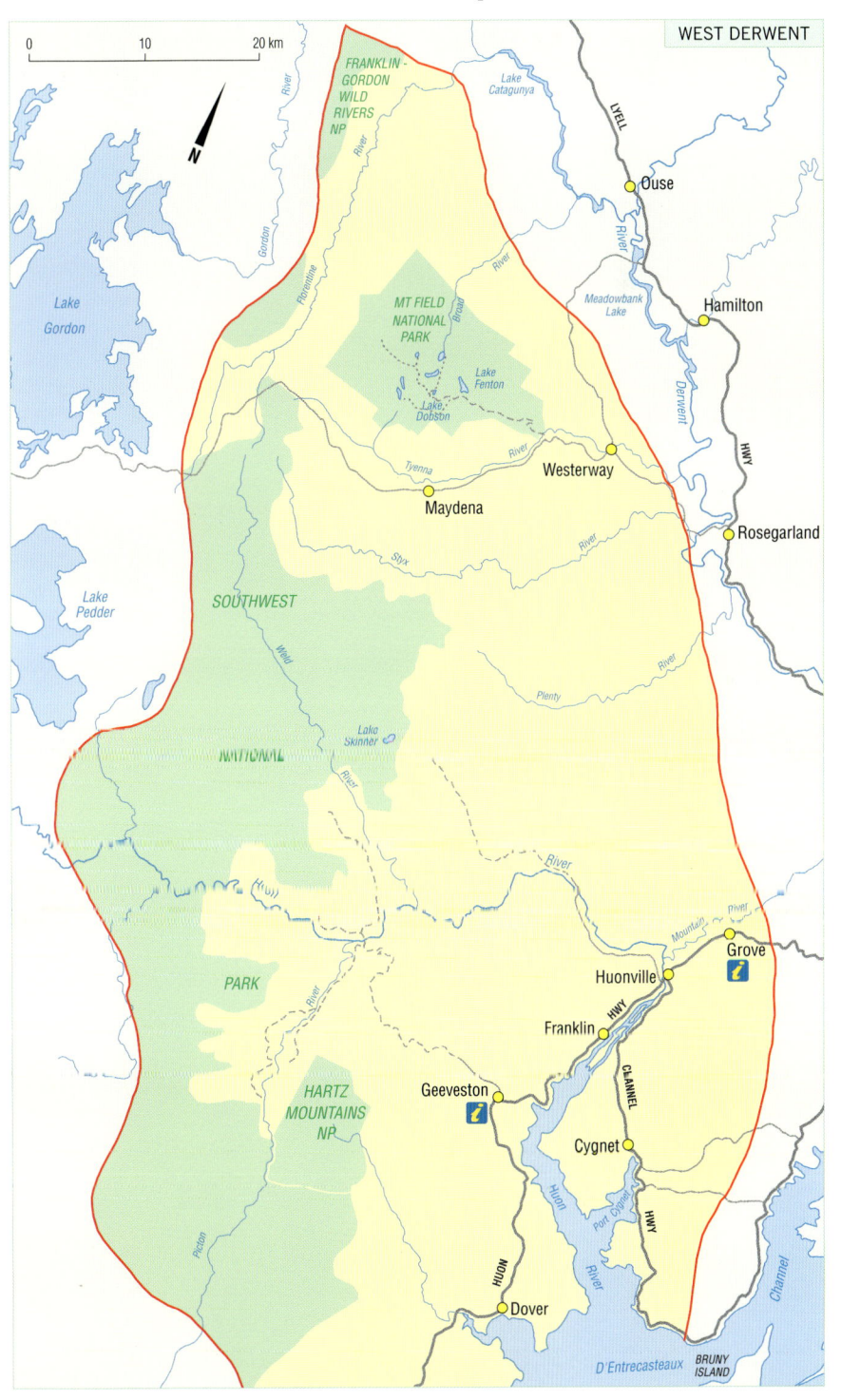

The Tyenna River is a prolific producer of trout

TASMANIA

INLAND FISHING CENTRAL HIGHLANDS REGION

Central Highlands Region

This mountainous region varies from 600 to 1200 m above sea level, with the landscape ranging from a high plateau in the east, jagged mountains in the west, and gentle foothills in the south. The weather is frequently cold and wet, with snow possible throughout the year.

Here an angler successfully lands a small rainbow trout on the northern rocks of Little Blue Lagoon

The highlands are literally dotted with artificial and natural lakes. Services and road networks are limited and often it is necessary to walk to reach the water. Even so, a number of excellent fishing locations can be comfortably reached by conventional car.

The very best and most popular trout waters are Arthurs Lake and Great Lake, which have well earned reputations for consistently producing good numbers of quality trout. Lakes Sorell and Crescent, formerly prime destinations, have been plagued by a number of environmental problems (chiefly arising from unprecedented low water) and face an uncertain future. Aside from these famous fisheries, anglers will do well to acquaint themselves with waters such as Bronte Lagoon, the Bradys chain of lakes, Lake Echo, Dee Lagoon, Lake St Clair, St Clair Lagoon and Little Pine Lagoon; all of which cater well for both shore-based and boat-based fishing. Anglers are advised to be prepared for extreme weather changes in the mountainous areas. Check the forecast before leaving and always carry some extra clothing if you intend walking longer distances.

GUIDE TO LOCAL FISH

- eel, short-finned
- redfin
- tench
- trout, brook
- trout, brown
- trout, rainbow

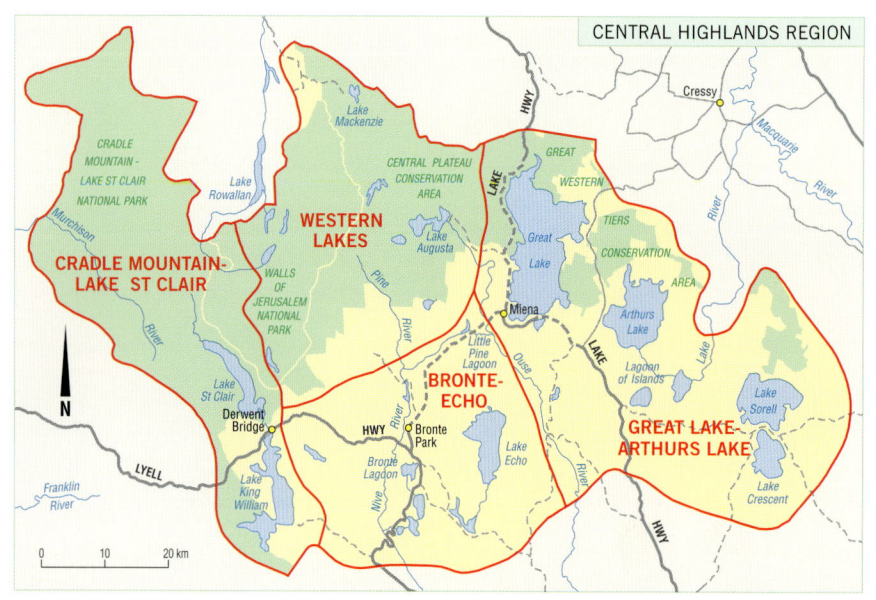

WHERE TO FISH

Central Highlands Region

GREAT LAKE–ARTHURS LAKE ● 254

The mighty Great Lake and Arthurs Lake are justifiably famous as consistent producers of quality trout, while the Lagoon of Islands and Penstock Lagoon are both capable of providing exceptional sport in the right season. Woods Lake is difficult to reach, but produces good trout. Stream fishing is limited in this area.

BRONTE–ECHO ● 255

Several hydro storages provide great fishing in this area. Bronte Lagoon, the Bradys–Binney–Tungatinah chain, Pine Tier Lagoon and Lake Echo are all productive lakes, while Little Pine Lagoon is a small but famous fly fishery. The Nive and Pine rivers can provide reasonable stream fishing, particularly above Pine Tier Lagoon.

WESTERN LAKES ● 256

This area features countless natural lakes and tarns in a wilderness setting, with an interconnecting system of streams. The great majority hold trout. Walking is all but essential to reach most waters; however, the western part is accessible in a few places by car. Most lakes are natural, with a couple of exceptions. Augusta and Ada are the hub of a renowned group of trout lakes casually referred to as the 'Nineteen Lagoons'.

CRADLE MOUNTAIN–LAKE ST CLAIR ● 257

Consisting of very high and rugged mountains, and subject to changeable weather, this area is centred on the famous Cradle Mountain–Lake St Clair National Park. The north of the park provides unremarkable angling, but Lake St Clair in the south, Australia's deepest lake, provides accessible fishing for good numbers of medium to good-sized trout in pristine surroundings. Just to the south, Lake King William holds numerous small trout.

FURTHER INFORMATION

Fishing and Boating The Inland Fisheries Service head office is at 6B Lampton Ave, Derwent Park, tel. (03) 6233 4010. An Inland Fisheries inspector is at Liawenee, tel. (03) 6259 8166. For information about boating safety and registration, contact Marine & Safety Tasmania, tel. (03) 6233 8801.

Tails on Evening

'I lifted the rod, and at once the ditch and surrounding water was a pandemonium of flying weed, splashing trout and a whirring reel ratchet.'

Of all the images that play before my mind's eye when I think of Tasmania, tailing trout are the strongest. 'Tailing' is a term used to describe the behaviour of trout searching the shallowest lake margins and marshes for food. For reasons not fully understood, Tasmanian trout seem particularly willing to forage among weedbeds or over newly-flooded flats, even where there is scarcely enough water to cover their bodies. Hence the term. these trout cannot avoid periodically sticking their tail-tips and dorsal fins out of the water. At times, when they tilt nose down, their entire tails wave in the air like a flag in the breeze. No wonder that this image remains so clearly in the memory!

Some of my favourite locations for tailing trout are to be found in the shallow lake margins of the Bronte–Echo area. Usually, tailers are best sought at dawn, when the lake shores have been undisturbed all night. But sometimes, sunset produces tailers, and one cool October evening, that was what I counted on. A westerly wind had robbed the day of warmth, and my companion and I held little hope of an evening rise to insects. So, rugged up with coats and mittens, we headed for a spot where the rising lake was inundating a grassy foreshore.

In our favour, the high water was flushing various creatures like worms and earwigs, a sure lure for hungry trout. But against us was the fact that the foreshore was riddled with depressions and ditches – the trout would be able to sneak around using the abundant patches of deeper water to conceal themselves. There would only be brief moments, when the trout crossed the shallow hummocks, that we could expect to see the fins and tails that would reveal them.

The sun disappeared behind the forested hills, and the afterglow reflected on the glassy lake margin, unbroken by the ripple of a moving trout. I searched vainly for that give-away dimple or protruding fin. Then at last, my eye caught a faint but unmistakable swirl far up a submerged ditch to my left. I removed my little Woolly Worm wet fly from the cork rod grip, and holding my rod with my right hand and fly in my left, I shuffled on my knees toward the ditch. At a distance of about 6 m, I stopped and stared. Nothing. The minutes ticked by, the icy water slowly numbing my knees through the waders.

Then just when I felt I could stand the discomfort no more, a large tail quietly slipped through the surface and casually waved at me. In an instant, I cast the Woolly Worm about a metre in front of the tail. It plopped through the surface and sank, the subtle line of my leader marking its location. Five seconds later, the water vaguely boiled in the vicinity of my fly, and then my leader surreptitiously sliced through the water. I lifted the rod, and at once the ditch and surrounding water was a pandemonium of flying weed, splashing trout and a whirring reel ratchet. Down the ditch and out into the lake shot the trout, with me stumbling somewhat stunned but elated behind it.

My struggle to control the now distant trout nearly ended in disaster when it swam between two posts, but fortunately it exited by the same route. Eventually, I was able to work line back onto the reel, and some ten minutes after the hook-up, a golden highland brown trout over 2 kg in weight grudgingly allowed itself to be beached on the grassy shore. I admired it in the torch light, before plucking the ridiculously tiny fly from its jaw and pushing it gently into the water. It sat there in the shallows for a second or two, then with a flick of the mighty tail that first gave it away, the trout was gone into the gathering night.

– *Philip Weigall*

TASMANIA

INLAND FISHING CENTRAL HIGHLANDS REGION

Great Lake–Arthurs Lake

Type of fishing
lake

Target fish
brown trout, rainbow trout

Conventional cars can reach several points on most of the lakes in this area, with boats handy to reach the more remote shores. A cool, often windy climate prevails, but a sheltered shore can be usually found except in the severest conditions. Highly regarded by locals and visitors alike, the area provides huge numbers of fish every year.

The north-western side of this area is dominated by the well-named **Great Lake**. Most visitors are bewildered by the sheer size and often barren appearance of this water, but in fact it regularly produces good catches of quality trout from dozens of bays and headlands, with fish succumbing to all angling techniques. The muddy **Shannon Lagoon** at the southern end of the lake has a famous history and is the subject of intensive efforts at rehabilitation, but in its present condition it is worth no more than a quick look en route to better waters. Not far from the Great Lake is **Arthurs Lake**. It is a little less daunting in size, and produces the greatest 'tonnage' of trout of any Tasmanian lake. Most are only of average size, but their abundance makes Arthurs a favourite destination. Again, all methods are successful under the right conditions. **Woods Lake** is a good fishery, but the access road is generally in poor condition so it is ignored by most anglers.

To the south, **Penstock Lagoon** and **Lagoon of Islands** are two highly regarded fly fisheries. Both have had ecological problems in recent years, which are being tackled with some success. When conditions are right, the weedy waters of Lagoon of Islands can produce browns and rainbows of trophy size, while Penstock fish are not quite as large, but still well worth the effort. Unfortunately, a population of redfin exists in the Lagoon of Islands.

Until the mid 1990s, **Lake Sorell** was one of the most popular and productive trout fisheries in Tasmania, while its sister water – **Lake Crescent** – was a highly regarded trophy-trout fishery. Unprecedented low water levels have since decimated both fisheries and the presence of carp (first documented in 1995) has further complicated efforts at rehabilitation. Both waters face an uncertain future.

Stream fishing is very limited and unimpressive in this area, with most lake inflows closed to angling.

Redfin
Also known as English perch, the redfin is an introduced species. There is a propensity to over breed and produce a 'stunt' fishery of tiddlers. While most of those caught would range from about 250 g to 1.5 kg, fish in excess of 3.5 kg have also been caught.

Fishing at Arthurs Lake

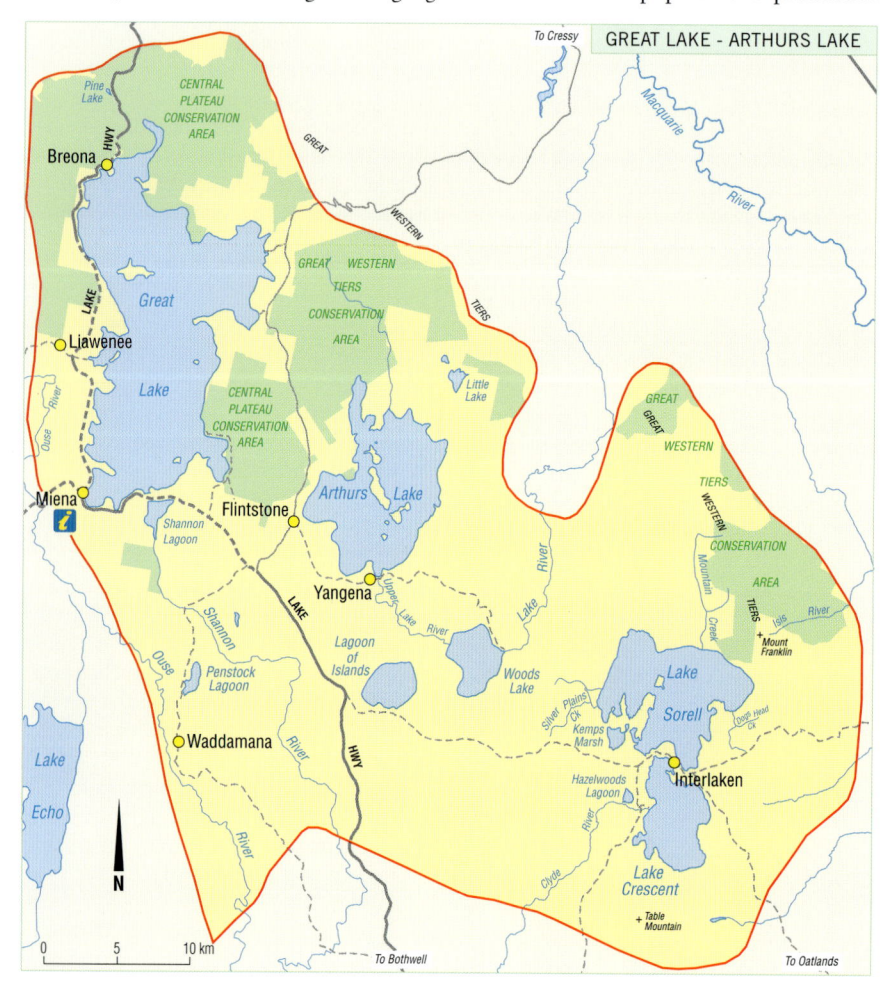

GUIDE TO LOCAL FISH

	Great Lake–Arthurs Lake	Bronte–Echo
eel	●	●
redfin	●	●
tench		●
trout, brown	●	●
trout, rainbow	●	●

INLAND FISHING CENTRAL HIGHLANDS REGION

TASMANIA

Bronte–Echo

Type of fishing
lake, river
Target fish
brown trout, rainbow trout

The terrain of this area is dominated by forested hills and mountains, with some partially cleared valleys. The weather can be changeable, though not as severe as further north or west. Most catchments have been extensively modified by hydro-electric schemes, resulting in reduced flows in the many rivers, but the creation of several top trout lakes. These artificial lakes are generally well accessed by roads, and although a boat is an advantage on some, most storages provide good shore-based fishing opportunities.

Bronte Lagoon is one of the most highly regarded waters in the area, particularly for fly fishing. Under the right conditions, its many shallow margins are ideal for 'tailers', trout feeding in water so shallow that their tails and fins are sometimes exposed, while rising fish are common during warm weather. Lure casters may find the weed frustrating, but some steeper shores yield good browns and rainbows under rough conditions. Tench exist in Bronte Lagoon, but are not often caught. Nearby **Bradys Lake**, and its 'sister' waters, **Lake Binney** and **Tungatinah Lagoon**, are underrated: they hold big populations of trout (despite competing populations of redfin), with the steeper shores ideal for lure and bait, with rising fish a good chance for fly fishers.

Car access is limited to one point on **Laughing Jack Lagoon**, in the north-west of this area. From there, walking or a boat is necessary. In the later half of the season, it is frequently low and unattractive to look at, but its browns are normally in excellent condition.

The clear, sheltered waters of **Pine Tier Lagoon**, north of Bronte Park, are regarded as a small fish water, but its huge population of trout makes it a good bet for less experienced anglers.

Further east, the shallow, windy **Little Pine Lagoon** is a fly-only water that is famous for 'tailers' in spring, and a summer mayfly hatch. Both events attract large numbers of anglers, but this water continues to produce plenty of good-sized browns.

Lake Echo is a vast storage that always holds plenty of good-sized trout, despite its uninviting appearance. Unfortunately, access is limited for those without a four-wheel drive, and boating is only suitable for large craft on its dangerously exposed waters. **Dee Lagoon**, to the south, is a very attractive lake with good access. It has a relatively high proportion of rainbows among the browns, and the average size of both species is very good. However, it is regarded as the most difficult fishery in the area, and is best for more experienced and dedicated anglers. Dee also contains plenty of stunted redfin.

Stream fishing options do not match the standard of the lakes, but the **Nive and Pine rivers** can provide reasonable stream fishing, particularly above Pine Tier Lagoon. Further west, the **Clarence River** and various canals open to fishing are also worth a look.

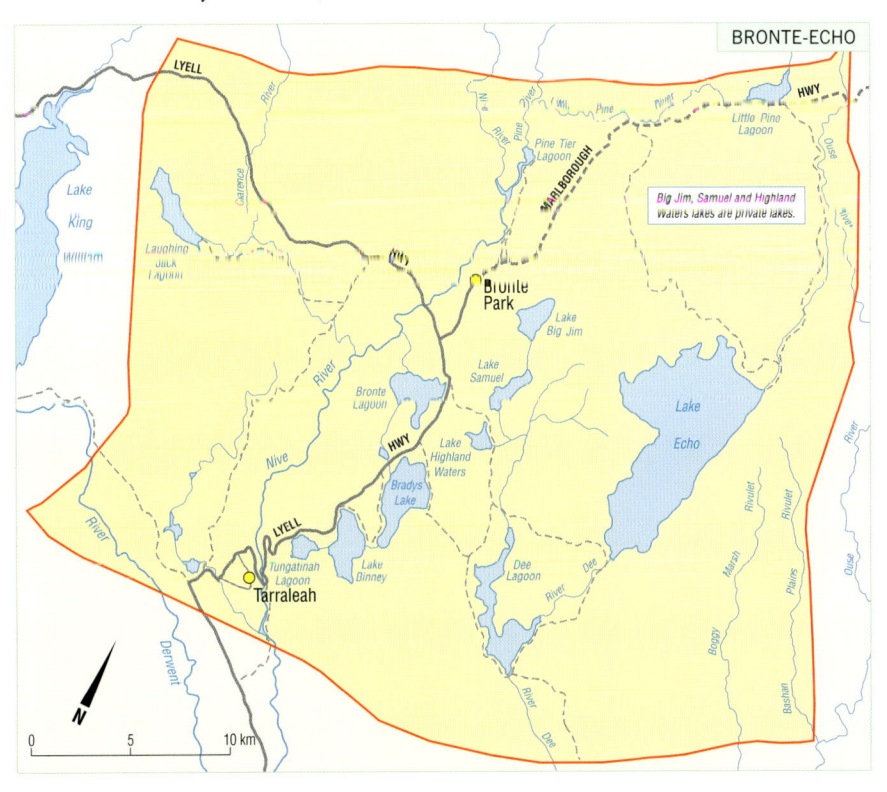

'Blue sky days' offer the promise of rising fish and polaroiding on lakes like Bronte Lagoon

INLAND FISHING CENTRAL HIGHLANDS REGION

Western Lakes

Type of fishing
lake, river

Target fish
brook trout, brown trout, rainbow trout

Perhaps Australia's greatest wilderness trout fishery exists in this area. Sometimes called 'Land of 3000 Lakes' or 'Central Plateau', it is a vast expanse of alpine country, mainly over 1000 m in elevation, dotted with countless lakes and tarns. Rainbow trout have not been terribly successful, but brown trout have colonised the great majority of waters: look for those lakes with limited spawning or stream access if you are prepared to work hard for a trophy or two, and apply the reverse for faster fishing for more modest trout.

The Western Lakes include many of Tasmania's most fragile trout waters. Regulations are being tailored to match the vagaries of individual lakes. Some waters are reserved for fly only while bait fishing is generally prohibited. Furthermore, many waters are now subject to more realistic catch limits; varying from five fish per angler per day to zero (catch-and-release).

As a general rule, lure casting is better suited to rough overcast conditions in this area, while fly fishing is the superior method under bright skies when polaroiding and casting to rising fish is practical. A fly fishing highlight is fishing to 'tailers'. 'Tailers' are fickle, but can be found in shallow, weedy lake margins during low light conditions.

The hilly western part of the Western Lakes is almost impossible to access except on foot. However, those prepared to devote time and careful planning to a trip will find numerous waters that contain good stocks of trout. The lakes and tarns that hold trout – even the best ones – are simply too numerous to name, while some others remain untitled. **Lakes Olive, Naomi, Fanny and Ball** are but a few that can produce excellent fishing.

As with this whole district, it is worth remembering that although phenomenal trouting occurs under perfect weather and water conditions, much more difficult circumstances are the norm. The fact that these lakes are lightly fished in no way guarantees easy fishing.

For the rainbow trout enthusiast, **Lake Meston** and **Junction Lake**, in the west, are rainbow-only waters accessible to fit bushwalkers, while **Clarence Lagoon**, a short walk from the end of a four-wheel drive track in the south, provides the only brook trout fishing on the plateau.

In the east, **Lake Augusta** and **Lake Ada** are the hub of a popular group of trout lakes casually referred to as the 'Nineteen Lagoons'. In the warmer months, it is usually possible to reach this area by car, though a short walk is often necessary to reach some lakes, or the best shore. The terrain is mostly flat with few trees and it is easy to become lost in bad weather.

As well as Augusta and Ada, **Double Lagoon, Lake Kay, Lake Botsford** and **Howes Lagoon Bay** are some favourites. These accessible waters average a 'catch per effort' that is comparable to that provided by more remote lakes on the plateau.

Lake Fergus is south of this cluster and requires a couple of hours walk to reach, but is highly regarded for its good population of medium-sized browns. As with the western part, large numbers of more remote lakes are good trout fisheries.

Pillans Lake and the **Julian Lakes**, to the north of this cluster, are also popular. Again, dozens of lakes and tarns are too abundant to name or identify, but most contain trout. **Lake Mackenzie**, on the northern edge of the plateau, is accessible by car to walkers heading into the Blue Peaks lakes area – a highly regarded system.

Stream fishing is possible in waters like the **Pine, Little and Nive rivers**, but is usually overshadowed by the lakes.

Stream fishing in the west is more promising than further east. The **Little Pine, James and upper Ouse rivers** can be well worth exploring.

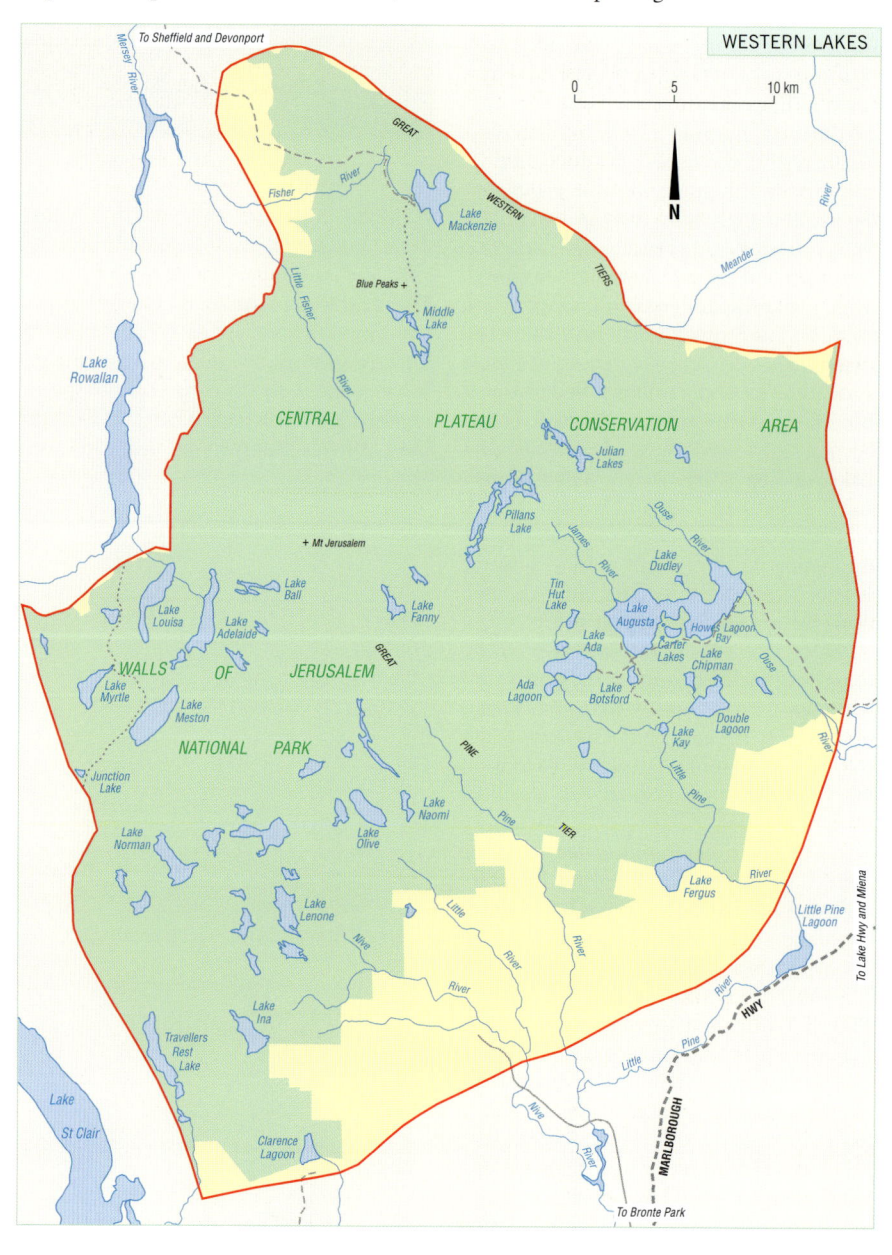

INLAND FISHING CENTRAL HIGHLANDS REGION

TASMANIA

Cradle Mountain– Lake St Clair

Type of fishing
lake, river
Target fish
brown trout, rainbow trout

The breathtaking mountain scenery of Cradle Mountain– Lake St Clair National Park provides a backdrop to some good trout fishing. Visitors should be prepared for an alpine climate, with plenty of rain and snow to be expected throughout the year. Only the north and south ends of the park are accessible by car, and strict regulations to protect the environment apply in this World Heritage area. No dogs or firearms are permitted, nor are wood fires, and bait fishing is prohibited within the national park. Check with rangers before setting out.

The most accessible water in the north of the park is **Lake Dove**. It provides some fishing for large numbers of relatively small trout.

The southern end of the park is dominated by **Lake St Clair**, Australia's deepest lake. The western and eastern shores are steep, inaccessible and offer minimal fishing opportunities in any case. Fortunately, the relatively flat southern shores are easily reached by car or a short walk, while the similar north shores can be accessed by the daily boat service. The typical 0.5 to 1.3 kg browns and rainbows are best fished for in the incredibly clear waters with fine fly gear, though spinning is worthwhile on rough or overcast days. **St Clair Lagoon** is a shallow, weedy backwater highly regarded by fly fishers. Several surrounding lakes like **Lake Petrarch**, **Shadow Lake** and **Forgotten Lake** offer fishing to keen walkers.

Just to the south of the park, the huge **Lake King William** is a hydro lake that features an ugly perimeter at low levels. Nevertheless, the crystal clear water holds a huge number of small trout, and the lake has one of the highest catch-per-effort rates in the state. The fishing is best when the lake is full, and at such times car access to the northern end is straightforward from tracks leading off the Lyell Highway.

A number of creeks and rivers throughout the area can provide fast stream fishing for small trout. The upper **River Derwent** is among the easiest to reach but it pays to get some local advice and to let someone know where you are going.

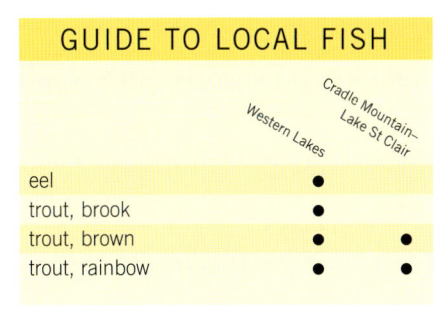

Lake Dove does not hold many big trout, but the scenery is superb

Black Spinner
The Black Spinner is an excellent dry fly in the Central Highlands on calm, mild days.

Red Tag
The Red Tag is a great all-purpose dry fly, and is particularly popular when sight fishing.

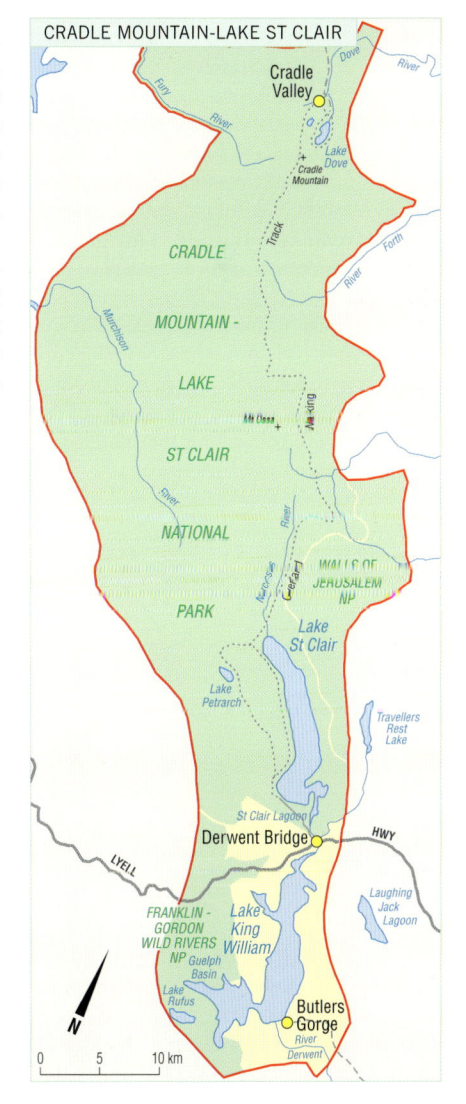

GUIDE TO LOCAL FISH

	Western Lakes	Cradle Mountain– Lake St Clair
eel	●	
trout, brook	●	
trout, brown	●	●
trout, rainbow	●	●

TASMANIA

INLAND FISHING NORTH-WEST AND WEST COAST REGION

North-west and West Coast Region

The west coast of Tasmania is mountainous, remote and subject to harsh weather throughout the year. Access is either difficult or virtually impossible away from the main highway networks, and generally the extensive effort required to reach inaccessible waters would not be worthwhile. Several good fisheries can be comfortably reached, however.

Access and services are very good along the north-west coastal fringe, but both gradually decline as one moves inland into the forested hill and mountain terrain. Numerous rivers and creeks flow through pasture and forest from the high rainfall 'back country', with hydro storages present in the east. Though not a first choice destination for interstate anglers, these waters are well patronised by locals.

The best stillwater is Lake Burbury near Queenstown, though lakes Pedder and Gordon are quite well respected. The lower reaches of the Henty, Pieman, Arthur and Gordon rivers are among the State's very best spring sea-trout fisheries.

The Franklin River headwaters typify the inhospitable wilderness of the west coast

WHERE TO FISH

North-west and West Coast Region

FRANKLIN–GORDON RIVERS ● 260
This area contains the famous Franklin and Gordon rivers – better known for their wild beauty than for their average-quality stream fishing. The lower reaches of the Gordon can produce excellent sea-run brown trout during spring for boat anglers. Very good fishing still exists today in Lake Pedder, although the boom years have passed. The weather-battered wilderness of the far south-west is totally without road access.

QUEENSTOWN–ARTHUR RIVER ● 261
Lake Burbury is the fishing mecca here, being easy to access in parts and producing huge numbers of medium-sized trout. Of the Pieman River storages, lakes Rosebery and Mackintosh provide reasonable trouting. The Pieman and Henty rivers are good spring sea-trout waters in their lower reaches, though access is limited for those without a four-wheel drive or boat. The large Arthur River system in the north offers limited stream fishing, with the Hellyer River perhaps the pick of rivers in this catchment.

DUCK–BLYTHE RIVERS ● 262
From Cape Grim through to the Blythe River, the fishing consists of numerous small to mid-sized streams flowing to the coast from partially cleared hill country. Most are fast, gravel-bottomed waters in their upper reaches, grading to slower and deeper pools toward the coast. Rivers like the Flowerdale, Inglis, Blythe and Cam all contain plenty of pan-sized trout, with some better sea-trout in the lowest reaches on occasions. The Duck River is a slower, richer river where larger fish around 1 kg are frequently caught.

LEVEN–MERSEY RIVERS ● 263
The rivers put on size in this district, and a couple of large lakes provide stillwater options. The River Leven offers many kilometres of quality trout water. The Mersey and the Forth have been extensively dammed, with resulting fluctuations in flow, but can still produce good trouting. Lakes Rowallan and Barrington offer consistent fishing, while the beautiful Lake Lea is a natural lake that can provide reasonable angling.

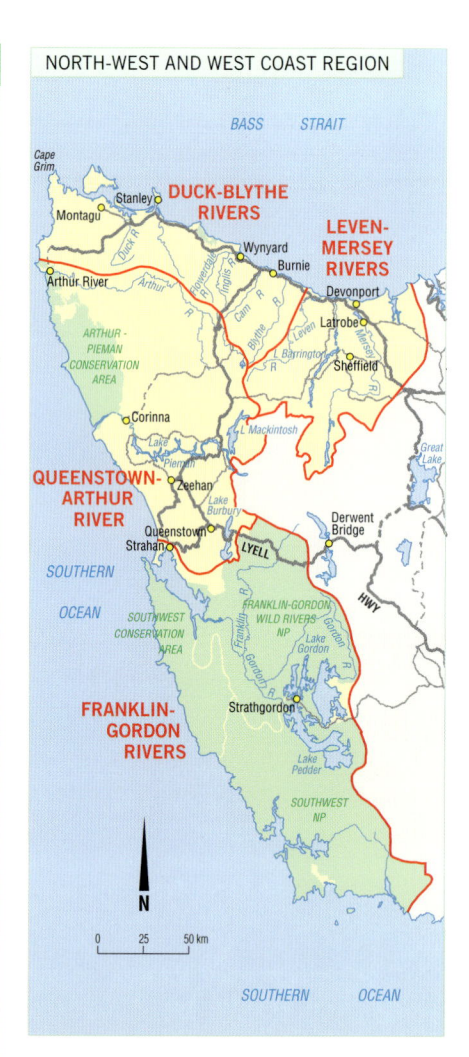

GUIDE TO LOCAL FISH

- blackfish, river
- eel, short-finned
- redfin
- trout, brook
- trout, brown
- trout, rainbow

FURTHER INFORMATION

Fishing and Boating The Inland Fisheries Service head office is at 6B Lampton Ave, Derwent Park, tel. (03) 6233 4140. For boating, contact the Port of Devonport Authority, tel. (03) 6424 0911.

Tourist centres Civic Centre Plaza, off Little Alexander St, Burnie, tel. (03) 6434 6111; 92 Formby Rd, Devonport, tel. (03) 6424 4466; 70 Gilbert St, Latrobe, tel. (03) 6426 2693; Pioneer Cres, Sheffield, tel. (03) 6491 1038; The Nut Chairlift, Browns Rd, Stanley, tel. (03) 6458 1286; The Esplanade, Strahan, tel. (03) 6471 7622; Cnr Hogg and Goldie sts, Wynyard, tel. (03) 6442 4143.

Great days on the Mersey

'In the still-early light it was possible to detect about twenty fish feeding at any one instant, hacking and slashing the surface of the glide to white water.'

The Mersey River, familiar to people arriving in Tasmania by ferry, has only a short tidal section, with Devonport at the seaward end and the smaller town of Latrobe at the upstream end of the broad mudflats cut by shallow channels. At Latrobe, the river's change is dramatic. Fresh oxygen-rich water from the mountains surges and ripples over rounded shingles between banks clothed in trees.

Just upstream of where this change takes place, I had an appointment to keep at first light of an October morning in 1970. As an expatriate Queenslander living in Devonport, my trout fishing forays till then had been rather pathetic affairs. With little knowledge, and no tuition, I would set forth into some incredibly rough and inaccessible spot with a spinning rod, and just very occasionally bring home an unlucky and immature river trout or two.

But this week an invitation had been issued by two experts. When we met, few words were said – it was, after all, my brief to watch. But a fly-rod equipped with reel, nylon filament line, and a very small hook, was thrust into my hand, and by torchlight we stumped down to the river.

The first stop was where a narrow backwater had formed beside the main stream. In the torchlight, we could see the large grey shadow of the school of minute whitebait resting in this haven after the labour of forcing their way up the rapid water from the estuary. With a small hand net we dipped out enough for our bait.

The two anglers took up position on opposite banks abreast of a strong downstream glide, whose broken surface was just becoming visible as dawn broke. I watched as Ned threaded a No. 10 hook through the back of a live bait, drew line from his reel and stood poised waiting for a fish to show within casting range. I saw no fish but the angler tensed, flicked the bait expertly some 5 m up into the stream, took up slack as the stiff current carried the struggling and injured whitebait downstream, then suddenly lifted the rod tip. *Then* I saw the fish.

Turmoil erupted as the 1-kg brown leapt and rolled and leapt again in the strong current, before diving deeper and trying for sanctuary upstream. But 9-lb nylon on a multiplying reel gives the angler more than an edge in such a battle, and that first fish was eventually landed.

It took perhaps 20 minutes for the first two fish to be caught, but quite suddenly the feeding activity of the trout, both residents and sea-running visitors, built to frenzied proportions. In the still-early light it was possible to detect about twenty fish feeding at any one instant, hacking and slashing the surface of the glide to white water. I tried desperately to put a bait in the right place. Totally inexperienced with a fly-rod, and never having cast nylon unless it had a healthy ball sinker on it, I seldom succeeded.

As daylight came, the catch-rate declined, the feeding ceased, and we took stock of our catch. My companions had twelve fish each; I miraculously had four!

Sadly the huge migrations of whitebait all but ceased in the 1970s, whether due to commercial over-fishing or to environmental factors, no one knows. A total ban was imposed on taking the tiny fish, and extravagant feeding frenzies such as these were no longer seen. But two years ago, the fragile recovery in whitebait numbers was sufficient to permit a very limited season.

One evening last spring I was visiting an old friend in Latrobe. Over a cup of coffee and a welcoming scotch he volunteered, 'You know, I saw something this morning I haven't see for twenty years. That ripple below the pump was alive with trout ripping into whitebait'. Great days!

– Neville Lester

TASMANIA

INLAND FISHING NORTH-WEST AND WEST COAST REGION

Franklin–Gordon Rivers

Type of fishing
lake, river
Target fish
brown trout

The far south-west is arguably the most inhospitable part of Tasmania. Sea-worthy boats can enter a few sheltered harbours on the wave-battered coast, but inland travel is limited to dedicated and well-equipped bushwalkers. The true fishing potential of some waters remains unknown, but it seems improbable that any trout fishing paradises lurk undiscovered. Those that are known seem mediocre at best.

Two major rivers, the **Gordon** and **Franklin**, drain the north of this wilderness. The Franklin and a major feeder, the **Collingwood**, can be accessed for short distances around the Lyell Highway, where they provide average stream fishing. The lower Gordon offers good sea-trout and some reasonable resident trout for those with boats. Elsewhere, the rivers can only be reached by raft, kayak or strenuous walking, and the fishing itself would not warrant the effort.

One of the few trout waters that can be comfortably reached by car is the massive **Lake Pedder**. The lake developed an international reputation for huge browns up to 10 kg or more during the first decade after its controversial flooding. However, this class of fish was dependent on the initial release of nutrients as inundated vegetation decomposed and the food chain boomed. Now stable, Pedder has reverted to less spectacular form, but it still produces plenty of trout in the 1 to 1.5 kg bracket, and remains quite popular despite frequent bad weather. The mid-summer mudeye migrations are a particular drawcard. Adjacent **Lake Gordon** is an ugly water that fluctuates dramatically, revealing dead trees and barren banks. It holds plenty of reasonable fish, but is not popular. Redfin and eels are also present in this lake.

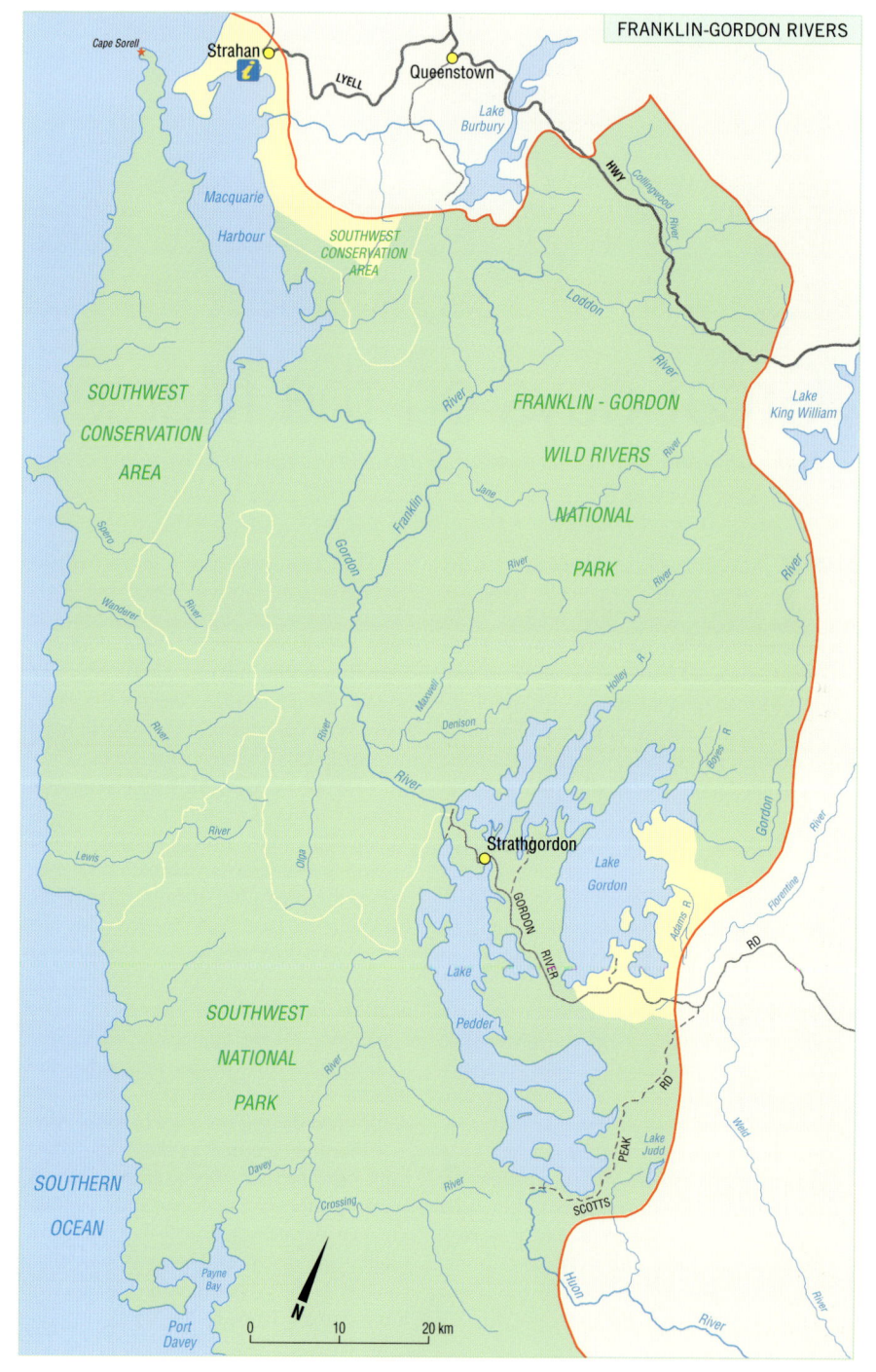

GUIDE TO LOCAL FISH

	Franklin-Gordon	Queenstown-Arthur River
blackfish, river		●
eel	●	●
redfin	●	
trout, brook		●
trout, brown	●	●
trout, rainbow	●	●

Pedder's heyday has passed, but the fishing is still very good

INLAND FISHING NORTH-WEST AND WEST COAST REGION

TASMANIA

Queenstown–Arthur River

Type of fishing
lake, river

Target fish
brook trout, brown trout, rainbow trout

Much of this area continues to be forested mountain wilderness, but some parts have been opened up by mining and hydro projects. The weather is unpredictable, and sustained cold and rainy conditions are common.

Lake Burbury near Queenstown is currently the most respected fishery. This enormous lake produces huge numbers of medium-sized browns and rainbows. Early hopes that this water would be 'another Pedder' have not been fulfilled, and most fish weight just 0.4 to 1.2 kg. However, during settled weather, reliable hatches of midges and mudeyes trigger phenomenal rises, which permit anglers to take good bags of fish. Good access in places, and proximity to Queenstown, mean it will probably remain popular. In the immediate vicinity of the town almost all waterways have been destroyed by mining. The **Queen and King rivers** have been turned into toxic drains below Queenstown.

The **Henty River** contains stream fish in its middle reaches, while the lower reaches are again well-regarded for spring sea-trout. A boat, four-wheel drive or walking is necessary to fish this section. **Lake Plimsoll** shows promise as a virtually unique brook trout fishery, as do some nearby lakes.

Two of the four hydro storages in the Pieman River Scheme, **Lake Rosebery** and **Lake Mackintosh**, are quite accessible, and have good reputations locally. The river itself is best fished in the reaches below the final storage dam, where sea-trout fishing is good, though a boat is necessary in most sections.

The large **Arthur River** and its tributaries in the north offer stream fishing, but access is often difficult. The trout are mostly small. The **Hellyer River** is perhaps the pick of rivers in this catchment. Blackfish are quite common in the Arthur system.

Elsewhere trout exist in numerous inaccessible streams and several small lakes, but for most anglers the quality of fishing seldom justifies the effort required to reach them.

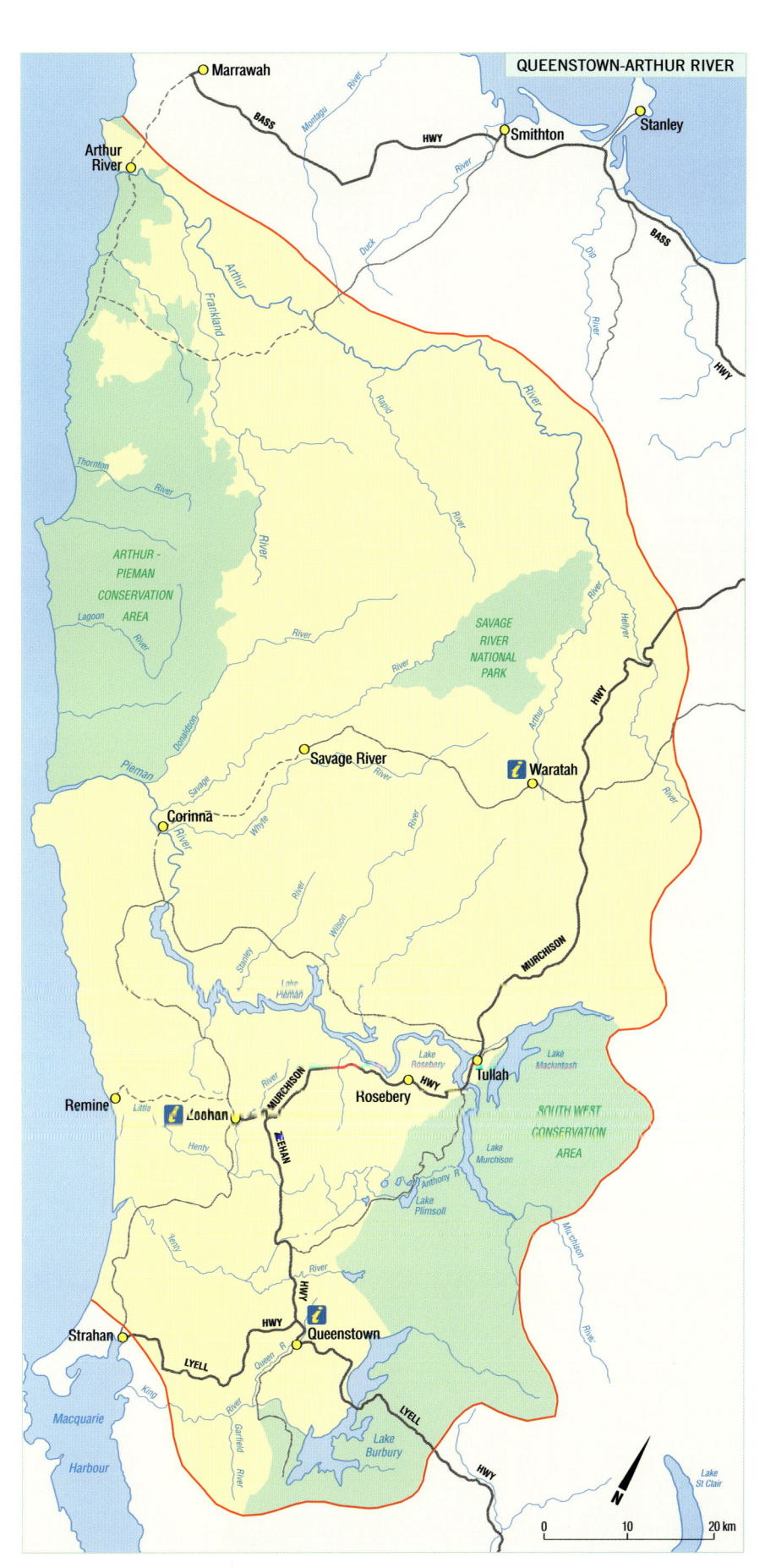

TASMANIA
INLAND FISHING NORTH-WEST AND WEST COAST REGION

Duck–Blythe Rivers

Type of fishing
river
Target fish
brown trout

This area attracts little attention from visiting trout anglers, yet there are plenty of stream fishing options, with typical river fish up to 0.5 kg quite abundant, and larger fish in places. Road access is good, with a mixture of private cleared country and state forest bordering most streams. The climate is generally not as inclement as in the centre and west.

The most westerly river of any consequence is the **Duck**, and it is also a good water for larger fish. Of slow to moderate flow, it is slightly cloudy and quite fertile. All fishing methods can produce results.

The **Flowerdale and Inglis rivers** are moderate-sized rivers of roughly similar characteristics. In the upper reaches, they are fast mountain streams bordered by forest and are quite comfortable to wade. Smallish stream fish are abundant. In the middle reaches, deep holes and overgrown steep banks prohibit easy fishing, but the size of the trout is more respectable. The lower reaches may produce some sea-trout fishing in spring.

The **Cam** and **Blythe** are smaller rivers consisting of quite overgrown pools and rapids for most of their length. The trout are seldom large, but quite plentiful. Sea-trout are a chance in their lowest reaches.

Numerous small creeks in the area also contain trout, though usually the size of the fish corresponds to the size of the creeks. Most streams in this area hold blackfish, and good populations exist where snaggy habitat is plentiful.

A few smaller lakes like the **Guide and Pet reservoirs** are of more interest to locals than visiting anglers.

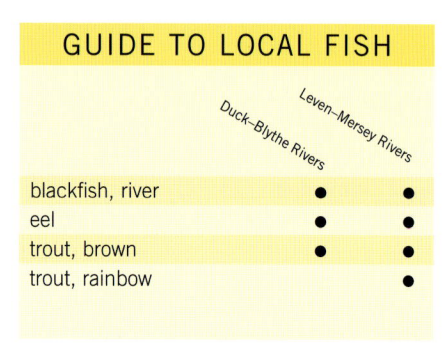

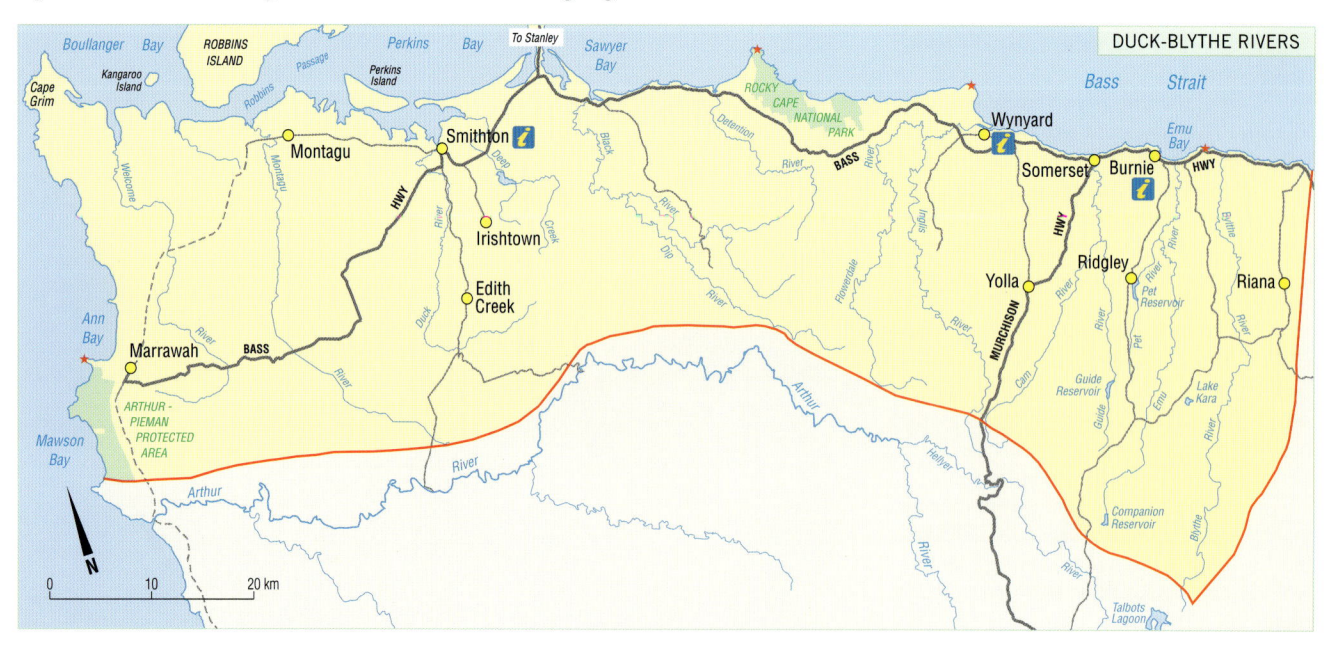

Good trout lurk among the willows of many streams on the north-west coast

GUIDE TO LOCAL FISH

	Duck-Blythe Rivers	Leven-Mersey Rivers
blackfish, river	●	●
eel	●	●
trout, brown	●	●
trout, rainbow		●

INLAND FISHING NORTH-WEST AND WEST COAST REGION

TASMANIA

Leven–Mersey Rivers

Type of fishing
lake, river

Target fish
brown trout, rainbow trout

Large catchments and high mountains in the headwaters have resulted in a number of substantial rivers. The **River Leven** is the most notable, being one of the few large Tasmanian rivers that has not been dammed. A very attractive stoney-bottomed fastwater, the Leven provides good trout fishing along most of its length. Only the massive Leven Canyon and the head-waters are inaccessible. Gunns Plains and Loongana Range are two areas that offer easy access and comfortable fishing. Leven trout are usually of modest size, though several exceptional specimens are taken each year. The lower reaches also produce reasonable sea-trout fishing.

Further east, the **Forth and Mersey rivers** have been extensively dammed by hydro schemes, with resulting fluctuations in flow. Both can still produce good fishing, however, and the lower reaches are noted sea-trout waters. The lower middle reaches of the Mersey are quite appealing and comfortable to fish despite reduced flows. **Lake Rowallan** and **Lake Barrington** are generally regarded as the best of several impoundments on these rivers. The fishing is seldom outstanding, but results are reasonably consistent. Barrington is particularly easy to reach.

The beautiful **Lake Lea**, in the west of this area, is a natural lake that returns modest bags of reasonable-sized trout, especially on lure and fly. Small streams like the **Don and Dasher rivers** can provide fast stream fishing for pan-sized trout and beetle patterns often work well for fly fishers. Blackfish can be found in some waters in this area.

Gum Beetle
Lake trout feed well on fallen gum beetles when they migrate through the forests on warm days.

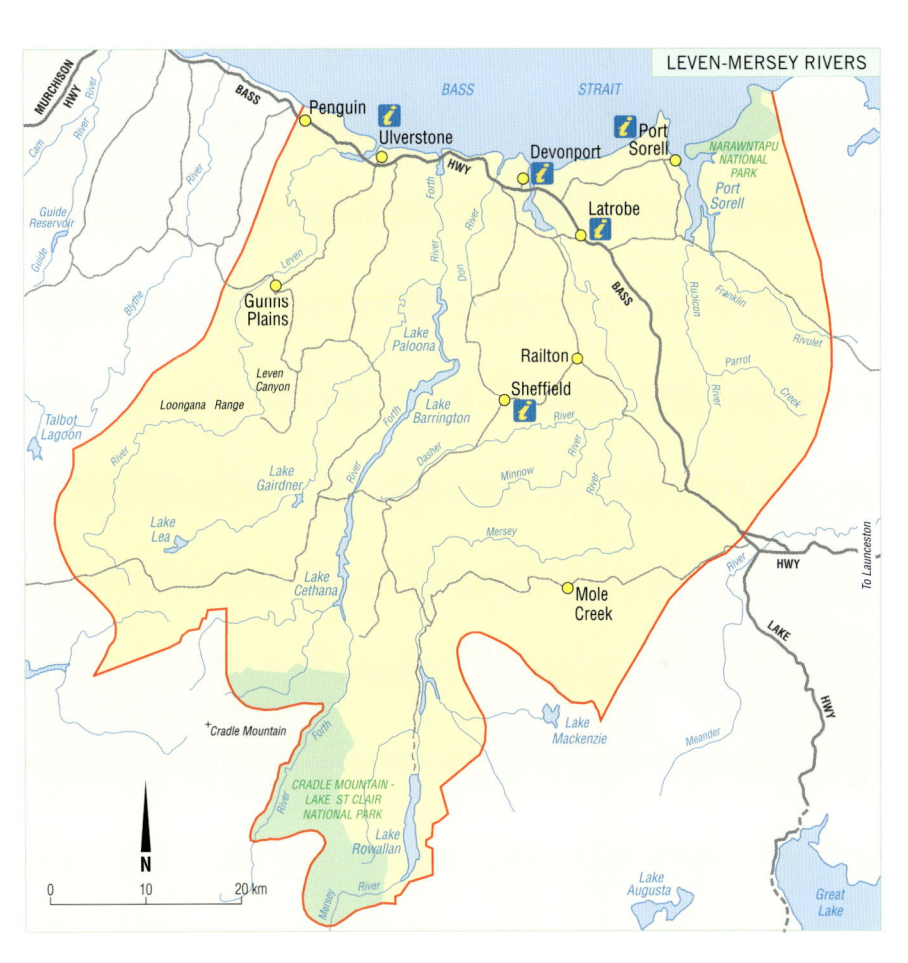

Abundant drowned timber is found in the fluctuating waters of Lake Rowallan. This impoundment is one of the better still waters in the Leven–Mersey area

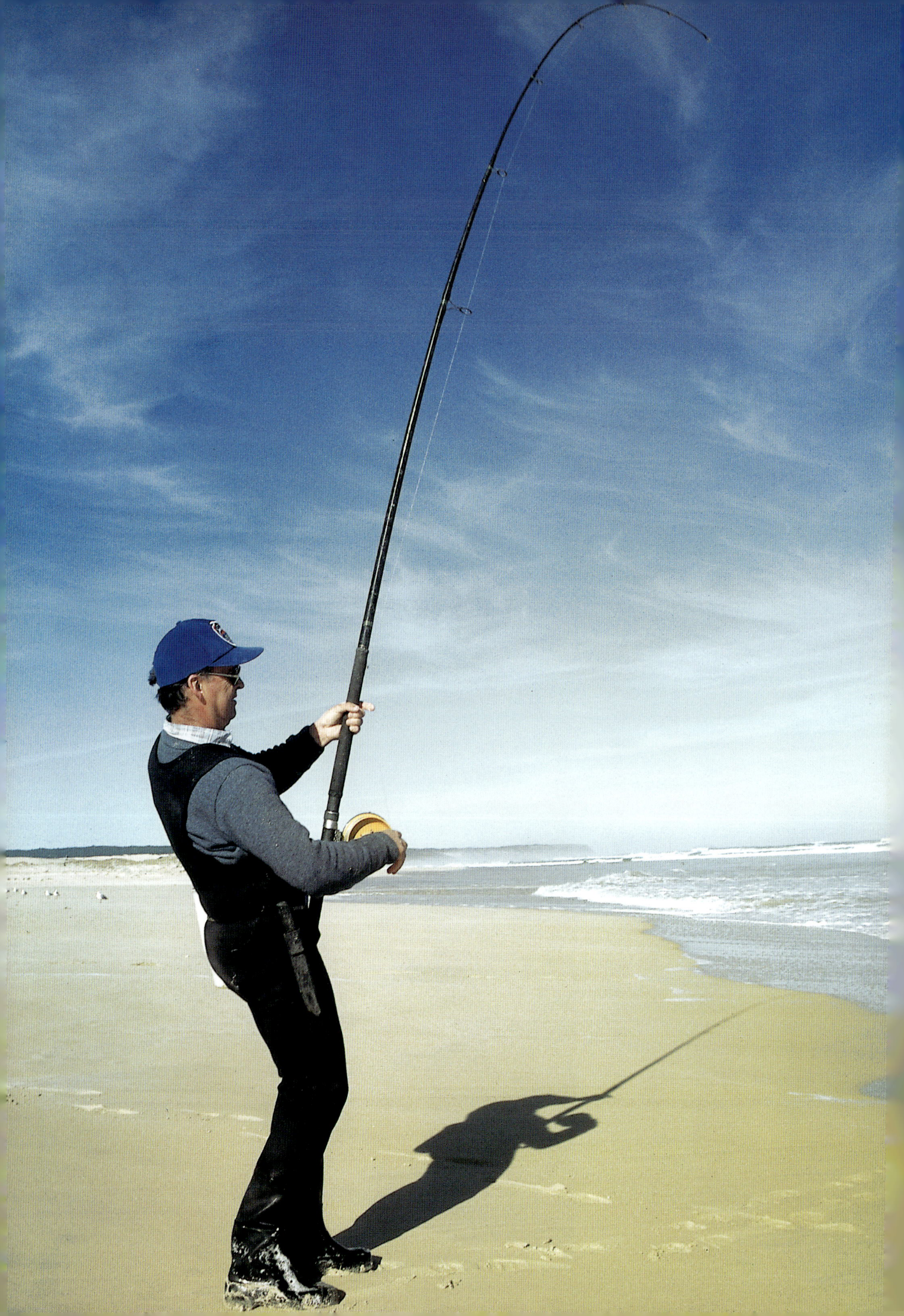

Contents

Coastal Fishing

Adelaide Region	268
South East Region	276
Port Lincoln Region	284

Inland Fishing

Murray River Region	293
Onkaparinga River Region	294
Broughton River Region	295

South Australia

Although South Australia has not been blessed with the inland fishing potential of most other States, its coastal areas offer some of the most productive angling in the country. The waters of both Spencer and St Vincent gulfs are a haven for small boat operators, while the many jetties and wharves enable anyone who owns a rod and reel to get among the action.

Fishing at Gunyah Beach near Port Lincoln

Estuary fishing in South Australia is somewhat limited, due to the paucity of true estuarine systems. Likely estuary species include bream, mullet, mulloway, salmon trout (juvenile Australian salmon) and sand whiting.

South Australia's gulfs, punctuated by shallow, clear-water bays, provide terrific fishing for a wide variety of inshore species. Some of the larger bays, and particularly those adjacent to population centres, are endowed with jetties maintained specifically for recreational angling.

Because most of the State's coastal waters front either Spencer or St Vincent gulfs, the rock fishing differs markedly from that of the eastern States. Instead of everything from luderick to tuna, South Australian rock hoppers make the most of species like snapper, salmon, sweep and silver trevally.

Outside of gulf waters, South Australia's beach fishing is superb. The west and far west coasts offer some of the best salmon and mulloway action in the country, while the Murray River mouth, south of Adelaide, is regarded as *the* place for mulloway on lures.

Although offshore anglers in South Australia will not find too many true game fish to tackle, they can locate giant snapper, huge King George whiting and a host of other great table fish. You don't need a big boat to fish offshore successfully in South Australia; just a bit of spare time and a modest rig will ensure a consistent supply of succulent fillets.

Freshwater fishing, though limited, still has surprises with small streams and rivers holding trout in excess of 4 kg. In addition to the main rivers, the River Torrens and many smaller streams are worth exploring.

SOUTH AUSTRALIA

Coastal Fishing

South Australia's coastal fishing varies markedly as you travel from the south-east to the far west. Those waters open to the Southern Ocean regularly yield fish of different variety to the Gulf coasts, providing a diversity of angling opportunities. While it is often an advantage to own a small boat, most anglers can find more than ample supplies of top-notch fish from land-based locations. For example, some of the biggest snapper in the country are taken regularly from the rocks at Whyalla, Wallaroo and even around Adelaide.

Anglers in South Australia are indeed a fortunate lot. They do not have to own a 6-m boat to catch their big snapper or King George whiting, nor do they have to own a mountain of expensive tackle. Their choices are varied, with many jetties along the Gulf shores, exciting surf fishing on both the south and west coasts and some first-rate reef fishing offshore from most coastal ports.

But the State's coastal fishing is not all snapper, whiting and other small varieties. If you enjoy a tussle with a decent shark, there are plenty of whalers and hammerheads within a short distance of a launching ramp, particularly in summer.

Adelaide anglers can take advantage of the Port Adelaide River system, which is virtually on their doorstep. Giant mulloway – some to more than 30 kg – are caught in the port each winter and the Outer Harbour shipping channel yields big snapper to a staggering 18 kg.

Despite fickle weather conditions, there is nearly always somewhere to go where a good catch of fish is virtually assured. The tackle shops are open from dawn to late evening, local baits are easy to obtain and South Australian anglers are a friendly lot, prepared to pass on local information to anyone, particularly visitors from interstate.

COASTAL FISHING

WHERE TO FISH
Along the coast

ADELAIDE REGION ● 268

In the Adelaide area, metropolitan jetties are popular venues with both young and casual anglers, while the Port Adelaide River and inshore waters yield quality table fish for either land-based or small boat anglers. Although a great base for offshore fishing, Yorke Peninsula also has a number of popular jetties for the land-based angler. Kangaroo Island has a broad range of options for the angler, from fishing the beaches and bays to game fishing.

SOUTH EAST REGION ● 276

This exposed and often windswept section of the South Australian coast provides a blend of angling opportunities. It is possible to tackle big mulloway in the surf, whiting from the inshore reefs or tuna and shark offshore. The potential of the South East is just waiting to be tapped.

PORT LINCOLN REGION ● 284

Port Lincoln Region shines above most others as an all-round angling centre. It does not matter what your angling preference is, you will find it in or around the town of Port Lincoln. Surf, rock, estuary, jetty – be prepared and take tackle to cover it all.

State regulations

Amateur fishing licences are not required for rod or handline fishing in South Australia. Fishing regulations, including minimum size limits and bag limits, are administered by the Department of Primary Industries (PIRSA) Fisheries, tel. (08) 8226 2311 or visit their web site www.pir.sa.gov.au

The department publishes the *Recreational Fishing Guide*, which is available from State Information, 77 Grenfell St, Adelaide or its office at 25 Grenfell St, marine and tackle outlets. The booklet identifies fishing regulations, minimum size limits, bag and boat limits as well as permitted devices. In addition there are totally protected species, closed seasons, aquatic and marine parks. Anglers should familiarise themselves with the regulations before fishing anywhere in the State.

COASTAL FISHING

SOUTH AUSTRALIA

Port Willunga beach: snapper and school mulloway are the main targets for surf anglers along this coast

Protected species

The following are totally protected in South Australia:

- all marine mammals
- leafy sea dragons
- blue crabs with eggs attached
- giant crabs with eggs attached
- rock lobsters with eggs attached

Boating regulations

Boating regulations are administered by the Department of Transport SA (Marine Group). The head office is at 64 Dale St, Port Adelaide, tel. (08) 8347 5001, or visit their web site www.marine.transport.sa.gov.au

Boating regulations are published in the *Recreational Boating Safety Handbook* available from Motor Registration offices and State Information at 77 Grenfell Street, Adelaide, tel. (08) 8204 1900.

All recreational boats fitted with an engine must be driven by a licenced operator. Boat operators licences and regulations governing minimum safety gear are strictly enforced.

All boat operators must familiarise themselves with current regulations before boating.

Transport South Australia Customer Service Centres in country areas can be accessed by phoning 13 1084.

Tide tables

Every angler should have a copy of tidal predictions for the area being fished as most fish behaviour is linked to tidal movement.

Ports Corp South Australia annually publish a booklet of tide tables for South Australian ports. The booklet also provides other general information that is useful to both anglers and boat operators. Included is a full listing of boat ramps giving ratings on road access, parking, ease of launch, shelter and additional comments. The booklet is available from Ports Corp, 296 St Vincent St, Port Adelaide; and State Information, 77 Grenfell St, tel. (08) 8204 1900; and boating and fishing tackle retail outlets.

FISHING TIP

Coastal and beach anglers can improve their catches by fishing the high tides that occur at dawn or dusk. This is when fish forage right along the waters edge in search of worms and small crustaceans that have died in the preceeding low tide. Under cover of diminished light, fish are not as timid as in full sunlight and bites can be hard and fast. Mullet in particular hug the shoreline in these conditions but large King George whiting, yellowfin whiting and garfish are frequently caught by the early angler at the edge. Even Adelaide's sheltered metropolitan beaches produce surprising dawn catches. Fresh baits of cockles and marine worms are the most effective with maggots the best for garfish.

GUIDE TO LOCAL FISH

BC	barracouta
B	bream, black
C	cod, rock
D	drummer, silver
F	flathead
FL	flounder
G	garfish
GR	groper, blue
KI	kingfish, yellowtail
LJ	leatherjacket
MA	mackerel
MO	morwong
M	mullet
MU	mulloway
NG	nannygai
SA	salmon, Australian
SH	shark, blue
SH	shark, bronze whaler
SH	shark, gummy
SH	shark, hammerhead
SH	shark, mako
SH	shark, school
S	snapper
SN	snook
SW	sweep
T	tailor
TF	tommy ruff
TR	trevally, silver
TU	tuna, southern bluefin
WA	warehou
W	whiting, King George
W	whiting, yellow-finned

Bag and size limits apply to most popular species. See the South Australian 'Recreational Fishing Guide' for details.

FURTHER INFORMATION

Fishing For full details on South Australia's fishing regulations, contact the Department of Primary Industries (PIRSA) Fisheries at 25 Grenfell St, Adelaide, tel. (08) 8226 2311, or one of its branch offices. The department publishes a regularly updated booklet, the 'Recreational Fishing Guide', which is available from any of its offices or on its web site www.pir.sa.gov.au

Boating The Department of Transport SA (Marine Group) head office is at 64 Dale St, Port Adelaide, tel. (08) 8347 5001; web site www.marine.transport.sa.gov.au The Department publishes the 'Recreational Boating Safety Handbook', which is available from its offices, from any Customer Service Centre throughout the State, or from its web site. The Bureau of Meteorology provides a recorded information service for current temperatures, forecasts and warnings. Call (08) 8366 2700 or visit its web site www.bom.gov.au/weather/sa

SOUTH AUSTRALIA

Adelaide Region

Although Adelaide boasts as many anglers per capita as any other city in Australia, the fishing here still has plenty to offer. The jetties along the metropolitan seaboard provide ample opportunities for shore-based fishers, while the protected waters of upper Gulf St Vincent are a haven for small boat operators.

Few, if any other, capital cities offer the shore-based angler such a diversity of options. In addition to the jetties along the metropolitan foreshore, there are many kilometres of wharves, breakwaters and beaches, most of which see thousands of young and enthusiastic anglers when the weather is suitable.

Excellent boat launching facilities are available both north and south of the city and there are several artificial reefs within easy boat reach. When the sea is too rough for outside fishing, the Port Adelaide River estuary provides a terrific small boat alternative, and the artificial West Lakes system is a bream fisher's paradise.

The waters of Gulf St Vincent are home to a variety of first-class table fish, the most significant of which are King George whiting, snapper, tommy ruff, mullet, bream, garfish and juvenile Australian salmon. Other great table fish which are caught around Adelaide are flathead, snook, leatherjacket, gummy shark and squid. Blue swimmer crabs are also abundant around weed beds and can be netted from boats or raked up in the shallows.

Weather

The prevailing winds in Adelaide are from the south-west. During the warmer months an

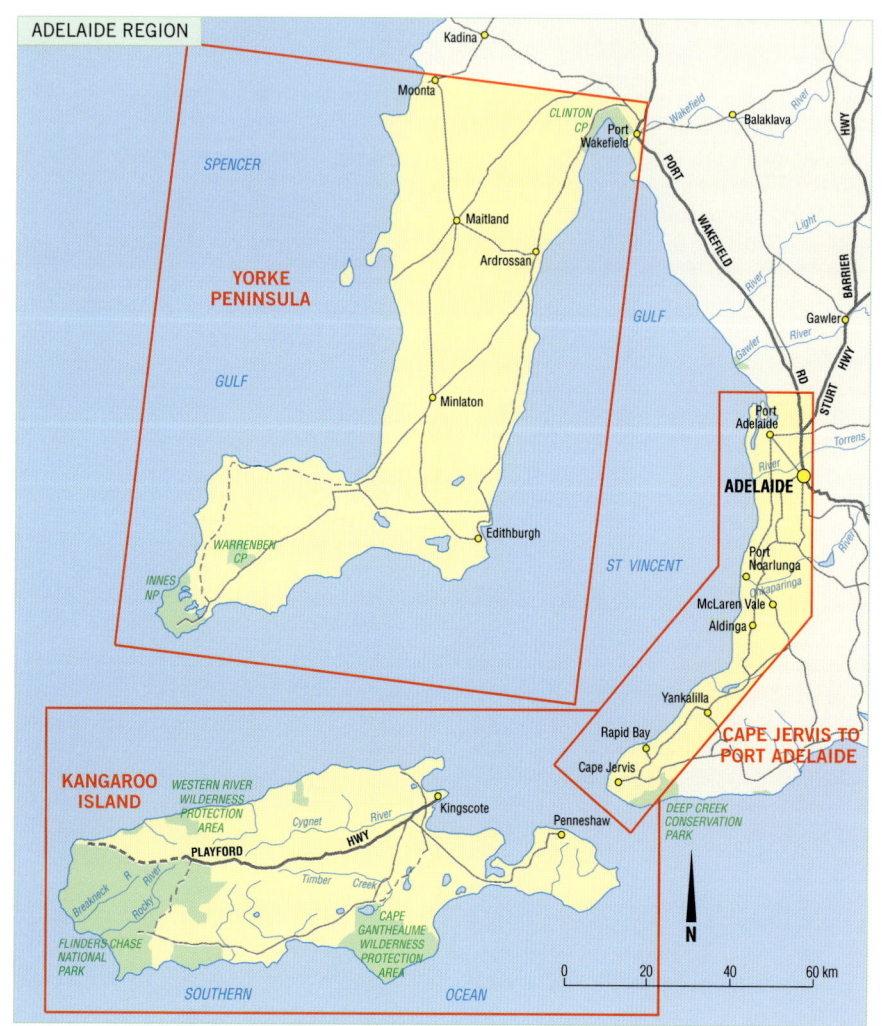

COASTAL FISHING ADELAIDE REGION

WHERE TO FISH

Adelaide Region

CAPE JERVIS TO PORT ADELAIDE ● 270
Also known as the Near South Coast, this region attracts thousands of anglers each year. Boat launching facilities are limited, but there is good rock and jetty fishing within easy access of the city. Rapid Bay Jetty, in particular, probably sees more anglers than any other pier in the State.

YORKE PENINSULA ● 272
This narrow strip of rural land essentially separates South Australia's two gulfs. Because of the peninsula's proximity to Adelaide, it draws thousands of anglers each month, many of whom have holiday houses dotted around its rocky shoreline. Once again, it is a jetty angler's paradise, as well as a great base for offshore fishing.

KANGAROO ISLAND ● 274
After Tasmania, Kangaroo Island is the second-largest island in Australia. It relies on agriculture for its major economic wellbeing, but in fishing terms it is considered the home of the King George whiting. There are some streams containing bream, mullet and salmon.

GUIDE TO LOCAL FISH

barracouta
bream
cod, rock
drummer, silver
flathead
flounder
garfish
groper
kingfish, yellowtail
leatherjacket
mackerel
mullet
mulloway
salmon, Australian
shark
snapper
snook
sweep
tailor
tommy ruff
trevally, silver
tuna, southern bluefin
whiting, King George
whiting, yellow-finned

COASTAL FISHING ADELAIDE REGION   SOUTH AUSTRALIA

Fishing for garfish from Port Noarlunga pier, which is a popular spot for local anglers

afternoon sea breeze, which can reach 20 to 25 knots, usually comes in about midday. Gulf St Vincent is relatively protected from the large ocean swells, but it does get a short chop, which can be uncomfortable for small boats. Always watch the west for signs of impending change in the weather, since changes can come in very quickly. Local radio stations broadcast regular updates. The Bureau of Meteorology has a recorded information service for forecasts and warnings on (08) 8366 2700 or visit its web site at www.bom.gov.au/weather/sa

Boating

The best boating facilities near Adelaide are about a half hour's drive out of the city, at North Haven, which offers a public boat ramp with floating pontoons and six ramps. It is protected by a breakwater and offers safe launching in all conditions. O'Sullivan Beach, about 45 minutes drive from the city, is the next best. Closest to the city is the West Beach boat ramp at Barcoo Rd. This multi-lane ramp offers all weather boat launch and retrieval and is an excellent land-based rock fishing platform.

FISHING TIP

If you find good fishing ground in a bay or estuary, it is a good idea to take note of where it is so you can return to the exact spot. The advent of technology with the Global Positioning System has helped anglers find favourite reefs and other fishing grounds with ease. For those without this technology, there is another method called triangulation, which uses landmarks to locate your desired area. By lining up three or four items on the land, be they a tree, a building, or something similar, you can easily return to the same position on another occasion. When you choose markers, go for big solid objects, such as buildings and trees, as these are easy to see and unlikely to change in a hurry. And remember to keep a note of the markers as a way of ensuring you are lining up the right objects each time.

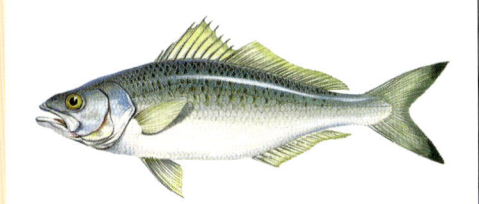

Tommy ruff

This fish is common in South Australian waters, inhabiting beaches, estuaries and the vicinity of rock walls. It gets its name from the rough feel of its scales.

FURTHER INFORMATION

Fishing and boating The Department of Primary Industries (PIRSA) Fisheries has offices at 25 Grentell St, Adelaide, tel. (08) 8226 2311. The Department of Transport SA (Marine Group) has offices at 64 Dale St, Port Adelaide, tel. (08) 8347 5001; Victor Harbor, tel. (08) 8553 2064; and Kingscote, tel. (08) 8553 2064.

Tourist centres South Australian Tourism Commission Travel Centre, 1 King William St, Adelaide, tel. (08) 8303 2033 or 1300 655 276; Aldinga Bay Holiday Village, The Esplanade, Aldinga Beach, tel. (08) 8556 5019; Ardrossan Bakery, 39 First St, Ardrossan, tel. (08) 8837 3015; Edithburgh Caravan Park, O'Halloran Pde, Edithburgh, tel. (08) 8852 6056; Kangaroo Island Visitor Information Centre, Howard Dve, Penneshaw, Kangaroo Island, tel. (08) 8553 1185; Main Rd, McLaren Vale, tel. (08) 8323 9944; Moonta Station Visitor Information Centre, Kadina St, Moonta, tel. (08) 8825 1891.

SOUTH AUSTRALIA

COASTAL FISHING ADELAIDE REGION

Cape Jervis to Port Adelaide

Type of fishing
beach, estuary, offshore, pier, reef, rock

Target fish
Australian salmon, garfish, mulloway, tommy ruff

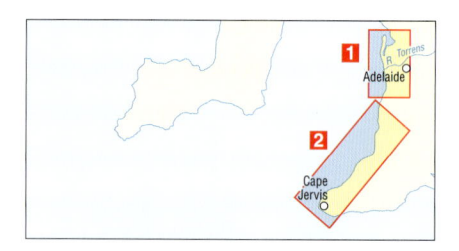

Gulf St Vincent is shallow and sandy, with the sea floor slowly shelving and only about 10 m of water under the boat in most fishing areas. Despite the protection of Kangaroo Island from ocean waves and swells, the bathtub effect of shallow water being disturbed by winds and storms means that the gulf can get rough at times, with choppy, bouncing waves. However, these waters, with their seagrass meadows, weed beds and shale areas, provide ideal breeding conditions for one of the most succulent fish in Australia, the King George whiting.

CAPE JERVIS TO PORT NOARLUNGA

The bulk of Kangaroo Island protects the west coast of the Fleurieu Peninsula and creates boating water unaffected by the Southern Ocean's swell. **Backstairs Passage**, between Cape Jervis and Kangaroo Island, can be turbulent, but is a great fishing area for snapper, Australian salmon and yellowtail kingfish. There is a boat ramp at **Cape Jervis** that can handle big boats at any stage of the tide. It is very busy between October and January when boat anglers head for the area of the snapper run, about 5 km out from the lighthouse.

Rapid Bay is very sheltered and its jetty is an outstanding venue, running out into deep water and providing wonderful fishing for flathead, Australian salmon and trevally. Tommy ruff and garfish often keep company in the winter, and squid specialists usually find a catch. Beach fishing here rewards with mulloway around the mouth of the creek, and Australian salmon, flathead and tommy ruff along the shore. **Wirrina Marina** offers an all weather boat ramp giving boat operators quick access to the waters around Second Valley and Rapid Bay as well as a land-based fishing option on the seaward side of the breakwaters. **Second Valley** jetty produces large catches of squid during the spawning run in September.

Normanville and **Carrickalinga** have jetty, beach and rock fishing, mainly for King George whiting, garfish and squid, with mulloway and snapper providing a change. Boats can be beach launched here in summer. There are bream around the entrances of the **Yankalilla and Bungala rivers**, and at the **Myponga River**. The Myponga Beach has fishing for flathead, mullet, mulloway, salmon and snapper, while the nearby rock ledges are very popular in summer with those after squid, tommy ruff and garfish. The towns of **Sellicks Beach**, **Aldinga Beach**, **Port Willunga** and **Maslin Beach** all have long, sandy stretches of beach, where small boats can be launched. Flathead, snapper and whiting are close inshore for boat anglers, with Australian salmon and school mulloway off the beaches. Fishing is not permitted in the Aldinga Reef Aquatic Reserve, a small area just south of Port Willunga, although anglers can launch from the beach and pass through to other areas.

The **Port Noarlunga Jetty** provides an unusual bonus for shore-based anglers as it runs right out to a reef. Although fishing is prohibited within 25 m of the reef, snapper, snook, sweep, flathead, tommy ruff, silver trevally, squid and garfish are all possibilities from the jetty. Big Australian salmon come in to the reef during winter, particularly during storms.

The entrance to the **Onkaparinga River** is just south of Port Noarlunga. Here there is brilliant bream fishing, particularly from late July to December, when the spawning run takes the fish around 10 km upriver. School mulloway, mullet and yellow-finned whiting are also in the lower reaches of the river.

ADELAIDE AND ENVIRONS

Artificial structures have transformed a good fishing area into a great one. The long piers have enabled fishing from the shore to be an excellent proposition. Two artificial reefs, off the beaches at Glenelg and Grange, have been built by the South Australian Department of Fisheries, leading to a concentration of fish into areas that can be easily accessed by boat. The reefs are brilliant whiting and snapper fisheries.

GUIDE TO LOCAL FISH

	Cape Jervis to Port Noarlunga	Adelaide and environs
(B) bream		●
(D) drummer		●
(F) flathead	●	●
(G) garfish	●	●
(KI) kingfish, yellowtail	●	●
(LJ) leatherjacket		●
(MA) mackerel	●	●
(M) mullet		●
(MU) mulloway	●	●
(SA) salmon, Australian	●	●
(SH) shark		●
(S) snapper	●	●
(SN) snook		●
(SW) sweep		●
(TF) tommy ruff	●	●
(TR) trevally	●	●
(W) whiting	●	●

COASTAL FISHING ADELAIDE REGION

SOUTH AUSTRALIA

There is plenty of room for anglers on the long piers, built to allow boats to tie up safely in any tide. The main piers thrusting into the gulf are at Brighton, Glenelg (in Holdfast Bay), Henley Beach, Grange, Semaphore and Largs Bay. The jetty at Port Stanvac is off limits to angling. The most likely catch is the tommy ruff, which schools in big numbers and can be caught right through the winter. Mullet also abound, along with garfish, snook and leatherjacket.

O'Sullivan Beach has an area protected by a breakwater where land-based anglers can get yellowtail kingfish, as well as snapper during winter storms and mulloway, bream, whiting, flathead and squid. There are mullet, flathead and tommy ruff along the beach.

There is deep water some 10 km off **Port Stanvac** where three barges were sunk in 1945. This unplanned artificial reef attracts snapper, trevally, flathead, mackerel and shark. **Marino Reef**, 2 km offshore from the Seacliff boat ramp, has whiting and leatherjacket. The Brighton Whiting Patch is off the **Brighton Jetty** and is very productive in winter.

Freds Ground (10 km out) and **Macs Ground** (6.5 km out) are offshore targets for Glenelg anglers seeking whiting and snapper over the reefs and rubble. **South Grange** is close inshore from the Grange Jetty, and **South Middle** is out from Tennyson.

There are good shore-based fishing spots along the coast, all with their own attractions: south of the pier at **Glenelg**; the **Patawalonga Entrance Groyne**; **West Beach**; the **Torrens outlet**; and **Tennyson**.

Port Adelaide encompasses the only big estuary in the area, that of the Port Adelaide River. Despite the industry and shipping, the estuary still provides good land-based and boat fishing. The shore-based anglers seem to have the best of it at times, with various wharves yielding abundant numbers of fish.

Squid are taken here, as well as mulloway and garfish. There are plenty of bream in the Para River system and in the **West Lakes** area. The Outer Harbor Wharves, near the entrance to the estuary, are off limits to fishing and Osborne Wharves (in front of the power station), once a popular spot, have been closed. Public access is denied to working wharves and these are fenced off.

The breakwater at Outer Harbor is appreciated by the rock anglers who converge there and fish into the night for snapper, mulloway and Australian salmon, with the occasional silver drummer showing up. The Black Pole area north of Outer Harbour is situated amongst numerous whiting patches. Tommy ruff, garfish, squid and crabs can also be caught here.

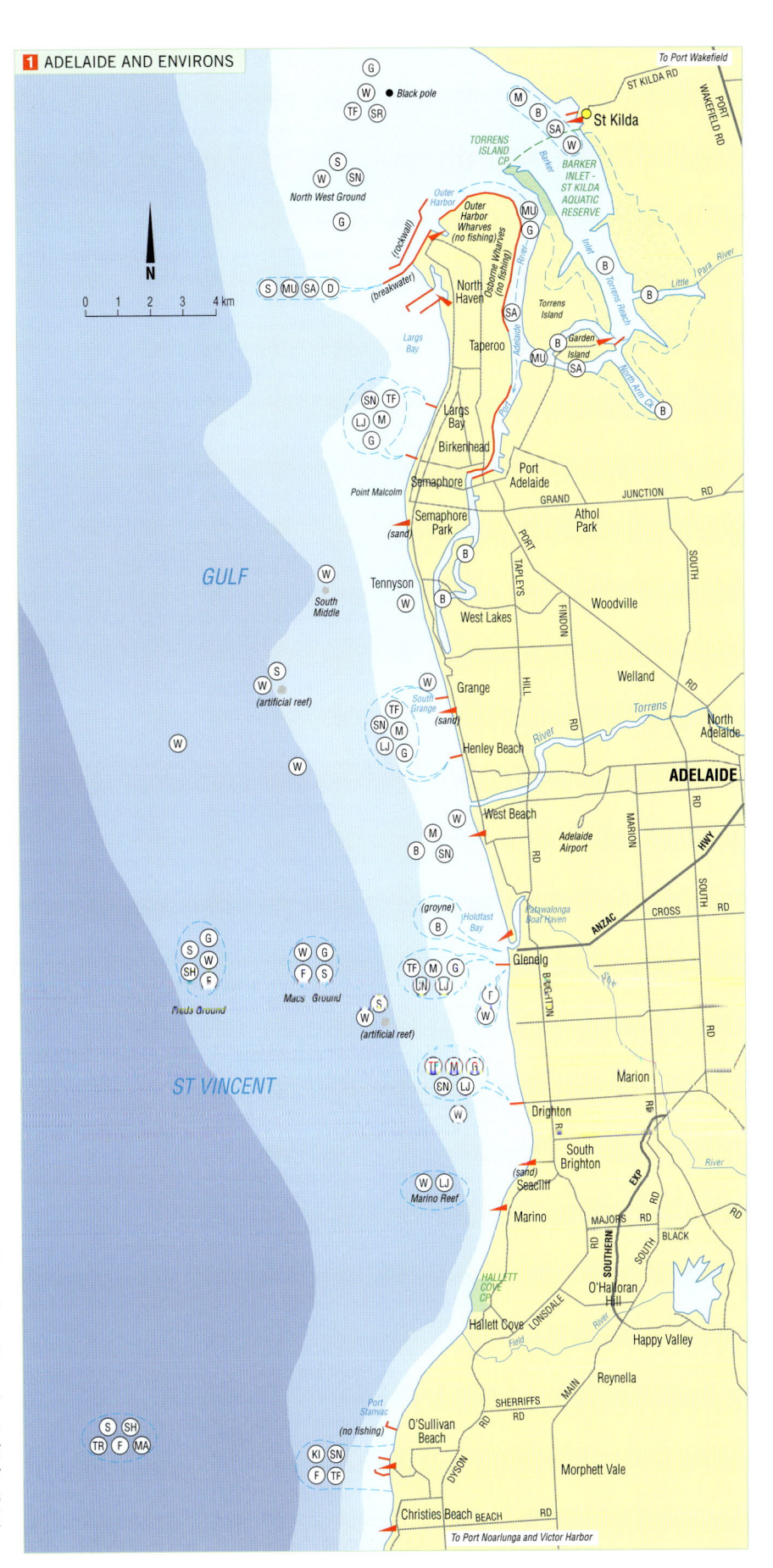

1 ADELAIDE AND ENVIRONS

SOUTH AUSTRALIA COASTAL FISHING ADELAIDE REGION

Yorke Peninsula

Type of fishing
bay, beach, jetty, offshore, rock
Target fish
Australian salmon, flathead, snapper, whiting

The shallow, clear waters on the north-western side of Gulf St Vincent are perfect for inshore boat fishing, and the boat ramp facilities extend down the coast. The main catches are snapper, whiting, flathead and Australian salmon. Tommy ruff and garfish are everywhere.

Around the north end of the gulf and the towns of **Port Wakefield**, **Port Clinton** and **Price**, the shallows and mangrove flats prohibit shore-based fishing and close-in boating, but boats can be taken to the offshore waters for whiting, snapper, mullet and Australian salmon. Hordes of blue swimmer crabs inhabit the flats during summer.

Ardrossan has one of the best all-tide boat ramps in this area, and good fishing inshore and from the jetty. Boat anglers will be trying for snapper, whiting, salmon, snook, mulloway and garfish. School mulloway are around the jetty in summer, with garfish and tommy ruff plentiful. Winter is the time for big tommy ruff and they are best fished at night. From **Rogues Point** to **Port Vincent** King George whiting is the target fish with snook, squid, blue swimmer crabs and tommy ruff in big numbers. Port Vincent has a wharf where bream and school mulloway can also be caught.

Stansbury has an all-weather, all-tide ramp and a long jetty. Huge amounts of squid are caught here, as well as from boats in the calm waters of **Oyster Bay**. Once again, flathead, tommy ruff, garfish and mullet can be caught from either jetty or beach.

Edithburgh has possibly the best jetty fishing in the area, with plenty of King George whiting, and snapper a strong possibility in the early morning and at dusk. Garfish, snook, squid and trevally are all around here.

Camping permit holders will be able to fish the bay at **Troubridge Point**, where tommy ruff, snapper, sweep, snook, flathead and mullet are close to shore and around the inshore rocks. Further west, towards Marion Bay, **Butlers Beach** is also a great rock and beach area, with mulloway off the beach.

Marion Bay offers access to deep water and reefs for species including big whiting to 1 kg, snapper, nannygai, kingfish and groper. The southern shoreline of the peninsula embraces Innes National Park, and is best fished when the winds are from the north. Tommy ruff, garfish, mullet, King George whiting and flathead are the targets at **Jollys Beach**, **Stenhouse Bay**, **Chinamans Hat Island** and **Cable Bay**.

The big, stumpy toe of the boot of Yorke Peninsula has the reputation of containing the best fishing water in Spencer Gulf. From **West Cape** to **Corny Point** the coastline is a running series of rock and beach locations, with some lovely sheltered bays for small craft fishing.

Pondalowie Bay is protected by its headland and **South Island** offshore. The long beach is at its best for fishing in the north, where the waves get through, but there are flounder, flathead, whiting, salmon and other species all along the beach. The island can be reached through shallow water at low tide, and fished, mostly on its southern side, for snapper, sweep and leatherjacket. The crossing should only be attempted in calm weather. Pondalowie Bay itself is also popular with boat anglers, who can fish its calm waters or near the rocks of South Island and **Middle Island** to the north.

Browns Beach has a reef along its entire length, renowned for salmon in winter and trevally in summer, but is also good for snapper, mullet, sweep and flathead. The beach to the south, reached by track from Browns Beach, has mulloway, salmon and shark. Submerged rocks at either end are good for snapper and sweep.

Little Beach and **High Cliff** can be reached by a turn-off from Marion Bay Road. Little Beach has submerged rocks offshore, which attract shark, salmon, snapper, sweep, whiting, flathead and sometimes schools of tailor. Snapper and trevally are the main catches from High Cliff.

Dust Hole beach is the exposed 8-km stretch of beach between High Cliff and Daly Head can be fished for salmon, shark, mulloway and flathead. The southern end, near High Cliff, has mullet in addition to these fish and whiting from the beach. The best fishing is in the middle of the beach, which can only be reached by foot. The rocks around **Daly Head** are good for salmon, sweep, snapper, flathead and mullet, while to the north, **Horseshoe Bay** can be fished for salmon, shark, flathead and snapper.

All these beaches can be subjected to strong swells when the wind is from the south, and care should be taken on rocks in these conditions.

Hardwicke Bay is a fine whiting area. There are little fishing shacks along the bay, with boats out in front that can be beach launched in a minute. There is a ramp at **Point Turton**, and a jetty where tommy ruff, garfish and squid, and the odd whiting, congregate. West of Point Turton, close inshore, are the best whiting patches in the bay.

Wardang Island, a 20-minute run from Port Victoria, has a lot of possibilities, although you will need a permit to land. Trolling for snook around the south of the island can lead also to picking up some snapper. Snook can be trolled from near the end of the jetty on the north-east side of the island, and there are big whiting in these waters as well. North of the island, out past the **Goose Islands**, are two reefs, which yield some of the best boat fishing in the gulf. The waters here are dangerous in westerly or southerly winds, but in good conditions whiting, trevally, sweep and snapper are abundant, along with shark. Fishing is prohibited in the Goose Islands Conservation Park and Aquatic Reserve within 100 m of the islands.

Port Hughes is a tiny town, with an excellent harbour, boat ramp and jetty. The hot spots here are some 6 km south-west at the submerged spit at Cape Elizabeth and about 15 km out near the Tiparra Reef Lighthouse. At **Cape Elizabeth** boat anglers can bottom fish for snapper, drift for whiting or flathead or berley up squid, tommy ruff and trevally. The **Tiparra Reef Lighthouse** (boats should only go in good weather) attracts whiting, snapper and garfish. Some 30 km out is the shipping channel, which runs to Whyalla and Port Pirie. There are big snapper here.

GUIDE TO LOCAL FISH

F	flathead
FL	flounder
G	garfish
LJ	leatherjacket
M	mullet
MU	mulloway
NG	nannygai
SA	salmon, Australian
SH	shark
S	snapper
SN	snook
SQ	squid
SW	sweep
T	tailor
TF	tommy ruff
TR	trevally
W	whiting

COASTAL FISHING ADELAIDE REGION

SOUTH AUSTRALIA

YORKE PENINSULA

0 5 10 15 km

There is no fishing within 100 m of the Goose Islands Conservation Park and Aquatic Reserve.

Waters: SPENCER GULF, GULF ST VINCENT, INVESTIGATOR STRAIT

Locations (north to south, west coast): Bird Islands, Walrus Rock, Warburton Point, Moonta Bay, Moonta, Port Hughes, Tiparra Reef Lighthouse, Tiparra Bay, Cape Elizabeth, The Gap, Point Warrene, Balgowan, Goose Islands Conservation Park and Aquatic Reserve, Red Cliffs, Snapper Point, Wardang Island, Bird Point, Point Gawler, Point Pearce, Port Victoria, Renowdens Rocks, Wauraltee Beach, Kemps Beach, The Bamboos, The Bushes, Port Rickaby, Barkers Rocks, Brown Point, Bluff Beach, Watsons Beach, Cockle Beach, Port Minlacowie, Sherrins Beach, Burners Beach, Levens Beach, Souttar Point, Hardwicke Bay, Daisy Beach, Dunn Point, Corny Point, Collins Beach, The Pines, Point Turton, Berry Bay, Point Deberg, Point Annie, Swincers Rocks, Horseshoe Bay, Daly Head, High Cliff, Little Beach, Browns Beach, Middle Island, South Island, West Cape, Pondalowie Bay, Reef Head, Emmes Reef, Jollys Beach, Stenhouse Bay, Chinamans Hat Island, Cable Bay, Marion Bay, Bullers Beach, Point Yorke, Treasure Cove, Point Davenport, Foul Bay, Point Gilbert, Waterloo Bay, Kemp Bay, Sturt Bay, Troubridge Hill, Troubridge Point, Troubridge Island, Troubridge Hill Aquatic Reserve (rod/handline fishing only)

Locations (east coast): Kulpara, Paskeville, Kainton, Port Arthur, Port Wakefield, Clinton CP, Port Clinton, Mangrove Point, Price, Arthurton, Maitland, Tiddy Widdy Beach, Ardrossan, Point Pearce Aboriginal Land, Urania, Rogues Point (sand), Pine Point (sand), Port Alfred, Black Point, Port Julia, Currumulka, Sheoak Flat Beach, Port Vincent, Minlaton, Beach Point, Oyster Bay, Stansbury, Oyster Point, Wool Bay, Yorketown, Port Giles, Giles Point, Salt Creek Bay, Edithburgh, Moorowie

Roads: PORT VICTORIA RD, MAITLAND RD, ARDROSSAN RD, STANSBURY RD, PORT RICKABY RD, BLUFF RD, CORNY POINT RD, WHITE HUT RD, GLEESONS RD, HUNDRED LINE RD, STENHOUSE BAY RD, MARION BAY RD, STURT BAY RD, SOUTH COAST RD, MOOROWIE RD

273

SOUTH AUSTRALIA | COASTAL FISHING ADELAIDE REGION

Kangaroo Island

Type of fishing
bay, beach, jetty, offshore, river, rock

Target fish
bream, garfish, mullet, Australian salmon, snapper, snook, tommy ruff

Kangaroo Island is just a few hours' drive and a ferry ride from Adelaide, but it is a wonderfully peaceful place given over to tourism, farming and fishing. There are many great fishing locations around the island and the anglers' choices range from peaceful river waters, rocks, beaches, jetties and bays, through to the game fishing Southern Ocean.

Kingscote has one of the most productive jetties in South Australia. It is one of the few jetties that yields King George whiting in consistent numbers, with the best results coming after dark. Tommy ruff, garfish, big snook, trevally, and squid are also taken at Kingscote and, if you are armed with the appropriate tackle, there are large whaler shark from the jetty as well. Kingscote provides convenient access to the Bay of Shoals, a shallow, protected inlet that abounds with whiting, Australian salmon, garfish, snook, squid and flathead. This is the ideal location for small boat operators, as it is sheltered in all but the worst weather.

Kingscote and the other major town, Penneshaw, face **Backstairs Passage**, and jetty anglers there have a chance at tommy ruff, garfish, snook and King George whiting. **Nepean Bay**, between the two towns, is good whiting ground and is sheltered from anything but a northerly. Snapper also stray in here from Backstairs Passage.

The bream are best fished when the rivers are landlocked, and among the many locations is the **Cygnet River**, south of Kingscote. **Emu Bay** close to Kingscote has a jetty and boat ramp. It produces similar species to Kingscote with the benefit of being sheltered when winds make Kingscote's Bay of Shoals uncomfortable and vice versa. From Emu Bay boaters can explore towards Stokes Bay for snapper, rock lobster and big whiting.

Small boat anglers enjoy the sheltered waters of the **American River** estuary, where the whiting is reliable. This area and **Kingscote** are bases for charter boat operators, who take anglers out among the sharks, southern bluefin tuna, and yellowtail kingfish.

Big King George whiting are around **Antechamber Bay**, which is good for bottom fishing. The **Chapman River**, which flows into the bay, has bream. Around on the south coast, **Mouth Flat Beach** and the beach at **Pennington Bay** have sweep, salmon and flathead as the main catches.

A jetty at **Vivonne Bay**, west of Cape Gantheaume, is not always sheltered, but good for tommy ruff, trevally, mackerel and snook. The beach at Vivonne Bay has reefs just offshore, submerged at high tide. Access to the beach is easy, and the gutters between the rocks can yield salmon and flathead. Mulloway and tailor are very rare. Bream can be sought in the creek behind the sandbar.

At **Cape Du Couedic**, on the southwest tip of the island, there is fishing from rocks, beach or the lighthouse jetty. The beach has mainly Australian salmon, the rocks have snapper, rock cod, sweep and groper, and the jetty has snook, Australian salmon, rock cod and barracouta.

There are some excellent land-based spots outside the main centres. **West Bay**, the westernmost point of the island, is a great rock fishing place, and heavy lines and gear are needed to deal with the potential of huge groper and big snapper. Sweep, rock cod, drummer and whiting are also around.

Just off the highway, on the northwestern shore, is **Harveys Return**. There are sweep and snapper from the rocks, and salmon, flathead and whiting from the beach. **Snug Cove**, to the east, requires a walk in of some 2 km, and access to the area is restricted, but there are very big whiting and drummer, along with an abundance of sweep, snook, snapper and trevally. On the northern coast, the **Middle River** and Western River hold bream.

A game boat anchored in idyllic surroundings in Snug Cove, Kangaroo Island

GUIDE TO LOCAL FISH

BC	barracouta
B	bream
C	cod, rock
D	drummer
F	flathead
G	garfish
GR	groper
KI	kingfish, yellowtail
MA	mackerel
M	mullet
MU	mulloway
SA	salmon, Australian
SH	shark
S	snapper
SN	snook
SQ	squid
SW	sweep
T	tailor
TF	tommy ruff
TR	trevally
TU	tuna
W	whiting

COASTAL FISHING ADELAIDE REGION

SOUTH AUSTRALIA

Fishing the beach at Western River Cove, on the north-western shore of Kangaroo Island

SOUTH AUSTRALIA

COASTAL FISHING SOUTH EAST REGION

South East Region

The section of coastline between Port MacDonnell and Victor Harbor is comprised mainly of dunes and flat surf beach, punctuated by the mouth of the Murray River near Goolwa. This is mulloway country for the surf specialist, but there is also first-rate offshore fishing when the southern bluefin tuna arrive in May and June.

The Coorong, nestled immediately behind the dunes of the surf beach and stretching for about 145 km along the State's south-east coast, is one of Australia's most beautiful and productive estuary systems. The inner Coorong is navigable by boat for over 60 km and the beach can be accessed by four-wheel drive.

Despite the fact that South Australian waters are not generously endowed with game fish, the south-eastern coast has some excellent offshore fishing, with southern bluefin tuna prevalent in the winter. This is also good shark fishing water.

One drawback is the weather, as the coast is pounded fairly incessantly with winds from the Southern Ocean. Anglers

The jetty at Beachport is a popular spot for local anglers, who fish here for mullet, tommy ruff, trevally, whiting, flathead, garfish and mulloway

COASTAL FISHING SOUTH EAST REGION   SOUTH AUSTRALIA

WHERE TO FISH

South East Region

PORT MACDONNELL TO KINGSTON S.E. ● 278

As well as being the State's premier lobster fishing area, the south-east coast boasts some terrific land-based and offshore angling. Mulloway and salmon can be caught from the beaches, while shark and bluefin tuna abound in the waters of the Southern Ocean. The southern ports and bays are not as protected as the gulf waters. Boat operators need to pay careful attention to weather reports.

THE COORONG ● 280

Recognised as one of the country's truly unique wildlife areas, the Coorong also yields top quality fishing for much of the year. The Tauwitchere and Mundoo channels are consistent producers of bream and school mulloway, while the Murray mouth itself is legendary among those who specialise in catching monster mulloway. The surf beach at Goolwa produces mullet, school mulloway and, of course, the much-loved Goolwa cockle. The surf beaches either side of the Murray mouth are accessed from Goolwa or from the crossings past Salt Creek via Meningie.

VICTOR HARBOR ● 282

Victor Harbor is South Australia's most popular tourist fishing destination. The jetty on Granite Island is a first-class venue, as is the small wharf at The Bluff. But it is Victor Harbor's offshore fishing that really attracts recreational anglers. Waitpinga and Parsons beaches, just a short drive away, offer superb surf fishing for salmon, mulloway and the occasional tailor.

Robe boat harbour is home to a large fishing industry: crayfish and shark are the main staples

reports before going out and stay ashore if warnings are current. It is also advisable to stay informed of any changes while on the water. Regular boating forecasts are broadcast by metropolitan and regional radio stations. The Bureau of Meteorology provides a recorded information service for current forecasts and warnings on (08) 8366 2700 or visit its web site at www.bom.gov.au/weather/sa

GUIDE TO LOCAL FISH

barracouta
bream
flathead
flounder
garfish
mackerel
morwong
mullet
mulloway
salmon, Australian
shark, blue
shark, hammerhead
shark, mako
snapper
snook
sweep
tailor
tommy ruff
trevally, silver
tuna, southern bluefin
warehou
whiting, King George

going out into these waters need a big seaworthy boat to cope with the winds and the ocean swell. The jetty and shore fishing opportunities along this coast make up for any lost boating time due to rough weather.

Weather

The south-east coast is exposed to fairly incessant winds off the Southern Ocean. Strong to gale force winds from the south are not uncommon and this can make for very rough seas. Always check weather

Boating

Ramps for small to medium boats can be found at Meningie, Beachport, Kingston S.E. and Robe. Ramps for boats of any size are at Goolwa, Blackfellows Caves and Port MacDonnell. Navigation around the Murray mouth at Goolwa can be hazardous due to sandbars, shifting sands and strong currents, and is not recommended without good local knowledge. Caution must also be exercised at the Port MacDonnell entrance due to an exposed reef and shallow water at low tide.

FURTHER INFORMATION

Fishing and boating The Department of Primary Industries (PIRSA) Fisheries has offices at 17 James Pl, Kingston S.E., tel. (08) 8767 2358 and at PIRSA, Jubilee Hwy East, Mount Gambier, tel. (08) 8724 2941. The Department of Transport SA (Marine Group) has offices at 64 Dale St, Port Adelaide, tel. (08) 8347 5001; and Victor Harbor, tel. (08) 8553 2064. There is a Marine Safety Officer stationed at 20 Cadell St, Goolwa, tel. (08) 8555 0144.

Tourist centres Millicent Rd, Beachport, tel. (08) 8735 8029; Signal Point River Murray Interpretative Centre, Goolwa Wharf, Goolwa, tel. (08) 8555 3488; The Big Lobster, Princes Hwy, Kingston S.E., tel. (08) 8767 2555; Millicent Tourist Information Centre, 1 Mount Gambier Rd, Millicent, tel. (08) 8733 3205; Lady Nelson Visitor and Discovery Centre, Jubilee Hwy East, Mount Gambier, tel. (08) 8724 9750; District Council of Grant, 5 Charles St, Port MacDonnell, tel. (08) 8739 2576; Robe Tourist Information Centre, Public Library, Mundy Tce, Robe, tel. (08) 8768 2465; Victor Harbor Tourist Information, Foreshore, adjacent to The Causeway, Victor Harbor, tel. (08) 8552 5738.

SOUTH AUSTRALIA

COASTAL FISHING SOUTH EAST REGION

Port MacDonnell to Kingston S.E.

Type of fishing
beach, lake, offshore, pier, reef, rock

Target fish
Australian salmon, garfish, mullet, shark, whiting

The South East offers excellent fishing for land-based and offshore anglers. Exposed to the Southern Ocean, this area has some wild weather, but those in boats able to cope with the waves can try offshore for tuna and shark. Australian salmon, mullet and mulloway can be caught from the beaches and jetties.

PORT MACDONNELL TO KINGSTON S.E.

Port MacDonnell, south of Mount Gambier, has a boat ramp and a harbour protected by a breakwater. It is now well known for the winter run of southern bluefin tuna. Professional charter services are available to chase this species. Anglers going out into these waters need a big seaworthy boat to cope with the winds and the ocean swell. There is a reef area just outside the harbour, worth exploring for snapper, morwong, King George whiting and

Most land-based anglers in Port MacDonnell fish the sheltered harbour waters, but outside there is some rock fishing for the more intrepid

Fishing for mullet off the long Beachport Jetty

garfish. The reef area extends along this coast for several kilometres to **Douglas Point**, but is best fished by boat. The best land-based fishing spots for reef fish in the area are the **Port MacDonnell Jetty, Carpenter Rocks** and **Cape Banks**. The long, lonely stretch of **Canunda Beach** is reached from Southend, further along the coast. This is a great mulloway area, mostly of school size. **Nora Creina Bay** is a renowned spot for Australian salmon.

North of Beachport and Robe is the small town of Kings Camp, protected by **Cape Jaffa**. The jetty is a terrific fishing area for tommy ruff, mullet, garfish and whiting, but the highlight of the area, for the boat anglers, is the **Margaret Brock Reef** and **North Rock**, which offer superb fishing less than 10 km offshore. Snapper, morwong, whiting, trevally and salmon are among the abundant reef fish. The town of **Kingston S.E.** is open to the sea in Lacepede Bay, and is the home port of the lobster fleet, which ties up at the pier. The arrival of the fleet brings the anglers out to try for mullet, attracted by the food scraps. Whiting, tommy ruff and garfish are around the pier, and big stingrays glide over the sandy sea floor. The drain between Cape Jaffa and Kingston S.E. is good for light surf fishing for flathead and whiting.

BEACHPORT

Beachport is a small and attractive fishing village retaining a number of sandstone cottages built in the 19th century. There is a boat ramp next to the town jetty, but **Rivoli Bay** and the offshore waters are subject to ocean swells. **Cape Buffon** at Southend and **Cape Martin** have land angling stands for salmon, whiting and trevally off the rocks. **Point William** at Beachport, and the sheltered cove known as the **Salmon Hole**, are

COASTAL FISHING SOUTH EAST REGION

SOUTH AUSTRALIA

salmon fishing areas. There are mullet off the beaches along this whole shoreline. There is whiting over weedy areas in the bay and also around **Cape Martin**, and in the small bay between the cape and **Snapper Point**. Sweep, snapper and flathead are also regular catches. The jetty can be fished for mullet near the shoreline, or further out for whiting, flathead, tommy ruff and garfish. The fishing is similar from the jetty at **Southend** at the other end of the bay.

ROBE

Robe, a picturesque holiday centre, is a charming and historic town with many delightful stone buildings. Once a major wool port, it is now the home of a commercial fishing fleet. Fishing in this area is of such a high standard that it attracts anglers from around the country. The rocky shores around **Cape Dombey** and to the south are fished for sweep. The breakwater and jetty around the cape near the town offer good fishing for garfish, mullet and trevally. The fishing fleet ties up in **Lake Butler**, which is reached by a channel from Guichen Bay. There is a lot of fun fishing for mullet in the lake and along the foreshore of the bay. The boat haven often holds schools of 2–3 kg mulloway in summer, in addition to bream. Salmon can also be caught from the shore at either end of **Hooper Beach**. The joined lakes of **Lake Battye**, **Lake Nunan** and **Pub Lake** are very close to town, and easy to fish for bream, which can be up to 2 kg. Prawn is the best bait and dusk is the best time to fish. **Guichen Bay** itself is essentially King George whiting territory, with flathead, sweep and snapper around the **Baudin Rocks**.

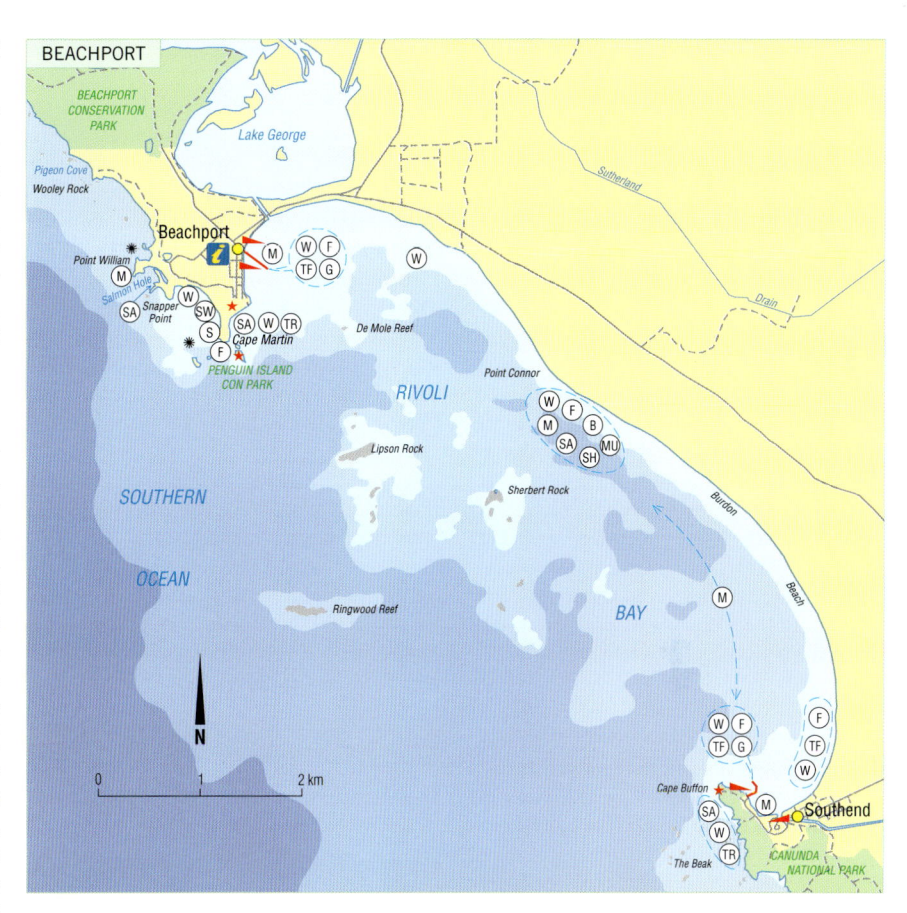

GUIDE TO LOCAL FISH

	Port MacDonnell to Kingston S.E.	Beachport	Robe
(B) bream		●	●
(F) flathead		●	●
(G) garfish	●	●	●
(MO) morwong	●		
(M) mullet	●	●	●
(MU) mulloway	●	●	●
(SA) salmon, Australian	●	●	●
(SH) shark	●	●	●
(S) snapper	●	●	●
(SW) sweep	●	●	●
(TR) tommy ruff	●	●	●
(TR) trevally	●	●	●
(W) whiting	●	●	●

SOUTH AUSTRALIA

COASTAL FISHING SOUTH EAST REGION

The Coorong

Type of fishing
beach, estuary, lake, river

Target fish
bream, flathead, flounder, mullet, mulloway

Renowned as a haven for waterbirds, the Coorong also offers excellent fishing, either from the beaches or a small boat. Around Hindmarsh Island the channels yield bream and school mulloway, while the Murray mouth attracts mulloway, some of exceptional size. Goolwa Surf Beach is a top fishing location, with flathead, bream and flounder. Goolwa cockles can be collected here, and from the sandy beaches of the Coorong (it is illegal to take them from 1 June to 31 October).

THE COORONG

The Coorong is a long chain of salt lagoons merging into an estuary, which runs for 145 km behind the ocean shoreline, separated from it only by a narrow peninsula of bush and sand dunes. It runs to the Murray mouth and joins the confluence of Lake Alexandrina and Lake Albert. This is all sandy, marshy bushland and still water, a magnificent haven for water birds and a quiet and fascinating fishing place, both in the Coorong itself and on the ocean side.

There are a few places where a crossing can be made but a four-wheel drive is needed to reach the ocean beach and make the most of the fishing. The turbulence of the ocean often churns the sand and makes the beach unfishable, but when the gutters are visible and the water reasonably calm there is great fishing for mulloway, Australian salmon, bream, whiting and shark. The most popular access point is **Tea Tree Crossing**, near Salt Creek, and there are others at **The 42 Mile** and **Jacks Point**. Salt Creek is one of the few places in this lonely, remote and strangely beautiful area where one can buy food, supplies, fuel, fishing tackle and bait – all at the general store.

The Coorong itself is ideal for small boat fishing, and boats can be beach launched from anywhere on this long stretch of water. There are several launching ramps at the north-western end, around Goolwa and Hindmarsh Island, but nothing in the shallower southern stretches. This area requires careful navigation in anything other than the shallowest draft 'tinnies' and punts, as it is full of sandbars and channels. The fishing is excellent, for land-based anglers as well as those in a boat, and school mulloway, bream, mullet, flathead and salmon are the main catches, with flounder spearing in the shallows. In mid to late summer, large numbers of school mulloway invade the Coorong and push far up into the inner lagoon. Fishing with pilchards along the channel to Policemans Point can be both productive and great fun.

GUIDE TO LOCAL FISH

	The Coorong	Goolwa
(B) bream	●	●
(F) flathead	●	●
(FL) flounder	●	●
(M) mullet	●	
(MU) mulloway	●	●
(SA) salmon, Australian	●	●
(SH) shark	●	●
(W) whiting	●	

The Coorong provides some of the most beautiful beaches in Australia. Access to this somewhat remote area is mainly by four-wheel drive. These anglers have made the crossing near Salt Creek

COASTAL FISHING SOUTH EAST REGION   SOUTH AUSTRALIA

GOOLWA

A freshwater barrage contains the Murray Basin area, but when it is opened to lower the river level, one of the great phenomenons of Australian fishing takes place. The outflow of dead fish and other aquatic food and debris attracts huge schools of mulloway for a feeding frenzy. Anglers line up at the **Murray mouth,** casting with lures or baits and catching some massive mulloway. These fish have been known to reach 40 kg. Naturally, a run-out tide is required for fishing the Murray mouth, as the mulloway lurk just outside, waiting for the strong current to push bait fish out into the ocean. When the big mulloway are on, it is a matter of baiting up, waiting for that screaming run and hanging on for dear life!

There are ramps to give boat access to this saltwater section – at the end of Barrage Road on the Sir Richard Peninsula, and on Hindmarsh Island, which is reached by bridge from Goolwa.

The best mulloway fishing time is after dark, but when the barrages are newly opened good catches can be made at any time. The mulloway can be caught on lures, with heavy metal models by far the most effective. However, recently there has been a tendency for anglers to drift large baits (either live fish or large fish fillets) out into the surf under polystyrene floats. Because of their line capacity, big game reels have emerged as the perfect tool for this style of fishing.

Goolwa Surf Beach is one of the best surf fishing locations in Australia, with plenty of flathead, bream, flounder and shark. A high bluff at **Surfers,** west of Goolwa Surf Beach, enables examination of the gutters and channels. The preferred bait is the Goolwa cockle, unique to the area and easily harvested by hand. To fish the surf well a four-wheel drive is needed to fully patrol the beach in search of the prevailing gutters and channels.

A fishing camp on Goolwa Beach. Limited four-wheel drive access is allowed to South Australian beaches

Goolwa cockles

Identical to the Victorian pippi, the Goolwa cockle is the natural diet of whiting as they forage for shellfish and crustaceans. This popular bait can be collected from the Goolwa Surf Beach or from the long sandy shores of the Younghusband Peninsula. Less energetic anglers can purchase supplies from bait shops.

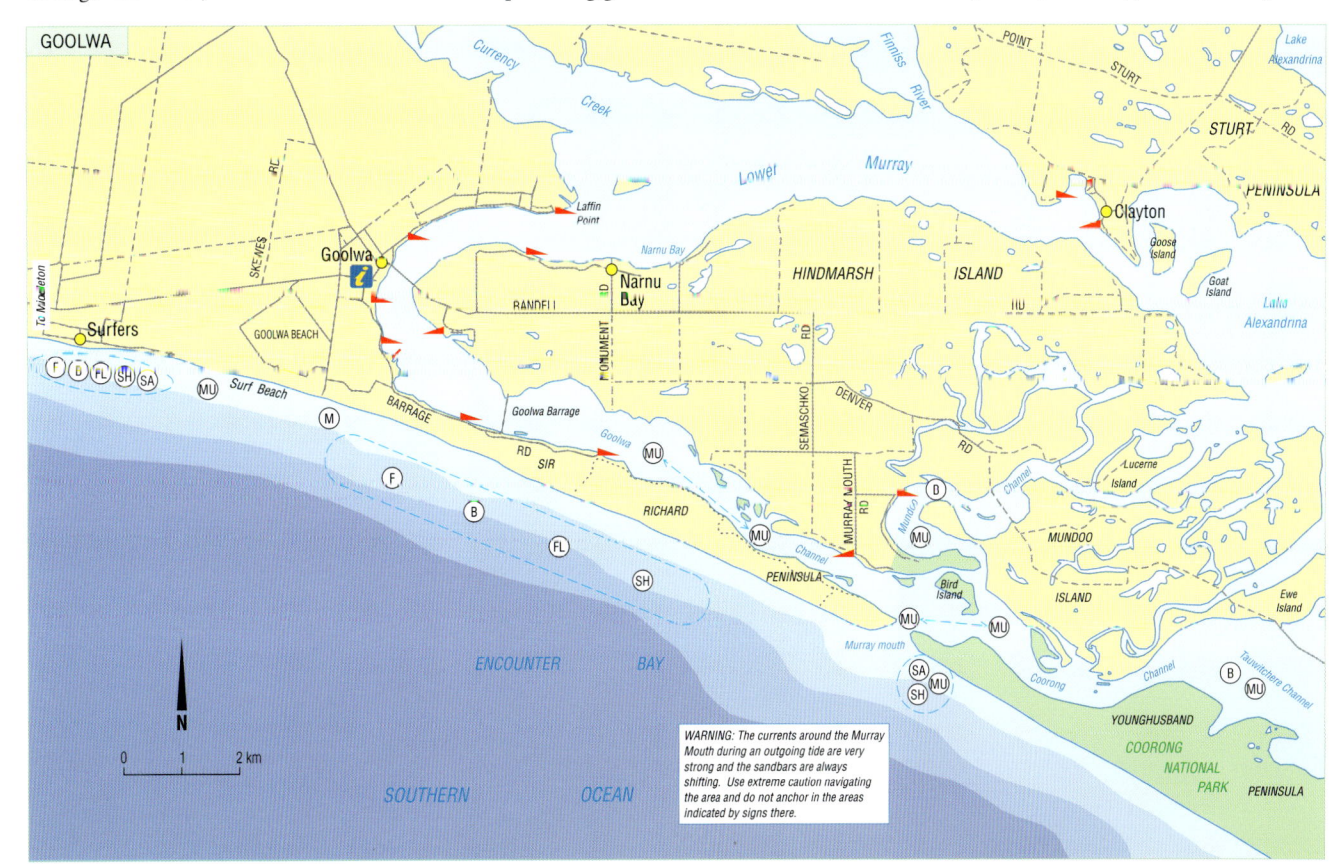

281

SOUTH AUSTRALIA
COASTAL FISHING SOUTH EAST REGION

Victor Harbor

Type of fishing
bay, beach, jetty, offshore, reef, river

Target fish
Australian salmon, garfish, snapper, trevally

GUIDE TO LOCAL FISH

(B)	bream
(F)	flathead
(G)	garfish
(M)	mullet
(MU)	mulloway
(SA)	salmon, Australian
(SH)	shark
(S)	snapper
(SN)	snook
(SQ)	squid
(SW)	sweep
(TF)	tommy ruff
(TR)	trevally
(W)	whiting

Fishing is a big part of the holiday attraction of Victor Harbor, as it is the base for a wide variety of fishing, and is easily reached from Adelaide. Jetty, rock, bay, river, surf and offshore fishing are all available in the area, with plenty of boat ramps, bait and tackle shops and charter operators to cater for the annual influx of up to 10 000 summer visitors. There is accommodation to suit all budgets, from camping grounds to modern motels.

The nearby town of **Port Elliot** is a convenient base to explore all that the area holds, and has its own fishing attractions. One of these is just short of the town of **Middleton**, where beach fishing into the deep channel behind the submerged reef will yield mulloway, whiting, sweep and flathead. The jetty in **Horseshoe Bay** is capable of creating a great moment in an angler's life as big mulloway are taken there at night, from waters that also abound in giant stingrays. Mullet, trevally and Australian salmon are other likely catches here. Close to shore are **Frenchman Rock** (out from Crockery Bay) and **Pullen Island**, where boat anglers can seek sweep and Australian salmon. Inshore there are Australian salmon at **Freeman Nob**, and Australian salmon, mulloway, flathead, shark and bream along **Boomer Beach**, particularly around **Chiton Rocks**, which are visible as this long beach reaches the outskirts of Victor Harbor. Snapper, snook and mullet are also around the rocks and the sunken reefs nearby. A tiny creek running back from the beach at **Watson Gap** can be explored for bream, as can the **Hindmarsh and Inman rivers**, which run through the town of Victor Harbor.

Victor Harbor is situated around **Encounter Bay**, which is relatively sheltered from the south-westerly swells flowing through the offshore waters. Garfish and Australian salmon are out in the middle of the bay, along with trevally.

The screwpile jetty at **Granite Island** is reached by a causeway, where a horse-drawn tram makes the journey to the island. The jetty is a reliable fishery for garfish, mullet and tommy ruff, with the occasional snapper a possibility. Big stingray and shark are sought out here by anglers with big tackle and serious intent. The causeway itself, a great tourist attraction, should not be overlooked by garfish anglers. Rock fishing is available from Granite Island and from the breakwater extending from the island. Use caution because the area is subject to large swells.

There is a lot of action around **Rosetta Harbour** and particularly Rosetta Head, also known locally as The Bluff. Garfish, whiting and trevally are in this sheltered harbour, while there are Australian salmon on the south side of **Wright Island** and snapper in the north.

Rosetta Head is particularly good for land-based anglers. **Whalers Wharf** has big squid as well as big mulloway, snapper, trevally, garfish and hordes of tommy ruff in

A small fishing boat returning from the close inshore fishing grounds around Wright Island

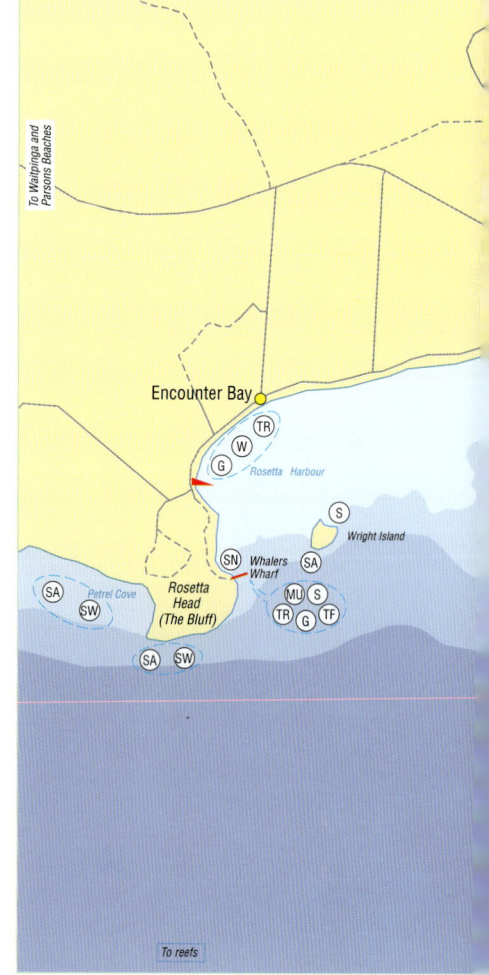

COASTAL FISHING SOUTH EAST REGION

SOUTH AUSTRALIA

the winter. There are snook and squid in the small bay near the wharf. Sweep and Australian salmon can be caught from many stands on **Rosetta Head** and around **Petrel Cove**.

Victor Harbor is a great base for some **offshore fishing** when the weather is stable and the Southern Ocean is relatively calm. Boats can be launched from Rosetta Harbour for reef areas that are around 10 km south of Rosetta Head. Snapper, mackerel, snook and silver trevally are over these reefs, with shark in attendance. In the winter warehou and barracouta add to the target species. A boat charter system takes anglers out to these reefs, so they can fish from a big deck and let someone else worry about the weather.

Those making for the reefs can detour to try for the snook and Australian salmon around **Seal Island**, which is a small outcrop some 3 km to the east of Rosetta Head.

West of Victor Harbor are **Parsons Beach** and **Waitpinga Beach**, which are outstanding for beach fishing. Night fishing for mulloway brings in some large specimens, but there is also opportunity for Australian salmon, flathead and tailor.

A fisherman checking nets near Whalers Wharf, with Wright Island in the background

283

SOUTH AUSTRALIA COASTAL FISHING PORT LINCOLN REGION

Port Lincoln Region

Originally mooted as the site for South Australia's capital city, Port Lincoln is situated on one of the country's most beautiful natural harbours. Liberally endowed with wharves and jetties, the town is a mecca for holiday anglers and is regularly used as a base for surf, rock, offshore and game fishing. Its white shark population is legendary among game anglers throughout the world.

The waters around the Eyre Peninsula are cold but clean and clear and have excellent fisheries especially for whiting

Port Lincoln is generally regarded as the 'capital city' of the Eyre Peninsula. Indeed, it makes a great base from which to fish lower Spencer Gulf, as well as the seemingly endless surf beaches stretching up the west coast to Ceduna and beyond. Big Australian salmon, monster mulloway, shark and tuna – this region has plenty of challenges for the keener angler. It is a long drive from Adelaide, but the results nearly always justify the journey.

Weather

Conditions in Spencer Gulf are generally good for boating. However, weather conditions can deteriorate rapidly. Monitor weather and forecasts while on the water. The Great Australian Bight is completely unprotected and subject to all the vicissitudes of the open sea. Regular boating forecasts are broadcast by metropolitan and regional radio stations. The Bureau of Meteorology has a recorded information line for forecasts and warnings on (08) 8366 2700 or visit its web site at www.bom.gov.au/weather/sa

Boating

Port Lincoln offers good boat ramp facilities in the bay, including an all-weather boat ramp with two launching ramps. The Lincoln Cove Marina is good in most weather conditions although you have to watch the northerlies. Generally the Boston Bay is safe and protected for recreational boating; there are no outstanding objects, and the reef outside the bay is well marked with buoys and lights. For further information, contact the local Marine Safety officer.

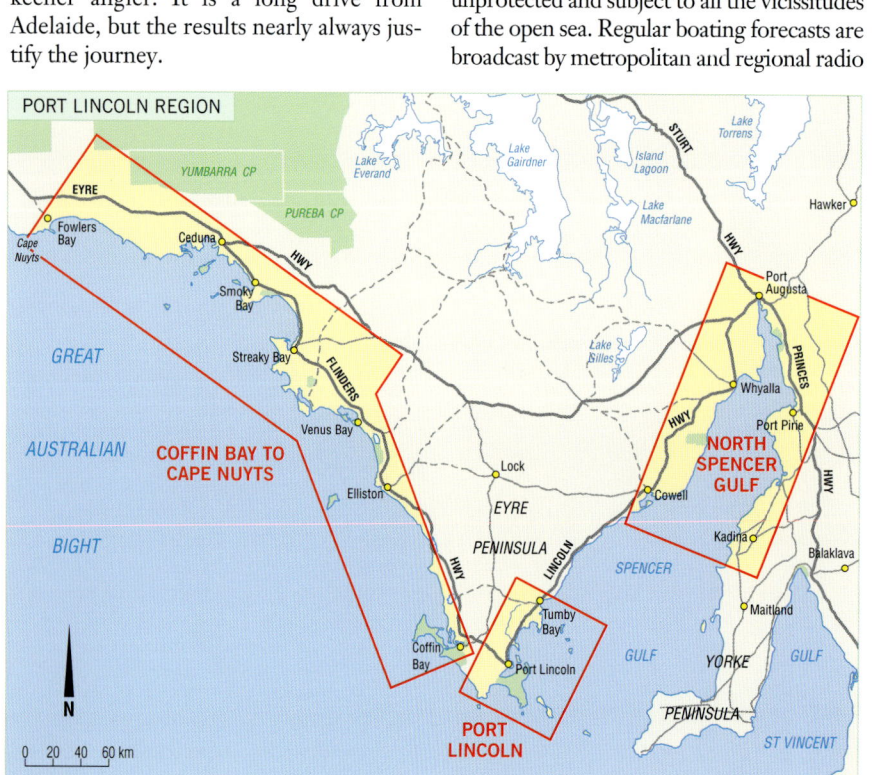

WHERE TO FISH

Port Lincoln Region

NORTH SPENCER GULF ● 286

Spencer Gulf, the larger of South Australia's two vast inlets, is renowned as the country's best snapper area. Whyalla, in particular, is a snapper hotspot, but big reds are also taken from Port Pirie, Port Augusta and Cowell. Most coastal towns feature well-maintained jetties, all of which yield tommy ruff, garfish, snook and other good table varieties.

PORT LINCOLN ● 288

The foot of Eyre Peninsula attracts more visiting anglers than any other part of the State. Port Lincoln's Boston Bay is well endowed with jetties and there are first-class launching facilities for trailer boat enthusiasts. The angling opportunities are many and varied in this region and include tackling salmon from rocks or beach, pulling bag limit hauls of big whiting around the offshore islands or trolling for tuna.

COFFIN BAY TO CAPE NUYTS ● 290

Known as the State's West Coast, this region is the surf angler's dream come true. Big salmon are caught near Elliston and Streaky Bay, but the most consistent catches come from the beaches west of Fowlers Bay. This is also mulloway country. Again, all jetties yield good fish and the whiting action in Venus, Smoky and Streaky bays is exceptional.

COASTAL FISHING PORT LINCOLN REGION

SOUTH AUSTRALIA

Fishing action at one of the many Port Lincoln jetties

Port Lincoln is famous for its tuna fleet, which regularly harvests the waters of the Great Australian Bight

FISHING TIP

When fishing the surf don't ignore the white water. The gutters are the places where big fish will wait in search of prey, but often the edges of the white water, where the water is froth on top but still clean below, will produce good catches of fish such as Australian salmon and mulloway. The best way to find holes, gutters and channels on a beach is to spend a few moments studying the beach from a high vantage point.

GUIDE TO LOCAL FISH

barracouta
bream
drummer, silver
flathead
flounder
garfish
groper
kingfish, yellowtail
leatherjacket
mackerel
mullet
mulloway
nannygai
salmon, Australian
shark, bronze whaler
snapper
snook
sweep
tailor
tommy ruff
trevally
tuna, southern bluefin
whiting, King George

FURTHER INFORMATION

Boating and fishing The Department of Primary Industries (PIRSA) Fisheries has offices at 25 Grenfell St, Adelaide, tel. (08) 8226 2311; 35 Frances Tce, Kadina, tel. (08) 8821 3242; Civic Centre, Tasman Tce, Port Lincoln, tel. (08) 8688 3488; and at PIRSA at 15 Bay Rd, Streaky Bay, tel. (08) 8626 1247. There is a Marine Safety officer stationed at Port Lincoln, tel. (08) 8347 5039 and Ports Corp South Australia has offices at Port Pirie, tel. (08) 8632 1455; Thevenard, tel. (08) 8082 0403 and Whyalla, tel. (08) 8645 3774.

Tourist centres Ceduna Gateway Visitor Information Centre, 58 Poynton St, Ceduna, tel. (08) 8625 2780; Beachcomber Agencies, The Esplanade, Coffin Bay, tel. (08) 8685 4057; District Council, Beach Tce, Elliston, tel. (08) 8687 9177; Station Visitor Information Centre, Kadina Rd, Moonta, tel. (08) 8825 1891; Wadlata Outback Centre, 41 Flinders Tce, Port Augusta, tel. (08) 8641 0793; Port Lincoln Tourist Information Centre, 3 Adelaide Pl, Port Lincoln, tel. (08) 8683 3544; Port Pirie Regional Tourism and Arts Centre, 3 Mary Elie St, Port Pirie, tel. (08) 8633 0439; Streaky Bay Motel, 15 Alfred Tce, Streaky Bay, tel. (08) 8626 1126; Whyalla Tourist Centre, Lincoln Hwy, Whyalla, tel. (08) 8645 7900.

SOUTH AUSTRALIA   COASTAL FISHING PORT LINCOLN REGION

North Spencer Gulf

Type of fishing
bay, jetty, offshore, reef, rock
Target fish
garfish, snapper, tommy ruff, whiting, yellowtail kingfish

The towns around Spencer Gulf are popular holiday destinations. Many of the sheltered bays offer excellent fishing. The gulf is renowned for its very big snapper and reliable fishing for King George whiting, yellowtail kingfish, garfish, tommy ruff and many other popular fish.

The bulk grain jetty at **Wallaroo**, on the Yorke Peninsula, is a land-based angler's dream, as a great variety of fish can be caught from here, including snapper in winter and spring. Other species include yellowtail kingfish, mulloway, snook, squid, garfish, mullet and tommy ruff. Dabbing garfish on calm, moonless nights using a spotlight and dab net is often very productive. Snapper and whiting are also around these areas. The offshore fishing is good, with the snapper best in summer and whiting in the winter. Blue swimmer crabs are abundant in summer.

Whyalla is considered to be the base for the best snapper fishing in Australia

Port Broughton has shallow and sheltered waters in the harbour or in nearby **Fisherman Bay**, providing reliable catches of whiting, garfish, squid, snook and snapper. The jetty and breakwater, which protects an all-weather ramp, can be crowded in the holiday season, particularly with children chasing tommy ruff, garfish, the odd whiting and squid.

There are some very good fishing areas between Port Pirie and Port Augusta at the head of the gulf. These shallow, confined waters stay warmer into the autumn season and the fish stay longer in their summer areas, down to the towns of **Port Broughton** in the east and **Cowell** in the west. Snapper, whiting, Australian salmon, flathead, yellowtail kingfish and bream can all be caught in this region. The big towns have bait and tackle facilities and plenty of advice from the locals.

Port Pirie is a big snapper area, but anglers have to compete with commercial fishing. Garfish, mullet, mulloway and whiting are among the catches in the **Port**

The confined waters around Port Augusta encourages the fish to stay longer in their summer areas

COASTAL FISHING PORT LINCOLN REGION

SOUTH AUSTRALIA

GUIDE TO LOCAL FISH

(B)	bream
(F)	flathead
(G)	garfish
(KI)	kingfish, yellowtail
(M)	mullet
(MU)	mulloway
(SA)	salmon, Australian
(SH)	shark
(S)	snapper
(SN)	snook
(SQ)	squid
(TF)	tommy ruff
(W)	whiting

Pirie River. Land anglers like to work from **Fishermans Jetty**.

Mulloway, whiting and snapper can be taken from **Port Augusta's wharves** or in the narrow confines of the gulf. The warm waters of the **power station outlet** attract fish, and hauls of mullet, garfish and bream can be taken. Big kingfish can be caught near the outlet in winter.

On the western side of Spencer Gulf the big regional town of **Whyalla** is considered to be the base for the best snapper fishing in Australia. The main areas to fish for them are in the shipping lanes leading to the harbour and in the shipping anchorage area offshore, and at the edge of the silt grounds in **False Bay**. There are a number of small artificial reefs around the harbour that also attract snapper. Rock anglers have their share of the action at **Black Point**, when the big winter seas bring in a bounty of snapper.

There are plenty of other fish in Whyalla waters, including whiting, snook and garfish inshore and salmon and yellowtail kingfish in the gulf. Bronze whaler and white pointer sharks also cruise in the gulf. For the less adventurous, there are blue swimmer crabs along the foreshore in summer.

Cowell is on **Franklin Harbour**, where the waters are protected and there are ideal launching facilities, either in the harbour or nearby Lucky Bay. As with Whyalla, there are blue swimmer crabs along the foreshore and a good variety of fish in the harbour, including snapper, whiting, garfish, tommy ruff, snook and mullet. The best snapper fishing is just inside the harbour entrance.

Further down the coast the towns of **Arno Bay** and **Point Neill** have whiting, snapper, garfish and tommy ruff in their reasonably protected inshore waters.

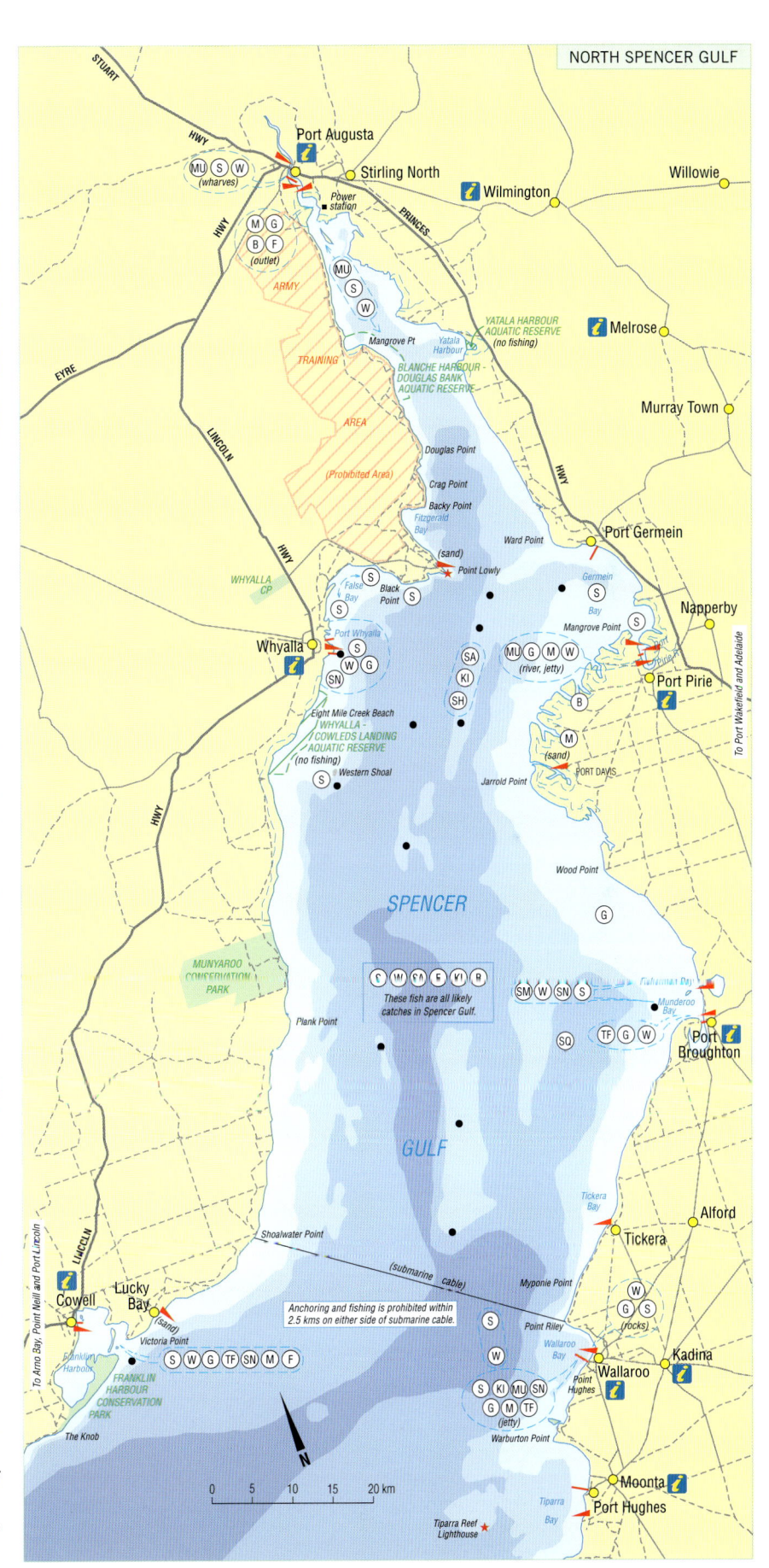

287

SOUTH AUSTRALIA

COASTAL FISHING PORT LINCOLN REGION

Port Lincoln

Type of fishing
bay, jetty, offshore, reef

Target fish
shark, snapper, snook, tommy ruff, whiting

Tumby Bay's greatest attraction is that it is the jumping-off place for the islands in the Sir Joseph Banks Group, but there is also good fishing inshore, with garfish, squid, tommy ruff and snook around the jetties and reasonable numbers of squid in the bay.

The Sir Joseph Banks Group can also be reached from Louth Bay and Port Lincoln. The islands are scattered along the coast and are a paradise for all kinds of angling, right up to heavy tackle fishing for sharks. Large boats are required in these waters. There are other big fish in these relatively underworked waters, including huge snapper and whiting, yellowtail kingfish, trevally, mackerel and barracouta.

Port Lincoln is a somewhat remote but beautiful city, located at the south of **Boston Bay**. This waterway is a lot bigger than Sydney Harbour, but the entrance in the past was considered unsafe for sailing vessels. Despite that it became an important grain port and is now the home of a big tuna fleet and a mecca for game anglers, who go well offshore after shark and southern bluefin tuna. Game charter operators are based in Lincoln Cove Marina. There are several jetties open to fishing, and the best – and longest – is the bulk grain jetty, known as **Brennans Wharf**. Here big snapper and Australian salmon top the catches of tommy ruff, trevally, mullet and snook. The smaller jetties have snook, mullet, garfish, squid and tommy ruff, with Kirton Point a venue for King George whiting. There are squid all along the foreshore, and whiting, snapper, snook and garfish for boat anglers in the bay. The ever popular tommy ruff can be taken in Lincoln Cove.

Boat anglers will find the best fishing down the west coast of **Boston Island** and to the west of the **Bickers Islands**, between Grantham Island and the coast and around **Horse Rock** in Proper Bay. The main catch is snapper, and there are plenty of whiting, trevally, snook, tommy ruff and sweep. Fishing pilchard baits outside the exclusion zones around tuna pens can result in snapper or even a free swimming wild tuna attracted to the area by the penned fish and regular feeding.

Sleaford Bay, 20 km south of Port Lincoln, is a big bay with a number of submerged reefs off the beach. Salmon are very prevalent in winter, and whiting and flathead are the main catches in summer. **Fishery Bay**, just south of Sleaford, is known for its salmon, whiting and mulloway, with snapper and sweep the targets from the rocks.

The great white shark is still a frequent visitor to the area. The species is now fully protected. Shark anglers must content themselves with bronze whalers.

Bronze whaler
This shark is found almost right around Australia. It inhabits offshore reefs, surf beaches, estuaries and bays.

GUIDE TO LOCAL FISH

BC	barracouta
F	flathead
G	garfish
KI	kingfish, yellowtail
MA	mackerel
M	mullet
MU	mulloway
SA	salmon, Australian
SH	shark
S	snapper
SN	snook
SQ	squid
SW	sweep
TF	tommy ruff
TR	trevally
TU	tuna
W	whiting

COASTAL FISHING PORT LINCOLN REGION   SOUTH AUSTRALIA

Carcharodon carcharias

Observing a 5-metre great white from the safety of a submerged steel cage has to be one of the most awesome experiences for any diver.

The great white shark is considered by many people, anglers included, as the most awesome marine creature roaming the oceans of the world. It grows to at least 7 m in length and has earned a fearsome reputation. It is at the top of the marine food chain with no serious predator threat. Carcharodon carcharias, as it is known to scientists, is essentially the perfect eating machine.

Back in the 1930s and 1940s, when heavy tackle game fishing was still in its infancy, Port Lincoln rocketed to stardom as its imposing population of great white sharks was discovered and publicised throughout the world. Legendary anglers like Zane Grey visited the area to seek record-sized sharks; before long Port Lincoln was as famous as Bermagui as a big game fishing destination. But it was Mildura market gardener, Alf Dean, who did more to promote heavy tackle shark fishing in South Australia than any other single angler. Dean broke world record after world record, often engaging in friendly rivalry with television and radio personality, Bob Dyer, who was also a white shark fanatic. Alf would charter local boats, often staying at sea for a week at a time until the big one turned up. He designed and made most of his own tackle and, within a relatively short period, developed the reputation of being the most respected and knowledgeable shark fisherman in the world. Indeed, his 2664-pound great white, captured in 1959, still stands as the all tackle world record for the species, and remains the heaviest game fish ever taken on rod and reel.

Today Port Lincoln is still regarded as the white shark capital of the world. When underwater sequences of large sharks were required for the making of the movie *Jaws*, Port Lincoln was the obvious choice from several possible locations worldwide. In fact, film crews have come from all parts of the globe to dive with and record the habits and characteristics of this incredible animal. Observing a 5-metre great white from the safety of a submerged steel cage has to be one of the most awesome experiences for any diver.

Alf Dean's contemporaries – members of the Game Fishing Club of South Australia – no longer do battle with enormous sharks offshore from Port Lincoln. Attitudes toward game fishing in general have undergone dramatic change in recent times and it is no longer acceptable for top-of-the-line predators like great whites to be slaughtered indiscriminately. In order to stop the decline in numbers, the great white shark is now a totally protected species.

Hopefully, with this philosophy now well in place, the greatest of all marine predators can look forward to a healthy future.

– *Shane Mensforth*

SOUTH AUSTRALIA

COASTAL FISHING PORT LINCOLN REGION

Coffin Bay to Cape Nuyts

Type of fishing
bay, beach, jetty, offshore, reef, rock
Target fish
Australian salmon, groper, snapper, whiting

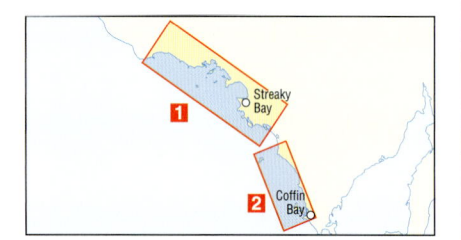

The coast of the Coffin Bay Peninsula and the Great Australian Bight is a delight for surf anglers. The string of beaches between Coffin Bay and Elliston yield King George whiting, while large Australian salmon are caught from the surf beaches along this coast. Venus and Streaky bays are sheltered and have jetties which offer excellent catches of whiting and a range of other species.

COFFIN BAY TO ELLISTON

The long sweep of coastline into the Great Australian Bight begins at the entrance to Coffin Bay, only a short drive across the peninsula from Port Lincoln. The waters here are a Chinese puzzle of bays – Coffin Bay leads to Port Douglas, which leads to Mount Dutton Bay and Kellidie Bay. The picturesque little town of Coffin Bay, which consists mainly of fishing shacks, a caravan park, a boat ramp and jetty, is opposite a narrow strip of water leading into Kellidie Bay, known as **The Ledge**. This is sheltered

Mulloway fishing on the remote coast between Point Sinclair and Fowlers Bay

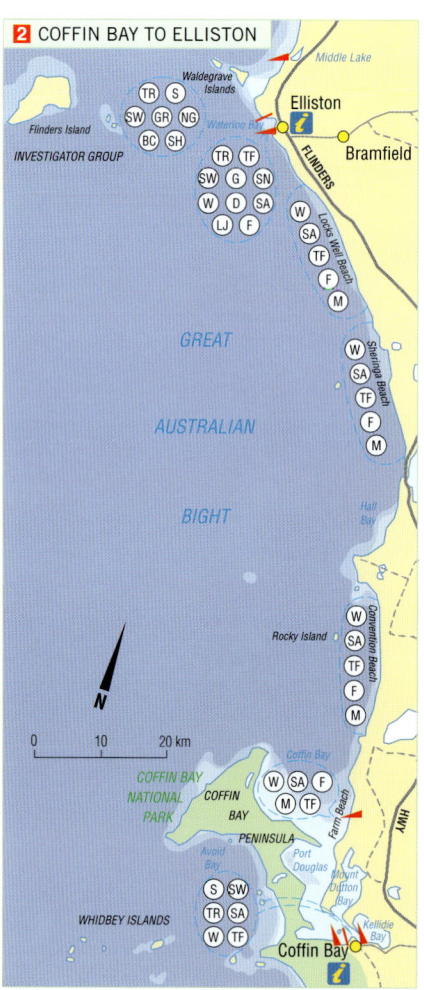

water with a reef running through it. Boat anglers anchor on the Coffin Bay side and cast into the reef for snapper, trevally, whiting, sweep and salmon. The jetty at Coffin Bay is a popular spot for trevally, whiting and tommy ruff. In this area **Kellidie Bay** is renowned for whiting.

The almost enclosed waters of Coffin Bay are an angler's paradise. Suitable for small boats and close to the town, anglers can still tackle snapper and even big yellowtail kingfish as well as the regular species.

The ledge is one of the rare rock fishing locations where parents can take the kids rock fishing in an area devoid of swells. Despite this, the ledge still produces quality fish like tommy ruff, garfish, trevally and whiting while the angler can sit on a deck chair at the edge of the rock platform.

Large yellowtail kingfish frequent the bay. Baits of live garfish or squid should be used if you sight one of these green-backed monsters. Look for signs like several fish jumping clear of the water as the kingfish pursue them.

Simply trolling a small lure around the bay almost guarantees a feed of tommy ruffs and Australian salmon, especially around the small islands known as the **Brothers**.

A series of beaches (**Farm Beach**, **Convention Beach**, **Sheringa** and **Locks Well**) are superb in their wild isolation, unspoiled and lightly fished. Farm Beach is reputed to be the best whiting fishery in the State, and all four can be fished for King George whiting, big Australian salmon, flathead, mullet and tommy ruff. Boats can be launched from the beach at Form Beach but a four-wheel drive vehicle is required.

Along the coast from the entrance to Coffin Bay are excellent surf beaches that are accessible with conventional vehicles. Australian salmon up to and even over 5 kg are the main target but mulloway, huge tommy ruffs over 1 kg, mullet, whiting, flathead and sharks are also frequently caught in these waters.

Convention Beach and Sheringa are two beaches where the Australian salmon is king. Beach conditions along this coast vary continually with massive amounts of moving sand covering or exposing reefs. Expect some tackle loss around the rocks.

Fourteen kilometres from Elliston towards Port Lincoln is the surf beach at Locks Well. It is arguably South Australia's most famous and reliable Australian salmon beach. There is a stairway of over 200 steps down to the beach where deep gutters can usually be found close to shore.

GUIDE TO LOCAL FISH

		Coffin Bay to Elliston	Venus Bay to Cape Nuyts
BC	barracouta	●	
D	drummer	●	●
F	flathead	●	●
FL	flounder		●
G	garfish	●	
GR	groper	●	
KI	kingfish, yellowtail	●	●
LJ	leatherjacket	●	
M	mullet	●	●
MU	mulloway	●	●
NG	nannygai	●	
SA	salmon, Australian	●	●
SH	shark	●	
S	snapper	●	
SN	snook	●	
SW	sweep	●	
T	tailor		●
TF	tommy ruff	●	●
TR	trevally	●	●
W	whiting	●	●

COASTAL FISHING PORT LINCOLN REGION — SOUTH AUSTRALIA

The town of **Elliston** on Waterloo Bay is a base for boat, jetty, beach and rock fishing. The jetty anglers will be after tommy ruff, garfish, squid, snook and leatherjacket, while the bay, in calm weather, can be a good place for snook, trevally, flathead and King George whiting. Sweep and drummer are around the rocks and the big Australian salmon, which are commonly caught in the 5-kg class, are the best of the beach prospects.

Larger boats can go out from the Elliston boat ramp to the islands of the **Investigator Group**, and troll along the south-east coast of **Flinders Island**. This area has huge sweep and groper, nannygai, trevally, snapper, barracouta, groper and big sharks.

VENUS BAY TO CAPE NUYTS

Venus Bay is a very popular holiday spot, and fishing is the main attraction. The bay is so sheltered that the conditions resemble that of an estuary. The tranquil conditions give boat anglers plenty of opportunities as they seek King George whiting, flathead, trevally and snapper. There are flounder in the shallows and mullet, flathead and whiting around the jetty. The outside coastline has the big seas of the Bight pounding in, providing pulse-racing prospects for beach anglers hoping for stirring battles with big Australian salmon, shark, whiting, flathead and the occasional mulloway. There are also many rock areas where snapper, groper, sweep and silver drummer can be sought.

A big blue groper caught off Ceduna

Bairds Bay is a narrow, shallow and sheltered bay with an island blocking swells from entering the bay. Fish abound in the bay which is evident by the number of professional line fishermen who operate there. Boat launching is from the beach but the water is calm and the sand firm.

Streaky Bay is a bigger town, but similarly attractive to anglers, with sheltered water close to the town, a boat ramp and a jetty from which snook, trevally, snapper, garfish, squid and tommy ruff can be caught. The highlight here is **Smooth Pool**, a rocky area some 30 km from town, between the coast and offshore reefs. It is a particularly good winter fishing place for Australian salmon, trevally and groper, with whiting and sweep adding to the catch in summer. In the right light, the angler can see the fish swimming around, with huge groper moving around the bottom and others species in large numbers.

The area between Streaky Bay and the head of the Bight (west of Cape Nuyts) is fairly remote and some of the locations can only be reached by rough driving, but the fishing remains consistently good. Boat fishing in the area depends on relatively quiet seas with King George whiting the premier fish in the inshore waters. But this whole coast has great rock and beach fishing. Australian salmon, tailor, mulloway, whiting and flathead are the prime beach species, while groper, silver drummer and snapper are taken from the rocks. The areas around **Haslam**, **Point Brown**, **Smoky Bay** and **Ceduna** are very accessible, but a four-wheel drive is needed for beaches beyond Ceduna and towards the head of the Bight.

Ceduna is the business centre of the far west, and its port town of **Thevenard** is both a general port for the produce of the area and the base for fishing and charter boat operations. Inshore boating in **Bosanquet Bay** and **Murat Bay** can bring big catches of whiting, snapper, trevally, garfish and squid. The shipping channel into Thevenard is a place for large snapper. There are good launching facilities, but they can be tricky at low tide in the shallow inshore waters. Crabs and squid are the main catches along the shoreline.

Major shore fishing locations beyond Ceduna are **Devonport Creek**, **Point Bell**, **Point Sinclair**, **Fowlers Bay** and **Scott Bay**. Fowlers Bay has a long jetty from which yellowtail kingfish are often caught during summer. Big tommy ruff, garfish and squid are also found around here. The headland is a good venue for Australian salmon, sweep and snapper. At Scott Bay a huge mulloway can be the catch of a lifetime.

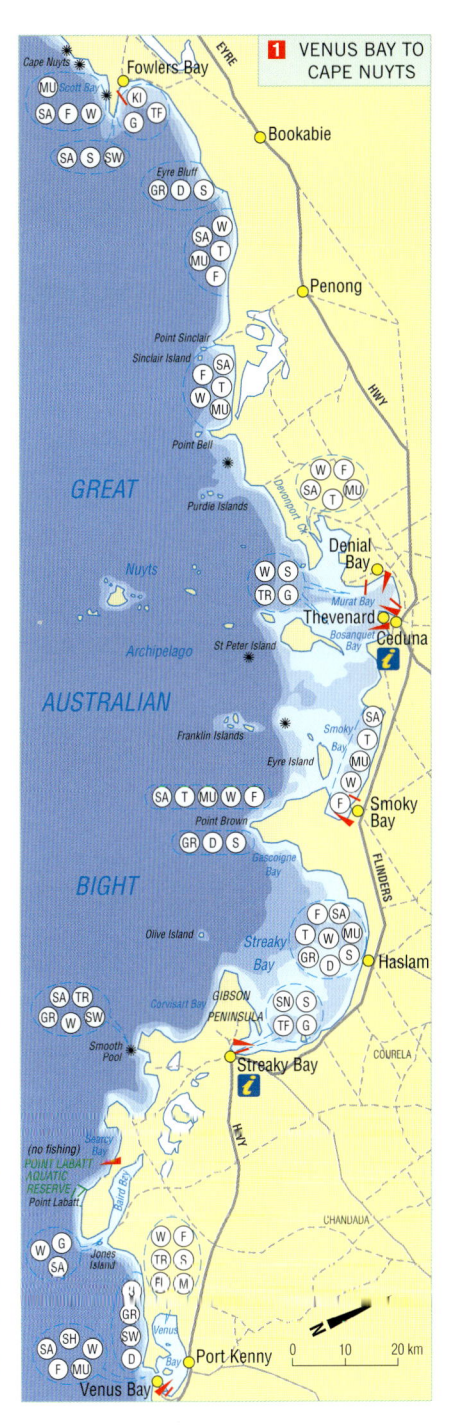

1 VENUS BAY TO CAPE NUYTS

While Australian salmon are always likely to be around, along with flathead and whiting, the big mulloway become the main target from this remote chain of beaches to the head of the Bight. The big seas keep shifting the sands here, and anglers must plot where the gutters are located. While fishing by day may be worthwhile, the best time is at dusk and night.

Four-wheel drives, beach buggies, complete camping equipment and trailers with freezers are required for serious fishing along this remote coast.

291

SOUTH AUSTRALIA

Inland Fishing

South Australia is generally recognised as being the driest State in the world's driest continent, so opportunities for freshwater fishers are very limited. Broadly speaking, there are two distinct groups of freshwater anglers – those who fish the Murray and those who specialise in trout.

The Murray River, of course, flows across the State from east to south-east, but upstream environmental influences mean that its water quality in the lower reaches is poor. The Broughton River, north of Adelaide, and the Onkaparinga River, south of Adelaide, stand alone as the most popular trout waters in the State.

There are a healthy number of lesser creeks and feeder systems to some of the more well known rivers and streams. Some of the least known waterways hold solid populations of brown and rainbow trout, redfin, Murray cod and golden perch.

Take the Broughton River for example. This river is regularly stocked with fry and fingerlings of both trout species but now this river also holds some very good size Murray cod and golden perch.

The Hutt River flows in the Broughton River downstream from the Spalding road bridge. Other lesser known streams holding good populations of trout and redfin, between Adelaide and the Broughton River are the Light River, the Wakefield River and Burra Creek. Surrounding Adelaide in the foothills are productive little streams for fishing such as the Torrens River's upper reaches, Sturt Creek and south of Adelaide are the Finnis, Bull Creek, the Inman and the Angas rivers.

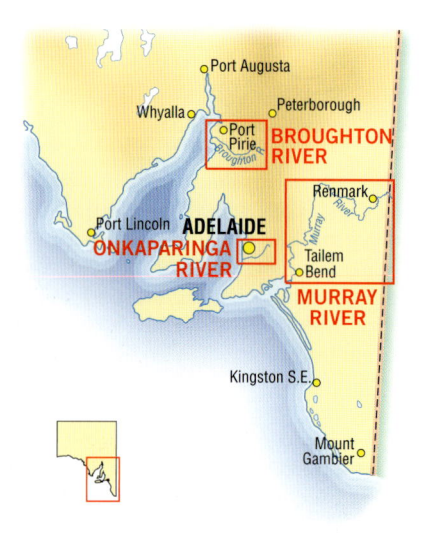

Protected species

In South Australia there is a total ban on the taking of the following freshwater species: Murray River crayfish, silver perch and catfish. Yabbies with eggs attached are also totally protected.

Boating regulations

Boating regulations in South Australia are covered by the Department of Transport SA (Marine Group). All motor boats require registration. Any type of motor boat must be driven by a licensed operator, regardless of its size or power, or whether it also operates under sail. Special permits are available to children between 12 and 16 years of age. These allow the holder to take charge of a motor boat less than 4 m in length and with a maximum speed of 10 knots or less under the supervision of a licensed holder. Other general rules are as follows:

- It is forbidden to dump any kind of waste from a boat. Noise pollution restrictions apply, particularly to residential areas along the Murray River.
- On the Murray River, speed must be reduced to 4 knots within 100 m of either side of a ferry crossing.
- When traversing a lock on the Murray, indicate to the lockmaster your intention to proceed by giving three long blasts (4 seconds each) on a whistle, portable air phone or other device, or waving a flag, or flashing a light. Do not come closer than 150 m to the lock until the lockmaster has given the signal to proceed, which is indicated by a green flag or a green fixed or flashing light.
- Some South Australian waters have speed restrictions, while others may exclude all boats or power boats. Watch out for signs.

Boating regulations are published in the 'Recreational Boating Safety Handbook' available from Motor Registration offices and the State Information office at 77 Grenfell St, Adelaide, tel. (08) 8204 1900.

INLAND FISHING

WHERE TO FISH

Inland

MURRAY RIVER REGION ● 293

The Murray remains an important fishery for natives despite degradation and the prevalence of introduced species.

ONKAPARINGA RIVER REGION ● 294

Proximity to Adelaide and healthy populations of fish make the Onkaparinga River popular with city-based anglers. Stocking of the water has been successful and trout have flourished.

BROUGHTON RIVER REGION ● 295

Like the Onkaparinga, the Broughton did not carry fish life of any significance until stocking took place. Regular stocking with trout has attracted fly fishers to the river, previously of little interest to anglers.

GUIDE TO LOCAL FISH

carp, European
catfish
cod, Murray
perch, golden
perch, silver
redfin
trout, brown
trout, rainbow

Bag and size limits apply. See the South Australian 'Recreational Fishing Guide' for details.

FURTHER INFORMATION

Fishing For full details on South Australia's fishing regulations, contact the Department of Primary Industries (PIRSA) Fisheries, 25 Grenfell St, Adelaide, tel. (08) 8226 2311, or one of its branch offices throughout the State.

Boating The Department of Transport SA (Marine Group) head office is at 64 Dale St, Port Adelaide, tel. (08) 8347 5001.

Tourist centres South Australian Tourism Travel Centre, 1 King William St, Adelaide, tel. (08) 8303 2033; Clare Valley Tourist Centre, Town Hall, 229 Main Rd North, Clare, tel. (08) 8842 2131; P.S. Marion Museum, Arnold Park, Randell St, Mannum, tel. (08) 8569 1303; Murray Bridge Information Centre, 3 South Terrace, Murray Bridge, tel. (08) 8532 2900; Tourist and Heritage Centre, 84 Murray Ave, Renmark, tel. (08) 8586 6704; 91 Railway Tce, Tailem Bend, tel. (08) 8572 4277.

SOUTH AUSTRALIA

INLAND FISHING MURRAY RIVER REGION

Murray River Region

The Murray River is undoubtedly South Australia's greatest inland waterway, but it is also one of the State's greatest tragedies.

Type of fishing
river
Target fish
golden perch, Murray cod

Up until the end of the 1960s the Murray ran clear, its native fish stocks were healthy and it consistently provided anglers with terrific catches. These days the river is discoloured and the introduced European carp have competed so strongly with the native species that catching a decent golden perch (callop) or Murray cod is the cause of much celebration.

Carp are still the main catch further upstream, but on occasions good bags of native varieties also can be caught. Large live baits, such as shrimps and yabbies, appear the best bet for those targeting golden perch or cod, but even these will be sucked down with relish by the carp. When the yabbies run in the summer months, the more remote, upstream locations definitely provide the best action as they are not so heavily fished.

In good seasons, when river levels fluctuate, yabbies are prolific throughout the river's lower reaches, and during the warmer months they provide a major source of attraction for drop netters.

The Murray's more accessible locations are Murray Bridge, Mannum and Swan Reach. At Murray Bridge there is a marina and at least four separately located boat ramps; Mannum has a number of concrete launching ramps and Swan Reach is also well provided with launching facilities. Further afield, Berri, Renmark, Loxton and Barmera see plenty of angling families during the course of a season. Murray River visitors can hire houseboats ('mobile' homes for some locals), which enable anglers a high degree of mobility; always a bonus when pursuing golden perch and cod.

The future of the Murray River and its native fish stocks is very much open to debate. If current trends are allowed to continue unchecked and water degradation is sustained, it is a good bet that the fragile natives will succumb in the not too distant future. There will always be carp to catch, but to lose the golden perch and Murray cod would be the ultimate tragedy.

FISHING TIP

Native fish on lures requires specialised techniques. Many top anglers put a larger set of treble hooks at the front of the lure and a smaller set at the rear. This is because of the way native fish feed. Golden perch and Murray cod suck in unsuspecting prey so most fish are taken at the broadest surface. It is the same with lures, which is why there is so much emphasis placed on the front treble.

Houseboating on the Murray is a pastime for many and a way of life for others

GUIDE TO LOCAL FISH

carp, European
cod, Murray
perch, golden

SOUTH AUSTRALIA

INLAND FISHING ONKAPARINGA RIVER REGION

Onkaparinga River Region

The Onkaparinga River, because of its proximity to Adelaide, receives its fair share of fishing pressure, but appears to cope quite well.

Type of fishing
river
Target fish
brown trout, golden perch, redfin

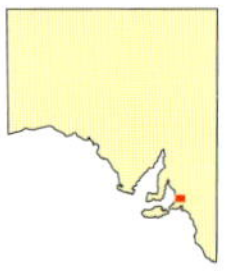

The 'Onk', as it is best known to Adelaide-based anglers, originates in the south Mount Lofty Ranges, then flows through Adelaide's southern suburbs and eventually enters Gulf St Vincent just south of the township of Port Noarlunga. It is the upstream reaches that attract the attention of fly fishers and freshwater lure tossers.

The Onkaparinga holds substantial populations of redfin, golden perch (callop) and both brown and rainbow trout which, due to the river's very healthy food supply, have flourished.

One of Adelaide's major water supplies, the Mount Bold Reservoir (fishing is prohibited in the dam), bisects the river near the town of Clarendon and it is in this general area that most Onkaparinga fishers begin a day's angling. Because redfin are numerous, small lures and spinners are very effective, particularly those with a flash of red. Unlike most waterways that hold redfin, the Onkaparinga fish are generally of good size and it is not unusual to bag specimens of up to 1 kg.

Trout will respond to the same lures, but they are by nature more difficult to tempt. Browns up to 3 kg have been caught in the upstream sections of the river. Indeed, there are still some monsters lurking in the less-accessible reaches, but these are invariably challenging fish. Blackberries can make access a frustrating experience. To be successful with trout offer them a lure or fly that resembles what they are feeding on.

The Onkaparinga River near Clarendon is a favoured freshwater fishing area for redfin as well as trout. Deep bankside foliage can make reaching the lighter-fished areas difficult

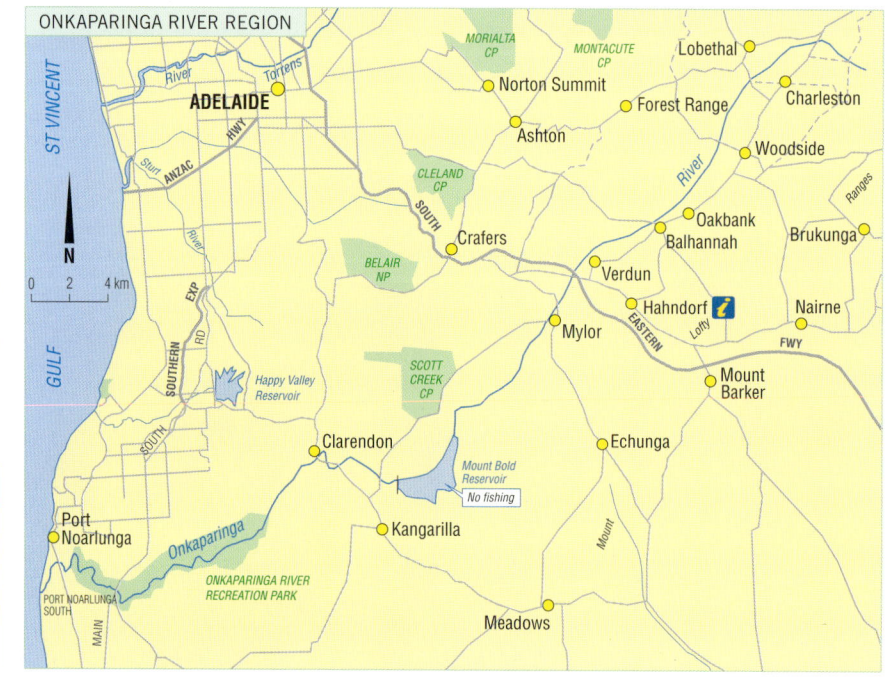

GUIDE TO LOCAL FISH

perch, golden
redfin
trout, brown
trout, rainbow

SOUTH AUSTRALIA

INLAND FISHING BROUGHTON RIVER REGION

Broughton River Region

As a result of stocking, it is now possible for anglers to catch both browns and rainbows from this previously barren waterway.

Type of fishing
river

Target fish
brown trout, rainbow trout

Like most of the rivers in this part of the State, the Broughton is not particularly convenient to fish. Reaching the deeper pools inevitably requires a lengthy walk, often through painfully annoying scotch thistles. It is also an area renowned for snake activity, so substantial footwear and a keen eye when negotiating long grass are a must.

Brown trout from the Broughton near Spalding

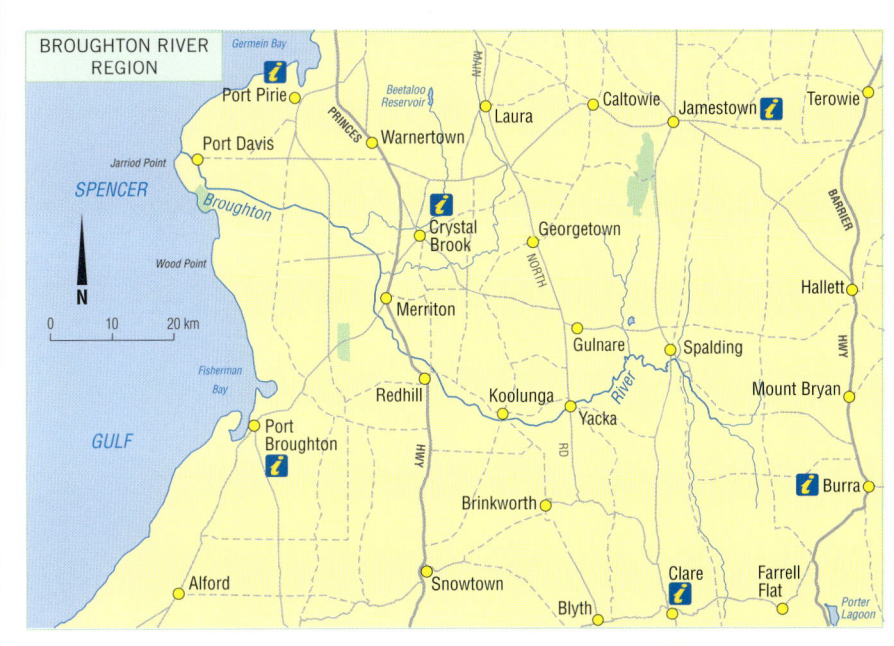

The Broughton originates just above the township of Spalding, in the State's mid north. Like most other northern streams, it is relatively deep and slow flowing. As is the case with practically all inland waterways in South Australia, the Broughton relies heavily on artificial stocking for the maintenance of its trout population. There is no natural spawning, so it makes sense to limit the number of trout taken from any single area. These days, the majority of anglers take just one fish for the table and return the rest. The river is regularly stocked with both brown and rainbow trout, both of which seem to have adapted to the environment.

Much of the waterway runs through private property, so it is essential to obtain the permission of the various land owners before venturing over fences or through gates.

The Broughton's brown trout population can be a frustrating proposition for anglers, particularly during the warmer months when the fish move into the river's deeper sections to escape the heat. Specimens of up to 4 kg or more can be seen cruising the pools at times, but trout of this size are cautious and difficult to tempt on any bait, natural or artificial.

Growth rates of the fish in this river are indeed healthy, as yabbies, shrimps and small native minnows are abundant. Although fly fishing purists generally frown on live baiting, it is a fact that a live yabby or minnow fished on light tackle is one of the deadliest techniques any angler can employ in the Broughton.

Spinning with artificial lures also can be effective at times, particularly on the rainbows. Recognised spinners such as the Celta or Mepps work well in the shallower runs, but small minnow lures like the Rapala CD5RT or Mini Fat Rap come into their own when working the deep, clear pools.

The towns of Spalding and Yacka are the major access points. A convenient option for those fishing the river for an extended period is to use the delightful town of Clare as a base, which has abundant services, including bait and tackle supplies, a range of accommodation, and is only half an hour's drive from the Broughton.

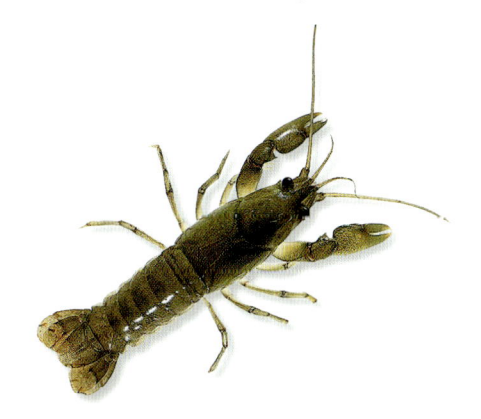

GUIDE TO LOCAL FISH

trout, brown
trout, rainbow

Yabbies
The yabby is a good freshwater bait for trout as well as Murray cod and golden perch. Remember to keep the size of the yabby matched to the size of the fish targeted.

295

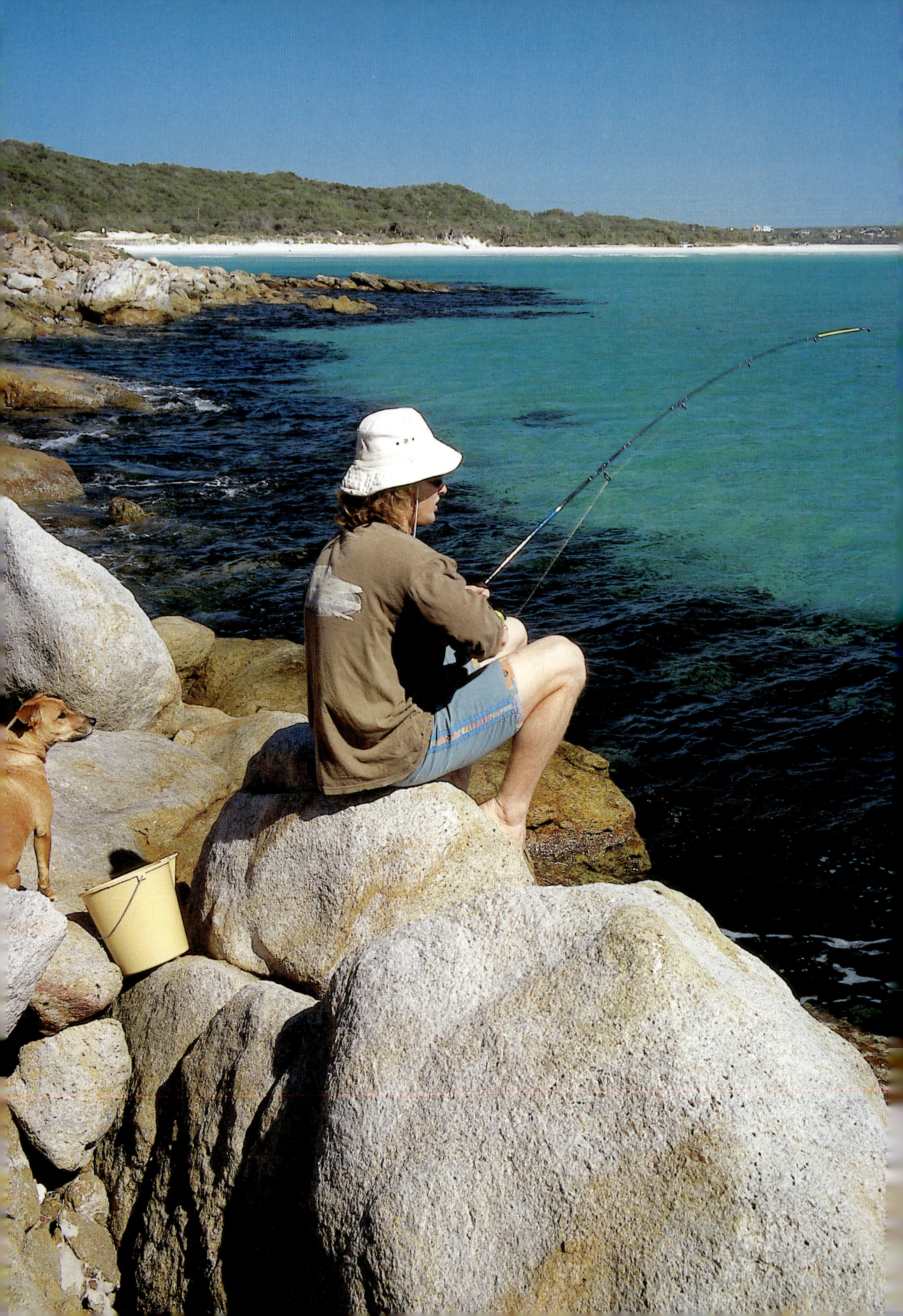

Contents

Coastal Fishing
Perth Region 300
Albany Region 308
Gascoyne–Kimberley Region 320

Inland Fishing
South-west Region 332
Kimberley Region 333

Western Australia

With 7000 kilometres of coastline, Western Australia offers an enormous breadth of fishing opportunities. There are waters as diverse as the Great Australian Bight, the deep blue Indian Ocean rolling in to the massive Zuytdorp Cliffs, cool trout streams bubbling through south-western karri forests and the tropical mangrove creeks of the Kimberley wilderness. This big State has it all.

Fishing near the mouth of the Bremer River, Bremer Bay

Along the coastline there is offshore fishing for superb bottom feeders wherever there are launching places. In the south, Westralian jewfish and pink snapper are the main fish caught, while further north members of the emperor family, coral trout and tuskfish reign supreme. The north-west has brilliant sport-fishing for fast pelagic fish such as Spanish mackerel and sailfish. Dinghy anglers in the south enjoy year-round inshore fishing for species such as tommy ruff and trevally. While Western Australia is not blessed with many estuaries, there is excellent fishing in the calm waters of Wilson, Nornalup, Leschenault and Peel Inlets and Harvey Estuary, and the lower reaches of rivers such as the Blackwood, Swan and Murchison, for black bream, tarwhine, tailor, whiting, flathead, flounder and mulloway.

For freshwater enthusiasts, trout and redfin can be caught in the overgrown streams and irrigation dams throughout the South-west. The fresh water of the Kimberley can provide exciting fishing for a variety of tropical species including barramundi, sooty grunter and catfish.

WESTERN AUSTRALIA

Coastal Fishing

The vastness of the West Australian coast presents many different challenges, not the least of which is the tyranny of distance. Anglers can fish in the comfort and safety of civilisation or be as adventurous as they like. There are exciting fishing opportunities to suit every taste, but those wanting to sample remote areas of the 'Wild West' should plan their trips with care. The nearest petrol station, food or water supply could be hours away.

State regulations

Western Australia has a wide range of fishing regulations that are designed to sustain and share the fish resources in the state. Depending on what you will be fishing for and where, it is important to understand all the rules and guidelines. There are rules regarding size and bag limits of species, boat limits, gear limits, possession limits and where you can fish as there are marine parks and sanctuary zones that also have separate rules applying to them. For up-to-date information you can visit the Fisheries Western Australia web site at www.wa.gov.au/westfish or ring (08) 9482 7333.

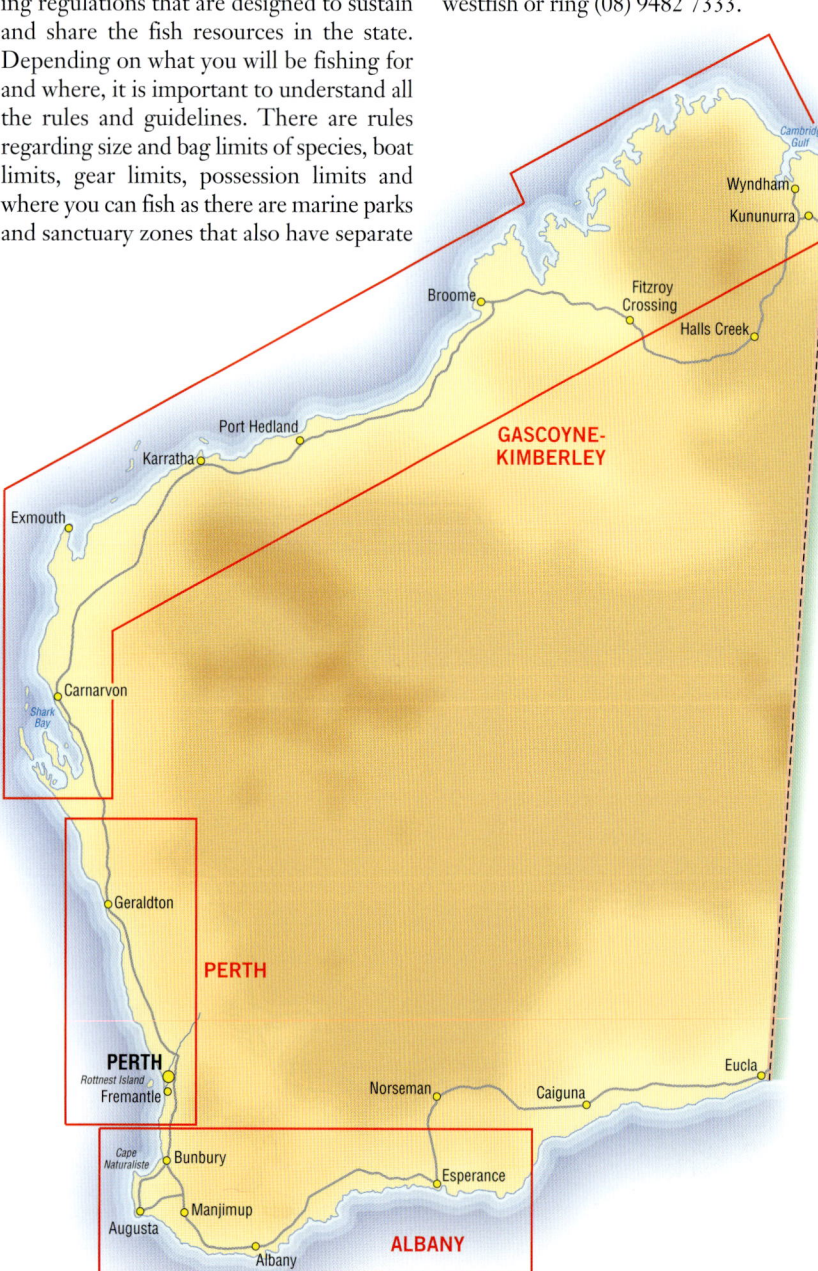

COASTAL FISHING

WHERE TO FISH
Along the coast

PERTH REGION ● 300

Perth has surf beaches to the north and south of the city, with tommy ruff, tailor and mullet; the Swan River estuary, where tailor and black bream can be found; and wonderful fishing around Rottnest Island and offshore locations reached by larger boats.

ALBANY REGION ● 308

This is a spectacular coastline, made up of sparkling white beaches, rocky headlands, quiet estuaries and inlets, and the enticing offshore islands of the Recherche Archipelago. Off Cape Naturaliste the waters are home to giant Westralian jewfish. This is a well-populated area, so facilities and services for anglers and travellers are comprehensive.

GASCOYNE–KIMBERLEY REGION ● 320

This enormous and varied region spans from Shark Bay to Cambridge Gulf, near the Northern Territory border. In between there is fishing for sailfish and Spanish mackerel from the huge cliffs of Point Quobba, sailfish around the islands of the Dampier Archipelago, barramundi, mangrove jack and catfish from the inlets and mangrove estuaries of the Kimberley.

FURTHER INFORMATION

Fishing For full details of fishing regulations and licencing in Western Australia, contact Fisheries Western Australia, 3rd floor, 168–170 St Georges Tce, Perth, tel. (08) 9482 7333, one of its 17 branch offices or see its web site at www.wa.gov.au/westfish The Department produces a number of brochures, books, magazines and videos about different aspects of fishing, which are available from any of its offices or its web site.

Boating The head office of the Maritime division of the Department of Transport is at 1 Essex St, Fremantle, tel. (08) 9216 8999. This Department has responsibility for transport, marine safety and coastal facilities. It publishes a 'Western Australian Boating Guide', and many other brochures and guides about boating safety and regulations. These are available from Department offices or its web site www.transport.wa.gov.au The Boating Industry Association can be contacted on tel. (08) 9271 9688. You will need tide charts in the north of the State, where tidal variations can be huge. The Bureau of Meteorology issues coastal forecasts several times daily. Call the Weathercall directory on 1900 926 113 for recorded information. Other sources are Weather by fax on 1800 061 436.

COASTAL FISHING

WESTERN AUSTRALIA

GUIDE TO LOCAL FISH

Code	Name	Code	Name	Code	Name
AJ	amberjack	SG	grunter, sooty	SH	shark, others
BD	barracuda	H	herring, oxeye	S	snapper, pink
BM	barramundi	MJ	jack, mangrove	QS	snapper, queen
BT	bonito	BJ	jewfish, black	S	snapper, red
B	bream, black	WJ	jewfish, Westralian	SN	snook
B	bream, yellowfin	KI	kingfish, yellowtail	SW	sweep
CF	catfish, estuary (cobbler)	LJ	leatherjacket	ES	sweetlip
CF	catfish, fork-tailed	MA	mackerel, blue	T	tailor
CO	cobia	MA	mackerel, grey	TA	tarwhine
C	cod	MA	mackerel, shark	TF	tommy ruff
C	cod, Chinaman	MA	mackerel, Spanish	TR	trevally, giant
DA	dart	MA	mackerel, spotted	TR	trevally, gold-spotted
DO	dolphin fish	ML	marlin, black	TR	trevally, golden
RE	emperor, red	ML	marlin, blue	TR	trevally, silver
ES	emperor, spangled (snapper, north-west)	M	mullet, sea	CT	trout, coral
		M	mullet, yelloweye	TP	trumpeter, yellowtail
FM	fingermark	MU	mulloway	TU	tuna, longtail
F	flathead	PI	pike	TU	tuna, southern bluefin
FL	flounder	Q	queenfish	TU	tuna, yellowfin
G	garfish	SL	sailfish	TK	tuskfish, blue
GR	groper, baldchin	SA	salmon, Australian	WH	wahoo
GR	groper, Queensland	TS	salmon, threadfin	W	whiting, King George
GR	groper, western blue	SM	samson fish	W	whiting, yellow-finned
		GS	shark, gummy		

Size and bag limits apply. Consult Fisheries WA guide, 'Fishing for the future' for details.

Protected species

There are several species that are protected in West Australian waters, and these are listed below:
- potato cod
- whale shark
- hump headed Maori wrasse
- leafy sea dragon
- great white shark
- All cods over 1200 mm in length.

If any of these species are accidentally caught they must be returned to the water as quickly as possible with little harm.

Boating regulations

No licence is required for boating in Western Australia. If you are under 17 years old, you need to obtain a Small Craft Proficiency Certificate or be accompanied by an adult. The boat must be registered with the Department of Transport. Interstate boats with current registration may operate in the State for three months before they require registration. More details are available at www.transport.wa.gov.au, including information on boating safety requirements and trip preparation.

ABORIGINAL LANDS

There are Aboriginal owned and controlled lands right throughout Western Australia, but those likely to affect the angler are concentrated along the coast north of Broome and across the Kimberley region.

Requests for access are common, particularly from anglers, and the first stop for both information and the necessary permits is the Aboriginal Lands Trust, Level 1, 197 St Georges Tce, Perth, tel. (09) 235 8000; website www.aad.wa.gov.au Permits may take between two and three weeks to process, so it is necessary to plan ahead.

There are some general rules that apply to those who wish to camp or fish on these lands. On arrival, visitors should go to the community office to advise the community members of their intentions. Requests to camp are nearly always granted, except during tribal and community events. It is important to keep to the main roads, and to camp only in designated areas. Rubbish should be removed, and the environment preserved in the state in which it was found.

Aerial view of Houtman Abrolhos Islands, the southernmost coral islands in the world

Spangled emperor

Also known as north-west snapper, this species is found in the northern half of Australia between Rottnest Island and northern New South Wales.

WESTERN AUSTRALIA

COASTAL FISHING PERTH REGION

Perth Region

Perth and Fremantle anglers have the huge estuary of the Swan River at their doorsteps. They can get out in boats or cast from jetties or points all around the river and right into the fringes of the central business district. There is wonderful surf fishing along the coastline, which really hots up when the tailor run in the summer, and the prolific tommy ruff reach their peak in autumn.

Perth and its environs have a Mediterranean-type climate that encourages an outdoor lifestyle. The Swan River winds through the city, widening to lake size at Perth and Melville Waters; and the Canning River provides an attractive waterway through the southern suburbs.

Weather

The waters around Perth are fairly protected by the offshore reefs and islands, which reduce the effect of the oceanic swells. Generally in summer there is a land breeze in the morning, followed by an afternoon sea breeze known as the Fremantle doctor. During the summer months the west coast trough may bring thunderstorms. In winter, the weather is usually influenced by low pressure systems or cold fronts, with the breeze turning north-west. The Bureau of Meteorology has recorded weather information by region. For a list of local service numbers call 1900 926 113. The bureau can be contacted on (08) 9263 2222 or visit its web site at www.bom.gov.au

Boating

The best launching areas around Perth are at Hillarys Boat Harbour, at Sorrento, which has an all-weather facility with six ramps, and at Woodman Point, which has four ramps and ample trailer parking. All boating hazards around Perth are clearly marked, as are most offshore reefs and islands. Always obtain an up-to-date chart and check the waters before you go out, or contact the Marine Operations Centre.

WHERE TO FISH

Perth Region

PERTH BEACHES ● 302

Perth is blessed with wonderful white-sand surf beaches, which fish well for tommy ruff throughout the year, tailor in spring and summer and yelloweye mullet in winter. Sand holes between the inshore reefs present great fishing for tarwhine and yellow-finned whiting in summer.

SWAN RIVER ● 304

There is good fishing in both the Swan and Canning rivers and right through to the port of Fremantle. The most common fish in the Swan estuary is tailor, although there is great black bream fishing in the lower reaches during winter and up around the Causeway in summer.

ROTTNEST ISLAND ● 305

Rottnest Island, 20 km off the coast, is wonderful for fishing as it has a series of small bays and rocky points, with many offshore reefs. It is renowned for catches of tommy ruff (Western Australian herring), and the autumn run of big Australian salmon.

GUILDERTON TO KALBARRI ● 306

This coast has some superb beach, rock and cliff fishing. Anglers are advised to carry a car topper or tow a bigger boat to make the most of the inshore reefs at places such as Jurien, Dongara, Geraldton and Port Gregory. They can try for a variety of fish from the coastal gorges around Red Bluff, south of Kalbarri.

GUIDE TO LOCAL FISH

- bonito
- bream, black
- catfish, estuary
- cod
- dolphin fish
- flathead
- flounder
- garfish
- groper, baldchin
- jewfish, Westralian
- kingfish, yellowtail
- mackerel, blue
- mackerel, shark
- mackerel, Spanish
- marlin, blue
- mullet, yelloweye
- mulloway
- pike
- salmon, Australian
- samson fish
- shark
- snapper, pink
- snapper, queen
- snapper, red
- snook
- sweetlip
- tailor
- tarwhine
- tommy ruff
- trevally, silver
- trout, coral
- tuna, southern bluefin
- tuna, yellowfin
- whiting, King George
- whiting, yellow-finned

Early morning bream fishing on the Swan River at Ashfield

COASTAL FISHING PERTH REGION

WESTERN AUSTRALIA

PERTH REGION

Jetty fishing is a popular recreation in and around the city of Perth

Westralian jewfish
Unique to West Australian waters, this fish is related to the pearl perch of eastern Australia. Found mainly in deeper coastal waters, it is much sought after for its fine table qualities.

FURTHER INFORMATION

Fishing and boating The head office of the Maritime division of the Department of Transport is at 1 Essex St, Fremantle, tel. (08) 9216 8999. Other offices are at 307 Marine Tce, Geraldton, tel. (08) 9921 3340; and Jurien Boat Harbour, Jurien, tel. (08) 9652 1323. Fisheries Western Australia has offices on the 3rd floor, 168–170 St Georges Tce, Perth, tel. (08) 9482 7333; 147 South Tce, Fremantle, tel. (08) 9335 6800; 68–75 Connell Rd, Geraldton, tel. (08) 9921 6800; and Jurien Bay Harbour Office Complex, Jurien Harbour, Jurien, tel. (08) 9682 1048.

Tourist centres Cervantes Service Station, cnr Aragon St and Seville St, Cervantes, tel. (08) 9652 7041; Dongara Library, 7 Waldeck St, Dongara, tel. (08) 9927 1404; Fremantle Visitor Information, Town Hall, Kings Square, Fremantle, tel. (08) 9431 7878; Bill Sewell Complex, Chapman Rd, Geraldton, tel. (08) 9921 3999; 102 Gingin Rd, Lancelin, tel. (08) 9655 1100; Grey St, Kalbarri, tel. (08) 9937 1104; Western Australian Tourist Centre, cnr Forrest Pl and Wellington St, Perth, tel. (08) 9483 1111; Henderson Ave, Settlement, Rottnest Island, tel. (08) 9372 9752; Information Office, Yanchep National Park, tel. (08) 9561 1004.

Perth Beaches

Type of fishing
beach, offshore, rock walls
Target fish
Australian salmon, tailor, tommy ruff, whiting

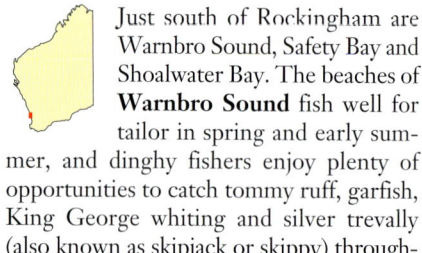

Just south of Rockingham are Warnbro Sound, Safety Bay and Shoalwater Bay. The beaches of **Warnbro Sound** fish well for tailor in spring and early summer, and dinghy fishers enjoy plenty of opportunities to catch tommy ruff, garfish, King George whiting and silver trevally (also known as skipjack or skippy) throughout the year. Big snapper enter both Warnbro Sound and **Cockburn Sound**, to the north, to spawn in spring; close-mouthed anglers who know the spots take sensational hauls of fish around 6 to 12 kg.

Rockingham, a large town situated at the southern end of Cockburn Sound, has jetties that are renowned for producing occasional big snapper, and mulloway in winter. The banks in the sound are fished for King George and sand whiting, silver trevally, mulloway, snapper and tailor.

There are many attractions for boat anglers offshore. West of Rockingham is **Coventry Reef**, best reached from boat ramps at Safety Bay. The reef is close to the surface and can be dangerous in heavy weather, when waves break over it. Good anchoring gear is essential and it is best to anchor in the mouth of the horseshoe-shaped reef. There are often big schools of Australian salmon in autumn – a worthy catch but likely to steal baits from the other targets of silver trevally, tailor, Westralian jewfish and snapper. Running north from the reef, **Five Fathom Bank** is a combination of reefs and shelves that abounds in snapper, whiting, silver trevally, Westralian jewfish, samson fish and queen snapper. The bank is some 5 km out from Garden Island and is 20 km long.

Garden Island has good reef and beach spots for land-based anglers seeking tarwhine, tailor, Australian salmon and tommy ruff. The naval base HMAS Stirling, around Careening Bay in the south-east of the island, and the Armaments Wharf in the north, are prohibited areas, although the rest of the island is open to the public. The causeway to the island also can only be used by navy personnel but the island can be reached by boat. Boat anglers fish on the ocean side of the Garden Island causeway for tommy ruff, snook, King George whiting,

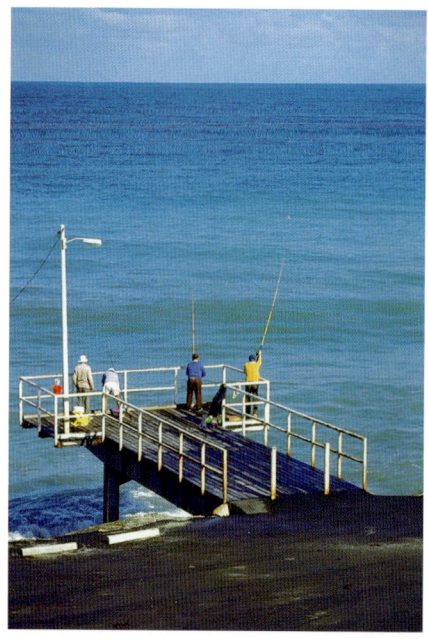

North Beach Jetty, a tommy ruff hot spot on Perth's north suburban coast

and, under the causeway, they fish for big silver trevally and tailor.

At **Woodman Point**, on the mainland north of Garden Island, the jetties and the groyne are good places to try for silver trevally, garfish, whiting and tommy ruff.

Perth beaches, shelving down into the strong surf, are seemingly ever-blessed by the brilliant Western Australian climate. There is hardly anywhere along this stretch of golden coast where you will not see an angler flinging a long cast out into the waves – often with a star sinker to counteract the turbulence. At times, especially when the tailor run is coming up the coast in spring, there will be a virtual forest of fishing rods along the foreshore.

The usual fishing times are dawn and dusk, and the fish are mainly tailor and tommy ruff, with tommy ruff at their peak during their spawning run in May. Other likely fish are silver trevally, garfish, whiting, Australian salmon and mulloway. The autumn arrival of big schools of Australian salmon, often over 5 kg each, can turn on superb spinning or baitfishing opportunities at places such as Cottesloe Groyne and Swanbourne Beach.

The main action is on the northern beaches, but **South Beach** is a handy venue for anglers in the southern suburbs and has its share of tailor, silver trevally, mulloway, tommy ruff and whiting. At **Port, Leighton and Cottesloe beaches**, the action on the beach is accompanied by the trolling activities from small boats patrolling behind the surf, usually with lures or mulie baits for tailor. At Cottesloe there is also fishing for tailor, garfish, silver trevally and tommy ruff on the reef at the end of the groyne. **Swanbourne Beach** and **Swanbourne Drain** have tailor, tommy ruff and mulloway all year round, whiting in summer, and tarwhine in winter.

Offshore, large reefs south and north of Rottnest Island fish well for Westralian jewfish, pink snapper, samson fish and big silver trevally. The west end of the island is a favourite trolling area for Spanish mackerel, yellowtail kingfish and yellowfin tuna in late summer and autumn, but care should be taken in periods of big swells. The deep waters of **Rottnest Trench**, 20 km west of the island, is productive blue marlin territory in late summer and autumn. Fish aggregating devices (FADs), installed in 100 fathoms on the edge of the trench, attract huge schools of brightly coloured dolphin fish in summer.

The groynes along the coast are focal points for shore fishing around Perth. Places such as **City Beach Groyne** produce good fishing all year round. Tailor, whiting and garfish, and the occasional mulloway, dominate catches in spring and summer, while autumn and winter are best for yelloweye mullet and the odd big tailor. Tommy ruff can be caught throughout the year.

Floreat Beach is a good night fishing spot for mulloway, with tailor, tommy ruff, whiting and small shark in summer, and **Herdsman Drain**, north of Floreat, for mulloway, tommy ruff and tailor, with whiting on summer nights and silver trevally in winter. Northwards to **Scarborough Beach** there are gutters and holes for tailor, mulloway, Australian salmon and whiting.

Trigg Point has an exposed reef and rocks that provide a fishing platform for tarwhine, tailor and silver trevally. In winter there are also big Australian salmon schools, and the inner and outer **Blue Holes**, right on the end of the point, are treacherous but famous for big salmon and tailor. North of Trigg Point there are reef holes that fish well at times for tommy ruff, whiting and tarwhine.

The various marinas along the coast of northern Perth offer shore-based anglers an alternative to the groynes for much the same results. **Hillarys Boat Harbour** and **Ocean Reef Marina** can be fished throughout the year for tommy ruff, with tailor, whiting, garfish and mulloway in the warmer months and yelloweye mullet at other times.

Opposite Hillarys Boat Harbour and running some 20 km north from Marmion Beach to Burns Beach are a series of small

COASTAL FISHING PERTH REGION

WESTERN AUSTRALIA

GUIDE TO LOCAL FISH

C	cod
G	garfish
GR	groper, baldchin
WJ	jewfish, Westralian
KI	kingfish, yellowtail
MA	mackerel
M	mullet
MU	mulloway
PI	pike
SA	salmon, Australian
SM	samson fish
SH	shark
S	snapper
QS	snapper, queen
SN	snook
T	tailor
TA	tarwhine
TF	tommy ruff
TR	trevally
TU	tuna
W	whiting

reefs called the **Marmion Reefs**, that are sometimes visible at low tide and often close to the surface. Again caution is required, but the fishing is terrific. The reefs are popular with small boat anglers, particularly where they are visible between Trigg Point and Burns Beach. The fishing is widely varied, with schools of yellow-finned whiting over the clean sand around the reefs and large numbers of tommy ruff and garfish. Silver trevally, tailor, snapper, samson fish, Westralian jewfish, Australian salmon and mackerel are all around these reef areas at various times of the year. There are plenty of launching ramps along the coast, with the main launching area being Hillarys Boat Harbour.

Further north, **Mindarie Keys** provide a platform for shore-based fishing as well as a place to launch to explore the offshore reefs. Fishing from the walls of the marina here rewards with the same species as at the boat harbours to the south – tailor, whiting, tommy ruff, mulloway, garfish and yellow-eye mullet.

Yanchep Beach has good year-round fishing. There is baitfishing for silver trevally, Australian salmon and tailor off the reef, and sinker fishing for mulloway, tailor and shark off the beach. At **The Spot**, between Yanchep and Two Rocks, the fishing is for big winter tailor and mulloway.

About 30 km off the coast and running west of Perth is **Direction Bank**, an important fishing area for the same wide variety of species as those on the Marmion Reefs.

303

WESTERN AUSTRALIA

COASTAL FISHING PERTH REGION

Swan River

Type of fishing
estuary, river

Target fish
black bream, flathead, flounder, mulloway, tailor

Spring and summer are the best times for boat fishing in the **Swan and Canning rivers**, when large schools of tailor roam the lower reaches as far up as the old brewery site and Canning Bridge. Trolling small lures is a great early morning and late afternoon pastime for surprisingly large fish early in the season, but the size usually drops dramatically in late summer. The best areas for trolling are along Blackwall Reach, in Freshwater Bay, close to shore near Applecross, Como and into the Canning River. Casting from shore with lightly weighted baits around Mosman Bay and Freshwater Bay can also be successful, particularly in the evening, but the fish will be smaller.

At the **Fremantle moles**, there is good fishing throughout the year, with tailor, whiting, garfish and mulloway in spring and summer, and in the colder months yellow-eye mullet and some tailor, with tommy ruff at all times. At **North Mole** it is also possible to spin or baitfish for big Australian salmon in autumn.

Large mulloway to 20 kg move into the deep water of **Blackwall Reach** and **Mosman Bay** each spring, and smaller fish to 6 kg run well upstream as far as Maylands, north-east of the city centre. Flathead, and to a lesser extent flounder, can be found in reasonable numbers along the channel edges of **Rocky Bay**, Mosman Bay and **Freshwater Bay**, with some flathead as far up as Maylands in mid-summer.

The river system is an excellent black bream fishery, with the fish spread right up as far as Caversham, in the Swan Valley, during summer but congregated around jetty piles downstream of the Causeway in winter. Fisheries Western Australia has introduced specific bag limits for black bream in the Swan and Canning rivers and their tributaries to protect fish stocks. The daily bag limits for black bream has been reduced from 20 to eight in the Swan and Canning rivers and their tributaries and the minimum legal length is 25 cm. For all other state waters, the daily bag limit remains at 20. Bloodworms, which can only be dug in designated sites on the foreshore, make first-class bait for bream and estuary catfish (cobbler), as do river prawns, which are usually gathered in drag nets over the muddy shallows on warm summer nights.

Southern blue-spotted flathead
This species resembles the dusky flathead in appearance. It is mostly caught by boat anglers, but land-based anglers can cast baits into bankside channels and weed beds in southern estuaries.

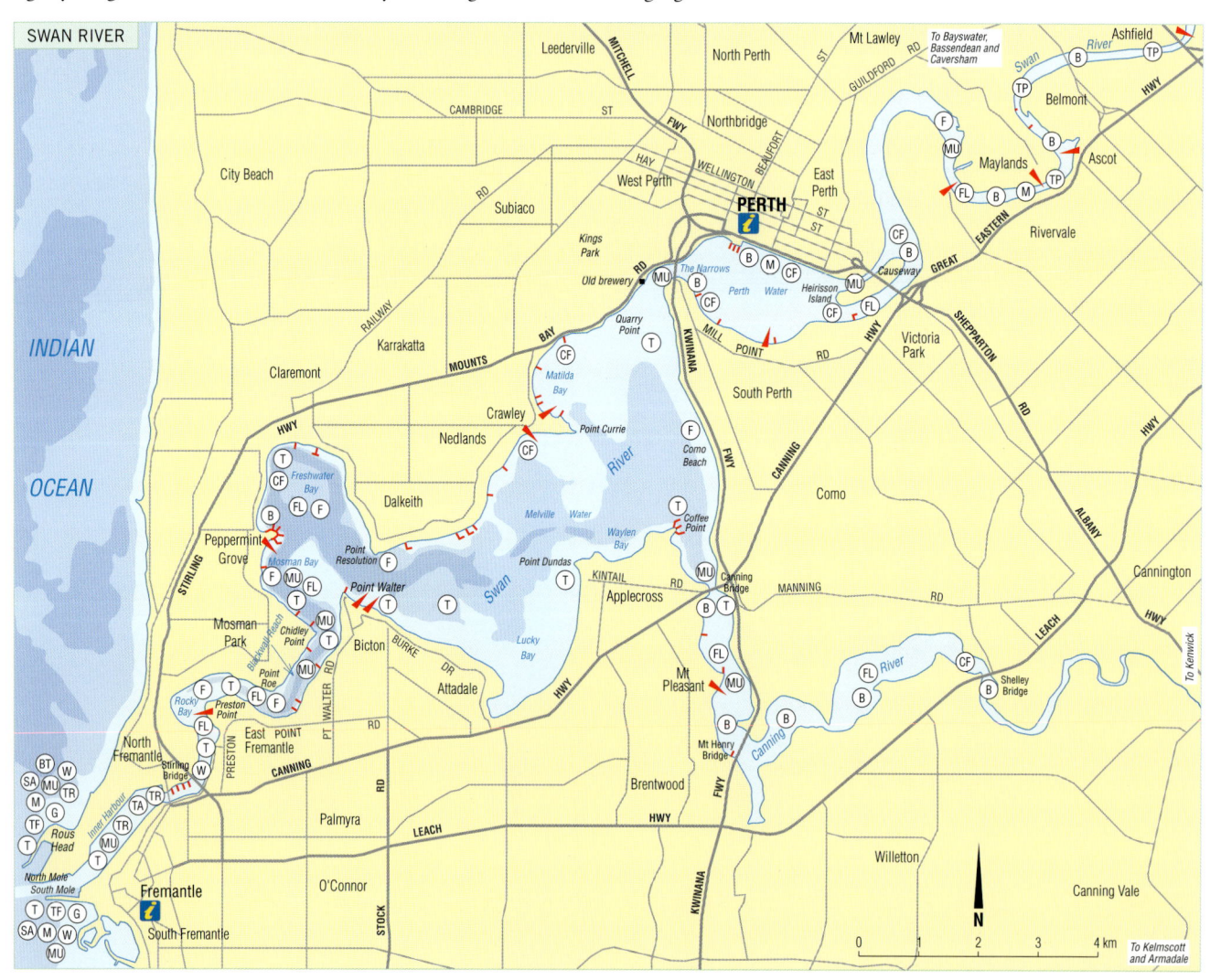

COASTAL FISHING PERTH REGION   WESTERN AUSTRALIA

Rottnest Island

Type of fishing
beach, reef, rock
Target fish
Australian salmon, tailor, silver trevally, tommy ruff, whiting

Rottnest Island, lying 20 km north-west of Fremantle, is a popular holiday destination. There are daily ferries from both Perth and Fremantle, and a variety of accommodation, including camping and resort facilities. The island is a public reserve – cars are not permitted and public transport is minimal, so most visitors either take their own bicycle or hire one there. The coastline of this low, sandy island is dotted with small bays and white beaches that are best explored by boat.

The clear waters around **Rottnest Island** are famous for their large numbers of tommy ruff, which reach their peak after spawning in late April and May. Berleying from the rocks almost anywhere around the island will usually attract plenty of these fish in short order at this time of year. King George and yellow-finned whiting, tarwhine, silver trevally and even the occasional mulloway haunt the sandy holes among the fringing reefs, and patches of white water over reefs are worth trying for tailor. **Natural Jetty**, **Salmon Bay** and **Armstrong Point** are among the most productive spots for mixed bags of fish, but the choice of fishing destination is often influenced by wind direction.

Boats anchored in Eagle Bay, at the north-west tip of Rottnest Island

Autumn is an exciting time at Rottnest, when the schools of Australian salmon arrive and hole up around the reefs of Salmon Bay, **West End** and **Ricey Beach**. Best fishing times for the salmon are usually dawn or dusk, and the big, powerful fish provide plenty of excitement on baitcast mulies (pilchards) and spinning, using both surface poppers and heavier chrome slice lures. In recent years there has been growing interest in the use of saltwater fly fishing tackle for the salmon. Fly fishers are also working flies for other species such as tommy ruff, tailor and trevally.

GUIDE TO LOCAL FISH

		Swan River	Rottnest Island
BT	bonito		●
B	bream	●	
CF	catfish, estuary	●	
F	flathead	●	
FL	flounder	●	
G	garfish	●	●
KI	kingfish, yellowtail		●
M	mullet	●	
MU	mulloway	●	●
SA	salmon, Australian	●	●
SM	samson fish		●
T	tailor	●	●
TA	tarwhine	●	●
TF	tommy ruff	●	●
TR	trevally	●	●
W	whiting	●	●

Radar Reef, on the south of West End, can be tremendous for fishing in periods of low swell. Australian salmon, tackle-busting yellowtail kingfish and even samson fish are regularly taken from the reef, and tailor occasionally, but few of the bigger specimens are landed in this rough terrain. Also towards the western end of the island, Fish Hook Bay and Eagle Bay both offer protected fishing in most winds. **Fish Hook Bay** is a consistent tommy ruff spot and good for Australian salmon in the season, while **Eagle Bay** provides tommy ruff and silver trevally. West of Eagle Bay are the **Cathedral Rocks**, and both the channel to the west and the pool east of the rocks can be great for Australian salmon at times.

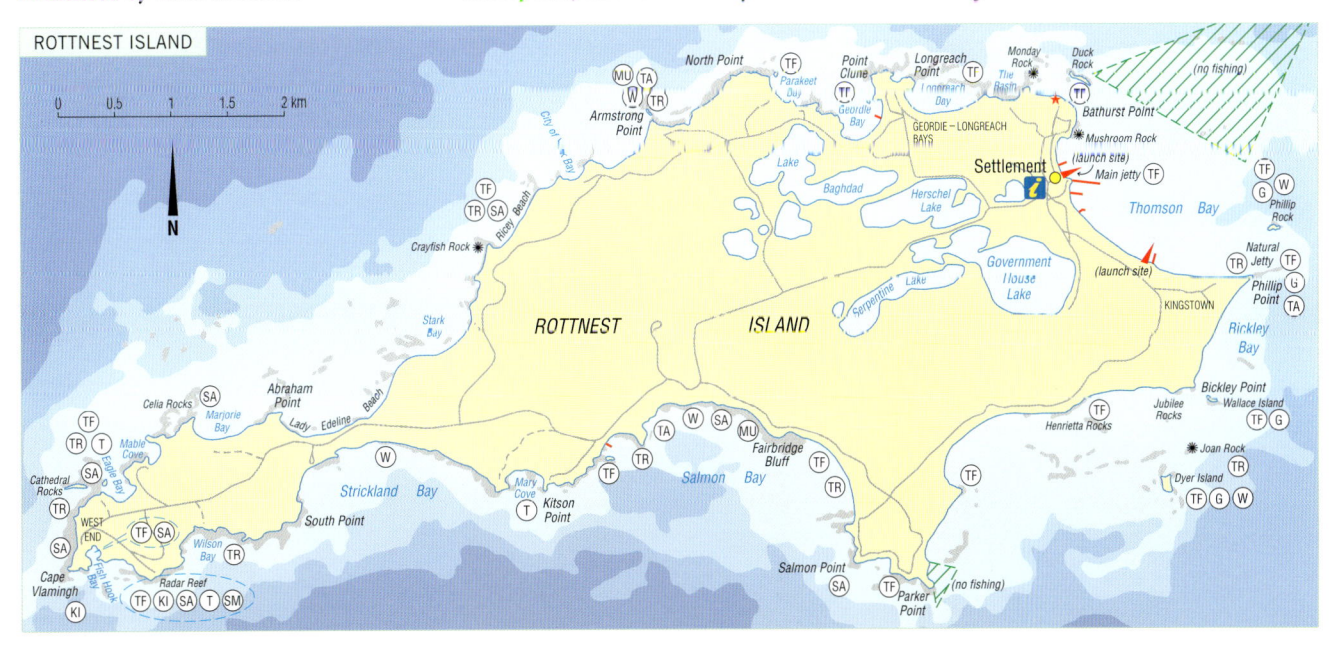

WESTERN AUSTRALIA — COASTAL FISHING PERTH REGION

Guilderton to Kalbarri

Type of fishing
beach, jetty, offshore, reef, river

Target fish
mulloway, silver trevally, tailor, Westralian jewfish

Road conditions in this area are good, and there are ample caravan parks and facilities, with the bonus that free camping is legal if it is outside a 16-km radius of a recognised camping ground. The fishing around the inshore reefs is very exciting, with snapper and Westralian jewfish the centre of attention. South of Kalbarri, anglers can fish from the coastal gorges for a variety of fish.

GUILDERTON TO KALBARRI

The first substantial stop north of Perth is **Guilderton**, at the mouth of the **Moore River**. Large numbers of smallish black bream and a few larger ones are spread throughout the river. The beach between the mouth and the groyne fishes well for tailor, tommy ruff, whiting and mulloway. North of the groyne is **Three Mile Reef**, a great early morning tailor spot. There is limited beach launching next to the groyne.

Further up the road at **Ledge Point** there is good tailor and mulloway fishing all year round, and jetty fishing for garfish, silver trevally and tommy ruff.

Lancelin is worth a visit for beach fishing for tailor, mulloway and shark, jetty fishing for tailor at night, and offshore fishing for silver trevally, mulloway, samson fish, Westralian jewfish and snapper.

From Lancelin it is a rough four-wheel drive to **Wedge Island**, the name of both a settlement on the mainland and a small island just offshore that can be reached with a boat launched off the sand. The fishing around the island for snapper, Westralian jewfish and mackerel, with silver trevally and tommy ruff on the surface, makes the trip well worthwhile. Beach fishing between Lancelin and **Cervantes** should bring catches of tailor and mulloway, but not all the beaches are easy to reach.

The jetties and the marina at **Jurien** are fished for silver trevally, tommy ruff, whiting and tailor, with samson fish and shark at night. There is beach fishing for tailor, mulloway and small shark on either side of the town, and at a good rock spot at **North Head**, 17 km to the north. The excellent boating facilities make Jurien a great launching point for offshore fishing. There is a line of reefs about 3 km offshore – an easy run for snapper, Spanish mackerel, silver trevally, baldchin groper and Westralian jewfish – and the wide grounds from 15 to 30 km out are alive with samson fish, Westralian jewfish, snapper, yellowfin tuna and the occasional cruising marlin.

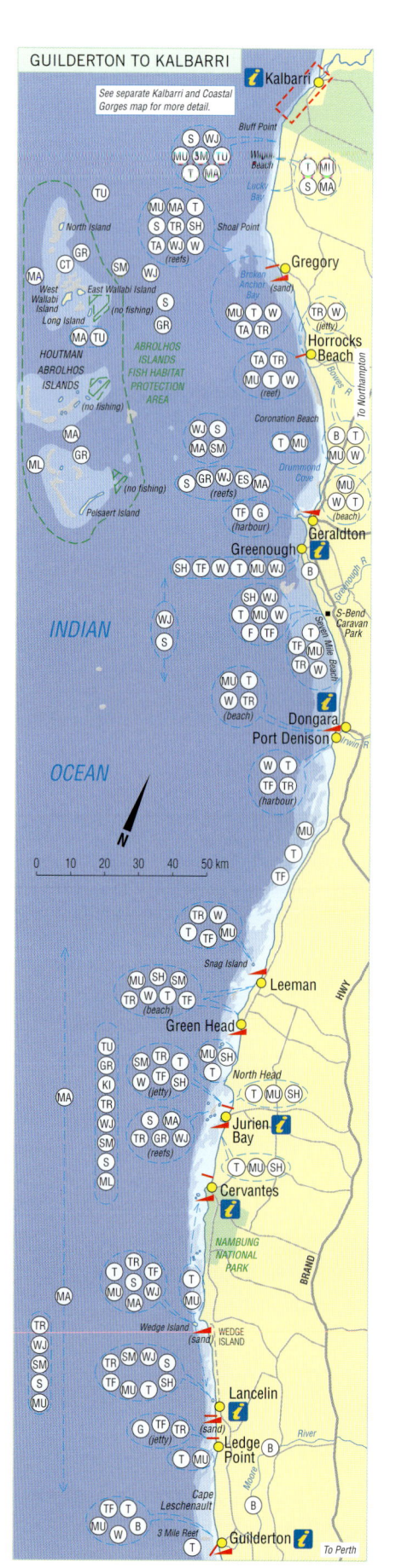

Fishing from the beach at Kalbarri can yield mulloway and tailor

COASTAL FISHING PERTH REGION — WESTERN AUSTRALIA

Green Head and **Leeman** have similar beach fishing, with **Snag Island** a nearby hot spot for silver trevally, whiting, tailor, tommy ruff and mulloway.

Further up the coast, the twin towns of **Port Denison** and **Dongara** are lobster fishing centres, and Port Denison has a sheltered harbour where whiting, tailor, tommy ruff and silver trevally can be caught. There is beach fishing just outside the entrance to the Irwin River for tailor, whiting and mulloway. To the north, **Seven Mile Beach** is a great rock spot for the same species. There are good boating facilities at these towns, and offshore reefs.

The coast behind S-Bend Caravan Park, south of the tiny historic settlement of **Greenough**, offers brilliant fishing almost all year round for big tailor, mulloway to 25 kg, whiting and shark. This is one of the few areas along the coast where Westralian jewfish to 15 kg are regularly taken from the shore. The **Greenough River** is fished for bream, with excellent tailor and mulloway fishing on the points outside the mouth.

Geraldton offers a wide variety of angling opportunities, from dinghy fishing in the harbour for tommy ruff and garfish, to beach fishing for tailor, mulloway and whiting. Inshore reefs and coral patches are renowned for turning up excellent catches of pink snapper, baldchin groper, Westralian jewfish, sweetlip and mackerel. Both **Drummond Cove** and **Coronation Beach**, to the north, produce good fishing for tailor and mulloway.

Offshore 50 km from Geraldton and Gregory lie the **Houtman Abrolhos Islands**. Spanish mackerel and yellowfin tuna are the main surface fish attractions for those with boats large enough to make the trip out, while Westralian jewfish, baldchin groper and coral trout are the best of the reef fish around the islands. As they are part of a reserve, tourists, including anglers, are not permitted to land on the islands, but this is a popular destination for several charter boats operating out of Geraldton.

Horrocks, 70 km north of Geraldton, has a small jetty for handline fishing for silver trevally and whiting – ideal for children – and a beach protected by a reef, which enables boats to be launched. The offshore reefs have good fishing for silver trevally, tarwhine, tailor, mulloway and whiting. A four-wheel-drive track takes you to the mouth of the **Bowes River**, where bream, tailor, mulloway and whiting can be found.

The tiny town of **Gregory** also has beach launching because a reef protects the shore and the jetty. The fishing inside the reef is for mulloway, tailor, silver trevally, whiting and tarwhine, while offshore fishing over reefs targets bottom-feeding species like Westralian jewfish and snapper. **Lucky Bay** and **Wagoe Beach** to the north are consistent tailor and mulloway spots, with great opportunities for snapper and mackerel from the shore in periods of low swell.

KALBARRI AND COASTAL GORGES

Kalbarri is a fishing town with a commercial fleet that brings in catches of rock lobster. For the recreational angler there are fishing possibilities in the Murchison River, from the beach, offshore or from the coastal gorges between Wagoe Beach and Red Bluff, for snapper, Westralian jewfish, mulloway, samson fish, tuna, tailor and Spanish mackerel.

Beyond Red Bluff to the south are the gorges, with exciting fishing for pink snapper and tailor at places like **Shell House**, **Goat Gulch**, **Eagle Gorge**, **Pot Alley Gorge** and **Mushroom Rock**. But a calm day is essential. **Wittecarra Creek** near Red Bluff is favoured by the locals, and some of the biggest tailor caught in the area come from the **Blue Holes**, just south of Kalbarri.

The **Murchison River** has fine bream and mulloway possibilities, with a four-wheel-drive track leading upstream to some good bank locations for bream fishing. The sand spit near the river mouth is a pleasant spot for whiting and tailor fishing, and **Chinaman Rock** on the southern side of the mouth will produce bigger tailor. Fishing off the beach will snare an occasional shark among the mulloway and tailor. **Oyster Reef**, north of the river mouth, and **Frustration Reef**, further north, are notable shore-based spots for tailor and large mulloway.

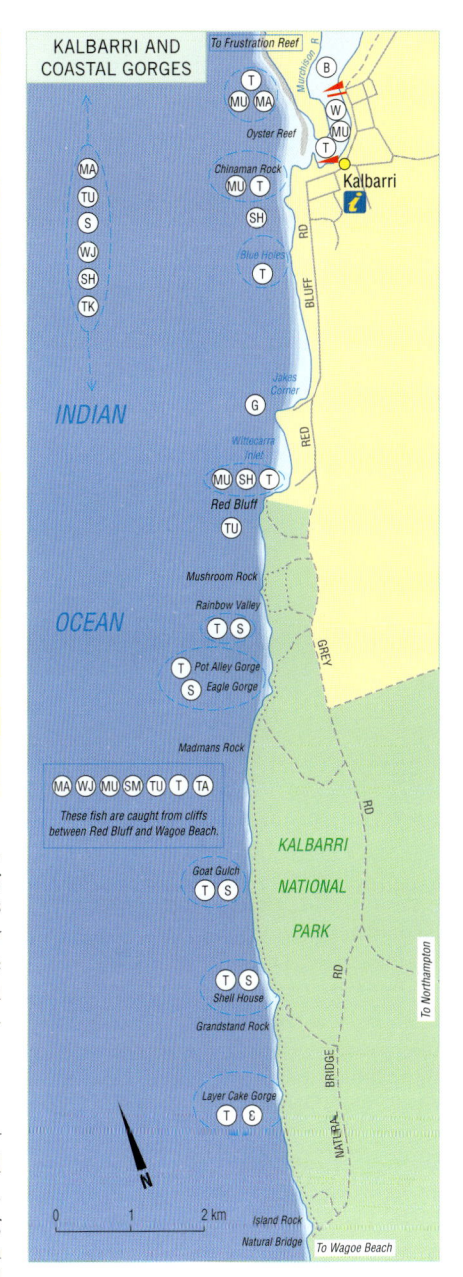

A boat ramp inside the mouth of the Murchison River allows easy launching for **offshore** anglers, but care must be taken in negotiating the entrance. Trolling for yellowfin tuna and mackerel is usually productive from Christmas to May, and there are many reefs for bottom fishing for Westralian jewfish, snapper and baldchin groper.

GUIDE TO LOCAL FISH

		Guilderton to Kalbarri	Kalbarri and Coastal Gorges
B	bream	●	●
F	flathead	●	
G	garfish	●	●
GR	groper, baldchin	●	●
WJ	jewfish, Westralian	●	●
KI	kingfish, yellowtail	●	
MA	mackerel	●	●
ML	marlin	●	
MU	mulloway	●	●
SM	samson fish	●	●
SH	shark	●	●
S	snapper	●	●
ES	sweetlip	●	
T	tailor	●	●
TA	tarwhine	●	●
TF	tommy ruff	●	
TR	trevally	●	●
CT	trout, coral	●	
TU	tuna	●	●
W	whiting	●	●

WESTERN AUSTRALIA

COASTAL FISHING ALBANY REGION

Albany Region

The sparkling clarity of the waters along the south coast of Western Australia means that anglers can see into many of the gutters and channels along the surf beaches, and the weed beds or rocky bottoms. They can sometimes even see the fish – mostly the tommy ruff, known locally as herring, that can be caught from beach and jetty, the Australian salmon and silver trevally that come close to the beaches, and the flathead, garfish and whiting that can be found close inshore.

The towering cliffs along the coastline of the Great Australian Bight finally drop back to ground level at Israelite Bay. This is the first genuine fishing location on a coast that boasts endless stark white surf beaches, spectacular rocky headlands, beautiful calm bays, estuaries and offshore islands – in short, something for everyone. Massive migrations of Australian salmon bring the shore fishing to life each year right along this coast, while Esperance is the home of the largest silver trevally (also known locally as skipjack) in Australia.

Offshore anglers can delight in catching striking red snapper, huge samson fish and queen snapper throughout the Recherche Archipelago. They can hook wily bream, King George whiting and flathead in the quiet waters of Nornalup Inlet or hunt the greatest prize of all, big Westralian jewfish, offshore from the rugged corner of Cape Naturaliste.

Weather

Weather patterns along the south coast of Western Australia are generally similar to those in coastal Victoria. During summer it experiences generally east to north-east winds, followed by fresh south-east breezes. In winter, the prevailing winds are north-east, with south-west changes that can be savage. Summer sea conditions can range from flat to a 2-m swell, and in winter the swells can reach 6 m. The best weather conditions for

WHERE TO FISH

Albany Region

ISRAELITE BAY TO MUNGLINUP BEACH ● 310

This starkly scenic stretch of coast takes in dozens of magnificent fishing spots. Huge silver trevally, large sharks, occasional giant tailor and hordes of Australian salmon draw beach anglers from afar. Boat fishing off Esperance ranges from King George whiting and tommy ruff in the bay to big samson fish offshore around the islands.

HOPETOUN TO TORBAY HEAD ● 312

Beautiful coastal scenery, including the spectacular harbours and sound at Albany, combines with brilliant fishing to make this a favourite area for anglers. Australian salmon, silver trevally, tommy ruff and shark run along most of this coast, and the sheltered waters around Albany are famous for prolific numbers of King George whiting and occasional visits by huge yellowfin tuna.

DENMARK TO POINT NUYTS ● 314

This is a beautiful coast for both shore and small boat fishing. Wilson Inlet and Nornalup Inlet provide wonderful light tackle opportunities for a range of quality small species, while the beaches are renowned for tommy ruff, Australian salmon, mulloway, tarwhine (silver bream) and King George whiting.

AUGUSTA TO CAPE NATURALISTE ● 316

Big seas and dangerous rocks are hallmarks of this coastline, but so too are great catches of large fish from the rocks and top-class offshore fishing for huge Westralian jewfish, snapper and silver trevally. Tremendous Australian salmon fishing can be had around Cape Naturaliste in late summer and spring, while the lower reaches of the estuary at Augusta are ever-reliable for yellow-finned whiting and tommy ruff.

BUNBURY AND MANDURAH ● 318

The most important land-based fishing platform in this area is the new Dawesville Channel, south of Mandurah, which can turn on exciting fishing for a range of species. The long white beaches between Bunbury and Mandurah are favourites with four-wheel-drive owners who like to get away from it all and catch tailor, tommy ruff, tarwhine and mulloway. Both the main towns have estuaries teeming with fish.

GUIDE TO LOCAL FISH

- bream, black
- catfish, estuary
- flathead, long-spined
- flathead, southern blue-spotted
- flounder, small-toothed
- garfish
- groper, western blue
- jewfish, Westralian
- kingfish, yellowtail
- leatherjacket
- mullet, yelloweye
- mulloway
- pike
- salmon, Australian
- samson fish
- shark, gummy
- shark, others
- snapper, pink
- snapper, queen
- snapper, red
- snook
- sweep
- tailor
- tarwhine
- tommy ruff
- trevally, silver
- trevally, others
- tuna, yellowfin
- whiting, King George
- whiting, yellow-finned

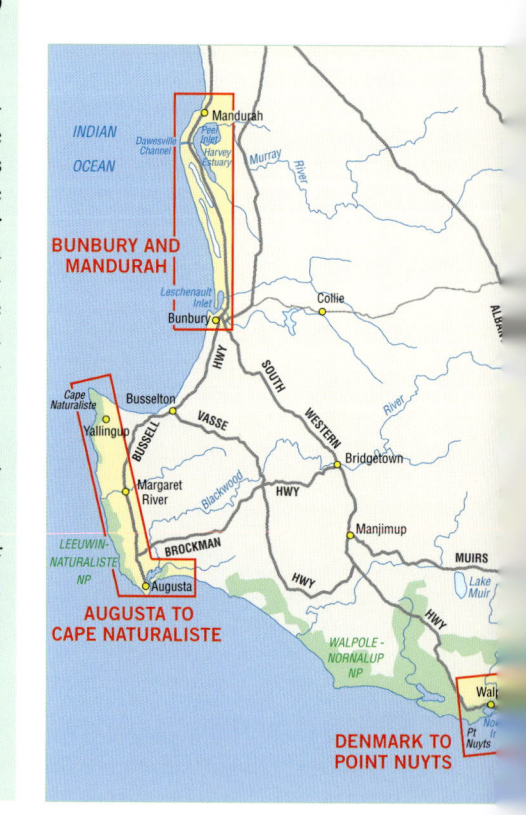

COASTAL FISHING ALBANY REGION

WESTERN AUSTRALIA

A typical remote south coast beach and a beautiful place to catch Australian salmon

boating are in the late summer and autumn months of February to April and sometimes May. For weather forecasts and information, ring the Weather Bureau on (08) 9263 2222.

Boating

There are many sheltered bays around Albany and Esperance that provide good conditions for recreational boating. Oyster Harbour has at present the best launching facilities, although at the time of writing new facilities are being built at Princess Royal Harbour, which will provide first-class boat ramps. Good launching facilities are also available at Bandy Creek, Esperance and Frenchman Bay. Otherwise along the coastline launching is mainly over the beach, with occasional shallow reefs. Around Esperance there are many offshore islands and semi-submerged reefs to beware of. Gain some local knowledge before you set out and refer to charts. For full details, contact your local marine officer.

FURTHER INFORMATION

Boating and fishing The Department of Transport has offices at Suite 1, Foreshore House, Proudlove Pde, Albany, tel. (08) 9841 3200; 11 Forrest Ave, Bunbury, tel. (08) 9791 1625; and 53 The Esplanade, Esperance, tel. (08) 9093 4814. Fisheries Western Australia has offices at 96 Stirling St, Bunbury, tel. (08) 9721 2688; 48 Bussell Hwy, Busselton, tel. (08) 9752 2152; Bandy Creek Boat Harbour, Esperance, tel. (08) 9071 1839; and 15 Leslie St, Mandurah, tel. (08) 9535 1240.

Tourist centres Old Railway Station, Proudlove Pde, Albany, tel. (08) 9841 1088; 70 Blackwood Ave, Augusta, tel. (08) 9758 0166; Bremer Bay Roadhouse, Gnombup Tce, Bremer Bay, tel. (08) 9837 4093; Old Railway Station, Carmody Pl, Bunbury, tel. (08) 9721 7922; Strickland St, Denmark, tel. (08) 9848 2055; Seymour Blvd, Dunsborough, tel. (08) 9755 3299; Museum Village, Dempster St, Esperance, tel. (08) 9071 2330; Hopetoun Tourist Information Centre, Chatterbox Crafts, Veal St, Hopetoun, tel. (08) 9838 3100; 75 Mandurah Tce, Mandurah, tel. (08) 9550 3999; Cnr Tunbridge Rd and Bussell Hwy, Margaret River, tel. (08) 9757 2911; Pioneer Cottages, Pioneer Park, Walpole, tel. (08) 9840 1111.

FISHING TIP

Casting into the wind can be difficult to master. Ideally you should keep your casting trajectory low. Another trick is to cast directly into the wind, rather than at an angle. This avoids a belly in the line and your lure or bait will travel further and more accurately.

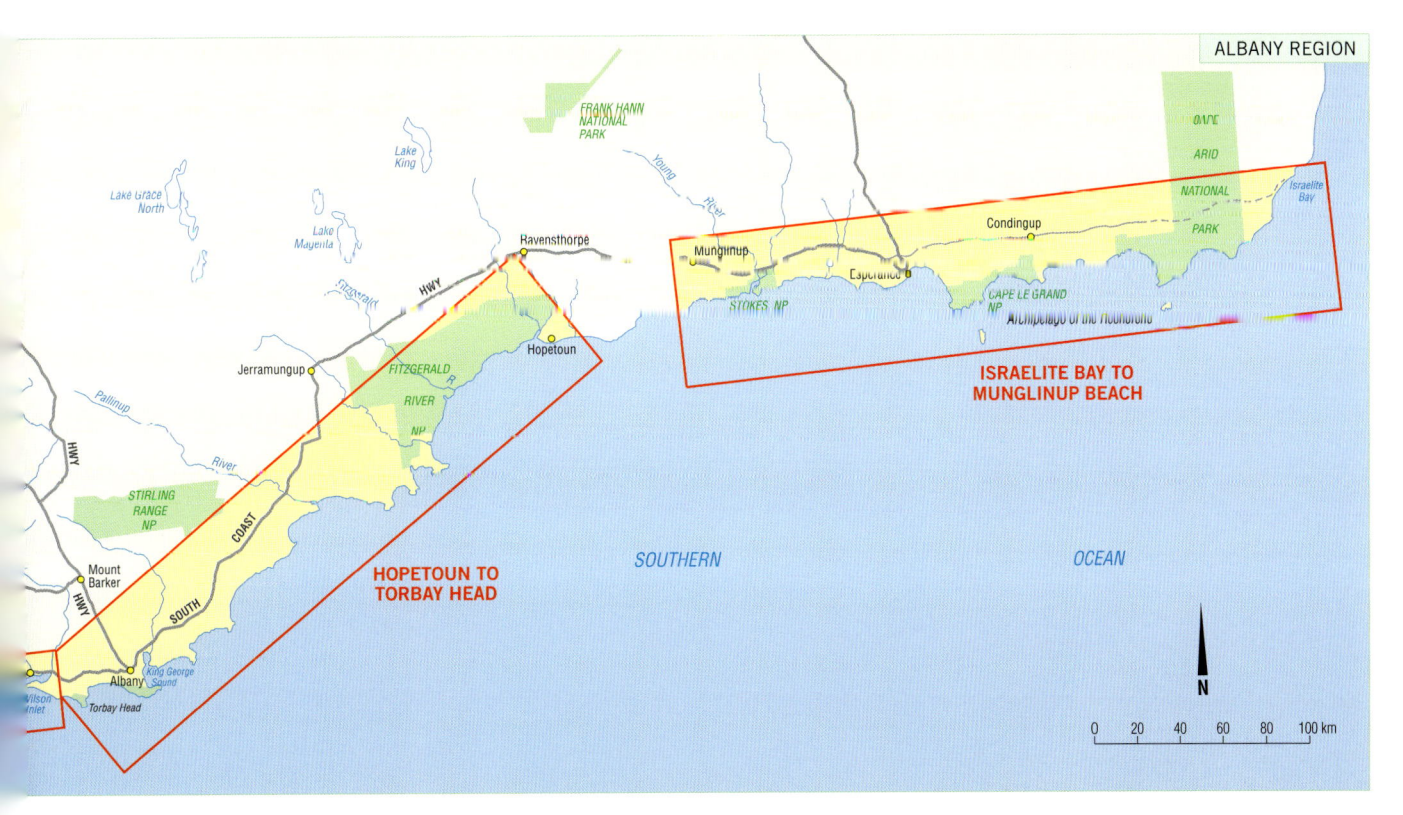

WESTERN AUSTRALIA　　　　　　　　COASTAL FISHING ALBANY REGION

Israelite Bay to Munglinup Beach

Type of fishing
beach, boat, offshore, rock
Target fish
Australian salmon, mulloway, queen snapper, red snapper, silver trevally

The spectacular and remote coast east of Esperance offers magnificent beach and rock fishing with four-wheel-drive access for most of the year, although some tracks are impassable in winter and it pays to check in Esperance before heading off to fish the area.

Poison Creek, between Cape Pasley and Cape Arid, is regarded as the most consistent Australian salmon spot on the whole coast, with the added bonus of plenty of mulloway and occasional big sharks. **Thomas River, Tagon Point, Kennedys Beach** and **Alexander Bay** are all great places for huge silver trevally, sometimes exceeding 5 kg; there are also Australian salmon, mulloway, shark and tommy ruff.

Duke of Orleans Bay is the most popular location east of Esperance, and one of the most beautiful bays along the coast. A large, well-appointed caravan park is close to the beach and anglers have a choice of boat fishing (launching off the beach), rock fishing or fishing from either the bay beaches or **Wharton Beach**, a little further west, where the great Australian salmon fishing attracts many anglers.

Lucky Bay is a prime location a little closer to Esperance and has a caravan park near the beach and easy beach launching. Beach and rock fishing are close by, with silver trevally, Australian salmon, tommy ruff, shark, tailor and mulloway off the beaches, and western blue groper, snapper, samson fish and silver trevally off the rocks.

Rock fishing comes to the fore at the magnificent **Cape Le Grand**, and there is protection on the lee sides of the high granite rocks, depending on the wind direction. **Le Grand Beach** has white sand that is firm enough for boat launching, so boat anglers can get out to the whiting patches and also target Westralian jewfish and snapper on the offshore reefs. There is easy access and camping. **Stockyard Creek**, 20 km along the beach east of Esperance, fishes well for gummy shark, Australian salmon, flathead and whiting. **Esperance**, the first sizeable town on this south-western coast, offers a marvellous combination of fishing. There is a succession of long white beaches, sandy coves and granite rock areas, with brilliant blue offshore waters, inviting exploration by boat anglers. There are plenty of launching, bait and tackle and charter boat facilities, and no end of advice from the locals, who seem to regard fishing as being as natural as breathing. At Esperance the beach barbecue is easy – you take everything to the beach, start the barbecue and then wander into the shallows and catch the fish! **Bandy Creek Boat Harbour**, at the eastern end of the township, often fishes well for King George whiting and bream, and the **Tanker Jetty**, just north of the town centre, is a popular spot for tommy ruff and squid. Charter boats operating from here take anglers out among the myriad islands of the **Recherche Archipelago** to catch big samson fish, queen snapper and red snapper.

Fishing for sand whiting

FISHING TIP

If you are missing bites, try letting the fish mouth the bait a little longer. If that doesn't work, drop back in hook size. Sometimes, rather than trying to hook a fish, it is better to let them hook themselves – so set your reel in gear on a light drag.

Silver trevally
Also known as skipjack trevally in Western Australia, the silver trevally inhabits the coastal waters of the southern half of Australia. It is generally found near reefs, often in schools, and you can anchor or drift over them, dropping baits or lures to catch fish up to 5 kg.

GUIDE TO LOCAL FISH

B	bream
F	flathead
GR	groper
WJ	jewfish, Westralian
MU	mulloway
SA	salmon, Australian
SM	samson fish
GS	shark, gummy
SH	shark, others
S	snapper
QS	snapper, queen
SN	snook
T	tailor
TF	tommy ruff
TR	trevally
TU	tuna
W	whiting

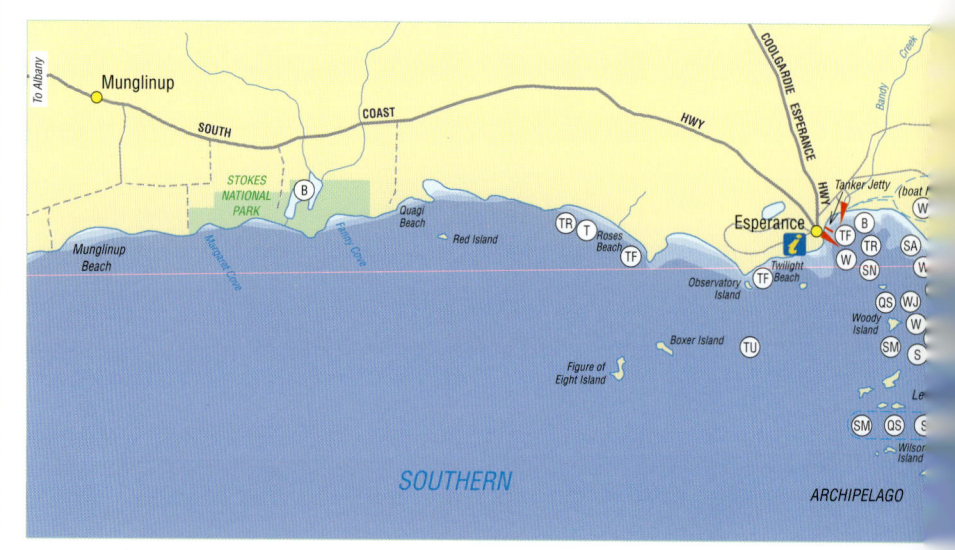

COASTAL FISHING ALBANY REGION

WESTERN AUSTRALIA

The spectacular and remote coast east of Esperance offers magnificent beach and rock fishing

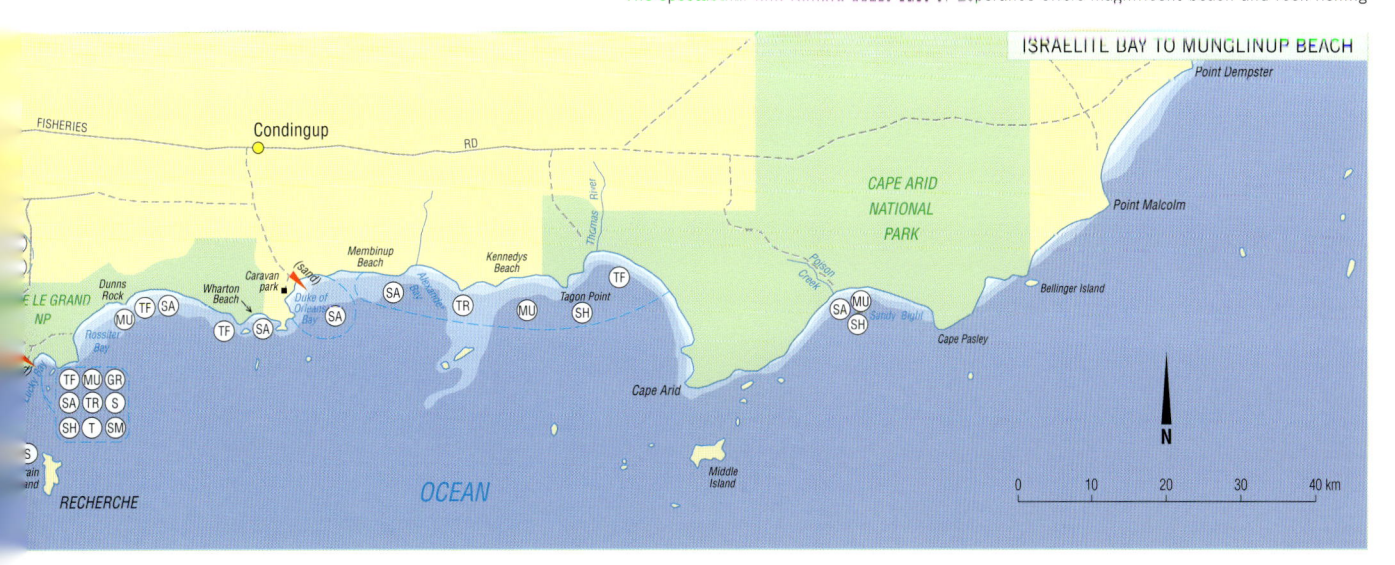

ISRAELITE BAY TO MUNGLINUP BEACH

WESTERN AUSTRALIA
COASTAL FISHING ALBANY REGION

Hopetoun to Torbay Head

Type of fishing
beach, estuary, offshore, river, rock

Target fish
Australian salmon, King George whiting, samson fish, silver trevally, tommy ruff

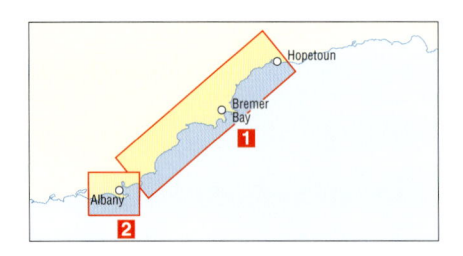

Two Peoples Bay has beach and rock fishing for a wide variety of species

This is a beautiful coast, with clear, blue water and a fascinating series of beaches, bays, inlets, rocky points and offshore islands. The national parks in the area can provide an added and relaxing interlude. The towns offer the angler good facilities, and the road network means that access to many top fishing spots is easy.

HOPETOUN TO CAPE VANCOUVER

Hopetoun is a tiny town that once flourished as a port for the inland goldfields. It has a substantial jetty and breakwater on the lovely **Mary Ann Haven**, which is fished for tommy ruff, garfish, whiting and silver trevally. The protected and beautifully white beaches in this area invite light tackle fishing for garfish, tommy ruff and Australian salmon. Five km west of the town there is a rough track that leads to good rock locations.

Several coastal rivers – the **Hamersley, Fitzgerald, Gairdner and Bremer** – are great fishing spots for black bream. A little north of the town of Bremer Bay there is a road to **Point Hood**, where there are beach and rock locations opposite the Doubtful Islands. A good road continues to the settlement of **Bremer Bay**, and there are tracks to the river and beach areas, where silver trevally, tommy ruff, whiting, Australian salmon and queen snapper can be sought. A 3-km track south of the town leads to **Point Gordon**, where big leatherjacket, western blue groper and sweep are caught from the rocks.

Dillon Bay and **Cape Knob** are reached by a track that leaves the main road 10 km west of Bremer Bay. Dillon Bay has Australian salmon and whiting, and Cape Knob has tommy ruff. This is an area of beautiful unspoilt beaches and rocks for anglers. Further west there is a good road to the **Pallinup River**, which is a fine bream location, with silver trevally, tommy ruff and Australian salmon from the beach at the mouth of the river.

Cheyne Beach is a notable place for Australian salmon, along with tommy ruff, snapper and trevally. The beaches west of Cape Riche can be fished for tommy ruff, silver trevally and Australian salmon.

Two Peoples Bay has beach fishing for salmon, tommy ruff and silver trevally, and rock fishing for silver trevally, snook, queen snapper, groper, tarwhine, sweep and shark.

The beaches with vehicle access, like Bremer, Cheyne and Two Peoples bays, are solid enough to beach launch small boats for offshore fishing. The water can be turbulent, and boat anglers should seek local advice. When the weather is right the fishing is superb for fish like snapper, queen snapper, tuna, trevally, samson fish and snook.

KING GEORGE SOUND

The town of Albany is built around soaring granite hills overlooking a magnificent vista of the sparkling blue waters of **King George Sound, Oyster Harbour** and **Princess Royal Harbour**. King George whiting are prolific in each of these bays; there are also tommy ruff, leatherjacket, flounder and garfish. Oyster Harbour has

COASTAL FISHING ALBANY REGION

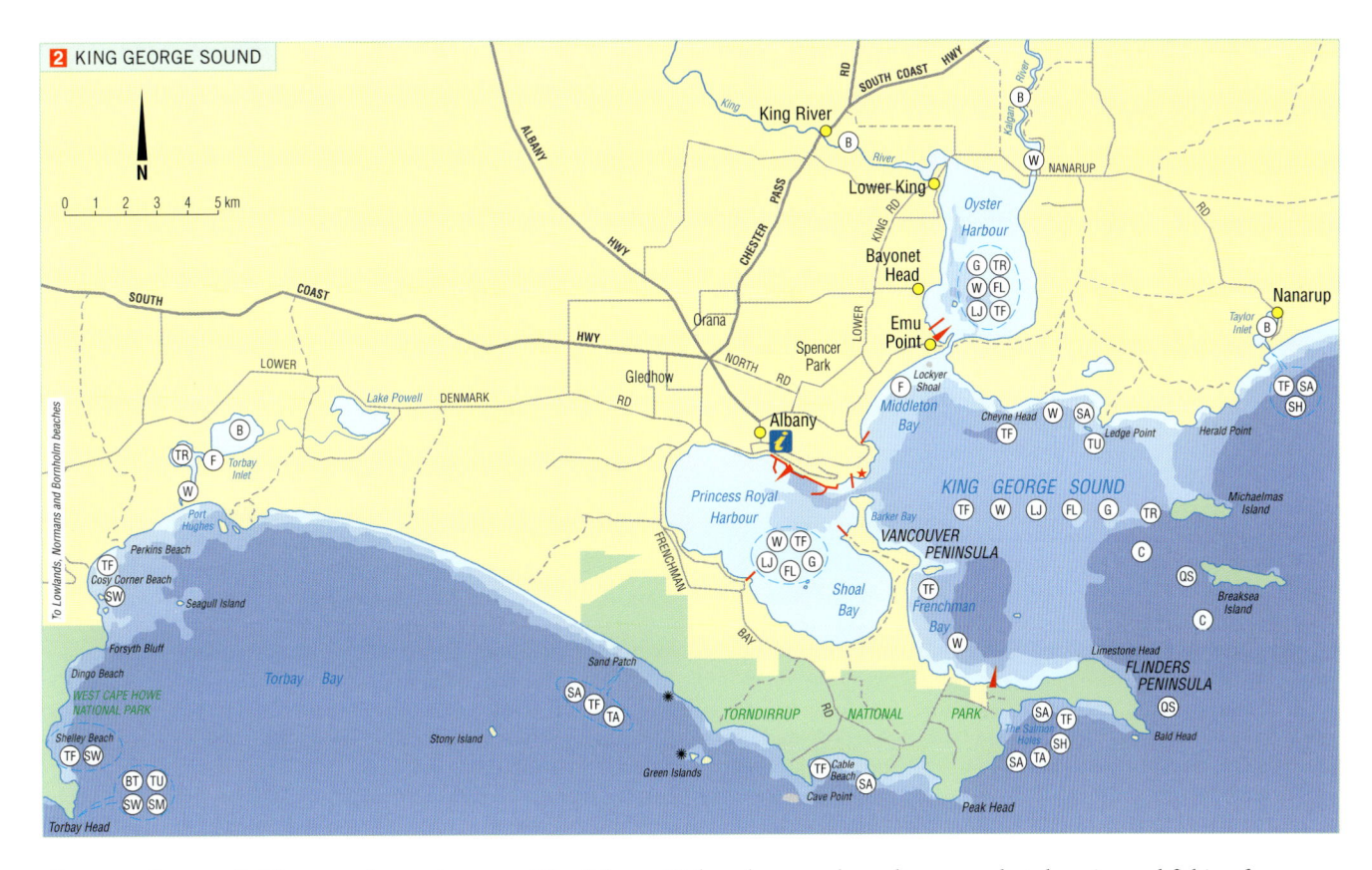

WESTERN AUSTRALIA

2 KING GEORGE SOUND

silver trevally as well. There are bream in the **Kalgan and King rivers**.

In recent years anglers have become aware of huge yellowfin tuna coming in quite close to shore in **King George Sound** in the autumn as they follow the mulie (pilchard) boats. A few have been caught to date and this exciting sport fishery is expected to develop in future years. Spinning with lead-head jigs around the sandbars in the harbours can produce some excellent flounder fishing. There are queen snapper and cod in the deeper water across the mouth of the sound.

The Salmon Holes, almost at the end of the Flinders Peninsula, is often brilliant for Australian salmon, tommy ruff, tarwhine and shark. **Cable Beach** has tommy ruff and Australian salmon, and there are tarwhine, tommy ruff and salmon at the **Sand Patch**, south-west of Albany (four-wheel drive only).

Torbay Inlet is a recognised black bream spot, especially near the floodgates, with chances of getting silver trevally, whiting and flathead as well.

At **Cosy Corner and Shelley beaches** there is fishing for tommy ruff and sweep. The rocks at **West Cape Howe** can be dangerous but there is good fishing for sweep, samson fish and sometimes tuna and bonito. Further west, **Normans, Bornholm and Lowlands beaches** (four-wheel drive only) are often very worthwhile for Australian salmon, tommy ruff and tarwhine.

Starkly beautiful Bornholm Bay near Albany fishes well for Australian salmon

GUIDE TO LOCAL FISH

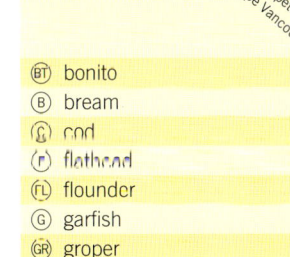

		Hopetoun to Cape Vancouver	King George Sound
BT	bonito		●
B	bream	●	●
C	cod	●	●
F	flathead		●
FL	flounder		●
G	garfish	●	●
GR	groper	●	
LJ	leatherjacket	●	●
SA	salmon, Australian	●	●
SM	samson fish	●	
SH	shark	●	●
S	snapper	●	
QS	snapper, queen	●	
SN	snook	●	
SW	sweep	●	●
TA	tarwhine	●	●
TF	tommy ruff	●	●
TR	trevally	●	●
TU	tuna	●	●
W	whiting	●	●

WESTERN AUSTRALIA

COASTAL FISHING ALBANY REGION

Denmark to Point Nuyts

Type of fishing
beach, offshore, river, rock

Target fish
Australian salmon, black bream, mulloway, tommy ruff

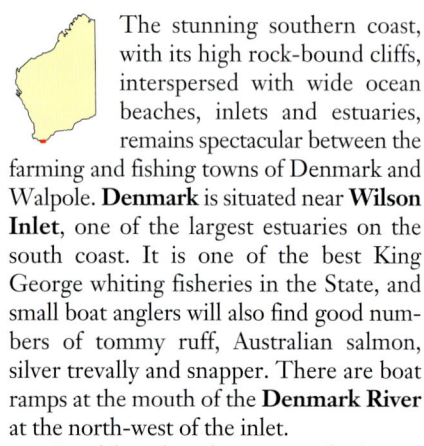

Early morning at Wilson Inlet, near Denmark

The stunning southern coast, with its high rock-bound cliffs, interspersed with wide ocean beaches, inlets and estuaries, remains spectacular between the farming and fishing towns of Denmark and Walpole. **Denmark** is situated near **Wilson Inlet**, one of the largest estuaries on the south coast. It is one of the best King George whiting fisheries in the State, and small boat anglers will also find good numbers of tommy ruff, Australian salmon, silver trevally and snapper. There are boat ramps at the mouth of the **Denmark River** at the north-west of the inlet.

Land-based anglers can try for bream from the banks of the **Hay, Denmark and Little rivers**, or fish from many points along **Inlet Drive**. This is a particularly fine location for family fishing, as children can play in the parks, and barbecue and picnic areas are near the fishing spots. Beach launching is also possible around the inlet.

Jacks Island and **Honeymoon Island** are two good places in the inlet, and a reef just east of Honeymoon Island is very productive. **Poisson Point** is a particularly favoured spot for land-based anglers for whiting, trevally, snapper, tommy ruff, tarwhine and Australian salmon. **Porpoise Rocks**, just off the point, should be tried by boat anglers. An exciting annual fishing event is when the snapper congregate inside the inlet just prior to the water breaking through the sandbar at the mouth. It is quite common for an angler to catch a bag limit of snapper weighing 2 to 3 kg each.

On the eastern side of the inlet, near the entrance, is **Palace Reef**, right on the shore, which can be fished by boat or from land for flathead and snapper. The ocean beach is magnificent, both for swimming and surfing, and anglers wanting to go offshore can take their four-wheel drives onto the hard sand and launch from there, going out mainly in search of snapper, Westralian jewfish, shark and snook. The beach anglers concentrate on Australian salmon, mulloway, tailor and tommy ruff, while the flat rocks provide good platforms from which to cast for Australian salmon, silver trevally, tailor and occasional samson fish.

In the area west of Denmark, **Madfish Bay** has Australian salmon, tommy ruff, tarwhine, trevally and whiting. Anglers can fish from the beach or the rocks in **Greens Pool** or **William Bay** for Australian salmon, tarwhine, King George whiting, mulloway and tailor. Greens Pool is a natural rock pool at the eastern end of William Bay where the fishing is also easy for tommy ruff and trevally. William Bay, a noted King George whiting spot, is an idyllic unspoiled area where anglers might be tempted to stay a few days. **Parry Beach**, at the western end of the bay, has the best of the beach fishing and sand suitable for beach launching.

Further west, **Irwin Inlet** is a good place to fish from either boat or land for King George whiting, tommy ruff, Australian salmon and silver trevally, and there is bream in the **Kent and Bow rivers**. The

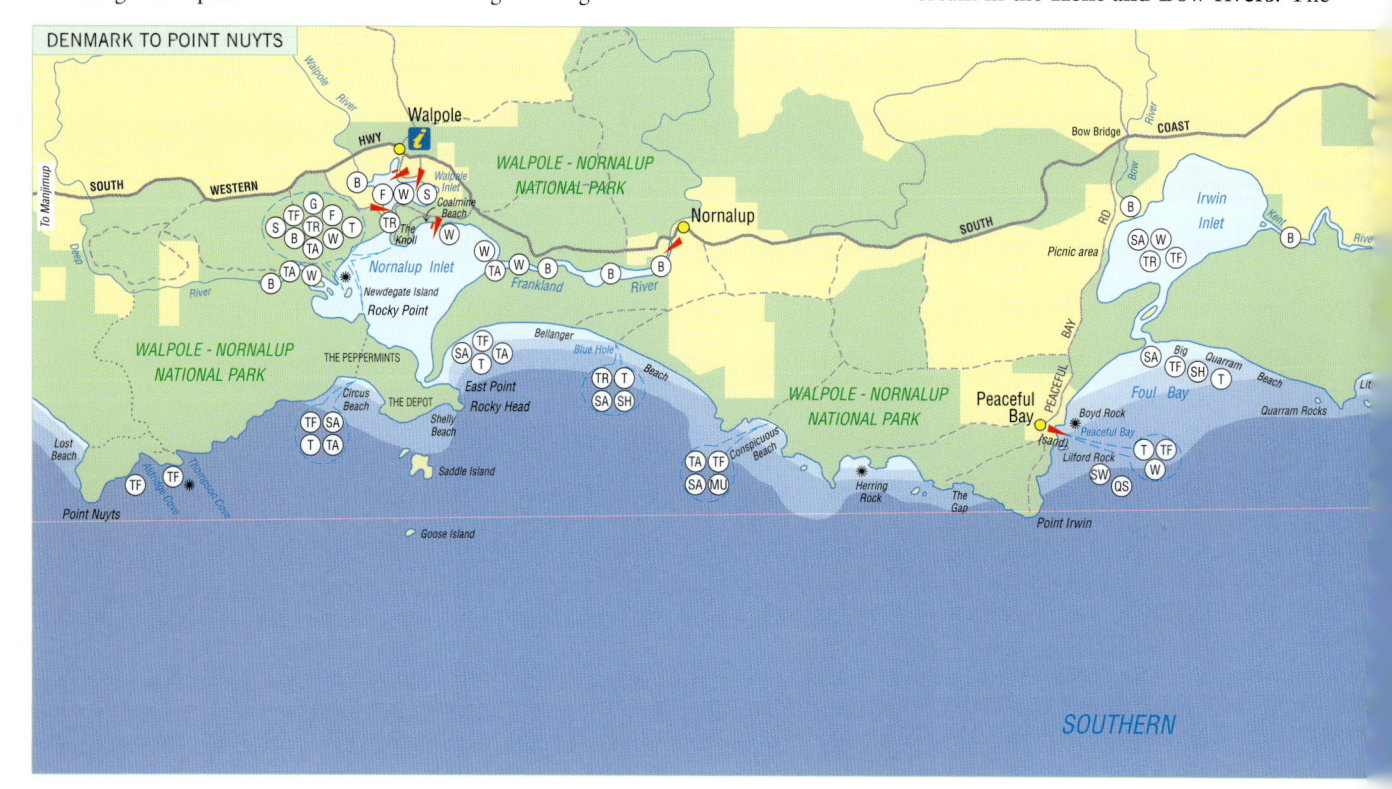

SOUTHERN

COASTAL FISHING ALBANY REGION   WESTERN AUSTRALIA

inlet is most accessible from a picnic area along Peaceful Bay Road, but boats launched from the ocean beach at **Peaceful Bay** can make their way into the inlet. The pretty bay is a good place for rock and beach fishing for King George whiting, tommy ruff, tailor and squid, but the settlement is also a base for four-wheel-drive trekking to nearby rock spots. **Conspicuous Beach**, further west again, is great for beach fishing and is an easy run by car from Peaceful Bay or from the South Coast Highway. From Nornalup, four-wheel-drive vehicles can reach the **Blue Hole** at Bellanger Beach and the ocean fishing for silver trevally, Australian salmon, tailor and shark.

The Walpole and Nornalup complex of inlets, river and ocean beaches, set in the beautiful karri country of the **Walpole-Nornalup National Park**, is a superb fishing area, with all facilities laid on. The National Park is a declared wilderness area, and no vehicles are permitted, so those wanting to fish the terrific beach locations of **Circus and Lost beaches**, or the rock areas at **Thompson and Aldridge coves** will have to walk. The easiest beach to reach is Circus Beach, as boats can tie up in Nornalup Inlet and anglers can walk across an isthmus known as **The Peppermints** to fish the beach for tommy ruff, Australian salmon, tailor and tarwhine. The large Nornalup Inlet is fed on either side by the **Frankland and Deep rivers**, and both are wonderful waters for tarwhine and black bream, with whiting straying in from the inlet. Boat anglers will find plenty of places in the inlet to try for bream, flathead, garfish, silver trevally, snapper, tailor, tarwhine, tommy ruff and whiting, particularly on the southern extremities of **The Knoll**, around **Newgate Island** and **Rocky Point**. There is a boat ramp at **Coalmine Beach** and the jetty nearby is one of the good land-based angling spots.

Walpole Inlet is reached by a channel from Nornalup Inlet, and this channel is a hot spot for whiting and flathead. Inside the waters are usually serene, and boats can drift for flathead on the banks, or explore the weed and rubble areas for whiting and snapper, among the usual estuary fish. There are three launching ramps and many land-based angling places, including the banks of the Walpole River, another bream fishery.

GUIDE TO LOCAL FISH	
B	bream, black
F	flathead
G	garfish
WJ	jewfish, Westralian
MU	mulloway
SA	salmon, Australian
SM	samson fish
SH	shark
S	snapper
QS	snapper, queen
SN	snook
SW	sweep
T	tailor
TA	tarwhine
TF	tommy ruff
TR	trevally
W	whiting

Rock fishing in Peaceful Bay

315

WESTERN AUSTRALIA

COASTAL FISHING ALBANY REGION

Augusta to Cape Naturaliste

Type of fishing
beach, jetty, offshore, reef, river, rock

Target fish
Australian salmon, samson fish, silver trevally, snapper, Westralian jewfish

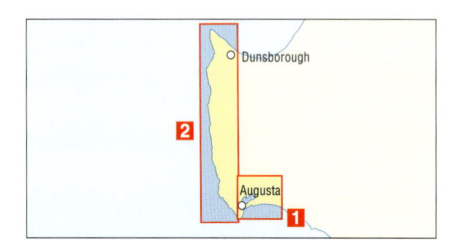

This is a rough, rugged and spectacular stretch of coast. Fishing at the many surf beaches can be excellent when the swell is not too high, as can fishing from the rock platforms that break up the stretch of beaches, but anglers need to take great care as this exposed coast can be treacherous in rough weather. The fishing over offshore reefs offers first-class action for species like Westralian jewfish, yellowtail kingfish, southern bluefin tuna and samson fish.

AUGUSTA

The sleepy little town of **Augusta** is picturesquely nestled on **Hardy Inlet**. The middle reaches of the **Blackwood River**, between Alexander Bridge and Molloy Island, produce good bream fishing for most of the year. The majority of anglers fishing in the inlet do so by boat. The estuary consistently produces big yellow-finned whiting, tommy ruff, tarwhine and flounder. There are jetties along the town foreshore where tommy ruff, garfish, squid and the occasional whiting are caught. **Ellis Street Jetty** can turn up superb big silver trevally after dark, and delightful fishing can be had for mixed bags of small species from the clean, white beach in an area known locally as the **Colour Patch**, named after a former popular delicatessen and cafe. Those who want to sample the abundant beach fishing cross the inlet by boat and then walk. Fishing from the beach can yield species such as mulloway and tailor.

There is plenty of whiting in Flinders Bay, and good fishing **offshore** for pike, Westralian jewfish and snapper. Offshore anglers have to use the Flinders Bay boat ramp at Barrack Point, as the mouth of the inlet can be very dangerous.

CAPE LEEUWIN TO CAPE NATURALISTE

Land-based anglers can also head to the west coast through the **Leeuwin–Naturaliste National Park**, along the Skippy Rock Road, to **Skippy Rock**. Here and around the **Cape Leeuwin lighthouse** the rock fishing can be good for tommy ruff, tailor, samson fish, shark, snapper and silver trevally. The seas can be dangerous all along this coast, so watch the weather. Boat anglers, too, must be mindful of the weather, but they can get out to Westralian jewfish over offshore reefs, and the King George whiting that live over the weed beds and soft-bottomed areas. Shark, snapper, queen snapper and silver trevally are among the catches in these offshore waters.

Further up the coast, **Deepdene** and **Cosy Corner** can be reached on another road from Augusta and have both beach and rock fishing for tommy ruff, Australian salmon and silver trevally.

Hamelin Bay is marked by the remains of an old jetty, but its fishing treasures are the eleven wrecks that lie beneath the waters, creating artificial reefs that attract Westralian jewfish, western blue groper, shark, yellowtail kingfish and snapper. Because the prevailing south-westerlies are lighter in summer, this is a better time for boat fishing, and the boat ramp makes access easy. This is also excellent territory for whiting.

The road north through the karri forests, with their wonderful wildflower displays in summer, has rough-track turnoffs to **Boranup**, the **Conto Spring Picnic Area**, **Bobs Hollow** and **Redgate**, where there are fine fishing beaches for Australian salmon, tailor, tommy ruff, mulloway and silver trevally.

Margaret River is well known as a wine district, but it also has good fishing. There is a boat ramp at **Prevelly** for offshore anglers, but weather and tremendous waves need to be respected despite the lure of the reef with its snapper, pike, Westralian jewfish, trevally, western blue groper and shark. The mouth of the Margaret River is good, particularly in summer, for tailor, mulloway, tommy ruff and Australian salmon, with reef fishing at low tide for silver trevally.

There is a boat ramp at **Cowaramup Bay**, some 12 km north of Margaret River, and the bay produces samson fish, silver trevally, Australian salmon, snook, tommy ruff and shark, which can be fished from the rocks. Westralian jewfish and snapper can be found outside the bay.

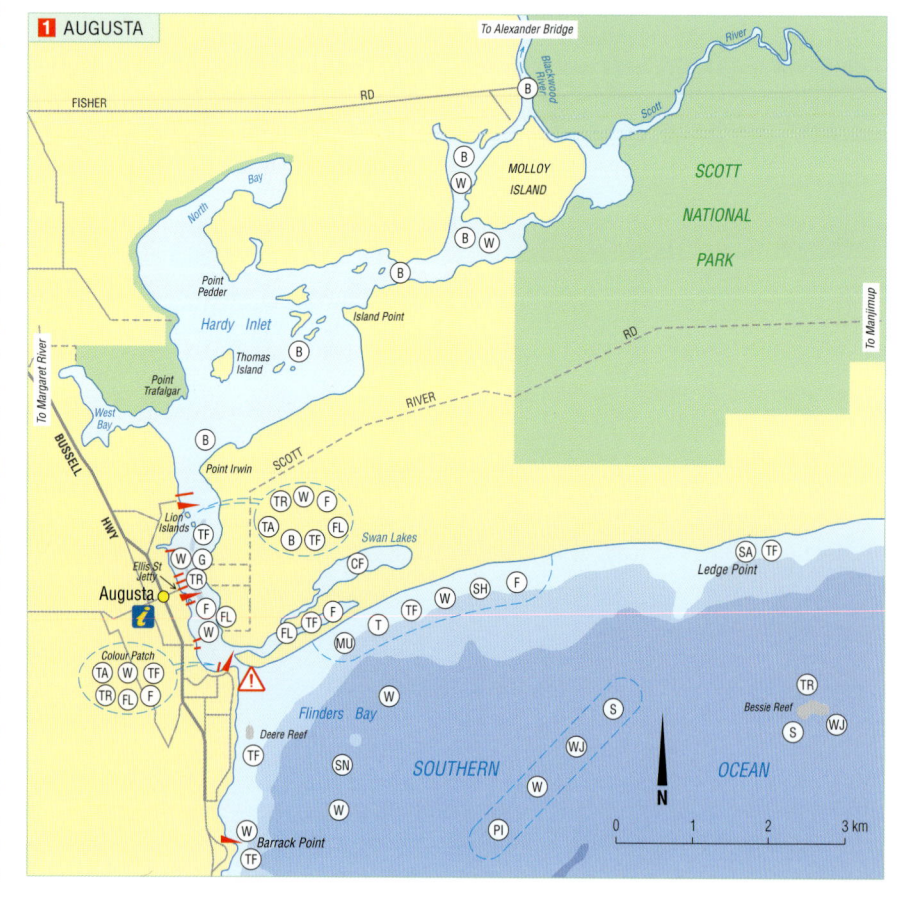

COASTAL FISHING ALBANY REGION

WESTERN AUSTRALIA

Canal Rocks, at the southern end of a small bay, is a great Australian salmon spot in autumn

Further north at **Injidup Point** and **Wyadup Rocks,** the land-based fishing is similar to that at Cowaramup Bay. In times of offshore winds anglers send their baits out into the deeper waters suspended from balloons. **Canal Rocks** attracts rock anglers for Australian salmon and tommy ruff, while there is year-round beach fishing at **Smiths Beach** for flathead, whiting, tailor, tommy ruff, flounder and mulloway, and lots of Australian salmon in winter. **Torpedo Rocks** offers excellent Australian salmon fishing in autumn, as well as samson fish, tommy ruff, pink snapper and Westralian jewfish. The town of **Yallingup** has great surf and great fishing. **Yallingup Beach** has close-in reefs where boat anglers can seek snapper, silver trevally and shark, while the beach has tarwhine, mulloway, tailor and flathead all year round.

Sugarloaf Rock, 10 km north, is very dangerous in any sort of sea but it offers spinning for tommy ruff, silver trevally, Australian salmon and samson fish. Westralian jewfish, snapper, shark and sweep can be caught using bottom-fishing gear.

At **Cape Naturaliste** there is a 2-km walk from the lighthouse to the rocks, but there is excellent tailor and Australian salmon fishing from here, with silver trevally, shark, tommy ruff and samson fish as well.

Around the corner, east of the cape, there is more shelter from the prevailing south-westerlies. A good rock location for tailor, silver trevally, salmon and snook is **The Docks**. In **Bunker Bay** there is beach fishing in more sheltered surroundings for Australian salmon, and tarwhine, flathead, whiting, mulloway and tommy ruff for most of the year. **Eagle Bay** and **Meelup** both offer beach, boat and rock fishing in beautiful locations. Boat launching is possible from the sand.

The town of **Dunsborough** has a boat ramp in the sheltered bay. There is reef fishing a few kilometres offshore, including **Four Mile Reef** and an artificial reef, for Westralian jewfish, samson fish and snapper. **Quindalup**, just east of Dunsborough, is good for big yellow-finned and King George whiting in the shallows, while the boat mooring area is often alive with squid.

The best fishing place in **Busselton** is the jetty, which is very busy in summer, with good catches of whiting, tommy ruff, squid and crabs for the anglers who crowd there during the holiday season. Hard-fighting bonito and the occasional tuna come in to the jetty in late summer, and mulloway can be expected on rough winter nights. There is beach fishing for tailor and tommy ruff, and some reefs offshore for Westralian jewfish, snapper and silver trevally.

GUIDE TO LOCAL FISH

		Augusta	Cape Leeuwin to Cape Naturaliste
(B)	bream	•	
(CF)	catfish	•	
(F)	flathead	•	•
(FL)	flounder	•	•
(G)	garfish	•	
(GR)	groper		•
(J)	jewfish, Westralian	•	•
(KI)	kingfish, yellowtail		•
(MU)	mulloway	•	•
(PI)	pike	•	
(SA)	salmon, Australian	•	•
(SM)	samson fish		•
(SH)	shark	•	•
(S)	snapper	•	•
(QS)	snapper, queen		•
(SN)	snook	•	•
(SW)	sweep		•
(T)	tailor	•	•
(TA)	tarwhine	•	•
(TF)	tommy ruff	•	•
(TR)	trevally	•	•
(TU)	tuna	•	
(W)	whiting	•	•

2 CAPE LEEUWIN TO CAPE NATURALISTE

WESTERN AUSTRALIA   COASTAL FISHING ALBANY REGION

Bunbury and Mandurah

Type of fishing
beach, estuary, jetty, offshore, river
Target fish
estuary catfish, mulloway, snapper, tailor, tommy ruff

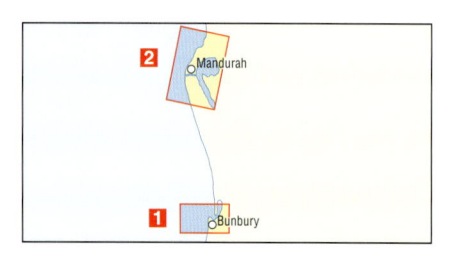

Mandurah's old road bridge, a favourite family fishing spot for decades

This stretch of coastline is an angler's paradise. There are towns with good facilities and plenty of spots easily accessed by those with two-wheel-drive cars, and even more for those with four-wheel drives. The range of species is large, too, with estuary and bay fish, rock and reef-dwellers and many offshore fish. This is a popular area for family holidays, and there are a number of places to choose from that offer enjoyable fishing and other activities for all members of the family.

BUNBURY

Bunbury, capital of the south-west, is situated on the Leschenault Inlet with two major rivers within the town precincts. These rivers plus a sheltered harbour, ocean beaches and interesting offshore waters make a bountiful fishing venue. The **Bunbury Back Beach** is easily reached and has excellent fishing for tailor, flathead, mulloway and shark. In winter, Australian salmon, tommy ruff and trevally are prevalent.

The harbour has a long breakwater that is often used by anglers, fishing outside for tailor, mulloway and snapper, and inside for tarwhine, garfish, whiting and tommy ruff, which are also available in the sheltered waters of the Inner Harbour. Boat anglers line up alongside the shipping channel inside Koombana Bay, seeking big mulloway, shark and bonito. The bigger craft also go offshore to fish for snapper, silver trevally, shark, West-ralian jewfish and tarwhine around the reefs.

The larger section of the shallow **Leschenault Inlet** is a popular place for small boat fishing and is famous for its big blue swimmer crabs, prawns during summer and large stocks of King George whiting. Garfish and tarwhine are also plentiful, and garfish can be berleyed up to the boat on still, moonlit nights. The rocks at the inlet entrance, known as **The Cut**, are a spot to try for mulloway, silver trevally, tommy ruff, tailor and Australian salmon.

Near the entrance to the estuary are the mouths of the **Preston and Collie rivers**. The Collie is bigger and is noted for its bream and mulloway. Collie Bridge and the east end of **Alexander Island** are good fishing places here, and there is a park along the southern side of the river that is ideal for fishing or a family outing.

North of Bunbury, **Binningup, Myalup and Preston ocean beaches** are easily reached and have excellent fishing for tailor, flathead, mulloway and shark. In winter, Australian salmon, tommy ruff and trevally are common catches.

MANDURAH AREA

Mandurah is a fast-growing holiday and retirement town set around a maze of waterways on **Harvey Estuary and Peel Inlet**. Pollution and over-fishing could cause problems without careful management, but fish resources are still good. To improve the health of the estuary, the **Dawesville Channel**, a huge engineering project 10 km south of Mandurah linking the estuary with the ocean, was completed in March 1994. The

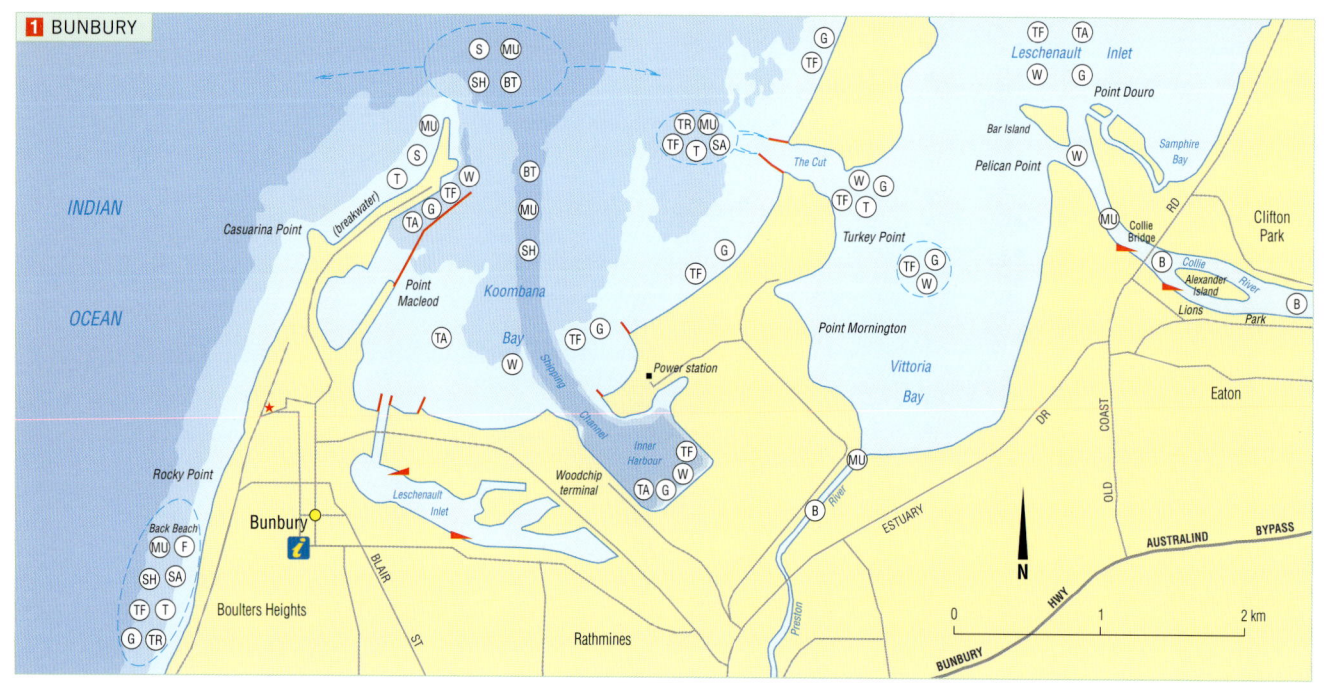

COASTAL FISHING ALBANY REGION　　　　WESTERN AUSTRALIA

200-m-wide channel has become renowned for tremendous catches of tailor, tommy ruff and small Australian salmon.

Travelling up the coast from Bunbury, the two ocean beaches of **White Hill** and **Tims Thicket** can be reached easily from the Old Coast Road, and are excellent places for flathead, tailor, mulloway and shark. The main catches in winter are Australian salmon, trevally and tommy ruff.

At Mandurah one of the most popular land-based spots is the old road bridge in the heart of town, which has a fishing platform underneath for anglers seeking tailor, mulloway, whiting, garfish and tarwhine. There are various jetties where the fishing is similar, and long breakwaters, where tarwhine, tommy ruff, yelloweye mullet and mulloway are the main catches. Prawns, estuary catfish and blue swimmer crabs are in the estuary and inlet, with the prawn run-out in the autumn attracting enthusiastic anglers armed with torches and nets. **Mary Street Lagoon** and the lagoon called **Dolphin Pool** are haunts of the estuary catfish – slimy, ugly and with poisonous spines, but with delicious flesh. There are excellent launching facilities in Mandurah and good offshore fishing for Westralian jewfish, snapper and King George whiting.

The **Murray River** has a complex of canals near its entrance, attracting bream, tommy ruff and yelloweye mullet.

North of Mandurah the beaches at **Silver Sands, San Remo, Madora** and **Singleton** have mulloway, tarwhine and Australian salmon, and are particularly good for tailor in summer.

GUIDE TO LOCAL FISH

		Bunbury	Mandurah Area
BT	bonito	●	
B	bream	●	●
CF	catfish		●
F	flathead	●	●
FL	flounder		●
G	garfish	●	●
WJ	jewfish, Westralian		●
M	mullet		●
MU	mulloway	●	●
SA	salmon, Australian	●	●
SH	shark	●	●
S	snapper	●	●
T	tailor	●	●
TA	tarwhine	●	●
TF	tommy ruff	●	●
TR	trevally	●	●
W	whiting	●	●

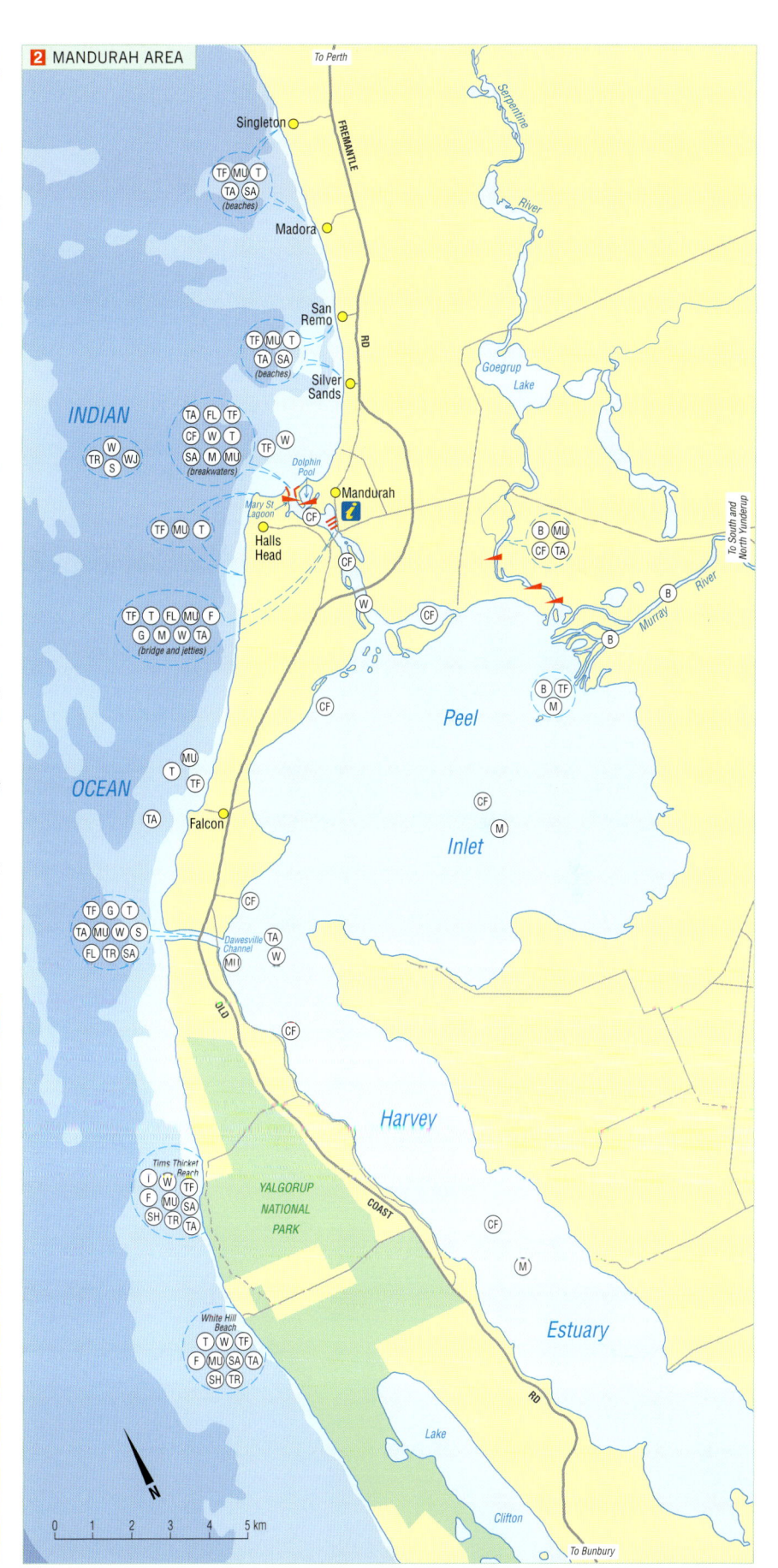

WESTERN AUSTRALIA

COASTAL FISHING GASCOYNE–KIMBERLEY REGION

Gascoyne–Kimberley Region

This vast region takes in the area from Shark Bay to the Northern Territory border, a distance that encompasses enormous coastal variety and fishing opportunities. From the massive cliffs of Point Quobba to the barren, scrubby islands of the Dampier Archipelago and the crocodile-infested tropical creeks of the Kimberley region, hard-fighting sportfish abound for both shore-bound and boat anglers.

Land-based fishing without equal is possible from the rock platforms of Steep Point and Point Quobba. Everything from sailfish to Spanish mackerel and big snapper are caught by anglers with their feet still on firm earth. Boat fishing both inside and outside the wondrous Ningaloo Reef can present fast and furious action with top quality pelagic and bottom species, while the waters of the Dampier Archipelago and those out from Broome are famous for their large numbers of spectacular sailfish.

The Kimberley region is the last frontier of true wilderness fishing, accessible for the most part only by boat. Fishing here is very much dependent on tides and local knowledge. For those wanting to experience real adventure, but without the necessary experience and equipment to do it safely on their own, excellent guided fishing charters can be organised from Broome or Kununurra.

Weather

The best time for fishing is during the winter months, when cooler currents attract game fish. During the wet season, from November to April, conditions for recreational fishing are generally poor and there is the chance of sudden squalls and thunderstorms. Temperatures can be very high during the Wet and much of the Kimberley region is totally inaccessible. Cyclones can affect coastal areas from November to May. For weather information or forecasts ring the Bureau of Meteorology, tel. (08) 9263 2222 or visit its website: www.bom.gov.au

WHERE TO FISH

Gascoyne–Kimberley Region

SHARK BAY • 322
The wide, shallow expanse of Shark Bay, with its myriad winding channels of old riverbeds, is a popular holiday destination for anglers who love to chase big pink snapper. Bordered on the seaward side by historic Dirk Hartog Island, with the massive Zuytdorp Cliffs in the south, Shark Bay is regarded as the melting pot of west coast fisheries, the place where tropical and temperate water fish meet.

CARNARVON TO EXMOUTH • 324
The fabulous rock fishing from the base of the Cape Cuvier cliffs attracts anglers from all over Australia. Anglers using spinning or ballooning rigs can try for Spanish mackerel and a wide variety of sportfish. Ningaloo Reef, near Exmouth, is a marine wonderland, with great fishing inside the reef and big black marlin, sailfish, mackerel and superb bottom species in the deep, blue water outside.

DAMPIER COAST • 326
The relatively unspoilt waters around the Dampier Archipelago abound with an outstanding range of fish. The great attraction is the abundance of sailfish, which leap from the water and can be trolled in many areas. The mangrove-lined coast, centring on the big mining town of Port Hedland, invites creek as well as offshore fishing.

BROOME TO CAMBRIDGE GULF • 328
Along the coast to Cape Leveque there are a number of excellent places for land-based angling and rich offshore waters. The remote and untamed coast from Derby to Cambridge Gulf is one of the few remaining areas for frontier fishing. Fishing the Kimberley is a unique experience that rewards with catches of barramundi and trevally of immense size.

Boating

The coast in this region is generally exposed to the Indian Ocean. There are numerous reefs that, although good for fishing, can be boating hazards, so it is important to have an up-to-date chart and seek local knowledge before you go out. For further information, contact the local marine officer at the Department of Transport.

COASTAL FISHING GASCOYNE–KIMBERLEY REGION — WESTERN AUSTRALIA

GUIDE TO LOCAL FISH

- amberjack
- barracuda
- barramundi
- bream
- catfish, fork-tailed
- cobia
- cod
- dart
- dolphin fish
- emperor, red
- emperor, spangled
- fingermark
- flathead
- garfish
- groper, baldchin
- herring, oxeye
- jack, mangrove
- jewfish, black
- kingfish, yellowtail
- mackerel, shark
- mackerel, Spanish
- marlin, black
- mulloway
- queenfish
- sailfish
- salmon, threadfin
- samson fish
- shark, others
- snapper
- sweetlip
- tailor
- tarwhine
- trevally, giant
- trevally, gold-spotted
- trevally, golden
- trout, coral
- tuna, longtail
- tuna, yellowfin
- wahoo
- whiting

Some basic safety rules for boat fishing include:
- Never fish alone.
- Check the weather.
- Always leave word of your destination and estimated time of return.
- If fishing strange waters try to go out with an experienced local first.
- Know the limitations of your boat and do not overload it.
- Stow your gear safely.
- If bad weather threatens, make for the shore and keep a lookout for the following warnings signs: clouds building up to windward; wind rising quickly; waves becoming bigger and the odd white cap appearing.

Creeks running into Roebuck Bay can be fished for species such as barramundi and mangrove jack

Sailfish

The sailfish is one of the number of sportfish collectively called billfish (other species include black, blue, white and striped marlin, spearfish and swordfish). The sailfish is distinguished by its enormous dorsal fin or 'sail', and is targeted by anglers because of its immense power and admirable fighting ability. It is found in the northern coastal waters of Australia, from as far south as Exmouth in Western Australia round to Moreton Bay in Queensland.

FISHING TIP

If you fish for a feed and are in the tropics, then preserving flesh quality is important. Once killed, all fish should be bled immediately and then gutted and washed. Leave the scales and skin on and lay the fish flat in a slurry of ice and salt water. An ice slurry mixture is a quicker chilling medium than straight ice and therefore the best method of storing fish.

FURTHER INFORMATION

Boating and fishing The Department of Transport has regional offices at Short St, Broome, tel. (08) 9193 5923; Fishing Boat Harbour, Carnarvon, tel. (08) 9941 1830; Lot 862, Maidstone Cres, Exmouth, tel. (08) 9949 2079; and Transport Centre, Welcome Rd, Karratha, tel. (08) 9185 5044. Fisheries Western Australia has district offices at Port of Pearls, 401 Port Dve, Broome, tel. (08) 9192 1121; Knight Tce, Denham, tel. (08) 9948 1210; Payne St, Exmouth, tel. (08) 9949 2755; and Unit 1/17–19 Crane Circle, Karratha, tel. (08) 9144 4337.

Tourist centres Cnr Broome Rd and Bagot St, Broome, tel. (08) 9192 2222; Robinson St, Carnarvon, tel. (08) 9941 1146; Coral Bay Arcade, Robinson St, Coral Bay, tel. (08) 9942 5988. Shark Bay Tourist Centre, 71 Knight Tce, Denham, tel. (08) 9948 1253; 2 Clarendon St, Derby, tel. (08) 9191 1426; Murat Rd, Exmouth, tel. (08) 9949 1176; 4548 Karratha Rd, Karratha, tel. (08) 9144 4600; East Kimberley Tourism House, Coolibah Dr, Kununurra, tel. (08) 9168 1177; Second Ave, Onslow, tel. (08) 9184 6644; 13 Wedge St, Port Hedland, tel. (08) 9173 1711; Old Gaol, Queen St, Roeburne, tel. (08) 9182 1060; Kimberley Motors, Lot 626, Great Northern Hwy, Wyndham, tel. (08) 9161 1281.

WESTERN AUSTRALIA COASTAL FISHING GASCOYNE–KIMBERLEY REGION

Shark Bay

Type of fishing
bay, beach, cliff, jetty, offshore, rock

Target fish
mackerel, pink snapper, tailor, whiting

The rock locations along the outside coast begin at **Zuytdorp Point** for fish such as snapper, tuna, mackerel and sailfish off the cliffs, and further out, spangled emperor. Like so many locations in this area, it is reached by four-wheel drive, and then on foot. The cliffs here, and all along the coast, rise high above the water. Fishing requires big game tackle, a steady nerve, a good sense of balance, an awareness of winds, waves and weather, and a refusal to take risks. The coast can be successfully fished all year round.

Steep Point is probably the most famous land-based fishing spot in Australia and is renowned among anglers around the world. Jutting out into the Indian Ocean, it is the westernmost point of continental Australia and an impressive platform for anglers who can look down from a great height to see the breakers hitting the rocks below. It attracts a passing parade of pelagic fish like Spanish mackerel, shark mackerel, amberjack, samson fish, yellowfin tuna, cobia, yellowtail kingfish and shark, with a lot of smaller fish around the rocks, like flathead, snapper, bream, trevally, mulloway and tailor. Many sailfish have been taken here – they can be seen leaping offshore – and a marlin catch is not unheard of. The prime time of the year for fishing at Steep Point is late December through to the end of March, when the weather is at its hottest. Not only are the mackerel at their best, but big yellowtail kingfish at the base of the rocks present a tremendous challenge.

Shark Bay is a fabulous fishing area and there are many other great rock fishing locations, and sheltered boating waters in the twin bays split by the Peron Peninsula. Bigger boats and charter boats go into the offshore channels for snapper or along the north and western shores of **Dirk Hartog Island** to troll for mackerel. Running through South Passage, offshore anglers can reach the open ocean and the abundant sailfish, tuna, mackerel and wahoo.

The main attraction for small boat anglers in the Shark Bay area is the run of pink snapper from May to August, which creates wonderful fishing around the deeper channels, reefs and little islands. Cod, whiting, mulloway and flathead are very prolific in the bays and channels.

Two good rock fishing locations on the Peron Peninsula are **Goulet Bluff**, for tailor and mulloway, and **Eagle Bluff**, for tailor. The main town of the area, **Denham**, is nearby, and caters well for anglers with tackle, bait, boat hire, charter boat and launching facilities. Whiting can be caught from the sandy areas in front of the town and squidding is popular from the two small jetties.

Access to Cape Peron is definitely by four-wheel drive only, and a stop at **Big Lagoon** on the way up can be worthwhile for whiting, flathead and snapper. At **Cape Peron North**, at the tip of the peninsula, there is shore fishing for snapper, mulloway, tailor and cod, and limited camping is available. Fishing is best in these bays at dusk or night on an incoming tide, but small boat anglers should be aware that these tides are strong.

Back down the east side of the peninsula, across from Denham, is **Monkey Mia**, where dolphins come in daily to be fed by tourists, and where the beach fishing is for whiting, mulloway and snapper. **Cape Rose** and nearby **Faure Island** are great night fishing locations, with the holes and channels around the island a haunt for snapper and mulloway. The world all-tackle game fishing record for cobia came from one of the channels not far out from Monkey Mia.

GUIDE TO LOCAL FISH

AJ	amberjack
B	bream
CO	cobia
C	cod
DO	dolphin fish
ES	emperor, spangled
F	flathead
GR	groper
H	herring, oxeye
KI	kingfish, yellowtail
MA	mackerel
ML	marlin
MU	mulloway
SL	sailfish
SM	samson fish
SH	shark
S	snapper
T	tailor
TA	tarwhine
TR	trevally
TU	tuna
WH	wahoo
W	whiting

An aerial view of Big Lagoon on Peron Peninsula

COASTAL FISHING GASCOYNE–KIMBERLEY REGION

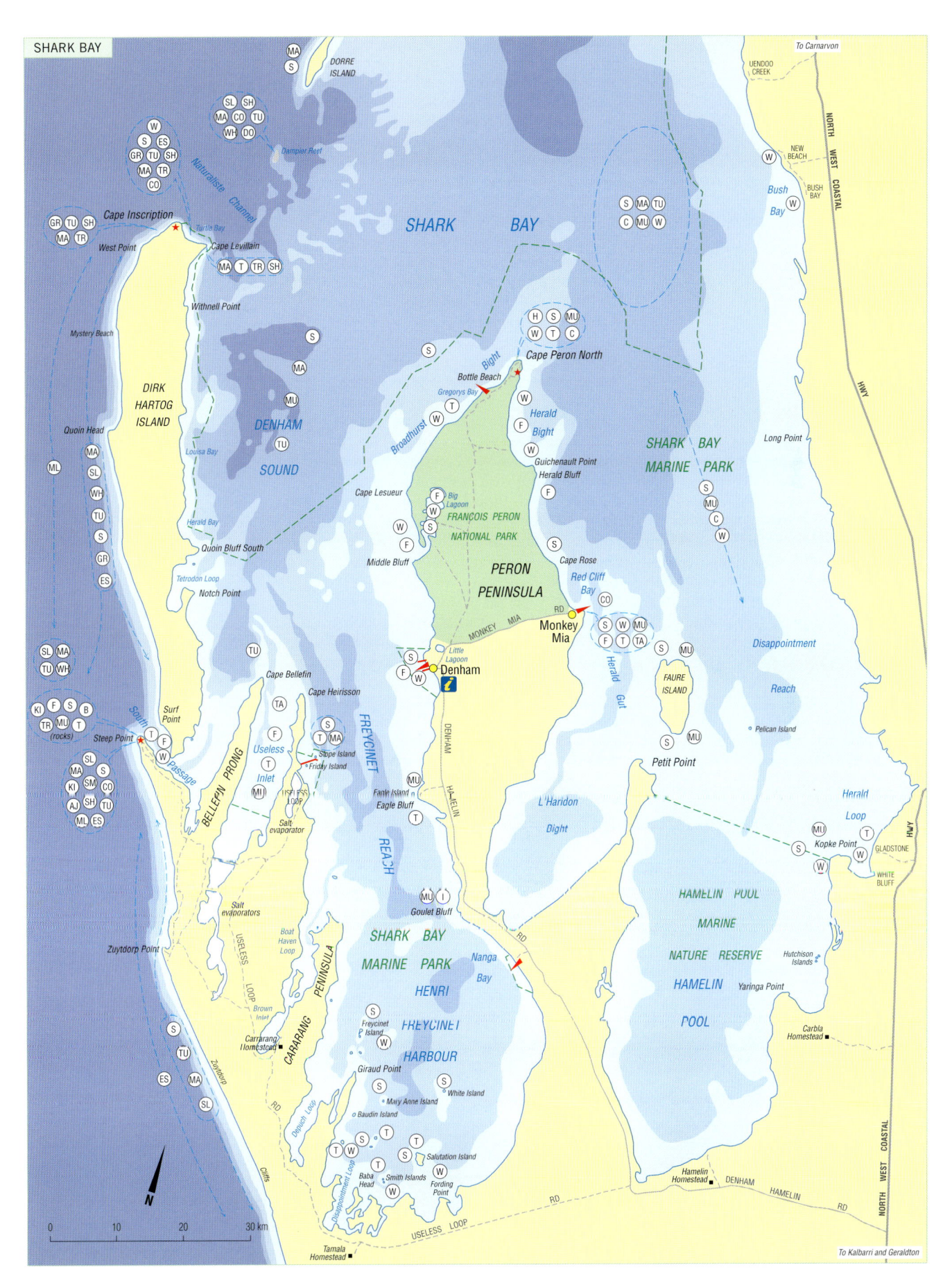

WESTERN AUSTRALIA

SHARK BAY

WESTERN AUSTRALIA COASTAL FISHING GASCOYNE–KIMBERLEY REGION

Carnarvon to Exmouth

Type of fishing
beach, cliff, jetty, offshore, reef, rock

Target fish
giant trevally, queenfish, spangled emperor

Carnarvon, on the northern extremity of Shark Bay, experiences the same mix of temperate and tropical water species as the bay. The area around Quobba Station is renowned for rock fishing venues such as Cape Cuvier, where anglers use spinning and gas ballooning rigs to target Spanish mackerel and a host of other game fish. Near Exmouth, there is good fishing on the reefs of the Ningaloo Marine Park.

CARNARVON TO POINT CLOATES

Babbage Island, at the mouth of the Gascoyne River at Carnarvon, has a long jetty running out into the Indian Ocean that is the focus for fishing in the town. From the jetty, anglers can fish for tailor, shark, bream and trevally, and try for big mulloway out in the deeper waters, though the jetty is sometimes closed to the public. There are mangrove jack in **Oyster Creek**, just south of Carnarvon, and in the mangrove area near the harbour. Nearby beaches such as **Miaboolya** are fished for tailor, mulloway, giant trevally and queenfish.

The Blowholes is a popular beach fishing place north of the town for Spanish mackerel, trevally, tuna, dart, shark and sailfish, and a tricky beach launching spot for the offshore fishing. **High Rock**, south of the Quobba Station homestead, is a formidable place, but it has been made less dangerous by the erection of a safety rail. Spinning for Spanish mackerel is popular here, as well as sending out baits under a gas balloon and attracting the mackerel to the bait skittering across the surface. There is accommodation at the station and the rock fishing for game fish in this area is among the best in the world. **Two Mile**, north of the homestead, can only be fished in favourable conditions. **Whistling Rock** is also a concern in rough seas, but is a good gas ballooning venue.

Further up the coast, about 20 km north of the homestead, are the legendary cliffs at **Cape Cuvier**, but care should be taken here as several lives have been lost to big seas hitting the rocks. Cliff gaffs are as essential in this area as the ballooning and spinning rigs that are used. The game fish includes shark, cobia, tuna, trevally, sailfish and amberjack, but the most common catch

An eroded ancient coral reef forms the rugged coastline at Point Quobba, about 70 km north of Carnarvon

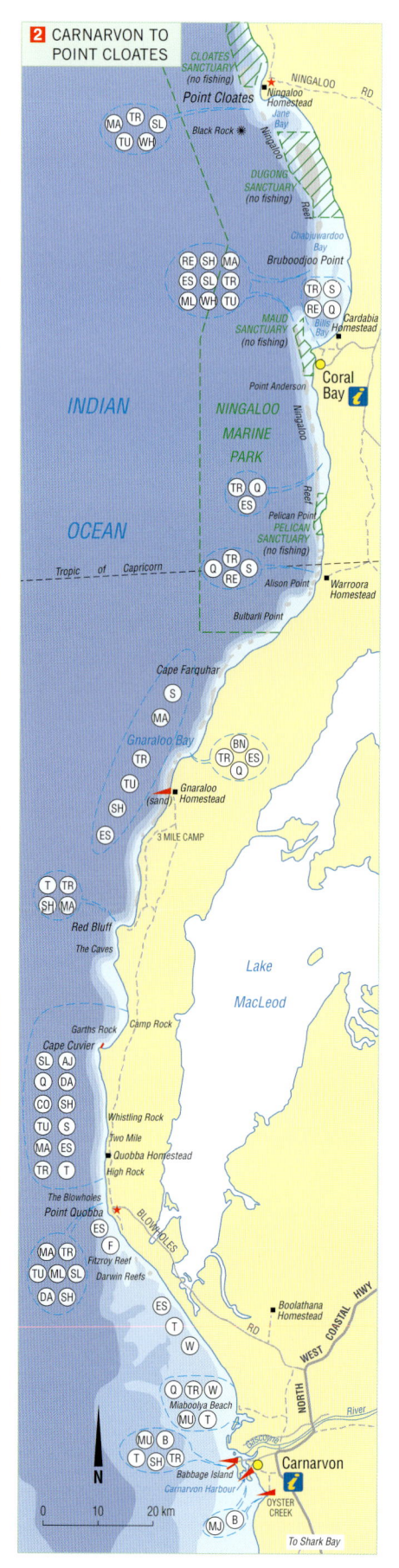

324

COASTAL FISHING GASCOYNE–KIMBERLEY REGION   WESTERN AUSTRALIA

GUIDE TO LOCAL FISH

		Ningaloo Marine Park and Exmouth	Carnarvon to Point Cloates
AJ	amberjack		•
BD	barracuda		•
B	bream	•	•
CO	cobia	•	•
C	cod	•	•
DA	dart	•	
RE	emperor, red	•	
ES	emperor, spangled	•	•
F	flathead	•	
MJ	jack, mangrove	•	•
MA	mackerel	•	•
ML	marlin	•	•
MU	mulloway	•	
Q	queenfish	•	•
SL	sailfish	•	•
SH	shark	•	
S	snapper	•	•
T	tailor	•	
TA	tarwhine		•
TR	trevally	•	•
TU	tuna	•	•
WH	wahoo	•	•
W	whiting	•	•

1 NINGALOO MARINE PARK AND EXMOUTH

is Spanish mackerel. **Garths Rock** requires a tough walk in, but is a fine location. **Camp Rock**, a little further north, can be reached by four-wheel drive and is one of the safer stands. Caves Rock also requires a hard walk. The beach at **Red Bluff** is quite accessible, and the sheltered platforms on the southern side are protected from southerly winds.

North of Red Bluff is **Gnaraloo Homestead**, which also caters for anglers, who can boat launch from the beach. Further north is **Warroora Homestead**, where there are trevally, red emperor, snapper and queenfish in the shallower waters.

Coral Bay has hotel, chalet and caravan park accommodation. Apart from the fishing, the attraction is the **Ningaloo Reef**, with glass-bottomed boats and snorkelling expeditions to look at the coral and brilliant tropical fish. The protecting reef makes this a great area for small boat fishing, for species like snapper, red emperor, spangled emperor, trevally and queenfish. Fishing is not allowed in the Maud Sanctuary, west of the town, so those wanting to fish inside the reef must head either north or south and keep a sharp eye out for coral bomboras. There is good bottom fishing outside the reef, and trolling for mackerel, marlin and sailfish. Reef fishing is possible from **Ningaloo Station**, with the permission of the owners.

NINGALOO MARINE PARK AND EXMOUTH

Exmouth is a well established town on the North West Cape, with excellent accommodation, a fine caravan and camping area and well-equipped charter boats. The fishing waters of the Ningaloo Reef area are within the **Ningaloo Marine Park** and special bag limits apply; anglers will need to check requirements locally or with the Fisheries Department. There is good fishing on the reefs for snapper, cobia, cod, wahoo, tuna, sailfish, mackerel, barracuda, spangled emperor, giant trevally and queenfish, while the calm gulf-side beaches consistently provide for whiting and bream.

At the tip of **North West Cape** spangled emperor, queenfish and trevally are the targets. Boats are launched at ramps such as those at Bundegi Beach and Tantabiddi Creek for reef fishing and the superb offshore fishing for queenfish, marlin, tuna, sailfish and spangled emperor. With the backup of a four-wheel drive and supplies, anglers can explore the virtually unfished mangrove creeks south of **Exmouth**.

North-east of Exmouth is the town of **Onslow**, where the tidal creeks can be fished for mangrove jack, bream and estuary cod. Onslow is the base for offshore fishing around the **Mackerel Islands**. Here the bottom and surface fishing is brilliant for coral trout, snapper, red emperor, spangled emperor, trevally, queenfish, Spanish mackerel, gold-spotted trevally, barracuda and many other species. There is accommodation, with boat and outboard supplied, on Thevenard Island, but bookings must be made through Mackerel Islands Holidays in Perth.

WESTERN AUSTRALIA — COASTAL FISHING GASCOYNE–KIMBERLEY REGION

Dampier Coast

Type of fishing
bay, beach, jetty, offshore, river

Target fish
queenfish, sailfish, Spanish mackerel, threadfin salmon, trevally

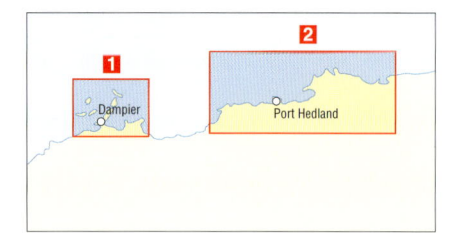

Lying offshore from the town of Dampier and within reach of small boats, the islands of the Dampier Archipelago offer an outstanding range of species in relatively unspoilt conditions. Sailfish and other game fish abound in the area. In spring there is a run of Spanish mackerel in Port Hedland harbour, and occasional schools of yellowtail tuna at other times. Boating anglers arriving for the first time need to take care. The submerged rocks and reefs combined with big tides can prove hazardous.

DAMPIER ARCHIPELAGO

Two rivers south-west of Dampier are accessible to anglers. The mouth of the **Fortescue River**, which is near James Point, attracts black jewfish, barramundi and threadfin salmon. Closer to Dampier, the **Maitland River** is fished in the reedy pools at the highway crossing for oxeye herring (tarpon), barramundi and trevally, with queenfish and trevally at the river entrance.

The **Dampier Archipelago** is a maze of islands out from Dampier. There is boat launching at Dampier from Hampton Harbour and a ramp that is suitable for small to medium-sized boats at Withnell Bay, on the Burrup Peninsula. There are big tides and submerged rocks and channels, so seek local advice before starting out. This is a relatively unspoilt area and the range of fish is outstanding, including queenfish, trevally, mackerel, red emperor, coral trout, shark, cobia and black jewfish. The great attraction is the abundance of sailfish, which leap from the water and can be trolled in many areas. One of the best trolling locations is between **Rosemary Island** and **Bare Rock**.

The best bottom fishing spots include the area around the natural gas pipeline in **Mermaid Sound**, for coral trout, spangled emperor, sweetlip, red emperor, and giant, golden and gold-spotted trevally, and **Madeleine Shoals**, at the northern tip of Legendre Island, for trevally, cod, shark, spangled emperor, sweetlip and red emperor.

While Dampier is the port for the iron ore mines in the region, most travellers stay at Karratha, the tourist centre. The best places to fish further east are at Point Samson and Cossack. The **Point Samson Beach** allows boat launching to fish for queenfish, Spanish mackerel, black jewfish and trevally. At **Cossack** the wharf is fished for trevally, mackerel and queenfish. There are many tidal creeks in the area, with queenfish, trevally, whiting and flathead at the entrances, and barramundi, oxeye herring and mangrove jack upstream.

PORT HEDLAND AND ENVIRONS

The mangrove-lined coast centring on the big mining town of Port Hedland invites creek as well as offshore fishing. The **Sherlock River**, about 120 km to the west of the town, is easily reached and is popular with anglers from both the Karratha and Port Hedland areas. Barramundi, mangrove jack, threadfin salmon and catfish are in good numbers here. Offshore from the Sherlock River is **Depuch Island**, where boat anglers gather, and sometimes camp, in

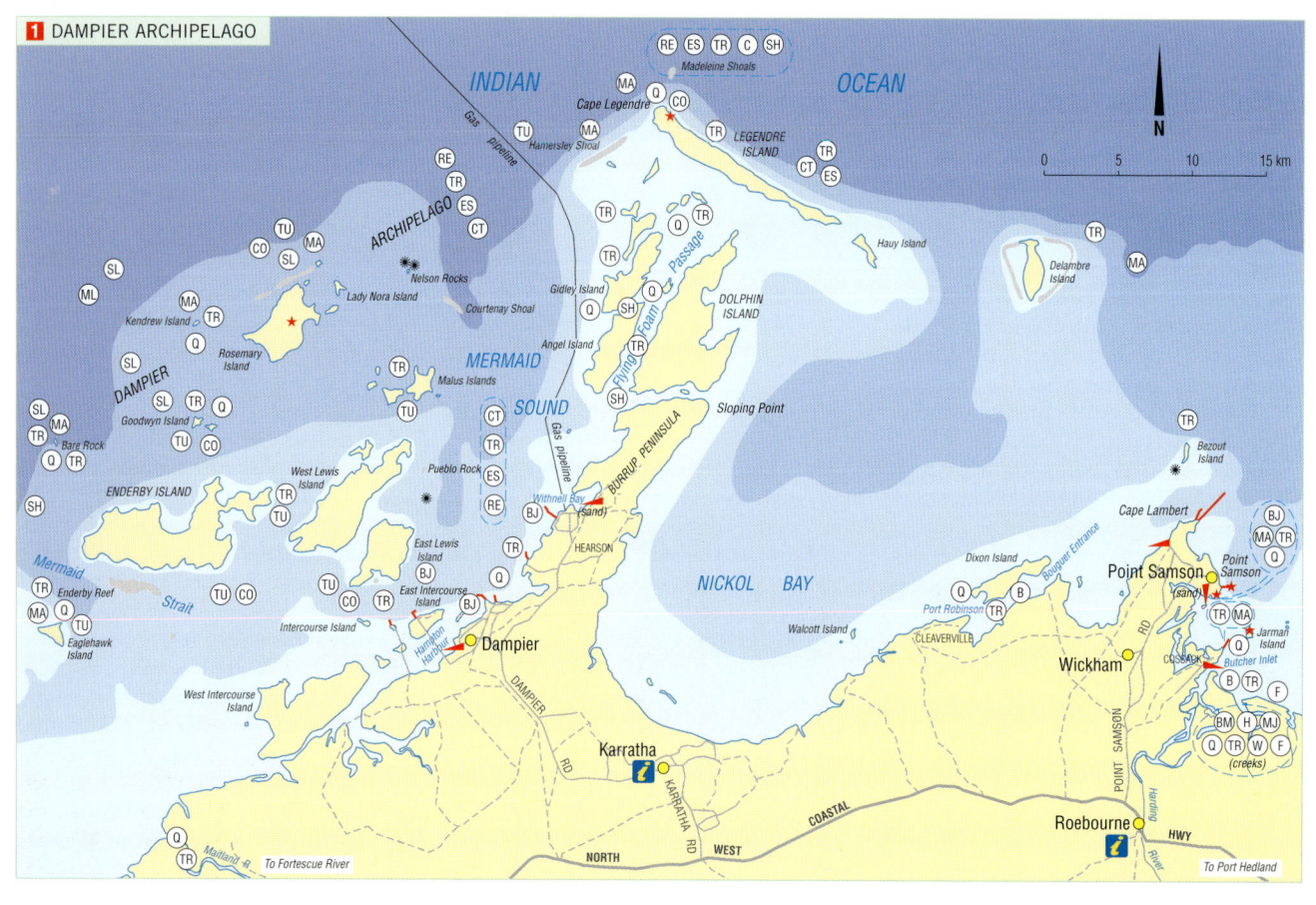

COASTAL FISHING GASCOYNE–KIMBERLEY REGION WESTERN AUSTRALIA

2 PORT HEDLAND AND ENVIRONS

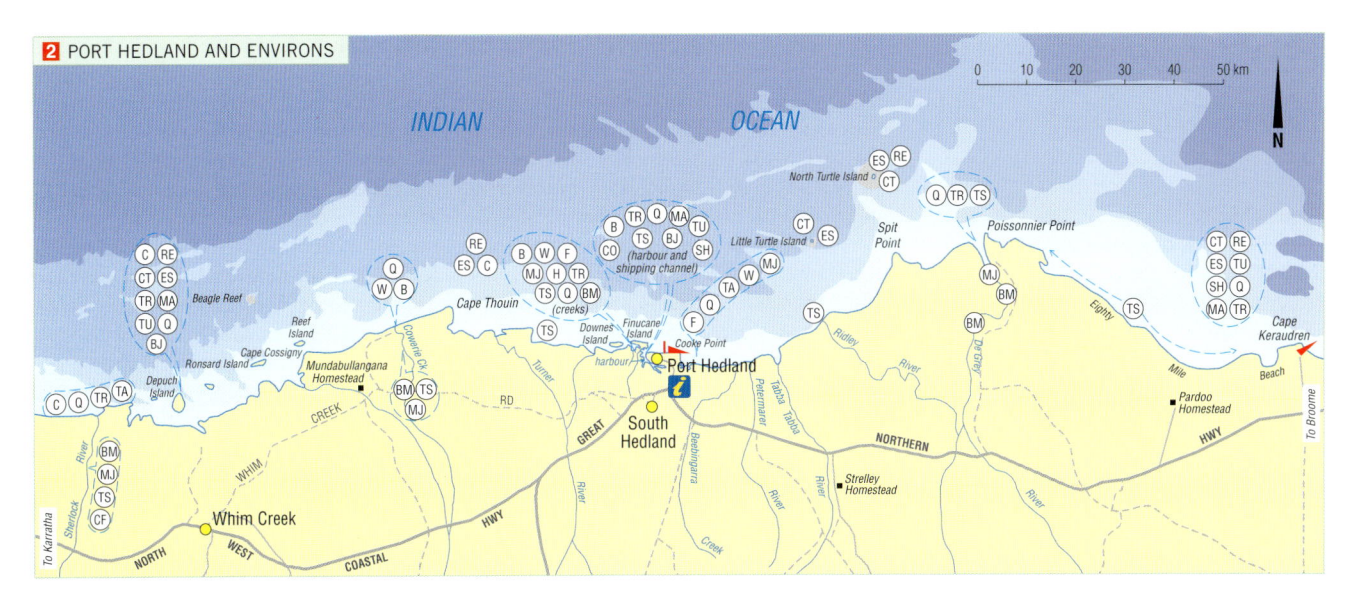

pursuit of the Spanish mackerel, longtail tuna, black jewfish, queenfish and trevally that cruise the waters.

Other creeks and bays in this area can only be reached by four-wheel drive, but **Cowerie Creek** is definitely worth the effort for the species around the entrance, such as queenfish, whiting and bream, as well as the barramundi, threadfin salmon and mangrove jack upriver.

Port Hedland harbour is a superb fishing area. Black jewfish offer a challenge around the jetty, as once they take a bait they often make a dash for the jetty piles, breaking the angler's line as a result. Schools of longtail tuna also come into the harbour, and a huge run of Spanish mackerel each spring has all the locals with small boats trolling up and down to get their share of the action. Perhaps the most sought-after fish are the threadfin salmon, which make a winter run. The best fishing for them is around the **Spoil Bank**, a sand spit just west of the jetty that is an underwater accumulation of material from channel dredgings. The shipping channel itself provides bottom fishing for black jewfish, bream and trevally, while trolling anglers target cobia, tuna, queenfish and mackerel. The coastal creeks opposite **Finucane Island** are good for boat fishing on an incoming tide, for threadfin salmon, queenfish and barramundi. Bream, whiting, flathead, mangrove jack, oxeye herring and trevally are also possible in these coastal creeks.

In the right place at the right time, mostly in winter, a haul of threadfin salmon is on the cards from **Eighty Mile Beach**, which is easily reached by road from the North West Coastal Highway. **Cape Keraudren**, at the eastern end of the beach, has a boat ramp for offshore fishing for trevally, mackerel, queenfish, tuna and bottom species such as red emperor and coral trout.

Evening jetty fishing at Point Samson, near Wickham

GUIDE TO LOCAL FISH

		Dampier Archipelago	Port Hedland and environs
BD	barracuda	●	
BM	barramundi	●	●
B	bream	●	●
CF	catfish	●	
CO	cobia	●	●
C	cod	●	●
RE	emperor, red	●	●
ES	emperor, spangled	●	●
F	flathead	●	●
H	herring, oxeye	●	●
MJ	jack, mangrove	●	●
BJ	jewfish, black	●	●
M	mackerel	●	●
ML	marlin	●	
Q	queenfish	●	●
SL	sailfish	●	
TS	salmon, threadfin	●	●
SH	shark	●	●
ES	sweetlip	●	●
TA	tarwhine	●	●
TR	trevally, giant	●	
TR	trevally, others	●	●
CT	trout, coral	●	●
TU	tuna	●	●
W	whiting		●

Broome to Cambridge Gulf

Type of fishing
bay, creek, jetty, offshore, reef, rock

Target fish
barramundi, red emperor, sailfish, threadfin salmon

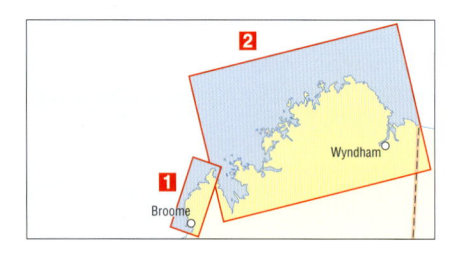

Stretching from Broome to the Northern Territory border, this area is one of the final frontiers for serious anglers. The pristine waters produce huge populations of great northern species such as queenfish and trevally. The less intrepid can drop a line from the Entrance Point Jetty at Broome and still not be disappointed.

BROOME

The fishing around Broome is magnificent. One of the most prolific sailfish grounds in the world is a mere 20 km or so offshore, and each July a tournament that attracts anglers from all over Australia is held here. The number of sailfish tagged and released can run into the hundreds. Broome is also one of the places where guided fishing trips into remote areas of the Kimberley can be arranged.

The shoreline of this old pearling town has tremendous tides, but the Town Beach boat ramp and the one at Entrance Point can be used at either high or low tides. Boat anglers need not go far, as a big hole only 150 m out from the jetty at **Entrance Point** is a famous black jewfish spot. The jetty itself is very popular for handliners with heavy lines, who also seek trevally and queenfish.

Creeks running into **Roebuck Bay** carry fork-tailed catfish, barramundi, mangrove jack, fingermark and threadfin salmon, while in the bay there are the wrecks of some Catalina flying boats, sunk during World War II, which have created reef conditions on an otherwise featureless bottom. **Roebuck Deep**, a channel some 2 km west of the town, is a good place to look for shark, black jewfish and fingermark. Rock anglers can try for the prevalent longtail tuna and mackerel at **Gantheaume Point**.

BROOME TO CAPE LEVEQUE

Disaster Rock, 13 km offshore to the south-west of Broome, attracts trevally, mackerel, tuna and barracuda, and there is bottom fishing for coral trout, red emperor and fingermark. Much further offshore, about 260 km, are the **Rowley Shoals**, which provide outstanding fishing for reef species and pelagics such as sailfish and tuna.

The excellent land spots and rich offshore waters north of Broome continue to be reasonably accessible to land-based anglers and boat launchers all the way to Cape Leveque. **Cape Boileau**, **Quondong Point**, **James Price Point**, **Coulomb Point**, **Cape Bertholet** and **Cape Baskerville** can all be reached and have good stocks of spangled emperor, queenfish, trevally and cod. Fishing is best on a rising tide. Permission is required to enter the **Aboriginal reserves** of Beagle Bay, including Cape Baskerville, and Lombadina, which covers One Arm Point and an area to the east of Lombadina Point.

North of Cape Baskerville are the **Lacepede Islands**, a group of sand islands

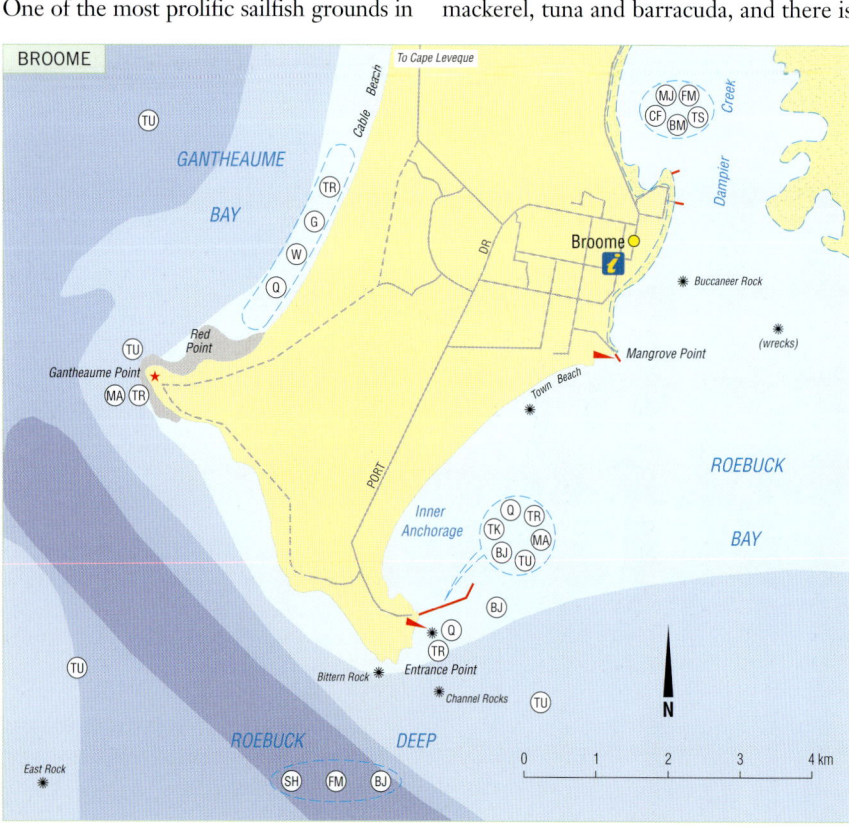

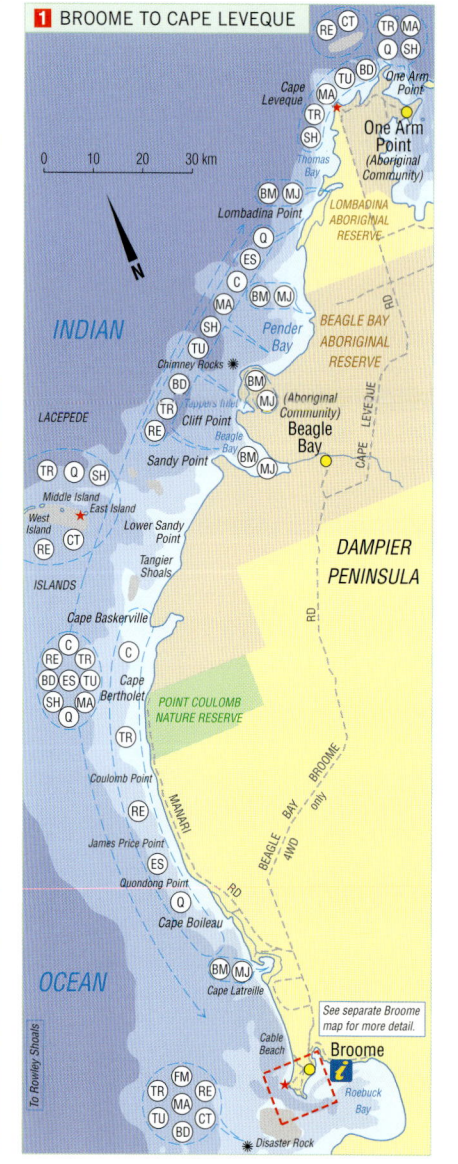

COASTAL FISHING GASCOYNE–KIMBERLEY REGION   **WESTERN AUSTRALIA**

surrounded by reefs and sandbars. Trevally and queenfish are the main species in the shallow waters, while pelagics circle the reefs and red emperor and coral trout are over the reefs in great numbers. There are numerous sharks in all these waters, demanding caution – along with patience as they steal catch after catch.

Beagle Bay, **Tappers Inlet**, **Pender Bay** and **Lombadina Point** have pelagics and reef fish such as red emperor, trevally, barracuda, tuna, shark, mackerel, cod, spangled emperor and queenfish in their sheltered waters. Barramundi and mangrove jack are up the bay creeks.

Both **Cape Leveque** and **One Arm Point** can have good land-based fishing for trevally and mackerel, and the offshore fishing is quite remarkable for both surface species and the main bottom species of red emperor and coral trout.

DERBY TO CAMBRIDGE GULF

This area, known as the Kimberley Coast, is one of the most remote, spectacular and untamed stretches of the Australian coastline. Just getting to the coast can be an adventure, and other than in the major coastal towns of Derby and Wyndham, it usually demands a four-wheel-drive vehicle in good condition.

Derby, nestled at the bottom of King Sound, has mostly muddy water, but there is reasonable fishing for threadfin salmon, shark and catfish from the town jetty. Small creeks to the north contain barramundi, mangrove jack, threadfin salmon and fingermark.

Much of the Kimberley is totally inaccessible during the wet season, at least from December to March, but during the dry season more intrepid travellers can get into isolated areas such as **Walcott Inlet** or **Port Warrender** and enjoy fishing beyond most people's wildest dreams. Huge barramundi, queenfish, cod, trevally of immense proportions and even big mackerel can be caught by anglers who have a car topper and can get a little offshore. **Wyndham** also has muddy inshore waters, but shark, catfish and threadfin salmon are possible from the wharf.

The entire Kimberley Coast and lower reaches of all rivers are the domain of large and dangerous saltwater crocodiles. Fishing in these areas needs to be approached with great caution. Excellent guided fishing trips, for as long a time and into as remote an area as you like, can be arranged from Kununurra, and this can be a way to enjoy the unique Kimberley experience without most of the risks. Tackle shops in the region should be able to supply the names and contact numbers for reputable guides.

The Kimberley coastline near Wyndham, much of which is totally inaccessible during the wet season

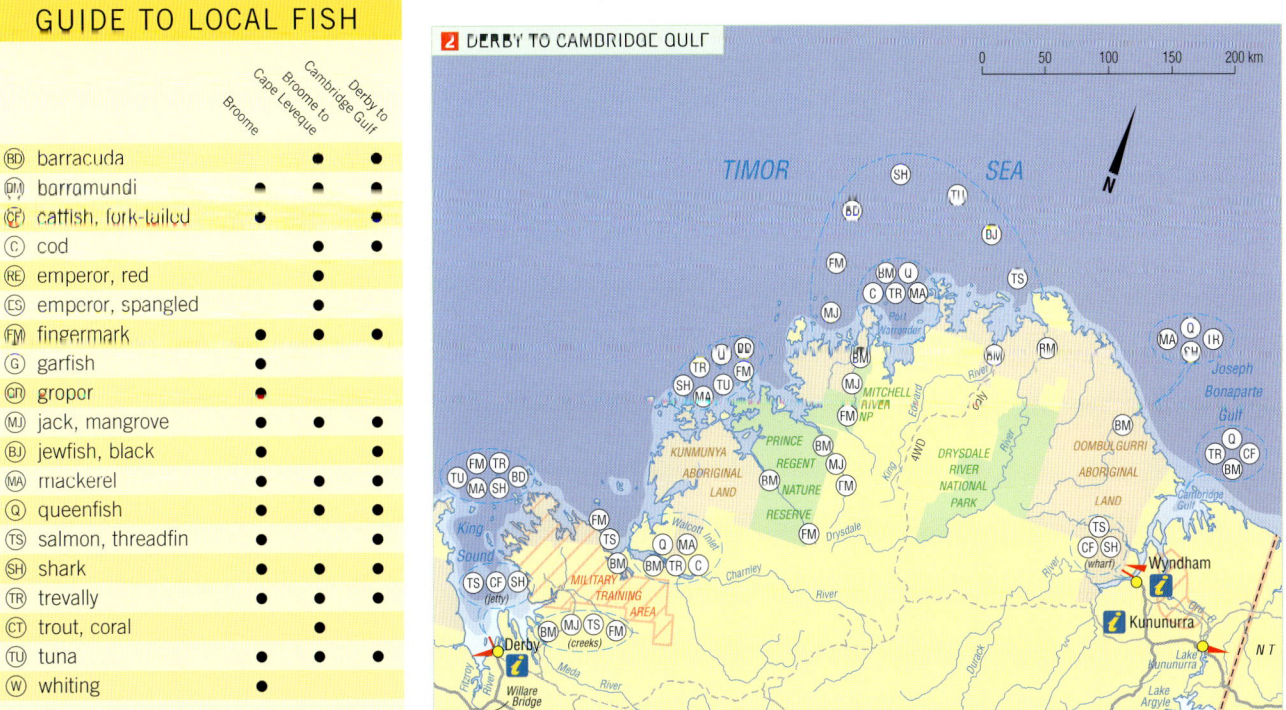

GUIDE TO LOCAL FISH

	Broome	Broome to Cape Leveque	Derby to Cambridge Gulf
(BD) barracuda		●	●
(BM) barramundi	●	●	●
(CF) catfish, fork-tailed	●		●
(C) cod		●	●
(RE) emperor, red		●	
(ES) emperor, spangled		●	
(FM) fingermark	●	●	●
(G) garfish	●		
(Gr) groper	●		
(MJ) jack, mangrove	●	●	●
(BJ) jewfish, black	●	●	●
(MA) mackerel	●	●	●
(Q) queenfish	●	●	●
(TS) salmon, threadfin	●		●
(SH) shark	●	●	●
(TR) trevally	●	●	●
(CT) trout, coral		●	
(TU) tuna	●	●	●
(W) whiting	●		

WESTERN AUSTRALIA

Inland Fishing

Western Australia is a vast, dry State, and except for the south-western corner and the rugged Kimberley region, it is generally flat and lacking the major inland waterways that are characteristic of the east coast. In between the productive northern and southern extremities there are some relatively short coastal rivers and streams, widely scattered and offering estuarine rather than true freshwater fishing.

In the karri and jarrah forests of the South-west corner of Western Australia a fragile but productive trout fishery survives thanks to annual stocking. The fishery comprises small rivers and streams flowing mostly through dense bushland, and a limited number of irrigation and farm dams in which both brown and rainbow trout have been stocked. Redfin have established themselves in many Southwest waterways, sometimes too successfully. The only native fish with any angling potential is the eel-tailed catfish (known as cobbler).

The wild and largely unpopulated Kimberley region has many rivers whose flow is generally dependent on the strength of the wet season. Here the barramundi is supreme, with sooty grunter, eel-tailed catfish and archer fish in the true freshwater stretches, and a wide variety of hard-fighting tropical species in the tidal-influenced lower reaches.

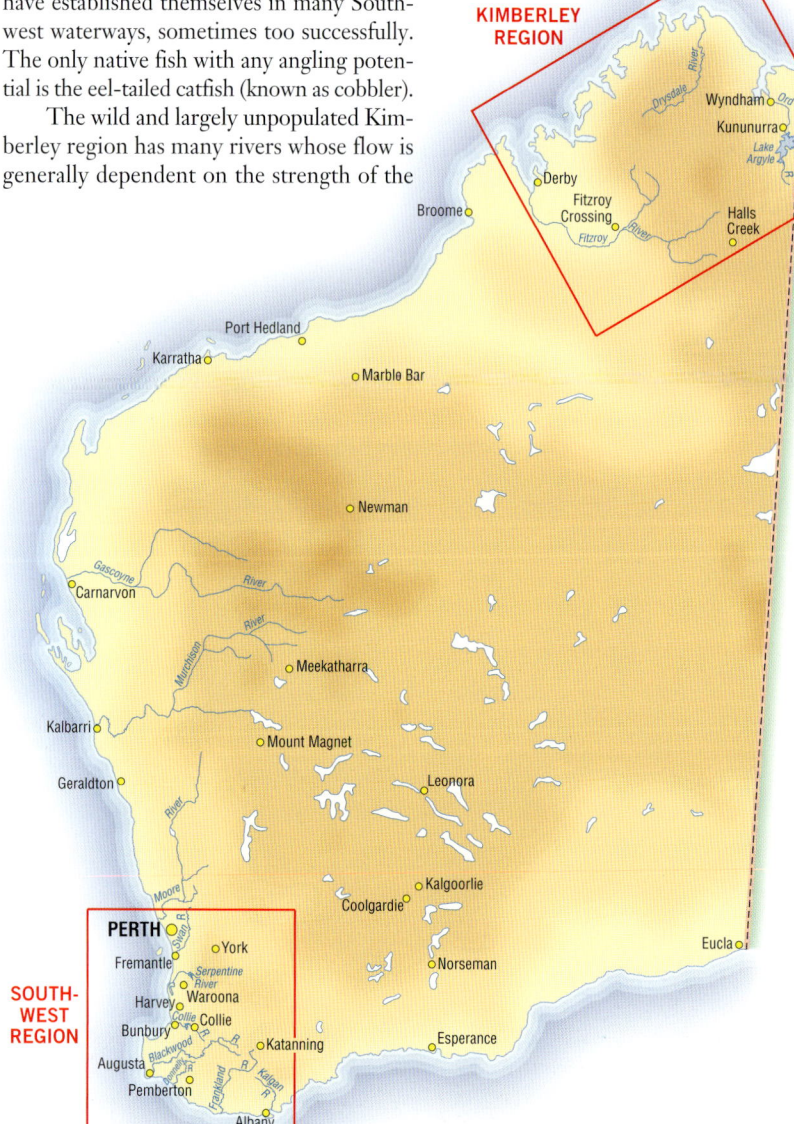

INLAND FISHING

WHERE TO FISH

Inland

SOUTH-WEST REGION • 332

The south-west corner stretching from Perth in the north down to Albany in the south is where populations of rainbow trout, brown trout and redfin perch can be found. Many of the major rivers and some of the irrigation dams are stocked with trout from the Pemberton Hatchery. The Warren, Donnelly, Blackwood, Collie, Brunswick and Murray rivers all produce fish during the season but fish best during steady water flows. Many of the smaller feeder streams of these major rivers are also productive trout spots with the Lefroy Brook and Hesters Brook a couple of the best fish producers. The large man-made irrigation water bodies that are stocked with trout and can be fished during the season are Waroona Dam, Drakesbrook Weir, Logues Brook Dam, Harvey Weir, Wellington Dam, Glen Mervin Dam and Big Brook Dam. The best redfin waters are Wellington Dam, Murray River, Warren River and Big Brook Dam. Closure of water bodies by Fisheries Western Australia varies from year to year so check regulations before wetting a line. Private waters can be accessed by joining the Western Australian Trout and Freshwater Angling Association. The association stocks numerous small farm dams.

KIMBERLEY REGION • 333

Many of the bigger rivers of the Kimberley have superb barramundi fishing along much of their length, with sooty grunter, oxeye herring and archer fish upstream, and mangrove jack, fingermark, threadfin salmon, pikey bream and queenfish adding to the variety as the rivers come under tidal influence. The Fitzroy and Ord rivers are the most accessible of the region, and south of Kununurra both Lake Kununurra and massive Lake Argyle offer consistently good, true freshwater fishing.

Fork-tailed catfish
Sometimes referred to as salmon catfish, the family includes blue salmon and threadfin salmon. They are estuarine and marine fish and can change their body colour to suit the environment.

INLAND FISHING

WESTERN AUSTRALIA

Runs under bridges are prime spots on the small streams around Pemberton

The coastal streams of the rest of the State are generally short and more brackish than fresh, offering first-class bream and estuary fishing in the southern half and a range of tropical opportunities in the north.

Freshwater regulations

You are required to have a licence to fish in freshwater in Western Australia, and depending on the species you are targeting you might need a special licence for that species. Check with Fisheries Western Australia about the licences required as well as size and bag limits for your catch and if there is a closed season. Freshwater fish can only be caught on a rod and line, and marron have special rules

GUIDE TO LOCAL FISH

- archer fish
- barramundi
- bream, black
- bream, pikey
- catfish, eel-tailed
- catfish, fork-tailed
- fingermark
- grunter, sooty
- herring, oxeye
- jack, mangrove
- marron
- queenfish
- redfin
- salmon, threadfin
- trout, brown
- trout, rainbow

Size and bag limits apply. Consult Fisheries WA guide, 'Fishing for the future' for details.

regarding methods of capture depending on which water body you will be fishing. As Western Australia is a dry State, the annual rainfall can have a devastating effect on the freshwater species, so open seasons and bag limits can change from year to year. To obtain up-to-date information visit the Fisheries Western Australia web site at www.wa.gov.au/westfish or ring (08) 9482 7333.

Boating rules

Unlike most other States, Western Australia does not require a licence to drive a boat, although with a few exemptions, all boats must be registered. Contact the Department of Transport for details.

Speed limits apply on many stretches of sheltered and inshore waters. These areas are marked by a sign indicating the speed limit in knots. As well as the limits applying to these specific areas, there are limits that can apply depending on circumstances. You must drop speed to 8 knots or less when in or around a mooring area, or within 45 m of the shore, a moored vessel, a person in the water, a jetty or wharf, and under the arch of a bridge. You must drop speed to 10 knots or less after dark everywhere on the Swan and Canning rivers (or a lower speed if in a speed-limited area).

Coastal rivers

While probably not offering true freshwater fishing, the coastal rivers between Esperance and Kalbarri generally hold good populations of black bream that venture up into the fresh water. Among the more renowned rivers are the Kalgan, Frankland, Blackwood, Collie, Serpentine, Swan, Moore and Murchison, all of which are capable of producing fish in the 1 to 2-kg range. The best fishing is generally around the upstream snags in summer, and in the lower reaches around jetty and bridge pilings after the rains have pushed the bream downstream.

FURTHER INFORMATION

Fishing and boating Offices of Fisheries Western Australia are Head Office on the 3rd floor, 168–170 St Georges Tce, Perth, tel. (08) 9482 7333; Suite 7, Frederick House, 70–74 Frederick St, Albany, tel. (08) 9841 7766; 96 Stirling St, Bunbury, tel. (08) 9721 2688; Port of Pearls, 401 Port Dve, Broome, tel. (08) 9192 1121; 48a Bussell Hwy, Busselton, tel. (08) 9752 2152; Bandy Creek Boat Harbour, Esperance, tel. (08) 9071 1839; 147 South Tce, Fremantle, tel. (08) 9335 6800; Hillarys Marina, Ground floor, Transport Building, 86 Southside Dve, Hillarys, tel. (08) 9448 6028; 15 Leslie St, Mandurah, tel. (08) 9535 1240. For full details on boating safety and regulations, contact the Maritime division of the Department of Transport, 1 Essex St, Fremantle, tel. (08) 9216 8999; or Short St, Broome, tel. (08) 9193 5923. The Boating Industry Association can be contacted on tel. (08) 9271 9688. The Department of Conservation and Land Management has offices at Broome, tel. (08) 9192 1036 and Kununurra, tel. (08) 9168 4200.

Tourist centres Old Railway Station, Proudlove Pde, Albany, tel. (08) 9841 1088; 70 Blackwood Ave, Augusta, tel. (08) 9758 0166; Old Railway Station, Carmody Pl, Bunbury, tel. (08) 9721 7922; Throssell Street, Collie, tel. (08) 9734 2051; 2 Clarendon St, Derby, tel. (08) 9191 1426; cnr Great Northern Hwy and Flynn Dr, Fitzroy Crossing, tel. (08) 9191 5355; Great Northern Hwy, Halls Creek, tel. (08) 9168 6262; South Western Hwy, Harvey, tel. (08) 9729 1122; Katanning Tourist Bureau, 54 Austral Tce and Clive St, Katanning, tel. (08) 9821 2634; East Kimberley Tourism House, Coolibah Dr, Kununurra, tel. (08) 9168 1177; Cnr Rose and Edward sts, Manjimup, tel. (08) 9771 1831; Cnr Bussell Hwy and Tunbridge Rd, Margaret River, tel. (08) 9757 2911; Karri Visitors Centre, Brockman St, Pemberton, tel. (08) 9776 1133; Kimberley Motors, Lot 626, Great Northern Hwy, Wyndham, tel. (08) 9161 1281; York Town Hall, 81 Avon Terrace, York, tel. (08) 9641 1301.

Oxeye herring

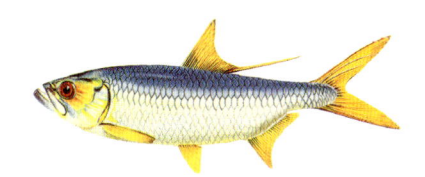

The oxeye herring is an active, shiny, large-scaled fish, mostly silver in colour and a great lure and fly taker. Also known as tarpon, this fish is fast and aerobatic when hooked on light tackle.

WESTERN AUSTRALIA

South-west Region

There are two main centres of trout fishing in the South-west, Pemberton and the Waroona–Harvey district, each offering uniquely Western Australian freshwater fishing.

Type of fishing
dam, river, stream

Target fish
brown trout, eel-tailed catfish, rainbow trout, redfin

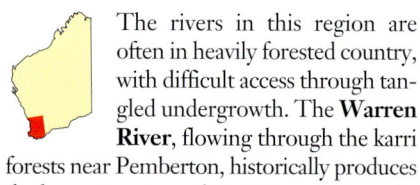

The rivers in this region are often in heavily forested country, with difficult access through tangled undergrowth. The **Warren River**, flowing through the karri forests near Pemberton, historically produces the largest trout caught in Western Australia each year. The river, like most in the area, consists of long pools between stretches of rapids, and the best fish invariably come from the fast-moving, well-oxygenated water of the rapids. Among the better known areas of white water are **Bannister Road** and **Moons Crossing**. Flies that imitate the large minnows of the area work well, and a big muddler minnow or parson's glory is a good starting point. **Lefroy Brook**, which flows through Pemberton and is the site of the State hatchery, eventually winds its way into the Warren and is a wonderful early-season fly fishery, but extensive damming of its catchment results in it almost drying up in the upper reaches from early summer. **Big Brook Dam**, on a tributary of the Lefroy, can produce good size browns and smaller rainbows, but suffers from an increasing redfin infestation.

The **Donnelly River**, about 25 km west of Pemberton, has consistently good early-season fishing for rainbows, especially upstream from Scotts Bridge on the Vasse Highway. Many small streams around Pemberton hold reasonable numbers of browns and rainbows, but getting access to the runs and the fish can involve a bit of work.

The **Blackwood River** and its tributaries carry good numbers of big fish in most years, but the main river is challenging to fish. The fish are in the fast-moving water and it pays to wait until the high, dirty waters of early spring have subsided before fishing this fascinating river. Of the tributaries, **Hester Brook** is the most consistent rainbow trout water, especially early in the season. There are also redfin here.

East of Bunbury, the huge **Wellington Reservoir** and the upper reaches of the **Collie River** are renowned as redfin habitats. Downstream of the dam, the Collie becomes a beautiful, cool trout water, regarded by many as the best summer fishery in the South-west. The rainbows average from 500 g to 1 kg and a handful of 2 to 3-kg fish are taken in most years.

The **Brunswick River** produces rainbow and brown trout but the fish seem to be concentrated in small areas, so much searching is required to find the hot spots. The **Harvey River** above **Harvey Weir** was once one of the best brown trout rivers in the State, but the construction of the new dam at the weir has seen it decline as a worthwhile fishery. **Stirling Dam** and the upper Harvey River are now off limits to anglers due to water catchment regulations, so the major fishable water body in the area is Harvey Weir where trout, perch and marron can still be found in good numbers.

Lake Navarino, just east of the town of Waroona, is better known as a redfin dam, although stocking of ex-hatchery brood fish trout in spring provides anglers with a chance of catching big fish for the first few weeks of the season. **Drakesbrook Weir** south-east of Waroona, has always fished well for redfin and recent consistent stocking with rainbow and brown trout is starting to pay dividends.

The **Murray River**, in the faster moving section through the Darling Range, fishes well for rainbows in spring and early summer, with some of the best runs downstream from the escarpment. Smaller streams to the south, such as **Samson Brook** and **McKnoe Brook**, carry small populations of rainbows and occasional browns.

Eel-tailed catfish are found through many of the rivers and streams and fishing at night with earthworms is the most favoured method. Marron, the largest freshwater crayfish native to the South-west, is regarded as a true delicacy. Considerable aquaculture efforts in recent years have resulted in its spread through a number of South-west rivers and dams. In 1987 marron catches dropped severely, and since then it has been subject to a short open season and stringent size and bag limits as well as gear restrictions. The traditional bushman's way of taking it with a bush pole and wire snare is finding favour and 'snare only' areas are increasingly being used as a conservation measure.

WESTERN AUSTRALIA

INLAND FISHING KIMBERLEY REGION

Kimberley Region

The freshwater sections of most rivers hold barramundi and sooty grunter where there are pools big enough to support them. Oxeye herring, archer fish and fork-tailed catfish are found in most streams.

Type of fishing
dam, river, stream
Target fish
barramundi, catfish, sooty grunter

Generally in this region, the more remote the river, the better the fishing will be. The most accessible and the most frequently fished rivers are the Fitzroy and Ord, although the Ord has a large quarantine area stretching downstream from a few kilometres below Kununurra.

The **Fitzroy River** is the State's foremost barramundi waterway and the accessible spots such as **Willare Bridge**, **Telegraph Pool** and beautiful **Geikie Gorge** further up the river produce good fishing on lures and live baits.

Kununurra is situated on the northern shore of Lake Kununurra, which is in turn north of the massive Lake Argyle. **Lake Kununurra** is a great water for light tackle fishing for sooty grunter to 2 kg and catfish.

Early-season fishing below the dam wall of Lake Kununurra on the Ord, just south of Victoria Highway crossing, turns up exceptional barramundi at times, as does **Ivanhoe Crossing** further downstream, and at other spots along the river between Wyndham and Kununurra.

Lake Argyle is an enormous body of water that empties into Lake Kununurra and then into the Ord, providing irrigation for the large fruit and vegetable farms of the region. A commercial fishery exists in Lake Argyle for very large fork-tailed catfish and there is plenty of scope for recreational fishing for the same species. Cherabin, a large freshwater prawn found in most of the Kimberley rivers, provides excellent eating or makes wonderful live bait for barramundi.

When fishing the northern rivers be very aware that you are in crocodile country. Do not clean fish on the water's edge, and stand well clear of the bank when fishing. Danger areas should have warning signs, but vandals tend to steal them. If you are unsure, contact the local office of the Department of Conservation and Land Management at Broome or Kununurra, or the Broome office of the Fisheries Department.

Canoe fishing on the upper King Edward River

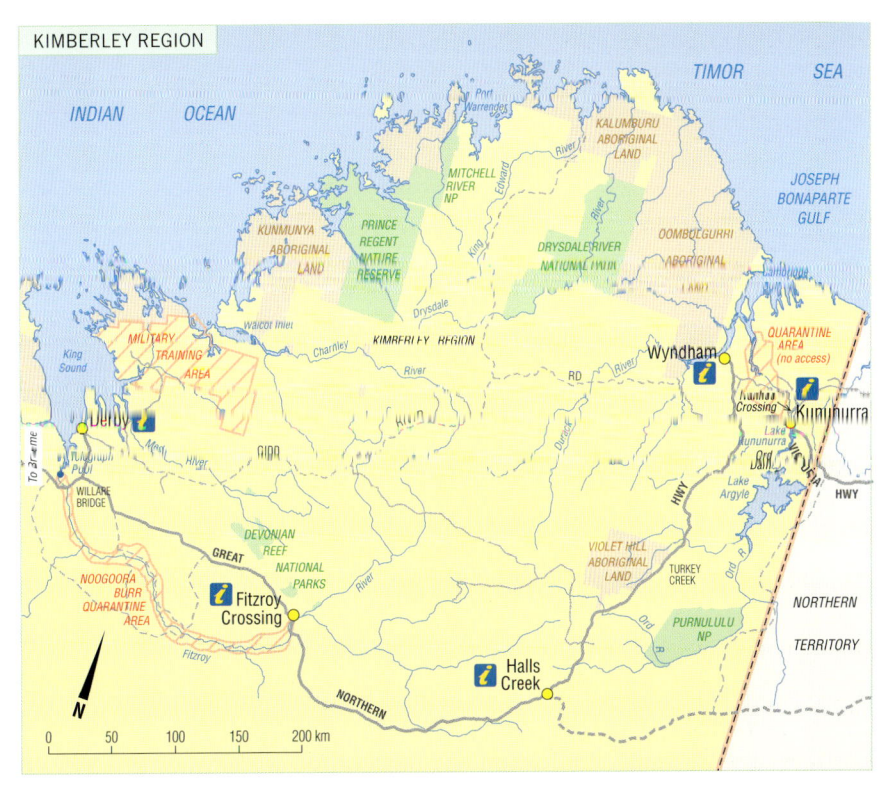

GUIDE TO LOCAL FISH

	South-west Region	Kimberley Region
archer fish		•
barramundi		•
bream, black	•	
bream, pikey	•	
catfish, eel-tailed	•	
catfish, fork-tailed		•
fingermark		•
grunter, sooty		•
herring, oxeye		•
jack, mangrove		•
queenfish		•
redfin	•	
salmon, threadfin		•
trout, brown	•	
trout, rainbow	•	

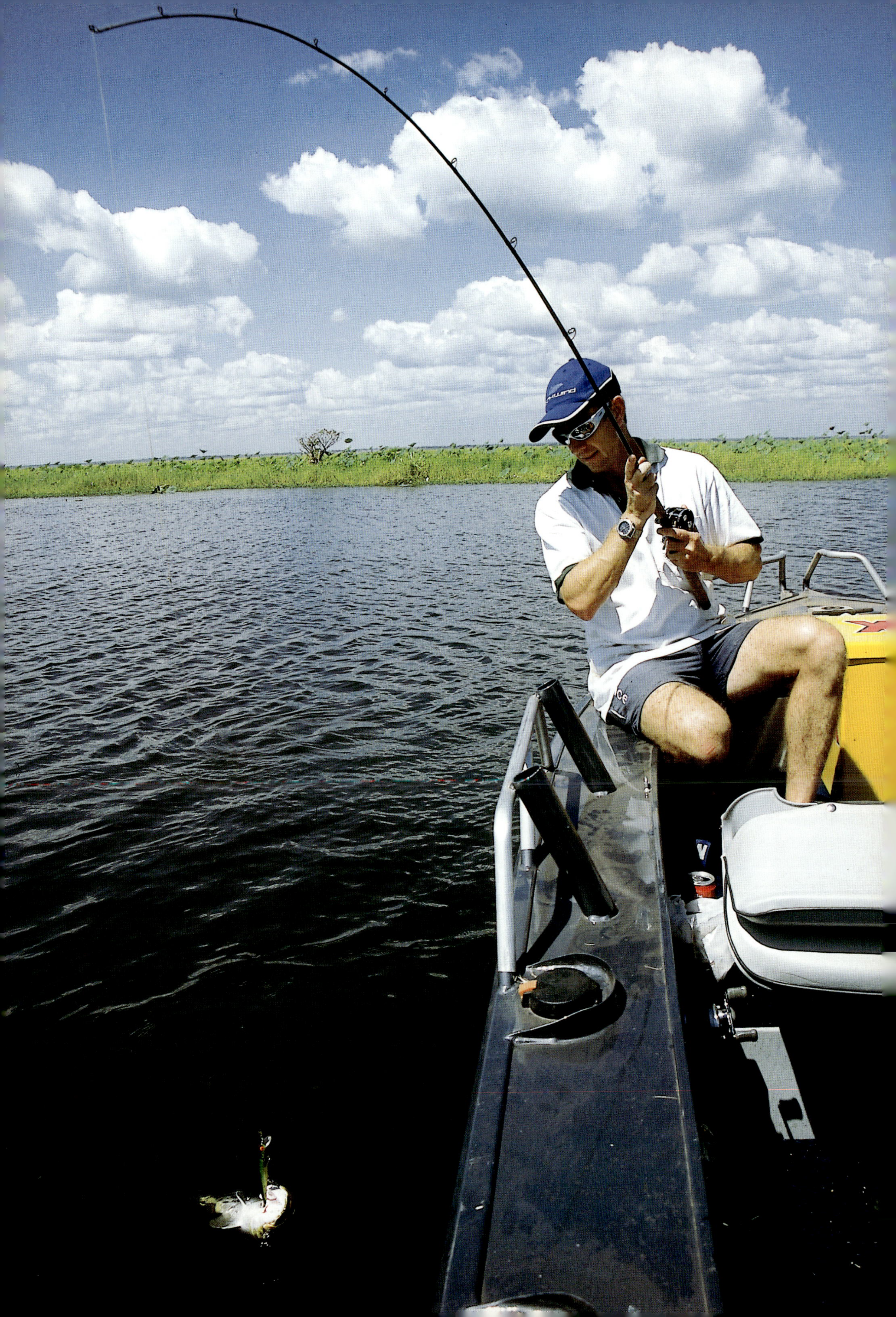

Coastal Fishing

Darwin Region	338
Gove Region	348

Inland Fishing

West Coast Rivers Region	354
Adelaide–Mary Rivers Region	356
Kakadu Region	358
East Coast Rivers Region	360

Northern Territory

The Northern Territory is one of the last great wilderness areas in the world. It is a place for big fish and memorable experiences. The Territory's distance from major population centres, combined with a huge tropical coastline and literally thousands of rivers, creeks and freshwater lagoons, point to a healthy recreational fishery where the quality of angling can be quite simply outstanding.

Fishing in Corroboree
Billabong on the Mary River

The Territory provides some of the best fishing in Australia. The coast has sheltered bays, estuaries, mangrove-lined creeks, offshore reefs and islands, and much of the fishing is easily reached from population centres. The inland has huge areas of wetlands, with rivers, billabongs and flood plains to be explored. In these outback environments the barramundi is king. Many inland visitors go on a guided camping and fishing tour to enjoy the camping life and get to the fishing spots with someone who has worked in the wilderness over the years. Barramundi, saratoga and sooty grunter stocks will be depleted by careless fishing, and it is a rule of the north that you retain fish only for the table, and catch and release the other fish.

There are remote and rugged areas that require a four-wheel drive vehicle but, except during the height of the wet season, there are plenty of excellent fishing locations that can be accessed in a two wheel drive vehicle. The Wet, however, renews the inland water system, and the best fishing conditions are in the months after the Wet, and then again late in the dry season.

Parts of the Territory, such as Arnhem Land, Bathurst and Melville islands and south of the Daly River, are designated Aboriginal land and a permit is required before entering these areas and fishing. Other fishing spots are on station properties and access is restricted or subject to permission. However, there are many inland waterways where permission to camp and fish is not required.

NORTHERN TERRITORY

Coastal Fishing

Whether you are targeting reef fish like fingermark (golden snapper) or red emperor, or chasing pelagics like Spanish mackerel or queenfish (leatherskin), the coast of the Northern Territory will give you more opportunities than just about anywhere else in Australia. This is virgin country, with very little commercial or recreational pressure. The real difficulty is access but, once you are on the water in a remote location, catching quality blue water fish is usually simply a matter of launching a boat and heading out.

The main attraction for most anglers visiting the Territory is the mighty barramundi but there are many other species available around the 3000 km of coastline. Great tropical sportfish such as the giant trevally, queenfish, threadfin salmon, black jewfish, and mangrove jack inhabit inshore waters and estuaries. Marlin, sailfish, mackerel, tuna and a huge variety of reef fish are available offshore.

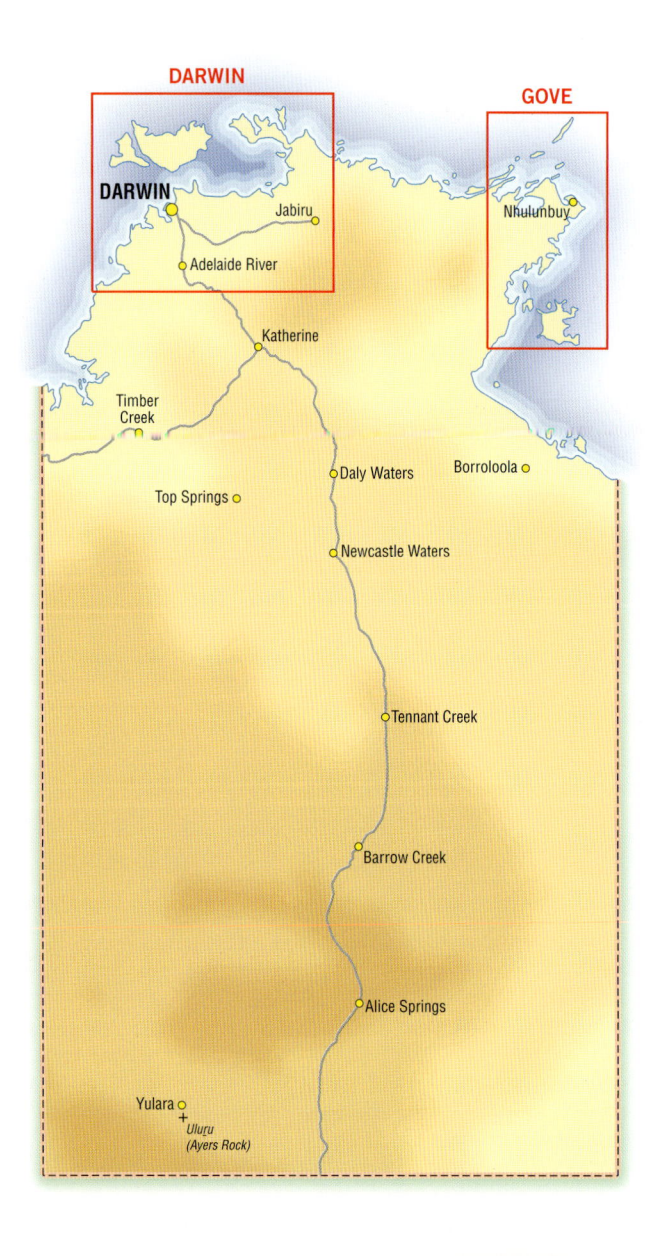

COASTAL FISHING

WHERE TO FISH

Along the coast

DARWIN REGION ● 338

Some of the best blue water fishing in Australia is available straight out of Darwin. You can fish from the shore or wharves of the city, take a car topper and explore the coastal estuaries, mangroves and sandbars, venture along the coast or to the offshore reefs by boat, or organise yourself a charter around the islands to go out game fishing.

GOVE REGION ● 348

The fishing on the east coast of Arnhem Land, based on the Gove Peninsula and Groote Eylandt, is legendary, but as access is difficult these great tropical waters remain scarcely touched. Nhulunbuy on the Gove Peninsula is the starting point. There is fishing all down this eastern coast; the popular fish are giant trevally, queenfish (leatherskin), mackerel, cobia and the occasional tuna. Black jewfish and fingermark (golden snapper) are taken from the harbour wharves, and sweetlip, coral trout and stripey are around the reefs. The islands in the region offer outstanding uncrowded fishing.

Tackle for the Territory

The most useful tackle is a good 6–8 kg casting rod coupled with a baitcaster or threadline reel. Baitcaster reels (the overhead style) are the most popular for catching barra and they are very versatile for most inland and offshore situations.

Strong handlines are often used by reef anglers but the above outfit will handle smaller reef species. Heavier gear will be necessary for larger reef fish such as the black jewfish. The best barramundi outfit is a 6–8 kg rod reel and line combination.

Rods should be around 1.7 m in length and suitable for casting lures to around 40 g. Small baitcasting or threadline reels that hold at least 150 m of 8 kg line are best. Good quality fishing lines of 6–8 kg breaking strain are generally used and braid lines are particularly suitable because of their small diameter and improved *feel*.

Use a double of main line around 1 m long tied with a spider hitch or bimini twist. Connect the double to a heavier monofilament leader of 15–20 kg using a suitable knot such as an Albright.

For barramundi, minnow style lures around 120 to 150 mm in length, which

COSTAL FISHING — NORTHERN TERRITORY

swim at around 3–4 m should be used when trolling the big rivers such as the Daly.

For casting at creek mouths and run-off gutters and casting for barramundi in the shallow estuaries, shallow-running, minnow-style lures with lots of *body roll* work best.

If fish are holding deep on larger creek run-offs, deep-diving minnow-style lures work and lead-head, rubber-tailed lures are also successful. Small minnow lures that swim to about 1 m are mostly used in the freshwater billabongs. Popper-style surface lures will take barramundi in some situations and provide sensational action on trevally and queenfish.

Tackle shops in the Northern Territory are well stocked and they are a great source of advice on the where, what and when of local fishing.

Territory regulations

Licences are not required for recreational fishing in the Northern Territory but a range of regulations are in place to ensure the quality of recreational fishing is maintained. Species-specific and general size and bag limits, equipment regulations and seasonal or area angling closures apply in some locations. Detailed fishing regulations are available from the Department of Primary Industry and Fisheries Recreational Fishing Office, tel. (08) 8999 2372 or check the web site at www.nt.gov.au/dpif/fisheries/recfish/recfish.shtml

Boating regulations

There are no requirements for licensing or registration of pleasure craft in the Northern Territory, although boaters must abide by minimum safety requirements. While at sea, you must observe the international boating regulations and carry the required boating equipment.

The requirements differ according to the size of the craft. For full details of requirements for recreational craft, contact the Department of Transport and Works, Marine Branch on (08) 8999 5253.

Navigation is often a problem in the Territory because of the lack of noticeable landmarks and anglers are advised to carry good navigation equipment. Those unfamiliar with the coastline should not venture far without an experienced guide. All vessels operating outside of sheltered waters and more than 2 miles (3.22 km) from the coastline are required by law to carry an approved EPIRB (Emer-gency Position Indicating Radio Beacon) with operating frequencies of 121.5 and 243 Mhz.

Red emperor

Highly rated as a table fish, red emperor is a much sought after species in tropical waters. Like many popular fish, this species is vulnerable to fishing pressure. Red emperor is mainly caught over heavy reef structure, where it inhabits the reef edge near the current influence.

ABORIGINAL LAND TRUSTS

Below are the relevant land councils in each region. Always allow at least ten working days for the processing of all permit applications.

Darwin Region

On the Territory's west coast there are two Aboriginal Land Trust areas: **Daly River/Port Keats** area and **Delissaville/Wagait/Larrakia** area. Permission is required to go onto this land, which includes the offshore Peron Islands. Permits are provided by the Northern Land Council in Darwin, tel. (08) 8920 5100, or by the Katherine office, tel. (08) 8972 2894. The Daly River/Port Keats Land Trust has a local office where permits may also be obtained, tel. (08) 8978 2355.

Bathurst and Melville islands make up the **Tiwi Land Council**. There are three designated areas on each island for angler camping. Permits can be obtained from the Amateur Fishermen's Association of the NT (AFANT), tel. (08) 8945 6455 or from the Tiwi Land Council, tel. (08) 8981 4898.

The **Gurig National Park** occupies the Cobourg Peninsula; permits to visit the area can be obtained from the Cobourg Peninsula Sanctuary Board, tel. (08) 8979 0244. The permits give permission for tourists to cross the Aboriginal Land Trust area of Arnhem Land in order to reach the peninsula, but those attempting the drive must keep to the designated route. The road is unsealed and open only during the dry months between May and October. There is a series of islands on the eastern side of the peninsula that are part of Arnhem Land, and boaters should not land without the correct permits.

Gove Region

The north east section of the Territory is part of the **Arnhem Land Aboriginal Land Trust**. Visitors who intend to drive to Gove through Arnhem Land must first seek permission from the Northern Land Council, tel. (08) 8920 5100. Once there, anglers wishing to fish beyond the township of Nhulunbuy can obtain a recreational permit locally from the Dhimurru Land Management & Aboriginal Corporation, tel. (08) 8987 3992. Access is limited to certain areas, and the islands north of the town are also subject to restrictions.

Those heading south to the areas on and around Groote Eylandt should contact the **Anindilyakawa Land Council**, tel. (08) 8987 6638. Groote is a mining settlement, with no tourist facilities. Most anglers who come to the island do so by invitation to participate in the popular annual fishing competition.

GUIDE TO LOCAL FISH

BD	barracuda
BM	barramundi
B	bream
CO	cobia
C	cod
RE	emperor, red
FM	fingermark
GR	groper
H	herring, wolf
MJ	jack, mangrove
BJ	jewfish, black
MA	mackerel, Spanish
MA	mackerel, spotted
MA	mackerel, others
ML	marlin, black
MF	moonfish
PF	parrotfish
Q	queenfish
SL	sailfish
TS	salmon, threadfin
SR	saratoga
SH	shark
SS	snapper, saddletail
SY	stripey
ES	sweetlip
TR	trevally, bigeye
TR	trevally, giant
TR	trevally, gold-spotted
TR	trevally, golden
CT	trout, coral
TU	tuna, longtail
TK	tuskfish

Bag and size limits apply. See the Department of Primary Industry and Fisheries guides for details.

FURTHER INFORMATION

Fishing The Fisheries Management head office of the Department of Primary Industry and Fisheries is at Berrimah Farm, Makagon Rd, Berrimah, tel. (08) 8999 2142. The department prints a number of free publications with details on regulations and information on fishing in the Northern Territory. They can be downloaded at www.nt.gov.au/dpif or ordered by tel. (08) 8999 2313.

Boating Tide charts are essential in the Top End, which has some of Australia's biggest tides. The range in Darwin Harbour can be greater than 7 m, leaving boat ramps high and dry on spring lows. Tide charts are available at the Darwin Port Corporation, GPO Box 390, Darwin 0801, tel. (08) 8922 0660. The Marine Branch, Department of Transport and Works is at 1st floor, Minerals House, 66 The Esplanade, Darwin, tel. (089) 8999 5285. It publishes guides to marine regulations and boating safety, which are available from its offices or its web site www.nt.gov.au/dtw/aboutus/branches/transport/marine

NORTHERN TERRITORY

COASTAL FISHING DARWIN REGION

Darwin Region

Some of the best blue water fishing in Australia is available straight out of Darwin. Head south, north or west, or simply go either way along the coast, and you're likely to find fishing as good as most 'city' anglers are ever likely to experience.

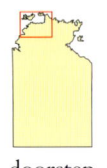

Launching facilities are excellent, with plenty of options for different weather conditions. And if worst comes to worst, you can fish right on Darwin's doorstep, along a 5-km stretch of coastline that is frequented by some terrific surface and bottom-dwelling species. If you are prepared to travel further afield, or tow a boat with a four-wheel drive to more remote coastal locations, you will find your efforts rewarded by an increased abundance of fish, and of a size to match their competitiveness.

Land-based anglers can fish from various points on the harbour foreshores and there are two wharves open to the public. These are at Stokes Hill and Mandorah. Both offer good fishing, especially during the dry season when mackerel and tuna come within casting distance. A fishing platform and artificial reef have been built at Stokes Hill wharf and there is a jetty beside the boat ramp at Nightcliff just outside the harbour.

Barramundi, salmon, mangrove jack, golden snapper and pikey bream are found around the tidal run-offs and creeks, in the harbour arms. For barramundi and salmon, these are best on the last two hours of the run-out tide and the first two hours of the run-in. Large black jewfish, golden snapper, cod, saddletail snapper, coral trout and tricky snapper are caught from the harbour's wrecks and reefs and pelagic fish such as queenfish and tuna are also available. Some good cobia have been caught at various locations. Succulent mud crabs are caught from many locations in the harbour.

Weather

Weather information is vital around this coastline since meteorological conditions can change dramatically and can also affect tidal conditions. Winds are generally light to moderate, usually from the east to south-east

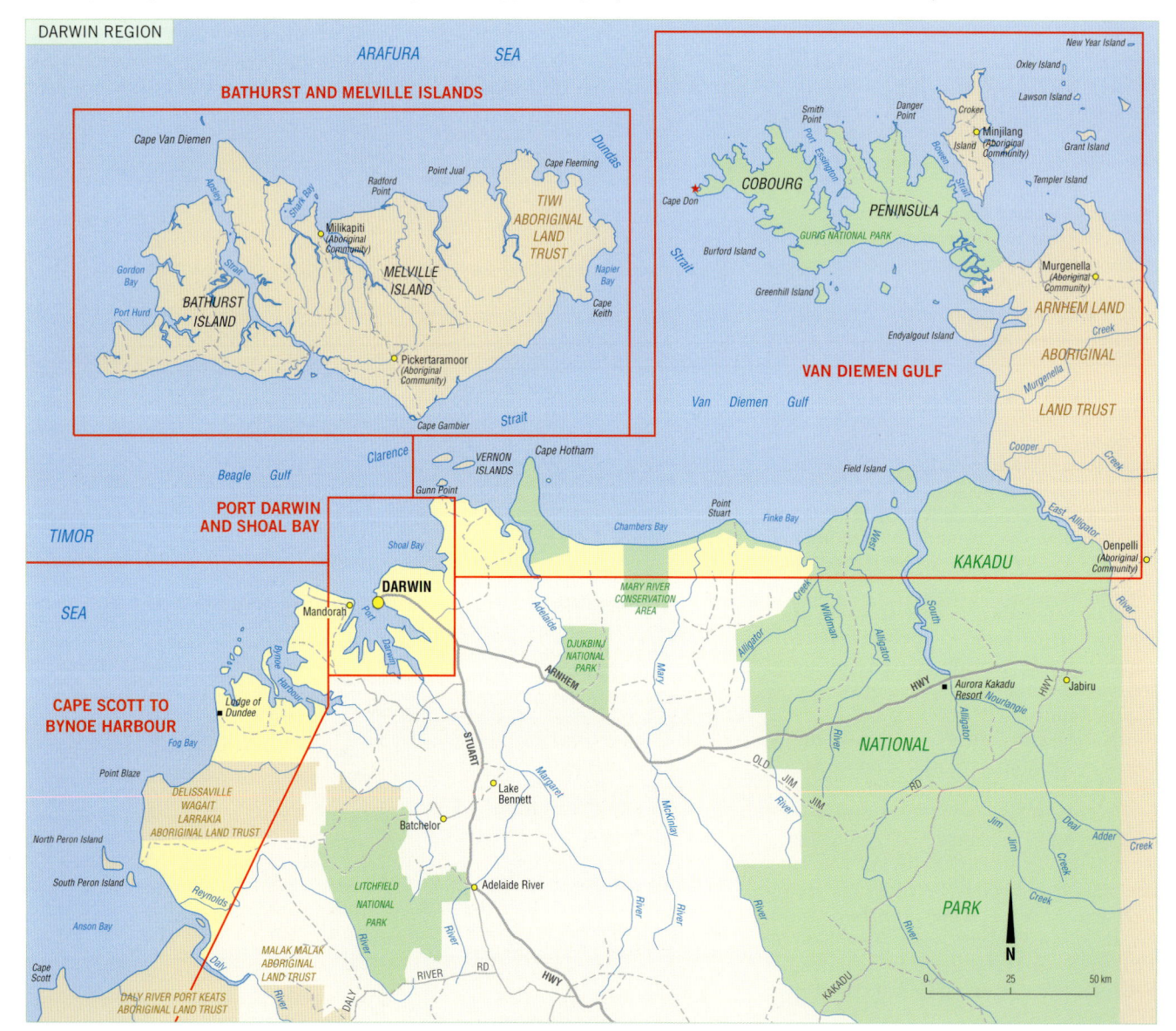

COASTAL FISHING DARWIN REGION

NORTHERN TERRITORY

WHERE TO FISH

Darwin Region

CAPE SCOTT TO BYNOE HARBOUR • 340

This area is punctuated by two locations: the famous Peron Islands, and the Lodge of Dundee, which provides reasonable boat access to the Perons. The fishing at the Perons is usually sensational, and the rest of the region has much to offer in the way of memorable angling opportunities.

PORT DARWIN AND SHOAL BAY • 342

Darwin is bordered by two major waterways: Darwin Harbour and Shoal Bay. In both these areas, and directly offshore from the northern capital, there are a variety, abundance and quality of fishing that cannot be matched by any other capital city.

BATHURST AND MELVILLE ISLANDS • 344

The Tiwi Islands, which is the collective term for Bathurst and Melville islands, are a day trip proposition for Darwin anglers in a large, fast power boat. Permits are required to go ashore, but offshore primitive angling skills will suffice to fill the creel.

VAN DIEMEN GULF • 346

The Van Diemen Gulf is like a big dish of dirty water – no matter what the tidal movement. But if you make the effort to travel down one of the big rivers to the gulf, and anchor on one of the many inshore reefs, big black jewfish, barramundi and fingermark (golden snapper) will keep you both busy and excited.

during the Dry (May–September), and from the north-east to the west in the Wet (October–April). Strong south-easterly winds can occur during the Dry, causing hazardous conditions for boaters. The north-west monsoon winds during the Wet are often strong enough for gale warnings to be issued and extremely heavy rains are common. Knowledge of the nature of cyclones and monsoon conditions generally is essential for anyone taking to the seas during this season. For information on weather 24 hours a day, call the Northern Territory Regional Office of the Bureau of Meteorology, tel (08) 8920 3826. Cyclone information can be obtained 24 hours a day by ringing 1300 659 211. Information is also available on the bureau's web site at www.bom.gov.au

Darwin blue water game fishers like to maximise their chances when trolling for sailfish and marlin

Boating

Tide charts are essential in the Top End, which has some of Australia's biggest tides. The range in Darwin Harbour can be greater than 7 m, leaving boat ramps high and dry on spring lows. Requests for tide charts may be made by phone or in writing to the Darwin Port Corporation and the Marine Branch, Department of Transport and Works. The Vernon Islands, north-east of Darwin, are particularly tricky for boaters in terms of navigation, so beware. There are good launching facilities in and around Darwin, and plenty of accessible launch sites in the more remote areas.

FURTHER INFORMATION

Fishing and boating The Fisheries Management head office of the Department of Primary Industry and Fisheries is at Berrimah Farm, Makagon Rd, Berrimah, tel. (08) 8999 2142. The Marine Branch, Department of Transport and Works is at 1st floor, Minmark House, 66 The Esplanade, Darwin, tel. (08) 8999 5285. The Darwin Port Corporation's postal address is GPO Box 390, Darwin 0801, tel. (08) 8922 0660.

Tourist centres Tourism Top End, cnr Mitchell & Knuckey sts, Darwin, tel. (08) 8936 2499, provides visitor information on fishing tours and all other attractions in the region, or see their website www.nttc.com.au. The Katherine Region Tourist Association, cnr Stuart Hwy and Lindsay St, Katherine, tel. (08) 8972 2650, provides a similar service for tourists passing through the town.

GUIDE TO LOCAL FISH

BD	barracuda
BM	barramundi
B	bream
CO	cobia
C	cod
RE	emperor, red
FM	fingermark
H	herring, wolf
MJ	jack, mangrove
BJ	jewfish, black
MA	mackerel, Spanish
MA	mackerel, spotted
M	mackerel, others
MI	marlin, black
MF	moonfish
PF	parrotfish
Q	queenfish
SL	sailfish
TS	salmon, threadfin
QU	saratoga
SH	shark
SS	snapper, saddletail
SY	stripey
ES	sweetlip
TR	trevally, giant
TR	trevally, others
CT	trout, coral
TU	tuna, longtail
TK	tuskfish

NORTHERN TERRITORY

COASTAL FISHING DARWIN REGION

Cape Scott to Bynoe Harbour

Type of fishing
bay, creek, estuary, offshore, reef, rock, shore

Target fish
barramundi, black jewfish, coral trout, fingermark, giant trevally, queenfish, red emperor, sailfish, Spanish mackerel, sweetlip, threadfin salmon

Cape Scott to Bynoe Harbour offers some of the best readily-accessible blue water fishing available to Darwin boating anglers. South of Point Blaze, at the north end of Anson Bay, the famous Peron islands seasonally provide refuge for a host of tropical pelagic and reef species. Closer to Bynoe Harbour, and to Darwin itself, islands such as Quail and Dum In Mirrie, and the vast Roche Reef, are popular for their scenery and their quality of fishing.

CAPE SCOTT TO POINT BLAZE

This area is difficult to reach. South of the Daly River the land is either Aboriginal Trust Land or remote cattle stations, passable only in the Dry on rough four wheel drive tracks. The access is by charter from the Lodge of Dundee up north, or by boat from the settlements up the Daly River. The fishing is superb – threadfin salmon, barramundi, queenfish, mangrove jack and fingermark are in the bays and entrances of the rivers. Offshore the reef fishing is excellent. **Cape Scott** and **Cape Ford** extend out to reefs and pinnacles that are visited by pelagics like mackerel, trevally, queenfish, tuna and occasionally sailfish. On the north side of Anson Bay are the **Peron islands**, which can be reached in the Dry through Labelle Downs Station to Channel Point (permission is required). Between **Channel Point** and the islands is a deep hole where the superb black jewfish are in abundance. The northern and western ends of North Peron Island have extensive reef areas carrying fingermark, red emperor, sweetlip and coral trout.

At low tide, the smaller sandy creeks in Fog Bay and Anson Bay are inaccessible to boats; but the incoming tide will often carry a school of barramundi and salmon

GUIDE TO LOCAL FISH

		Cape Scott to Point Blaze	Bynoe Harbour
BD	barracuda	●	
BM	barramundi	●	●
C	cod	●	
RE	emperor, red	●	●
FM	fingermark	●	●
H	herring, wolf	●	
MJ	jack, mangrove	●	●
BJ	jewfish, black	●	
MA	mackerel, Spanish	●	●
MA	mackerel, others	●	
Q	queenfish	●	●
SL	sailfish	●	
TS	salmon, threadfin	●	●
SY	stripey	●	
ES	sweetlip	●	●
TR	trevally, giant	●	●
TR	trevally, others	●	●
CT	trout, coral	●	●
TU	tuna	●	
TK	tuskfish	●	

The **Bateman Shoal**, about 8 km south of North Peron Island, has reef fish including fingermark, sweetlip, coral trout and red emperor, and pelagics such as Spanish mackerel, longtail tuna, giant trevally and sailfish, which are very prevalent in these waters. Barramundi and queenfish are in the causeway between the islands and around the rocks on the southern shore of South Peron Island. Black jewfish roam the waters around the northern shore. Further north, **Point Blaze** is a great area for inshore reef fishing and offshore fishing for mackerel and sailfish.

COASTAL FISHING DARWIN REGION   NORTHERN TERRITORY

A catch of fingermark taken wide of Dundee Beach to the west of Bynoe Harbour

BYNOE HARBOUR

The fishing is now closer to Darwin and available even to shore anglers. On the northern side of the harbour, boats can be beach launched off Pioneer Beach, Rankin Point or Raft Point. On the southern side, there are boat ramps at McKenzie Arm and the Lodge of Dundee. These last ramps provide the easiest run to **Dum In Mirrie Island**, **Grose Island** and the **Quail Island group**. These islands are surrounded by reefs and sandy shallows, requiring careful boating. Queenfish are around the sandbars, and are best caught by trolling minnows or poppers. Mackerel and trevally cruise around the reefs, while fingermark, red emperor, sweetlip and coral trout are abundant in places. A prime pelagic area is **Lorna Shoals**, north-west of these islands, with mackerel, shark, cobia, sailfish and tuna attracted to the aggregation of reef fish over the area.

Bynoe Harbour runs into many fingers of mangrove creeks. Barramundi, mangrove jack and fingermark are around the mangroves and rock bars. The north-eastern tip of Indian Island has rocky points where anglers can troll for queenfish, which are prevalent in these waters. They are also close to the beaches at **Raft Point** and **Rankin Point**. Black jewfish can be located in a deep hole (a fish-finder is a great aid) between Rankin Point and Indian Island. The coastline around **Masson Point** and **Burge Point** allows land casting for threadfin salmon and fingermark.

Charles Point is a long run up from Bynoe Harbour but only 20 km west of Darwin by boat. Just off the point are a number of pinnacles, reefs and rocks, which are frequented by black jewfish, fingermark and assorted reef fish. In the shallow bay between Charles Point and Gilruth Point there is an extensive reef area, frequented by queenfish and occasionally wolf herring, which are inclined to jump into a boat by mistake and terrify the occupants with their pointed snapping teeth.

Land anglers can cast into **Two Fella Creek** or other small creeks along the Cox Peninsula for barramundi, mangrove jack, fingermark and threadfin salmon.

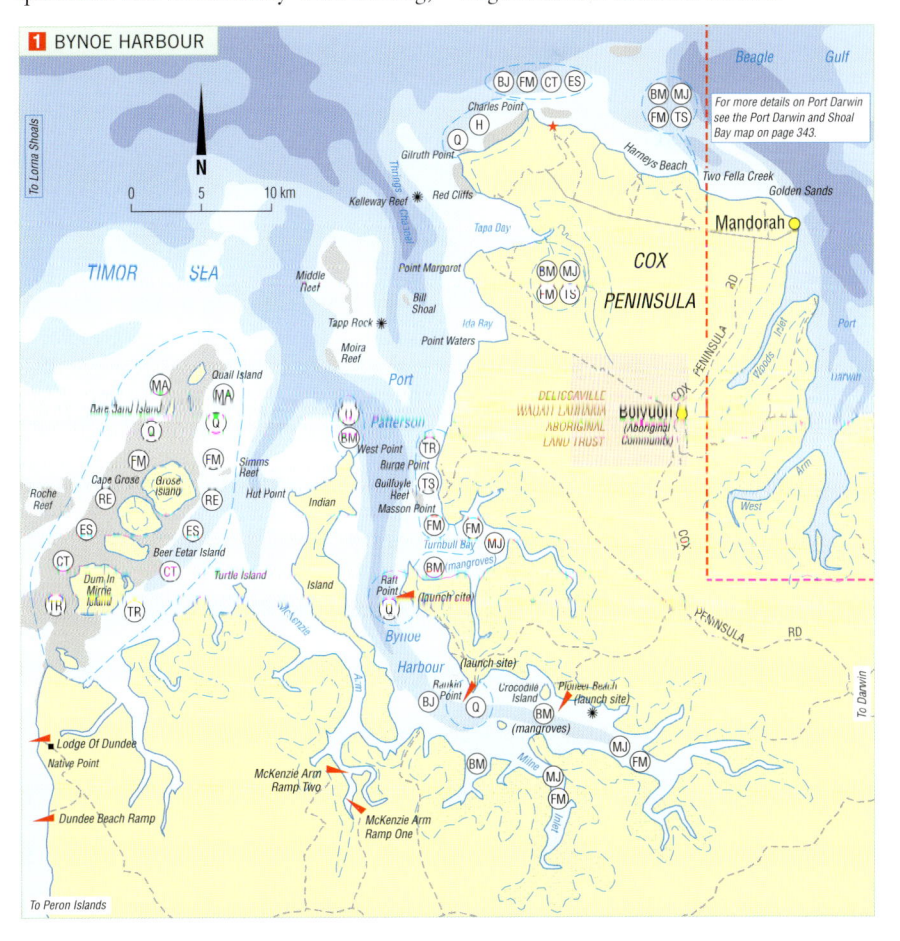

341

NORTHERN TERRITORY
COASTAL FISHING DARWIN REGION

Port Darwin and Shoal Bay

Type of fishing
bay, creek, reef, rock, wharf
Target fish
barramundi, black jewfish, fingermark, queenfish, Spanish mackerel, trevally, tuna

Sheltered from all but a howling north-westerly, **Port Darwin** is a very productive fishing area, made all the more exciting by sunken wrecks that act as artificial reefs. On the north-west headland, near the town of Mandorah, is the tiny **wreck of the *Mandorah Queen***, a local haunt for black jewfish. Beaches in this area can be fished for queenfish, trevally and threadfin salmon.

Most harbour wrecks lie in a rough east-west line between Talc Head and Shell Islands (off the East Arm boat ramp). Big jewfish, fingermark and cod are on these reefs. Boat ramps are all down the eastern side of the port, which breaks into the **East Arm**, **Middle Arm** and **West Arm** and in turn into mangrove-lined creeks. These are all good fishing areas for barramundi and fingermark.

Darwin's **wharves**, clustered around the harbour and on the city peninsula, are great fishing spots. Tuna and queenfish are often the main catch, and barramundi are a possibility, particularly at night, when they are attracted towards the lights. Big black jewfish are also caught off the wharves.

During the Dry, pelagics such as northern bluefin tuna, queenfish, giant trevally, barracuda and mackerel come around **East Point** and **Lee Point**, north of the harbour. Big Spanish mackerel are the most prevalent and can be taken trolling, spinning with lures or live baiting amid berley. Both land and boat anglers can get some action here, and there is always a chance of barracuda, trevally, queenfish and tuna.

Further afield, boat anglers can find great fishing on the **Fenton Patches**, in Beagle Gulf, some 20 km north of West Point. The ridges of sand and reef carry hordes of bait fish at times and therefore attract pelagics such as Spanish mackerel, giant trevally and sailfish. The creation of a complex of artificial reefs has further enhanced the fishing possibilities. Black jewfish, fingermark, moonfish, giant trevally and queenfish are regular foragers, with Spanish and spotted mackerel in good numbers, and black marlin and sailfish as exotic, big-tackle extras.

Hope Inlet, to the north-east of Port Darwin, is mainly a boat fishing area, as the low mangrove swamps do not invite exploration on foot. Boats can be launched at **Buffalo Creek**, and anglers can fish Shoal Bay, particularly the famous **Micket and King creeks** and the **Howard River** for saltwater barramundi. In the creeks, barramundi congregate in the deeper sections late in the dry season. Micket and King creeks are on Naval land and entry is restricted. Permits to enter can be obtained by ringing (08) 8935 4002. King Creek produces black jewfish in any holes deeper than 5 m. Other fish in Hope Inlet include queenfish, mangrove jack and fingermark. The area is popular for anglers searching for a feed of mud crabs. The most accessible shore fishing is along the banks of Buffalo Creek itself.

One in the boat and one hooked up – Spanish mackerel just outside Darwin Harbour

Fishing from the rocks in Darwin Harbour

GUIDE TO LOCAL FISH

(BD)	barracuda
(BM)	barramundi
(C)	cod
(FM)	fingermark
(ML)	jack, mangrove
(BJ)	jewfish, black
(MA)	mackerel, Spanish
(MA)	mackerel, spotted
(ML)	marlin, black
(MF)	moonfish
(Q)	queenfish
(SL)	sailfish
(TS)	salmon, threadfin
(TR)	trevally, giant
(TR)	trevally, others
(TU)	tuna, longtail

Black jewfish
The black jewfish is the northern cousin of the mulloway. It grows to 50 kg and is often encountered in schools of 10 to 15-kg fish. It frequents sunken wrecks, jetties and deep holes adjacent to river and creek mouths.

COASTAL FISHING DARWIN REGION

NORTHERN TERRITORY

PORT DARWIN AND SHOAL BAY

0 5 10 km

BEAGLE GULF

Fenton Patches

To Charles Point Patches

SHOAL BAY

GUNN POINT FORESTRY RESERVE

Lee Point

Old Man Rock

Casuarina

Buffalo Creek

Micket Creek

SHOAL BAY PENINSULA

King Creek

Hope Inlet

Howard River

Nightcliff

Ludmilla Creek

East Point

EAST POINT REEF AQUATIC RESERVE

Coconut Grove

Vesteys Beach

Fannie Bay

Winnellie

Berrimah

STUART HWY

CHARLES DARWIN NP

West Point

Mandorah

Mandorah Queen (wreck)

Mindil Beach

Emery Point

Larrakeyah

DARWIN

Lameroo Beach

Darwin Harbour

Frances Bay

Sadgroves Creek

Talc Head

Wrecks

Weed Reef

PORT DARWIN

Wrecks

Middle Point

North Shell Island

South Shell Island

East Arm

Palmerston

Howard Springs

COX PENINSULA RD

Woods Inlet

Swires Bluff

Channel Island

Middle Arm

West Arm

Elizabeth River

343

NORTHERN TERRITORY
COASTAL FISHING DARWIN REGION

Bathurst and Melville Islands

Type of fishing
bay, beach, creek, estuary, offshore, reef

Target fish
barramundi, black jewfish, coral trout, fingermark, giant trevally, mangrove jack, marlin, queenfish, red emperor, sailfish, Spanish mackerel, sweetlip, threadfin salmon

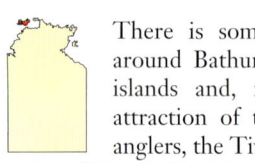

There is some great fishing around Bathurst and Melville islands and, recognising the attraction of their waters for anglers, the Tiwi Land Council and traditional Aboriginal landowners, in association with the Amateur Fishermen's Association of the NT (AFANT), have established streamlined access and permit procedures. Six areas have been designated for angler camping – three are located on Melville Island and three on Bathurst Island. Permits can be obtained from AFANT and need to be applied for at least one week in advance of intended visits. Contact AFANT on (08) 8945 6455.

Port Hurd is a large estuary system with three arms, breaking down into mangrove-lined creeks. This is a typical Northern Territory scenario and the fishing is in keeping, with barramundi, mangrove jack, queenfish and fingermark sometimes taking a back seat to prolific threadfin salmon, one of the finest table fish in the land. There is good fishing in the creeks for barramundi, while black jewfish is targeted in the open estuary waters. The beach in front of the lodge is probably the most comfortable beach location in Australia, and threadfin salmon, queenfish, black jewfish and bream are the targets.

North of Gordon Bay, there are reefs around **Clift Island**, which yield barramundi and fingermark. The steep drop-off at the western end is fished for its healthy population of Spanish mackerel, queenfish and giant trevally. **Gullala Creek**, running from the top end of the bay, is barramundi, mangrove jack and threadfin territory. Reefs and rocks all the way up to **Deception Point** allow good boat fishing, but care must be taken to avoid the rocks off the point. **Apsley Strait**, which runs between the islands, is excellent for barramundi and jewfish, but is dangerously rocky and is best fished on neap tides because of the strong tidal flow.

These sorts of reef and rock hazards continue past **Cape Van Diemen**, although those who know these waters will lead anglers to good fishing for queenfish, trevally, barracuda, mackerel, fingermark and black jewfish around the reefs. The creeks

Snake Bay can be fished both from the shore and by boat

The west shore of Melville Island, at the entrance to Apsley Strait, offers excellent fishing

GUIDE TO LOCAL FISH

BD	barracuda
BM	barramundi
B	bream
CO	cobia
C	cod
FM	fingermark
MU	jack, mangrove
BJ	jewfish, black
MA	mackerel, Spanish
MA	mackerel, others
ML	marlin
MF	moonfish
Q	queenfish
SL	sailfish
TS	salmon, threadfin
SR	saratoga
SS	snapper, saddletail
SY	stripey
ES	sweetlip
TR	trevally, giant
TR	trevally, others
CT	trout, coral
TU	tuna

COASTAL FISHING DARWIN REGION NORTHERN TERRITORY

flowing into **Snake Bay** have silver barramundi in great numbers, and upstream among the lily pads, there are large numbers of saratoga, as well as freshwater barramundi.

The entrances to the **Aliu and Tuanunaku rivers**, which cleave deep down into the island, are surrounded by fringing reefs carrying fingermark, stripey, bream and cod. There are also big mackerel, queenfish and giant trevally around the reefs with barramundi, threadfin salmon and bream in the estuaries. The rivers produce all of the north's freshwater species such as archer fish, sooty grunter and oxeye herring. The Tuanunaku opens out into **Brenton Bay**, which holds plenty of barramundi, with fingermark, queenfish and giant trevally around the reefs.

The entire eastern side of Melville Island is subject to some fairly uncomfortable easterly sea breezes, including the trade winds that roar up from the south-east. The area is best fished just before the Wet, when the prevailing winds are from the west. Napier Bay on the far east is guarded by Soldier Point and Cape Keith and provides great fishing for barramundi, threadfin salmon, queenfish and trevally.

Further out there is outstanding reef fishing over the **Hinkler Patches** and **Beagle Shoals**. Fingermark, trevally and queenfish are the most prolific species in these remote, undisturbed waters.

Goose Creek on Melville Island has a healthy population of saratoga that most anglers are content to catch and then release

345

NORTHERN TERRITORY

COASTAL FISHING DARWIN REGION

Van Diemen Gulf

Type of fishing
creek, estuary, reef, rock

Target fish
barramundi, black jewfish, coral trout, fingermark, mangrove jack, queenfish, Spanish mackerel, threadfin salmon

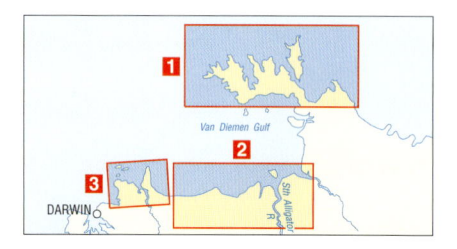

The long stretch of coast from Darwin to the East Alligator River has a lot of fishing water, but exploring the possibilities often means long river runs to the sea. Boat ramps are sometimes concrete constructions, but sometimes are launch sites only. It is not always possible to get a trailer boat into the water from these ramps.

GUNN POINT TO CAPE HOTHAM

The **Vernon Islands** can be reached by launching from Gunn Point (car toppers only) or the boat ramp in Leaders Creek, although the Leaders Creek option may be too distracting, with its barramundi, threadfin salmon, and black jewfish, for anglers to bother to make the 20-km journey to the islands. Similarly, those launching car toppers from Gunn Point can fish the **Blue Hole**, which is a very productive location inside the reef and can only be reached from its sea side via the channel inside South West Vernon Island. Anglers must enter on the top half of the tide and can be caught inside during low tide.

Those who go out will find three mangrove-covered islands, threaded by narrow creeks, which carry mangrove jack, barramundi, threadfin salmon and fingermark. The creeks can only be entered and fished on a high tide, and they are lonely and mosquito-ridden places to be if you are trapped by the tidal run-out.

The reefs around the atolls are also fished at high tide for stripey, fingermark and moonfish, while trevally is the most prevalent of the cruising fish. The deep channel inside **South West Vernon Island** is a jewfish hotspot on neap tides. The Vernons feature fast currents, deep channels around the reefs, and conditions requiring good boat handling.

Further east, the **Adelaide River** can be reached by launching at Leaders Creek. Beach launching at Point Stephens is closer, but only recommended at high tide in still conditions. A concrete ramp has been built in Salt Water Arm providing easy access to the lower reaches of the Adelaide River. This is a huge river, giving way to long freshwater stretches. Its estuary is excellent for fingermark, barramundi and cod. There are deep holes near the mouth of the river where black jewfish can be caught at low tide.

Cape Hotham is also accessed from Leaders Creek, but the run is about 20 km. There are offshore rocks and reefs around the cape, and the area fishes well, particularly for black jewfish, fingermark, cod and stripey. There are tiny creeks along the cape, and threadfin salmon in their thousands sometimes enter these creeks on fast-rising tides. There is good bottom-fishing around **Ruby Island** on its western side for fingermark, black jewfish, cod and stripey, but anglers need to be aware of shallow reefs that become exposed at low tide.

CHAMBERS BAY TO EAST ALLIGATOR RIVER

On the eastern side of Chambers Bay is a series of major rivers. The **Mary River** entrance can be reached by an hour or more of boat running from Shady Camp. However, the fishing is generally poor due to dirty water. **West Alligator Head**, at the mouth of the West Alligator River, can be reached from the Arnhem Highway by those with four-wheel-drive vehicles and roof topper boats. Trailer boats can only be launched near the Aurora Kakadu Resort on the **South Alligator** or at Cahills Crossing on the **East Alligator**, with a three-hour

GUIDE TO LOCAL FISH

	Gunn Point to Cape Hotham	Chambers Bay to East Alligator River	Cobourg Peninsula
(BD) barracuda			●
(BM) barramundi	●	●	●
(B) bream			●
(CO) cobia			●
(C) cod	●		●
(FM) fingermark	●	●	●
(MJ) jack, mangrove	●		●
(BJ) jewfish, black	●	●	●
(MA) mackerel, Spanish			●
(MA) mackerel, others	●		●
(ML) marlin			●
(MF) moonfish	●		●
(PF) parrotfish			●
(Q) queenfish	●		●
(SL) sailfish			●
(TS) salmon, threadfin	●	●	●
(SS) snapper, saddletail			●
(SY) stripey	●		●
(ES) sweetlip			●
(TR) trevally, giant	●		●
(TR) trevally, others	●	●	●
(CT) trout, coral	●		●
(TU) tuna	●		●
(TK) tuskfish			●

COASTAL FISHING DARWIN REGION   NORTHERN TERRITORY

run to the entrances. Munmarlary Landing, on the South Alligator, is a closer landing spot, but the road up from Kakadu Village is rough at the best of times and submerged during the Wet.

Reef fishing is quite brilliant just outside the **West Alligator and South Alligator entrances** with the black jewfish and fingermark mingling with other reef fish and concentrations of threadfin salmon. **Field Island**, north of the South Alligator entrance, is a recognised hot spot for reef fish.

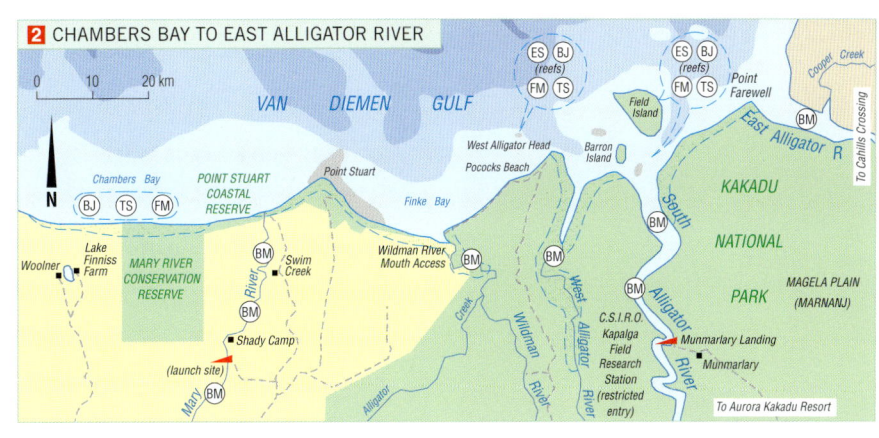

COBOURG PENINSULA

Gurig National Park covers the Cobourg Peninsula and is managed by the Northern Territory Parks and Wildlife Commission and local Aboriginal people. To protect this pristine wilderness area, only a limited number of visitors are permitted each year. To obtain a permit to enter Gurig, contact the Cobourg Peninsula Sanctuary Board, tel. (08) 8979 0244. Accommodation and guided fishing are available on the peninsula at Gurig Nature Experience on Cape Don and Seven Spirits Bay Resort. Cabins are available for rent at Smith Point.

On Cobourg's south-west coast there is a series of protected bays – **Aiton, Silvid, Shamrock and Shark bays**, reached by a large boat journeying around Cape Don. Fishing is for queenfish, mackerel and trevally around the fringing reefs, fingermark and cod on the bottom, and barramundi and mangrove jack up the creeks.

The boat ramp at Black Point allows access to Port Essington and to the sea and offshore islands. Around **Cape Don** is an expanse of coral reefs and rock pinnacles where reef fish abound, but the area requires careful navigation. Queenfish, giant trevally, Spanish mackerel, tuna and barracuda are around the bomboras. **Allaru Island** is a hot spot for trevally and mackerel. The deep bays in the area can be trolled for queenfish, giant trevally and barracuda.

Port Essington is big and sheltered, with sometimes wonderful fishing. Queenfish and trevally roam along the headlands, particularly around **Record Point**, in the south-east corner of the bay. A number of creeks can be explored for mangrove jack and barramundi. There are reefs just north of the port within easy reach, which yield fingermark, cod, coral trout and stripey.

To the east of Port Essington are the **Sandy Islands**, which are fished for their large populations of giant trevally, Spanish mackerel and queenfish, and reef fish such as fingermark, sweetlip and coral trout. The run around to **Croker Island** requires calm seas. Around the island there are reef varieties (sweetlip, fingermark, saddletail snapper and coral trout) and pelagics (sailfish, cobia, queenfish, barracuda, marlin and mackerel). There is also creek fishing near the settlement of **Minjilang**, but permits are again required. Also, bear in mind that the whole of the Cobourg Peninsula is surrounded by a marine park. Other than Territory-wide restrictions, no specific regulations apply here.

There are a number of small islands flung out to the east that are accessible to charters and those with experienced guides. **Oxley Island** has a small estuary and an offshore area to the north-west, **Bramble Rocks**, where Spanish mackerel gather before and during the wet season. **Lawson, Grant and New Year islands** have pelagic fish such as giant trevally, queenfish, Spanish mackerel, longtail tuna, marlin and sailfish, as well as reef species such as coral trout, fingermark, moonfish, tuskfish, parrotfish and cod.

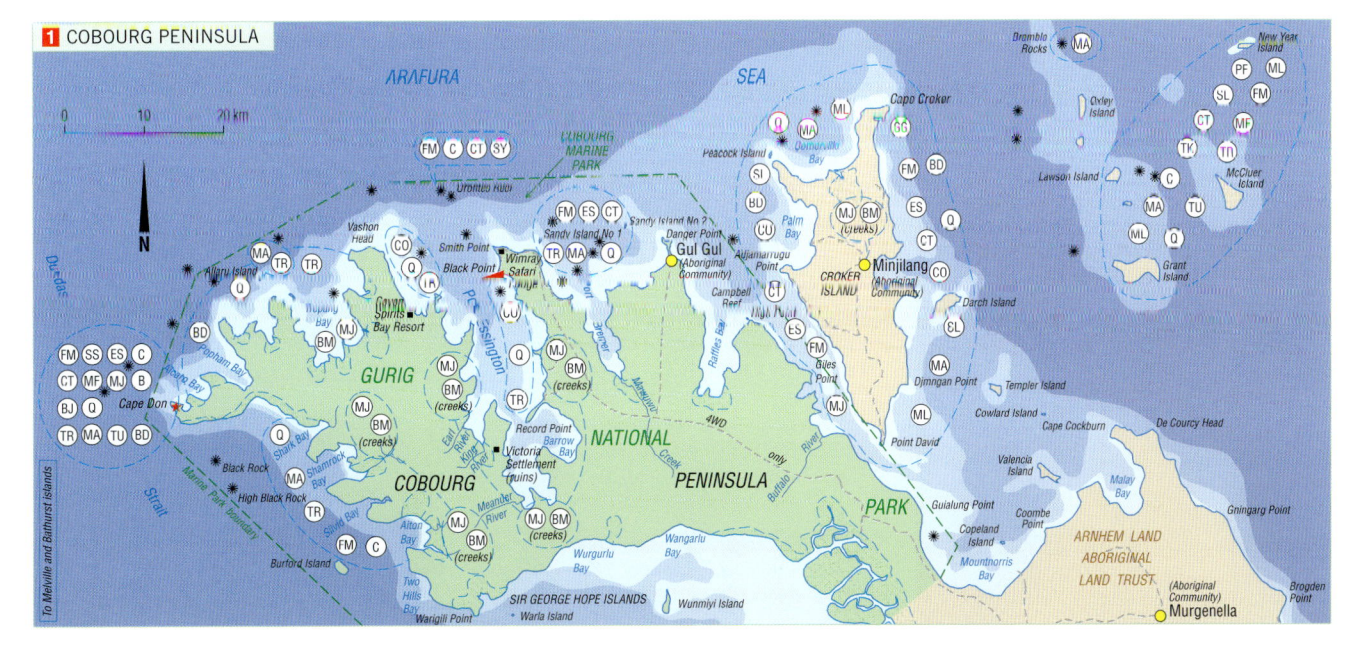

NORTHERN TERRITORY

COASTAL FISHING GOVE REGION

Gove Region

The rich blue waters and the white sandy beaches of the many islands in this region are symptomatic of reduced tidal flows compared to elsewhere along the Northern Territory coast. Commonly referred to as the north-east Arnhem Land coast, it rates as one of the greatest light-to-medium sportfishing areas in Australia.

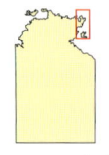

This remote north-eastern corner of the Northern Territory is where the Gulf of Carpentaria and the Arafura Sea converge, which may well explain why the region is home to such an abundance and variety of tropical reef, pelagic and estuarine species.

Aboriginal land

Much of the Gove region is Aboriginal land and permission is required before visiting. Permits may be obtained from the Northern Land Council, PO Box 42921, Casuarina NT 0811, tel. (08) 8920 5100. Permits for Groote Eylandt may be obtained from the Anindilyakwa Land Council at Alyangula on Groote Eylandt, tel. (08) 8987 6638.

Weather

Winds in this area are generally light to moderate, usually from the east to south-east during the Dry (May–September), and from the north to the north-west in the Wet (October–April). Sometimes during the Dry the south-easterlies can be very stiff, and a strong wind or gale warning will be issued. The north-west monsoon winds during the Wet can also be strong and are often accompanied by extremely heavy rain. Boaters must be aware of the high risk of cyclones and of the very temperamental monsoon conditions that occur during this season. For information on weather 24 hours a day, call the Northern Territory Regional Office of the Bureau of Meteorology, tel. (08) 8982 4711. For cyclone warnings and general weather updates, tel. 11 542, or tune into the local radio stations.

Boating

The inexperienced are advised to seek out guides or charters in order to explore these waters. The best fishing spots are very remote, and some areas are uncharted. The straits between the Wessel Islands are particularly dangerous. The islands stretching to the north and south of Gove are Aboriginal land and boats should not dock without prior permission. See Aboriginal Land Trusts, on page 337 for more details.

FURTHER INFORMATION

Fishing and boating The Fisheries Management head office of the Department of Primary Industry and Fisheries is at Berrimah Farm, Makagon Rd, Berrimah, tel. (08) 8999 2142. The Marine Branch, Department of Transport and Works is on the 1st floor, Minerals House, 66 The Esplanade, Darwin, tel. (08) 8999 5285. The Darwin Port Corporation's postal address is GPO Box 390, Darwin 0801, tel. (08) 8922 0660.

Tourist centres Gove Tourist Information Association, Gove Resort Hotel, 12 Westall St, Nhulunbuy, tel. (08) 8987 1777.

WHERE TO FISH

Gove Region

EAST ARNHEM LAND • 350

The red bauxite cliffs along the Gove Peninsula give a clue to the huge deposits further inland and the purpose of the mining township of Nhulunbuy. When they are not working, many of the locals head out to adjacent islands to fish for red emperor or Spanish mackerel, or cast lures in the sandy estuaries for barramundi and mangrove jack. To them, this place is very special.

GUIDE TO LOCAL FISH

BD	barracuda
BM	barramundi
CO	cobia
C	cod
RE	emperor, red
FM	fingermark
MU	jack, mangrove
BJ	jewfish, black
MA	mackerel, Spanish
MA	mackerel, others
ML	marlin, black
PF	parrotfish
Q	queenfish
SL	sailfish
TS	salmon, threadfin
SY	stripey
ES	sweetlip
TR	trevally, giant
TR	trevally, golden
CT	trout, coral
TU	tuna, longtail
TK	tuskfish

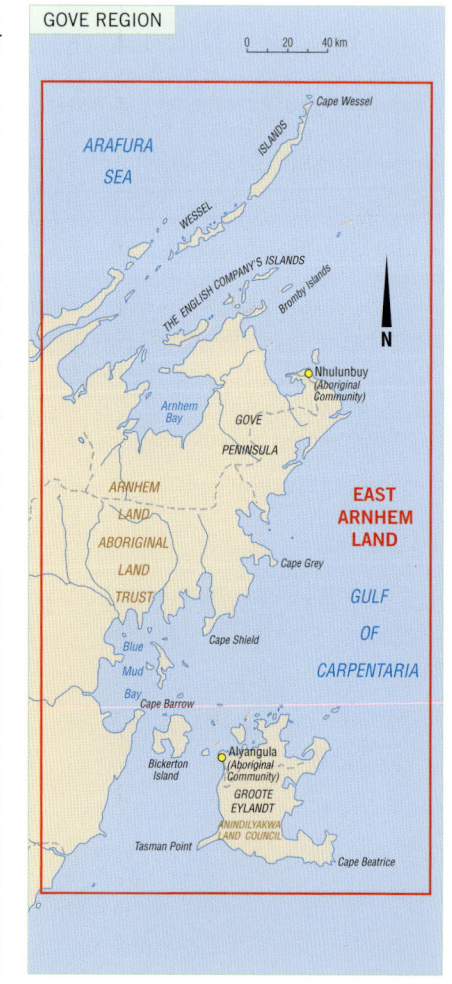

Around the Gove Peninsula extra-large giant trevally are regularly encountered on trolled lures. This one was released after providing excellent sport

COASTAL FISHING GOVE REGION   NORTHERN TERRITORY

Gove marlin . . . or barramundi?

I was aboard the comfortable mothership *Iron Lady* at the invitation of owner Dan Bergano and my Nhulunbuy mate, Roger Gentle, who were trying to prove up the billfish potential off north-east Arnhem Land. Our objective was to explore the waters around Wessel Islands and look for marlin and sailfish.

We had Roger's 7.3 m game boat *Solitaire* in tow along with his Quintrex 4.3 m Top Ender set up to tackle the big sportfish such as the mackerel and trevally species which are plentiful around these picturesque islands.

Our exploration of the islands was successful as far as sailfish were concerned but, although we had raised and fought some nice marlin, all had been lost. On our way back to Gove, Brad Goodings and I were having a fish around the Bombies for coral trout, trolling with our usual barra baitcasting tackle over the coral bombies in water from 4 m to 8 m deep. We were trolling Killalure River Rats and RMG Scorpions which are more familiar on barra waters.

We were trolling a channel between two small islands when I felt a *tap tap* on my lure which felt like our lures had tangled. I wound my lure in a few metres and I was just asking Brad to pull his in a bit when his prized old barra rod went into a full bend.

'You got a fish on mate?' I asked.

'There's something there, but it's not fighting – it's just a dead weight,' he replied.

'I'll just stop the boat and you wind it in mate.'

Brad had no resistance as he wound in the 6 kg monofilament line on his little baitcaster. The water was exceptionally clear and, with the polarised sunglasses I was wearing, I could see right down into the water.

As Brad continued to wind in slack line I saw something that really surprised me – it looked like a huge Spanish mackerel. When the fish was only about 15 m away I got a real shock. I looked at Brad and said: 'Mate you've hooked a marlin! Hang on because, when it realises it's hooked, all hell's going to break loose.'

This was a hefty marlin and Brad's ancient rod and tiny reel had about as much chance of holding it as my wife's tabby had of pulling down a water buffalo. The marlin swam closer to the boat before it figured out that something was not quite right. It was a spectacular sight as 3 m and 150 kg of angrily lit-up marlin took to the air right beside our boat. We could see the lure hanging from its bill like a tooth pick. It seemed to stay in the air for an age, carving up the water around the boat with its tail dancing before crashing back in and screaming away from us.

We took off after the fish but it quickly turned and charged off in another direction, making it impossible for Brad to keep up with the little reel. The marlin took to the air again and charged across the surface but, by this time, the inevitable had happened and Brad's line had been snapped, probably cut by the fish's huge tail.

We weren't really disappointed that we had lost the fish but we were amazed that we had encountered such a large marlin relatively close to the coast in such shallow water. We were stunned that it had decided to have a go at a barra lure. It speaks volumes for the quality of fishing in these pristine waters.

– *Alex Julius*

NORTHERN TERRITORY
COASTAL FISHING GOVE REGION

East Arnhem Land

Type of fishing
beach, offshore, reef, wharf

Target fish
barracuda, giant trevally, mackerel, marlin, sailfish, queenfish, red emperor

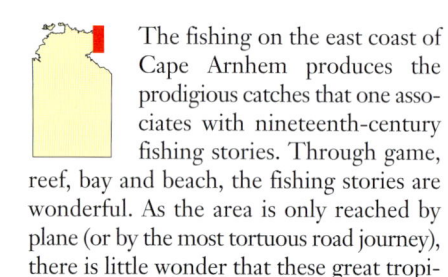

The fishing on the east coast of Cape Arnhem produces the prodigious catches that one associates with nineteenth-century fishing stories. Through game, reef, bay and beach, the fishing stories are wonderful. As the area is only reached by plane (or by the most tortuous road journey), there is little wonder that these great tropical waters remain scarcely touched.

Most of the north-east coast of the Territory is Aboriginal land, and permits are essential for anglers wishing to fish the area.

CAPE WESSEL TO GROOTE EYLANDT

The pristine waters in this very remote area provide some of the best tropical sportfishing in Australia. Black marlin, sailfish, high-flying queenfish, huge Spanish mackerel, monster giant trevally, red emperor, golden snapper and coral trout are all plentiful. Offshore the big action for reef fish and pelagics really starts. The prevailing easterly winds have to be considered by boat anglers, but once at your destination there is a lot of protection from the lee coasts of the islands.

The **Wessel Islands** are a long finger running out to sea about 80 km north-west of the Gove Peninsula. This is an area you can only reach on a charter boat or with a guide. At Cape Wessel, at the very far north-east of the island chain, the deep waters are frequented by trevally, tuna, marlin, sailfish, mackerel and other pelagics. The western side of Marchinbar Island, sheltered from the prevailing easterly winds in the dry season, is a series of bays and beaches where queenfish, golden and giant trevally are the target fish. **Hole in the Wall** and **Cumberland Strait**, two gaps in the Wessel Islands, offer outstanding lure fishing for reef fish such as coral trout, tuskfish, cod and fingermark. Hole in the Wall is very dangerous and should only be attempted with an experienced navigator on board.

Apart from the Wessels, **Truant Island** is the most distant of the islands around the Gove Peninsula, some 70 km north-east of the harbour. It rivals the

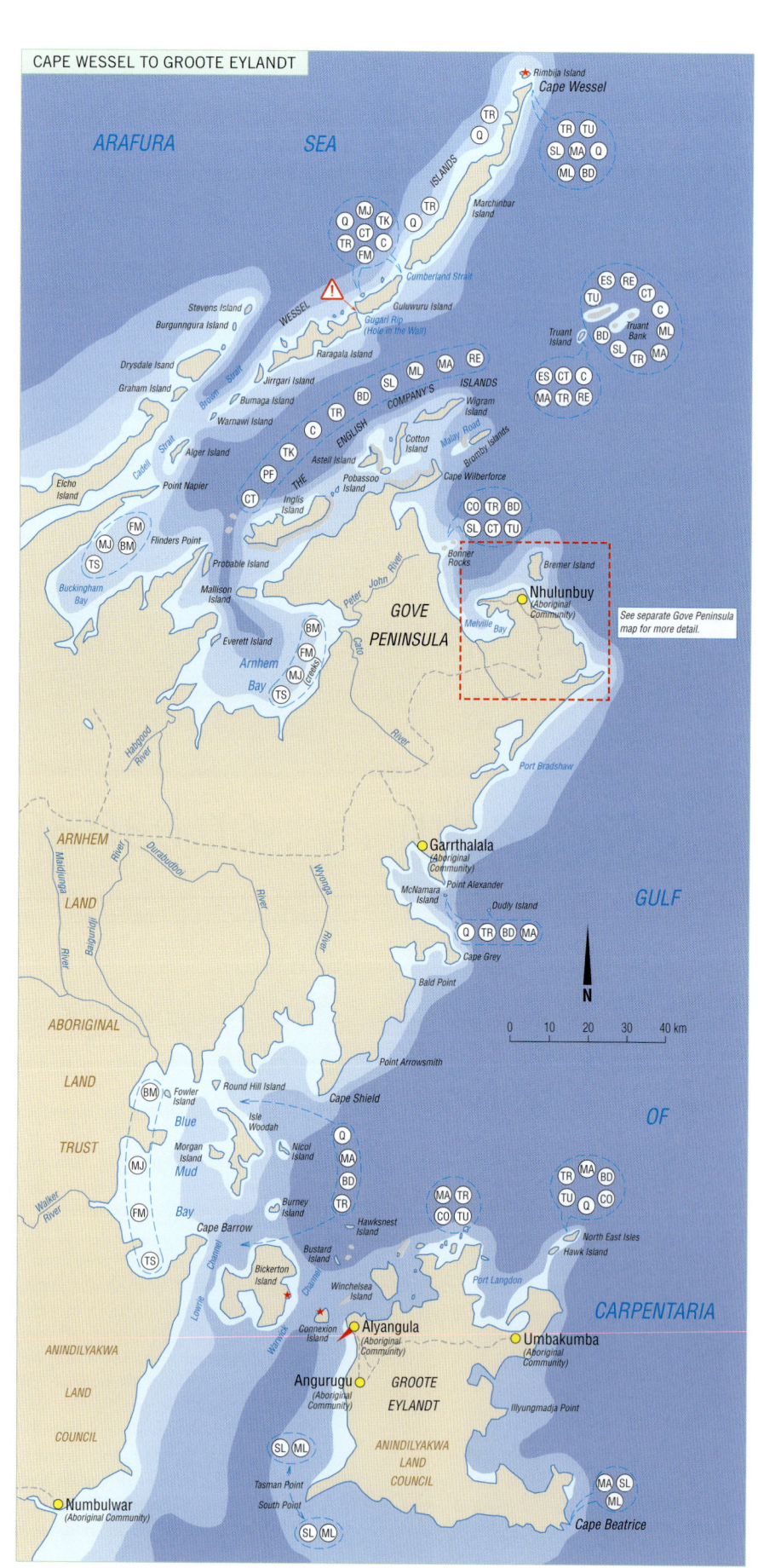

COASTAL FISHING GOVE REGION — NORTHERN TERRITORY

Wessels for its reef fishing (red emperor, coral trout and cod) and sportfishing (mackerel and giant trevally). Nearby, the **Truant Bank** is a great reef area, comprising red emperor and coral trout among the many reef fish, and Spanish mackerel, golden trevally, giant trevally, barracuda and tuna in the area. It is also frequented by black marlin and sailfish.

To the north-west of Gove Harbour is a series of small islands grouped under the name of the **English Company's Islands**, where reefs and rocky headlands extend the fishing through reef fish such as coral trout, red emperor, tuskfish, parrotfish and cod to big pelagics such as mackerel, barracuda, sailfish, marlin and trevally species. Gove residents favour the **Bromby Islands** for camping and as a fishing base for expeditions around the islands, once again after appropriate permits have been obtained.

Bonner Rocks, between Cape Wilberforce and Gove, carry reef fish, cobia, golden trevally and barracuda.

A series of islands between the Gove Peninsula and Groote Eylandt each have abundant queenfish, giant and golden trevally and barracuda, with a school of mackerel always a chance.

The **North East Isles** are the focus for game fishing off Groote Eylandt, producing trevally, queenfish, longtail tuna, mackerel and cobia in large numbers. Groote Eylandt itself is Aboriginal land and can only be visited with a permit and a place to stay, as there are no tourist facilities on the island. Each year the Groote Eylandt Game and Sport Fishing Club hosts a competition and accommodation can be arranged with locals for the out-of-town participants. At **South Point**, on the south-western end, sailfish and marlin are regular catches during the months of November and December.

GOVE PENINSULA

The attractive mining town of **Nhulunbuy** on the Gove Peninsula is the starting point for the various fishing experiences. Close to home, a visit to the **Town Beach** can begin the action, with giant trevally and queenfish close inshore and mackerel and cobia fairly regular visitors among the pelagics. There is fishing all down this eastern coast, with some shore casting for mackerel and the occasional tuna, from **Cape Wirawawoi**, **Rainbow Cliff**, **Rocky Point** and **Cape Arnhem** and a string of beaches, all yielding trevally and queenfish.

The Gove Harbour wharves add the welcome options of shore fishing for black jewfish and fingermark. The reef species out in the harbour include sweetlip, coral trout and stripey. Just outside the harbour are the **West Woody and East Woody islands**, which attract queenfish, giant and golden trevally, barracuda and mackerel.

Closer in, to the north-east of Gove, is **Bremer Island**, which is thick with reef fish and pelagics. Big tuna and sailfish move through these waters. Reef fish are plentiful, but some species carry the toxin ciguatera, which can cause severe illness in humans. Predatory pelagics also carry the disease and anglers are advised to seek local knowledge on what fish can be eaten in the Nhulunbuy area.

Truant Island requires a permit to land. In this case, permission was obtained to hold the Gove Game Classic from the idyllic island

GUIDE TO LOCAL FISH

		Cape Wessel to Groote Eylandt	Gove Peninsula
(BD)	barracuda	•	•
(BM)	barramundi	•	•
(CO)	cobia	•	•
(C)	cod	•	
(RE)	emperor, red	•	•
(FM)	fingermark	•	•
(MU)	jack, mangrove	•	
(BJ)	jewfish, black	•	•
(MA)	mackerel, Spanish	•	•
(MR)	mackerel, others	•	•
(ML)	marlin, black	•	
(PF)	parrotfish	•	
(Q)	queenfish	•	•
(SL)	sailfish	•	
(TS)	salmon, threadfin	•	
(SY)	stripey		•
(ES)	sweetlip	•	•
(TR)	trevally, giant	•	•
(TR)	trevally, golden	•	•
(CT)	trout, coral	•	•
(TU)	tuna, longtail	•	•
(TK)	tuskfish	•	•

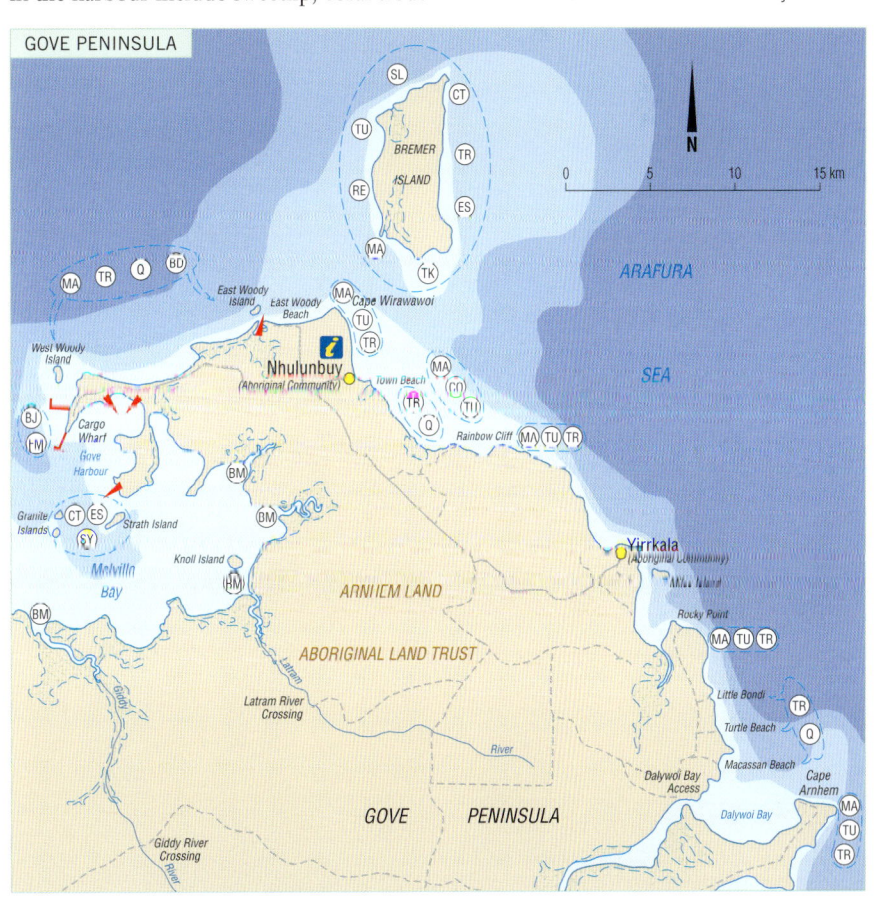

NORTHERN TERRITORY

Inland Fishing

The Wet is the lifeblood of the Northern Territory, filling its network of rivers and streams, which overflow into billabongs and flood plains to become great lakes of the inland. The rivers wash to the coast, flushing out detritus and small marine animals, and assisting the passage of those creatures, like the freshwater barramundi, which are called to a change of habitat. The best fishing is just after the Wet and at the end of the Dry.

The brimming Territory rivers fish well as the first flush of water spreads through the system. They are flooded by the Wet, renewed and full of life, and recede slowly through the eight months of the Dry. Those eight months coincide with the northern winter, when the day temperatures are balmy and the nights are crisp and cool.

Many government-accredited professional guides now operate fishing safaris in the Territory. Through them, anglers from other parts of Australia and aboard can have all the equipment, the travel, the camping and the sport laid on, without worrying about the hazards that can beset beginners.

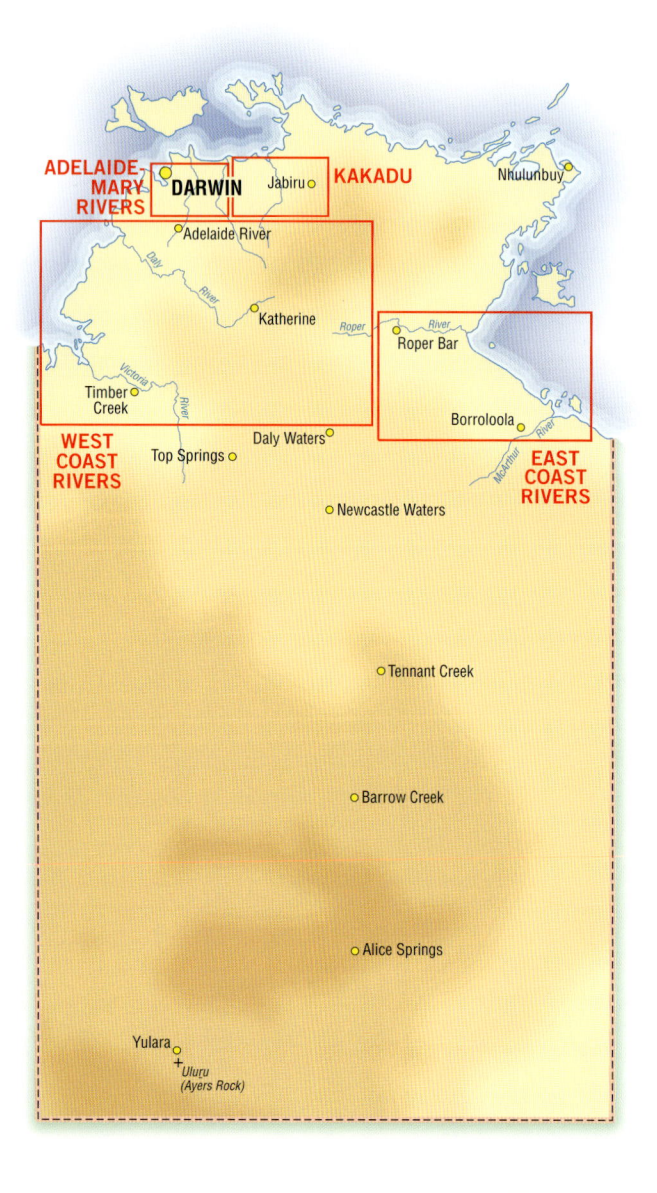

WHERE TO FISH

Inland

WEST COAST RIVERS REGION ● 354
The western region of the Top End combines both the grandeur and ruggedness of the Kimberley with the lush flowing plains of the tropical wetlands. It contains a spider web of largely pristine waterways that delineate boundaries between pastoral properties, Aboriginal lands and national parks.

ADELAIDE–MARY RIVERS REGION ● 356
Small land-locked waterways and vast meandering rivers are the basis of inland fishing in this region. They may be close to the far north's capital city, but they are a rich aquatic and terrestrial habitat. The wetlands of the Mary and Adelaide rivers may change mood with the seasons, but they remain the lifeblood of a vast and healthy population of the Territory's great barramundi.

KAKADU REGION ● 358
Kakadu National Park is a World Heritage area, and it contains several major angling rivers. Although fishing is prohibited in parts of Kakadu, those areas where anglers are welcome are probably the best. From the turbulent and mud-lined tidal river mouths to the pandanus-fringed, placid lagoons, Kakadu is a fishing destination no Territory-bound angler can afford to pass by.

EAST COAST RIVERS REGION ● 360
The greatest difference between the eastern or gulf side of the Territory and the rest of the Top End is tidal variation. The eastern region experiences minimal, although at times erratic, tidal movement. As a consequence, the rivers are smaller. They are, however, numerous, and extremely clear due to restricted tidal fluctuation.

The north's inland fishing tends to springboard from the highway and river crossings. This is genuine wilderness territory, sometimes impassable in the Wet and with rough tracks extending the range of movement in the Dry. It makes sense that the fishing should focus, for the most part, around places that can be reasonably reached by all-weather roads.

There are, however, many fishing places that can be reached by four-wheel drive and by boat and others, on Aboriginal land or station properties, that require permission.

INLAND FISHING

NORTHERN TERRITORY

Essentially the fishing in the north is best just after the Wet, and at the end of the Dry, when the receding waters and increasing water temperatures mobilise the fish into an aggressive feeding pattern.

Crocodile warning

Crocodiles abound in Northern Territory inland waters. Saltwater crocodiles are the most dangerous, and capable of travelling up the rivers for distances of 300 km or more. Crocodiles are a protected species and must not be harmed or killed. It is essential that anglers observe these basic safety measures.
- Do not clean fish on or near the water's edge.
- Do not stand or wade in the water for longer than necessary.
- Clean up rubbish immediately.
- Set up camp a good away distance from the river bank.

Fishing regulations

Licences are not required for recreational fishing but regulations exist to ensure the quality of recreational fishing is maintained. Species-specific and general size and bag limits, equipment regulations and seasonal or area angling closures apply in some locations. Detailed regulations are available from the Department of Primary Industry and Fisheries Recreational Fishing Office, tel. (08) 8999 2372 or check the web site at www.nt.gov.au/dpif/fisheries/recfish/recfish.shtml

Big tidal rivers

Some of the best barramundi fishing action is found in the Top End's big tidal rivers in the dry season, which usually runs from late March to June. Fish congregate at floodwater run-offs and creek mouths as the wet season floods start to recede and are caught casting lures to them. Trolling around underwater snags and rock bars in the big rivers produces excellent fishing as the floodwaters fall further and the waters clear.

Freshwater lagoons

Late in the dry season from September to November is the best time to fish the Territory's beautiful inland billabongs, although expert fishing guides produce excellent catches during the cooler months in the middle of the dry season.

Barramundi

The barramundi is Australia's top native sportfish and the Northern Territory has some of the best barramundi fishing in the world. Barramundi are aggressive predators and great fighting fish and anglers who experience their strong runs, high jumps, and rod bending lunges rate them as world-class sportfish. There are lots of big barramundi in the Territory and it is not uncommon to catch 10 kg-plus barramundi with plenty of fish weighing 20 kg or more landed each year.

Barramundi frequent inshore rocks and headlands, coastal estuaries and creeks, big rivers and inland billabongs. They can be caught using a wide range of lures – casting and trolling – and a variety of baits can be successful. The barramundi is also a fantastic opponent for the fly fisher. It can be caught all year round in the right locations and using the right fishing techniques.

Recreational barramundi fishing is well protected by a sensible approach to fishery management and a responsible attitude by anglers. The pressure of commercial fishing is limited and rivers like the Daly, Mary, Roper and those in Kakadu National Park are closed to commercial fishing as are the waters of Darwin Harbour and Shoal Bay. Bag limits which strongly promote catch and release fishing are also in place. A properly-organised barramundi fishing trip in the Territory will almost always result in quality fish.

Boating regulations

There are no requirements for licensing or registration of pleasure craft in the Northern Territory, although boaters must abide by minimum safety regulations. Regulations specify the equipment that must be carried in particular areas. For full details of requirements for recreational craft, contact the Department of Transport and Works, Marine Branch on (08) 8999 5253.

GUIDE TO LOCAL FISH

- archer fish
- barramundi
- catfish
- cod, sleepy
- fingermark
- herring, oxeye
- jack, mangrove
- jewfish, black
- mullet
- salmon, threadfin
- saratoga
- shark
- sooty grunter

Bag and size limits apply. See the Northern Territory Department of Primary Industry and Fisheries guides for details.

ABORIGINAL LAND TRUSTS

West Coast Rivers Region

The land around the township of Daly River is part of the **Malak Malak Aboriginal Land Trust**, which comes under the jurisdiction of the Northern Land Council. Anglers do not need permission to travel in by road or to fish the river, but those wishing to explore the surrounding country can contact one of the local fishing lodges to arrange the necessary permits.

Near Katherine there are **Beswick and Jawoyn Aboriginal land trusts**. Permits are required to enter these areas and can be obtained from the Northern Land Council in Darwin, tel. (08) 8920 5100, or from the Katherine office, tel. (08) 8972 2894.

East Coast Rivers Region

On the southern side of the Roper River is the **Marra Aboriginal Land Trust**. The township of Boorroola, further south, lies in the heart of the **Narwinbi Aboriginal Land Trust** on the McArthur River. The roads in both areas are public so no permits are required to travel through, but those wishing to explore further must first contact the Northern Land Council either in Darwin, tel. (08) 8921 5100 or Katherine, tel. (08) 8972 2894, for the necessary permits.

FURTHER INFORMATION

Fishing The Fisheries Management head office of the Department of Primary Industry and Fisheries is located at Berrimah Farm, Makagon Rd, Berrimah, tel. (08) 8999 2142. The Department prints a number of free publications with details on regulations and information on fishing in the Northern Territory. They can be downloaded at www.nt.gov.au/dpif or ordered by tel. (08) 8999 2313.

Boating Further information on pleasure boating is available from the Boating Safety Officer, tel. (08) 8999 5253, of the Marine Branch, Department of Transport and Works, 1st floor, Minerals House, 66 The Esplanade, Darwin. It publishes guides to marine regulations and boating safety which are available from its offices or its web site www.nt.gov.au/drw/aboutus/branches/transport/marine Information about boat ramps can be obtained from the Recreational Fishing Officer, Fisheries Management, Berrimah Farm, Makagon Rd, Berrimah, tel. (08) 8999 2142.

Tourist centres The Lakes Resort and Caravan Park, Doris Rd, Berry Springs, tel. (08) 8988 6277; McArthur River Caravan Park, Robinson Rd, Borroloola, tel. (08) 8975 8734; Tourism Top End, cnr Mitchell & Knuckey sts, Darwin, tel. (08) 8936 2499; Bowali Visitors Centre, Kakadu National Park Headquarters, Kakadu Hwy, Kakadu National Park, tel. (08) 8938 1120; Kakadu Resort, Arnhem Hwy, Kakadu, tel. (08) 8979 0166; Katherine Region Tourist Association, cnr Stuart Hwy and Lindsay St, Katherine, tel. (08) 8972 2650; Lake Bennett Wilderness Resort, 152 Chinner Rd, Lake Bennett, tel. (08) 8976 0960.

NORTHERN TERRITORY

INLAND FISHING WEST COAST RIVERS REGION

West Coast Rivers Region

The western region of the Top End combines the grandeur of the Kimberley with the tropical wetlands. It contains a spider web of largely pristine waterways that delineate boundaries between pastoral properties, Aboriginal lands and national parks.

Type of fishing
river, waterhole

Target fish
barramundi, sooty grunter, threadfin salmon

The rivers running to the west coast are in drier country, an area of plains dotted with gum trees, boabs and spinifex and broken by bare, rocky hills. The main access highway is the Victoria Highway, which branches from the Stuart Highway at Katherine and runs to Kununurra and the Ord River region in Western Australia.

The **Keep River Crossing**, to the north of the Keep River National Park, can be reached from Kununurra (in Western Australia) by travelling north along an unsealed road. The road is submerged during the Wet. It is a remote but popular fishing spot, with a good range of inland species, such as barramundi, sleepy cod, archer fish and sooty grunter; in the tidal waters threadfin salmon and shark can also be caught. Boats can be launched at Keep River Crossing. There are also plenty of opportunities for shore anglers.

Some of the Territory's biggest barramundi come from the Victoria River – and enough 20 kg-plus fish are caught there each year to keep anglers coming back regularly. This is a big-tidal river and fishing is best on neap tides where there is not so much water movement and the water is relatively clear. Local knowledge is the key to fishing success.

The focus for access to the Victoria River is **Timber Creek**. Supplies and fishing gear can be obtained here, and boats launch at Big Horse Creek for trips up or down the **Victoria River**, which is strewn with lurking rock bars and requires a cautious approach. Boating anglers heading down the Victoria can enter **Angalarri**

Discreet inland lagoons along the west coast are often worth a cast for barramundi and sooty grunter

River but are advised to stay upstream of the Baines River junction, which can only be traversed at high tide due to extensive mud bars. Fishing safaris with professional guidance are conducted from Timber Creek, and anglers are advised to explore the intricacies of this largest of Territory rivers with a guide first before venturing out on their own. South-east of Timber Creek, a track runs into the Gregory National Park, giving access to fishing on the **East Baines River** at Limestone Gorge or at Bullita Outstation. The Victoria River can also be fished much further upstream, launching at the Victoria River Roadhouse, also on the Victoria Highway, near the tiny settlement of Victoria River. While the fishing may be just as productive, there are fewer waters to explore. Barramundi, sooty grunter, archer fish, sleepy cod and oxeye herring are all caught in these systems.

Just near Katherine, the superb **Katherine Gorge** is the backdrop to one of the Territory's best fisheries. Boats can be launched at the gorge, but there is a limit to motor size of 10 hp. Boats with bigger engines can launch at the town of Katherine, and the river is productive for a couple of months after the Wet but still capable of producing small barramundi through the Dry, particularly below the **Low Level Bridge**. **Knotts Crossing**, 5 km north of the town, is another good fishing place, particularly for land-based anglers.

Fishing at Mataranka, 107 km south-east of Katherine on the Stuart Highway, is focussed around the **Mataranka Homestead Tourist Resort**. The fishing waters are the **Elsey Creek**, **Roper Creek** and **Waterhouse River**, with a number of holes in the Elsey National Park along the upper Roper River. There are restrictions on outboard motor sizes during the Dry (10 hp).

North-west of Katherine on the Stuart Highway, at Hayes Creek, a turnoff to the west will lead to fishing at **Douglas River Crossing**, and a track further on takes you to **Lukies Farm** (about 30 km). This is on Grimaldi Station, so you need to check in at the homestead first. It is a bit further to the **Oolloo Crossing** on the Daly River. Lukies and Oolloo have boat launching facilities.

The **Daly River system** is much closer to Darwin, and is known for its big barramundi, so it attracts most of the fishing interest in this western region. The township of Daly River and nearby lodges providing accommodation, boat hire and fishing tours are reached by turning off the Stuart Highway at Adelaide River or Hayes Creek, then taking the Daly River Road. On the way, there are some good stopping places to prospect from the shore at the **Adelaide River Crossing** and the **Reynolds River Crossing**. Once at the Daly River, boats can be launched at a concrete ramp below Woolianna and the Daly River Crossing, which is also a famous spot for land-based barramundi fishing. The water is brackish right up to Browns Creek, so there is a variety of salt-water as well as inland species to be caught. Archer fish, sooty grunter, catfish, sleepy cod, threadfin salmon, barramundi and shark can all be found in these waters.

GUIDE TO LOCAL FISH

archer fish
barramundi
catfish
cod, sleepy
herring, oxeye
salmon, threadfin
shark
sooty grunter

INLAND FISHING WEST COAST RIVERS REGION

NORTHERN TERRITORY

The Territory's barramundi is renowned for its fighting ability. This one does battle on the lower Daly River

NORTHERN TERRITORY

INLAND FISHING ADELAIDE–MARY RIVERS REGION

Adelaide– Mary Rivers Region

The freshwater fishing around Darwin is both easily reached and varied, with several dams and lakes adding to the possibilities. In Darwin itself, there are many operators of guided fishing tours.

Type of fishing
billabong, dam, flood plain, river
Target fish
barramundi, oxeye herring, saratoga

South-east of Darwin, at **Berry Springs**, there is boat launching into the **Blackmore and Darwin rivers**. **The Lakes Tourist Resort**, between Berry Springs and the Stuart Highway, offers a chance of a barramundi, and the restriction to electric outboard motors only adds to the peace of the scene.

Following the Stuart Highway south, it leads to the **Manton River Crossing** and the big **Manton Dam**, which has excellent launching facilities. Manton Dam has been stocked with barramundi, which have grown to a legal size (55 cm). Further south, the **Lake Bennett Holiday Resort**, at Lake Bennett, offers accommodation and good fishing nearby in the Adelaide River.

North of the Stuart Highway, beyond Howard Springs, the **Howard River Crossing** is an easy day trip from Darwin for family fishing. Further down the river there are boat hire and launching facilities at Shoal Bay Boat Hire. In the upper tidal reaches, pools form among the rocks at high tide and barramundi are caught regularly.

The big **Adelaide and Mary rivers**, both to the east of Darwin, attract serious wetland and river fishing. These rivers expand into big lagoon systems in the Wet. The usual point of entry, especially for the inexperienced, is by the boat ramp at the **Adelaide River Bridge** on the Arnhem Highway. The fishing is both upstream and downstream, but is really only worth the effort while flood waters are receding after the Wet. Scotts Creek Crossing on Scotts Creek can also be reached by turning off the Arnhem Highway, some 10 km east of the

A good barramundi catch on the Mary River

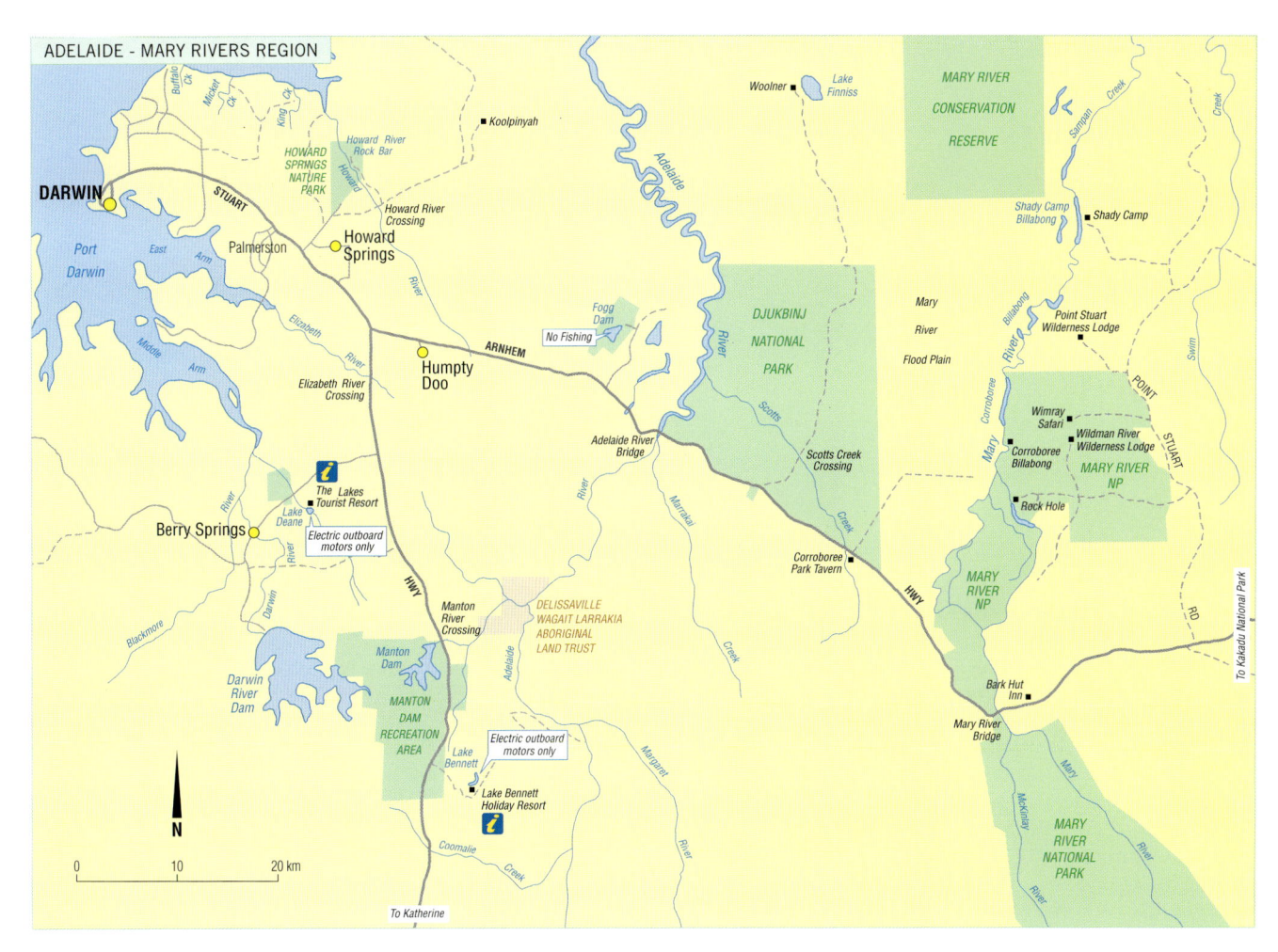

INLAND FISHING ADELAIDE–MARY RIVERS REGION   NORTHERN TERRITORY

Adelaide River Bridge, and this location marks the westernmost habitat for saratoga on the Australian mainland.

The **Mary River** and its flood plain are equally prolific for barramundi, sleepy cod, saratoga and oxeye herring. The **Corroboree Billabong** area can be reached by two wheel drive. There is good road access via the Arnhem Highway. Turn off just west of the Corroboree Park Tavern. At Corroboree Billabong, houseboats, hire boats and bait and tackle are available, and there is a concrete boat ramp. Corroboree is a beautiful lagoon. At more than 20 km in length, it is the largest landlocked waterway in the Northern Territory. Although its diverse wildlife and tropical ambience provide a perfect backdrop for barramundi fishing, in recent years its prolific population of saratoga has attracted specialised fly fishers from all over the world. Guided fishing can be arranged through Hot Spot Fishing Tours in Darwin, tel. (08) 8983 2167.

Further north is a renowned barramundi spot, **Shady Camp**. Each year after the Wet, huge barramundi move up the river to Shady Camp and feed at high tide on the deep bends. Boats can be hired here, but guided fishing, arranged before you arrive, is best. There are restrictions on tackle that may be used close to the barrage wall at Shady Camp Billabong. The barrage is a concrete causeway constructed to prevent salt water going any further up-river. For shore anglers, the Shady Camp barrage is hard to beat for barramundi anywhere in the Territory, but watch out for crocodiles.

MARY RIVER REGULATIONS

Because of its proximity to Darwin, the Mary is one of the Territory's most fished rivers and specific bag limits, equipment regulations and seasonal area closures are in place to ensure a healthy fishery. Details are available from the Department of Primary Industry and Fisheries Recreational Fishing Office, tel. (08) 8999 2372 or check the web site at www.nt.gov.au/dpif/fisheries/recfish/recfish.shtml

Saratoga are a common catch in Corroboree Lagoon

GUIDE TO LOCAL FISH

barramundi
cod, sleepy
herring, oxeye
saratoga

357

NORTHERN TERRITORY   INLAND FISHING KAKADU REGION

Kakadu Region

This is the heart of Northern Territory fishing, so beautiful and unspoiled that it has a World Heritage listing.

Type of fishing
billabong, flood plain, lagoon, river
Target fish
barramundi, oxeye herring, sooty grunter, threadfin salmon

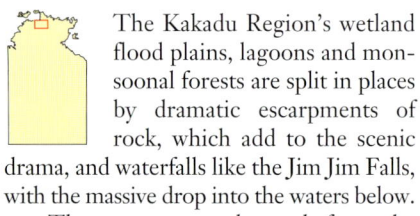

The famous Cahills Crossing on the East Alligator River. It is standing room only in the middle of the dry season as barramundi enthusiasts try their luck. Watch out for crocodiles

The Kakadu Region's wetland flood plains, lagoons and monsoonal forests are split in places by dramatic escarpments of rock, which add to the scenic drama, and waterfalls like the Jim Jim Falls, with the massive drop into the waters below.

The entrance to the park from the Darwin side is on the Arnhem Highway, which runs through the Aurora Kakadu Resort, some 47 km from the entrance, and continues on to Jabiru. From west to east, the first fishing area is the **Wildman River**. Just past the park entrance, a road runs north to **Two Mile Hole**, and passes a track turning right, which meanders up to two further spots – **Four Mile Hole** and **Alecs Hole**. The stretch to the last two places is passable only in the dry season. These

The South Alligator River is held in high regard for the size of its barramundi population

billabongs fish well late in the Dry. They each have camping grounds, and boats may be easily launched. The most effective fishing method is trolling, but casting to the bases of the fringing palms is also effective.

A major waterway in the Territory, the **South Alligator River**, crosses the Arnhem Highway 2 km east of the Aurora Kakadu Resort. Before the bridge, the river gets a lot of attention from casual land-based anglers fishing for barramundi from a road culvert during the Wet. A concrete boat ramp provides access to the river at the bridge. The fishing either side of the bridge is in a big, mangrove-lined river, with a tidal range of 5 to 6 m. Boat fishing can be very good for barramundi, but only while the river is receding in March to May. Camping is not permitted at or near the launching area, but anglers can stay at the Aurora Kakadu Resort, which offers camping and special anglers' packages in unit accommodation.

Above the tidal part of the South Alligator River there is one of the most beautiful water areas of the park, and most bountiful for anglers. The mangroves give way to paperbark and barringtonia trees if you head upriver during the Wet through the flood plain to **Bucket, Red Lily and Alligator billabongs**. These waters are best fished when the first floods begin to fill the flood plains and billabongs, and towards the end of the dry season. During the dry season, the barramundi tend to lie low in the colder water, but persistence and skill will often yield a fish or two.

The same could be said for Yellow Waters. The settlement of **Cooinda**, within the **Yellow Waters** area, has a motel and camping ground, boat launching and boat and tackle hire, and bank fishing when the water is not too high. Fishing from a boat with lures is best. Despite being heavily fished, these billabongs are still productive.

About 30 km south-west, along the Jim Jim Road from the Kakadu Highway, the **South Alligator Crossing** and the **Kunkamoula Billabong** both have boat launching facilities and good fishing. South-east of here, along the Kakadu Highway, are **Long Billabong** and **Shovel Billabong**, both with launching facilities.

To the east, the flood plains of the **Nourlangie Creek** extend down to the South Alligator River in the Wet, so this area can be reached by boat. During the Dry, the wetlands only extend as far as the Nourlangie Billabongs.

The flood plains and billabongs of the **Nourlangie, Malabanbandju, Baroalba, Muirella Park and Sandy creeks** provide fine fishing. In the flood there will be fish around weed and grass areas and sunken trees and logs. In the Dry, Nourlangie Creek is full of sunken logs that create stations for the barramundi and other fish. At low tide the mouths of secondary creeks can be hot spots.

The Magela Creek Crossing, northeast of the town of Jabiru, is the limit for vehicles during the Wet. The **Magela Creek** and its flood plain can provide great fishing just after the Wet, with the best fishing in the mouth of the creek and up the creek at the fork. There are many lagoons on the Magela flood plain, but these have been closed temporarily due to infestation by the noxious floating weed, salvinia.

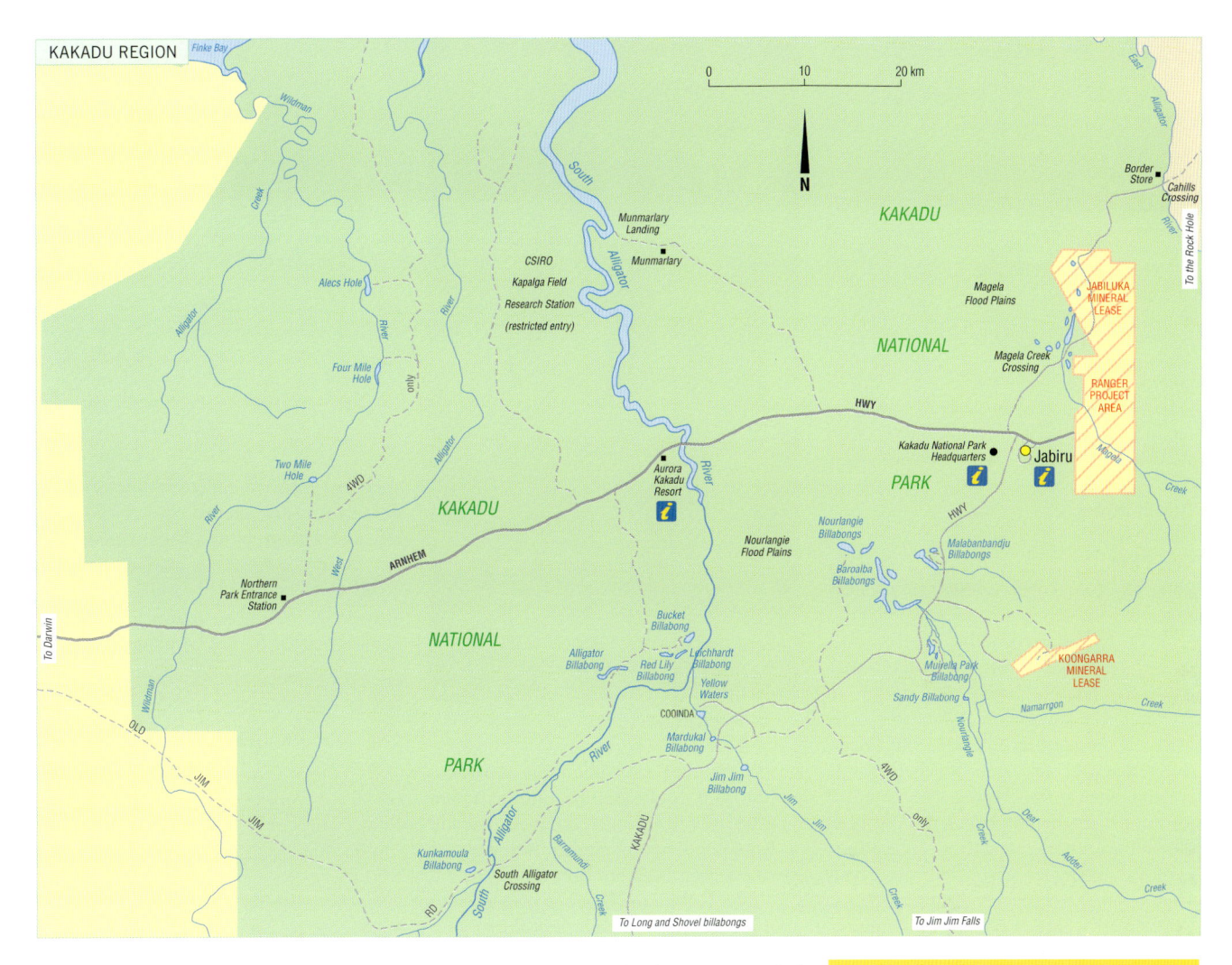

INLAND FISHING KAKADU REGION — NORTHERN TERRITORY

Visitors should check with Kakadu park rangers on the status of access, and always be careful not to transport salvinia to unaffected areas.

In the far north-east corner of Kakadu National Park, the **East Alligator River** enters the park from Arnhem Land, and forms the boundary between Arnhem Land and the park in its run to the sea. Above the entry point fishing is off limits, unless you have a permit. But the flood plain complex washes well into Kakadu, through the Magela Creek and its surrounding flood plain.

In the Dry, vehicles can go from Magela Creek Crossing through to **Cahills Crossing**, where boats can be launched into the East Alligator. Downstream the barramundi fishing can be wonderful for a short period after the Wet, with many species, including barramundi, sleepy cod, sooty grunter and oxeye herring, depending on how far you travel down. There is a rock bar some 5 km downstream from the crossing that is unnavigable at low tide. On the rising tide it produces catfish, shark, barramundi and threadfin salmon, feeding on the incoming mullet that are impeded by the rocks.

There is good camping near Cahills Crossing, and land-based fishing around the crossing, but be wary on the causeway, where there has been a fatal crocodile attack. This is big barramundi territory, with the tide sweeping the salt water up the river and down again, twice a day, bringing saltwater barramundi up to the Crossing and driving the freshwater fish upriver.

Just downstream from the point where the East Alligator enters Kakadu, there is a deep and permanent pool known as the **Rock Hole**, which fishes well at times and is a beautiful place, with the Arnhem Land escarpment rising from the edge of the pool. Between here and Cahills Crossing, the East Alligator River is full of snags, worth casting into for barramundi and generally producing for the whole of the dry season.

The whole of this country is very scenic, fringing the Arnhem Land escarpment, and has patches of rainforest, mingled with the pools and billabongs, which become a flooded plain during the Wet. Many anglers stay at the big and well-serviced camping ground, exploring these fabulous waterways on daily excursions.

Remember that **cast nets and beach seines** are prohibited in the Kakadu National Park. Due to the prevalence of large crocodiles it is an offence to clean or fillet a fish within 50 m of a waterway in the park. Fishing and boating regulations in Kakadu can also be different from the rest of the Territory. Information can be obtained by ringing park management on (08) 8938 1100.

GUIDE TO LOCAL FISH

- barramundi
- catfish
- cod, sleepy
- herring, oxeye
- mullet
- salmon, threadfin
- shark
- sooty grunter

NORTHERN TERRITORY   INLAND FISHING EAST COAST RIVERS REGION

East Coast Rivers Region

The eastern rivers of the Territory flow into the Gulf of Carpentaria through flat and sparse country where cattle roam on huge station properties. In the Wet, some of the rivers branch out into flood plains, but there is none of the lush scenery of Kakadu.

Type of fishing
estuary, river

Target fish
archer fish, barramundi, saratoga, sooty grunter

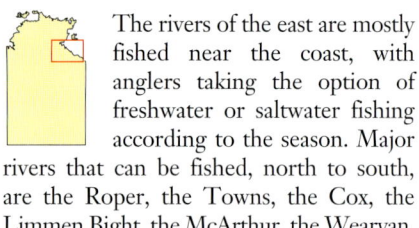

The rivers of the east are mostly fished near the coast, with anglers taking the option of freshwater or saltwater fishing according to the season. Major rivers that can be fished, north to south, are the Roper, the Towns, the Cox, the Limmen Bight, the McArthur, the Wearyan, the Robinson and the Calvert. The Roper Highway branches east from the Stuart Highway at Mataranka and runs 174 km to Roper Bar, where there are camping and launching facilities. The bar marks the confluence of the fresh water and the salt water in the **Roper River**. Upstream from the bar there is fine fishing for barramundi, sooty grunter, sleepy cod, saratoga and archer fish. The **Hodgson River** flows into the Roper's tidal area, but has freshwater fishing upstream. Launching ramps for the Hodgson are at the Hodgson River Crossing and the Rocky Bar Crossing. The tidal section of the river is basically a barramundi habitat, with mangrove jack and fingermark also present.

Boats launch into the **Towns River** at Towns River Crossing. It is mostly tidal water, fishing wonderfully for barramundi and there is a fine camping spot.

The **Cox River** meets the Roper Highway at the Cox River Crossing and then joins the **Limmen Bight River** for the run to the coast. There are both launch sites and camp sites around this area, and there is salt water below the Cox River Crossing and freshwater above.

The township of Borroloola is on the **McArthur River** and there are boat ramps in the town. The lower reaches have barramundi, black jewfish, fingermark, salmon

Towns River action

and mangrove jack, while there are barramundi and sooty grunter in the upper reaches. There is good camping downriver at King Ash Bay, and guided fishing excursions are available from Borroloola.

The **Robinson River** is reached by a four wheel drive track south of Borroloola, and is a top barramundi location.

Access to the **Calvert River** is possible through the Pungalina Station, and at various other spots along the river. Permission should be obtained first from the Borroloola Holiday Resort in Borroloola.

All these rivers need careful navigation as they contain rock and sand bars, sand flats and channels.

There are a number of other fishing places in the region, based on station properties. Anglers are welcome, but require permission from stations to camp and fish. From the Cox River south they are **Nathan River Station, Lorella Station, Billengarrah Station** and **Broadmere Station** (accessible from the Carpentaria Highway west of Cape Crawford). East of Borroloola there is **Manangoora Station, Seven Emu Station** and **Pungalina Station**, with **Wollogorang Station** close to the Queensland border. All have rough launching facilities onto rivers or creeks.

The Northern Territory offers wild frontier fishing the equal of anywhere in the world. However, local knowledge and tropical fishing skills are often not part of a southern visitor's repertoire. It is sound advice for visitors on that big Territory fishing adventure to book a fishing guide for a day or two right at the start of a trip, in order to glean the skills and a bit of local knowledge to enhance the prospects of angling success for the duration of the visit.

Lures
Successful barramundi lures come in a variety of colours, shapes, sizes and swimming depths but minnow-style lures like this produce the most fish. Lure choice depends on fishing location, water depth, fish activity and prey.

FISHING TIP

Super braids or gelspun lines are popular with anglers using lures. These lines are more sensitive and finer in diameter than equivalent breaking strain monofilament. Due to their lack of stretch you can detect a subtle strike more easily, and because they are thinner in diameter there is less water drag, which preserves the action of lures and allows them to swim deeper.

Barramundi
Australia's premier native sportfish is adept at turning up in just about any place where there is water in the Top End. Favourite habitats include estuarine rocky outcrops, mangrove creeks, tidal rivers and freshwater lagoons.

GUIDE TO LOCAL FISH

archer fish
barramundi
cod, sleepy
fingermark
jack, mangrove
jewfish, black
salmon, threadfin
saratoga
sooty grunter

INLAND FISHING EAST COAST RIVERS REGION

NORTHERN TERRITORY

The Roper River, rising east of Katherine in the West Coast Rivers Region, is nevertheless classed as an East Coast river. Mataranka Falls, in the upper reaches near Mataranka, provides good sport for barramundi and saratoga

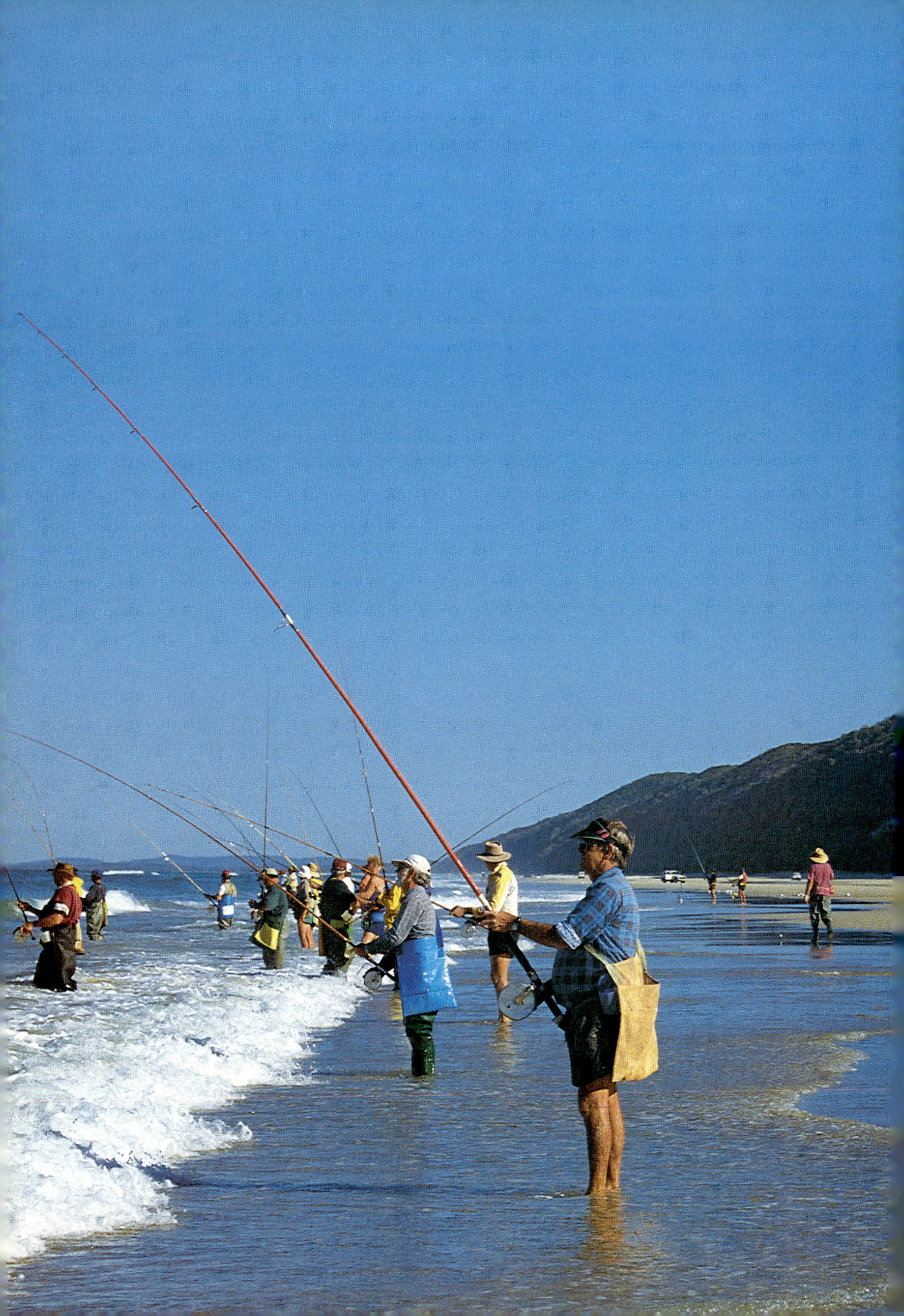

Coastal Fishing

Brisbane Region	366
Cairns Region	380
Townsville Region	392
Rockhampton Region	402

Inland Fishing

Northern Region	416
Southern Region	418

Queensland

Queensland offers a wonderful destination for the angler. A tropical climate, breathtaking scenery and a brilliant variety of fishing come together in an irresistible combination. Whether you are into light tackle sportfishing, big game fishing or fly fishing, there are enough destinations and species to cater to your needs.

Surf fishing for tailor is popular with Queensland anglers

The coast is the chief attraction. Cairns is now a world-famous location for black marlin and other big game fishing, while the Great Barrier Reef provides fertile ground for a dazzling array of reef and bottom fish, in an environmentally spectacular setting. On the Cape, there are pristine wilderness areas, and the fishing for tropical exotics around the river mouths is unsurpassed. The region stretching north and south of Brisbane continues to surprise with its capacity to produce large numbers of fish, despite the ever-increasing pressures of population, with beach fishing being one of the highlights.

Inland fishing has gone ahead in recent years with the stocking of impoundments, offering yet another perspective on the Queensland scene. Anglers can now fish for species such as Australian bass, golden perch and Murray cod throughout the south-east of the State.

QUEENSLAND

Coastal Fishing

The Queensland coast offers inexhaustible opportunities for the angler, with everything from estuary fishing for barramundi and mangrove jack, to the chase for giant marlin. There is a lifetime of fishing to be done along the Great Barrier Reef, where exotic reef species compete for attention with the spectacular array of game fish, while further north the remote regions of Cape York provide a frontier experience for those seeking barramundi, queenfish and giant trevally.

State regulations

The principal legislation that deals with fishery matters in Queensland is the *Fisheries Act 1994* and the *Fisheries Regulation 1995*. The agency responsible for management of most recreational fishing activities is the Queensland Fisheries Service.

No licence is required for saltwater recreational fishing. Closed seasons, bag and size limits apply. Consult 'Guidelines for Recreational Fishing in Queensland – Tidal Waters'.

For the full details of any rules concerning fishing activities, contact Queensland Fisheries Service on 13 2523 or see their website: www.dpi.qld.gov.au For information concerning restricted areas in the Great Barrier Reef Marine Park, contact the Great Barrier Reef Marine Park Authority.

Protected species

There are certain species of fish protected throughout Queensland. These include: ceratodus or lungfish; helmet, trumpet and clam shells; female mud and blue swimmer crabs; whales; porpoises; dugongs; dolphins; turtles and egg-bearing spanner crabs; bugs and slipper lobsters.

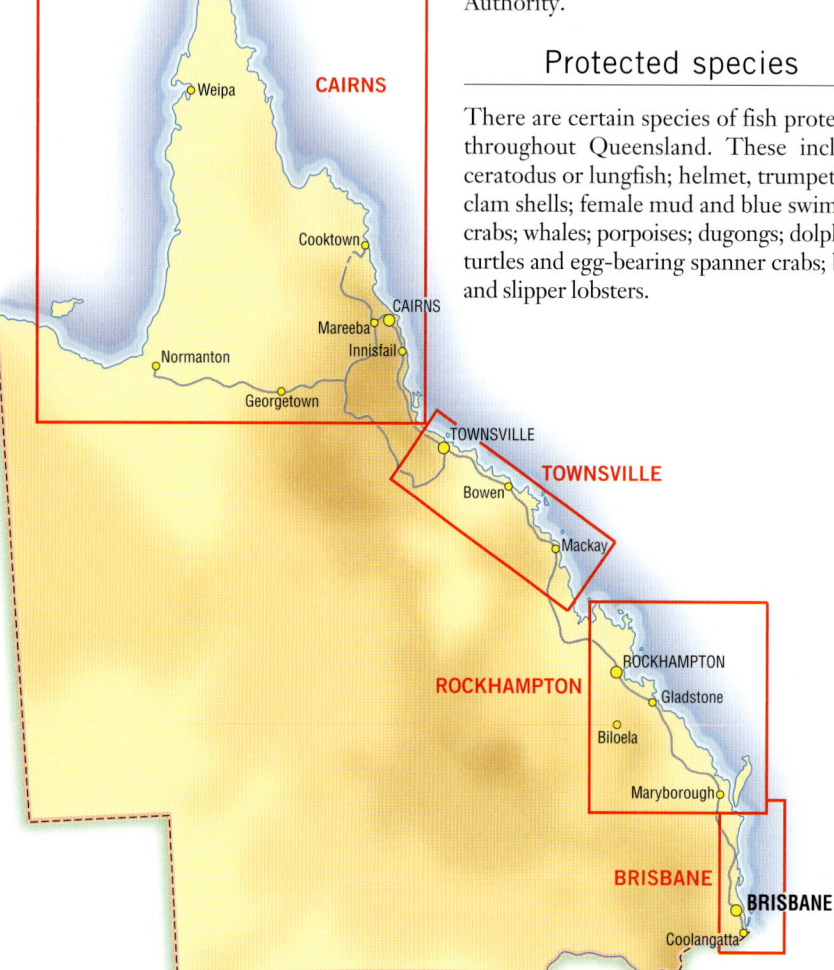

COASTAL FISHING

WHERE TO FISH
Along the coast

BRISBANE REGION ● 366

Brisbane's semi-tropical climate and the relaxed lifestyle means that there is great enthusiasm for the excellent local fishing. The warm tropical currents provide a tempting mix of temperature and tropical fish. Estuary, coastal, reef and offshore fishing are all possibilities here.

CAIRNS REGION ● 380

Tropical Cairns is a departure point for the northern wilderness of Cape York and the Gulf. It is also a major centre for charter boats going out to the Great Barrier Reef, and deepwater game fishing, especially for black marlin.

TOWNSVILLE REGION ● 392

In the Townsville region, the mangrove estuaries on the coastline are renowned for barramundi and mangrove jack. Just off the coast are the wonders of the Whitsundays and a host of other coastal islands, with their waters teeming with mackerel, queenfish, trevally and others. The Great Barrier Reef is well offshore, and has a variety of reef and pelagic fish for those with the time to travel there.

ROCKHAMPTON REGION ● 402

The pristine bays and rocky peninsulas of Shoalwater Bay and its islets lead on to the beaches and islands further south. The Keppel Islands are a tropical paradise at the very south of the tropics. There are the mangrove creeks around Curtis Island and The Narrows. The tailor at Fraser Island are legendary, and the nearby Great Sandy Strait has a large variety of estuary species in the mangrove channels.

The Great Barrier Reef Marine Park

The Great Barrier Reef is the largest system of coral on earth, stretching for almost 2300 km along the north-east coast of Queensland, and encompassed in a marine park covering 348,700 sq km, making it the world's most extensive protected marine area. It has 2900 individual reefs of greatly varying sizes, providing a superb habitat for over 1500 fish species, 215 bird species and 6 breeding species of turtle. Its World Heritage listing confirms its status as an area of enormous environmental significance.

COASTAL FISHING

QUEENSLAND

GUIDE TO LOCAL FISH

(AJ)	amberjack	(BJ)	jewfish, black	(SH)	shark, hammerhead
(BD)	barracuda	(SJ)	jewfish, silver	(SH)	shark, shovelnose
(BM)	barramundi	(JF)	Job-fish, rosy	(S)	snapper
(BA)	bass, Australian	(KI)	kingfish, yellowtail	(SY)	stripey
(BT)	bonito	(LT)	long tom	(ES)	sweetlip, grass
(B)	bream, black	(LU)	luderick	(ES)	sweetlip, red-throated
(B)	bream, pikey	(MA)	mackerel, grey	(T)	tailor
(B)	bream, yellowfin	(MA)	mackerel, school	(TA)	tarwhine
(CO)	cobia	(MA)	mackerel, shark	(TL)	teraglin, jew
(C)	cod, estuary	(MA)	mackerel, Spanish	(TL)	teraglin, silver
(C)	cod, yellow-spotted rock	(MA)	mackerel, spotted	(TR)	trevally, bigeye
(C)	cod, potato	(ML)	marlin, black	(TR)	trevally, giant
(C)	cod, rock	(ML)	marlin, blue	(TR)	trevally, golden
(DA)	dart	(ML)	marlin, striped	(TR)	trevally, gold-spotted
(DO)	dolphin fish	(MO)	morwong	(TU)	tuna, mackerel
(RE)	emperor, red	(M)	mullet, sea	(CT)	trout, coral
(ES)	emperor, spangled	(MU)	mulloway	(TU)	tuna, northern bluefin
(FM)	fingermark	(NG)	nannygai	(TU)	tuna, striped
(F)	flathead, dusky	(PF)	parrotfish	(TU)	tuna, yellowfin
(F)	flathead, sand	(MP)	perch, Moses	(TK)	tuskfish
(F)	flathead, others	(PP)	perch, pearl	(WH)	wahoo
(GR)	groper, Queensland	(Q)	queenfish	(W)	whiting, sand
(H)	herring, oxeye	(SL)	sailfish	(W)	whiting, trumpeter
(MJ)	jack, mangrove	(TS)	salmon, threadfin	(WR)	wrasse, Maori
(JA)	javelin fish	(SH)	shark, bronze whaler		

Size and bag limits apply. Consult 'Guidelines for Recreational Fishing in Queensland – Tidal Waters'.

The Great Barrier Reef Marine Park Authority tries to ensure that a balance is maintained between the principles of conservation and the concept of reasonable use of the Reef by a wide range of users, including anglers, charter groups, scientists and tourists. To facilitate this the Reef has been divided into zones that have regulations that reflect their particular status as areas of scientific interest, preservation or general use. For the angler, the most important zone areas are those where line fishing is either prohibited or restricted. Official maps are widely available, and those planning to spend any amount of time on the Reef are advised to become familiar with the restrictions in the areas they wish to explore. Detailed maps also appear on information boards at nearly all the public boat ramps along the coast. Areas that are off-limits are clearly shown, as are those that are subject to restrictions on activities such as bait netting and spearfishing. Check with the Great Barrier Reef Marine Park Authority for the latest information on areas off-limits to fishing. The Further Information box also provides details of organisations able to provide maps or details of fishing and boating regulations in these areas. For information on the islands of the Great Barrier Reef, contact Tourism Queensland on (07) 3535 3535.

Boating regulations

Licensing and registration are compulsory for certain vessels and operators. Contact a Queensland Transport Customer Service Centre or the Boating Registration and Licensing Hotline for details. Speed limits apply on the water throughout the State. EPIRBs (Emergency Positioning Indicating Radio Beacon) are compulsory for all boats with motors of 3 kw or more. Safety equipment is compulsory for most vessels. Check these requirements with Queensland Transport or the Queensland Boating and Fisheries Patrol office on (07) 3224 2282.

ABORIGINAL LANDS

There are areas of Aboriginal land throughout the State that are managed by different resident communities, and rules about access vary greatly. The roads are in most cases public and therefore open to general use, but visitors wishing to fish and camp should first seek permission from the relevant body. The Cape York Land Council, tel. (07) 4053 9222, is a good place to start for initial inquiries. Several groups have begun to make provisions to accommodate the growing influx of tourists to this remote region.

For more details see the information box on p. 414.

FURTHER INFORMATION

Fishing & boating *The Queensland Boating and Fisheries Patrol (a part of the Department of Primary Industries) enforces boating and fishing regulations and provides information on rules, regulations, licences and permits. The head office is on the 2nd floor, 80 Ann St, Brisbane, tel. 13 2523 or (07) 3224 2282; website www.dpi.qld.gov.au The Queensland Fisheries Service, tel. 13 2523, publishes a pamphlet on recreational fishing in the State, listing all regulations for tidal and non-tidal waters, which can be obtained from Queensland Boating and Fisheries Patrol offices, some bait and tackle shops and marine dealers.*

The Great Barrier Reef Marine Park Authority at 2–68 Flinders St, Townsville, tel. (07) 4750 0700, can supply zoning maps and guidelines for use of the Park. Maps can also be obtained from some tourist centres, some bait and tackle shops and all Queensland Parks and Wildlife Service offices.

The Environmental Protection Agency is at the Naturally Queensland Information Centre (NQIC), Ground floor, 160 Ann St, Brisbane, tel. (07) 3227 8187. NQIC can provide information on recreational fishing in national parks and protected areas, reef boating and fishing guidance, and Moreton Bay tide times. To report an injured or dead dugong, turtle, whale or dolphin call 1300 360 898.

Queensland Transport controls recreational boating. It publishes a boating safety handbook and various marine safety brochures. Contact their Maritime Division head office on (07) 3860 3500. The Boating Registration and Licensing Hotline is 13 2380.

QUEENSLAND

Brisbane Region

In many ways Brisbane has the best fishing of any Australian capital city, and the semi-tropical climate stimulates an enviable relaxed lifestyle, part of which includes the highest per capita boat ownership in the country and great enthusiasm for the region's excellent fishing.

Local anglers often do not go far on holidays, because the fishing is no better further north or further south. Many southern residents heading north on holiday drive right past exactly what they are looking for when they pass through the Brisbane Region. The huge estuary of Moreton Bay and the warm tropical currents of summer provide a great mix of temperature and tropical fish.

Fishing in the Brisbane Region changes with the seasons, with tropical species like sailfish and mackerel being present in the warmer months, and sub-tropical species like bream and tailor predominating in catches over winter. There is also freshwater fishing for Australian bass and blue water fishing for marlin and sailfish.

The sandy islands, Moreton and North and South Stradbroke, shelter an enormous semi-estuarine mangrove system between Brisbane's southernmost suburbs and the northern extent of the Gold Coast. This area is relatively pristine despite its location between two densely populated urban areas. Most of southern Moreton Bay is only accessible by boat.

WHERE TO FISH
Brisbane Region

TIN CAN INLET AND SUNSHINE COAST ● 368
The sheltered waters of Tin Can Inlet and the renowned Rainbow Beach are famous for good catches of fish, from bream to mackerel. The beautiful Sunshine Coast has great fishing all year round. The mouth of the Mooloolah River is a protected entrance giving small boat anglers safe passage to offshore reefs. There is a great mixture of temperate and tropical species available in rivers and from rocks, beaches and offshore. In spring the estuaries produce some of the biggest flathead in Australia with fish over 80 cm common.

MORETON BAY AND BRISBANE RIVER ● 372
Moreton Bay is a huge body of fertile water on the doorstep of Brisbane. It produces good quantities of fish all year, with tremendous variety. Species vary from the small, delicious trumpeter whiting (winter whiting) right through to sailfish and black marlin. The Brisbane River is an excellent bream fishery and a range of estuary species can be sought from the river banks, rock walls and wharves near the city.

JUMPINPIN AND GOLD COAST ● 376
The Jumpinpin, Southport and Coolangatta areas provide good estuary and offshore fishing with legendary bream runs each winter and monster flathead in spring. The Southport Broadwater is a fairly good whiting ground, and provides access to offshore reefs frequented by snapper, with pearl perch and rosy Jobfish in deep water. The area is establishing itself as a major game fishing centre for marlin.

Gatherings of anglers at Teewah Beach can signify a tailor fishing bonanza

Weather

South-easterly winds can dominate in summer and produce large swells. The most southerly section of the Queensland coast is affected by winter and early spring westerlies, which can reach gale force, but winter generally coincides with calm conditions and good bottom fishing. There is a chance of tropical cyclones any time between December to May, but usually they have weakened significantly by the time they reach the area, while winter storms occasionally bring gales and heavy rain. Afternoon and evening thunderstorms occur in the late spring and summer months. Watch for weather updates on television and radio news or get online with the Bureau of Meteorology: www.bom.gov.au

COASTAL FISHING BRISBANE REGION

QUEENSLAND

GUIDE TO LOCAL FISH

- amberjack
- bass, Australian
- bonito
- bream, black
- cobia
- cod, estuary
- cod, others
- dart
- dolphin fish
- flathead, dusky
- jack, mangrove
- Job-fish, rosy
- kingfish, yellowtail
- luderick
- mackerel, school
- mackerel, Spanish
- mackerel, spotted
- marlin, black
- marlin, blue
- marlin, striped
- mulloway
- parrotfish
- perch, pearl
- sailfish
- shark, bronze whaler
- shark, hammerhead
- shark, shovelnose
- snapper
- sweetlip
- tailor
- teraglin
- trevally
- tuna, mackerel
- tuna, longtail
- tuna, striped
- tuna, yellowfin
- wahoo
- whiting, sand
- whiting, trumpeter

Hooked onto a big Spanish mackerel near Wolf Rock, out from Double Island Point

A fine catch of estuary cod

Boating

All entrances in this region, except those inside Moreton Bay and the Mooloolah River, involve the crossing of a bar. Visitors are advised to seek local advice before attempting a crossing. On the Gold Coast the entrances at Jumpinpin, Currumbin and Tallebudgera are particularly shallow. The Gold Coast Seaway is a safe, deep water access in most conditions. Entrances on the Sunshine Coast at Caloundra, the Maroochy River, the Noosa River and the Wide Bay Bar at the southern end of Fraser Island, should also be approached with caution. Moreton Bay has numerous sandbanks that can be hazardous to boating. Seek local advice and refer to local charts.

Many of the major beaches in the Brisbane Region, such as Noosa Beach, contain bathing reserves where boats must stay 400 m offshore. Shark control measures are in place on many popular beaches. Boat operators should stay well clear of marker buoys indicating shark nets and drum lines.

FURTHER INFORMATION

Fishing and boating The head office of the Queensland Boating and Fisheries Patrol is at Marine Operations Base, MacArthur Ave East, Pinkenba, tel. (07) 3860 3502. Other offices are at Sea World Dr, Main Beach, Gold Coast, tel. (07) 5583 5500, Parkyn Pde, Mooloolaba, tel. (07) 5444 4599; and Russell St, Noosaville, tel. (07) 5449 7555.

Tourist centres Marketing Information Booth, Queen St Mall, Brisbane, tel. (07) 3006 6290; Tourism Queensland, Level 10, 30 Makerston St, Brisbane, tel. (07) 3406 5400; Caloundra Tourist Information Centre, 7 Caloundra Rd, Caloundra, tel. (07) 5491 0202; Redlands Tourism Information Centre, 152 Shore St West, Cleveland, tel. (07) 3821 0057; Gold Coast Tourism Bureau Information Kiosk, Griffith St, Coolangatta, tel. (07) 5536 7765, cnr Sixth Ave and Aerodrome Rd, Maroochydore, tel. (07) 5479 1566; Hastings St roundabout, Noosa Heads, tel. (07) 5447 4988; North Stradbroke Island Visitors Centre, Junner St, Dunwich, North Stradbroke Island, tel. (07) 3409 9555; Rainbow Beach Rd, Rainbow Beach, tel. (07) 5486 3227; Redcliffe Tourist Information Centre, Pelican Park, Hornibrook Esplanade, Redcliffe, tel. (07) 3284 3500; Gold Coast Tourism Bureau Information Kiosk, Cavill Walk, Surfers Paradise, tel. (07) 5538 4419.

Tin Can Inlet and Sunshine Coast

Type of fishing
beach, estuary, jetty, offshore, reef

Target fish
bream, flathead, mackerel, tailor

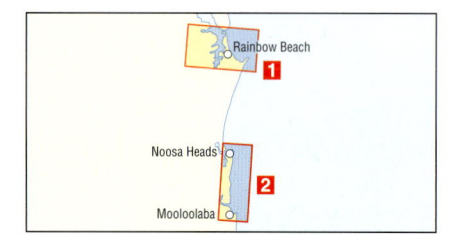

A string of beautiful beaches rimmed by the blue waters of the Pacific stretches from Rainbow Beach southwards to Bribie Island to form the Sunshine Coast. These beaches, and the numerous rivers, are famous for producing good catches of fish such as tailor, bream, whiting and flathead. The major towns are Noosa Heads, Maroochydore, Mooloolaba and Caloundra, with year-round fishing available and safe ocean access via the Mooloolah River entrance.

TIN CAN INLET AND RAINBOW BEACH

The waters in **Tin Can Inlet** are sheltered and offer protected fishing in all but the windiest weather. The inlet is shallow and the sandbanks and channels provide an ideal habitat for bream, flathead and whiting. Care must be taken at low tides.

Kauri Creek, north-west of the entrance to the inlet, produces big whiting, flathead and bream on the sand flats. A few mangrove jack can be caught here by lure fishing or live baiting around the oyster rocks.

Inskip Point, at the north-eastern entrance, is the site of a ferry crossing to Fraser Island. It is a good whiting spot in summer, with dart, bream and spotted mackerel also taken in this season. It is also a reliable place for tailor, bream and mulloway in winter. **Pelican Bay** has tailor, mulloway, bream and cod in winter and early summer, while the banks around **Pannikin Island** can be fished for whiting and mackerel. The **Teebar Ledge** is a renowned cod spot, with whiting and flathead also around the banks.

Teebar and **Snapper creeks**, running into the west of the inlet, are the places to search for mangrove jack.

The main channel, running down the centre of the inlet and curving in to Snapper Creek, is frequented by a mixture of bottom fish, such as cod, flathead and young snapper (known as squire). Similar fish are at the **Parrot Hole**, just below the southern point of Snapper Creek. The channel continues all the way down to the head of the inlet, at **Poverty Point**. The banks begin to close in here, and abound with mud crabs. Whiting, sweetlip and bream can be caught all around the sandbanks.

The town of **Rainbow Beach** is placed mid-way along its famous beach, the southern end of which is protected by Double Island Point. There are gutters all along the beach for anglers seeking bream, whiting, flathead and dart. Gatherings of anglers can signify a tailor fishing bonanza. There are places on the beach to launch a boat for those with experience who wish to head out into Wide Bay to seek mackerel and snapper.

Wolf Rock, offshore to the north of Double Island Point, is a bombora that gives way to an area of pinnacles and rubble extending out to sea from the north-east angle of the point. It is snapper, cod and sweetlip ground, with large Spanish mackerel, cobia, mackerel tuna and other pelagics over and around the reef, especially in autumn.

Double Island Point is a brilliant rock fishing spot. Bream, trevally, sweetlip, dart, mulloway, Spanish and spotted mackerel, yellowtail kingfish and tailor are all regularly landed off the rocks. This area has tremendous land-based game fishing potential but

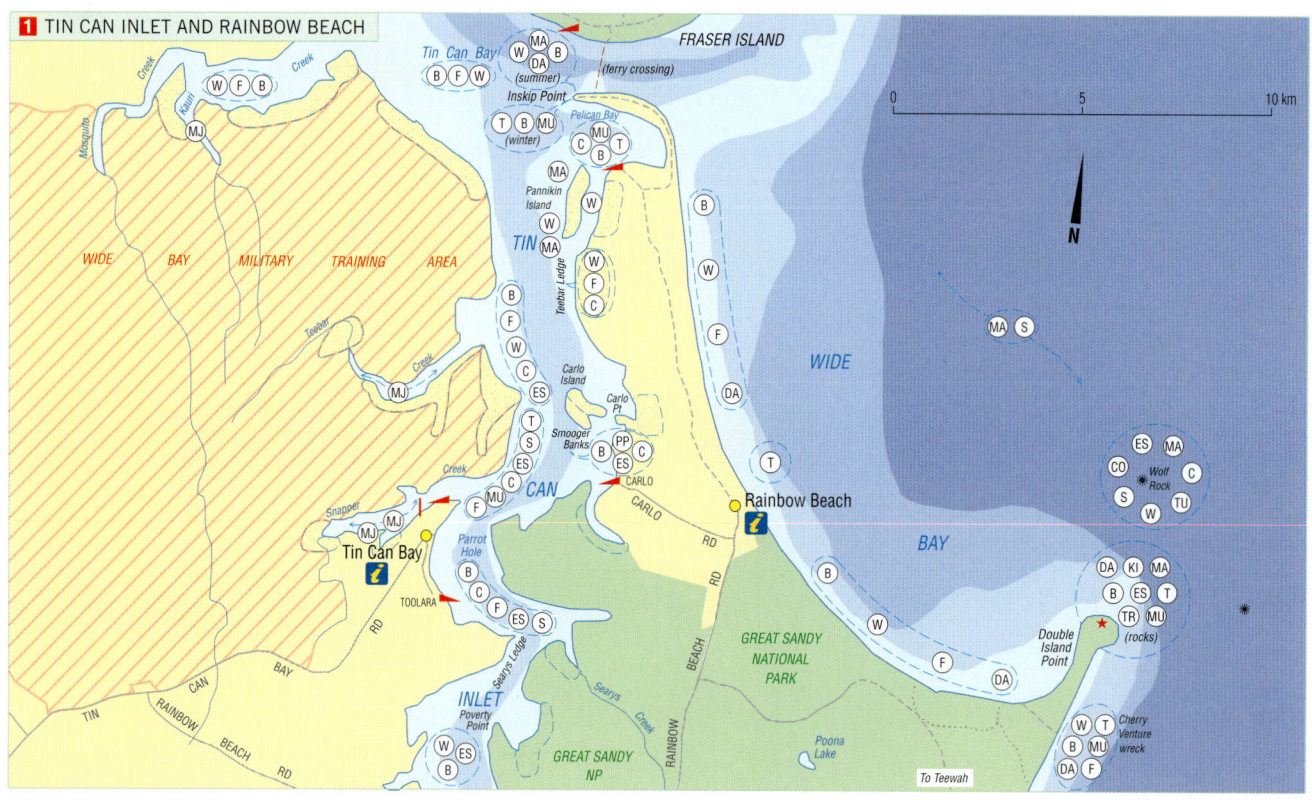

COASTAL FISHING BRISBANE REGION

QUEENSLAND

Fishing at Teewah Beach, which is also the four-wheel-drive pathway to Fraser Island

can be dangerous. As always, approach these rocks with caution if a swell is running. Fatalities have occurred here. To the south, the wreck of the *Cherry Venture* marks a gutter holding tailor, whiting, bream, dart, flathead and mulloway.

SUNSHINE COAST

Although this is a rapidly growing holiday area, the beach, rock and offshore fishing remains excellent, and it is easy to get out to sea from the deep and protected entrance of the Mooloolah River at Mooloolaba.

Off the coast, between Sunshine and Coolum beaches, are several reefs, all 2 km or more out from shore. **Chardons Reef** is some 7.5 km east out from the northern end of Sunshine Reef and offers snapper, sweetlip, cod, pearl perch, Spanish and spotted mackerel. **Sunshine Reefs, Victor Bailey Reef, Castaways Reef** and **Hancock Shoal** all hold mackerel, snapper, sweetlip and cod.

From **Peregian Beach** to **Point Arkwright**, gutter formations occur all along the beaches. Anglers will have to spend some time looking for channels and gutters, or get local information, as the sands are subtly shifted by wave action. Flathead, whiting, bream and dart are the staple fish, with mulloway and tailor in winter.

Point Arkwright, near the town of Coolum Beach, has a reef called the **Arkwright Shoal** extending about 2.5 km out to sea. This has snapper, sweetlip, Spanish and spotted mackerel and mulloway are out over the reef.

Running from Noosa Heads to Mooloolaba, some 35 km offshore, is a very big reef area known as the **Barwon Banks**. The reef rises from 60 m depth to some 30 m, and then drops off to 80 m on the eastern side and produces sweetlip, pearl perch, parrotfish and snapper. The inner reef edges are cruised by Spanish mackerel, wahoo, cobia and yellowfin tuna, while the drop-off can be trolled for black marlin and sailfish. This is an excellent game fishing ground and is regularly fished by charter boats operating from Mooloolaba.

Reefs easily reached by boats launched at Mooloolaba are the **Inner Gneerings** and **Outer Gneerings** off Maroochydore. The Inner Gneerings is a reef area just a few kilometres out from the Maroochy River, which fishes well for snapper and sweetlip over the bottom at 10 to 20 m depth, and for Spanish mackerel. Nearby is a blinker buoy marking the beginning of the shipping channel to Brisbane, which is a great attractor for yellowtail kingfish and amberjack. About 5 km north-east from the Inner Gneerings is the Outer Gneerings, with similar fishing to the inner reef. The **Gneering Shoal**, between the Inner and Outer Gneerings, is an area for caution as occasionally waves break over it in bad weather.

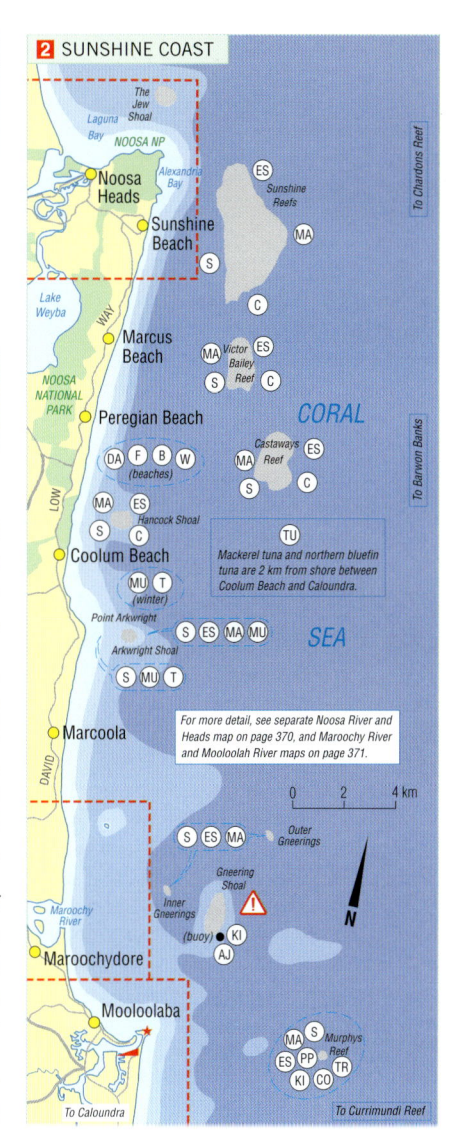

Murphys Reef is about 7 km due east of Mooloolaba, with depths of 20 to 30 m. The occasional pearl perch may be part of the targeted haul of snapper, sweetlip, Spanish mackerel, trevally, cobia and yellowtail kingfish. Mackerel tuna and northern bluefin tuna also move along an 'alley' some 2 km from shore between Coolum Beach and Mooloolaba, and this is popular trolling ground. Wahoo, marlin and the magnificent sailfish are further out, on the 50-m line.

Currimundi Reef, just near the Currimundi shore, carries a good mixture of reef fish and pelagics including sweetlip, snapper, Spanish mackerel, cobia and yellowtail kingfish.

GUIDE TO LOCAL FISH

	Tin Can Inlet and Rainbow Beach	Noosa River and Heads	Sunshine Coast	Maroochy River	Mooloolah River
(A) amberjack			•		
(B) bream	•	•	•	•	•
(C) cobia		•	•		
(D) cod		•		•	
(DA) dart	•	•	•	•	
(F) flathead	•	•	•	•	
(M) jack, mangrove	•	•	•	•	
(KI) kingfish, yellowtail		•	•		
(LU) luderick			•	•	•
(MA) mackerel	•	•	•	•	•
(MU) mulloway	•	•	•	•	
(PP) perch, pearl	•	•			
(S) snapper	•	•	•		
(ES) sweetlip	•	•	•		
(T) tailor	•	•	•	•	
(TR) trevally	•	•	•		
(TU) tuna	•	•	•		
(W) whiting	•	•	•	•	•

2 SUNSHINE COAST

369

COASTAL FISHING BRISBANE REGION

NOOSA RIVER AND HEADS

The 80-km-long **Teewah Beach**, spectacularly beautiful and noted for its coloured sands, is also a four-wheel-drive pathway to Fraser Island. There are gutters all along the beach, and bream, whiting, flathead and dart are here in summer, with tailor and mulloway in winter. The southern end of Teewah Beach at Noosa Heads is a good mulloway spot at night, has tailor and bream in winter, and whiting and dart in summer.

Noosa Heads is a booming and sophisticated resort area. With its river, lakes and a national park virtually adjacent to the town, it is a beautiful place. The Noosa River estuary is one of the safest in Australia, and the fishing is quite good. In winter target fish include bream, whiting and flathead, while in the summer big whiting dominate, with bream and flathead still around in reduced numbers. Mulloway, tailor, trevally and mangrove jack are the target fish, and prawns and mud crabs add to the abundance.

The breakwall is the last remaining luderick spot as one heads north. The bar at Noosa Heads can be dangerous, and requires experience. Fishing beyond the bar can be rewarding, with big tailor catches possible on the run-out tide during winter, and bream on the rising tide. On the north side of the river is a bay, a great winter bream area, with the inland side of the bay, known as **The Snags**, being the premier bream spot in the river. Great hauls are taken in winter, and this area continues to fish well for flathead and whiting through the year. Opposite the bay is a deep water hole, which yields big bream and mulloway, particularly at night. The best flathead in the river are in a channel between sandbanks off **Munna Point**, which is a very popular shore-based fishing spot for flathead and whiting all year round, and for bream in winter.

In **Noosa Sound**, bream, trevally and mangrove jack are found around the rocks. Upriver, the channel deepens past Munna Point, and the drop-off, near the jetty, is a station for flathead, with whiting and bream also present. The channel continues to fish well near its banks. A landing opposite **Goat Island** is one of the best bream spots in the river. Areas outside **Doonella Lake** and either end of Goat Island are reliable for bream, flathead and whiting, as is the reedy area on the way to Sheep Island.

Weyba Creek winds its way down to Noosa Sound from **Lake Weyba**, a reasonably large area of water offering whiting and mud crabs. Anglers take a stand on the bridges over Weyba Creek, seeking mangrove jack, bream, whiting and flathead.

The Noosa National Park provides some of the best rock fishing in Queensland. The access is excellent provided you do not mind a bit of a walk, although the rocks within 50 m of the carpark are a stand for good yields of tailor and bream, with a chance of big mulloway at night. Moving away from Noosa Heads, the **Boiling Pot** (also called the Witches Cauldron), a short walk from the carpark, is a fine spot for tailor, with a chance of mulloway.

Dolphin Point attracts mulloway, trevally, yellowtail kingfish, tailor and bream, while the **Fairy Pools** outcrop is a safe area offering shelter from south-westerlies and fishing well for tailor, mulloway, bream and trevally. **Hells Gates** at Noosa Head is the best mulloway spot in this fine rock fishing area, and is best fished with live or fresh bait. Tailor and bream are also in the washes and big Spanish mackerel, yellowtail kingfish and longtail tuna are readily available for the live bait enthusiast.

The rock fishing spots in the south of the park area are best reached from the Sunshine Beach end. Just south of Alexandria Bay, **Oyster Rocks** is a superb tailor stand in winter, bringing in good hauls, with mulloway, trevally, Spanish mackerel and longtail tuna also available. **Lion Rock** is a fine bream spot, with fish such as snapper, sweetlip and luderick over the submerged rocks, and mulloway and tailor at dawn and dusk. The **Paradise Caves** area fishes well for tailor, bream, mulloway, sweetlip and whiting.

There are several good reefs offshore from Noosa Heads. To the north, about 2 km from the Noosa River entrance, **Halls Reef** is about 1 km out to sea. Spanish mackerel, spotted mackerel, snapper and sweetlip are the target fish. To the north-east of the town, and about 2 km north of Noosa Head, is **The Jew Shoal**, carrying the same fish species, and a further 5 km on the same heading is **North Reef**, an extensive reef

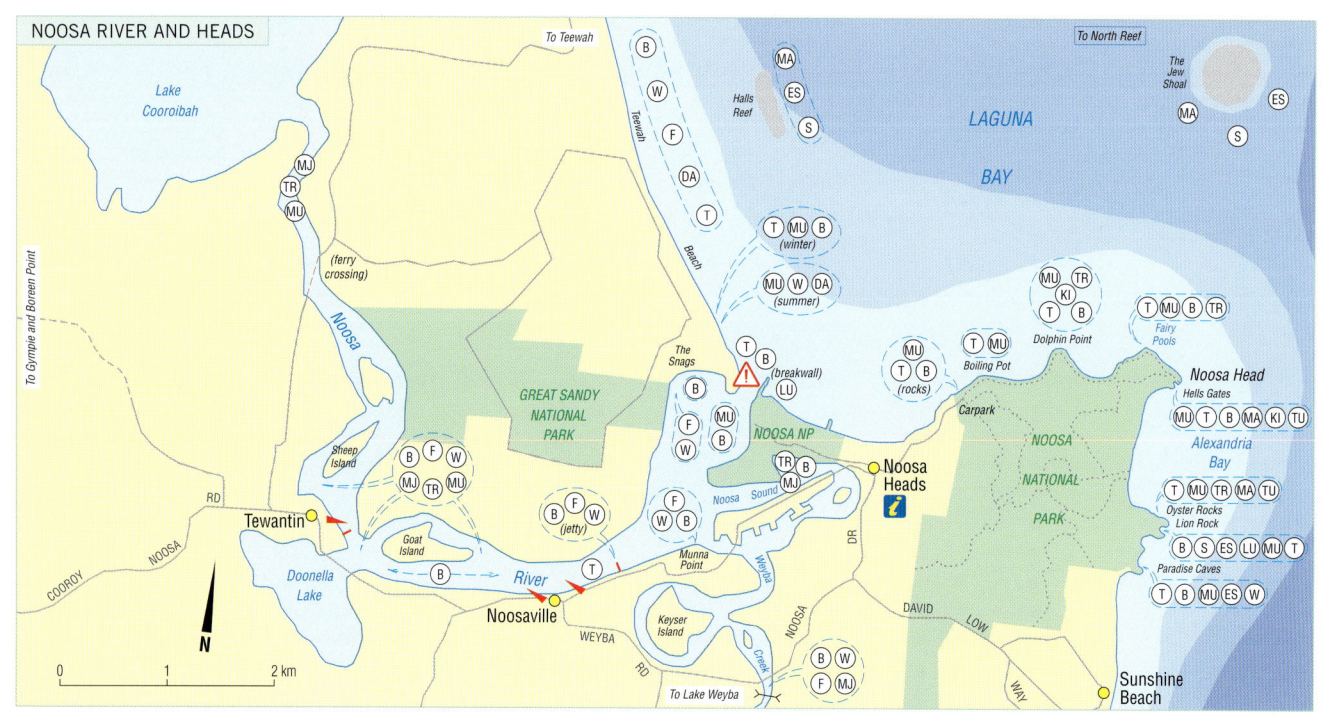

COASTAL FISHING BRISBANE REGION

QUEENSLAND

Rock fishing at sunset, Maroochydore

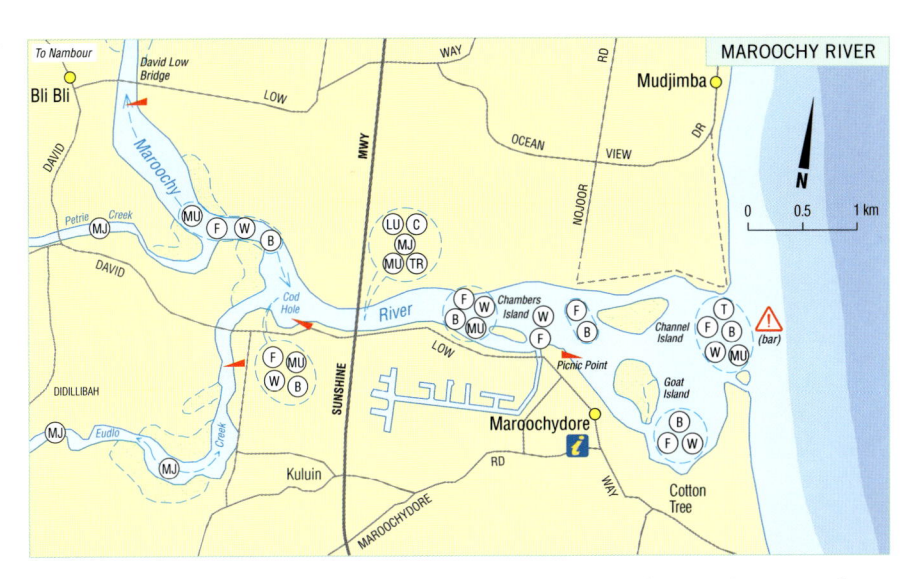

area with many pinnacles, with the target fish being red emperor, Spanish and spotted mackerel, snapper and sweetlip.

MAROOCHY RIVER

While the bar and the surf at the **Maroochy River** entrance preclude taking a boat out to sea, the shallow estuary is a productive fishing area. It is a great source of the estuary anglers' preferred bait – worms and yabbies from the sand flats and live herring. There are sand flats and channel formations right through the system, with whiting, flathead and bream the most abundant fish, but also opportunities for mulloway, mangrove jack and tailor. There is good land-based fishing on both the north and south side of the entrance for flathead, tailor, bream, whiting and mulloway.

Channel Island and **Goat Island** lie across the estuary, linked by a sand flat. Inside Channel Island, flathead and bream can be found around the mangroves and snags. The southern point of Goat Island is a good place to anchor and fish for bream, flathead and whiting.

Around **Chambers Island** there is sandy-bottomed water carrying whiting and flathead, while the channel in the river as it runs down to the motorway bridge can be explored for school mulloway, flathead, whiting and bream. The bridge itself widens the options, as mulloway, estuary cod, mangrove jack, trevally and luderick are around this area. Past the bridge a bay called the **Cod Hole** fishes well on the incoming tide for mulloway, big flathead, whiting and bream, and this continues up to the David Low Bridge.

Eudlo and **Petrie creeks** are good places to explore in the mangroves and mud for crabs and mangrove jack. The **Maroochy River** north of the David Low Bridge is mostly boating water.

MOOLOOLAH RIVER

The **Mooloolah River** has been sculpted into a maze of canals near its entrance to provide prestige waterfront living, and this has had some negative effects on the fishing, but there are still fish to be caught.

Inside the entrance, bream are attracted to the wharf area, where the fishing fleet moors. Big flathead are also here, especially on a run-out tide. There are similar fish further down the river at the Wharf Marina, where luderick are also fished from the wharf. Around the bridges anglers can try for mulloway, trevally and bream, either from the bridges or around the nearby sand flats. Flathead and whiting are common along the river. Mangrove jack are caught by trolling, lure casting and live baiting in the upper reaches and around the rock walls. There is plenty of yabby, worm and herring bait, and mud crabs are still quite common, especially after heavy rain.

Outside the entrance, the northern breakwater fishes well for bream, spotted mackerel, tailor and flathead. The rocks at **Point Cartwright** are visited by a wide range of inshore fish and pelagics. Mulloway, bream, trevally, school mackerel, tailor and luderick are close in, while Spanish mackerel, longtail tuna and mackerel tuna cruise by.

From **Point Cartwright** to as far south as **Caloundra** the beaches are heavy with surfers, but there are good fishing possibilities at dawn and dusk for flathead, whiting, dart and bream. The gutters are more pronounced in these areas when the waves carve into them in heavy weather, so the best fishing is on falling seas.

QUEENSLAND

COASTAL FISHING BRISBANE REGION

Moreton Bay and Brisbane River

Type of fishing
beach, estuary, game, reef, rock

Target fish
bream, flathead, mackerel, whiting

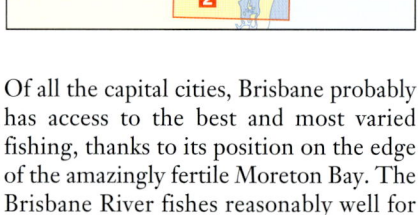

Heading for Moreton Island's Big Sandhills, an ideal place to fish or simply enjoy the view

GUIDE TO LOCAL FISH

		Moreton Bay North	Moreton Bay South	Brisbane River
AJ	amberjack	●		
B	bream	●	●	●
CO	cobia	●	●	
C	cod	●		●
DA	dart	●	●	
DO	dolphin fish	●		
F	flathead	●	●	●
MJ	jack, mangrove	●		
KI	kingfish, yellowtail	●	●	
LU	luderick		●	●
MA	mackerel	●	●	
ML	marlin	●	●	
MU	mulloway	●	●	●
PF	parrotfish	●	●	
SL	sailfish	●		
SH	shark			
S	snapper	●	●	
ES	sweetlip	●	●	
T	tailor	●	●	
TL	teraglin	●		
TR	trevally		●	
TU	tuna	●		
WH	wahoo	●		
W	whiting	●	●	

Of all the capital cities, Brisbane probably has access to the best and most varied fishing, thanks to its position on the edge of the amazingly fertile Moreton Bay. The Brisbane River fishes reasonably well for estuary species, particularly bream.

MORETON BAY NORTH

Moreton Bay action begins in the beach areas and shallows of **Caloundra**, where bream fishing in winter is excellent. Off Caloundra, the **Fairway Buoy** and **Bray Rock** are yellowtail kingfish haunts, with cobia and Spanish and spotted mackerel also encountered in summer. Some of the best spots are off **Golden Beach** and the channel between the mainland and Bribie Island, called **Pumicestone Passage**, shallow in places, but navigable down its whole 30-km length inside Bribie Island. Yabby baits for whiting and bream are collected from the large sandbank inside the head of Bribie Island. Whiting, bream and flathead are the prolific fish in the passage, with mangrove jack a possibility inside the mainland creeks. Best places to fish on the mainland side are in and around **Bells Creek**, in the **Tripcony Bight** area and around the **bridge to Bribie Island** in the south, where there are also mulloway. On the island side, the bream are around **Poverty Creek**, **Gallagher Point** and off the ledge around the southern town of **Bongaree**. The **Donnybrook** area offers whiting, bream, flathead, tailor and school mulloway as well as the occasional mangrove jack.

At the southern end of the island there can be large numbers of whiting in **Deception Bay**, while there is also great fishing for whiting from the beaches all along the eastern and southern sides of the island, particularly at dawn and dusk. The bay is heavily fished by boating anglers. Boats can be launched from the ramps at Scarborough Boat Harbour, which provide access to the reefs out from Castlereagh Point. This area is noted for its snapper, sweetlip, cod, bream, flathead and sometimes school mackerel. The water is shallow and very rocky, requiring little sinker weight with baits of pilchards, garfish, squid and yabbies.

Boat anglers outside **Bribie Island** usually have good fishing around the shipping channel beacons, which attract yellowtail kingfish, cobia, spotted mackerel and tuna species. The Bribie Banks are the sandbanks that sit out on the 40-metre mark and stretch between Bribie Island and Cape Moreton on the northern tip of Moreton Island. They are famous as sailfish ground and are also home to small black marlin between December and April.

Moreton Island can be reached by boat or by taking a four-wheel drive over to the island on the vehicular ferry. Extensive sandbanks between the south of Bribie Island and the north of Moreton Island should be avoided by larger boats, but they are no problem to small fishing boats.

A superb reef fishing area extends out from Cape Moreton, however **Flinders**

The Tangalooma 'wrecks' provide sheltered fishing for boat anglers at Moreton Island

COASTAL FISHING BRISBANE REGION

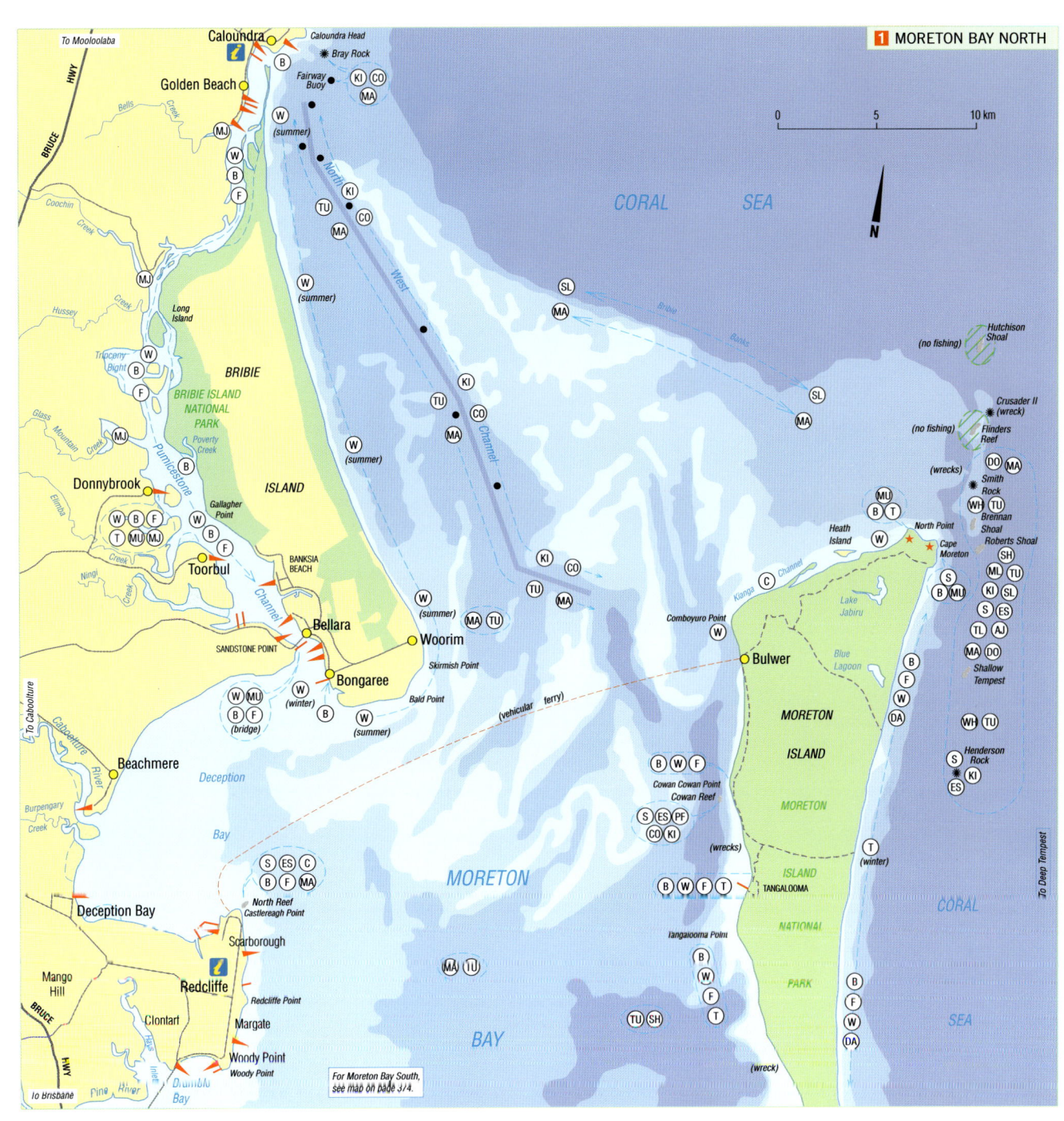

QUEENSLAND

1 MORETON BAY NORTH

Reef and **Hutchison Shoal** are now Marine Sanctuaries and fishing is banned within 500 metres. Sunken wrecks add extra holding areas for fish. The reef seam extends south-east through the **Brennan** and **Roberts shoals, Shallow Tempest, Deep Tempest** and **Henderson Rock**. Reef fish like snapper, sweetlip, teraglin and amberjack are quite common and Spanish mackerel in summer and autumn. Dolphin fish, wahoo, sailfish, juvenile black marlin and tuna species are common targets for game anglers between December and April.

Around Moreton Island itself the rocks below **Cape Moreton Lighthouse** have good land-based positions to fish for snapper, bream and mulloway, while nearby **North Point** provides fishing for mulloway, bream and tailor. The **Kianga Channel** in the north-west carries cod in its deeper sections. Further south, the **Comboyuro Point** area has big sand whiting. The Cowan Reef lies about 200 m off the beach at Cowan Cowan Point and is extremely productive for fish such as snapper, sweetlip, parrotfish, cobia and yellowtail kingfish. The bay south of Tangalooma Point, and the **Big Sandhills** and the **Blue Hole** (see map on page 374) are all good boat spots for bream, whiting, tailor and flathead.

The best land-based spots from which to fish on the west side of Moreton Island are **Cowan Cowan Point, Tangalooma Jetty, Days Gutter** and **Reeders Point**. Whiting, bream and flathead are the targets, but whiting is the bonanza catch in the summer. The east coast is surf rod territory, with gutters forming all along the beach, particularly after heavy weather. There are tailor in winter and bream, flathead, whiting and dart all year round.

373

QUEENSLAND

COASTAL FISHING BRISBANE REGION

MORETON BAY SOUTH

The sheltered waters around Brisbane are heavily fished commercially, but they still produce pelagics such as spotted mackerel, shark, longtails and mackerel tuna for the recreational angler. There are many gutters and holes throughout the bay, with whiting, bream and flathead in and around the gutters and drop-offs, and mulloway and snapper mainly in deep areas. A big area of the bay, offshore from Dunwich on North Stradbroke Island to the south-east of Moreton Island, contains sandy shallows, which must be carefully navigated by larger craft. Ocean-bound boats must first negotiate the Rous Channel, which runs between Moreton and South Stradbroke islands, and then leads out into the highly dangerous South Passage. This bar must never be attempted without local guidance, because the channels are ill-defined. **Days Gutter**, inside the south-western tip of Moreton Island, is a secure anchorage for those making the journey to the northern reefs.

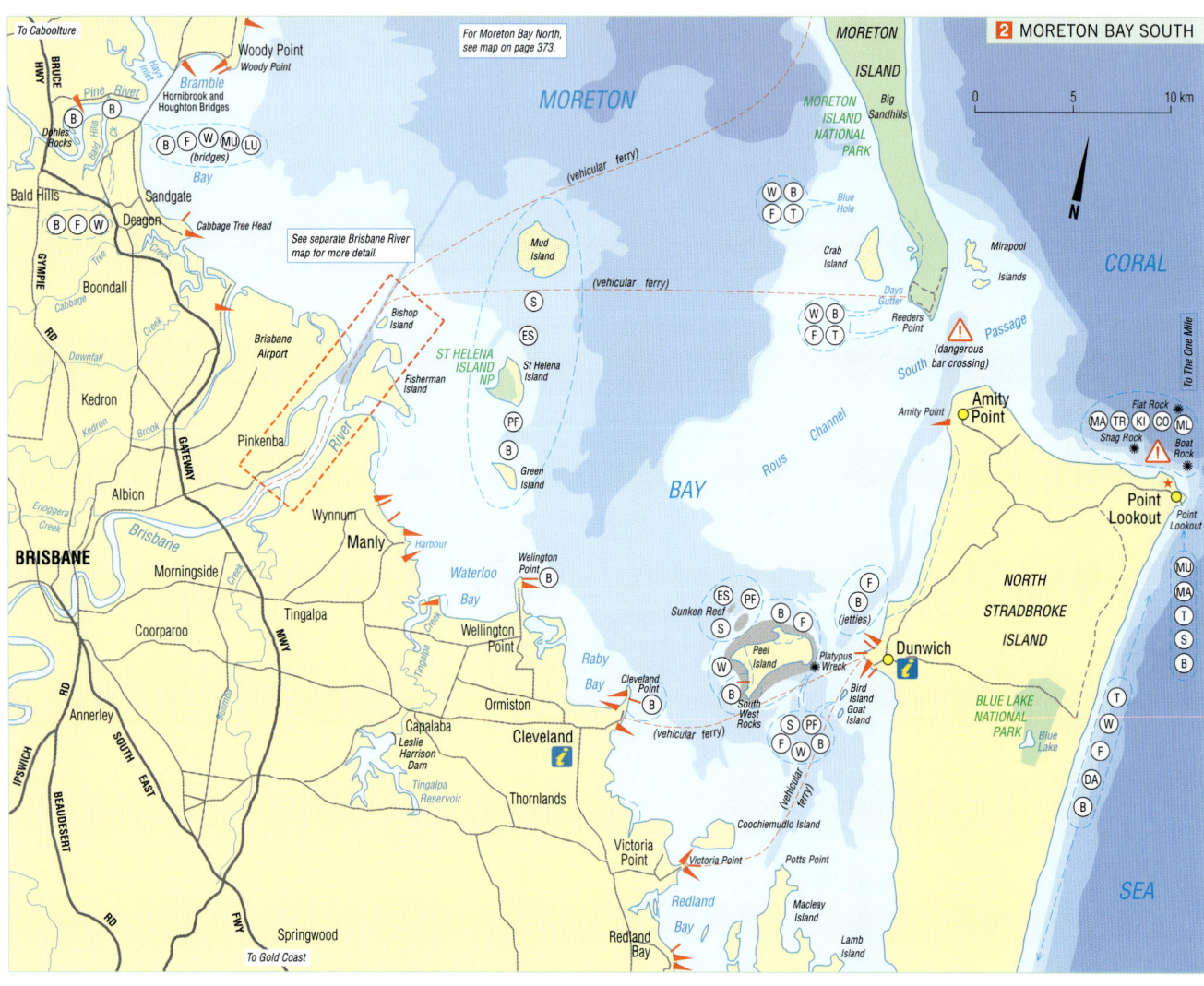

Days Gutter, Moreton Island: anglers clean their catch of squire (small snapper), caught over the reefs off Point Lookout

COASTAL FISHING BRISBANE REGION QUEENSLAND

Spanish mackerel
Spanish mackerel, often called narrow-barred Spanish mackerel in Queensland, are prevalent in all the State's coastal waters and their distribution extends across the top of Australia and south to Geraldton. It is an especially good eating fish.

Winding in the big one at Woody Point Jetty, Redcliffe, Brisbane

The sandbanks in this area create fishing grounds for flathead, whiting, bream and tailor.

Peel Island is surrounded by gutters, reefs, banks and channels. **Sunken Reef** and the surrounding reef areas on the north-west coast of the island carry reasonable quantities of young snapper, bream, sweetlip and parrotfish, while the shallower areas have whiting, bream and flathead. Some of the hottest spots around Peel Island are **South West Rocks** for big bream at night, the *Platypus* wreck for snapper, parrotfish, flathead, whiting and bream, **Bird Island** and **Goat Island** for snapper, whiting, parrotfish, bream and flathead, and the jetty on Peel Island for good bream. Land anglers use the **jetties around Dunwich** for bream and flathead, and squid can be caught at night.

On **North Stradbroke Island** the beach fishing is good for tailor, whiting, flathead, dart and bream. **Point Lookout**, at the north-east tip, is brilliant for rock fishing for mulloway, Spanish mackerel, snapper, bream and tailor. North of Point Lookout are **Flat Rock, Shag Rock** and **Boat Rock**, great attractors of Spanish mackerel, trevally, yellowtail kingfish, marlin and cobia. Anglers fishing these areas should take great care as there is a significant current. Some 3.5 km north-east of Flat Rock is the **One Mile**, the biggest of a number of reefs in the area, all of which hold snapper, sweetlip and teraglin.

The **Pine River** is at the northern edge of Brisbane. It winds through mangroves and is heavily fished, but remains a fairly productive area. A good spot for the land-based angler is the old **Hornibrook Highway Bridge**. It gets crowded and is best fished at night for bream, flathead, whiting, luderick and mulloway. The bridges are best fished around periods of slack water. The south bank fishes well, particularly around the mouth of **Bald Hills Creek**. Bream is the main catch, along with flathead and whiting. Opposite Bald Hills Creek, around the remains of an old jetty, is another fine bream spot. **Dohles Rocks**, at Pine River, is also good.

Moving southwards from Bribie Island, the coast is mostly sand flats and mangroves, and is not conducive to fishing. South of the Brisbane River entrance, land-based anglers fish the jetties at **Wellington Point** and **Cleveland Point** for bream and squid. Out from the river the eastern sides of **Mud, St Helena** and **Green islands** have fringing corals and are bottom-fished for snapper, sweetlip, parrotfish and bream.

BRISBANE RIVER

The **Brisbane River** is an excellent bream fishery in autumn and winter, and some of the best spots to fish are the rock walls at **Bishop Island, Luggage Point** and **Pinkenba**, and from the **wharves at the tanker and cargo terminal**. The Luggage Point and Pinkenba walls can be fished either from the bank or from a boat. It is a fair walk for the bank-based anglers, and parts of the Pinkenba wall can be under water during the spring tides. The best fishing is at night when the bream come in close to feed at the walls, and it is important to put your bait in close to the wall. Other fish around the walls are luderick, flathead, school mulloway and estuary cod. The best baits are undoubtedly live yabbies and live fish. Berleying with chicken pellets definitely improves catches.

Further up the river the fishing declines along with the water quality, although it is worth trying for the big mulloway around the city bridges at night on the top of the tide in the winter months.

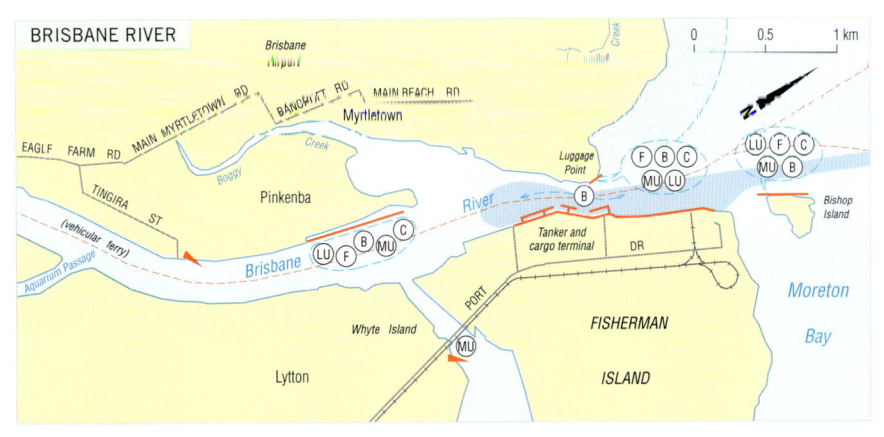

QUEENSLAND   COASTAL FISHING BRISBANE REGION

Jumpinpin and Gold Coast

Type of fishing
beach, creek, estuary, jetty, reef, rock
Target fish
bream, flathead, tailor, whiting

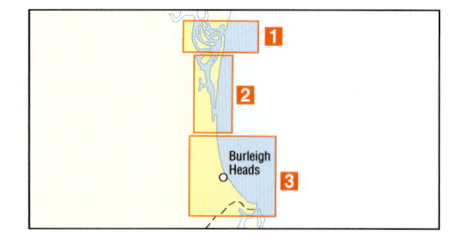

Between Moreton Bay and the Gold Coast, the Jumpinpin area is celebrated for its superb bream and flathead catches. The Gold Coast provides good fishing in both the Broadwater, its draining rivers and offshore. The estuary has undergone massive development in the past decade and continues to be commercially netted. Despite this it still provides reasonable fishing for bream, whiting and flathead. Productive offshore grounds can be safely reached via the Gold Coast Seaway.

JUMPINPIN

The **Jumpinpin area** is a maze of mangrove-covered sand islands. They have been created as a type of delta as the sediment from nearby rivers is deposited before the water is released between the North Stradbroke and South Stradbroke islands. The channels move around with the volume of water going through the system, so it is best to have an up-to-date chart, and to time departures and returns with rising waters. It is a place of sheltered backwaters and clean beaches, safe from all but the worst weather, and ideal for staying out overnight in an anchored boat (but watch the tides) or tying up and camping on land.

Lure fishing for flathead, South Stradbroke Island

The low, sandy ground around Jumpinpin is not conducive to road building, and roads to the only public boat ramps, at Cabbage Tree Point and Jacobs Well, can be crowded with cars, boats and trailers on weekends. There are private ramps nearby where vehicles and trailers can be left under security by those planning an extended trip.

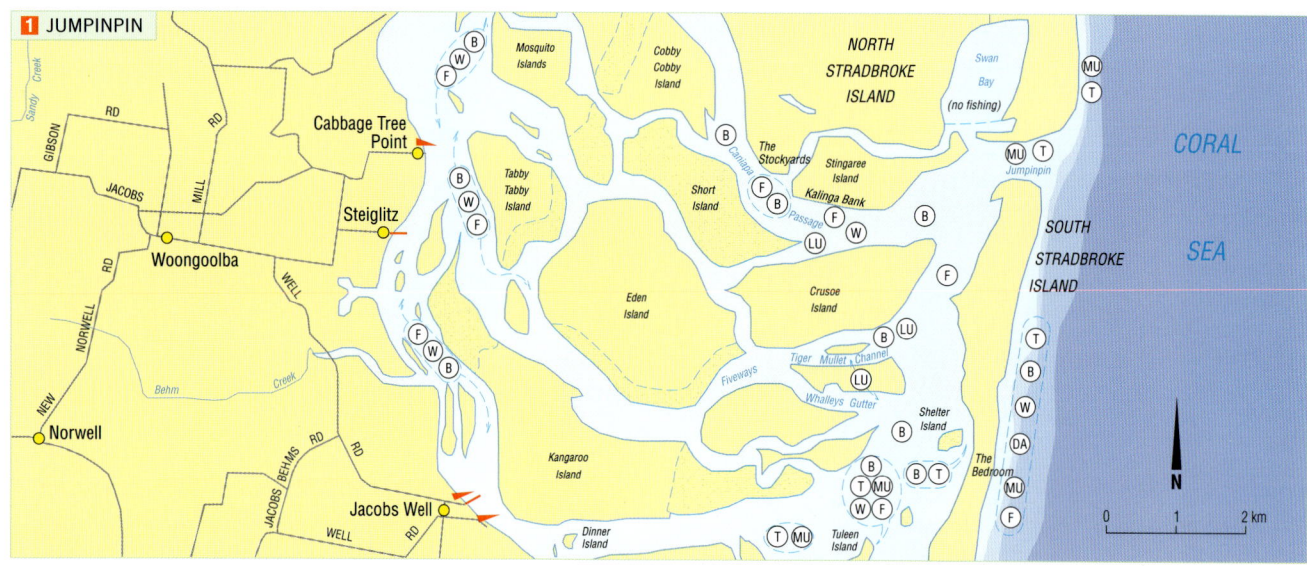

COASTAL FISHING BRISBANE REGION QUEENSLAND

Blue swimmer crab
Often incorrectly called the sand crab, the blue swimmer is one of the best-known crab species in Australia. Although present in estuarine and salt waters around the entire coastline, it is mainly caught in southern Queensland, Spencer Gulf in South Australia, and around Carnarvon and south of Perth in Western Australia.

The shores on either side of the Jumpinpin entrance have ready supplies of mulloway and shoals of chopper tailor (small tailor). Swan Bay, just around the corner on the northern side, is a marine reserve closed to all fishing activity.

In the **western channels** of the area, near the towns of Cabbage Tree Point and down to Jacobs Well, bream, flathead and whiting are the most commonly caught fish, as they are throughout the system, and the myriad of bank channels and gutters make prospecting for them exciting. Generally spring is the best time for flathead, summer for whiting, and the area is justly famous for its bream run in winter.

The flathead can be huge. The best spots are fished by drifting on the tide, and include the **sandbanks** between South Stradbroke and Crusoe islands, **Kalinga Bank** on the southern side of Stingree Island and **Caniapa Passage** just inside Short Island. There are also some bream hot spots in this part of the system. The area known as **The Stockyards** and the north shore of **Crusoe Island** are both very productive. During the cooler months, the eastern tip of **Short Island** is the best place to look for luderick.

One of the most popular camping and anchorage places, behind the head of South Stradbroke, is called **The Bedroom**. Campers here can walk across the South Stradbroke Island to the **ocean beaches**, where there is excellent fishing for tailor, whiting, bream, dart, mulloway and flathead. On the inland side, the channels opposite The Bedroom are fished for bream and tailor. The southern sides of **Tiger Mullet Channel** and **Whalleys Gutter** both hold bream. To the north of **Tuleen Island** whiting, flathead and bream are everywhere there is a likely gutter, bank or weed bed. Tailor and mulloway are also often found in this southern channel area.

SOUTHPORT BROADWATER

The Southport Broadwater is a system of canals lined with houses, and outside most houses there are boats. The **Gold Coast Seaway**, which allows the system to be flushed out more fully than before, provides good deep water offshore access. The new conditions have brought pelagics like yellowtail kingfish, trevally and occasional Spanish mackerel into a system once largely reserved for flathead, whiting and bream.

The breakwalls of the Seaway entrance and **Wave Break Island**, which sits inside the entrance, have created a great shore-based fishing area and provide a habitat for luderick, bream, tailor and mulloway, while the deep water at the wall attracts the pelagics. The safe entrance now also allows easy access to the outside reefs and game fishing grounds.

Within the Broadwater, whiting, flathead, bream, mulloway and mangrove jack are the targets. It is a fishing area for light tackle, and the preferred baits are freshly collected worms, yabbies and soldier crabs. Fishing at dawn and dusk gets the best results, sometimes huge catches of whiting in the summer, with bream in winter and flathead best in spring. When the flathead come in to spawn, trolling big lures is an extremely effective way to take them.

The Gold Coast Seaway provides safe passage for boat anglers heading for the productive offshore grounds

GUIDE TO LOCAL FISH

	Jumpinpin	Southport Broadwater	Surfers Paradise to Coolangatta
(AJ) amberjack			•
(BT) bonito			•
(B) bream	•	•	•
(CO) cobia			•
(C) cod		•	
(DA) dart	•		•
(F) flathead	•	•	•
(M) jack, mangrove		•	•
(KI) kingfish, yellowtail		•	•
(U) luderick	•	•	•
(MN) mackerel		•	•
(MU) mulloway	•	•	•
(PF) parrotfish			•
(PP) perch, pearl			•
(SH) shark		•	
(S) snapper			•
(T) tailor	•	•	•
(TL) teraglin			•
(TR) trevally		•	•
(TU) tuna		•	•
(W) whiting	•	•	•

QUEENSLAND

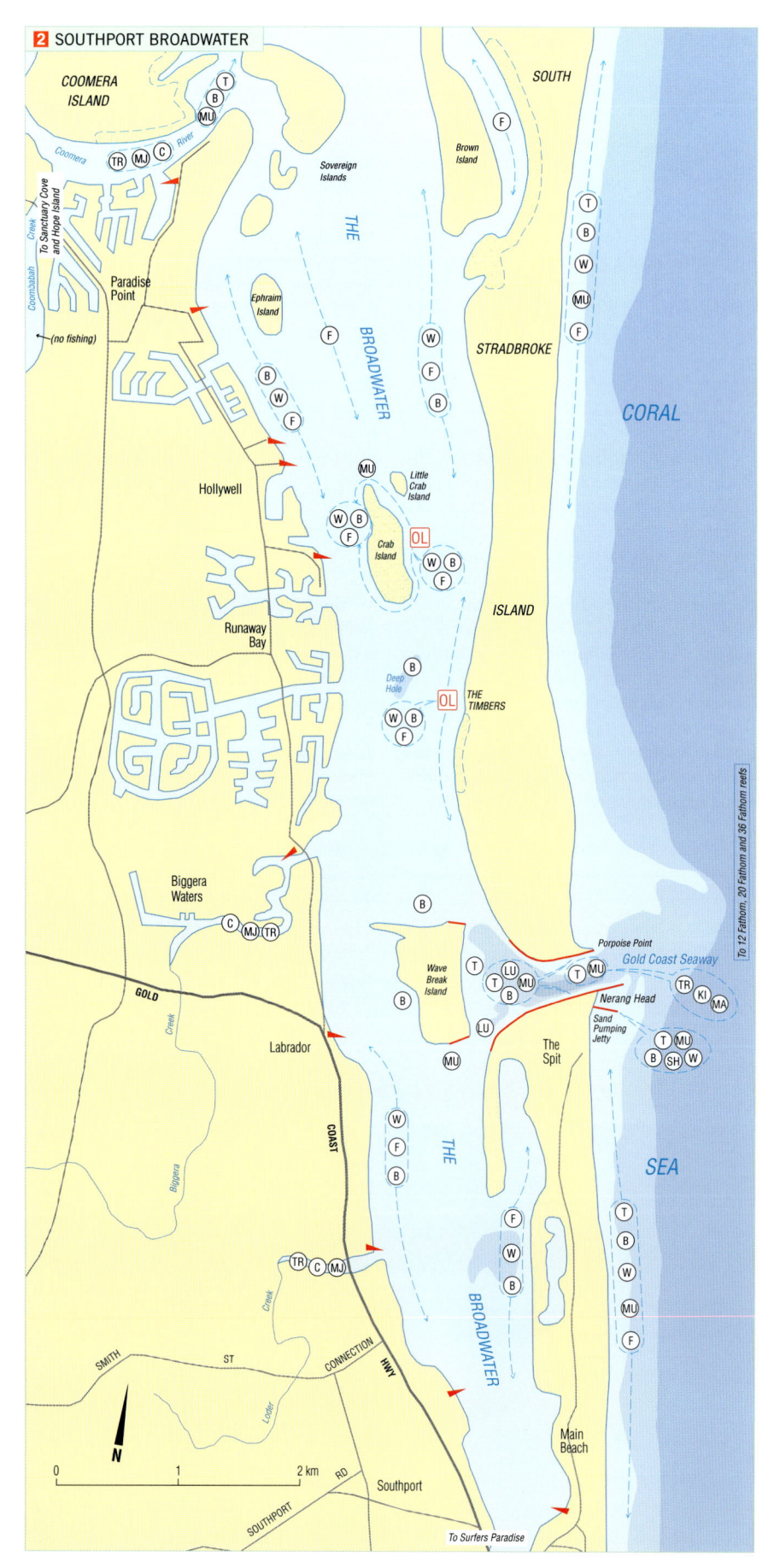

COASTAL FISHING BRISBANE REGION

Where the **Coomera River** enters the Broadwater, just north of Sovereign Island, there is a 8-m-deep hole that produces mulloway, bream and tailor. The channel near **Brown Island** is one of the best flathead areas in the estuary. The inside shore of South Stradbroke Island is good drifting and trolling ground for flathead. Around **Ephraim Island** there are many banks and channels that can be prospected with success. **Crab Island** is surrounded by oyster leases. The adjacent channels around them have whiting, bream and flathead. The **Deep Hole** is found east of Runaway Bay. This area is now silted up but still produces good bream in winter. The **oyster leases** along South Stradbroke Island attract bream and flathead.

Up the rivers, and away from the canals, there are likely to be mangrove jack, cod and trevally around rocky banks and bridges.

Immediately outside and to the south of the Gold Coast Seaway, the **Sand Pumping Jetty** provides a safe land base from which tailor, big mulloway, bream, whiting and hammerhead and shovelnose sharks are regularly caught. The beach anglers target tailor, bream, whiting, mulloway and flathead in the gutters.

Offshore reefs include 12 Fathom Reef, only 2 km out from the entrance, 20 Fathom Reef about 8 km out, and 36 Fathom Reef about 25 km out. Near the reefs, marlin, cobia, Spanish mackerel, yellowtail kingfish and amberjack are best caught by trolling lures or by deep drifting or trolling live baits. Snapper, pearl perch and teraglin are caught over the deeper reefs.

SURFERS PARADISE TO COOLANGATTA

The tourist strip around Surfers Paradise provides surprisingly good beach fishing, particularly during the cooler months. Bream, dart, whiting and tailor are all here in good numbers.

Along the coast the best rock fishing spots are **Burleigh Heads** for tailor; the **Tallebudgera retaining wall** for tailor, mulloway, bream and flathead; the retaining walls at **Palm Beach** and **Currumbin** for tailor; **Currumbin Rock** for mackerel, bream, tailor, luderick; **Elephant Rock** for tailor and bream; **Flat Rock** for tailor and bream, but dangerous in high seas; and **Snapper Rocks** at Point Danger for bream, tailor, Spanish mackerel and cobia.

The bridges over both the **Tallebudgera** and **Currumbin creeks** attract a lot of anglers. The highway bridge at Tallebudgera is the most versatile, with

COASTAL FISHING BRISBANE REGION

bream, flathead, whiting and mangrove jack around the area. Both creeks have yabby banks upstream for bait gathering, and are pleasant for bank fishing for whiting, bream and flathead. Small boats can be used in the estuary areas.

All reefs in this area produce spotted and Spanish mackerel, snapper, mackerel tuna and bonito. Boat anglers heading to sea from the Tallebudgera Creek can access **The Gravel Patch** (5 km offshore). Out from Currumbin is **Palm Beach Reef**, famous for its summer run of spotted mackerel. The more adventurous can head for more distant areas such as the **24 Fathom** and **32 Fathom reefs**, where there is reasonable fishing for snapper, teraglin, cobia, Spanish mackerel and yellowtail kingfish.

Pumping bait from the sands of Tallebudgera Creek

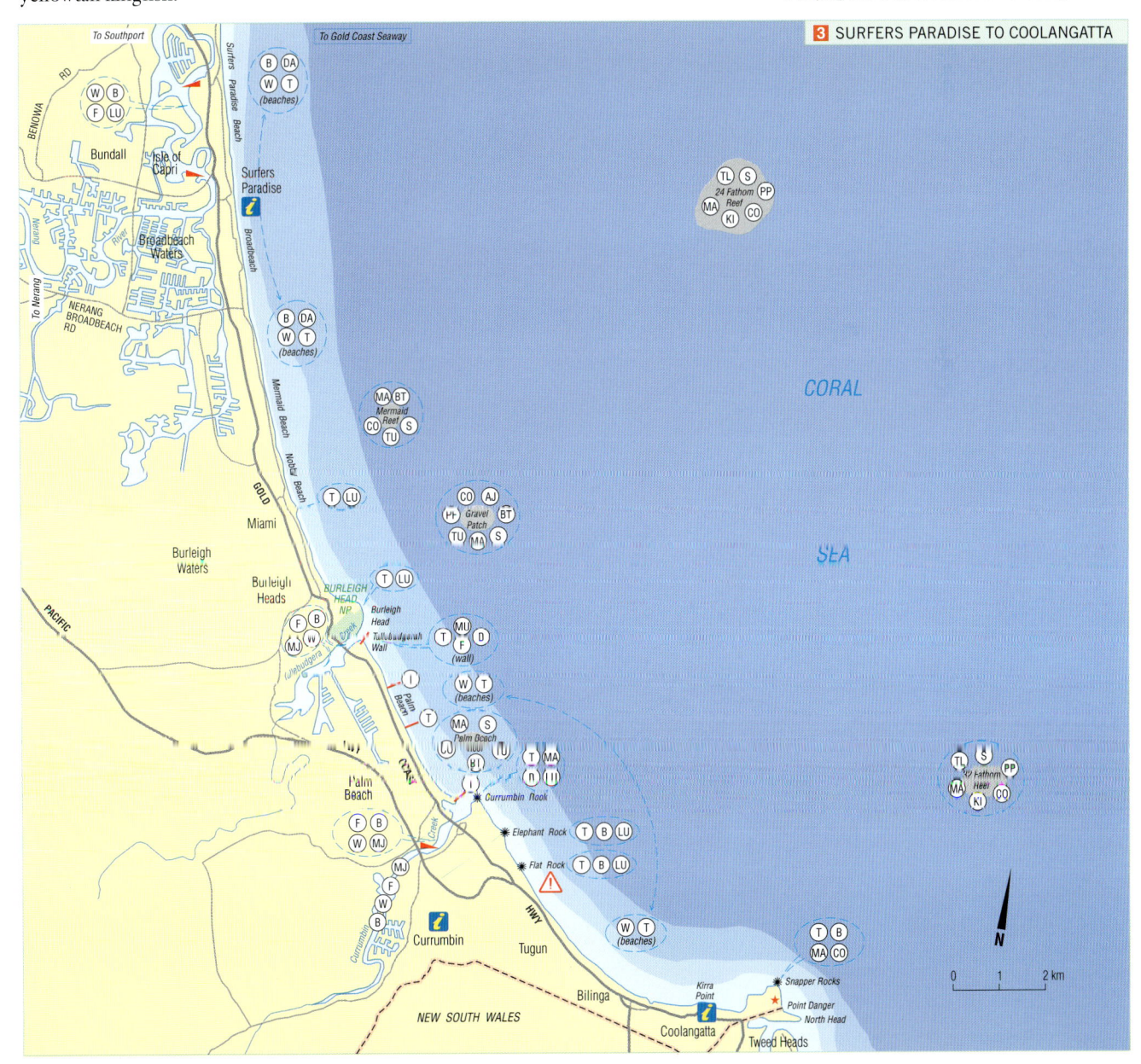

3 SURFERS PARADISE TO COOLANGATTA

QUEENSLAND

COASTAL FISHING CAIRNS REGION

Cairns Region

Cairns is in the exotic tropics and is the black marlin capital of the world. It is also the jumping-off point to some of the world's most pristine wilderness areas on Cape York and in the Gulf of Carpentaria. The infrastructure of the city is unashamedly geared towards tourism, the spin-off being an excellent selection of fishing guides and charter boats.

Because of Cairns' reputation as a fishing mecca, visiting anglers have high expectations. It must be remembered that the coastal strip to Tully and Cardwell has been settled for as long as most places in the south. The tropical exotics like barramundi, fingermark, mangrove jack and queenfish are certainly present, but as elsewhere require some work to catch. The easiest way of learning where to fish and how is to go out for a day with a local fishing guide.

This is not the case in the Gulf country and on Cape York. Even population centres like Weipa and Karumba have memorable fishing. This area has what fishing dreams are made of if you have a well-equipped four-wheel drive, some good maps and a small boat. Weipa is a one-hour flight from Cairns and is serviced by an array of motherships and fishing guides for all budgets.

The magnetism of the Great Barrier Reef is renowned worldwide. It is closest to the coast north of Cairns and is easily fished on day trips either in your own boat or from a charter boat. The reef acts as a barrier to the ocean, so big swells are not a problem. Coral trout, red emperor and nannygai are here and those with a sportfishing inclination can tangle with anything from monster Spanish mackerel to enormous giant trevally and small (or large) marlin.

WHERE TO FISH

Cairns Region

GULF AND CAPE YORK ● 382

It is possible to fly into centres in the Gulf and Cape York country like Weipa, Bamaga or Karumba, hire a four-wheel drive and boat and go fishing. Most people, however, come in their own four-wheel drive. This is remote country so plan accordingly. The fishing makes it all worthwhile.

COOKTOWN TO CAIRNS ● 386

Here the reef hugs the coast to seaward; to the west the ranges crowd a narrow coastal plain. Cooktown and Port Douglas are gateways to great fishing offshore, and the Bloomfield and Daintree rivers provide wonderful estuary fishing. Anglers will also find good fishing from beaches that can be accessed. If you don't have a boat then take a charter because the experience outweighs the cost.

INNISFAIL–MOURILYAN AREA ● 390

This section of coast is the wettest part of Australia and, although short, rivers here like the Russell, the Mulgrave and the Tully all carry tremendous amounts of fresh water during the Wet. Fish during the Dry (the southern winter) for best results.

HINCHINBROOK ISLAND AREA ● 391

Hinchinbrook Island is separated from the mainland by the complexity of a mangrove maze called Hinchinbrook Channel. With relatively few access points, except near Cardwell in the north and Lucinda in the south, Hinchinbrook, like much of North Queensland, is for boat fishing only. Larger trailer-sized boats are safest because some of Hinchinbrook's waters are expansive.

FISHING TIP

Many pelagic species such as tuna and marlin are highly sensitive to water temperature and quality so finding the right water temperature can be a critical factor in a successful day's outing. For example, some tuna species such as yellowfin are best sought when the water temperature is above 20 degrees Celsius. However, if the water gets too warm these fish can be equally difficult to find.

COASTAL FISHING CAIRNS REGION

QUEENSLAND

GUIDE TO LOCAL FISH

- archer fish
- barracuda
- barramundi
- bream, pikey
- catfish
- cobia
- cod, estuary
- cod, others
- dart
- emperor, red
- fingermark
- flathead
- herring, giant
- herring, oxeye
- jack, mangrove
- javelin fish
- jewfish, black
- Job-fish
- long tom
- mackerel, grey
- mackerel, school
- mackerel, Spanish
- mackerel, spotted
- marlin, black
- nannygai
- queenfish
- sailfish
- salmon, threadfin
- shark
- sweetlip
- trevally
- trevally, giant
- trout, coral
- tuna, mackerel
- tuna, longtail
- tuna, yellowfin
- whiting

Hinchinbrook Island: the mangrove-lined Hinchinbrook Channel offers a variety of inshore and estuary fish

Weather

The Cairns Region is tropical and has two seasons, the Wet (December to March) and the Dry (June to September). During the Wet the heaviest falls are roughly from Christmas to Easter, when virtually the entire Gulf and all of Cape York are cut off by floods. Over January and February major bitumen roads are sometimes cut around Cairns as well. The start and end of the Dry (late April, May, June, then October, November and early December) are the best times of the year to fish in northern Queensland.

One or two tropical cyclones per year may affect parts of this whole region from December to April. People in boats need to be particularly aware of any tropical cyclone threat during this period. Monsoonal weather is normal from late December through to March, particularly in the north. The winds are often squally westerly or north-westerly and accompanied by local thunderstorms. From about May to October the water is often affected by very strong south-east trade winds. During the Dry, the trade winds blow persistently, exceeding 20 knots for weeks on end, curtailing offshore trips and even making creek fishing difficult. The trades are at their worst over the southern winter (June to September).

Weather forecasts are readily available from newspapers, radio and television in Cairns, but basically non-existent north and west of this population centre. The Bureau of Meteorology provides specialised forecasts and advice for small ships on its website: www.bom.gov.au

Coastal weather information is available on 1300 360 426.

Boating

On the east coast the trade winds rule all boating activities and there are periods when trips out to the reef are out of the question for days on end. All reef areas are hazardous so it is important to be aware of them and to use proper navigation charts in these waters. Seek local advice about conditions.

To the north and west of Cairns, roads are generally unsuitable for towing boats and so on the Cape and in the Gulf country most fishing is from car-topped boats. In such remote areas you need to be able to launch a boat over rocks, beaches and down steep banks, sometimes carrying boat, motor and all your equipment some distance to the water.

Boating self-sufficiency is required in the Gulf of Carpentaria due to its isolation and limited rescue facilities. Take plenty of fuel, water and spare parts and advise someone of your movements. Communication can be difficult; VHF radio may not get a response, so if entering these waters for long periods HF radio is recommended. Mobile phones will not work unless linked to satellite. CDMA coverage is planned. In some areas in the Gulf of Carpentaria navigation along the shoreline is restricted by shallow water. Beware of crocodiles and stingers throughout this region.

FURTHER INFORMATION

Fishing and boating Queensland Boating and Fisheries Patrol (Department of Primary Industries) has offices at 64–66 Tingira St, Portsmith, Cairns, tel. (07) 4035 0700; Inlet St, Port Douglas, tel. (07) 4099 5160; 38 Victoria Pde, Thursday Island, tel. (07) 4069 1772; 8 Palmer St, The Point, Karumba, tel. (07) 4745 9233. For information on zoning maps and guidelines for marine parks, the Environmental Protection Agency has an office at 2–4 McLeod St, Cairns, tel. (07) 4046 6602. The Great Barrier Reef Marine Park Authority in Townsville, tel. (07) 4750 0700, can also supply zoning maps and guidelines for Marine Park use. Maps are also available from some tourist centres, some bait and tackle shops and all Queensland Parks and Wildlife Service offices. The Boating Registration and Licensing Hotline is tel. 13 2380.

Tourist centres Tourism Tropical North Queensland, 51 The Esplanade, Cairns, tel. (07) 4051 3588; Cape Tribulation Tourist Information Centre, Mason Store, Cape Tribulation, tel. (07) 4098 0070; Cooktown Tourism, Charlotte St, Cooktown, tel. (07) 4069 6100; Daintree Tourist Information Centre, 5 Stewart St, Daintree, tel. (07) 4098 6133; Hinchinbrook Island Ferries, Bruce Hwy, tel. (07) 4066 8270; Port Douglas Tourist Information Centre, 23 Macrossan St, Port Douglas, tel. (07) 4099 5599.

Gulf and Cape York

Type of fishing
estuary, offshore, reef, river, rock, wharf

Target fish
barramundi, black jewfish, mangrove jack, queenfish

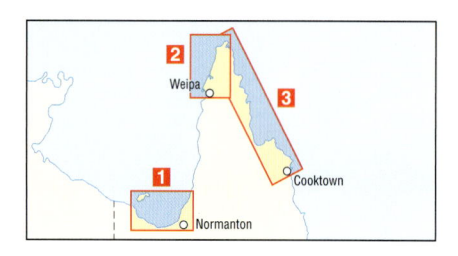

The Gulf of Carpentaria and Cape York are among the last frontiers for the travelling angler. Most places require a boat for best results. There is river and creek fishing and excellent offshore sportfishing for queenfish, mackerel, tuna and trevally. The entire Gulf of Carpentaria is shallow and serves as one of Australia's largest fish nurseries.

GULF COUNTRY

Burketown is one of the few towns in the flat, inhospitable Gulf country. There are access roads leading towards this area from the east coast or from Mount Isa, but they fall 100 km or more short of this destination, and it is then four-wheel-drive bashing on roads that are often impassable during the wet season (the southern summer). The safe driving months are in the mid-year dry season (the southern winter).

Birri Beach, Mornington Island

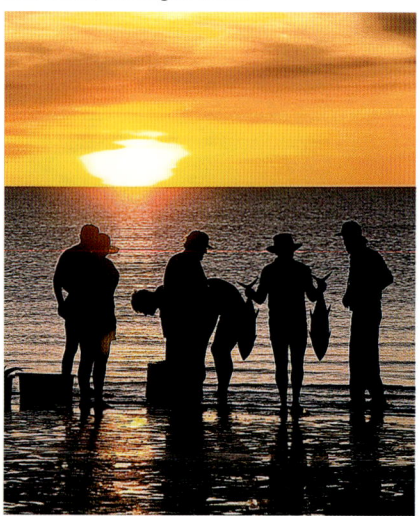

Visitors should have good camping gear, food and water, petrol, motor and tyre spares, plenty of fishing equipment, a lot of insect repellent, and the patience to endure being stranded for any one of a dozen reasons. Saltwater crocodiles are prevalent in the river, so swimming should not be attempted, and care should be taken when near the water on foot, and especially when cleaning fish.

But the fishing is so interesting that it is worthwhile making the trip to this remote place. **Burketown** is strategically placed for fishing both in the Gulf and along the rivers. It is just outside the extensive mangrove area that runs from the coast, and is situated on the Albert River, between the Nicholson and Leichhardt River. In the brackish estuary waters there is good fishing for mangrove jack, barramundi and catfish. You really need a boat here, but bank or jetty fishing is possible at Burketown.

Barramundi is the main target fish in the estuaries, where it shares the water with mangrove jack, estuary cod, threadfin salmon, small queenfish and trevally. Out to sea there are big queenfish, javelin fish, fingermark, black jewfish, trevally, whiting and flathead. There is large-scale netting of barramundi and threadfin salmon in the Gulf, so amateur anglers suffer from shrewd competition. **Escott Lodge**, only 16 km west of Burketown, caters for anglers, giving them guided access to some 300 km of nearby waterways, both fresh and tidal. Rods, boats and vehicles can be hired, and flights can be arranged to the Wellesley Islands.

Anglers staying at the **Birri Fishing Resort** on Mornington Island and the **Sweers Island Resort** can take advantage of the superb fishing around the Wellesley Island group. The islands are not fished commercially, other than that by the prawn fleet, and the seas abound with fish – coral trout, sweetlip, red emperor, queenfish, mackerel, trevally and cod over the reefs; queenfish, mackerel, cobia, barracuda and tuna in the inshore waters; barramundi and mangrove jack in the creeks. An area near

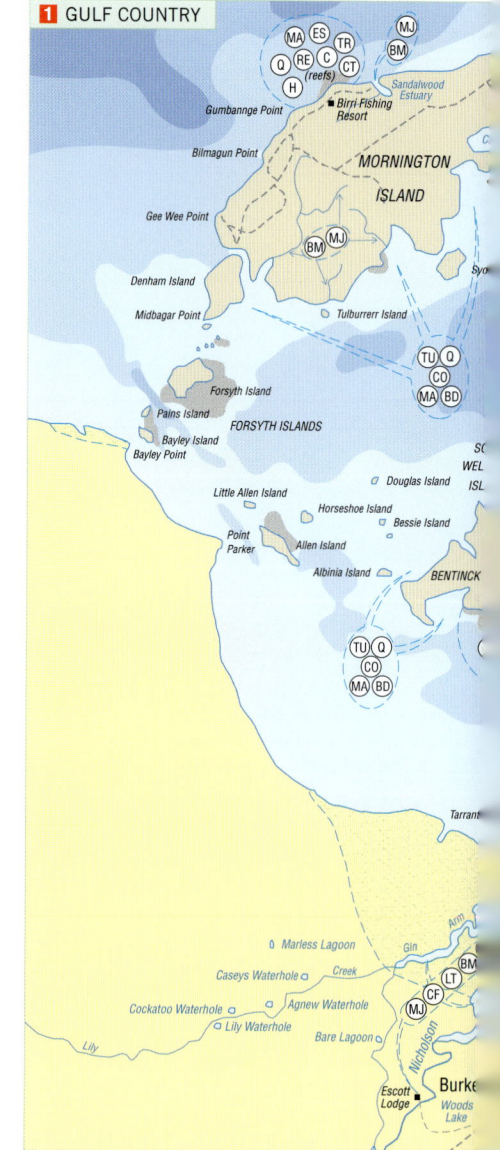

GUIDE TO LOCAL FISH

		Gulf Country	Cape York West	Cape York East
BD	barracuda	●		●
BM	barramundi	●	●	●
B	bream, pikey	●	●	
CF	catfish	●		
CO	cobia		●	●
C	cod, estuary	●	●	●
C	cod, others	●	●	●
RE	emperor, red			●
FM	fingermark	●	●	
F	flathead	●		
H	herring, giant	●		
MJ	jack, mangrove	●	●	●
JA	javelin fish	●		
BJ	jewfish, black	●	●	
LT	long tom	●		
MA	mackerel	●	●	●
ML	marlin, black			●
Q	queenfish	●	●	●
TS	salmon, threadfin	●	●	
ES	sweetlip	●	●	●
TR	trevally	●	●	●
CT	trout, coral	●	●	●
TU	tuna	●		●
W	whiting	●		

COASTAL FISHING CAIRNS REGION

the Birri Fishing Resort is the best place for the hard-fighting giant herring.

Karumba is the home port of the big prawn fishing fleet that plies the gulf. Road travel from the east coast is usually fine, but roads between Normanton and Karumba can become impassable in wet season floods. Karumba is at the head of a vast delta of rivers, creeks, anabranches, mangrove swamps and wetlands. The crocodiles and mosquitoes are prolific, but the river fishing within a few kilometres of the town can be good for the estuary species, particularly barramundi. There are coach services from the east coast, and accommodation, camping, boat hire, charter boats and bait and tackle are available.

There are shore fishing spots on the **Flinders** and **Bynoe rivers**, 35 km and 25 km, respectively, west of Karumba. There are also spots on the **Norman River**, close to the town, and around **Karumba Point**, where anglers anticipate the javelin fish run in April.

CAPE YORK WEST

With the right equipment, careful planning and enough time, fishing on Cape York is a wonderful experience. The major ingredients are a four-wheel drive and a small sturdy boat that can be launched without using a boat ramp, ample supplies of fuel, food and the necessities of camping. Some of the most exciting fishing action is in the mangrove-lined rivers, although the river estuaries and offshore have much to offer the angler. Light tackle provides some sport in this part of the world as the black jewfish, queenfish, barramundi and mangrove jack are great fighters, causing a lot of lost tackle.

In the Dry, when four-wheel-drive access opens up the peninsula, it is possible to get to the remote rivers, such as **Watson**, **Coleman** and **Staaten**. The fishing is prolific, but the land is the preserve of the Kowanyama, Pormpuraaw and Aurukun Aboriginal communities, and permission must be gained before camping or fishing on the land.

Weipa is much easier to reach, as you can travel by plane or road. Roads are also well maintained and the town has modern facilities. It is one of the few places on the peninsula where shore-based fishing rivals that for the boat anglers. The rocks near the **Evans Landing** boat ramp are a good stand for threadfin salmon, pikey bream, barramundi and queenfish. The **Andoom**

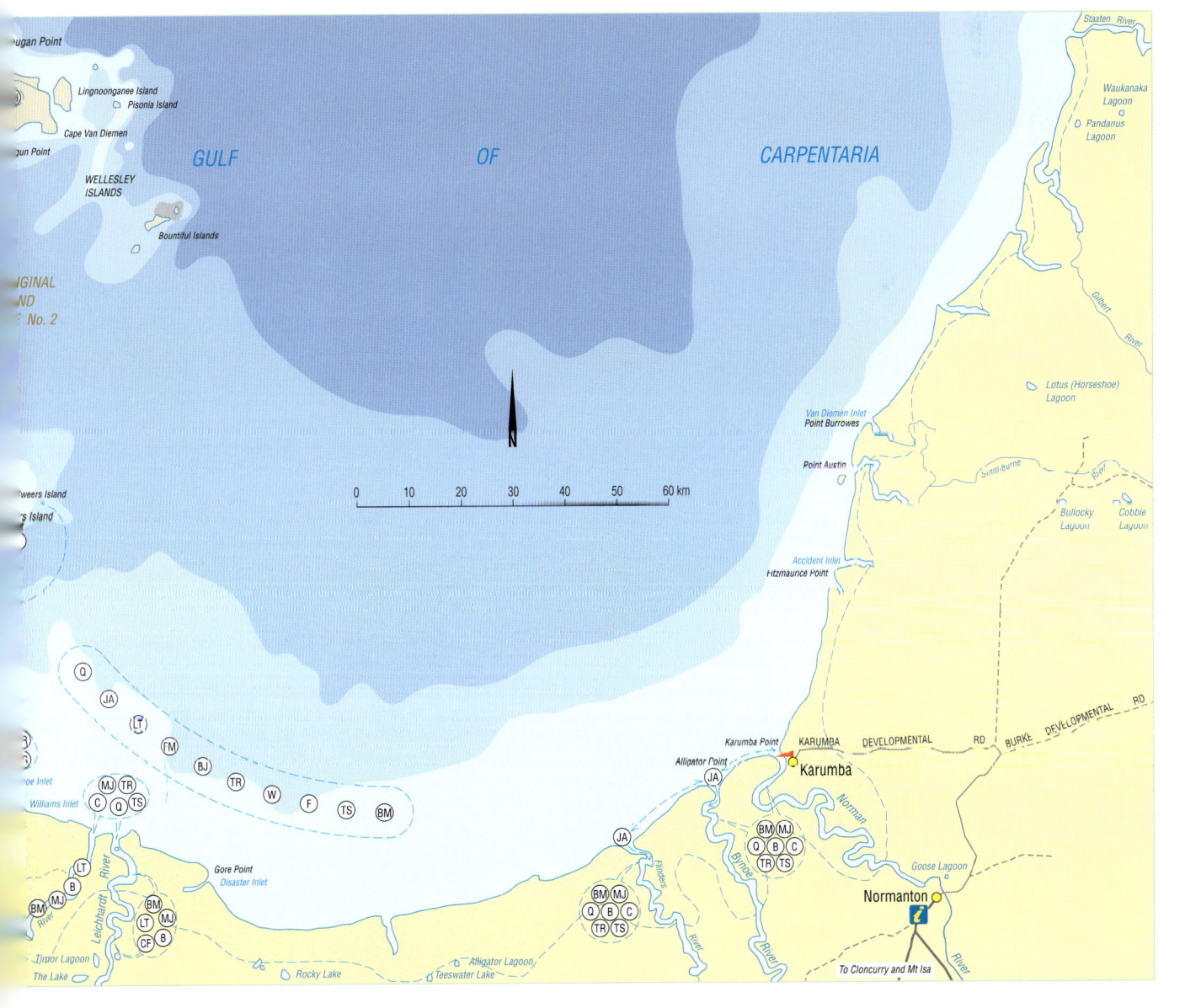

QUEENSLAND — COASTAL FISHING CAIRNS REGION

Bridge has a reputation for the size and fighting power of the black jewfish taken from the deep water beneath, with 15 kg being average.

There are plenty of accessible rivers in the area. The **Embley** and **Mission rivers** flow into Albatross Bay, while not far to the north of Weipa the **Wenlock** and **Ducie rivers** flow into Port Musgrave. The greatest sport of all in the north is exploring such rivers for barramundi, mangrove jack, archer fish, estuary cod, pikey bream and trevally. In the river estuaries the targets change to fingermark, queenfish and threadfin salmon. Fishing charters are available into either rivers or the sea. Both lures and bait are options here.

Near the tip of Cape York, the major river is the **Jardine**, which runs clear and has wonderful white sandy beaches near its mouth. It flows almost the entire width of the Cape, from east to west, and has such a strong flow of fresh water, originating in the large swamp to the east, that salt water can scarcely penetrate from the west, even on the strongest tides. It runs clean and hard over a sandy bed, mangrove-lined towards the coast and with tidal creeks that allow continued exploration. Boats can be launched at the ferry crossing on the road to Cape York, but it is a long trip in very shallow water to reach the river mouth. Barramundi are here, where the salt water backs up in the Dry. At the end of the Wet, trevally, giant queenfish, Spanish mackerel and threadfin salmon will strike at either bait or lures on a rising tide at the mouth of the river.

There is good boat fishing all along this coast. Offshore catches can include black jewfish, cobia, coral trout, sweetlip, cod and trevally. At **Mutee Head**, to the east of the Jardine River, there is plenty of action when the black jewfish are on the bite around the piles of the old jetty. Both the Jardine and Mutee Head are easily reached from the town of Bamaga. It has a general store and an airstrip with regular commercial services and anglers have plenty of facilities.

A further 5 km north of Bamaga is **Seisia**, with good facilities for the angler, including charter and guide services, caravan park and boat hire. One of the highlights is the town wharf known affectionately as the 'pier without peer'. Here shoals of herring gather around the pylons and are preyed upon by mackerel, trevally, queenfish and black jewfish. Much of the land in this region is controlled by either Aboriginal or Torres Strait Islander communities and while there are no problems with access, visitors should only camp at the grounds in Seisia or at the fishing lodges to the north.

The best camping in this area is beside the lodge at Punsand Bay where camp sites overlook a beautiful beach with the islands of Torres Strait on the horizon. The Pajinka Lodge is only 400 m from the tip of Cape York, and there is a camping ground here as well. The rocky promontories around **Cape York** are all fine fishing platforms from August to October, with queenfish, trevally, Spanish mackerel, coral trout and sweetlip, normally best taken by boat. Trolling around the tip, some 500 m offshore, should produce good catches of trevally, Spanish mackerel and queenfish.

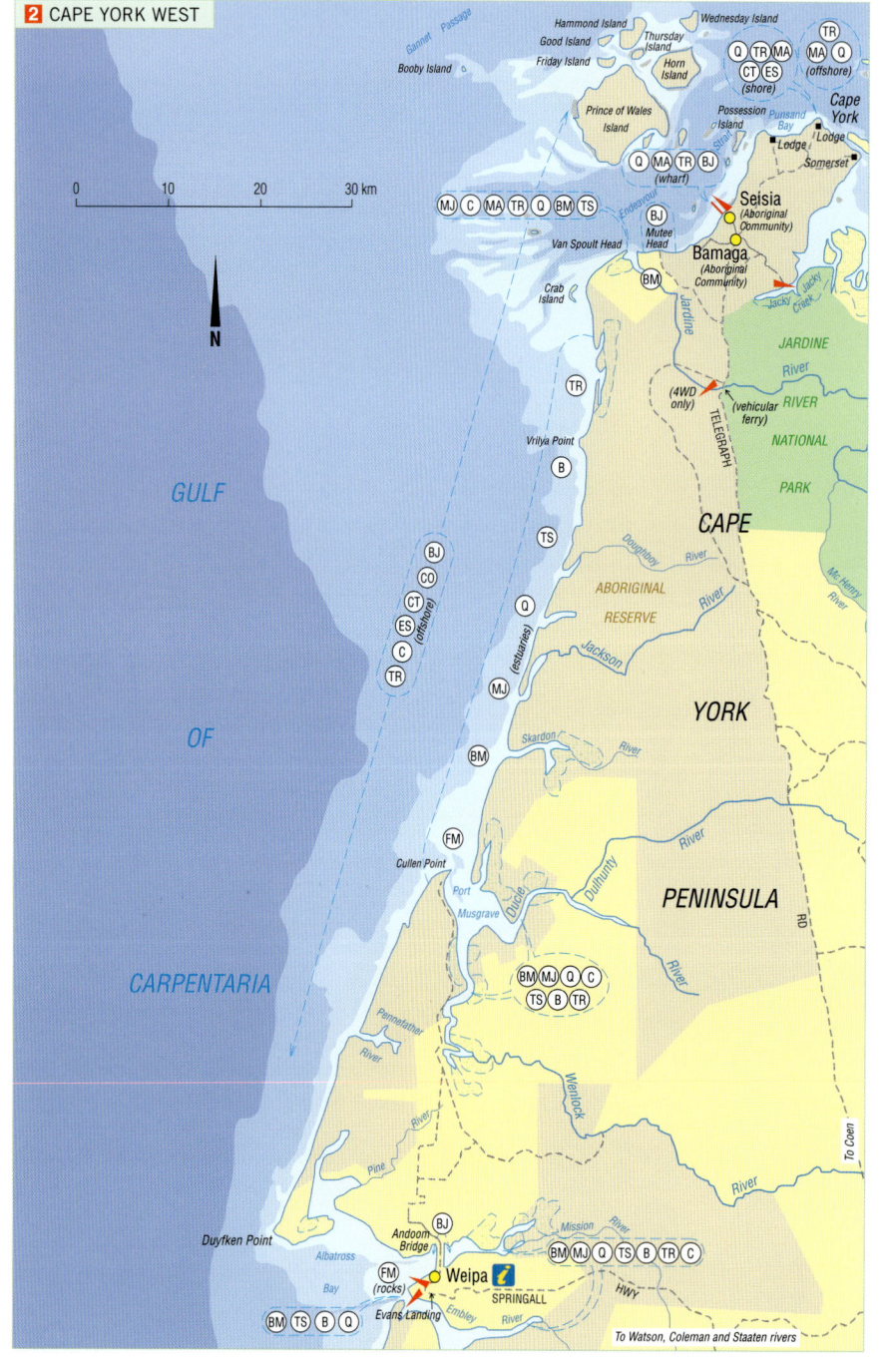

CAPE YORK EAST

From Cape York to Cooktown there are many roads and tracks turning off into the bush from the Peninsula Developmental Road, leading to mining settlements, Aboriginal communities and other properties by the coast. There may be brilliant fishing, but without local knowledge you may be in danger in this rugged terrain. Without prior

COASTAL FISHING CAIRNS REGION

Collecting bait in the Jacky Jacky system

permission you cannot turn up expecting to be allowed access for fishing.

The best way to fish the coast is by sea, cruising the coast in a substantial vessel like a motor yacht, and having a small craft on board so you can explore the coastal waterways. The offshore coral reefs with scores of fish, including coral trout, sweetlip and queenfish, are virtually unfished. Several operators take fishing parties up the coast.

If you are travelling by land, there are more accessible and better known places to fish down the east coast.

Albany Island is about 10 km southeast of the tip of Cape York. On the mainland, four-wheel-drive visitors will find bush camping with no facilities at the abandoned settlement of Somerset. There is superb fishing around the island or from Fly Point, 2 km east of Somerset, for land-based anglers. Queenfish, trevally and Spanish mackerel can be taken from the point, and the range of fish widens for boat anglers to tuna, barracuda, cobia and cod.

There is a boat ramp less than 15 km south-east of Bamaga at Jacky Jacky Creek, which enters **Kennedy Inlet** on the eastern side of Cape York. Several reefs in the open part of the inlet can be fished for fingermark, sweetlip and coral trout, but most of the inlet is a maze of channels through the mangroves, and care must be taken to avoid getting lost. The target species here is fingermark, with mangrove jack and barramundi less prevalent.

Portland Roads is a lot further south, reached by 100 km of rough road branching from the Peninsula Development Road about 20 km north of the Archer River roadhouse. Portland Roads is a small settlement in the lee of Cape Weymouth, and is a great place for queenfish and trevally in and around the bay. There is a jetty and boat launching, and the mouth of the Pascoe River, a little further north, has river species such as mangrove jack and barramundi. The Lockhart River Aboriginal Community manages land in this area, and while the roads are open to all, there are restrictions on camping and fishing in this area. Visitors can camp in the Iron Range National Park, but must obtain a permit from the entry gate first.

Over 200 km further south is the **Lakefield National Park**. This is a vast area, with the **Morehead, Hann** and **Normanby rivers** and their many tributaries flowing into Princess Charlotte Bay. It is best reached by turning off the Peninsula Developmental Road at the Musgrave roadhouse. This provides access to the north of the National Park, bordering the bay. The vast flood plains of these rivers provide fascinating fishing among the lily lagoons, particularly for barramundi, or in the estuaries. **Princess Charlotte Bay** and **Bathurst Head**, just to the east, are both renowned for the barramundi fishing. If you drive up from the south into the park, through Laura, one of the best fishing places is **Kalpowar Crossing**. There are many camping places in the park.

There are a number of tracks that lead off the road between **Cape Melville** and **Cooktown**, where it is safe in the dry season to explore some coastal fishing spots. The Hope Vale Aboriginal community controls land along this strip and visitors are advised to check restrictions in these areas before camping or fishing.

Lizard Island, north-east of Cooktown and offshore from Lookout Point, became famous as a base for giant black marlin fishing. There is great light tackle fishing on the reefs for coral trout, red emperor and sweetlip.

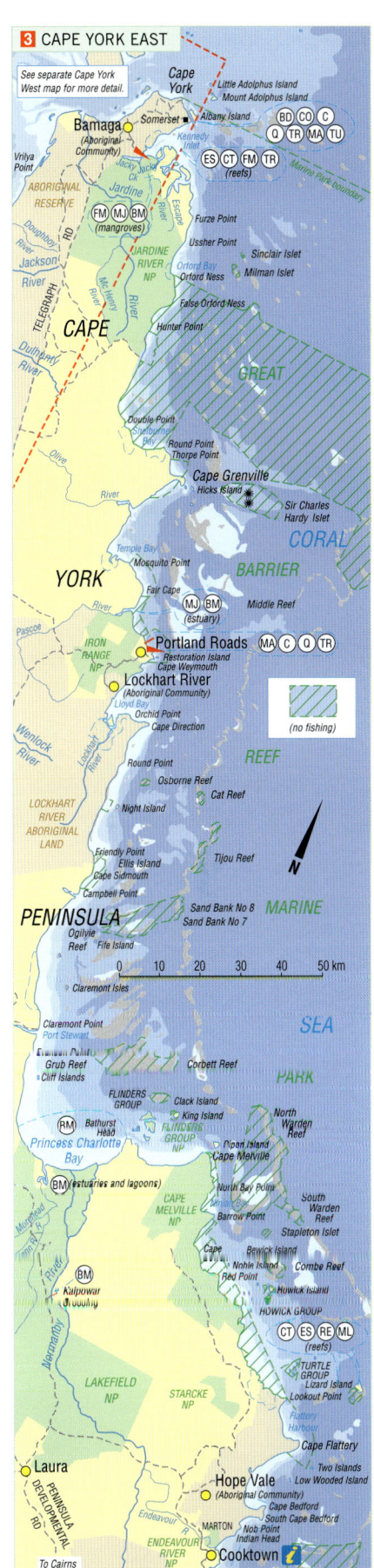

Cooktown to Cairns

Type of fishing
beach, estuary, offshore, reef, river
Target fish
barramundi, fingermark, mackerel, mangrove jack, marlin, trevally

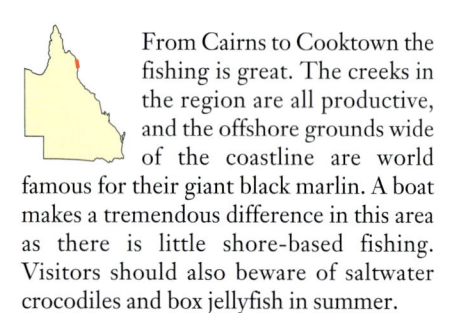

From Cairns to Cooktown the fishing is great. The creeks in the region are all productive, and the offshore grounds wide of the coastline are world famous for their giant black marlin. A boat makes a tremendous difference in this area as there is little shore-based fishing. Visitors should also beware of saltwater crocodiles and box jellyfish in summer.

Land-based anglers find the old jetty structure at Archer Point a great fish attractor

COOKTOWN TO CAIRNS AREA

Cooktown is a place where it seems that catching a big fish is inevitable, even if you are an absolute beginner. The town faces on to the Endeavour River and there is great fishing along the foreshores at the entrance. The simplest fishing method is to drop a net into the water to collect your 'sardine' bait (not a real sardine but a species of herring that schools around any wharf in the north), and then put one on a hook live. There are trevally, mackerel, queenfish and even barramundi in the area. The **Endeavour River** runs through the old town, which was Queensland's

Fishing the Endeavour River, Cooktown

second-largest town in the gold rush days, and the **Annan River** is nearby to the south. These rivers hold barramundi, fingermark, mangrove jack and trevally. Freshwater species such as oxeye herring (tarpon) and jungle perch are found well up the rivers. There are plenty of bank fishing spots, as well as good boat fishing. Both the Endeavour and Annan rivers are stocked regularly with barramundi.

There are coral reefs just offshore at Cooktown with abundant fishing and, further out, marlin along the reef's outer edge. Just 15 km south of Cooktown is **Archer Point**, which can be reached by a track during the dry season. The rocky headlands are a great place to spin off the rocks, seeking trevally, queenfish, mackerel, cod and fingermark. A broken-down jetty just inside the point is also a magnet for fish.

As a safe anchorage for boats plying the Cape York waters, the isolated **Bloomfield River** gets quite a lot of boating and fishing traffic. The river runs into **Weary Bay**, near the settlement of Ayton. The river's journey begins in mountainous rainforest country and ends in dense mangroves. Although it is a short river it is ideal for fishing, as a small boat can take you almost to the headwaters, into the habitat of jungle perch. In the saltwater area the mangroves can be explored for barramundi and mangrove jack, while at the river mouth there are beaches and rock shelves from which to spin for trevally and queenfish, and a large area of sand flats and channels that can be drifted for these species. There are camping areas nearby and fishing trips can sometimes be arranged by lodge operators to the **Pickersgill, Ruby** and **Escape reefs**.

The area around Cairns is known as the **Marlin Coast**, and draws big game anglers from all over the world to pit themselves against the mighty black marlin that cruise the deep waters out past the reefs. Sophisticated charter boats are on hand for those who yearn for this exciting fishing. There are many other light tackle game fish closer inshore, including tuna, Spanish mackerel, sailfish and small black marlin. The reefs, islands and cays studding the waters create shelves, gutters, rubble bottoms, sand flats and drop-offs to attract fish. The reef fish include fingermark, barracuda, school mackerel, Spanish mackerel, Job-fish, coral trout, sweetlip, nannygai and red emperor.

The Low Islets, in the northern part of Trinity Bay, are among several continental islands in the area lying close to the coast. Although fishing is prohibited around the islands themselves, the inshore reefs to the east at **Dayman Point** are hot spots for anglers. Most inshore species, such as coral trout, sweetlip, trevally, mackerel and nannygai, can be found there.

Reef areas require careful navigation, both visually and with depth sounding. Maps are available, but some areas, particularly north of Port Douglas, have not been subject to detailed soundings. Close-in reefs abound in the Port Douglas area. **Wentworth** and **Egmont reefs** are particularly accessible and attract mackerel, tuna and bottom feeders like coral trout, sweetlip and nannygai.

COASTAL FISHING CAIRNS REGION

QUEENSLAND

GUIDE TO LOCAL FISH

	Cooktown to Cairns Area	Daintree River	Port Douglas	Trinity Inlet
(BD) barracuda	●			●
(BM) barramundi	●	●	●	●
(B) bream, pikey	●	●	●	
(C) cod	●			
(RE) emperor, red	●			
(FM) fingermark	●	●	●	●
(H) herring, oxeye		●		
(MJ) jack, mangrove	●	●		
(BJ) jewfish, black	●			
(JF) Job-fish	●			
(MA) mackerel	●		●	
(ML) marlin, black	●			
(NG) nannygai	●			
(Q) queenfish	●	●	●	●
(SL) sailfish	●			
(TS) salmon, threadfin	●			●
(ES) sweetlip	●			
(TR) trevally	●	●	●	●
(CT) trout, coral	●			
(TU) tuna	●		●	

Inshore trolling and drifting is productive right along this coast. Spanish mackerel and black jewfish are the targets between May and October, while queenfish, trevally, cod and fingermark are fished all year round. Rock anglers also target these inshore species. There are good prospects along Trinity Bay at **Yule Point, Slip Cliff Point, Buchan Point** and **Taylor Point**.

There is a chain of continental islands close to shore along this part of the coast, including **Double Island** in Trinity Bay, and **Fitzroy Island** south-east of Cape Grafton, which provide a focus to the prolific inshore fishing. The reefs inshore at Double Island and the channel inshore at Fitzroy Island, known as **Wide Bay**, are hot spots.

Yorkeys Knob, just north of Cairns, is famous for its big barramundi, while closer to Cairns the banks of the **Barron River** may be fished for fingermark, barramundi and pikey bream. Beach fishing for threadfin salmon, queenfish and trevally is excellent on **Holloways Beach** and **Machans Beach**.

Most reef anglers leave from the Cairns area, and they have a wide choice of locations within 50 km including **Oyster Reef, Upolu Reef and Cay, Arlington Reef, Thetford, Moore, Elford** and **Sudbury reefs**, and **Stagg Patches**. Stagg Patches and Upolu are coral cays, so it is possible, when the tides are right, to stretch your legs for a while in the middle of a day's fishing.

COOKTOWN TO CAIRNS

QUEENSLAND   COASTAL FISHING CAIRNS REGION

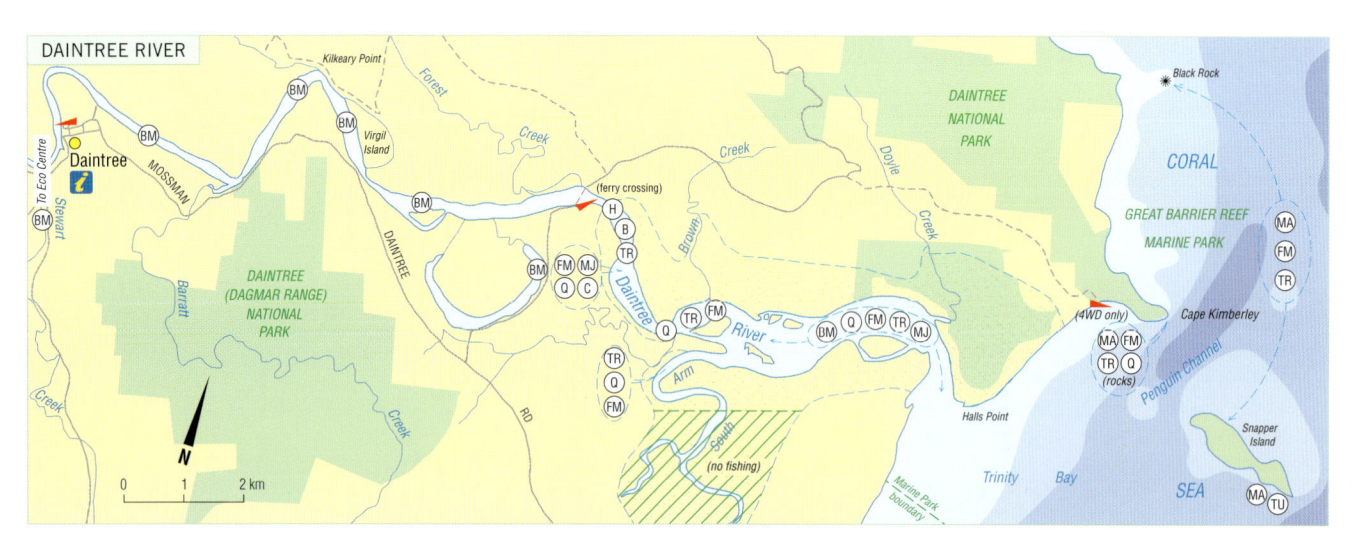

DAINTREE RIVER

The Daintree can be classed as equal to the more northerly tropical rivers, and if it has lost something due to a recent increase in fishing pressure from the locals and tourists in the fast-growing north, it has the advantage that it can be easily reached in the family car. The river, less than three hours' drive north of Cairns, has two boat ramps, one next to the vehicular ferry downstream, and one in the town of Daintree. Boats may be hired from the Eco Centre, 3 km southwest of the township. Remember to observe the crocodile warning signs.

A little north of the mouth of the Daintree River, there is good reef fishing around **Black Rock**, with Spanish mackerel, fingermark and giant trevally among the target fish. Closer to the Daintree's mouth, the rocks at **Cape Kimberley** are a good spot for mackerel, fingermark, trevally and queenfish. Small boats can be beach launched in the lee of the cape for offshore fishing. **Snapper Island** has a deep gutter on its southern side that attracts schools of bait, and in turn large numbers of Spanish mackerel and longtail tuna.

The Daintree is a big river, meandering through the rainforest and down into mangrove lowlands before reaching the coast. The broadwater areas close to the river mouth are patrolled by a wide variety of fish including queenfish, barramundi, fingermark, trevally and mangrove jack. These are best fished at dawn and dusk. Upstream and in the South Arm (note closed areas), there are deep holes that are excellent for fingermark, queenfish and trevally, especially at dawn or dusk. Below the ferry crossing pikey bream, oxeye herring, trevally, queenfish, fingermark, mangrove jack and cod are all possibilities. The best time to fish this lower part of the river is on a run-out tide, and the best months for the whole river are September to February. There is ample live bait to be caught on the mudflats and in the weedy areas. In the upper freshwater reaches above the ferry, the Daintree carries tropical coastal river species such as barramundi. Jungle perch and sooty grunter are much further upriver.

The Daintree River, with its mangrove-lined banks, is a great habitat for barramundi and other tropical coastal river species

COASTAL FISHING CAIRNS REGION

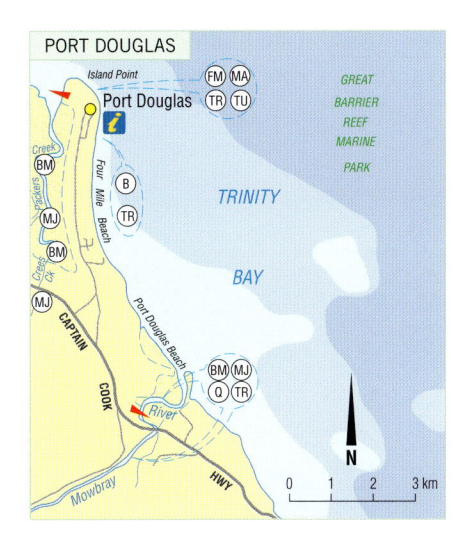

QUEENSLAND

PORT DOUGLAS

Tourism has awakened this once-sleepy northern town, and boat hire, launching ramps and availability of bait make fishing the small waterways comparatively easy. **Packers Creek**, and its tributary **Crees Creek**, run into the mangroves near the very glamorous marina area. One minute you are among million-dollar yachts, and the next you are a world away, hemmed in by mangroves, close enough to them to work both sides of the river at once. Live prawns and lures are best, particularly on a run-out tide at dawn and dusk; barramundi and mangrove jack are the most sought-after fish.

Land anglers can fish from **Island Point**, which is best reached from Four Mile Beach. The fishing is good in the summer months for barramundi, mackerel, fingermark, giant trevally and tuna, spinning with lures or live baiting. **Four Mile Beach** fishes best at its northern end for pikey bream and trevally.

South of Port Douglas boats can be launched into the **Mowbray River**, just off the Captain Cook Highway. You can fish from boats on either side of the bridge, and catches include barramundi, mangrove jack, queenfish and trevally.

TRINITY INLET

The best fishing around **Cairns** is virtually in the heart of the city in **Trinity Inlet** and its tributaries, which wind and snake through the dense mangrove flats on the city's southern side, virtually hidden from the smart hotels, restaurants and shops only a few kilometres away. The wide variety of fish includes mangrove jack, barramundi, fingermark, pikey bream, trevally, black jewfish, queenfish, barracuda, oxeye herring and threadfin salmon.

Heading out to Fitzroy Island for some light tackle sportfishing, with big Spanish mackerel the target

The inlet is a vast tidal estuary, with channels, sandbanks and mudbanks creating both recognisable fishing spots and a harvest of baits. Local anglers prefer live prawn, as it will catch almost anything in the estuary, but herring and mullet are also easily netted. Because of the mangroves, fishing is done by boat, except in the wharf area close to **Cairns Harbour**, but even this is restricted by the presence of a busy fishing fleet. The main launching ramp is at the Marlin Jetty, but there are ramps that can be reached by roads cutting through the mangroves in the upper recesses of the creek. Mud crabs and prawns also abound in this environment, with the mud crabs mostly being caught in set pots. A bonanza of prawns occurs when the heavy summer rains wash them down to the mudflats in the harbour. The prawns are taken in the inlet by cast net. Besides its charter fleet, Cairns has an excellent range of fishing guide services.

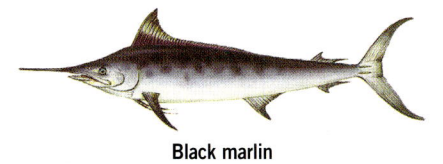

Black marlin

Also known as Pacific black marlin and silver marlin, the black marlin is found throughout northern waters and as far south as Tasmania in the east and Albany in the west.

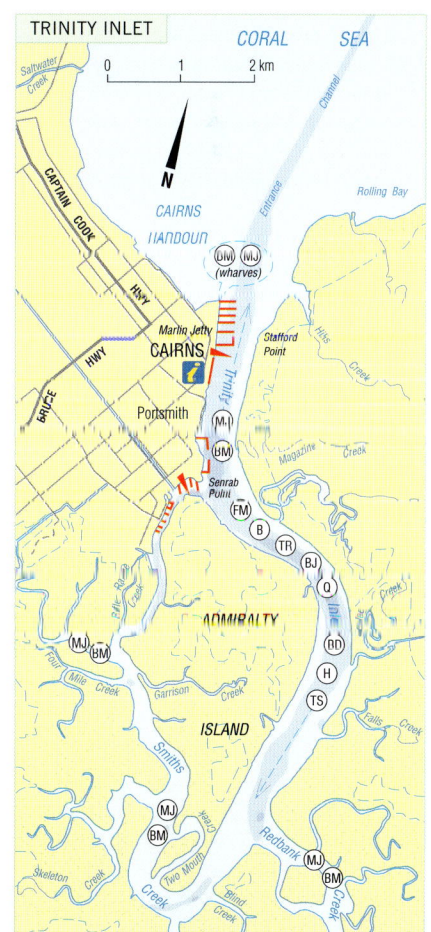

389

QUEENSLAND COASTAL FISHING CAIRNS REGION

Innisfail–Mourilyan Area

Type of fishing
estuary, island, reef, river, rock
Target fish
barramundi, mackerel, queenfish, trevally

This section of coastline has deepwater anchorage at Mourilyan harbour and great inshore fishing for Spanish and spotted mackerel in season. Mission Beach and Kurrimine Beach are excellent stopping points.

HIGH ISLAND TO TULLY HEADS

The main attraction to anglers are the offshore reefs and superb tropical islands. **Arthur Patches** and **Howie**, **Pearl** and **Feather reefs** are the most accessible reefs, reached from either the Bramston Beach or Flying Fish Point ramps, with coral trout, sweetlip, nannygai and red emperor.

Mourilyan Harbour has a boat ramp leading to deep inshore water. Boat anglers seek barramundi as their main catch here, with trevally and queenfish also possible.

Launching from the ramps at Kurrimine Beach, Mission Beach and South Mission Beach should only be attempted at high tide, as the water is very shallow here. The best launching for fishing around Dunk, Bedarra and the Family Islands is from Hull Heads or Tully Heads. The estuaries at **Hull Heads** and in the **Tully River** provide some good fishing, with mangrove jack, barramundi, fingermark, trevally and javelin fish. Small fish may be cast netted or yabbies can be pumped from the mudflats to provide live bait. Spinning with minnow lures is popular.

The islands are the magnet here, and they are easily reached by boat. The seaward side of **Dunk Island** fishes well for queenfish, giant trevally and Spanish mackerel among the surface fish, while coral trout and sweetlip are the bottom feeders. Adventurous anglers can cast lures in the shallow, reefy terrain for a mix of hard-fighting reef species ranging from cod to coral trout. There is camping for boat anglers at the northern end of Dunk, and a good anchorage nearby. About 25 km north-east of Dunk, **near Beaver Reef**, small black marlin and sailfish can be found as they move southwards during July and August. Fishing is banned on the reef itself.

The rest of the **Family Islands**, south of Dunk Island, are good places to troll for pelagics, mostly spotted and Spanish mackerel. The best spots are on the eastern shores, particularly around land that projects into the marine highways. Lure casting and live baiting can also be successful close inshore.

RUSSELL HEADS

The waters of the Mulgrave and Russell rivers offer some of the most exciting fishing waters in the State, culminating at Russell Heads. There is no road access to the area, so boat anglers have these waters to themselves after they launch into the Mulgrave River at Deeral Landing, off the Bruce Highway, north of Innisfail.

At the heads and in the **Mutchero Inlet** (the joint outlet to the sea for the Mulgrave and Russell rivers), the prime fish is the queenfish. The entrance carries whiting, pikey bream and dart as the main species, while the deep channel on the northern side of the inlet produces fingermark and pikey bream. Flathead and pikey bream are around the sand flats on the southern side. At the confluence of the two rivers, around **Mud Island**, queenfish, javelin fish, mangrove jack, estuary cod, threadfin salmon and pikey bream are the targets. Mutchero Inlet has been restocked with barramundi. Special fishing regulations are in place from time to time. Check in Cairns before fishing. Further upstream, barramundi, mangrove jack and oxeye herring are joined by freshwater species such as sooty grunter, catfish, archer fish and jungle perch.

Offshore from Russell Heads there is superb fishing for Spanish and spotted mackerel around the **Frankland Islands: High, Normanby, Mabel, Round** and **Russell**. A rocky terrace at **Bramston Point**, south of Mutchero Inlet, allows fishing for queenfish and trevally.

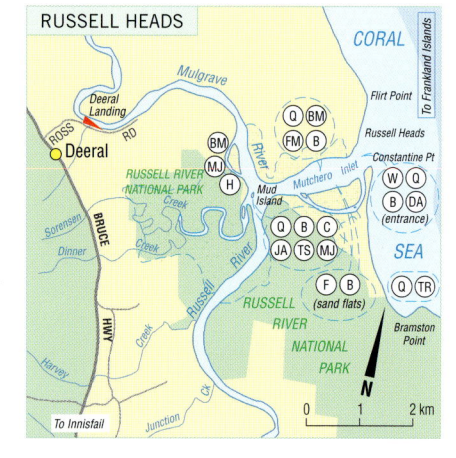

COASTAL FISHING CAIRNS REGION   QUEENSLAND

Hinchinbrook Island Area

Type of fishing
creek, estuary, jetty, reef

Target fish
barramundi, javelin fish, mackerel, mangrove jack, tuna, queenfish, trevally, threadfin salmon

Hinchinbrook presents a spectacular sight from the mainland, towering and jungle-covered and surrounded by rocky islets and the sparkling sea. The Hinchinbrook Channel, with its mangrove-covered islets and inlets, is a magnetic attraction for boat anglers, as it offers a variety of inshore fish and estuary species, all within sheltered water. The jumping-off points for this fishing experience are the towns of Cardwell and Lucinda. A ban on commercial gill netting in the channel to protect dugong has had a positive impact on the barramundi and threadfin salmon.

In **Cardwell**, land-based anglers must be content with the jetty, or the creeks that cross the Bruce Highway. Trevally, queenfish, long tom, mackerel and barramundi can be caught from the town jetty and in the channels of the Port Hinchinbrook development.

Offshore from Cardwell is the tiny **Goold Island**. It is bounded by deep water and attracts mackerel, tuna, trevally and queenfish. The reef area running off it can be fished for coral trout, cod, red emperor and sweetlip. The nearby Brook Islands are protected areas and fishing is prohibited.

In the **Hinchinbrook Channel**, the main catches are barracuda, trevally and queenfish. Half-way down, the channel breaks up into a maze of small islands and mangrove-lined channels. The trolling target is fingermark, but there are also trevally, estuary cod, barramundi, queenfish, javelin fish, pikey bream, threadfin salmon, oxeye herring and mangrove jack. Lure casting to suitable structures will result in estuary cod, mangrove jack and barramundi.

The seaward side of Hinchinbrook Island is hospitable to boat anglers only in the calmest of weather. Offshore reefs are frequented by Spanish mackerel, trevally, queenfish, spotted mackerel, coral trout and sharks. The best area is between **Cape Sandwich** and **Channel Rock**. Mackerel, trevally and fingermark can also be found in Shepherd Bay. In the north, the many creeks running into **Missionary Bay** carry barramundi, pikey bream, mangrove jack, estuary cod, trevally and queenfish.

At **Lucinda**, anglers can try for barramundi, long tom, queenfish, mackerel and trevally from the jetty. At the **Herbert River**, estuary cod, small barramundi, threadfin salmon and mangrove jack can be found. Boat anglers heading north to Hinchinbrook from here should be aware of the marked channels, as many have been brought undone by the sand flats and mudbanks.

GUIDE TO LOCAL FISH

		High Island to Tully Heads	Russell Heads	Hinchinbrook Island Area
BD	barracuda			●
BM	barramundi	●	●	●
B	bream, pikey		●	●
CF	catfish			
C	cod, estuary		●	●
C	cod, others			●
DA	dart		●	
RE	emperor, red	●		●
FM	fingermark	●	●	●
F	flathead		●	
H	herring, oxeye		●	●
MJ	jack, mangrove	●	●	●
JA	javelin fish	●	●	●
LT	long tom			●
MA	mackerel			●
MA	mackerel, Spanish	●		
MA	mackerel, spotted	●		
ML	marlin	●		
NG	nannygai	●		
Q	queenfish	●	●	●
SL	sailfish	●		
TS	salmon, threadfin		●	●
SH	shark			●
ES	sweetlip	●	●	●
TR	trevally	●	●	●
TR	trevally, giant	●		
CT	trout, coral	●		●
TU	tuna			●
W	whiting		●	

QUEENSLAND

COASTAL FISHING TOWNSVILLE REGION

Townsville Region

The fishing interest here focuses on the Whitsundays and several extensive mangrove systems. The Barrier Reef is well offshore, almost beyond the reach of trailer boats.

This coast is dry compared to the Cairns Region. Rivers tend to be small and are often very shallow. The Palm Islands and the famous Whitsundays are both boating paradises for anyone with an offshore boat and enough navigation experience. The many creeks among the mangroves in Cleveland Bay, Bowling Green Bay and Upstart Bay are the places to go for some of the best barramundi and mangrove jack fishing on the east coast. The offshore waters from Bowling Green Bay have become popular for light tackle game fishing, particularly for small marlin, mackerel and tuna.

Weather

The Townsville Region has heavy monsoonal summer rains and a low winter and spring rainfall. Tropical cyclones often occur along this section of the coast. The south-east trade winds that blow for much of the remainder of the year are moderate to strong. They can curtail boating for days on end during June to August. Moderate afternoon sea breezes are common in inshore areas. A day on the water means wearing hats, sunglasses and plenty of protective cream. The Bureau of Meteorology has current information on its website: www.bom.gov.au or call the Queensland Transport boating weather information lines on: 1300 360 426 for boating weather; 1300 360 427 for marine weather warnings.

Boating

It is about 40 nautical miles out to the reef from Townsville and Bowen, so boats going there need to carry ample

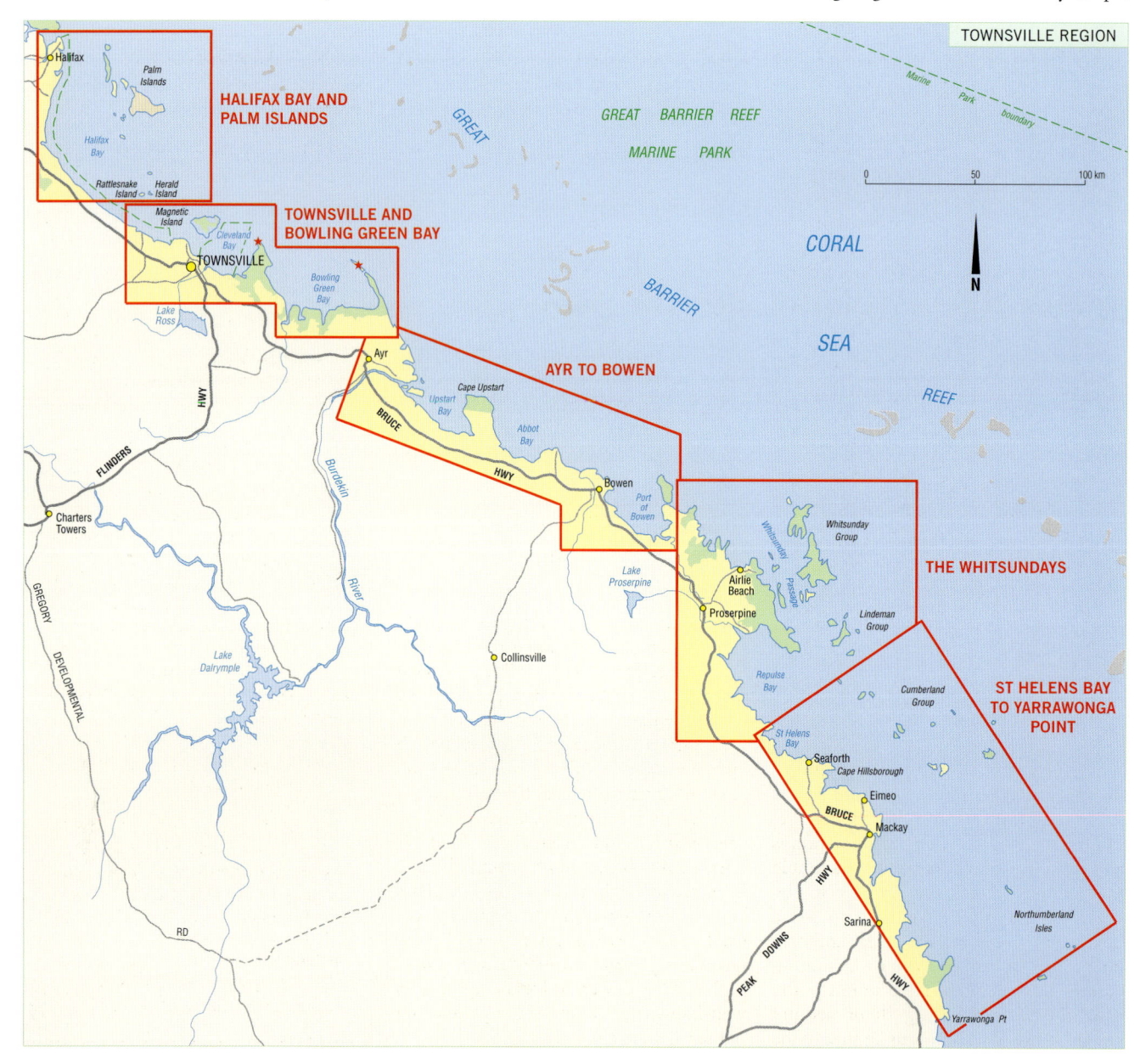

COASTAL FISHING TOWNSVILLE REGION   QUEENSLAND

WHERE TO FISH

Townsville Region

HALIFAX BAY AND PALM ISLANDS ● 394

The Palm Islands off Ingham and a group of smaller islands in Halifax Bay, including Herald and Rattlesnake islands, are real hotspots for mackerel, queenfish and trevally. Reef fish are here, too, including the prized red emperor in deeper water around the Palm Islands.

TOWNSVILLE AND BOWLING GREEN BAY ● 395

Both Cleveland Bay and Bowling Green Bay contain numerous mangrove creeks, all of which hold healthy populations of barramundi and mangrove jack. Some of the best barramundi fishing near Townsville is right in town in the harbour.

AYR TO BOWEN ● 396

The mighty Burdekin is by far the largest river in this area. Its estuary fishing is excellent. On the other side of Upstart Bay, in the lee of Cape Upstart itself, the fishing is even better. Bowen has some of the best sportfishing for queenfish, trevally and mackerel to be found in the north.

THE WHITSUNDAYS ● 398

Superlatives abound about the Whitsundays. To fish the whole group would be impossible in a single lifetime. No one ever fishes the Whitsundays once.

ST HELENS BAY TO YARRAWONGA POINT ● 400

The Mackay area has much to offer and gems like Cape Hillsborough and sleepy fishing villages like Eimeo keep regular visitors coming back. A little further north the area between St Helens and Seaforth and the islands close inshore is well worth a look.

fuel. It is also important to keep an eye on the weather. There are boat ramps suitable for large craft in Townsville, Shutehaven and Bowen. Smaller ramps and those in the creeks are more suitable for 'tinnies'. Tides vary greatly in the area, particularly at Mackay, so some boat ramps are short and steep, and care needs to be taken when launching vessels. Also be careful to monitor the tidal flow when fishing in or around creeks. Note that some launch sites in the Townsville Region are difficult to locate when returning into a late afternoon sun.

A large part of Halifax Bay is zoned a defence area and entry may be restricted during defence operations. Check with Queensland Boating and Fisheries before entering the area. There is a no-boating area off Townsville main beach, although line fishing is permitted. Care should be exercised around Salamander Reef, at Cleveland Point south of Townsville, as it is unmarked by beacons. Gloucester Pass and the bottom end of Edgecumbe Bay are shallow so beware of tides. Edwin Rocks, near Grassy Island, is exposed but not lit at night. The Bowen-Whitsunday area is well-known for diving activity so watch out for diving flags.

GUIDE TO LOCAL FISH

- barracuda
- barramundi
- bream
- bream, pikey
- cobia
- cod, estuary
- cod, others
- dart
- emperor, red
- emperor, spangled
- fingermark
- flathead
- herring, oxeye
- jack, mangrove
- javelin fish
- jewfish, black
- Job-fish
- long tom
- mackerel, grey
- mackerel, Spanish
- mackerel, spotted
- marlin, black
- nannygai
- parrotfish
- queenfish
- sailfish
- salmon, threadfin
- shark
- snapper
- sweetlip
- trevally, bigeye
- trevally, giant
- trevally, golden
- trevally, gold-spotted
- trout, coral
- tuna, mackerel
- tuna
- tuna, yellowfin
- whiting

FISHING TIP

A great way to see and fish the Whitsundays is to charter a 'bareboat'. Several companies offer access to fleets of 'drive yourself' boats – from small sailing boats to large motor cruisers. Bareboats offer the luxury of on-water accommodation, right at your fishing spot, and that spot can be wherever you wish.

You can either fish off the bareboats, off the tenders they provide or off your own trailerboat, that you can tow behind you as you cruise around. Basic tuition is part of the package, however, if you are not confident, captains can be arranged.

Longtail tuna

Also known as northern bluefin, the longtail tuna is a popular sportfish along the State's coastal waters. In Moreton Bay and other more northerly locations, this fish may be spun or fly fished from a boat. Essentially a sportfish, longtail tuna are poor table fare.

FURTHER INFORMATION

Fishing and boating The Queensland Boating and Fisheries Patrol (Department of Primary Industries) has offices at Able Point Marina, Airlie Beach, tel. (07) 4746 7003; 6 Herbert St, Bowen, tel. (07) 4786 3444; 7 Haigh St, Ingham, tel. (07) 4776 1611; DPI Building, Tennyson St, Mackay, tel. (07) 4967 8724; and 60 Ross St, Townsville, tel. (07) 4772 7311. The Great Barrier Reef Marine Park Authority is at 2-68 Flinders St, Townsville, tel. (07) 4750 0700. For information on fishing and boating regulations in State and Commonwealth marine parks, including zoning maps and guidelines, contact the Environmental Protection Agency, tel. (07) 4046 6602. Zoning maps are also available from some tourist centres, some bait and tackle shops and all Queensland Parks and Wildlife Service offices. The Boating Registration and Licensing Hotline is tel. 13 2380.

Tourist centres Tourism Whitsundays, Bruce Hwy, Proserpine, tel. 4945 3711; 161 Bruce Hwy, Ayr, tel. (07) 4783 9097; 12 Williams St, Bowen, tel. (07) 4786 4494; Bruce Hwy, Ingham, tel. (07) 4776 5211; Mackay Tourism and Development Bureau, 320 Nebo Rd, Mackay, tel. (07) 4952 2677; Magnetic Island Tourist Bureau, 26 The Grove, Nelly Bay, tel. (07) 4778 5256; Highway Information Centre, Bruce Hwy, Stuart, Townsville, tel. (07) 4778 3555; Mall Information Centre, Flinders Mall, Townsville, tel. (07) 4721 3660; Townsville Enterprise Ltd, Enterprise House, 6 The Strand, Townsville, tel. (07) 4771 3061; Butterfly World Information Centre, 1337 Bruce Hwy, Yabulu, tel. (07) 4778 6003.

QUEENSLAND COASTAL FISHING TOWNSVILLE REGION

Halifax Bay and Palm Islands

Type of fishing
beach, offshore, reef
Target fish
coral trout, mackerel, queenfish, sweetlip

The Palm Islands group, and the nearby Herald and Rattlesnake islands, a little further south in Halifax Bay, are an easy run out from the coast, either from Taylors Beach, Allingham or Balgal. These beaches are easily reached from the Bruce Highway near Ingham, but the waters are shallow, and launching must wait for the tide.

Halifax Bay is a good place to try for queenfish, trevally, javelin fish or fingermark and the beaches offer limited fishing for bream, whiting or flathead.

The **Palm Islands group**, with a number of small islands clustered around Orpheus and Great Palm islands, are all coral-fringed and provide good fishing for the main target fish on the reefs – sweetlip, coral trout, red emperor and mackerel. The Spanish and spotted mackerel are more common on the seaward side of the islands, which can be fished only in calm conditions. Headlands and bomboras are good places to cast lures for queenfish and giant trevally.

Balgal is a favoured ramp for Townsville anglers, due to its close proximity to Herald Island. Those launching here must take care to fix on a bearing or recognisable feature on the flat foreshores of Halifax Bay, for it is hard to distinguish the creek mouths and ramps on the return trip.

Mackerel are the main fish around **Herald and Rattlesnake islands**, with spotted, grey and Spanish mackerel all found in these waters. Reef fish are also present. There is a sand spit on Herald Island, which enables a stopover, either to camp or to wait for the right tide back at the Balgal ramp. Trolling is the most popular method, but setting up a berley trail and using baits is also effective for the mackerel.

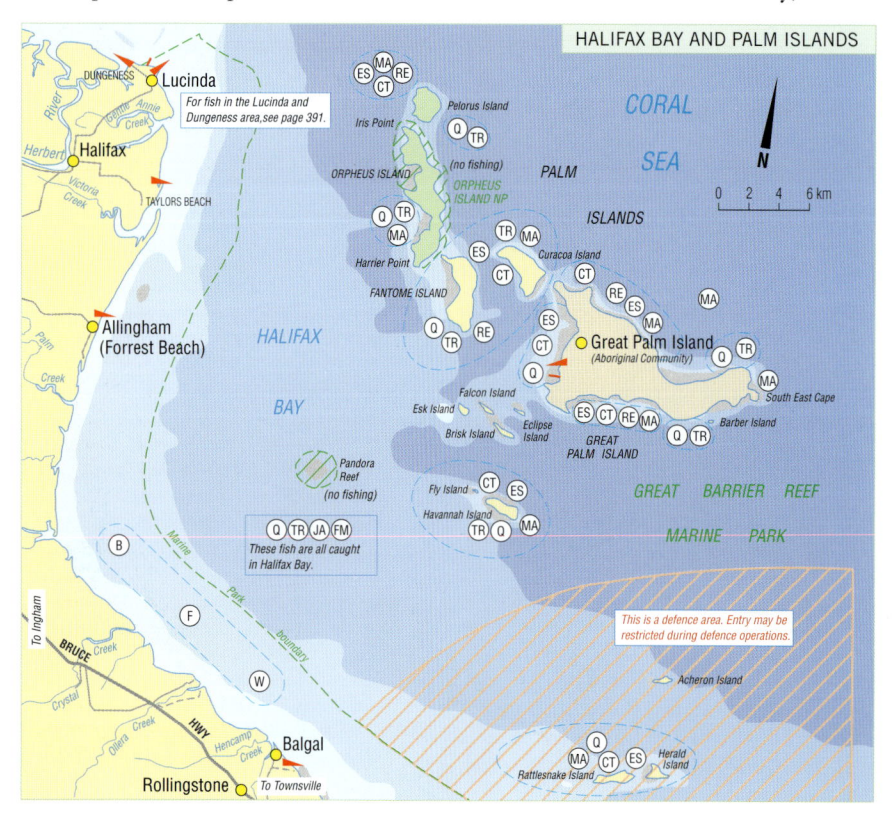

The sandbar at Herald Island is a popular camping spot for anglers

GUIDE TO LOCAL FISH

		Halifax Bay and Palm Islands	Townsville	Bowling Green Bay
BM	barramundi		●	●
B	bream	●	●	
C	cod		●	
RE	emperor, red	●		
FM	fingermark	●	●	●
F	flathead	●		
MJ	jack, mangrove			●
JA	javelin fish	●	●	●
MA	mackerel	●	●	●
ML	marlin			●
Q	queenfish	●	●	●
SL	sailfish			●
TS	salmon, threadfin			●
ES	sweetlip	●	●	
TR	trevally, giant	●	●	
TR	trevally, others	●	●	●
CT	trout, coral	●	●	
W	whiting	●		

COASTAL FISHING TOWNSVILLE REGION   QUEENSLAND

Townsville and Bowling Green Bay

Type of fishing
bay, estuary, harbour, offshore

Target fish
barramundi, marlin, sailfish, trevally

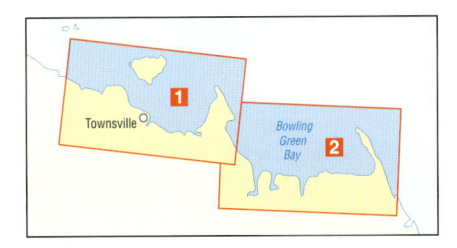

The coastal waters between Townsville and Cape Bowling Green provide a wide variety of options for anglers. Magnetic Island is a good starting point and is easily accessed from Townsville, and the harbour at Ross Creek has some quite good barramundi fishing. Cape Bowling Green has a reputation as one of the finest light tackle marlin grounds in the world.

TOWNSVILLE

The fishing around Townsville is centred on the Ross River, Ross Creek, Cleveland Bay and Magnetic Island. **Ross Creek** is the main boat harbour at Townsville, and fishing from its stone walls can be quite productive, with the chance of bream, barramundi and trevally. The **Ross River** has barramundi, mangrove jack, queenfish, javelin fish, fingermark and threadfin salmon. Best results are near low tide at dawn or dusk, and lures and baits both work well. Several weirs on the Ross River have been stocked with barramundi and offer an excellent chance of catching fish over the 10 kg mark.

Cleveland Bay itself is well worth exploring by boat. There are extensive mangrove areas around the creek entrances, which produce estuarine species such as mangrove jack and barramundi.

Magnetic Island, virtually a seaside suburb of Townsville, is only a 29-minute catamaran ride across Cleveland Bay. The outside coast, where fishing is best, should be avoided in heavier weather. Mackerel and queenfish can be sought around the points, while coral trout, cod and trevally are concentrated in some of the sheltered bays.

BOWLING GREEN BAY

Bowling Green Bay is situated just to the south-east of Townsville. It has sheltered waters between Cape Ferguson and Cape Bowling Green, with fingermark, queenfish, trevally, threadfin salmon and javelin fish the prime targets. A series of mangrove creeks empties into the bay. Mangrove jack, barramundi and other estuarine fish are abundant in these waters.

The Haughton River and Baratta Creek are the main streams and the entire system is well serviced with ramps.

Cape Bowling Green is regarded as one of the best inshore areas in Australia for marlin and sailfish, found close in to the eastern side of the cape or as far out as 20 km. The best way to locate them is to find bait schools with an echo sounder, or look for birds feeding from the schools. Trolling or drifting with live baits is the most effective fishing method. The western side of the spit offers a safe anchorage.

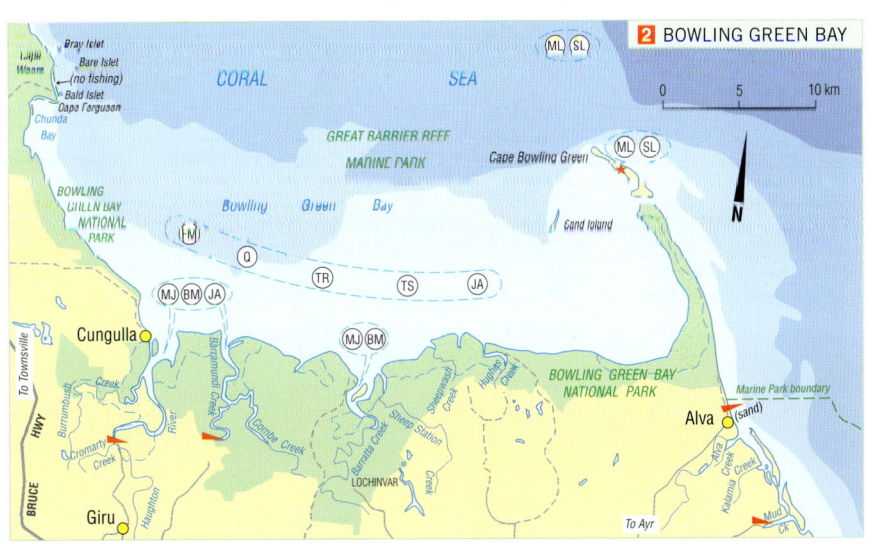

Large barramundi caught in the Townsville Harbour

QUEENSLAND
COASTAL FISHING TOWNSVILLE REGION

Ayr to Bowen

Type of fishing
bay, beach, estuary, jetty, offshore, rock
Target fish
mackerel, mangrove jack, queenfish, trevally

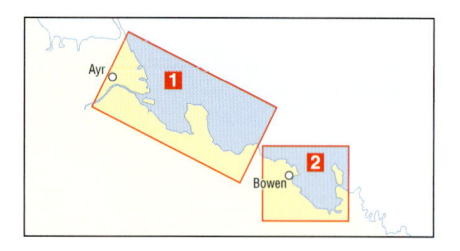

The town of Ayr is situated in sugarcane country on the northern side of the Burdekin delta. The strip of coastline between Ayr and Bowen can provide fantastic tropical sportfishing. There is also quite good barramundi fishing in season. The Burdekin River is a good starting point for visiting anglers. Bowen, exactly half-way between Mackay and Townsville, offers charter fishing and day trips to Stone Island.

AYR TO EURI CREEK

The Burdekin is one of Queensland's main rivers, barrelling down from the inland to break up and filter through islands and mudflats out into Upstart Bay. It runs between the towns of Ayr and Home Hill. The settlement of Groper Creek, on the south bank of the river near the coast, has a boat ramp, fuel and food, and there is another ramp on Rita Island.

To keep your boat out of the mud, and to find out where the fish are, you need good knowledge of the area, or need to ask questions of the locals. The river is virtually unnavigable at low tide. As with any shallow estuary there are drop-offs where the flathead station themselves, weedy patches frequented by whiting and bream and, in the deeper waters, fish like barramundi, fingermark, black jewfish, threadfin salmon and javelin fish.

Cape Upstart is a famous haunt for light tackle game fishing. There is also excellent fishing in Upstart Bay and, if conditions are bad, some sheltered fishing in the lee of the bay and in the numerous creeks. **Upstart Bay** has barramundi, queenfish and fingermark, and the beautiful beaches are worth fishing for threadfin salmon and trevally. But the best feature is the mangrove area at the south-eastern end of the bay, where creeks meander into the sea, allowing lure tossing and bait casting for mangrove jack and barramundi.

Cape Upstart is rocky and rugged on its exposed north and eastern faces where pelagics like Spanish mackerel, queenfish, mackerel tuna and longtail tuna congregate. Lure tossing may yield queenfish, giant trevally or even mackerel, and offshore anglers can troll for all these fish with baits or lures, or drift along the current lines.

The shipping jetty at **Abbot Point** is closed to anglers but attracts a lot of fish, so boat anglers can launch from Grays Bay at Cape Edgecumbe or from Bowen (see map on page 397). Trevally, queenfish, mackerel and cobia are around the jetty, and the angler's main difficulty is getting them clear of the jetty pylons. Beyond Abbot Point, **Euri Creek** runs through mangrove country, and can be entered at both ends of the tide. Those who make the 10-km journey from Bowen can catch mangrove jack, pikey bream, trevally, fingermark and javelin fish.

Golden trevally and juvenile
Although giant trevally are possibly more often targeted in this area, golden trevally, a related species, is also in these waters. It is a stubborn fighter and excellent table fare.

BOWEN

Bait fish mass in the Bowen area before the northern wet season, and mackerel, tuna, cobia, queenfish and giant trevally move through here to feed. These fish come close enough to offer a good chance for anglers lure tossing or bait fishing from the rocks between **Cape Edgecumbe** and **Dalrymple Point**. An old slipway at Dalrymple Point allows casting into deep water for these species.

The harbour at **Bowen** has a number of land-based angling locations that can

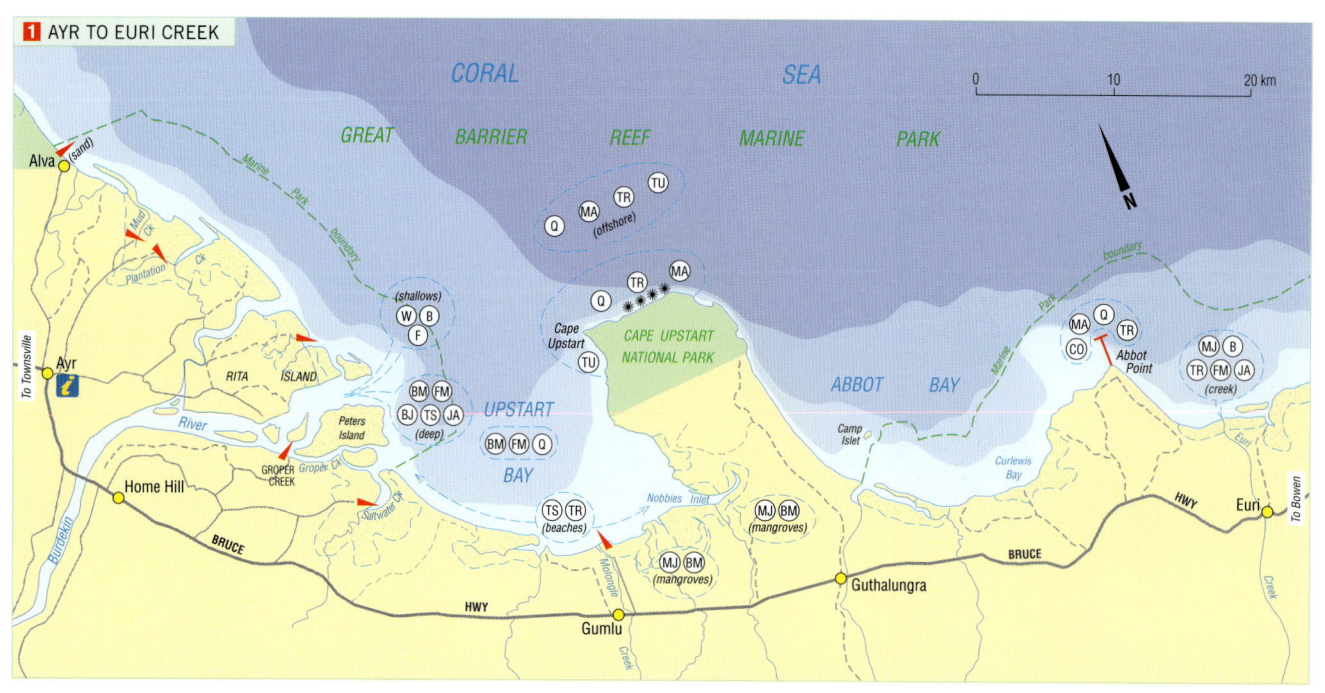

COASTAL FISHING TOWNSVILLE REGION
QUEENSLAND

GUIDE TO LOCAL FISH

	Ayr to Euri Creek	Bowen
(BM) barramundi	•	•
(B) bream	•	•
(B) bream, pikey	•	•
(CO) cobia	•	•
(FM) fingermark	•	•
(F) flathead	•	•
(H) herring, oxeye	•	•
(MJ) jack, mangrove	•	•
(JA) javelin fish	•	•
(F) jewfish, black	•	
(MA) mackerel, Spanish	•	•
(MA) mackerel, spotted	•	•
(Q) queenfish	•	•
(TS) salmon, threadfin	•	
(TR) trevally, giant	•	•
(TR) trevally, others	•	•
(TU) tuna	•	•
(W) whiting	•	•

produce big fish. Mangrove jack and bream are the main catches around the rock walls, while the town jetty is a great family spot, where bream and flathead mingle with the trevally and mackerel.

Adelaide Point, south-east of Bowen, has rock spots for casting for the queenfish, Spanish and spotted mackerel and trevally that come in on big tide runs. Just out from **Duck Creek** are some extensive weedy flats, frequented by whiting at high tide.

Boat anglers in this area have plenty of interesting options for creek, offshore or bay fishing. Oxeye herring is a regular in the bay, particularly around the boat harbour, and mackerel and queenfish are common catches. **Stone, Thomas** and **Poole islands** are all close in and provide brilliant fishing, either with bait or lures, for mackerel, tuna, queenfish and trevally. Bait fish school around the islands, particularly around the points and bomboras. **Shoalwater Bay**, on the southern side of Stone Island, contains a number of bomboras that attract giant trevally and queenfish.

There are small creeks between Bowen and White Cliffs, which can be entered (and left) at high tide. Bream, javelin fish, whiting, flathead, mangrove jack and trevally are among the possibilities here. **Eden Creek** and **Gregory River** at the southern end of Edgecumbe Bay are bigger, but can still only be entered at high tide. They are the best places in the area for barramundi and javelin fish.

Bait fishing on the Great Barrier Reef

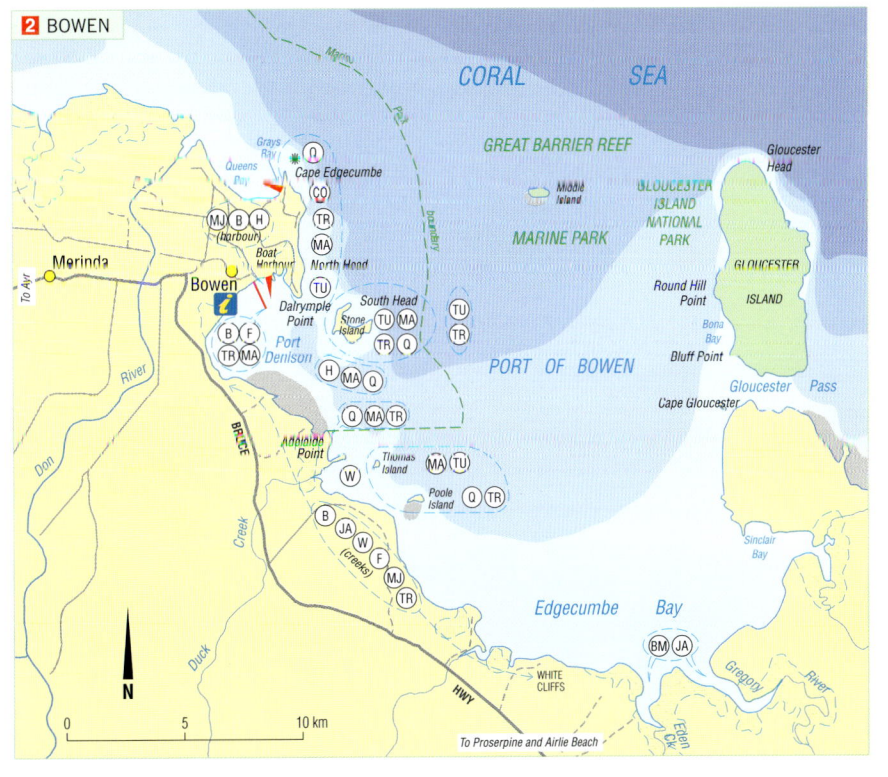

The Whitsundays

Type of fishing
bay, beach, jetty, offshore, reef
Target fish
coral trout, mackerel, queenfish, sweetlip, trevally

The jewel of the Great Barrier Reef is the Whitsunday Islands group. It is known for its resorts, but they take up only a tiny proportion of its area. The rest is left to sailing enthusiasts and boat anglers, many of them hiring their crafts for a cruising holiday. There are many sheltered moorings, but the best fishing is on the seaward side of the islands, with game fish in abundance.

On the mainland there is good fishing from Airlie Beach, Pioneer Point and Shutehaven. **Mandalay Point**, to the north-east of Airlie Beach, favours lure tossing for reef species like coral trout, estuary cod, sweetlip, trevally and queenfish. **Pioneer Point** has a strong tidal flow between the mainland and offshore rocks, carrying bait fish that attract queenfish and trevally.

Shute Harbour is one of the busiest waterways in Australia, but it carries big schools of bait fish and these attract trevally, Spanish mackerel and cod, which can be caught by live baiting from the jetty. Neap tides fish best in this region, rather than the very strong flow of the spring tides.

Airlie Beach, where the waters of the Whitsundays can be fished without leaving the mainland

Hook Island has two long and completely protected inlets, **Nara** and **Macona**, on its southern side. Fishing here can yield bream, trevally and some reef fish such as sweetlip and cod. The reefs between the two inlets carry spangled emperor, long tom, trevally, coral trout and cod, with queenfish just outside the reef, but it is forbidden to fish within 100 m of the observatory. **Hook Passage** offers a combination of reef fishing for coral trout and sweetlip or trolling for mackerel and big trevally. The eastern side of Hook Island fishes well, either trolling for mackerel or queenfish, or lure tossing over the reefy areas. The best reef area is **Mackerel Bay**, where coral trout, sweetlip, long tom, parrotfish and cod are on offer. **Pinnacle Point** receives the brunt of tide and weather, but there is trolling in reasonable conditions for big Spanish mackerel, tuna, marlin, sailfish, cobia and queenfish.

West of Hook Island, the best reef fishing in the Whitsunday group is at **Langford Reef**, the habitat of spangled emperor, coral trout, nannygai, Job-fish, long tom and sweetlip. The preferred technique over the coral is to cast lures like poppers and small metal spoons. Cruising outside the reef are mackerel, tuna, trevally, barracuda and queenfish.

Hayman Island attracts pelagics to its eastern side, and has a large coral reef – great for lure tossing for spangled emperor, long tom, big trevally and big coral trout.

Two island groups close in to the mainland are the cluster around **South Molle Island** and **Dent and Hamilton islands**. Resort dwellers on South Molle are able to catch reef fish such as coral trout, while trolling around the island can yield queenfish, trevally, cod and mackerel. Hamilton Island's best areas are Crab Bay and Driftwood Bay, where the targets are big cod, trevally and coral trout.

The largest island in the Whitsundays is **Whitsunday Island** and it invites both reef and deepwater fishing. On the south-western side of the island, trevally, queenfish and tuna congregate between **Cid Harbour** and **Reef Point**. The western side also carries trevally and queenfish, best sought by trolling with lures, or lure tossing. Baitfishing over the reefs works best for coral trout and sweetlip. The **Gulnare Inlet** sends a wedge of water into the island. It is shallow but has mangrove jack and bream.

On the south-eastern side of the island, **Hill Inlet** has sand flats that have created a habitat for dart, whiting and trevally. Further inland the inlet is virtually an estuary and supports populations of bream, mangrove jack and javelin fish. Between Whitsunday and Haslewood islands is the narrow **Solway Pass**, which creates deep water and a powerful tidal flow. It is a great place for surface fishing with baits or lures for queenfish and trevally, particularly around **Martin Inlet** and **Frith Rock**. The nearby channel between Haslewood and

GUIDE TO LOCAL FISH

BD	barracuda
BM	barramundi
B	bream
CO	cobia
C	cod
C	cod, estuary
DA	dart
RE	emperor, red
ES	emperor, spangled
FM	fingermark
MJ	jack, mangrove
JA	javelin fish
JF	Job-fish
LT	long tom
MA	mackerel, Spanish
MA	mackerel, others
ML	marlin
NG	nannygai
PF	parrotfish
Q	queenfish
SL	sailfish
SH	shark
ES	sweetlip
TR	trevally
CT	trout, coral
TU	tuna
W	whiting

COASTAL FISHING TOWNSVILLE REGION

QUEENSLAND

Teague islands has great fishing over the coral for coral trout, sweetlip, Job-fish and other reef species.

The eastern side of Whitsunday Island generally has terrific fishing offshore for queenfish, trevally and mackerel and, in **Apostle Bay**, for reef fish like sweetlip.

Deloraine Island, in the north-east of the group, should be fished only on a calm day. The western side of the island is great for reef fish while further out there are large trevally, mackerel, queenfish and shark.

Further south on the mainland is **Cape Conway**, north of the wide and sometimes rough expanse of **Repulse Bay**. Queenfish, mackerel, trevally and tuna come close to the cape, while queenfish, fingermark and whiting are in the bay. The **Proserpine** and **O'Connell rivers**, as well as various creeks, flow into the bay and bream, javelin fish fingermark, mangrove jack and barramundi are in the estuaries.

The **Lindeman Group of islands** is 15 km or so east of Cape Conway, and is the habitat of both reef fish (coral trout, sweetlip and long tom) and pelagics (mackerel, queenfish and trevally). The long run out from Shute Harbour or Repulse Bay means there is less fishing traffic here than in the Whitsundays.

St Helens Bay to Yarrawonga Point

Type of fishing
bay, beach, estuary, offshore, reef, rock

Target fish
barramundi, mackerel, mangrove jack, snapper, trevally

The Mackay coast can be a bit difficult for boating, as the coastal sand flats make boat ramps generally unstable at low tide. The tides can rise 5 or 6 m. Fishing close in to the shore on a run-out tide and casting into the channels can, however, bring big hauls of flathead.

There are shallow creeks running into mangrove areas, notably in **St Helens Bay**, where estuary species such as barramundi, mangrove jack and fingermark dwell. A number of islets are close to shore here, easily reached from the St Helens boat ramp, and promising excellent fishing for mackerel and tuna, with some reef fishing close in for sweetlip and coral trout.

There are a number of excellent land locations along this part of the coast. Spots on either side of **McBrides Point** can be fished for sweetlip, coral trout, red emperor, cod and parrotfish, or pelagics such as Spanish mackerel and trevally. At low tide it is possible to walk to **Wedge Island** to fish the eastern side for these same fish.

Fishing at Percy Island for mackerel

Constant Creek runs into **Sand Bay**, and there is good fishing, especially around the creek, for estuary species such as barramundi, threadfin salmon, fingermark, queenfish, javelin fish, mangrove jack and pikey bream. Closer to Mackay there are rocky ledges at **Shoal Point, Eimeo** and **Slade Point**, where queenfish, trevally, mackerel and tuna can be sought with lures and baits.

Offshore, to the east, is the **Cumberland Group of islands** with **Brampton Island** closest in. These are a 30-km run from Mackay, but there are several safe anchorages to allow an overnight stay. There are fringing reefs and shoals here that make bottom fishing attractive, particularly as snapper can be caught right at the northern limit of its range. Other reef fish are sweetlip, coral trout and Job-fish; black marlin, sailfish, mackerel, queenfish and trevally are in the deeper waters.

The big sugar town of **Mackay** is on the **Pioneer River**, which practically drains out at low tide. A channel has been cut from the boat ramp to the sea, but fishing the river is possible only on the high tide, with barramundi, threadfin salmon and mangrove jack the targets. Sooty grunter have been released in the river upstream in the fresh water and are thriving.

In the Port of Mackay, the extensive harbour walls provide good fishing for trevally, queenfish, bream, black jewfish, javelin fish, mangrove jack and tuna.

GUIDE TO LOCAL FISH

BM	barramundi
B	bream
C	cod
RE	emperor, red
FM	fingermark
F	flathead
MJ	jack, mangrove
JA	javelin fish
BJ	jewfish, black
JF	Job-fish
MA	mackerel
ML	marlin, black
NG	nannygai
PF	parrotfish
Q	queenfish
SL	sailfish
TS	salmon, threadfin
S	snapper
ES	sweetlip
TR	trevally
CT	trout, coral
TU	tuna

Just south-east of the harbour is the most productive fishing area. The east of **Flat Top Island** has reef fishing for sweetlip, nannygai and coral trout. Big schools of various species of tuna and mackerel move past Flat Top and Round Top islands. **Oyster Rock**, closer in, is also a fish attractor. **Bakers Creek**, south of Mackay, is typically shallow and mangrove-lined and has barramundi, threadfin salmon and mangrove jack.

The coastline south of Mackay is characterised by mangrove-lined creeks and estuaries, where barramundi is always a possible catch. Rock and beach fishing add to the variety.

For a couple of days per year the waters around **Hay Point** provide some extraordinary fishing for snapper. At **Hay Reef**, out from Hay Point, black jewfish are the target, with good numbers of sweetlip, coral trout, trevally and Job-fish.

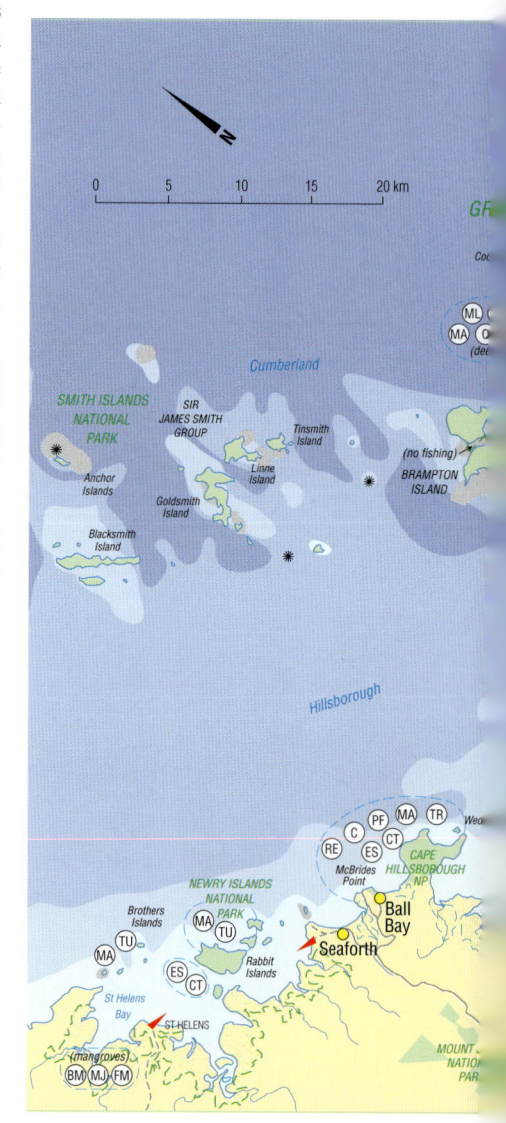

COASTAL FISHING TOWNSVILLE REGION   QUEENSLAND

Cape Palmerston is at the head of a national park, but there are four-wheel-drive tracks to the area. There are mangrove estuaries on the western side of the cape. Rock fishing platforms provide good spots for lure casting and bait fishing, mostly for mackerel and tuna.

East of Cape Palmerston are the **Northumberland Islands**, comprising the Beverley, Bedwell and Percy island groups. All attract mackerel and tuna, and are mangrove-lined, so inshore fishing may yield barramundi, mangrove jack, trevally, queenfish and fingermark. The **Beverley Group** is the closest, with the **Bedwell** and **Percy groups** 40 km offshore. Expeditions to these places can launch further south at Carmila, Clairview and St Lawrence and the rewards are coral trout, Job-fish, sweetlip and cod on the reefs, and mackerel and tuna around the islands, with sailfish and young black marlin available in season.

The bays at Cape Hillsborough National Park provide good fishing for barramundi and mangrove jack

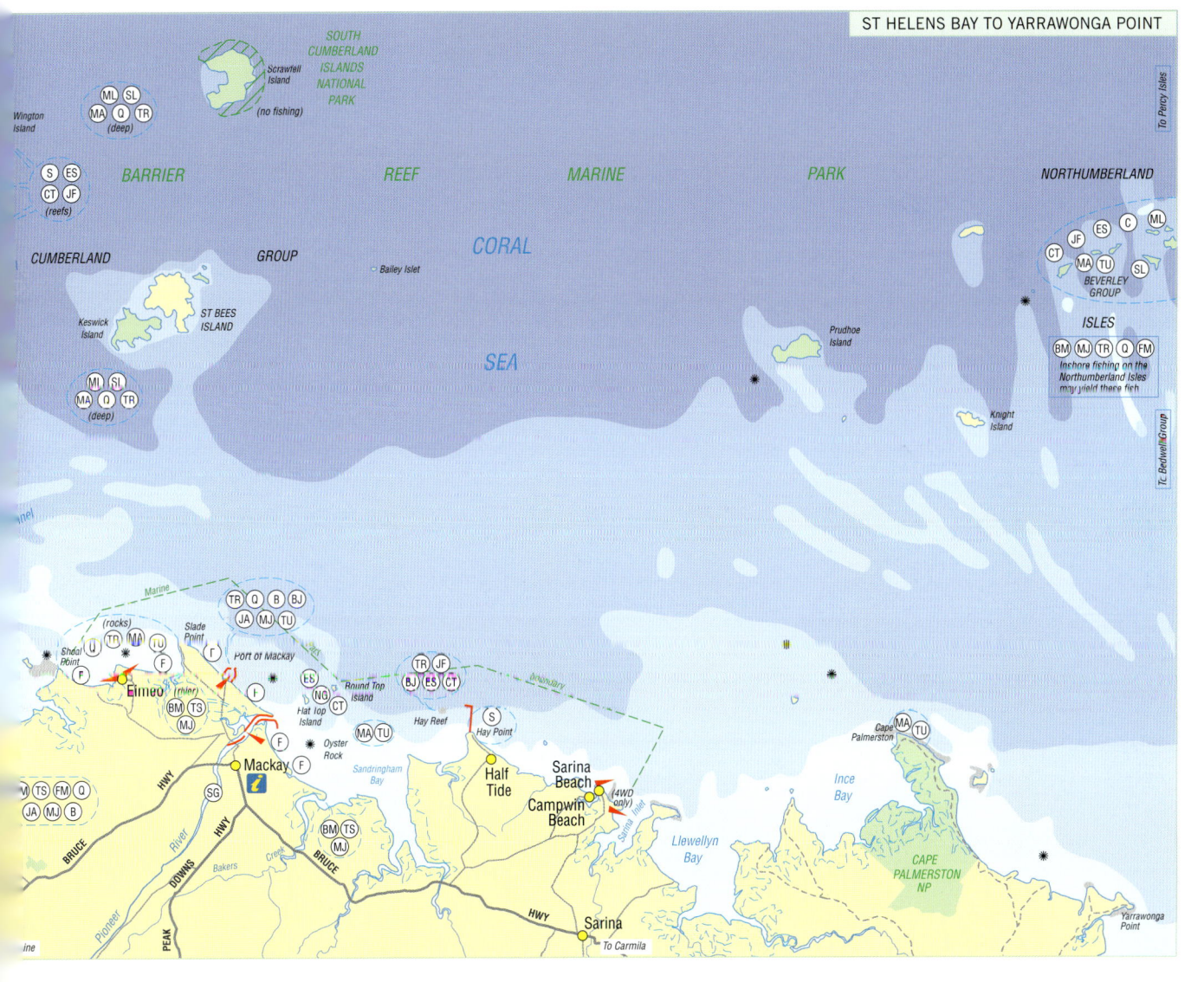

QUEENSLAND

COASTAL FISHING ROCKHAMPTON REGION

Rockhampton Region

With the sandy expanses of Hervey Bay and the extensive mangrove wetlands of The Narrows and Great Sandy Strait, the Rockhampton Region would have enough to offer. But there is also beach fishing on Fraser Island, the easily accessible Keppel Group of islands and all the wonderful beaches and rocks in between.

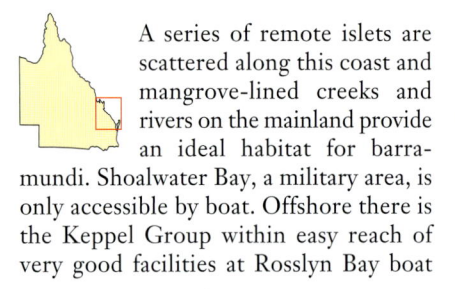

Fishing for spotted mackerel

A series of remote islets are scattered along this coast and mangrove-lined creeks and rivers on the mainland provide an ideal habitat for barramundi. Shoalwater Bay, a military area, is only accessible by boat. Offshore there is the Keppel Group within easy reach of very good facilities at Rosslyn Bay boat harbour. Hervey Bay and Fraser Island provide wonderful fishing in the south of the region.

Weather

This section of coastal Queensland has a lower rainfall than the north. South-easterly winds prevail for most of the year, but westerlies affect the south of the region in the winter months. In spring and summer, moderate afternoon sea breezes are common, and afternoon thunderstorms may cross the coast. The Bureau of Meteorology broadcasts severe thunderstorm warnings on local radio stations.

Current weather information is available from the Bureau on their website: www.bom.gov.au or call Queensland Transport boating weather information lines: 1300 360 426 for boating; 1300 360 427 for marine weather warnings.

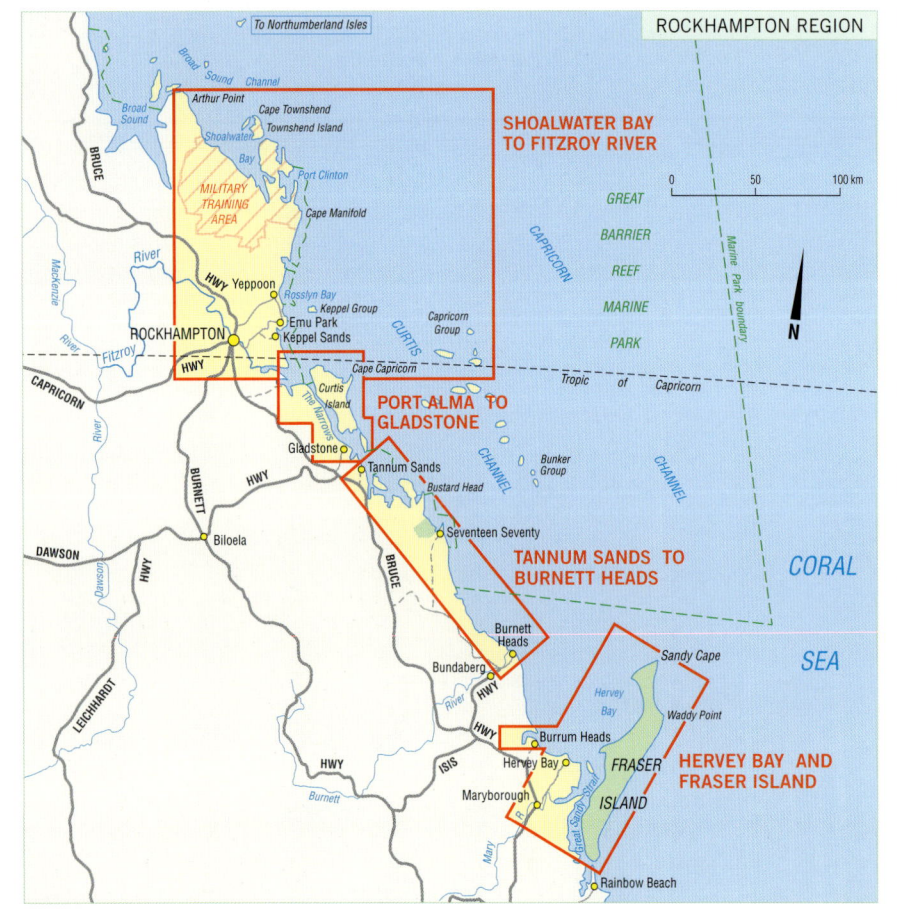

WHERE TO FISH

Rockhampton Region

SHOALWATER BAY TO FITZROY RIVER ● 404
Shoalwater Bay, thanks to the closure of overland access by the military, remains an almost untouched area, with queenfish, trevally and mackerel in the bay. The rest of the coast south to the Fitzroy River comprises small holiday villages on either side of the large town of Yeppoon, where there is fishing for a variety of species, including threadfin salmon, flathead, mackerel and mulloway. The Keppel Group of islands has big pelagics in the deeper water.

PORT ALMA TO GLADSTONE ● 406
Curtis Island shelters a mangrove-lined channel called The Narrows. The many creeks and inlets here abound with barramundi, mangrove jack and mud crabs. In the Port of Gladstone, despite the huge alumina plant, there is good boat fishing in a large area of relatively sheltered water, with queenfish and trevally the main targets.

TANNUM SANDS TO BURNETT HEADS ● 408
This stretch of coast is somewhat remote and access can be difficult. There are mangrove jack and barramundi in the rivers and creeks, largely accessed by four-wheel drive. Rocky areas along the coast can be fished for snapper, sweetlip and mackerel. Mud crabs are prolific in the area.

HERVEY BAY AND FRASER ISLAND ● 410
Tailor fishing along the eastern beach of Fraser Island is legendary, but the fishing for bream, whiting and dart is also very worthwhile. The area has become a popular venue for salt water fly fishing for golden trevally and marlin. Hervey Bay and especially the Great Sandy Strait have many good reef fishing spots. Estuary species can be found in the multitude of channels among the mangroves lining the strait.

COASTAL FISHING ROCKHAMPTON REGION   QUEENSLAND

GUIDE TO LOCAL FISH

- barramundi
- bream
- catfish
- cobia
- cod
- dart
- emperor, red
- fingermark
- flathead, dusky
- herring, oxeye
- jack, mangrove
- javelin fish
- kingfish, yellowtail
- mackerel, school
- mackerel, Spanish
- mackerel, spotted
- morwong
- mullet
- mulloway
- nannygai
- queenfish
- salmon, threadfin
- shark, bronze whaler
- shark, school
- shark, others
- snapper
- sweetlip
- trevally, giant
- trevally, golden
- trout, coral
- tuna, longtail
- whiting, sand

Fishing Expo held on Fraser Island

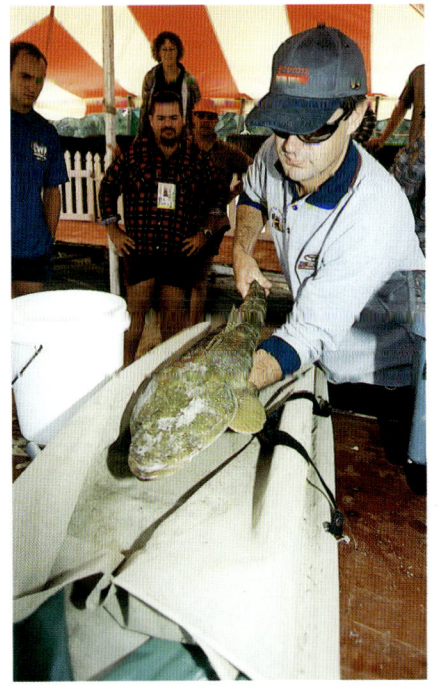

Launching a boat off Fraser Island

Boating

This coastline is very isolated. Take plenty of fuel, water, a radio and an EPIRB and tell somebody where you are going. There are limited safe anchorages so watch the weather very carefully.

In the Shoalwater Bay military training area, defence exercises for naval ships, aircraft and troops are held regularly, and parts or all of the bay may be closed. Check with the Rockhampton office of the Boating and Fisheries Patrol before any proposed fishing expedition.

Beware of extensive sandbars at the mouth of the Fitzroy River. The Narrows between Curtis Island and the mainland, from the Fitzroy River mouth to Gladstone Harbour, is navigable only at high water. The Great Sandy Strait is mostly a shallow sandy area with one main shipping channel, which is well buoyed. Remain within this channel if you are unfamiliar with the area. Be cautious crossing the Wide Bay Bar south of Fraser Island.

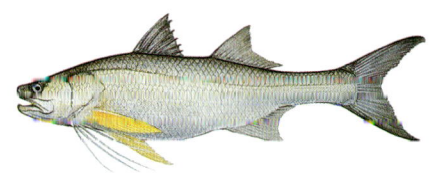

Threadfin salmon

This fish is found in tropical inshore waters and estuaries. The blue threadfin species is also known as Rockhampton salmon, giant threadfin and bluenose salmon. The king threadfin species is commonly called Burnett salmon or king salmon in Queensland. Its table qualities are greatly underrated.

FISHING TIP

When fishing the surf don't ignore the white water. The gutters are the places where big fish will wait in search of prey, but often the edges of the white water, where the water is still clean below but froth on top, will produce good catches of fish such as tailor, salmon, mullet and bream. The best way to find holes, gutters and channels on a beach is to spend a few moments studying the beach from a high vantage point.

FURTHER INFORMATION

Fishing and boating The Queensland Boating and Fisheries Patrol has offices at Alf O'Rourke Dve, Gladstone Marina, Gladstone, tel. (07) 4972 0699; Enterprise St, Bundaberg, tel. (07) 4131 5851; Buccaneer Ave, Urangan, Hervey Bay, tel. (07) 4125 3989. For information on zoning maps and guidelines for marine parks, contact The Great Barrier Reef Marine Park Authority at 2–68 Flinders St, Townsville, tel. (07) 4750 0700. Maps can also be obtained from some tourist centres, some bait and tackle shops and all Queensland Parks and Wildlife Service offices. The Boating Registration and Licensing Hotline is 13 2380.

Tourist centres Bryan Jordan Dve, Gladstone, tel. (07) 4972 9922; 30 Ferry St, Maryborough, tel. (07) 4121 4111; The Spire, Gladstone Rd, Rockhampton, tel. (07) 4927 2055; Dreamtime Cultural Centre, Yaamba Rd, Rockhampton, tel. (07) 4936 1655; Boyne Tannum Information Centre, Ocean St, Tannum Sands, tel. (07) 4973 8062; 10 Bideford St, Torquay, tel. (07) 4142 9609; Capricorn Coast Tourist Information Centre, Ross Creek Roundabout, Yeppoon, tel. (07) 4939 4888.

Shoalwater Bay to Fitzroy River

Type of fishing
bay, beach, estuary, offshore, reef, river, rock

Target fish
barramundi, bream, flathead, threadfin salmon, tuna, whiting

The **Shoalwater Bay** area is the first good fishing water on this part of the coast, but it is under the control of the defence forces, with no overland access allowed. A large seaworthy boat with a range of at least 100 km is necessary to access the area between Shoalwater Bay and Corio Bay. Launch from St Lawrence, to the north-west, or from Rosslyn Bay near Yeppoon. You need a dinghy to explore the estuaries and creeks.

SHOALWATER BAY TO FITZROY RIVER

Those who go to Shoalwater Bay by boat must obtain a permit from the army, but can fish in relatively unspoilt waters for barramundi, mangrove jack and other estuarine species around the shores, queenfish and trevally in the bay, and pelagics like mackerel and tuna around the islands.

Outside the bay, **Split, Dome and Delcomyn islands**, and other small islands, can be fished for Spanish mackerel and tuna in the deeper waters, and snapper, sweetlip and nannygai on the reefs in Pearl Bay.

Further south, both **Peaked Island** (also known as Perforated Island) and **Flat Island** require a run of about 60 km north from Rosslyn Bay boat harbour, but the reef fishing is superb for red emperor, coral trout, sweetlip and snapper, while the surrounding waters are rich with Spanish mackerel, giant trevally, cobia and tuna. The reefs around **Conical Rocks** and **Corroboree Island** (just north-west of North Keppel Island) are much more accessible, and invite trolling and baitfishing outside the reef areas for trevally, mackerel, cobia and tuna, and drifting over the reefs for sweetlip, snapper and coral trout.

The **Keppel Group**, and the many rocks and islands that surround it, are an easy run from Rosslyn Bay, but wind will cause steep, choppy waves in these shallow waters, creating uncomfortable and dangerous boating conditions. In winter, school and spotted mackerel and longtail tuna move through Keppel Bay. Whiting, bream and flathead are caught close to the Keppels. The deeper water beyond the Keppels is roamed by big pelagics like Spanish mackerel, cobia and giant trevally. Small boats can pull in to sheltered anchorages at both North Keppel and Great Keppel islands. Overnight accommodation is available for anglers wishing to explore the rocks and islands further offshore. Some of these are surrounded by reefs holding snapper, sweetlip and coral trout, and all attract

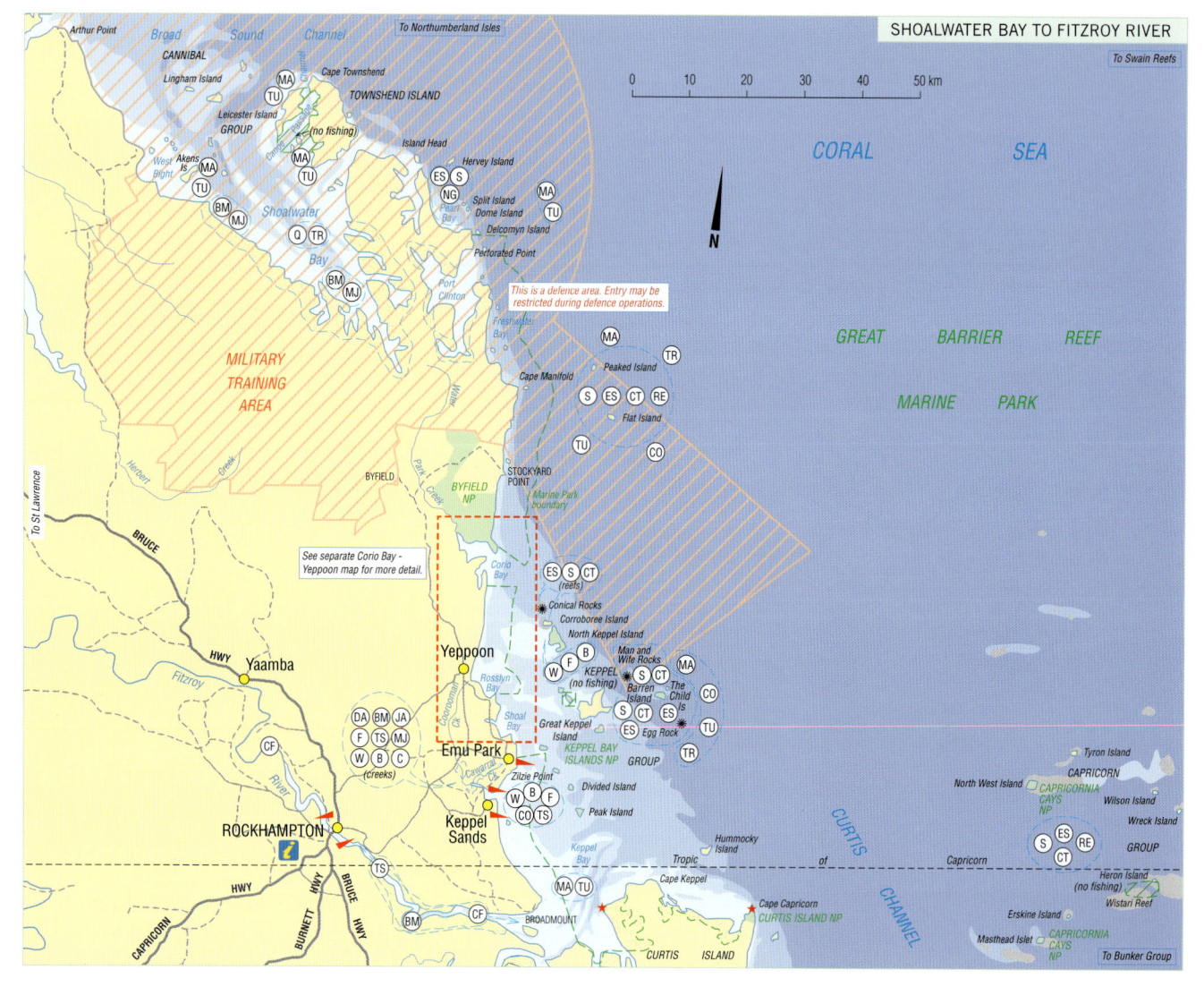

COASTAL FISHING ROCKHAMPTON REGION — QUEENSLAND

concentrations of Spanish and school mackerel, cobia, trevally and tuna.

The small town of **Emu Park** gives good access to rock fishing, especially from **Zilzie Point**, for whiting, bream, flathead, threadfin salmon and cobia.

It is not far south to the **Coorooman–Cawarral creek** system. This area is more reminiscent of a New South Wales estuary, with sand bars and channel at the entrance, and a complex of some ten creeks. There are whiting and flathead around the sandbanks. Near the boat ramp, and further in, land and boat anglers can fish for barramundi, estuary cod, bream, dart and threadfin salmon. Barramundi, javelin fish and mangrove jack are in the smaller tributaries.

The **Fitzroy River estuary**, from the coast to Rockhampton, has a big population of catfish, but is also heavily fished for barramundi and threadfin salmon. A barrage at Rockhampton prevents movement of the barramundi upstream and the upper reaches of the river are inhabited by catfish. Fishing is banned at the barrage but excellent barramundi fishing is available below the exclusion zone – right in the middle of town.

The **Swain Reefs**, on the outer and southernmost edge of the Great Barrier Reef, are offshore some 210 km north-east from Rosslyn Bay. These reefs are a wonderful fishing area for a charter trip or for those with big, seaworthy boats, equipped with radio and on-board sleeping and eating facilities. Most of the charter companies operate out of Gladstone. The main target fish are coral trout, sweetlip and red emperor, while trevally and mackerel predominate among the pelagics. The reefs require careful navigation, as the only landmark structures are towers on **Gannet Cay** and a wreck on **Horseshoe Reef**. Experts advise travelling only between 9 a.m. and 3 p.m., when the submerged parts of the reefs can be seen clearly. Boats should tie up well before sunset.

CORIO BAY–YEPPOON

There is some beach angling along the **Nine Mile Beach** and **Farnborough Beach**, north and south of the entrance to Corio Bay. The targets are whiting, bream, flathead, dart and threadfin salmon. At the south end of Nine Mile Beach, around Water Park Point, there is rock fishing for mulloway, trevally, tuna, mackerel, dart, queenfish and cod.

Corio Bay has good fishing, but access to the area is not very good. It is not advisable to bring trailer boats in here, but tinnies on top of a vehicle are no trouble. The bay itself has many sand flats, but there are channels leading to the two prolific creeks, **Water Park Creek** and **Fishing Creek**. In the centre of the bay and in the lower reaches of the channels is a wonderful assortment of inshore and estuary fish. Oxeye herring, barramundi, bream, flathead, threadfin salmon, whiting, dart, mangrove jack and queenfish are here in large numbers, and the yabby bait to tempt them is on the sand flats. Barramundi can be found in the entrances to the creeks, along with whiting, bream and flathead.

Light tackle lure fishing and saltwater fly fishing are also productive here. Fly fishers work eight and 10 weight outfits with intermediate or sinking lines in conjunction with baitfish and shrimp patterns to good effect in this area. Lure fishers use floating and sinking lures. The best results come when the lure is worked, that is the retrieve rate is varied to imitate a wounded or fleeing baitfish.

At **Yeppoon** there are rocks on either side of the entrance to Ross Creek, which can be fished for school mackerel and cod, as well as whiting, flathead, bream and threadfin salmon. **Rosslyn Bay** provides one of the most easily fished land-based angling spots in the area. At **Double Head** and the two sea walls of the harbour the fishing outside is for bream, threadfin salmon, flathead, school mackerel, tuna, mulloway and cod. Inside the bay there are barramundi, bream, threadfin salmon, whiting, cod, school mackerel and bait fish. Several rock bomboras off the eastern wall are havens for trevally and queenfish. **Causeway Lake**, south of Rosslyn Bay, has easily accessible and sheltered fishing for flathead, whiting, bream and barramundi.

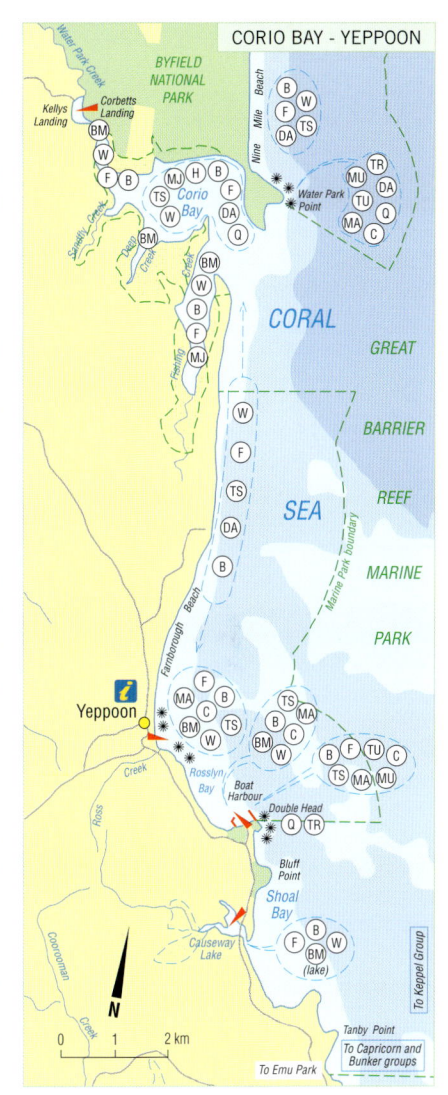

The offshore boating waters in this area are among the richest in Queensland. The species available are generally prolific and of good size, whether bottom bouncing or trolling for pelagics. At Yeppoon the launching ramp is accessible for only three hours each side of high tide, so it is best to launch from the safe harbour at Rosslyn Bay. There are charter operations from the bay leaving for some of the outlying reefs such as the Capricorn and Bunker groups, and the more distant Swain Reefs. Some of these charters stay at sea for several days, while anglers and divers make use of smaller boats.

GUIDE TO LOCAL FISH

	Shoalwater Bay to Fitzroy River	Corio Bay–Yeppoon
(BM) barramundi	•	•
(B) bream	•	•
(F) catfish	•	
(CO) cobia	•	
(C) cod	•	•
(DA) dart	•	•
(RE) emperor, red	•	
(F) flathead	•	•
(H) herring		•
(MJ) jack, mangrove	•	
(JA) javelin fish	•	
(MA) mackerel	•	•
(MU) mulloway	•	•
(NG) nannygai	•	
(Q) queenfish	•	•
(TS) salmon, threadfin	•	•
(S) snapper	•	
(ES) sweetlip	•	
(TR) trevally	•	•
(CT) trout, coral	•	
(TU) tuna	•	•
(W) whiting	•	•

CORIO BAY – YEPPOON

QUEENSLAND   COASTAL FISHING ROCKHAMPTON REGION

Port Alma to Gladstone

Type of fishing
estuary, offshore, reef, rock, wharf
Target fish
bream, flathead, queenfish, trevally

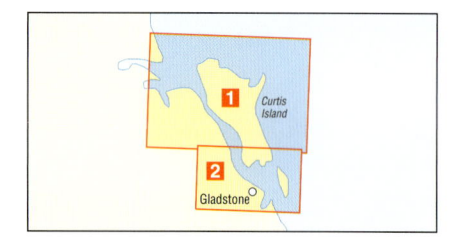

Fishing around Curtis Island for species such as mangrove jack, flathead, whiting and bream

A feature of this area is The Narrows, an enormous mangrove wetlands system in very pristine condition, unpolluted and commercially undeveloped. Boats capable of going offshore can go out around Cape Keppel on Curtis Island to Hummocky Island and Cape Capricorn. Curtis Island provides protection from the prevailing south-easterly winds, so it is quite safe for fairly small craft to make the trip provided that plenty of fuel is carried and general commonsense safety procedures are followed.

PORT ALMA AND THE NARROWS

The **Fitzroy River, Casuarina** and **Raglan creeks, Kamiesh Pass**, and the **Connor** and **Deception creeks** flow into a shallow area of flats and channels, best explored by boats launched at Port Alma. These estuary waters are fished for bream, flathead and spotted javelin fish, and plenty of mud crabs can be harvested as well. Kamiesh Pass also has threadfin salmon, trevally, queenfish, mullet and javelin fish. From the entrance of the Fitzroy River south to Gladstone is **The Narrows**, a mangrove-lined passage that includes a maze of tidal creeks on both sides. It stretches for 60 km and is the habitat of both tropical and temperate fish. The Narrows is basically the southern limit for good barramundi fishing, particularly at the junctions of the main channel and the off-shoot creeks. Mangrove jack, trevally, queenfish, spotted javelin fish, flathead and mullet are also present in these waters.

Curtis Island has limited land-based fishing, because land is privately owned.

Hummocky Island, offshore from Port Alma and 10 km north-east of Cape Keppel, is surrounded by marvellous water for trolling or drifting with live baits and lures. Yellowtail kingfish, cobia, trevally, Spanish mackerel and other pelagics are prolific. Most of the 20 km or so from the ramp to this area is protected by Curtis Island from the prevailing south-east winds.

GUIDE TO LOCAL FISH

	Port Alma and The Narrows	Gladstone
(BM) barramundi	●	●
(B) bream	●	●
(CO) cobia		●
(C) cod	●	●
(F) flathead	●	●
(MJ) jack, mangrove	●	●
(JA) javelin fish	●	●
(MA) mackerel	●	●
(MO) morwong		●
(M) mullet	●	●
(MU) mulloway	●	●
(Q) queenfish	●	●
(TS) salmon, threadfin	●	●
(S) snapper		●
(ES) sweetlip		●
(TR) trevally	●	●
(CT) trout, coral		●
(TU) tuna		●
(W) whiting	●	●

COASTAL FISHING ROCKHAMPTON REGION — QUEENSLAND

2 GLADSTONE

From Station Point to **Cape Keppel**, mulloway and trevally are the main fish, along with whiting, bream, flathead, threadfin salmon and queenfish. South-east of Cape Keppel, in two inlets known as **The Lagoons** and **Yellow Patch**, there are some protected waters where bream, whiting and flathead find shelter. At **Cape Capricorn**, at the north-east of the island, and nearby **Rundle Island** there is bottom fishing over reefs for coral trout, sweetlip and snapper. Offshore from Cape Capricorn there is deep water ideal for trolling for mackerel, trevally and queenfish.

GLADSTONE

The **Calliope River** reaches the coast near the big industrial city of Gladstone, creating a delta of mangrove creeks and sand flats. The hot water outlet from the power station near the boat ramp is a top spot for barramundi and threadfin salmon. Flathead, mangrove jack, bream and spotted javelin fish can also be found in this area.

To reach the northern waters of the port, boat anglers have to navigate the channels through the sandbanks. There is a car ferry service from Gladstone to Southend on Curtis Island on Friday, Saturday and Sunday. All roads on the island are suitable only for four-wheel-drive vehicles. The long stretch from Black Head down to North Entrance is ideal for anglers seeking cod, trevally and queenfish. North Entrance, especially around tiny **Rat Island**, is excellent for bream and whiting.

Facing Island shelters the Port of Gladstone. The island has rocks and a number of reefs at its north and south ends that attract fish like cod, snapper and trevally; morwong and mackerel are possible catches around the reef fringes.

The deeper port area has good land-based angling, particularly from **Barney Point** and **South Trees wharves**, with mulloway and barramundi the main targets, along with trevally, queenfish and bream. There is some good fishing around **South Trees Island** and **Boyne Island**. Whiting are among the weed patches, and there are discernible gutters for flathead and bream around the shorelines. Ramps at Boyne Island and Tannum Sands provide the easiest launching for the deep shipping channel, which runs through **Port Curtis** and carries school mackerel, cobia, trevally, queenfish and tuna. Gladstone is the best launching place for boat anglers wanting access to the offshore reefs. Charter fishing vessels regularly leave here for the Swain Reefs, 210 km north-east of Rosslyn Bay (see Shoalwater Bay to Fitzroy River area).

About 60 km east of Gladstone are a chain of reefs and islands generally known as the **Capricorn** and **Bunker groups** which include the **Fairfax Islands, Lady Musgrave Island** and **Lady Elliot Island**. There are certain areas around Lady Musgrave and Lady Elliot islands where you are not permitted to fish. Charter boats visit the area regularly. Over the reefs there are red emperor, sweetlip, snapper and cod, and the surrounding waters, according to the season, have Spanish and school mackerel, yellowtail kingfish, trevally, cobia and tuna.

Prawns

There are a number of prawn species in Australia, inhabiting mangrove areas, mud flats, sand channels, sea grass and open waters. They can be collected by dragging the area with a scoop net and are an ideal bait for fish such as bream, whiting, barramundi and mangrove jack.

QUEENSLAND — COASTAL FISHING ROCKHAMPTON REGION

Tannum Sands to Burnett Heads

Type of fishing
beach, estuary, offshore, river, rock
Target fish
bream, flathead, mackerel, whiting, yellowtail kingfish

The **Tannum Sands** area has the largest commercial mud crab operation in Australia. Gigantic specimens inhabit the mangrove swamps. Wild Cattle Creek, which cuts Wild Cattle Island off from the mainland, has barramundi, queenfish, flathead, whiting and mangrove jack. There are also lots of yabbies in the sand spits. Flathead are in the shallow channels, particularly on a receding tide.

The mouth of the **Boyne River** near the caravan park, and the **John Oxley Bridge** over the Boyne River, are best fished on the run-in tide for whiting and flathead using yabby bait. An exposed rock near the ramp within the estuary north of Tannum Sands is excellent for bream, whiting, queenfish and mangrove jack, and an outcrop that is exposed at low tide marks a position for flathead and bream on a run-out tide.

Bustard Head, south-east of Tannum Sands, projects out into deep water and is a natural attractor for pelagics. It is one of the best land-based angling spots on this coast, and also attracts boat anglers launching at either Turkey Beach, around to the west in Rodds Harbour, or the town of Seventeen Seventy to the south-east. Spanish mackerel and schools of spotted mackerel come through in early summer, and there are big numbers of yellowtail kingfish and queenfish in autumn and winter, and giant trevally and cobia in summer. Yellowtail kingfish in the winter and cobia in summer can be attracted in the washes by popper lures, cast from the rock ledges. The area from **Turkey Beach** to **Seventeen Seventy** is very remote and has few facilities. Be well prepared with spare fuel, water, food and shelter. For those who wish to stay overnight, there is an anchorage within Pancake Creek, just west of Clews Point, and another in Round Hill Creek at Seventeen Seventy.

Tranquil waters at Seventeen Seventy

Seventeen Seventy is a base for four-wheel-drive access to the coastal creeks. North of the town, **Middle** and **Eurimbula creeks** are well worth a visit for anglers seeking mangrove jack, flathead, bream and whiting.

At **Round Hill Head**, a little north of Seventeen Seventy, there is good land-based angling for passing pelagics such as Spanish mackerel, spotted mackerel, yellowtail kingfish, queenfish, trevally and cobia.

This area has a number of shallow estuaries and beaches that provide boat or land-based fishing. Boat ramps are all easily reached. In the south are two substantial estuaries, Baffle Creek and the Kolan River. **Baffle Creek** can be fished from a land location or by wading near Winfield, but most fishing is done by boat. The channels, weed and holes provide good habitats for flathead, whiting, spotted javelin fish and bream, with mangrove jack further upriver. The estuary entrances will also yield threadfin salmon, the best sporting fish in the region. There are plenty of yabbies to be pumped, and they are the best bait for the whiting and bream that are prevalent all along this coast. Pilchards are best for the other species. Mud crabs are prolific in all the estuaries and rivers.

The **Burnett River** is the biggest river in the area and has bream and whiting to some 20 km upriver, almost to Bundaberg.

In the Burnett Heads area, at **South Head** there is a protected boat harbour and ramp near the entrance, with launching ramps capable of carrying large boats. The rock walls at the mouth of the river attract a congregation of bream in winter.

Further along the coast, **south of Burnett Heads**, are some good rocky areas

Launching is from the sand at Bargara and a four-wheel drive is mandatory

COASTAL FISHING ROCKHAMPTON REGION

QUEENSLAND

GUIDE TO LOCAL FISH

BD	barramundi
B	bream
CO	cobia
F	flathead
MJ	jack, mangrove
JA	javelin fish
KI	kingfish, yellowtail
MA	mackerel
Q	queenfish
TS	salmon, threadfin
S	snapper
ES	sweetlip
TR	trevally
W	whiting

where snapper, sweetlip and school mackerel can be caught in summer. **Bargara**, a coastal satellite town of Bundaberg, has a sand ramp on the beach, but a four-wheel drive is required. Boat anglers head for **Two Mile Rock** offshore, where they fish for spotted and Spanish mackerel, cobia, trevally and yellowtail kingfish. The **Elliot River** and its estuary, south-east of Bundaberg, can be relied on for whiting, flathead and bream, and there is a ramp at Riverview. Outside the estuary there are inshore reefs, some only a few hundred metres out. Sweetlip, snapper and cod can be found over the reef, and mackerel and trevally in the surrounding waters. A ramp in **Theodolite Creek**, to the north of Woodgate, provides access to the fishing for bream, whiting and spotted javelin fish in the estuary. A ramp at **Woodgate** is exposed to wave action, but boats can launch here in calm weather for an artificial reef just offshore. Mackerel, yellowtail kingfish and cobia can be caught around this reef, while snapper, sweetlip and coral trout can be targeted from over the reef itself.

Mud crab
The mud crab is found in estuarine waters, mangrove areas and mud flats of tropical Queensland, and along the northern coastal reaches of New South Wales. The outer shell turns red during cooking.

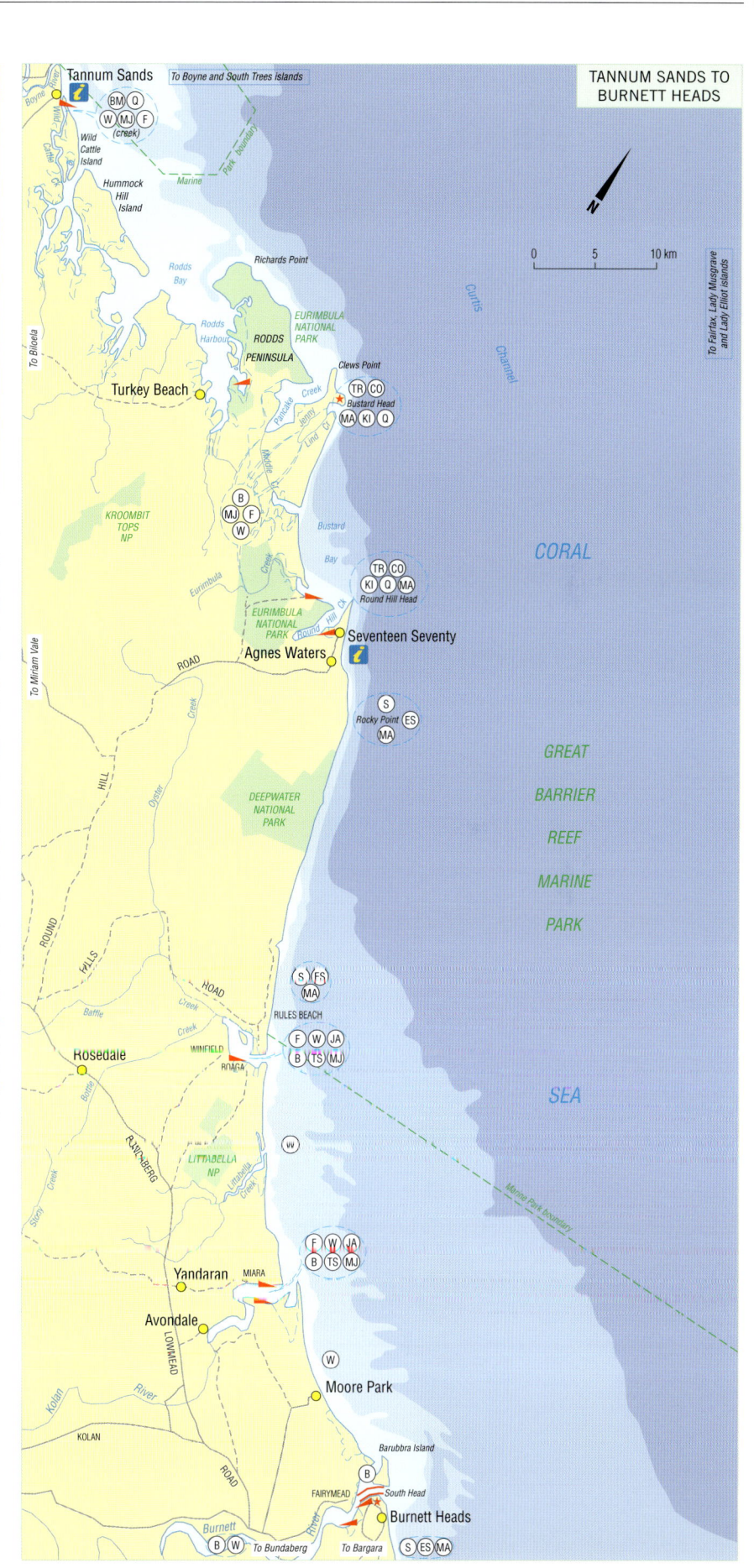

TANNUM SANDS TO BURNETT HEADS

Hervey Bay and Fraser Island

Type of fishing
beach, estuary, pier, reef, river, rock

Target fish
bream, flathead, javelin fish, tailor, threadfin salmon, whiting

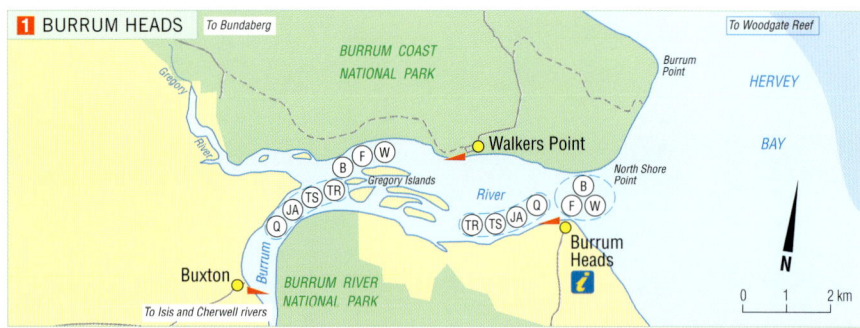

The Hervey Bay and Fraser Island area continues to live up to its reputation as being prolific and safe for virtually every type of fishing. Hervey Bay and the Great Sandy Strait are a boat angler's paradise. Within their relatively safe waters there are large and small islands, tidal flats, mangrove creeks, reefs, sand flats and a vast number of submerged ledges.

The main Hervey Bay fish are large sand whiting, locally referred to as bluenose. They are a prized table fish. Commercial fishing is banned along the beaches of Hervey Bay township, but the fishing is great for recreational anglers. Fishing for Spanish mackerel is banned in Platypus Bay, the eastern area of Hervey Bay, between Rooney Point and Moon Point on Fraser Island. This is due to the high incidence of ciguatera poisoning.

BURRUM HEADS

Burrum Heads is a town on a big sand shallow estuary at the confluence of the Gregory and Burrum rivers, on the south-west coast of Hervey Bay. Like most estuaries in this area, it has extensive sand flats and channels, with plenty of bream, flathead, javelin fish and whiting. There are boat ramps on either side of the estuary and boat anglers can drift for javelin fish, threadfin salmon and trevally around the sands and the **Gregory Islands**. There are yabby banks around the islands that are good for bait gathering. Bank-based anglers can fish from the sand spit, which extends well out from the mouth of the river.

HERVEY BAY TOWNSHIP

Hervey Bay township is situated at the southern end of the bay, at the entrance to Great Sandy Strait. The best spot to fish is the remarkable **Urangan Pier**, at Dayman Point, which fishes well for whiting, particularly in the peak period of spring. The whiting anglers use local bloodworm and yabby baits. They fish the outer gutter at low tide, and as the tide floods in, the fish move into the inner gutter to feed. Land-based anglers can also catch whiting, along with bream, from **Shelly Beach**, the **Urangan Steps**, just west of the Urangan Pier, and the **Great Sandy Strait Marina** walls.

Bait fish – hardyheads, garfish and herring – swarm under the Urangan Pier and attract pelagics. The outer end of the pier is in deep water and the game anglers gather here, baiting up with live herring,

Fishing Hervey Bay for spotted mackerel

GUIDE TO LOCAL FISH

		Burrum Heads	Hervey Bay Township	Fraser Island Area
B	bream	•	•	•
C	cod			•
DA	dart			•
F	flathead	•	•	•
G	garfish			•
MJ	jack, mangrove			•
JA	javelin fish	•		•
MA	mackerel		•	•
MO	morwong		•	•
MU	mulloway		•	•
PF	parrotfish			•
Q	queenfish		•	•
TS	salmon, threadfin	•	•	•
SH	shark		•	•
S	snapper		•	•
ES	sweetlip			•
TR	tailor		•	•
TR	trevally	•	•	•
TU	tuna		•	•
W	whiting	•	•	•

COASTAL FISHING ROCKHAMPTON REGION   QUEENSLAND

to cast for queenfish, school mackerel, Spanish mackerel, trevally and tuna.

The run out to the islands east of the Hervey Bay township requires care at low tide, as the northern entrance to Great Sandy Strait has shallows and sandbanks. Fierce winds can cause dangerous sea conditions, especially if the wind is against the tidal flow, which is very strong.

At the tiny **Round Island**, between Urangan and Big Woody Island, the reef can be fished for parrotfish, sweetlip and snapper. But the main target for boat anglers from Hervey Bay township is **Big Woody Island**, where the best fishing is on the north-eastern side. Reefs here, known as **The Graves**, are fished for reef species such as snapper, sweetlip, morwong, parrotfish and mulloway. A little further to the east there is a big artificial reef, which is a great attraction for the same reef species. Trevally and mackerel are among the pelagics outside the reef.

Between Big Woody Island and Fraser Island is **Little Woody Island**, with reefs on its eastern side, and with a rocky area at its northern tip, attracting flathead, whiting and bream. There are a number of holes and ledges around Little Woody Island, which are also worth exploring.

Yellowfin bream
Often known as silver bream or sea bream, this species inhabits the coastal and estuarine waters of the Queensland coast, south of Townsville.

Boat anglers at Wathumba Creek, on the north west coast of Fraser Island. Whiting, bream and flathead are the main target fish in these waters

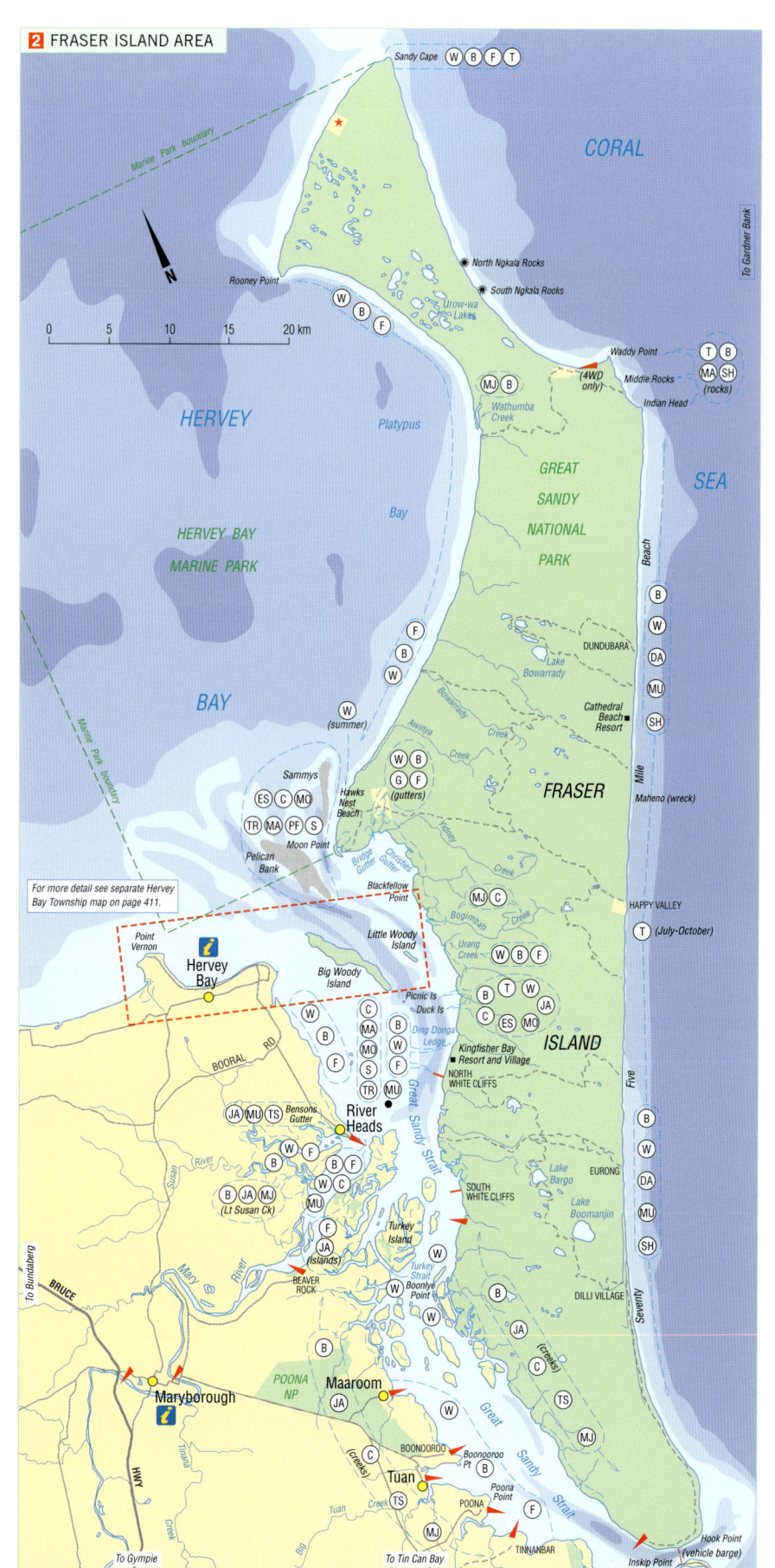

QUEENSLAND
COASTAL FISHING ROCKHAMPTON REGION

FRASER ISLAND AREA

Fraser Island, the largest sand island in the world, is split by creeks that often stream across the beaches in wet periods, creating treacherous conditions for four-wheel-drive vehicles. Generally the beaches are the island's highways, although there are some inland tracks to carry visitors from east to west. Anglers with their four-wheel drives come by ferry, and have over 150 km of ocean beach on the eastern side at their disposal.

Sandy Cape, at the far north-east of the island, is fairly remote, but its beaches fish well for whiting, bream, flathead and tailor. A large part of the north end of Fraser Island has been closed to four-wheel-drive traffic, as part of the land management of the Great Sandy National Park. The restricted area is from Wathumba Creek on the west coast around to the Sandy Cape lighthouse. Keen anglers will have to walk, or get there by boat. There is still vehicle access north of Ngkala Rocks, on the east coast, subject to tides and sea conditions.

At the north end of the Seventy Five Mile Beach there are great rock spots: **Waddy Point, Middle Rocks** and **Indian Head** attract tailor, bream, mackerel and shark. Boat anglers launch into the bay behind Waddy Point to explore the offshore reefs and the **Gardner Bank**, some 15 to 20 km to the east. Queensland Fisheries Service applies a seasonal closure on tailor in certain areas for spawning.

It is the beach fishing on the ocean side of Fraser Island, especially the northern half of the **Seventy Five Mile Beach**, that attracts large numbers of anglers. These beaches are famous for the northern run of tailor between July and October. Anglers patrol the beach in four-wheel drives, looking for good gutter formations and signs of tailor schools – wheeling and diving birds, 'boiling' water and congregations of other anglers casting out, usually with gang-hooked pilchards. Although this time of year sees a frenzy of fishing activity, there is good fishing year round for bream, whiting, dart, mulloway and whaler shark. Sandworms and pippis (known locally as 'eugaries') are abundant for bait along this mighty beach.

The beaches on the **west of Fraser Island**, facing the Great Sandy Strait, are broken by many creeks, and vehicle access is limited. The boat and land-based fishing is wonderful all along the west coast. Four-wheel drives can travel no further north than **Wathumba Creek**, where there is a good camping area with most facilities;

COASTAL FISHING ROCKHAMPTON REGION QUEENSLAND

Anglers casting for tailor at Maheno *wreck, on Fraser Island's famous Seventy Five Mile Beach*

you should check with the barge operator when you arrive on Fraser Island to gauge the state of the beach between Moon Point and Wathumba. It is worth the long trip to Wathumba for the beach fishing, but all the coast between Rooney Point and Moon Point can yield whiting, bream and flathead. Spanish mackerel caught in this area, however, must not be eaten, because of the risk of ciguatera poisoning. There are good campsites beside Awinya and Bowarrady creeks and plenty of yabby patches for bait along the entire coast.

Hawks Nest Beach, just north of Moon Point, has great fishing for sand whiting. The reefs (**Pelican Bank and Sammys**) and ledges around **Moon Point** have to be fished by boat. They are heavily fished for sweetlip, cod, morwong, parrotfish, snapper and other reef species. **Bridge Gutter** and **Christies Gutter**, out from the mouth of Yidney Creek, yield whiting, bream and flathead. You can also fish these gutters by wading from the shore of Fraser Island.

Directly east of Little Woody Island, some of the best land-based fishing spots are **Bogimbah Creek**, which has mangrove jack and cod, and **Urang Creek**, with whiting, bream and flathead the possible catches from the banks near the sea.

South of the Big Woody Island, near the Kingfisher Bay Resort and Village, **North White Cliffs** jetty is good for bream, whiting and flathead, and **Ding Donga Ledge**, is ideal for the same fish from the beach.

The main north–south channel of Great Sandy Strait is well marked with port and starboard beacons. On both sides of the narrowing strait there are fascinating mangrove-lined creeks, the domain of bream, javelin fish, cod and threadfin salmon. There is always the chance, too, of catching the more elusive mangrove jack.

Dotted along this coast are the small settlements of **Tinnanbar, Poona, Tuan, Boonooroo** and **Maaroom**, which all have boat ramps. The target fish in the channels next to the sandbanks is whiting, and they share the water with bream and flathead. Some of the best whiting fishing is at **Poona Point, Boonooroo Point**, in the channels around **Boonlye Point**, and the southern end of **Turkey Strait**, which is to the west of **Turkey Island**, but all sandbanks with flowing water at their edge are good prospects.

The middle section of Great Sandy Strait is studded with mangrove-covered islands and mudflats, and has a tidal range of over 3 m on the spring tides. This has a significant effect on the one true estuary in the Hervey Bay system, that of the **Mary River** and its tributaries. The Mary River has a huge estuary, which is supplemented by the much smaller Susan River. The estuary breaks into mangrove creeks, with sand flats and islands, creating recognisable fishing places but also creating navigating difficulties. If anglers lose track of time and tide, there is the possibility of being stranded high and dry. The estuary has bream, cod, flathead and whiting at its entrance, near the boat ramp and ferry landing at **River Heads**. You will only need to move the boat a few yards from the ramp to get to some prime fishing water, between the ramp and the beacon in the middle of the river. There is a hole here, close to the low-water mark, that carries big mulloway.

The **Susan River** branches north from the Mary just inside the entrance and winds through islands and sand flats, which provide ideal conditions for bream, flathead and whiting. At the point of convergence with the first creek, **Bensons Gutter**, there is good fishing for javelin fish, mulloway and threadfin salmon. **Little Susan Creek**, a narrow, mangrove-lined waterway joining the Mary and Susan rivers, can be fished along its length for bream, javelin fish and mangrove jack.

Mangrove-covered islands in the Mary River create stations for flathead and javelin fish. They can be easily reached from a boat ramp at Beaver Rock, on the south side of the river.

Channels that run through a maze of sandbanks and low mangrove islands are the norm from **River Heads township to Hervey Bay**, and they can be drifted for bream, flathead and whiting, with a possible diversion for catching sand crabs or yabbies for bait.

The waters between River Heads and Big Woody Island can be trolled or drifted for mackerel and trevally. Banks around **Picnic Island** and **Duck Island** can be explored for bream, school tailor, whiting and javelin fish. Reef fish like cod, sweetlip and morwong are also around the islands.

413

QUEENSLAND

Inland Fishing

Inland fishing in Queensland is concentrated in a number of areas, many situated vast distances from population centres, but offering great variety to those willing to make the trip. There are the tropical coastal rivers of the north; the northern lakes, dams, pools and flood plains; the temperate rivers and impoundments of the south (below a line west from Rockhampton); and the slow, turbid rivers that flow from the western slopes of the Great Dividing Range towards the centre of Australia.

One of the best times to fish the northern rivers is after the Wet, when the rivers are still running hard but falling. In these conditions it is necessary to have good anchoring equipment to hold station against the flow. Other than at this time of the year, the rivers and the many well-stocked lakes and dams are generally tranquil.

A useful item of equipment, if you are to get the best of the inland waters, is a boat. Large and powerful rigs are not really suitable, however, as the main requirements for an inland boat are portability and manoeuvrability. Northern anglers should also be equipped with a four-wheel drive vehicle.

WHERE TO FISH

Inland

NORTHERN REGION ● 416

There are literally hundreds of rivers running to the coast north of Mackay, and nearly all of them provide superb inland fishing for species such as sooty grunter, jungle perch and barramundi. The isolated rivers of the Cape York's west coast are just as productive, with the spectacular scenery adding further incentive for those attempting the long journey.

SOUTHERN REGION ● 418

Up until twenty years ago the inland fishing in the south of the State was limited, but with the introduction of stocked impoundments a welcome regeneration has taken place. Anglers can now fish the dams and lakes, as well as the rivers, for a large variety of southern and northern species, and not be disappointed.

ABORIGINAL LANDS

There are areas of Aboriginal land throughout the State that are managed by different resident communities, and rules about access vary greatly. The roads are in most cases public and therefore open to general use, but visitors wishing to fish and camp should first seek permission from the relevant body. The Cape York Land Council, tel. (07) 4053 9222, is a good place to start for initial inquiries. Several groups (listed below) have begun to make provisions to accommodate the growing influx of tourists to this remote region.

Wellesley Island Group Apart from Sweers Island, the whole of the Wellesley Island Group is Aboriginal land. Visitors are welcome provided they stay at the Birri Fishing Resort on Mornington Island, tel. (07) 4745 7277.

Kowanyama Kowanyama is open to limited recreational fishing and an active management plan ensures that the fishing resources are carefully maintained. There are camping sites available for a small fee and permission to visit should be sought in advance, tel. (07) 4060 5155.

Mapoon Visitors can camp at designated spots along the coast at Mapoon. Camping fees apply and permits can be obtained directly from the council office at Red Beach, tel. (07) 4090 9124.

Injinoo The Injinoo community controls areas of land from the Jardine River north to the tip of the Cape. It also manages the Jardine River ferry, which for most people provides the only road access. Visitors pay $80.00 return per car and there are no other camping fees or permits required. For information contact the Injinoo Community Council, tel. (07) 4069 3252.

INLAND FISHING

QUEENSLAND

Inland fishing: Kalpowar Crossing on the Normanby River, north-west of Cooktown

State regulations

A recreational licence is not required for freshwater fishing in Queensland however, there is a schedule of 17 impoundments that are covered by a user-pays 'Stocked Impoundment Permit'. Permits can be purchased at any Post Office and cost $7 a week/$35 a year. Funds raised from the sale of permits are returned to the fishery in the form of fingerlings, ensuring improving fishing in the future.

Declared noxious species, such as carp and tilapia must be destroyed and not returned to the water.

Lungfish are a fully protected species in Queensland, as are Mary River cod in their natural habitat of the Mary River catchment.

Closed seasons apply for several species, including Australian bass and barramundi. Minimum size limits and bag limits also apply for most popular freshwater fish. Protected or undersized fish that are caught must be returned to the water immediately. You can obtain a brochure covering Queensland freshwater regulations at most tackle stores or by calling the Queensland Fisheries Service on 13 2523.

Licensing and registration are compulsory for certain operators and vessels. A minimum level of safety equipment is also mandatory. For details, contact 13 2380.

Exercise care on inland waters as there may be hazards, such as tree stumps just below the surface, and crocodiles in the northern rivers. The water levels in dams and impoundments in Queensland can get very low during drought seasons.

GUIDE TO LOCAL FISH

- archer fish
- barramundi
- bass, Australian
- catfish, eel-tailed
- catfish, fork-tailed
- cod, Murray
- cod, sleepy
- eel, long-finned
- eel, short finned
- garfish, northern
- grunter, leathery
- grunter, sooty
- herring, oxeye
- long tom, freshwater
- jack, mangrove
- perch, golden
- perch, jungle
- perch, silver
- saratoga, northern
- saratoga, southern
- sawfish
- shark

Protected species

Ceratodus, also known as lungfish, is a fully protected species throughout Queensland.

Mary River cod is a protected species, but there are special rules in relation to the taking of Mary River cod in some areas. The details of those rules can be found in the *Fisheries Regulation 1995* or the 'Guidelines for Recreational Fishing in Queensland'.

FURTHER INFORMATION

Fishing & boating The head office of the Queensland Boating and Fisheries Patrol is on the 2nd floor, 80 Ann St, Brisbane, tel. 13 2523 or (07) 3224 2282, and its Brisbane Operations Base is at MacArthur Ave East, Pinkenba, tel. (07) 3860 3506. There are a number of offices throughout the State. The main offices concerned with inland areas are at cnr Bowen St and Spencer St, Roma, tel. (07) 4622 9920; Landsborough Hwy, Longreach, tel. (07) 4658 4400; Yeppoon Rd, Rockhampton, tel. (07) 4936 0211; 64–66 Tingira St, Cairns, tel. (07) 4052 7404; and The Point, Karumba, tel. (07) 4745 9142. The Boating Registration and Licensing Hotline is 13 1477.

The Queensland Fisheries Service is located on the 2nd floor, 80 Ann St, Brisbane, tel. 13 2523. The Service publishes 'Guidelines for Recreational Fishing in Queensland', a pamphlet on recreational fishing in the State listing all regulations for tidal and non-tidal waters which can be obtained from Queensland Boating and Fisheries Patrol offices, some bait and tackle shops and marine dealers.

Queensland Transport controls recreational boating and can provide information on boating safety. It publishes a boating safety handbook, and various marine safety brochures. Contact the Maritime Division head office, tel. (07) 3860 3500, or the Boating Registration and Licensing Hotline, tel. 13 2380.

Tourist centres Old Post Office Gallery, Herberton Rd, Atherton, tel. (07) 4091 4222; Boulia Library and Information Centre, Herbert St, Boulia, tel. (07) 4746 3386; cnr Bourbong St and Mulgrave St, Bundaberg, tel. (07) 4152 2333; Burke Shire Council, Musgrave St, Burketown, tel. (07) 4745 5100; Graeme Andrews Parkland, Charleville, tel. (07) 4654 3057; Mosman St, Charters Towers, tel. (07) 4752 0314; Pharmaceutical Museum, Churchill St, Childers, tel. (07) 4126 1994; Mary Kathleen Memorial Park, Cloncurry, tel. (07) 4742 1361; Centenary Park, Cunnamulla, tel. (07) 4655 2481; Thomas Jack Park, Drayton St, Dalby, tel. (07) 4662 1066; Claremont St, Emerald, tel. (07) 4982 4142; McLean St, Goondiwindi, tel. (07) 4671 2653; Gray St, Hughenden, tel. (07) 4741 1021; Shire Offices, Julia St, Julia Creek, tel. (07) 4746 7166; South Burnett Visitor Information Centre, Haly St, Kingaroy, tel. (07) 4162 3199; Qantas Park, Eagle St, Longreach, tel. (07) 4658 3555; Riversleigh Fossils Centre, Marion St, Mount Isa, tel. (07) 4749 1555; Shire Offices, cnr Haig St and Landsborough St, Normanton, tel. (07) 4745 1166; cnr Goldring St & Flinders Hwy, Richmond, tel. (07) 4741 3429; Ruthven St, Toowoomba, tel. (07) 4639 3797.

Northern Region

Most freshwater fishing in the north requires a lot of planning. The fishing water can often be in a distant location, where there are few amenities like general stores, motels, service stations and bait and tackle shops. Mostly it is boat fishing country, with land-based angling limited to places like bridges and river crossings, or near towns and camp sites.

Type of fishing
lagoon, lake, river

Target fish
archer fish, barramundi, catfish, jungle perch, saratoga, sooty grunter

The northern angler should be equipped with a four-wheel-drive vehicle, a trailer boat or a car topper, camping gear, spare parts for the vehicle, and a good supply of lures, hooks, rods, reels, spools of line and other fishing equipment. The fish are usually bigger than in the south, so tougher tackle is required.

The Cape York Peninsula has some superb stretches of inland water all the way up the western Gulf coast – rivers such as the **Jardine, Wenlock, Watson and Coen**, the **Mitchell and its tributaries**, and the **Staaten–Wyabba complex**. This area also has, after the Wet, chains of lagoons and flooded wetlands that can be explored by boat. Bank fishing spots can also be found along these waterways.

The most targeted fish is the freshwater barramundi, darker in colour than its saltwater counterpart. It is likely to be located in the same sort of places as other freshwater fish: near objects like fallen trees, rocks, weedy banks and around snags and lily pads. It tends to feed in the early morning and at dusk, and to lie low during the day.

Other northern fish are the northern saratoga, sooty grunter, archer fish, the fork-tailed catfish and jungle perch. Mangrove jack and oxeye herring also move well up into the freshwater zone, and incidental catches include freshwater long tom, long-finned eel, shark and sawfish.

GUIDE TO LOCAL FISH

- archer fish
- barramundi
- catfish, eel-tailed
- catfish, fork-tailed
- eel, long-finned
- grunter, sooty
- herring, oxeye
- jack, mangrove
- long tom, freshwater
- perch, jungle
- saratoga, northern
- sawfish
- shark

The eating quality of all these fish is determined by their environment. Fish living in lagoons and swamps and under rainforest canopies are likely to have a 'muddy' taste compared to those inhabiting clear sand and gravel-bottom rivers and streams.

Flowing into Princess Charlotte Bay, on the north-east coast, are the **Morehead, Kennedy** and **Normanby rivers**, all with stretches of fresh water. Some of the most accessible freshwater lagoons are in Lakefield National Park, close to roads and tracks. North of the great fishing area of Kalpowar Crossing are **Blue Lagoon**, the **Whiphandle waterholes** and the **White Lily** and **Red Lily lagoons**. From Kalpowar south to Laura are **Catfish Waterhole, Kennedy Bend Waterhole, Eight Mile Lagoon** and **Six Mile Waterhole**.

The rivers that run into the south-east corner of the Gulf of Carpentaria, such as the **Norman, Bynoe, Flinders, Leichhardt, Gregory and Nicholson**, flow through mangrove swamps near the coast and through flat lands, which become virtually impassable in the Wet, but are veined with rivers, creeks and lagoons after the Wet, the best time for fishing.

The rivers on the more settled eastern coast, from around Mossman to Mackay, are better suited to the land-based angler, who can find a shore location or wade upstream in some rivers, searching for barramundi, archer fish, catfish, sooty grunter and jungle perch. Rivers here include the **Daintree, Russell, North Johnstone, South Johnstone** and **Tully rivers**, all of which are quite short.

South-west of Cairns on the Atherton Tableland, **Lake Tinaroo** and **Lake Koombooloomba** have excellent fishing for world record class barramundi, and sensational fishing for the big inland fighter, sooty grunter. Lake Tinaroo's barramundi are exempt from closed seasons and maximum size limits when processed through the tagging stations on-site.

Light tackle lure fishing is popular in freshwater regions

INLAND FISHING NORTHERN REGION — QUEENSLAND

The **Burdekin** is a big river, if only when it flows during the annual rains. It runs through flat and dry country, and sooty grunter, archer fish and eel-tailed catfish are the main targets for anglers. **Lake Dalrymple**, the storage area of the Burdekin Falls Dam on the Burdekin River, holds a natural population of sooty grunter, and is stocked with barramundi.

To the west of the region, near Mount Isa, **Lake Moondarra** has sooty grunter. There is fishing for this same fish at **Lake Julius**, to the north, and camping facilities near the lake.

Fishing one of the many rainforest streams, Cape York

QUEENSLAND

INLAND FISHING SOUTHERN REGION

Southern Region

The southerly coastal areas carry the fish of more temperate waters and are much more accessible to the land-based angler than the northern streams. However, a boat will generally make fishing easier and will yield better results.

Type of fishing
dam, lake, river

Target fish
Australian bass, golden perch, Murray cod, silver perch

South of Mackay, barramundi and mangrove jack become less prevalent in the freshwater stretches of the coastal rivers, and are replaced by southern saratoga, silver perch, northern garfish (also known as snub-nosed garfish), Australian bass and Mary River cod. Long-finned eels are found throughout the eastern coastal rivers, while short-finned eels are concentrated in the far south-east of the State.

The southern saratoga, like its northern cousin, is a great sportfish, usually feeding close to the surface. It is highly susceptible to lures, particularly the noisy poppers. It is found most often in the **Fitzroy–Dawson river complex**, which enters the sea at Rockhampton. Further south, some impoundments on the **Mary** and **Brisbane rivers** have been stocked with small numbers of saratoga, but of these, only Lake Borumba and Cania Reservoir provide good fishing for this species.

Bass are in inland waters **south of Hervey Bay**. Some of the best streams are those behind the Sunshine Coast (the upper reaches of the **Noosa River** are considered the best bass waters in the State) and those flowing into the Pumicestone Passage, between Bribie Island and the mainland. In the lower freshwater reaches, the northern garfish is prevalent and best fished around weed beds. It takes small insect or shrimp baits from the surface.

The waterways of the inland, such as the **Condamine, Maranoa, Warrego, Barcoo and Thomson rivers and Cooper Creek**, are generally slow moving. Often these waters dry into strings of waterholes, but occasionally they flow strongly, and once in a while they flood. Most commonly, however, they are mud-coloured and placid. Baitfishing is the predominant method in these less than clear waters. Bank-based anglers often throw in a yabby, frog or worm bait in the 'set and forget' method, while they enjoy a snooze or a picnic under the trees.

The staple fish of the Condamine, Maranoa and Warrego rivers are Murray cod, golden perch (yellowbelly) and eel-tailed catfish. The catfish is a bottom feeder and responds more to baits than lures. It was once despised for its ugly appearance and poisonous spines, but has come to be known as a fine table fish. Silver perch is found mostly in running water, feeding in mid-water.

The big development for Queensland anglers has been the growth of the number of impoundments – dams, reservoirs and lakes – into which fish have been released. These have been stocked with a variety of species such as silver perch, southern saratoga, bass, golden perch and Murray cod,

Australian bass thrive in Queensland's southern impoundments

Australian bass
In Queensland, this native fish naturally inhabits the freshwater reaches of rivers in the south-east of the State. It has recently been established in freshwater dams through artificial stocking and grows to 4 kg.

while eel-tailed catfish and spangled perch occur naturally. Check to ensure that you have the correct boating and/or Stocked Impoundment Permit before fishing.

Lake Maraboon, south-west of Emerald, has both southern and northern fish species, with Murray cod and golden perch fishing well alongside the more tropical varieties such as leathery grunter, and eel-tailed catfish. South-east towards Bundaberg, **Cania Reservoir** and **Lake Monduran** are well set up with facilities for camping anglers. Cania has superb fishing for bass, silver perch and saratoga.

Boondooma Reservoir and **Bjelke-Petersen Dam** are both within an hour's drive of the township of Kingaroy. Facilities are available at both dams and the fishing is for bass, and golden perch that come in at around the 4-kg mark. **Lake Awoonga** is the Gladstone water storage and has been

GUIDE TO LOCAL FISH

barramundi
bass, Australian
catfish, eel-tailed
catfish, fork-tailed
cod, Mary River
cod, Murray
eel, long-finned
eel, short-finned
garfish, northern
grunter, leathery
grunter, sooty
jack, mangrove
perch, golden
perch, silver
perch, spangled
saratoga, southern

INLAND FISHING SOUTHERN REGION QUEENSLAND

The muddy waters of the Barcoo River (part of the Eyre River system) can yield catfish and golden perch

well stocked with barramundi. The lake also has a big population of fork-tailed catfish that can plague anglers. Camping and restaurant facilities are available.

Lake Somerset and **Lake Wivenhoe** are water supply dams for the city of Brisbane with great fishing and facilities. Golden and silver perch and bass feature strongly, along with an enormous population of fork-tailed catfish. Combustion motors are not allowed on Wivenhoe, while Somerset is open to all forms of propulsion after a South-East Queensland Water Co. permit is purchased on site.

Cressbrook Dam and **Cooby Creek Reservoir** near Toowoomba are another two water supply areas. Both produce good quantities of cod and silver and golden perch, but both are subject to boating regulations, which visiting anglers need to be aware of (information boards at public ramps outline details). Experts predict an excellent future for these places, particularly Cressbrook.

South of Brisbane, and heading west, there are a series of lakes offering mixed prospects. **Advancetown Lake** (electric only), **Lake Maroon** and **Lake Moogerah** all have good fishing for bass and golden perch. **Glen Lyon Dam**, on the border of New South Wales, is renowned for its attractive and well-maintained camping area. A user-pays permit must be obtained before fishing.

419

IDENTIFYING YOUR CATCH

IDENTIFYING YOUR CATCH

FISH	LOCATION/DESCRIPTION	FISHING METHOD
ALBACORE *Thunnus alalunga* *Also known as longfin tuna.*	Found in offshore waters and usually in schools, the albacore is recognised by its exceptionally long pectoral fins, which extend well beyond the second dorsal. Although it can grow to 40 kg, it is commonly captured at 2 to 5 kg. The fish is irridescent blue along the top with a silvery belly. It is prized for its fight, particularly when encountered in a large school. Its table quality is also excellent, the meat being almost white when cooked, whereas the meat of other tunas is mostly red and oily.	This fish is mostly caught by trolling or jigging with lures, live baiting with yellowtail or slimy mackerel, or drift fishing with berley and bait of cubed fish flesh. It inhabits the warm ocean currents in waters well offshore.
BARRACOUTA *Thyrsites atun* *Also known as axehandle, couta, pickhandle.*	The barracouta is a pelagic, schooling, cold-water fish. When caught in warmer waters it is rarely good eating because of parasitic worms and 'milky' flesh, but it is a regularly sold commercial species in Australia's south. This long, slender fish is fast and voracious but even a 1.5 m specimen will not weigh much more than 5 or 6 kg. It is blue-black on top, fading down the sides to a silvery belly. The black dorsal fin is long and low, and the protruding jaws are lined with large, needle-sharp teeth.	Barracouta will bite anything (a piece of red or white rag, even a bare shiny hook), but is usually fished by trolling or casting with whitebait, bacon rind, fish strips, or a variety of lures. A trace is necessary because of its teeth.
BARRACUDA *Sphyraena barracuda* *Also known as cuda, dingo fish.*	The barracuda inhabits tropical estuaries and creeks as juveniles, and beaches and reefs as adults. It has a generally silver body, sometimes with brown bands and with distinct spots toward the tail. Its teeth are large and dagger-like, and it can attain 1.7 m and some 25 kg. Handling a well-toothed fish of this size requires care and common sense. No kitchen prizes here, particularly as the bigger fish are known to be linked with cases of ciguatera poisoning (when caught off the east coast). Even the small fish are best returned and not eaten.	This fish is mostly caught incidentally, because its food value is low and its fight, while brutal, is of only short duration. A wire trace can save lures too expensive to lose, while heavy mono will suffice for bait fishing when the only loss is likely to be a hook and sinker.
BARRAMUNDI *Lates calcarifer* *Also known as barra, giant perch.*	One of Australia's favourite fish, the barramundi is a respected angling opponent and good eating. Reportedly reaching 1.5 m and 50 kg, the majority caught weigh less than 6 kg. It travels from fresh to salt water to spawn and, while in salt water, is silvery and bronze. Landlocked fish are generally darker, they don't fight as well, and their table quality is inferior. Almost all barramundi less than 5 years of age are male and some become female at a certain size, so large fish are vitally important brood stock.	Barramundi respond best to live bait or lures, but will also take well-presented strip baits. Line sizes from 4 to 10 kg are appropriate and boat fishing, either trolling or casting, is the most favoured method.
BASS, AUSTRALIAN *Macquaria novemaculata* *Also known as bass, perch.*	This native freshwater fish hits lures and baits with an aggression out of proportion to its size, and it fights hard when hooked. It naturally inhabits southern and eastern coastal freshwater and estuarine river systems, but has recently also been established in freshwater dams and impoundments through artificial stocking. Bass prey on insects, shrimp, small fish, frogs and earthworms, and favour snaggy corners and bank sides strewn with logs, reeds and boulders. They require brackish water to spawn in late winter.	Anglers now fish for bass with lures instead of baits. Lures work just as well, are more fun to fish with, and suit catch and release fishing. Trolling and lure casting work well in both rivers and impoundments. As a sportfish, bass is usually released on capture.

IDENTIFYING YOUR CATCH

FISH	LOCATION/DESCRIPTION	FISHING METHOD

BLACKFISH, ROCK
Girella elevata

Also known as black drummer, blackfish, pig.

The rock blackfish grows to around 8 kg, but the most common catch ranges from 1 to 2 kg. It is a dark, rotund, small-mouthed herbivorous species with the occasional urge to eat meat, and with the ability to romp happily in rocky water rough enough to smash lesser fish to a pulp. It is found all along the east coast of Australia from Noosa Heads in Queensland to Victoria, but not in western Victoria or South Australia. Its western relative, *G. tephraeops*, is found on coastal reefs of south-western Western Australia.

Serious rock blackfish anglers use stout rods, sidecast reels and line from 10 to 20 kg. Bobby corks help to minimise tackle losses, and hooks should be double or triple X strong in sizes from #1 to 2/0.

BONITO
Sarda australis

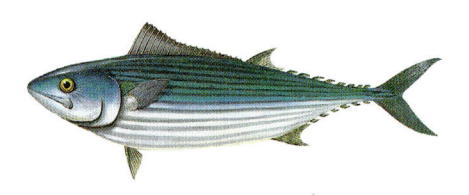

Also known as bonnie, horse mackerel, horsie.

Found in coastal waters of New South Wales, southern Queensland and southern Western Australia, this member of the tuna family has horizontal dark stripes on its back and sides, differing from the similar oriental bonito (*S. orientalis*), a west coast species, striped only on its upper half. Another species, Watson's leaping bonito (*Cybiosarda elegans*), is found in east coast waters and is characterised by a high dorsal fin, belly stripes and broken wavy markings from shoulder to tail on its back.

Strip baits or small live fish can be used, but bonito is best caught by trolling or casting with lures: usually small chromed metal slices, swimming minnows or saltwater flies. Top time is dawn. Bonito frequent wash areas of headlands and inshore islands.

BREAM, BLACK
Acanthropagrus butcheri

Also known as southern black bream, southern bream.

Black bream is the most commonly found member of this family in southern waters. It favours estuaries and inshore waters where it feeds on various marine worms, crustacea, shellfish, juvenile molluscs and fin-fish. Anglers can expect to catch a few good-sized examples of this fine table fish in any southern estuary. Its body colour varies between dull gold and silvery olive-brown. Similar in colouration but of different body shape, the pikey bream (*A. berda*), is found only in the tropics.

Light lines from 2 to 6 kg, depending on terrain, and baits of worms, nippers or even tuna strips are best. Black bream (and pikey bream) will also attack small lures if they are accurately cast and worked close to structures where these fish lie in wait.

BREAM, YELLOWFIN
Acanthropagrus australis

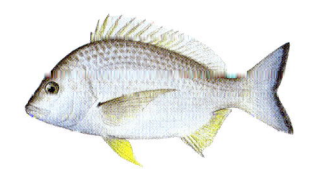

Also known as eastern black bream, sea bream, silver bream, surf bream.

Yellowfin bream has a much narrower geographical range than black bream. This handsome silver fish has bright to dull yellow pelvic and anal fins. The head is more sharply pointed than the black bream and the clear to yellowish tail has a distinct black trailing edge. It inhabits surf beaches as well as estuaries in northern and central New South Wales, and Queensland. In common with other members of the bream family, it becomes extremely cunning as it matures. It is a popular table fish.

Popular baits include live nippers, live or dead crabs, prawns, shrimp, live marine worms, strip baits of fish flesh, squid or octopus or whole pippis or other shellfish. Yellowfin bream will also take small lures.

CARP, EUROPEAN
Cyprinus carpio

Also known as common carp.

This fish is extremely widespread, from the sub-tropics to the alpine regions of Victoria, New South Wales and, recently, Tasmania. Of the various imported species of fish introduced into Australian waters, carp is considered the greatest pest. It is neither a good table fish nor a good sportfish, and it threatens the habitat of many native species. Its feeding techniques stir up silt, which reduces the oxygen output of native aquatic plants and smothers the eggs of trout and native fish. Popular with some anglers but certainly not all.

Carp respond to berleying and fishing with baits of maggots, sweet corn, dough, bardi grubs or scrubworms. Fisheries regulations in enlightened States require that once caught, carp should never be put back.

IDENTIFYING YOUR CATCH

FISH	LOCATION/DESCRIPTION	FISHING METHOD

CATFISH, EEL-TAILED
Tandanus tandanus

Also known as dewfish, freshwater catfish, kenaru, freshwater jewfish.

Eel-tailed catfish occur in various forms; the *Tandanus* species is found throughout the inland and coastal freshwater of much of south and eastern Australia. It has thrived in many water supply impoundments. This species is usually mottled grey to russet brown and averages 1 to 2 kg. Like many catfish, the dorsal and pectoral spines can inflict nasty wounds. It needs careful handling when brought in. Despite its appearance, the catfish is considered by some to be a prize table fish, once the skin has been peeled away.

Catfish is not generally caught on lure or fly. It is more usually targeted with baits of peeled crayfish tail, a bunch of worms or bardi grub. Fish these baits on light line with a running sinker rig over a shelving soft bottom, especially at night.

CATFISH, FORK-TAILED
Arius leptaspis

Also known as croaker, salmon catfish.

Fork-tailed catfish are collectively referred to as salmon catfish, and common among several species are: the one illustrated here, *Arius leptaspis*, the blue (*A. graffei*), the threadfin (*A. armiger*), the lesser salmon catfish (*A. berneyi*) and the small-mouthed salmon catfish (*Cinetodus froggatti*). They are all freshwater, estuarine or marine fish and inhabit tropical waters. The fork-tailed catfish can change its body colour to suit its environment. The males of some species hold the eggs in their mouths.

Essentially a bottom feeder, this species will take most fish flesh baits and can also be taken on lures. It will often take lures intended for other fish, such as barramundi. Line from 4 to 6 kg and a medium weight baitcaster or threadline outfit is ideal.

COBIA
Rachycentron canadus

Also known as black king, black kingfish, cobe, crab-eater, ling, sergeant fish.

The cobia is a handsome game fish, found in oceanic waters from temperate to sub-tropical climes. It frequents areas around navigation beacons, deepwater wharves, headlands, offshore islands and over reefs. It is blackish-brown with a creamy stripe along its sides, and its streamlined shape can lead anglers to mistakenly identify it as a shark. Growing to over 50 kg and being common between 10 and 20 kg, cobia is recognised as one of the toughest fighting fish in Australian waters.

Cobia is taken by trolling, jigging or casting lures toward washes and island corners, drifting live baits over reefs or from ocean rock locations. Lines should be around 10 to 15, or even up to 24 kg. Traces of 40 to 60-kg nylon will suffice.

COD, ESTUARY
Epinephelus coioides

Also known as brown-spotted rock cod, greasy cod, north-west groper.

In Australia the name 'cod' has been given indiscriminately to a large number of fish including members of the Serranidae family. This family has a number of species, including estuary cod (*E. coioides*), the most common at around 2 to 4 kg, but growing in excess of 50 kg. Others include the black cod (*E. damelli*), the Queensland groper (*E. lanceolatus*) and the potato cod (*E. tukula*). In New South Wales, estuary cod, black cod and Queensland groper are all totally protected.

Cod are common captures in tidal creeks, large inshore bays, and around some headlands and island groups. A short trace of heavy nylon or wire is advisable.

COD, MURRAY
Maccullochella peeli peeli

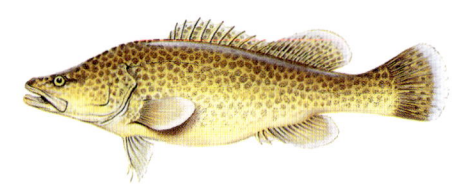

Also known as goodoo, Murray, codfish.

Considered to be the largest and most famous native freshwater table fish (although those caught by anglers usually average from 6 to 8 kg), the Murray cod is actually found well beyond the confines of the Murray River, being distributed throughout the Murray–Darling Basin. It has also been stocked in many popular impoundments and now has a wide distribution through Queensland, New South Wales and Victoria. Related species include the protected trout cod, the Clarence River cod, the Mary River cod and the protected eastern cod.

Cod will take lures, flies and baits. Tackle should be 4 to 10 kg depending on the terrain; in the Murray River, where the fish are big, 15 kg is not too heavy. They can be taken by trolling or casting lures, bottom fishing or 'bobbing' baits of bardi grub, worms or crayfish.

IDENTIFYING YOUR CATCH

FISH	LOCATION/DESCRIPTION	FISHING METHOD
DART, SWALLOWTAIL *Trachinotus coppingeri* *Also known as billy lids, dart, surf trevally.*	A thin, deep-bodied and agile fish, the swallowtail dart is commonly found along surf beaches swimming among the waves with great speed and dexterity. It will snatch at baits, but when hooked, will hang out there with tenacity beyond its size. A relative, the common dart *(T. botla)*, is found in Western Australia and a smaller, spotted east coast cousin, the black-spotted dart *(T. bailloni)*, has a distribution that overlaps that of the swallowtail.	Dart will take beachworm and pippi baits, or thin strips of fish flesh, and even small lures on occasion. Light beach rods with 3 to 7-kg line are suitable. Cast towards any deep holes adjacent to broken water and move the bait or lure steadily.
DOLPHIN FISH *Coryphaena hippurus* *Also known as dollies, dorado, Mahi Mahi.*	The dolphin fish, not related to the mammalian dolphin, is one of the most beautiful species of fish; its colours vary from blue to green, and silver to gold. Its dorsal fin stretches from the top of the head to the tail butt, and it has tremendous speed and agility. Preferring warmer waters, it is found northward from New South Wales in the east and from Bunbury in the west. The average size of this species is 2 to 5 kg, but may exceed 25 kg.	Dolphin fish tend to school near reefs, or fish aggregating devices such as fish trap buoys, floating objects like rafts, weed, logs or even a length of rope. Troll or cast lures or whole fish baits so they travel past such 'habitats'.
DORY, JOHN *Zeus faber* *Also known as St. Peter's fish, dories, johnnies.*	The john dory visits central New South Wales estuaries each winter and becomes an inshore angling target. The related mirror dory *(Zenopsis nebulosus)* and silver dory *(Cyttus australis)* are only obtained by commercial deep trawling. Aside from its habit of taking inshore winter holidays, the john dory can be distinguished from its relatives by a dark 'thumbprint' either side of its body and by the long spines on its dorsal fin. It is one of Australia's best table fish.	Squid strips, fish flesh or live prawns are good, but the best bait is a small live yellowtail with its tail fin clipped, and suspended under a float on a sharp 3/0 or 4/0 suicide hook. A take is indicated by the float moving out and down steadily.
DRUMMER, SILVER *Kyphosus sydneyanus* *Also known as buffalo bream.*	The silver drummer *(K. sydneyanus)* is a streamlined fish with a dull metallic hue. Often caught from ocean rocks in rough seas, it is quite a brawler when hooked. The popularity of this tough tenacious fighter relates to its fighting qualities rather than its table quality. It has relatives such as the western buffalo bream *(K. cornelii)* and low-finned drummer *(K. vaigiensis)*. The silver drummer is very popular in South Australia.	The silver drummer is found around reefs and rocky shores, and hence the need to avoid snags and to prevent the fish reaching rocky hideaways when making its run. It is best fished for with a paternoster rig using baits of bread, cunjevoi and abalone gut.
EEL, SHORT-FINNED *Anguilla australis* *Also known as freshwater eel, silver eel.*	A freshwater species that migrates to salt water to spawn, the short-finned eel is common in dams, swamps, rivers and estuaries throughout much of eastern Australia, including Tasmania, and extending offshore to Lord Howe and Norfolk islands, and New Zealand. Olive-green to brown in colour, it grows in excess of 6 kg and over 1 m in length. This eel will eat almost anything that presents itself, whether alive or dead, but is essentially carnivorous.	Baitfishing with fish strips, worms or bardi grubs is best. Hooks can be 1/0 to 2/0, rigged with a small running sinker. Use 4 to 6-kg line or risk having the line broken by the eel's vigorous struggles, particularly when it is about to be landed.

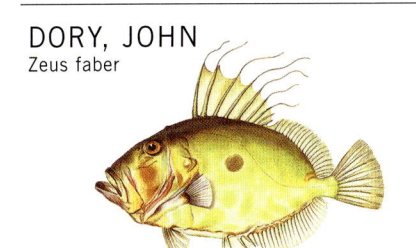

IDENTIFYING YOUR CATCH

FISH	LOCATION/DESCRIPTION	FISHING METHOD
EMPEROR, RED *Lutjanus sebae*  *Also known as emperor, government bream, red (juvenile pictured).*	 Like many prime species of fish, red emperor is vulnerable to fishing pressure and can be quickly fished down to a level where large fish are difficult to find. It is found often in 30 to 35 m of water on heavy reef structure, where it inhabits the reef edge near the current influence. It is distributed throughout the tropics and is a prized fish of the Great Barrier Reef. It is rarely found in temperate waters. Red emperor is a highly rated table fish commonly caught at sizes of 1 to 6 kg.	Use fresh fillet baits suspended close to the bottom, just off the down-current edge of a fairly vertical shelf of reef. A 10-kg line on a rod is a realistic minimum, with handlines around 40 kg. Sinker weight should suit the current and depth.
EMPEROR, SPANGLED *Lethrinus nebulosus*  *Also known as iodine bream, yellow sweetlip, north-west snapper.*	 A handsome fish with a yellow-golden body with blue spots, the spangled emperor is renowned for its excellent table quality. Average size is from 2 to 3 kg with good specimens reaching 6 kg. Other common emperors are the long-nosed emperor (*L. olivaceous*) and the yellow-tailed emperor (*L. atkinsoni*). The spangled emperor is found in northern waters from southern Queensland in the east around to southern Western Australia. It prefers a loose rocky bottom of gravel or broken coral and inhabits shallow reefs.	Bottom fishing on anchor with a paternoster rig and cut baits is best. The fish will occasionally strike at jigs worked near the bottom. Best baits include fish, crab, prawn and squid.
FLATHEAD, DUSKY *Platycephalus fuscus*  *Also known as black flathead, flatty, lizard.*	 Of the fourteen common species of flathead in Australian waters, the largest by far is the dusky flathead. This elongated fish takes its name from the colour of its head. It is common in estuaries along the east coast from around the Whitsundays in Queensland to as far south as Victoria. Growing to 15 kg, it is more commonly encountered from 1 to 3 kg. Dusky flathead is a bottom dweller, usually found in shallow water (1 to 6 m) in estuaries, bays and surf beaches.	From a boat, drift baits of fish strip or whole prawns, rigged to bounce along the bottom behind a sinker heavy enough to stir up sediment. From shore, flick out into deep channels and allow the tide to sweep the bait around. It responds well to lures or saltwater flies.
FLATHEAD, SOUTHERN BLUE-SPOT *Platycephalus speculator*  *Also known as yank flathead, long nose, sandies (incorrect), shovel nose.*	 This fish inhabits the Victorian coastline from New South Wales to South Australia, and also the waters of northern Tasmania and southern Western Australia. The southern blue-spot species resembles the dusky in appearance and occupies a similar range of habitats. It is commonly caught by drift fishing over sand and it is distinguished by the dark bars across its back. In Port Phillip Bay, Victoria, it is the predominant 'larger' specimen caught. It is an excellent table fish.	Strip baits of fish, or prawns, whole small fish, etc. are best, but lures will also work. Mostly caught by boat anglers, but land-based anglers can cast baits into bankside channels and across weed beds in southern estuaries.
FLOUNDER, SMALL-TOOTHED *Pseudorhombus jenysii* 	 The flounder begins life with an eye on each side of its head, but metamorphoses into adulthood with both eyes on the same side. The small-toothed flounder is found in both eastern and Western Australia, is dark coloured and carries five to six eye-like blotches spread around the body. Other species include the large-toothed, elongated, long-snouted and green-back flounders. They are common in southern estuaries, and are considered to be fine table fish.	Flounder may be speared in some States, but are usually caught with lines from 2 to 4 kg, small long shanked hooks and small pieces of bait, fished on the bottom from a drifting boat. Popular baits include fish strips, peeled prawn, marine worms or whitebait.

IDENTIFYING YOUR CATCH

FISH	LOCATION/DESCRIPTION	FISHING METHOD
GARFISH, EASTERN SEA *Hyporhamphus australis* *Also known as garie, beakie, red beak.*	The slender, bony sea garfish is a common species on the east coast, targeted both for bait and food. The flesh, despite its small size and large number of bones, is keenly sought for its outstanding flavour. A southern form, *H. melanochir*, is similar in all respects to *H. australis* but grows larger, to the delight of South Australian and Victorian anglers. The garfish is found around jetties and other estuary and bay structures, and is most active in the summer and autumn months.	Sea garfish can be readily line-caught, and are also netted professionally. To catch garfish, berley with bran or bread, and use small baits of fish or prawn flesh (or dough), on tiny long shanked hooks on a float rig.
GROPER, BLUE *Achoerodus viridis* *Also known as bluey.*	The eastern blue groper inhabits the waters of mid-Queensland and New South Wales and commonly grows to around 15 kg. A western species, *A. gouldii*, also exists, distributed from South Australia around into Western Australia, and can grow in excess of 30 kg. The western female is greenish, the eastern is reddish brown (called red groper), and the juveniles of both are a grey-brown in colour.	To withstand the tug of war involved in landing a groper, use heavy line, extra strong hooks from 1/0 to 6/0 to carry the large favoured baits of cunjevoi, red crab or abalone gut, and a powerful rod. The fish is usually caught by land-based fishing from rocks.
GRUNTER, SOOTY *Hephaestus fuliginosus* *Also known as black bream, sooties.*	This species generally weighs around half a kilogram but will grow in excess of 4 kg, at which size it is a formidable opponent on light tackle. The sooty grunter is but one form of the large and varied grunter family known for its pugnacious nature. It is found in both inland and coastal fresh water from near Emerald in Queensland, northwards over the Top End and south to the Kimberley region. Drift or walk the banks of tropical freshwater rivers and cast to places like snags, overhanging foliage, corners and deep holes.	Sooty grunter will attack lures as readily as baits, and are a lot more fun on artificials. A light threadline to bait casting outfit with 2 to 4-kg line is enough to handle this fish.
HAIRTAIL *Trichiurus lepturus* *Also known as Australian hairtail, Cox's hairtail, largerhead hairtail.*	The hairtail is a long fish with a fearsomely toothed head, a scaleless body and a tail tapering to a thin, thread-like end. The body colour is a brilliant silver, like polished chrome. This fish is found in coastal bays and estuaries of Australia's east and west coasts. Growing in excess of 2 m and weighing over 4 kg as an adult, the hairtail is most active at night. Usually found in deep holes in estuaries, but unpredictable as to when it will bite, it provides exciting sport for anglers.	Most regular hairtail anglers use from 4 to 10-kg line, a 1/0 to 4/0 hook, and always with a short (15-cm) wire trace as insurance against those teeth. Favoured baits include fillet of yellowtail or slimy mackerel and whole or half pilchards.
HERRING, OXEYE *Megalops cyprinoides* *Also known as tarpon.*	Found in tropical water, from far northern New South Wales, throughout Queensland and across the Gulf of Carpentaria to the Northern Territory, this species is an active, shiny, large-scaled fish, mostly silver in colour, and a great lure and fly taker. It provides a light-tackle diversion for anglers taking a break from barramundi and saratoga. Oxeye are commonly fished for sport as they are very fast and resist until exhausted. It is not highly regarded for its table quality and is usually released unharmed.	Best caught using casting lures, especially small lead-headed jigs with either feather, fibre or soft plastic tails. Larger specimens will take small swimming plugs, and small surface poppers are also particularly useful, whether cast with fly tackle or spinning gear.

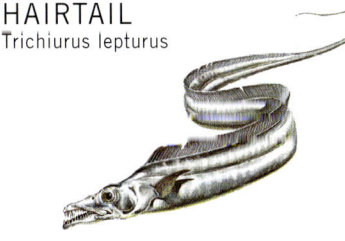

IDENTIFYING YOUR CATCH

FISH	LOCATION/DESCRIPTION	FISHING METHOD

JACK, MANGROVE
Lutjanus argentimaculatus

Also known as creek red bream, dog bream, red bream, jack, mangrove snapper, rock barramundi.

Mangrove jack is common throughout the tropical north, as far south as Coffs Harbour in the east and Exmouth in the west. A dark red, powerfully built fish, mangrove jack up to 3 kg are prevalent in tidal creeks and estuaries. Larger fish tend to move out into bays and on to onshore reefs. Some monster specimens of 11 kg or more have been taken from offshore reefs in New South Wales. A good table fish, it should not be confused with red bass (which has a distinctive 'pit' in front of each eye), which is often toxic.

Mangrove jack has canine teeth, sharp spines and gill blades. It lives around oyster-encrusted rocks, mangrove roots and various other line-cutting structures. Line classes upwards of 6 kg are adequate. The fish will hit lures, baits or flies, then dash for cover.

JAVELIN FISH
Pomadasys kaakan

Also known as barred grunter, trumpeter, spotted grunter, spotted javelin fish.

This fish's other common name, grunter, evolved because of its habit of emitting loud grunting sounds on capture. The name 'javelin' fish comes from the heavy spear-like anal fin that is capable of inflicting severe wounds on anglers who handle this fish carelessly. Commonly found in estuarine rivers, especially close to the sea, javelin fish live in far northern New South Wales, Queensland and the Northern Territory and parts of Western Australia. This fish is great table fare and good sport on reasonable tackle.

Fish strips or prawn baits are best. Most anglers fish with 6 to 10-kg tackle and just enough sinker weight to get the bait down in a tidal run. Because the javelin often lives near line-cutting structures, a heavier trace of 25 kg is sometimes used.

JEWFISH, BLACK
Protonibea diacanthus

Also known as spotted croaker, spotted jewfish, croaker.

A fish of northern waters, especially within the Northern Territory, the black jewfish is a darker coloured member of the same family as the southern mulloway. It also carries scattered dark blotches over much of its body. It has a predilection for reef areas, sunken wrecks and deepwater wharves in northern harbours. A predator of the first order, this fish loves nothing more than a large live bait (half a kilo is not too big). It is caught by dropping baits down and hanging on.

Heavy handlines are normal gear, as the runs, when they come, are short and sizzling, and you either stop your fish or lose it. Rod and reel fishing is possible, but usually only when the fish have congregated over a relatively clear space of bottom.

JEWFISH, LITTLE
Johnius vogleri

Also known as silver jewfish.

The little jewfish is smaller than its two heavyweight relatives, the mulloway and the black jewfish. It is often mistaken for a juvenile mulloway, but there are distinguishing features, notably that the little jewfish is always fatter for a given length than the southern mulloway. The little jewfish is significantly lighter in colour and lacks the dark blotches of the black jewfish as well. *J. vogleri* is found in deep holes or near vertical structures such as wharves or bridges, in northern latitudes only.

Use live baits of mullet, herring or prawns in tropical rivers and creeks. A running sinker rig with a large slab bait can be almost as effective, particularly if taken from a freshly caught mullet or pike.

JEWFISH, WESTRALIAN
Glaucosoma herbraicum

Also known as dhufish (incorrect), jewie, West Australian jewfish.

Related to the pearl perch of eastern Australia, this magnificent table fish is much larger, lives in generally deeper water and is the sole province of lucky Western Australian anglers – hence its common name. It is generally confined to coastal waters between Shark Bay and the beginnings of the Great Australian Bight, and so is unfamiliar to most eastern anglers. Anglers fishing the east coast would think they had died and gone to heaven if they hauled in one of these massive fish!

Stout handlines with a lot of sinker weight in the rig, and preferably lines with minimal stretch are best. Use fish strip baits, skinned octopus or squid, if absolutely fresh. Change baits every so often if there are no bites – freshness is that important!

IDENTIFYING YOUR CATCH

FISH	LOCATION/DESCRIPTION	FISHING METHOD

JOB-FISH, ROSY
Pristipomoides filamentosus

Also known as king snapper, rosy snapper.

Plentiful within the warmer waters of Queensland and far northern New South Wales, the rosy Job-fish is also caught around Lord Howe Island, and off Australia's north-western continental shelf. Growing in excess of 7 kg, it is a handsome, top-grade table species, with the same colouration as adult snapper, but much more streamlined. Related to the small-toothed Job-fish (*Aphareus furca*) and green Job-fish (*Aprion viriscens*), it is known for its sad look and hence the biblical reference in its common name.

Fished for over reefs in 50 m or more of depth, the rosy Job-fish bites best on cut fish baits at night, and is an excellent table fish as are all Job-fish. Solid tackle with 10-kg line or even higher is useful due to the depth of water it inhabits.

KINGFISH, YELLOWTAIL
Seriola lalandi

Also known as bandit, hoodlum, king.

A fish of exciting power and glamorous appearance, it has the nasty habit of taking lures and bait rigs and refusing to give them back. This very popular sportfish can be caught off the rocks or from a boat. It is usually associated with reef areas and often schools. It is found in waters from southern Queensland, to New South Wales, Victoria, South Australia and as far west as Shark Bay in Western Australia. Growing to 50 kg or better, this species averages from 4 to 10 kg.

Use lures, strip baits, cube baits or live baits, fished over reef, around deepwater wharf pylons and channel markers, from boats or the ocean rocks. Berley works well. The selection of a breaking strain in line should reflect the size and strength of the fish.

LEATHERJACKET, TOOTHBRUSH
Acanthaluteres vittiger

Also known as jackets, pale brown leatherjacket.

Leatherjacket is easily recognised by the prominent dorsal spine above the eyes, which in some species, including *A. vittiger*, folds completely into a groove when not in use. Its other distinguishing feature is the leathery skin rather than scales. It is a peaceful breed of fish that mooches around reef and weed beds grazing daintily with its small but chisel-toothed mouth. The toothbrush leatherjacket is commonly found around southern Australia, from Coffs Harbour, New South Wales, to Western Australia's Jurien.

The shearing teeth make long shank hooks necessary. Baits should be small and soft, such as peeled prawn, fish flesh, skinned octopus or squid meat. An unweighted or lightly weighted bait allowed to sink slowly is the best method.

LONG TOM, SLENDER
Strongylura leiura

Also known as hornpike long tom, needlefish.

The long tom has jaws of equal length, studded with rows of tiny, needle-sharp teeth. The slender long tom is distinguished by the black bar on the side of the head. It is found in Australia's northern and temperate waters, and is related to the barred long tom (*Ablennes hians*), which is purely tropical, the stout long tom (*Tylosurus gavialoides*) and the crocodilian long tom (*Tylosurus crocodilus*), the last two being much larger fish and found in both tropical and temperate waters.

Long tom are surface cruisers, preying on small fish, which they herd and slash at in spectacular fashion. They are easy to draw strikes from with small lures, but not so simple to hook, there being little soft tissue among all those teeth.

LUDERICK
Girella tricuspidata

Also known as blackfish, darkie, nigger.

A fish of the estuaries and inshore rocks mainly along the eastern seaboard, luderick is most commonly found in New South Wales. This chunky little fish is usually encountered around a half to 1.5 kg. Essentially vegetarian, the luderick will take baits of marine worms, prawns and nippers on occasion. A good table fish if prepared correctly, it is often kept alive in net bags, then bled, cleaned and skinned immediately before the angler leaves for home.

Float fishing is best with green weed or sea lettuce baits from the ocean rocks, river breakwalls or within estuaries from bank or boat. The float is weighted with either running barrels, beans or crimped split shot, and hooks should be small.

IDENTIFYING YOUR CATCH

FISH	LOCATION/DESCRIPTION	FISHING METHOD

MACKEREL, SHARK
Grammatorcynus bicarinatus

Also known as large-scaled tuna, scaly mackerel, sharkie.

The southern limits to the distribution of this tropical species are around Fraser Island in the east and Steep Point, near Shark Bay, in the west. Shark mackerel comprises much of the Western Australian rock angler's catch on lures north of Shark Bay. Usual shark mackerel sizes are from 2 to 6 kg, but can double that. Whole (up to 12 kg in size), it is a prized trolling bait for giant marlin off Cairns. A distinguishing feature of the shark mackerel is its double lateral line. It takes its name from the shark-like smell when gutted.

Lure casting from ocean rocks is best in Western Australia. Trolling around inner reef edges is best from about Gladstone north. They respond to either lures or baits of garfish, mullet and pike. Suitable line classes are from 4 to 8 kg; wire trace is essential.

MACKEREL, SLIMY
Scomber australasicus

Also known as blue mackerel, common mackerel, slimies.

This speedy little baitfish is excellent live or cut bait for larger quarry such as snapper, mulloway, yellowtail kingfish and tuna. Usually caught from 15 to 25 cm in length, this species prefers cooler areas and often forming extensive surface shoals. It is most common inshore in the southern half of Australia, where it schools over reefs, around islands and headlands, and occasionally enters bays. Its skin is soft and slippery to touch – hence its common name.

Light handlines or flick rods are used to cast tiny metal lures or flies, small pieces of cut bait or multi-hook live bait jigs. These fish respond to berley and can be kept alive in a large container of sea water, provided the water is constantly exchanged.

MACKEREL, SPANISH
Scomberomorus commerson

Also known as narrow-barred mackerel, narrow-barred Spanish mackerel, Spaniards, Spanish.

The largest member of the mackerel family and a fast swimming oceanic species, the Spanish mackerel can grow to 30 kg or more, but is commonly encountered around 5 to 10 kg. It ranges throughout the tropics and as far south as Montague Island on the east coast and Rottnest Island in the west. A streamlined fish, it is all about speed and slicing power. Its serrated rows of dagger-like teeth interlock like shears. It is an extremely popular game fish and fair table food.

Mackerel teeth mean wire traces are a must, or at least ganged hooks. Mackerel can be trolled, or spun to with lures, especially surface poppers. They love live baits as well, and dead baits are useful. Mackerel usually hit first to maim the bait then come back to inhale it.

MACKEREL, SPOTTED
Scomberomorus munroi

Also known as Japanese mackerel, snook, spottie, Australian spotted mackerel.

As its common name indicates, numerous small spots on its body distinguish this species. The spotted mackerel frequents a similar area to Spanish mackerel (*S. commerson*), although it rarely moves further south than Forster, on the New South Wales coast. Slightly smaller than the Spaniard, it averages around 3 to 5 kg, with a really big fish being around 8 or 9 kg and probably coming from a north Queensland offshore reef. Found offshore in schools, its presence is usually signalled by wheeling and diving birds.

Trolling lures or live baits, or drifting with live or cut baits over inshore plateaus of reefs is best. Mackerel teeth mean wire trace is essential or at least ganged hooks. This fish will often move up a berley trail behind an anchored boat.

MARLIN, BLACK
Makaira indica

Also known as black, silver marlin, silver.

Black marlin is a fast swimming, highly prized big game fish. Available offshore right down the east and west coasts of Australia, the black marlin becomes less common the further south you go. In Queensland and throughout much of New South Wales, marlin of various sizes are regular summer visitors to waters as shallow as 40 m or less. Many game fishers suspect big fish inhabit deeper offshore trenches year round. The largest known aggregation of giant black marlin is around the Great Barrier Reef north of Cairns.

Giant black marlin of 500 kg are taken trolling large baits well offshore. Smaller blacks, around 100 kg, are regularly taken closer inshore. Boat anglers troll large skirted lures, bibless minnows or whole fish baits – either dead or alive.

IDENTIFYING YOUR CATCH

FISH	LOCATION/DESCRIPTION	FISHING METHOD

MARLIN, BLUE
Makaira nigricans

Also known as blues, Indo-Pacific blue marlin.

The blue marlin inhabits much the same waters as the black marlin (*M. indica*), but is less common and appears to prefer the deep, oceanic currents and to be more tolerant of cooler water temperatures. It has been caught as far south as Storm Bay in Tasmania. It is a prized game fish, and some anglers consider it a tougher opponent than equivalent sized black marlin. Large blue marlin have been captured offshore of Bermagui, south of Sydney. Once hooked, a marlin of any size will put up a tremendous fight.

Lure fishing works best, especially over deep offshore canyons where the bigger fish prowl. Lures need to be large, as do the rods, reels and line classes, as when hooked, big blue marlin are capable of stripping over 1000 m of line from a reel.

MARLIN, STRIPED
Tetrapturus audax

Also known as stripey.

Far more prevalent along the eastern seaboard than in the west, the striped marlin is generally a lighter built fish than either the black or blue of the same length. It makes up for this lack of bulk by being the most spectacular of all the billfish when hooked, often racing across the sea making immense leaps. It is not unknown for a prime adult striped marlin to jump more than thirty times during a fight, and twenty consecutive jumps are common. It takes its name from the bluish stripes that extend across its body.

Small trolled live baits, such as slimy mackerel and yellowtail, are favoured. Trolling an array of skirted lures intended for blue marlin will often land this fish. It will respond to live baits cast across its path when cruising the surface.

MORWONG, BLUE
Nemadactylus douglasii

Also known as grey morwong, mowie.

Commonly found throughout the inshore coastal reef waters of southern Queensland, all of New South Wales and the eastern part of Victoria, the blue morwong is also an occasional catch in Tasmania's warmer northern waters. A fish that favours moderately deep reef areas and rubble bottom, morwong is a popular charter-boat fish for handline anglers bouncing baits off the bottom. While not highly rated as a sporting fish, despite its size and fight, it is a fair table fish.

It is best caught with baits of fish strip and peeled prawn, fished as close to the vertical edges of reefs as is practicable. As charter boats drift fish, such precision is not always achieved, but anglers in charge of their own craft should do a better job.

MULLET, SAND
Myxus elongatus

Also known as lano, sandie, tallegalane.

The sand mullet is widespread throughout New South Wales and South Australia, and occasionally in southern Western Australia. A solid-bodied streamlined fish, with a straight back, large eye and small, pointed snout, it also has a large black spot at the base of the pectoral fin. Its rows of well-developed teeth distinguish it from other members of the mullet family. Caught mostly from sand flat areas in estuaries or from beaches, sand mullet is excellent bait for larger fish, but also a good table fish in its own right.

Small baits of fish flesh, peeled prawn, marine worms or dough are best. These can be fished on the bottom, or unweighted, but more success will be enjoyed if you berley heavily with bread and fish these baits under a slim quill float. Hooks should be small.

MULLET, SEA
Mugil cephalus

Also known as bully mullet, hardgut mullet, poddy mullet, grey mullet.

The sea mullet is a much larger mullet than most, growing to an astonishing 8 kg or more, but is rarely seen above 2 kg. It is a temperate species of fish that spends part of its life in freshwater reaches of coastal rivers and lakes. It travels to sea as an adult and runs up the east coast in huge schools for annual spawning migrations. The eggs are carried southwards until the young have developed enough to enter bays and harbours. These bully mullet are a common catch in coastal rivers of New South Wales.

Float fishing in estuaries is best, or fishing baits on the bottom in either estuaries or surf. It forages in freshwater reaches of rivers over weed beds, but can be caught on small trout flies. It is not easy to tempt and is rarely taken by line in Western Australia.

431

IDENTIFYING YOUR CATCH

| FISH | LOCATION/DESCRIPTION | FISHING METHOD |

MULLET, YELLOWEYE
Aldrichetta forsteri

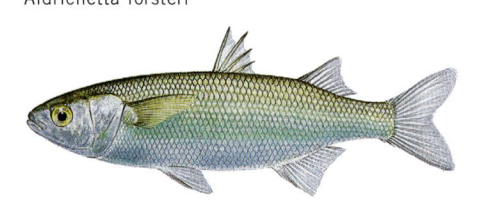

Also known as pilch.

A similar fish to sand mullet, this species is distinguished by a rounder back, absence of the black spot near the pectoral fins and having a large, prominent yellow eye. It shares similar distribution to the sand mullet, but is found much further west. In Western Australia it is known as 'pilch', and is taken from both estuary and surf. The yelloweye mullet is predominant in Victoria where it is a major part of the surf angling catch. It is a good table fish, with firm white fillets ideal for cooking.

In the surf the paternoster rig is best using small pieces of fresh tuna, or better still, pippis, mussel or other shell baits. The yelloweye mullet responds well to berley and is found in gutters close to shore and in estuaries.

MULLOWAY
Argyrosomus hololepidotus

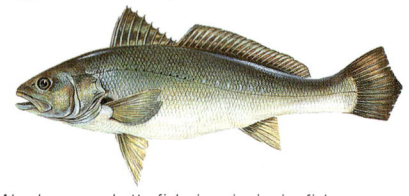

Also known as butterfish, jew, jewie, jewfish, river kingfish, soapie (juvenile).

Known by a host of confusing names, this large species is a predator of major southern estuarine river and lake systems, surf beaches and offshore reefs. Growing in excess of 50 kg, most adult mulloway are caught between 10 and 15 kg. The smaller juveniles, up to 4 kg, are known as 'soapies' because of their soft flesh. They will often follow squid and sometimes develop a fixation for these cephalopods. The mulloway is considered an important sportfish and respected for its table quality, particularly in South Australia.

Use strip baits in the surf; live baits of pike, yellowtail scad, slimy mackerel, or mullet, in estuaries or over reefs. Hooks should be 5/0 to 8/0, lines from 6 to 10 kg, but over reefs or from the rocks, 15 to 20-kg line may be more sensible. Mulloway will also take lures.

NANNYGAI
Centroberyx affinis

Also known as 'gai, goat (nanny-goat), nanny, redfish.

A deepwater species found in New South Wales, Victoria and Tasmania, the nannygai is a prime commercial fish occasionally caught by anglers fishing deep reefs for snapper or morwong. The nannygai is conspicuous by its colouring, which is deep pink to red with metallic-silvery tints. An acceptable to good table fish, growing over 2 kg but being common at about half that size, nannygai is also a prized live bait for yellowfin tuna. A similar species, the red snapper (*C. gerrardi*), is found in southern waters.

Strip baits of fish flesh, mounted on hooks from 1/0 to 4/0 are best, as this small fish has a large mouth. Rigs commonly are of the paternoster type, with a large sinker hung below several short dropper lines, each carrying its own hook and bait.

PERCH, ESTUARY
Macquaria colonorum

Also known as Australian perch, freshwater perch, perch.

Estuary perch is found in the brackish reaches of coastal fresh water from around Lismore in New South Wales, down the southern New South Wales and Victorian coast and around to the Murray mouth in South Australia. Some isolated populations also exist in northern Tasmania. Similar to bass (*M. novemaculata*) in appearance and habit, this fish will be found relating strongly to snags, creek mouths, reefs and rock-wall structures in mid to upper estuarine sections of coastal rivers.

The perch loves baits of live prawns, crickets, worms, tiny poddy mullet and crabs, but will occasionally take trolled, or cast, lures and flies. Its activity is quite tide-related, and tide changes and either dawn or dusk are prime fishing times.

PERCH, GOLDEN
Macquaria ambigua

Also known as callop, yellowbelly.

Naturally occurring throughout the Murray–Darling system in New South Wales, and southern Queensland, into Victoria and South Australia, the golden perch has also been artificially stocked in a number of alpine and coastal drainage impoundments. Stocky, deep-bodied fish, goldens commonly range from 1 kg to 3 kg in rivers and farm dams, and can reach 5 or 10 kg in major impoundments. It is a popular fish with anglers for its table quality.

Baits of crayfish, bardi grub and shrimp are effective, as are diving lures with the capability of diving to 3 to 5 m. Casting or trolling lures around suitable stands of drowned timber is effective in impoundments. Bait fishing is more effective in turbid (muddy) rivers.

IDENTIFYING YOUR CATCH

FISH	LOCATION/DESCRIPTION	FISHING METHOD

PERCH, JUNGLE
Kuhlia rupestris

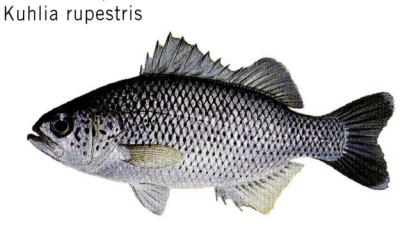

Also known as junglies, rock flagtail, mountain trout.

A tropical freshwater native fish, the jungle perch is found in northern coastal streams, usually in estuaries, but it moves freely into fresh water. It is silvery with reddish brown markings and some black colouration on the second dorsal fin and tail fin. Its relatively slow breeding cycle, coupled with the fact that its habitat is under threat in Queensland, means its future is in jepopardy. If you can find a jungle perch at all, it will probably be half a kilo or so, much less than its one-time common weight of 1 to 2 kg.

Strictly a catch and release proposition. Jungle perch show a willingness to strike at lures and baits, particularly surface lures, and will take small swimming plugs as used for sooty grunter or bass. Please fish with barbless hooks.

PERCH, MACQUARIE
Macquaria australasica

Also known as mackas, Macquarie, mountain perch, silvereye, black bream.

The Macquarie perch is a shy, cryptic fish of freshwater streams. Competition from introduced species and the erection of weirs and dams restricting its spawning grounds have caused the reduction in numbers. The best places to catch a Macquarie perch are in Lake Dartmouth and the upper Mitta Mitta River in Victoria. While it does exist in some New South Wales rivers such as the Lachlan, Nepean and Shoalhaven, its threatened status means it is totally protected in that State.

A light paternoster rig with worm or mudeyes as bait is best. Also good is jigging small spoons around sunken timber, using tiny minnow lures or trout flies. The fish is usually found in between 5 to 10 m of water around trees in Lake Dartmouth.

PERCH, MOSES
Lutjanus russelli

Also known as Moses sea perch, Moses snapper, black-spot sea perch.

The Moses perch is a similar fish to fingermark and is often confused with that fish. It is probably the dominant species of the two in Western Australia. Found around inshore reefs and mangroves in tropical estuaries, it is more prevalent across the top of Australia. It is usually found in pairs or small groups, sometimes hiding under ledges or gutters. The Moses perch is reasonably small, averaging between 400 g and 1.5 kg, and is frequently considered a nuisance fish by amateur anglers hoping to catch larger fish.

Moses perch can be caught on lures and with both dead and live bait. Lures cast close to mangroves and meant for barramundi or mangrove jack can induce strikes from Moses perch.

PERCH, PEARL
Glaucosoma scapulare

Also known as eastern pearl perch, pearlie, nannygai.

This species frequents offshore deep water over rubble beds and low reef areas. It is found from central Queensland through northern New South Wales, to as far south as Newcastle. Those caught usually average around 1 to 2 kg. It has a deep, laterally compressed body, large eye and a black-skinned bony extension to the top of the gill cover. Beneath the thin black membrane, this bony plate is pearly – hence its common name. It is widely regarded as one of Australia's best table fish.

Only fresh fish strip baits are likely to be taken, or small squid. Hooks of 3/0 to 6/0 are suitable, with lines usually being 4 to 8 kg on rods and 15 to 20 kg for handlines.

PERCH, SILVER
Bidyanus bidyanus

Also known as bidyan, black bream, silvers.

The natural distribution of this fish is throughout the Murray–Darling Basin, but it has been translocated to impoundments throughout southern Queensland, much of New South Wales and into Victoria, with minor stockings in parts of South Australia. Once considered the carp of the inland, silver perch are now rare in rivers. Silver perch prefer timbered and weedy water with moderate depth and good clarity. The silver perch is an acceptable table fish, having firm, dry, white flesh.

Best baits are worms, grubs, crickets, grasshoppers, mudeyes and yabbies. Riverine dwellers seem to prefer small wobbling or spinning lures, but larger impoundment fish can fall for lures aimed at golden perch or Murray cod.

433

IDENTIFYING YOUR CATCH

FISH	LOCATION/DESCRIPTION	FISHING METHOD

PERCH, STRIPEY SEA
Lutjanus carponotatus

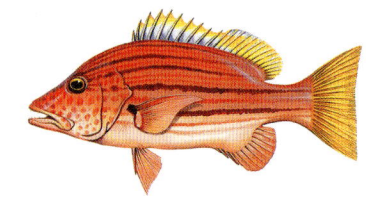

Also known as stripey snapper, stripey.

Not to be confused with *Microcanthus strigatus*, also known as stripey, the *L. carponotanus* species has brown and yellow lateral stripes on a silver body. It is commonly around 1 kg or just under, but can reach in excess of 2 kg. It has the typical humped Lutjanid head shape and large canine teeth. Spread along the coast from central Queensland throughout the tropics, it is a voracious, aggressive fish that will charge out and strike at lures, baits or virtually anything small enough to be edible. It is not great eating.

Cast small lures across shallow coral outcrops or fish strip baits over reef areas and jiggle them, about an arm's length off the bottom. Stout mono traces are a good idea.

PIKE, LONG-FINNED
Dinolestes lewini

The long-finned pike grows in excess of 2 kg but is common at less than 1 kg. Often confused with the smaller seapike (*Sphyraena obtusata*), it is best distinguished by the longer length of its anal fins and is a more stoutly bodied fish. Distributed throughout the mid to southern coastlines of Australia, it is variously described as a poor food fish, a bait-stealing pest, an entertaining light-tackle lure chaser, but most importantly, as a prime live bait for large yellowtail kingfish, mulloway and snapper.

Small whole fish such as whitebait, fish strips or lures, moved erratically in the manner of wounded bait fish is best. Its dagger-like teeth mean a short trace of heavier nylon is useful. Trolling from boats and also lure casting from rocks is common.

QUEENFISH
Scomberoides commersonianus

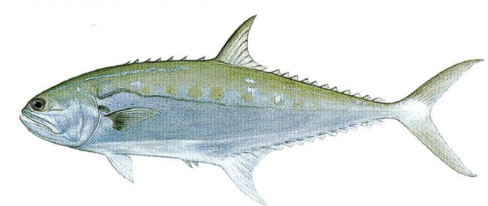

Also known as leatherskin, queenie, skinnyfish, skinny.

A fish of the tropical north, 'queenfish' is the term now coming into popular usage to describe both the giant leatherskin (*S. commersonianus*) and the related *S. lysan*. A member of the trevally family, queenfish school and attack with the same ferocity as their shorter more blunt-shaped cousins. To both the consternation and delight of anglers they often leap clear of the water in a repeated, cartwheeling motion. Queenfish move at great speed, put up a good fight when hooked and are a fair table fish.

Troll the gaps between coral islands, or drift over reefs and around shallow bomboras casting chrome lures or surface poppers. These fish are fun on tackle from 4 to 6 kg.

REDFIN
Perca fluviatilis

Also known as English perch, reddies, redfin perch.

The redfin, an introduced species, has a propensity to overbreed and produce what is called a 'stunt' fishery of voracious tiddlers. If kept in check by predators, the redfin can grow to a respectable size and is quite good food and fair sport too. Its track record of taking over to the detriment of native species means it should never be stocked or returned to the water once caught. This fish has now infiltrated most of the eastern States' fresh water, petering out in the warmer waters of Queensland.

Any freshwater bait, such as worms, crickets, mudeyes, yabbies or bardi grubs, is best. They will take almost any small lure or fly, particularly small metal fish-shaped lures, jigged in deep water over schools located by echo sounder.

SAILFISH
Istiophorus platypterus

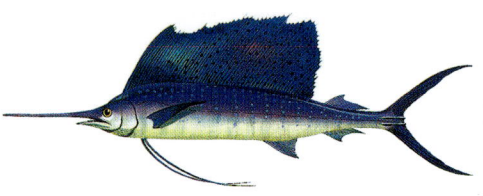

Also known as sails.

Found throughout Queensland and the Top End, and south as far as Exmouth in Western Australia, the sailfish is most plentiful off the Pilbara coast in the west and in the east in Moreton Bay and throughout the island complexes of the Great Barrier Reef. This most elegant of the billfish family is a prized game fish, which has in recent years become a regular target for anglers in small boats. Fish in the 20 to 40-kg bracket will gather in schools around reefs or sandy tidal bays where currents aggregate bait fish.

A Queensland technique is to locate a pod of midwater bait on the sounder, jig up a supply on multihook baitjigs and either rig these for trolling, or present them as live baits on casting tackle to surface swimming sailfish.

IDENTIFYING YOUR CATCH

FISH	LOCATION/DESCRIPTION	FISHING METHOD

SALMON, AUSTRALIAN
Arripis trutta

Also known as bay trout, blackback, cockie salmon, colonial salmon, kahawai, salmon trout, sambo.

Prized more as a fighting fish than table fare, the Australian salmon is no relation to the European salmon. It moves in schools, leaving sheltered estuary and inlet waters in its second or third year for beach, reef and ocean rock environments. The two species are the eastern salmon (*A. trutta*), which is commonly 2 to 4 kg, and a western salmon (*A. truttaceus*), which can easily top 8 kg. Adult salmon are silvery with an olive-grey back, while juvenile salmon have brown markings on their backs and sides.

Favourite baits are beach and bloodworms, pilchards, garfish, pippis and a variety of lures and saltwater flies. The bite of a salmon can be indecisive and its mouth is soft, so sharp hooks and a careful hand are needed to avoid it tearing free.

SALMON, THREADFIN
Eleutheronema tetradactylum

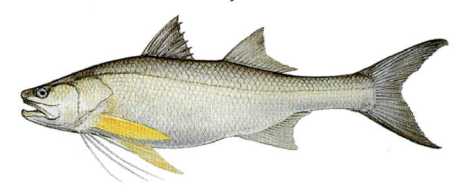

Also known as Burnett River salmon, king salmon, putty nose, giant threadies.

Threadfin salmon come in a few different colours – silver, golden and blue – and the little ones (blue), from 1 to 4 kg, are found throughout north Queensland. Strongholds of the bigger, more golden and silver fish, from 4 kg to over 20 kg, are found in the remote waters of the Top End. Threadfin are as fast as barramundi, and turn and jump with even more style and grace. They like estuarine and shallow bay waters, and are not averse to feeding in conditions that you might think are too muddy. They are excellent eating.

Baits of live prawns and small live fish are taken with relish at creek mouths on a high but falling tide, as are various minnow-style lures. Large, bushy saltwater flies can be cast to sighted fish cruising in the shallows.

SAMSON FISH
Seriola hippos

Also known as sambos, samsons, sea kingfish.

The samson fish can vary considerably in shape and colour, causing much confusion. Often mistaken for a differently coloured yellowtail kingfish, the samson fish is generally stouter in build and uniformly bronze to grey-green across the back. Common in Western Australia it inhabits the coastal waters of Australia's east and west coasts. It is found over reefs and in water to 50 m in depth, and can top 40 kg. This large powerful game fish fights savagely when hooked; it is an excellent table fish, particularly when juvenile.

Bottom fish with large, live or strip baits of squid or fish, or cast, jig or troll lures. Lines can be from 6 to 8 kg but should more probably be 10 to 15, with 24-kg line. Samson fish respond to berley.

SARATOGA, EASTERN
Scleropages leichardti

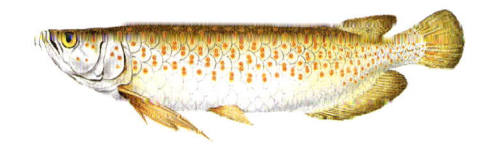

Also known as Dawson River barramundi, spotted barramundi, toga.

This smaller of the two saratogas, averaging 1 to 3 kg, is distributed throughout central Queensland fresh water from about Fairbairn Dam, near Emerald, up to the tip of Cape York. This species favours pandanus-lined creeks and billabongs, but has adapted to warm water storages with reed and rush-bed edges. Only smaller saratoga are suitable for the table as the large fish tend to be flavourless and coarsely textured. Anglers should treat them as a 'catch and release' species as they are a very long living fish.

Troll or cast swimming minnows, bladed lures or surface poppers. In tight-pocket water pinpoint presentation works best. Lines of 4 to 6 kg are ideal, and traces of heavier nylon, roughly twice the mainline thickness, are suitable.

SARATOGA, GULF
Scleropages jardini

Also known as toga, northern spotted barramundi.

Distributed across the Top End through Arnhem Land, but petering out west and south of Darwin, the gulf saratoga also extends into the western drainage areas of lower Cape York. It is usually caught around 3 to 4 kg, with exceptional fish reaching 6 or 7 kg. It can be distinguished from the Dawson River saratoga by the red crescent-shaped markings on its scales. Saratoga fishing is edge fishing: the edges of riverbanks, billabong cut-backs, drowned stands of paperbarks and pandanus forests.

Casting with lures and flies is effective. Work poppers at dawn and dusk or in shady areas, and toss sinking lures like rattling spots and soft plastics into lily patches.

IDENTIFYING YOUR CATCH

FISH	LOCATION/DESCRIPTION	FISHING METHOD

SERGEANT BAKER
Aulopus purpurissatus

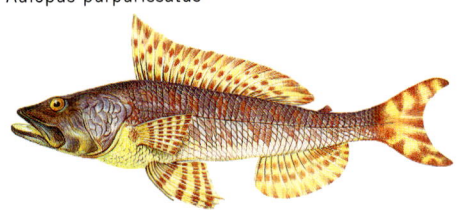

Also known as sarge.

Plentiful on both deep and inshore coastal reefs throughout much of the lower two-thirds of the continent, the sergeant baker commonly sits perched tripod-like on its fins, on boulders, reef bottoms or in crevices. It can be caught from boats or ocean rocks, and in some exceptionally deep and clean harbours, such as Jervis Bay in New South Wales. This fish apparently takes its common name from a sergeant with the First Fleet, who reportedly first spotted it. They are a reasonable table fish.

Use fish baits, and allow the bait to settle where rock bottom turns to sand. Also put lures close to the bottom where this fish spends most of its time.

SHARK, BRONZE WHALER
Carcharinus brachyurus

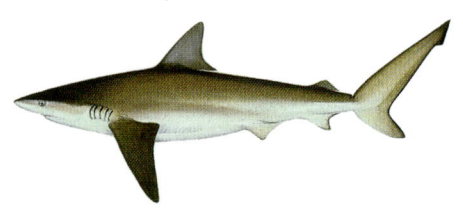

Also known as cocktail shark, copper shark, whaler.

One of many 'whaler' sharks, the bronze whaler is perhaps the best known, by reputation if not personal encounter. A potentially dangerous shark to swimmers, it is inquisitive, aggressive and when excited, quite fearless. Found with related species almost all around Australia, it roams between offshore reefs, surf beaches, estuaries and bays, and along the ocean rocks. It can be targeted by land-based gamefishers from piers and rocks. It is happy to switch from being a hunter to a scavenger as the need arises.

Use large, live or dead, whole fish baits, or large slabs of cut bait, squid, fish heads, or whatever, suspended under a balloon for a float. Large forged game hooks and traces of 7 to 49-strand cable wire are usually employed.

SHARK, SCHOOL
Galeorhinus galeus

Also known as greyboy, grey shark, snapper shark, tope.

Together with the gummy shark (*Mustelus antarcticus*), pencil shark (*Hypogaleus hyugaensis*) and whiskery shark (*Furgaleus macki*), the school shark does not attack swimmers. Unlike the gummy shark, however, it has small sharp teeth that can inflict a painful bite to a careless angler's hands. It is found offshore and within enclosed waters from Brisbane, throughout New South Wales, Victoria and Tasmania, to South Australia and just north of Perth in Western Australia. It is a small species of around 1 m in length.

Most often trawled or long-lined by professionals, this shark will take fish-flesh baits in estuaries or over shallow reefs. It is a common catch along north-eastern Victorian beaches and estuaries.

SNAPPER
Pagrus auratus

Also known as cockney bream, red bream, reddies, schnapper, squire (juvenile).

The snapper is widely distributed from central Queensland, throughout New South Wales, Victoria and the two gulf regions of South Australia, into Western Australia as far north as Shark Bay. Inhabiting inshore to moderate-depth reefs, snapper is also found in major estuaries and bays. The juveniles inhabit bays and estuaries as nurseries, but the adult fish will enter large bays such as Port Phillip in Victoria. The biggest snapper are found in the gulf waters of South Australia and Shark Bay, Western Australia.

Fresh baits of whole or cut fish or squid, or live baits, such as yellowtail scad, slimy mackerel and garfish are best. Use needle sharp hooks from 2/0 to 6/0, line of 4 to 8 kg and a running sinker rig with a minimum of sinker weight. Berley helps.

SNOOK
Sphyraena novaehollandiae

Also known as pike, short-finned seapike.

This member of the pike family inhabits cool southern waters from around Port Stephens, New South Wales, southward around the coast to Island Point in Western Australia. Favouring shallow waters to 20 m with sand to weed bottoms, the snook preys upon small bait fish, juvenile squid and various crustaceans. It is often found in the same places over periods of weeks or even years, in season. Fish average under 1 kg, but can reach over 2 kg. It is a very popular angling species in South Australia.

Small fish strip baits or even lures are taken, it being best to 'jig' the offering. A trace of heavier monofilament can help. Use bluebait or whitebait presented on linked #1 to 2/0 hooks.

IDENTIFYING YOUR CATCH

FISH	LOCATION/DESCRIPTION	FISHING METHOD

SWEEP
Scorpis aequipinnis

Also known as sea sweep.

Juvenile sweep inhabit the New South Wales coastal estuaries and close inshore on the rocks where it is regarded as a nuisance. Larger specimens are found over reefs. In Victoria and South Australia sweep can grow in excess of 2 kg. These fish are good table fare and on some parts of the coast highly sought after by anglers. Sweep seem to favour the tip of breaking water near the edge of bomboras and the like. Drifting in a boat close to the white water of breaking reefs can make serious sweep fishing a dangerous proposition.

Regular sweep anglers berley over shallow reefs. Small hooks, baited with peeled prawn, squid or fish flesh are drifted down on lightly weighted rigs.

SWEETLIP, GRASS
Lethrinus laticaudis

Also known as brown sweetlip, snapper bream, grass emperor.

The grass sweetlip is an attractive, powerful fish of exceptional table value. Its distribution ranges from temperate to tropical waters, favouring rocky or coral reefs according to latitudes, and the species is apt to follow warm coastal currents in summer from its usual tropical haunts as far south as central New South Wales. Common in sizes from 2 to 3 kg, sweetlip may surpass 6 kg, but such fish are rare these days as fishing pressure mounts on tropical coral reefs.

Present fresh bait close to, but just off, the bottom. Use leadhead jigs, tipped with baits of squid or fish strip, to get the bait down past the swarming lesser fry. This rig, however, must be 'worked' or jigged up and down.

SWEETLIP, RED-THROATED
Lethrinus miniatus

Also known as red-throated emperor, sweetlip, sweetlips emperor, tricky snapper.

The attractive, powerful, red-throated sweetlip is one of the most common of the Lethrinidae family of emperors and sweetlips. It ranges from temperate to tropical waters, favouring rocky or coral reefs according to latitudes and is apt to follow warm coastal currents south from its usual tropical haunts to central New South Wales. Common in sizes from 1 to 2 kg, sweetlip rarely surpass 4 kg. It provides excellent eating but it has been associated with ciguatera – in north-eastern regions only.

Fresh bait presented just off the bottom is best. Leadhead jigs tipped with squid or fish strip baits can be used to ensure the bait is not taken by other fish on the way down. If using this rig, it must be jigged up and down.

TAILOR
Pomatomus saltatrix

Also known as chopper (juvenile), pomba, skipjack.

A saltwater favourite found throughout New South Wales, southern Queensland and the Western Australian coast south of Shark Bay, the tailor seldom attains more than 4 kg. Fish of 9 or 10 kg create a sensation when caught. Tailor frequent surf beaches, rocky headlands, offshore islands and wash areas, and can often be seen tearing up the surface under a canopy of screeching sea birds. The Fraser Island tailor run is the best known in Australia.

Troll tidelines and the edges of ocean rock washes, and also cast with lures, or whole fish baits on gangod hook rigs, usually comprised of three, four or even five hooks from 2/0 to 5/0 in size.

TARWHINE
Rhabdosargus sarba

Also known as silver bream.

This member of the same family as bream and snapper has a smaller, slightly undershot mouth and a pattern of golden, wavy, horizontal lines on a silver background, which distinguish it from the similar looking yellowfin bream. Tarwhine is distributed throughout shallow reef, surfline and estuary environments, from southern Queensland, throughout New South Wales, Victoria, part of South Australia and southern Western Australia. Fish over 2 kg are occasionally caught, but half to 1 kg is the average size.

Baits of marine worms or prawns, nippers or shrimp are effective, particularly at coastal lake entrances during a prawn run. Tarwhine also inhabit the surf and will take baits of pippi. Hooks need to be slightly smaller than for an equivalent-sized bream.

IDENTIFYING YOUR CATCH

FISH	LOCATION/DESCRIPTION	FISHING METHOD
TERAGLIN *Atractoscion aequidens* *Also known as trag, teraglin-jew.*	The southern teraglin is similar in appearance to the juvenile mulloway, but where the mulloway's tail is convex, that of the teraglin is concave, almost crescent shaped. It is commonly found from just south of Fraser Island in Queensland to Bermagui in New South Wales, and over reefy bottom in depths of something around 60 m. This species is related to the silver teraglin *(Otolithes ruber)* found in more tropical waters and sometimes called 'wiretooth' or 'yankee whiting'. Both species are top-rate table fish.	Use baits of fish strip mounted on two linked 5/0 hooks on a short trace below a running sinker. This rig is night-fished over suitable reef area – full moon is best. Handlines around 15 to 20 kg are necessary as a lost fish can put the school off the bite.
TOMMY RUFF *Arripis georgianus* *Also known as Australian herring, ruff, tommy rough.*	A member of the same family as the Australian salmon, the tommy ruff (so-called because of the rough feel of its scales) is a small fish distributed widely through southern Western Australia and across South Australia. Often confused with juvenile Australian salmon, it can be distinguished by its larger eye and black-tipped tail. The tommy ruff is an important recreational fishing species along beaches, in estuaries and from rocky groynes, often schooling in vast numbers and hitting baits or small lures voraciously.	Small hooks, size 4 to 8 baited with fish flesh, prawns, or specially bred bait maggots are best. Rigs commonly incorporate some form of berley dispenser, into which an oily mix of bread, pollard fish flesh and tuna oil is pressed.
TREVALLY, GIANT *Caranx ignobilis* *Also known as lowly trevally, turrum.*	This fish is a strong opponent on any line class and is a slab of raw swimming power weighing in excess of 30 kg. A surface hit from one of these fish is awesome and the run is often unstoppable. The giant trevally is distributed throughout the tropics and is occasionally found in more southern waters on the east and west coasts during summer, a result of following the warm currents. It prefers rocky corners of reefs, partially submerged bomboras or the narrow tide-race passages between tropical islands and coral formations.	Baits of dead or live fish, or whole squid, or a variety of lures, especially surface poppers, are best. Troll or cast these and retrieve them quickly over or past preferred habitat. Giant trevally sometimes band up in packs and savage schools of smaller fish.
TREVALLY, GOLDEN *Gnathanodon speciosus* *Also known as golden.*	Golden trevally is a tropical species and one of the most attractive in the family. It is found in the warmer coastal waters of northern Australia and along the coast of Western Australia. Life colours are often silvery, but on capture this fish's flanks turn a more distinctive rich gold, with greenish hues across the back. A distinctive dark stripe runs down through the eye. Common from 5 to 8 kg, this fish grows in excess of 30 kg and more than 1 m long. It is a powerful, stubborn fighter and excellent table fare.	This trevally will take baits of fish flesh, crustaceans and small live fish, but is much better sport if pursued on lures, either jigged, trolled or cast. It will sometimes attack with such ferocity that a carelessly held rod can be torn from the angler's grasp.
TREVALLY, SILVER *Pseudocaranx dentex* *Also known as blurter, croaker, silver, skipjack trevally, skippy, white trevally.*	By far the most common trevally in cooler southern waters, this fish is normally caught in sizes ranging from juveniles weighing half a kilogram in estuaries, to adults from 3 to 5 kg around reefs and open headlands. The silver trevally is distributed from southern Queensland through New South Wales and into Victoria, extending southward to Tasmania and westward through South Australia into Western Australia and as far north as North West Cape. It is renowned as an excellent table fish.	Use strip baits of fish or squid, whole peeled prawns or small chrome lures. The fish often school offshore over reefs in 5 to 40 m of water. Depending on local conditions, you can anchor or drift over them, drop baits or lures, and expect to capture fish up to 5 kg.

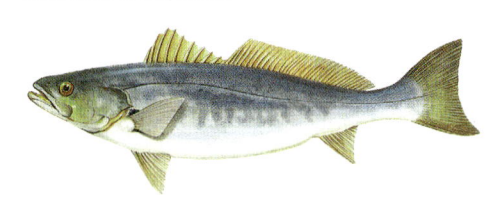

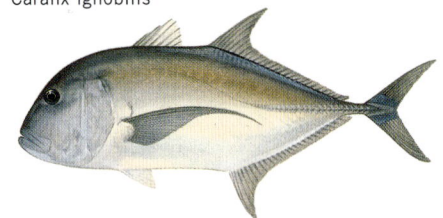

IDENTIFYING YOUR CATCH

FISH	LOCATION/DESCRIPTION	FISHING METHOD

TROUT, BROOK
Salvelinus fontinalis

Also known as brookies, brook char.

Brook trout, actually a form of North American char, were first introduced in the 1870s, but have not acclimatised with the same success as browns and rainbows. Their distribution is patchy in most alpine regions of Australia, notably within Lake Jindabyne, and some streams within the New England area of New South Wales. One of the most important populations is present in Tasmania's Clarence Lagoon. Common sizes are between half a kilo and 2 kg.

Flies, bait or lures can be used. In lakes, they respond to fly fishing from the bank perhaps more readily than to other methods, and opinion is divided whether bait fishing or fly fishing is better in streams.

TROUT, BROWN
Salmo trutta

Also known as brownie, brown, German trout, Englishman.

The brown trout originated in Europe and has been successfully introduced into New South Wales and Victoria, with Tasmania having perhaps some of the best wild, brown trout fishing in the world. Nearly all alpine regions capable of sustaining trout have been stocked with browns, most notably Lake Eucumbene in New South Wales, which has a successful spawning run most winters into the Eucumbene River. Browns are commonly caught from half a kilo up to 2 kg, but can exceed 5 kg in some waters.

The best methods are wet or dry fly fishing, spinning with small-bladed lures, or using Glo-bugs and trailing nymph rigs on fish that gather in pre-spawning aggregations. Browns also readily take baits of worms, yabbies, mudeyes, live crickets and grasshoppers.

TROUT, CORAL
Plectropomus maculatus

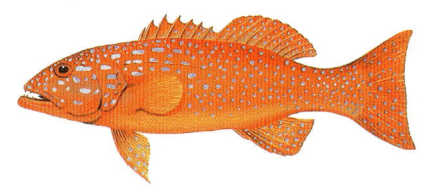

Also known as coastal trout, island coral trout, leopard cod trout.

The coral trout is one of the most prized sport and table fish of the north. It inhabits both inshore and outer reefs, the larger fish being found on the most seaward extremities or most remote locations. It is stout, with an amazing range of colouration, the most common of which is a bright red body carrying electric blue spots that become larger and more scattered towards the head. Fish larger than 8 kg have been implicated in ciguatera cases, when caught off the Great Barrier Reef. Western Australia does not have ciguatera.

Suspend baits just off the bottom and pay great attention to precise anchoring. Alternatively, large surface poppers can be cast over coral shallows, skipping them back over the drop-off into deeper water. When hooked, trout run like an express train.

TROUT, RAINBOW
Oncorhynchus mykiss

Also known as bows, rainbows, sea-run trout, steelhead.

This flashy, attractively coloured fish needs artificial stocking to maintain numbers. This is due to the fact that it spawns after the brown trout and the results are less productive. Distributed widely throughout Tasmania, Victoria and alpine regions of New South Wales, the rainbow seems to prefer faster, rocky streams, and deeper, colder lakes. It is also found in certain areas of South Australia and Western Australia. This fish commonly attains 1 to 2 kg, but is capable of growing to 6 kg or more.

Best methods are bait fishing, trolling and spinning for most small to average fish, and fly fishing for the large specimens. Trolling very early in the morning is preferred once the warmer weather arrives.

TRUMPETER, BASTARD
Latridopsis forsteri

Also known as silver trumpeter.

This species is said to have earned its common name because it is difficult to catch. It is found in the cool marine environments of the southern states, inhabiting areas from deep offshore reefs to shallow rocky inshore waters. Its distribution is similar to the Tasmanian trumpeter (*Latris lineata*), but it is often found in shallow waters while the Tasmanian is not. The bastard trumpeter is not a large fish, averaging 1 to 2 kg, whereas the Tasmanian can grow to well over 10 kg. Both are good table fish.

Not a common catch on hook and line, but best baits include crab, prawn and squid fished on or near the bottom. The Tasmanian trumpeter is often taken on bait or jigs fished on the bottom in deep water from 20 to 160 m.

439

IDENTIFYING YOUR CATCH

FISH	LOCATION/DESCRIPTION	FISHING METHOD

TUNA, LONGTAIL
Thunnus tonggol

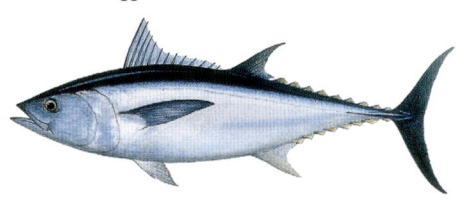

Also known as northern bluefin tuna, northern blue.

This species is common at 10 to 15 kg and is known to exceed 40 kg. It has a similar distribution to mackerel tuna. It is regularly taken each summer and autumn by rock anglers in New South Wales who use live bait with slimy mackerel, garfish or yellowtail scad. In Moreton Bay and various other more northerly Queensland locations, it may be spun for from boats by approaching surface feeding schools. Of only passable food value, northern blues are essentially a sportfish or a source of bait.

Best methods include lure casting or live baiting from either ocean rocks, large river breakwalls, or boats. Some anglers berleying and cubing for yellowfin tuna around Bermagui have taken exceptional specimens of this fish, to 35 kg or better, on live baits.

TUNA, MACKEREL
Euthynnus affinis

Also known as kawakawa, mack tuna, mack, oriental bonito.

The mackerel tuna is a robust, tapering fish found in northern New South Wales, Queensland, Northern Territory and the west coast of Western Australia. A fish of both open ocean and inshore waters, it often schools with Spanish and spotted mackerel. In spring, schools of this fish gather inshore to harass glass bait fish and may enter large bays. However, these incursions are not as common as they once were, due perhaps to natural cycles of abundance and scarcity, or overfishing.

Lure casting metal lures such as those that imitate small bait fish is successful from boats or ocean rocks. Also fishing small live fish under a bobby cork is useful when they are not evident. Trolling is not a preferred option.

TUNA, SOUTHERN BLUEFIN
Thunnus maccoyii

Also known as southern blue.

A more rotund and stocky tuna, the southern bluefin is one of the largest marine game fish in southern Australia. It was once a profitable and rich fishing resource of Australia's southern oceans. Overfishing and poor resource management led to the collapse of southern bluefin stocks. It is found in coastal offshore waters throughout southern Australia, from southern New South Wales to the coast of Western Australia. An acceptable barbecue fish, the main use of southern bluefin is for canned tuna.

Lures, live baits and strip baits are best. It is normally taken by trolling small feather jigs at a fairly fast troll speed. At times it is best to lure cast from a boat. Taking from shore is rare.

TUNA, STRIPED
Katsuwonis pelamis

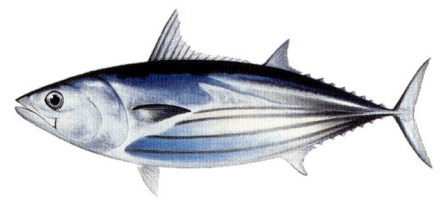

Also known as skipjack tuna, stripey.

Striped tuna are found usually in large schools all around Australia, particularly in coastal waters of southern Australia. Commonly trolled from the 100-m line off coastlines from Queensland through New South Wales to Tasmania, this species is a vital intermediate forage link in the food chain between small ocean species and the larger game fish. Although well regarded as a sportfish, it is of poor food value unless steamed commercially, and is most often killed for bait or berley.

Spinning or trolling with lures from a boat is best, but it can be taken from the shore with long casts by rock anglers. Lines can be down to 3 or 4 kg, but reels must have good drags and carry enough line to exhaust this determined and powerful little battler.

TUNA, YELLOWFIN
Thunnus albacares

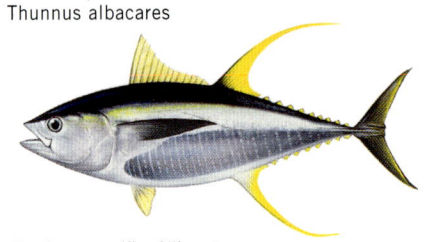

Also known as 'fin, Allison tuna.

An important commercial species, which in angling terms has come to mean 'a threatened resource', yellowfin tuna has been targeted more in the last twenty years than in the previous hundred, probably because of the aggravated decline of southern bluefin. Found all around Australia, yellowfin comes within reach of coastal anglers most often in late summer and early autumn, when fish can vary between 15 to 50 kg. Known to grow in excess of 100 kg, this is a magnificent food and sportfish.

Best methods include trolling lures or live fish, such as striped tuna and frigate mackerel, or skipping dead rigged garfish. Cubing – a technique of feeding baits and berley out into a current – practised from an anchored boat is very successful.

IDENTIFYING YOUR CATCH

FISH	LOCATION/DESCRIPTION	FISHING METHOD
TUSKFISH, VENUS *Choerodon venustus*  *Also known as bluebone tuskfish, venus parrotfish.*	 The Venus tuskfish is a member of the wrasse family and not hard to recognise due to its bright colouring of purples, silver and pink. This fish is found along the east coast, north of Sydney, and across the top half of Australia. Its size varies from 2 to 5 kg, with larger specimens reaching 7 to 8 kg. Another species (*C. rubescens*), found in Western Australia between Coral Bay and Geographe Bay, grows to over 10 kg. Both species are superb fish to eat.	Baits of crab and cut fish are best, with double extra strong hooks and lines. Rod and reel anglers might get by with 15 to 25-kg line on the smaller fish, which average around 5 to 6 kg, but the big adults can require heavy handlines.
WAHOO *Acanthocybium solandri*  *Also known as Doctor Hoo, 'hoo.*	 A tropical species of fish, loosely related to the mackerels, wahoo is found around coral reef areas of northern New South Wales, Queensland and Exmouth in Western Australia. It strays as far south as Sydney and the Sir Joseph Young Banks off Nowra, when warm northerly currents create the sparkling clean, deep blue ocean water in which you would expect to see this fish. The wahoo's speed and willingness to put up a fight make it a game fish of international note. The average size is about 15 kg.	Rarely caught from shore, it is usually encountered when trolling lures from a boat. Lures must be rigged on wire. Be prepared in the event of an accidental strike. Wahoo earn the ire of many marlin anglers, being capable of severing a carefully rigged marlin bait.
WHITING, KING GEORGE *Sillaginodes punctata*  *Also known as black whiting, South Australian writing, spotted whiting.*	 The King George whiting, the largest and tastiest of the whiting family, is plentiful in Victoria, South Australia and southern Western Australia. It is only an occasional capture in New South Wales and Tasmania. It is native to the shallow grassy flats with sand and mud bottom, although some larger fish prefer scattered offshore reefs. It grows to an impressive 60 cm or more, which translates into weights in excess of 2 kg. An important commercial catch, it is an excellent table fish.	Baits of mussel, pippi, skinned squid and octopus tentacle, live marine worms and pink nippers are all used. Hooks need to be small, but this can mean up to #1 or 1/0 for the larger fish, and #6 to #4 for the average size. Line need only be 3 to 4 kg.
WHITING, SAND *Sillago ciliata*  *Also known as bluenose whiting, sandie, silver whiting, summer whiting.*	 Abundant on the east coast, the sand whiting is commonly caught by anglers. It is found along the east coast from Cape York, south along the New South Wales coast and into the East Gippsland–Lakes Entrance region of Victoria. Tasmania has a few on the eastern seaboard. Common from half to three quarters of a kilo, the sand whiting can grow in excess of 1 kg and has sweet tasting, firm flesh. It is a willing, straightforward biter on most marine worm and shellfish baits, and is fun to catch.	Small-gape long shanked hooks from #6 to #2 are usual in estuaries; bigger beach fish will take baits on a size #1 if hungry enough. Good baits are bloodworms, squirt worms, beachworms, garden worms, pippis, cockles, mussels and small soldier crabs.
WRASSE, CRIMSON-BANDED *Pseudolabrus gymnogenis*  *Also known as white spotted parrotfish.*	 This commonly encountered fish is one of several species known as parrotfish, so-called because of the formation of the front teeth, which form parrot-like shears. A related species, the rosy wrasse (*P. psittaculus*) is fairly common in reef areas of coastal Victoria and Tasmania. The white-spotted parrotfish commonly attains weights of 1 kg, but may be caught at several times that size. It is found on reefs from 2 m to 30 m in depth, and can dominate rock fishing captures. It is a fair table fish.	Use strips of fish flesh, presented near or on the bottom. It is best targeted in shallow water by dropping baits close to natural rock walls and using minimum weight to enable the bait to sink slowly.

COOKING YOUR CATCH

COOKING YOUR CATCH

Hook to Cook

The preparation stage is never as enjoyable as the act of fishing itself. However, the correct preparation will go some way towards making the eating as enjoyable as the sport. From hook to cook (spear to smear), the three most important steps are killing, cleaning and storing. Every fish killed deserves to be killed quickly and humanely, cleaned efficiently, stored responsibly, cooked thoughtfully and eaten slowly.

Most people have probably never been lucky enough to eat a fish that is really fresh. A fresh fish is one that has been caught, landed and killed quickly and without stress. It has been bled and gutted in clean water using a clean knife. Straight after the cleaning it has been laid in a slurry of ice and salt water (equal parts of each) in an esky or similar and cooked before the ice melts.

This is truly an experience worth trying because there's nothing quite like it, and once you have experienced the flavour, no other fish will taste the same. Fresh fish has the most wonderful taste, smell and texture, and is also very nutritious. If your fish is not fresh, all these other attributes are affected.

FISH FLESH

In cooking, the flesh is the part of the fish in which we are obviously most interested. In some fish, such as john dory, the flesh accounts for only 25 per cent of the whole fish. However, the fish carcass should not be wasted. Heads and bones, for instance, can be used to make fish stocks and soups.

Fish flesh is easily digested and is generally delicate in texture. It should never be overcooked or dried out. The muscles are fragile and the muscle fibres break down quickly when heated. It is a nutritious food, rich in protein and vitamins, low in carbohydrates and cholesterol. Because the essences, or the aromatic juices, are so subtle in fish, short simple cooking techniques are best. Fish rarely improves from long cooking or the addition of strong flavours.

Fish species vary in flavour, and generally the whiter-fleshed fish have milder flavours, while the darker-fleshed fish are richer in taste and require more technique in preparation and cooking. Fish quality is better out of the spawning season, during which time both texture and taste are adversely affected. Know your fish and learn about its habits, both in the water and in the pan.

John dory fillets account for only 25 per cent of the whole fish

SCALING

Start at the tail

Scrape, using short strokes toward the head

KILLING YOUR FISH

There has been much research done in this area, and yet nobody is sure whether fish suffer pain as we do. However, it is known that fish do experience stress, which in turn releases lactic acid to the blood supply and consequently has a detrimental effect on texture and taste. Apart from the undesirable affect on table quality, the fish does not deserve to suffer, and it is to everyone's advantage to kill quickly. How best to do it? The Japanese use the phrase 'ike jima' to describe the quick death experienced by all tuna for the sashimi market. A pointed instrument is used to pith (to deliver a quick blow to) the brain. However, the angler needs to be aware that the brain is not in the same place in all species of fish, and it takes practice to get it right every time.

Generally, one quick blow to the top of the head with a blunt instrument (often referred to as a 'priest' in fishing parlance) will kill the fish outright. A piece of hardwood, an old hammer, a cut-down axe or mattock handle will suffice – something that fits comfortably in your hand and can be accurately struck to the top of the fish's head. If you can't bring yourself to do this, cut its throat and bleed it, or throw it back while it is still alive. If you plan to return the fish to the water, handle it as little as possible because the slime coating on the fish protects it from exposure to various diseases. If you want to catch fish for the sport rather than for the eating, a good practice is to use flattened or barbless hooks, so that returning the fish to the water is simply a matter of releasing the pressure on the hook.

COOKING YOUR CATCH

CLEANING

To remove head, slide serrated knife in behind gill

Cut through bone and repeat on other side

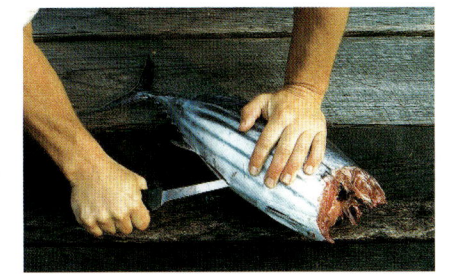

(Remove head.) Slip point of filleting knife in vent

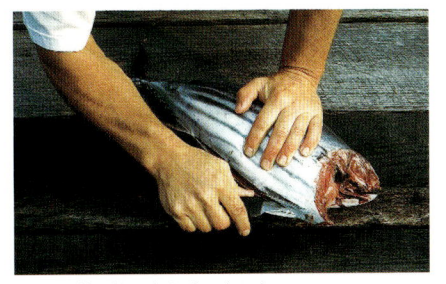

Push knife through to head end

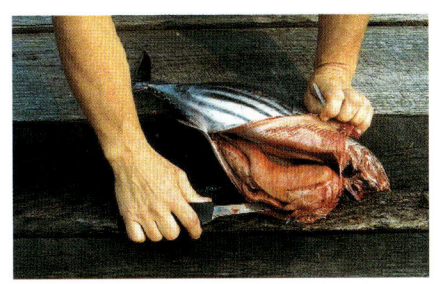

Open up to expose gut

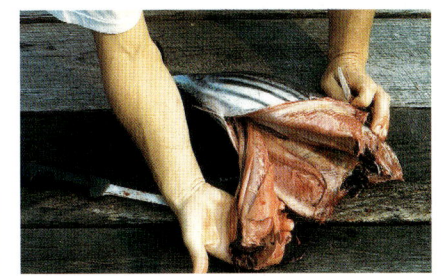

Grab what you can and remove

CLEANING YOUR FISH

All fish should be bled immediately after they have been killed, and then gutted and washed. Scaling and skinning the fish can be safely left until you are ready to prepare the fish for cooking. The skin and scales help extend the life of the flesh, and skin can be removed later in one swift action with a knife.

Bleeding To bleed most fish, cut the throat below the gills and bend the head back, which in turn breaks the spine. To remove the gut, lay the fish on its side, insert the point of the knife into the vent and slit the stomach open, turning the knife towards the centre of the gills. Using a knife, a spoon or your hand, forcefully pull out everything that is inside. Remove any blood vessels along the inside of the backbone and cut out any other red meat (in the case of white-fleshed fish), gills, etc. It is these red meats that speed up the decaying process if left in or on the fish. If you are at sea or upriver, throw the guts over the side. If you are onshore, keep the good bits of offal for bait and dispose of the rest thoughtfully; buried, they make great fertiliser for the garden.

Washing Once gutted, the flesh of the fish is exposed to attack by bacteria and it is very important to wash the fish thoroughly in clean water. If you are at sea or on a lake, up a river or on rocks, chances are that your water is clean. The worst place for fish cleaning is on or around slipways and loading ramps. These areas are alive with germs, spilt fuel, old bait, old fish guts, and other decomposing remains. Wash the insides of the fish out thoroughly and rinse the outside of the fish with clean water and leave the slime, scales and skin on the fish to help preserve the flesh.

If you leave cleaning and gutting your fish until returning to land, there is a chance that the gases emitted from the gut will begin to spoil and taint the flesh. It is for this reason that the cleaning and gutting is best done as soon as possible after killing your fish.

STORING YOUR FISH

Fish is best consumed as soon as possible after being caught. Fresh fish should never be put in any sort of a bag. Plastic, paper and even hessian speeds up the decaying process. Leave the scales and skin on and lay the fish flat in a slurry of ice and salt water (a ratio of 1:1). An ice slurry mixture is a quicker chilling medium than straight ice and therefore the best method of storing fish. If rigor mortis (stiffening) sets in, do not try to straighten the fish. This will only tear the flesh and speed up the decaying process. If the water is changed daily and the ice replaced, cleaned and gutted fish should keep in reasonable condition for up to 14 days. In a domestic refrigerator, with an average temperature of 1° C to 5° C, fish will keep fresh for 3 days. It will not be worth eating after 5 days.

If freezing your fish, they should be put into plastic bags prior to freezing. If storing in a domestic freezer (–18° C to –23° C), frozen fish should be eaten within 3 months. Temperatures ranging between –23° C and –30° C cause the water content in fish to change to ice crystals, rupturing the cells, and resulting in loss of flavour and nutrients.

Commercial freezers operate at temperatures below –30° C, which maintains flavour and nutrients. They can therefore provide a superior frozen product to the home-frozen fish. This is another reason to eat your fish fresh from the ocean. It follows that you should catch less fish and fish more often.

Remember, some fish species do not freeze well. Trevally, a delicious fish fresh, is almost inedible after freezing. Some fish that do freeze well are: those belonging to the Salmonidae family, such as trout; deepwater fish such as fingermark and orange roughy (sea perch); and firm, white-fleshed fish such as snapper.

It should also be noted that the warmer the climate, the quicker the degeneration of the fish flesh. In the tropical north of Australia it is mandatory to get your fish cleaned, gutted and onto ice within 5 to 15 minutes of capture. Further south, in the colder climates, the urgency is reduced somewhat, although as a general rule, 'the sooner the better'.

Fish can be stored in a slurry of ice and salt water

COOKING YOUR CATCH

Cuts for Cooking

The size of the fish and the size of your cooking utensil will determine the method of preparing the fish. Generally, big fish can be cut into steaks and smaller fish are better suited to filleting. All fish can be cooked whole, but the size of the oven and pan will limit your options.

WHOLE FISH

Fish cooked whole are best if medium-sized, ranging up to about 3 kg. Whole fish are easy to cook, but they must be gutted and cleaned. The skin and scales can be retained during cooking; afterwards the skin will peel off, exposing the lovely moist flesh.

Leaving the head on during cooking is optional. The head does not improve the cooking. It is merely left on for appearance. Some people like the look of the whole fish; others savour the little pockets of flesh around the eyes. One thing to remember is that if the head is left on after killing, it will speed up the process of natural decomposition. If the head is removed, it is worth keeping to add to the other bones to make a wonderful fish stock, ideal for soups and sauces to complement fish dishes.

FISH STEAKS OR CUTLETS

Fish steaks or cutlets are best cut from larger fish of 3 to 10 kg in size. Use a knife with a serrated edge. Lay the fish on its side on a bench and start at the tail end. Cut off the tail by using a sawing action. Work your way along the fish, cutting steaks of about 30 mm thick. Cut thicker steaks at the tail end and thinner portions where the body gets larger. Steaks can be cooked by any of the suggested cooking methods on page 448. The fish most commonly cut into steaks include tuna, snapper, salmon and tailor.

FISH FILLETS

Smaller fish are better filleted. Some fillets like john dory and silver dory will keep their shape better if cooked with the skin on. However, a fish such as flathead is better with the skin removed. Fish such as bream, dory, whiting, trout and flathead are ideal for filleting. Bream is the easiest fish to fillet.

Filleting The fish must be gutted and cleaned before filleting, but scaling and skinning is easiest after the filleting process. Filleting of most fish can be done in the following way.

- Slip a very sharp knife in behind the gills (which are the side fins closest to the head).
- Cut through the bone. Turn the fish over and repeat this action on the other side. Remove the head.
- Cut flesh near the tail, down to the backbone. Lay the knife flat and slide it towards the head end, making sure the knife is working away from you.
- Turn the fish over and repeat the process.

Skinning fish fillets The majority of fish are easier to skin after filleting.

- Lay the fillet on a bench, skin side down.
- Grab the skin at the very tip of the tail end with your fingers or a pair of pliers and slip the knife in on the flesh.
- Cut down until you feel the skin.
- In one motion cut along the skin towards the wide end of the fillet.

Skinning whole fish There are some fish, such as leatherjacket, red morwong and flounder, that are easily skinned while still whole. If you are careful, you should end up with a fish with no skin and no torn flesh.

- With the point of a knife, cut the skin right around the perimeter of the body where it joins all fins, including a slit across the tail.
- Slip the knife in under the skin at the end of the tail and make a pocket big enough to get hold of the skin with either your fingers or a pair of pliers.
- Simply peel the skin gently back towards the head.

USEFUL TIP

Use a filleting knife to cut fish flesh and a serrated knife to saw through bone.

FILLETING A SMALL FISH

Slip knife in and down until stopped by bone

Change position and cut, keeping knife flat

Continue to cut along the bone

SKINNING A SMALL FISH FILLET

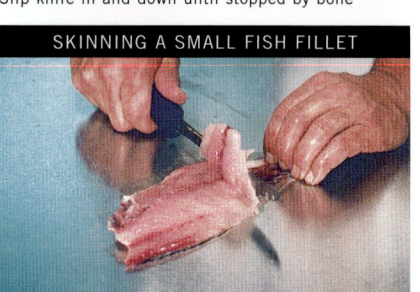

Place fillet skin side down

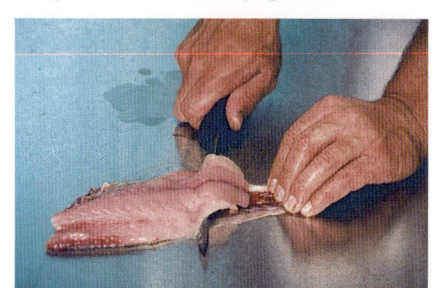

Cut through flesh to the skin

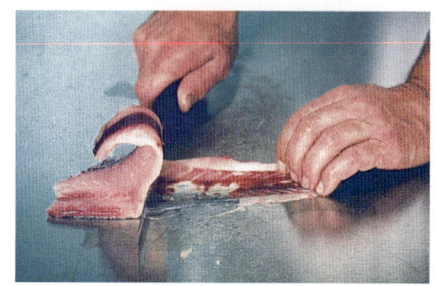

Flatten knife and slide along skin

COOKING YOUR CATCH

FISH STEAKS

Remove gills

Remove any traces of red meat

Using serrated knife, start at tail

Saw through bone to other side

Cut steaks more thickly at tail end

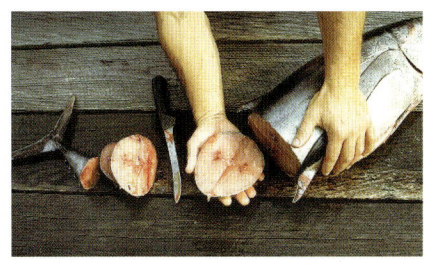

Cut steaks more thinly as body gets bigger

FILLETING A LARGE FISH

(Remove head.) Slip knife in and down to bone

Run knife along swiftly

Continue along bone

Slip fingers in to aid progress

Keep knife flat against backbone

Lift up fillet and finish cut

SKINNING A LARGE FISH FILLET

Fillet must be skin side down

Hold tail end and cut flesh to skin

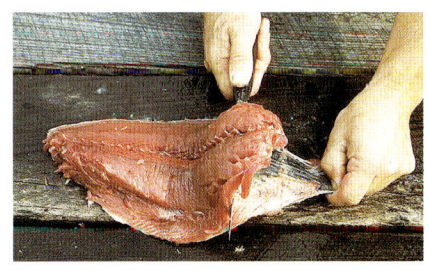

Run knife along flesh, keeping knife flat

Keep firm grip on skin

Fold back flesh

Pull skin against knife to finish off

447

Cooking Methods

Fish fall into several categories, each suiting particular cooking methods. The light white-fleshed fish, such as bream, flounder, whiting, john dory, mulloway and ling are all best suited to frying or gentle baking. The darker, oilier fish with a stronger flavour, including kingfish, mullet, tuna, gemfish and tailor, are better grilled, poached or braised.

Fresh fish flesh is reasonably translucent, becoming opaque or whitish when cooked. At this stage the flesh will flake along the muscle and release a clear juice. Once cooked the fish should be served immediately. Remember, the flesh will continue to cook a little when removed from the heat, so always serve fish firm and juicy, not firm and dry.

The following cooking methods and recipes are suggestions only. However, like the selection of a particular wine, anything goes. It is up to the individual palate. Why not experiment; you will discover that most fish can be cooked by any method. Just remember, it takes great chefs and even greater recipes to make something out of a second-rate fish. Really fresh fish only needs a simple recipe.

FRYING

Frying fish can be carried out by either of two methods: panfrying, also known as shallow frying; and deepfrying, which is the style used in fish and chip shops. Both frying techniques are suited to most fish species. However, in panfrying, the fish only needs a light dusting of flour before being placed gently into the hot cooking agent. In the case of deepfrying, the fish needs to be coated in batter or breadcrumbs to benefit from the oil saturation.

GRILLING

This is a method of cooking where the fish is either placed on a grill over a fire or placed under a griller. In the latter case, the heat source is above the food, and the heat is generally very severe. It is an ideal cooking method for people requiring a diet with no added fat. Alternatively, grilling can be done on a barbecue. Generally, the severe form of heat of the barbecue is ideal for all fish. Delicate-fleshed fish benefit from a little basting with butter or oil. Darker, fattier types of fish grill well without added fats, but a squeeze of lemon and some grated peppercorns will enhance the flavour.

When grilling fish, care must be taken not to overcook or dry out the fish and constant attention and basting with a little oil or butter will help. Leaving the skin on can also protect the flesh from drying out too quickly. The recipe on page 450 will work equally well with mullet, tailor, coral trout, estuary cod, threadfin salmon and pearl perch, to name but a few.

BAKING

This is one of the simplest ways to cook a whole fish, particularly a large specimen. The fish should be buttered on the outside, laid on a baking tray with a little liquid in the bottom, and moist baked.

POACHING

This is not a commonly used cooking method in Australia but it is suited to delicate-fleshed fish. In poaching, the cooking liquid is generally water, with an onion, bay-leaf and clove added. The water should only just simmer. Poaching is a great way to cook a whole fish, which can be served hot or cold. Served with a sauce, it is ideal for lunch.

STEAMING

This is the easiest method of cooking without the addition of any fats. The fish are laid out on a rack over water that must be boiled to maintain a constant temperature above 100° C. Bamboo steamers are ideal or a colander sitting over a saucepan of water will do. A tight-fitting lid is required or enough aluminium foil to seal in the steam. This method of cooking is quite quick, and a fillet takes only a few minutes.

BRAISING

Braising is a cooking method generally done in a large pot or casserole dish with a lid, or a baking tray, which is later covered with foil. The fish should be placed in the casserole, on a bed of vegetables, and barely covered with fish stock or wine, covered with a lid, and slowly simmered in the oven or over a very gentle heat on a stove, or on the hot coals of an open fire. In the oven, most fish will require slow cooking at 180° C for at least 1 hour. This method of cooking is best for fish that will improve with the addition of the subtle flavours of vegetables and wine.

The bed of vegetables is often referred to as a mirepoix, and comprises coarsely chopped vegetables and herbs cooked in butter. Shark and nannygai lend themselves to braised dishes with tomato and fennel. Large mulloway and eel (eel is becoming increasingly available live and chilled) can also be braised.

SMOKING

There are two forms of smoking: hot smoke and cold smoke. Recent research has shown that cold smoking can form perfect conditions for the incubation of harmful bacteria. Hot smoking, however, is safe, and the technique is described on page 452. This method was first employed to preserve fish, but the flavours imparted by the wood and smoke make fish cooked this way worth trying.

MARINATING

This is another form of preserving fish, but is also a way of imparting additional flavours to the flesh of what might normally be a fairly bland-tasting fish. You can use either a liquid marinade (a mixture of oil, acid – vinegar, wine or citrus juice – and spices), in which the fish will soak for several hours prior to cooking, or a dry marinade, made up of salts, sugar and spices. The dry marinade mix is sprinkled heavily over the fish flesh, which needs to be turned regularly over a period of 48 hours. The result will be a fish ready for eating, which has required no cooking. The Cajun style of marinating uses chilli, cumin and coriander, before cooking the fish over a very high heat. The 'blackened' result is attractive and particularly flavoursome.

STOCK, SOUP, PATTIES AND PIES

Good stock is made from good bones and fish offcuts, which must always be fresh. Pies and patties can be made from fresh uncooked fish pieces or from cooked leftovers. By adding herbs and spices, and eggs and flour, you can make crumbed patties or pastry-topped pies, all great hot or cold for picnics or that next fishing trip.

UNLESS OTHERWISE STATED, RECIPES SERVE 4.

Fried Fish

It is very important to control the temperature of the cooking agent when panfrying fish. It must be kept very hot but must not burn. For this reason oil is preferable to butter, but if care is taken, a little butter added to the oil just before cooking will provide the fish with that wonderful buttery flavour. Clarified butter (ghee) is also ideal. The oil should be almost smoking before adding the fish, which must be perfectly dry (wipe it with a paper towel). Dust the fish with flour and place it gently in the hot oil. Whole fish will take about 5 minutes on each side; fillets will take 2 or 3 minutes. Fish such as flathead, ling, whiting, barramundi, flounder, bream and leatherjacket can be cooked in this way.

PANFRIED TROUT WITH ALMONDS

1 CUP MILK
SALT
PEPPER
4 TROUT
4 TABLESPOONS FLOUR
3 TABLESPOONS OIL
150 G BUTTER
1 CUP FLAKED OR SLICED ALMONDS
1 TABLESPOON FRESHLY CHOPPED PARSLEY
2 LEMONS, CUT IN HALF TO SERVE

Panfried trout with almonds

Pour the milk into a shallow dish and season with salt and pepper. Dip each trout in the milk and then roll in the flour. Heat the oil in a pan and, when hot, add 50 g of butter. When the butter has melted, add the trout and cook until golden on each side. This will take about 5 minutes. Remove to serving plates. In a separate pan, heat the remaining butter. Add the almonds and carefully heat and stir until golden brown. Tip butter and almond mixture over the trout, add the chopped parsley and serve.

Panfried john dory

PANFRIED JOHN DORY

4 JOHN DORY FILLETS (SKIN ON)
50 G PLAIN FLOUR
60 G BUTTER, MELTED
OIL, FOR COOKING
PINCH OF PAPRIKA
SALT
WHITE PEPPERCORNS

Dry fillets with a paper towel and dust each one with flour. Holding the tip of the tail end, dip the floured fillet into the melted butter, making sure to coat both sides. Heat a little oil in a frying pan. When hot, gently lay fillets skin-side down in pan and sprinkle with paprika. Fry gently over a low heat until the flesh is just firm. This will take 2 to 3 minutes. Place a lid over the pan for the last minute to ensure even cooking. Season with a little salt and freshly ground white peppercorns.

Deepfried Fish

Deepfried fish should be coated with batter before cooking. It is important that the temperature of the oil should be kept constant at 180°C to 190°C. To check the temperature of the hot oil, simply drop a little batter into it. If the oil is hot enough, the batter will instantly come to the top of the oil and start bubbling and cooking. If the batter sinks, the oil is too cold. Some fish that are particularly suited to deepfrying include shark, snapper, blue grenadier, garfish, morwong, mulloway, red emperor, estuary cod, sweetlip, warehou and trevally.

BATTER FOR FISH

1 CUP WATER OR BEER
2 EGGS
1 TEASPOON OLIVE OIL
½ TEASPOON SALT
½ TEASPOON GROUND WHITE PEPPER
1 TABLESPOON CORNFLOUR
1 ½ CUPS PLAIN FLOUR

Beat the water and eggs and add the oil, salt and pepper. Gradually add the cornflour and plain flour, beating constantly as you do so. Let the batter sit for at least 1 hour before using. When ready, heat the oil to 180° C – 190° C, and check the temperature as discussed above. Dry your fish fillets completely, dust them with flour and then dip them into the batter. Wipe off any excess batter on the edge of the bowl. Gently and carefully slip the battered fish into the hot oil, taking care not to splash yourself. Cook for 5 to 10 minutes: 5 minutes for small fillets, 10 minutes for large, thicker fillets.

COOKING YOUR CATCH

Grilled Fish

GRILLED TUNA

4 TUNA STEAKS
4 TABLESPOONS OLIVE OIL
1 LEMON, SLICED

Herb butter
150 G BUTTER, AT ROOM TEMPERATURE
1 TABLESPOON FRESHLY CHOPPED CHIVES
1 TABLESPOON FRESHLY CHOPPED PARSLEY
1 TABLESPOON WORCESTERSHIRE SAUCE
SALT
PEPPER

To make the herb butter, whisk the soft butter until creamy. Add all the other ingredients and mix until well blended. Roll like a sausage in foil and refrigerate until firm. When ready to use, slice off in 25-mm rounds and remove the foil. Brush the tuna with oil and place under a hot grill. Baste steaks with more oil as they begin to dry out. Turn over after 3 minutes, baste again and grill for 3 minutes more. Remove from the griller and place on a plate with a slice of herb butter. Serve with slices of lemon.

Grilled tuna

Baked Fish

Baking fish is a wonderful way of keeping a reasonably delicate piece of fish intact. Something as small and delicate as a whiting fillet can be dusted with flour, dipped in a bowl with a few tablespoons of melted butter, then laid on a tray and baked in an oven that has been preheated to 180° C. Bake for 5 minutes or until the flesh is firm to touch. Larger whole fish can be treated the same way (2 kg will take about 35 minutes, 3 kg about 45 minutes). Try baking albacore, whiting, dory, barramundi, trout, flounder, snapper, nannygai or Australian salmon.

FISH ON THE SPOT

All you need is a fire, a fish (cleaned) and some foil, and you do not really need the foil if you like that charcoal flavour.

Find a safe spot for lighting a fire. You need to establish a reasonable-sized log blaze in order to be left with good coals when the flames have died down. Wrap a whole fish in foil, place it gently in the coals and cover it with more coals. Allow it to cook until the flesh falls away from the bone when poked with a stick – 10 minutes or so should do it. If you are cooking without foil, simply put the whole fish on the coals and proceed in the same way.

For flavour variations when cooking the fish in foil, you can add butter, onion, garlic, lemon slices, tomato, bay-leaves, thyme and peppercorns – separately or in combinations, wrapped inside the foil. A few potatoes thrown into the coals and you will quite possibly end up with a fish dish that the great chefs dream about.

BAKED WHOLE FISH

1 WHOLE FISH, CLEANED
SALT
PEPPER
4 SHALLOTS, FINELY CHOPPED
1 CUP DRY WHITE WINE
2 TABLESPOONS FRESH BREADCRUMBS
2 TABLESPOONS FRESHLY CHOPPED PARSLEY
25 G BUTTER

Preheat the oven to 220° C. Make a few cuts across the fish flesh with a knife, place in an ovenproof dish and season with salt and pepper. Sprinkle the chopped shallots over the fish and add the wine. Sprinkle the breadcrumbs and parsley over the fish and dot with small pieces of butter. Bake for 25 to 30 minutes, with par-boiled vegetables.

COOKING YOUR CATCH

FISH IN FOIL

4 SQUARES ALUMINIUM FOIL (LARGE ENOUGH
TO WRAP AROUND FISH)
2 TABLESPOONS OLIVE OIL
4 SMALL WHOLE FISH, CLEANED
3 CLOVES GARLIC, FINELY CHOPPED
3 MEDIUM-SIZED TOMATOES, DICED
1 TABLESPOON FINELY CHOPPED PARSLEY
SALT
PEPPER
4 BAY LEAVES

Preheat the oven to 180° C. Brush one side of the foil squares with some olive oil. Place one fish on each piece of foil. In a bowl, mix the garlic, tomato and parsley together and season with salt and pepper. Spoon an equal amount onto each fish. Place a bay leaf on each seasoning mound and dribble the remaining oil over the top. Wrap the foil so as to completely encase the fish and its seasonings. Place in the oven for 10 to 15 minutes or sit in the ashes of a fire for 5 to 10 minutes.

Steamed fish

RICE STUFFING FOR BAKED WHOLE FISH

½ CUP OLIVE OIL
1 ONION, FINELY CHOPPED
½ CUP WHITE WINE
2 TABLESPOONS FRESHLY CHOPPED PARSLEY
1 TABLESPOON TOMATO PASTE
SALT
PEPPER
1 CUP RICE
JUICE OF ½ LEMON

Tip half the oil into a pan and heat. Add the onion and sauté in the oil. Add the wine, parsley, tomato paste, salt and pepper to taste, and bring to the boil. Add the rice and cook until the liquid evaporates and the rice is partly cooked. Allow to cool a little, and then the add the lemon juice. The stuffing is now ready to put into the cavity of your fish before cooking it whole.

Baked fish in foil

Poached and Steamed

Poaching requires a constant and gentle simmering of liquid, which should only just cover the fish that is cooking in it. The poaching liquid should never boil and care must be taken in removing the fish after cooking as it will be very fragile. A bamboo skewer thrust through the tail and then in through the head can hold the fish in position while poaching and give a handle to remove it from the liquid after cooking. Trout, flathead, garfish, snapper, rosy Job-fish and john dory are ideal fish for poaching.

Steaming is the easiest method of cooking fish quickly without the addition of any fats. All that is needed is a little boiling water in the bottom of a saucepan, a colander or bamboo steamer sitting over the water and a tight-fitting lid or enough aluminium foil to seal in the steam. Fish suited to steaming include whiting, trout, golden perch, sweetlip, Westralian jewfish, red emperor and estuary cod.

STEAMED FISH WITH BABY VEGETABLES

4 x 100 G FISH FILLETS OR CUTLETS
300 ML FISH STOCK
150 ML CREAM
½ TEASPOON FRESHLY CHOPPED CHIVES
½ TEASPOON FRESHLY CHOPPED DILL
SELECTION OF BABY VEGETABLES

Quarter-fill a saucepan with water and bring to the boil. Place the fish fillets in a steamer or other perforated container, such as a colander, over the saucepan. Fit lid, or cover with foil, and steam for about 3 minutes for fillets, 4 to 5 minutes for cutlets and 5 minutes for a whole small fish. The fish will cook thoroughly without turning. When the fish is cooked the flesh should be firm to touch. Carefully remove from the steamer.

In a small saucepan bring the fish stock to the boil and cook the baby vegetables in the hot stock. This will take a few minutes. Remove the vegetables from the stock and keep warm. Continue to boil the stock for a few minutes to reduce slightly. Add the cream, chives and dill to the fish stock and stir. Place the fish on a plate, surround it with vegetables and spoon the sauce over the top.

COOKING YOUR CATCH

Braised Fish

BRAISED LUDERICK

1 SMALL TO MEDIUM-SIZED FISH (½ – 2 KG)
1 LITRE WINE, WATER OR FISH STOCK
(OR COMBINATION)

Mirepoix
1 TABLESPOON OLIVE OIL
1 CARROT, FINELY CHOPPED
1 STICK CELERY, FINELY SLICED
1 ONION, FINELY CHOPPED
1 BAY LEAF
2 SPRIGS THYME
2 SPRIGS PARSLEY

To make the mirepoix, heat the olive oil in a pan until smoking hot. Toss in all the ingredients, remove from the heat and stir until the sizzling stops. Spoon the cooked herbs and vegetables into the bottom of the dish being used to braise the fish.

Lay the fish on the bed of vegetables and add enough wine to almost cover the fish. Seal with a lid and simmer gently for 1 hour. The longer and slower the cooking, the more the vegetable flavours will enhance the flavour of the fish.

Smoked Fish

Hot smoked fish can have the most wonderful flavour, depending on the natural oils in the fish and the type of sawdust used during smoking. For seafood the best wood is apple. Next time you are near an apple orchard find out if you can buy some wood. Dry it out and run an electric planer over it. Gather the sawdust that results. You can experiment with different wood types until you find flavours you like. Sawdust or wood chips, in many flavours, can be obtained from your local tackle shop. Beware of some woods such as pine as they can give off undesirable chemicals that impart an unpleasant taste to the fish. In some cases the substances are even poisonous.

The following 'recipe' gives instructions on how to hot smoke a fish in a kitchen using the stove (gas or electric). Note that once fish is smoked it should still be kept refrigerated and treated as a perishable product. Some prized fish for smoking are Atlantic salmon, trevally, mullet, warehou, tailor, trout, snapper, tuna and eel.

2 BAKING TRAYS OF EQUAL SIZE
1 CAKE COOLING RACK
SAWDUST (OR WOOD CHIPS)
FISH
OIL FOR BASTING
HERBS AND SPICES (OPTIONAL)

Sprinkle a layer of sawdust over the bottom of a baking tray, sit the rack on the sawdust and lay the fish on the rack. Brush the fish with oil. Put the other baking tray upside down on top and place this little smoke house over a gentle flame or electric hotplate. To maintain a steady source of smoke, the heat needs to be 80° C to 90° C. The smoking process can take 30 to 60 minutes, depending on the size of the fish. Fish should feel firm to touch. Oil can be brushed on several times during the process to maintain moisture in a dry-fleshed fish. Herbs and spices in small quantities can be added to the smoking wood to impart flavour.

Braised luderick

SMOKED TROUT SALAD

SERVES 2
1 SMOKED TROUT
MIXED SALAD GREENS
½ RED CAPSICUM, SLICED
HANDFUL SNOWPEAS
FAVOURITE DRESSING

Smoked fish makes a wonderful addition to a salad. Simply place your choice of salad greens in a bowl with some sliced capsicum for colour and some snowpeas for crunch. Break the fish flesh into bite-sized pieces and add to the bowl. Toss with your favourite dressing.

Smoked trout salad

Marinated Fish

A marinade is a pickling liquid with aromatic flavours. Its use can tenderise the flesh and enhance the flavour by the addition of herbs, spices, fruits and wine. Fish suited to this process include Australian salmon, mackerel, mullet, trout, red emperor and tuna. Crustaceans such as rock lobster and bugs are also popular. The recipe below for gravlax is a Scandinavian speciality of raw salmon cured in a dill marinade.

Gravlax

GRAVLAX

1 TABLESPOON SEA SALT (OR OTHER SALT WITHOUT ADDED CHEMICALS)
¾ TABLESPOON SUGAR
½ TEASPOON FRESHLY GROUND WHITE PEPPER
2 TABLESPOONS COARSELY CHOPPED FRESH DILL, WITH STEMS
500 G SALMON FILLET, WITH SKIN ON
½ TABLESPOON DILL SEED, COARSELY CHOPPED

Mix the salt, sugar and pepper and rub the fish flesh with the mixture. Place one salmon fillet flesh side up in a steel or plastic container and sprinkle dill over the top. Lay next fillet on top of the other and repeat. Place the fish in the refrigerator for two days. Turn at least twice a day and baste with juices that are formed. Cut salmon in very thin slices, down onto the skin, and serve with a coarse dark bread, like pumpernickel, and salad or pickled vegetables. An easy sauce of mustard-flavoured sour cream with mustard seeds is a good accompaniment.

Fish Stock and Soup

A good fish stock is a fairly simple thing to make, but the ingredients must be incredibly fresh and sweet to make a stock that will form the basis for your soups and sauces.

FISH STOCK

1.5 KG WHOLE FISH, CLEANED (GILLS AND GUTS REMOVED, BUT HEADS INTACT)
2.5 LITRES WATER
2 STICKS CELERY, SLICED
2 MEDIUM-SIZED ONIONS, SLICED
2 MEDIUM-SIZED CARROTS, SLICED
1 TEASPOON CRACKED PEPPERCORNS
½ BOTTLE DRY WHITE WINE

Bring all the ingredients to a rapid boil and remove any scum that appears on the surface. Boil for 15 minutes. Do not boil for longer than this because a bitterness will start to exude from the fish bones. Strain the stock, return the liquid to the pot and bring to a simmer.

When the reserved meat and bones have cooled enough to handle, separate the flesh from the bones and return the flesh to the liquid stock. Continue to simmer until the liquid has been reduced by half. Strain and refrigerate or freeze until required. Do not season with salt or pepper at this stage.

Fish soup

FISH SOUP

3 TABLESPOONS OLIVE OIL
2 CLOVES GARLIC, FINELY CHOPPED
1 LARGE ONION, FINELY CHOPPED
JUICE OF 1 LEMON
3 RIPE TOMATOES, PEELED AND CHOPPED
750 ML FISH STOCK (OR WATER)
1 KG ASSORTED FISH (INCLUDING SOME SHELLFISH SUCH AS MUSSELS, PRAWNS, ETC.)
SALT
PEPPER

Heat the oil in a saucepan, toss in the garlic and onion and lightly sauté until clear, making sure not to brown. Add the lemon juice, tomato and water. Break the fish into bite-sized pieces and add to the saucepan. Do not add the shellfish at this stage. Simmer gently for 15 minutes.

Strain the liquid stock into a pot. Remove the flesh from the bones and skin and return it, with the vegetables, to the stock. Now add the shellfish, simmer for 5 minutes, season and serve. This soup is delicious with toasted bread that has been rubbed with a raw garlic clove prior to toasting.

Fish Patties and Pies

BABY SNAPPER PIE

50 G BUTTER
1 MEDIUM-SIZED ONION, ROUGHLY CHOPPED
1 MEDIUM-SIZED CARROT, FINELY CHOPPED
50 G FLOUR
3 CUPS MILK
PINCH OF NUTMEG
SALT
WHITE PEPPER
200 G FRESHLY CHOPPED BEANS, OR PEAS
500 G COOKED FISH FLESH, CUT INTO BITE-SIZE PIECES (LEFTOVERS ARE IDEAL)
1 TABLESPOON WHITE WINE OR CREAM (OPTIONAL)
PUFF PASTRY OR 75 G GRATED TASTY CHEESE

Melt the butter in a saucepan and add chopped onion. Sauté for a few minutes and add carrot. Sprinkle the flour over the vegetables and stir thoroughly, continuing to stir for a few minutes as the flour and vegetables cook. Do not allow the flour to brown. Pour in the milk and mix thoroughly. Lower the heat to a simmer, stirring constantly until the milk has absorbed all the flour and the mixture has thickened. Season with the nutmeg, salt and pepper. Allow to cool.

In a saucepan, boil a little water and add beans or peas. Cook for 1 or 2 minutes. Arrange the fish in the bottom of a pie dish and season with a little salt. Add lightly blanched greens and cover with vegetable mixture.

At this stage, you can either cover the vegetables with pastry or grated cheese. If using pastry, first paint the side of the pie dish with egg wash. Place a layer of puff pastry over the dish, press the edges into the dish with a fork and trim off the excess. Brush the top with a little beaten egg or milk, prick some holes in the pastry with a fork, and place in a moderate oven (about 180° C) and bake until pastry is crisp and golden. It will take 15 to 20 minutes.

If your preference is for a cheese topping, simply sprinkle the top of the vegetable mixture with grated cheese. Place in a moderate oven (about 180° C) and bake until the cheese has melted and turned golden brown. This takes about 15 to 20 minutes.

Baby snapper pie

Black bream cakes

BLACK BREAM CAKES

250 G COOKED FISH FILLET
250 G COOKED POTATO, MASHED
1 EGG WHITE, ROUGHLY BEATEN
1 TABLESPOON FRESHLY CHOPPED PARSLEY
1 TABLESPOON FRESHLY CHOPPED CHIVES
SALT
PEPPER
A LITTLE FLOUR
1 EGG YOLK, BEATEN (OPTIONAL)
½ CUP BREADCRUMBS (OPTIONAL)
BUTTER OR OIL FOR COOKING

Break the fish into small pieces and combine with the mashed potato in a bowl. Add the roughly beaten egg white and mix thoroughly with a fork. Add the parsley and chives, and season with salt and pepper to taste.

Using your hands, roll the mixture into desired shapes – small balls, patties or croquettes. Place the flour, egg yolk and breadcrumbs in three separate dishes. Roll each fish cake in the flour. You can cook the cakes at this stage, or first roll them in egg yolk and coat them with breadcrumbs.

Melt some butter (or heat a little oil) in a pan. When hot, put in the cakes. Cook gently for a few minutes until lightly browned. Turn over and brown the other side. Serve with freshly cooked vegetables.

Index of Place Names

This is an index to the place names in the Where to Fish section.

Abbotsford Wharf NSW 58
Abbott Point QLD 396
Abercrombie River NSW 141, 144, 145
Aberfoyle River NSW 134
Acheron Ledge NSW 114
Acheron River Vic. 205
Adelaide SA 266, 268–9, 270–1
Adelaide Bay Tas. 239
Adelaide Point QLD 397
Adelaide River NT 346, 352, 354, 356
Adelaide River Bridge NT 356
Adelaide River Crossing NT 354
Advancetown Lake QLD 419
Adventure Bay Tas. 228
Aire River Vic. 187, 190, 208, 212
Aireys Inlet Vic. 188
Airforce Beach NSW 71
Airlie Beach QLD 398
Aiton Bay NT 347
Akuna Bay NSW 48
Albany WA 298, 308, 309, 312, 330
Albany Island QLD 385
Albatross Bay QLD 384
Albert River QLD 382
Aldinga Beach SA 270
Aldinga Reef Aquatic Reserve SA 270
Aldridge Cove WA 315
Alecs Hole NT 358
Alexander Bay WA 310
Alexander Island WA 318
Alexandria Bay QLD 370
Aliu River NT 345
Allaru Island NT 347
Alligator Billabong NT 358
Allingham Beach QLD 394
Allyn River NSW 136, 138
Alonnah Tas. 228
Altona Bay Vic. 163
American River SA 274
Anderson Bay Tas. 234, 244
Anderson Inlet Vic. 178, 179, 181
Andoom Bridge QLD 383–4
Angalarri River NT 354
Angas River SA 292
Angels Beach NSW 70
Anglers Rest Vic. 200
Anglesea Vic. 186, 188
Anglesea River Vic. 188
Angourie Beach NSW 72
Anna Bay NSW 93
Annabella Reef Vic. 191
Annan River QLD 386

Anneaura wreck Vic. 164
Anonyma Shoal Vic. 162
Anson Bay NT 340
Ansons Bay Tas. 218, 230, 236
Antechamber Bay SA 274
Antwerp Vic. 215
Apollo Bay Vic. 186, 187, 189
Apostle Bay QLD 399
Applecross WA 304
Apsley River NSW 133, 134
Apsley River Tas. 242, 245
Apsley Strait NT 344
'Aquarium Hole' Vic. 162
Arafura Sea NT 348
Archer Point QLD 386
Ardrossan SA 272
Arkwright Shoal QLD 369
Arlington Reef QLD 387
Armstrong Point WA 305
Arnhem Land NT 336, 337
Arno Bay SA 287
Arrawarra Creek NSW 74
Arrawarra Headland NSW 74
Arthur Bay Tas. 239
Arthur Patches QLD 390
Arthur River Tas. 232, 258, 261
Arthur the Great buoy Vic. 164
Arthurs Lake Tas. 240, 246, 252, 254
Artillery Rocks Vic. 189
Ashford NSW 135
Aslings Beach NSW 124
Aspendale Vic. 162
Audley Weir NSW 63, 130
Aughinish Rocks NSW 118
Augusta WA 308, 316
Aurora Channel Vic. 174
Austinmer NSW 102
Australian Capital Territory 126, 147, 148
Avalon NSW 52
Avalon Vic. 164
Avenue River Tas. 237
Avoca Beach NSW 99
Avoca River Vic. 208, 210, 211
Avon River Vic. 175
Awinya Creek QLD 413
Ayr QLD 396
Ayton QLD 386

Babbage Island WA 324
Baby Reef NSW 90
Back Creek NSW 80
Back Lagoon NSW 123
Back Water Vic. 168
Backstairs Passage SA 270, 274
Baffle Creek QLD 408
Baines River NT 354

Bairds Bay SA 291
Bairnsdale Vic. 166–7
Bakers Creek QLD 400
Balcombe Bay Vic. 158
Bald Hills Creek QLD 375
Balgal Beach QLD 394
Ballast Heap NSW 63
Ballina NSW 64, 65, 70–1
Balls Head NSW 58, 59
Balmain NSW 59
Balnarring Vic. 182
Bamaga QLD 380, 384, 385
Bancroft Bay Vic. 172–3
Bandy Creek WA 309, 310
Bannister Road WA 332
Bantry Bay NSW 55
Bar Beach NSW 118
Bar Point NSW 48
Baragoot Beach NSW 121
Baratta Creek QLD 395
Barcoo River QLD 418
Bare Bluff NSW 74
Bare Island NSW 60
Bare Rock WA 326
Bargara QLD 409
Barham River Vic. 189
Barney Point QLD 407
Barneys Point Bridge NSW 67
Baroalba Creek NT 358
Baronda Head NSW 122
Barrack Point NSW 105
Barrack Point WA 316
Barragga Point NSW 121
Barrenjoey Head NSW 48, 52
Barrington River NSW 136, 137
Barrington Tops NSW 126, 134, 136, 137, 138
Barron River QLD 387
Barrys Bay NSW 82
Barwon Banks QLD 369
Barwon Heads Vic. 158, 165
Barwon River NSW 152
Barwon River Vic. 165, 208, 212
Basin Point Vic. 191
Bass Islet NSW 108
Bass Point NSW 100, 104, 105
Bass River Vic. 183
Bass Strait Tas. 218, 230, 232
Bastion Point Vic. 168
Bateau Bay NSW 98
Batehaven NSW 114
Bateman Shoal NT 340
Batemans Bay NSW 112, 113, 114
Bathurst NSW 141, 142, 143
Bathurst Head QLD 385
Bathurst Island NT 337, 339, 344

Battery Point NSW 103
Baudin Rocks SA 279
Bawley Point NSW 110, 111
Baxters Beach Vic. 178
Bay of Shoals SA 274
Beachport SA 277, 278–9
Beagle Bay NSW 114
Beagle Bay WA 328, 329
Beagle Gulf NT 342
Beagle Shoals NT 345
Beardy Waters NSW 134
Beares Beach NSW 120
Beaumaris Bay Vic. 162
Beauty Point NSW 55
Beauty Point Tas. 235
Beauty Point Road Jetty NSW 119
Beaver Reef QLD 390
Beaver Rock QLD 413
Bedarra Island QLD 390
Bedwell Group QLD 401
Beecroft Peninsula NSW 100, 108
Bega NSW 128, 131
Bega River NSW 122, 131
Bell Point Vic. 172, 173
Bell Reef Vic. 165
Bellambi NSW 100
Bellambi Point NSW 102
Bellanger Beach WA 315
Bellarine Bank Vic. 164
Bellarine Peninsula Vic. 158, 165
Bellinger River NSW 78–9, 129
Bells Creek QLD 372
Bemm River Vic. 166, 170, 198
Ben Buckler NSW 60
Ben Chifley Dam NSW 143
Benambra Creek Vic. 200
Bendoc River Vic. 198
Bendolba NSW 138
Bengello Beach NSW 116
Bennetts Beach NSW 92
Bensons Gutter QLD 413
Bentley Point Vic. 176
Bents Basin NSW 130
Bermagui NSW 118, 120
Bermagui River NSW 120
Berowra Creek NSW 48, 51
Berriedale Bay Tas. 226
Berry Springs NT 356
Berrys Canal NSW 107
Betka River Vic. 168
Bevans Island NSW 104
Beverley Group QLD 401
Bicheno Tas. 218, 230, 236, 237
Bickers Islands SA 288
Big Badja River NSW 148

Big Ben Rock NSW 94
Big Bight Vic. 171
Big Brook Dam WA 330, 332
Big Gibber Headland NSW 90, 91
Big Greeny Ledge NSW 60
Big Hill Point NSW 82, 83
Big Horse Creek NT 354
Big Island (Clyde River) NSW 114
Big Island (Port Kembla) NSW 103
Big Island (Port Stephens) NSW 92
Big Lagoon WA 322
Big River Vic. 200, 205
Big Rock NSW 106–7
Big Sandhills QLD 373
Big Waterhouse Lake Tas. 244
Big Woody Island QLD 411, 413
Bilgola Beach NSW 52
Bilgola Head NSW 52
Billengarrah Station NT 360
Binalong Bay Tas. 236
Bingara NSW 135
Bingie Bingie Point NSW 116
Binningup Beach WA 318
Bird Island QLD 375
Birdie Beach NSW 88, 96–7
Birdie Island NSW 74
Birri Fishing Resort QLD 382–3
Bishop Island QLD 375
Bishops Rock Vic. 193
Bittangabee Bay NSW 125
Bjelke-Petersen Dam QLD 418
Black Head (Ballina) NSW 70
Black Head (Gerroa) NSW 100, 107
Black Head (Tuncurry) NSW 87
Black Head QLD 407
Black Point NT 347
Black Point SA 287
Black Pole SA 271
Black Rock NSW 113, 114
Black Rock QLD 388
Black Rock Vic. 159, 162
Black Rocks (South West Rocks) NSW 81
Black Rocks (Wooyung) NSW 66
Blackfellows Caves SA 277
Blackheath Creek NSW 143
Blackman Bay Tas. 220, 224
Blackmans Lagoon Tas. 242, 244
Blackmore River NT 356
Blacknose Point Vic. 192
Blackwall Point NSW 59
Blackwall Reach WA 304

455

INDEX   BLACKWOOD RIVER WA – CAPE YORK PENINSULA QLD

Blackwood River WA 297, 316, 330, 331, 332
Blairgowrie Vic. 160
Blakes Channel Vic. 183
Blind Bight Vic. 185
Bloomfield River QLD 380, 386
Blossom Point NSW 91
Blowering Reservoir NSW 147, 150
Blowhole Point NSW 100, 106
Blue Hole NSW 67
Blue Hole NT 346
Blue Hole QLD 373
Blue Hole Vic. 191
Blue Hole WA (Bellanger Beach) 315
Blue Holes (Kalbarri) WA 307
Blue Holes (Trigg Point) WA 302
Blue Lagoon QLD 416
Blue Rock Lake Vic. 202, 206
Bluff Head NSW 55
Bluff Point (Lake Victoria) Vic. 174
Bluff Point (Western Port) Vic. 184
Bluff River Tas. 245
Blythe River Tas. 258, 262
Boambee Beach NSW 75, 76, 78
Boambee Creek NSW 78
Boat Harbour NSW 62
Boat Harbour Tas. 232
Boat Rock QLD 375
Bobs Bay Vic. 170
Bobs Hollow WA 316
Bobundara Creek NSW 146, 149
Bodalla NSW 131
Bogan River NSW 152
Bogangar Beach NSW 66
Bogimbah Creek QLD 413
Bogola Head NSW 118
Boiling Pot QLD 370
Bokhara River NSW 152
Bombah Point NSW 90
Bombala River NSW 149
Bombo Beach NSW 106
Bonang River Vic. 198
Bongaree QLD 372
Bonner Rocks NT 351
Bonnet Rock Vic. 159
Bonnievale Spit NSW 63
Bonville Creek NSW 78
Boolambayte Lake NSW 90
Boomer Beach SA 282
Boomer Island Tas. 224
Boondelbah Island NSW 92
Boondooma Reservoir QLD 418
Boonlye Point QLD 413
Boonooroo Point QLD 413
Booroopki Swamp Vic. 215
Booti Booti Beach NSW 87
Borang Lake NSW 117
Boranup WA 316
Bornholm Beach WA 313
Borroloola NT 360

Bosanquet Bay SA 291
Boston Bay SA 284, 288
Boston Island SA 288
Botany Bay NSW 42, 44, 60–1
Bottle and Glass Point NSW 57
Bottom Lake Vic. 168
Bouchier Channel Vic. 184
Boulder Point Tas. 238
Boulton Channel Vic. 184
Bournda Island NSW 122
Bow River WA 314
Bowarrady Creek QLD 413
Bowen QLD 392, 393, 396–7
Bowes River WA 307
Bowling Green Bay QLD 392, 393, 395
Box Head NSW 98, 99
Boyds Bay Bridge NSW 67
Boyds Beach NSW 106
Boyne Island QLD 407
Boyne River QLD 408
Bradys Lake Tas. 255
Bramble Rocks NT 347
Brampton Island QLD 400
Bramston Beach QLD 390
Bramston Point QLD 390
Bray Rock QLD 372
Break O'Day River Tas. 240, 242, 246
Breakwater Pier Vic. 163
Bream Hole NSW 75
Breckenridge Channel NSW 86
Bredbo River NSW 148
Bremer Bay WA 312
Bremer Island NT 351
Bremer River WA 312
Brennan Shoal QLD 373
Brennans Wharf SA 288
Brenton Bay NT 345
Bribie Banks QLD 372
Bribie Island QLD 368, 372, 375, 418
Brid River Tas. 234, 244
Bridge Gutter QLD 413
Bridgewater Bay Vic. 193
Bridgewater Causeway Tas. 226
Bridport Tas. 218, 230, 234
Brighton Jetty SA 271
Brighton Pier Vic. 159, 162
Brighton Wharf NSW 60
Brighton Whiting Patch SA 271
Brisbane QLD 364, 366, 367, 372, 375
Brisbane River QLD 366, 372, 375, 418
Brisbane Water NSW 44, 46–7
British Admiral Reef Tas. 238
Broadmere Station NT 360
Brodribb River Vic. 171, 198
Brogo Reservoir NSW 128, 131
Brogo River NSW 131
Broken Bay NSW 42, 46, 48, 51
Broken Creek Vic. 204
Broken Head NSW 69
Broken River Vic. 204, 198

Bromby Islands NT 351
Bronte Lagoon Tas. 252, 255
Brook Islands QLD 391
Brooklyn Dam NSW 130
Brooks Reef NSW 109
Broome WA 320, 328
Brooms Head NSW 72
Brothers Islands SA 290
Brou Beach NSW 116
Brou Lake NSW 116
Broughton Creek NSW 107, 131
Broughton Island NSW 88, 92, 93
Broughton River SA 292, 295
Broulee Bay NSW 112
Broulee Beach NSW 115
Broulee Island NSW 115
Brown Island QLD 378
Brown Mountain NSW 147
Browns Beach SA 272
Browns Creek NT 354
Brumbys Creek Tas. 240, 242, 246
Brunswick Heads NSW 64, 65, 66, 68
Brunswick River NSW 42, 64, 68, 129
Brunswick River WA 330, 332
Bruny Island Tas. 218, 220, 228
Brush Island NSW 111
Brushy Lagoon Tas. 246
Buchan Point QLD 387
Buchan River Vic. 198
Bucket Billabong NT 358
Buckland River Vic. 202, 204
Buckley Falls Vic. 212
Buckwong Creek Vic. 200
Budawang Range NSW 131
Budgewoi Lake NSW 88, 96
Buffalo Creek NT 342
Buffalo River Vic. 202, 204
Bull Creek SA 292
Bull Ring Vic. 168
Bullita Outstation NT 354
Bullock Island Vic. 172
Bunbury WA 308, 318, 332
Bunbury Reef Vic. 189
Bundara River Vic. 200
Bundegi Beach WA 325
Bunga Head NSW 121
Bungala River SA 270
Bungan Beach NSW 52
Bunker Bay WA 317
Bunker Group QLD 407
Bunker Reefs QLD 405
Bunurong Marine Park Vic. 181
Bunyip River Vic. 207
Burdekin River QLD 393, 396, 417
Burge Point NT 341
Burketown QLD 382
Burleigh Heads QLD 378
Burnett Heads QLD 402, 408
Burnett River QLD 408
Burnie Tas. 232

Burns Beach WA 302, 303
Burns Point NSW 71
Burra Creek SA 292
Burrah Burrah Point NSW 91
Burrewarra Point NSW 114, 115
Burrier NSW 128, 131
Burrill Lake NSW 110
Burrinjuck Dam NSW 140, 141, 145
Burrum Heads QLD 410
Burrum River QLD 410
Burrup Peninsula WA 326
Bushrangers Bay NSW 105
Busselton WA 317
Bustard Head QLD 408
Butchers Creek NSW 143
Butchers Jetty Vic. 193
Butlers Beach SA 272
Buxton Point Tas. 223
Bynoe Harbour NT 340, 341
Bynoe River QLD 383, 416
Byron Bay NSW 64, 68, 69

Cabarita Point NSW 58
Cabbage Tree Creek Vic. 171
Cabbage Tree Island NSW 92
Cabbage Tree Point QLD 376, 377
Cable Bay SA 272
Cable Beach WA 313
Cahills Crossing NT 346, 359
Cairn Curran Reservoir Vic. 208, 210
Cairns QLD 380, 381, 386, 389, 416
Calabash Bay NSW 48
Calliope River QLD 407
Caloundra QLD 367, 368, 371, 372
Calvert River NT 360
Cam River Tas. 258, 262
Cambalong Creek NSW 146, 149
Cambridge Gulf WA 298, 320
Camden Haven NSW 76, 77, 84–5
Camden Haven River NSW 129
Camden Point NSW 84
Camel Rock NSW 119
Cameron Inlet Tas. 239
Camp Cove NSW 57
Camp Rock WA 325
Campaspe River Vic. 194, 205
Campbell Channel Vic. 174
Campbells Creek Vic. 190
Campbells River NSW 143
Canal Rocks WA 317
Candle Creek NSW 51
Cania Reservoir QLD 418
Caniapa Passage QLD 377
Canning River WA 300, 304, 331
Canton Beach NSW 97
Canunda Beach SA 278
Cape Arid WA 310
Cape Arnhem NT 350, 351
Cape Banks NSW 60
Cape Banks SA 278

Cape Barren Island Tas. 230
Cape Baskerville WA 328
Cape Bertholet WA 328
Cape Boileau WA 328
Cape Bowling Green QLD 395
Cape Buffon SA 278
Cape Byron NSW 64, 69
Cape Capricorn QLD 406, 407
Cape Conran Vic. 167, 171
Cape Conway QLD 399
Cape Cuvier WA 320, 324–5
Cape Dombey SA 279
Cape Don NT 347
Cape Du Couedic SA 274
Cape Edgecumbe QLD 396
Cape Elizabeth SA 272
Cape Ferguson QLD 395
Cape Ford NT 340
Cape Gantheaume SA 274
Cape Grafton QLD 387
Cape Green NSW 112, 124
Cape Grim Tas. 258
Cape Hauy Tas. 224
Cape Hillsborough QLD 393
Cape Horn Vic. 168
Cape Hotham NT 346
Cape Jaffa SA 278
Cape Jervis SA 270
Cape Keith NT 345
Cape Keppel QLD 406
Cape Keraudren WA 327
Cape Kimberley QLD 388
Cape Knob WA 312
Cape Le Grand WA 310
Cape Leeuwin lighthouse WA 316
Cape Leveque WA 320, 328, 329
Cape Martin SA 278, 279
Cape Melville QLD 385
Cape Moreton QLD 372, 373
Cape Naturaliste WA 298, 308, 317
Cape Nelson Vic. 192, 193
Cape Nuyts SA 291
Cape Otway Vic. 186, 190
Cape Palmerston QLD 401
Cape Pasley WA 310
Cape Paterson Vic. 181
Cape Patton Vic. 189
Cape Peron WA 322
Cape Riche WA 312
Cape Rose WA 322
Cape Sandwich QLD 391
Cape Scott NT 340
Cape Sir William Grant Vic. 192
Cape Upstart QLD 393, 396
Cape Van Diemen NT 344
Cape Wessel NT 350
Cape Weymouth QLD 385
Cape Wilberforce NT 351
Cape Wirawawoi NT 351
Cape Woolamai Vic. 183
Cape York Peninsula QLD 364, 380, 381, 382, 383–5, 414, 416

456

CAPEL SOUND VIC. – DILLON BAY WA

Capel Sound Vic. 160
Capricorn Group QLD 407
Capricorn Reefs QLD 405
Captain Cook Bridge NSW 61
Captains Point Vic. 168
Carcoar Lake NSW 141, 145
Cardwell QLD 380, 391
Careening Bay WA 302
Carisbrook Creek Vic. 189
Carls Reef NSW 93
Carlton River Tas. 220, 224
Carmila QLD 401
Carnarvon WA 320, 324
Carpenter Rocks SA 278
Carrickalinga SA 270
Carrow Brook NSW 139
Carrum Drain Vic. 162
Castaways Reef QLD 369
Castle Cove Vic. 190
Castlereagh Point QLD 372
Castlereagh River NSW 152
Casuarina Creek QLD 406
Casuarina Sands NSW 148
Cat Bay Vic. 183
Catagunya Lake Tas. 250
Cataract Dam NSW 131
Cataraqui Point Tas. 238
Catfish Waterhole QLD 416
Cathedral Rocks WA 305
Cattai Bridge NSW 85
Cattai Creek NSW 130
Causeway Lake QLD 405
Cave Beach NSW 108
Caversham WA 304
Ceduna SA 284, 291
Cemetery Beach Vic. 178
Cemetery Bight Vic. 168
Cemetery Point NSW 119
Cerberus Breakwater Vic. 159
Cervantes WA 306
Chaffey Dam NSW 133, 135
Chambers Bay NT 346
Champers Island QLD 371
Chandler River NSW 134
Changle Shoal NSW 75
Channel Island QLD 371
Channel Point NT 340
Channel Rock QLD 391
Chaos bombora NSW 71
Chapman River SA 274
Chardons Reef QLD 369
Charles Point NT 341
Charlotte Head NSW 76, 86, 87
Cherry Venture wreck QLD 369
Cheyne Beach WA 312
Chichester Dam NSW 138
Chichester River NSW 136, 138
Chinaman Rock WA 307
Chinamans Beach NSW 71
Chinamans Hat Island SA 272
Chinamans Point NSW 114
Chinderah NSW 67
Chinnock Lagoon NSW 122
Chiton Rocks SA 282
Chittaway Point NSW 97

Chowder Head NSW 57
Christies Gutter QLD 413
Christmas Island Tas. 238
Cid Harbour QLD 398
Circular Head Tas. 232
Circus Beach WA 315
City Beach Groyne WA 302
City Rocks NSW 125
Clairview QLD 401
Clare SA 295
Clarence Lagoon Tas. 256
Clarence River NSW 64, 72, 129
Clarence River Tas. 255
Clarence Town NSW 138
Clarendon SA 294
Clarkes Beach NSW 69
Clarkes Point Reserve NSW 58
Clarrie Hall Dam NSW 129
Cleveland Bay QLD 392, 393, 395
Cleveland Point QLD 375, 393
Clews Point QLD 408
Clift Island NT 344
Close Reef NSW 81
Cloudy Bay Tas. 228
Clovelly Baths NSW 60
Cluny Lagoon Tas. 250
Clybucca Creek NSW 80
Clyde River NSW 112, 114, 128, 131
Clyde River Tas. 240, 248, 250
Coal Creek NSW 51
Coal River Tas. 248, 250
Coalmine Beach WA 315
Coba Point NSW 48
Cobourg Peninsula NT 337, 347
Cobungra River Vic. 200
Cochrane Dam NSW 147
Cockatoo Island (Sydney) NSW 59
Cockatoo Island (Tuncurry) NSW 86
Cockaynes Channel Vic. 184
Cockburn Sound WA 302
Cockle Channel NSW 46
Cockle Creek Tas. 228
Cockrone Lake NSW 99
Cod Hole NSW 99
Cod Hole QLD 371
Cod Splat Vic. 192
Coen River QLD 416
Coffin Bay SA 290
Coffs Creek NSW 75
Coffs Harbour NSW 64, 65, 74, 75, 78
Coila Creek NSW 117
Coila Lake NSW 112, 117
Colchis Creek Tas. 236
Coleman River QLD 383
Coleraine Vic. 208, 214
Coles Bay Tas. 218, 220, 222
Coles Channel Vic. 165
Coliban River Vic. 205
Collaroy NSW 52
Collie River WA 318, 330, 331, 332

Collingwood River Tas. 260
Collis Wall NSW 72
Colo River NSW 130
Colour Patch WA 316
Combienbar River Vic. 198
Comboyuro Point QLD 373
Comerong Bay NSW 107
Como WA 304
Condamine River QLD 418
Congo Point NSW 116
Conical Rocks QLD 404
Conjola Beach NSW 109
Conjola Creek NSW 131
Connor Creek QLD 406
Connors Beach NSW 81
Conspicuous Beach WA 315
Constant Creek QLD 400
Conto Spring Picnic Area WA 316
Convention Beach SA 290
Cooby Creek Reservoir QLD 419
Coogee Beach NSW 60
Cooinda NT 358
Cook Island NSW 66
Cooks River NSW 60
Cooktown QLD 380, 385, 386
Coolangatta QLD 366
Coolum Beach QLD 369
Coolumbooka River NSW 149
Cooma Creek NSW 148
Coomera River QLD 378
Cooper Creek QLD 418
Cooper Island NSW 117
Copeton Dam NSW 133
Coral Bay WA 325
Corindi Beach NSW 74
Corindi River NSW 74
Corinella Vic. 178, 182, 183, 184
Corio Bay QLD 404, 405
Corio Bay Vic. 158, 164
Corner Basin Vic. 156
Corner Inlet Vic. 166, 167, 177
Corny Point SA 272
Coronation Beach WA 307
Corrigans Beach NSW 114
Corroboree Billabong NT 357
Corroboree Island QLD 404
Corryong Vic. 200
Corunna Lake NSW 118–19
Corvette Hole Vic. 164
Cosgrove Reservoir Vic. 210, 211
Cossack WA 326
Cosy Corner WA 313, 316
Cottage Point NSW 51
Cottesloe Beach and Groyne WA 302
Coulomb Point WA 328
Coventry Reef WA 302
Cow Rock NSW 48
Cowan Cowan Point QLD 373
Cowan Creek NSW 44, 48, 51
Cowan Reef QLD 373
Cowaramup Bay WA 316
Cowdroys Beach NSW 122
Cowell SA 284, 286

Cowerie Creek WA 327
Cowes Vic. 178, 183
Cowra NSW 145
Cox Peninsula NT 341
Cox River NT 360
Coxs River NSW 140, 142, 143
Crab Bay QLD 398
Crab Island QLD 378
Crabneck Point NSW 98
Cradle Mountain–Lake St Clair National Park Tas. 252, 257
Craigbourne Dam Tas. 248, 250
Crampton Island NSW 111
Crawfish Rock Vic. 184
Crayfish Point Tas. 226
Crees Creek QLD 389
Cremorne Bay Tas. 224
Crescent Head NSW 76, 83
Cressbrook Dam QLD 419
Crib Point Vic. 185
Crockery Bay SA 282
Croker Island NT 347
Cronulla NSW 44, 62
Crookhaven River NSW 107
Crookwell Reservoir NSW 141, 144
Crookwell River NSW 141, 144
Crowdy Head NSW 77, 85
Crusoe Island QLD 377
Cudgegong River NSW 141, 142
Cudgen Creek NSW 66
Cudgera Creek NSW 66
Cudgeree Island NSW 104
Cudgewa Creek Vic. 194, 200
Culburra NSW 100, 106
Culgoa River NSW 152
Cumberland Group QLD 400
Cumberland River Vic. 189
Cumberland Strait NT 350
Cunningham Pier Vic. 164
Cunninghame Arm Vic. 172
Curalo Lagoon NSW 124
Curdies River Vic. 187, 190, 208, 212
Curleys Bay NSW 107
Curracurrang NSW 102
Currie Tas. 230
Curries River Dam Tas. 246
Currimundi Reef QLD 369
Currumbin QLD 367, 378
Currumbin Creek QLD 378–9
Currumbin Rock QLD 378
Curtis Island QLD 364, 402, 403, 406, 407
Cuttagee Lake NSW 120–1
Cygnet Tas. 228
Cygnet River SA 274

Daintree River QLD 380, 388, 416
Dalmeny NSW 116
Dalrymple Point QLD 396
Daly Head SA 272
Daly River NT 337, 340, 353, 354
Dampier WA 326

Dampier Archipelago WA 298, 320, 326
Dandongadale River Vic. 204
Dangar Island NSW 48
Danjera Dam NSW 131
Dargo River Vic. 199
Dark Hole NSW 53
Darling Range WA 332
Dart River Vic. 201
Darwin NT 336, 337, 338–9, 341, 356
Darwin River NT 356
Darwin wharves NT 342, 353
Dasher River Tas. 263
Dawes Point NSW 58
Dawesville Channel WA 308, 318–19
Dawn Fraser Pool NSW 58
Dayman Point QLD 386, 410
Days Gutter QLD 373, 374
Dead Mans Hole NSW 103
Dean Reservoir Vic. 210, 211
Death Hole NSW 81
Deception Bay QLD 372
Deception Creek QLD 406
Deception Point NT 344
Deddick River Vic. 198
Dee Lagoon Tas. 252, 255
Dee Why Beach NSW 52
Deep Creek NSW 53
Deep Creek Vic. 207
Deep Hole QLD 378
Deep Lake Vic. 212
Deep River WA 315
Deep Tempest QLD 373
Deepdene WA 316
Deepwater River NSW 133, 134
Deeral Landing QLD 390
Delatite River Vic. 205
Delcomyn Island QLD 404
Delegate River NSW 149
Delegate River Vic. 198
Deloraine Island QLD 399
Denham WA 322
Denhams Beach NSW 114
Deniliquin NSW 139
Denmark River WA 314
Denmark WA 308, 314
Dent Island QLD 398
D'Entrecasteaux Channel Tas. 218, 220, 228–9
Depot Beach NSW 111
Depuch Island WA 326–7
Derby WA 320, 329
Derwent River Tas. 218, 220, 226–7, 240, 248, 250, 257
Deua River NSW 131
Devils Gorge NSW 108
Devils Hole Vic. 171
Devonport Tas. 233, 234
Devonport Creek SA 291
Diamond Head NSW 85
Diggers Beach NSW 75
Dignams Creek NSW 119
Dillon Bay WA 312

457

INDEX

DING DONGA LEDGE QLD – GILRUTH POINT NT

Ding Donga Ledge QLD 413
Direction Bank WA 303
Dirk Hartog Island WA 320, 322
Disaster Bay NSW 124, 125
Disaster Rock WA 328
Discovery Bay VIC. 193
Dobroyd Head NSW 54, 55
Dock Lake VIC. 208, 215
Doctors Rocks NSW 60
Dodds Island NSW 67
Dodges Ferry TAS. 224
Dohles Rocks QLD 375
Dolans Bay Wharf NSW 63
Dolls Point NSW 60
Dolphin Point QLD 370
Dolphin Pool WA 319
Dome Island QLD 404
Don River TAS. 263
Don River VIC. 207
Dongara WA 300, 307
Donkeys NSW 60
Donnelly River WA 330, 332
Donnybrook QLD 372
Doonella Lake QLD 370
Dora Creek NSW 95, 130
Double Bay NSW 57
Double Creek Arm VIC. 168
Double Head QLD 405
Double Island QLD 387
Double Island Point QLD 368–9
Double Lagoon TAS. 256
Doubtful Islands WA 312
Douglas Point SA 278
Douglas River TAS. 237
Douglas River Crossing NT 354
Dover TAS. 228
Dowardee Island NSW 92
Drakesbrook Weir WA 330, 332
Dreamtime Beach NSW 66
Driftwood Bay QLD 398
Dromana VIC. 158, 161
Droughty Point TAS. 226
Drummond Cove WA 307
Ducie River QLD 384
Duck Arm VIC. 174
Duck Bay TAS. 218, 230, 232
Duck Creek NSW 100, 103, 104–5
Duck Creek QLD 397
Duck Island QLD 413
Duck Island VIC. 165
Duck River TAS. 232, 258, 262
Duckmaloi River NSW 143
Duke of Orleans Bay WA 310
Dum In Mirrie Island NT 340, 341
Dumaresq Island Bridge NSW 85
Dumaresq River NSW 133, 135
Dunalley TAS. 224
Dunbogan Beach NSW 84
Dungog NSW 138
Dunk Island QLD 390
Dunsborough WA 317
Dunwich QLD 374, 375
Durras NSW 114

Durras Lake NSW 100, 111
Dust Hole Beach SA 272
Dutchmans Beach NSW 92
Dutton Trout Hatchery NSW 134

Eagle Bay WA 305, 317
Eagle Bluff WA 322
Eagle Gorge WA 307
Eagle Point VIC. 173
Eagle Rock VIC. 188
Eaglehawk Neck TAS. 224
East Alligator River NT 346–7, 359
East Arm NT 342
East Arm VIC. 183
East Baines River NT 354
East Cove TAS. 228
East Derwent TAS. 250
East Devonport Beach TAS. 233
East Gresford NSW 138
East Point NT 342
East Wall NSW 75
East Woody Island NT 351
Eastern View VIC. 188
Ebor NSW 134
Eden NSW 42, 112–13, 124
Eden Creek QLD 397
Edgecumbe Bay QLD 393, 397
Edith Breaker NSW 91
Edithburgh SA 272
Edward River NSW 152
Edwards Point VIC. 165
Edwin Rocks QLD 393
Egmont Reef QLD 386
Eight Mile Lagoon QLD 416
18-metre line VIC. 158, 161
Eighty Mile Beach WA 327
Eimeo QLD 393, 400
Eleanor Bluffs NSW 48
Elephant Rock NSW 60
Elephant Rock QLD 378
Elford Reef QLD 387
Elizabeth Beach NSW 87
Elizabeth Channel VIC. 183
Elizabeth River TAS. 246
Elliot River QLD 409
Elliot River VIC. 189
Ellis Street Jetty WA 316
Elliston SA 284, 290, 291
Elmore Weir VIC. 205
Elsey Creek NT 354
Elsey National Park NT 354
Elsmore NSW 135
Elwick Bay TAS. 226
Elwood Canal VIC. 159
Embley River QLD 384
Emerald Beach NSW 65
Emigrant Creek NSW 71
Emmaville NSW 135
Empire Bay NSW 46
Emu Bay SA 274
Emu Bay TAS. 232
Emu Creek VIC. 207
Emu Park QLD 405
Encounter Bay SA 282
Endeavour River QLD 386

English Company's Islands NT 351
Entrance Point WA 328
Ephraim Island QLD 378
Errinundra River VIC. 198
Erskine River VIC. 189
Escape Reef QLD 386
Escott Lodge QLD 382
Esmeralda Cove NSW 93
Esperance WA 308, 309, 310, 331
Eucumbene River NSW 146, 151
Eudlo Creek QLD 371
Euri Creek QLD 396
Eurimbula Creek QLD 408
Evans Head NSW 64, 65, 70, 71
Evans Landing QLD 383
Evans River NSW 64
Eves Ravine NSW 108
Exmouth WA 320, 324, 325
Explosives Pier VIC. 164
Eyre Peninsula SA 284

Facing Island QLD 407
Fairfax Islands QLD 407
Fairhaven Beach VIC. 188
Fairway Buoy QLD 372
Fairy Pools QLD 370
False Bay SA 287
Family Islands QLD 390
Farm Beach SA 290
Farnborough Beach QLD 405
Farquhar Inlet NSW 85
Faure Island WA 322
Fawkner beacon VIC. 162
Feather Reef QLD 390
Fenton Patches NT 342
Fidos Reef NSW 66
Field Island NT 347
Fig Tree Point NSW 55
Fingal Bay NSW 93
Fingal Beach NSW 66
Fingal Head NSW 64, 66
Finnis River SA 292
Finucane Island WA 327
Fish Hook Bay WA 305
Fish River NSW 143
Fish Rock NSW 76, 81
Fisheries Beach NSW 124
Fisherman Bay SA 286
Fishermans Bay NSW 63
Fishermans Jetty SA 287
Fishermans Landing (Inverloch) VIC. 181
Fishermans Landing Arm (Lake Tyers) VIC. 171
Fishermens Jetty VIC. 165
Fishery Bay SA 288
Fishing Creek QLD 405
Fitzgerald River WA 312
Fitzroy Falls Reservoir NSW 131
Fitzroy Island QLD 387
Fitzroy River QLD 402, 403, 405, 406
Fitzroy River VIC. 192, 193, 214

Fitzroy River WA 330, 333
Five Dock Point NSW 58
Five Fathom Bank WA 302
Flagstaff Point NSW 103
Flannagan Island VIC. 172
Flat Island QLD 404
Flat Rock (Ballina) NSW 70
Flat Rock (Hastings Point) NSW 66
Flat Rock (Pippi Beach) NSW 72
Flat Rock (Terrigal) NSW 99
Flat Rock (Currumbin) QLD 378
Flat Rock (North Stradbroke Island) QLD 375
Flat Rock VIC. 193
Flat Rock Island NSW 114
Flat Top Island QLD 400
Flathead Spit NSW 80
Fleurieu Peninsula SA 270
Flinders VIC. 183
Flinders Bay WA 316
Flinders Bight VIC. 182
Flinders Island SA 291
Flinders Island TAS. 218, 230–1, 239
Flinders Islet NSW 103
Flinders Peninsula WA 313
Flinders Reef QLD 372–3
Flinders River QLD 383, 416
Flint and Steel Bay NSW 48
Flint and Steel Point NSW 51
Floreat Beach WA 302
Florence Bay VIC. 171
Florentine River TAS. 251
Flowerdale River TAS. 258, 262
Fly Point QLD 385
Flying Fish Point QLD 390
Folly Point NSW 55
Ford River VIC. 190, 208
Forestier Peninsula TAS. 224
Forgotten Lake TAS. 257
Form Beach SA 290
Forresters Beach NSW 98
Forster NSW 76, 86
Forster Channel NSW 86
Fortescue Bay TAS. 224
Fortescue River WA 326
Forth River TAS. 218, 230, 232–3, 258, 263
Forty Baskets Beach NSW 54
Four Mile Beach QLD 389
Four Mile Hole NT 358
Four Mile Reef NSW 120
Four Mile Reef WA 317
Four Springs Lake TAS. 246
Four Ways NSW 117
Fowlers Bay SA 284, 291
Frankland Islands QLD 390
Frankland River WA 315, 331
Franklin TAS. 228
Franklin Channel VIC. 177
Franklin Harbour SA 287
Franklin River TAS. 258, 260
Franklin Sound TAS. 230, 239
Frankston VIC. 161, 162

Fraser Island QLD 364, 367, 368, 370, 402, 403, 410, 411, 412–13
Frasers Rock NSW 72
Frederick Henry Bay TAS. 220, 224
Freds Ground SA 271
Freeburn Island NSW 72
Freeman Nob SA 282
Freestone Point TAS. 223
Fremantle WA 300, 304
French Island VIC. 179, 183, 184
Frenchman Bay WA 309
Frenchman Rock SA 282
Frenchs Narrows VIC. 171
Freshwater Bay WA 304
Freycinet National Park TAS. 220
Freycinet Peninsula TAS. 222
Frith Rock QLD 398
Frustration Reef WA 307
Frying Pan Arm NSW 151
Furneaux Group TAS. 239
Furnell VIC. 170

Gabo Island VIC. 168
Gairdner River WA 312
Gallagher Point QLD 372
Gannet Cay QLD 405
Gantheaume Point WA 328
Gap Beach NSW 81
Gara River NSW 133, 134
Garden Bay NSW 114
Garden Island WA 302
Garden Point TAS. 224
Gardner Bank QLD 412
Gardners Channel VIC. 183
Garie Beach NSW 102
Garths Rock WA 325
Gascoyne River WA 324
Geehi Dam NSW 151
Geehi River NSW 150
Geelong VIC. 164, 212
Geikie Gorge WA 333
Gellibrand River VIC. 187, 190, 208, 212
Gellibrand Shoal VIC. 163
Gem Pier VIC. 163
Genoa River VIC. 168
Gentle Anne Channel VIC. 185
George River TAS. 236, 244
George Town TAS. 234, 235, 246
Georges Bay TAS. 230, 236, 244
Georges Head NSW 57
Georges River NSW 42, 44, 61, 130
Geraldton WA 300, 307
Gerringong NSW 100
Gerroa NSW 42, 100, 106, 107
Giants Causeway NSW 66
Gibbo River VIC. 200
Gibraltar Rock NSW 81
Gibsons Steps VIC. 190
Gillards Beach NSW 122
Gilruth Point NT 341

458

INDEX

Gippsland Lakes VIC. 156, 166, 167, 172–3
Gipsy Point VIC. 168
Gladesville Bridge NSW 59
Gladstone QLD 402, 403, 405, 406, 407
Glen Innes NSW 134, 135
Glen Lyon Dam QLD 419
Glen Marvin Dam WA 330
Glenbawn Dam NSW 136, 138, 139
Glenelg Beach SA 270, 271
Glenelg River VIC. 186, 193, 194, 208, 214
Glennies Creek NSW 139
Gloucester Pass QLD 393
Gloucester River NSW 136, 137
Gloucester Tops NSW 136
Gnaraloo Homestead WA 325
Gneering Shoal QLD 369
Goalen Head NSW 121
Goat Gulch WA 307
Goat Island (Boolambayte Lake) NSW 90
Goat Island (Sydney) NSW 59
Goat Island (Maroochy River) QLD 371
Goat Island (Moreton Bay) QLD 375
Goat Island (Noosa River) QLD 370
Godfreys Beach TAS. 232
Godwin Island NSW 86
Gogleys Creek NSW 84
Gogleys Lagoon NSW 84
Gold Coast QLD 366, 376–9
Gold Coast Seaway QLD 367, 376, 377
Golden Beach QLD 372
Goobarragandra River NSW 150
Goodradigbee River NSW 145, 148
Googong Dam NSW 148
Goold Island QLD 391
Goolwa SA 277, 280, 281
Goose Islands SA 272
Gordon Bay NT 344
Gordon Bight VIC. 171
Gordon River TAS. 258, 260
Gosford NSW 46
Goulburn NSW 141, 144
Goulburn River VIC. 194, 202, 205
Goulburn Weir VIC. 194, 202, 205
Goulet Bluff WA 322
Gove Peninsula NT 336, 348, 350, 351
Governor Island TAS. 237
Graces Shore NSW 48
Grahamstown Dam NSW 130
Grange Beach SA 270, 271
Grange Jetty SA 271
Granite Island SA 277, 282
Grannys Rock NSW 99

Grant Island NT 347
Grantham Island SA 288
Grants Beach NSW 84
Grants Point TAS. 236
Grantville VIC. 184
Grasshopper Island NSW 111
Grassy TAS. 238
Grassy Creek VIC. 188
Grassy Head NSW 79
Grassy Island QLD 393
Grassy Point VIC. 165
Grays Bay QLD 396
Grays Point NSW 63
Great Barrier Reef QLD 364–5, 380, 398, 405
Great Forester River TAS. 240, 242, 244
Great Keppel Island QLD 404
Great Lake TAS. 240, 252, 254
Great Oyster Bay TAS. 218, 220, 222–3, 245
Great Palm Island QLD 394
Great Sandy National Park QLD 412
Great Sandy Strait QLD 364, 402, 403, 410, 413
Great Taylors Bay TAS. 228
Green Cape NSW 112, 124, 125
Green Head WA 307
Green Island (Lake Conjola) NSW 109
Green Island (South West Rocks) NSW 80, 81
Green Island QLD 375
Green Light Wedding Cake NSW 57
Green Point (Angourie) NSW 72
Green Point (Durras) NSW 114
Green Point (Hawkesbury) NSW 48, 51
Green Point TAS. 224
Green Rock NSW 108
Greenhill Lake VIC. 213
Greenough WA 307
Greenough River WA 307
Greens Pool WA 314
Greenwell Point NSW 107
Greenwich Sailing Club NSW 59
Gregory Islands QLD 410
Gregory WA 307
Gregory National Park NT 354
Gregory River QLD 397, 410, 416
Groote Eylandt NT 336, 337, 351
Groper Creek QLD 396
Groper Islet NSW 74
Grose Island NT 341
Grotto Point NSW 55
Guerrilla Bay NSW 115
Guichen Bay SA 279
Guide Reservoir TAS. 262
Guilderton WA 300, 306
Gulf of Carpentaria QLD 364, 380, 381, 382–3, 416

Gulf St Vincent SA 268, 269, 270, 272, 294
Gullala Creek NT 344
Gulnare Inlet QLD 398
Gungarlin River NSW 151
Gunn Point NT 346
Gunnamatta VIC. 160
Gunnamatta Bay NSW 63
Gunns Plains TAS. 263
Gunsight Reef NSW 92–3
Gunyah Point NSW 48
Gurig National Park NT 337, 347
Guy Fawkes River NSW 133, 134
Guyra NSW 133, 134
Gwydir River NSW 133, 135

Hacking River NSW 63, 130
Half Moon Bay NSW 58
Half Moon Bay VIC. 162
Half Tide Inlet NSW 71
Halifax Bay QLD 393, 394
Halls Reef QLD 370
Hamelin Bay WA 316
Hamersley River WA 312
Hamilton Island QLD 398
Hampton Harbour WA 326
Hancock Shoal QLD 369
Hanging Rock Lake VIC. 207
Hann River QLD 385
Happy Jacks Pondage NSW 151
Harcourt Reservoir VIC. 210, 211
Hardwicke Bay SA 272
Hardy Inlet WA 316
Hardys Bay Jetty NSW 46
Harrington NSW 77, 85
Hartz Mountains National Park TAS. 228
Harvey Estuary WA 318
Harvey River WA 332
Harvey Weir WA 330, 332
Harveys Return SA 274
Haslam SA 291
Haslewood Island QLD 398
Hastings Point NSW 66
Hastings River NSW 76, 82, 83, 129
Hat Head NSW 76, 81
Haughton River QLD 395
Haunted Stream VIC. 199
Hawkesbury River NSW 42, 44, 48, 50, 51, 99, 130
Hawks Nest NSW 88, 92
Hawks Nest Beach QLD 413
Hay NSW 152
Hay Point QLD 400
Hay Reef QLD 400
Hay River WA 314
Haycock Point NSW 123
Haycock Reach NSW 51
Hayley Reef VIC. 189
Hayman Island QLD 398
Helens Rock VIC. 191
Hells Gate NSW 86
Hells Gates QLD 370
Hellyer River TAS. 258, 261

Hen and Chicken Bay NSW 58
Henderson Lagoon TAS. 237
Henderson Rock QLD 373
Henley Beach SA 271
Henty River TAS. 240, 258, 261
Hepburn Lagoon VIC. 208, 210, 211
Herald Island QLD 393, 394
Herbert River QLD 391
Herdsman Drain WA 302
Herdsmans Cove TAS. 226
Hervey Bay QLD 402, 410–11, 413, 418
Hesters Brook WA 330, 332
High Cliff SA 272
High Island QLD 390
High Rock WA 324
Hill Inlet QLD 398
Hillarys Boat Harbour WA 300, 302, 303
Hinchinbrook Channel QLD 380, 391
Hinchinbrook Island QLD 380, 391
Hindmarsh Island SA 280, 281
Hindmarsh River SA 282
Hinkler Patches NT 345
Hobart TAS. 218, 220, 226, 250
Hodgson River NT 360
Hole in the Wall NSW 52
Hole in the Wall NT 350
Hollands Landing VIC. 174, 175
Holloways Beach QLD 387
Home Hill QLD 396
Honeymoon Island WA 314
Honeysuckle Island NSW 119
Hook Island QLD 398
Hook Passage QLD 398
Hooper Beach SA 279
Hope Inlet NT 342
Hopetoun WA 308, 312
Hopetoun Channel VIC. 172
Hopkins River VIC. 187, 190–1, 194, 208, 213
Hornibrook Highway Bridge QLD 375
Horrocks WA 307
Horse Island NSW 117
Horse Rock SA 288
Horse Shoe Beach NSW 94
Horseshoe Bay (Victor Harbor) SA 282
Horseshoe Bay (Yorke Peninsula) SA 272
Horseshoe Beach NSW 110
Horseshoe Reef QLD 405
Horsham VIC. 194, 215
Houtman Abrolhos Islands WA 307
Hovell Pile VIC. 158, 160
Howard River NT 342
Howard River Crossing NT 356
Howard Springs NT 356
Howes Lagoon Bay TAS. 256
Howie Reef QLD 390

Howqua River VIC. 194, 203, 205
Hull Heads QLD 390
Hume NSW 152
Hummocky Island QLD 406
Hungry Head NSW 79
Hungry Point NSW 63
Hunter Island TAS. 232
Hunter River NSW 94, 136, 137, 138–9
Hunter Rock NSW 123
Hunters Bay NSW 57
Huon River TAS. 218, 228, 248, 251
Huonville TAS. 228
Hutchison Shoal QLD 373
Hutt Gully VIC. 188
Hutt River SA 292

Illawong Bay NSW 51
Iluka NSW 64, 72
Indi River NSW 150
Indi River VIC. 200
Indian Head QLD 412
Indian Island NT 341
Ingham QLD 393, 394
Inglis River TAS. 258, 262
Ingoldsby Reef VIC. 186, 188
Injidup Point WA 317
Inlet Drive WA 314
Inman River SA 282, 292
Inner Gneerings Reef QLD 369
Innes National Park SA 272
Inscription Point NSW 62
Inside Channel VIC. 184
Inskip Point QLD 368
Inverloch VIC. 178, 181
Investigator Group SA 291
Iron Gates NSW 71
Iron Peg NSW 69
Iron Range National Park QLD 385
Ironhouse Point TAS. 237
Irwin Inlet WA 314–15
Irwin River WA 307
Isabella River NSW 143
Island Bend Dam NSW 146
Island Point QLD 389
Israelite Bay WA 308, 310
Isthmus Bay TAS. 228
Ivanhoe Crossing WA 333

Jacks Island WA 314
Jacks Point SA 280
Jacksons Creek VIC. 207
Jacky Jacky Creek QLD 385
Jacobs Well QLD 376, 377
Jaggers Beach NSW 120
James Point WA 326
James Price Point WA 328
James River TAS. 256
Jamieson Creek VIC. 189
Jamieson River VIC. 194, 205
Jardine River QLD 384, 416
Jemmys Point VIC. 172

459

INDEX

JENOLAN RIVER NSW – LEVEN RIVER TAS.

Jenolan River NSW 143
Jeparit Vic. 215
Jerimbut Point NSW 120
Jerrys Plains NSW 139
Jerusalem Bay NSW 48, 51
Jervis Bay NSW 100, 108
Jetty Beach NSW 75
Jewfish Bay NSW 61
Jewfish Point NSW 61
Jews Head NSW 125
Jibbon Bombora NSW 102
Jimmies Island NSW 112, 115
Jingellic Vic. 200
Joe Crafts Creek NSW 48
Joes Island Vic. 184
Joggly Point NSW 71
Johanna Vic. 190
John Bull Light Vic. 168
John Oxley Bridge QLD 408
Johnsonville Vic. 173
Jollys Beach SA 272
Jolong NSW 60
Jones Island NSW 85
Jordan River Tas. 250
Juan Rocks NSW 69
Julian Lakes Tas. 256
Julian Rocks Aquatic Reserve NSW 64
Julieann NSW 60
Jumpinpin QLD 366, 367
Junction Lake Tas. 256
Juno Point NSW 48, 51
Jurien WA 300, 306

Kakadu National Park NT 352, 353, 358–9
Kalang River NSW 76, 79
Kalbarri WA 300, 306, 307, 331
Kalgan River WA 313, 331
Kalimna Vic. 172
Kalinga Bank QLD 377
Kalpowar Crossing QLD 385, 416
Kamiesh Pass QLD 406
Kananook Creek Vic. 159
Kangaroo Island SA 266, 268, 270, 274–5
Kangaroo Lake Vic. 211
Kangaroo Valley NSW 131
Kangarutha Point NSW 122
Karratha WA 326
Karuah River NSW 92, 130
Karumba QLD 380, 383
Karumba Point QLD 383
Katherine NT 354
Katherine Gorge NT 354
Katoomba NSW 143
Kauri Creek QLD 368
Kedumba River NSW 143
Keep River Crossing NT 354
Keep River National Park NT 354
Kellidie Bay SA 290
Kellys Bush Reserve NSW 58
Kemps Corner NSW 80, 81
Kendalls Beach NSW 106

Kennedy Bend Waterhole QLD 416
Kennedy Inlet QLD 385
Kennedy River QLD 416
Kennedys Beach WA 310
Kennett River Vic. 189
Kent River WA 314
Keppel Bay QLD 404
Keppel Group QLD 364, 402, 404
Kerford Road Pier Vic. 162
Kettering Tas. 228
Khancoban Pondage NSW 151
Kiah Inlet NSW 124
Kiama NSW 42, 100, 106
Kianga Channel QLD 373
Kianga Lake NSW 116
Kianinny Bay NSW 122, 123
Kiewa River Vic. 194, 196, 201
Killarney Beach Vic. 191
Killiecrankie Bay Tas. 239
Kimberley WA 297, 320, 328, 330, 333
Kimberley Coast WA 329
King Ash Bay NT 360
King Creek NT 342
King George Sound WA 312–13
King Island Tas. 218, 230–1, 238, 261
King Parrot Creek Vic. 205
King River Tas. 261
King River Vic. 194, 202, 204
King River WA 313
King Sound WA 329
Kingaroy QLD 418
Kingfisher Bay Resort QLD 413
Kings Camp SA 278
Kingscliff Beach NSW 66
Kingscote SA 274
Kingston SA 277, 278
Kirk Point Vic. 163
Kirton Point SA 288
Kitty Miller Bay Beach Vic. 183
Knotts Crossing NT 354
Koetong Creek Vic. 200
Kolan River QLD 408
Konong Wootong Reservoir Vic. 208, 214
Koombana Bay WA 318
Korogoro Point NSW 81
Kourung Gourung Point NSW 46
Kow Swamp Vic. 211
Kowmung River NSW 143
Kunkamoula Billabong NT 358
Kununurra WA 320, 329, 330, 333
Kurnell Peninsula NSW 44, 61, 62
Kurrimine Beach QLD 390
Kybeyan River NSW 146, 148
Kydra Creek NSW 146, 148
Kyogle NSW 129

La Trobe Creek Vic. 190
La Trobe River Vic. 175, 202, 206
Lacepede Bay SA 278
Lacepede Islands WA 328–9
Lachlan River NSW 144, 145, 152
Lady Barron Tas. 230, 239
Lady Bay Vic. 174, 191
Lady Beach NSW 57
Lady Elliot Island QLD 407
Lady Julia Percy Island Vic. 187, 192, 193
Lady Musgrave Island QLD 407
Lady Robinsons Beach NSW 60
Lagoon Head NSW 110, 111
Lagoon of Islands Tas. 252, 254
Lagoon Pier Vic. 162
Lake Ada Tas. 252
Lake Albert NSW 152
Lake Argyle WA 330, 333
Lake Augusta Tas. 252, 256
Lake Awoonga QLD 418–19
Lake Ball Tas. 256
Lake Barrington Tas. 240, 258, 263
Lake Bathurst NSW 144
Lake Battye SA 279
Lake Bennet NT 356
Lake Binney Tas. 255
Lake Boga Vic. 211
Lake Bolac Vic. 208, 213
Lake Borumba QLD 418
Lake Botsford Tas. 256
Lake Brewster NSW 152
Lake Bullen Merri Vic. 194, 208, 212
Lake Burbury Tas. 240, 258, 261
Lake Burragorang NSW 141, 143, 144
Lake Burrendong NSW 141, 142
Lake Burrumbeet Vic. 208, 213
Lake Butler SA 279
Lake Canobolas NSW 142
Lake Cargelligo NSW 152
Lake Caval NSW 152
Lake Centenary NSW 152
Lake Charlegrark Vic. 215
Lake Charm Vic. 211
Lake Colac Vic. 212
Lake Conjola NSW 100, 108, 109
Lake Copeton NSW 133, 135
Lake Corringle Vic. 171
Lake Craven Vic. 190
Lake Crescent Tas. 252, 254
Lake Dalrymple QLD 417
Lake Dartmouth Vic. 194, 196, 200, 201
Lake Dobson Tas. 248, 251
Lake Dock Vic. 208, 215
Lake Dove Tas. 257
Lake Dulverton Tas. 250
Lake Echo Tas. 252, 255
Lake Eildon Vic. 194, 202, 205
Lake Elingamite Vic. 212
Lake Eppalock Vic. 194, 202, 205
Lake Ettrick Vic. 212

Lake Eucumbene NSW 146, 151
Lake Fanny Tas. 256
Lake Fenton Tas. 251
Lake Fergus Tas. 256
Lake Forbes NSW 152
Lake Fyans Vic. 208, 215
Lake George NSW 141, 144
Lake Gillear Vic. 190, 208, 213
Lake Glenmaggie Vic. 206
Lake Gordon Tas. 258, 260
Lake Hamilton Vic. 214
Lake Hope NSW 84
Lake Hume Vic. 194, 200, 201
Lake Illawarra NSW 100, 103, 104–5
Lake Inverell NSW 135
Lake Jindabyne NSW 146, 149, 151
Lake Julius QLD 417
Lake Kay Tas. 256
Lake Keepit NSW 133, 135
Lake King Vic. 166, 167, 173
Lake King William Tas. 240, 252, 257
Lake Koombooloomba QLD 416
Lake Kununurra WA 330, 333
Lake Lea Tas. 258, 263
Lake Leake Tas. 242, 246
Lake Learmonth Vic. 208, 213
Lake Lyell NSW 140, 143
Lake Mackenzie Tas. 256
Lake Mackintosh Tas. 258, 261
Lake Macquarie NSW 42, 88, 89, 94, 95
Lake Maraboon QLD 418
Lake Maroon QLD 419
Lake Meston Tas. 256
Lake Modewarre Vic. 208, 212
Lake Mokoan Vic. 204
Lake Monduran QLD 418
Lake Moogerah QLD 419
Lake Moondarra QLD 417
Lake Mulwala NSW 152
Lake Mulwala Vic. 204
Lake Munmorah NSW 88, 96
Lake Murdeduke Vic. 208, 212
Lake Nagambie Vic. 205
Lake Naomi Tas. 256
Lake Navarino WA 332
Lake Nillahcootie Vic. 204
Lake Nunan SA 279
Lake Oberon NSW 143
Lake Olive Tas. 256
Lake Parramatta NSW 130
Lake Pedder Tas. 240, 258, 260
Lake Petrarch Tas. 257
Lake Pine Vic. 208, 215
Lake Plimsoll Tas. 261
Lake Purrumbete Vic. 194, 208, 212
Lake Repulse Tas. 250
Lake River Tas. 242, 246
Lake Rosebery Tas. 258, 261
Lake Rowallan Tas. 240, 258, 263

Lake St Clair NSW 136, 139
Lake St Clair Tas. 252, 257
Lake Somerset QLD 419
Lake Sooley NSW 144
Lake Sorell Tas. 252, 254
Lake Talbot NSW 152
Lake Tali Karng Vic. 206
Lake Tinaroo QLD 416
Lake Tooliorook Vic. 208, 212
Lake Toolondo Vic. 194
Lake Trevallyn Tas. 246
Lake Tyers Vic. 156, 171
Lake Victoria Vic. 166, 174–5
Lake Wallace Vic. 215
Lake Wallerawang (Wallis) NSW 140, 141, 142, 143
Lake Wartook Vic. 215
Lake Wellington Vic. 167, 175
Lake Wendouree Vic. 212
Lake Weyba QLD 370
Lake William Hovell Vic. 202, 204
Lake Windamere NSW 141, 142
Lake Winslow Vic. 213
Lake Wivenhoe QLD 419
Lake Wyangala NSW 140, 141, 143, 145
Lakefield National Park QLD 385, 416
Lakes Entrance Vic. 166, 167, 172
Lakes Tourist Resort NT 356
Lancelin WA 306
Lane Cove River NSW 59
Lang Lang Vic. 184
Langford Reef QLD 398
Lansdowne River NSW 129
Largs Bay SA 271
Lauderdale Tas. 224
Laughing Jack Lagoon Tas. 255
Launceston Tas. 218, 230, 234, 235, 246
Laurieton NSW 77, 84
Lauriston Reservoir Vic. 205
Lavinia Point Tas. 238
Lawrence Rocks Vic. 192, 193
Lawson Island NT 347
Le Grand Beach WA 310
Leaders Creek NT 346
Ledge Point WA 306
Lee Breakwater Vic. 192, 193
Lee Point NT 342
Leeman WA 307
Leeuwin–Naturaliste National Park WA 316
Lefroy Brook WA 330, 332
Legendre Island WA 326
Leichhardt River QLD 382, 416
Leighton Beach WA 302
Lemon Tree Passage NSW 92
Lennox Head NSW 64, 69
Lerderderg River Vic. 207
Leschenault Inlet WA 297, 318
Leven Canyon Tas. 263
Leven River Tas. 240, 258, 263

INDEX

Levys Beach Vic. 191
Lewis Channel Vic. 177
Lewisham Tas. 224
Liffey River Tas. 246
Light River SA 292
Lilli Pilli Baths NSW 63
Lilli Pilli Headland NSW 114
Lillies Island NSW 67
Lime Bay Tas. 224
Limeburners Bay Vic. 158, 164
Limeburners Creek NSW 83
Limestone Creek Vic. 200
Limestone Gorge NT 354
Limmen Bight River NT 360
Lincoln Cove SA 284, 288
Lindeman Group QLD 399
Lintern Channel NSW 46
Lion Rock QLD 370
Lithgow NSW 141, 143
Little Bay NSW 80
Little Beach (Hat Head) NSW 81
Little Beach (Little Bay) NSW 60
Little Beach SA 272
Little Forester River Tas. 234, 244
Little Greeny Ledge NSW 60
Little Head NSW 52
Little Island NSW 92
Little Marley Beach NSW 102
Little Murray River Vic. 211
Little Muttonbird Island NSW 75
Little Pine Lagoon Tas. 240, 252, 255
Little Pine River Tas. 256
Little Plains River NSW 149
Little Reef NSW 52
Little River NSW 143
Little River Tas. 256
Little River WA 314
Little Seal Rocks NSW 91
Little Shark Island NSW 80
Little Sirius Cove NSW 57
Little Susan Creek QLD 413
Little Swanport River Tas. 223, 245
Little Taylors Bay Tas. 228
Little Wall NSW 71
Little Waterhouse Lake Tas. 244
Little Wobby Beach NSW 48
Little Woody Island QLD 411, 413
Little Yarra River Vic. 207
Liverpool NSW 130
Lizard Island QLD 385
Lobster Beach NSW 46
Loch Sport Vic. 166, 174, 175
Locks Well Beach SA 290
Loddon River Vic. 208, 210, 211
Lodge of Dundee NT 339, 340, 341
Loelia Channel Vic. 160
Logans Beach Vic. 191
Logues Brook Dam WA 330
Lombadina Point WA 328, 329
Long Billabong NT 358

Long Point (Macquarie River) NSW 142
Long Point (Myall Lakes) NSW 91
Long Point Tas. 237
Long Reef NSW 45
Long Reef Point NSW 52
Longnose Point NSW 48
Lonsdale Bay Vic. 165
Loongana Range Tas. 263
Lorella Station NT 360
Lorna Shoals NT 341
Lorne Vic. 186, 189, 194
Lost Beach WA 315
Lostock Dam NSW 136, 138
Louth Bay SA 288
Loutit Bay Vic. 189
Low Head Tas. 234
Low Islets QLD 386
Low Level Bridge NT 354
Lowlands Beach WA 313
Lucinda QLD 380, 391
Lucky Bay (Esperance) WA 310
Lucky Bay (Gregory) WA 307, 310
Lucky Bay SA 287
Luggage Point QLD 375
Lukies Farm NT 354
Luna Park NSW 58
Lunawanna Tas. 228
Lyalls Channel Vic. 184

Maaroom QLD 413
Mabel Island QLD 390
Macalister River Vic. 175, 202, 206
McArthur River NT 360
Macauleys Headland NSW 75
McBrides Point QLD 400
Macdonald River NSW 134
McEacherns Rocks Vic. 193
McHaffief Point Vic. 183
Machans Beach QLD 387
Macintyre River NSW 133, 135
Mackay QLD 393, 396, 400, 414, 416, 418
McKenzie Arm NT 341
Mackenzies Point NSW 60
Mackerel Bay QLD 398
Mackerel Islands WA 325
McKnoe Brook WA 332
Maclaughlin River NSW 146, 149
Maclean NSW 72
MacLean Bay Tas. 237
Macleay River NSW 76, 77, 80, 129
McLennan Strait Vic. 166, 175
McLoughlins Beach Vic. 166, 167, 176
McMahons Point NSW 58
MacMasters Beach NSW 99
McMillan Strait Vic. 166, 174
Macona Inlet QLD 398
Macquarie River NSW 141, 142, 143, 152

Macquarie River Tas. 240, 242, 243, 246
Macquarie Rivulet NSW 104
Macs Ground SA 271
Madeleine Shoals WA 326
Madfish Bay WA 314
Madora Beach WA 319
Magela Creek NT 358, 359
Magic Triangle NSW 125
Magnetic Island QLD 395
Mahers Landing Vic. 181
Maianbar NSW 63
Main Beach NSW 69
Maitland NSW 136, 139
Maitland River WA 326
Malabanbandju Creek NT 358
Malabar Creek NSW 116
Mallacoota Vic. 156, 167, 168–9
Malmsbury Reservoir Vic. 205
Malpas Dam NSW 133, 134
Manangoora Station NT 360
Mandalay Point QLD 398
Mandorah Queen wreck NT 342
Mandorah Wharf NT 338
Mandurah WA 308, 318–19
Mangrove Creek NSW 44, 50, 51, 130
Manilla River NSW 135
Manly Dam NSW 130
Manly Point NSW 54
Manly Wharf NSW 54
Manning Point NSW 85
Manning River Estuary NSW 76, 77, 84, 85, 130
Manns Beach Vic. 176
Manton Dam NT 356
Manton River Crossing NT 356
Maranoa River QLD 418
Marchinbar Island NT 350
Marengo Vic. 187, 189
Margaret Brock Reef SA 278
Margaret River WA 316
Maria Island Tas. 220, 222, 223
Maria River NSW 83
Maribyrnong River Vic. 158, 162, 202, 207
Maringa Creek Vic. 172
Marino Reef SA 271
Marion Bay SA 272
Marion Bay Narrows Tas. 220
Marley Beach NSW 102
Marley Head NSW 102
Marlin Coast QLD 386
Marlin Jetty QLD 389
Marlo Vic. 166, 171
Marmion Beach WA 302
Marmion Reefs WA 302–3
Maroochy River QLD 367, 369, 371
Maroochydore QLD 368, 369
Maroubra Beach NSW 60
Marsden Head NSW 106
Marshalls Creek NSW 68
Martin Inlet QLD 398
Mary Ann Haven WA 312

Mary River NT 346, 352, 353, 356, 357
Mary River QLD 413, 415, 418
Mary Street Lagoon WA 319
Marys Rock NSW 66
Maslin Beach SA 270
Masson Point NT 341
Mataranka NT 354, 360
Maud Sanctuary WA 325
Mayers Point NSW 90
Maylands WA 304
Meadowbank Lake Tas. 240, 248, 250
Meander River Tas. 240, 242, 246
Medeas Cove Tas. 236
Meelup WA 317
Melbourne Vic. 156, 158–9, 207
Melville Island NT 337, 339, 344
Melville Waters WA 300
Memorial Wall NSW 68
Menindee Lakes NSW 152
Meningie SA 277
Mercury Passage Tas. 218, 220, 223
Merewether Beach NSW 94
Merimbula NSW 42, 113, 123
Merimbula Lake NSW 123
Merimbula Wharf NSW 122, 123
Mermaid Reef NSW 77, 85
Mermaid Sound WA 326
Merri River Vic. 187, 190, 194, 208, 213
Merry Beach NSW 111
Mersey River Tas. 218, 230, 233, 240, 258, 259, 263
Metung Vic. 166, 173
Miaboolya Beach WA 324
Micalo Island NSW 72
Micket Creek NT 342
Middle Arm NT 342
Middle Bank Vic. 179
Middle Beach NSW 122
Middle Channel Vic. 185
Middle Creek QLD 408
Middle Ground Reef NSW 108
Middle Harbour NSW 44, 54–5
Middle Head NSW 57
Middle Island NSW 92
Middle Island SA 272
Middle Lagoon NSW 122
Middle Reef NSW 94
Middle River SA 274
Middle Rocks QLD 412
Middle Wall NSW 72
Middleton SA 282
Midge Channel Vic. 166
Mills Reef Vic. 193
Mindarie Keys WA 303
Minerva Reef Vic. 192
Minjilang NT 347
Minnamurra NSW 100, 106
Minnamurra River NSW 100, 106
Minnie Water NSW 64, 72, 73

Missingham Bridge NSW 70
Mission Beach QLD 390
Mission River QLD 384
Missionary Bay QLD 391
Mitchell River QLD 416
Mitchell River Vic. 166, 173, 194, 196, 196, 199
Mitchells Island NSW 85
Mitta Mitta River Vic. 194, 196, 200, 201
Mogareka Inlet NSW 122
Moggs Creek Vic. 188
Moggs Ledge Vic. 188
Mole River NSW 133, 135
Molineaux Point NSW 60, 61
Mollymook Beach NSW 110
Molong NSW 142
Molonga River NSW 148
Mona Vale Headland NSW 52
Monkey Mia WA 322
Montague Island NSW 112, 118, 120
Monument Point NSW 80
Mooball Beach NSW 66
Mooloolaba QLD 368, 369
Mooloolah River QLD 366, 367, 368, 369, 371
Moon Point QLD 410, 413
Moonan Brook NSW 138
Moonee Beach NSW 74
Moonee Creek NSW 74
Moons Crossing WA 332
Moorabool Reservoir Vic. 212
Moorabool River Vic. 212
Moore Reef QLD 387
Moore River WA 306, 331
Moppy River NSW 136, 137
Moras Creek Vic. 200
Mordialloc Creek Vic. 159
Mordialloc Pier Vic. 162
Morehead River QLD 385, 416
Moreton Bay QLD 366, 367, 372–5, 376
Moreton Island QLD 366, 372, 373, 374
Morna Point NSW 93
Mornington Island QLD 382
Mornington Pier Vic. 158, 161
Morpeth NSW 138
Morrisons Fault Line Vic. 158, 161
Moruya River NSW 112, 116
Morwell River Vic. 202, 206
Mosman Bay WA 304
Mosquito Bay NSW 114
Mosquito Channel Vic. 183
Moulting Lagoon Tas. 222
Mount Bold Reservoir SA 294
Mount Eliza Vic. 158, 161
Mount Emu Creek Vic. 213
Mount Field National Park Tas. 240, 248, 251
Mount Martha Vic. 158, 161
Mounts Bay Vic. 189
Mourilyan Harbour QLD 390

461

INDEX

MOUTH FLAT BEACH SA – PIG ISLAND NSW

Mouth Flat Beach SA 274
Mowarry Point NSW 125
Mowbray River QLD 389
Moyne River VIC. 191, 214
Mud Island (Brisbane) QLD 375
Mud Island (Russell Heads) QLD 390
Mud Island (Port Phillip) VIC. 160
Mud Islands (Lake Tyers) VIC. 171
Mudgee NSW 141, 142
Muirella Park Creek NT 358
Mulgrave River QLD 380, 390
Mullet Creek NSW 104
Mullimburra Point NSW 116
Mummuga Lake NSW 116
Mundoo Channel SA 277
Munglinup Beach WA 308, 310
Mungo Brush NSW 90
Munmarlary Landing NT 347
Munna Point QLD 370
Munyang River NSW 151
Murat Bay SA 291
Murchison River WA 297, 307, 331
Murphys Reef QLD 369
Murrah Head NSW 121
Murrah Lagoon NSW 121
Murrah Lake NSW 120–1
Murrah River NSW 131
Murramarang Beach NSW 111
Murray River NSW 152
Murray River SA 277, 280, 281, 292–3
Murray River VIC. 194, 196, 200, 201, 211, 215
Murray River WA 319, 330, 332
Murrindindi River VIC. 205
Murrumbidgee River NSW 145, 146, 147, 148, 150, 152
Murwillumbah NSW 67, 129
Mushroom Rock WA 307
Muswellbrook NSW 139
Mutchero Inlet QLD 390
Mutee Head QLD 384
Muttonbird Island NSW 75
Muzzelwood Inlet NSW 151
Myall Lakes NSW 42, 88, 90–1
Myall River NSW 88, 90, 92
Myalup Beach WA 318
Mylestom NSW 79
Myponga Beach SA 270
Myponga River SA 270
Myrtle Beach NSW 114
Mystery Bay NSW 118–19

Nabiac NSW 130
Nagambie VIC. 194, 202
Nambucca Heads NSW 76, 78, 79
Nambucca River NSW 79, 129
Namoi River NSW 134, 135
Napier Bay NT 345
Nara Inlet QLD 398
Naracoopa TAS. 238

Narara Creek NSW 46
Nariel Creek VIC. 194, 200
Narooma NSW 112, 116, 118
Narooma Bar NSW 113, 120
Narrabeen Lakes NSW 44, 52, 53
Narrabeen NSW 52
Narrandera NSW 152
Narrawong VIC. 186, 193
Nathan River Station NT 360
Nathans Point VIC. 188
Nattai River NSW 143
Natural Jetty WA 305
Nelligen NSW 114
Nelson VIC. 193
Nelson Bay NSW 92
Nelson Lagoon NSW 122
Nepean Bay SA 274
Nepean River NSW 48, 130
Neranie Head NSW 90
Nerong NSW 90
Never Fail (Jervis Bay) NSW 108
Neverfail (Port Macquarie) NSW 82
Nerverfail Island NSW 50
New Brighton NSW 66
New Year Island NT 347
New Year Island TAS. 238
New Zealand Beach NSW 71
Newcastle NSW 88, 94
Newcastle Beach NSW 94
Newgate Island WA 315
Newlands Arm VIC. 174
Newlyn Reservoir VIC. 208, 210, 211
Newport NSW 52
Ngkala Rocks QLD 412
Nhulunbuy NT 336, 337, 348, 351
Niangala NSW 134
Nicholson River QLD 382, 416
Nicholson River VIC. 166, 173, 194, 196, 199
Niemur River NSW 152
Nightcliff NT 338
Nile River TAS. 246
Nine Mile Beach QLD 405
Nine Mile Beach TAS. 222–3
Nine Mile Reef NSW 66
Nineteen Lagoons TAS. 252, 256
Ninety Mile Beach VIC. 171, 172
Ningaloo Marine Park WA 324, 325
Ningaloo Reef WA 320, 325
Ningaloo Station WA 325
Nive River TAS. 252, 255, 256
Nobbys Beach NSW 94
Noland Bay TAS. 234
Noojee VIC. 206
Noosa Heads QLD 368, 369, 370
Noosa National Park QLD 370
Noosa River QLD 367, 370, 418
Noosa Sound QLD 370
Nora Creina Bay SA 278

Norah Head NSW 97
Norfolk Bay TAS. 224
Norman River QLD 383, 416
Normanby Island QLD 390
Normanby River QLD 385, 416
Normans Beach WA 313
Normanville SA 270
Nornalup Inlet WA 297, 308, 315
Norries Head NSW 66
North Arm VIC. 185
North Beach (Port Macquarie) NSW 82
North Beach (Shark Bay) NSW 72
North Creek NSW 70
North East Isles NT 351
North East River TAS. 239
North Entrance QLD 407
North Esk River TAS. 240, 242, 246
North Harbour Aquatic Reserve NSW 54
North Haven Bridge NSW 84
North Haven SA 269
North Head (Batemans Bay) NSW 114
North Head (Sydney) NSW 52, 54
North Head WA 306
North Johnstone River QLD 416
North Keppel Island QLD 404
North Mole WA 304
North Peron Island NT 340
North Point QLD 373
North Point TAS. 232
North Reef QLD 370–1
North Riordan Shoal NSW 71
North Rock NSW 74
North Rock SA 278
North Shore rocks VIC. 158
North Solitary Island NSW 74
North Stradbroke Island QLD 366, 374, 375, 376
North West Cape WA 325
North West Solitary Island NSW 74
North White Cliffs jetty QLD 413
Northbridge Marina NSW 55
Northumberland Islands QLD 401
Nortons Basin NSW 130
Nourlangie Creek NT 358
Nowa Nowa Arm VIC. 171
Nowra NSW 131
Nowra Hill Ground NSW 108
Numbaa Island NSW 107
Numeralla River NSW 146, 148
Nungurner VIC. 172
Nymboida River NSW 128, 129

Oaky Beach NSW 114
Oaky River NSW 134
Obelisk Beach NSW 57
Oberon NSW 143

O'Briens Point VIC. 193
Observation Head NSW 114
Ocean Beach NSW 46
Ocean Grove VIC. 165
Ocean Reef Marina WA 302
Ocean Street Bridge NSW 53
O'Connell River QLD 399
O'Keefes Point NSW 107
Old Beach TAS. 226
Old Gladesville Bridge NSW 58
Olinda Creek VIC. 207
Omadale Brook NSW 138
One Arm Point WA 328, 329
One Man Rock NSW 72
One Mile Reef QLD 375
Onkaparinga River SA 270, 292, 294
Onslow WA 325
Ooloo Crossing NT 354
Opossum Bay TAS. 226
Orange NSW 142
Orara River NSW 129
Ord River WA 330, 333
Orford Rivulet TAS. 223
Orford TAS. 218, 220, 222
Orpheus Island QLD 394
Osborne wharves SA 271
O'Sullivan Beach SA 269, 271
Otago Bay TAS. 226
Ourimbah Creek NSW 97
Ouse River TAS. 240, 248, 249, 250, 256
Outer Gneerings Reef QLD 369
Outer Harbour SA 266, 271
'Outer Spuds' VIC. 162
Ovens River VIC. 194, 202, 204
Oxley Island NT 347
Oxley Wild Rivers National Park NSW 134
Oyster Bay SA 272
Oyster Creek WA 324
Oyster Harbour WA 309, 312–13
Oyster Reef QLD 387
Oyster Reef WA 307
Oyster Rock (Mackay) QLD 400
Oyster Rocks (Noosa Heads) QLD 370
Ozone Jetty VIC. 165

P2 buoy VIC. 163
Packers Creek QLD 389
Paddys River NSW 150
Painkalac Creek VIC. 188
Palace Reef WA 314
Pallinup River WA 312
Palm Beach NSW 52
Palm Beach QLD 378
Palm Beach Reef QLD 379
Palm Islands QLD 392, 393, 394
Palmers Island NSW 72
Pambula NSW 113
Pambula Lake NSW 123
Pambula River NSW 123
Pancake Creek QLD 408
Pannikin Island QLD 368

Paradise Caves QLD 370
Park Beach NSW 75
Parker River VIC. 189
Paroo River NSW 152
Parramatta River NSW 58
Parramatta wreck NSW 48
Parrot Hole QLD 368
Parry Beach WA 314
Parsons Bay TAS. 224
Parsons Beach SA 277, 283
Pascoe River QLD 385
Patawalonga Entrance Groyne SA 271
Paterson River NSW 136, 138, 139
Patriarch Inlet TAS. 239
Patterson Lakes VIC. 162
Patterson River VIC. 158
Paynesville VIC. 166, 174
Peaceful Bay WA 315
Peach Tree Creek VIC. 170
Peaked Island QLD 404
Pearl Bay NSW 55
Pearl Bay QLD 404
Pearl Reef QLD 390
Pedro Point NSW 116
Peel Inlet WA 297, 318
Peel Island QLD 375
Pejar Dam NSW 141, 144
Pelican Bank Reef QLD 413
Pelican Bay QLD 368
Pelican Island NSW 97
Pelican Point NSW 97
Pelican Point VIC. 170
Pemberton WA 332
Pender Bay WA 329
Penguin Head NSW 108
Penneshaw SA 274
Pennington Bay SA 274
Penstock Lagoon TAS. 252, 254
Percy Island QLD 401
Peregian Beach QLD 369
Perforated Island QLD 404
Perkins Bay TAS. 218, 230, 232
Perkins Beach NSW 103, 104
Peron Islands NT 339, 340
Peron Peninsula WA 322
Perseverance wreck VIC. 161
Perth WA 298, 300, 302–3, 330
Pet Reservoir TAS. 262
Peterborough VIC. 186, 190
Petrel Cover SA 283
Petrie Creek QLD 371
Phillip Island VIC. 178, 179, 156, 183
Phoques Bay TAS. 238
Piano Rocks NSW 71
Piccaninny Point TAS. 237
Pickersgill Reef QLD 386
Picnic Arm VIC. 174
Picnic Island QLD 413
Picton River TAS. 251
Pieman River TAS. 240, 258
Piersons Point TAS. 226
Pig Island NSW 107

Pigeon Point NSW 90
Pillans Lake TAS. 256
Pilot Beach NSW 84
Pimlico Island NSW 71
Pindari Dam NSW 133, 135
Pine Creek NSW 78
Pine Island NSW 148
Pine Lake VIC. 208, 215
Pine River QLD 375
Pine River TAS. 252, 255, 256
Pine Tier Lagoon TAS. 252, 255
Pinkenba QLD 375
Pinnace Channel VIC. 160
Pinnacle Point QLD 398
Pioneer Beach NT 341
Pioneer Point QLD 398
Pioneer River QLD 400
Pipeclay Point NSW 53
Pipers River TAS. 234
Pippi Beach NSW 72
Pirates Bay TAS. 224
Pitt Water TAS. 224
Pittwater NSW 44, 45, 48, 51
Pittwater Road Bridge NSW 53
Platypus Bay QLD 410
Platypus wreck QLD 375
Plenty River TAS. 248, 251
Plover Island NSW 73
Point Arkwright QLD 369
Point Bailly TAS. 223
Point Bell SA 291
Point Blaze NT 340
Point Brown SA 291
Point Cartwright QLD 371
Point Cook VIC. 159, 163
Point Danger QLD 378
Point Danger VIC. 192
Point Dickinson NSW 120
Point Gellibrand VIC. 163
Point Gordon WA 312
Point Grey VIC. 189
Point Henry VIC. 164
Point Hood WA 312
Point Lillias VIC. 158, 164
Point Lonsdale VIC. 158, 165
Point Lookout QLD 375
Point Neill SA 287
Point Nepean VIC. 160
Point Nuyts WA 308, 314
Point Perpendicular NSW 76, 84–5
Point Piper NSW 57
Point Pleasure NSW 114
Point Plomer NSW 82
Point Puer TAS. 224
Point Quobba WA 298, 320
Point Samson WA 326
Point Sinclair SA 291
Point Stephens NT 346
Point Turton SA 272
Point Upright NSW 110, 111
Point William SA 278
Point Wilson VIC. 162, 164
Poison Creek WA 310
Poisson Point WA 314

Polblue Creek NSW 138
Policemans Point SA 280
Polly McQuinn Dam VIC. 205
Pondalowie Bay SA 272
Pontoon Rocks NSW 70
Poole Island QLD 397
Poona QLD 413
Poona Point QLD 413
Popran Creek NSW 50
Porpoise Rocks WA 314
Porpoise Wall NSW 70–1
Port Adelaide River SA 266, 268, 271
Port Albert VIC. 166, 167, 176
Port Alma QLD 402, 406
Port Arthur TAS. 224
Port Augusta SA 284, 286, 287
Port Beach WA 302
Port Broughton SA 286
Port Campbell VIC. 186, 190, 194
Port Clinton SA 272
Port Curtis QLD 407
Port Cygnet TAS. 228
Port Dalrymple TAS. 218, 230, 234
Port Darwin NT 342
Port Davies TAS. 239
Port Denison WA 307
Port Douglas QLD 380, 386, 389
Port Elliot SA 282
Port Esperance TAS. 228
Port Essington NT 347
Port Fairy VIC. 186, 187, 191
Port Gregory WA 300
Port Hacking NSW 42, 44, 62–3
Port Hedland WA 320, 326–7
Port Hughes SA 272
Port Huon TAS. 228
Port Hurd NT 344
Port Jackson NSW 44, 54, 56–7
Port Keats 337
Port Kembla NSW 100, 103
Port Lincoln SA 266, 284, 288, 289
Port MacDonnell SA 277, 278
Port Macquarie NSW 76, 77, 82–3
Port Melbourne VIC. 162
Port Musgrave QLD 384
Port Noarlunga SA 270, 294
Port Phillip Bay VIC. 156, 158, 160–3
Port Pirie River SA 286–7
Port Pirie SA 284, 286
Port Sorell TAS. 218, 230, 234
Port Stanvac SA 271
Port Stephens NSW 42, 88, 92–3
Port Victoria SA 272
Port Vincent SA 272
Port Wakefield SA 272
Port Warrender WA 329
Port Welshpool VIC. 177
Port Willunga SA 270
Portarlington VIC. 158, 165

Portland VIC. 186, 192
Portlands Roads QLD 385
Portsea VIC. 158
Portsea Pier VIC. 160
Post Office gutter VIC. 184
Pot Alley Gorge WA 307
Potato Point NSW 116
Potter Point NSW 62
Pottsville Beach NSW 66
Poverty Creek QLD 372
Poverty Point QLD 368
Preston Beach WA 318
Preston River WA 318
Pretty Point NSW 115
Prevelly WA 316
Price SA 272
Prickly Point NSW 51
Primrose Sands TAS. 224
Prince George Light VIC. 165
Princess Charlotte Bay QLD 385, 416
Princess Royal Harbour WA 309, 312
Proper Bay SA 288
Proserpine River QLD 399
Prosser Bay TAS. 223
Prosser River TAS. 220, 223, 245
Pub Lake SA 279
Pullen Island SA 282
Pulpit Point NSW 59
Pulpit Rock NSW 125
Pumicestone Passage QLD 372, 418
Punchs Reef TAS. 226
Pungalina Station NT 360
Punsand Bay QLD 384
Putty Beach NSW 99
Pykes Creek Reservoir VIC. 207
Pyrmont wharves NSW 58

Quail Island NT 340, 341
Quakers Hat NSW 55
Quarantine Bay NSW 124
Quarantine Beach NSW 54
Queen River TAS. 261
Queens Domain TAS. 226
Queens Head NSW 76, 82
Queens Lake NSW 84
Queens Wharf NSW 94
Queensborough River VIC. 198
Queenscliff VIC. 158, 165
Queenstown TAS. 261
Quiet Corner VIC. 162
Quindalup WA 317
Quobba Station WA 324
Quondong Point WA 328

RAAF Jetty VIC. 159, 163
Racecourse Beach NSW 110
Racecourse Head NSW 82
Racecourse Island NSW 82
Radar Reef WA 305
Raft Point NT 341
Raglan Creek QLD 406
Rainbow Beach QLD 366, 368

Rainbow Cliff NT 351
Ralphs Bay TAS. 226
Ramsgate Baths NSW 60
Rankin Point NT 341
Rapid Bay SA 268, 270
Rat Island QLD 407
Rattlesnake Island QLD 393, 394
Raymond Island VIC. 174
Raymond Terrace NSW 138
Recherche Archipelago WA 298, 308, 310
Recherche Bay TAS. 228
Record Point NT 347
Red Bluff (Cape Cuvier) WA 325
Red Bluff (Kalbarri) WA 300, 307
Red Bluff Hotel VIC. 159
Red Hill Headland NSW 71
Red Light Wedding Cake NSW 57
Red Lily Billabong NT 358
Red Lily Lagoon QLD 416
Red Point (Port Kembla) NSW 103
Red Point (Twofold Bay) NSW 125
Red Point VIC. 183
Red Rock Headland NSW 74
Redbill Beach TAS. 237
Redgate WA 316
Redground Dam NSW 141, 144
Reeders Point QLD 373
Reedy Island NSW 117
Reef Point QLD 398
Reeve Channel VIC. 172
Refuge Bay NSW 48
Regatta Island NSW 86
Reids Flat NSW 145
Rennies Beach NSW 110
Repton NSW 79
Repulse Bay QLD 399
Retreat River NSW 143
Reynolds River Crossing NT 354
Rhyll VIC. 178, 183
Ricey Beach WA 305
Richmond Beach NSW 114
Richmond River NSW 42, 64, 70, 71, 129
Ricketts Point VIC. 162
Rifle Butts VIC. 189
Rigby Island VIC. 172
Rileys Island NSW 46
Ringarooma River TAS. 240, 244
Rippleside Jetty VIC. 164
Rita Island QLD 396
River Heads QLD 413
Riverview QLD 409
Rivoli Bay SA 278
Robbins Island TAS. 232
Robbins Passage TAS. 232
Robe SA 277, 278, 279
Roberts Shoal QLD 373
Robertsons Beach VIC. 176
Robinson River NT 360
Roche Reef NT 340

Rock Flat Creek NSW 146, 148
Rock Hole NT 359
Rockhampton QLD 405, 418
Rockingham WA 302
Rocklands Reservoir VIC. 193, 208, 214
Rocky Bar Crossing NT 360
Rocky Bay WA 304
Rocky Cape TAS. 232
Rocky Point NT 351
Rocky Point WA 315
Rocky Valley Dam VIC. 201
Rodds Harbour QLD 408
Roebuck Bay WA 328
Roebuck Deep WA 328
Rogues Point SA 272
Rooney Point QLD 410, 413
Roper Bar NT 360
Roper Creek NT 354
Roper River NT 353, 354, 360
Rosa Gully NSW 60
Rose Bay NSW 57
Rose River VIC. 204
Rosebud VIC. 158, 160
Rosemary Island WA 326
Rosetta Harbour SA 282, 283
Roseville Bridge NSW 55
Ross Creek QLD 395, 405
Ross River QLD 395
Rosslyn Bay QLD 402, 404, 405, 407
Rottnest Island WA 298, 300, 302, 305
Rottnest Trench WA 302
Round Hill Creek QLD 408
Round Hill Head QLD 408
Round Island (Great Sandy Strait) QLD 411
Round Island (Russell Heads) QLD 390
Round Top Island QLD 400
Rous Channel QLD 374
Rowley Shoals WA 328
Royal National Park NSW 42, 102
Royston River VIC. 205
Rubicon River TAS. 234
Rubicon River VIC. 205
Ruby Island NT 346
Ruby Reef QLD 386
Rum Island NSW 75
Runaway Bay QLD 378
Rundle Island QLD 407
Russell Heads QLD 390
Russell Island QLD 390
Russell River QLD 380, 390, 416
Rye Ocean Beach VIC. 160
Rylstone Weir NSW 141, 142

Safety Bay WA 302
Sailors Bay NSW 55
St Andrews VIC. 160
St Clair Lagoon TAS. 252
St George River VIC. 189
St Georges Basin NSW 109

INDEX ST HELENA ISLAND QLD – SUNDAY ISLAND VIC.

St Helena Island QLD 375
St Helens QLD 393
St Helens TAS. 218, 230, 236
St Helens VIC. 158
St Helens Bay QLD 400
St Helens Point TAS. 236
St Huberts Island Bridge NSW 46
St Kilda Pier VIC. 162
St Lawrence QLD 401, 404
St Leonards Pier VIC. 165
St Patricks River TAS. 246
St Pauls River TAS. 246
Salamander Bay NSW 92
Salamander Reef QLD 393
Salisbury NSW 138
Salmon Bay WA 305
Salmon Hole SA 278
Salt Creek SA 277, 280
Salt Pan Creek NSW 55
Salt Water Arm NT 346
Saltwater Creek (Green Cape) NSW 125
Saltwater Creek (Wooli) NSW 74
Saltwater River TAS. 224
Sammys Reef QLD 413
Samson Brook WA 332
San Remo Beach WA 319
San Remo VIC. 178, 183
Sand Bar Beach NSW 91
Sand Bay QLD 400
Sand Patch WA 313
Sand Pumping Jetty QLD 378
Sandon River NSW 42, 64, 73
Sandridge Beach VIC. 162
Sandringham VIC. 162
Sandshoes Beach NSW 62
Sandy Bay TAS. 226
Sandy Cape QLD 412
Sandy Creek NT 358
Sandy Islands NT 347
Sandy Point NSW 117
Sara River NSW 134
Saucy Creek NSW 149
Sawtell NSW 76, 78
Sawtell Island NSW 78
Sawtell River VIC. 185
Sawyer Bay TAS. 232
Scamander TAS. 237
Scamander River TAS. 242, 245
Scarborough Beach WA 302
Scarborough Boat Harbour QLD 372
Schouten Passage TAS. 222
Scotchmans Creek NSW 50
Scotland Island NSW 48
Scott Bay SA 291
Scotts Bridge WA 332
Scotts Creek NSW 85
Scotts Creek NT 356
Scotts Creek Crossing NT 356–7
Scotts Head NSW 79
Scrub Point VIC. 184
Seacombe VIC. 175
Seaford Pier VIC. 162
Seaforth QLD 393

Seagull Point NSW 87
Seagull Rocks NSW 68
Seaham Weir NSW 130
Seal Island SA 283
Seal Island VIC. 176
Seal Rocks NSW 88, 90
Seal Rocks TAS. 230
Secheron Point TAS. 226
Second Bluff NSW 72
Second Valley Jetty SA 270
Seisia QLD 384
Selfs Point TAS. 226
Sellicks Beach SA 270
Semaphore SA 271
Sentry Box Reach NSW 51
Serpentine Falls NSW 134
Serpentine River NSW 133
Serpentine River WA 331
Settlement Point TAS. 239
Seven Creeks VIC. 205
Seven Emu Station NT 360
Seven Mile Beach (Charlotte Head) NSW 87
Seven Mile Beach (Gerroa) NSW 107
Seven Mile Beach (Lennox Head) NSW 69
Seven Mile Beach WA 307
Seventeen Seventy QLD 408
Seventy Five Mile Beach QLD 412
Severn River NSW 133, 135
Seymour VIC. 202, 205
Shadow Lake TAS. 257
Shady Camp NT 346, 357
Shag Rock NSW 69
Shag Rock QLD 375
Shakey NSW 60
Shallow Crossing NSW 131
Shallow Inlet VIC. 178, 179, 180
Shallow Tempest QLD 373
Shamrock Bay NT 347
Shannon Lagoon TAS. 254
Shannon River TAS. 249
Shark Bay NSW 64, 72
Shark Bay NT 347
Shark Bay WA 298, 320, 322–3, 324
Shark Hole VIC. 160
Shark Island (Macleay River) NSW 80
Shark Island (Port Jackson) NSW 57
Shark Island (Port Stephens) NSW 93
Shark Point NSW 60
Sharps Beach NSW 70
Shaving Point VIC. 173
Shaw Creek VIC. 206
Shaw River VIC. 214
Shaws Bay NSW 70
Sheep Island NSW 90
Sheep Island QLD 370
Shell House WA 307
Shell Islands NT 342
Shelley Beach WA 313

Shellharbour NSW 100, 104, 105
Shelly Beach (Charlotte Head) NSW 87
Shelly Beach (Nambucca Heads) NSW 79
Shelly Beach (Port Macquarie) NSW 83
Shelly Beach QLD 410
Shelly Beach VIC. 193
Shelly Beach Head NSW 72
Shelly Point NSW 91
She-Oak Creek VIC. 189
Shepherd Bay QLD 391
Shepparton VIC. 202
Sheringa Beach SA 290
Sherlock River WA 326
Shoal Bay NT 339, 342, 353
Shoal Point QLD 400
Shoalhaven River NSW 42, 100, 106, 107, 128, 131
Shoalwater Bay (Bowen) QLD 397
Shoalwater Bay (Rockhampton) QLD 364, 402, 403, 404
Shoalwater Bay WA 302
Short Island QLD 377
Short Point NSW 123
Short Point Beach NSW 122
Shortland Bluff VIC. 165
Shovel Billabong NT 358
Shute Harbour QLD 398, 399
Shutehaven QLD 393, 398
'Siberia' VIC. 162
Sigma wreck NSW 93
Silver Beach NSW 61
Silver Sands Beach WA 319
Silvid Bay NT 347
Simpsons Creek NSW 68
Singapore Deep VIC. 177
Singleton Beach WA 319
Singleton NSW 139
Sir Richard Peninsula SA 281
Sisters Beach TAS. 232
Six Mile Waterhole QLD 416
Skenes Creek VIC. 189
Skippy Rock WA 316
Slade Point QLD 400
Sleaford Bay SA 288
Slip Cliff Point QLD 387
Sloop Lagoon TAS. 236
Sloop Reef TAS. 236
Sloping Island TAS. 224
Smiths Beach WA 317
Smiths Lake NSW 90
Smithton TAS. 232
Smoky Bay SA 284, 291
Smoky Cape NSW 76, 80, 81
Smooth Pool SA 291
Snag Island WA 307
Snake Bay NT 345
Snake Channel VIC. 166
Snake Island VIC. 176
Snapper Creek QLD 368
Snapper Hole NSW 79

Snapper Island NSW 114
Snapper Island QLD 388
Snapper Point SA 279
Snapper Point (Coastal Lakes) NSW 96
Snapper Point (Merry Beach) NSW 111
Snapper Rock NSW 71
Snapper Rocks QLD 378
Snowy Creek VIC. 201
Snowy River NSW 149, 151
Snowy River VIC. 171, 194, 196, 198
Snug Cove SA 274
Soldier Point NT 345
Soldiers Point NSW 48
Solitary Islands NSW 42, 73, 74
Solway Pass QLD 398
Somers VIC. 182
Sorrento VIC. 158, 160
Sorrento WA 300
South Alligator River NT 346, 347, 358
South Arm TAS. 226
South Beach NSW 68
South Beach WA 302
South Channel (Lakes Entrance) VIC. 172
South Channel (Port Phillip) VIC. 158, 160, 172
South Cove NSW 93
South Era Beach NSW 102
South Esk River TAS. 240, 242, 246
South Grange SA 271
South Head (Malua Bay) NSW 114–15
South Head (Sydney) NSW 44, 45, 57, 60
South Head QLD 408
South Island SA 272
South Johnstone River QLD 416
South Middle SA 271
South Mission Beach QLD 390
South Molle Island QLD 398
South Passage QLD 374
South Passage WA 322
South Peron Island NT 340
South Point NT 351
South Riordan Shoal NSW 71
South Solitary Island NSW 65, 74
South Stradbroke Island QLD 366, 374, 376, 377, 378
South Trees Island QLD 407
South Trees Wharf QLD 407
South West Arm NSW 63
South West National Park TAS. 228
South West Rocks NSW 76, 80
South West Rocks QLD 375
South West Solitary Island NSW 74
South West Vernon Island NT 346
Southend QLD 407

Southend SA 279
Southport TAS. 228
Southport Broadwater QLD 366, 377–8
Southport Lagoon TAS. 220
Sovereign Island QLD 378
Sow and Pigs Reef NSW 44, 45, 57
Spalding SA 295
Spectacle Island NSW 59
Spencer NSW 50, 51
Spencer Gulf SA 272, 284, 286–7
Spencers Creek NSW 80
Spencers Hole NSW 66
Spit Bridge NSW 55
Splashy NSW 99
Split Island QLD 404
Split Rock Dam NSW 133, 135
Split Solitary Island NSW 74
Spoil Bank WA 327
Spring Bay TAS. 222, 223
Spur Wall NSW 68
Square Head NSW 114
Staaten River QLD 383
Stagg Patches QLD 387
Stand Up Point TAS. 224
Stanley Wharf TAS. 232
Stansbury SA 272
Station Creek NSW 74
Station Pier VIC. 162
Station Point QLD 407
Station Point VIC. 189
Steel Bay VIC. 174
Steep Point WA 320, 322
Stenhouse Bay SA 272
Stewarts River NSW 129
Stieglitz TAS. 236
Stinging Tree Point NSW 91
Stirling Dam WA 332
Stockton Beach NSW 88, 93
Stockyard Creek WA 310
Stokes Hill Wharf NT 338
Stone Island QLD 396, 397
Stony Point NSW 94
Stony Point VIC. 182, 183, 185
Storm Bay TAS. 220, 224, 226
Stotts Island NSW 67
Streaky Bay SA 284, 290, 291
Stringree Island QLD 377
Stuarts Point NSW 80
Sturt Creek SA 292
Styx River NSW 133, 134
Styx River TAS. 248, 251
Sudbury Reef QLD 387
Sue City NSW 150
Suffolk Park Beach NSW 64, 69
Sugarloaf Bay (Middle Harbour) NSW 55
Sugarloaf Bay (Seal Rocks) NSW 90
Sugarloaf Reservoir VIC. 207
Sugarloaf Rock WA 317
Suicide Point NSW 52
Sunday Island VIC. 176

464

INDEX

SUNKEN REEF QLD – VENUS BAY SA

Sunken Reef QLD 375
Sunshine Beach QLD 369, 370
Sunshine Coast QLD 366, 367, 368, 369, 418
Sunshine Reefs QLD 369
Surf Beach NSW 106
Surfers Paradise QLD 378
Surprise Point TAS. 238
Surrey River VIC. 186, 192, 193, 214
Susan River QLD 413
Sussex Inlet NSW 100, 108–9
Swain Reefs QLD 405, 407
Swampy Plains River NSW 150
Swan Bay QLD 377
Swan Bay VIC. 158, 165
Swan Island Point VIC. 165
Swan Lake NSW 109
Swan River TAS. 223, 245
Swan River WA 297, 298, 300, 304, 331
Swanbourne Beach WA 302
Swansea Bridge NSW 89
Swansea Channel NSW 95
Swansea Heads NSW 89
Swansea TAS. 223, 245
Sweers Island Resort QLD 382
Sydenham Inlet VIC. 166, 170
Sydney Harbour NSW 42, 44, 54–9
Symonds Channel VIC. 160

Tabbigai NSW 62
Table Rock VIC. 162
Tabourie Creek NSW 111
Tabourie Lake NSW 111
Tabourie Point NSW 111
Tacoma NSW 97
Tagon Point WA 310
Tahara Bridge VIC. 214
Talbingo Reservoir NSW 146, 150
Talbot Reservoir VIC. 210, 211
Talc Head NT 342
Tallaberga Island VIC. 168
Tallebudgera Creek QLD 378–9
Tallow Beach NSW 69
Tallowa Dam NSW 128, 131
Tamar River TAS. 218, 230, 234–5
Tambo Bluff VIC. 173
Tambo River VIC. 166, 173, 194, 198, 199
Tamboon Inlet VIC. 166, 170
Tamworth NSW 135
Tangalooma Jetty QLD 373
Tangalooma Point QLD 373
Tanjil River VIC. 206
Tanker Jetty WA 310
Tankerton Jetty VIC. 183
Tannum Sands QLD 402, 407, 408
Tantabiddi Creek WA 325
Tantangara Creek NSW 150–1
Tantangara Reservoir NSW 146, 151

Tappers Inlet WA 329
Tarago Reservoir VIC. 207
Tarago River VIC. 207
Taranna TAS. 224
Tarban Creek NSW 58
Tarbay Gully NSW 50
Taroona TAS. 226
Tarourga Lake NSW 116
Tarra River VIC. 206
Tarwin River VIC. 178, 181, 206
Tasman Bridge TAS. 226
Tasman Island TAS. 224
Tathra NSW 112, 122
Tathra Head NSW 123
Tathra Wharf NSW 42, 112, 122–3
Tatlows Beach TAS. 232
Tauwitchere Channel SA 277
Taylor Point QLD 387
Taylors Bay NSW 57
Taylors Beach QLD 394
Tea Gardens NSW 92
Tea Tree Crossing SA 280
Tea Tree Rivulet TAS. 245
Teague Island QLD 399
Tee Tree Point NSW 123
Teebar Creek QLD 368
Teebar Ledge QLD 368
Teewah Beach QLD 370
Telegraph Pool WA 333
Tenterfield Creek NSW 133, 135
Terrigal NSW 88, 98, 99
Terrigal Lagoon NSW 99
The Arch NSW 82
The Basket beacon VIC. 185
The Bay NSW 80
The Bedroom QLD 377
The Blessings NSW 60
The Blowhole NSW 83
The Blowholes WA 324
The Blue Hole NSW 107
The Bluff SA 277
The Boneyard NSW 106
'The Butts' VIC. 163
The Causeway WA 300, 304
'The Chair' beacon VIC. 164
The Cobblers NSW 102
The Coorong SA 276, 277, 280–1
The Cut VIC. 173
The Cut WA 318
The Cutting VIC. 191
The Docks WA 317
The Entrance NSW 88, 97
The Fish Pond TAS. 232
The Five Islands NSW 103
The Forks NSW 75
The 42 Mile SA 280
The Gap NSW 60
The Gardens TAS. 230, 236
The Gravel NSW 93
The Gravel Patch QLD 379
The Graves QLD 411
The Gulf NSW 100, 102
The Gutter NSW 60

The Horseshoe NSW 111
The Island NSW 81
The Jew Bite NSW 81
The Jew Shoal QLD 370
The Knoll WA 315
The Ladders NSW 108
The Lagoons QLD 407
The Lakes Tourist Resort NT 356
The Ledge NSW 69
The Ledge SA 290
'The Magpie' VIC. 162
The Mahogonys VIC. 170
The Narrows (Lakes Entrance) VIC. 172
The Narrows (Mallacoota) VIC. 168
The Narrows QLD 364, 402, 403, 406
The Nobbies VIC. 178, 183
The Nut TAS. 232
The Pass NSW 69
The Peppermints WA 315
The Pinnacle (Little Reef) NSW 60
The Pinnacles Reef (Cape Hawke) NSW 87
The Point NSW 69
The Pumping Station VIC. 189
The Rip VIC. 160
The Rip Bridge NSW 46
The Salmon Holes WA 313
The Shallows (Jervis Bay) NSW 108
The Shallows (Tuggerah) NSW 97
The Sir Joseph Banks Group SA 288
The Skillion NSW 88, 99
The Slot NSW 120
The Snags QLD 370
The Spot NSW 80
The Spot WA 303
The Stairs NSW 82
The Step (Wallis Lake) NSW 86–7
The Steps (Lake Conjola) NSW 109
The Sticks NSW 123
The Stockyard NSW 86
The Stockyards QLD 377
The Trap NSW 60
The Vines NSW 48
Theodolite Creek QLD 409
Thetford Reef QLD 387
Thevenard Island WA 325
Thevenard SA 291
Third Beach NSW 81
32 Fathom Reef QLD 379
36 Fathom Reef QLD 378
Thomas Island QLD 397
Thomas River WA 310
Thompson Cove WA 315
Thompson Creek Dam NSW 140, 143
Thomson Reservoir VIC. 206

Thomson River QLD 418
Thomson River VIC. 202, 206
Thredbo River NSW 146, 151
Three Hummocks Island TAS. 232
Three Mile Dam NSW 151
Three Mile Reef WA 306
Thunder Point VIC. 191
Tiger Mullet Channel QLD 377
Tilba Beach NSW 119
Tilba Road Bridge NSW 119
Timbarra River NSW 128, 129
Timbarra River VIC. 199
Timber Creek NT 354
Tims Thicket Beach WA 319
Tin Can Inlet QLD 366, 368
Tinnanbar QLD 413
Tintaldra VIC. 200
Tiparra Reef Lighthouse SA 272
Tiwi Islands NT 337, 339, 344–5
Tocumwal NSW 152
Tollgate Islands NSW 114
Tomaga River NSW 115
Tomaree Head NSW 92
Tonalli River NSW 143
Tonys Island NSW 67
Toolondo Reservoir VIC. 208, 215
Tooma Pondage NSW 151
Tooma River NSW 150
Tooms Lake TAS. 242, 246
Toonumbar Dam NSW 129
Toora VIC. 177
Tooradin VIC. 185
Tooram Stones VIC. 191, 213
Toowoomba QLD 419
Toowoon Point NSW 97
Top Lake VIC. 168
Toragy Point NSW 116
Torbay Inlet WA 313
Torpedo Rocks WA 317
Torquay VIC. 165
Torrens River SA 292
Tortoise Head VIC. 183
Toumbaal Creek NSW 73
Towamba River NSW 124, 131
Town Beach NT 351
Town Beach WA 328
Towners Hole NSW 66
Towns River NT 360
Townsville QLD 392, 393, 394, 395, 396
Towong VIC. 200
Town Point NSW 60
Tranmere TAS. 226
Treachery Head NSW 90
Trevallyn Tailrace TAS. 235
Triabunna TAS. 218, 220, 222, 223, 245
Trial Bay Gaol NSW 80
Triangle Island NSW 50
Trigg Point WA 302, 303
Trinity Bay QLD 386, 387
Trinity Inlet QLD 389
Tripcony Bight QLD 372
Troubridge Point SA 272
Trousers Point TAS. 239

Truant Bank NT 351
Truant Island NT 350–1
Trumpeter Bay TAS. 228
Tuan QLD 413
Tuanunaku River NT 345
Tuckers Island NSW 79
Tuggerah Beach NSW 97
Tuggerah Lake NSW 42, 88, 96, 97
Tuglow River NSW 143
Tuleen Island QLD 377
Tullaroop Reservoir VIC. 211
Tully QLD 380
Tully Heads QLD 390
Tully River QLD 380, 390, 416
Tumbulgum NSW 67
Tumby Bay SA 288
Tumut River NSW 150
Tuncurry NSW 76, 86
Tungatinah Lagoon TAS. 255
Tura Head NSW 122
Turimetta Head NSW 52
Turingal Head NSW 122
Turkey Beach QLD 408
Turkey Island QLD 413
Turkey Strait QLD 413
Turkeys Nest Wall NSW 72
Turon River NSW 142
Tuross Lake NSW 112, 113, 117
Tuross River NSW 117, 131
Turpin Falls VIC. 205
Tweed Coast NSW 64, 66–7
Tweed Heads NSW 65, 66
Tweed River NSW 42, 66, 67
12 Fathom Reef QLD 378
Twelve Mile Reef NSW 120
20 Fathom Reef QLD 378
24 Fathom Reef QLD 379
Twin Holes NSW 81
Two Fella Creek NT 341
Two Mile Hole NT 358
Two Mile WA 324
Two Mile Rock QLD 400
Two Peoples Bay WA 312
Two Rocks WA 303
Twofold Bay NSW 112, 124–5
Tyenna River TAS. 240, 248, 251

Ukerebagh Island NSW 67
Ulladulla Harbour NSW 110
Ulverstone TAS. 232
Upolu Reef and Cay QLD 387
Upper Coliban Reservoir VIC. 205
Upper Yarra Reservoir VIC. 207
Upstart Bay QLD 392, 393, 396
Urang Creek QLD 413
Urangan Pier QLD 410
Urangan Steps QLD 410
Urquhart Bluff VIC. 188
Urunga NSW 76, 78–9

Vacy NSW 138
Van Diemen Gulf NT 339, 346–7
Vee Beach NSW 79
Venus Bay SA 284, 290, 291

465

Venus Bay Vic. 156, 178, 181
Vernon Islands NT 339, 346
Victor Bailey Reef QLD 369
Victor Harbor SA 277, 282–3
Victoria River NT 354
Violet Hill NSW 90
Vivonne Bay SA 274

Waddy Point QLD 412
Wagga Wagga NSW 152
Wagoe Beach WA 307
Wagonga Head NSW 118
Wagonga Inlet NSW 112, 113, 118
Wagstaff Point NSW 46
Wairo Beach NSW 111
Waitpinga Beach SA 277, 283
Wajurda Point NSW 122
Wakefield River SA 292
Wakool River NSW 152
Walcha NSW 134
Walcott Inlet WA 329
Walker Channel TAS. 232
Walker Island TAS. 232
Walker Point Vic. 174
Walkers Beach NSW 106, 107
Walkerville Vic. 180
Wallacia NSW 130
Wallaga Lake NSW 118, 119
Wallagaraugh River NSW 131
Wallagaraugh River Vic. 168
Wallagoot Lake NSW 122
Wallamba River NSW 130
Wallangra NSW 135
Wallarah Creek NSW 96
Wallaroo SA 286
Wallis Island NSW 86
Wallis Lake NSW 76, 86
Walpole Inlet WA 315
Walpole–Nornalup National Park WA 315
Walsh Bay NSW 58
Walwa Vic. 200
Walwa Creek Vic. 200
Wamberal Lagoon NSW 98
Wamberal Point NSW 98
Wandandian Creek NSW 131
Wannon Falls Vic. 214
Wannon River Vic. 214
Wapengo Lake NSW 112, 120–1
Waranga Reservoir Vic. 194, 202, 205
Waratah Bay NSW 48

Waratah Bay Vic. 156, 178, 179, 180
Wardang Island SA 272
Warden Head NSW 110
Wardlaws Point TAS. 237
Warilla Beach NSW 104–5
'Warmies' Vic. 162
Warnbro Sound WA 302
Warneet Vic. 185
Warners Bay NSW 95
Waroona WA 332
Waroona Dam WA 330
Warrego River NSW 152
Warrego River QLD 418
Warrell Creek NSW 79
Warren River WA 330, 332
Warriewood Ledges NSW 52
Warrnambool Vic. 186–7, 190–1, 213
Warroora Homestead WA 325
Wasp Island NSW 114
Watchbox Creek Vic. 205
Wategos Beach NSW 69
Water Park Creek QLD 405
Water Park Point QLD 405
Waterhouse River NT 354
Waterloo Bay SA 291
Waterloo Point TAS. 223
Wathumba Creek QLD 412–13
Watson Gap SA 282
Watson River QLD 383, 416
Watson Taylors Lake NSW 84
Wattamolla Bay NSW 102
Watts Reef NSW 61
Waubs Bay TAS. 237
Waubs Gulch TAS. 237
Wave Break Island QLD 377
Wayatinah Lagoon TAS. 250
Weary Bay QLD 386
Wearyan River NT 360
Webber Point TAS. 223
Webbs Creek NSW 130
Wedding Cakes NSW 44, 57
Wedge Island QLD 400
Wedge Island WA 306
Wedge Point Vic. 159, 163
Wee Jasper NSW 145
Weipa QLD 380, 383, 384
Weld River TAS. 248, 251
Wellesley Group QLD 382
Wellington Dam WA 330, 332
Wellington Point QLD 375
Wellington River Vic. 206

Wenlock River QLD 384, 416
Wentworth Falls NSW 143
Wentworth Reef QLD 386
Wentworth River Vic. 199
Werri Beach NSW 106
Werribee River Vic. 158, 163, 202, 207
Wessel Islands NT 348, 349, 350
West Alligator Head NT 346
West Alligator River NT 346, 347
West Arm NT 342
West Bay SA 274
West Beach SA 269, 271
West Cape SA 272
West Cape Howe WA 313
West End WA 305
West Gate Bridge Vic. 162
West Head NSW 48
West Head Vic. 183
West Lakes SA 268
West Point NT 342
West Woody Island NT 351
Western Beach Vic. 164
Western Port Vic. 156, 178–9, 182–5
Western River SA 274
Weyba Creek QLD 370
Whale Beach (Pittwater Beaches) NSW 52
Whale Beach (Twofold Bay) NSW 124
Whalers Wharf SA 282–3
Whalleys Gutter NSW 377
Wharf Marina QLD 371
Wharton Beach WA 310
Whiphandle Waterholes QLD 416
Whistler Point TAS. 238
Whistling Rock WA 324
White Cliffs QLD 397
White Hill Beach WA 319
White Lily Lagoon QLD 416
Whites Head NSW 64, 69
Whitsunday Island QLD 398, 399
Whitsundays Group QLD 364, 392, 393, 398–9
Whyalla SA 284, 287
Wide Bay (Cairns) QLD 387
Wide Bay (Fraser Island) QLD 367, 403
Wide Bay (Rainbow Beach) QLD 368

Wide Reef NSW 81
Wild Cattle Creek QLD 408
Wild Cattle Island QLD 408
Wild Dog Creek Vic. 189
Wildman River NT 358
Willare Bridge WA 333
William Bay WA 314
Williams River NSW 130, 136, 138, 139
Williamsons Beach Vic. 178
Williamstown Vic. 163
Willoughby Bay NSW 55
Wilson Inlet WA 297, 308, 314
Wilson Point Vic. 174
Wilson River NSW 129
Wilsons Promontory Vic. 177, 180
Wimmera River Vic. 208, 215
Windang Island NSW 100, 103, 104
Windermere TAS. 235
Windy Gap NSW 81
Wineglass Bay TAS. 222
Winfield QLD 408
Wingan Inlet Vic. 170
Wirrina Marina SA 270
Wisemans Ferry NSW 50, 130
Witches Cauldron QLD 370
Withnell Bay WA 326
Wittecarra Creek WA 307
Wolf Rock QLD 368
Wollogorang Station NT 360
Wollomombi River NSW 133, 134
Wollondilly River NSW 141, 143, 144
Wollongbar 1 wreck NSW 69
Wollongong NSW 100, 103
Wolseley Street Wharf NSW 58
Wommin Bay NSW 66
Wonboyn Beach NSW 125
Wonboyn Lake NSW 113, 125
Wonboyn River NSW 125
Wongungarra River Vic. 199
Wonnangatta River Vic. 199
Woodgate QLD 409
Woodman Point WA 300, 302
Woods Lake TAS. 252, 254
Woody Head NSW 72
Woolamai Vic. 156, 178
Woolaston Weir Vic. 213
Woolgoolga Beach NSW 74
Woolgoolga Creek NSW 74

Wooli NSW 64, 74, 75
Wooli Wooli River NSW 74, 75
Woolooware Bay NSW 61
Wooloweyah Lagoon NSW 72
Wooyung Beach NSW 66
Worang Point NSW 124, 125
Woronora River NSW 61
Woy Woy NSW 46
Wright Island SA 282
Wrights Point NSW 59
Wyadup Rocks WA 317
Wybalenna TAS. 239
Wybung Head NSW 88, 96
Wye River Vic. 189
Wyndham WA 329, 333
Wyong Creek NSW 130
Wyong River NSW 97

Yacaaba Head NSW 92
Yacka SA 295
Yackandandah Creek Vic. 201
Yagon Gibber Headland NSW 91
Yagon Reef NSW 91
Yallingup Beach WA 317
Yamba NSW 64, 72
Yambuk Lake Vic. 193
Yanakie Landing Vic. 177
Yanchep Beach WA 303
Yankalilla River SA 270
Yaringa Harbour Vic. 185
Yarra River Vic. 158, 162, 202, 207
Yarrangobilly River NSW 150
Yarrawonga Weir NSW 152
Yass NSW 141, 145
Yass River NSW 145
Yeerung Estuary Vic. 171
Yellow Patch QLD 407
Yellow Rock Inlet NSW 79
Yellow Waters NT 358
Yeomans Bay NSW 48, 51
Yeppoon QLD 404, 405
Yidney Creek QLD 413
Yorke Peninsula SA 266, 268, 272–3, 286
Yorkeys Knob QLD 387
Yule Point QLD 387
Yum Point NSW 119
Yumbool Point NSW 98

Zilzie Point QLD 405
Zuytdorp Cliffs WA 320, 322
Zuytdorp Point WA 322